INTEGRATED CME PROJECT

# Mathematics III

PEARSON

**The Center for Mathematics Education Project was developed at Education Development Center, Inc. (EDC) within the Center for Mathematics Education (CME), with partial support from the National Science Foundation.**

**Education Development Center, Inc.
Center for Mathematics Education
Newton, Massachusetts**

This material is based upon work supported by the National Science Foundation under Grant No. ESI-0242476, Grant No. MDR-9252952, and Grant No. ESI-9617369. Any opinions, findings, and conclusions or recommendations expressed in this material are those of the author(s) and do not necessarily reflect the views of the National Science Foundation.

Cover Art: 9 Surf Studios; Peter Sterling/Getty Images, Inc.

Taken from:
*CME Project: Geometry, Algebra 2, Algebra 1, Precalculus*
By the CME Project Development Team

Published by Pearson Education, Inc.
Upper Saddle River, New Jersey 07458

*CME Common Core Additional Lessons: Precalculus, Algebra 2*
By the CME Project Development Team

Published by Pearson Education, Inc.
Upper Saddle River, New Jersey 07458

CME Project Development Team

***Lead Developers:*** Al Cuoco and Bowen Kerins

***Core Development Team:*** Anna Baccaglini-Frank, Jean Benson, Nancy Antonellis D'Amato, Daniel Erman, Paul Goldenberg, Brian Harvey, Wayne Harvey, Doreen Kilday, Ryota Matsuura, Stephen Maurer, Nina Shteingold, Sarah Sword, Audrey Ting, Kevin Waterman. ***Others who contributed include:*** Elena Kaczorowski, Matt McLeod, Joe Obrycki, Carrie Abrams Ott, and William Thill.



This special edition published in cooperation with Pearson Learning Solutions.



Pearson Learning Solutions, 501 Boylston Street, Suite 900, Boston, MA 02116
A Pearson Education Company
www.pearsoned.com

Printed in the United States of America

2 3 4 5 6 7 8 9 10 V011 18 17 15 14 13

3338000585786D

000200010271656492

CP

PEARSON

ISBN 10: 1-256-69476-2
ISBN 13: 978-1-256-69476-2

# Contents in Brief

# Introduction to the CME Project

The CME Project, developed by EDC's Center for Mathematics Education, is a new NSF-funded high school program, organized around the familiar courses of algebra 1, geometry, algebra 2, and precalculus. The CME Project provides teachers and schools with a third alternative to the choice between traditional texts driven by basic skill development and more progressive texts that have unfamiliar organizations. This program gives teachers the option of a problem-based, student-centered program, organized around the mathematical themes with which teachers and parents are familiar. Furthermore, the tremendous success of NSF-funded middle school programs has left a need for a high school program with similar rigor and pedagogy. The CME Project fills this need.

The goal of the CME Project is to help students acquire a deep understanding of mathematics. Therefore, the mathematics here is rigorous. We took great care to create lesson plans that, while challenging, will capture and engage students of all abilities and improve their mathematical achievement.

## The Program's Approach

The organization of the CME Project provides students the time and focus they need to develop fundamental mathematical ways of thinking. Its primary goal is to develop in students robust mathematical proficiency.

- The program employs innovative instructional methods, developed over decades of classroom experience and informed by research, that help students master mathematical topics.
- One of the core tenets of the CME Project is to focus on developing students' Habits of Mind, or ways in which students approach and solve mathematical challenges.
- The program builds on lessons learned from high-performing countries: develop an idea thoroughly and then revisit it only to deepen it; organize ideas in a way that is faithful to how they are organized in mathematics; and reduce clutter and extraneous topics.
- It also employs the best American models that call for grappling with ideas and problems as preparation for instruction, moving from concrete problems to abstractions and general theories, and situating mathematics in engaging contexts.
- The CME Project is a comprehensive curriculum that meets the dual goals of mathematical rigor and accessibility for a broad range of students.

## About CME

EDC's Center for Mathematics Education, led by mathematician and teacher **Al Cuoco,** brings together an eclectic staff of mathematicians, teachers, cognitive scientists, education researchers, curriculum developers, specialists in educational technology, and teacher educators, internationally known for leadership across the entire range of K–16 mathematics education. We aim to help students and teachers in this country experience the thrill of solving problems and building theories, understand the history of ideas behind the evolution of mathematical disciplines, and appreciate the standards of rigor that are central to mathematical culture.

# Contributors to the CME Project

**National Advisory Board** The National Advisory Board met early in the project, providing critical feedback on the instructional design and the overall organization. Members include

**Richard Askey,** University of Wisconsin
**Edward Barbeau,** University of Toronto
**Hyman Bass,** University of Michigan
**Carol Findell,** Boston University
**Arthur Heinricher,** Worcester Polytechnic Institute
**Roger Howe,** Yale University
**Barbara Janson,** Janson Associates
**Kenneth Levasseur,** University of Massachusetts, Lowell
**James Madden,** Louisiana State University, Baton Rouge
**Jacqueline Miller,** Education Development Center
**James Newton,** University of Maryland
**Robert Segall,** Greater Hartford Academy of Mathematics and Science
**Glenn Stevens,** Boston University
**Herbert Wilf,** University of Pennsylvania
**Hung-Hsi Wu,** University of California, Berkeley

**Core Mathematical Consultants** **Dick Askey, Ed Barbeau**, and **Roger Howe** have been involved in an even more substantial way, reviewing chapters and providing detailed and critical advice on every aspect of the program. Dick and Roger spent many hours reading and criticizing drafts, brainstorming with the writing team, and offering advice on everything from the logical organization to the actual numbers used in problems. We can't thank them enough.

**Teacher Advisory Board** The Teacher Advisory Board for the CME Project was essential in helping us create an effective format for our lessons that embodies the philosophy and goals of the program. Their debates about pedagogical issues and how to develop mathematical topics helped to shape the distinguishing features of the curriculum so that our lessons work effectively in the classroom. The advisory board includes

**Jayne Abbas, Richard Coffey, Charles Garabedian, Dennis Geller, Eileen Herlihy, Doreen Kilday, Gayle Masse, Hugh McLaughlin, Nancy McLaughlin, Allen Olsen, Kimberly Osborne, Brian Shoemaker,** and **Benjamin Sinwell**

**Field-Test Teachers** Our field-test teachers gave us the benefit of their classroom experience by teaching from our draft lessons and giving us extensive, critical feedback that shaped the drafts into realistic, teachable lessons. They shared their concerns, questions, challenges, and successes and kept us focused on the real world. Some of them even welcomed us into their classrooms as co-teachers to give us the direct experience with students that we needed to hone our lessons. Working with these expert professionals has been one of the most gratifying parts of the development—they are "highly qualified" in the most profound sense.

California **Barney Martinez**, Jefferson High School, Daly City; **Calvin Baylon** and **Jaime Lao**, Bell Junior High School, San Diego; Colorado **Rocky Cundiff**, Ignacio High School, Ignacio; Illinois **Jeremy Kahan**, **Tammy Nguyen**, and **Stephanie Pederson**, Ida Crown Jewish Academy, Chicago; Massachusetts **Carol Martignette, Chris Martino,** and **Kent Werst**, Arlington High School, Arlington; **Larry Davidson**, Boston University Academy, Boston; **Joe Bishop** and **Carol Rosen**, Lawrence High School, Lawrence; **Maureen Mulryan**, Lowell High School, Lowell; **Felisa Honeyman**, Newton South High School, Newton Centre; **Jim Barnes** and **Carol Haney**, Revere High School, Revere; New Hampshire **Jayne Abbas** and **Terin Voisine**, Cawley Middle School, Hooksett; New Mexico **Mary Andrews**, Las Cruces High School, Las Cruces; Ohio **James Stallworth**, Hughes Center, Cincinnati; Texas **Arnell Crayton**, Bellaire High School, Bellaire; Utah **Troy Jones**, Waterford School, Sandy; Washington **Dale Erz, Kathy Greer, Karena Hanscom,** and **John Henry**, Port Angeles High School, Port Angeles; Wisconsin **Annette Roskam**, Rice Lake High School, Rice Lake.

Special thanks go to our colleagues at Pearson, most notably Elizabeth Lehnertz, Joe Will, and Stewart Wood. The program benefits from their expertise in every way, from the actual mathematics to the design of the printed page.

# 1 Functions and Polynomials

# Sequences and Series

# 3 Statistical Inference

# Trigonometry

# Analyzing Trigonometric Functions

6

# Complex Numbers and Polynomials

# 7 Polynomial and Rational Functions

# 8 Exponential and Logarithmic Functions

9

# Optimization and Geometric Modeling

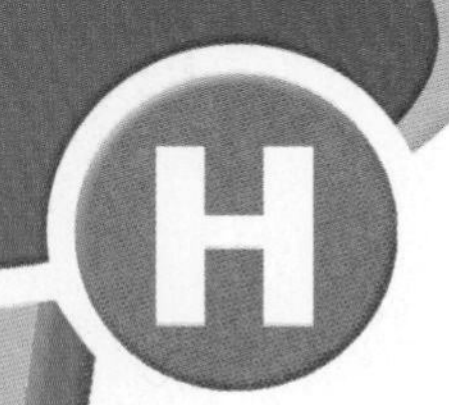

# Honors Appendix

# CME Project Student Handbook

## What Makes CME Different

Welcome to the CME Project! The goal of this program is to help you develop a deep understanding of mathematics. Throughout this book, you will engage in many different activities to help you develop that deep understanding. Some of these instructional activities may be different from ones you are used to. Below is an overview of some of these elements and why they are an important part of the CME Project.

## The Habits of Mind Experience

Mathematical Habits of Mind are the foundation for serious questioning, solid thinking, good problem solving, and critical analysis. These Habits of Mind are what will help you become a mathematical thinker. Throughout the CME Project, you will focus on developing and refining these Habits of Mind.

### Developing Habits of Mind

**Develop thinking skills.** This feature provides you with various methods and approaches to solving problems.

You will develop, use, and revisit specific Habits of Mind throughout the course. These include

- **Process** (how you work through problems)
- **Visualization** (how you "picture" problems)
- **Representation** (what you write down)
- **Patterns** (what you find)
- **Relationships** (what you find or use)

Developing good habits will help you as problems become more complicated.

**Habits of Mind**

**Think.** These special margin notes highlight key thinking skills and prompt you to apply your developing Habits of Mind.

## Minds in Action

Discussion of mathematical ideas is an effective method of learning. The Minds in Action feature exposes you to ways of communicating about mathematics.

Join Sasha, Tony, Derman, and others as they think, calculate, predict, and discuss their way towards understanding.

### Minds in Action

*Sasha, Tony, and Derman have just skimmed through their* Mathematics III *book.*

**Sasha** Did you notice the student dialogs throughout the book?

**Derman** Sure did!

**Tony** They talk and think just the way we do.

**Sasha** I know! And they even make mistakes sometimes, the way we do.

**Tony** But I like how they help each other to learn from those mistakes. I bet they use the Habits of Mind I saw all over the book, too.

**Sasha** That's great! They should help a lot.

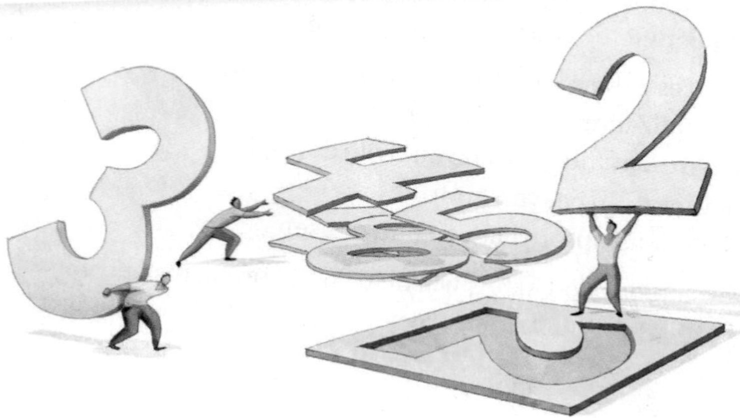

# Exploring Mathematics

Throughout the CME Project, you will engage in activities that extend your learning and allow you to explore the concepts you learn in greater depth. Two of these activities are In-Class Experiments and Chapter Projects.

## In-Class Experiment

In-Class Experiments allow you to explore new concepts and apply the Habits of Mind.

You will explore math as mathematicians do. You start with a question and develop answers through experimentation.

## Chapter Projects

Chapter Projects allow you to apply your Habits of Mind to the content of the chapter. These projects cover many different topics and allow you to explore and engage in greater depth.

### Chapter Projects
### Using Mathematical Habits

Here is a list of the Chapter Projects and page numbers.

# Using your CME Book

To help you make the most of your CME experience, we are providing the following overview of the organization of your book.

## Focusing your Learning

In *Mathematics III*, there are 9 chapters, with each chapter devoted to a mathematical concept. With only 9 chapters, your class will be able to focus on these core concepts and develop a deep understanding of them.

Within each chapter, you will explore a series of Investigations. Each Investigation focuses on an important aspect of the mathematical concept for that chapter.

# The CME Investigation

The goal of each mathematical Investigation is for you to formalize your understanding of the mathematics being taught. There are some common instructional features in each Investigation.

## Getting Started

You will launch into each Investigation with a Getting Started lesson that activates prior knowledge and explores new ideas. This lesson provides you the opportunity to grapple with ideas and problems. The goal of these lessons is for you to explore—not all your questions will be answered in these lessons.

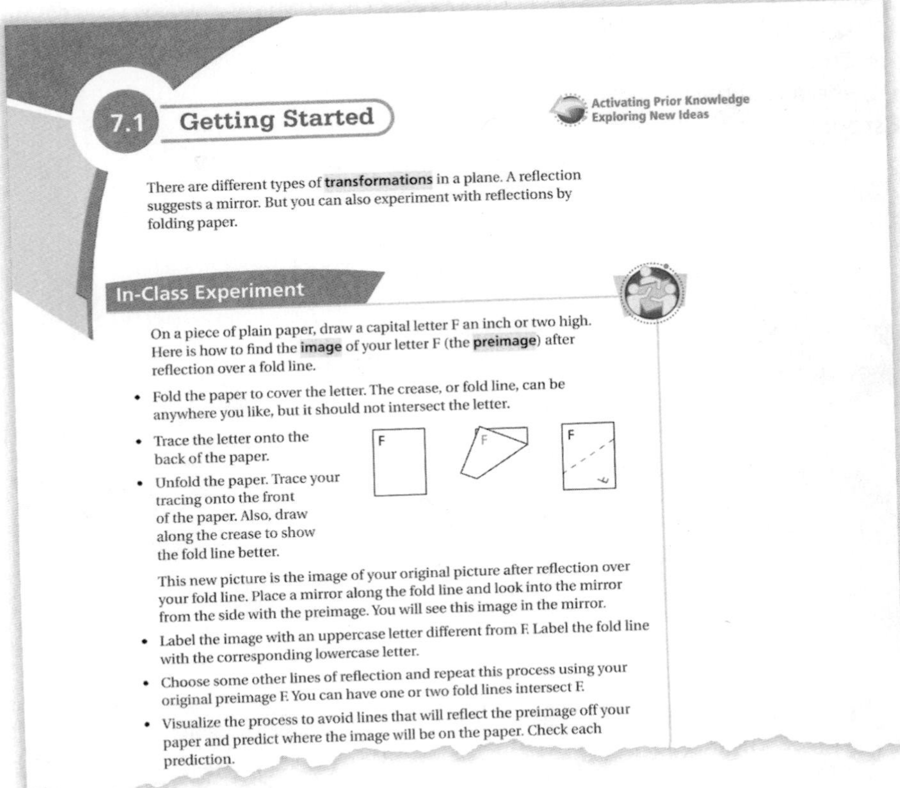

7.1 Getting Started

Activating Prior Knowledge
Exploring New Ideas

There are different types of **transformations** in a plane. A reflection suggests a mirror. But you can also experiment with reflections by folding paper.

In-Class Experiment

On a piece of plain paper, draw a capital letter F an inch or two high. Here is how to find the **image** of your letter F (the **preimage**) after reflection over a fold line.

- Fold the paper to cover the letter. The crease, or fold line, can be anywhere you like, but it should not intersect the letter.
- Trace the letter onto the back of the paper.
- Unfold the paper. Trace your tracing onto the front of the paper. Also, draw along the crease to show the fold line better.

This new picture is the image of your original picture after reflection over your fold line. Place a mirror along the fold line and look into the mirror from the side with the preimage. You will see this image in the mirror.

- Label the image with an uppercase letter different from F. Label the fold line with the corresponding lowercase letter.
- Choose some other lines of reflection and repeat this process using your original preimage F. You can have one or two fold lines intersect F.
- Visualize the process to avoid lines that will reflect the preimage off your paper and predict where the image will be on the paper. Check each prediction.

## Learning the Mathematics

You will engage in, learn, and practice the mathematics in a variety of ways. The types of learning elements you will find throughout this course include

- **Worked-Out Examples** that model how to solve problems
- **Definitions and Theorems** to summarize key concepts
- **In-Class Experiments** to explore the concepts
- **For You to Do** assignments to check your understanding
- **For Discussion** questions to encourage communication
- **Minds in Action** to model mathematical discussion

# Communicating the Mathematics

## Minds in Action

### Student dialogs

By featuring dialogs between characters, the CME Project exposes you to a way of communicating about mathematics. These dialogs will then become a real part of your classroom!

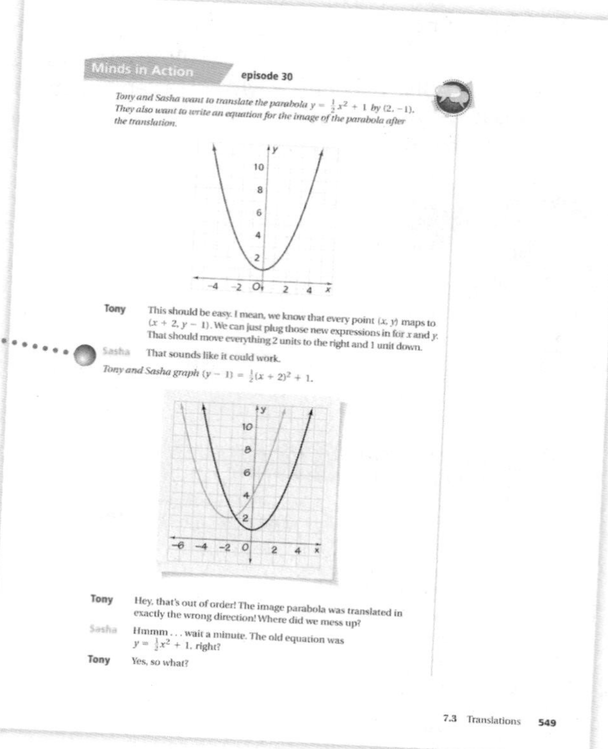

Minds in Action episode 30

*Tony and Sasha want to translate the parabola $y = \frac{1}{2}x^2 + 1$ by $(2, -1)$. They also want to write an equation for the image of the parabola after the translation.*

**Tony** This should be easy. I mean, we know that every point $(x, y)$ maps to $(x + 2, y - 1)$. We can just plug those new expressions in for $x$ and $y$. That should move everything 2 units to the right and 1 unit down.

**Sasha** That sounds like it could work.

*Tony and Sasha graph $(y - 1) = \frac{1}{2}(x + 2)^2 + 1$.*

**Tony** Hey, that's out of order! The image parabola was translated in exactly the wrong direction! Where did we mess up?

**Sasha** Hmmm . . . wait a minute. The old equation was $y = \frac{1}{2}x^2 + 1$, right?

**Tony** Yes, so what?

7.3 Translations 549

# Reflecting on the Mathematics

At the end of each Investigation, Mathematical Reflections give you an opportunity to put ideas together. This feature allows you to demonstrate your understanding of the Investigation and reflect on what you learn.

# Practice

The CME Project views extensive practice as a critical component of a mathematics curriculum. You will have daily opportunities to practice what you learn.

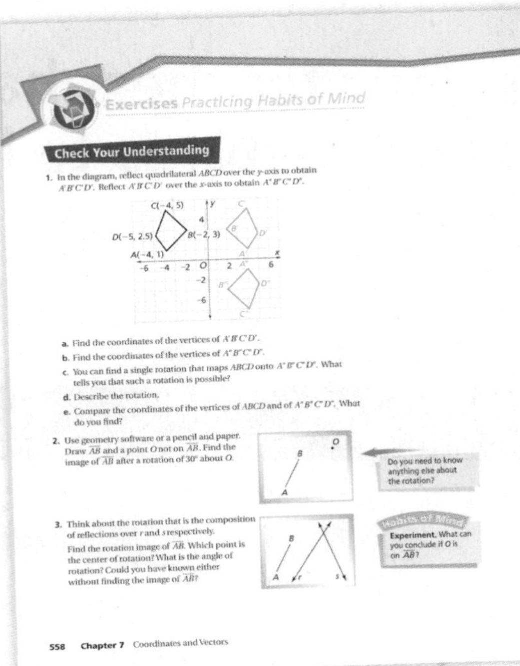

Exercises Practicing Habits of Mind

Check Your Understanding

1. In the diagram, reflect quadrilateral $ABCD$ over the $y$-axis to obtain $A'B'C'D'$. Reflect $A'B'C'D'$ over the $x$-axis to obtain $A''B''C''D''$.



a. Find the coordinates of the vertices of $A'B'C'D'$.
b. Find the coordinates of the vertices of $A''B''C''D''$.
c. You can find a single rotation that maps $ABCD$ onto $A''B''C''D''$. What tells you that such a rotation is possible?
d. Describe the rotation.
e. Compare the coordinates of the vertices of $ABCD$ and of $A''B''C''D''$. What do you find?

2. Use geometry software or a pencil and paper. Draw $\overline{AB}$ and a point $O$ not on $\overline{AB}$. Find the image of $\overline{AB}$ after a rotation of 30° about $O$.

Do you need to know anything else about the rotation?

3. Think about the rotation that is the composition of reflections over $r$ and $s$ respectively. Find the rotation image of $\overline{AB}$. Which point is the center of rotation? What is the angle of rotation? Could you have known either without finding the image of $\overline{AB}$?

Habits of Mind
**Experiment.** What can you conclude if $O$ is on $\overline{AB}$?

558 **Chapter 7** Coordinates and Vectors

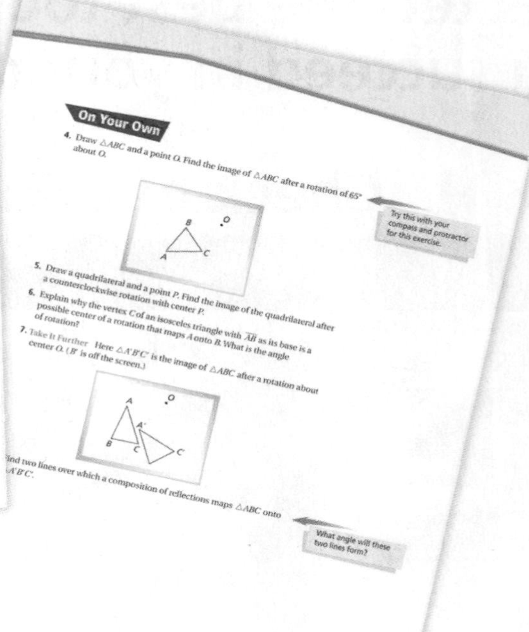

On Your Own

4. Draw $\triangle ABC$ and a point $O$. Find the image of $\triangle ABC$ after a rotation of 65° about $O$.

Try this with your compass and protractor for this exercise.

5. Draw a quadrilateral and a point $P$. Find the image of the quadrilateral after a counterclockwise rotation with center $P$.
6. Explain why the vertex $C$ of an isosceles triangle with $\overline{AB}$ as its base is a possible center of a rotation that maps $A$ onto $B$. What is the angle of rotation?
7. Take It Further Here $\triangle A'B'C'$ is the image of $\triangle ABC$ after a rotation about center $O$. ($B'$ is off the screen.)

…ind two lines over which a composition of reflections maps $\triangle ABC$ onto …$A'B'C'$.

What angle will these two lines form?

7.4 Rotations 559

### Check Your Understanding

Assess your readiness for independent practice by working through these problems in class.

### Maintain Your Skills

Review and reinforce skills from previous lessons.

### On Your Own

Practice and continue developing the mathematical understanding you learn in each lesson.

### *Also Available*

An additional Practice Workbook is available separately.

## With **SuccessNet Plus** your teachers have selected the best tools and features to help you succeed in your classes.

### Check out SuccessNet Plus

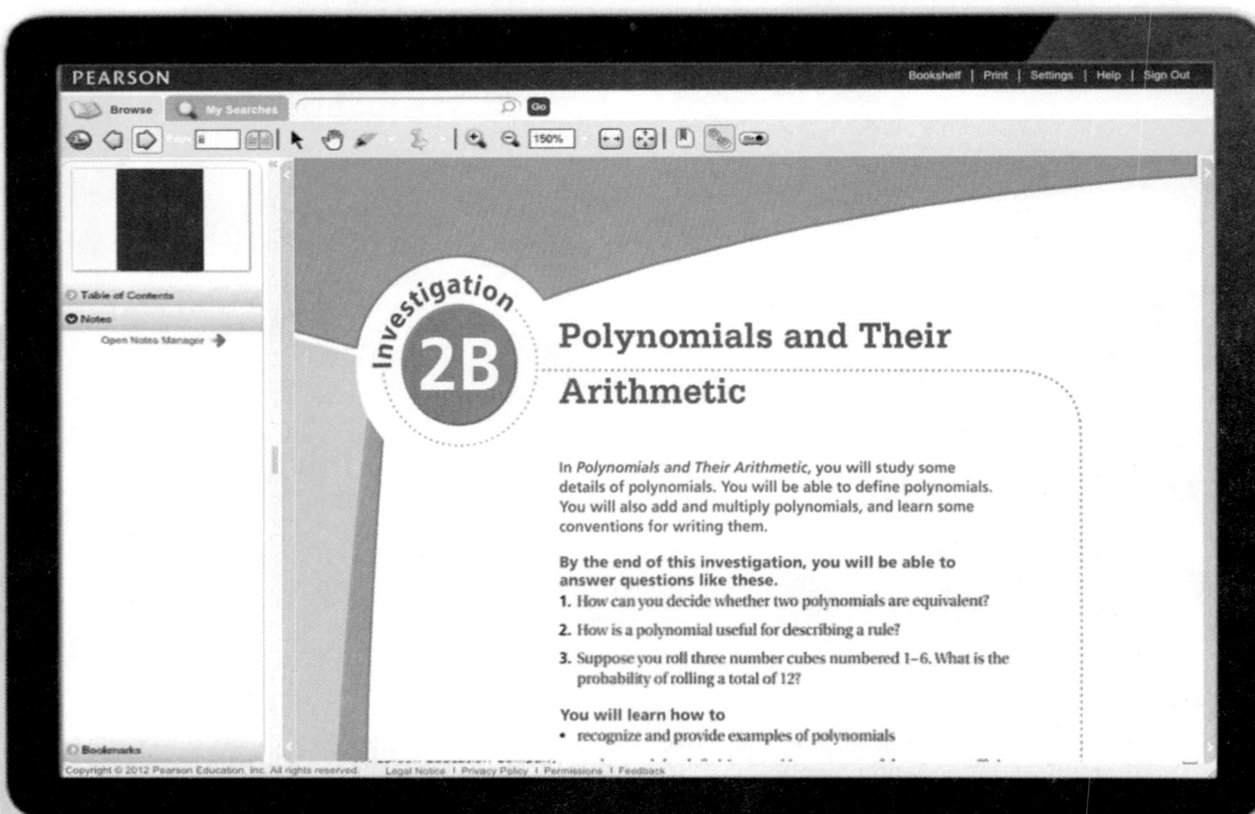

## Log-in to www.successnetplus.com to find:

- **an online Pearson eText version of your textbook**
- **extra practice and assessments**
- **worksheets and activities**
- **multimedia**

Check out the TI-Nspire™ Technology Handbook on p. 817 for examples of how you can use handheld technology with your math learning!

Chapter
1
Investigations at a Glance
1A Making It Fit
1B Factors, Roots, and Zeros
1C Advanced Factoring

# Functions and Polynomials

Mathematics has a remarkable relationship with the natural world. Often a table of observations of two related quantities matches a mathematical function. Examination of this function can reveal the relationship between the two quantities.

Suppose you throw a ball up into the air and measure its height at different times. Suppose further that you make a table with columns for the time elapsed since the throw and the height observed at that time. There is a quadratic function that matches this table.

If you measure the velocity of the ball at several times and make a table of time and the ball's velocity, a linear function matches the table. The linear function shows that the upward velocity of the ball decreases at a constant rate, eventually becoming negative as the ball stops rising and begins to fall back down.

The functions tell you what is happening to the ball. A scientific explanation tells why the function has the structure it does and what the coefficients and roots of the polynomial mean.

## Vocabulary and Notation

- coefficient
- cubic polynomial
- degree of a monomial
- degree of a polynomial
- difference of cubes
- Lagrange interpolation
- linear polynomial
- monomial
- parameter
- polynomial
- quadratic formula
- quadratic polynomial
- quartic polynomial
- quintic polynomial
- quotient
- rational expression
- remainder
- sum of cubes
- $\mathbb{Q}$ (the rational numbers)
- $\mathbb{Z}$ (the integers)

# 1.0 Anatomy of a Polynomial

It can be difficult to understand the definition of a polynomial without first seeing some examples. The following are all polynomials.

| | | |
|---|---|---|
| $x^2 - 1$ | $3x + 5y + 1$ | $2x^3 - 9x^4 - 3x + 2$ |
| $\frac{6}{7}x^3 - 8x^2 + 1$ | $\frac{3}{7}x + \frac{1}{2}$ | $y^2 - x^3 - xy$ |
| $x$ | $x^3 - 8x^2 + 1$ | $3$ |

As you can see from the examples, a polynomial is a sum of one or more terms. Each term is called a monomial.

### *Definitions*

**A monomial is the product of a number, the coefficient, and one or more variables raised to nonnegative integer powers.**

The coefficient can be any real number. Most of the polynomials you will work with in this chapter will have integer or rational coefficients.

The **degree of a monomial** with only one variable is the exponent of the variable. If a monomial has more than one variable, the degree is the sum of the exponents of each variable.

## Example 1

**Problem** Name the coefficient, variable, and degree of each monomial.

**a.** $3x^2$ **b.** $-4a^5$ **c.** $b^3$

**d.** $-\frac{1}{2}$ **e.** $7x^3y^5$

**Solution**

| | Coefficient | Variable | Degree |
|---|---|---|---|
| **a.** $3x^2$ | 3 | $x$ | 2 |
| **b.** $-4a^5$ | $-4$ | $a$ | 5 |
| **c.** $b^3$ | 1 | $b$ | 3 |
| **d.** $-\frac{1}{2}$ | $-\frac{1}{2}$ | none | 0 |
| **e.** $7x^3y^5$ | 7 | $x$ and $y$ | $3 + 5 = 8$ |

Although there is not a variable in the expression, you can write $-\frac{1}{2}$ as $-\frac{1}{2}x^0$. Remember that any expression raised to the 0 power equals 1. Also, you can use any variable in this expression since there is not any context given.

You can define a polynomial as the sum of any number of monomials like these. Sometimes, a polynomial is made up of only one monomial.

| | Coefficient | Variables | Degree |
|---|---|---|---|
| $7x^3y^5$ | 7 | $x, y$ | 3 in $x$<br>5 in $y$ |

## Definition

A **polynomial** is a monomial or a sum of two or more monomials.

## Facts and Notation

There are many conventions for polynomials—conventions that have to do with the way people prefer to do things rather than with the algebra. You will use the following conventions in this book.

- Coefficients can be any real number. However, most of the polynomials in this book will have integer coefficients. Unless explicitly stated otherwise, assume that all coefficients are integers.
- Polynomials can have any number of variables. However, most polynomials in this book are of one variable. Unless explicitly stated otherwise, assume that *polynomial* means a polynomial of a single variable.

You can think of a polynomial such as $ax^2 + bx + c$ as a polynomial in 4 variables: $a$, $b$, $c$, and $x$. However, in most cases in this book, the polynomial is in $x$, with the other letters being unknown coefficients. The text is explicit about which letters are variables and which letters are unknown coefficients.

An unknown coefficient is also known as a **parameter**.

## Definition

The **degree of a polynomial** is the greatest degree among all the monomials in the polynomial.

Here are some examples.

- $13x^5 - 9x^3 + \frac{2}{5}x^2 + \frac{1}{7}x - 13$ has degree 5.
- $\frac{13}{2}y - 4y^2 + 9$ has degree 2.
- $2s$ has degree 1.
- 17 has degree 0 (think of $17x^0$).

There are special names for some polynomials in one variable.

| Degree | Type of Polynomial |
|---|---|
| 1 | linear |
| 2 | quadratic |
| 3 | cubic |
| 4 | quartic |
| 5 | quintic |

## For Discussion

Find polynomials that satisfy each condition. If it is impossible to satisfy the condition, explain why.

1. a cubic polynomial with three terms, all of different degrees
2. a linear polynomial with two terms, both of different degrees
3. a linear polynomial with three terms, all of different degrees

Polynomials have an arithmetic that is very similar to the arithmetic of numbers. In fact, since each variable is just a placeholder for a number, you might expect that all of the operations of number arithmetic would apply to polynomials. You may also think the basic rules apply the same way.

## For You to Do

For Problems 4–7, is each result always a polynomial? Explain.

4. sum of two polynomials
5. product of two polynomials
6. difference of two polynomials
7. quotient of two polynomials

Adding polynomials is like adding any expressions. You combine the like terms to make a simplified expression. Two terms in a polynomial are like terms when they meet the following conditions.

- All variables are the same.
- The exponents of the variables are the same.

| Terms | Variable | Exponent | Like Terms |
|---|---|---|---|
| $7x^3$ | $x$ | 3 | |
| $3x^3$ | $x$ | 3 | yes |
| $2x^5$ | $x$ | 5 | |
| $11x$ | $x$ | 1 | no |
| $x^2$ | $x$ | 2 | |
| $3y^2$ | $y$ | 2 | no |

The expressions $3x^3$ and $3x^4$ are not like terms even though they have the same coefficient. Explain.

## Example 2

**Problem** Calculate the sum and product of $x^2 - 6x + 5$ and $3x + 7$.

**Solution** Calculate the sum by combining like terms.

$$\begin{aligned}(x^2 - 6x + 5) + (3x + 7) &= (x^2 - 6x + 5) + (3x + 7)\\ &= x^2 - 6x + 3x + 5 + 7\\ &= x^2 + (-6 + 3)x + (5 + 7)\\ &= x^2 - 3x + 12\end{aligned}$$

Calculate the product by expanding. Then collect like terms.

$$\begin{aligned}(x^2 - 6x + 5)(3x + 7) &= 3x(x^2 - 6x + 5) + 7(x^2 - 6x + 5)\\ &= 3x^3 - 18x^2 + 15x + 7x^2 - 42x + 35\\ &= 3x^3 + ((-18) + 7)x^2 + (15 - 42)x + 35\\ &= 3x^3 - 11x^2 - 27x + 35\end{aligned}$$

Expand by multiplying everything in the first polynomial by 3x. Then multiply by 7 and combine. What is another way to expand?

## For Discussion

**8.** Which basic rules of algebra do you use to combine like terms?

## For You to Do

**9.** What's Wrong Here? Jacob and Anna subtracted these polynomials. They got different answers.

$$3x^2 - 7x + 1 \text{ and } 10x^3 - x^2 + 3x$$

**Jacob**

$$\begin{aligned}(3x^2 - 7x + 1) - (10x^3 - x^2 + 3x) &= 3x^2 - 7x + 1 - 10x^3 - x^2 + 3x\\ &= -10x^3 + 2x^2 - 4x + 1\end{aligned}$$

**Anna**

$$\begin{aligned}(3x^2 - 7x + 1) - (10x^3 - x^2 + 3x) &= 3x^2 - 7x + 1 - 10x^3 + x^2 - 3x\\ &= -10x^3 + 4x^2 - 10x + 1\end{aligned}$$

Who is correct? What mistake did the other person make?

**Habits of Mind**

**Check your work.** Plug any number into the two expressions and subtract the results. Then plug the same number into each of the answers that Jacob and Anna found. If the results are different, you know that the answer is incorrect. If they are the same, you have evidence that they might be correct.

## For You to Do

Expand each expression. Combine like terms to get a polynomial answer. Be careful of negative signs!

**10.** $3x^2 - 7x + 1 - 2(10x^3 - x^2 + 3x)$

**11.** $(3x - 1)(x^2 + 2x + 5)$

## In-Class Experiment

Develop two theorems that answer the following questions.

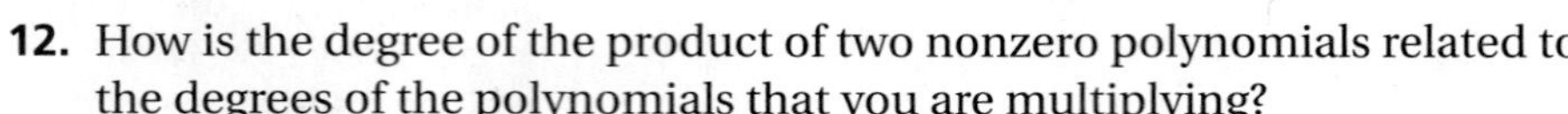

**12.** How is the degree of the product of two nonzero polynomials related to the degrees of the polynomials that you are multiplying?

Why is it important that the polynomials be nonzero?

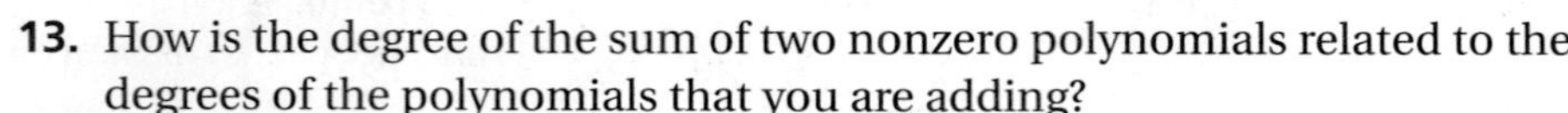

**13.** How is the degree of the sum of two nonzero polynomials related to the degrees of the polynomials that you are adding?

Here are some polynomials that you can use to develop your theorems.

- $x^2 + 4x + 5$
- $-2x^5 + 7x - 1$
- $3x + 7$
- $7x^3 - 2x^2 + 1$
- $2x^5 + 5$
- $14x$
- $9$
- $x^9 + x^3 + 1$
- $4x^3 + 2x + 1$

## Exercises Practicing Habits of Mind

### Check Your Understanding

1. Find two polynomials with a sum and product that have the following degrees. If you cannot find the polynomials, explain why.
   **a.** The sum has degree 3 and the product has degree 6.
   **b.** The sum has degree 4 and the product has degree 2.
   **c.** The sum has degree 4 and the product has degree 4.
   **d.** The sum has degree 2 and the product has degree 1.

2. Take It Further Find two polynomials with a sum that has degree 1 and a product that has degree 4. If you cannot find the two polynomials, explain why.

3. **a.** Find two polynomials with the same degree that have a sum of $3x^2 + 7x + 4$.
   **b.** Find two polynomials with different degrees that have a sum of $3x^2 + 7x + 4$.
   **c.** Find two polynomials that have a sum of 4.
   **d.** Find two polynomials that have a product of $x^2 - 1$.

4. Write About It How does the degree of a polynomial compare to the degree of that polynomial squared? Support your conjecture with at least three examples.

## On Your Own

**5.** Find two polynomials that meet each condition.

**a.** The product has degree 6.

**b.** The product has degree 1.

**c.** The sum has degree 4 and the product has degree 6.

**6. a.** Use $p(x) = x^2 + 4x + 9$. Find a polynomial $r(x)$ such that $p(x) + r(x) = 2x^2 - 6x + 14$.

**b.** Find a polynomial $s(x)$ such that $p(x) + s(x) = 2x^2 + 14$.

**c.** Find a polynomial $t(x)$ such that $p(x) + t(x)$ has degree 2 and $p(x) \cdot t(x)$ has degree 3.

**7.** Find the value of $a$ such that $(x + a)(x + 3) = x^2 + 5x + 6$ is an identity. Copying and completing the expansion box at the right may be helpful.

| | $x$ | $+3$ |
|---|---|---|
| $x$ | ■ | ■ |
| $a$ | ■ | ■ |

**8.** **Standardized Test Prep** Use $q(x) = 2x - 3$ and $r(x) = 2x^2 + 3x - 5$. Find $s(x) = q(x) + r(x)$ and $p(x) = q(x) \cdot r(x)$.

**A.** $s(x) = 2x^2 + 5x + 8$ and $p(x) = 4x^3 + 12x^2 - 19x + 15$

**B.** $s(x) = 2x^2 + 5x + 8$ and $p(x) = 4x^3 - x + 15$

**C.** $s(x) = 2x^2 + 5x - 8$ and $p(x) = 4x^3 - 19x + 15$

**D.** $s(x) = 2x^2 + 5x - 8$ and $p(x) = 4x^3 - 19x - 15$

**9.** **Write About It** Suppose you need to explain the phrase *like terms* to a student who has never heard it before. Write a definition of like terms. Explain how you add and subtract them. Be as precise as possible.

**10.** Suppose you make a frame for a square photo. The frame is 2 inches wide. Find the area of the frame if the photo has the following dimensions.

**a.** 3 in. by 3 in.

**b.** 9 in. by 9 in.

**c.** $x$ in. by $x$ in.

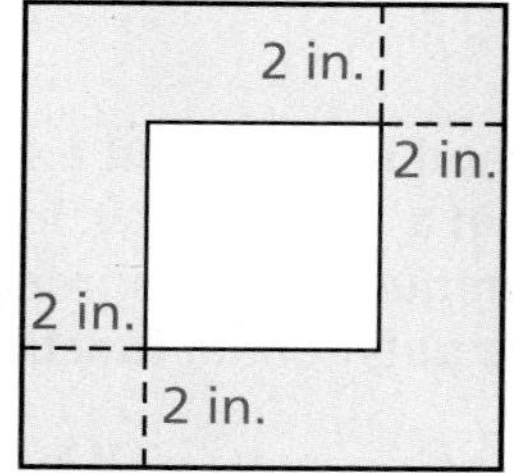


The area of the border does not include the area of the picture.

If each side of the photo is 6 inches, the area of the border is $(6 + 4)^2 - 6^2$ square inches.

## Maintain Your Skills

For Exercises 11–13, expand and combine like terms.

**11. a.** $(x + 1)^2 - x^2$ **b.** $(x + 1)^3 - x^3$

**c.** $(x + 1)^4 - x^4$ **d.** $(x + 1)^5 - x^5$

**12. a.** $(x + y)^2 - y^2$ **b.** $(x + y)^3 - y^3$

**c.** $(x + y)^4 - y^4$

**13. a.** $x(x - 1) + x$ **b.** $x(x - 1)(x - 2) + x(x - 1)$

**c.** $x(x - 1)(x - 2)(x - 3) + x(x - 1)(x - 2)$

# Making It Fit

**In previous courses, you learned how to find a simple function that fits a table if the inputs increase in a regular way. In *Making It Fit,* you will learn a general-purpose technique called Lagrange interpolation. You can use this technique to fit a polynomial function to any table.**

**By the end of this investigation, you will be able to answer questions like these.**

1. How can you find a polynomial that agrees with a table?
2. How can you find two different functions that agree with the same table?
3. What number comes next in the sequence 1, 4, 9, . . . ?

**You will learn how to**

- fit polynomials to tables
- work with linear combinations

**You will develop these habits and skills:**

- Use linear combinations of polynomials to determine new polynomials.
- Use zeros of polynomials to determine factors of polynomials.
- Find several functions that agree with a given table.
- Predict the results of calculations without having to carry them out.

In this latticework, pairs of apple-tree branches suggest polynomial-function graphs that agree at one point.

# 1.01 Getting Started

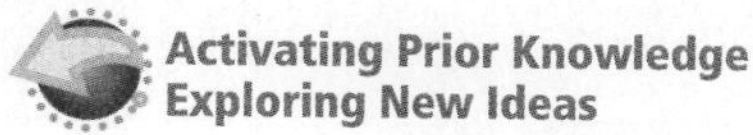


In previous courses, you learned some techniques for finding polynomial functions that agree with tables. Usually the tables started with 0 and had inputs that increased by 1. How do you handle inputs that are not arranged that way? What do you do if the inputs do not follow a simple pattern? Suppose you have to work with a graph like this.

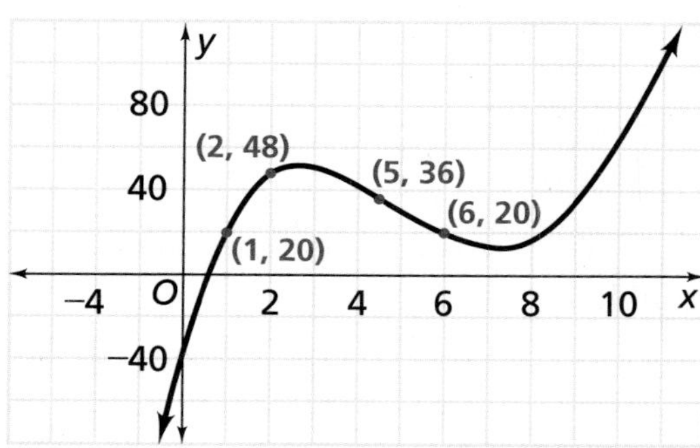


In this investigation, you will learn *Lagrange interpolation*. This technique will handle any data set that can come from a polynomial function.

## For You to Explore

In Problems 1–3, find a polynomial function that agrees with each table.

How can you check that the functions you find actually agree with the tables?

**1.**

| $n$ | $f(n)$ |
|---|---|
| 2 | 5 |
| 5 | 11 |
| 7 | 15 |

**2.**

| $n$ | $g(n)$ |
|---|---|
| 2 | 6 |
| 5 | 30 |
| 7 | 56 |

**3.**

| $x$ | $h(x)$ |
|---|---|
| 2 | 10 |
| 5 | 55 |
| 7 | 105 |

**4. a.** Find a quadratic function that agrees with the following table.

| $x$ | $k(x)$ |
|---|---|
| 1 | 0 |
| 3 | 0 |

**b.** Is the function you found the only quadratic function that agrees with the table? If it is, explain why. If not, find another one.

5. Find a quadratic function that agrees with each table.

a.

| $x$ | $j(x)$ |
|---|---|
| 1 | 20 |
| 3 | 0 |
| 6 | 0 |

b.

| $x$ | $n(x)$ |
|---|---|
| 1 | 0 |
| 3 | 12 |
| 6 | 0 |

c.

| $x$ | $m(x)$ |
|---|---|
| 1 | 0 |
| 3 | 0 |
| 6 | 60 |

d. Copy and complete the following table.

| $x$ | $j(x) + n(x) + m(x)$ |
|---|---|
| 1 | ■ |
| 3 | ■ |
| 6 | ■ |

6. Find a quadratic function $f$ that agrees with this table.

| $x$ | $f(x)$ |
|---|---|
| 1 | 20 |
| 3 | 12 |
| 6 | 60 |

7. Find a polynomial function $k$ that agrees with this table.

| $x$ | $k(x)$ |
|---|---|
| 1 | 10 |
| 3 | 12 |
| 6 | 45 |

8. Find a polynomial function $t$ that agrees with this table.

| $x$ | $t(x)$ |
|---|---|
| 1 | 84 |
| 5 | 48 |
| 8 | 42 |

9. Find a quadratic function $f$ such that the graph of $f$ contains the points in the graph.

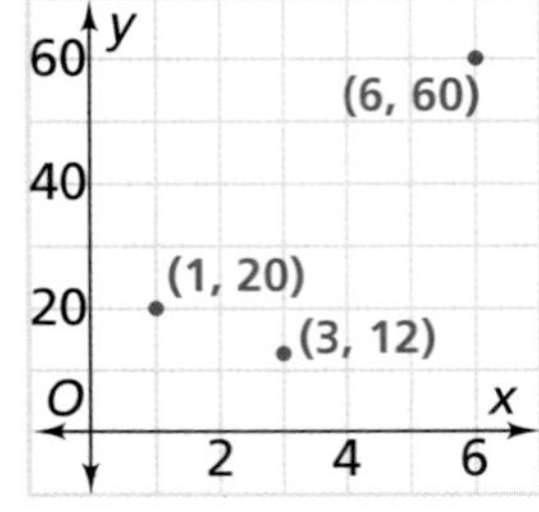

## Exercises *Practicing Habits of Mind*

### On Your Own

**10.** Suppose $f(x) = A(x - 1)(x - 4) + B(x - 1)(x - 6) + C(x - 4)(x - 6)$ for some numbers $A$, $B$, and $C$.

Sketch the graph of $f$.

**a.** Find the numbers $A$, $B$, and $C$ such that the graph of $f$ contains the points $(1, 45)$, $(4, 12)$, and $(6, 60)$.

**b.** Find the normal form of the polynomial that defines $f$.

**11.** Find a function that agrees with this table.

| x | r(x) |
|---|---|
| 1 | 45 |
| 4 | 12 |
| 6 | 60 |

**12.** Consider these two functions.

$$f(x) = 3x + 1$$
$$g(x) = 3x + 1 + 7(x - 1)(x - 2)(x - 4)(x + 1)$$

**a.** Copy and complete the following table.

| x | f(x) | g(x) |
|---|---|---|
| −2 | ■ | ■ |
| −1 | ■ | ■ |
| 0 | ■ | ■ |
| 1 | ■ | ■ |
| 2 | ■ | ■ |
| 3 | ■ | ■ |
| 4 | ■ | ■ |
| 5 | ■ | ■ |

**b.** On which inputs do $f$ and $g$ agree?

**c.** Are the inputs you found in part (a) the only inputs on which $f$ and $g$ agree? Explain.

**d.** Find the normal form of the polynomial that defines $g$.

**e.** Sketch the graphs of $f$ and $g$.

13. Let $f(x) = 4x - 3$.

**a.** Find a polynomial function that agrees with $f$ for the input 2 but differs from it for every other input.

**b.** Find a polynomial function that agrees with $f$ for the inputs 2, 5, and 7 but differs from $f$ for every other input.

## Maintain Your Skills

Suppose $f(x) = A(x - 1)(x - 4) + B(x - 1)(x - 6) + C(x - 4)(x - 6)$ for some numbers $A$, $B$, and $C$. For Exercises 14–18, use the information given about $f$ to do parts (a)–(d).

**a.** Find $A$, $B$, and $C$.

**b.** Find the normal form of the polynomial that defines $f$.

**c.** Sketch the graph of $f$.

**d.** Take It Further Find the minimum or maximum output of $f$.

**14.**

| $x$ | $f(x)$ |
|---|---|
| 1 | 60 |
| 4 | −18 |
| 6 | 20 |

**15.**

| $x$ | $f(x)$ |
|---|---|
| 1 | 60 |
| 4 | −18 |
| 6 | 10 |

**16.** The graph of $f$ contains (1, 0), (4, 6), and (6, 30).

**17.** The graph of $f$ contains (1, 0), (4, 6), and (6, −30).

**18.**

| $x$ | $f(x)$ |
|---|---|
| 1 | 30 |
| 4 | −6 |
| 6 | −30 |

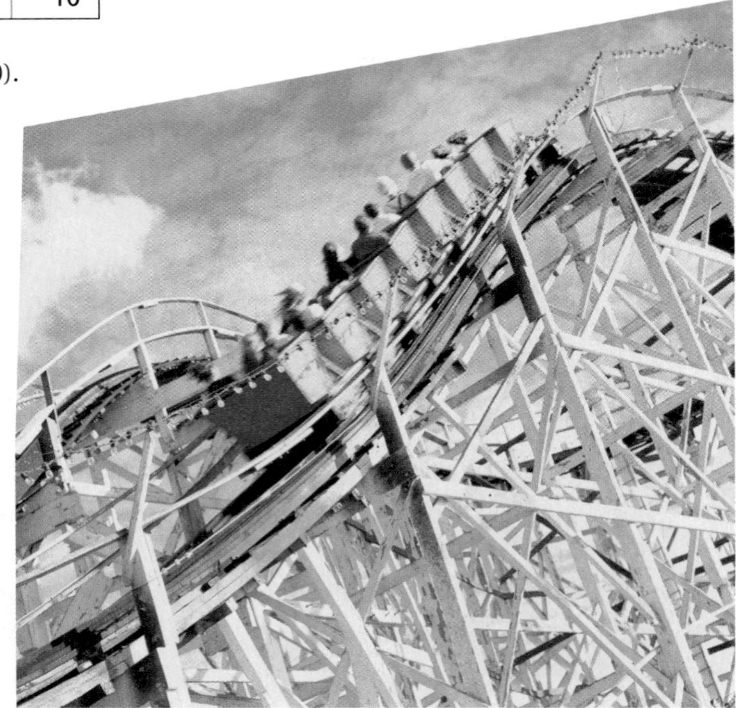

The cars are approaching the roller coaster's maximum.

# 1.02 Lagrange Interpolation—Fitting Polynomial Functions to Tables

In previous courses, you found rules to match the entries in tables. You developed some methods for fitting functions to tables. The methods were not general for two reasons.

- Most of the tables had inputs that started with 0 and increased by 1 in each row.
- The methods relied on your ability to spot patterns.

In this lesson you will develop a way of matching the values in a table for any $n$ distinct points using a polynomial of degree less than $n$. If you just rely on cleverness, it can be hard to find a function that agrees with a table (very hard for some tables), so it is very useful to have a method that will work for all tables.

The polynomial you get using this method may not be the simplest function that matches the $n$ values in your table. It may look so messy that you want to use a computer or calculator to simplify it. But the method always works. Given a table, you will be able to find a function every time. And if the simplest function that matches the table is a polynomial, the method gives you the unique simplest rule for the table.

You learned that a constant first difference means there is an exact linear fit. A constant nonzero second difference means there is an exact quadratic fit.

You will prove that the rule you get is unique in a later lesson.

## Minds in Action

*Derman and Sasha are working on Problem 6 from the Getting Started lesson.*

Table A

| Input, x | Output, f(x) |
|---|---|
| 1 | 20 |
| 3 | 12 |
| 6 | 60 |

**Derman** I wish a couple of these outputs were 0. Then this would be easy.

**Sasha** Derman, that gives me an idea. We could split up Table A this way.

*Sasha writes the following three tables on the board.*

| x | g(x) |
|---|---|
| 1 | 20 |
| 3 | 0 |
| 6 | 0 |

+

| x | h(x) |
|---|---|
| 1 | 0 |
| 3 | 12 |
| 6 | 0 |

+

| x | j(x) |
|---|---|
| 1 | 0 |
| 3 | 0 |
| 6 | 60 |

**Sasha** I can find polynomials that fit these tables. Look what happens if we add $g(x) + h(x) + j(x)$.

| x | g(x) + h(x) + j(x) |
|---|---|
| 1 | 20 + 0 + 0 = 20 |
| 3 | 0 + 12 + 0 = 12 |
| 6 | 0 + 0 + 60 = 60 |

We're back to Table A. So if we can figure out polynomials that fit the three simpler tables, we can get a polynomial that fits Table A. Let's look at the first table.

| x | g(x) |
|---|---|
| 1 | 20 |
| 3 | 0 |
| 6 | 0 |

Let's start with $x \mapsto (x - 3)(x - 6)$. At least that agrees with our table for $x = 3$ and $x = 6$.

**Derman** Well, in that function, $1 \mapsto 10$, so that doesn't agree with the table.

**Sasha** OK, what about a multiple of that function? Try $g(x) = A(x - 3)(x - 6)$ for some $A$. Let's figure out what $A$ has to be in order for $g(1)$ to be 20.

$$20 = g(1) = A(1 - 3)(1 - 6)$$
$$20 = A(-2)(-5)$$
$$20 = 10A$$
$$A = 2$$

So $g(x) = 2(x - 3)(x - 6) = 2x^2 - 18x + 36$.

**Derman** OK, that works. And $h(x)$ could be $B(x - 1)(x - 6)$ for some number $B$. Then I can figure out what $B$ is.

$$12 = h(3) = B(3 - 1)(3 - 6)$$
$$12 = B(2)(-3)$$
$$12 = -6B$$
$$B = -2$$

So $h(x) = -2(x - 1)(x - 6) = -2x^2 + 14x - 12$.

**Habits of Mind**

**Determine the process.** How might Sasha have known that $x \mapsto (x - 3)(x - 6)$ agrees with their table for $x = 3$ and $x = 6$? How does Derman know that $1 \mapsto 10$?

Do you agree with Derman that $g(x) = 2(x - 3)(x - 6)$ works?

**Sasha** While you were doing that, I figured out a function for the last table.

$$j(x) = 4(x - 1)(x - 3) = 4x^2 - 16x + 12$$

**Derman** Adding $g(x) + h(x) + j(x)$, we get $f(x) = 4x^2 - 20x + 36$.

And here is its graph.

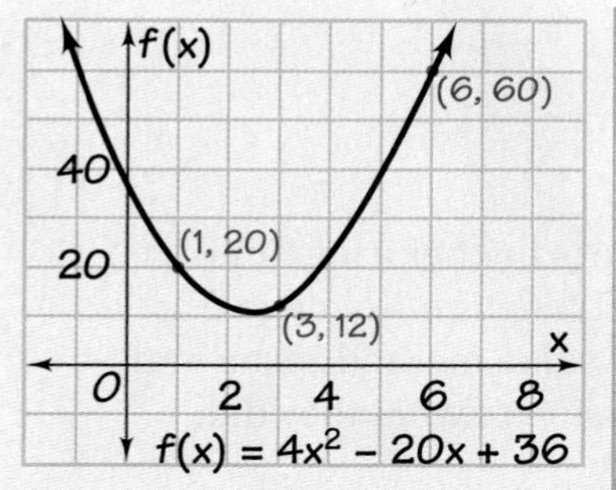


**Habits of Mind**

**Establish a process.** How can you check that the function $f(x)$ fits the original table?

**Sasha** Hey, if we write $f(x)$ without expanding all the pieces, we can see more.

*Sasha writes an equation on the board.*

$$f(x) = 2(x - 3)(x - 6) - 2(x - 1)(x - 6) + 4(x - 1)(x - 3)$$

**Derman** That looks much more complicated.

**Sasha** Yes, but it lets you see the way it all works. Look what happens if you replace $x$ with 1.

**Derman** Oh yeah—everything disappears except the first bit.

**Sasha** So, if we had another table with inputs 1, 3, and 6, and if the output for 1 were 30, I could change the $2(x - 3)(x - 6)$ to $3(x - 3)(x - 6)$.

**Derman** And you could adjust the other numbers to make this expression work for any table with inputs 1, 3, and 6. So I guess the complicated form is pretty useful.

Why would Sasha change the 2 to a 3?

## For You to Do

1. Find a polynomial function with a graph that contains (1, 80), (3, 36), and (6, 30).

Remember to check that the polynomial you find actually agrees with the input-output pairs.

## Example

**Problem** Suppose you have the following table.

| Input, $x$ | Output, $f(x)$ |
|---|---|
| 1 | 20 |
| 2 | 48 |
| 5 | 36 |
| 6 | 20 |

If you graph the data, you can determine that there is neither a linear nor a quadratic fit. So, you are looking for a polynomial function—of degree at least 3—that agrees with the table. You can use the same method Sasha and Derman used. Here is a somewhat streamlined version of what they did.

**Solution** Suppose the following strange rule gives a function $f(x)$. You will determine the numbers $A$, $B$, $C$, and $D$ later.

> Notice that, no matter what the values for *A*, *B*, *C*, and *D* are, this function cannot have degree greater than 3.

$$\begin{aligned} f(x) = {} & A(x-1)(x-2)(x-5) + B(x-1)(x-2)(x-6) \\ & + C(x-1)(x-5)(x-6) + D(x-2)(x-5)(x-6) \end{aligned}$$

Why would anyone write a function this way? This is just a sum of functions, like the sum of functions Sasha and Derman found. Now you can find expressions for $f(1)$, $f(2)$, $f(5)$, and $f(6)$.

$$\begin{aligned} f(1) &= A(1-1)(1-2)(1-5) + B(1-1)(1-2)(1-6) \\ &\quad + C(1-1)(1-5)(1-6) + D(1-2)(1-5)(1-6) \\ &= 0 + 0 + 0 + D(1-2)(1-5)(1-6) \\ &= D(-1)(-4)(-5) \\ &= -20D \end{aligned}$$

In the same way, you can find $f(2)$, $f(5)$, and $f(6)$.

$$f(2) = C(2-1)(2-5)(2-6) = 12C$$
$$f(5) = B(5-1)(5-2)(5-6) = -12B$$
$$f(6) = A(6-1)(6-2)(6-5) = 20A$$

But you know $f(1)$, $f(2)$, $f(5)$, and $f(6)$. They are in the table.

$$f(1) = 20 = -20D, \text{ so } D = -1$$
$$f(2) = 48 = 12C, \text{ so } C = 4$$
$$f(5) = 36 = -12B, \text{ so } B = -3$$
$$f(6) = 20 = 20A, \text{ so } A = 1$$

By substituting in these values, you find a formula for $f(x)$.

$$\begin{aligned} f(x) = {} & (x-1)(x-2)(x-5) - 3(x-1)(x-2)(x-6) \\ & + 4(x-1)(x-5)(x-6) - 1(x-2)(x-5)(x-6) \end{aligned}$$

Too messy, you say. But a CAS can simplify this with no trouble. You could too, if you needed to. The formula simplifies to

$$f(x) = x^3 - 16x^2 + 69x - 34$$

This is a well-behaved cubic that agrees with the table. How is this similar to the method Sasha and Derman used?

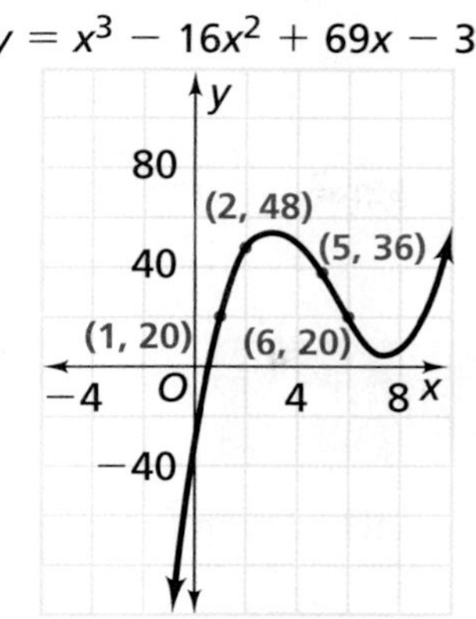


Here is the graph.

This method of finding a polynomial to agree with a table is **Lagrange interpolation.**

## For You to Do

**2.** Use Lagrange interpolation to find a polynomial function with a graph that contains (1, 20), (2, 48), and (5, 36).

## Historical Perspective

Joseph-Louis Lagrange was born in Turin, Italy, in 1736, and died in Paris, France, in 1813. His interest in advanced mathematics began when he read a calculus book by Edmond Halley (of Halley's comet fame).

Lagrange was a professor of geometry at the Royal Artillery School in Turin from 1755 (at age 19) to 1766 and helped to found the Royal Academy of Sciences there in 1757. In 1766, when Leonhard Euler left his post as director of the Berlin Academy of Sciences, Lagrange succeeded him. In 1787, Lagrange left Berlin to become a member of the French Academy of Sciences, where he remained for the rest of his career.

Lagrange contributed many results and techniques to the field of algebra. Lagrange interpolation is one of these contributions. Another contribution was a new proof that every integer is the sum of the squares of at most four integers. His interest in physics and mechanics led him to devise a new way of writing down Newton's laws of motion.

Joseph-Louis Lagrange

# Exercises Practicing Habits of Mind

## Check Your Understanding

In Exercises 1–4, find a polynomial function that agrees with each table.

**1.**

| Input | Output |
|---|---|
| 1 | 12 |
| 2 | 8 |
| 4 | 36 |

**2.**

| Input | Output |
|---|---|
| 1 | 2 |
| 2 | 11 |
| 3 | 20 |

**3.**

| Input | Output |
|---|---|
| 1 | 2 |
| 2 | 11 |
| 3 | 28 |

**4.**

| Input | Output |
|---|---|
| 1 | 1 |
| 2 | 22 |
| 3 | 61 |
| 4 | 124 |

**5.** Sasha has a method for solving Exercise 4. She writes $f(x) = A + B(x - 1) + C(x - 1)(x - 2) + D(x - 1)(x - 2)(x - 3)$. Then she uses $f(1) = 1$ to find $A$, $f(2) = 22$ to find $B$, and so on.

**a.** Find $A$, $B$, $C$, and $D$ using Sasha's method.

**b.** Do you get the same rule for $f$ as you got in Exercise 4?

**6.** **Write About It** Sometimes, when you might expect a cubic, Lagrange interpolation produces a polynomial of lesser degree. How might this happen? (*Hint:* You can use Exercise 2 as an example.)

A curved underground hose joining 4 sprinkler heads could suggest a unique polynomial function of degree 3 or less.

## On Your Own

**7.** A radio show offers a prize to the first caller who can predict the next term in this sequence.

$$\{1, 2, 4, 8, 16\}$$

**a.** What do you get if you use common sense?

**b.** What do you get if you use Lagrange interpolation? (You will need a CAS for this one.)

8. Find a polynomial function that agrees with this table.

| Input | Output |
|---|---|
| 1 | −6 |
| 3 | 166 |
| 6 | 7159 |
| 8 | 31,291 |
| 9 | 56,938 |
| 12 | 243,787 |

9. **Write About It** Explain Lagrange interpolation in your own words.

10. Suppose you have a table that has five entries. What is the greatest possible degree of polynomial that you would need to match the table using Lagrange interpolation? What is the least possible degree of polynomial that you would need?

For Exercises 11 and 12, sketch the graphs!

11. Find a nonconstant polynomial function $h$ such that

$$h(1) = h(2) = h(3) = h(4) = 0$$

12. Find a nonconstant polynomial function $j$ such that

$$j(1) = j(2) = j(3) = 3$$

13. **Standardized Test Prep** Tony has the graph of a cubic function through the four points $(-2, 0)$, $(0, -6)$, $(1, -12)$, and $(3, 30)$. He has written the following formula to approximate the function.

$$\begin{aligned} f(x) &= Ax(x-1)(x-3) + B(x+2)(x-1)(x-3) \\ &\quad + Cx(x+2)(x-3) + Dx(x+2)(x-1) \end{aligned}$$

If the value of $C$ is 2 and the value of $D$ is 1, what are the values of $A$ and $B$?

**A.** $A = -1, B = 0$ **B.** $A = 0, B = -1$

**C.** $A = 1, B = -1$ **D.** $A = 1, B = 1$

14. You may know a formula for the sum of the numbers from 1 to $n$. If you do not know it, you can figure it out. You can model the sum of the first $n$ numbers with a recursively defined function $s$.

$$s(n) = \begin{cases} 1 & \text{if } n = 1 \\ s(n-1) + n & \text{if } n > 1 \end{cases}$$

**a.** Explain why the recursion above yields the following sum.

$$s(n) = 1 + 2 + 3 + \cdots + (n-1) + n$$

This is the sum of the integers between 1 and $n$.

**b.** Make a table of $s(n)$. Find a simple polynomial function $S$ that agrees with $s$ for all values in your table.

**15.** Take It Further Use the method in Exercise 14 to find a formula for the sum of the squares between 1 and $n$. The recursive function below gives the sum of the squares of the numbers from 1 to $n$.

$$q(n) = \begin{cases} 1 & \text{if } n = 1 \\ q(n-1) + n^2 & \text{if } n > 1 \end{cases}$$

Find a closed-form polynomial function $Q$ that agrees with $q$.

## Maintain Your Skills

**16.** For each function $f$, find $f(5)$ and $f(7)$. Then write $f$ in normal form.

**a.** $f(x) = \frac{6}{7-5}(x-5) + \frac{3}{5-7}(x-7)$

**b.** $f(x) = \frac{12}{7-5}(x-5) + \frac{-20}{5-7}(x-7)$

**c.** $f(x) = \frac{b_2}{7-5}(x-5) + \frac{b_1}{5-7}(x-7)$

**d.** Take It Further Suppose $f(x) = \frac{b_2}{a_2 - a_1}(x - a_1) + \frac{b_1}{a_1 - a_2}(x - a_2)$. Find $f(a_1)$ and $f(a_2)$. Write $f$ in normal form.

**17.** For each function $f$, find $f(3)$, $f(5)$, and $f(7)$. Then write $f$ in normal form.

**a.** $f(x) = \frac{6}{(7-3)(7-5)}(x-3)(x-5) + \frac{4}{(5-3)(5-7)}(x-3)(x-7) + \frac{9}{(3-5)(3-7)}(x-5)(x-7)$

**b.** $f(x) = \frac{16}{(7-3)(7-5)}(x-3)(x-5) + \frac{-9}{(5-3)(5-7)}(x-3)(x-7) + \frac{29}{(3-5)(3-7)}(x-5)(x-7)$

**c.** $f(x) = \frac{b_3}{(7-3)(7-5)}(x-3)(x-5) + \frac{b_2}{(5-3)(5-7)}(x-3)(x-7) + \frac{b_1}{(3-5)(3-7)}(x-5)(x-7)$

**d.** Take It Further Suppose $f(x) = \frac{b_3}{(a_3 - a_1)(a_3 - a_2)}(x - a_1)(x - a_2) + \frac{b_2}{(a_2 - a_1)(a_2 - a_3)}(x - a_1)(x - a_3) + \frac{b_1}{(a_1 - a_2)(a_1 - a_3)}(x - a_2)(x - a_3)$. Find $f(a_1)$, $f(a_2)$, and $f(a_3)$.

Write $f$ in normal form.

# 1.03 Agreeing to Disagree—Finding Functions with Specific Values

More than one polynomial function can agree with the inputs and outputs in a table.

## Minds in Action

*Tony and Sasha are looking at Table A.*

**Table A**

| Input | Output |
|---|---|
| 1 | 4 |
| 2 | 6 |
| 3 | 8 |
| 4 | 10 |

**Tony** Sure, $h(x) = 2x + 2$ is a polynomial function that works. But I think there are other functions that agree with the table. I couldn't write down a rule, but I can draw a graph. Look.

*Tony draws on the board.*

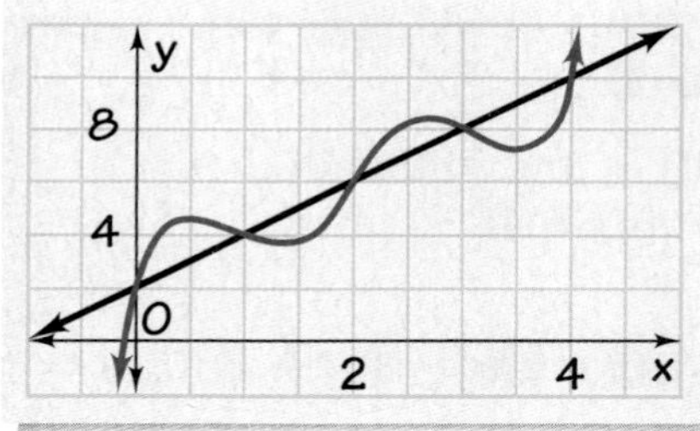


**Sasha** Well, that looks like the graph of a function, all right, but how do you know it's the graph of a *polynomial* function? Can you find a polynomial that's not linear and that goes through the points you get from the table?

Why might Sasha say this "looks like the graph of a function"?

**Tony** Hmm . . . sure! I just add another input to the table. Let's say 5. Then I make the output something other than $2 \cdot 5 + 2$. I'll make it 13.

Table A

| Input | Output |
|---|---|
| 1 | 4 |
| 2 | 6 |
| 3 | 8 |
| 4 | 10 |
| 5 | 13 |

**Tony and Sasha** . . . and then use Lagrange interpolation!

**Sasha** So, all those problems on the standardized tests that ask you to find the next term in a sequence are misleading—*any* number could be the next term in a sequence.

**Tony** The test writers must not know about Lagrange interpolation.

## For You to Do

1. Find a polynomial function that agrees with Tony's extension of Table A.

A CAS might be helpful here.

*Tony and Sasha are still thinking about the original Table A.*

**Sasha** I think I have another way to trick the table, a way that might be easier than Lagrange interpolation. We know that $x \mapsto 2x + 2$ fits what we have. If I add to that another polynomial that outputs zero for the inputs 1, 2, 3, and 4, the result will still produce the outputs of Table A.

**Tony** How are you going to find a function like that?

**Sasha** I remember we did that a few days ago.

*Sasha thumbs through her notebook.*

**Sasha** Here it is: Exercise 11 from Lesson 1.02. This will do the trick.

$$x \mapsto (x - 1)(x - 2)(x - 3)(x - 4)$$

**Tony** So $r(x) = 2x + 2 + (x - 1)(x - 2)(x - 3)(x - 4)$ will agree with Table A. And it is not linear—it has degree 4.

Why does Tony's polynomial have degree 4?

**Sasha** So will $t(x) = 2x + 2 + 3(x - 1)(x - 2)(x - 3)(x - 4)$ and $q(x) = 2x + 2 + 275(x - 1)(x - 2)(x - 3)(x - 4)$.

For that matter,
$x \mapsto 2x + 2 + (\text{any polynomial}) \cdot (x - 1)(x - 2)(x - 3)(x - 4)$
will work.

**Tony** I think we're onto something. I wonder if every polynomial function that agrees with the table can be built by this method.

**Sasha** We need to think about that.

## For Discussion

2. Can you write the polynomial Tony got using Lagrange interpolation in Sasha's form below? Explain.

   $x \mapsto 2x + 2 + (\text{any polynomial}) \cdot (x - 1)(x - 2)(x - 3)(x - 4)$

## Developing Habits of Mind

**Establish a process.** You can use Tony and Sasha's new method to find a polynomial that agrees with a given function on any finite set of inputs but that takes on a different specific value at some other input. For example, suppose you want a function $f$ that agrees with $x \mapsto 3x$ for $x$-values of 1, 3, and 4, but you want $f(2)$ to be 12. Start with the following equation.

$$f(x) = 3x + A(x - 1)(x - 3)(x - 4)$$

This function agrees with $x \mapsto 3x$ for $x$-values of 1, 3, and 4. Then you can figure out $A$ from the equation below.

$$12 = f(2) = 3 \cdot 2 + A(2 - 1)(2 - 3)(2 - 5)$$

## For You to Do

**3.** Find the value of $A$.

**4.** Find a function that agrees with $x \mapsto 3x$ at 1, 3, and 5 but that takes on the value 21 at $x = 2$.

## Check Your Understanding

**1.** Graph the functions $f$ and $h$ with equations $f(x) = 2x + 2 + 3(x - 1)(x - 2)(x - 3)$ and $h(x) = 2x + 2$. List the points where the graphs intersect.

**2.** Find and graph two different functions $j$ and $k$ that agree with $h(x) = 2x + 2$ for $x$-values of 1, 2, and 3. How can you produce more functions like these?

**3.** Consider the function with outputs 1, 3, and 5 for $x = 1, 2, 3$.

**a.** If someone asked you to come up with the next term, what would you say? What simple rule could define this function?

**b.** Give another possible next term and the rule that produces it.

**c.** Find a rule that gives 19 as the next term.

**d.** Find a rule that gives 1 as the next term.

4. Suppose you see the following problem on a multiple-choice test.

What is the next number in the sequence?

2, 4, 6, . . .

**A.** 0 **B.** 8 **C.** 10 **D.** 80

Show that any of these answers could be correct. To do this, you may want to set up tables like the one at the right.

| Input | Output |
|---|---|
| 1 | 2 |
| 2 | 4 |
| 3 | 6 |
| 4 | ■ |

5. Use the following rules to play the Polynomial Game. This game requires at least three players.

- Choose one player to be the Polynomial Keeper. The other players are the Finders.
- The Polynomial Keeper writes down a (secret) polynomial function and gives one input-output pair to the Finders.
- The Finders guess a polynomial function. If they are successful, the Keeper gets one point. If they are not successful, the Keeper gives them another input-output pair.
- The Keeper continues to give out pairs until the Finders figure out the polynomial. The Keeper scores one point for every pair the Finders need to figure out the polynomial. Then the Keeper becomes a Finder and a new Keeper is chosen.
- The player with the most points at the end of the game wins.

**a.** How many points is a Keeper likely to get for a quadratic function?

**b.** How many points is a Keeper likely to get for a quintic function? A quintic function is a polynomial of degree 5.

**c.** How many points is a Keeper likely to get for a polynomial of degree $n$?

## On Your Own

For Exercises 6–9, find a function that agrees with the given function for the given inputs but is not equal to the given function. Graph your function and the given function on the same set of axes. Identify the points where the graphs intersect.

**6.** $x \mapsto 3x - 1;\ x = 0, 1, 2, 3$

**7.** $x \mapsto 3x - 1;\ x = 0, 1, 2, 3, 4$

**8.** $x \mapsto 4 - x^2;\ x = 0, 1, 2, 3$

**9.** $x \mapsto 4 - x^2;\ x = 0, 1, 2, 3, 4$

10. Is there another linear function that agrees with $x \mapsto 3x - 1$ at the inputs 1 and 2? Explain.

11. **a.** Is there another quadratic function that agrees with $x \mapsto 4 - x^2$ at the inputs 1 and 2? Explain.

    **b.** Is there another quadratic function that agrees with $x \mapsto 4 - x^2$ at the inputs 1, 2, and 3? Explain.

12. **Write About It** Describe two methods for finding a function that agrees with $x \mapsto x^2$ at $x = 1, 2,$ and 3 and that takes on the value 7 at $x = 4$.

13. **Standardized Test Prep** You are given three points on a line. You wish to find a function that has the same values as the linear function at those three points but is different everywhere else. What is the least possible degree of a polynomial function through those points?

    **A.** 2 **B.** 3
    **C.** 4 **D.** 5

14. **Write About It** Is there a nonconstant polynomial that takes on the value 0 at every integer? Explain.

## Maintain Your Skills

15. Expand each product. Describe and explain at least two patterns among the coefficients in the collection of answers.

    **a.** $(x - 1)(x - 2)$
    **b.** $(x - 1)(x - 2)(x - 3)$
    **c.** $(x - 1)(x - 2)(x - 3)(x - 4)$
    **d.** $(x - 1)(x - 2)(x - 3)(x - 4)(x - 5)$
    **e.** $(x - 1)(x - 2)(x - 3)(x - 4)(x - 5)(x - 6)$
    **f.** $(x - 1)(x - 2)(x - 3)(x - 4)(x - 5)(x - 6)(x - 7)$
    **g.** $(x - 1)(x - 2)(x - 3)(x - 4)(x - 5)(x - 6)(x - 7)(x - 8)$

Use each answer to help you get the next one.

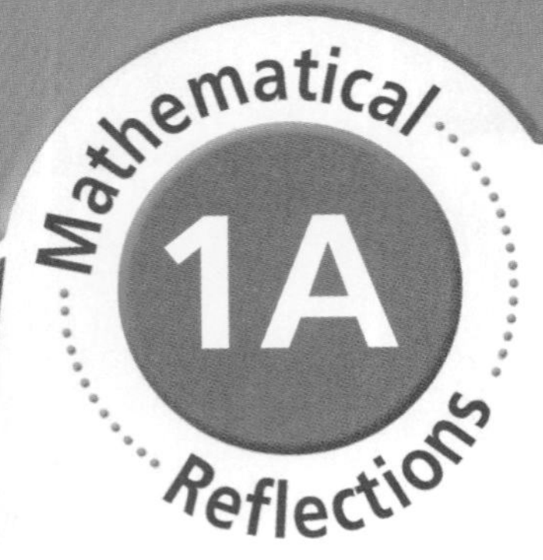


**In this investigation, you learned how to use linear combinations of polynomials to determine new polynomials and find polynomials that agree with a given table. These exercises will help you summarize what you have learned.**

In Exercises 1 and 2, find a polynomial function that agrees with each table.

**1.**

| Input | Output |
|---|---|
| 1 | 3 |
| 2 | 7 |
| 4 | 21 |

**2.**

| Input | Output |
|---|---|
| 1 | 4 |
| 3 | 40 |
| 5 | 156 |

**3.** Find a nonconstant polynomial $h$ such that $h(1) = h(2) = h(4) = 7$.

**4.** Find a polynomial function that agrees with $x \rightarrow x^3 - x$ at $x = 1, 2,$ and 3 but has the value 0 at $x = 4$.

**5.** Take It Further Suppose you define the function $q$ for nonnegative integers using the following rule.

$$q(x) = \begin{cases} 1 & \text{if } x = 0 \\ q(x-1) + 3x^2 - x + 1 & \text{if } x > 0 \end{cases}$$

Find a polynomial function that agrees with $q$ on its domain.

**6.** How can you find a polynomial that agrees with a table?

7. How can you find two different functions that agree with the same table?

8. What number comes next in the sequence 1, 4, 9, . . . ?

## Vocabulary

In this investigation, you learned this term. Make sure you understand what it means and how to use it.

- **Lagrange interpolation**

Through any three noncollinear points there is a unique polynomial of degree 2 with a graph that fits the points.

# Factors, Roots, and Zeros

In *Factors, Roots, and Zeros,* you will discover some important facts about polynomials and polynomial functions. You will study the connection between the zeros of a polynomial function and the factors of the polynomial. You may have already learned the "form-implies-function" principle:

> If you can transform one polynomial into another with the basic rules of algebra, the polynomials define the same function.

In this investigation, you will see a partial converse:

> If two polynomial functions agree for enough inputs (depending on their degree), then they are equivalent under the basic rules of algebra.

**By the end of this investigation, you will be able to answer questions like these.**

1. How are the zeros of a polynomial related to its factors?
2. How can you tell if two polynomials are equivalent without using the form-implies-function principle?
3. What is the greatest-degree polynomial you need to fit a table with four inputs?

**You will learn how to**

- understand the relationship between roots and factors of a polynomial
- divide polynomials by monic linear polynomials
- state and use the Remainder Theorem and the Factor Theorem
- check that two polynomials of degree $n$ are equivalent by checking $n + 1$ function values
- write the general form of a function that fits a table

**You will develop these habits and skills:**

- Make conjectures and create proofs.
- Formalize previous experiences.
- Connect the algebra in this investigation to Lagrange interpolation.

A blacksmith puts specific points of iron stock into place along a bending jig. Identical curves result.

# 1.04 Getting Started

These exercises look like ordinary calculations, but they give a preview of some important themes in this investigation.

## For You to Explore

1. Suppose $f(x) = (x - 5)(x - 3)(x^2 - 1) + 219$.
   a. Find $f(5)$.
   b. List four values of $x$ for which $f(x) = 219$.
2. a. Find a nonconstant polynomial that agrees with the table at the right. You do not need to find the normal form.

| $x$ | $q(x)$ |
|---|---|
| 1 | 0 |
| 3 | 0 |

   b. What is the degree of the polynomial you found in part (a)?
   c. Find a nonconstant polynomial that agrees with the table at the right. You do not need to find the normal form.

| $x$ | $r(x)$ |
|---|---|
| 1 | 0 |
| 3 | 0 |
| 5 | 0 |
| 7 | 0 |
| 9 | 0 |

   d. What is the degree of the polynomial you found in part (c)?
3. a. Find two different polynomials $j(x)$ and $g(x)$ such that the degree of each polynomial is greater than 1 and $j(5) = g(5) = 0$.
   b. Suppose $h(x) = j(x) - g(x)$. What is $h(5)$?
4. Use the three functions below. Find the degree of each polynomial.
   $t(x) = x^5 - 1$ $\quad u(x) = x^5 + x^2 + 3$ $\quad v(x) = x^4 + 7$
   a. $t(x) + u(x)$
   b. $t(x) - u(x)$
   c. $t(x) + v(x)$
   d. $t(x) - v(x)$
   e. $t(x) \cdot u(x)$
5. Find $k$ if $m(x) = (x - 8)\left(7x^3 + 12x^2 - 13x + \frac{22}{5}\right) + 7(k + 1)$ and $m(8) = 21$.
6. Find a polynomial $g(x)$ such that $x^3 - 1 = (x - 1)g(x)$.
7. Show that if $n$ is a positive integer,
   $x^n - 1 = (x - 1)(x^{n-1} + x^{n-2} + \cdots + x^2 + x + 1)$.

This is an important identity that you will use throughout this course.

# Exercises *Practicing Habits of Mind*

## On Your Own

**8.** Suppose $h(x) = (x - 1)(x + 3)(x^5 + x^4 + x^3 + x^2 + x + 1) + 5x - 2$.

**a.** For what inputs $a$ can you easily find $h(a)$ without using a calculator?

**b.** Find the output of $h$ for each of your answers to part (a).

**9.** If $a$ is some fixed number, find the normal form of $(x - a)(x^2 + ax + a^2)$.

**10.** If $a$ is some fixed number, find the normal form of $(x - a)(x^3 + ax^2 + a^2x + a^3)$.

**11.** Find a polynomial $g(x)$ such that $\frac{x^5 - 1}{x - 1} = g(x)$.

**Habits of Mind**

**Look for patterns.** What is a general result suggested by Exercises 9 and 10?

## Maintain Your Skills

In Exercises 12–14, expand each expression and write the result in normal form.

**12.** $(x^2 - 1)(x^4 + x^2 + 1)$

**13.** $(x^3 - 1)(x^6 + x^3 + 1)$

**14.** $(x^4 - 1)(x^8 + x^4 + 1)$

**Go Online**
**Video Tutor**
www.successnetplus.com

# 1.05 Polynomial Division

After you learned to multiply numbers, you learned to "undo" multiplication with division. The same thing can be done with polynomials. If you know that $x^3 + 10x^2 + 18x - 35 = (x + 5)(x^2 + 5x + 7)$, then you also know that $\frac{x^3 + 10x^2 + 18x - 35}{x + 5} = x^2 + 5x - 7$.

When you divide one polynomial by another, you get a quotient and a remainder. In the example above, the quotient is $x^2 + 5x - 7$ and the remainder is 0.

## Example

**Problem** Find the quotient and the remainder when you divide $x^3 + 2x^2 + 4x + 6$ by $x - 2$.

**Solution** You can do a calculation that looks just like long division.

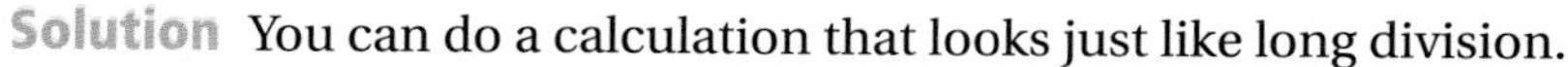

$$
\begin{array}{r|l}
 & x^2 + 4x + 12 \\
\hline
x - 2 & x^3 + 2x^2 + 4x + 6 \\
 & x^3 - 2x^2 \\
\hline
 & \quad 4x^2 + 4x + 6 \\
 & \quad 4x^2 - 8x \\
\hline
 & \qquad 12x + 6 \\
 & \qquad 12x - 24 \\
\hline
 & \qquad\qquad 30
\end{array}
$$

So, the quotient is $x^2 + 4x + 12$ and the remainder is 30.

For information on dividing polynomials, see the TI-Nspire Handbook, p. 817.

**Habits of Mind**

**Establish a process.** In the long division process, how do you know when to stop?

## For You to Do

1. Find the quotient and the remainder when you divide $x^3 + 2x^2 + 4x + 10$ by $x - 2$.
2. If $g(x) = x^3 + 2x^2 + 4x + 10$, what is $g(2)$?
3. Find a polynomial $q(x)$ and a number $r$ such that $x^3 + 2x^2 + 4x + 10 = (x - 2)q(x) + r$.

When you divide 37 by 7, the quotient is 5 and the remainder is 2.

$$
\begin{array}{r|l}
 & 5 \\
\hline
7 & 37 \\
 & 35 \\
\hline
 & \ \ 2
\end{array}
$$

You can summarize the division by writing $37 = 7 \cdot 5 + 2$.

You could also say $37 = 7 \cdot 4 + 9$.

$$
\begin{array}{r|l}
 & 4 \\
\hline
7 & 37 \\
 & 28 \\
\hline
 & \ \ 9
\end{array}
$$

While $37 = 7 \cdot 4 + 9$ is correct, this is not standard division. When you divide, the remainder must be less than the divisor (less than 7, in this example). In general, an important property of integers is the Euclidean Property.

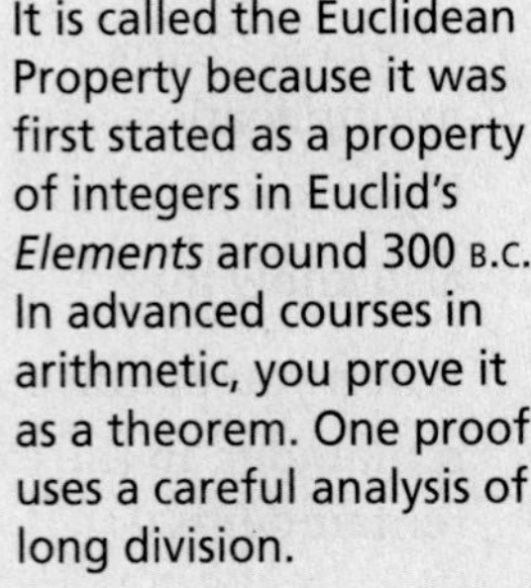

It is called the Euclidean Property because it was first stated as a property of integers in Euclid's *Elements* around 300 B.C. In advanced courses in arithmetic, you prove it as a theorem. One proof uses a careful analysis of long division.


### Property Euclidean Property

**Given positive integers $a$ and $b$, there are unique nonnegative integers $q$ (the quotient) and $r$ (the remainder) such that**

- $b = a \cdot q + r$
- $0 \leq r < a$

In the example above, $b = 37$, $a = 7$, $q = 5$, and $r = 2$.

There is a Euclidean Property for polynomials, too. It comes from the fact that you can divide and get a remainder with degree less than the degree of the divisor. In the example, the result is an identity.

$$x^3 + 2x^2 + 4x + 6 = (x - 2)(x^2 + 4x + 12) + 30$$

## For You to Do

4. Use the basic rules of algebra to show that $(x - 2)(x^2 + 4x + 12) + 30$ is, in fact, equal to $x^3 + 2x^2 + 4x + 6$.
5. If $h(x) = x^3 + 2x^2 + 4x + 6$, find $h(2)$.

### Property Euclidean Property for Polynomials

**Given polynomials $f(x)$ and $g(x)$, there are unique polynomials $q(x)$ (the quotient) and $r(x)$ (the remainder) such that**

- $f(x) = g(x) \cdot q(x) + r(x)$
- $\deg(r(x)) < \deg(g(x))$

## Developing Habits of Mind

**Use an equation to represent a process.** The identity $f(x) = g(x) \cdot q(x) + r(x)$ is just another way to state the division.

$$\begin{array}{r|l} & q(x) \\ \hline g(x) & f(x) \\ & \underline{g(x) \cdot q(x)} \\ & r(x) \end{array}$$

The polynomial $g(x)$ is the divisor. It is what gets divided into $f(x)$. The condition $\deg(r(x)) < \deg(g(x))$ guarantees that the degree of the remainder is less than the degree of the divisor.

## For You to Do

**6.** Using the above notation, find $q(x)$ and $r(x)$ if $f(x) = 2x^3 - 7x^2 - 8x - 34$ and $g(x) = x - 5$.

The most important case for this investigation is when the divisor is of the form $x - a$ for some number $a$. Suppose $f(x)$ is a polynomial and you divide it by $x - a$. Then the remainder has degree less than 1, so it must be a constant. The constant turns out to be very useful. It is equal to $f(a)$. Here are the details.

Working with greater-degree divisors is important, especially in calculus. In general, though, it is more important to be able to reason about the division process than to be skilled at carrying it out.

### *Theorem 1.1 The Remainder Theorem*

**If you divide a polynomial $f(x)$ by $x - a$, where $a$ is a number, the remainder is the number $f(a)$.**

**Proof** First look at a concrete example. Use the polynomial from the example at the beginning of the lesson. Suppose $f(x) = x^3 + 2x^2 + 4x + 6$ and you divide it by $x - 2$.

$$\begin{array}{r}
x^2 + 4x + 12 \\
x - 2 \overline{)\, x^3 + 2x^2 + 4x + 6} \\
\underline{x^3 - 2x^2 \qquad\qquad} \\
4x^2 + 4x + 6 \\
\underline{4x^2 - 8x \qquad} \\
12x + 6 \\
\underline{12x - 24} \\
30
\end{array}$$

So you can summarize the division by writing

$$f(x) = x^3 + 2x^2 + 4x + 6 = (x - 2)(x^2 + 4x + 12) + 30$$

Use the far right side as the form that defines $f$.

$$\begin{aligned}
f(2) &= (2 - 2)(2^2 + 2x + 12) + 30 \\
&= 0 \cdot (\text{some number}) + 30 \\
&= 30
\end{aligned}$$

The proof amounts to carrying out this argument generally, without using specific polynomials. It goes this way.

Suppose you divide $f(x)$ by $x - a$. The remainder is a number, because you are dividing by $x - a$. You cannot stop until you get a polynomial of degree less than 1 (that is, a constant). Call the remainder $r$. The main point of the theorem is that the remainder $r$ is the same as $f(a)$. So the division looks like this.

$$\begin{array}{r}
q(x) \\
x - a \overline{)\qquad f(x)} \\
\underline{(x - a)q(x)} \\
r
\end{array}$$

You can summarize the division by writing $f(x) = (x - a)q(x) + r$.

Now replace $x$ with $a$.

$$\begin{aligned} f(a) &= (a - a) \cdot q(a) + r \\ &= 0 \cdot (\text{some number}) + r \\ &= r \end{aligned}$$

So, $f(a) = r$.

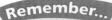

The remainder $r$ is a number, so it does not change when you replace $x$ with $a$.

## Developing Habits of Mind

**Think about it another way.** You can restate the Remainder Theorem this way.

If $f(x)$ is a polynomial and $a$ is a number, then there exists a polynomial $q(x)$ such that $f(x) = (x - a)q(x) + f(a)$.

## For You to Do

**7.** Find the quotient and the remainder when you divide $f(x) = x^3 + x^2 + x$ by $x - 2$.

**8.** Find $f(2)$.

**9.** What are the zeros of $f$?

**Remember...**

The zeros of $f$ are the numbers $a$ that make $f(a) = 0$.

# Exercises *Practicing Habits of Mind*

## Check Your Understanding

**1. a.** Find the quotient and the remainder when you divide $h(x) = x^3 + 2x^2 - 3x - 6$ by $x + 2$.

**b.** Use your result to find $h(-2)$.

**2.** Find the remainder of $x^{105} + x + 1$ divided by $x - 1$.

**3.** Find the remainder of $x^{105} + x + 1$ divided by $x + 1$.

Long division takes too long in these cases. Some CAS systems will have trouble, too.

4. Suppose $(x - 10)$ divides evenly into some polynomial $P(x)$. What is $P(10)$?

5. At Sasha's party, Tony presents the following puzzle: "I'm thinking of a number. If I divide it by 3, the remainder is 2. If I divide it by 5, the remainder is 3. If I divide it by 7, the remainder is 1. What's my number?"

   a. What number might Tony be thinking of?

   b. Is there more than one integer that fits Tony's puzzle? If so, name two of them. If not, explain why.

6. Later that night, Derman takes the floor and presents the following puzzle: "I'm thinking of a polynomial. If I divide it by $x - 3$, the remainder is 16. If I divide it by $x - 5$, the remainder is 42. If I divide it by $x - 7$, the remainder is 84. What's my polynomial?"

   a. What polynomial might Derman be thinking of?

   b. Is there more than one polynomial that fits Derman's puzzle? If so, name two of them. If not, explain why.

## On Your Own

7. a. Find the quotient and the remainder when you divide $f(x) = x^3 + x^2 + x$ by $x + 2$.

   b. Find $f(-2)$.

8. Find the remainders when you divide each polynomial by $x - 3$.

   a. $x^3 - 1$
   b. $x - 1$
   c. $x^2 + x + 1$
   d. $x^4 + x^2 + 1$
   e. $(x^4 + x^2 + 1)(x - 1)$
   f. $x^4 + x^3 + x^2$

**Habits of Mind**

**Consider more than one strategy.** Is long division really necessary?

9. Suppose that $f$ and $g$ are polynomials and that $f(2) = 5$ and $g(2) = -4$. Find the remainder when you divide each of the following polynomials by $x - 2$.

   a. $3f + g$

   b. $fg^2$

   c. $(x^2 + x + 1)f(x) + g(x)$

The leftover dough between the cookies is the remainder.

10. Suppose $f(x) = 5(x - 2)^3 + 3(x - 2)^2 - 6(x - 2) + 8$.

a. What is $f(2)$?

b. What is the remainder when you divide $f(x)$ by $x - 2$?

c. Suppose $g(x)$ is the quotient when you divide $f(x)$ by $x - 2$. What is $g(2)$?

d. What is the remainder when you divide $g(x)$ by $x - 2$?

e. Suppose $h(x)$ is the quotient when you divide $g(x)$ by $x - 2$. What is $h(2)$?

f. What is the remainder when you divide $h(x)$ by $x - 2$?

g. Suppose $m(x)$ is the quotient when you divide $h(x)$ by $x - 2$. What is $m(2)$?

h. What is the remainder when you divide $m(x)$ by $x - 2$?

Go Online
www.successnetplus.com

11. **Standardized Test Prep** Let $g(x) = x^3 - 12x^2 + 21x + 98$ and $g(-2) = 0$. Find the zeros of $g(x)$.

A. $-2$ and $-7$

B. $-2$ and $7$

C. $2$ and $-7$

D. $2$ and $7$

12. **Take It Further** Suppose $f(x)$ is a polynomial such that $f(2) = 5$ and $f(3) = 7$. What is the remainder when you divide $f(x)$ by $(x - 2)(x - 3)$?

13. Find numbers $B$, $C$, and $D$ such that
$x^3 + x^2 - 8x + 13 = (x - 1)^3 + B(x - 1)^2 + C(x - 1) + D$.

14. Suppose $P(x) = x^3 - 3x^2 + 2x + 5$. Use the Remainder Theorem to show that $P(x) - P(7)$ is divisible by $x - 7$.

15. **Take It Further** Suppose $P(x)$ is any polynomial and $a$ is a number. Use the Remainder Theorem to show that $P(x) - P(a)$ is divisible by $x - a$.

## Maintain Your Skills

16. Find each quotient.

a. $\frac{x^2 - 1}{x - 1}$ b. $\frac{x^3 - 1}{x - 1}$ c. $\frac{x^4 - 1}{x - 1}$ d. $\frac{x^5 - 1}{x - 1}$ e. $\frac{x^{12} - 1}{x - 1}$

17. Suppose $f(x) = 2x^2 + 5x - 1$. Simplify each expression.

a. $\frac{f(x) - f(1)}{x - 1}$ b. $\frac{f(x) - f(2)}{x - 2}$ c. $\frac{f(x) - f(3)}{x - 3}$

d. $\frac{f(x) - f(4)}{x - 4}$ e. $\frac{f(x) - f(5)}{x - 5}$ f. $\frac{f(x) - f(6)}{x - 6}$

What is the pattern?

# 1.06 The Factor Theorem

Suppose you want to find all roots of the equation below.

$$x^3 + 4x^2 - 9x - 36 = 0$$

You can start by factoring the left side of the equation.

$$x^3 + 4x^2 - 9x - 36 = (x^2 - 9)(x + 4) = (x - 3)(x + 3)(x + 4)$$

Suppose $a$ is a root of the equation. Then $a^3 + 4a^2 - 9a - 36 = 0$.

By the form-implies-function principle, $(a - 3)(a + 3)(a + 4) = 0$.

By the Zero Product Property, one of the factors must be 0.

$$a - 3 = 0 \text{ or } a + 3 = 0 \text{ or } a + 4 = 0$$

If $a - 3 = 0$, then $a = 3$. If $a + 3 = 0$, then $a = -3$. If $a + 4 = 0$, then $a = -4$. So, the roots of the equation are 3, $-3$, and $-4$. Notice that each root $a$ of the equation corresponds to a factor $(x - a)$ of the polynomial on the left side. This happens for any root.

**Remember...**

The form-implies-function principle says that if two expressions are the same under the basic rules of algebra, then they define functions that produce the same output for the same input.

The Zero Product Property states that if $ab = 0$, then at least one of the numbers $a$ and $b$ has to be zero.

### *Theorem 1.2 The Factor Theorem*

**Suppose $f(x)$ is a polynomial. Then the number a is a root of the equation $f(x) = 0$ if and only if $x - a$ is a factor of $f(x)$.**

## For Discussion

**1.** Use the Remainder Theorem to prove the Factor Theorem.

## For You to Do

**2.** Suppose $p(x)$ is a polynomial of degree 3 with three zeros at $x = 1, 2,$ and 3. Find $p(x)$ if $p(5) = 48$.

There are many corollaries to the Factor Theorem that have a wide range of applications in algebra. Here are a few.

### *Corollary 1.2.1*

**A polynomial of degree $n$ can have at most $n$ distinct real-number zeros.**

**Proof** Suppose $f(x)$ is a polynomial of degree $n$ and $a$ is a zero. Then, by the Factor Theorem, there is a polynomial $q(x)$ such that

$$f(x) = (x - a)q(x)$$

Because the degree of a product is the sum of the degrees (see Problem 4 from Lesson 1.04), the degree of $q(x)$ has to be $n - 1$.

Suppose $b$ is another zero of $f(x)$, different from $a$. Then, using the above equation,

$$0 = f(b) = (b - a)q(b)$$

Since $b - a \neq 0$, $q(b) = 0$ by the Zero Product Property. Apply the Factor Theorem and the result of Problem 4 from Lesson 1.04. There is a polynomial $p(x)$ of degree $n - 2$ such that

$$q(x) = (x - b)p(x)$$

Substituting $f(x) = (x - a)q(x)$, you have

$$f(x) = (x - a)(x - b)p(x)$$

Keep doing this until you run out of real zeros.

$$f(x) = (x - a)(x - b)(x - c)\ldots\ell(x)$$

The polynomial $\ell(x)$ has no real zeros. Since the degree of $f(x)$ is $n$, the sum of the degrees on the right side must be $n$. Since each zero of $f(x)$ contributes 1 to this sum, there can be at most $n$ of them.

## For You to Do

**3.** Carefully write out the steps for applying this proof to $f(x) = x^3 - 2x^2 - x + 2$.

### *Corollary 1.2.2*

**If two polynomials of degree $n$ agree at $n + 1$ inputs, they are identical.**

## For Discussion

**4.** Prove Corollary 1.2.2. Why might you call Corollary 1.2.2 the "function-implies-form" principle?

## Developing Habits of Mind

**Use a different process to get the same answer.** Corollary 1.2.2 will save you time and effort. It provides an alternative to the form-implies-function principle.

For example, suppose you have two polynomials of degree 5. You want to show that they will always give the same output for a given input. One way to do that is to show that they are equivalent under the basic rules of algebra. Another way is to show that they agree at six inputs. Corollary 1.2.2 says that, if two fifth-degree polynomials agree for six inputs, they are automatically identical. That is, they are equivalent under the basic rules.

So, to check that two polynomial functions are equal for all real inputs, all you have to do is to show that they agree on enough inputs. *Enough* means 1 more than their degree. This is quite a remarkable fact. It is not often that only a few checks of a result guarantee the result for infinitely many other cases.

### *Corollary 1.2.3*

**A polynomial of degree $n$ is completely determined by its output values for $n + 1$ inputs.**

## Minds in Action

*Tony and Sasha are picking up where they left off in Lesson 1.03.*

**Tony** So, we have a way to build as many polynomials as we want that agree with this table for $f(x) = 2x + 2$.

| x | f(x) |
|---|---|
| 1 | 4 |
| 2 | 6 |
| 3 | 8 |
| 4 | 10 |

**Sasha** Right. We just take another function of the form

$$r(x) = 2x + 2 + (\text{something}) \cdot (x - 1)(x - 2)(x - 3)(x - 4).$$

And I think this is the only way to get such a function.

**Tony** Me too, but I don't see why.

**Sasha** Suppose we have a function $g(x)$ that agrees with $f$ on the table. Then if I subtract $g(x)$ from $f(x)$, I get a polynomial that outputs zero for all the input values in the table.

| x | f(x) | g(x) | f(x) − g(x) |
|---|---|---|---|
| 1 | 4 | 4 | 0 |
| 2 | 6 | 6 | 0 |
| 3 | 8 | 8 | 0 |
| 4 | 10 | 10 | 0 |

What do we know about a polynomial that has 1, 2, 3, and 4 as zeros?

**Tony** We know it looks like

$$(\text{something}) \cdot (x - 1)(x - 2)(x - 3)(x - 4)$$

Why do they know this?

**Sasha** Right. So,

$$f(x) - g(x) = (\text{something}) \cdot (x - 1)(x - 2)(x - 3)(x - 4)$$

So . . .

**Tony** Oh.

$$f(x) = g(x) + (\text{something}) \cdot (x - 1)(x - 2)(x - 3)(x - 4)$$

and $g(x)$ comes from our method. Very smooth.

*Derman enters the discussion.*

**Derman** But I have another function that agrees with $f$ at 1, 2, 3, and 4.

Look.

$$d(x) = 338 - 698x + 490x^2 - 140x^3 + 14x^4$$

## For You to Do

**5.** Write Derman's function in a way that shows how it comes from Tony and Sasha's method.

# Exercises Practicing Habits of Mind

## Check Your Understanding

1. What is the greatest number of real roots a polynomial of degree 2 can have? Explain.

2. If two linear polynomials agree at two points, then Corollary 1.2.2 says that they must be identical. If two quadratic polynomials agree at three points, then they must be identical, and so on. For each pair of polynomials, decide if the polynomials are identical using this idea of checking $n + 1$ points.

   **a.** $P(x) = x^4 - x^2 - 2$ and $R(x) = (x^2 + 1)(x^2 - 2)$

   **b.** $P(x) = x(x + 1)(x - 1)$ and $R(x) = x - x^3$

   **c.** $P(x) = (x + 3)^2 - 7$ and $R(x) = x^2 + 6x + 2$

3. Find the value of $a$ such that $x - 1$ is a factor of $x^3 + ax^2 - x + 5$.

4. Find numbers $a$ and $b$ such that $x^2 + x - 6$ is a factor of $x^4 + x^3 - ax^2 - bx + a - b$.

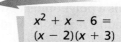

> $x^2 + x - 6 =$
> $(x - 2)(x + 3)$

5. Solve the equation $x^4 + x^3 - 7x^2 - x + 6 = 0$.

6. Establish the following identity.

$$(x - 1)(x - 3) + (x - 2)(x - 3) + (x - 1)(x - 2) = 3x^2 - 12x + 11$$

7. Establish the following identity.

$$\frac{20}{(1 - 3)(1 - 6)}(x - 3)(x - 6) + \frac{12}{(3 - 1)(3 - 6)}(x - 1)(x - 6) + \frac{60}{(6 - 1)(6 - 3)}(x - 1)(x - 3) = 4x^2 - 20x + 36$$

> Can you do Exercises 6 and 7 without expanding the left sides?

8. Find the normal form of $P(x)$.

$$P(x) = \frac{(x - 1)(x - 2)}{(3 - 1)(3 - 2)} + \frac{(x - 1)(x - 3)}{(2 - 1)(2 - 3)} + \frac{(x - 2)(x - 3)}{(1 - 2)(1 - 3)}$$

## On Your Own

9. Find the number $a$ such that $x - 1$ is a factor of $x^3 + ax^2 - x + 8$.

10. Find numbers $a$ and $b$ such that $x^2 + x - 6$ is a factor of $x^4 + x^3 - ax^2 - bx + 2a + b$.

> **Go Online**
> www.successnetplus.com

11. Solve the equation $x^4 + x^3 - 10x^2 - 4x + 24 = 0$.

12. Suppose $f(x) = 4 - 4x + 13x^2 - 12x^3 + 3x^4$. Show that each statement is true.

    **a.** $x - 2$ is a factor of $f(x)$.

    **b.** $(x - 2)^2$ is a factor of $f(x)$.

    **c.** If $f(x) = (x - 2)q(x)$, then $x - 2$ is a factor of $q(x)$.

13. Establish the following identity.

$$x^n - a^n = (x - a)(x^{n-1} + ax^{n-2} + a^2x^{n-3} + a^3x^{n-4} + \cdots + a^{n-2}x + a^{n-1})$$

14. Suppose that $r$ is a number and $f(x) = a_nx^n + a_{n-1}x^{n-1} + \cdots + a_1x + a_0$.

**a.** Show that $f(x) - f(r) = (x - r)g(x)$ for some polynomial $g$.

**b.** Take It Further Write an expression for $g$.

15. Use Exercise 14 to prove the Remainder Theorem.

16. Here is a table for the sum of the first $n$ squares.

A cubic polynomial function gives the sum of the first $n$ squares. Find a cubic that agrees with this table.

| $n$ | $1^2 + 2^2 + \cdots + n^2$ |
|---|---|
| 1 | 1 |
| 2 | 5 |
| 3 | 14 |
| 4 | 30 |
| 5 | 55 |
| 6 | 91 |

17. Standardized Test Prep The function $f(x)$ is a polynomial of degree 4. The function $p(x) = (x + a)^2$ is a factor of $f(x)$. Which of the following is NOT always true?

**A.** $f(x) = (x + a) \cdot$ (something else) $+ r(x)$, where $r(x) = 0$

**B.** $f(a) = 0$

**C.** The trinomial $x^2 + 2ax + a^2$ is a factor of $f(x)$.

**D.** The degree of the function $h(x)$ defined by the equation $f(x) = p(x) \cdot h(x)$ is 2.

**Habits of Mind**

**Look for relationships.** How is Exercise 13 a generalization of Exercise 7 from Lesson 1.04?

## Maintain Your Skills

18. Suppose $f(x) = (x^2 + 1)(x - 1)(x - 2)(x - 3)(x - 4)$. Find the factored form of each expression.

**a.** $\dfrac{f(x)}{x - 1}$

**b.** $\dfrac{f(x)}{(x - 1)(x - 2)}$

**c.** $\dfrac{f(x)}{x - 3}$

**d.** $\dfrac{f(x)}{x - 4}$

**e.** $\dfrac{f(x)}{(x - 1)(x - 2)(x - 3)}$

**f.** $\dfrac{f(x)}{(x - 1)(x - 2)(x - 3)(x - 4)}$

19. Graph each function.

**a.** $f(x) = (x - 1)(x - 3)$

**b.** $g(x) = (x - 1.5)(x - 2.5)$

**c.** $h(x) = (x - 1.8)(x - 2.2)$

**d.** $k(x) = (x - 1.9)(x - 2.1)$

**e.** $\ell(x) = (x - 2)^2$

**In this investigation, you learned how to divide polynomials by linear polynomials and how to use the Remainder Theorem and the Factor Theorem. You also learned about the relationship between roots and factors of polynomials. These exercises will help you summarize what you have learned.**

1. Find the polynomial $g(x)$ such that $x^8 - 1 = (x - 1)g(x)$.
2. Find the polynomial $g(x)$ such that $x^8 - 1 = (x - 1)(x + 1)g(x)$.
3. Find the remainder of $x^{105} - 3x + 1$ divided by $x + 1$.
4. Find numbers $B$ and $C$ such that $x^2 + 2x = (x - 1)^2 + B(x - 1) + C$.
5. Take It Further Find numbers $r$ and $s$ if $(x - 2)^2$ is a factor of $2x^3 + rx^2 + sx + 4$.
6. How are the zeros of a polynomial related to its factors?
7. How can you tell if two polynomials are equal without using the form-implies-function principle?
8. What is the greatest-degree polynomial you need to fit a table with four inputs?

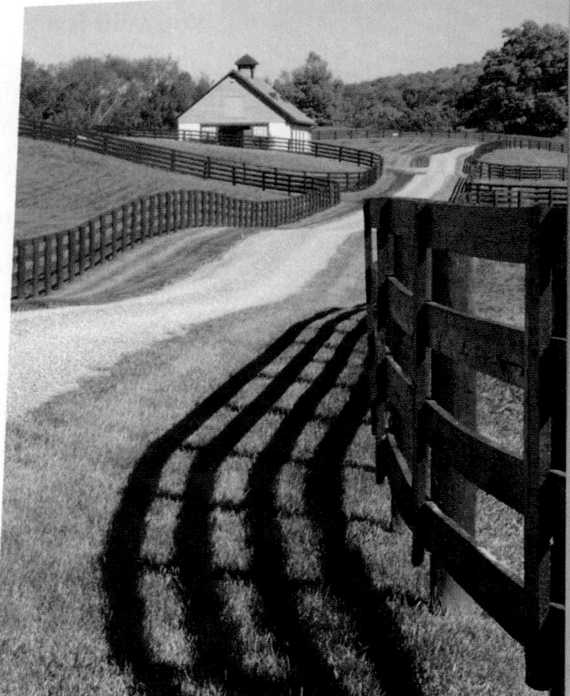

The posts determine a unique fence line. A set of points can determine a unique function.

## Vocabulary

In this investigation, you learned these terms. Make sure you understand what each one means and how to use it.

- **quotient**
- **remainder**

# Advanced Factoring

In *Advanced Factoring*, you will develop some advanced factoring methods. Many of them depend on the connection between roots and factors. Factoring a polynomial is important because it simplifies the problem of finding the zeros of the polynomial.

**By the end of this investigation, you will be able to answer questions like these.**

1. How do you factor nonmonic quadratics?
2. How do you factor differences and sums of cubes?
3. Does $x^4 + 4$ factor over $\mathbb{Z}$?

**You will learn how to**

- factor polynomials by scaling
- factor polynomials using the differences and sums of squares
- factor polynomials using the differences and sums of cubes
- factor polynomials using grouping
- factor polynomials by identifying quadratic-like or cubic-like polynomials
- factor polynomials by finding roots

**You will develop these habits and skills:**

- Rearrange polynomials into more useful forms. Sometimes a factored form of a polynomial is more useful than an expanded form.
- Use several techniques for factoring polynomials.

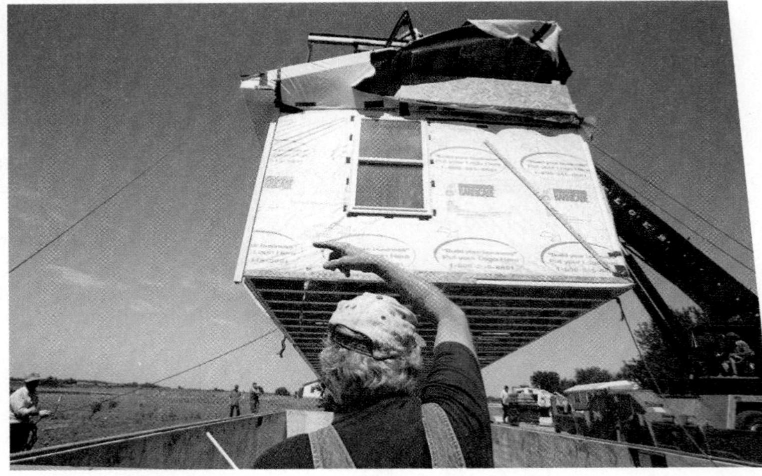

Breaking a house into parts makes it easier to move. Breaking a polynomial into factors makes it easier to identify roots.

# 1.07 Getting Started

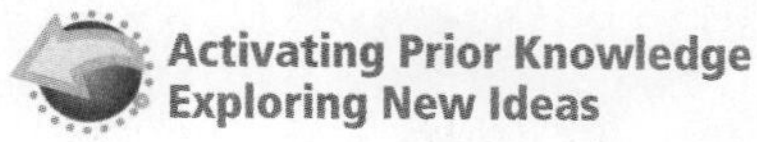


The following problems and exercises ask you to review some ideas from previous courses and to preview some ideas from this investigation.

You can decide if a problem or exercise is a review, a preview, or both.

## For You to Explore

1. Factor each quadratic polynomial over $\mathbb{Z}$. If a polynomial does not factor, explain why not.

   a. $x^2 + 10x + 25$

   b. $x^2 + 10x + 24$

   c. $z^2 + 10z + 23$

   d. $u^2 + 10u + 21$

   e. $y^2 + 10y + 26$

The symbol $\mathbb{Z}$ means the integers.

2. Factor each polynomial over $\mathbb{Z}$. If a polynomial does not factor, explain why not.

   a. $x^2 + 18x + 45$

   b. $4x^2 + 36x + 45$

   c. $(x - 3)^2 + 18(x - 3) + 45$

   d. $z^2 - 121$

   e. $9u^2 - 121$

   f. $(y + 5)^2 - 121$

   g. $y^2(y + 5) - 4(y + 5)$

   h. $y^2(y + 5) - 3(y + 5)$

3. Suppose $\alpha$ and $\beta$ are roots of this equation.

$$x^2 - 6x + 5 = 0$$

   Find each value.

   a. $\alpha + \beta$

   b. $\alpha\beta$

4. Suppose $\alpha$ and $\beta$ are two numbers with a sum of 6 and a product of $-3$. Show that $\alpha$ and $\beta$ are roots of the equation $x^2 - 6x - 3 = 0$.

# Exercises *Practicing Habits of Mind*

## On Your Own

**5.** Factor these quadratic polynomials over $\mathbb{Z}$. If a polynomial does not factor, explain why not.

**a.** $x^2 + 6x + 5$ **b.** $x^2 - 6x + 9$ **c.** $x^2 + 12x + 20$

**d.** $x^2 + 10x - 20$ **e.** $x^2 - 5x - 24$ **f.** $x^2 + 10x + 30$

**Habits of Mind**

**Look for patterns.** Generalize the identities you find.

**6.** Find the normal form for each polynomial.

**a.** $(x - 1)(x^2 + x + 1)$ **b.** $(x + 1)(x^2 - x + 1)$

**7.** Factor each polynomial over $\mathbb{Z}$.

**a.** $x^3 - 1$ **b.** $x^3 + 1$ **c.** $x^3 - 8$

**d.** $x^3 + 8$ **e.** $8x^3 - 1$ **f.** $8x^3 + 1$

**g.** $x^3 - a^3$ **h.** $x^3 + a^3$ **i.** $(x + 1)^3 - 1$

**j.** $(x - 1)^3 + 1$

In parts (g) and (h), *a* stands for an integer.

**8.** Show that if the equation $x^2 - 10x + 7 = 0$ has roots $p$ and $q$, then the following statement must be true.

$$p + q = 10 \quad \text{and} \quad pq = 7$$

Is the converse true?

**9.** Find a quadratic equation with solutions $3 + \sqrt{7}$ and $3 - \sqrt{7}$.

**10.** Find $A$, $B$, $C$, and $D$ such that

$$-37 + 40x - 18x^2 + 3x^3 = A(x - 2)^3 + B(x - 2)^2 + C(x - 2) + D$$

## Maintain Your Skills

**11.** Find the normal form for each polynomial.

**a.** $x^2 - 9$ **b.** $(2x)^2 - 9$

**c.** $9 - x^2$ **d.** $(x + 1)^2 - 9$

**e.** $(x + 1)^2 - x^2$ **f.** $(x^2 + 1)^2 - x^2$

**g.** $(x^2 + 1)^3 - x^3$ **h.** $(x^2 + 1)^3 - x^6$

**12.** Factor each polynomial over $\mathbb{Z}$.

**a.** $x^2 - 9$ **b.** $(2x)^2 - 9$

**c.** $9 - x^2$ **d.** $(x + 1)^2 - 9$

**e.** $(x + 1)^2 - x^2$ **f.** $(x^2 + 1)^2 - x^2$

**g.** $(x^2 + 1)^3 - x^3$ **h.** $(x^2 + 1)^3 - x^6$

# 1.08 Quadratics

In previous courses, you learned to factor quadratic polynomials in order to solve quadratic equations. Most of the quadratics you factored were monic—the coefficient of $x^2$ was 1. In this lesson, you will build on the methods you used to factor monics to find the factors of any quadratic polynomial. The new methods will extend to polynomials of higher degrees.

> Factoring to solve was the original motivation for factoring, but, like most topics in mathematics, factoring has become an interesting problem in its own right.

First, you will quickly review the basic factoring techniques for monic quadratics. If you want to factor $x^2 - 7x + 12$, you look for two numbers with sum of 7 and a product of 12. To understand why you do this, suppose the equation is in factored form.

$$x^2 - 7x + 12 = (x - r)(x - s)$$

If you multiply out the right side, you get

$$x^2 - 7x + 12 = x^2 - (r + s)x + rs$$

> Make sure you know how to multiply out the right side.

So, in this case, $r + s = 7$ and $rs = 12$.

## For You to Do

**1.** Factor $x^2 - 7x + 12$.

Now, what can you do if the quadratic is not monic? A good mathematical habit is to make use of something you already know how to do. The scaling method is a good example of this habit.

You can scale up to make a process—such as removing bunny ears—easier to do. After you have fixed the problem, you can scale back down.

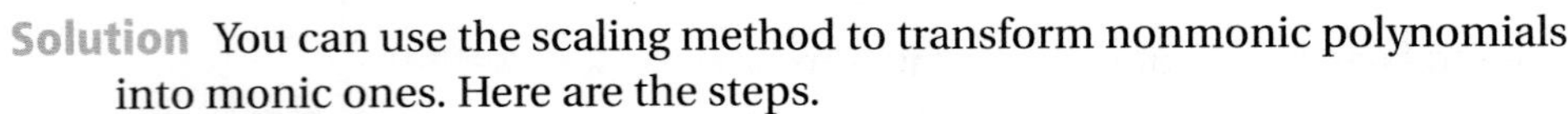

## Example

**Problem** Factor $6x^2 + 11x - 10$.

**Solution** You can use the scaling method to transform nonmonic polynomials into monic ones. Here are the steps.

**Step 1** Multiply the polynomial by 6 to make the leading coefficient a perfect square.

$$6(6x^2 + 11x - 10) = 36x^2 + 11 \cdot 6x - 60 = (6x)^2 + 11(6x) - 60$$

**Step 2** Think of $6x$ as the variable. Let $z = 6x$.

$$z^2 + 11z - 60$$

**Step 3** This expression factors.

$$z^2 + 11z - 60 = (z + 15)(z - 4)$$

**Step 4** Replace $z$ with $6x$.

$$(6x + 15)(6x - 4)$$

So

$$\begin{aligned} 6(6x^2 + 11x - 10) &= (6x + 15)(6x - 4) \\ &= 3(2x + 5) \cdot 2(3x - 2) \\ &= 6(2x + 5)(3x - 2) \end{aligned}$$

**Step 5** Divide both sides by 6 to obtain the factored form.

$$6x^2 + 11x - 10 = (2x + 5)(3x - 2)$$

**Habits of Mind**

**Look for relationships.** Dividing by 6 undoes the multiplication by 6 that you did in Step 1.

## Developing Habits of Mind

**Change variables.** This idea of chunking part of an expression into one unit is very useful in mathematics. You can say that $(2x)^2 + 18(2x) + 45$ is a monic quadratic in $2x$. This means that if you think of $2x$ as the variable instead of $x$, the quadratic looks monic.

## For You to Do

2. Factor $6x^2 - 31x + 35$.

## For Discussion

3. State the scaling method as an algorithm, a sequence of steps that describes exactly what to do.

# Exercises Practicing Habits of Mind

## Check Your Understanding

1. Factor each polynomial.
   a. $9x^2 + 18x - 7$
   b. $6x^2 - 31x + 35$
   c. $15x^2 + 16x - 7$
   d. $9x^2 + 62x - 7$
   e. $-18x^2 - 65x - 7$
   f. $-18x^2 + 61x + 7$
   g. $9x^4 + 62x^2 - 7$
   h. $25 - 4x^2$
   i. $18x^3 - 61x^2 - 7x$

For more on factoring polynomials, see the TI-Nspire Handbook, p. 817.

2. Factor each polynomial.
   a. $9x^2 + 18xy - 7y^2$
   b. $6x^2 - 31xy + 35y^2$
   c. $15x^2 + 16xa - 7a^2$
   d. $9x^2 + 62xb - 7b^2$
   e. $-18x^2 - 65xa - 7a^2$
   f. $-18x^2 + 61xy + 7y^2$
   g. $25y^2 - 4x^2$
   h. $18x^3 - 61x^2y - 7xy^2$

## On Your Own

3. Factor each polynomial.
   a. $4x^2 - 13x + 3$
   b. $4x^2 - 8x + 3$
   c. $4x^2 + 4x - 3$
   d. $4(x + 1)^2 + 4(x + 1) - 3$
   e. $4x^4 - 13x^2 + 3$
   f. $4(x - 1)^4 - 13(x - 1)^2 + 3$
   g. $4(x - 1)^{12} - 13(x - 1)^6 + 3$
   h. $(x^2 + 1)^2 - x^2$

4. Solve $2x - \frac{3}{x} = 5$ for $x$.

5. In the equation $x^2 - 6x + 7 = 0$, let $z = x - 3$.
   a. Express the equation in terms of $z$.
   b. Solve the equation for $z$.
   c. Use the result from part (b) to solve the original equation.

If $z = x - 3$, then $x = z + 3$.

6. Standardized Test Prep Sasha has a number of rules for factoring quadratic polynomial of the form $ax^2 + bx + c$. Which of the following is NOT always true?

A. If $a > 0$ and $c < 0$, then one real root is positive and one real root is negative.

B. If $a = 1$ and $b < 0$ and $d$ and $e$ are the roots, with $|d| > |e|$, then $(x - d)$ is a factor of the polynomial.

C. If $a$ is an integer greater than 1, then multiplying $c$ by $a^2$ converts the polynomial into a monic polynomial.

D. If $a$, $b$, and $c$ are integers and all are greater than zero, then any real roots, if they exist, are less than zero.

7. Derman wants to use the scaling method to factor $18x^2 + 7x - 1$. He multiplies the polynomial by 2 to make 18 a perfect square. Will this work?

## Maintain Your Skills

8. Solve each pair of equations and compare the solutions.

How are the equations in each pair related?

a. $x^2 - 8x + 7 = 0$ and $x^2 - 24x + 63 = 0$

b. $2x^2 + 11x - 21 = 0$ and $2x^2 + 22x - 84 = 0$

c. $2x^2 + 11x - 21 = 0$ and $2x^2 + 33x - 189 = 0$

d. $2x^2 + 11x - 21 = 0$ and $2x^2 + 55x - 525 = 0$

e. $2x^2 + 11x - 21 = 0$ and $x^2 + 11x - 42 = 0$

f. $3x^2 + 16x - 35 = 0$ and $x^2 + 16x - 105 = 0$

g. $3x^2 + 16x - 32 = 0$ and $x^2 + 16x - 96 = 0$

9. Find an equation with solutions scaled in each of the following ways.

a. 7 times the solutions of $x^2 - 8x + 7 = 0$

b. 7 times the solutions of $2x^2 + 11x - 21 = 0$

c. 2 times the solutions of $2x^2 + 11x - 21 = 0$

d. 3 times the solutions of $3x^2 + 11x - 21 = 0$

e. 5 times the solutions of $5x^2 + 11x - 21 = 0$

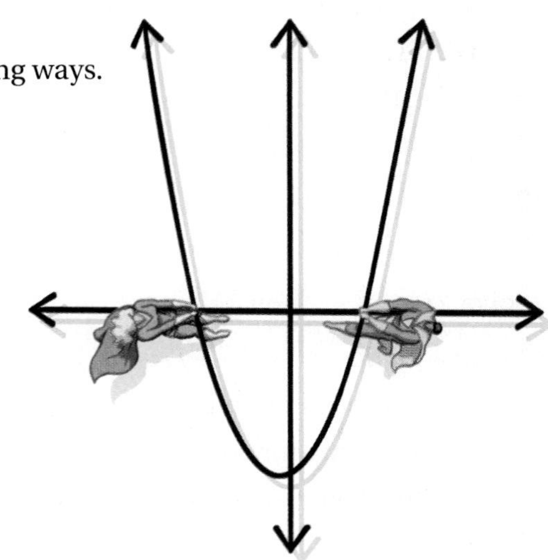

# 1.09 Factoring Cubes

In previous courses, you learned some basic identities that allow you to factor most quadratics that factor over $\mathbb{Z}$. Some of these identities included

- the difference-of-squares identity

$$x^2 - y^2 = (x - y)(x + y)$$

- the perfect-square identities

$$x^2 + 2xy + y^2 = (x + y)^2$$
$$x^2 - 2xy + y^2 = (x - y)^2$$

- the sum-and-product identity

$$x^2 - (a + b)x + ab = (x - a)(x - b)$$

Only one of these perfect-square identities is really necessary.

Equipped with these identities, the **quadratic formula,** the Factor Theorem, and the scaling method, you can tackle any quadratic, often in more than one way.

If all else fails, you can use the quadratic formula to get the roots.
$x = \frac{-b \pm \sqrt{b^2 - 4ac}}{2a}$
If the roots are rational numbers, you can factor the quadratic over $\mathbb{Z}$.

But how can you handle cubics?

In this lesson, you will learn some methods for factoring certain cubics. There is a formula, similar to the quadratic formula, that you can use to find the roots, and therefore the factors, of any cubic. But this cubic formula often leads to solutions that are in such an unrecognizable form that they are useless, so factoring special cubics is still worthwhile. Besides, it is fun.

## Sums and Differences of Cubes

By now, you have seen the following theorem several times in exercises.

### *Theorem 1.3*

**The following identities show the factoring for the difference of cubes and the sum of cubes.**

- $x^3 - y^3 = (x - y)(x^2 + xy + y^2)$
- $x^3 + y^3 = (x + y)(x^2 - xy + y^2)$

**Habits of Mind**

**Look for relationships.** You need only one of these identities.

## For Discussion

1. Prove Theorem 1.3.

## For You to Do

**2.** Factor $x^3 - 27$ and $8x^3 + 27$ over $\mathbb{Z}$.

## Example 1

**Problem** Factor $(x + 1)^3 - 1$ over $\mathbb{Z}$.

**Solution** You can look at this two different ways.

**Method 1** Difference of Cubes

If you chunk things together and think of $x + 1$ as $z$, you get

$$z^3 - 1 = z^3 - 1^3$$

By Theorem 1.3, you can factor this as a difference of cubes.

$$z^3 - 1^3 = (z - 1)(z^2 + z + 1)$$

Now replace $z$ with $(x + 1)$ and simplify.

$$\begin{aligned}(z - 1)(z^2 + z + 1) &= ((x + 1) - 1)((x + 1)^2 + (x + 1) + 1)\\ &= x\left((x^2 + 2x + 1) + (x + 1) + 1\right)\\ &= x(x^2 + 3x + 3)\end{aligned}$$

Since $x^2 + 3x + 3$ does not factor over $\mathbb{Z}$, this is the factored form.

**Method 2** Expand and Simplify

For this method, you just expand $(x + 1)^3$, subtract 1, simplify, and factor the result.

$$\begin{aligned}(x + 1)^3 &= (x + 1)(x + 1)^2\\ &= (x + 1)(x^2 + 2x + 1)\\ &= x^3 + 2x^2 + x + x^2 + 2x + 1\\ &= x^3 + 3x^2 + 3x + 1\end{aligned}$$

So

$$(x + 1)^3 - 1 = (x^3 + 3x^2 + 3x + 1) - 1 = x^3 + 3x^2 + 3x$$

Now factor out the common factor of $x$.

$$x^3 + 3x^2 + 3x = x(x^2 + 3x + 3)$$

**Habits of Mind**

**Check your work.** It is a good thing that both methods give the same answer, because there is only one factorization of a polynomial over $\mathbb{Z}$.

## For You to Do

**3.** Factor $(3x + 2)^3 + 8$ over $\mathbb{Z}$.

### Grouping

Grouping is a technique in which you gather a few terms of a polynomial together so that you can factor that piece. Sometimes the factors of that piece are also factors of the whole polynomial.

You can apply grouping to any polynomial. Cubics with four terms are convenient because sometimes you can group them in pairs.

## Example 2

**Problem** Factor the following two polynomials over $\mathbb{Z}$.

**a.** $x^3 - 8x^2 + 4x - 32$

**b.** $x^3 - 2x^2 + x - 2$

**Solution**

**a.** Factor $x^3 - 8x^2 + 4x - 32$.

Group the first two terms and the last two terms together.

$$x^3 - 8x^2 + 4x - 32 = (x^3 - 8x^2) + (4x - 32)$$

Factor out the common factor in each group.

$$(x^3 - 8x^2) + (4x - 32) = x^2(x - 8) + 4(x - 8)$$

Each group has a factor of $x - 8$, so you can pull it out.

$$x^2(x - 8) + 4(x - 8) = (x - 8)(x^2 + 4)$$

The polynomial $x^2 + 4$ does not factor over $\mathbb{Z}$, so you are done.

If $f(x) = x^3 - 8x^2 + 4x - 32$, what is $f(8)$?

**b.** Factor $x^3 - 2x^2 + x - 2$.

Just for variety, group the first and third terms together, and then the second and fourth terms.

$$x^3 - 2x^2 + x - 2 = (x^3 + x) + (-2x^2 - 2)$$

Factor out the common factor in each group.

$$(x^3 + x) + (-2x^2 - 2) = x(x^2 + 1) - 2(x^2 + 1)$$

Each group has a factor of $x^2 + 1$, so you can pull it out.

$$x(x^2 + 1) - 2(x^2 + 1) = (x - 2)(x^2 + 1)$$

The polynomial $x^2 + 1$ does not factor over $\mathbb{Z}$, so you are done.

If $f(x) = x^3 - 2x^2 + x - 2$, what is $f(2)$?

## For You to Do

4. Factor $x^3 - 2x^2 + x - 2$ another way: Group the first two terms together and the last two terms together.

## For Discussion

5. Factor the expression $(r + s)^3 - 3rs(r + s)$ by grouping.
6. Use your factoring to establish the identity below.

$$(r + s)^3 - 3rs(r + s) - \left(r^3 + s^3\right) = 0$$

## Developing Habits of Mind

**Consider more than one strategy.** Some warnings:

- Not all cubics can be factored by grouping, but they may still factor. For example, you can try every grouping combination for $2x^3 - 13x^2 + x + 21$ and nothing will work, but it still factors.

$$2x^3 - 13x^2 + x + 21 = (2x - 3)\left(x^2 - 5x - 7\right)$$

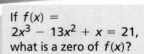

If $f(x) = 2x^3 - 13x^2 + x = 21$, what is a zero of $f(x)$?

- Sometimes a combination of methods can be useful. For example, look at the following polynomial.

$$27x^3 + 27x^2 + 9x + 1$$

Grouping the first and second terms looks promising, but it does not lead anywhere. You can group the first and last terms, factor that pair as a sum of cubes, and then factor out the common factor from the middle two terms.

$$\begin{aligned} 27x^3 + 27x^2 + 9x + 1 &= \left(27x^3 + 1\right) + 27x^2 + 9x \\ &= (3x + 1)((3x)^2 - (3x) + 1) + 9x(3x + 1) \\ &= (3x + 1)\left(9x^2 - 3x + 1\right) + 9x(3x + 1) \\ &= (3x + 1)\left(9x^2 - 3x + 1 + 9x\right) \\ &= (3x + 1)\left(9x^2 + 6x + 1\right) \\ &= (3x + 1)(3x + 1)^2 \\ &= (3x + 1)^3 \end{aligned}$$

So $27x^3 + 27x^2 + 9x + 1$ is a perfect cube.

## Find a Root, Find a Factor

The Factor Theorem sets up a correspondence between roots and factors. For cubics, if you can find a root $a$ of the equation $f(x) = 0$, you have found a factor of $f(x)$, namely $x - a$. So, you know $f(x) = (x - a)g(x)$, where $g(x)$ is a quadratic. And you know how to handle quadratics.

## Minds in Action

*Sasha and Tony are trying to factor $x^3 - 8x^2 + 22x - 21$ over $\mathbb{Z}$.*

**Tony** We can factor $x^3 - 8x^2 + 22x - 21$ if we can solve the equation $x^3 - 8x^2 + 22x - 21 = 0$. Do you have any ideas about roots? They could be anything.

**Sasha** Let's use the trick of working backward. Suppose we have a root $a$. Then $x - a$ is a factor, so we'd get something like

$$x^3 - 8x^2 + 8x + 21 = (x - a)(rx^2 + sx + t)$$

for integers $r$, $s$, and $t$.

**Tony** I know that $r$ would have to be 1, because if you multiplied it back out, the leading term would be $rx^3$. May be we could figure out the other coefficients in the same way.

**Sasha** I'm looking at the constant term. It would have to be $-at$. So, $-at = 21$, and $at = -21$.

Why does the constant term have to be $-at$?

*Derman joins the discussion.*

**Derman** Well, there are millions of pairs of numbers with a product of $-21$. Like $-100$ and $\frac{21}{100}$, for example. Or $\frac{21}{\sqrt{2}}$ and $\sqrt{2}$.

**Sasha** Yes, Derman, but $a$ and $t$ have to be integers. That narrows the field.

**Tony** Right. We're basically looking at factors of 21. So $a$ can only be 1, 3, or 7.

**Sasha** Or their opposites. So, we only have six numbers to try. Let's do it.

*They split up the numbers—three for Sasha, two for Tony, and one for Derman.*

**Tony** I've got it: 3 is a root. So, $x - 3$ is a factor. Now we can either figure out $s$ from $x^3 - 8x^2 + 8x + 21 = (x - 3)(x^2 + sx - 7)$, or we can use long division.

Why is the second factor $x^2 + sx - 7$?

*They try it both ways and get the same answer.*

**Tony** So here's how it factors.

$$x^3 - 8x^2 + 8x + 21 = (x - 3)(x^2 - 5x - 7)$$

**Derman** Does the quadratic factor some more?

## For You to Do

7. What are the roots of $x^2 - 5x - 7$?
8. Answer Derman's question from the dialog.

## For Discussion

9. Can you use the scaling method to turn nonmonic cubics into monic cubics? Try it with $2x^3 - 13x^2 + x + 21$.

## For You to Do

10. Find all real roots of $2x^3 - 13x^2 + x + 21$.

# Exercises *Practicing Habits of Mind*

## Check Your Understanding

1. Prove the following theorem that shows how to cube a binomial.

### *Theorem 1.4*

**The following are identities.**

- $(x + y)^3 = x^3 + 3x^2y + 3xy^2 + y^3$
- $(x - y)^3 = x^3 - 3x^2y + 3xy^2 - y^3$

2. Factor each polynomial over $\mathbb{Z}$.

   **a.** $x^3 - 64$ **b.** $x^3 + 64$ **c.** $27x^3 - 64$

   **d.** $27x^3 + 64$ **e.** $(x + 1)^3 - 64$

   **f.** $(2x - 3)^3 + 64$ **g.** $x^3 + 3x^2 - 9x - 27$

   **h.** $x^3 + ax^2 - a^2x - a^3$ **i.** $x^2 - (3x + 1)^2$

   **j.** $x^2 - y^2 + 2yz - z^2$ **k.** $x^3 - 4x^2 - 31x + 70$

   **l.** $x^3 - 4x^2y - 31xy^2 + 70y^3$ **m.** $(x + 1)^3 - 3x(x + 1)$

3. Use the scaling method to transform $5x^2 + 3x^2 + 3x - 2$ into a monic cubic. Then use the transformed cubic to factor $5x^3 + 3x^2 + 3x - 2$.

## On Your Own

4. Factor each polynomial over $\mathbb{Z}$.

   a. $x^3 - 27$
   b. $x^3 + 27$
   c. $64x^3 - 27$
   d. $64x^3 + 27$
   e. $(x - 1)^3 - 125$
   f. $(2x - 3)^3 + 125$
   g. $x^3 + 5x^2 - 25x - 125$
   h. $5x^3 - 7x^2 + 7x - 2$
   i. $x^4 - (3x + 1)^4$
   j. $x^2 - y^2 - 2yz - z^2$
   k. $(x + 1)^3 + x^3$
   l. $x^3 - 3x^2 + 3x - 2$
   m. $x^3 - 3x^2z + 3xz^2 - 2z^3$
   n. $x^3 - 12x^2 + 48x - 64$

**Go Online**
www.successnetplus.com

5. Factor $x^3 - 15x - 4$ over $\mathbb{Z}$.

6. Factor $(x - 1)^3 - 15(x - 1) - 4$ over $\mathbb{Z}$.

7. **Take It Further** Factor $x^4 - x^3 - 2x^2 + x + 1$ over $\mathbb{Z}$.

8. **Standardized Test Prep** What is the difference $(x + 4)^3 - (x^3 + 4^3)$?

   A. $x^2 - 4x + 4$
   B. $x^2 - 4x + 16$
   C. $3x^2 + 48$
   D. $12x^2 + 48x$

## Maintain Your Skills

9. Find the normal form of each polynomial.

   a. $x + 1$
   b. $(x + 1)^2$
   c. $(x + 1)^3$
   d. $(x + 1)^4$
   e. $(x + 1)^5$

What patterns do you see?

# 1.10 Pippins and Cheese—More Factoring Techniques

There are many more methods of factoring, some of them quite involved. You will learn about a few more very beautiful ones later. For now, you will look at three more topics to round out the discussion.

> I will make an end of my dinner; there's pippins and cheese to come.
>
> —William Shakespeare

## Quadratic-like and Cubic-like Polynomials

In Exercise 3a from Lesson 1.08, you factored this quadratic.

$$4x^2 - 13x + 3 = (4x - 1)(x - 3)$$

Then in Exercise 3e, you factored this fourth-degree polynomial.

$$4x^4 - 13x^2 + 3$$

One way to factor is to notice that this is a quadratic in $x^2$.

$$4x^4 - 13x^2 + 3 = 4(x^2)^2 - 13(x^2) + 3$$

So, if you let $z = x^2$, you have the same form as in Exercise 3a.

$$4z^2 - 13z + 3 = (4z - 1)(z - 3)$$

Now $z = x^2$, so you can convert to a polynomial in $x$.

$$4x^4 - 13x^2 + 3 = \left(4x^2 - 1\right)\left(x^2 - 3\right)$$

Then $4x^2 - 1$ factors some more over $\mathbb{Z}$, but $x^2 - 3$ does not.

**Remember...**

A fourth-degree polynomial is a quartic. Some people call a quartic that is a quadratic in $x^2$ a biquadratic.

## For You to Do

1. Factor $9x^4 - 37x^2 + 4$ over $\mathbb{Z}$.

There are other kinds of quadratic-like polynomials—polynomials that are quadratic in some power of $x$.

## Example 1

**Problem** Factor $x^6 - 7x^3 - 8$ over $\mathbb{Z}$.

**Solution** Is it a sixth degree polynomial? Well, yes, but it is a quadratic in $x^3$.

$$x^6 - 7x^3 - 8 = (x^3)^2 - 7(x^3) - 8$$

This is like $z^2 - 7z - 8$, where $z = x^3$. Write $z^2 - 7z - 8 = (z - 8)(z + 1)$.

## For You to Do

**2.** Finish the example. Replace $z$ with $x^3$ and finish the factorization.

So, some polynomials are quadratic-like. And some are cubic-like.

## Example 2

**Problem** Factor $x^9 - 8x^6 + 4x^3 - 32$ over $\mathbb{Z}$.

**Solution** This is a cubic in $x^3$.

$$x^9 - 8x^6 + 4x^3 - 32 = (x^3)^3 - 8(x^3)^2 + 4(x^3) - 32$$

Let $z = x^3$. Then you get $x^9 - 8x^6 + 4x^3 - 32 = z^3 - 8z^2 + 4z - 32$.

In Example 2 from Lesson 1.09, you factored this cubic by grouping.

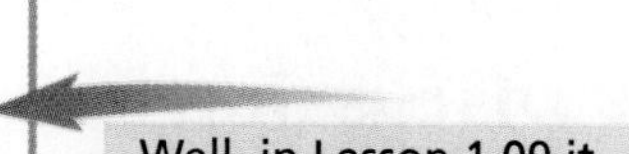

Well, in Lesson 1.09 it was a different variable.

$$z^3 - 8z^2 + 4z - 32 = (z - 8)(z^2 + 4)$$

Now replace $z$ with $x^3$.

$$(z - 8)(z^2 + 4) = (x^3 - 8)((x^3)^2 + 4) = (x^3 - 8)(x^6 + 4)$$

The polynomial $x^3 - 8$ factors as a difference of cubes.

$$(x^3 - 8) = (x - 2)(x^2 + 2x + 4)$$

So you have $x^9 - 8x^6 + 4x^3 - 32 = (x - 2)(x^2 + 2x + 4)(x^6 + 4)$.

## For Discussion

**3.** Are you done? Does either $x^2 + 2x + 4$ or $x^6 + 4$ factor over $\mathbb{Z}$?

## Difference of Squares in Disguise

There is a class of biquadratics that you can factor as the difference of two squares if you add and subtract a perfect square. Here is how it works.

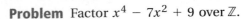

## Example 3

**Problem** Factor $x^4 - 7x^2 + 9$ over $\mathbb{Z}$.

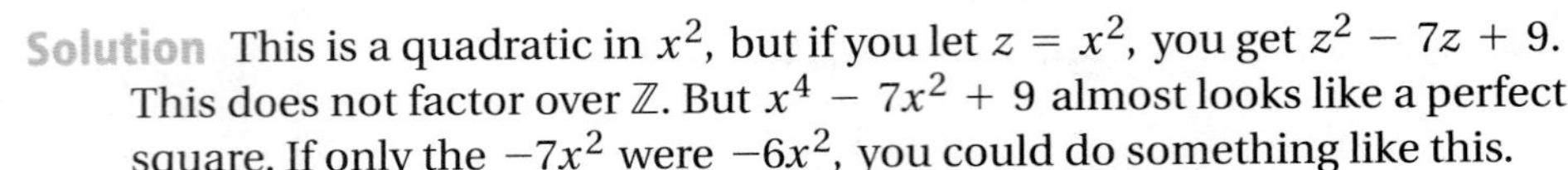

**Solution** This is a quadratic in $x^2$, but if you let $z = x^2$, you get $z^2 - 7z + 9$. This does not factor over $\mathbb{Z}$. But $x^4 - 7x^2 + 9$ almost looks like a perfect square. If only the $-7x^2$ were $-6x^2$, you could do something like this.

$$x^4 - 6x^2 + 9 = (x^2 - 3)^2$$

Well, you can make the middle term $-6x^2$ by adding and subtracting $x^2$.

$$x^4 - 7x^2 + 9 = x^4 - 6x^2 + 9 - x^2 = (x^2 - 3)^2 - x^2$$

That did it. This is a difference of squares, so now you can factor it.

$$x^4 - 7x^2 + 9 = (x^2 - 3)^2 - x^2 = (x^2 - 3 - x)(x^2 - 3 + x)$$

Can you factor either of these factors any more?

You can write each factor in normal form.

$$x^4 - 7x^2 + 9 = (x^2 - x - 3)(x^2 + x - 3)$$

## For You to Do

**4.** Factor $x^4 + 4$ over $\mathbb{Z}$.

## For Discussion

**5.** Suppose you want to factor $x^6 - 1$ over $\mathbb{Z}$. You have at least two ways to do it:

- as a difference of squares

$$\begin{aligned} x^6 - 1 &= (x^3)^2 - 1 \\ &= (x^3 - 1)(x^3 + 1) \\ &= (x - 1)(x^2 + x + 1)(x + 1)(x^2 - x + 1) \end{aligned}$$

- as a difference of cubes

$$\begin{aligned} x^6 - 1 &= (x^2)^3 - 1 \\ &= (x^2 - 1)((x^2)^2 + (x^2) + 1) \\ &= (x - 1)(x + 1)(x^4 + x^2 + 1) \end{aligned}$$

These look like two different factorizations. Are they?

## Factoring Over Extensions

Throughout this investigation, the verb *factor* has meant "to factor over $\mathbb{Z}$." If you allow for polynomials with real-number coefficients, some polynomials that do not factor over $\mathbb{Z}$ will factor over $\mathbb{R}$. For example, $x^2 - 3$ is irreducible over $\mathbb{Z}$, but if you "move up" to $\mathbb{R}$, you can factor it.

$$x^2 - 3 = (x - \sqrt{3})(x + \sqrt{3})$$

Factoring over $\mathbb{R}$ is often the right setting for applying the Factor Theorem.

Another way to say that a polynomial does not factor over $\mathbb{Z}$ is to say that a polynomial is *irreducible* over $\mathbb{Z}$.

Sometimes you have to search a larger set of objects to find what you are looking for.

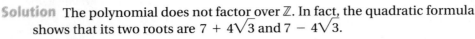

## Example 4

**Problem** Factor $x^2 - 14x + 1$ over $\mathbb{R}$.

**Solution** The polynomial does not factor over $\mathbb{Z}$. In fact, the quadratic formula shows that its two roots are $7 + 4\sqrt{3}$ and $7 - 4\sqrt{3}$.

Check that the quadratic formula gives these roots.

The Factor Theorem says that if $7 + 4\sqrt{3}$ is a root, $(x - (7 + 4\sqrt{3}))$, or $(x - 7 - 4\sqrt{3})$, must be a factor.

Similarly, another factor must be

$$(x - (7 - 4\sqrt{3})) = (x - 7 + 4\sqrt{3})$$

Since the original is a monic quadratic, the factorization must be

$$x^2 - 14x + 1 = (x - 7 - 4\sqrt{3})(x - 7 + 4\sqrt{3})$$

## For You to Do

6. Expand the product $(x - 7 - 4\sqrt{3})(x - 7 + 4\sqrt{3})$. (*Hint:* Why is this equal to $(x - 7)^2 - 48$?)

## For Discussion

7. Find real numbers $a$ and $b$ such that $(a + b\sqrt{3})^2 = 7 + 4\sqrt{3}$.
8. Find four real roots for the equation $x^4 - 14x^2 + 1 = 0$.

# Exercises Practicing Habits of Mind

## Check Your Understanding

**1.** Factor each polynomial over $\mathbb{Z}$.

**a.** $x^4 - x^2 - 6$

**b.** $x^6 - 9x^3 + 8$

**c.** $x^4 - 16$

**d.** $x^6 - 8$

**e.** $x^4 - 16y^4$

**f.** $x^6 + 8$

**g.** $x^4 - 9x^2 + 16$

**h.** $x^4 + x^2 + 1$

**2.** Factor each polynomial over $\mathbb{R}$.

**a.** $x^2 - 2x - 4$

**b.** $x^2 - x - 1$

**3.** Find a polynomial with integer coefficients that has a zero for each given value.

**a.** $2 + \sqrt{3}$

**b.** $2 - \sqrt{3}$

**c.** Take It Further $\sqrt{2} + \sqrt{3}$

**4.** Can a polynomial be irreducible over $\mathbb{Z}$ but factor over $\mathbb{Q}$? Explain.

Think of quadratics, for example. The symbol $\mathbb{Q}$ means the rational numbers.

## On Your Own

**5.** Factor each polynomial over $\mathbb{Z}$.

**a.** $x^4 - 11x^2 + 28$

**b.** $x^6 - 6x^3 + 9$

**c.** $x^6 - 27$

**d.** $x^6 + 3x^4 + 3x^2 + 1$

**e.** $x^4 + 9x^2 + 25$

**f.** $x^4 - 3a^2x^2 + a^4$

**g.** $x^6 - 1$

**h.** $x^8 - 1$

**6.** Solve each equation.

**a.** $\sqrt{x} = 7$

**b.** $\sqrt{x - 3} = 7$

**c.** $\sqrt{x - 3} = \sqrt{78}$

**d.** $\sqrt{x - 3} = \sqrt{x^2 - 15}$

**e.** Take It Further $\sqrt{2x - 5} - \sqrt{x - 2} = 2$

7. Derman is thinking about For Discussion Problem 5. He says, "I have a third way to factor $x^6 - 1$. I remember it from a homework problem a long time ago.

$$x^6 - 1 = (x - 1)(x^5 + x^4 + x^3 + x^2 + x + 1)$$

This is different from both answers."

Is Derman's factorization really different?

Go Online
www.successnetplus.com

8. **Standardized Test Prep** What is the greatest number of binomial factors over $\mathbb{Z}$ that you can use in a product to get $x^4 - 1$?

**A.** 2

**B.** 3

**C.** 4

**D.** 5

9. **Take It Further** Find real numbers $a$ and $b$ such that

$$x^4 + x^3 + x^2 + x + 1 = (x^2 + ax + 1)(x^2 + bx + 1)$$

## Maintain Your Skills

10. Factor each polynomial over $\mathbb{Z}$.

**a.** $1 + x + x^2 + x^3$

**b.** $1 + x + x^2 + x^3 + x^4 + x^5$

**c.** $1 + x + x^2 + x^3 + x^4 + x^5 + x^6 + x^7$

**d.** $1 + x + x^2 + x^3 + x^4 + x^5 + x^6 + x^7 + x^8 + x^9$

Is there a general method here?

# 1.11 Rational Expressions

Polynomials have an arithmetic that is similar to the arithmetic of ordinary integers. In both systems, you can add, subtract, multiply, and divide, and these operations obey the same basic rules. You also have long division in both systems. You can use these facts to show that you can factor anything (into primes for an integer and into irreducibles for a polynomial) in exactly one way.

There may be more than one way to carry out the factorization, but there will only be one final result.

Factoring polynomials is useful when you want to solve polynomial equations. Factoring integers is useful when you want to do arithmetic with fractions. That is, when you want to simplify a fraction and when you want to add two fractions.

## For You to Do

1. Just for old-time's sake, simplify $\frac{25,725}{86,625}$.
2. Find the sum $\frac{18}{49} + \frac{5}{21}$.

Because polynomials have an arithmetic (the basic rules of algebra) that is so much like the arithmetic of $\mathbb{Z}$, you can do arithmetic with fractions of polynomials.

## Example 1

**Problem** Simplify $\frac{x^2 - 5x + 6}{x^2 - 9}$.

**Solution**

$$\begin{aligned}\frac{x^2 - 5x + 6}{x^2 - 9} &= \frac{(x-3)(x-2)}{(x-3)(x+3)} \\ &= \frac{\cancel{(x-3)}(x-2)}{\cancel{(x-3)}(x+3)} \\ &= \frac{(x-2)}{(x+3)}\end{aligned}$$

Notice that this expression is equivalent to the original everywhere except at $x = 3$. At $x = 3$, the original rational expression was undefined, but this new expression is equal to $\frac{1}{6}$ at $x = 3$.

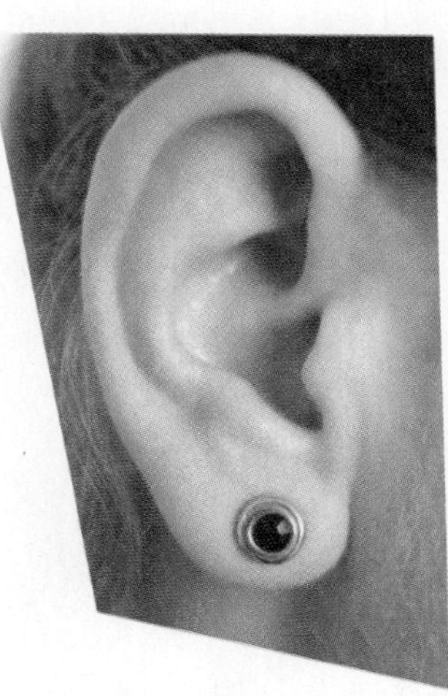

When you get your ear pierced, your ear remains the same everywhere except at one point.

## For You to Do

3. Simplify $\frac{x^3 - 1}{x^2 - 1}$.

## Example 2

**Problem** Write this sum as a single rational expression.

$$\frac{5x + 1}{x^2 - 1} + \frac{3}{x - 1} + \frac{2}{x + 1}$$

**Solution** Just as with integers, you need to find a common denominator. Since $x^2 - 1 = (x - 1)(x + 1)$, all three denominators are factors of $x^2 - 1$. You can use that expression as the denominator. Multiply each fraction by a form of 1 that makes its denominator $x^2 - 1$.

$$\begin{aligned}\frac{5x + 1}{x^2 - 1} + \frac{3}{x - 1} + \frac{2}{x + 1} &= \frac{5x + 1}{x^2 - 1} + \frac{3}{x - 1} \cdot \frac{(x + 1)}{(x + 1)} + \frac{2}{x + 1} \cdot \frac{(x - 1)}{(x - 1)} \\ &= \frac{5x + 1}{x^2 - 1} + \frac{3(x + 1)}{x^2 - 1} + \frac{2(x - 1)}{x^2 - 1} \\ &= \frac{(5x + 1) + 3(x + 1) + 2(x - 1)}{x^2 - 1} \\ &= \frac{10x + 2}{x^2 - 1} \\ &= \frac{2(5x + 1)}{x^2 - 1}\end{aligned}$$

**Habits of Mind**

**Think about it more than one way.** If you are thinking of the polynomials as expressions, you call fractions like these **rational expressions.** If you are thinking of the polynomials as functions, you call them rational functions.

## For You to Do

4. Write this difference as a single rational expression.

$$\frac{10}{x + 2} - \frac{6}{x - 2}$$

## Exercises Practicing Habits of Mind

### Check Your Understanding

**1.** Simplify each rational expression.

**a.** $\dfrac{15x}{5x^2}$ **b.** $\dfrac{x^2 - y^2}{(x + y)}$

**c.** $\dfrac{x^2 - y^2}{(x + y)^2}$ **d.** $\dfrac{x^2 - 1}{x^4 - 1}$

**e.** $\dfrac{2x^2 + x - 6}{3x^2 + 4x - 4}$ **f.** $\dfrac{3 - x - 3x^4 + x^5}{3 - x - 3x^3 + x^4}$

**2.** Let $f(x) = \dfrac{2x^2 + x - 6}{3x^2 + 4x - 4}$.

Suppose you define $g(x)$ by the same fraction, except the fraction is in simplest form. How do the graphs of $f(x)$ and $g(x)$ compare?

**3.** Write each sum as a single rational expression.

**a.** $\dfrac{b}{b - a} + \dfrac{a}{a - b}$

**b.** $\dfrac{1}{(x - a)(a - b)} + \dfrac{1}{(x - b)(b - a)}$

**4.** Write each sum as a single rational expression.

**a.** $\dfrac{1 + 2x}{3x - 3} + \dfrac{5 - x}{x^2 - 5x + 4}$

**b.** $\dfrac{2}{x - 3} - \dfrac{2}{x + 3} - \dfrac{1}{x}$

**c.** $\dfrac{1}{(a - b)(b - c)} + \dfrac{1}{(b - c)(c - a)} + \dfrac{1}{(c - a)(a - b)}$

**5.** Take It Further Find numbers $A$ and $B$ such that

$$\frac{1}{(x - 1)(x - 3)} = \frac{A}{(x - 1)} + \frac{B}{(x - 3)}$$

### On Your Own

**6.** Simplify each rational expression.

**a.** $\dfrac{x^2 - 1}{x - 1}$ **b.** $\dfrac{x^4 - 1}{x^2 - 1}$ **c.** $\dfrac{x^6 - 1}{x^3 - 1}$

**d.** $\dfrac{x^8 - 1}{x^4 - 1}$ **e.** $\dfrac{x^{10} - 1}{x^5 - 1}$

7. Write each expression as the quotient of two polynomials.

a. $1 + \frac{1}{x-1} - \frac{1}{1+x}$

b. $1 - \frac{2}{1+x^2}$

c. $\frac{1}{x-2} - \frac{1}{x-1}$

d. $\frac{1}{2(x-3)} - \frac{1}{x-2} + \frac{1}{2(x-1)}$

e. $\frac{2}{(x-1)^2} + \frac{1}{x-1} - \frac{1}{x-2}$

8. **Take It Further** Find numbers $A$ and $B$ such that

$$\frac{1}{(x-1)(x-2)} = \frac{A}{x-1} + \frac{B}{x-2}$$

9. **Standardized Test Prep** What is $\frac{x^2 - 9x + 20}{-x^2 + 6x - 8}$ written in lowest terms?

A. $\frac{x-5}{2-x}$

B. $\frac{x-5}{x-2}$

C. $\frac{x-4}{x-2}$

D. $\frac{x-5}{x-4}$

## Maintain Your Skills

10. Simplify each rational expression.

Go Online
Video Tutor
www.successnetplus.com

a. $\frac{x^3 - 1}{x - 1}$

b. $\frac{x^4 - 1}{(x-1)(x+1)}$

c. $\frac{x^5 - 1}{x - 1}$

d. $\frac{x^6 - 1}{(x-1)(x+1)(x^2+x+1)}$

e. $\frac{x^8 - 1}{(x-1)(x+1)(x^2+1)}$

f. $\frac{x^9 - 1}{(x-1)(x^2+x+1)}$

g. $\frac{x^{10} - 1}{(x-1)(x+1)(x^4+x^3+x^2+x+1)}$

h. $\frac{x^{12} - 1}{(x-1)(x+1)(x^2+x+1)(x^2+1)(x^2-x+1)}$

11. **Take It Further** Suppose that $f(x) = \frac{1}{(x-1)(x-2)}$. Find each value.

a. $f(3) + f(4) + f(5)$

b. $f(3) + f(4) + f(5) + f(6)$

c. $f(3) + f(4) + f(5) + f(6) + f(7)$

d. $f(3) + f(4) + f(5) + f(6) + f(7) + \cdots + f(23)$

e. $f(3) + f(4) + f(5) + f(6) + f(7) + \cdots + f(n)$ (in terms of $n$)

## Mathematical Reflections 1C

**In this investigation, you learned to factor polynomials by scaling, by finding roots, by using the sums and differences of squares and cubes, by grouping, and by identifying quadratic-like or cubic-like polynomials. These questions will help you summarize what you have learned.**

**1.** Factor each polynomial.

**a.** $6x^2 - x - 15$ **b.** $6x^2 + x - 15$ **c.** $35x^2 + 79x + 42$

**2.** Factor each polynomial over $\mathbb{Z}$.

**a.** $x^3 - 125$ **b.** $x^3 + 125$

**c.** $27x^3 - 64$ **d.** $27x^3 + 64$

**e.** $(x - 1)^3 - 27$ **f.** $(2x - 3)^3 + 27$

**g.** $x^3 + 3x^2 - 9x - 27$ **h.** $x^3 - 4x^2 + 4x - 3$

**i.** $x^4 - (2x + 1)^4$ **j.** $x^2 - y^2 + 2yz - z^2$

**3.** Factor each polynomial over $\mathbb{Z}$.

**a.** $35x^4 + 79x^2 + 42$ **b.** $6x^6 + x^3 - 15$

**c.** $x^4 - 81$ **d.** $x^6 - 27$

**e.** $4x^4 - 5x^2 + 1$ **f.** $x^4 + 5x^2 + 9$

**4.** For each number, find an equation with integer coefficients that has that number as a solution.

**a.** $\sqrt{5}$ **b.** $\sqrt{5} + \sqrt{7}$

**c.** Take It Further $3 + \sqrt{5} + \sqrt{7}$

**5.** Write each expression as a single rational expression.

**a.** $1 - \dfrac{x + 2}{x^2 + x + 1}$

**b.** $1 - \dfrac{2}{3(1 + x)} + \dfrac{2(x - 2)}{3(1 - x + x^2)}$

**6.** How do you factor nonmonic quadratics?

**7.** How do you factor differences and sums of cubes?

**8.** Does $x^4 + 4$ factor over $\mathbb{Z}$?

### Vocabulary and Notation

In this investigation, you learned these terms and symbols. Make sure you understand what each one means and how to use it.

- **difference of cubes**
- **quadratic formula**
- **rational expression**
- **sum of cubes**
- **$\mathbb{Z}$ (the integers)**
- **$\mathbb{Q}$ (the rational numbers)**

Chapter 1

# Review

Go Online
www.successnetplus.com

In **Investigation 1A,** you learned how to

- use linear combinations of polynomials to determine new polynomials
- use zeros of polynomials to determine factors of polynomials
- find polynomials that agree with a given table

*The following questions will help you check your understanding.*

**1.** Find a nonconstant polynomial function $h$ such that $h(1) = h(3) = h(4) = 0$.

**2.** Find a polynomial function $f$ in normal form that agrees with this table.

| Input | Output |
|---|---|
| 1 | −24 |
| 3 | 16 |
| 4 | 9 |
| 5 | −8 |

**3. a.** Find a quadratic function $g$ that agrees with $f: x \mapsto 3x - 5$ only at inputs $x = -1$ and $x = 2$.

**b.** Sketch the graphs of $f$ and $g$ on the same set of axes.

In **Investigation 1B,** you learned how to

- understand the relationship between roots and factors of polynomials
- divide polynomials by monic linear polynomials
- state and use the Remainder Theorem and the Factor Theorem
- write the general form of a function that fits a table

*The following questions will help you check your understanding.*

**4. a.** Find the quotient and remainder when you divide $p(x) = x^3 - 8x^2 + 3x - 5$ by $x + 3$.

**b.** Use your answer to find $p(-3)$.

**5.** Find the number $a$ such that $x - 2$ is a factor of $p(x) = x^3 + 3x^2 + 4x + a$.

**6.** Find the numbers $B$ and $C$ such that $x^2 - 8x = (x - 1)^2 + B(x - 1) + C$.

In **Investigation 1C,** you learned how to

- factor polynomials by scaling and by finding roots
- factor polynomials using the sums and differences of squares and cubes
- factor polynomials by grouping and by identifying quadratic-like or cubic-like polynomials

*The following questions will help you check your understanding.*

**7.** Factor each polynomial over $\mathbb{Z}$.

**a.** $4x^2 + 4x - 3$

**b.** $6x^2 + 23x + 21$

**c.** $36x^2 - 49y^2$

**d.** $3(x - 2)^2 + 5(x - 2) + 2$

**e.** $x^3 + 8$

**f.** $x^3 - 2x^2 + 3x - 6$

**8.** Factor each polynomial over $\mathbb{R}$.

**a.** $x^4 - 2x^2 + 1$

**b.** $x^2 - x - 4$

**9.** Write each expression as a single rational expression.

**a.** $\dfrac{2}{x - 4} + \dfrac{x}{x + 4}$

**b.** $2 - \dfrac{x + 3}{x - 2}$

Chapter 1

## Chapter Test

### Multiple Choice

**1.** Suppose the graph of $f: x = A(x-2)(x-3)$ contains the points $(2, 0)$, $(3, 0)$, and $(4, -6)$. What is the value of $A$?

**A.** $-6$

**B.** $-3$

**C.** $-\frac{1}{3}$

**D.** 3

**2.** When you divide $p(x) = 2x^3 - 3x^2 + 5x - 1$ by $x - 2$, what is the remainder?

**A.** $-1$

**B.** 0

**C.** 13

**D.** 36

**3.** Which expression is the factored form of $x^3 - 8$?

**A.** $(x+2)(x^2+2x+4)$

**B.** $(x-2)^3$

**C.** $(x-2)(x^2+2x+4)$

**D.** $(x-2)(x^2+4x+4)$

### Open Response

**4.** Find a polynomial function in normal form that agrees with the table.

| Input, $x$ | Output, $f(x)$ |
|---|---|
| 1 | 4 |
| 2 | $-2$ |
| 3 | 20 |

**5. a.** Find the quotient and remainder when you divide $f(x) = 2x^3 + 4x^2 - 5x + 6$ by $x - 3$.

**b.** Use your answer to find $f(3)$.

**6.** Factor each polynomial over $\mathbb{Z}$.

**a.** $8x^2 + 22x + 15$

**b.** $x^4 - 13x^2 + 36$

**c.** $x^3 + 1$

**7.** Find the difference.

$$\frac{x}{x+3} - \frac{3}{x-2}$$

**8.** How are the zeros of a polynomial related to its factors?

Chapter
2
Investigations at a Glance
2A The Need to Sum
2B Sum Identities
2C Arithmetic and Geometric Sequences and Series
2D Pascal's Triangle and the Binomial Theorem

# Sequences and Series

If you win \$1,000,000 in a state lottery, it is often buried in the contest rules that the prize is not really a check for \$1,000,000. Instead, it is \$50,000 a year for 20 years. Is your prize really worth \$1,000,000?

No, it is not. If you got the \$1,000,000 at the time you won the lottery, you might be able to invest it safely for at least a 6% return. That would give you not just \$50,000 a year, but \$60,000 a year, and not just for 20 years, but forever!

So your prize is not worth \$1,000,000. How much is it worth? What is its present value? To find the present value of the lottery prize, assuming you invest it at an interest rate of 6%, you can compute this sum.

$$50{,}000 + 50{,}000\left(\frac{1}{1.06}\right) + 50{,}000\left(\frac{1}{1.06}\right)^2 + \cdots + 50{,}000\left(\frac{1}{1.06}\right)^{19}$$

That expression is an example of a geometric series. You can write it more compactly.

$$\sum_{k=0}^{19} 50{,}000\left(\frac{1}{1.06}\right)^k$$

And even though it is not really worth \$1,000,000, you can see why the lottery does not advertise a big $\sum_{k=0}^{19} 50{,}000\left(\frac{1}{1.06}\right)^k$ prize. It is just not as impressive!

## Vocabulary and Notation

- arithmetic sequences
- arithmetic series
- Bernoulli's formulas
- closed-form definition
- common difference
- common ratio
- definite sum
- difference table
- Euclid's method
- figurative number
- Gauss's method
- geometric sequence
- geometric series
- identity
- indefinite sum
- index
- limit
- Pascal's Triangle
- recursive definition
- repeating decimal
- sequence
- series associated with $f$
- slope
- term
- $\sum_{k=0}^{n} f(k)$ (summation)
- $\binom{n}{k}$ (the $n$th row, $k$th column entry of Pascal's triangle)

## 2.0 Two Types of Definitions

Look at the table below.

**Table H**

| Input | Output |
|---|---|
| 0 | 3 |
| 1 | 8 |
| 2 | 13 |
| 3 | 18 |
| 4 | 23 |

You can describe a function that agrees with this table in more than one way. For example,

- If the input $n$ is zero, the output is 3. To get the next output, add 5 to the previous output.
- $g(n) = 5n + 3$

### Developing Habits of Mind

**Look for patterns.** In previous coursework, you learned that Table H itself is a function. The set of possible inputs is $\{0, 1, 2, 3, 4\}$ and nothing else. When you think of the table as a function, you can write $H(2) = 13$, but $H(6)$ is not defined.

In this lesson, you are looking for something different—a way to express some regularity in the table. Finding and describing a pattern can allow you to extend the domain from $\{0, 1, 2, 3, 4\}$ to a larger set of numbers. Both bulleted descriptions above do this. When you match a table with a polynomial or another simple rule, you are uncovering a hidden relationship in the numbers. This is something that mathematicians really prize.

You learned that the domain of a function is *the set of allowable inputs.*

### For You to Do

1. When the input is 9, what is the output of each of the two functions described above?
2. Can you use each function to find the output when the input is $-2$? Explain.

## *Facts and Notation*

A function definition such as "$g(n) = 5n + 3$" is a **closed-form definition.** A closed-form definition lets you find any output $g(n)$ for any input $n$ by direct calculation.

A function definition such as "$f(0) = 3$ and any output is 5 more than the previous output" is a **recursive definition.** Recursive definitions are useful for expressing patterns in the outputs of a function. The notation below is a useful way to write a recursive definition.

$$f(n) = \begin{cases} 3 & \text{if } n = 0 \\ f(n-1) + 5 & \text{if } n > 0 \end{cases}$$

Notice that $f$ is a recursive function and $g$ is a closed-form function. Do the two definitions give the same function?

## Developing Habits of Mind

**Use a model.** The closed-form definition below matches Table H from the previous page.

$$g(n) = 5n + 3$$

You can build a computer or calculator model for function $g$ in your function-modeling language. Then you can experiment with the model. You can do the following:

- Evaluate the function.
- Graph the function.
- Make a table of the function in a spreadsheet window.

It is a good habit to build models like these for the functions you use, especially when you want to get a feel for how the functions behave.

How you build a model depends on your computer or calculator. See the TI-Nspire™ Handbook, p. 817.

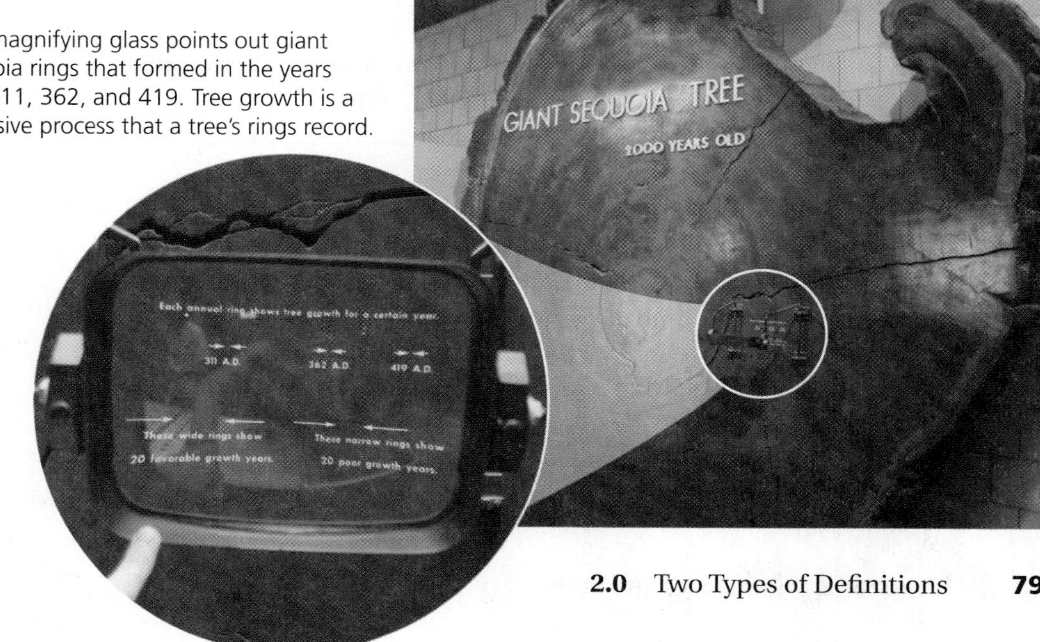


The magnifying glass points out giant sequoia rings that formed in the years A.D. 311, 362, and 419. Tree growth is a recursive process that a tree's rings record.

## For You to Do

3. Build a model for $g$ in your function-modeling language.
4. Make a table of your model for inputs between 0 and 10.
5. Graph your model in your graphing environment.

A recursive definition lets you calculate any output in terms of previous outputs. The simplest kind of recursive definition for a function $f$ tells you how to compute $f(n)$ for an integer $n$ in terms of $f(n - 1)$. You need a place to start. The definition below tells you to start at 3 (when $n = 0$) and to add 5 to get from one output to the next.

$$f(n) = \begin{cases} 3 & \text{if } n = 0 \\ f(n-1) + 5 & \text{if } n > 0 \end{cases}$$

Read the second line as "the current output is the previous output plus five." This recursively defined function fits all the entries in Table H.

- $f(0) = 3$, because $n = 0$
- $f(1) = f(1 - 1) + 5 = f(0) + 5 = 3 + 5 = 8$
- $f(2) = f(2 - 1) + 5 = f(1) + 5 = 8 + 5 = 13$

## For You to Do

You can use function-modeling language to model a recursive definition. Your technology may even provide a template like the one below. For help, see the TI-Nspire™ Handbook, p. 817.

Recursive definitions tell you how the outputs are related. Closed-form definitions tell you how inputs are related to outputs. Each tells you something interesting. In some cases, you can convert one to the other.

$$\text{define } f(n) = \begin{cases} \blacksquare, \blacksquare \\ \blacksquare, \blacksquare \end{cases}$$

You just fill in the boxes.

$$\text{define } f(n) = \begin{cases} 3, & \text{if } n = 0 \\ f(n-1) + 5, & \text{if } n > 0 \end{cases}$$

6. Build a model for $f$ and experiment with it. What numbers will $f$ accept as inputs? Explain. How does $g$ compare to $f$?

### Difference Tables

A **difference table** can help you see patterns that lead to recursive definitions. Use Table H from earlier in this lesson.

**Table H**

| Input | Output |
|---|---|
| 0 | 3 |
| 1 | 8 |
| 2 | 13 |
| 3 | 18 |
| 4 | 23 |

To make a difference table, add a third column marked with the $\Delta$ symbol. Write the difference between one output and the next in the third column.

The $\Delta$ symbol is the capital Greek letter delta. It represents change or difference.

| Input | Output | $\Delta$ |
|---|---|---|
| 0 | 3 | $8 - 3 = \mathbf{5}$ |
| 1 | 8 | $13 - 8 = \mathbf{5}$ |
| 2 | 13 | $18 - 13 = \mathbf{5}$ |
| 3 | 18 | $23 - 18 = \mathbf{5}$ |
| 4 | 23 | |

The differences are exactly what you need to write a recursively defined function that matches Table H. In this case, all the differences are the same number, 5. The following recursive definition fits Table H.

$$f(n) = \begin{cases} 3 & \text{if } n = 0 \\ f(n-1) + 5 & \text{if } n > 0 \end{cases}$$

In some tables the differences are not constant, as in the table below.

**Table D**

| Input, *n* | Output, *d*(*n*) | $\Delta$ |
|---|---|---|
| 0 | 0 | 3 |
| 1 | 3 | 5 |
| 2 | 8 | 7 |
| 3 | 15 | 9 |
| 4 | 24 | 11 |
| 5 | 35 | 13 |
| 6 | 48 | |

You can still use the $\Delta$ column to find a recursive function that matches the table. Here is a recursive definition for *d*.

What function matches the $\Delta$ column?

$$d(n) = \begin{cases} 0 & \text{if } n = 0 \\ d(n-1) + 2n + 1 & \text{if } n > 0 \end{cases}$$

## For You to Do

**7.** Show that the function *d* fits Table D.

## Exercises *Practicing Habits of Mind*

### Check Your Understanding

For Exercises 1–3, use Table B.

**Table B**

| Input, *n* | Output, *B*(*n*) |
|---|---|
| 0 | 0 |
| 1 | 2 |
| 2 | 6 |
| 3 | 12 |
| 4 | 20 |

**1.** Make a difference table for Table B.

**2.** Decide whether each recursive definition fits Table B.

**a.** $b(n) = \begin{cases} 0 & \text{if } n = 0 \\ b(n-1) + 2 & \text{if } n > 0 \end{cases}$

**b.** $b(n) = \begin{cases} 0 & \text{if } n = 0 \\ b(n-1) + 2(n-1) & \text{if } n > 0 \end{cases}$

**c.** $b(n) = \begin{cases} 0 & \text{if } n = 0 \\ b(n-1) + 2n & \text{if } n > 0 \end{cases}$

**d.** $b(n) = \begin{cases} 2 & \text{if } n = 0 \\ b(n-1) + 2n & \text{if } n > 0 \end{cases}$

**3.** Decide whether each closed-form definition fits Table B.

**a.** $b(n) = 2n$

**b.** $b(n) = n^2 + n$

**c.** To find each output, take the input and multiply by one more than the input.

**d.** $b(n) = 2^{n+1} - 2$

For Exercises 4–6, copy and complete each difference table.

**4.**

| Input | Output | Δ |
|---|---|---|
| 0 | 5 | 6 |
| 1 | 11 | ■ |
| 2 | 19 | 10 |
| 3 | ■ | 15 |
| 4 | ■ | |

**5.**

| Input | Output | Δ |
|---|---|---|
| 0 | ■ | 3 |
| 1 | ■ | 3 |
| 2 | ■ | 3 |
| 3 | ■ | 3 |
| 4 | 18 | |

**6.**

| Input | Output | Δ |
|---|---|---|
| 0 | 5 | −3 |
| 1 | ■ | ■ |
| 2 | 17 | ■ |
| 3 | ■ | −5 |
| 4 | −1 | |

**7.** Use the recursive definition below.

$$f(n) = \begin{cases} 1 & \text{if } n = 0 \\ n \cdot f(n-1) & \text{if } n > 0 \end{cases}$$

**a.** Find the values of $f(1)$ through $f(6)$ for this function.

**b.** What preprogrammed function on your calculator agrees with $f$?

**8.** The table at the right is an incomplete input-output table for a function.

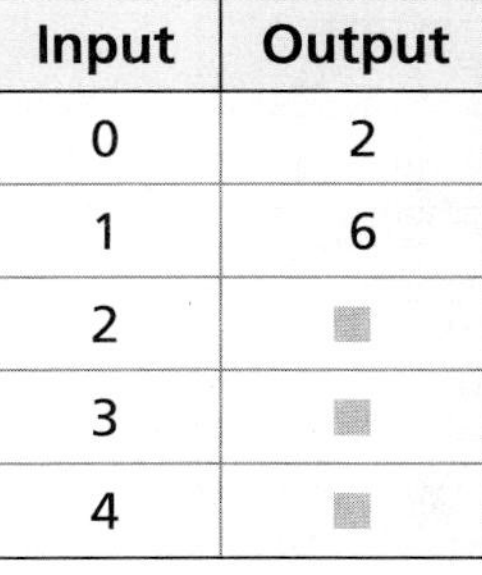

| Input | Output |
|---|---|
| 0 | 2 |
| 1 | 6 |
| 2 | ■ |
| 3 | ■ |
| 4 | ■ |

You can use each rule to complete the table. Make a completed table for each rule.

**a.** To get each output, take the previous output and add four.

**b.** To get each output, take the previous output and multiply by three.

**c.** $n \mapsto 2(3^n)$

**d.** To get each output, take the input, multiply by four, and then add two.

**9.** **Write About It** Consider the tables used in this lesson. Find three tables that are related. Describe how they are related. You may find it helpful to make difference tables.

**Remember...**

$a^0 = 1$ for any nonzero number $a$, so $3^0 = 1$.

## On Your Own

The *triangular numbers* are numbers determined by the pattern shown below. The number of dots in a triangular pattern with $n$ dots on a side is the $n$th triangular number.

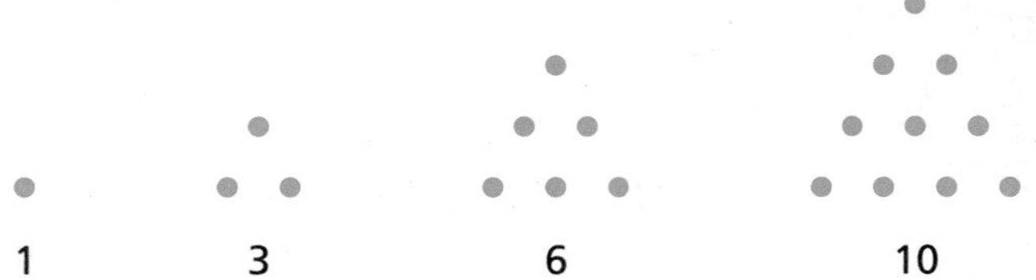


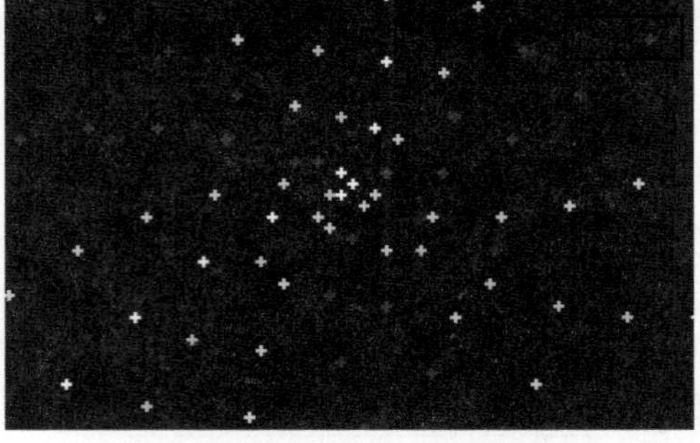

This pattern results when you arrange the counting numbers in a spiral and color the triangular numbers.

Here is a table for the triangular numbers.

| Side Length | Number of Dots |
|---|---|
| 0 | 0 |
| 1 | 1 |
| 2 | 3 |
| 3 | 6 |
| 4 | 10 |
| 5 | 15 |

**10.** Make a difference table for the triangular numbers.

**11.** **a.** Write a recursive function definition that fits the table of triangular numbers.

**b.** Take It Further Find a closed-form definition for a function that generates the triangular numbers.

**12.** **a.** Copy and complete the difference table below.

| Input, $x$ | Output, $ax + b$ | Δ |
|---|---|---|
| 0 | $b$ | ■ |
| 1 | $a + b$ | ■ |
| 2 | $2a + b$ | ■ |
| 3 | $3a + b$ | ■ |
| 4 | $4a + b$ | ■ |
| 5 | $5a + b$ | |

**b.** Find a formula for $f(x + 1) - f(x)$ when $f(x) = ax + b$.

You can define $f(x) = ax + b$ in your computer algebra system (CAS) and ask for $f(x + 1) - f(x)$. Make sure you have not assigned any values to $a$, $b$, or $x$.

**13. a.** Copy and complete the difference table below.

| Input, $x$ | Output, $ax^2 + bx + c$ | $\Delta$ |
|---|---|---|
| 0 | $c$ | ■ |
| 1 | $a + b + c$ | ■ |
| 2 | $4a + 2b + c$ | ■ |
| 3 | $9a + 3b + c$ | ■ |
| 4 | $16a + 4b + c$ | ■ |
| 5 | $25a + 5b + c$ | |

**b.** Find a formula for $f(x + 1) - f(x)$ when $f(x) = ax^2 + bx + c$.

**Habits of Mind**

**Look for relationships.** What is the connection between the two parts of this exercise?

**14.** Standardized Test Prep Find the output of the function $g(n)$ below for the input $n = 4$.

$$g(n) = \begin{cases} 1 & \text{if } n = 1 \\ g(n - 1) + 2n - 1 & \text{if } n > 1 \end{cases}$$

**A.** 1 **B.** 4

**C.** 10 **D.** 16

## Maintain Your Skills

**15.** In each table below, the input-output pairs represent points on the graph of a linear function. Find the slope of each graph.

**a.**

| Input | Output |
|---|---|
| 0 | −7 |
| 1 | −4 |
| 2 | −1 |
| 3 | 2 |
| 4 | 5 |
| 5 | 8 |

**b.**

| Input | Output |
|---|---|
| 0 | −7 |
| 1 | −11 |
| 2 | −15 |
| 3 | −19 |
| 4 | −23 |
| 5 | −27 |

**c.**

| Input | Output |
|---|---|
| 0 | 2 |
| 1 | $1\frac{1}{2}$ |
| 2 | 1 |
| 3 | $\frac{1}{2}$ |
| 4 | 0 |
| 5 | $-\frac{1}{2}$ |

**d.** Describe how you can find the slope of a linear function when you have a table for the function in which the inputs are consecutive integers.

**Remember...**

**Slope** is the ratio of the change in the $y$-coordinates to the change in the $x$-coordinates.

# The Need to Sum

**In *The Need to Sum,* you will explore sums. You will add a sum column to tables and find function rules to match the sum column. You will learn methods to calculate sums more easily.**

**By the end of this investigation, you will be able to answer questions like these.**

1. Describe Gauss's method for summing all integers from 1 to $n$.
2. Find a formula for $\sum_{j=0}^{n} 2^j$ in terms of $n$.
3. Evaluate $\sum_{j=1}^{5} 4j$.

**You will learn how to**

- make a sum table for a function and write a closed-form rule for the sum column where appropriate
- use Gauss's method to find the sum of a sequence with a constant difference between successive terms
- use Euclid's method to find the sum of a sequence with a constant ratio between successive terms
- expand $\Sigma$ notation or convert an expanded sum back to $\Sigma$ notation

**You will develop these habits and skills:**

- Reason logically to understand how both Gauss's method and Euclid's method work, and choose which method to use for finding a particular sum.
- Visualize a sum geometrically to make sense of an algebraic pattern.
- Generalize a result from a series of numerical examples.

You can use $\Sigma$ notation to describe sums with patterns, such as the total volume of successively smaller slices of watermelon.

# 2.01 Getting Started

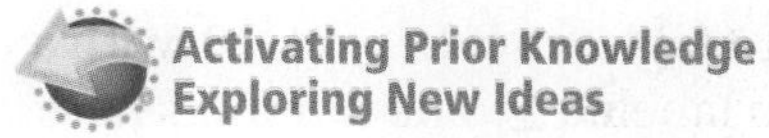


For some problems, you need to look at the sums of all the outputs as well as the individual outputs.

## For You to Explore

Emile got a letter in the mail saying that a wealthy relative had left him an inheritance. At a meeting the next week, a lawyer read the following statement.

To Emile, because he likes math problems, I leave a choice. He can have one of two inheritances. He must make his choice before leaving the office today.

**Option 1** A starting amount of $10,000 and then, for the next 26 years, an annual payment at the end of each year that is $1000 more than the amount he received the previous year.

For each option, there is a total of 27 payments.

**Option 2** A starting amount of one cent and then, for the next 26 years, an annual payment at the end of each year that is twice the amount he received in the previous year.

Luckily, Emile brought his calculator to the meeting.

**1.** Suppose $f(n)$ is the amount of money Emile gets in Year $n$ under Option 1 and $g(n)$ is the amount of money he gets in Year $n$ under Option 2. Year 0 is the year in which Emile chooses one of the options and gets his first payment.

**a.** Find closed-form rules for $f(n)$ and $g(n)$.

**b.** For what values of $n$ is $f(n) < g(n)$?

**c.** For what values of $n$ is $f(n) > g(n)$?

**Habits of Mind**

**Check your units.** When you compare the two functions, do not forget that you probably calculated $f$ in dollars and $g$ in cents.

**2.** Suppose $F(n)$ is the total amount of money Emile has received after $n$ years under Option 1, and $G(n)$ is the total amount of money he has received after $n$ years under Option 2.

**a.** Make a table of values for $F(n)$ with inputs 0 through 5.

**b.** Make a table of values for $G(n)$ with inputs 0 through 5.

**c.** For what values of $n$ is $F(n) < G(n)$?

**d.** For what values of $n$ is $F(n) > G(n)$?

**3. a.** Write a closed-form rule for $F(n)$.

**b.** Write a closed-form rule for $G(n)$.

**4.** If you were Emile, which option would you choose? Explain.

Here is a table from Lesson 2.0, with a new column labeled $\Sigma$. The numbers in the $\Sigma$ column are just the running totals of the outputs.

A closed-form rule for the $\Sigma$ column in this case is $n \mapsto (n + 1)^2$.

| $n$ | $f(n)$ | $\Sigma$ |
|---|---|---|
| 0 | 1 | 1 |
| 1 | 3 | 4 |
| 2 | 5 | 9 |
| 3 | 7 | 16 |
| 4 | 9 | 25 |
| 5 | 11 | 36 |

The symbol $\Sigma$ is based on the capital Greek letter *sigma*. In mathematics, you often use $\Sigma$ to stand for "sum."

5. **a.** Copy the table at the right. Add a $\Sigma$ column to the table.

   **b.** Find a closed-form rule for the $\Sigma$ column.

| $n$ | $h(n)$ |
|---|---|
| 0 | 0 |
| 1 | 2 |
| 2 | 4 |
| 3 | 6 |
| 4 | 8 |
| 5 | 10 |

## Exercises Practicing Habits of Mind

### On Your Own

6. Ken and Maggie both start with 50 chips. One of them rolls a number cube. If the number is even, Maggie gives Ken that many chips. If the number is odd, Ken gives Maggie that many chips.

   The table shows how many chips Maggie gains for each roll. If she loses chips, she records this as a negative gain.

   **a.** Copy Maggie's table. Add a column that shows how many chips she has after each move.

   **b.** Is this a fair game? Explain.

**Maggie's Table**

| Roll | Gain |
|---|---|
| 1 | 5 |
| 2 | −2 |
| 3 | −4 |
| 4 | 3 |
| 5 | −6 |
| 6 | 1 |
| 7 | −6 |

For Exercises 7–9, copy each table. Add a $\Sigma$ column. Find a closed-form rule for the $\Sigma$ column.

You can use a spreadsheet to make $\Sigma$ columns. See the TI-Nspire™ Handbook, p. 817.

**7.**

| $n$ | $t(n)$ |
|---|---|
| 0 | 1 |
| 1 | 9 |
| 2 | 90 |
| 3 | 900 |
| 4 | 9000 |

**8.**

| $n$ | $h(n)$ |
|---|---|
| 0 | 5 |
| 1 | 5 |
| 2 | 5 |
| 3 | 5 |
| 4 | 5 |

**9.**

| $n$ | $g(n)$ |
|---|---|
| 0 | −1 |
| 1 | 1 |
| 2 | 3 |
| 3 | 5 |
| 4 | 7 |
| 5 | 9 |

**10.** At the beginning of a bus route, 10 people get on the bus. At the first stop, 3 more people get on. At the second stop, 2 people get off and 5 others get on. At the third stop, 1 person gets off. At the next stop, 3 get off and 4 get on. At the next stop, 2 get on and 5 get off. At the next stop, 3 get on. How many passengers are on the bus?

**11.** A bakery manager asks employees to keep at least 6 dozen muffins in the display case at all times. The counter clerk has to keep track of the sales as well as how many muffins the baker brings out from the kitchen. Copy the table below. Add a $\Sigma$ column to answer the questions.

| Time | Baked or Bought | Amount |
|---|---|---|
| 6:00 A.M. | Baked | 144 |
| 6:10 A.M. | Bought | 12 |
| 6:25 A.M. | Bought | 2 |
| 6:45 A.M. | Bought | 24 |
| 7:00 A.M. | Bought | 5 |
| 7:15 A.M. | Baked | 24 |
| 7:30 A.M. | Bought | 36 |
| 8:15 A.M. | Baked | 12 |
| 8:25 A.M. | Bought | 6 |
| 8:30 A.M. | Bought | 24 |

**a.** What was the total number of muffins in the case after the 8:30 A.M. count?

**b.** Did the clerk ever allow the total muffin count to go below the manager's requirement? If so, when?

Suppose that in Problem 1, the will gives Emile a third option.

**Option 3** There is a starting amount of $0 and then, for the next 26 years, an annual payment at the end of each year that is the square of the year (1, 2, and so on) times $100.

**12.** Suppose $h(n)$ is the amount of money Emile gets in Year $n$ under Option 3.

**a.** What is a closed form for $h(n)$?

**b.** Compare $h(n)$ to the functions $f(n)$ and $g(n)$ from Problem 1. For what values of $n$ is each inequality true?

$h(n) < f(n)$

$h(n) > f(n)$

$h(n) < g(n)$

$h(n) > g(n)$

**13.** Suppose $H(n)$ is the total amount of money Emile gets after $n$ years under Option 3. For what values of $n$ is each inequality true?

**a.** $H(n) < F(n)$

**b.** $H(n) > F(n)$

**c.** $H(n) < G(n)$

**d.** $H(n) > G(n)$

## Maintain Your Skills

**14.** Copy and complete the following difference tables. Write a closed-form rule for each function.

| $n$ | $F(n)$ | $\Delta$ |
|---|---|---|
| 0 | 1 | ■ |
| 1 | 4 | ■ |
| 2 | 9 | ■ |
| 3 | 16 | ■ |
| 4 | 25 | ■ |
| 5 | 36 | |

| $n$ | $T(n)$ | $\Delta$ |
|---|---|---|
| 0 | 1 | ■ |
| 1 | 10 | ■ |
| 2 | 100 | ■ |
| 3 | 1000 | ■ |
| 4 | 10,000 | ■ |
| 5 | 100,000 | |

| $n$ | $H(n)$ | $\Delta$ |
|---|---|---|
| 0 | 5 | ■ |
| 1 | 10 | ■ |
| 2 | 15 | ■ |
| 3 | 20 | ■ |
| 4 | 25 | ■ |
| 5 | 30 | |

# 2.02 Gauss's Method and Euclid's Method

Many stories are told about the mathematician Carl Friedrich Gauss. According to one story, one of his teachers gave Gauss and some classmates a problem to keep them busy for a while. The teacher asked the students to add all of the integers from 1 to 100. In just a few moments, Gauss wrote the number 5050 on his paper, and he was right!

## Minds in Action

*For her history class, Sasha is doing a project about Gauss's life.*

**Sasha** So, Gauss had to solve the following problem.

Add up the integers from 1 to 100.

He probably did something like this.

You can write the sum two ways.

$$S = 1 + 2 + 3 + 4 + \cdots + 100$$
$$S = 100 + 99 + 98 + 97 + \cdots + 1$$

Some people believe that he just added all the numbers up in his head.

Add the first numbers of each sum together, then the second numbers, then the third ones, and so on, and you'll get

$$\begin{array}{cccccccccccccccc} & S & = & 1 & + & 2 & + & 3 & + & 4 & + & \cdots & + & 100 \\ & \downarrow & & \downarrow & & \downarrow & & \downarrow & & \downarrow & & & & \downarrow \\ + & S & = & 100 & + & 99 & + & 98 & + & 97 & + & \cdots & + & 1 \\ \hline & 2S & = & 101 & + & 101 & + & 101 & + & 101 & + & \cdots & + & 101 \end{array}$$

There are one hundred 101's altogether, so

$$2S = 100 \cdot 101$$
$$S = 5050$$

## For You to Do

Gauss found a way to add up the first 100 integers. Use his method to find the following sums.

1. Add up all integers from 1 to 371, inclusive.
2. Add up all integers from 0 to 789, inclusive.

**Gauss's method** allows you to add up certain kinds of lists of numbers. The method works when the numbers add up in the same way forward and backward. Not all sequences of numbers have this property.

For example, suppose $g(n) = 3^n$. A table for $g$ looks fairly regular.

| $n$ | $g(n)$ |
|---|---|
| 0 | $3^0 = 1$ |
| 1 | $3^1 = 3$ |
| 2 | $3^2 = 9$ |
| 3 | $3^3 = 27$ |
| 4 | $3^4 = 81$ |
| 5 | $3^5 = 243$ |

How would you add up all the outputs of $g$ between 1 and, say, $3^5$? You might try Gauss's method.

$$S = 1 + 3 + 3^2 + 3^3 + 3^4 + 3^5$$

$$S = 3^5 + 3^4 + 3^3 + 3^2 + 3 + 1$$

$$\begin{array}{rrcrcrcrcrcrcr} & S & = & 1 & + & 3 & + & 9 & + & 27 & + & 81 & + & 243 \\ & \downarrow & & \downarrow & & \downarrow & & \downarrow & & \downarrow & & \downarrow & & \downarrow \\ + & S & = & 243 & + & 81 & + & 27 & + & 9 & + & 3 & + & 1 \\ \hline & 2S & = & 244 & + & 84 & + & 36 & + & 36 & + & 84 & + & 244 \end{array}$$

These sums are not all the same, so Gauss's trick does not work. What can you do?

## Example

**Problem** Add up the numbers $3^0 + 3^1 + 3^2 + 3^3 + 3^4 + 3^5$.

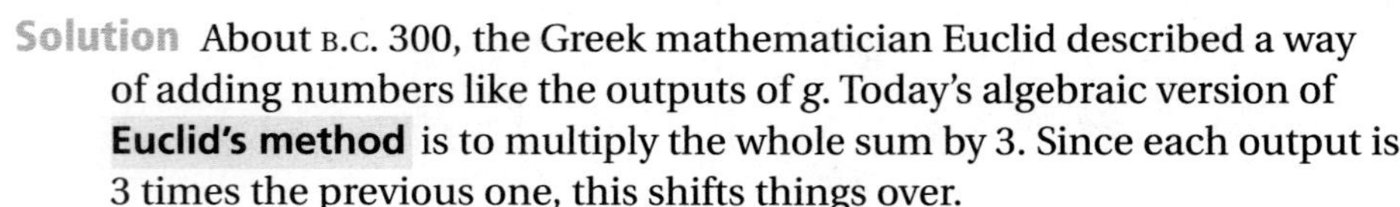

**Solution** About B.C. 300, the Greek mathematician Euclid described a way of adding numbers like the outputs of $g$. Today's algebraic version of **Euclid's method** is to multiply the whole sum by 3. Since each output is 3 times the previous one, this shifts things over.

$$\begin{array}{rcrcrcrcrcrcrcr} S & = & 3^0 & + & 3^1 & + & 3^2 & + & 3^3 & + & 3^4 & + & 3^5 & & \\ 3S & = & & & 3^1 & + & 3^2 & + & 3^3 & + & 3^4 & + & 3^5 & + & 3^6 \end{array}$$

Now subtract the top sum from the bottom one.

$$\begin{array}{rrcrrcrcrcrcrcr} & 3S & = & & & 3^1 & + & 3^2 & + & 3^3 & + & 3^4 & + & 3^5 & + & 3^6 \\ - & S & = & - & 3^0 & - & 3^1 & - & 3^2 & - & 3^3 & - & 3^4 & - & 3^5 & & \\ \hline & 2S & = & - & 3^0 & & & & & & & & & & + & 3^6 \end{array}$$

Almost everything cancels. You get the following result.

$$2S = -1 + 3^6$$

$$S = \frac{3^6 - 1}{2} = 364$$

Euclid described his method in Book IX, Proposition 35 of *Elements*. He based his demonstration on the theory of proportions.

## For You to Do

Use Euclid's method to find each sum.

**3.** $1 + 2 + 2^2 + 2^3 + \cdots + 2^{12}$

**4.** $5^3 + 5^4 + 5^5 + 5^6 + 5^7 + 5^8$

## Exercises *Practicing Habits of Mind*

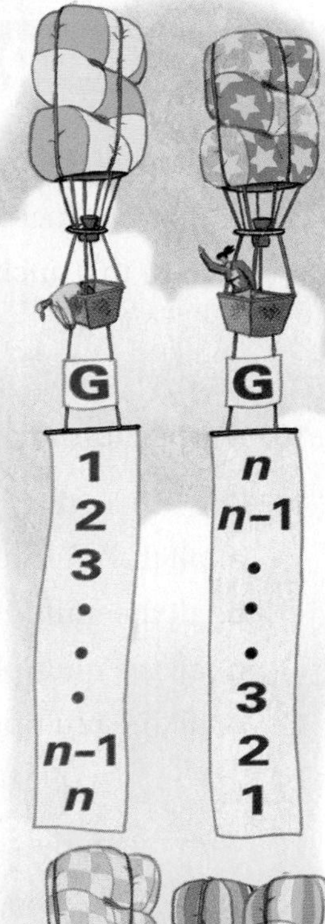


### Check Your Understanding

**1.** Use Gauss's method to find a formula for each sum.

**a.** Add up all the integers from 0 to $n$.

**b.** Add up all the integers from 1 to $n$.

**c.** Add up all the integers from 0 to $n - 1$.

**2.** Add up the even integers in each range.

**a.** 0 to 4, inclusive **b.** 0 to 10, inclusive **c.** 0 to 1000, inclusive

**3.** Add up the odd integers in each range.

**a.** 1 to 7, inclusive **b.** 1 to 13, inclusive **c.** 1 to 999, inclusive

**4.** Find a formula for each sum.

**a.** the even integers from 0 to $2n$ **b.** the odd integers from 1 to $2n + 1$

**5.** Use Euclid's method to find each sum.

**a.** $2^5 + 2^6 + 2^7 + \cdots + 2^{15}$

**b.** $3 \cdot 2^5 + 3 \cdot 2^6 + 3 \cdot 2^7 + \cdots + 3 \cdot 2^{15}$

**c.** $\frac{9}{10} + \left(\frac{9}{10}\right)^2 + \left(\frac{9}{10}\right)^3 + \cdots + \left(\frac{9}{10}\right)^{10}$

**d.** $\frac{9}{10} + \frac{9}{10^2} + \frac{9}{10^3} + \cdots + \frac{9}{10^{10}}$

**e.** $1 - \frac{1}{2} + \left(\frac{1}{2}\right)^2 - \left(\frac{1}{2}\right)^3 + \cdots - \left(\frac{1}{2}\right)^7$

**6. Write About It**

**a.** Give three sequences of numbers for which Gauss's method works. What do they have in common?

**b.** Give three sequences of numbers for which Euclid's method works. What do they have in common?

**7.** Suppose $r$ is some number. Find a formula for each sum.

**a.** $1 + r + r^2 + \cdots + r^n$ **b.** $a + ar + ar^2 + \cdots + ar^n$

## On Your Own

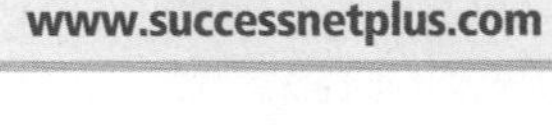


8. Add up all the integers in each range.
   a. $-4$ to 0, inclusive
   b. $-10$ to 0, inclusive
   c. $-1000$ to 0, inclusive
9. Find a formula for the sum of the integers from $-n$ to 0.
10. Adapt a formula or formulas to find the sum of the integers from $-10$ to 8.
11. **Take It Further** Find a formula for each sum.
    a. all the multiples of 3 from 0 to $3n$
    b. all the multiples of 5 from 0 to $5n$
    c. all the multiples of 7 from 0 to $7n$
    d. all the multiples of $k$ from 0 to $kn$
12. Let $f(n) = \left(\frac{1}{2}\right)^1 + \left(\frac{1}{2}\right)^2 + \left(\frac{1}{2}\right)^3 + \cdots + \left(\frac{1}{2}\right)^n$. Make a table for $f$ starting with the initial term $f(1) = \frac{1}{2}$. Find a closed form for $f(n)$.
13. Let $g(n) = \left(\frac{1}{2}\right)^0 + \left(\frac{1}{2}\right)^1 + \left(\frac{1}{2}\right)^2 + \left(\frac{1}{2}\right)^3 + \cdots + \left(\frac{1}{2}\right)^n$. Make a table for $g$ starting with the initial term $g(0) = \left(\frac{1}{2}\right)^0 = 1$. Find a closed form for $g(n)$.
14. **Standardized Test Prep** Rod went to a party. The host asked each guest to shake hands with every other guest exactly once. The next morning Rod's mother asked him how many guests attended the party. He forgot the number, but he remembered the host announced there had been 78 handshakes. How many guests attended the party?

    **A.** 10 **B.** 11 **C.** 12 **D.** 13

## Maintain Your Skills

15. Use Gauss's method to add up the integers in each range.
    a. 3 to 5, inclusive
    b. 55 to 60, inclusive
    c. 5 to 80, inclusive
    d. $-7$ to 150, inclusive
    e. $-31$ to 131, inclusive
    f. $n$ to $m$, inclusive

# 2.03 Ways to Visualize Sums

Many people like to think in images. Here are two In-Class Experiments that help you "see" what is going on with Gauss's and Euclid's methods.

## In-Class Experiment

Suppose $f(n) = n$. The diagram at the right represents the first five outputs of $f$. The outputs are the number of squares in the towers.

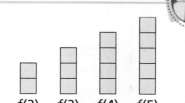

$f(1)$ $f(2)$ $f(3)$ $f(4)$ $f(5)$

Now you want to add these up, so you can think of pushing the towers together to form a staircase. Then you want to count the number of blocks that make up the staircase.

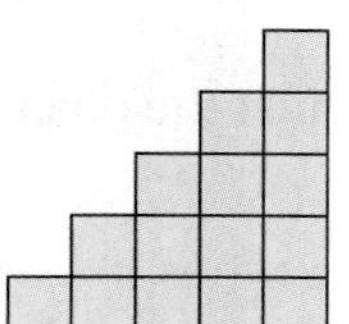

**Step 1** Make two copies of the staircase above. Cut out the two copies of the staircase, made up of the blocks that you want to count. For now, just draw diagrams for the staircase that goes from $f(1)$ to $f(5)$.

**Step 2** Flip one of the copies.

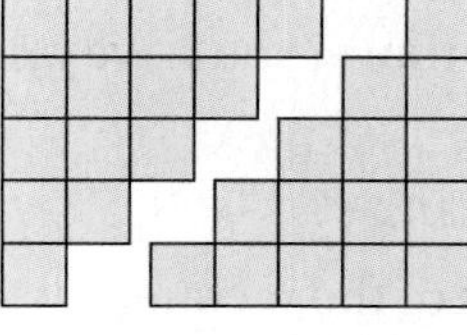

**Step 3** Push them together to make a rectangle.

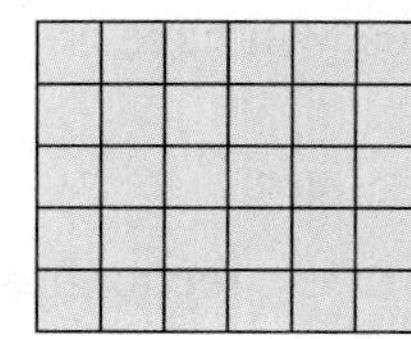

1. Find the height and length of the resulting rectangle. What is its area?
2. How many blocks are in the original staircase?
3. Use the staircase method to find $1 + 2 + 3 + 4 + 5 + 6$.

Euclid's method applies to functions in which each output is a multiple of the previous one, such as $f(n) = 3^n$. If that multiple is between 0 and 1, you can picture what is going on by ripping up a piece of paper.

**Remember...**

The function $f(n) = 3^n$ is an exponential function.

## In-Class Experiment

Get a piece of paper. Call the area of the paper 1.

**Step 1** Take your piece of paper and fold it in half. Cut it into two pieces.

**Step 2** Place one half on the desk in front of you. Keep the other half in your hand.

**Step 3** Repeat Steps 1 and 2 using just the piece of paper that is in your hand now.

Repeat this process a few more times.

**4.** After doing Steps 1 and 2 three times, you have one rectangle in your hand and three on the desk.

**a.** What is the area of each rectangle?

**b.** What is the sum of the areas of the rectangles on the desk?

**Remember...**

The area of the original sheet was 1.

**5.** After doing Steps 1 and 2 eight times, you have one rectangle in your hand and eight on the desk.

**a.** What is the area of each rectangle?

**b.** What is the sum of the areas of the rectangles on the desk?

**6.** After doing Steps 1 and 2 $n$ times, you have one rectangle in your hand and $n$ rectangles on the desk.

**a.** What is the area of each rectangle?

**b.** What is the sum of the areas of the rectangles on the desk?

## Developing Habits of Mind

**Consider more than one strategy.** There are two useful ways to visualize the algebraic pattern that results when you find the product below.

$$P = (1 - x)(1 + x + x^2 + x^3 + x^4)$$

One is the telescoping sum model and the other is the shifting model.

The telescoping method works as follows.

$$\begin{aligned} P &= (1 - x)(1 + x + x^2 + x^3 + x^4) \\ &= (1 - x) + (x - x^2) + (x^2 - x^3) + (x^3 - x^4) + (x^4 - x^5) \\ &= 1 - x + x - x^2 + x^2 - x^3 + x^3 - x^4 + x^4 - x^5 \\ &= 1 + (-x + x) + (-x^2 + x^2) + (-x^3 + x^3) + (-x^4 + x^4) - x^5 \\ &= 1 - x^5 \end{aligned}$$

The terms telescope as shown.

The shifting method works as follows.

$$\begin{aligned} P &= 1(1 + x + x^2 + x^3 + x^4) - x(1 + x + x^2 + x^3 + x^4) \\ &= 1 + x + x^2 + x^3 + x^4 - (x + x^2 + x^3 + x^4 + x^5) \\ &= 1 - x^5 \end{aligned}$$

Shift and subtract.

**Remember...**

You saw and used the general identity in Chapter 1.

**Habits of Mind**

**Detect the key characteristics.** Each method corresponds to a different application of the Distributive Property.

## Exercises Practicing Habits of Mind

### Check Your Understanding

1. Referring to the second In-Class Experiment, Cori says, "If I add the areas of all these rectangles, I will never have a sum of more than the area of the piece of paper I started with."

   David replies, "That can't be right! If you repeat the process more times, you'll get more rectangles and the total area will grow."

   Who do you think is correct? Explain.

2. Take It Further When Emma does the second In-Class Experiment, she puts half of the paper (area = 1) on the table and keeps half for herself. She then cuts in half the piece that she kept, and again puts half on the table and keeps half for herself. Now, suppose that Emma repeats this process forever and ever. Explain why this suggests the following.

$$\frac{1}{2} + \frac{1}{4} + \frac{1}{8} + \frac{1}{16} + \frac{1}{32} + \frac{1}{64} + \cdots = 1$$

3. Use the staircase method to calculate each sum.

   a. $1 + 2 + 3 + \cdots + 23 + 24$

   b. $1 + 2 + 3 + \cdots + 55 + 56$

   c. $1 + 2 + 3 + \cdots + 79 + 80$

   d. $1 + 2 + 3 + \cdots + 122 + 123$

   e. Use the staircase method to find a closed form for the following sum.

$$1 + 2 + 3 + \cdots + (n-2) + (n-1) + n$$

4. Expand each product.

   a. $(1-r)(1+r)$

   b. $(1-r)(1+r+r^2)$

   c. $(1-r)(1+r+r^2+r^3)$

   d. $(1-r)(1+r+r^2+r^3+\cdots+r^n)$

Exercise 4 was more than just an exercise in algebraic calculation. The results give you the following identity.

$$(1-r)(1+r+r^2+r^3+\cdots+r^n) = 1 - r^{n+1}$$

You can divide both sides by $1 - r$.

$$1 + r + r^2 + r^3 + \cdots + r^n = \frac{1-r^{n+1}}{1-r}$$

This is an algebraic identity. It holds for any value of $r$ that is allowed, which means all values of $r$ such that $r \neq 1$. This formula allows you to add up certain sequences of numbers without working through the details of Euclid's method each time.

**Remember...**

You saw this identity in Chapter 1.

5. Use the formula above to find each sum.

   a. $1 + \frac{2}{3} + \left(\frac{2}{3}\right)^2 + \left(\frac{2}{3}\right)^3 + \cdots + \left(\frac{2}{3}\right)^8$

   b. $1 + \frac{1}{4} + \left(\frac{1}{4}\right)^2 + \left(\frac{1}{4}\right)^3 + \cdots + \left(\frac{1}{4}\right)^8$

   c. $1 + 10 + 10^2 + 10^3 + \cdots + 10^{10}$

6. Show that $\frac{1-r^{n+1}}{1-r}$ is the same as $\frac{r^{n+1}-1}{r-1}$.

**Habits of Mind**

**Make strategic choices.** When would it be more convenient to use the $1 - r$ form? When would the $r - 1$ form be more convenient? Explain.

## On Your Own

7. Standardized Test Prep What is the sum $1 + \frac{3}{4} + \left(\frac{3}{4}\right)^2 + \left(\frac{3}{4}\right)^3 + \left(\frac{3}{4}\right)^4$ rounded to two decimal places?

   A. 2.15 B. 2.73 C. 3.05 D. 3.29

**8.** The diagram represents the first four outputs for a function $s$.

**a.** Make a table for $s$, including a $\Sigma$ column.

**b.** Find a closed form for $s(n)$.

**c.** Use a "cut and paste" argument to find a closed form for the $\Sigma$ column.

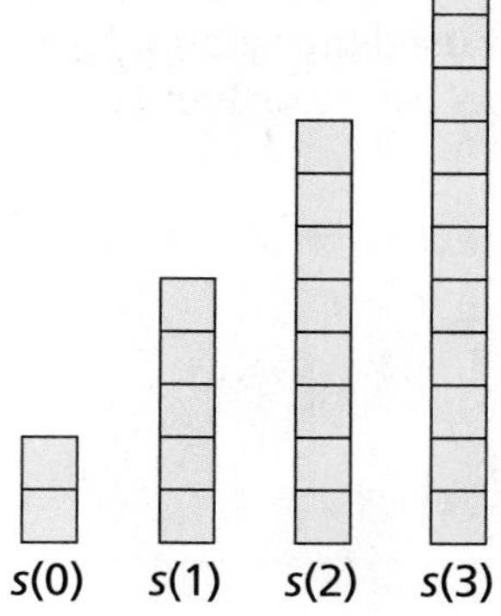


**9.** Use any piece of paper. Call its area 1. Follow these steps.

**Step 1** Fold the paper in your hand into thirds. Cut it into 3 pieces.

**Step 2** Put one piece in Pile 1, put one piece in Pile 2, and keep one piece in your hand.

**Step 3** Repeat Steps 1 and 2 with just the piece of paper that is in your hand.

This is similar to, but not exactly the same as, the last cutting activity you did.

Repeat this process a few more times.

**a.** After completing Steps 1 and 2 twice, you have two pieces of paper in each stack. What is the area of the paper in your hand? What is the sum of the areas of the rectangles in each pile?

**b.** After completing Steps 1 and 2 three times, what is the area of the paper in your hand? What is the sum of the areas of the rectangles in each pile?

**c.** After completing Steps 1 and 2 $n$ times, what is the area of the paper in your hand? What is the sum of the areas of the rectangles in each pile?

**d.** Take It Further Suppose you could do this process infinitely many times. Estimate the sum of the areas of the rectangles in each pile.

**10.** What is a closed form for $\frac{1}{3} + \frac{1}{9} + \frac{1}{27} + \cdots + \frac{1}{3^n}$?

## Maintain Your Skills

**11.** Find each sum.

**a.** $1 + 2 + 1$

**b.** $1 + 2 + 3 + 2 + 1$

**c.** $1 + 2 + 3 + 4 + 3 + 2 + 1$

**d.** $1 + 2 + 3 + 4 + 5 + 4 + 3 + 2 + 1$

**e.** $1 + 2 + \cdots + 23 + 24 + 25 + 24 + 23 + \cdots + 2 + 1$

**f.** $1 + 2 + 3 + \cdots + (n - 1) + n + (n - 1) + 3 + 2 + 1$

## 2.04 The $\sum$ Notation

You have been looking at ways to find sums—to add up sequences of numbers. You have already used the symbol $\sum$ to describe sums in a table. You can also use this symbol as a shorthand notation to describe the sum of a sequence.

For now, think of a *sequence* as a list of numbers. The elements of this list are *terms*.

### Example

**Problem** Find the sum of $2i$ as $i$ goes from 1 to 4, that is, $\sum_{i=1}^{4} 2i$.

**Solution**
$$\sum_{i=1}^{4} 2i = 2 \cdot 1 + 2 \cdot 2 + 2 \cdot 3 + 2 \cdot 4$$
$$= 2 + 4 + 6 + 8$$
$$= 20$$

**Problem** Find the sum of $2k + 3$ as $k$ goes from 0 to 5, that is, $\sum_{k=0}^{5} (2k + 3)$.

**Solution**
$$\sum_{k=0}^{5} (2k + 3) = (2 \cdot 0 + 3) + (2 \cdot 1 + 3) + (2 \cdot 2 + 3)$$
$$+ (2 \cdot 3 + 3) + (2 \cdot 4 + 3) + (2 \cdot 5 + 3)$$
$$= 3 + 5 + 7 + 9 + 11 + 13$$
$$= 48$$

**Problem** Find the sum of $2^k$ as $k$ goes from 0 to 5, that is, $\sum_{k=0}^{5} 2^k$.

**Solution**
$$\sum_{k=0}^{5} 2^k = 2^0 + 2^1 + 2^2 + 2^3 + 2^4 + 2^5$$
$$= 1 + 2 + 4 + 8 + 16 + 32 = 63$$

You can model functions with $\sum$ notation. See the TI-Nspire Handbook, p. 817.

This is a general form of the notation.

$$\sum_{k=0}^{n} f(k) = f(0) + f(1) + \cdots + f(n)$$

final value → $n$; function to sum → $f(k)$; **index** variable → $k$; starting value → $0$

Go Online
www.successnetplus.com

### For You to Do

Write each sum using $\sum$ notation.

1. $2 + 4 + 6 + 8 + 10 + 12 + 14 + 16 + 18 + 20$
2. $1 + 4 + 9 + 16 + 25$

# Exercises Practicing Habits of Mind

## Check Your Understanding

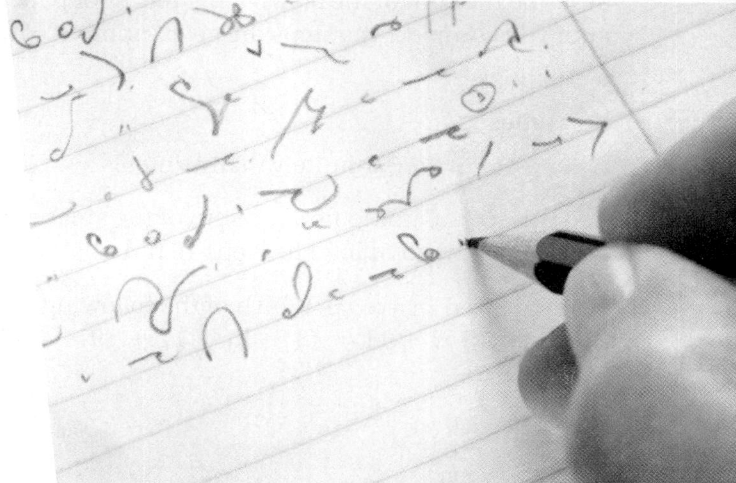

Shorthand allows you to write sentences more easily. $\sum$ notation allows you to write sums more easily.

**1.** Evaluate each sum.

**a.** $\sum_{j=0}^{6} (3j + 4)$

**b.** $\sum_{i=1}^{324} 1$

**c.** $\sum_{i=0}^{4} i$

**d.** $\sum_{i=12}^{45} i$

**2.** Ms. Take wrote Exercise 1 on the board. When Robin copied part (a), he accidentally changed all the $j$'s to $i$'s. Will Robin still get the correct answer? Explain.

**3.** Write each sum using $\sum$ notation.

**a.** $1 + 4 + 9 + 16 + 25 + \ldots + n^2$

**b.** $1 + 1 + 1 + 1 + 1 + 1$

**c.** $1 + 2 + 3 + 4 + 5 + 6 + 7 + 8 + 9 + 10$

**4.** In Exercise 2 from Lesson 2.03, Emma cuts sheets of paper in half. Use $\sum$ notation to describe the sum of the areas of the pieces of paper on the table after Emma completes the steps the given number of times.

**a.** 10 times

**b.** $n$ times

**c.** Take It Further infinitely many times

**5.** Use your calculator to find the sum of the areas of the paper on the table after Emma completes the steps 10 times.

**Habits of Mind**

**Experiment.** In Exercises 4 and 5, you have to picture cutting the paper 10 times. Can you actually cut it 10 times?

## On Your Own

6. For Exercise 9 in Lesson 2.03, you cut paper in thirds. Use $\sum$ notation to describe the sum of the areas of the pieces of paper in each pile on the table after you complete the steps the given number of times.

   a. 10 times

   b. $n$ times

   c. **Take It Further** infinitely many times

7. Use your calculator to find the sum of the areas of the pieces of paper on the table after you complete the steps 10 times.

8. **Standardized Test Prep** Which of the following sums is equivalent to $3 + 5 + 7 + 9 + 11 + 13 + 15 + 17 + 19$?

   A. $\sum_{i=1}^{9} (2i + 1)$

   B. $\sum_{i=1}^{19} (2i - 1)$

   C. $1 + \sum_{i=1}^{9} 2i$

   D. $2 \cdot \sum_{i=0}^{8} (i + 3)$

## Maintain Your Skills

9. Evaluate each sum. Look for patterns and general methods.

   a. $\sum_{j=1}^{4} (5j - 1)$

   b. $\sum_{j=4}^{10} (5j - 1)$

   c. $\sum_{k=1}^{4} (5k - 1)$

   d. $\sum_{i=0}^{6} 2i$

   e. $\sum_{k=1}^{6} k(k + 1)$

   f. $\sum_{i=0}^{15} 1$

   g. $\sum_{i=0}^{16} 1$

   h. $\sum_{i=1}^{15} 1$

**Habits of Mind**

**Look for patterns.** While evaluating a sum, see if you can use sums you have already evaluated. Which sums can you find using Gauss's method? Which can you find using Euclid's? Which can you find using arithmetic or other methods?

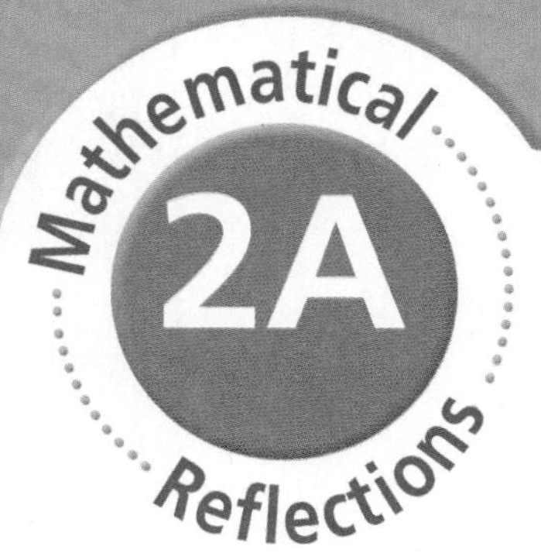


**In this investigation, you learned to make a sum table for a function, write closed-form rules for the sum column, and use $\sum$ notation. You used Gauss's method to find the sum of a sequence with constant differences and Euclid's method to find the sum of a sequence with constant ratios. These exercises will help you summarize what you have learned.**

**1.** Copy and complete the following sum table. Find a closed-form rule for the $\sum$ column.

| $n$ | $g(n)$ | $\Sigma$ |
|---|---|---|
| 0 | −3 | ■ |
| 1 | 1 | ■ |
| 2 | 5 | ■ |
| 3 | 9 | ■ |
| 4 | 13 | ■ |
| 5 | 17 | ■ |

$$\sum_{i=1}^{4}\left(\frac{1}{2^i}\right) = \frac{15}{16}$$

**2.** Let $S = \frac{1}{3} + \frac{2}{3} + \frac{4}{3} + \cdots + \frac{256}{3}$.

**a.** Explain why you can use Euclid's method to find the sum $S$.

**b.** Find $S$ using Euclid's method. Show your work.

**3.** Write an expression in $\sum$ notation for the sum in Exercise 2.

**4.** Find each sum.

**a.** odd integers 3 to 33, inclusive

**b.** powers of 4 from $4^0$ to $4^{11}$

**5.** Find each sum.

**a.** $\sum_{i=1}^{8}\left(\frac{1}{2}\right)^i$

**b.** $\sum_{k=0}^{8}(9 - 3k)$

**6.** Describe Gauss's method for summing all integers from 1 to $n$.

**7.** Find a formula for $\sum_{j=0}^{n} 2^j$ in terms of $n$.

**8.** Evaluate $\sum_{j=1}^{5} 4j$.

## Vocabulary and Notation

In this investigation, you learned these terms and symbols. Make sure you understand what each one means and how to use it.

- **Euclid's method**
- **Gauss's method**
- **index**
- $\sum_{k=0}^{n} f(k)$ **(summation)**

# Sum Identities

In *Sum Identities*, you will evaluate definite sums and find closed-form formulas for indefinite sums. You will learn identities that help you simplify sums. You will also use sums and these identities to find functions that agree with tables.

**By the end of this investigation, you will be able to answer questions like these.**

1. What is $\sum_{k=0}^{25} (k + 6^k)$?
2. What is a recursive rule for the series associated with $f(n) = 3n + 6$ having initial term $f(0)$?
3. What is a closed form for the following recursive rule?

$$f(n) = \begin{cases} 5 & \text{if } n = 0 \\ f(n-1) + 2n^2 + 3n + 2 & \text{if } n > 0 \end{cases}$$

**You will learn how to**

- find closed-form expressions for indefinite sums and use them to evaluate definite sums
- develop a list of $\Sigma$ identities and recognize situations in which you can apply them
- find closed-form expressions for the series associated with a function

**You will develop these habits and skills:**

- Visualize a complicated sum as a combination of different simpler sums.
- Generalize the steps in calculating definite sums to find a closed form for an indefinite sum.
- Reason logically using a recursive definition of a function to develop a closed-form definition.

To complete the stack, she needs (4 + 3 + 2 + 1) cups.

# 2.05 Getting Started

Activating Prior Knowledge
Exploring New Ideas

Look for patterns as you do the following problems.

## For You to Explore

**1.** Copy and complete each table.

**a.**

| $n$ | $f(n)$ | $\Sigma$ |
|---|---|---|
| 0 | −2 | ■ |
| 1 | 3 | ■ |
| 2 | 8 | ■ |
| 3 | 13 | ■ |
| 4 | 18 | ■ |
| 5 | 23 | ■ |

**b.**

| $n$ | $g(n)$ | $\Sigma$ |
|---|---|---|
| 0 | 0 | ■ |
| 1 | 2 | ■ |
| 2 | 4 | ■ |
| 3 | 6 | ■ |
| 4 | 8 | ■ |
| 5 | 10 | ■ |

**c.**

| $n$ | $f(n) + g(n)$ | $\Sigma$ |
|---|---|---|
| 0 | −2 | ■ |
| 1 | 5 | ■ |
| 2 | ■ | ■ |
| 3 | ■ | ■ |
| 4 | ■ | ■ |
| 5 | ■ | ■ |

**d.**

| $n$ | $2f(n)$ | $\Sigma$ |
|---|---|---|
| 0 | −4 | ■ |
| 1 | 6 | ■ |
| 2 | ■ | ■ |
| 3 | ■ | ■ |
| 4 | ■ | ■ |
| 5 | ■ | ■ |

**e.**

| $n$ | $3g(n)$ | $\Sigma$ |
|---|---|---|
| 0 | 0 | ■ |
| 1 | 6 | ■ |
| 2 | ■ | ■ |
| 3 | ■ | ■ |
| 4 | ■ | ■ |
| 5 | ■ | ■ |

**f.**

| $n$ | $f(n) \cdot g(n)$ | $\Sigma$ |
|---|---|---|
| 0 | 0 | ■ |
| 1 | 6 | ■ |
| 2 | ■ | ■ |
| 3 | ■ | ■ |
| 4 | ■ | ■ |
| 5 | ■ | ■ |

**2.** Calculate each sum.

**a.** $\sum_{j=1}^{5} 1$ **b.** $\sum_{j=1}^{5} j$ **c.** $\sum_{j=1}^{5} 2j$ **d.** $\sum_{j=1}^{5} 3j$

**e.** $2\sum_{j=1}^{5} j$ **f.** $3\sum_{j=1}^{5} j$ **g.** $\sum_{j=1}^{5} (j + 1)$ **h.** $\sum_{j=1}^{5} j^2$

**i.** $\left(\sum_{j=1}^{5} j\right)^2$ **j.** $\sum_{j=6}^{10} j$ **k.** $\sum_{j=1}^{10} j$

# Exercises Practicing Habits of Mind

## On Your Own

**3.** Tony is filling in a table like those in Problem 1.

| n | q(n) | Σ |
|---|---|---|
| 0 | 5 | 5 |
| 1 | 8 | 13 |
| 2 | 11 | 24 |
| 3 | 14 | 38 |
| 4 | 17 | 55 |
| 5 | 20 | 75 |

Tony says, "I can tell that $q(n)$ is linear. And I think $\Sigma$ is a quadratic function of the inputs."

**a.** Show that $q(n)$ is a linear function.

**b.** Show that in this table, $\Sigma$ is a quadratic function of the inputs.

**c.** Is it true that the $\Sigma$ column in a table of any linear function is quadratic? Explain.

## Maintain Your Skills

**4. a.** Copy and complete each table. The numbers in the $\Sigma$ column are just the running totals of the outputs in the $\Delta$ column.

| *n* | *f*(*n*) | Δ | Σ |
|---|---|---|---|
| 0 | 0 | 1 | 1 |
| 1 | 1 | 3 | 4 |
| 2 | 4 | ■ | ■ |
| 3 | 9 | ■ | ■ |
| 4 | 16 | ■ | ■ |
| 5 | 25 | | |

| *n* | *g*(*n*) | Δ | Σ |
|---|---|---|---|
| 0 | 1 | ■ | ■ |
| 1 | 2 | ■ | ■ |
| 2 | 5 | ■ | ■ |
| 3 | 10 | ■ | ■ |
| 4 | 17 | ■ | ■ |
| 5 | 26 | | |

| *n* | *h*(*n*) | Δ | Σ |
|---|---|---|---|
| 0 | 5 | ■ | ■ |
| 1 | 6 | ■ | ■ |
| 2 | 9 | ■ | ■ |
| 3 | 14 | ■ | ■ |
| 4 | 21 | ■ | ■ |
| 5 | 30 | | |

**b.** What is going on here?

# 2.06 Definite and Indefinite Sums

You have already learned at least two methods for finding certain kinds of sums. Using Gauss's method, Euclid's method, and a few new methods that you will learn in this investigation, you can solve very complicated sums.

## Minds in Action

*Sasha and Derman are working on evaluating* $\sum_{i=1}^{25} (3i + 2)$.

**Derman** I've got this one. $5 + 8 + 11 + 14 + \cdots$

**Sasha** Derman, we *could* figure out the 25 numbers and add them up. But let's try arranging the terms differently instead of writing out the whole list.

*Sasha starts writing on the board.*

$$\sum_{i=1}^{25} (3i + 2) = (3 \cdot 1 + 2) + (3 \cdot 2 + 2) + (3 \cdot 3 + 2) + (3 \cdot 4 + 2) + \cdots + (3 \cdot 25 + 2)$$

**Sasha** Now rearrange the numbers, grouping all the "$3 \times$" terms together and all the 2's together.

$$(3 \cdot 1 + 3 \cdot 2 + 3 \cdot 3 + 3 \cdot 4 + \cdots + 3 \cdot 25) + \underbrace{2 + 2 + \cdots + 2}_{25\text{ 2's}}$$

Factor out a 3 from the first part of the sum.

$$3(1 + 2 + 3 + 4 + \cdots + 25) + \underbrace{2 + 2 + \cdots + 2}_{25\text{ 2's}}$$

**Derman** I get it! You have three times the sum of the integers from 1 to 25, plus 25 two's.

- The sum of the integers from 1 to 25 is $\frac{25 \cdot 26}{2}$.
- 25 two's is $25 \cdot 2$ or 50.

So, the sum is $3 \cdot \frac{25 \cdot 26}{2} + 25 \cdot 2$, which simplifies to 1025.

You can summarize Sasha's method this way.

- Collect all the terms with a common factor of 3, factor out the 3, and use Gauss's method.
- Collect all the 2's, figure out how many there will be, and multiply.

## For You to Do

Use Sasha's method to evaluate each sum.

1. $\sum_{k=1}^{30}(3k + 2)$

2. $\sum_{k=1}^{13}3^k$

3. $\sum_{k=0}^{10}(f(k) + g(k))$, where $f(n) = 5n - 1$ and $g(n) = 2n + 3$

4. $\sum_{k=0}^{12}f(k)$, where $f(n) = 5n - 1$

Write out each sum and rearrange it so that you can use the method of Gauss or the method of Euclid.

In all the problems so far, you knew where to start summing and where to stop. Sums like that are **definite sums.** Sometimes you have an **indefinite sum,** such as $\sum_{k=1}^{n}(3k + 2)$, where $n$ is a variable.

With an indefinite sum, you cannot find a number equal to the sum, but you can find a closed-form expression for it.

## Example

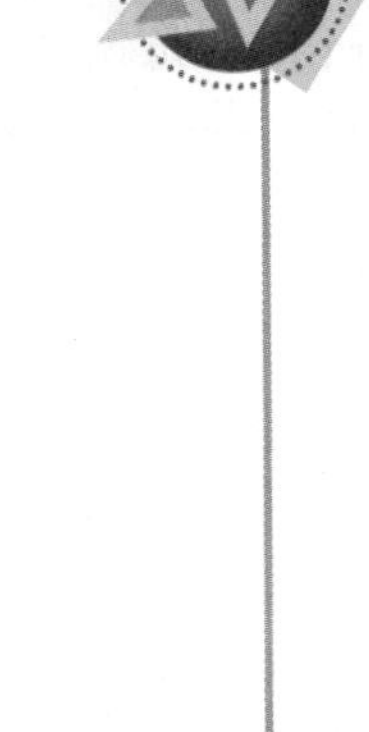

**Problem** Find a closed form for $\sum_{k=1}^{n}(3k + 2)$.

**Solution**

$$\begin{aligned}\sum_{k=1}^{n}(3k + 2) &= (3 \cdot 1 + 2) + (3 \cdot 2 + 2) + \ldots + (3 \cdot n + 2)\\ &= (3 \cdot 1 + 3 \cdot 2 + 3 \cdot 3 + 3 \cdot 4 + \cdots + 3 \cdot n)\\ &\quad + \underbrace{2 + 2 + \cdots + 2}_{n\ 2\text{'s}}\\ &= 3(1 + 2 + \ldots + n) + 2n\\ &= 3 \cdot \frac{n(n+1)}{2} + 2n\\ &= \frac{3n^2 + 7n}{2}\end{aligned}$$

What good are indefinite sums? Well, if you can find a closed form for one, you can just plug numbers into that closed form to get values for many definite sums. For example, you know

$$\sum_{k=1}^{n}(3k + 2) = \frac{3n^2 + 7n}{2}$$

So you can say with certainty that

$$\sum_{k=1}^{20}(3k + 2) = \frac{3 \cdot 20^2 + 7 \cdot 20}{2} = 670$$

You can also use indefinite sums to define new functions from old ones.

### Definition

**Given a function $f$ having a domain that contains the nonnegative integers, the series associated with $f$ is the function defined on nonnegative integers by**

$$F(n) = \sum_{k=0}^{n} f(k) = f(0) + f(1) + f(2) + \cdots + f(n)$$

If you use a spreadsheet, you can make a summation column to tabulate the associated series. See the TI-Nspire Handbook, p. 817.

So, the series associated with $f$ is a running total of the outputs of $f$. For example, in Exercise 3 from Lesson 2.05, the $\Sigma$ column gives the outputs for the series associated with the function $q$.

### Definition

**An identity is a statement that two expressions that may seem different are actually equivalent under the basic rules of algebra.**

## Minds in Action

*Derman is looking at his solutions to Problem 2 in Lesson 2.05.*

**Derman** I found that my answers to a lot of these were the same. For instance, $\sum_{j=1}^{5} 2j = 2\left(\sum_{j=1}^{5} j\right)$. I wonder if it's true for any $n$ that $\sum_{j=1}^{n} 2j$ is the same as $2\left(\sum_{j=1}^{n} j\right)$?

**Sasha** You mean, you wonder if you've found an identity?

In the Check Your Understanding exercises, you will get to investigate this very question, and others like it.

# Exercises Practicing Habits of Mind

## Check Your Understanding

**1.** Consider the statements below. Some of them are identities. Others are not, even though they may look as though they are true. Explore the statements and discover exactly which are identities and which are not.

In these exercises, $n$ is some integer.

**a.** $\sum_{k=1}^{n} 2k \stackrel{?}{=} 2\sum_{k=1}^{n} k$

**b.** $\sum_{k=0}^{n} 2f(k) \stackrel{?}{=} 2\sum_{k=0}^{n} f(k)$

**c.** $\sum_{k=1}^{n} k^2 \stackrel{?}{=} \left(\sum_{k=1}^{n} k\right)^2$

**d.** $\sum_{k=0}^{n} k \stackrel{?}{=} \frac{n(n+1)}{2}$

**e.** $\sum_{k=1}^{n} k \stackrel{?}{=} \frac{n(n+1)}{2}$

**f.** $\sum_{k=0}^{n} 1 \stackrel{?}{=} n + 1$

**g.** $\sum_{k=1}^{n} 1 \stackrel{?}{=} n$

**h.** $\sum_{k=1}^{n} 1^2 \stackrel{?}{=} \left(\sum_{k=1}^{n} 1\right)^2$

**i.** $\sum_{k=0}^{n} g(k)f(k) \stackrel{?}{=} \left(\sum_{k=0}^{n} g(k)\right) \times \left(\sum_{k=0}^{n} f(k)\right)$

**j.** $\sum_{k=0}^{n} r^k \stackrel{?}{=} \frac{r^{n+1} - 1}{r - 1}$, where $r \neq 1$

**k.** $\sum_{k=0}^{n} (f(k) + g(k)) \stackrel{?}{=} \sum_{k=0}^{n} f(k) + \sum_{k=0}^{n} g(k)$

**2.** Use Sasha's method from the dialog to evaluate the two sums in each part.

**a.** $\sum_{k=1}^{16} (3k + 2)$, $\sum_{k=0}^{16} (3k + 2)$

**b.** $\sum_{k=1}^{13} 2 \cdot 3^k$, $\sum_{k=0}^{6} 2 \cdot 3^k$

**c.** $\sum_{k=0}^{12} (f(k) - g(k))$, $\sum_{j=5}^{12} f(j)$, where $f(n) = 5n - 1$ and $g(n) = 2n + 3$

**3.** Find each sum.

**a.** $\sum_{k=1}^{5} (2k - 1)$

**b.** $\sum_{k=1}^{10} (2k - 1)$

**c.** $\sum_{k=6}^{10} (2k - 1)$

**d.** Find a closed form for $\sum_{k=1}^{n} (2k - 1)$.

**e.** Use the closed form for $\sum_{k=1}^{n} (2k - 1)$ to calculate $\sum_{k=1}^{1000} (2k - 1)$.

Or find a closed form for the series associated with $x \mapsto 2x - 1$.

## On Your Own

**4.** Find a closed form for the series associated with the function $f$, where $f(x) = 5x - 1$.

**5.** Use the closed form from Exercise 4 to find each sum.

**a.** $\sum_{k=0}^{23} (5k - 1)$ **b.** $\sum_{k=0}^{7} (5k - 1)$

**6.** Find a closed form for $\left(\sum_{k=0}^{n} 5k\right) - 1$.

**7.** Find each sum.

**a.** $\sum_{k=0}^{5} 7$ **b.** $\sum_{k=1}^{6} 7$

**c.** Find a closed form for $\sum_{k=1}^{n} 7$. **d.** Find a closed form for $\sum_{k=0}^{n-1} 7$.

**8.** Suppose $a$ and $b$ are numbers. What is a closed form for $\sum_{k=1}^{n} (ak + b)$, in terms of $a$ and $b$?

**9.** Find each sum.

**a.** $\sum_{k=0}^{4} 9 \cdot 10^k$ **b.** $\sum_{k=0}^{12} 9 \cdot 10^k$ **c.** $\sum_{k=5}^{12} 9 \cdot 10^k$

**d.** Find a closed form for $\sum_{k=0}^{n} 9 \cdot 10^k$.

**10.** Standardized Test Prep Which expression is a closed form for $\sum_{k=0}^{n} \left(\frac{2}{3}\right)^k$?

**A.** $\dfrac{1 - \left(\frac{2}{3}\right)^{n+1}}{3}$ **B.** $3\left(1 - \left(\frac{2}{3}\right)^{n+1}\right)$ **C.** $3 - \left(\frac{1}{3}\right)^{n+1}$ **D.** $\dfrac{\left(\frac{2}{3}\right)^{n+1} - 1}{\frac{1}{3}}$

## Maintain Your Skills

**11.** Consider the statements below. Some of them are identities. Others are not, even though they may look as though they are true. Explore the statements and discover which are identities and which are not.

In these exercises, $m$ and $n$ are integers.

**a.** $\sum_{k=1}^{m} f(k) + \sum_{k=m+1}^{n} f(k) \stackrel{?}{=} \sum_{k=1}^{n} f(k)$, where $m < n$

**b.** $\sum_{k=1}^{n} ck^2 \stackrel{?}{=} c\sum_{k=1}^{n} k^2$, where $c$ is any real number

**c.** $\sum_{k=1}^{n} k(k + 1) \stackrel{?}{=} \sum_{k=1}^{n} k^2 + \sum_{k=1}^{n} k$

**d.** $\sum_{k=1}^{n} k(k + 1) \stackrel{?}{=} \left(\sum_{k=1}^{n} k\right) \times \left(\sum_{k=1}^{n} (k + 1)\right)$

# 2.07 $\Sigma$ Identities

Take stock of what you have done so far. There are several $\Sigma$ identities that are so useful that you can list them in a theorem and refer to them by name. You have seen most of these in Exercise 1 of Lesson 2.06. And, as you go on, you will add to this list.

### *Theorem 2.1*

The following are identities.

- Factors come out.

$$\sum_{k=0}^{n} cf(k) = c \times \sum_{k=0}^{n} f(k), \text{ where } c \text{ is any real number}$$

- The sigma of a sum is the sum of the sigmas.

$$\sum_{k=0}^{n} (f(k) + g(k)) = \sum_{k=0}^{n} f(k) + \sum_{k=0}^{n} g(k)$$

- Splitting up a sum

$$\sum_{k=0}^{n} f(k) = \sum_{k=0}^{m} f(k) + \sum_{k=m+1}^{n} f(k), \text{ where } 0 < m < n$$

- Add a bunch of ones.

$$\sum_{k=0}^{n} 1 = n + 1 \quad \text{or} \quad \sum_{k=1}^{n} 1 = n$$

- Think Gauss.

$$\sum_{k=0}^{n} k = \frac{n(n+1)}{2}$$

- Think Euclid.

$$\sum_{k=0}^{n} r^k = \frac{r^{n+1} - 1}{r - 1}$$

**Habits of Mind**

**Detect the key characteristics.** You can use the first two identities together under the name *linearity*.

It is a good idea to put these identities on a poster or in your notes.

## For Discussion

1. Why are the "add a bunch of ones" identities different depending on whether the summation starts at $k = 0$ or $k = 1$?
2. How does a change of starting point from $k = 0$ to $k = 1$ affect the identities listed above as "Think Gauss" and "Think Euclid"?

## Example

**Problem** Evaluate $\sum_{k=0}^{8}(3k+2)$.

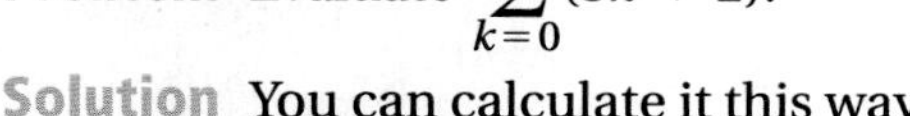

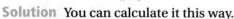

**Solution** You can calculate it this way.

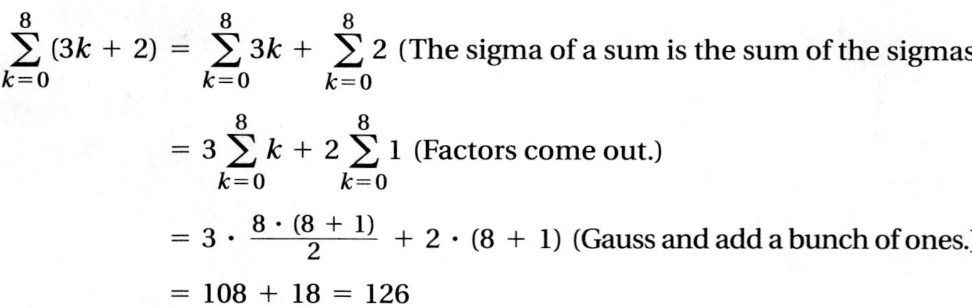

$$\begin{aligned}\sum_{k=0}^{8}(3k+2) &= \sum_{k=0}^{8}3k + \sum_{k=0}^{8}2 \text{ (The sigma of a sum is the sum of the sigmas.)}\\ &= 3\sum_{k=0}^{8}k + 2\sum_{k=0}^{8}1 \text{ (Factors come out.)}\\ &= 3\cdot\frac{8\cdot(8+1)}{2} + 2\cdot(8+1) \text{ (Gauss and add a bunch of ones.)}\\ &= 108 + 18 = 126\end{aligned}$$

**Problem** Find a closed form for $\sum_{k=0}^{n}(3k+2)$.

**Solution**

$$\begin{aligned}\sum_{k=0}^{n}(3k+2) &= \sum_{k=0}^{n}3k + \sum_{k=0}^{n}2 \text{ (The sigma of a sum is the sum of the sigmas.)}\\ &= 3\sum_{k=0}^{n}k + 2\sum_{k=0}^{n}1 \text{ (Factors come out.)}\\ &= 3\cdot\frac{n(n+1)}{2} + 2(n+1) \text{ (Gauss and add a bunch of ones.)}\end{aligned}$$

This is an example of an indefinite sum.

The last expression in the solution above is a fine way to represent the closed form for the sum. If you want, however, you can transform it even more.

$$\begin{aligned}\sum_{k=0}^{n}(3k+2) &= 3\frac{n(n+1)}{2} + 2(n+1)\\ &= \frac{3n(n+1)+4(n+1)}{2}\\ &= \frac{(n+1)(3n+4)}{2}\end{aligned}$$

Notice that if you substitute $n = 8$ in this formula, you get 126. This agrees with the earlier result. And, you can use this formula for the indefinite sum to do other definite sums, such as the following.

$$\sum_{k=0}^{205}(3k+2) = \frac{(205+1)(3\cdot 205+4)}{2} = 63{,}757$$

### Habits of Mind

**Use a different process to get the same answer.** Your CAS can evaluate finite and indefinite sums. See the TI-Nspire Handbook on p. 817. But it is important to know how to use the sigma identities to break down complicated sums into simpler ones. Besides, why should the calculator have all the fun?

## For You to Do

Evaluate each sum.

**3.** $\sum_{k=1}^{30}(3k-2)$

**4.** $\sum_{k=1}^{n}(6k-4)$, in terms of $n$

Jakob Bernoulli (1654–1705) was a member of a remarkable Swiss family that produced many mathematicians and scientists. Jakob studied the formulas for the sums of powers. These sums are the series associated with the functions $x \mapsto x^m$ for positive integers $m$. Johan Faulhaber published them in his 1631 work *Academia Algebrae.*

Jakob Bernoulli

These sums are

$$\sum_{k=0}^{n} k = 0 + 1 + 2 + 3 + \cdots + n$$

$$\sum_{k=0}^{n} k^2 = 0^2 + 1^2 + 2^2 + 3^2 + \cdots + n^2$$

$$\sum_{k=0}^{n} k^3 = 0^3 + 1^3 + 2^3 + 3^3 + \cdots + n^3$$

$$\sum_{k=0}^{n} k^4 = 0^4 + 1^4 + 2^4 + 3^4 + \cdots + n^4$$

$$\vdots$$

$$\sum_{k=0}^{n} k^m = 0^m + 1^m + 2^m + 3^m + \cdots + n^m$$

You have seen a closed form for the first sum. Bernoulli studied all such sums. His definitive results were published in his book *Ars Conjectandi* in 1713, after his death. The coefficients in these formulas are related to an important sequence called the Bernoulli numbers. This book calls these formulas **Bernoulli's formulas** in his honor. Here are just the first few of the formulas Bernoulli gave.

$$\sum_{k=0}^{n} k = \frac{n(n+1)}{2}$$

$$\sum_{k=0}^{n} k^2 = \frac{n(n+1)(2n+1)}{6}$$

$$\sum_{k=0}^{n} k^3 = \frac{n^2(n+1)^2}{4}$$

$$\sum_{k=0}^{n} k^4 = \frac{n(n+1)(2n+1)(3n^2+3n-1)}{30}$$

$$\sum_{k=0}^{n} k^5 = \frac{n^2(n+1)^2(2n^2+2n-1)}{12}$$

It is useful to add these formulas to your list of $\Sigma$ identities.

Bernoulli liked to brag that he could find the sum of the tenth powers of the first thousand numbers in less than 10 minutes. He would have been amazed at how his methods have continued to evolve over the last 300 years. A calculator uses Bernoulli's formulas and can find the sum of the first thousand tenth powers in seconds.

$$\sum_{k=0}^{1000} k^{10} = 91{,}409{,}924{,}241{,}424{,}243{,}424{,}241{,}924{,}242{,}500$$

None of this would have been possible without the work of mathematicians such as Bernoulli.

## For You to Do

Use Bernoulli's formulas to evaluate each sum.

5. $\sum_{j=1}^{45} (4j + 3)$

6. $\sum_{k=0}^{100} (2k^2 + 1)$

Find a formula for each series.

7. $\sum_{j=1}^{n} (4j + 3)$

8. $\sum_{j=0}^{n} (4j + 3)$

## Exercises *Practicing Habits of Mind*

### Check Your Understanding

1. Evaluate $\sum_{k=1}^{50} 5(k + 1)$.

2. Evaluate each sum using the method in the example.

   a. $\sum_{k=0}^{16} (3k - 2)$ b. $\sum_{k=0}^{13} \left(\frac{1}{2}\right)^k$ c. $\sum_{k=1}^{13} \left(\frac{1}{2}\right)^k$

3. Suppose $f(n) = 5n - 1$ and $g(n) = 2n + 3$. Evaluate each sum.

   a. $\sum_{k=0}^{12} f(k)$ b. $\sum_{k=0}^{12} (f(k) + g(k))$

   c. $\sum_{k=0}^{12} (3f(k) + g(k))$ d. $\sum_{j=5}^{12} f(j)$

## On Your Own

Go Online
www.successnetplus.com

4. Use the $\Sigma$ identities in Theorem 2.1 to evaluate each sum.

a. $\sum_{j=1}^{12} (5j - 1)$
b. $\sum_{j=7}^{12} (5j - 1)$
c. $\sum_{j=1}^{n} (5j - 1)$
d. $\sum_{j=0}^{7} 2^j$
e. $\sum_{j=0}^{7} 3 \cdot 2^j$
f. $\sum_{j=0}^{n} 3 \cdot 2^j$

Suppose you have a mystery function $f$, and all you know is a formula for its associated series.

$$\sum_{k=0}^{n} f(k) = n^2 - 3n$$

5. Find each sum.

a. $\sum_{k=0}^{10} f(k)$
b. $\sum_{k=5}^{10} f(k)$
c. $\sum_{k=1}^{11} f(k - 1)$
d. $\sum_{k=0}^{10} (3f(k) + 5^k)$

6. a. Find a polynomial $g$ that agrees with $f$ for all integers $n > 0$.

b. Take It Further Is there more than one polynomial $g$ that works? Explain.

Suppose you have a mystery function $g$, and all you know is a formula for this indefinite sum.

$$\sum_{k=0}^{n} g(k) = 2n^2 - 5n$$

7. Find each sum.

a. $\sum_{k=0}^{10} g(k)$
b. $\sum_{k=5}^{10} g(k)$
c. $\sum_{k=1}^{11} g(k - 1)$
d. $\sum_{k=0}^{10} (3g(k) + 7^k)$

8. a. Find a polynomial $h$ that agrees with $g$ for all integers $n > 0$.

b. Take It Further Is there more than one polynomial $h$ that works? Explain.

9. What is the sum of all the multiples of 3 that are greater than 1 and less than 1000?

10. Use Bernoulli's formulas to evaluate each sum.

a. $\sum_{k=1}^{30} k(k + 1)(k + 2)$
b. $\sum_{k=1}^{100} (3k^2 + 5k - 7)$

**11.** Find a formula for each indefinite sum.

**a.** $\sum_{k=0}^{n} k(k+1)$ **b.** $\sum_{k=0}^{n} k(k+1)(k+2)$

**c.** $\sum_{k=0}^{n} k(k+1)(k+2)(k+3)$

**12.** Evaluate each definite sum.

**a.** $\sum_{j=12}^{45} (4j+3)$ **b.** $5 + 9 + 13 + 17 + 21 + \cdots + 201$

**c.** $\sum_{k=1}^{36} k(k+1)$ **d.** $1 - 2 + 3 - 4 + 5 - \cdots - 1000$

**e.** $1 - 2 + 4 - 8 + 16 - \cdots + 1024$

**13.** Use Bernoulli's formulas to evaluate each sum.

**a.** $\sum_{k=1}^{5} 2k^3$ **b.** $\sum_{k=1}^{30} (k-1)^3$ **c.** $\sum_{k=1}^{30} (k+1)^3$ **d.** $\sum_{k=7}^{30} (k+2)^3$

**14.** Standardized Test Prep Which of the following closed-form formulas can you use to find the sum of all perfect squares less than or equal to 100?

**A.** $\dfrac{n(n-1)^2}{2}$ **B.** $\dfrac{10^3\left(1-\left(\frac{1}{10}\right)^{n+1}\right)}{3}$

**C.** $\dfrac{n(n+1)(2n+1)}{6}$ **D.** $\dfrac{n^2(n+1)^2}{4}$

## Maintain Your Skills

**15.** **a.** Copy and complete each table. The numbers in the $\Sigma$ column are just the running totals of the outputs in the $\Delta$ column.

| $n$ | $f(n)$ | $\Delta$ | $\Sigma$ |
|---|---|---|---|
| 0 | 0 | 2 | 2 |
| 1 | 2 | 4 | 6 |
| 2 | 6 | ■ | ■ |
| 3 | 12 | ■ | ■ |
| 4 | 20 | ■ | ■ |
| 5 | 30 | | |

| $n$ | $g(n)$ | $\Delta$ | $\Sigma$ |
|---|---|---|---|
| 0 | 1 | ■ | ■ |
| 1 | 3 | ■ | ■ |
| 2 | 7 | ■ | ■ |
| 3 | 13 | ■ | ■ |
| 4 | 21 | ■ | ■ |
| 5 | 31 | | |

| $n$ | $h(n)$ | $\Delta$ | $\Sigma$ |
|---|---|---|---|
| 0 | 5 | ■ | ■ |
| 1 | 7 | ■ | ■ |
| 2 | 11 | ■ | ■ |
| 3 | 17 | ■ | ■ |
| 4 | 25 | ■ | ■ |
| 5 | 35 | | |

**b.** What is going on here?

# 2.08 Tables and Figurate Numbers

In earlier lessons, you looked at tables like this one.

| $n$ | $g(n)$ |
|---|---|
| 0 | 7 |
| 1 | 8 |
| 2 | 10 |
| 3 | 13 |

**Remember...**

In Chapter 1, you studied Lagrange Interpolation, a method for fitting a function to any table. This lesson develops another method.

Your goal was to find a function that agreed with the table. Finding a closed-form function that agrees with a table is not always easy. But sometimes it is fairly easy to find a recursively defined function. For example, you can add a $\Delta$ column.

As you saw in Chapter 1, there are many functions (even polynomial functions) that agree with this table.

| $n$ | $g(n)$ | $\Delta$ |
|---|---|---|
| 0 | 7 | 1 |
| 1 | 8 | 2 |
| 2 | 10 | 3 |
| 3 | 13 | |

This leads to a function $g$, defined on positive integers, that agrees with the table above.

$$g(n) = \begin{cases} 7 & \text{if } n = 0 \\ g(n-1) + n & \text{if } n > 0 \end{cases}$$

You can sometimes use the ideas in this investigation to find a closed form for recursively defined functions. You can call this method *unstacking*.

You can "unstack" the nesting dolls until you reach the smallest doll.

## Example

**Problem** Find a closed-form definition for a function $G$, defined on all of $\mathbb{R}$, that agrees with $g$.

**Solution**

**Step 1** Calculate $g(5)$ the way a computer would.

$$g(5) = g(4) + 5 \qquad \text{but } g(4) = g(3) + 4 \qquad \text{so}$$

$$= g(3) + 4 + 5$$

$$= g(2) + 3 + 4 + 5$$

$$= g(1) + 2 + 3 + 4 + 5$$

$$= g(0) + 1 + 2 + 3 + 4 + 5$$

$$= 7 + 1 + 2 + 3 + 4 + 5$$

So $g(5) = 7 + 1 + 2 + 3 + 4 + 5$.

**Step 2** Now, write $g(6)$ and $g(7)$ in the same form, just to get in the rhythm of the calculation.

**Step 3** So, you can also write $g(n)$ using $\Sigma$ notation.

$$g(n) = 7 + 1 + 2 + 3 + \cdots + n = 7 + \sum_{k=1}^{n} k$$

**Step 4** Use Gauss's method to write $\sum_{k=1}^{n} k$ in a closed form.

**Step 5** Now you can write a closed form for $G(n)$.

**Habits of Mind**

**Make a connection.** This is just the hockey stick property of difference tables from *Mathematics II.*

## For You to Do

1. Complete the missing calculations in the Example above.

## For Discussion

Tony is looking for a closed-form function $F(n)$ that agrees with the function $f(n)$ below.

$$f(n) = \begin{cases} 3 & \text{if } n = 0 \\ f(n-1) + 6n^2 + 2n + 5 & \text{if } n > 0 \end{cases}$$

Tony says, "After I unstacked $f(n)$, I ended up with

$$F(n) = 3 + 6\sum_{k=1}^{n} k^2 + 2\sum_{k=1}^{n} k + 5\sum_{k=1}^{n} 1."$$

Sasha circles the coefficients and draws some arrows.

$$f(n) = \begin{cases} \textcircled{3} & \text{if } n = 0 \\ f(n-1) + \textcircled{6}n^2 + \textcircled{2}n + \textcircled{5} & \text{if } n > 0 \end{cases}$$

$$F(n) = \textcircled{3} + \textcircled{6}\sum_{k=1}^{n} k^2 + \textcircled{2}\sum_{k=1}^{n} k + \textcircled{5}\sum_{k=1}^{n} 1$$

2. Does this happen for all functions like $f(n)$? Explain.
3. Find a closed form for $f$.

### Figurate Numbers

Since the time of the Pythagoreans, around 500 B.C., people have classified numbers according to geometric shapes. The diagrams below show examples of **figurate numbers.** The triangular numbers are the numbers of dots needed to make up the equilateral triangles shown below.

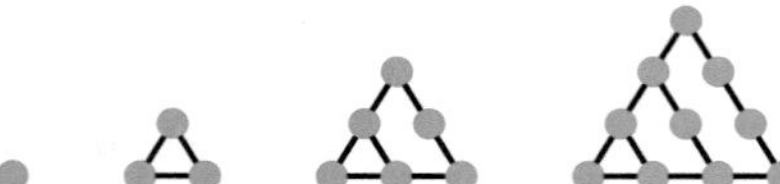

The square numbers are the numbers of dots needed to make up the squares shown below.

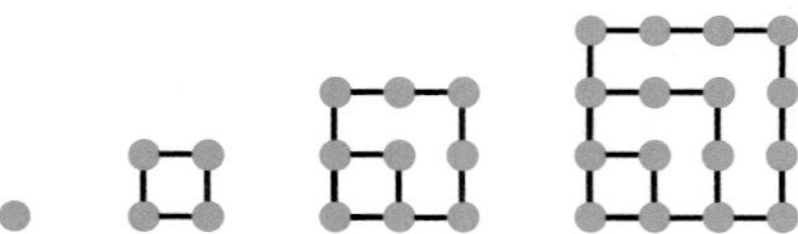

And there are pentagonal numbers, hexagonal numbers, and so on.

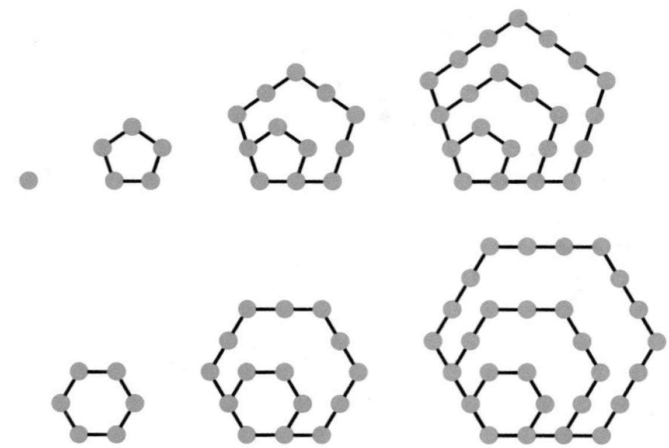

## For You to Do

You can use the recursive definition below to find the $n$th triangular number.

$$t(n) = \begin{cases} 1 & \text{if } n = 1 \\ t(n-1) + n & \text{if } n > 1 \end{cases}$$

**4.** Verify that this recursive formula is correct for the diagrams above.

**5.** Find a closed form for the triangular numbers.

## Check Your Understanding

In these exercises, *a closed-form definition for a function* means a closed-form definition for a function defined on all of $\mathbb{R}$. Also, *a closed-form definition for a function $H$ that agrees with $h$* means a closed-form definition for a function $H$ that agrees with $h$ for all nonnegative integers.

**1.** Use the recursive definition for the function $h$ below.

$$h(n) = \begin{cases} 3 & \text{if } n = 0 \\ h(n-1) + n & \text{if } n > 0 \end{cases}$$

Find a closed-form definition for a function $H$ that agrees with $h$.

**2.** This table shows values of a function $q$.

| $n$ | $q(n)$ | $\Delta$ |
|---|---|---|
| 0 | 32 | ■ |
| 1 | 34 | ■ |
| 2 | 38 | ■ |
| 3 | 44 | |

**a.** Find a recursively defined formula for $q(n)$ that agrees with the table.

**b.** Find a closed-form definition for a function $Q$ that agrees with your function from part (a).

**3.** Find a closed form for this recursive definition.

$$s(n) = \begin{cases} 1 & \text{if } n = 1 \\ s(n-1) + (2n-1) & \text{if } n > 1 \end{cases}$$

## On Your Own

Go Online
www.successnetplus.com

**4.** Use this recursive definition of the function $m$.

$$m(n) = \begin{cases} 28 & \text{if } n = 0 \\ m(n-1) + 2n - 1 & \text{if } n > 0 \end{cases}$$

Find a closed-form definition for a function $M$ that agrees with the function $m$.

**5.** Copy this table for a function $s$.

| $n$ | $s(n)$ | $\Delta$ |
|---|---|---|
| 0 | 7 | ■ |
| 1 | 8 | ■ |
| 2 | 12 | ■ |
| 3 | 21 | |

**a.** Complete the $\Delta$ column. Use it to find a recursive formula for $s(n)$.

**b.** Find a closed-form definition for a function $S$ that agrees with your function $s$.

**6.** Use this recursive definition of a function $t$.

$$t(n) = \begin{cases} 1 & \text{if } n = 0 \\ t(n-1) + 2^n & \text{if } n > 0 \end{cases}$$

**a.** Express $t(n)$ as a sum of powers of 2.

**b.** Find a closed-form definition for a function $T$ that agrees with $t$.

**7.** This table for some function $g$ has a $\Delta$ column. Nina spilled ink over most of the $g(n)$ column.

| $n$ | $g(n)$ | $\Delta$ |
|---|---|---|
| 1 | 12 | 5 |
| 2 | | 6 |
| 3 | | 7 |
| 4 | | 8 |
| 5 | | |

**a.** What is $g(5)$?

**b.** How did you find it?

**c.** Find a recursive formula for $g(n)$.

**d.** Find a closed-form definition for a function $G$ that agrees with $g$.

**8.** **Standardized Test Prep** Which of the following expressions is a closed-form rule for the recursively defined function below?

$$f(n) = \begin{cases} 5 & \text{if } n = 0 \\ f(n-1) + 8n^3 & \text{if } n > 0 \end{cases}$$

**A.** $8n^3(n+1)^2$ **B.** $5 + 4n(n+1)$

**C.** $8n^3 8n^3(n+1)^2$ **D.** $5 + 2n^2(n+1)^2$

**9. a.** Find two triangular numbers that are also square numbers.

**b.** **Take It Further** Are there more than two such numbers?

**10. a.** Find a recursive formula $p(n)$ to describe the pentagonal numbers.

**b.** Find a closed-form definition for a function $P$ to describe the pentagonal numbers.

**11. a.** Find a recursive formula $h(n)$ to describe the hexagonal numbers.

**b.** Find a closed-form formula $H(n)$ to describe the hexagonal numbers.

## Maintain Your Skills

**12.** Let $T(n)$ be a formula for the $n$th triangular number. Show that $T(n-1) + T(n) = S(n)$. In other words, show that if you add two consecutive triangular numbers, you get a square number.

Here is a picture of the tetrahedral numbers. Notice that each level is made up of a triangular number of dots.

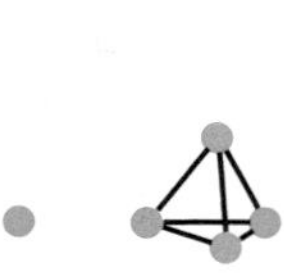

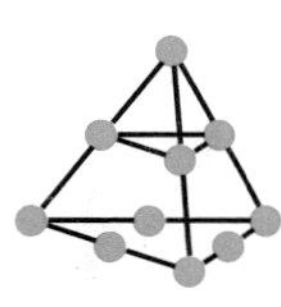

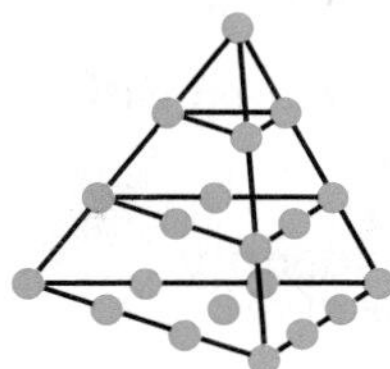

Let $T(n)$ be the $n$th triangular number. You can use the recursive formula below for the tetrahedral numbers.

$$a(n) = \begin{cases} 1 & \text{if } n = 1 \\ a(n-1) + T(n) & \text{if } n > 1 \end{cases}$$

**13. a.** Find a recursive definition for $a(n)$ that does not depend on $T(n)$.

**b.** Find a closed-form function definition for a function $A$ that agrees with the tetrahedral numbers at positive integers.

**In this investigation, you learned to find closed-form definitions for indefinite sums and to use the definitions to evaluate definite sums, develop and use $\sum$ identities, and find closed-form expressions for the series associated with a function. These questions will help you summarize what you have learned.**

**1.** Evaluate each sum.

**a.** $\sum_{k=2}^{21}(2k - 4)$

**b.** $\sum_{k=3}^{10}(2 \cdot 5^k)$

**2.** Find a closed form for each indefinite sum.

**a.** $\sum_{k=0}^{n}(2k - 4)$

**b.** $\sum_{k=0}^{n}(2 \cdot 5^k)$

**3.** Suppose you know $\sum_{j=0}^{n} f(j) = 3n^2 + 4$ for a mystery function $f$.

| $n$ | $f(n)$ | $\Sigma$ |
|---|---|---|
| 0 | 4 | 4 |
| 1 | 3 | ■ |
| 2 | ■ | 16 |
| 3 | ■ | ■ |
| 4 | ■ | ■ |
| 5 | ■ | ■ |

**a.** Copy and complete the table above for $f$.

**b.** Find a polynomial $g$ that agrees with $f$ for all integers $n > 0$.

**4.** Find a closed form for the series associated with $h(n) = 3 - 8n$, having initial term $h(0)$.

**5. a.** Explain why you can write the $\sum$ identity "Think Euclid" as $\sum_{k=0}^{n} r^k = \frac{1 - r^{n+1}}{1 - r}$.

**b.** Find a closed form for $\sum_{k=2}^{n} r^k$.

6. What is $\sum_{k=0}^{25} (k + 6^k)$?

7. What is a recursive rule for the series associated with $f(n) = 3n + 6$, having initial term $f(0)$?

8. What is a closed form for the following recursive rule?

$$f(n) = \begin{cases} 5 & \text{if } n = 0 \\ f(n-1) + 2n^2 + 3n + 2 & \text{if } n > 0 \end{cases}$$

## Vocabulary

In this investigation, you learned these terms. Make sure you understand what each one means and how to use it.

- **Bernoulli's formulas**
- **definite sum**
- **figurate number**
- **identity**
- **indefinite sum**
- **series associated with *f***

# Arithmetic and Geometric Sequences and Series

**In *Arithmetic and Geometric Sequences and Series,* you will explore the properties of arithmetic and geometric sequences. You will also investigate the series associated with arithmetic and geometric sequences.**

**By the end of this investigation, you will be able to answer questions like these.**

1. What is an arithmetic sequence?
2. What is a geometric series?
3. How do you write the repeating decimal 0.121212121 . . . as a fraction?

**You will learn how to**

- find a closed-form representation for an arithmetic sequence and its associated series
- find a closed-form representation for a geometric sequence and its associated series
- determine whether a geometric sequence has a limit, and if it does, how to find the limit
- convert a repeating decimal into an exact fraction

**You will develop these habits and skills:**

- Visualize arithmetic and geometric series to better understand their behavior.
- Think about extreme cases as values of $n$ become very large or as terms in a sequence become very small.
- Reason logically to understand, write, and analyze proofs.

You can use a geometric sequence with common ratio $\frac{1}{2}$ to model the number of teams in each round of a single-elimination tournament.

# 2.09 Getting Started

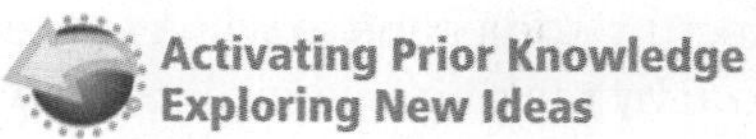


## For You to Explore

Here are tables and graphs for functions $K$ and $L$.

1. a. Make a difference table for each function.

   b. Describe functions $K$ and $L$ as completely as you can.

**Table K**

| $n$ | $K(n)$ |
|---|---|
| 0 | 3 |
| 1 | 8 |
| 2 | 13 |
| 3 | 18 |
| 4 | 23 |

**Table L**

| $m$ | $L(m)$ |
|---|---|
| 0 | 3 |
| 1 | 9 |
| 2 | 15 |
| 3 | 21 |
| 4 | 27 |

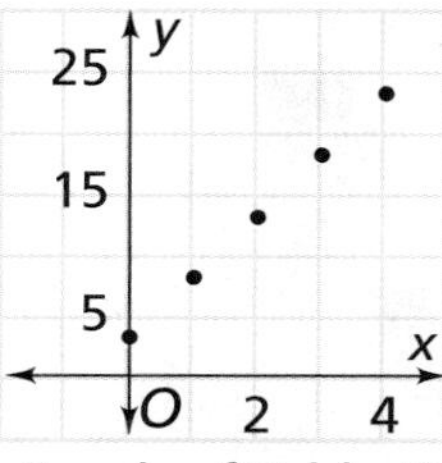

Graph of Table K

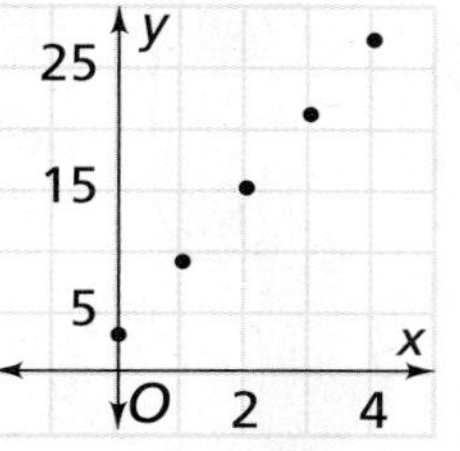

Graph of Table L

2. Thor and Pandora are bouncing a ball. Thor drops the ball from a height of 2 meters. Each time it bounces, Pandora measures the height of the bounce. The following table shows the results of this experiment.

| Number of Bounces | Height (m) |
|---|---|
| 0 | 2.00 |
| 1 | 1.68 |
| 2 | 1.41 |
| 3 | 1.19 |
| 4 | 1.00 |
| 5 | 0.84 |
| 6 | 0.71 |

   a. Find a recursive rule for determining the height of a bounce based on the previous height.

   b. How high would the ball bounce on its 100th bounce? Do you think Pandora would be able to measure this height?

Does the ball ever stop bouncing?

3. Lisa is collecting soda cans to win a contest. She is storing her soda cans in her bedroom by making a stack like the one shown here. If she begins with a base of 75 soda cans (the number of cans that will fit across the length of her room), how many cans will she have in her finished stack?

4. Find the missing terms in each sequence. The ratio between each term and the previous one is constant. For each sequence, find this common ratio.

   **a.** $1, 2, 4, ■, 16, ■, ■, \ldots$

   **b.** $1, -2, 4, ■, 16, ■, ■, \ldots$

   **c.** $1, -1, 1, ■, ■, ■, \ldots$

   **d.** $2, 6, 18, ■, ■, \ldots$

   **e.** $4, 1, \frac{1}{4}, ■, ■, \ldots$

   **f.** $-1, \frac{2}{3}, -\frac{4}{9}, ■, \ldots$

## Exercises *Practicing Habits of Mind*

### On Your Own

**5.** Suppose a snail moves 5 inches up a tree every day and 2 inches down the tree every night. In the morning of Day 0, the snail starts on the ground.

**a.** Write a function for the snail's height in the morning and another function for the snail's height in the evening.

**b.** Does either of these functions have a constant $\Delta$ column? Explain.

**c.** If the tree is 40 feet tall, on what day does the snail reach the top?

**6.** The function $F(n)$ has a constant difference. Copy and complete the following table.

| $n$ | $F(n)$ | $\Delta$ |
|---|---|---|
| 0 | 8 | ■ |
| 1 | ■ | ■ |
| 2 | ■ | ■ |
| 3 | ■ | ■ |
| 4 | 12 | |

**7.** A health club charges \$70 for the first month's membership fee and reduces the monthly fee by \$2 each month after that. What is the total membership fee for an entire year?

### Maintain Your Skills

**8.** How many multiples of 9 are between each pair of numbers?

**a.** 2 and 22 **b.** 2 and 62 **c.** 2 and 1000

**d.** 2 and $n$, where $n$ is some integer greater than 2

**9.** How many multiples of 3 are strictly between each pair of numbers?

**a.** 2 and 22 **b.** 45 and 62 **c.** 45 and 1000

**d.** integers $m$ and $n$, where $n$ is greater than $m$

## 2.10 Arithmetic Sequences and Series

Until now, a sequence has been a list of numbers. Another way to think about a **sequence** is as a function with a domain that is the set of nonnegative integers. So sequences are nothing new. If the domain of a function is {0, 1, 2, 3, 4, 5, . . . }, then it is a sequence. For example, the function defined by $f(n) = 2n^2 + 3n + 5$ is a sequence, if you restrict its domain. You can then list the outputs of the function "in sequence."

$$\{f(0), f(1), f(2), f(3), f(4), \ldots\} = \{5, 10, 19, 32, 49, \ldots\}$$

The outputs of the function are the **terms** of the sequence. In this case, the initial term is 5, the next term is 10, and the fourth term is 32.

In this example, $f(0)$ is the initial term. Sometimes, you want the domain to be all integers $n$ that are greater than 1, and then the initial term is $f(1)$.

**Habits of Mind**

**Detect the key characteristics.** In Chapter 1, you saw that to define a function, you must specify the domain. If the domain is the nonnegative integers, the function is a sequence.

### Minds in Action

*Tony is working on Problem 1 from Lesson 2.09.*

**Tony** $K(m)$ and $L(m)$ have a lot in common.

Table K

| n | K(n) | Δ |
|---|---|---|
| 0 | 3 | 5 |
| 1 | 8 | 5 |
| 2 | 13 | 5 |
| 3 | 18 | 5 |
| 4 | 23 | |

Table L

| m | L(m) | Δ |
|---|---|---|
| 0 | 3 | 6 |
| 1 | 9 | 6 |
| 2 | 15 | 6 |
| 3 | 21 | 6 |
| 4 | 27 | |

There's a constant difference of 5 in Table K.

There's a constant difference of 6 in Table L.

The two functions are defined on the set {0, 1, 2, 3, 4}.

Functions like $K(n)$ and $L(m)$ are special sequences called *arithmetic sequences*. They are defined by the property that their Δ columns are constant.

When you use *arithmetic* as an adjective, the accent is on the third syllable: arithMETIC.

The constant value of an arithmetic sequence's Δ column is the *common difference d* for that sequence. The formal definition is on the following page.

### Definitions

A sequence is an **arithmetic sequence** if

- its domain is the set of integers $n \geq 0$
- there is a number $d$, the **common difference** for the sequence, such that

$$f(n) = f(n-1) + d \text{ for all integers } n > 0$$

**Habits of Mind**

**Detect the key characteristics.** You can also call arithmetic sequences *linear sequences.* Do their graphs suggest why? Is there an algebraic reason?

**Examples of Arithmetic Sequences**

| Initial term | $d$ | Sequence | Formula and Domain |
|---|---|---|---|
| $a(0) = 3$ | 3 | 3, 6, 9, 12, . . . | $a(n) = 3(n+1)$ for all $n \geq 0$ |
| $b(1) = 10$ | −1 | 10, 9, 8, 7, . . . | $b(n) = 11 - n$ for all $n \geq 1$ |
| $w(3) = 180$ | 180 | 180, 360, 540, . . . | $w(n) = 180(n-2)$ for all $n \geq 3$ |

## For You to Do

**1.** In an arithmetic sequence, $f(0) = 8$ and $f(1) = 12$. Write out the first several terms of such a sequence. Is there any other arithmetic sequence with first term 8 and second term 12?

You can denote the terms of a sequence by subscripts $t_0, t_1, t_2, \ldots$ Here, the ninth term is $t_8$. Explain.

**2.** Suppose $r$ is an arithmetic sequence with $r(5) = 8$ and $r(12) = 29$.

**a.** What is the common difference?

**b.** Find $r(9)$.

**c.** Find a closed form for $r$.

**d.** Is 78,209,756 a term of $r$? If so, what term is it? If not, explain why you think it is not.

**3.** Give two different examples of an arithmetic sequence with common difference 0. How would you describe an arithmetic sequence with common difference 0?

## For Discussion

**4.** Suppose $f$ is an arithmetic sequence with initial term $f(0) = a$ and common difference $d$. Find a closed form for $f(n)$ in terms of $a$ and $d$.

**Habits of Mind**

**Establish a process.** It might help you to make a table for the sequence.

**5.** Suppose $g$ is an arithmetic sequence with initial term $g(1) = b$ and common difference $d$. Find a closed form for $g(n)$ in terms of $b$ and $d$.

## Arithmetic Series

Every arithmetic sequence has an associated arithmetic series.

### Definition

**If the sequence $t$ is an arithmetic sequence with initial term $t(0)$, the associated series $T$ defined on integers $n$, such that $n \geq 0$ by $T(n) = \sum_{k=0}^{n} t(k)$ is an arithmetic series.**

**Remember...**

If $f$ is any function, the function defined on nonnegative integers by $n \mapsto \sum_{k=0}^{n} f(k)$ is the series associated with $f$.

## Example

**Problem** Consider the arithmetic sequence in Table K. The initial term is $f(0) = 3$. The common difference is 5. A closed form is $f(n) = 3 + 5n$.

Find a closed form for $F(n) = \sum_{k=0}^{n} f(k)$.

**Solution**

$$\begin{aligned}\sum_{k=0}^{n} (3 + 5k) &= \sum_{k=0}^{n} 3 + \sum_{k=0}^{n} 5k \\ &= 3(n + 1) + 5 \cdot \frac{n(n + 1)}{2} \\ &= \frac{(5n + 6)(n + 1)}{2}\end{aligned}$$

## For You to Do

Here is Table L again.

| $m$ | $L(m)$ | $\Sigma$ |
|---|---|---|
| 0 | 3 | ■ |
| 1 | 9 | ■ |
| 2 | 15 | ■ |
| 3 | 21 | ■ |
| 4 | 27 | ■ |

6. Copy the table and complete the $\Sigma$ column.
7. Find a closed form for the sequence.
8. Find a closed form for the series.

# Exercises Practicing Habits of Mind

## Check Your Understanding

**1.** In an arithmetic sequence, the first term is 8 and the $n$th term is 12. Find the common difference.

**2.** Can the numbers 1, $\frac{1}{2}$, and $\frac{1}{3}$ belong to the same arithmetic sequence? If so, give an example of such a sequence. If not, explain why not.

**3.** Can you find three numbers that cannot all belong to the same arithmetic sequence? If so, give an example. If not, explain why not.

**4.** For each table,

- Copy the table and complete the $\Sigma$ column.
- Find a closed form for the sequence.
- Find a closed form for the series.

**a.**

| $n$ | $q(n)$ | $\Sigma$ |
|---|---|---|
| 0 | 9 | ■ |
| 1 | 15 | ■ |
| 2 | 21 | ■ |
| 3 | 27 | ■ |
| 4 | 33 | ■ |

**b.**

| $n$ | $p(n)$ | $\Sigma$ |
|---|---|---|
| 0 | 12 | ■ |
| 1 | 7 | ■ |
| 2 | 2 | ■ |
| 3 | −3 | ■ |
| 4 | −8 | ■ |

**5.** In an arithmetic sequence, $f(0) = 8$ and $f(2) = 12$. Write the first several terms of such a sequence. Is there any other arithmetic sequence with first term 8 and third term 12?

**6.** Consider the arithmetic sequence $g$ with $g(0) = 2$ and common difference 3.

**a.** Write the first four terms of $g$.

**b.** Write the first four terms of the series $G$ associated with $g$.

**c.** Find closed forms for $g(n)$ and for the associated series $G(n)$.

**7.** For each sequence with the given initial term and constant difference,

- tabulate the sequence and the associated series
- find closed forms for the sequence and the associated series

**a.** $t(0) = 5, d = 9$ **b.** $h(0) = 7, d = -4$ **c.** $t(0) = 6, d = \frac{1}{2}$

8. Let $f(n) = a + dn$, where $a$ is the initial term and $d$ is the common difference.

a. Copy and complete this table in terms of $a$ and $d$.

| $n$ | $f(n)$ | $\Sigma$ |
|---|---|---|
| 0 | $a$ | ■ |
| 1 | $a + d$ | ■ |
| 2 | ■ | $3a + 3d$ |
| 3 | ■ | ■ |
| 4 | ■ | ■ |
| 5 | ■ | ■ |

b. Find a closed form for the series associated with $f$.

## On Your Own

9. Suppose $f$ is an arithmetic sequence with initial term $f(0) = 3$ and common difference 6.

a. Find $f(8)$.

b. Find a closed form for $f$.

c. Is 78,209,756 a term of $f$? If so, what term is it? If not, explain why not.

10. How would you describe the arithmetic sequence with initial term $f(0) = 1$ and common difference 1?

11. Show that the average of any three consecutive integers is equal to the middle number.

The diameters, in inches, of the cake's layers are part of an arithmetic sequence with initial term 6 and common difference 2.

**12.** Consider an arithmetic sequence $t$. Show that any term $t(n)$ is the average of the one before it, $t(n-1)$, and the one after it, $t(n+1)$.

In other words, in an arithmetic sequence, each term starting with the second one is the arithmetic mean of the preceding term and the following term. That is where the name "arithmetic sequence" comes from.

**13.** Below is an illustration of the first three pyramidal numbers. Each layer is a square.

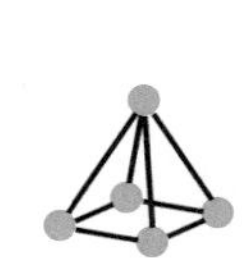

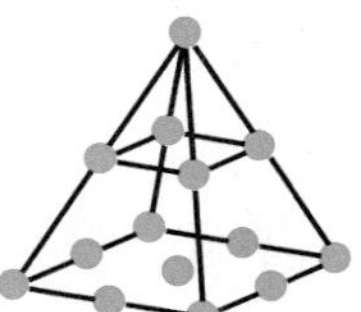

**a.** Use this illustration to list the first five pyramidal numbers.

You count the dots here.

**b.** What series does the total number of dots in each figure represent? Is this series an arithmetic series? Explain.

**c.** Find the closed form for the number of dots $n$ in a pyramid that is $n$ rows high.

**d.** How many dots are in a pyramid ten levels high?

**14.** An arithmetic sequence with terms $a(1), a(2), \ldots, a(5)$ satisfies both $a(1) + a(3) + a(5) = -12$ and $a(1) \cdot a(3) \cdot a(5) = 80$. Find the terms in this sequence.

Some of these exercises have more than one solution.

**15.** In an arithmetic sequence with a difference $d$, the product of the second term and $d$ is 30. The sum of the third and fifth terms is 32. Find the first three terms in this sequence.

**16.** Give an example of a sequence with a $\Delta$ column that is an arithmetic sequence. Find a closed form for your sequence.

**17.** Give an example of a sequence with a $\Sigma$ column that is an arithmetic sequence. Find a closed form for your sequence.

**18.** Can the $\Sigma$ column of an arithmetic sequence ever be arithmetic? Explain.

**19.** The sum of the first and fifth terms of an arithmetic sequence is $\frac{5}{3}$. The product of the third and fourth terms of the same sequence is $\frac{65}{72}$. Find the sum of the first 17 terms of this sequence.

**20.** Standardized Test Prep Let $G(n) = \sum_{k=0}^{n} g(k)$, where $g(n) = 5 - 3n$. What is the value of $G(3)$?

**A.** $-4$ **B.** $-3$ **C.** $-1$ **D.** 2

Use this array for Exercises 21 and 22.

$$\begin{array}{cccccccc} 1 & 2 & 3 & 4 & 5 & \cdots & k \\ 2 & 2 & 3 & 4 & 5 & \cdots & k \\ 3 & 3 & 3 & 4 & 5 & \cdots & k \\ 4 & 4 & 4 & 4 & 5 & \cdots & k \\ 5 & 5 & 5 & 5 & 5 & \cdots & k \\ \vdots & \vdots & \vdots & \vdots & \vdots & \ddots & \\ k & k & k & k & k & & k \end{array}$$

**21.** You can continue the pattern of numbers above indefinitely down and to the right. Let $S(n)$ be the number of entries that are less than or equal to $n$ in this array.

So $S(2) = 4$ because there are one 1 and three 2's for a total of 4 entries.

**a.** Find a sequence $s(n)$ such that $S(n) = \sum_{k=1}^{n} s(k)$. Is $s$ an arithmetic sequence? Explain.

**b.** Find a closed form for $S(n)$.

**22.** Take It Further Let $G(n)$ be the sum of all of the entries in the array above that are less than or equal to $n$.

So $G(2) = 2 + 2 + 2 + 1 = 7$. It is the sum of the one 1 and the three 2's.

**a.** Find a sequence $g(n)$ such that $G(n) = \sum_{k=1}^{n} g(k)$. Is $g$ an arithmetic sequence? Explain.

**b.** Find a closed form for $G(n)$.

## Maintain Your Skills

**23.** Suppose $t$ is the sequence given by $t(n) = (n + 1)2^n$.

**a.** Make a table for $t$ for $n = 0$ through $n = 5$.

**b.** Add a column to the table for the values of the ratio $\frac{t(n)}{t(n-1)}$.

**c.** Is $t$ an arithmetic sequence? Is the definition of each of its terms as $t(n) = (n + 1)2^n$ enough to decide? Explain.

**d.** Find a closed form for $\sum_{k=0}^{n} t(k)$.

To evaluate the indefinite sum, see the TI-Nspire Handbook, p. 817.

# 2.11 Geometric Sequences and Series

There are other types of sequences and series besides arithmetic sequences and series.

## In-Class Experiment

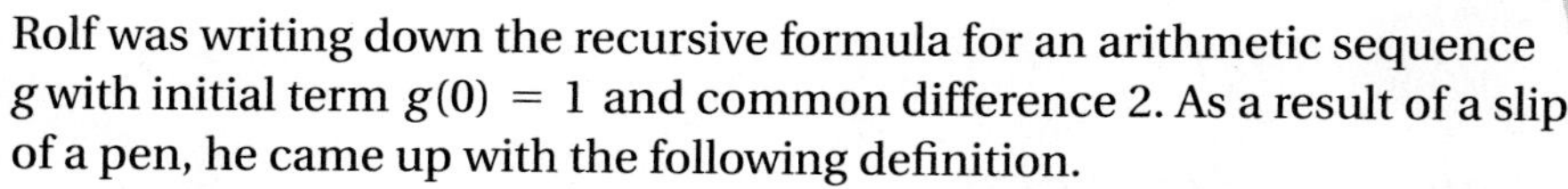

Rolf was writing down the recursive formula for an arithmetic sequence $g$ with initial term $g(0) = 1$ and common difference 2. As a result of a slip of a pen, he came up with the following definition.

$$g(n) = \begin{cases} 1 & \text{if } n = 0 \\ g(n-1) \cdot 2 & \text{if } n > 0 \end{cases}$$

1. **a.** Make a table and write down a few entries for $g$.
   **b.** Is $g$ an arithmetic sequence? Explain.
   **c.** Write a closed form for $g(n)$.

2. **a.** Add a $\Delta$ column to the table for $g$. Describe a pattern in the $\Delta$ column.
   **b.** Add a $\Sigma$ column to the table for $g$. Describe a pattern in the $\Sigma$ column.

3. **a.** Add a ratio column to the table for $g$.

| $n$ | $g(n)$ | $\frac{g(n+1)}{g(n)}$ |
|---|---|---|
| 0 | 1 | $\frac{2}{1} = 2$ |
| 1 | 2 | ■ |
| 2 | 4 | ■ |
| 3 | ■ | ■ |
| 4 | ■ | ■ |

   **b.** Describe a pattern in the ratio column.

**Remember...**

Instead of what you must add to one output to get the next one, this column gives what you must multiply each output by to get the next one.

Functions like the ones that Rolf built and that Thor and Pandora recorded in Exercise 2 from Lesson 2.09 are *geometric sequences*. To be a geometric sequence, a function has to have two properties.

- It is a sequence, meaning a function defined on the nonnegative integers.
- The ratio column is constant.

Here is a formal definition.

### Definitions

A sequence is a **geometric sequence** if

- its domain is the integers $n \geq 0$
- there is a number $r \neq 0$, called the **common ratio,** such that

$$f(n) = r \cdot f(n-1) \text{ for all integers } n > 0$$

Compare this definition with the definition of arithmetic sequence in Lesson 2.10.

**Examples of Geometric Sequences**

| Initial Term | $r$ | Sequence | Formula and Domain |
|---|---|---|---|
| $a(0) = 3$ | 3 | 3, 9, 27, 81, ... | $a(n) = 3^{n+1}$ for all $n \geq 0$ |
| $b(1) = 1$ | −1 | 1, −1, 1, −1, ... | $b(n) = (-1)^{n-1}$ for all $n \geq 1$ |
| $c(0) = 8$ | $\frac{1}{2}$ | 8, 4, 2, 1, ... | $c(n) = \frac{8}{(2^n)}$ for all $n \geq 0$ |

## For You to Do

**4.** Suppose $t$ is a geometric sequence.

**a.** If $t(3) = 100$ and $t(5) = 10{,}000$, what is $t(4)$?

**b.** If $t(3) = 100$ and $t(5) = 4$, what is $t(4)$?

**c.** If $t(n-1) = a$ and $t(n+1) = b$, what is $t(n)$?

There could be more than one possibility for $t(4)$.

**5.** Write down the first four terms of a geometric sequence $g$ with the given initial term and common ratio.

**a.** $g(0) = 5,\ r = 2$

**b.** $g(0) = 5,\ r = -2$

**c.** $g(0) = 5,\ r = 1$

**d.** $g(0) = 5,\ r = \frac{1}{2}$

## Geometric Series

Just as an arithmetic sequence has an associated arithmetic series, a geometric sequence has an associated *geometric series.*

### Definition

**If the sequence $g$ is a geometric sequence with initial term $g(0)$, the associated series $G(n) = \sum_{k=0}^{n} g(n)$ is a geometric series.**

## For You to Do

Suppose you have a table for a geometric sequence $t$. You can make a table for the series associated with $t$ by adding a $\Sigma$ column.

| $n$ | $t(n)$ | $\Sigma$ |
|---|---|---|
| 0 | 3 | 3 |
| 1 | 6 | 9 |
| 2 | 12 | 21 |
| 3 | 24 | 45 |
| 4 | 48 | 93 |
| 5 | 96 | 189 |

**6.** Find both closed and recursive forms for $t$.

**7.** Find both closed and recursive forms for the associated series $T(n) = \sum_{k=0}^{n} t(k)$.

**8.** What is $\sum_{k=0}^{18} t(k)$?

# Exercises Practicing Habits of Mind

## Check Your Understanding

1. Find $g(7)$ for each geometric sequence.

   a. $g(1) = 5,\ r = 2$
   b. $g(1) = 5,\ r = -2$
   c. $g(1) = 5,\ r = 1$
   d. $g(1) = 5,\ r = \frac{1}{2}$
   e. $g(5) = 18,\ g(6) = 9$
   f. $g(3) = 12,\ g(5) = 30$
   g. $g(6) = 6,\ g(8) = 54$
   h. $g(5) = 6,\ g(9) = 54$

2. Can a sequence be geometric and arithmetic at the same time? Explain.

3. **Write About It** Write at least four pairs of sequences. A pair will consist of an arithmetic sequence $a$ and a geometric sequence $g$ with the same initial term and the common difference of $a$ equal to the common ratio of $g$. For example,

   $$a(1) = 2, 5, 8, 11, 14, \ldots$$

   $$g(1) = 2, 6, 18, 54, 162, \ldots$$

   Both sequences have initial term 2. The common difference for the arithmetic series $a$ is 3. The common ratio for geometric series $g$ is 3.

   Compare the behavior of sequences in each pair. Do both sequences increase or decrease?

> Make sure you have first terms, common differences, and common ratios with various signs and values.

4. Let $s(n) = 5 \cdot \left(\frac{1}{2}\right)^n$.

   a. Find a formula for $\sum_{i=0}^{n} s(i)$.
   b. Use the formula to find $\sum_{i=0}^{15} s(i)$.

## On Your Own

5. Write a closed-form definition for a function that generates each sequence in Exercise 1.

> That is, write a formula for $g(n)$.

6. **Standardized Test Prep** Suppose $a(n)$ is a geometric sequence with initial term $a(0) = 6$ and common ratio $\frac{3}{2}$. What is the value of $a(5)$?

   A. $\frac{15}{2}$
   B. $\frac{243}{32}$
   C. $\frac{27}{2}$
   D. $\frac{729}{16}$

7. Draw a square. Connect the midpoints of the sides of this square to form another square. Connect the midpoints of the sides of the second square to form the next one. You can continue to make more squares in this pattern.

   a. If the side length of the first square you draw is 1, what is the side length of the second square? Of the third square?

> **Go Online**
> www.successnetplus.com

b. Do these lengths form a geometric sequence? Explain. If they do, what are the first term and the common ratio of this geometric sequence?

c. If the area of the first square you draw is 1, what is the area of the second square? Of the third square?

d. Do these areas form a geometric sequence? Explain. If they do, what are the first term and the common ratio of this geometric sequence? If they do not, what kind of a sequence do they form?

e. **Take It Further** Prove that connecting the midpoints of the sides of a square really gives you another square.

**8.** a. Turn a blank piece of $8\frac{1}{2}$ in.-by-11 in. paper lengthwise and draw a 45° angle in the bottom left corner of the paper.

b. Draw a small square, $\frac{1}{2}$ in. on each side, with one side on the horizontal side of the angle and a vertex on the other side of the angle.

c. Extend the right side of this square vertically until it intersects the sloping side of the 45° angle. Draw a second square with this segment as its left side, as shown.

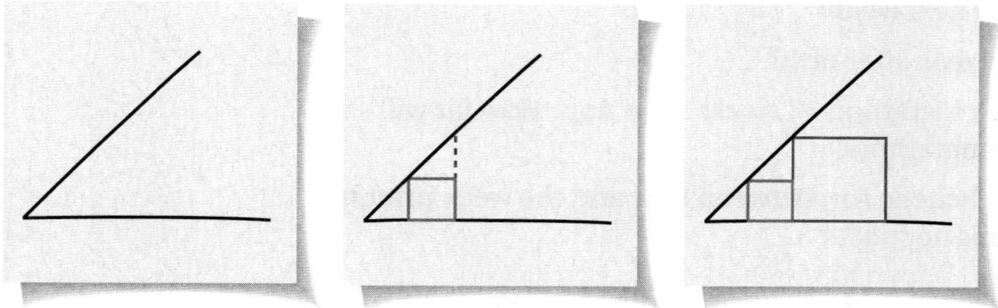

d. Continue the process to draw two more squares.

e. What are the lengths of the sides of the four squares?

f. Find at least two geometric sequences in the diagram.

**9.** An old tale tells of a king who was tricked into paying an outrageous amount for a favor. The king was to pay by placing 1 grain of rice on the first square of a chessboard, 2 on the second square, 4 on the third square, 8 on the fourth square, and keep doubling the amount this way until all 64 squares had rice. The king thought this might take several pounds of rice.

a. How many grains of rice would the king place on the last (64th) square?

b. In all, how many grains of rice would the king place on the chessboard?

c. If there are 8000 grains of rice in a pound, how many pounds of rice did the king have to pay for the favor?

10. Suppose you make up a joke. On Day 1, you tell your two best friends. They cannot stop laughing. The next day (Day 2), each of them tells two people, who also love the joke. On Day 3, the four people who heard the joke the day before all tell two new people. And so it continues. Each day, everyone who heard the joke yesterday tells two people who have never heard the joke. How quickly does the joke spread?

   a. How many people hear the joke for the first time on the 8th day?

   b. In all, how many people have heard the joke by the end of the 8th day?

   c. How long would it take all the students in your school to hear the joke?

   d. How long would it take all the students in your town or city to hear the joke?

   e. How long would it take everyone in the world to hear the joke?

> You can also model the spread of disease with geometric series, but the spread of jokes is more pleasant to think about.

> Assume there are about 6 billion people in the world.

11. To keep from getting in a rut, many athletes challenge themselves. Suppose Michelle runs 5 miles this week. She gives herself this challenge. In any week, she will never run a shorter distance than she did the week before, and she will try to increase her distance 10% each week.

   a. How far will Michelle run next week?

   b. How far will she run the week after next?

   c. Michelle plans to run in a marathon 32 weeks from now. How far will she run the week before the marathon?

   d. What total mileage will Michelle run between now and the week prior to the marathon, if she keeps her pact?

Do you remember this exercise from Lesson 2.01?

A wealthy relative left Emile an inheritance. The will read as follows.

To Emile, because he likes math problems, I leave a choice. He can have one of two inheritances.

**Option 1** A starting amount of \$10,000 with an annual payment at the end of each year that is \$1000 more than the amount he received the previous year, for the next 26 years

**Option 2** A starting amount of one cent with an annual payment at the end of each year that is twice the amount he received in the previous year, for the next 26 years

Year 0 is the year in which Emile chooses an option and gets his first payment.

To find the total Emile gets under Option 1, you can sum an arithmetic series. After $n$ years, he will get

$$10{,}000 + 11{,}000 + 12{,}000 + 13{,}000 + \cdots + (10{,}000 + 1{,}000n)$$

To find the total Emile gets under Option 2, you can sum a geometric series. After $n$ years, he will get

$$0.01 + 0.02 + 0.04 + 0.08 + \cdots + (0.01) \cdot 2^n$$

**12.** **a.** What is $n$? That is, what is the last term you would add in each series?

**b.** Sum the arithmetic series to find the total Emile gets with Option 1.

**c.** Sum the geometric series to find the total Emile gets with Option 2.

Remember Thor and Pandora? They dropped a ball from a height of 2 meters and measured the height of each bounce. The following table shows the results of this experiment.

| Number of Bounces | Height (m) |
|---|---|
| 0 | 2.00 |
| 1 | 1.68 |
| 2 | 1.41 |
| 3 | 1.19 |
| 4 | 1.00 |
| 5 | 0.84 |
| 6 | 0.71 |

One question you might ask is what total distance the ball travels in, say, 100 bounces? The problem is more complicated than it might seem at first. Exercises 13–17 will help you answer this question.

13. First, just think about the distance the ball falls. Do not worry about the distance it travels bouncing up. When the ball first drops, it falls 2 meters. How far does it fall after the first bounce? After the second bounce? After the third bounce?

14. You saw that the bounce height was actually close to a geometric sequence. So you can rewrite your answers above as 2 meters, $2x$ meters, $2x^2$ meters, and $2x^3$ meters. What is the common ratio $x$?

15. To find the distance the ball falls in 100 bounces, you have to find this sum.

$$2 + 2x + 2x^2 + 2x^3 + \cdots + 2x^{100}$$

The value of $x$ is whatever you found in Exercise 13. What is the sum?

16. What is the total distance the ball travels upward? Use any method you like to find out that total distance.

17. Find the total distance the ball travels upward and downward. Do you think your answer would be different if you calculated the distance for 1000 bounces instead? Explain.

## Maintain Your Skills

18. Zeno starts 24 feet from a wall. He jumps half the distance to the wall. Then he jumps halfway across the remaining distance to the wall. Then he jumps half of that.

    a. How far does Zeno travel after 3 jumps? How far is he from the wall?

    b. How far does Zeno travel after 6 jumps? How far is he from the wall?

    c. How far does Zeno travel after $n$ jumps? How far is he from the wall?

    d. Will Zeno ever get to the wall if he keeps up this "jumping halfway" scheme?

This is a variation on a famous problem known as Zeno's paradox, named for a Greek mathematician who lived in the 400's B.C.

# 2.12 Limits

For some sequences and series, as the input values increase, the output values get closer and closer to a certain number.

## In-Class Experiment

1. Suppose $f(n) = \frac{1}{2^n}$, and $f$ is defined on the integers $n$ such that $n \geq 1$.

| $n$ | $f(n)$ |
|---|---|
| 1 | $\frac{1}{2^1} = \frac{1}{2}$ |
| 2 | $\frac{1}{2^2} = \frac{1}{4}$ |
| 3 | $\frac{1}{2^3} = \frac{1}{8}$ |
| 4 | $\frac{1}{2^4} = \frac{1}{16}$ |
| 5 | $\frac{1}{2^5} = \frac{1}{32}$ |

   **a.** How large do you have to make $n$ to be sure that $f(n)$ is within 0.1 of 0?

   **b.** How large do you have to make $n$ to ensure that $f(n)$ is within 0.01 of 0?

   **c.** How large do you have to make $n$ to ensure that $f(n)$ is within 0.001 of 0?

2. Copy the table above and add a $\Sigma$ column. Use it to answer these questions.

   **a.** Suppose $F(n)$ is the series associated with $f$.

$$F(n) = \sum_{k=1}^{n} f(k) = \frac{1}{2} + \frac{1}{4} + \frac{1}{8} + \cdots + \frac{1}{2^n}$$

   Find a closed form for $F(n)$.

   **b.** How large do you have to make $n$ to be sure that $F(n)$ is within 0.1 of 1?

   **c.** How large do you have to make $n$ to ensure that $F(n)$ is within 0.01 of 1?

   **d.** How large do you have to make $n$ to ensure that $F(n)$ is within 0.001 of 1?

You say that the sequence in Problem 1 of the In-Class Experiment has a **limit**, or ultimate value, of 0. This means that if you make $n$ large enough, you can make $f(n)$ as close as you want to 0.

Similarly, the series in Problem 2 has a limit of 1. If you make $n$ large enough, you can make $F(n)$ as close as you want to 1.

## For Discussion

3. In Problem 1, is there any value of $n$ for which $f(n) = 0$? In what sense is 0 a limit for the sequence?

4. In Problem 2, is there any value of $n$ for which $F(n) = 1$? In what sense is 1 a limit for the series?

5. Can a sequence ever have more than one limit? Explain.

## Minds in Action

*Tony, Sasha, and Derman are working on the following questions.*

**Question 1** Suppose $g$ is a geometric sequence with first term $g(0) = 1$ and common ratio $\frac{1}{5}$. Does $g$ have a limit? If so, what is it?

**Question 2** Using the same function $g$, does the associated series have a limit? If so, what is it?

**Sasha** Let's try making a table for $g$, so we can see what's going on.

**Tony** I've already filled in values up to $n = 3$.

| n | g(n) |
|---|---|
| 0 | 1 |
| 1 | $\frac{1}{5}$ |
| 2 | $\frac{1}{25}$ |
| 3 | $\frac{1}{125}$ |

**Derman** Look—the outputs get smaller and smaller! They seem to approach 0, so I guess that's the limit.

**Sasha** It's not enough to say "they seem to approach 0." In order to say that the limit of the sequence is 0, we have to show that we can get as close as we want to 0. I mean, if we pick any number close to 0, we then have to find an $n$ such that $g(n)$ is even closer to 0 than our number.

**Tony** Yes, look at this.

To get within 0.1 of 0, let $n = 2$.

$$g(2) = \left(\frac{1}{5}\right)^2 = \frac{1}{25} < 0.1$$

To get within 0.01 of 0, let $n = 3$.

$$g(3) = \left(\frac{1}{5}\right)^3 = \frac{1}{125} < 0.01$$

To get within 0.001 of 0, let $n = 5$.

$$g(5) = \left(\frac{1}{5}\right)^5 = \frac{1}{3125} < 0.001$$

Since you can get as close as you want to 0 by making $n$ large enough, 0 is the limit of the sequence.

**Derman** Look—it seems that for every three steps in this process, we get another two places of accuracy. If that's true, I'm sure that the terms of the sequence converge to 0.

**Sasha** OK, so what's the answer to Question 2? I think we should find a formula for the associated series. We have $g(n) = \left(\frac{1}{5}\right)^n$, so we can write out $G(n)$ like this.

$$\begin{aligned} G(n) &= \sum_{k=0}^{n} g(k) \\ &= \sum_{k=0}^{n} \left(\frac{1}{5}\right)^k \\ &= \frac{1 - \left(\frac{1}{5}\right)^{n+1}}{1 - \frac{1}{5}} \\ &= \frac{1}{1 - \frac{1}{5}}\left(1 - \left(\frac{1}{5}\right)^{n+1}\right) \\ &= \frac{1}{\frac{4}{5}}\left(1 - \left(\frac{1}{5}\right)^{n+1}\right) \\ &= \frac{5}{4}\left(1 - \left(\frac{1}{5}\right)^{n+1}\right) \end{aligned}$$

**Derman** Then I'll use the fact that $G(n) = \frac{5}{4}\left(1 - \left(\frac{1}{5}\right)^{n+1}\right)$ to fill in a $\Sigma$ column.

| n | g(n) | Σ |
|---|---|---|
| 0 | 1 | $\frac{5}{4}\left(1-\frac{1}{5}\right)$ |
| 1 | $\frac{1}{5}$ | $\frac{5}{4}\left(1-\frac{1}{25}\right)$ |
| 2 | $\frac{1}{25}$ | $\frac{5}{4}\left(1-\frac{1}{125}\right)$ |
| 3 | $\frac{1}{125}$ | $\frac{5}{4}\left(1-\frac{1}{625}\right)$ |
| 4 | $\frac{1}{625}$ | $\frac{5}{4}\left(1-\frac{1}{3125}\right)$ |

**Tony** Well, $1 - \frac{1}{25}$ is within 0.1 of 1, $1 - \frac{1}{125}$ is within 0.01 of 1, and $1 - \frac{1}{3125}$ is within 0.001 of 1. Now it's clear that as $n$ gets larger, the factor $\left(1 - \left(\frac{1}{5}\right)^{n+1}\right)$ gets closer and closer to 1. It's equal to 1 minus a tiny number.

**Sasha** Right, so you can get as close as anyone wants to $\frac{5}{4}$ by making $n$ large enough. So the limit of the series is $\frac{5}{4}$.

## Habits of Mind

**Look for relationships.** If $g$ is a geometric sequence with first term $g(0) = a$ and common ratio $r$, then $g(n) = ar^n$, and

$$\sum_{k=0}^{n} g(k) = a \sum_{k=0}^{n} r^k = a\left(\frac{1 - r^{n+1}}{1 - r}\right)$$

You can rewrite this as $\frac{a}{1 - r}(1 - r^{n+1})$. This is equivalent to the "Think Euclid" identity multiplied by the constant $a$.

## For You to Do

Suppose $a = 12$. Pick three values for $r$ from this list.

$$2, \frac{1}{2}, \frac{1}{3}, -1, -3, -\frac{1}{2}, -\frac{1}{3}, \frac{3}{8}, \frac{9}{8}, 10$$

6. For each $r$-value you select, decide whether the following series has a limit.

$$\sum_{k=0}^{n} g(k) = \frac{12}{1-r}(1 - r^{n+1})$$

7. If it does, say what the limit is. If it does not, explain why not.
8. If $r = 1$, what happens with the formula? Does the series have a limit? Explain.

## For Discussion

9. Explain how you can tell, just based on the value of $r$, if a geometric series has a limit.
10. Can an arithmetic series have a limit? Does the limit depend on the first term, the common difference, or both? Explain.

## Exercises *Practicing Habits of Mind*

### Check Your Understanding

1. For each geometric sequence described, do the following.
   - Write the first four terms of the sequence.
   - Write the first four terms of the series associated with the sequence.
   - Decide if the series has a limit.
   - If the series does have a limit, give that number.

   a. first term 7 and common ratio $\frac{2}{9}$
   b. first term 100 and common ratio $\frac{1}{2}$
   c. first term $\frac{3}{4}$ and common ratio 2
   d. first term 1 and common ratio 1

**2.** Pat and Sam are out for some exercise. They start off on a mile-long path. Sam starts walking at a steady rate. Pat starts running twice as fast as Sam walks. Pat runs to the end of the mile, runs back to Sam, turns around and runs to the end of the mile, turns around and runs to Sam, and so on. All the while Sam walks steadily along, laughing at Pat.

When Sam reaches the end of the mile-long path, how far has Pat run?

## On Your Own

**3.** The diagrams below show the first three stages of the Koch curve. The segment of Stage 0 gets replaced by four segments, each $\frac{1}{3}$ the length of the original segment and arranged as shown in Stage 1. The same rule applies to each segment of Stage $n$ as you pass to Stage $n + 1$.

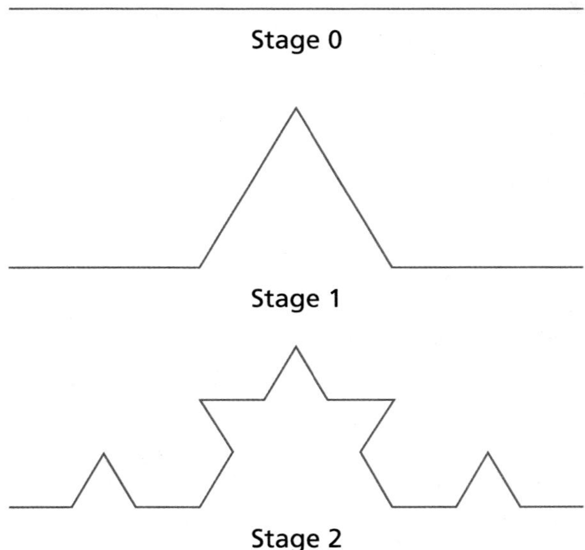


**a.** Draw the next stage.

**b.** Assume you start with length 1 at Stage 0. Find the length of the curve at Stages 1–3.

**c.** Find a closed form for the length of the curve at stage $n$.

**d.** Does the perimeter have a limit? That is, as $n$ increases, does the perimeter of Stage $n$ approach some fixed number, or does it increase without bound?

**4.** You can close the shape at each stage by adding line segments. The diagram below shows closed shapes for Stage 1 and Stage 2. Then you can find the area within the curve.

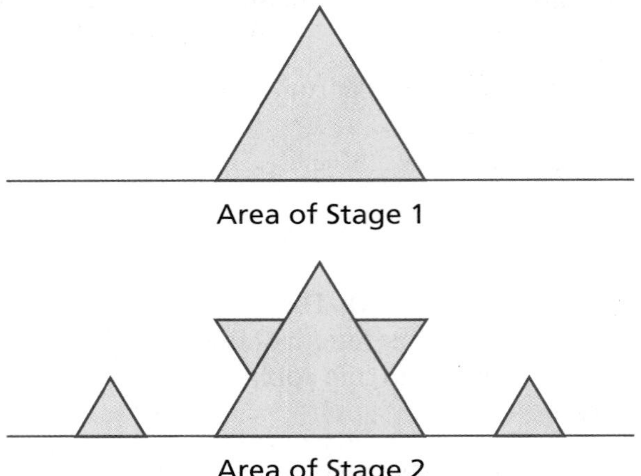

Area of Stage 1

Area of Stage 2

Assume that for Stage 1 above, the area is 1 square unit.

**a.** Find the area within the curve at Stages 2–4.

**b.** What is the area at Stage $n$?

**c.** Does the area have a limit? That is, as $n$ increases, does the area of Stage $n$ approach some fixed number, or does it increase without bound?

**5.** You can line up the squares shown in the diagram below on the left to make an infinite staircase, shown below on the right. The first square is 1 by 1. The second square is $\frac{2}{3}$ by $\frac{2}{3}$. Each successive square is $\frac{2}{3}$ the height of the previous square.

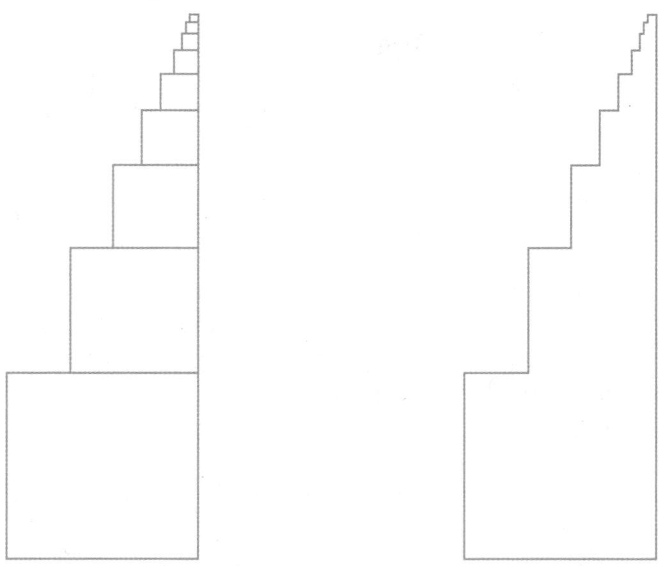

**a.** Find the area of the staircase. **b.** Find the perimeter of the staircase.

6. To make the figure at the right, you connect the midpoints of the sides of a square of area 1 to form an inner square. You shade two opposite corners. You then repeat the process for the smaller square. Suppose you repeat this process an infinite number of times. Use a geometric series to find the total area of the shaded region. Does your answer make sense?

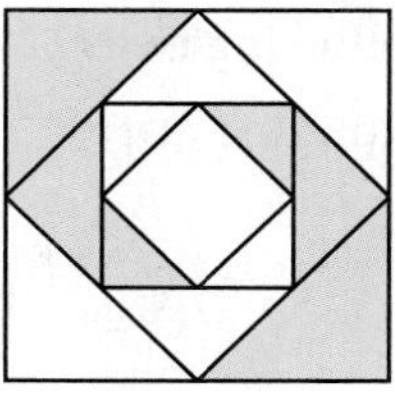

7. **Standardized Test Prep** What is the limit of the following geometric series?

$$1 + \frac{3}{5} + \frac{9}{25} + \frac{27}{125} + \frac{81}{625} + \cdots$$

**A.** $\frac{3}{2}$ **B.** 2 **C.** $\frac{5}{2}$ **D.** 3

## Maintain Your Skills

8. Achilles and the tortoise run a race. Since Achilles is a faster runner (in fact, he can run 10 times faster than the tortoise), he gives the tortoise a 10-meter head start.

   During the time it takes Achilles to run 10 meters, the tortoise covers 1 meter. Thus, the tortoise now has a 1-meter lead. During the time it takes Achilles to run another 1 meter, the tortoise runs 0.1 meter. Thus, the tortoise still has a 0.1-meter lead.

   As Achilles runs the next 0.1 meter of the race, the tortoise goes 0.01 meter. Therefore, as small as the lead may be, the tortoise is still ahead in the race.

   Does this mean Achilles never catches up to the tortoise? Explain.

9. **Take It Further** Suppose you divide a 3 inch-by-3 inch square into nine smaller squares and shade the center square. You then partition each unshaded square into nine squares and shade their centers. If you continue this process forever, how much area is shaded? (Note: The figures below are not full size.)

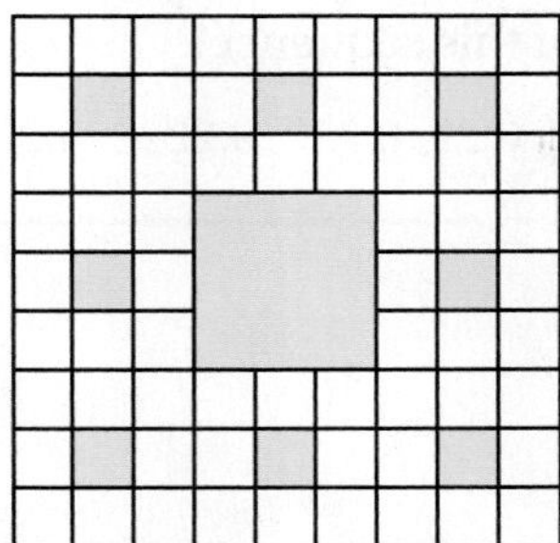

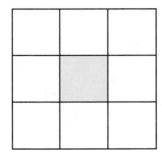

## 2.13 Repeating Decimals

You have learned the following two things in this investigation.

- If $g$ is a geometric sequence $g(n) = a \cdot r^n$, then the formula for the associated series is

$$G(n) = \sum_{k=0}^{n} g(k) = \frac{a}{1-r}(1 - r^{n+1})$$

- If the common ratio of a geometric sequences is between $-1$ and 1—that is, $-1 < r < 1$—then the associated series has a limit. That limit is $\frac{a}{1-r}$.

Some decimals are geometric series. You can use the above facts to find fractions equivalent to them. For example, the decimal 0.2222 is

$$\frac{2}{10} + \frac{2}{100} + \frac{2}{1000} + \frac{2}{10{,}000} = \frac{2}{10} + \frac{2}{10^2} + \frac{2}{10^3} + \frac{2}{10^4}$$
$$= \frac{2}{10} + \frac{2}{10}\left(\frac{1}{10}\right) + \frac{2}{10}\left(\frac{1}{10}\right)^2 + \frac{2}{10}\left(\frac{1}{10}\right)^3$$

This is the sum of four terms of a geometric sequence with first term $\frac{2}{10}$ and common ratio $\frac{1}{10}$. You can use the formula below for the sum of $n + 1$ terms of a geometric series to get a fraction equivalent to 0.2222.

$$\left(\frac{a}{1-r}\right)(1 - r^{n+1})$$

**Remember...**

If $|r| < 1$, then as $n$ gets very large, $|r^{n+1}|$ gets very small. In fact, it gets arbitrarily close to 0. So the factor of $(1 - r^{n+1})$ gets very close to 1. If $(1 - r^{n+1})$ is very close to 1, then $G(n)$ is very close to $\frac{a}{1-r}$.

Why are there $n + 1$ terms?

### For You to Do

1. Think about the sequence that represents 0.2222.
   a. What is the initial term $a$?
   b. What is the common ratio $r$?
   c. What is $n$?
   d. Use the formula above to find a fraction equivalent to 0.2222.
2. Show that the following equations are true.

$$0.22222 = \frac{2}{9}\left(1 - \left(\frac{1}{10}\right)^5\right)$$

$$0.222222 = \frac{2}{9}\left(1 - \left(\frac{1}{10}\right)^6\right)$$

3. What is the limit of this sequence?

$$\{0.2, 0.22, 0.222, 0.2222, 0.22222, 0.222222, \ldots\}$$

**Remember...**

When you write 0.222 . . . or $0.\overline{2}$, what you mean is the limit of the sequence.

## Developing Habits of Mind

**Think about it another way.** This is another way to think about **repeating decimals.** What you really want in Problem 3 above is the infinite decimal 0.222 . . . . Call this $x$. Then

$$10x = 2.22222\ldots$$
$$x = 0.22222\ldots$$

Subtract. You get $9x = 2$, so $x = \frac{2}{9}$.

What the argument really says is if 0.2222 . . . stands for anything, it has to stand for a number that when multiplied by 10, gives two more than itself. That is the 2.22222. . . . The only number with this property is $\frac{2}{9}$.

This trick does, in fact, work. You can use it to convert repeating decimals to fractions. But it rests on some properties of limits that you will not learn until you study calculus.

The important point is that the repeating decimal stands for something in the first place. Suppose you have an infinite string of 9's to the left of the decimal place.

$$\ldots 999999.00\ldots$$

See where this leads you. In these calculations, make the decimal point large, as in 9**.**0, so it is distinct from an ordinary decimal point.

Let $x = \ldots 9999.000\ldots$

Then

$$x = \ldots 99999.000\ldots$$
$$10x = \ldots 99990.000\ldots$$

Subtract. You get $-9x = 9$, so $x = -1$.

That cannot be right. So a string of 9's to the left of the decimal point does not name a real number. You cannot call it $x$ and do algebra with it.

To be safe, use geometric series when dealing with repeating decimals. For example, think of the decimal 0.12121212 . . . as a series with first term $\frac{12}{100}$ and common ratio $\frac{1}{100}$.

Sometimes you can only successfully complete an action by going in a certain direction.

# Exercises Practicing Habits of Mind

## Check Your Understanding

**1.** Consider the repeating decimal 0.123123123. . . .

**a.** What is the initial term $a$?

**b.** What is the common ratio $r$?

**c.** Write this repeating decimal as a fraction.

**2.** Write each repeating decimal as a fraction.

**a.** 0.121212 . . .

**b.** 0.807807807 . . .

**c.** 0.0123123123 . . .

**d.** 0.075123123123 . . .

## On Your Own

**3.** Write each repeating decimal as a fraction.

**a.** 0.09090909 . . .

**b.** 0.0370370370 . . .

**c.** 0.0522222 . . .

Go Online
www.successnetplus.com

**4.** Shannon says, "I know the series $1 + 2 + 4 + 8 + \cdots$ keeps increasing. But if I call it $x$, watch what happens.

$$2x = 2 + 4 + 8 + 16 + \cdots$$

$$x = 1 + 2 + 4 + 8 + \cdots$$

Subtract and I get $x = -1$."

Shannon is confused. What would you say to help?

**5.** Standardized Test Prep Which fraction is equivalent to the repeating decimal $0.25714\overline{714}$?

**A.** $\frac{8563}{33,300}$

**B.** $\frac{25,689}{99,000}$

**C.** $\frac{25,714}{99,900}$

**D.** $\frac{25,714}{99,999}$

## Maintain Your Skills

**6.** Write each repeating decimal as a fraction.

**a.** 0.111 . . .

**b.** 0.222 . . .

**c.** 0.333 . . .

**d.** 0.444 . . .

**e.** 0.555 . . .

**f.** 0.666 . . .

**g.** 0.777 . . .

**h.** 0.888 . . .

**i.** 0.999 . . .

In this investigation, you learned to find closed forms for arithmetic and geometric sequences and their associated series. The following exercises will help you summarize what you have learned.

1. An arithmetic sequence $s$ has second term 8 and fifth term 1.
   - a. Explain why there is only one sequence that meets these requirements.

   For the sequence, find each of the following.
   - b. the common difference
   - c. the 28th term
   - d. a closed form
2. An arithmetic sequence $g$ has $g(0) = -10$ and common difference 4.
   - a. Make a $\Sigma$ table for $g(n)$ for $n$-values 0 through 5.
   - b. Find a closed form for the sequence.
   - c. Find a closed form for the associated series.
3. Repeat Exercise 1 replacing *arithmetic sequence* with *geometric sequence.* In part (b), replace *common difference* with *common ratio.*
4. Repeat Exercise 2 replacing *arithmetic sequence* with *geometric sequence* and *common difference* with *common ratio.*
5. Derman wins a "million-dollar" prize, which he knows is not really worth \$1,000,000. Instead of a check for \$1,000,000, he is going to get \$50,000 per year for 20 years. He wants to know what the present value of his prize is.
   - a. Use $\sum_{k=0}^{19} 50{,}000\left(\frac{1}{1.06}\right)^k$ to find the present value. Assume a 6% interest rate.
   - b. Suppose Derman is able to invest his money with an 8% rate of return. Would the present value of his prize be more or less than the amount you found for a 6% rate? Find the new present value to check your estimate. Explain why the interest rate affects the present value in the way it does.
6. What is an arithmetic sequence?
7. What is a geometric series?
8. How do you write the repeating decimal 0.121212121 . . . as a fraction?

## Vocabulary

In this investigation, you learned these terms. Make sure you understand what each one means and how to use it.

- **arithmetic sequence**
- **arithmetic series**
- **common difference**
- **common ratio**
- **geometric sequence**
- **geometric series**
- **limit**
- **repeating decimal**
- **sequence**
- **term**

# Pascal's Triangle and the Binomial Theorem

In *Pascal's Triangle and the Binomial Theorem*, you will explore the patterns in Pascal's Triangle. You will find patterns in the triangle and learn how the numbers in the triangle are related to powers of polynomials.

**By the end of this investigation, you will be able to answer questions like these.**

1. What is the sum of the entries in row 10 of Pascal's Triangle?
2. What is the expanded form of $(2d + 7)^8$?
3. What is the coefficient of $x^7y^3$ in the expansion of $(x + y)^{10}$?

**You will learn how to**

- generate Pascal's Triangle and evaluate the $n$th row, $k$th column entry as $\binom{n}{k}$
- notice and explain patterns in Pascal's Triangle
- use the Binomial Theorem for expanding expressions of the form $(a + b)^n$

**You will develop these habits and skills:**

- Seek invariants or regularity in calculation to develop a conjecture.
- Reason logically to prove conjectures.
- Apply previous results in new contexts.

There are $\binom{30}{2}$ ways to choose 2 socks from a pile of 30 socks.

# 2.14 Getting Started

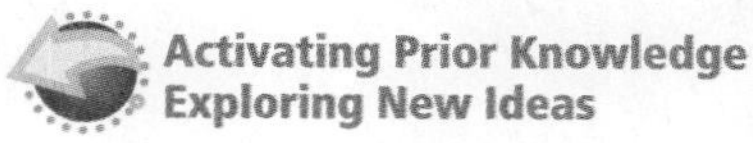


You can find many patterns in the sums of sums and in the powers of polynomials.

## For You to Explore

For Problems 1–5, use this big, but simple, table.

| $n$ | $f(n)$ | $\Sigma$ | $\Sigma\Sigma$ | $\Sigma\Sigma\Sigma$ | $\Sigma\Sigma\Sigma\Sigma$ |
|---|---|---|---|---|---|
| 1 | 1 | ■ | ■ | ■ | ■ |
| 2 | 2 | ■ | ■ | ■ | ■ |
| 3 | 3 | ■ | ■ | ■ | ■ |
| 4 | 4 | ■ | ■ | ■ | ■ |
| 5 | 5 | ■ | ■ | ■ | ■ |
| 6 | 6 | ■ | ■ | ■ | ■ |
| 7 | 7 | ■ | ■ | ■ | ■ |
| 8 | 8 | ■ | ■ | ■ | ■ |
| 9 | 9 | ■ | ■ | ■ | ■ |
| 10 | 10 | ■ | ■ | ■ | ■ |

**1.** Copy and complete the table.

**2.** Find, describe, and explain several patterns in your table.

**3.** Find a closed form for $f$.

**4. a.** What is $\sum_{k=1}^{7} f(k)$?

**b.** What is $\sum_{k=1}^{1000} f(k)$? Explain.

**c.** Find a closed form for $\sum_{k=1}^{n} f(k)$.

**5. a.** Find a closed form for the $\Sigma\Sigma$ column.

**b.** Find a closed form for the $\Sigma\Sigma\Sigma$ column.

**c.** Where have you seen these closed forms before? What can you predict as a closed form for the $\Sigma\Sigma\Sigma\Sigma$ column?

# Exercises Practicing Habits of Mind

## On Your Own

**6.** Expand each expression.

**a.** $(a + b)^2$

**b.** $(a + b)^3$

**c.** $(a + b)^4$

**d.** $(a + b)^5$

**e.** $(a + b)^6$

**f.** What patterns do you observe?

> **Habits of Mind**
>
> **Look for patterns.** Use the answer to each part to help you with the next one.

**7.** Use your result from Exercise 6c to expand $(M + N)^4$, where $M = 2d$ and $N = 7$.

**8.** Expand each expression.

**a.** $\left(\frac{1}{4}r + \frac{3}{4}s\right)^2$

**b.** $\left(\frac{1}{4}r + \frac{3}{4}s\right)^3$

**c.** $\left(\frac{1}{4}r + \frac{3}{4}s\right)^4$

**d.** $\left(\frac{1}{4}r + \frac{3}{4}s\right)^5$

## Maintain Your Skills

**9. a** Find the first five powers of 99.

**b.** What patterns do you notice?

**10.** Tony is looking at differences of cubes. He says, "Let's see.

$$1^3 - 0^3 = 1 - 0 = 1$$

$$2^3 - 1^3 = 8 - 1 = 7$$

$$3^3 - 2^3 = 27 - 8 = 19$$

$$4^3 - 3^3 = 64 - 27 = 37$$

"I'm going to make a $\Sigma$ table for these differences and see what happens."

| n | $(n+1)^3 - n^3$ | $\Sigma$ |
|---|---|---|
| 0 | 1 | 1 |
| 1 | 7 | 8 |

Use Tony's idea to find the sum of the first 20 differences of cubes starting with $1^3 - 0^3$. The last one is $20^3 - 19^3$.

# 2.15 Pascal's Triangle

This triangular table below is **Pascal's Triangle.** It is a very famous triangle, named after mathematician Blaise Pascal, who is known for his studies of the relationships in the triangle.

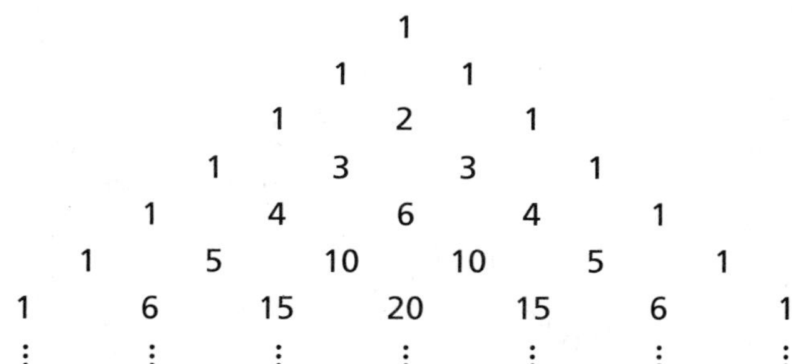

Pascal's Triangle shows up in many different areas of mathematics, including combinatorics. You will spend some time getting familiar with it and finding some of the many beautiful patterns it contains. You will also use it in other parts of this book, and in other mathematics courses throughout your life. An interesting thing to do with Pascal's Triangle is to see how many different patterns you can see in the rows and the columns of the triangle.

Some people might even call it fun!

## For Discussion

1. If you have seen Pascal's Triangle before, discuss anything you remember about it. What do the numbers represent?
2. What patterns can you find in the entries of Pascal's Triangle?
3. Describe in words how to find any entry in Pascal's Triangle.
4. Describe how Pascal's Triangle is related to the table in this investigation's Getting Started lesson.

You can label the entries of Pascal's Triangle with their row and column numbers, this way.

$$\binom{n}{k}$$

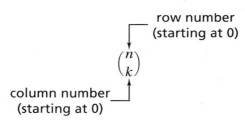

The horizontal entries are the rows. The diagonals are the columns. Usually you number the first column and the first row 0.

The top number $n$ is the row number, starting with 0.

The bottom number $k$ is how far you go across in a row, starting with 0. So you label the entries in the sixth row this way.

row number (starting at 0)

$$\binom{n}{k}$$

column number (starting at 0)

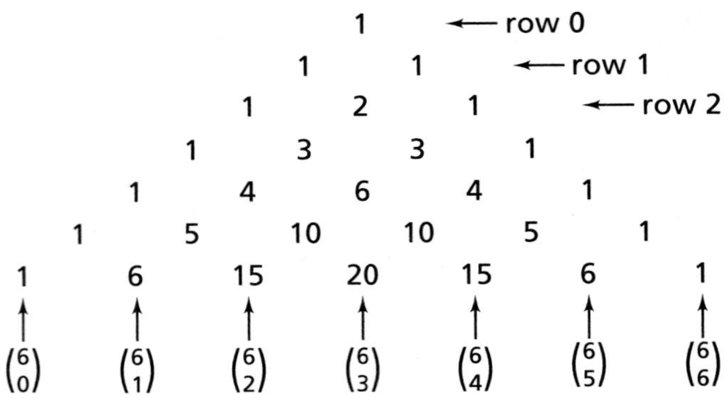

1 ← row 0
1 1 ← row 1
1 2 1 ← row 2
1 3 3 1
1 4 6 4 1
1 5 10 10 5 1
1 6 15 20 15 6 1

$\binom{6}{0}$ $\binom{6}{1}$ $\binom{6}{2}$ $\binom{6}{3}$ $\binom{6}{4}$ $\binom{6}{5}$ $\binom{6}{6}$

## For You to Do

5. Find the value of each entry in the triangle.

   a. $\binom{17}{1}$ b. $\binom{14}{14}$ c. $\binom{19}{0}$

6. Find all $n$ and $k$ such that $\binom{n}{k} = 15$.

Pascal's Triangle seems to have a kind of hockey stick property. If you draw a hockey stick on the triangle, the sum of the numbers on the handle is equal to the number on the tip.

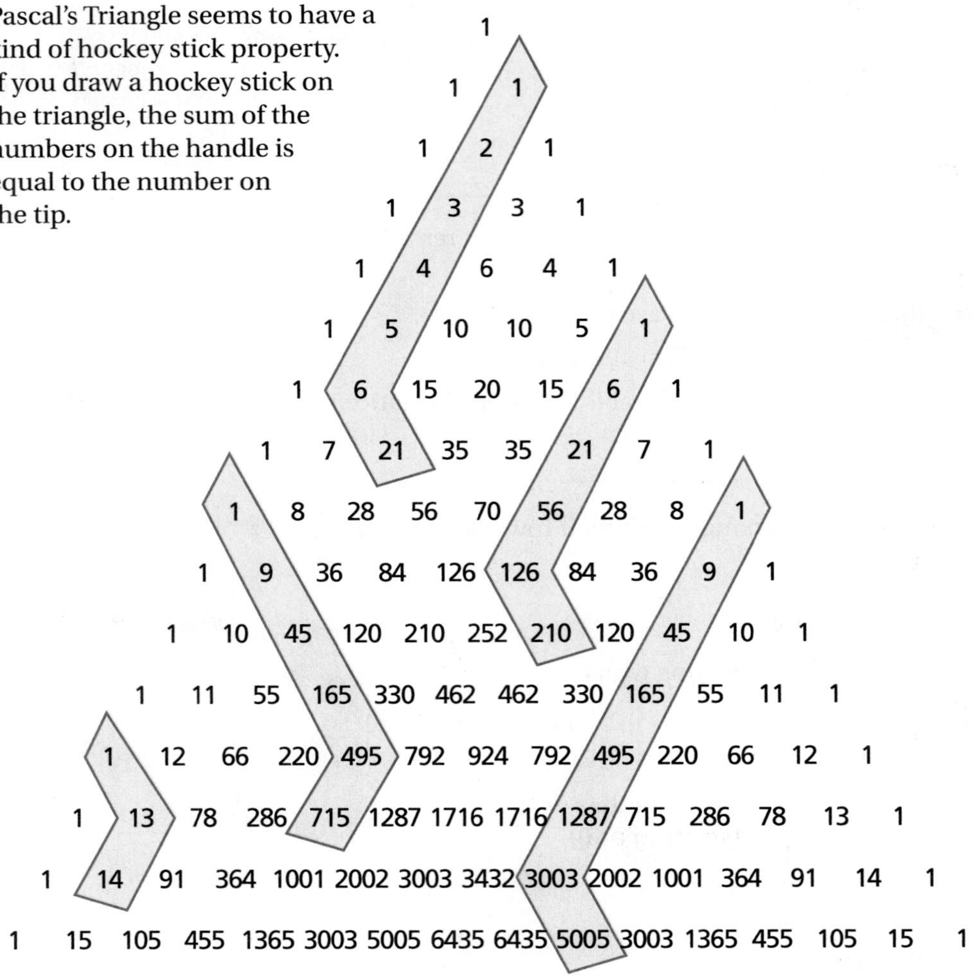

1
1 1
1 2 1
1 3 3 1
1 4 6 4 1
1 5 10 10 5 1
1 6 15 20 15 6 1
1 7 21 35 35 21 7 1
1 8 28 56 70 56 28 8 1
1 9 36 84 126 126 84 36 9 1
1 10 45 120 210 252 210 120 45 10 1
1 11 55 165 330 462 462 330 165 55 11 1
1 12 66 220 495 792 924 792 495 220 66 12 1
1 13 78 286 715 1287 1716 1716 1287 715 286 78 13 1
1 14 91 364 1001 2002 3003 3432 3003 2002 1001 364 91 14 1
1 15 105 455 1365 3003 5005 6435 6435 5005 3003 1365 455 105 15 1

## For Discussion

7. Does the hockey stick have to start on a one, or can it start anywhere in the triangle?
8. Does it matter if the hockey stick points left or right?
9. Does it matter if the hockey stick points up or down?
10. Explain the hockey stick property based on how you construct Pascal's Triangle.

## For You to Do

11. Write the hockey stick property as an identity involving sums and the numbers $\binom{n}{k}$.

## Exercises Practicing Habits of Mind

### Check Your Understanding

1. Evaluate each sum.

   a. $\sum_{k=0}^{5} \binom{5}{k}$ b. $\sum_{k=0}^{6} \binom{6}{k}$ c. $\sum_{k=0}^{7} \binom{7}{k}$ d. $\sum_{k=0}^{n} \binom{n}{k}$

2. **Write About It** Explain why you get the sum you found in part (d) of Exercise 1. Think about how you get the numbers in Pascal's Triangle, or about what you know they represent.

### On Your Own

3. Investigate the number of odd numbers in each row of Pascal's Triangle. If you continued the triangle out to row 64, how many odd numbers would you find in this row? In row 100? Explain.

**Remember...**

You start counting at row 0, so row 100 is really the 101st row you write down.

4. Make three copies of the diagram below. Write in the values of Pascal's Triangle on your copies. You will use your copies to explore patterns in Pascal's Triangle.

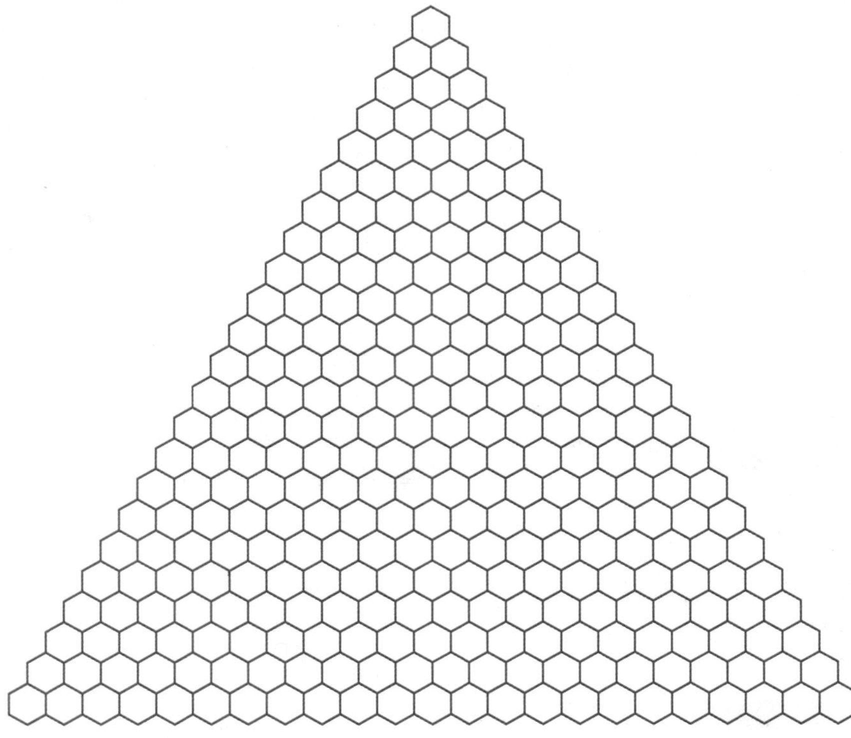

a. On one copy, color the odd numbers one color and the even numbers another color. Describe the patterns you find.

b. You can divide the integers up into three categories when you divide them by 3: those that leave a remainder of 1, those that leave a remainder of 2, and those that can be divided evenly by 3. On the second copy of the diagram, color each of these kinds of numbers a different color. Describe the patterns you find.

c. If you divide integers by 4, how many different kinds of numbers do you get? On the third copy of the diagram, color each of them a different color. Describe the patterns you find.

5. **Standardized Test Prep** The following list gives the first eight entries in the 15th row of Pascal's Triangle.

1 15 105 455 1365 3003 5005 6435

What is the value of $\binom{17}{6}$ in Pascal's Triangle?

**A.** 6188 **B.** 8008 **C.** 12,376 **D.** 19,448

6. **Take It Further** In Lesson 2.14, you found the closed forms for $f$, $\Sigma f$, $\Sigma\Sigma f$, and $\Sigma\Sigma\Sigma f$, where $f(n) = n$. You can see these functions along diagonals in Pascal's Triangle.

Find a closed form for $\underbrace{\Sigma\Sigma\Sigma\Sigma \ldots \Sigma}_{k \text{ times}} f(n)$.

$f$, $\Sigma f$, $\Sigma\Sigma f$, $\Sigma\Sigma\Sigma f$, $\Sigma\Sigma\Sigma\Sigma f$

1
1 1
1 2 1
1 3 3 1
1 4 6 4 1
1 5 10 10 5 1
1 6 15 20 15 6 1
1 7 21 35 35 21 7 1
1 8 28 56 70 56 28 8 1
1 9 36 84 126 126 84 36 9 1
1 10 45 120 210 252 210 120 45 10 1
1 11 55 165 330 462 462 330 165 55 11 1
1 12 66 220 495 792 924 792 495 220 66 12 1
1 13 78 286 715 1287 1716 1716 1287 715 286 78 13 1
1 14 91 364 1001 2002 3003 3432 3003 2002 1001 364 91 14 1
1 15 105 455 1365 3003 5005 6435 6435 5005 3003 1365 455 105 15 1

## Maintain Your Skills

7. Find the values of $m$ and $n$ that satisfy each equation.

**a.** $\binom{9}{4} = \binom{8}{4} + \binom{8}{m}$

**b.** $\binom{3}{2} = \binom{2}{2} + \binom{2}{m}$

**c.** $\binom{14}{8} = \binom{13}{8} + \binom{13}{m}$

**d.** $\binom{100}{15} = \binom{m}{15} + \binom{m}{n}$

# 2.16 The Binomial Theorem

In Exercise 6 of Lesson 2.14, you found some of these expansions.

$(a + b)^0 = 1$

$(a + b)^1 = a + b$

$(a + b)^2 = a^2 + 2ab + b^2$

$(a + b)^3 = a^3 + 3a^2b + 3ab^2 + b^3$

$(a + b)^4 = a^4 + 4a^3b + 6a^2b^2 + 4ab^3 + b^4$

$(a + b)^5 = a^5 + 5a^4b + 10a^3b^2 + 10a^2b^3 + 5ab^4 + b^5$

$(a + b)^6 = a^6 + 6a^5b + 15a^4b^2 + 20a^3b^3 + 15a^2b^4 + 6ab^5 + b^6$

Compare the coefficients of these polynomials to the entries of Pascal's Triangle.

```
            1
          1   1
        1   2   1
      1   3   3   1
    1   4   6   4   1
  1   5  10  10   5   1
1   6  15  20  15   6   1
```

In fact, you find the coefficients for any binomial expansion $(a + b)^n$ in Pascal's triangle. The Binomial Theorem states this relationship.

### Theorem 2.2 The Binomial Theorem

For $n \geq 0$,

$$(a + b)^n = \binom{n}{0}a^nb^0 + \binom{n}{1}a^{n-1}b^1 + \binom{n}{2}a^{n-2}b^2 + \cdots + \binom{n}{k}a^{n-k}b^k + \ldots + \binom{n}{n-1}a^1b^{n-1} + \binom{n}{n}a^0b^n$$

**Go Online**
www.successnetplus.com

You must admit, this connection is rather unexpected! But, as is usually the case in mathematics, it is no coincidence. The real question to ask is, "Why is there a connection?"

## Developing Habits of Mind

**Establish a process.** To see why this pattern holds, look closely at an example—multiplication by $(x + 1)$. Suppose you want to expand

$$(x + 1)(x^5 + 3x^4 + 7x^3 + 2x^2 + x + 1)$$

By the Distributive Property, this equals

$$\begin{aligned} &x \cdot (x^5 + 3x^4 + 7x^3 + 2x^2 + x + 1) + 1 \cdot (x^5 + 3x^4 + 7x^3 + 2x^2 + x + 1) \\ &\quad = (x^6 + 3x^5 + 7x^4 + 2x^3 + x^2 + x) + (x^5 + 3x^4 + 7x^3 + 2x^2 + x + 1) \\ &\quad = x^6 + 4x^5 + 10x^4 + 9x^3 + 3x^2 + 2x + 1 \end{aligned}$$

Notice that the original polynomial has these coefficients.

1 3 7 2 1 1

To find the coefficients of the product, you can simply add Pascal-style, as follows.

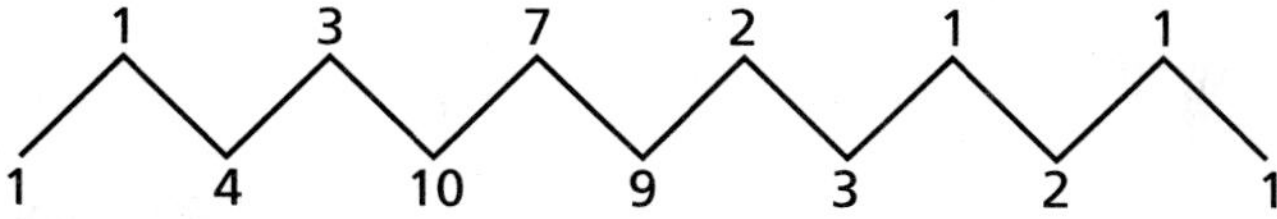


You should convince yourself why this method works. Look at another example. Suppose you want to expand

$$(x + 1)(7x^4 + 2x^3 + x^2 + 3x + 1)$$

You can obtain the coefficients of the product as follows.

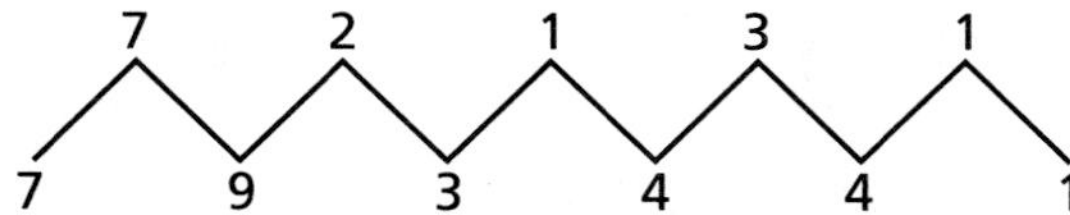


So the product is

$$7x^5 + 9x^4 + 3x^3 + 4x^2 + 4x + 1$$

## For Discussion

1. Use the discussion above to explain why the fifth row of Pascal's Triangle gives the coefficients of $(x + 1)^5$, assuming that you know that the fourth row gives the coefficients of $(x + 1)^4$. (*Hint:* $(x + 1)^5 = (x + 1)(x + 1)^4$, and you already know what $(x + 1)^4$ looks like.)

# Exercises Practicing Habits of Mind

## Check Your Understanding

1. Use the Binomial Theorem to expand each binomial. Use your CAS to verify your answers.

   a. $(x + y)^7$ b. $(x + 2y)^5$

2. Consider the expansion of $(a + b)^8$.

   a. What is the coefficient of the term $a^3b^5$?

   b. What other term or terms share this coefficient?

   c. Which terms do not share their coefficients with any other terms?

3. Determine the coefficient of each term below in the expansion of $(x + y)^{10}$.

   a. $x^3y^7$ b. $xy^9$ c. $x^5y^5$

You certainly should use your CAS to help evaluate these, but do not ask it to find all 11 terms! Use what you know, too, so the CAS does not have to do everything.

## On Your Own

4. Compute the alternating sum below.

$$\binom{5}{0} - \binom{5}{1} + \binom{5}{2} - \binom{5}{3} + \binom{5}{4} - \binom{5}{5}$$

   This is the alternating sum of the numbers in the fifth row of Pascal's Triangle. What is the sum if the row number $n$ is 6 instead of 5? If $n$ is 11 instead of 5?

5. Write a polynomial that you can factor in the form $(a + b)^n$, satisfying the following criteria:

   - The constant term is not 1.
   - There is exactly one variable $x$.
   - There are at least five terms.

6. Simplify $(\sqrt{3} + \sqrt{2})^{100}(\sqrt{3} - \sqrt{2})^{100}$.

7. Standardized Test Prep What is the coefficient of the $x^3$ term in the expansion of $(a + b)^n$, where $a = 2x$, $b = -1$, and $n = 4$?

   A. $-32$ B. $-4$ C. 24 D. 21

## Maintain Your Skills

**8.** Write About It Look at the pattern in the powers of 11.

$$11^2 = 121$$

$$11^3 = 1331$$

$$11^4 = 14{,}641$$

Look at this more closely. You have $11^4 = 11^3 \times 11$, and since $11^3 = 1331$, you get

$$\begin{array}{r} 1\,3\,3\,1 \\ \times \quad\quad 1\,1 \\ \hline 1\,3\,3\,1 \\ 1\,3\,3\,1\phantom{\,1} \\ \hline 1\,4\,6\,4\,1 \end{array}$$

Or you can calculate Pascal-style.

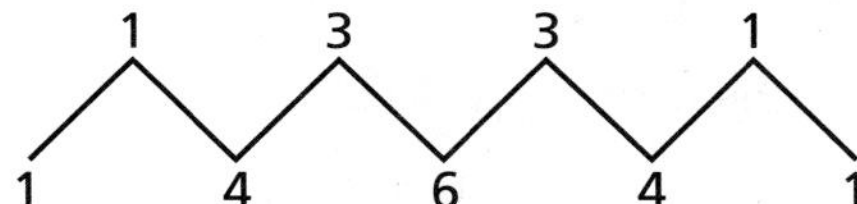


Now you may be tempted to conclude that $11^5 = 15{,}101{,}051$, but, in fact, $11^5 = 161{,}051$. What went wrong? Did anything really go wrong here?

**9. a.** Write out the first 7 powers of 101.

**b.** Write out the first 7 powers of 1001.

## Historical Perspective

Pascal's Triangle gets its name from Blaise Pascal, a famous French mathematician who wrote *Traité du triangle arithmétique* in 1654. Pascal showed many uses of the triangle and proved many things about its number patterns. He was not, however, the first person to discover or write about the triangle. The triangle was known in India as early as 1068—nearly 600 years before Pascal wrote his *Traité*. A mathematician named Bhattotpala used it to compute combinations of as many as sixteen things. The triangle was also known in China, probably as early as 1100, when Chia Hsien used something similar for finding binomial coefficients. It was certainly known there by 1303, when Chu Shih-Chieh used the triangle at the right.

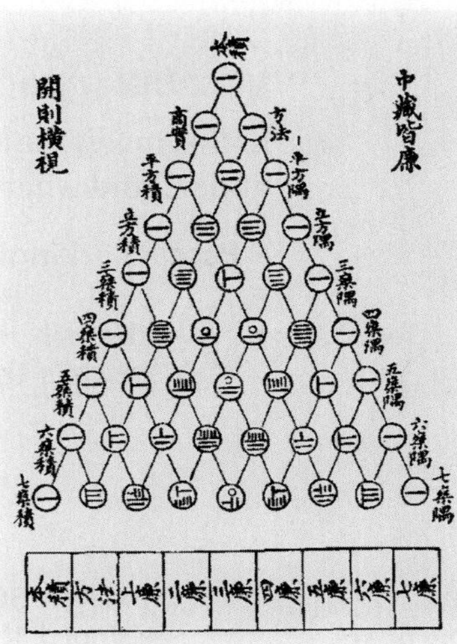

The triangle of Chu Shih-Chieh

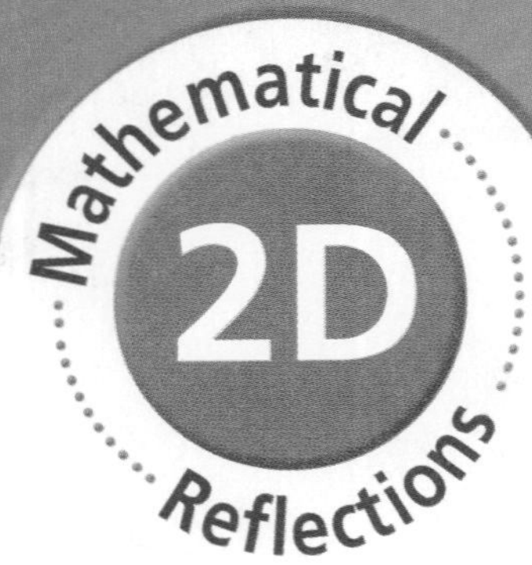


**In this investigation, you learned to generate Pascal's Triangle, to find and explain patterns in Pascal's Triangle, and to use the Binomial Theorem to expand expressions. These exercises will help you summarize what you have learned.**

1. Give an example of the hockey stick property of Pascal's Triangle in which the sum on the tip is 20.
2. Find all values of $m$ that satisfy each equation.
   - **a.** $\binom{m}{1} = 27$
   - **b.** $\binom{24}{m} = 1$
   - **c.** $\binom{m}{31} = 32$
   - **d.** $\binom{m}{4} + \binom{m}{5} = \binom{19}{5}$
3. Make an input-output table for the function $b(n) = \binom{n}{2}$ for $n = 2$ to $n = 6$. Find a polynomial function $p(n)$ that matches your table for $b(n)$, even if you continue the table.
4. Multiply $(x + 1)(5x^5 + 3x^4 - 2x^3 + 4x^2 + 6x - 7)$.
5. You can factor the polynomial below into the form $(a + b)^5$.

   $$32x^5 - 80x^4 + cx^3 - 40x^2 + 10x - 1$$

   Find $a$, $b$, and $c$.
6. What is the sum of the entries in row 10 of Pascal's Triangle?
7. What is the expanded form of $(2d + 7)^8$?
8. What is the coefficient of $x^7y^3$ in the expansion of $(x + y)^{10}$?

## Vocabulary and Notation

In this investigation, you learned this term and this symbol. Make sure you understand what each one means and how to use it.

- **Pascal's Triangle**
- $\binom{n}{k}$ **(the *n*th row, *k*th column entry of Pascal's triangle)**

If you have 30 socks and 6 of them are striped, the probability of randomly choosing a matching pair of striped socks is $\binom{6}{2} \div \binom{30}{2}$.

# Review

Go Online
www.successnetplus.com

In **Investigation 2A,** you learned how to

- make a sum table for a function and write a closed-form rule for the sum column where appropriate
- use Gauss's method to find the sum of a sequence with a constant difference between successive terms
- use Euclid's method to find the sum of a sequence with a constant ratio between successive terms
- expand $\Sigma$ notation or convert an expanded sum back to $\Sigma$ notation

*The following exercises will help you check your understanding.*

**1.** Copy and complete the following sum table. Find a closed-form rule for the $\Sigma$ column.

| $n$ | $g(n)$ | $\Sigma$ |
|---|---|---|
| 0 | 1 | ■ |
| 1 | 2 | ■ |
| 2 | 6 | ■ |
| 3 | 18 | ■ |
| 4 | 54 | ■ |
| 5 | 162 | ■ |

**2.** Suppose $S = 3 + 6 + \cdots + 96$.

**a.** If there is a constant difference between successive terms, what is the value of $S$? Use Gauss's method.

**b.** If there is a constant ratio between successive terms, what is the value of $S$? Use Euclid's method.

**3. a.** Evaluate $\sum_{j=0}^{3} 3^j$.

**b.** Evaluate $\sum_{k=1}^{5} (k + 2)$.

**c.** Use $\Sigma$ notation to write an expression for $S = \frac{1}{2} + 1 + \frac{3}{2} + 2 + \cdots + 6$.

In **Investigation 2B,** you learned how to

- find closed-form expressions for indefinite sums and use them to evaluate definite sums
- develop a list of $\Sigma$ identities and recognize situations in which you can apply them
- find closed-form expressions for the series associated with a function

*The following exercises will help you check your understanding.*

**4.** Use the definitions below.

$$S(n) = \sum_{k=0}^{n} (4 - 3k)$$

$$T(n) = \sum_{k=0}^{n} \left(\frac{1}{2}\right)^k$$

**a.** Find a closed form for $S(n)$.

**b.** Find a closed form for $T(n)$.

**c.** Use the closed form for $S(n)$ to find $\sum_{k=0}^{100} (4 - 3k)$.

**d.** Use the closed form for $T(n)$ to find $\sum_{k=0}^{4} \left(\frac{1}{2}\right)^k$.

**5.** Find a closed form for the series associated with $g(n) = 4 - 5n$, with initial term $g(0)$.

In **Investigation 2C,** you learned how to

- find a closed-form representation for an arithmetic sequence and its associated series
- find a closed-form representation for a geometric sequence and its associated series
- determine whether a geometric sequence has a limit, and if it does, how to find it
- convert a repeating decimal into an exact fraction

*The following exercises will help you check your understanding.*

**6.** Suppose $f$ is a sequence with initial term $f(0) = 5$.

| $n$ | $f(n)$ | $\Sigma$ |
|---|---|---|
| 0 | 5 | 5 |
| 1 | ■ | ■ |
| 2 | ■ | ■ |
| 3 | ■ | ■ |
| 4 | ■ | ■ |
| 5 | ■ | ■ |

**a.** • Copy and complete the table if $f$ is an arithmetic sequence with a constant difference of 2.

- Find a closed form for the sequence.
- Find a closed form for the series $F(n) = \sum_{k=0}^{n} f(k)$.
- Find $f(10)$ and $F(10)$.

**b.** • Copy and complete the table if $f$ is a geometric sequence with a constant ratio of 2.

- Find a closed form for the sequence.
- Find a closed form for the series $F(n) = \sum_{k=0}^{n} f(k)$.
- Find $f(10)$ and $F(10)$.

**7.** For each geometric sequence $t$, do the following:

- Write the first four terms of the sequence.
- Find $T(0)$, $T(1)$, $T(2)$, and $T(3)$, where $T(n) = \sum_{k=0}^{n} t(k)$ is the series associated with the sequence.
- Decide if the series has a limit.
- If the series does have a limit, find it.

**a.** first term 10 and common ratio $\frac{1}{10}$

**b.** second term 3 and fifth term $\frac{81}{8}$

**8.** Write each repeating decimal as a fraction.

**a.** 0.151515...

**b.** 0.100100100...

In **Investigation 2D,** you learned how to

- generate Pascal's Triangle and write the $n$th row, $k$th column entry as $\binom{n}{k}$
- notice and explain patterns in Pascal's Triangle
- use the Binomial Theorem to expand expressions of the form $(a + b)^n$

*The following exercises will help you check your understanding.*

**9. a.** Make a copy of Pascal's Triangle through Row 5.

**b.** On your copy, show two examples of the hockey stick property in which the sum on the tip is 10.

**c.** Find the value of $\binom{4}{2} + \binom{5}{4}$.

**10. a.** What is the expanded form for $(3x + 2)^5$?

**b.** What is the coefficient of $x^2y^4$ in the expansion of $(x + 2y)^6$?

Chapter 2

# Test

Go Online
www.successnetplus.com

## Multiple Choice

**1.** What is the sum of the odd integers from 7 to 55, inclusive?

**A.** 62  **B.** 775

**C.** 850  **D.** 1550

**2.** Suppose $\binom{j}{1} = 5$. What is $j$?

**A.** 0  **B.** 4

**C.** 5  **D.** 6

**3.** Which number is equivalent to 0.999 . . . ?

**A.** 0  **B.** $\frac{1}{9}$

**C.** $\frac{999}{1000}$  **D.** 1

**4.** In an arithmetic sequence, the second term is 9 and the eighth term is 33. What is the third term?

**A.** 4  **B.** 12

**C.** 13  **D.** 17

**5.** What is the coefficient of $x^4y^5$ in the expansion of $(x + y)^9$?

**A.** $\binom{5}{4}$

**B.** $\binom{4}{5}$

**C.** $\binom{9}{1}$

**D.** $\binom{9}{5}$

## Open Response

**6.** Find each sum.

**a.** $\sum_{k=0}^{10} (7 - 4k)$

**b.** $\sum_{j=0}^{8} \left(\frac{1}{3}\right)^j$

**c.** $\sum_{k=3}^{12} 4k$

**7.** Find a closed form for each indefinite sum.

**a.** $\sum_{k=0}^{n} (6k + 2)$  **b.** $\sum_{k=0}^{n} (k^2 + 1)$

**8.** Find a recursive rule and a closed-form rule for the series associated with $h(n) = 4 - 6n$, having initial term $h(0)$.

**9.** A geometric sequence $h$ has $h(0) = 18$ and common ratio $\frac{1}{3}$.

**a.** Make a $\Sigma$ table for $h(n)$ for $n = 0$ through $n = 4$.

**b.** Find a closed form for the sequence.

**c.** Find a closed form for the associated series.

**10.** You can factor the polynomial below into the form $(a + b)^7$.

$$x^7 - 14x^6 + 84x^5 + cx^4 + 560x^3 - 672x^2 + 448x - 128$$

Find $a$, $b$, and $c$.

**11.** What is a geometric series?

Chapter
3
Investigations at a Glance
3A Probability and Decision-Making
3B Expectation and Variation
3C Designing Experiments
3D The Normal Distribution

# Statistical Inference

Although there is much variation between individuals, populations are often quite consistent. Probability and statistics allow you to quantify a population and make predictions about it.

In this picture of a school of fish, you see that this fish can be yellow or red but the yellow occurs more frequently. Is that true of this type of fish in general or just this school of fish? You can use probability and statistics to quantify this information accurately.

## Vocabulary and Notation

- Bernoulli trial
- confidence interval
- control group
- cumulative density function
- deviation
- event
- expected value, $E(X)$
- experiment
- experimental probability
- frequency, $|A|$
- independent
- margin of error
- mean absolute deviation
- mean squared deviation, or variance, $\sigma^2$
- mutually exclusive
- normal distribution, $N(\mu, \sigma)$
- observational study
- outcome
- population parameter
- probability density function
- probability distribution
- probability histogram
- probability of an event
- random sampling
- random variable
- root mean squared deviation, or standard deviation, $\sigma$
- sample proportion
- sample space
- sample statistic
- sample survey
- spread
- theoretical probability
- treatment group
- unit normal distribution, $N(0,1)$
- $z$-score

# Probability and Decision-Making

**In *Probability and Decision-Making,* you will learn basic probability definitions and rules. You will discover connections between probability and Pascal's Triangle. You will model a variety of experiments with polynomials. You will calculate the likelihood of each outcome in an experiment, and also predict the average outcome of an experiment.**

**By the end of this investigation, you will be able to answer questions like these.**

1. If you are to roll four number cubes, what is the probability they sum to 12?
2. What is expected value?
3. How can you use polynomials to solve probability problems?

**You will learn how to**

- calculate probabilities of simple random events
- build a set of equally likely outcomes for a probability experiment
- find a polynomial to model a probability experiment and interpret expansions of its powers
- calculate the expected value of a random variable

**You will develop these habits and skills:**

- Visualize the process of a probability experiment in order to count its outcomes.
- Reason from definitions, such as for *mutually exclusive* and *independent,* and apply them to probability situations.
- Understand the domains and ranges of various functions related to probability, including random variables, frequency, expected value, and probability functions.

# 3.01 Getting Started

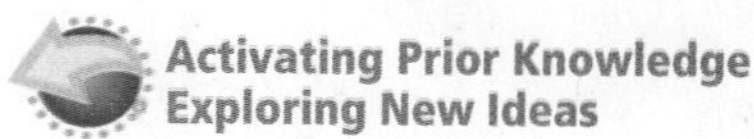


Considering all possible outcomes is a good habit when calculating probabilities. If you know all possible outcomes in an experiment, you can find the likelihood of any particular outcome occurring.

## For You to Explore

1. When you flip a coin three times, there are eight possible outcomes. For example, one outcome is heads-tails-heads. Write out the eight outcomes. Determine how many outcomes are in each category.

   a. no heads  b. one head  c. two heads  d. three heads

2. There are 16 possible outcomes when you flip a coin four times. For example, one outcome is heads-tails-heads-heads. Write out the 16 outcomes. Determine how many outcomes are in each category.

   a. no heads  b. one head  c. two heads
   d. three heads  e. four heads

3. You are to flip a coin five times.

   a. Write down the ten different ways you could flip two heads and three tails.
   b. What is the probability that you flip two heads and three tails?

4. Expand each of these expressions.

   a. $(t + h)^2$  b. $(t + h)^3$  c. $(t + h)^4$  d. $(t + h)^5$

One of the outcomes is "heads, tails, tails, heads, tails" but you might prefer to write it as HTTHT.

See the TI-Nspire™ Handbook on p. 817, for instructions on how to expand these expressions with a CAS.

If the survival rate for turtle eggs is 38%, how many are expected to hatch from a nest of 120 eggs?

## Exercises *Practicing Habits of Mind*

### On Your Own

**5.** Write out the first eight rows of Pascal's Triangle. Count your rows so that the third row is

$$1 \quad 3 \quad 3 \quad 1$$

**6.** Determine the probability that if you flip a coin eight times, you will flip exactly four heads and four tails. Explain in detail how you arrived at your answer.

**7. a.** Picture two spinners that are equally likely to land on any integer between 1 and 5, inclusive. List all 25 ways the spinners could land if you spin them both.

> Here is one way: first spinner 3, second spinner 4. And here is another, different way: first spinner 4, second spinner 3.

**b.** Find the probability that the two numbers spun do not share a common factor greater than 1.

**c.** Repeat parts (a) and (b) for two spinners that are equally likely to land on any integer between 1 and 6, inclusive. For this, there are 36 outcomes.

**d.** Repeat parts (a) and (b) for two spinners that are equally likely to land on any integer between 1 and 7, inclusive.

**8. a.** If you flip a fair coin 240 times, how many heads would you expect?

**b.** Guess the probability of getting exactly this many heads.

**9. a.** If you roll a fair number cube 240 times, how many ones would you expect?

> You may assume that a number cube has the numbers 1 through 6 on its faces, unless stated otherwise.

**b.** Guess the probability of getting exactly this many ones.

### Maintain Your Skills

**10.** For each value of $n$, you are to pick an integer at random from 1 to $n$. What is the probability it will be a perfect square?

**a.** $n = 10$ **b.** $n = 100$ **c.** $n = 1000$ **d.** $n = 10{,}000$

**e.** What is happening "in the long run" (as $n$ grows larger without bound)?

# 3.02 Probability and Pascal's Triangle

In this section you will learn some basic definitions and rules of probability. If you have not done so already, start to think about how you can count the possible outcomes of experiments more efficiently.

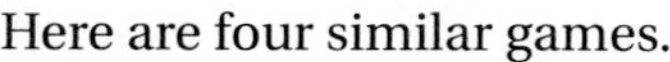

## In-Class Experiment

Here are four similar games.

**Game 1:** Flip two coins. If you get exactly two heads, you win.

**Game 2:** Flip three coins. If you get exactly two heads, you win.

**Game 3:** Flip four coins. If you get exactly two heads, you win.

**Game 4:** Flip five coins. If you get exactly two heads, you win.

1. Which game gives you the greatest probability of winning?

You can use probability theory to determine how likely it is that an event will occur. Consider a multiple-choice question with five options. Only one is right. If you guess randomly, the probability of getting the correct answer is $\frac{1}{5}$. The probability of getting an incorrect answer is $\frac{4}{5}$.

## Example

**Problem** Roll two different-colored number cubes. Find the probability of each event.

**a.** At least one number cube shows a 5.

**b.** The sum of the numbers is exactly 5.

**Solution** One way to proceed is to write out the *sample space*, the entire list of possible outcomes. Since each number cube has 6 possible outcomes, there are 36 total outcomes for this experiment.

| | 1 | 2 | 3 | 4 | 5 | 6 |
|---|---|---|---|---|---|---|
| 1 | (1,1) | (1,2) | (1,3) | (1,4) | **(1,5)** | (1,6) |
| 2 | (2,1) | (2,2) | (2,3) | (2,4) | **(2,5)** | (2,6) |
| 3 | (3,1) | (3,2) | (3,3) | (3,4) | **(3,5)** | (3,6) |
| 4 | (4,1) | (4,2) | (4,3) | (4,4) | **(4,5)** | (4,6) |
| 5 | **(5,1)** | **(5,2)** | **(5,3)** | **(5,4)** | **(5,5)** | **(5,6)** |
| 6 | (6,1) | (6,2) | (6,3) | (6,4) | **(6,5)** | (6,6) |

**a.** The 11 highlighted outcomes have at least one 5. So, the probability of rolling at least one 5 is

$$P\text{ (at least one 5)} = \frac{\text{number of successful outcomes}}{\text{total number of outcomes}} = \frac{11}{36}$$

**b.** Make a second table showing the sums of the numbers on the two number cubes.

| + | 1 | 2 | 3 | 4 | 5 | 6 |
|---|---|---|---|---|---|---|
| **1** | 2 | 3 | 4 | **5** | 6 | 7 |
| **2** | 3 | 4 | **5** | 6 | 7 | 8 |
| **3** | 4 | **5** | 6 | 7 | 8 | 9 |
| **4** | **5** | 6 | 7 | 8 | 9 | 10 |
| **5** | 6 | 7 | 8 | 9 | 10 | 11 |
| **6** | 7 | 8 | 9 | 10 | 11 | 12 |

The 4 highlighted outcomes each show a sum of 5. So, the probability of rolling a sum of exactly 5 is $\frac{4}{36}$ or $\frac{1}{9}$.

## For You to Do

**2.** Find the probability that when rolling two number cubes, the sum is less than or equal to 5.

Several definitions come in handy when talking about probability problems.

### *Definitions*

**The sample space is a set. Its elements are outcomes.**

**An event is a subset of the sample space, a set of outcomes. $|A|$ denotes the number of outcomes in event $A$.**

***P*(*A*), the probability of an event *A*, is the number of outcomes in *A*, divided by the number of outcomes in the sample space *S*.**

$$P(A) = \frac{\text{number of outcomes in } A}{\text{total number of outcomes}} = \frac{|A|}{|S|}$$

An *outcome* could be anything, such as "rolling a 3" or "heads, heads, tails." The situation determines the appropriate outcomes.

This definition of probability depends on the assumption that all outcomes in the sample space are equally likely. You cannot use this definition when the outcomes are not equally likely.

When rolling a number cube, there are six outcomes in the sample space, all equally likely. One outcome is "roll the number 5." An event might be "roll a prime number." There are three outcomes in this event, so $P(\text{roll a prime number}) = \frac{3}{6}$ or $\frac{1}{2}$.

Often, there are shortcuts to counting either the number of outcomes in an event, or the number of outcomes in the sample space. The sample space for rolling two number cubes has $6 \times 6 = 36$ outcomes since there are six ways each number cube can land.

## Minds in Action

*Derman and Sasha are working on Game 4 from the In-Class Experiment.*

**Derman** We want to find the probability of getting exactly two heads when you flip five coins.

**Sasha** All right, so we need to know the number of outcomes with exactly two heads, and the total number of outcomes in the sample space.

**Derman** I think the probability should be 1 out of 6.

**Sasha** Oh?

**Derman** Well, you could get 0 heads, 1 head, 2, 3, 4, or 5 heads. Six ways it could happen. It's 1 out of 6.

**Sasha** Wait, wait, wait. That's not going to work, those things would have to be equally likely. But I'm not convinced that they are.

**Derman** Well, flipping a coin is equally likely: heads or tails.

**Sasha** Right. So start from there. Five coin flips.

**Derman** The total number of outcomes is . . . I think it's 32, 2 to the fifth.

**Sasha** That's a much better sample space. The probability's got to be something out of 32, then. Now we just have to figure out how many of those 32 outcomes have exactly two heads.

**Derman** I'll make a list . . .

| | | |
|---|---|---|
| HHTTT | TTTHH | THTHT |
| HTHTT | HTTTH | HTTHT |
| THHTT | THTTH | TTHHT |

**Derman** Nine! It's nine out of 32.

**Sasha** You missed one: TTHTH. It's ten.

**Derman** It's hard to know the list is complete. There must be a better way to count these.

**Sasha** It's two H's out of a total of five spots.

**Derman** Ohh . . . just like a combination! From Chapter 2, I know that 10 is in Pascal's Triangle.

**Sasha** Hey, nice. Five flips and two H's. So the number of ways should be 5 choose 2, which is 10.

**Derman** So the probability is 10 out of 32. Guess it wasn't 1 out of 6 after all.

**Remember...**

The notation for "five choose 2" is $\binom{5}{2}$ or ${}_5C_2$. You can calculate it as $\frac{5!}{2! \cdot 3!}$.

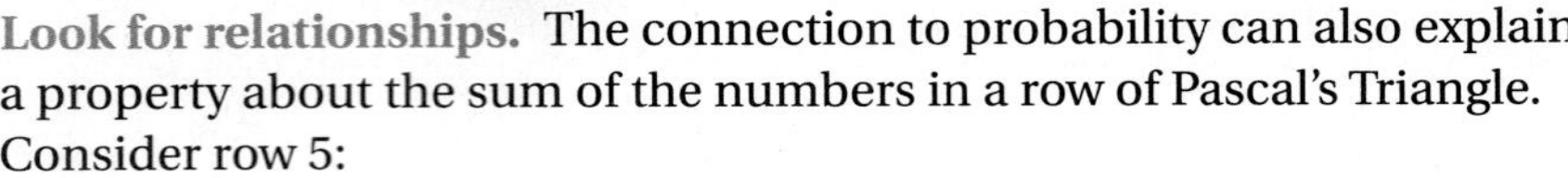

## Developing Habits of Mind

**Look for relationships.** The connection to probability can also explain a property about the sum of the numbers in a row of Pascal's Triangle. Consider row 5:

$$1 \quad 5 \quad 10 \quad 10 \quad 5 \quad 1$$

When you toss five coins, these numbers show up as the number of ways to get 0 heads, 1 head, 2 heads, and so on. For example, the probability of getting no heads when you flip five coins is $\frac{1}{32}$, since there is 1 successful outcome out of 32 total. Now look at the sum of all the probabilities.

$$\frac{1}{32} + \frac{5}{32} + \frac{10}{32} + \frac{10}{32} + \frac{5}{32} + \frac{1}{32}$$

If you toss five coins, you have to get *some* number of heads from 0 to 5. If you add up the probability of getting 0 heads, 1 head, 2 heads, 3 heads, 4 heads, and 5 heads, you have covered all the possibilities. Also, there is no overlap between these events. When you count the number of heads, the answer cannot be 2 *and* 4. So, the sum of these probabilities must be 1.

$$\frac{1}{32} + \frac{5}{32} + \frac{10}{32} + \frac{10}{32} + \frac{5}{32} + \frac{1}{32} = 1$$

This happens with any row of Pascal's Triangle. The sum of the numbers in the $n$th row of Pascal's Triangle is $2^n$, which equals the total number of outcomes when tossing $n$ coins.

## For You to Do

**3.** Which is more likely, flipping exactly 3 heads in 10 coin flips, or flipping exactly 4 heads in 5 coin flips?

Here are two additional terms that apply to events.

### *Definitions*

Two events $A$ and $B$ are **mutually exclusive** if they do not share any outcomes in the same sample space: whenever $P(A \text{ and } B) = 0$. If $A$ and $B$ are mutually exclusive, then $P(A \text{ or } B) = P(A) + P(B)$.

Two events $A$ and $B$ are **independent** if the result from one event has no effect on the other. If $A$ and $B$ are independent, then $P(A \text{ and } B) = P(A) \cdot P(B)$.

Consider rolling a single number cube. Rolling a 5 and rolling a 6 are mutually exclusive: you cannot do both at once. To find the probability of rolling a 5 or 6, add the probabilities of rolling each.

$P(5 \text{ and } 6) = 0$
$P(5 \text{ or } 6) = P(5) + P(6)$

Consider rolling two number cubes. The probability of rolling a 5 on the first number cube is $\frac{1}{6}$. The probability of rolling a 6 on the second number cube is also $\frac{1}{6}$. These events are independent: the result for the second number cube does not rely in any way on the result for the first number cube. So, the probability of rolling a 5 on the first number cube and a 6 on the second number cube is $\frac{1}{6} \cdot \frac{1}{6} = \frac{1}{36}$.

## Developing Habits of Mind

**Extend the process.** The rule for $P(A \text{ or } B)$ is slightly different when $A$ and $B$ share outcomes. For any events $A$ and $B$,

$$P(A \text{ or } B) = P(A) + P(B) - P(A \text{ and } B)$$

One way to look at this is with a Venn diagram.

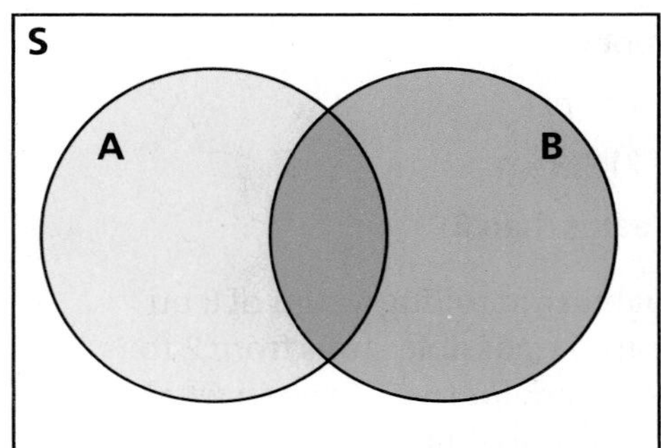


Let $S$ be the sample space. In the diagram, the entire yellow circle represents event $A$. The entire blue circle represents event $B$. The green intersection of the two circles (where the yellow and blue overlap) represents the event ($A$ and $B$). The union of the two circles represents the event ($A$ or $B$).

In the diagram, this union is the part that is either yellow or blue, or is both yellow and blue. How could you compute the area of this colored region? You cannot just add the area of the entire yellow circle and the area of the entire blue circle. If you were to do this, you would double-count the middle green area, where the two circles intersect. So, subtract that green area from the sum and you will get the correct area.

Note that if $A$ and $B$ are mutually exclusive, $P(A \text{ and } B) = 0$. Then you do not have to take the intersection into account. This makes sense, since for mutually exclusive events $P(A \text{ or } B) = P(A) + P(B)$.

You can find probabilities for more than two overlapping events by using the inclusion-exclusion principle. For three events $A$, $B$, and $C$, first add the probabilities of the events. Next subtract all the intersections of pairs of events. Then add back in the intersection of *triples* of events.

$$\begin{aligned} P(A \text{ or } B \text{ or } C) = {} & P(A) + P(B) + P(C) \\ & - P(A \text{ and } B) - P(A \text{ and } C) - P(B \text{ and } C) \\ & + P(A \text{ and } B \text{ and } C) \end{aligned}$$

What happens if *A*, *B*, and *C* are mutually exclusive?

You can extend this principle to find probabilities for any number of overlapping events.

# Exercises *Practicing Habits of Mind*

## Check Your Understanding

1. Determine each probability.
   - **a.** *P*(flip 1 coin, heads)
   - **b.** *P*(flip 2 coins, both heads)
   - **c.** *P*(roll a number cube and get an odd number)
   - **d.** *P*(roll a number cube and get an even number)
   - **e.** *P*(roll a number cube and get a negative number)
   - **f.** *P*(roll two number cubes and get a sum of 2)
   - **g.** *P*(roll two number cubes and get a sum greater than 2)
2. **What's Wrong Here?** Russ says that the probability of rolling a sum of 8 on two number cubes should be $\frac{1}{11}$, since there are 11 possible sums from 2 to 12. "It works for one number cube, so it should work for two." Explain what is wrong with his reasoning, and find the correct probability.
3. If you flip a coin six times, how many different ways are there for the result to be 2 heads and 4 tails? Write them out.
4. Calculate the value of $\binom{6}{2}$. Explain how your result relates to the work in Exercise 3.
5. Use the expansion of $(t + h)^6$ to find the total number of ways you could flip 3 heads and 3 tails in a sequence of six coin tosses.
6. **Take It Further** Suppose you are to roll a number cube three times. Find the probability that the sum of the numbers will be 8.

## On Your Own

7. Make a game where the probability of winning is about $\frac{1}{3}$. Explain clearly how the game is played, and what the winning condition is. The best games are simple to play but complex in their potential outcomes.

> So, one game would be "Roll a number cube. If it comes up 1 or 2, you win." But you can make something more interesting!

8. You flip a coin eight times.
   - **a.** Explain why there are 256 outcomes in the sample space.
   - **b.** What is the most likely number of heads? How likely is it to occur?
9. Find the probability that if you flip nine coins, you will get exactly six heads and three tails.

10. In a carnival game, you roll a standard number cube and flip a coin. The coin has a 0 on one side, and a 5 on the other side. Your score is the sum of the values that appear on the number cube and the coin.

a. You win the game if you score 10 points or more. Find the probability that you win the game.

b. The man running the carnival says that every score from 1 to 11 is equally likely. Is he right? Explain.

11. Consider the set $S$ of ordered pairs $(x, y)$ such that $x$ and $y$ are both integers between 1 and 8, inclusive, and $x \geq y$.

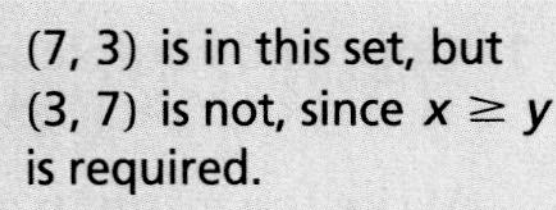

(7, 3) is in this set, but
(3, 7) is not, since $x \geq y$
is required.


a. How many such ordered pairs are there?

b. If you are to pick an ordered pair $(x, y)$ at random, what is the probability that $x$ and $y$ do not have any common factor greater than 1?

c. In the coordinate plane, plot all the ordered pairs $(x, y)$ in $S$ that do not have any common factor greater than 1.

12. Repeat Exercise 11 with the integer pairs satisfying $1 \leq y \leq x \leq 9$.

13. **Take It Further** Flip a coin 10 times, keeping score as follows. If you flip heads, you get one point. If you flip tails, you are in "danger." If you flip tails twice in a row, you "bust," lose all your points, and the game ends.

a. What is the probability you survive all ten flips without busting?

b. What is the average score players achieve in this game?

14. **Standardized Test Prep** In the sample space for rolling two number cubes, how many outcomes will have neither a one nor a two on either cube?

**A.** 16 **B.** 18 **C.** 20 **D.** 24

## Maintain Your Skills

15. This is $F_5$, the *Farey sequence* of order 5:

$$\frac{0}{1}, \frac{1}{5}, \frac{1}{4}, \frac{1}{3}, \frac{2}{5}, \frac{1}{2}, \frac{3}{5}, \frac{2}{3}, \frac{3}{4}, \frac{4}{5}, \frac{1}{1}$$

$F_5$ is all fractions from 0 to 1, inclusive, with denominators less than or equal to 5. It is written in increasing order with fractions in lowest terms.

Find the number of elements in $F_n$. Copy and complete the table for $n$ from 1 to 10, inclusive. Describe any patterns you find.

| $n$ | Number of elements in $F_n$ |
|---|---|
| 1 | 2 |
| 2 | 3 |
| 3 | ■ |
| 4 | ■ |
| 5 | 11 |

# 3.03 Polynomial Powers

You can use Pascal's Triangle to quickly count the number of each type of outcome for coin-flip experiments. But what about other experiments, like rolling a number cube or answering multiple-choice questions? This lesson explores the use of polynomials to solve probability problems.

## For You to Do

1. Copy and complete the expansion box below to find the expanded form of $(x + x^2 + x^3 + x^4 + x^5 + x^6)^2$.

   Write the result in ascending powers of $x$.

| $\cdot$ | $x$ | $x^2$ | $x^3$ | $x^4$ | $x^5$ | $x^6$ |
|---|---|---|---|---|---|---|
| $x$ | ■ | ■ | ■ | ■ | ■ | ■ |
| $x^2$ | ■ | ■ | $x^5$ | ■ | ■ | ■ |
| $x^3$ | ■ | ■ | ■ | ■ | ■ | ■ |
| $x^4$ | ■ | ■ | ■ | ■ | ■ | ■ |
| $x^5$ | ■ | $x^7$ | ■ | ■ | ■ | ■ |
| $x^6$ | ■ | ■ | ■ | ■ | ■ | $x^{12}$ |

2. When you roll two number cubes, what is the probability that the sum of the numbers will be exactly 5?

**Remember...**

You first used expansion boxes as a way to keep track of all the terms when you were multiplying two expressions.

## Developing Habits of Mind

**Recognize a similar process.** Consider the table from Lesson 3.02, with the 36 possible outcomes for the sum when rolling two number cubes.

| + | 1 | 2 | 3 | 4 | 5 | 6 |
|---|---|---|---|---|---|---|
| 1 | 2 | 3 | 4 | 5 | 6 | 7 |
| 2 | 3 | 4 | 5 | 6 | 7 | 8 |
| 3 | 4 | 5 | 6 | 7 | 8 | 9 |
| 4 | 5 | 6 | 7 | 8 | 9 | 10 |
| 5 | 6 | 7 | 8 | 9 | 10 | 11 |
| 6 | 7 | 8 | 9 | 10 | 11 | 12 |

This table and the one from For You To Do are nearly identical, and they should be! Think about how you might get an $x^5$ in the expansion: multiply two terms like $x^2$ and $x^3$, or $x^4$ and $x^1$. In all, there are four ways to do this. Now think about how you get a 5 from the sum of the numbers on two cubes: roll a 2 and a 3, or a 4 and a 1. There are four ways to do this, too. It works because when you multiply polynomials, you are adding exponents.

So, you can use the polynomial $(x + x^2 + x^3 + x^4 + x^5 + x^6)$ to model the results when rolling a number cube with the numbers 1 through 6 on it.

Consider this frequency chart, listing the number of ways to get each sum when rolling two number cubes:

The **frequency** of an event $A$ is the number of outcomes in $A$. The frequency of the event "roll a sum of 10 on two number cubes" is 3, since there are 3 different outcomes with sum 10. In shorthand, $|A| = 3$.

| Roll | 2 | 3 | 4 | 5 | 6 | 7 | 8 | 9 | 10 | 11 | 12 |
|---|---|---|---|---|---|---|---|---|---|---|---|
| Frequency | 1 | 2 | 3 | 4 | 5 | 6 | 5 | 4 | 3 | 2 | 1 |

Compare it to the result when squaring the polynomial that models a number cube roll:

$$(x + x^2 + x^3 + x^4 + x^5 + x^6)^2 =$$

$$1x^2 + 2x^3 + 3x^4 + 4x^5 + 5x^6 + 6x^7 + 5x^8 + 4x^9 + 3x^{10} + 2x^{11} + 1x^{12}$$

The expansion gives the same frequency information. There is one way to make $x^2$, two ways to make $x^3$, and so on. The table analyzing the sample space is really the same as the expansion box multiplying the polynomials.

Polynomials come in handy when exploring sample spaces that are too complex to list by hand. The sample space for rolling two number cubes has 36 outcomes, but the sample space for rolling four number cubes has $6^4 = 1296$ outcomes. This is tough to build by hand, but a CAS can quickly perform the corresponding polynomial expansion.

See the TI-Nspire Handbook on p. 817, for details on how to expand polynomials.

$$(x + x^2 + x^3 + x^4 + x^5 + x^6)^4 =$$

$$x^{24} + 4x^{23} + 10x^{22} + 20x^{21} + 35x^{20} + 56x^{19}$$
$$+ 80x^{18} + 104x^{17} + 125x^{16} + 140x^{15} + 146x^{14} + 140x^{13}$$
$$+ 125x^{12} + 104x^{11} + 80x^{10} + 56x^9 + 35x^8 + 20x^7 + 10x^6 + 4x^5 + x^4$$

This expansion gives a lot of information. For example, there are exactly 80 ways to roll a sum of 18 on four number cubes. Since there are $6^4 = 1296$ outcomes, $P(\text{rolling a sum of 18}) = \frac{80}{1296}$.

## Example

A spinner has five wedges of equal area. The wedges are labeled with the numbers 1, 2, 3, 3, and 8.

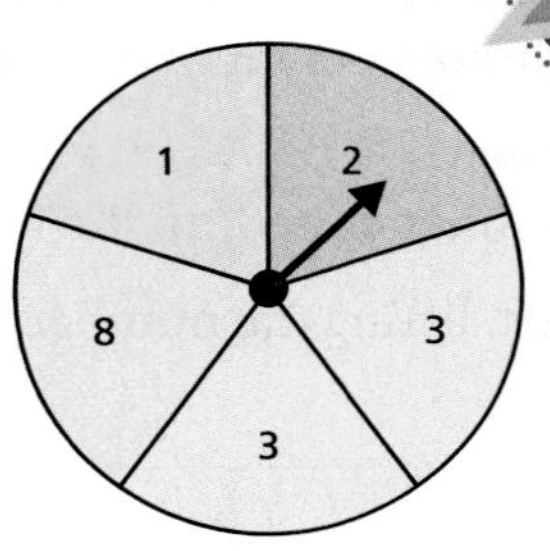


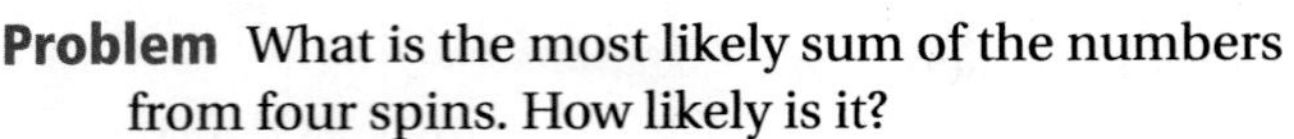

**Problem** What is the most likely sum of the numbers from four spins. How likely is it?

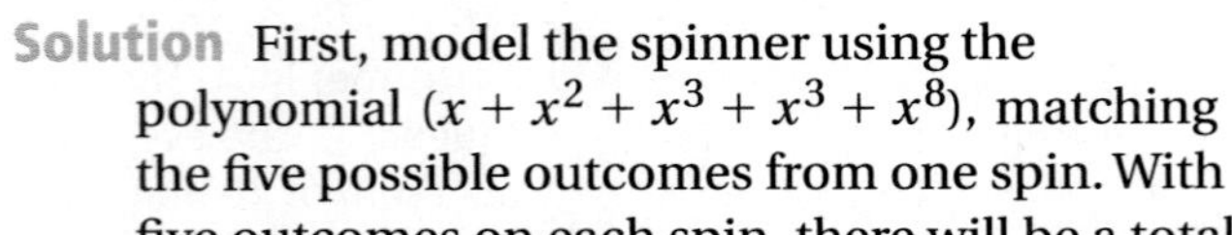

**Solution** First, model the spinner using the polynomial $(x + x^2 + x^3 + x^3 + x^8)$, matching the five possible outcomes from one spin. With five outcomes on each spin, there will be a total of $5^4 = 625$ outcomes from four spins.

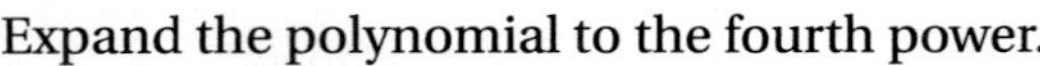

Expand the polynomial to the fourth power.

$$(x + x^2 + x^3 + x^3 + x^8)^4 =$$
$$x^{32} + 8x^{27} + 4x^{26} + 4x^{25} + 24x^{22} + 24x^{21} + 30x^{20}$$
$$+ 12x^{19} + 6x^{18} + 32x^{17} + 48x^{16} + 72x^{15} + 52x^{14} + 36x^{13}$$
$$+ 28x^{12} + 36x^{11} + 56x^{10} + 56x^9 + 49x^8 + 28x^7 + 14x^6 + 4x^5 + x^4$$

Each coefficient is the frequency for a specific sum, indicated by the exponent. The greatest coefficient is 72. There are 72 ways to make a sum of 15. The probability of this sum occuring is $\frac{72}{625}$, since there are $5^4 = 625$ total outcomes.

**Habits of Mind**

**Look for a relationship.** You could also write the polynomial as $(x + x^2 + 2x^3 + x^8)$. What does the coefficient 2 mean here?

## For You to Do

**3.** A second similar spinner has the numbers 2, 4, 6, 6, 16. What is the most likely sum from four spins?

**4.** Let $f(x) = (x + x^2 + x^3 + x^3 + x^8)^4$. What is the value of $f(1)$?

You can model other situations using polynomials as well. To model a coin flip, use the polynomial $(t + h)$ as seen in Lesson 3.01. Look at this expansion:

$$(t + h)^5 = t^5 + 5t^4h + 10t^3h^2 + 10t^2h^3 + 5th^4 + h^5$$

You can interpret this as, "There is one way to get five tails, then five ways to get four tails and one head, then ten ways to get three tails and two heads . . ."

To model a multiple-choice question with one right answer and three wrong answers use the polynomial $(r + w + w + w)$, or $(r + 3w)$. Here is another expansion:

$$(r + 3w)^5 = r^5 + 15r^4w + 90r^3w^2 + 270r^2w^3 + 405rw^4 + 243w^5$$

**Habits of Mind**

**Represent the situation.** An appropriate choice of letters can be helpful. Here, you use $t$ and $h$ for tails and heads. You use $r$ and $w$ for right and wrong answers.

You can use the expression to show that on five questions, there are 270 different ways to get exactly two right and three wrong answers. The total number of outcomes in the sample space is the sum of the coefficients.

$$1 + 15 + 90 + 270 + 405 + 243 = 1024 = 4^5$$

So, $P(\text{2 right and 3 wrong}) = \frac{270}{1024} \approx 0.2637$.

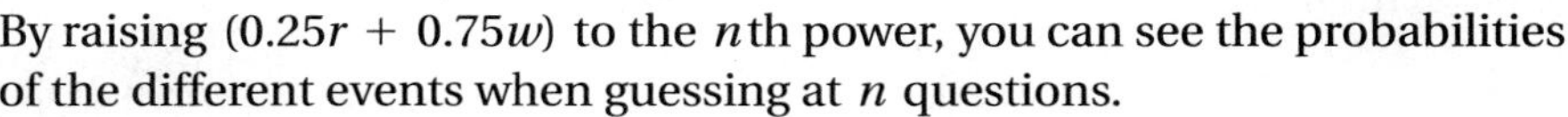

## Developing Habits of Mind

**Extend the process.** The polynomials you have seen so far are helpful in counting outcomes, but you can use a variation to calculate the probability directly. For example, by raising $(r + 3w)$ to powers, you can see how many ways there are to get right and wrong answers to a multiple-choice test. But the probability of getting a question right is $\frac{1}{4} = 0.25$ and the probability of getting it wrong is $\frac{3}{4} = 0.75$.

By raising $(0.25r + 0.75w)$ to the $n$th power, you can see the probabilities of the different events when guessing at $n$ questions.

Consider the expansion of $(0.25r + 0.75w)^5$.

$$0.000977r^5 + 0.014648r^4w + 0.087891r^3w^2 + 0.263672r^2w^3 + 0.395508rw^4 + 0.237305w^5$$

Expand using the Binomial Theorem or a CAS.

Now each coefficient gives the probability of each event occurring, rather than its frequency. The probability of getting 2 right and 3 wrong is the coefficient of the $r^2w^3$ term.

You can also obtain more information by evaluating the polynomial. For example, take the polynomial for rolling a number cube, $p(x) = x + x^2 + x^3 + x^4 + x^5 + x^6$. The output $p(1) = 6$ gives the total number of outcomes. Also, $(p(1))^3$ equals $6^3 = 216$. This is the total number of outcomes when rolling three number cubes.

But consider $p(-1) = 0$ and how it is built term by term. Let $x = -1$. Then $x^k = 1$ if $k$ is even and $x^k = -1$ if $k$ is odd. So, $p(-1) = 0$ means there are just as many even numbers on a number cube as odd numbers.

Now look at $(p(-1))^4$. It also equals zero, but models the sum of four number cubes. So, there are just as many ways to roll an odd sum from four number cubes as an even sum. This is pretty surprising, but you can verify it using the expansion on page 185. In fact, it must be true no matter how many number cubes are thrown.

One important thing to remember is that the method of polynomial powers is useful when performing the same experiment several times. Experiments involving coins, number cubes, and spinners are good examples. Picking a committee or drawing balls out of a bingo machine are not good examples, since the experiment changes over time. To see this, think about drawing a bingo number. When you draw that number, you remove it from the machine. You have fewer numbers for the next draw.

# Exercises *Practicing Habits of Mind*

## Check Your Understanding

**1.** The polynomial on page 185 gives the distribution of possible sums for rolling four number cubes.

**a.** Build a histogram showing the frequency for each outcome, from 4 to 24.

**b.** Explain why there are exactly as many ways to roll a sum of 5 as there are ways to roll a sum of 23.

**2.** Suppose you roll three number cubes. Calculate the probability that the sum of the numbers will be greater than 10.

**3.** On an unusual number cube the "1" face has a 10 instead.

**a.** Find a polynomial that models one roll of this number cube.

**b.** In four rolls, what is the most likely sum? How likely is it?

The six faces on this number cube have the numbers 2, 3, 4, 5, 6, and 10.

**4.** On another number cube the "6" face has a 5 instead.

**a.** Explain why the polynomial $p(x) = x + x^2 + x^3 + x^4 + 2x^5$ models one roll of this number cube.

**b.** In four rolls, what is the most likely sum? How likely is it?

The six faces on this number cube have the numbers 1, 2, 3, 4, 5, and 5.

**5.** Consider the number cube from Exercise 4 and its corresponding polynomial $p$.

**a.** Expand $q(x) = (p(x))^2$. What does $q$ represent?

**b.** Find the value of $q(1)$.

**c.** There are 36 outcomes when rolling this number cube twice. How many more ways are there to roll an even sum than an odd sum?

**d.** Find the value of $q(-1)$.

**6.** A board game has a spinner with the numbers 1 through 10 on it. All numbers are equally likely. As you near the end of the game, you have 18 spaces left to move.

**a.** Find the probability that you spin a total of *at least* 18 on just two spins.

**b.** Find the probability that you spin a total of *at least* 18 on three spins.

**c.** Find the probability that you spin a total of *at least* 18 on four spins.

## On Your Own

7. A spinner has the five numbers 0, 1, 2, 2, and 7.
   a. Find a polynomial to model one spin.
   b. What is the most likely sum of the numbers from four spins. How likely is it?

8. Avery takes a multiple-choice test with six questions. There are five choices per question. He guesses at each question.
   a. What is the probability that Avery guesses correctly on the first question? on the second question?
   b. What is the probability that Avery guesses correctly on all six questions?
   c. Write a polynomial expansion to model this situation.
   d. Find the probability that Avery guesses correctly on exactly two of the six questions.

9. A local market has a prize wheel. Lucky customers can spin the wheel to win free fish. On one spin, it is possible to win 1 fish, 2 fish, 3 fish, or 10 fish.
   a. What is the average number of fish the market can expect to give away, per spin?
   b. Three customers spin the wheel. What is the most likely total number of fish that they win? How likely is this?

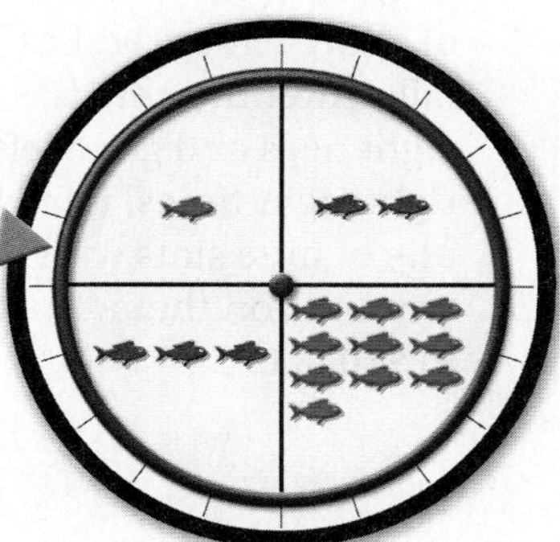

10. Take It Further Ten customers spin the Wheel of Fish from Exercise 9. Find the probability that the total number of fish they win is even.

11. Use a coordinate grid with $1 \le x \le 10, 1 \le y \le 10$. Plot all 55 points with integer coordinates $(x, y)$ in this range with $x \ge y$. Use one color if the two numbers share a common factor greater than 1. Use a second color if they do not.

12. You are to choose two integers $x$ and $y$ between 1 and 10, inclusive, with $x \ge y$. Use your plot from Exercise 11. Determine the probability that the pair of integers will have no common factor greater than 1.

13. Standardized Test Prep Which of the following is the sum of the entries in the 12th row of Pascal's Triangle?

    **A.** 12!  **B.** $6^6$  **C.** $2^{12}$  **D.** ${}_{12}P_2$

## Maintain Your Skills

14. Write out $F_{10}$, the Farey sequence of order 10.

15. Take a coordinate grid with $0 \le x \le 10, 0 \le y \le 10$. Plot all points $(x, y)$ in this range where the fraction $\frac{y}{x}$ is in $F_{10}$, the Farey sequence of order 10. Compare the results to Exercise 11.

**Remember...**

The *Farey sequence* of order *n* is all fractions between 0 and 1 in lowest terms with denominators less than or equal to *n*, written from least to greatest.

## 3.04 Expected Value

The expected value for a game is how much you could expect to win per game, on average. It is not necessarily the most likely amount you would win in any one game. Instead, if you played many times over, your average score would approach this expected value in the long run.

### In-Class Experiment

On game shows and at school carnivals, the game of Plinko is a often favorite. Suppose on one game show all the player has to do is drop a chip, and they can win up to $10,000. Here is a simplified version of the Plinko board:

Whenever the chip hits a peg, it has a 50-50 chance of going left or right as it falls. After the chip has hit eight pegs and gone left or right eight times, it falls into one of nine slots with dollar amounts on them, from $0 to $10,000.

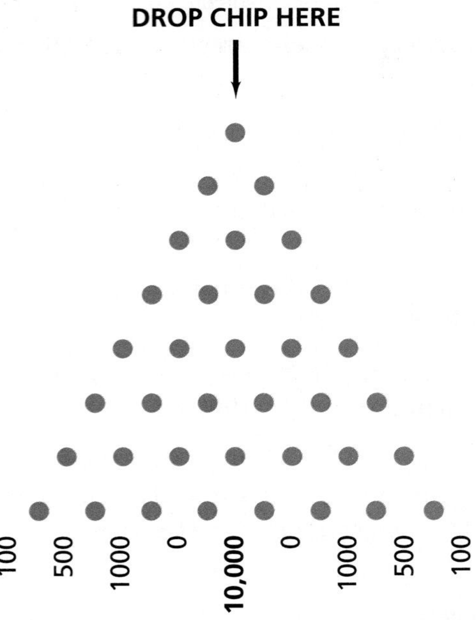


1. Describe the relationship between the falling chip and coin flipping.
2. Write a polynomial, raised to a power, to model this game.
3. Find the probability that the chip falls into the center slot for a $10,000 win.
4. Find the probability that the chip falls into a $0 slot. Note there are two such slots.
5. What is the probability of winning $1000? $500? $100?
6. How much, on average, would you win per chip if you were to keep playing this game for a long, long time?

The sample space here has 256 outcomes. Why?

## Minds in Action

*A student is thinking about the last problem from the In-Class Experiment.*

**Wendy** Let me answer a simpler question first: let's say you paid me \$10,000 if I flip a coin heads, and \$0 if it's tails. I've got a $\frac{1}{2}$ chance to make heads, so it should be \$5000 per flip, on average.

So now let me look at this bigger problem. I'll focus on the \$10,000 first. Every time I drop a chip, there's a $\frac{70}{256}$ chance of getting the 10 grand. If you sat me there all day dropping chips, I can find the average by multiplying.

$$\$10{,}000 \cdot \frac{70}{256} \approx \$2734$$

So if everything else was zeros, that would be my average.

But I could win some smaller amounts of money. There's a $\frac{56}{256}$ chance of hitting \$1000. I'll do the same thing:

$$\$1000 \cdot \frac{56}{256} \approx \$219$$

So, I'll build a table for all the options.

| Win | Probability | Win × Probability |
|---|---|---|
| \$10,000 | $\frac{70}{256}$ | \$2734 |
| \$1000 | $\frac{56}{256}$ | \$219 |
| \$500 | $\frac{16}{256}$ | \$31 |
| \$100 | $\frac{2}{256}$ | \$1 |
| \$0 | whatever | \$0 |

I'm not sure what to do now, I think I'll just add the dollar values. On average, I'd expect to win around \$2985 per chip, if you let me sit there all day and drop chips. Not a bad day's work.

Often, it makes sense to assign a number to each outcome of an experiment, such as "3" instead of "rolling a 3 on the number cube," or "2" instead of "heads, tails, heads, tails, tails" or "10,000" instead of "the chip falls in the middle slot." Each set of these numerical assignments is a random variable, and typically uses a capital letter like $X$ or $Y$.

Wendy's method calculates the *expected value* of a random variable.

A **random variable** is a function whose inputs are outcomes, and whose outputs are numbers.

### *Definition*

**The expected value of a random variable $X$ is the sum when each value of $X$ is multiplied by its probability. The typical notation is $E(X)$.**

$$E(X) = \sum_i x_i \cdot p_i$$

**where the $x_i$ are the values of the random variable, and the $p_i$ are the probabilities of the values, respectively. An alternative notation is**

$$E(X) = \sum_i s_i \cdot P(X = s_i)$$

**where $P(X = s_i)$ is the probability that the random variable $X$ takes on the value $s_i$.**

> **Remember...**
>
> $\sum_i x_i \cdot p_i$ means to add the products of all the different possible $x$'s and their corresponding $p$'s. It is the same as writing $\sum_{i=1}^{n} x_i \cdot p_i$ There are $n$ different outcomes, so there are $n$ products to add.

The definition is a mouthful, but the Plinko game is a good example. For the Plinko board, each $x_i$ is a dollar value. Each $p_i$ is the probability of hitting that value.

## Example

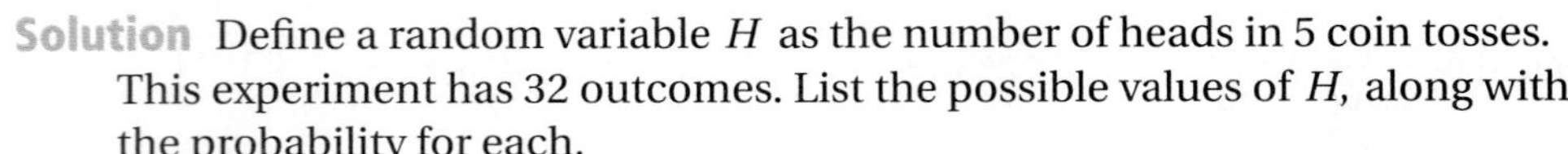

**Problem** Toss five coins. What is the expected value for the number of heads?

**Solution** Define a random variable $H$ as the number of heads in 5 coin tosses. This experiment has 32 outcomes. List the possible values of $H$, along with the probability for each.

> **Remember...**
>
> A random variable takes in outcomes and returns numbers. For example, one outcome is $a$ = "heads, tails, heads, tails, tails." The random variable $H$ takes in that outcome and returns the number 2, $H(a) = 2$.

| Number of Heads | Probability |
|---|---|
| 0 | $\frac{1}{32}$ |
| 1 | $\frac{5}{32}$ |
| 2 | $\frac{10}{32}$ |
| 3 | $\frac{10}{32}$ |
| 4 | $\frac{5}{32}$ |
| 5 | $\frac{1}{32}$ |

Calculate expected value. Multiply each value of $H$ by its probability. Then add the results.

| Number of Heads | Probability | Product |
|---|---|---|
| 0 | $\frac{1}{32}$ | 0/32 |
| 1 | $\frac{5}{32}$ | 5/32 |
| 2 | $\frac{10}{32}$ | 20/32 |
| 3 | $\frac{10}{32}$ | 30/32 |
| 4 | $\frac{5}{32}$ | 20/32 |
| 5 | $\frac{1}{32}$ | 5/32 |
| **Total** | | **80/32** |

The expected value is $\frac{80}{32}$, which simplifies to $\frac{5}{2}$.

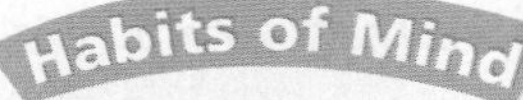


**Check the result.** Does $\frac{5}{2}$ make sense as the average number of heads when flipping five coins?

## Developing Habits of Mind

**Use a different process.** You might have thought about the Plinko game in a different way. You could add up all the money you would win from each path. There are 2 ways to win \$100, 16 ways to win \$500, 56 ways to win \$1000, and 70 ways to win \$10,000. The total winnings from all the different paths is

$$2 \cdot \$100 + 16 \cdot \$500 + 56 \cdot \$1000 + 70 \cdot \$10{,}000 = \$764{,}200$$

This is the total value for all 256 paths, so the average would have to be

$$\frac{\$764{,}200}{256} \approx \$2985.16$$

This gives the correct result! Both methods are valid. It comes down to whether you prefer to count probabilities or frequencies. The result Wendy comes up with is

$$\frac{2}{256} \cdot \$100 + \frac{16}{256} \cdot \$500 + \frac{56}{256} \cdot \$1000 + \frac{70}{256} \cdot \$10{,}000$$

The distributive law shows that both these results must be identical. So, you can also calculate the expected value by taking the sum of all the outputs from the random variable, then dividing by the total number of outcomes. The expected value is the mean result from the random variable.

For example, the expected value of the numeric result when rolling one number cube is the mean of the numbers on the six faces.

$$\frac{1 + 2 + 3 + 4 + 5 + 6}{6} = 3.5$$

## Minds in Action

*Tony and Derman look at Exercise 9 from Lesson 3.03.*

**Tony** So, it's a wheel with 1, 2, 3, and 10 fish on it. And we want to know the average from one spin.

**Derman** I'll just add and divide. The sum is . . . 16. So the average is 4.

**Tony** Sounds good. Now what about two spins?

**Derman** I think it's going to be 8. Two times four. Two spins, 4 fish each?

**Tony** I'm not sure it works that way. Let's just write out the sample space. There are only 16 ways it can go.

**Derman** A table it is.

| + | 1 | 2 | 3 | 10 |
|---|---|---|---|---|
| 1 | 2 | 3 | 4 | 11 |
| 2 | 3 | 4 | 5 | 12 |
| 3 | 4 | 5 | 6 | 13 |
| 10 | 11 | 12 | 13 | 20 |

**Tony** Cool. I'm going to add all these numbers then divide by 16. Since the sample space is small, I won't bother making a frequency table.

The sum is 128. So, the expected value for two spins is 128 over 16 . . . hey, you were right! It is 8.

**Derman** It was bound to happen sometime. If I'm right, for three spins the expected value should be 12. The table's going to be a mess!

**Tony** Well, we should use a polynomial power instead. The outcomes are 1, 2, 3, and 10, so the polynomial for one spin should be

$$(x^1 + x^2 + x^3 + x^{10})$$

**Derman** Isn't $x^1$ just $x$?

**Tony** I like writing $x^1$, it makes it more clear where it came from. I'd do that for $x^0$ instead of writing 1.

**Derman** Fair enough. And we raise that to the third power, since it's three spins. Expand that and . . .

**Tony** Let's write that out.

## For You to Do

**7.** Complete the work from the dialog. Write out the expansion of $(x^1 + x^2 + x^3 + x^{10})^3$, then use it to show that the expected value for three spins is 12.

# Exercises *Practicing Habits of Mind*

## Check Your Understanding

Alice, Bev, Craig, and Dawn sit at a table for four in no particular order. Rey, the host of the party, tells them their seats are assigned at the table and shows them the chart.

**Habits of Mind**

**Make a list.** There are 24 possible ways for the four guests to sit down. Do you see why there are 24 possible outcomes? Try listing them.

1. **a.** What is the probability that all four of them are already in the right seat?

   **b.** What is the probability that all four of them are in the *wrong* seat?

2. On average, how many of the four will be sitting in the right seat?

3. Suppose a Plinko board has a center hole worth $20,000.

   Find the average amount a player will win, per chip, in the long run.

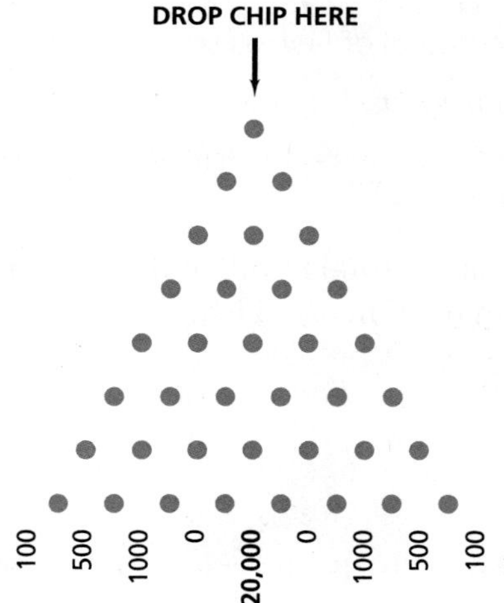


This is another way to say, "Calculate the expected value" for this new version of the game.

4. **What's Wrong Here?** Daisuke had trouble calculating the expected number of heads when tossing three coins.

   Daisuke: I built the table with each outcome and its probability, then added it up. I got the probabilities from the Getting Started lesson. I could use Pascal's Triangle to get them, too.

| Number of Heads | Probability | Product |
|---|---|---|
| 0 | $\frac{1}{8}$ | $\frac{0}{8}$ |
| 1 | $\frac{3}{8}$ | $\frac{3}{8}$ |
| 2 | $\frac{3}{8}$ | $\frac{6}{8}$ |
| 3 | $\frac{1}{8}$ | $\frac{3}{8}$ |
| Total | | $\frac{12}{8}$ |

Daisuke: But it doesn't make sense to me to get $\frac{12}{8}$ as the answer: that's one and a half, and I thought probability was never supposed to be more than one.

What would you say to Daisuke? Has he made a mistake in the calculation?

5. Avery is taking a six-question multiple choice test, with five choices for each question. He guesses at each question.

   a. Expand the polynomial $(0.2r + 0.8w)^6$. What do the results represent?

   b. Find the expected value for the number of questions Avery gets right when taking the test.

6. Three customers spin the Wheel of Fish as seen in Exercise 9 on page 189.

   a. Use a polynomial expansion to find the frequency of each outcome.

   b. Find the probability that the market will give away fewer than 10 total fish to these three customers.

On one spin, the possible outcomes are 1, 2, 3, and 10 fish.

7. Find the expected value for the total number of fish the market gives away when four customers spin the Wheel of Fish.

## On Your Own

8. In this lesson's In-Class Experiment, you calculated the expected value for dropping one Plinko chip. Now suppose you drop five chips.

   a. What is the expected value, in dollars, for the first chip? the second chip? the third chip?

   b. What is the expected value for the total earned from all five chips?

9. Find the expected value for the number of heads when tossing six coins.

10. a. Find the expected value for the sum when rolling two number cubes.

    b. Find the expected value for the sum when rolling three number cubes.

11. **Take It Further**

    a. Find the expected value for the *product* when rolling two number cubes.

    b. Find the expected value for the product when rolling three number cubes. How could you use a polynomial here?

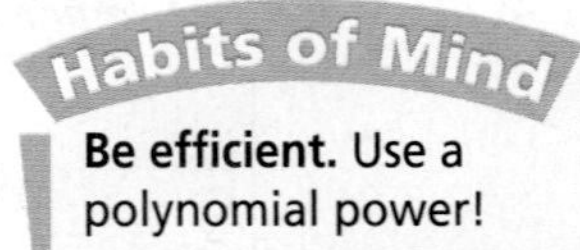


**Be efficient.** Use a polynomial power!

Suppose a friend gives you five envelopes, each with a different address on it. You are to put one of five different letters in each envelope. But you have no idea which letter is for which person, so you stuff them in at random.

**12.** What is the probability that all five envelopes contain the right letter?

This exercise is in the same style as Exercises 1 and 2. You might want to think of this as five people and five seats.

**13.** What is the probability that exactly four envelopes contain the right letter?

**14.** What is the probability that all five envelopes contain the wrong letter?

**15.** Find the expected value for the number of letters correctly addressed.

**16.** **Standardized Test Prep** A student randomly guesses on a true-false combinatorics test with five questions. Which of the following is the probability that the student will score at least 80%?

**A.** $\frac{5}{32}$ **B.** $\frac{3}{16}$ **C.** $\frac{1}{4}$ **D.** $\frac{1}{2}$

## Maintain Your Skills

**17.** Copy and complete this table using your work from previous lessons.

| $n$ | Number of Elements in $F_n$ | Relatively Prime Pairs |
|---|---|---|
| 1 | 2 | ■ |
| 2 | ■ | ■ |
| 3 | ■ | 4 |
| 4 | ■ | ■ |
| 5 | 11 | ■ |
| 6 | ■ | ■ |
| 7 | ■ | 18 |
| 8 | ■ | ■ |
| 9 | ■ | ■ |
| 10 | 33 | ■ |

Here, $F_n$ is the Farey sequence of order $n$. *Relatively prime pairs* refers to the number of pairs that have no common factors greater than 1 as plotted in Exercise 11 on page 189.

**Habits of Mind**

**Look for relationships.** Look for a simpler method than writing out the entire sequence $F_{30}$.

**18.** **Take It Further** Find the number of elements in $F_{30}$, the Farey sequence of order 30. Your goal is only to find the number of elements, not list them all.

# 3.05 Lotteries

One application of expected value is a lottery. There are several different kinds of lotteries. In some lotteries, expected value can be directly calculated, while others require an approach based on combinations.

## Scratch Tickets

State lotteries print batches of tickets, some of which are prize winners. Players pay to get a ticket. Most tickets lose, but some tickets are worth hundreds or thousands of dollars.

Here is the distribution from a scratch ticket game where each ticket costs $1.

| Payout | Frequency |
|---|---|
| $1 | 163,500 |
| $2 | 62,800 |
| $4 | 20,945 |
| $8 | 4,189 |
| $12 | 4,189 |
| $50 | 5,621 |
| $100 | 128 |
| $1,000 | 4 |
| $0 (lose) | 995,324 |
| **Total** | **1,256,700** |

Most of the tickets lose. Only a small percentage give the player more money than the price of the ticket.

How much is the average ticket worth in this game? To find this, calculate the expected value.

The random variable is the dollar value (payout) of the ticket, from 0 to 1000. The sample space is all 1,256,700 tickets. The expected value is the sum of each payout, multiplied by its probability.

| Payout | Frequency | Product |
|---|---|---|
| 1 | 163,500 | 163,500 |
| 2 | 62,800 | 125,600 |
| 4 | 20,945 | 83,780 |
| 8 | 4,189 | 33,512 |
| 12 | 4,189 | 50,268 |
| 50 | 5,621 | 281,050 |
| 100 | 128 | 12,800 |
| 1,000 | 4 | 4,000 |
| 0 (lose) | 995,324 | 0 |
| **Total** | **1,256,700** | **754,510** |

The expected value is $\frac{754{,}510}{1{,}256{,}700}$, very close to 60 cents. This lottery ticket actually costs $1, so roughly 60% of the money paid for tickets is returned to players as prizes, while 40% is kept by the state that runs this lottery.

## Example

In a 6-ball lottery a player picks six numbers, from 1 to 42. Then a machine draws six balls at random from a set of 42 numbered balls. The order of the drawing does not matter. The amount the player wins depends on how many of the numbers match numbers on their ticket.

The sample space has $\binom{42}{6} = 5{,}245{,}786$ elements.

This table shows the possible outcomes and their frequencies.

| Matches | Frequency | Payout |
|---|---|---|
| 0 correct | 1,947,792 | \$0 (loss) |
| 1 correct | 2,261,952 | \$0 (loss) |
| 2 correct | 883,575 | \$0 (loss) |
| 3 correct | 142,800 | \$1 |
| 4 correct | 9,450 | \$75 |
| 5 correct | 216 | \$1,500 |
| 6 correct | 1 | \$2,000,000 jackpot |
| **Total** | **5,245,786** | |

**Problem** A ticket in this lottery costs \$1. Find the expected value for one ticket.

**Solution** Multiply the frequencies by the payouts.

| Matches | Frequency | Payout | Product |
|---|---|---|---|
| 0 correct | 1,947,792 | 0 | 0 |
| 1 correct | 2,261,952 | 0 | 0 |
| 2 correct | 883,575 | 0 | 0 |
| 3 correct | 142,800 | 1 | 142,800 |
| 4 correct | 9,450 | 75 | 708,750 |
| 5 correct | 216 | 1,500 | 324,000 |
| 6 correct | 1 | 2,000,000 | 2,000,000 |
| **Total** | **5,245,786** | | **3,175,550** |

Note that the majority of the payouts go to the single jackpot winner (if there is one). Overall the expected value is

$$\frac{3{,}175{,}550}{5{,}245{,}786} \approx 0.6054$$

The \$1 ticket is worth just over 60 cents, so the lottery earns an average profit of nearly 40 cents per dollar played.

## For You to Do

**1.** Suppose the lottery is considering changing the rules to give a $5 prize for 3 numbers correct. What would happen to the expected value of a ticket? Would the lottery still be profitable for whoever is running it?

**Habits of Mind**

**Use what you know.** Try modifying the information from the table.

### Combinatorics and Lotteries

You can determine the frequencies in the previous example by counting combinations. Picture the 42 balls in the lottery drawing. The player picks 6 numbers, dividing the 42 balls into two categories: 6 that they want to see, and 36 others that they do not want to see.

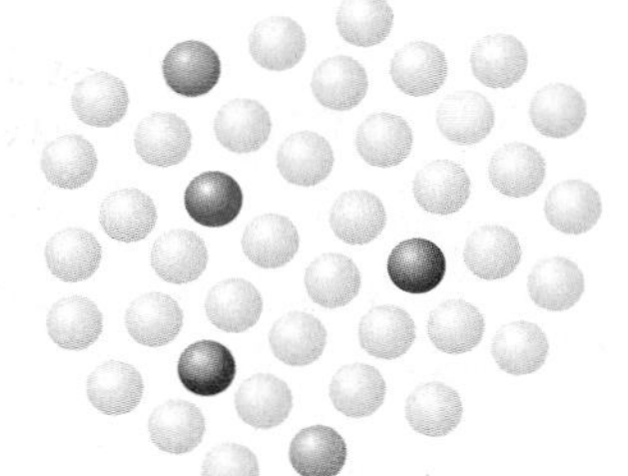

Suppose you want to know how many different ways there are to get exactly four balls correct in the lottery drawing. Well, out of the 6 balls the player wants to see, the machine draws 4. That can happen $\binom{6}{4}$ ways. But the machine also draws 2 of the "other" balls. That can happen $\binom{36}{2}$ ways. So, the number of ways to get exactly four balls correct is

$$\binom{6}{4} \cdot \binom{36}{2} = 15 \cdot 630 = 9450$$

You can use this approach for any count between 0 and 6.

| Matches | Frequency |
|---|---|
| 0 correct | $\binom{6}{0} \cdot \binom{36}{6} = 1{,}947{,}792$ |
| 1 correct | $\binom{6}{1} \cdot \binom{36}{5} = 2{,}261{,}952$ |
| 2 correct | $\binom{6}{2} \cdot \binom{36}{4} = 883{,}575$ |
| 3 correct | $\binom{6}{3} \cdot \binom{36}{3} = 142{,}800$ |
| 4 correct | $\binom{6}{4} \cdot \binom{36}{2} = 9{,}450$ |
| 5 correct | $\binom{6}{5} \cdot \binom{36}{1} = 216$ |
| 6 correct | $\binom{6}{6} \cdot \binom{36}{0} = 1$ |

**Remember...**

You can calculate combinations like $\binom{36}{2}$ using the nCr function on a calculator, or by using the factorial formula:

$$\binom{n}{k} = \frac{n!}{k!(n-k)!}$$

Note that the total number of outcomes is $\binom{42}{6}$ since there are 42 balls and 6 are picked. This leads to a theorem about combinations.

### *Theorem 3.1 Vandermonde's Identity*

**Let $r \leq n$ be nonnegative integers. Then**

$$\binom{n}{r} = \sum_{k=0}^{r} \binom{r}{k} \cdot \binom{n-r}{r-k}$$

**This method can be used to analyze most ball-drawing lottery games.**

## Developing Habits of Mind

**Study the difference.** Larger multi-state lotteries now exist, typically using these rules:

- First, a machine draws five balls from a set.
- Second, another machine draws the sixth ball (the "bonus ball") from a second set of balls, a completely different group.

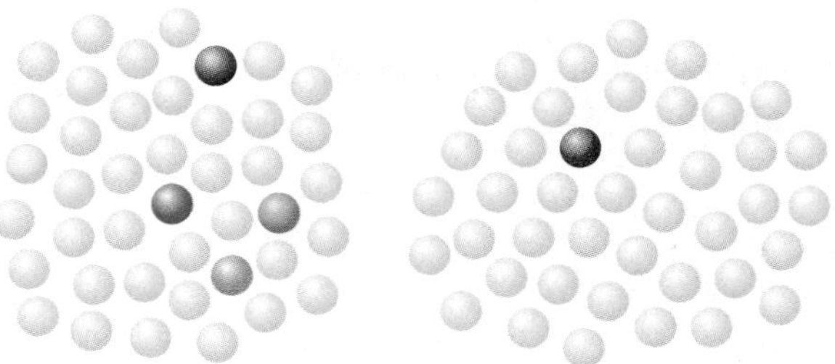

In order to win the jackpot, the player must get all five regular balls correct, plus the bonus ball. What effect does the existence of the bonus ball have on the sample space? Consider a game with 42 balls for the regular drawing, and a new set of 42 balls for the "bonus."

The size of the sample space becomes

$$\binom{42}{5} \cdot \binom{42}{1}$$

since 5 balls are chosen from the first set of 42, then 1 ball is chosen from the second set. While it may not seem like much of a difference, this has a huge effect on the size of the sample space.

$$\text{sample space for 6-ball lottery} = \binom{42}{6} = 5{,}245{,}786$$

$$\text{sample space with bonus ball} = \binom{42}{5} \cdot \binom{42}{1} = 35{,}728{,}056$$

The sample space is roughly 7 times bigger. It is much less likely a player will win. As of April 2008, one multi-state lottery had a sample space of over 146 million, while another had a sample space of over 175 million!

Think about flipping a coin 27 times in a row, and having all 27 coin flips come up heads. This would happen once every 134 million tries. In other words, flipping 27 heads in a row is *more* likely to happen than buying a winning ticket in either of these multi-state lotteries.

## For Discussion

**2.** A multi-state lottery could increase its sample space by adding more balls to either the regular pool or the "bonus" pool. How many more regular-pool balls would be needed to double the sample space? How many more "bonus" balls would be needed to double the sample space?

# Exercises Practicing Habits of Mind

## Check Your Understanding

1. A 5-ball lottery has 55 numbered balls. A player selects five numbers. Then, five of the balls are drawn by a machine.

   Copy and complete this frequency table.

| Matches | Frequency |
|---|---|
| 0 correct | ■ |
| 1 correct | 1,151,500 |
| 2 correct | ■ |
| 3 correct | ■ |
| 4 correct | ■ |
| 5 correct | 1 |

2. Find the expected value for the number of balls a player will correctly match in the 5-ball lottery presented in Exercise 1.

3. Suppose an interstate lottery has a 5-ball component with 55 balls, and then a bonus ball from a separate set of 42 balls. This table lists the payouts for this lottery.

| Ticket Type | Frequency | Payout |
|---|---|---|
| 5 balls + bonus | 1 | Jackpot |
| 5 balls + no bonus | 41 | $200,000 |
| 4 balls + bonus | 250 | $10,000 |
| 4 balls + no bonus | 10,250 | $100 |
| 3 balls + bonus | 12,250 | $100 |
| 3 balls + no bonus | 502,250 | $7 |
| 2 balls + bonus | 196,000 | $7 |
| 1 ball + bonus | 1,151,500 | $4 |
| Bonus only | 2,118,760 | $3 |
| Losing ticket | 142,116,660 | $0 |
| **Total outcomes** | **146,107,962** | |

   The base jackpot for this lottery is $16,000,000. Find the expected value of a $1 ticket in this lottery.

4. The jackpot in the game from Exercise 3 may grow as high as $100 million!

   a. Suppose the jackpot is worth $m$ million dollars. Find the expected value of a ticket, in terms of $m$.

   b. If the jackpot is $100 million, what is the expected value of a ticket?

   c. How high must the jackpot be for the expected value to be greater than $1 per ticket?

The jackpots that lotteries report are actually much more than the money that they pay out or that a player would get. A player has to pay taxes on winnings. Also, the lottery pays the jackpot over many years, not all up front. In fact, it is rare for the jackpot to grow above $100 million in most lotteries.

5. **Take It Further** A second multistate lottery has a 5-ball component with 56 balls, and then a bonus ball from a separate set of 46 balls.

   Copy and complete this table for the frequency of each payout.

| Ticket Type | Frequency | Payout |
|---|---|---|
| 5 balls + bonus | 1 | Jackpot |
| 5 balls + no bonus | ■ | $250,000 |
| 4 balls + bonus | ■ | $10,000 |
| 4 balls + no bonus | 11,475 | $150 |
| 3 balls + bonus | ■ | $150 |
| 3 balls + no bonus | ■ | $7 |
| 2 balls + bonus | ■ | $10 |
| 1 ball + bonus | ■ | $3 |
| Bonus only | ■ | $2 |
| Losing ticket | 171,306,450 | $0 |
| **Total outcomes** | **175,711,536** | |

   Then, find the expected value of a $1 ticket at the base jackpot of $12 million.

6. A state-run raffle offers a number of prizes. A total of 500,000 tickets are available. Each ticket costs $20. These prizes are available:

| Payout | Frequency |
|---|---|
| $1,000,000 | 4 |
| $100,000 | 5 |
| $10,000 | 8 |
| $5,000 | 8 |
| $1,000 | 500 |
| $100 | 2000 |
| $0 (lose) | 497,475 |

   Find the expected value of a $20 raffle ticket.

## On Your Own

Go Online
www.successnetplus.com

7. Consider the 6-ball lottery with 42 balls from this lesson. Find the expected value for the number of balls that a player will correctly match.

8. Consider the following prize distribution from a large scratch ticket game.

| Payout | Frequency |
|---|---|
| $10,000,000 | 10 |
| $1,000,000 | 130 |
| $25,000 | 130 |
| $10,000 | 1,820 |
| $1,000 | 33,670 |
| $500 | 109,200 |
| $200 | 336,700 |
| $100 | 1,791,335 |
| $50 | 1,310,400 |
| $40 | 2,620,800 |
| $25 | 7,862,400 |
| $20 | 7,862,400 |
| $0 (lose) | 43,585,545 |
| **Total tickets** | **65,520,000** |

a. Find the expected value of one ticket.

b. Each ticket costs $20. If all tickets are sold, how much profit will be made by the state running this lottery?

9. A 6-ball lottery in Italy is the largest of its kind with 90 balls to pick from. A player wins a prize in this lottery if they get at least 3 of the 6 numbers right. What is the probability of winning a prize in this lottery?

10. Use the Internet to find information on a lottery or scratch ticket game. Determine the expected value on a ticket in that game.

**11.** Suppose a friend gives you six envelopes, each with a different address on it. You are to put one of six different letters in each envelope. But you have no idea which letter is for which person, so you stuff them in at random. You hope at least some of the envelopes contain the correct letter.

This frequency table lists the number of different permutations with 0 correct envelopes, 1 correct, and so on.

| Number Correct | Frequency |
|---|---|
| 0 | 265 |
| 1 | 264 |
| 2 | 135 |
| 3 | 40 |
| 4 | 15 |
| 5 | 0 |
| 6 | 1 |

**a.** What is the total number of outcomes in this sample space?

**b.** Find the expected value for the number of correct envelopes.

**12.** Standardized Test Prep A bag contains 16 red chips and 4 blue chips. Amy picks one chip. After returning the chip to the bag and remixing the chips, she reaches in a second time and picks one chip. If Amy is paid as shown in the table, what is the expected value of the amount she will win?

| Outcome | Payout |
|---|---|
| Two blue | wins $10 |
| One blue, one red | wins $1 |
| Two red | loses $1 |

**A.** loses at least $1 **B.** loses less than $1 **C.** Breaks even

**D.** wins less than $1 **E.** wins at least $1

## Maintain Your Skills

**13.** The numbers 7, 21, and 35 appear in the 7th row of Pascal's Triangle. These numbers are unusual in that they form an arithmetic sequence: add 14 to 7 to get 21, then add another 14 to get 35. Or, put another way, 21 is the mean of 7 and 35.

**a.** Find the next time this occurs in Pascal's Triangle.

**b.** Take It Further If $\binom{n}{k}$ is the mean of $\binom{n}{k-1}$ and $\binom{n}{k+1}$, find a relationship between $n$ and $k$.

**In this investigation, you calculated probabilities using Pascal's Triangle and polynomial powers. You also learned about expected value and its uses. The following questions will help you summarize what you have learned.**

1. How can you use the expansion of $(t + h)^5$ to find the probability of getting exactly two heads on five coin tosses?
2. **a.** Al wins a game if he flips a coin heads, and rolls less than a six on a number cube. What is the probability that Al wins the game?

   **b.** Beth wins a game if she flips a coin tails, or (after flipping heads) if she rolls a six on a number cube. What is the probability that Beth wins the game?
3. A wheel has the numbers 5 through 100 on it, in multiples of 5. What is the expected value of one spin of this wheel?
4. A 5-ball state lottery uses 49 balls. What is the probability of getting exactly four of the five balls correct?
5. A wheel has the numbers 1, 2, 3, and 6 on it. After spinning the wheel four times, what is the most likely total?
6. If you are to roll four number cubes, what is the probability they sum to 12?
7. What is expected value?
8. How can you use polynomials to solve probability problems?

## Vocabulary and Notation

In this investigation, you learned these terms and symbols. Make sure you understand what each one means and how to use it.

- **event**
- **expected value, $E(X)$**
- **frequency, $|A|$**
- **independent**
- **mutually exclusive**
- **outcome**
- **probability of an event**
- **random variable**
- **sample space**

If the survival rate for a hatchling to make it to the sea is 32%, how many in a group of 46 are expected to reach the sea?

# Expectation and Variation

**In *Expectation and Variation*, you will learn how to calculate an interval of values that you are likely to obtain when you perform an experiment involving data.**

**By the end of this investigation, you will be able to answer questions like these.**

1. How can you calculate the standard deviation for a large set of data?
2. What happens to the mean, variance, and standard deviation if an experiment is repeated a second time?
3. What is the mean and standard deviation for the number of heads on 400 coin flips?

**You will learn how to**

- calculate expected value, mean absolute deviation, variance, and standard deviation
- calculate statistics for compound events, including repeated experiments

**You will develop these habits and skills:**

- Interpret statistics in order to compare two data sets or make predictions.
- Understand $\Sigma$ notation and apply $\Sigma$ theorems.
- Reason deductively to prove relationships in statistics such as the "machine formula."

When flipping coins, you expect to get about half heads and half tails. The actual number of heads and tails cannot be predicted but the amount of variation can be calculated.

# 3.06 Getting Started

Here is an opportunity to explore how well you would do if you guessed at every question on a multiple-choice test.

## For You to Explore

1. On a separate piece of paper, take this multiple-choice test. For each of the 20 questions, select choice A, B, C, D, or E. Only one answer is correct. After the test, your class can compile the scores and build a histogram of the data.

   Oops, the questions are missing. Good luck!

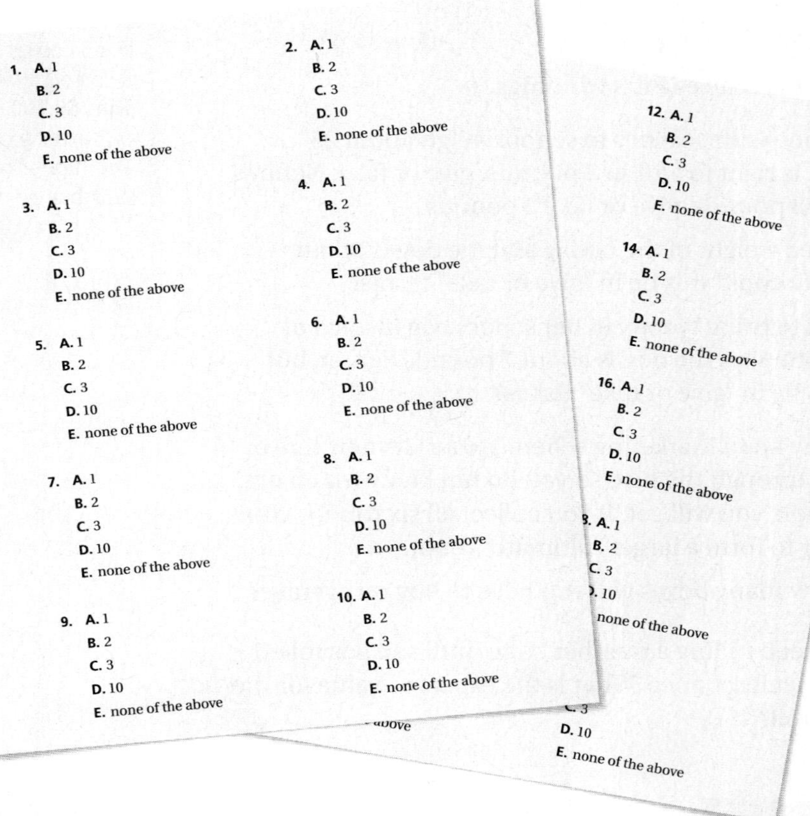


2. On average, how many questions would you expect each person in your class to get right? Explain.

3. **a.** Build a histogram for the number of questions each person in your class answered correctly.

   **b.** What percent of the class got between 2 and 6 correct, inclusive?

## Exercises Practicing Habits of Mind

### On Your Own

**4.** Bill is a contestant on a game show. On this show, Bill gets a random integer $n$ between 1 and 75. He then guesses whether the next number (picked from the remaining numbers) will be higher or lower. If Bill is correct, he wins \$100 times the new number. Bill's plan is to win as much money as possible. Determine whether Bill should pick higher or lower in each of the following cases.

**a.** $n = 25$ **b.** $n = 38$ **c.** $n = 39$ **d.** $n = 42$

**e.** Describe a strategy that maximizes Bill's winnings.

So, he wins only \$300 if a 3 comes out after a correct guess, but he wins \$6,700 if a 67 comes out after a correct guess. The higher numbers are worth a lot more!

**5.** Nancy estimates that the books she carries to school weigh about 25 pounds. Nancy figures she is right to within 3 pounds, give or take. Nancy's dog Woody weighs about 18 pounds, give or take 2 pounds.

**a.** Nancy says the combined weight of the books and the dog is about 43 pounds. How accurate could this be in "give or take" terms?

**b.** One day, Nancy decides to bring Woody in her school bag instead of books (a lighter load!). She says the dog is about 7 pounds lighter, but how accurate could this be in "give or take" terms?

**6.** Take It Further A company has a marketing scheme to sell its new line of toy robots. You cannot see through the box, so you do not know which one of the six equally likely robots you will get. If you collect all six robots, you can connect them together to form a larger "ultimate" robot.

To collect all six robots, how many boxes will you have to buy on average?

**7.** Take It Further Bree will keep rolling a number cube until she has rolled each number (1 through 6) at least once. What is the expected value for the number of times Bree will roll?

### Maintain Your Skills

**8.** Calculate each sum.

**a.** $\sum_{k=1}^{9} k$ **b.** $\sum_{k=1}^{9} k^2$ **c.** $\sum_{k=1}^{9} \frac{k^2}{9}$

**d.** $\sum_{k=1}^{9} \frac{(k-5)^2}{9}$ **e.** $\sqrt{\sum_{k=1}^{9} \frac{(k-5)^2}{9}}$

## 3.07 Variance and Standard Deviation

When you do an experiment repeatedly, it is likely that your results will cluster around the expected value of the experiment. You can measure how well they cluster by calculating the standard deviation.

### In-Class Experiment

As the winner of a contest, you get to pick one of three spinners and spin it. You will earn \$1 multiplied by the number you spin.

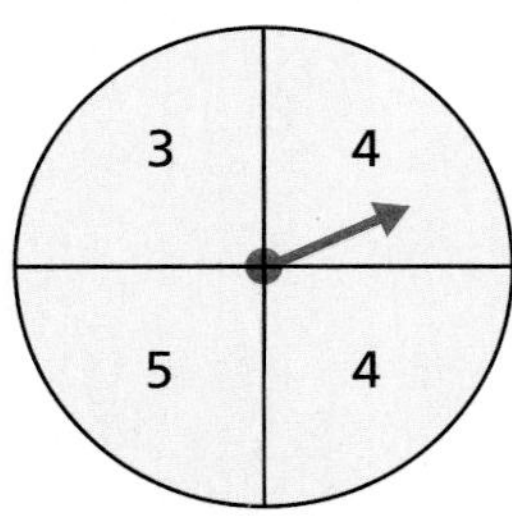


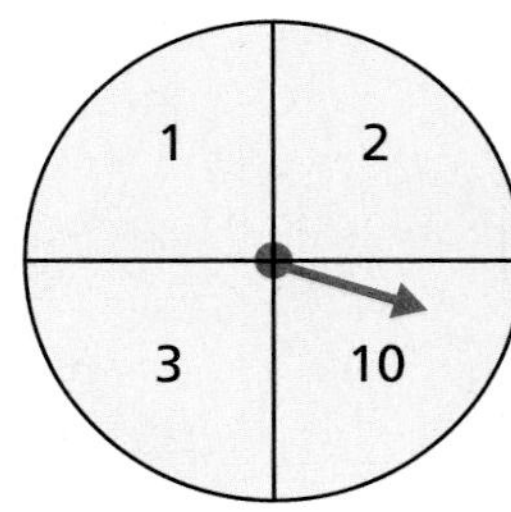


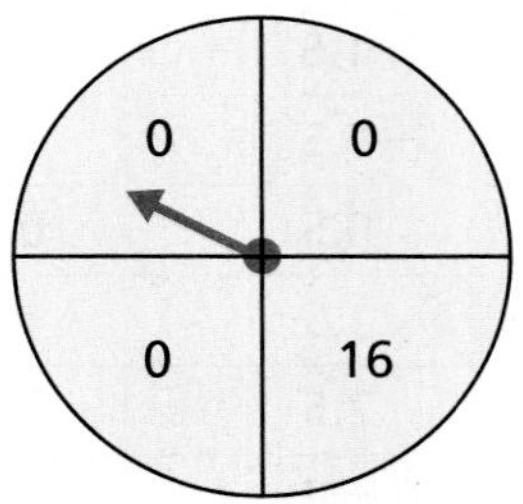


**1.** For each spinner, calculate the expected value of the spin. Which spinner would you choose? Explain your choice. Would your answer change if you were spinning for \$10,000 multiplied by the spin?

Suppose for a random variable $X$, the $n$ outputs $x_1$ through $x_n$ are all equally likely. Then, as you learned in Investigation 3A, the expected value $E(X)$ is equal to the mean $\overline{x}$.

$$E(X) = \frac{x_1 + x_2 + \cdots + x_n}{n} = \frac{\sum_i x_i}{n} = \overline{x}$$

With equally likely outcomes, the expected value and the mean are interchangeable. So, both $E(Y)$ and $\overline{y}$ denote the expected value for random variable $Y$ with equally likely outcomes.

The three spinners in the In-Class Experiment each have the same expected value. But there are major differences in the **spread** of each. Most measures of spread start by calculating the **deviation** of each result from the mean. For example, if $X$ is the random variable corresponding to the value on one number cube roll, its possible values are 1, 2, 3, 4, 5, and 6. Its mean is $\overline{x} = 3.5$. The table at the right calculates the deviations for each result.

| x | Deviation $x - \overline{x}$ |
|---|---|
| 1 | −2.5 |
| 2 | −1.5 |
| 3 | −0.5 |
| 4 | 0.5 |
| 5 | 1.5 |
| 6 | 2.5 |

Deviation may be positive, negative, or zero.

## For You to Do

**2.** For each spinner in the In-Class Experiment, calculate the deviations from the mean. Then calculate the sum of the deviations.

Three common measures of spread arise from deviations. You can use these measures to judge how wide a distribution is, or to compare distributions. A larger spread means the distribution is wider.

**Habits of Mind**

**Understand the process.** For each of these measures of spread, the name will tell you how to calculate it.

The first measure of spread is the **mean absolute deviation.** Calculate it by finding the absolute value of each deviation, then finding the mean of these numbers.

| $x$ | Deviation $x - \bar{x}$ | $\|x - \bar{x}\|$ |
|---|---|---|
| 1 | −2.5 | 2.5 |
| 2 | −1.5 | 1.5 |
| 3 | −0.5 | 0.5 |
| 4 | 0.5 | 0.5 |
| 5 | 1.5 | 1.5 |
| 6 | 2.5 | 2.5 |
| | **Total** | **9** |

The mean absolute deviation for one number cube roll is $\frac{9}{6} = \frac{3}{2} = 1.5$.

The second measure is the **mean squared deviation.** Calculate it by finding the square of each deviation, then finding the mean of these numbers.

| $x$ | Deviation $x - \bar{x}$ | $(x - \bar{x})^2$ |
|---|---|---|
| 1 | −2.5 | 6.25 |
| 2 | −1.5 | 2.25 |
| 3 | −0.5 | 0.25 |
| 4 | 0.5 | 0.25 |
| 5 | 1.5 | 2.25 |
| 6 | 2.5 | 6.25 |
| | **Total** | **17.5** |

The mean squared deviation for one number cube roll is $\frac{17.5}{6} = \frac{35}{12} \approx 2.917$. Note that you can express the mean squared deviation as

$$\frac{\sum_i (x_i - \bar{x})^2}{n}$$

The third measure is the **root mean squared deviation.** Calculate it by finding the square root of the mean squared deviation. The root mean squared deviation for one number cube roll is approximately 1.708.

## Developing Habits of Mind

**Reason about calculations.** Why would anyone use the root mean squared deviation if it is just the square root of another measure? The biggest reason is units. Squaring changes the units, so the mean squared deviation is not in the same units. Consider the second spinner from the In-Class Experiment, with outcomes 1, 2, 3, and 10 and mean 4. Include the units (dollars).

| Payout $x$ | Deviation $x - \bar{x}$ | $(x - \bar{x})^2$ |
|---|---|---|
| \$1 | −3 dollars | 9 square dollars |
| \$2 | −2 dollars | 4 square dollars |
| \$3 | −1 dollar | 1 square dollar |
| \$10 | 6 dollars | 36 square dollars |
| | **Total** | **50 square dollars** |

The mean squared deviation is $\frac{50}{4} = 12.5$ square dollars! By taking the square root, the result is in dollars again.

Of the three measures of spread, the last two are so common that they have shorter names. **Variance** is the shorter, more common name for mean squared deviation. **Standard deviation** is the common name for root mean squared deviation. You may want to remember the longer names, because they reveal the calculations involved and make an underlying relationship more clear:

**Standard deviation is the square root of variance**

Standard deviation is a good measure of the spread of data. Most data will be within one standard deviation of the mean. For example, the mean height for adult women is 63.5 inches. The standard deviation is 2.5 inches. Most adult women are between 61 and 66 inches tall. 61 and 66 are each one standard deviation away from the mean of 63.5.

See the TI-Nspire Handbook on p. 817 for details on how to calculate variance and standard deviation.

### *Definitions*

The *variance* $\sigma^2$ for a data set $\{x_1, x_2, \ldots, x_n\}$ is given by

$$\sigma^2 = \frac{\sum_i (x_i - \bar{x})^2}{n}$$

where $\bar{x}$ is the mean of the data set.

The *standard deviation* $\sigma$ for a data set is the square root of the variance and is given by

$$\sigma = \sqrt{\frac{\sum_i (x_i - \bar{x})^2}{n}}$$

These same formulas apply when you view the data as the outputs of a random variable $X$ (rather than as just a set of outcomes). If the outputs $x_i$ are all equally likely, the expected value $E(X)$ is equal to the mean $\overline{x}$. So, you can write the variance as

$$V(X) = E\left((X - E(X))^2\right)$$

A short formula for variance exists: variance is "the mean of the squares minus the square of the mean." Often, this is easier to calculate. For a number cube roll of 1 through 6 consider the following calculations.

When you compute the variance using this easier calculation, you are using the "machine formula."

- The *mean of the squares* is $(1 + 4 + 9 + 16 + 25 + 36)$ divided by 6, which is $\frac{91}{6}$.
- The *square of the mean* is $\left(\frac{7}{2}\right)^2 = \frac{49}{4}$.
- The difference between these is $\frac{91}{6} - \frac{49}{4} = \frac{35}{12}$. This is the same value for the variance that you calculated using the mean squared deviation.

Below is a proof that this short formula follows from the definition of mean squared deviation, by using binomial expansion and some properties of sums.

**Proof**

$$\begin{aligned}
\frac{\sum_i (x_i - \overline{x})^2}{n} &= \frac{\sum_i (x_i^2 - 2x_i\overline{x} + \overline{x}^2)}{n} \\
&= \sum_i \frac{x_i^2}{n} - 2\sum_i \frac{x_i\overline{x}}{n} + \sum_i \frac{\overline{x}^2}{n} \\
&= \sum_i \frac{x_i^2}{n} - 2\overline{x}\sum_i \frac{x_i}{n} + \overline{x}^2\sum_i \frac{1}{n} \\
&= \sum_i \frac{x_i^2}{n} - 2\overline{x}^2 + \overline{x}^2 \\
&= \sum_i \frac{x_i^2}{n} - \overline{x}^2 \\
&= \overline{x^2} - \overline{x}^2
\end{aligned}$$

## For Discussion

3. For each step in the deviation of the machine formula, give a justification. Why is it okay to pull $\overline{x}$ out of the sum? Where does the $\overline{x}^2$ come from in the middle term? How does the $\sum_i \frac{1}{n}$ just disappear?

# Exercises *Practicing Habits of Mind*

## Check Your Understanding

A standard number cube has the numbers 1 through 6. You know from this lesson that the numbers on the faces have the following statistics.

mean $\bar{x} = 3.5$

mean absolute deviation $= 1.5$

mean squared deviation (variance) $\sigma^2 = \frac{35}{12} \approx 2.917$

root mean squared deviation (standard deviation) $\sigma = \sqrt{\frac{35}{12}} \approx 1.708$

For each nonstandard number cube listed below, calculate each of these:

**a.** the mean

**b.** the mean absolute deviation

**c.** the variance

**d.** the standard deviation

**1.** A number cube with the numbers 2, 3, 4, 5, 6, 7

**2.** A number cube with the numbers 2, 4, 6, 8, 10, 12

**3.** A number cube with the numbers 1, 2, 3, 4, 5, 5

**4.** A number cube with the numbers 3, 3, 3, 3, 3, 3

**5.** Write About It

**a.** When you add a constant $c$ to each element in a data set, what happens to the mean, mean absolute deviation, variance, and standard deviation? Give an additional example using a new data set.

**b.** When you multiply each element of a data set by a constant $k$, what happens to the mean, mean absolute deviation, variance, and standard deviation? Give an additional example using a new data set.

6. This frequency table gives the results when 500 students took the 20-question multiple choice test from the Getting Started lesson.

| Score | Frequency |
|---|---|
| 0 | 5 |
| 1 | 34 |
| 2 | 74 |
| 3 | 100 |
| 4 | 100 |
| 5 | 85 |
| 6 | 59 |
| 7 | 29 |
| 8 | 10 |
| 9 | 4 |
| 10+ | 0 |

This is a data set with 500 elements! Think about how you might simplify the calculation. Since this is a frequency table, the mean is not the average of 5, 34, 74, . . . , but the mean of 0, 0, 0, 0, 0, 1, 1, 1, 1, . . . , 8, 9, 9, 9, 9.

Find the mean and standard deviation for this data.

7. **Take It Further** Use algebra and what you know about sums to prove the claims made in Exercise 5.

8. When you roll two standard number cubes, there are 36 possible outcomes. Calculate the mean, mean absolute deviation, variance, and standard deviation for the sum of the numbers rolled for all 36 possible outcomes. Compare to the results from the numbers on one number cube.

## On Your Own

9. Define a random variable for a coin flip as follows. The random variable $X$ equals 1 if the coin flip is heads. It equals 0 if the coin flip is tails.

   a. Calculate $E(X)$, the expected value for $X$.

   b. Calculate the deviation for $X$ for each possible outcome.

   c. Calculate the mean absolute deviation, the variance, and the standard deviation for the number of heads on one coin flip.

How often will $X = 1$? How often will $X = 0$? Remember, deviation can be negative.

10. Define a random variable for two coin flips as follows. The random variable $Y$ equals 2 if both coins are heads, 1 if exactly one coin is heads, and 0 if both coins are tails.

    a. Calculate $E(Y)$, the expected value for $Y$.

    b. Calculate the deviation for $Y$ for each of the four outcomes.

    c. Calculate the mean absolute deviation, the variance, and the standard deviation for the number of heads on two coin flips.

11. Your class should have data for the 20-question test from the Getting Started lesson. Each element in the data set is the number of correct answers for a particular student. For your class's data, find the mean, mean absolute deviation, variance, and standard deviation.

This might be a good place to use the machine formula for variance: the mean of the squares, minus the square of the mean.

12. Consider this set of 16 sums from Derman's table in Lesson 3.04.

| + | 1 | 2 | 3 | 10 |
|---|---|---|---|---|
| **1** | 2 | 3 | 4 | 11 |
| **2** | 3 | 4 | 5 | 12 |
| **3** | 4 | 5 | 6 | 13 |
| **10** | 11 | 12 | 13 | 20 |

**a.** Build a second table with each element's deviation from the mean.

**b.** Find the mean absolute deviation and the mean squared deviation for the 16 sums.

**c.** Which is larger, the mean absolute deviation or the standard deviation?

13. What's Wrong Here? Dani thinks that adding deviations is useful.

Dani: Why do we have to do absolute value or squaring? It seems like we should be able to just find the deviations from the mean, then add them up. Done, and done.

Make an argument to convince Dani that adding the deviations is not a helpful calculation.

14. Find the mean, mean absolute deviation, variance, and standard deviation for the data set $\{1, 2, 3, 4, 5, 6, 7, 8, 9, 10\}$.

**Go Online**
www.successnetplus.com

15. Take It Further In terms of $n$, find formulas for the mean, mean absolute deviation, variance, and standard deviation for the data set $\{1, 2, 3 \dots, n\}$.

16. Standardized Test Prep The table shows the frequency of each score possible in a game. Find the (mean, variance) for the score.

| Score | Frequency |
|---|---|
| −5 | 2 |
| 0 | 1 |
| 1 | 2 |
| 2 | 1 |

**A.** $\left(-\frac{1}{3}, \frac{10}{3}\right)$ **B.** $\left(-\frac{1}{3}, \frac{25}{3}\right)$

**C.** $\left(-1, \frac{10}{3}\right)$ **D.** $\left(-1, \frac{25}{3}\right)$

## Maintain Your Skills

17. Find the variance for each data set.

**a.** $\{1, 1, 1, 2, 2, 11\}$ **b.** $\{1, 1, 1, 8, 8, 11\}$

**c.** $\{1, 1, 1, 11, 11, 11\}$ **d.** $\{1, 1, 1, n, n, 11\}$

## 3.08 Adding Variances

You can view two separate experiments as one big experiment. If you do, there is a way to combine information about the two experiments to find the expected value and variance of the one big experiment.

### In-Class Experiment

Here are two spinners. One is from the previous lesson, and the other one is a new one.

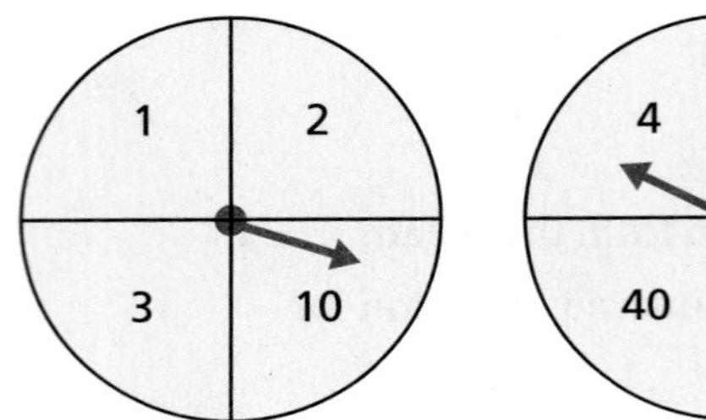

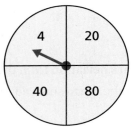

In this game, you spin each spinner once. Let $Z$ be the random variable defined by the sum of the values on the two spinners.

1. Find the mean, mean absolute deviation, mean squared deviation, and root mean squared deviation for the values when spinning each spinner.
2. Use polynomial expansion to quickly find the 16 possible values for the random variable $Z$.
3. Find the mean, mean absolute deviation, mean squared deviation, and root mean squared deviation for $Z$.

**Remember...**

The mean squared deviation and the root mean squared deviation are more commonly called the *variance* and *standard deviation*.

An investment manager adds variances to find the overall risk of an investment portfolio.

## Minds in Action

*Sasha and Derman are working on the In-Class Experiment.*

**Derman** Let's start playing the game.

**Sasha** Derman! We can't do this by playing. We'd have to play thousands of times. This is about what will happen *on average*.

**Derman** So, how are we supposed to do that?

**Sasha** Come on, Derman. You can look back at the last lesson if you've forgotten how to find any of these things.

**Derman** Alright, I'm going to find the mean for each spinner by averaging. The mean for the first spinner is 4. The mean for the second spinner is 36. So, the mean for $Z$, when you add them, should be 40.

**Sasha** That seems like it makes sense.

**Derman** I'm making a list of the 16 possible results . . . hey, it worked!

**Sasha** That was a good idea.

**Derman** Alright, on to the next one. The mean absolute deviation for the first spinner is 3 . . . and for the second spinner is 24 . . . so for $Z$ it should be 27.

**Sasha** Did you calculate it?

**Derman** I added 3 and 24.

**Sasha** Let's just check, I'm not so sure this time. Unfortunately . . . you lose. It's 24, not 27.

**Derman** What? It worked for the mean, it's supposed to work on everything. Do it again.

**Sasha** Derman. It's still 24. I think it only works for the mean. Not everything adds like that.

**Derman** Alright, alright, what about the variance?

**Sasha** The variance for the first spinner is 12.5. The variance for the second spinner is 808.

**Derman** So the variance for $Z$ will be 820.5.

**Sasha** You wish. You can't just add these things.

**Derman** Au contraire. *I* win. It *is* 820.5. Exactly.

*Sasha, baffled, performs the calculation.*

**Sasha** Wow! You're kidding me. I can't believe that worked. Does that always work? That would be amazing. I've gotta see why.

Sasha and Derman suspect that mean and variance are additive.

## Example

**Problem** Find the mean and variance for the sum when tossing two standard number cubes. Compare to the mean and variance for the value from tossing one number cube.

**Solution** You calculated the mean and variance for one number cube in Lesson 3.07. The mean is 3.5. The variance is $\frac{35}{12} \approx 2.917$.

For the sum of the numbers on two number cubes, expand the polynomial $(x + x^2 + x^3 + x^4 + x^5 + x^6)^2$ or make a table of the 36 outcomes in the sample space, as you did in Investigation 3A.

| + | 1 | 2 | 3 | 4 | 5 | 6 |
|---|---|---|---|---|---|---|
| **1** | 2 | 3 | 4 | 5 | 6 | 7 |
| **2** | 3 | 4 | 5 | 6 | 7 | 8 |
| **3** | 4 | 5 | 6 | 7 | 8 | 9 |
| **4** | 5 | 6 | 7 | 8 | 9 | 10 |
| **5** | 6 | 7 | 8 | 9 | 10 | 11 |
| **6** | 7 | 8 | 9 | 10 | 11 | 12 |

Determine the expected value by building a frequency table as in Lesson 3.04.

| Sum | Frequency | Product |
|---|---|---|
| 2 | 1 | 2 |
| 3 | 2 | 6 |
| 4 | 3 | 12 |
| 5 | 4 | 20 |
| 6 | 5 | 30 |
| 7 | 6 | 42 |
| 8 | 5 | 40 |
| 9 | 4 | 36 |
| 10 | 3 | 30 |
| 11 | 2 | 22 |
| 12 | 1 | 12 |
| **Total** | **36** | **252** |

See the TI-Nspire Handbook on p. 817 for help in using a spreadsheet to perform these calculations.

The expected value is $\frac{252}{36} = 7$.

Use a similar table to calculate the mean squared deviation. Here, multiply each squared deviation by the frequency of the outcome.

| Sum | Frequency | Deviation $x - \bar{x}$ | Deviation$^2$ | Freq · Dev.$^2$ |
|---|---|---|---|---|
| 2 | 1 | −5 | 25 | 25 |
| 3 | 2 | −4 | 16 | 32 |
| 4 | 3 | −3 | 9 | 27 |
| 5 | 4 | −2 | 4 | 16 |
| 6 | 5 | −1 | 1 | 5 |
| 7 | 6 | 0 | 0 | 0 |
| 8 | 5 | 1 | 1 | 5 |
| 9 | 4 | 2 | 4 | 16 |
| 10 | 3 | 3 | 9 | 27 |
| 11 | 2 | 4 | 16 | 32 |
| 12 | 1 | 5 | 25 | 25 |
| **Total** | **36** | | | **210** |

The variance (mean squared deviation) is $\frac{210}{36} = \frac{35}{6} \approx 5.833$.

Note that both the mean and variance for the sums when rolling two number cubes are exactly double the mean and variance for the values of one number cube.

**Habits of Mind**

**Visualize.** Think about what the table might look like if it had 36 rows so each outcome had its own line. The result for ways to roll a 4 is multiplied by three, since there are three ways to roll a 4. The result for 11 is multiplied by two, since there are two ways an outcome of 11 can occur.

## For You to Do

**4.** Take a guess at the mean and variance for the sums of the numbers when rolling three number cubes.

### Proving It

The proofs that mean and variance add are complicated. Keep this picture in mind for what the combined sample space looks like when the sample spaces of two random variables $X$ and $Y$ are combined:

| + | $x_1$ | $x_2$ | ... | $x_n$ |
|---|---|---|---|---|
| $y_1$ | $x_1 + y_1$ | $x_2 + y_1$ | ... | $x_n + y_1$ |
| $y_2$ | $x_1 + y_2$ | $x_2 + y_2$ | ... | $x_n + y_2$ |
| $y_3$ | $x_1 + y_3$ | $x_2 + y_3$ | ... | $x_n + y_3$ |
| $\vdots$ | $\vdots$ | $\vdots$ | $\ddots$ | $\vdots$ |
| $y_m$ | $x_1 + y_m$ | $x_2 + y_m$ | ... | $x_n + y_m$ |

### *Theorem 3.2*

**Let $Z$ be the random variable defined by adding the results of independent random variables $X$ and $Y$. Then**

- **The expected value, or mean, of $Z$ is the sum of the expected values for $X$ and $Y$, and**
- **The variance, or mean squared deviation, of $Z$ is the sum of the variances for $X$ and $Y$.**

**Proof** First, prove the property for the mean. Let $\bar{x}$ be the mean for $X$ with $n$ outcomes and $\bar{y}$ be the mean for $Y$ with $m$ outcomes. (See the table on page 221.) Of the $mn$ outcomes for $Z$, each value $x_1$ through $x_n$ occurs $m$ times, one for each $y$-pairing. Each value $y_1$ through $y_m$ occurs $n$ times. So, the mean for random variable $Z$ is as follows.

$$\begin{aligned}\bar{z} &= \frac{m(x_1 + x_2 + \cdots + x_n) + n(y_1 + y_2 + \cdots + y_m)}{mn} \\ &= \frac{m(x_1 + x_2 + \cdots + x_n)}{mn} + \frac{n(y_1 + y_2 + \cdots + y_m)}{mn} \\ &= \frac{(x_1 + x_2 + \cdots + x_n)}{n} + \frac{(y_1 + y_2 + \cdots + y_m)}{m} \\ &= \bar{x} + \bar{y}\end{aligned}$$

The proof for the variance uses the machine formula from Lesson 3.07. You want to show that $V(Z) = V(X) + V(Y)$. But the machine formula states that the variance is the mean of the squares less the square of the means. So, the goal is to show that

$$\overline{z^2} - \bar{z}^2 = (\overline{x^2} - \bar{x}^2) + (\overline{y^2} - \bar{y}^2)$$

Rewrite $\bar{z}$ as $\bar{x} + \bar{y}$ and expand. The left side becomes

$$\begin{aligned}\overline{z^2} - \bar{z}^2 &= \overline{z^2} - (\bar{x} + \bar{y})^2 \\ &= \overline{z^2} - (\bar{x}^2 + 2\bar{x} \cdot \bar{y} + \bar{y}^2)\end{aligned}$$

Think about how to calculate $\overline{z^2}$. First square each possible value of $Z$. Then add the squares and divide by $mn$ at the end. Each value of $Z$ is of the form $x_i + y_j$ for some $i$ and $j$, so its square is $x_i^2 + 2x_iy_j + y_j^2$. Think about how many times each number appears. The number of terms is $mn$. Each $x_i^2$ appears $m$ times, each $y_j^2$ appears $n$ times, and every possible pair of $x_iy_j$ occurs once. So,

$$\begin{aligned}\overline{z^2} &= \frac{m\left(\sum_i x_i^2\right) + n\left(\sum_j y_j^2\right) + 2\sum_i \sum_j x_iy_j}{mn} \\ &= \frac{\sum_i x_i^2}{n} + \frac{\sum_j y_j^2}{m} + 2\frac{\sum_i \sum_j x_iy_j}{mn} \\ &= \overline{x^2} + \overline{y^2} + 2\overline{xy}\end{aligned}$$

**Remember...**

$\bar{x}$ is the same as $E(X)$, the expected value of the random variable $X$. For example, if $X$ is the value when rolling a number cube, $\bar{x} = E(X) = 3.5$.

**Habits of Mind**

**Try a specific case.** This proof may seem clearer if you try working it out completely for a small example, say $m = 3$ and $n = 4$.

When you see $\sum_i \sum_j x_i y_j$, that means that you sum all the products $x_iy_j$ over all $i$ and $j$, in other words, match every $x_i$ with every $y_j$.

$$\overline{z^2} - \overline{z}^2 = \overline{x^2} + \overline{y^2} + 2\overline{xy} - \overline{x}^2 - 2\overline{x} \cdot \overline{y} - \overline{y}^2$$
$$= \left(\overline{x^2} + \overline{x}^2\right) + \left(\overline{y^2} - \overline{y}^2\right) + 2\overline{xy} - 2\overline{x} \cdot \overline{y}$$
$$= V(X) + V(Y) + 2\overline{xy} - 2\overline{x} \cdot \overline{y}$$

This is very close to what you want to show. However, you still need to show that $\overline{xy} = \overline{x} \cdot \overline{y}$ (the mean of the product is the product of the means). This is true whenever $X$ and $Y$ are independent random variables. The proof of this fact is left as Exercise 14. Once this is known, the proof is complete: the variance of $Z$ is the sum of the variances of $X$ and $Y$.

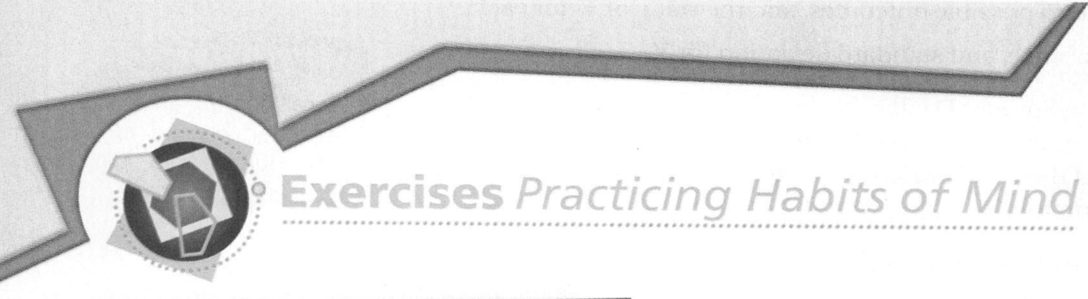

## Exercises *Practicing Habits of Mind*

### Check Your Understanding

1. a. Use a polynomial power to write a frequency table for the sums when rolling three number cubes.
   b. Find the mean for the sums when rolling three number cubes.
   c. Using the mean, find the variance and standard deviation for the sums when rolling three number cubes.
   d. How many times as large is the variance for the sums for three number cubes than the variance for one number cube?
   e. How many times as large is the standard deviation for the sums for three number cubes than the standard deviation for the values from rolling one number cube?

2. Find the mean, variance, and standard deviation for the values when spinning each spinner.

   a. Spinner A

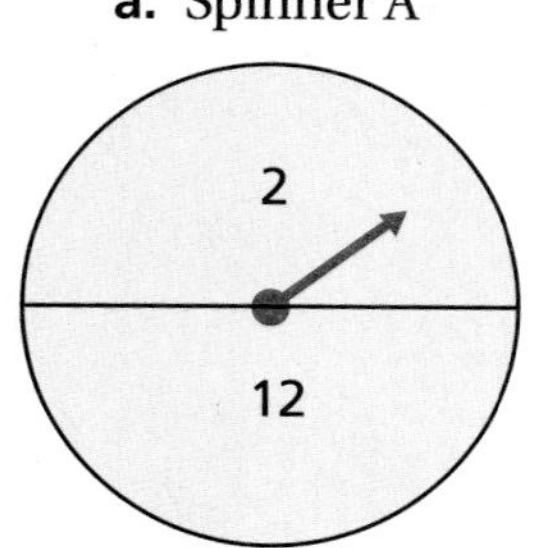


   b. Spinner B

   c. Spinner C

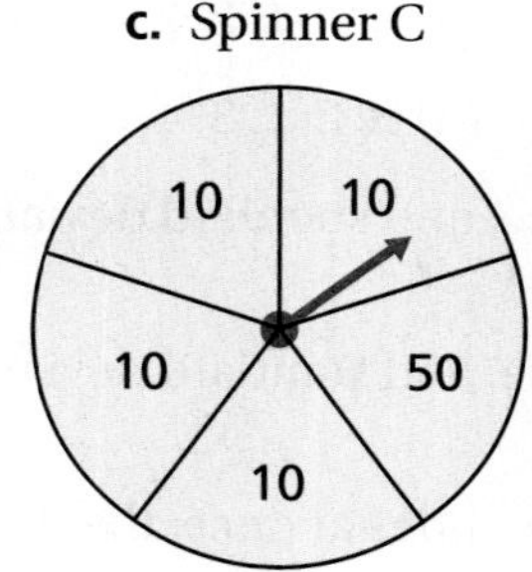

3. Consider spinners A and B from Exercise 2. Let $X$ be the random variable defined as the sum of the values when spinning A and B once each.

   a. Build a table of the 10 possible values of $X$.

   b. Find the mean, variance, and standard deviation of $X$.

4. Consider spinners B and C from Exercise 2. Let $Y$ be the random variable defined as the sum of the values when spinning B and C once each.

   a. Build a table of the 25 possible outcomes, and the value of $Y$ for each.

   b. Find the mean, variance, and standard deviation for $Y$.

**Remember...**

Recall how variance is related to standard deviation.

5. Suppose the values on Spinner D have standard deviation 8. Also, the values on Spinner E have standard deviation 15. Let $Z$ be the random variable defined as the sum of the values when spinning $D$ and $E$ once each. What is the standard deviation for $Z$?

6. a. Calculate the mean absolute deviation for each spinner $A$, $B$, and $C$ in Exercise 2.

   b. Calculate the mean absolute deviation for $X$, the random variable for the resulting sum of spinning A and B.

   c. Calculate the mean absolute deviation for $Y$, the random variable for the resulting sum of spinning B and C.

   d. What pattern, if any, emerges for the mean absolute deviation of the combined spinners?

7. **Write About It** The additive property of variance is sometimes called the "Pythagorean Theorem of Statistics." Why do you suppose this is, in light of the results from Exercises 3 through 5?

## On Your Own

8. Consider two number cubes with different numbers on their faces:

   Cube 1: 1, 2, 2, 3, 3, 4

   Cube 2: 1, 3, 4, 5, 6, 8

   a. Find the mean, variance, and standard deviation for the result when rolling Cube 1 once.

   b. Find the mean, variance, and standard deviation for the result when rolling Cube 2 once.

   c. If you roll both number cubes at once, there are 36 outcomes. Find the mean, variance, and standard deviation for the sum when rolling the two number cubes.

**9.** Here is an experiment: Roll a standard number cube. Spin Spinner A from Exercise 2. Then, add the numbers that result.

Find the mean, variance, and standard deviation for each of the 12 possible outcomes.

See if you can do this exercise without writing out the 12 outcomes.

**10.** Take It Further Kevin is challenged to roll a sum of 15 from standard number cubes. He can choose how many number cubes to roll. How many number cubes gives Kevin the best chance of rolling a sum of 15?

**11.** What's Wrong Here? Cayle looked at the data from Exercise 12 in Lesson 3.07:

| + | 1 | 2 | 3 | 10 |
|---|---|---|---|---|
| **1** | 2 | 3 | 4 | 11 |
| **2** | 3 | 4 | 5 | 12 |
| **3** | 4 | 5 | 6 | 13 |
| **10** | 11 | 12 | 13 | 20 |

Cayle: I know this data comes from two spins of that fish wheel with 1, 2, 3, 10 on it. And I know the standard deviation for one spin is about 3.54. So, the standard deviation for two spins should be $3.54 + 3.54$, just over 7. But I am *not* getting that answer! I've checked it three times.

Explain what went wrong here, and how the correct standard deviation could be calculated.

**12.** Jane is designing a game of chance for her school's Random Fair. It costs 50 cents to play Jane's game. The player flips a coin. Then the player rolls a number cube. If the player gets heads on the coin flip, the number cube result is multiplied by 20 cents. That money is the prize. If the player gets tails on the coin flip, though, the number cube result is multiplied by 5 cents. Although everyone takes away some money, most people do not make back the price of the game.

**a.** List the sample space for Jane's game as a set of equally likely outcomes.

**b.** Calculate the expected value for Jane's game. Will Jane's game make money for the fair over time?

**c.** Calculate the variance and standard deviation for Jane's game.

**d.** What's Wrong Here? Jane wants to check her variance calculation by computing it two ways. In the first way, she uses the data and the machine formula. In the second way, she adds the variance for one coin flip to the variance for one number cube roll. The two methods do not give the same result. Where did Jane go wrong?

13. The variance for one spin of the Wheel of Fish with the numbers 1, 2, 3, and 10 is 12.5.

a. Calculate the variance and standard deviation for the sum of two spins.

b. Calculate the variance and standard deviation for the sum of three spins.

c. Verify that your answers to part (b) are correct by calculating the sum of three spins for all 64 outcomes, then calculating the variance for the data.

14. Consider the following table for the product of independent random variables $X$ and $Y$.

| $\cdot$ | $x_1$ | $x_2$ | $\cdots$ | $x_n$ |
|---|---|---|---|---|
| $y_1$ | $x_1 \cdot y_1$ | $x_2 \cdot y_1$ | $\cdots$ | $x_n \cdot y_1$ |
| $y_2$ | $x_1 \cdot y_2$ | $x_2 \cdot y_2$ | $\cdots$ | $x_n \cdot y_2$ |
| $y_3$ | $x_1 \cdot y_3$ | $x_2 \cdot y_3$ | $\cdots$ | $x_n \cdot y_3$ |
| $\vdots$ | $\vdots$ | $\vdots$ | $\ddots$ | $\vdots$ |
| $y_m$ | $x_1 \cdot y_m$ | $x_2 \cdot y_m$ | $\cdots$ | $x_n \cdot y_m$ |

Show that the mean of the products is the product of the means for the original random variables. That is,

$$\overline{xy} = \overline{x} \cdot \overline{y}$$

This completes the proof given in the lesson.

15. **Standardized Test Prep** For a random positive integer less than 1001, what is the probability that the number is neither divisible by 2 nor 5?

**A.** 0.1 **B.** 0.4 **C.** 0.5 **D.** 0.6

## Maintain Your Skills

16. Suppose you are to pick an integer at random. Find the probability of each event.

a. The number is not divisible by 2.

b. The number is not divisible by 5.

c. The number is neither divisible by 2 nor 5.

d. The number is divisible by 2 *or* 5 (or both).

17. Suppose you are to pick an integer at random. Find the probability that it is divisible by 4 or 13 (or both).

18. **Take It Further** Find some other values of $p$ and $q$ so that $\frac{p}{q}$ is the probability that an integer chosen at random is divisible by $p$ or $q$ (or both).

# 3.09 Repeated Experiments

Suppose you define a random variable $Z$ as the sum of two independent random variables $X$ and $Y$. In the previous lesson, you learned that the mean and variance of $Z$ are the sum of the means and variances of $X$ and $Y$. This knowledge can help you quickly calculate important statistics, especially the standard deviation for many consecutive trials of the same kind of experiment.

## For Discussion

1. Suppose you flip 100 coins. What is the average number of heads you would expect? Would 40 heads seem reasonable? What about 65 heads?

## In-Class Experiment

2. Flip 100 coins and count the total number of heads. Record your data along with all other data the class collects. What percent of the data was between 40 and 60 heads, inclusive? between 45 and 55 heads?

In Exercise 9 in Lesson 3.07 you found the mean, variance, and standard deviation for one coin flip. Recall for that experiment, a head counts as 1. A tail counts as 0. The mean is $\frac{1}{2}$, the variance is $\frac{1}{4}$, and the standard deviation is $\sqrt{\frac{1}{4}} = \frac{1}{2}$.

For two coin flips, there are four possible outcomes: HH, HT, TH, and TT. The mean number of heads is 1, which is twice the mean for one coin flip. This table calculates the variance:

Here, "HT" means that the first flip is heads, and the second flip is tails. HT and TH are two different outcomes.

| Outcome | Number of Heads | Deviation | Deviation$^2$ |
|---|---|---|---|
| HH | 2 | 1 | 1 |
| HT | 1 | 0 | 0 |
| TH | 1 | 0 | 0 |
| TT | 0 | −1 | 1 |
| **4 outcomes** | | | 2 |

The variance is $\frac{2}{4} = \frac{1}{2}$, which is twice the variance for one coin flip. The standard deviation is the square root of the variance, so it is $\sqrt{\frac{1}{2}} = \frac{\sqrt{2}}{2} \approx 0.707$.

## For You to Do

3. Consider three coin flips, with eight possible outcomes. Verify that the variance of the number of heads is exactly $\frac{3}{4}$.

Each coin flip adds $\frac{1}{2}$ to the mean number of heads tossed, and $\frac{1}{4}$ to the variance. The additive rules for mean and variance give these results for the number of heads in $n$ coin flips:

$$\text{mean: } \tfrac{1}{2}n$$

$$\text{variance: } \tfrac{1}{4}n$$

$$\text{standard deviation: } \sqrt{\tfrac{1}{4}n} = \tfrac{1}{2}\sqrt{n}$$

In Lesson 3.07, you learned that most data will be within one standard deviation of the mean.

For 100 coin flips, the standard deviation for the number of heads is $\frac{1}{2}\sqrt{100} = 5$. Most of the time you flip 100 coins, the number of heads will be between 45 and 55, one standard deviation away from the mean.

In a theoretical statistics course, you would prove that most of the data will be within one standard deviation of the mean. For now, your experiments should be enough.

Did most of your class flip between 45 and 55 heads in the In-Class Experiment? Did everyone?

The fact that mean and variance add can help you make similar observations about other repeated experiments. While most data will fall within one standard deviation of the mean, results outside this interval are likely.

### Two Kinds of Probability

As you learned in Investigation 3A, the probability of an event is the number of outcomes in that event, divided by the total number of outcomes in the sample space. This is known as **theoretical probability.** You use this kind of probability when the properties of an experiment are clear.

But many probability questions are not clear-cut. What is the probability that it will rain tomorrow? What is the probability that Teri will make her next free throw? In many cases where randomness is present, you have no way to determine the exact properties of the experiment. In these situations, experimental probability is all you can compute.

The **experimental probability** of an event is the number of times the event occurred, divided by the number of trials. If Teri has made 37 of 50 free throws, the experimental probability is $\frac{37}{50} = 0.74$. You might say that Teri has a 74% chance of making her next free throw. Experimental probability is more prone to change than theoretical probability. Maybe Teri had especially good or bad luck on her 50 shots. The greater the number of trials, the more accurate an experimental probability becomes.

## Developing Habits of Mind

**Make connections.** The result of a random experiment is rarely exactly equal to the expected value. If you flip 100 coins, getting exactly 50 heads is pretty unlikely. But the properties of mean and standard deviation can explain an important concept. Over time, experimental probability will come closer and closer to theoretical probability.

As the number of trials grows, the mean and standard deviation are both growing, because the mean and the variance (the square of the standard deviation) are additive. But the mean grows by the factor $n$. Also, the standard deviation grows by the factor $\sqrt{n}$. This means that the ratio

$$\frac{\text{standard deviation}}{\text{mean}}$$

gets smaller as $n$ grows. Consider 100 coin flips. The mean number of heads is 50. The standard deviation is 5 heads. Most of the time you flip 100 coins, the results will fall between $50 - 5 = 45$ and $50 + 5 = 55$ heads.

Now consider 2500 coin flips. The mean number of heads is 1250, and the standard deviation is 25 heads. Most of the time when you flip 2500 coins, the results will fall between $1250 - 25 = 1225$ and $1250 + 25 = 1275$ heads.

The spread is widening, but only when you consider the number of heads. If you consider the ratio of heads, the spread is narrowing. Most of the time you flip 100 coins, the ratio of heads will be between 0.45 and 0.55. But for 2500 flips, this spread narrows:

$$\frac{1225}{2500} \leq \text{ratio of heads} \leq \frac{1275}{2500}$$

$$0.49 \leq \text{ratio of heads} \leq 0.51$$

So most of the time you flip 2500 coins, you will get between 49% and 51% heads. If you continue to increase the number of coin flips, you can get the numbers as close to 50% as you like.

Equaling the expected value may even be impossible. It's impossible to roll a number cube and get 3.5, but that is the expected value.

### Habits of Mind

**Make strategic choices.** Why is 2500 flips a better choice here than 1000?

## For You to Do

**4.** What is the mean and standard deviation for the number of heads in 10,000 coin flips? Most of the time, the percentage of heads would be within what range?

# Exercises *Practicing Habits of Mind*

## Check Your Understanding

1. Avery answers one multiple-choice question with five options. He guesses. He scores a 1 if he is right, a 0 if he is wrong. Find the mean, variance, and standard deviation for the score on one question.

2. Avery answers two multiple-choice questions, still five options, still guessing.

   a. What is the probability that Avery scores a 2? a 1? a 0?

   b. Find the mean, variance, and standard deviation for the score on two questions.

3. Find the mean, variance, and standard deviation for the score on three multiple-choice questions with five options each.

4. A multiple-choice test has 20 questions, each with five options. Find the mean, variance, and standard deviation for the score on all 20 questions.

5. Find the variance and standard deviation for the number of heads when flipping each of the following.

   a. one coin
   b. two coins
   c. four coins
   d. nine coins
   e. 100 coins

6. You flip a coin 36 times. The result is 10 heads and 26 tails.

   a. Find the standard deviation for the number of heads tossed when flipping 36 coins.

   b. Is it particularly unusual to get only 10 heads? Use the standard deviation to decide.

   c. Take It Further Suppose you are to flip a fair coin 36 times. Find the probability that you get exactly 10 heads and 26 tails.

7. Take It Further An experiment has probability of success $p$.

   a. Find the mean, variance, and standard deviation for the number of successes in one such experiment (in terms of $p$).

   b. Find the mean, variance and standard deviation for the number of successes in $n$ such experiments (in terms of $n$ and $p$).

Check that your answers are correct for $p = \frac{1}{2}$. What if $p = 0$?

## On Your Own

8. A spinner has the numbers 25, 50, 75, and 100. Find the variance and standard deviation for the sum of each number of spins.
   a. one spin
   b. two spins
   c. four spins
   d. 100 spins

9. Find the variance and standard deviation for the number of sixes you get when rolling each number of number cubes.
   a. one number cube
   b. two number cubes
   c. four number cubes
   d. nine number cubes
   e. $n$ number cubes

10. You roll a number cube 50 times. The sum of the rolls is 165. Is this a particularly unusual result? Use the standard deviation to decide.

11. Take It Further
    a. You are to roll $n$ number cubes and count the number of sixes. Find the smallest integer $n$ so that the standard deviation is an integer.
    b. You are to roll $n$ number cubes and sum the results. Find the smallest positive integer $n$ so that the standard deviation is an integer.

12. A board game has a spinner with numbers 1 to 10.
    a. Find the mean and standard deviation when spinning this spinner 100 times.
    b. Would it be unlikely for you to get a total of 600 in 100 spins? Explain.

**13. Write About It** In a new promotion, 100 people will spin the Wheel of Fish for prizes. The manager of the market is hoping that no more than 500 fish will be given away. Is this a likely outcome? Use the standard deviation to decide.

**Remember...**

The Wheel of Fish has the numbers 1, 2, 3, 10 on it. The mean for one spin is 4, and the variance is 12.5.

**14. Standardized Test Prep** For each play of a game, the mean is 1 and the standard deviation is 1. Which of the following pairs of numbers represents the (mean, standard deviation) for 100 plays?

**a.** (1, 100)

**b.** (10, 100)

**c.** (100, 1)

**d.** (100, 10)

## Maintain Your Skills

**15.** You are to roll five number cubes. Find the probability that you roll

**a.** no sixes.

**b.** exactly one six.

**c.** exactly two sixes.

**d.** more than two sixes.

**16.** Expand $\left(\frac{1}{6}s + \frac{5}{6}n\right)^5$. How can you use this expansion to help answer the questions in Exercise 15?

**In this investigation, you calculated variance and standard deviation, which give you some sense of how much your results vary from the average outcome, or expected value, of an experiment. You then tailored these calculations to repeated experiments. The following questions will help you summarize what you have learned.**

1. If you guess on a 25-question multiple-choice test with five options, what is the expected number of correct answers? What is the standard deviation?
2. Find the variance for this set: {1, 2, 5, 7, 10, 11}.
3. A number cube has the numbers 1, 2, 2, 3, 3, and 4 on it. Find the mean, variance, and standard deviation for each random variable.
   a. the value of one roll of this number cube
   b. the sum of two rolls of this number cube
4. You are to roll 15 number cubes. Find the probability of getting no more than two sixes.
5. How can you calculate the standard deviation for a large set of data?
6. What happens to the mean, variance, and standard deviation if an experiment is repeated a second time?
7. What is the mean and standard deviation for the number of heads on 400 coin flips?

## Vocabulary and Notation

In this investigation, you learned these terms and symbols. Make sure you understand what each one means and how to use it.

- **experimental probability**
- **mean absolute deviation**
- **mean squared deviation, or variance, $\sigma^2$**
- **root mean squared deviation, or standard deviation, $\sigma$**
- **spread**
- **theoretical probability**

# Designing Experiments

In *Designing Experiments,* you will learn how to test whether or not a statistical claim is true, and ways to distinguish several methods of gathering data for statistical analysis.

**By the end of this investigation, you will be able to answer questions like these.**

1. How might you decide if a coin is fair or unfair?
2. What are some differences between sample surveys, experiments, and observational studies?
3. 100 fair coins are flipped. What is the mean and standard deviation for the number of coins that come up heads?

**You will learn how to**

- decide if a mathematical model is consistent with results from a simulation
- identify Bernoulli trials and compute statistics for them
- determine potential sources of bias in surveys and studies

**You will develop these habits and skills:**

- Construct and analyze representations of data, including two-way tables, dot plots, and histograms
- Use combinations to determine the probabilities of events
- Learn the difference between correlation and causation
- Reason about calculations
- Generalize from repeated reasoning

# 3.10 Getting Started

It is hard to be completely random. This lesson will ask you to make truly random data, but also to try to make a believable fake.

## For You to Explore

1. *Fake* the results of flipping a coin 240 times as a sequence of 1's and 0's. Write heads as 1, tails as 0, and make the order of the fake flips clear. Do not use any computer, calculator, or anything that could be used to make the random numbers.
2. Now, *make* the results of flipping a coin 240 times. Write heads as 1, tails as 0, and make the order of the real flips clear. Seriously, make it: flip a coin 240 times and write down the results as a sequence. Use the same format you used when making the fake results so that only you will know which result is real and which is fake.
3. Make a test you could use to decide whether a list someone gives you is real or fake.
4. Exchange lists with a classmate and run your test on their lists. Did your test correctly decide which was real and which was fake?

## On Your Own

5. Use your test on each of these seven data sets to decide whether each is real or fake.

**a.**

1 0 0 1 0 1 1 1 1 0 0 0 1 1 0 1 0 0 0 1 0
1 0 1 0 0 0 0 1 1 0 1 0 0 1 0 1 0 0 0 1 1
1 0 1 0 1 1 0 1 0 1 1 0 0 0 1 1 0 1 0 0 0
1 0 0 0 1 0 1 0 0 1 0 1 1 0 0 0 0 1 0 1 1
1 0 0 0 1 0 1 1 0 0 0 1 1 1 1 0 1 0 0 1 1
1 1 1 0 0 1 1 0 0 0 0 1 1 1 1 0 0 1 1 0 0
0 0 1 1 0 0 0 1 1 1 1 0 0 0 1 1 0 1 0 1 0
0 0 0 0 1 0 1 1 0 0 0 1 1 1 1 1 1 0 0 1 0
0 1 0 0 1 1 0 0 1 1 1 0 1 0 1 1 0 0 1 0
0 1 1 0 0 1 1 0 1 0 1 1 1 1 0 0 0 1 0 1
1 0 1 0 0 0 1 1 1 1 0 1 0 1 1 0 0 1 1 0
1 0 0 1 1 0 1 0 0 1 1 0 0 1 0 0 1 0 0 1

**b.** ↓

| | | | | | | | | | | | |
|---|---|---|---|---|---|---|---|---|---|---|---|
| 0 | 0 | 1 | 0 | 0 | 1 | 0 | 1 | 1 | 0 | 1 | 0 |
| 0 | 1 | 1 | 1 | 1 | 1 | 0 | 1 | 0 | 0 | 1 | 0 |
| 0 | 0 | 1 | 1 | 1 | 0 | 1 | 0 | 1 | 1 | 1 | 1 |
| 0 | 0 | 1 | 1 | 1 | 1 | 1 | 0 | 0 | 0 | 0 | 0 |
| 0 | 0 | 0 | 0 | 1 | 1 | 0 | 1 | 0 | 0 | 1 | 0 |
| 0 | 0 | 0 | 1 | 1 | 1 | 1 | 0 | 1 | 1 | 0 | 0 |
| 0 | 1 | 0 | 0 | 1 | 0 | 0 | 1 | 0 | 0 | 0 | 0 |
| 1 | 0 | 1 | 0 | 0 | 1 | 0 | 0 | 0 | 0 | 0 | 1 |
| 0 | 1 | 1 | 0 | 1 | 1 | 1 | 0 | 0 | 1 | 1 | 1 |
| 1 | 1 | 0 | 1 | 0 | 0 | 1 | 0 | 0 | 0 | 1 | 1 |
| 1 | 0 | 0 | 1 | 0 | 0 | 1 | 1 | 1 | 1 | 1 | 0 |
| 1 | 0 | 0 | 1 | 0 | 1 | 0 | 0 | 1 | 1 | 0 | 0 |
| 1 | 1 | 1 | 0 | 1 | 1 | 1 | 1 | 1 | 1 | 1 | 0 |
| 1 | 0 | 0 | 1 | 1 | 1 | 1 | 1 | 0 | 1 | 0 | 1 |
| 0 | 1 | 0 | 0 | 0 | 1 | 1 | 1 | 1 | 1 | 0 | 0 |
| 0 | 1 | 1 | 1 | 1 | 1 | 1 | 0 | 0 | 0 | 0 | 1 |
| 1 | 0 | 1 | 0 | 1 | 0 | 0 | 0 | 1 | 1 | 0 | 1 |
| 1 | 1 | 0 | 0 | 1 | 1 | 0 | 1 | 1 | 0 | 0 | 0 |
| 1 | 1 | 1 | 0 | 1 | 1 | 0 | 1 | 0 | 0 | 1 | 0 |
| 1 | 0 | 1 | 0 | 0 | 0 | 0 | 0 | 0 | 1 | 1 | 1 |

**c.**

0 0 1 0 0 1 1 0 0 0 1 1 1 1 1 0 1 0 0 1 0 1 1 0
1 1 1 0 0 1 1 0 0 0 1 1 1 0 1 1 0 1 0 1 1 0 0 1
0 1 0 1 1 1 0 1 0 0 1 1 0 1 0 1 0 1 1 0 1 0 0 0
1 0 1 1 0 1 1 0 0 1 1 1 1 1 1 0 0 1 0 1 1 0 1 0
0 0 0 0 0 0 1 0 0 1 0 1 1 0 1 1 0 1 0 0 1 1 1 1
0 1 1 0 1 0 1 1 1 1 0 1 0 0 0 0 1 0 1 0 1 0 1 0
0 1 0 1 0 1 0 1 0 1 1 1 0 0 0 1 0 0 1 0 1 0 0 0
1 0 0 1 1 1 0 1 1 0 1 0 1 1 0 0 1 0 1 0 0 1 0 1
0 1 0 0 1 0 0 0 1 1 1 0 1 0 0 1 0 1 0 1 0 1 1 1
1 1 0 0 1 0 0 1 1 1 0 0 0 1 0 0 0 0 0 0 1 0 1 1

## Exercises Practicing Habits of Mind

**d.**

0 0 1 0 0 1 0 1 1 0 0 0 1 0 1 0 0 1 1 1 0 1 1 0 0 1 1 0 1 1
0 1 1 1 0 0 1 0 0 1 1 1 0 1 1 0 0 0 1 0 0 1 1 0 0 1 0 0 0 0
0 1 1 1 1 1 0 0 0 0 1 0 0 0 1 1 1 0 1 1 0 0 1 0 1 0 0 1 1 0
0 0 0 0 0 1 1 0 1 0 0 0 1 1 0 1 1 0 0 1 0 1 1 1 0 1 0 0 0 1
1 0 0 1 1 0 1 1 0 0 0 1 0 0 1 0 1 1 1 0 1 0 0 1 0 1 0 0 1 1
1 0 0 1 1 0 1 0 1 1 1 0 1 1 0 0 0 1 1 1 0 0 1 0 1 1 0 1 0 1
0 1 1 0 0 1 1 0 0 1 1 1 0 1 0 1 0 0 1 1 1 1 1 1 0 0 1 0 0 1
0 1 1 1 1 1 1 0 0 0 1 0 0 1 1 0 1 0 0 1 0 0 1 0 1 1 1 0 1 0

**e.**

0001 0001 0110 1100 1100 1110
0100 0010 1100 0111 0001 1111
1110 0110 0001 1000 1111 0110
0110 1000 0010 1010 0110 1001
0111 0001 0110 0000 0100 1110
0110 0010 1011 1110 0101 0100
0100 0101 0001 0010 0101 0101
0100 1010 0000 0010 0001 1010
1101 0010 0100 1011 1110 1111
1111 0011 0011 1010 1100 1000

**f.**

111010110011011111111101
111111010110100100000000
010000100000110011000010
000011010010101010101011
110101011101000010110010
111000000000101110111101
011011001000101010101001
100000100111000011011100
101101011001001100111010
101100101001111001100000

**g.**

→

1 1 0 0 0 0 1 0 1 1 0 1
0 0 1 1 1 0 0 1 0 0 0 0
1 1 1 0 0 1 0 0 1 1 1 1
0 0 1 1 0 0 0 1 0 1 1 1
0 1 1 0 0 1 0 0 0 1 1 0
0 1 1 1 1 0 0 1 0 1 1 0
1 0 0 0 0 1 0 1 1 1 1 0
0 1 1 0 0 1 0 0 0 0 1 1
1 0 0 1 0 1 1 1 0 0 0 0
1 1 0 1 0 1 1 1 0 0 1 0
0 0 1 0 0 0 1 1 0 1 0 0
1 1 1 0 1 1 0 0 0 1 1 1
1 1 1 1 0 0 1 0 1 0 0 0
1 1 0 0 1 0 1 1 1 1 0 0
1 0 1 1 0 1 0 0 0 0 1 1
0 1 0 0 0 0 1 1 0 1 0 0
1 0 1 1 1 0 1 0 0 0 0 0
1 0 1 1 1 0 0 1 0 1 1 1
0 0 1 0 0 0 1 1 0 1 1 1
0 0 1 0 0 0 1 1 0 1 0 0

**6.** Using what you have learned from testing real and fake data, construct a more believable fake set of 240 coin flips.

## Maintain Your Skills

**7.** Gary built a test by counting the number of "swaps," the number of times a sequence of heads and tails switches from heads to tails, or from tails to heads.

**a.** In a coin-flipping sequence, what is the probability that any coin flip should result in a swap?

**b.** In 240 coin flips, about how many swaps should occur?

**c.** Estimate the number of swaps that would cause you to say that a set of 240 coin flips was fake.

# 3.11 Experiments and Simulations

Often mathematicians and scientists want to determine whether or not a particular item or treatment is really effective. Examples of products that may claim benefits include a new drug, a fuel additive, a new variety of corn, or a speed-reading technique. In any situation, some randomness occurs and is expected. Even when we see an impact from the item, how do we know that the item caused the effect and it wasn't random?

## For Discussion

1. Suppose your friend flips a coin and it lands showing heads. Do you believe the coin is a fair coin?
2. Suppose your friend flips the coin twice in a row and it shows heads both times. Do you believe the coin is fair?
3. What if the coin is flipped 15 times in a row and it shows heads every time? Do you believe the coin is fair?

When the coin comes up heads enough times in a row, we start to suspect the coin is not fair. The field of statistics has grown up around questions like, "How many heads do I need to get in a row before I should think the coin is not fair?" In this lesson, we will explore this idea in the context of a scientific study.

Statisticians do not answer questions like these as definitively as you might expect. Instead of saying "The coin is rigged!", they are more likely to say something like "The coin is probably not fair." or "The evidence suggests we reject the idea the coin is fair."

## For Discussion

A TV commercial advertises the "amazing power of magnetic power bands." In this commercial, the advertiser claims that wearing magnetic power bands will improve athletes' balance. Is it possible to find scientific evidence to support this claim?

A university researcher in sports medicine decides to test this claim. Forty-eight college athletes volunteer and participate in the study. At the beginning of the study, each athlete's name is written on a slip of paper. The researcher mixes up all of the 48 names and randomly selects 24 of them. These 24 subjects are assigned to the Magnet Group. The remaining subjects are assigned to the Control Group. The name for this process is *randomization*. The athletes are not told whether they are in the Magnet Group or the Control Group.

In a scientific study, the *control group* does not receive the treatment. This allows the researcher to compare subjects who received the treatment to those who did not.

4. Why might randomization of subjects be important for a study such as this one?

5. The researcher considered randomizing by having all 48 students line up, and then having the first athlete flip a coin. The athlete is placed in the Magnet Group if heads is flipped and in the Control Group if tails is flipped. The next athlete in line flips the coin, and this continues until there are 24 students in either the Magnet Group or the Control Group. Then the remaining students are placed in the group that has not yet been filled. Why might the researcher reject this plan for randomization?

6. Why would the researcher not tell the athletes which group they have been assigned to?

Once the students are randomly assigned to either the Magnet Group or the Control Group (without knowing which group they are in), each student is given a wristband. If the student was assigned to the Magnet Group, the wristband contains power magnets. If the student was assigned to the Control Group, the wristband has the same weight as the Magnet Group wristband but no power magnets.

Each student is given two hours for the body to "adjust" to the power magnets, and then takes a balance test designed by the researcher.

Here is a table with some of the information from the study filled in:

| | Passed Balance Test | Failed Balance Test | Total |
|---|---|---|---|
| **Magnet** | | | 24 |
| **Control** | | | 24 |
| **Total** | 36 | 12 | 48 |

## For You to Do

7. Suppose that there is *little or no evidence* that the magnets are effective in improving balance. Complete the table with possible values under this assumption.

8. Are there other ways to complete the table such that there is little or no evidence that the magnets are effective in improving balance? Describe any changes that could be made while maintaining little or no evidence in the effectiveness of the magnets.

9. Suppose that there is *strong evidence* that the magnets are effective in improving balance. Complete the table with possible values under this assumption.

10. Are there other ways to complete the table such that there is strong evidence that the magnets are effective in improving balance? Describe any changes that could be made while maintaining strong evidence in the effectiveness of the magnets.

11. Suppose that there is *possible evidence* that the magnets are effective in improving balance. Complete the table with possible values. Could there be different answers to this question?

The idea that there could be a range of possible values for *strong evidence, possible evidence,* and *little or no evidence* is an important idea, but how can these ranges be mathematically justified? Given a set of initial conditions, any outcome is theoretically possible. A fair coin could flip heads 15 times in a row, or everyone in the Magnet Group could have passed the balance test without magnets. In order to more accurately interpret our results, we need to know how likely different outcomes are assuming randomness. To do this, we can use a *simulation*.

## Minds in Action

*Tony, Sasha, and Derman are discussing their ranges of values for strong evidence, possible evidence, and little or no evidence of magnet effectiveness.*

**Derman** So now that we have the different ranges, we just see which category the actual data fall in, right?

**Sasha** But how do we know our ranges are correct? Maybe they are really far off.

**Tony** Well, the *little or no evidence* category makes sense. If the magnets don't work, half of the athletes who passed the balance test should be from the Magnet Group and the other half should be from the Control Group.

**Derman** Yeah, 18 and 18!

**Sasha** But even if the magnets don't work, we won't necessarily get 18 and 18 each time. Maybe we get 19 and 17.

**Derman** Well, sure, but the magnets still won't work with 19 and 17.

**Sasha** But what about 20 and 16?

**Derman** Umm, they probably don't work . . . I think—

**Sasha** What about 21 and 15? Then do they work?

**Derman** Maybe, I don't know. If the number gets high enough, then we think they work, right?

**Tony** Right, but how high is high enough? And what about those middle numbers, like 20 and 21? Are those *no evidence* or *possible evidence*? How can we tell?

**Sasha** Let's run a simulation to replicate this experiment, assuming the power magnets don't work.

**Derman** Why would we do that?

**Sasha** We want to rule out luck as a cause for the data we got. But to do this, we need to get a plausible range of values for the number of people from the Magnet Group who passed the balance test if the magnets don't work, and everything is just random.

**Tony** Okay, I see. If the number of athletes in the Magnet Group who passed the balance test is too high to be caused by random chance, then we can probably rule out luck as a cause for the high value. Something else must have caused the high value . . .

**Derman** Well, maybe the Magnet Group had the better balancers in the first place.

**Sasha** Maybe, but we randomly assigned everybody into one of the two groups. For that reason, the balance levels of each group are probably the same entering the treatments.

**Derman** Oh, I see—the two groups in the experiment are as similar as possible before entering the treatments.

**Sasha** Right, so if the percent of passers in the Magnet Group is too high to be caused by chance, then we can probably conclude that the magnets work!

**Tony** Cool! So we need to know how likely it is to get 18, or 19, or 20, or 21, etc. . . . That seems hard to calculate directly. Let's create a simulation.

## For Discussion

**12.** How should this simulation work? Describe a possible way to set up and carry out this simulation.

*Tony, Sasha, and Derman are discussing their idea for this simulation.*

**Tony** We have 48 people in our experiment altogether, so we need something with a lot of choices. How about a deck of cards?

**Sasha** Okay, suppose you let a red card be someone in the Magnet Group, and a black card is someone in the Control Group. How would we represent somebody who passed and somebody who failed?

**Derman** Wait, aren't there 52 cards in a deck?

**Tony** That's true. Well, let's leave out two red cards and two black cards—then we have 48.

**Sasha** So if I shuffle the cards, then deal out 36—those ones passed the test, and the rest failed.

**Derman** Then what?

**Sasha** Then I count out how many red cards I dealt to figure out how many people in the Magnet Group would have passed the test. That's replicating the situation where the power magnets don't work.

**Tony** Because the only thing making someone from each group pass or fail the balance test is random chance. Cool! Let's try it.

**Derman** This will be faster if we all do the simulation. Here are two more decks of cards.

**Sasha** Great! Let's each simulate this 30 times and keep track of the number of people from the Magnet Group who pass the balance test.

*Tony, Sasha, and Derman each run the simulation 30 times. They graph their individual data in the dot plots shown below.*

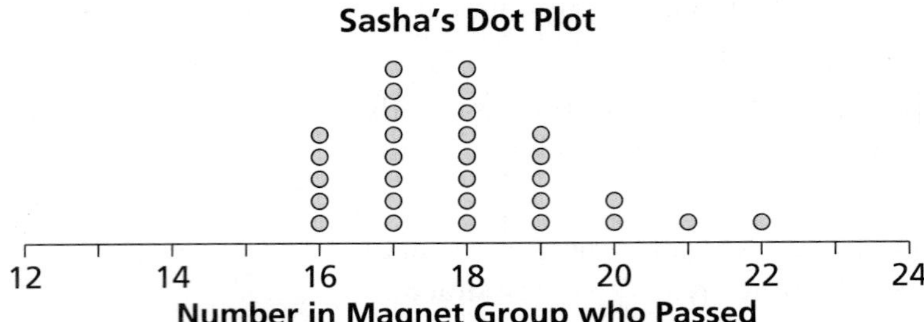


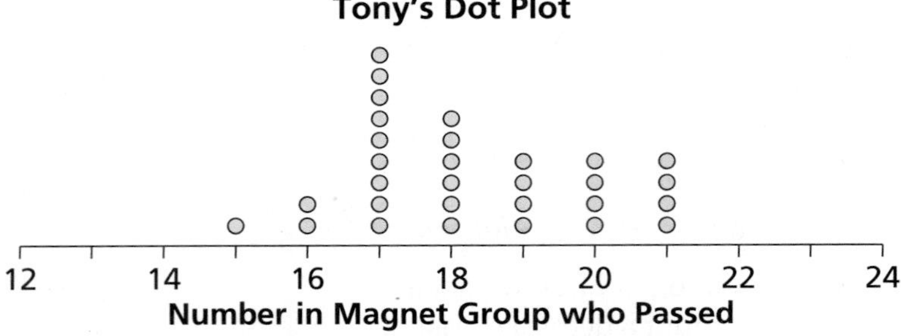


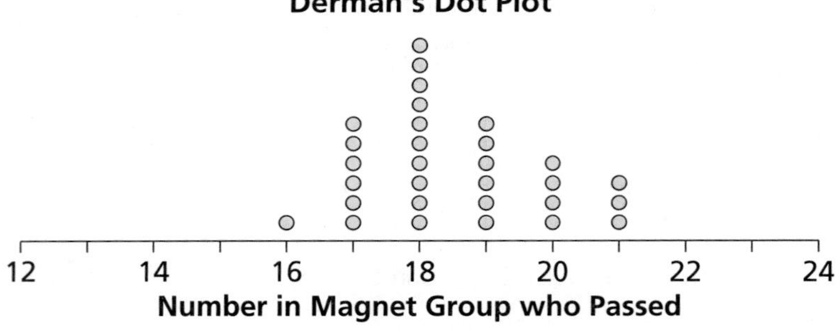

## For You to Do

**13.** How many times out of 30 did Sasha have 17 athletes in the Magnet Group pass the balance test?

**14.** How many times out of 30 did Tony have 17 athletes in the Magnet Group pass the balance test?

**15.** Neither Sasha, Tony, nor Derman had a simulation where 23 athletes in the Magnet Group passed the balance test. Does this mean it is impossible for 23 athletes in the Magnet Group to pass the balance test? Explain.

**16.** In the actual experiment, 21 of the 24 athletes in the Magnet Group passed the test. Based on these simulations of 30 trials, what would you conclude? Do you believe the power magnets assist balance?

**17.** What makes it difficult to make a definite conclusion?

Even though we might consider 90 trials a fairly large number of simulations, we usually will need more, depending on the frequency of particular outcomes and the number of possible outcomes. Using a computer, Sasha replicated the card simulation many more times. Here is a histogram of her results:

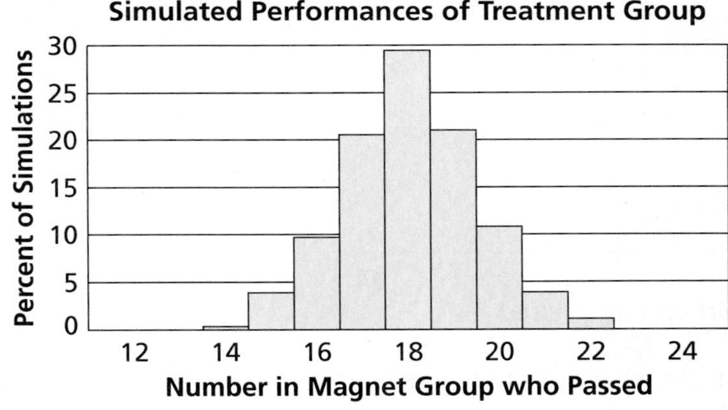


## For You to Do

**18.** Do you believe having 21 of 24 athletes in the Magnet Group pass the balance test is sufficient evidence that power magnets improve balance? Explain.

## Exercises *Practicing Habits of Mind*

### Check Your Understanding

1. Using Sasha's histogram, create a range of values for the number of athletes in the Magnet Group who passed the balance test showing the following. Justify your answers with evidence from the histogram.

   a. *little or no evidence* that the magnets work

   b. *possible evidence* that the magnets work

   c. *strong evidence* that the magnets work

2. What number of athletes in the Magnet Group who passed the balance test would convince you that the magnets had a *detrimental* effect on balance? Justify your answer.

Some synonyms for *detrimental* are *adverse, harmful,* and *negative*.

3. The mode of Tony's dot plot data is 17 athletes in the Magnet Group who passed the balance test.

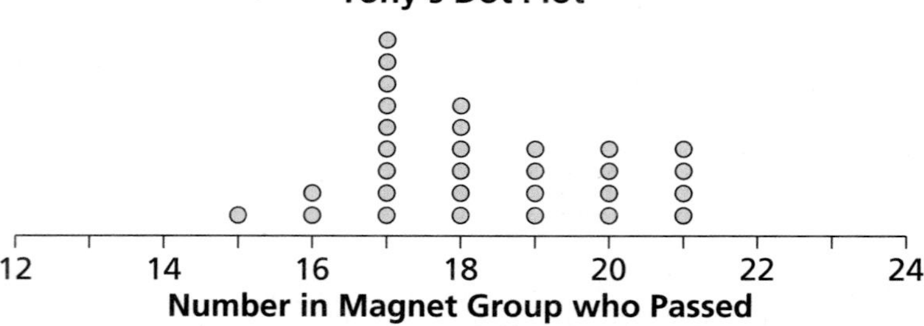


   a. Tony ran his simulations assuming all subjects had the same chance to pass the balance test. How many athletes from the Magnet Group should Tony expect to pass the balance test?

   b. Did Tony do something wrong with his simulations? Explain.

4. Can the university researcher know for sure whether or not power magnets improve balance as a result of an experiment like this one? Explain.

### On Your Own

5. **What's Wrong Here?** Tony and Sasha have 15 playing cards: 10 black and 5 red. Two cards will be selected without replacement from this group. Tony and Sasha are interested in the number of red cards drawn. Sasha proposes the following simulation: use a calculator to randomly generate 0, 1, or 2, with this number representing the number of red cards drawn. Why is this not a good simulation for this scenario?

6. Heidi suspects a number cube with numbers 1 through 6 is weighted such that "1" occurs more often than it should. To test this, she rolls the number cube five times, and four of the five times the number "1" is rolled.

   a. Design a simulation to replicate this situation.

   b. Carry out your simulation 100 times. Record your data as you go.

   c. Create a histogram of your results.

   d. Do you believe this number cube is fair? Explain.

7. A dropout prevention program is being pilot-tested at a high school. The guidance counselors have identified 20 seniors as being at risk for dropping out and have randomly divided them into two equal groups. One group will participate in the program and the other will not. At the end of the year, 15 of the 20 students graduate from high school.

   a. Explain why a valid simulation for this scenario is to generate a random list of 5 whole numbers and count the number of odd numbers that occur. This number represents the number of students in the prevention program who did not graduate from high school.

   b. Carry out this simulation 50 times. Create a histogram for these data.

8. A fair coin is flipped eight times. Without running a simulation, determine the probability of getting each number of heads.

   a. 8

   b. 7

   c. 4

9. A new meditation exercise has been advertised to "significantly improve memory." Thirty-six volunteers agree to participate in a study to test this claim and are divided equally into two groups: the Treatment Group and the Control Group.

   a. Describe an effective and valid way to randomize the participants into the Treatment Group and Control Group.

   b. Describe what should occur if a participant is in the Treatment Group or Control Group.

**c.** Overall, 15 of the participants in the study improved their score on a memory test. Consider the partially completed table below. Complete the table under each of the following conditions.

- *little or no evidence* the meditation exercise improves memory
- *possible evidence* the meditation exercise improves memory
- *strong evidence* the meditation exercise improves memory

| | Improved Memory | Did Not Improve Memory | Total |
|---|---|---|---|
| **Treatment** | | | 18 |
| **Control** | | | 18 |
| **Total** | 15 | 21 | 36 |

**d.** Design a simulation for this scenario.

**e.** Carry out this simulation 100 times. Record your data and create a histogram of the results.

**f.** Revisit your answer to part (c) above, and create a range of values for the number of participants from the Treatment Group who improved their memory that demonstrates each of the following.

- *little or no evidence* the meditation exercise improves memory
- *possible evidence* the meditation exercise improves memory
- *strong evidence* the meditation exercise improves memory

**g.** In the experiment, 10 out of the 18 participants in the Treatment Group successfully improved their memory. Do you believe the claim in the advertisements to be valid? Explain.

## Maintain Your Skills

**10.** Suppose you repeatedly flip a fair coin. Find the probability of getting each result.

**a.** a head on your first flip

**b.** 2 heads on your first 2 flips

**c.** 3 heads on your first 3 flips

**d.** $n$ heads on your first $n$ flips

**11.** For what values of $n$ is the probability of getting $n$ heads on your first $n$ flips of a coin less than 1%?

# 3.12 Bernoulli Trials

A **Bernoulli trial** is an experiment with two outcomes, *success* and *failure*. You have seen several examples of Bernoulli trials: flipping a coin heads, answering a multiple-choice question correctly, rolling a six. A Bernoulli trial has a probability of success $p$, so the probability of failure is $1 - p$.

**Habits of Mind**

**Look for a relationship.** Why must the probability of failure be $1 - p$?

## Example 1

**Problem** Consider a Bernoulli trial with probability of success $p = 0.2$. In three trials, what is the probability of exactly two successes?

Some examples of Bernoulli trials with probability of success 0.2: correctly answering a multiple-choice question with 5 choices, spinning a 1 or 2 on a spinner with 1–10, or a baseball player getting a hit.

**Solution**

**Method 1** Write out all eight possible outcomes. Determine the probability of each. Then, add the probabilities that have exactly two successes. Use S for success and F for failure.

| Outcome | Probability | Product |
|---|---|---|
| SSS | $0.2 \cdot 0.2 \cdot 0.2$ | 0.008 |
| **SSF** | $\mathbf{0.2 \cdot 0.2 \cdot 0.8}$ | **0.032** |
| **SFS** | $\mathbf{0.2 \cdot 0.8 \cdot 0.2}$ | **0.032** |
| SFF | $0.2 \cdot 0.8 \cdot 0.8$ | 0.128 |
| **FSS** | $\mathbf{0.8 \cdot 0.2 \cdot 0.2}$ | **0.032** |
| FSF | $0.8 \cdot 0.2 \cdot 0.8$ | 0.128 |
| FFS | $0.8 \cdot 0.8 \cdot 0.2$ | 0.128 |
| FFF | $0.8 \cdot 0.8 \cdot 0.8$ | 0.512 |

The probability is the sum for all the outcomes with exactly two successes: 0.096, or 9.6%.

**Method 2** Use combinatorics to identify the number of different outcomes, with exponents that correspond to the number of successes and failures.

For this experiment, there are $\binom{3}{2} = 3$ different orderings for 2 successes and 1 failure. Each success has probability 0.2, while each failure has probability 0.8. The probability for exactly two successes is

$$\binom{3}{2} \cdot (0.2)^2 \cdot (0.8)^1 = 0.096$$

In general, the probability of exactly $k$ successes in $n$ trials for this experiment is given by

$$\binom{n}{k} \cdot (0.2)^k \cdot (0.8)^{n-k}$$

since there are $k$ successes and $(n - k)$ failures.

**Method 3** The binomial $(0.2s + 0.8f)$ models one trial. Raising this binomial to the third power gives all the probabilities:

$$(0.2s + 0.8f)^3 = 0.008s^3 + 0.096s^2f + 0.384sf^2 + 0.512f^3$$

The probability of two successes and one failure can be read by looking at the coefficient of the $s^2f$ term. The coefficient is 0.096.

## For Discussion

1. Given $p = 0.2$ as in Example 1, find the probability that there will be at least one success in the three trials. Is there more than one way to do this?

To calculate the mean and variance for a Bernoulli trial, assign 1 as the value of a success and 0 as the value of a failure. Using the calculation method from Lesson 3.04, find the mean by multiplying each value by its probability. The probability of a success is $p$. The probability of a failure is $(1 - p)$.

**Habits of Mind**

**Make strategic choices.** This way, the sum of the values for $n$ trials will be the number of successes.

| Value | Probability | Product |
|---|---|---|
| 1 (success) | $p$ | $p$ |
| 0 (failure) | $1 - p$ | 0 |
| Total | | $p$ |

The mean for a single Bernoulli trial is the probability of its success. Since the mean is additive, in $n$ trials the expected number of successes will be $np$. For example, on a 20-question multiple-choice test with 5 choices per question, you would expect (on average) to get 4 out of 20 if you were completely guessing throughout the test.

$n = 20$ and $p = 0.2$, so $np = 4$.

What about variance? Variance is mean squared deviation. Here, the deviation is taken from the mean $p$. Each squared deviation is multiplied by its probability.

| Result | Deviation | Deviation² | Probability | Product |
|---|---|---|---|---|
| 1 (success) | $1 - p$ | $(1 - p)^2$ | $p$ | $p(1 - p)^2$ |
| 0 (failure) | $-p$ | $p^2$ | $1 - p$ | $p^2(1 - p)$ |
| Total | | | | $p(1 - p)$ |

This result for variance matches earlier results. For a coin flip, the variance is $0.5(1 - 0.5) = 0.25$. If an outcome is impossible $(p = 0)$ or guaranteed $(p = 1)$, the variance is zero.

Since variance is additive, in $n$ trials the variance is $np(1 - p)$. As before, the standard deviation is the square root of the variance.

### *Facts and Notation*

**Consider a Bernoulli trial with probability of success $p$. In $n$ trials, the mean, variance, and standard deviation for the number of successes are as follows.**

$$\text{mean } \bar{x} = np$$
$$\text{variance } \sigma^2 = np(1 - p)$$
$$\text{standard deviation } \sigma = \sqrt{np(1 - p)}$$

**These formulas all rely on the fact that mean and variance are additive.**

> **Habits of Mind**
>
> **Try a specific case.** With $n = 20$ and $p = 0.2$ like a 20-question multiple-choice test, $\bar{x} = 4$ and $\sigma \approx 1.789$. Most people guessing on this test will get between 2 and 6 correct.

## Example 2

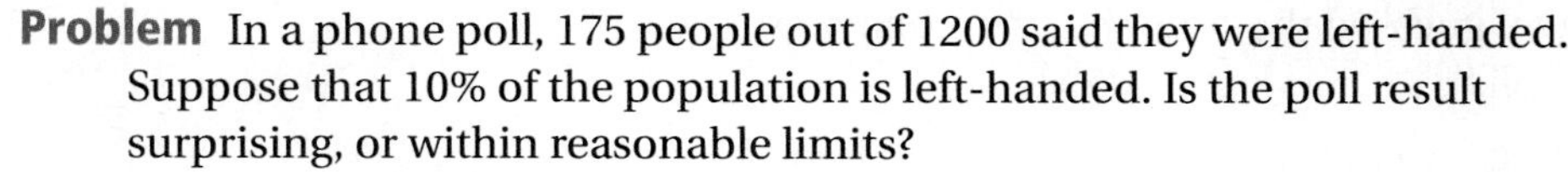

**Problem** In a phone poll, 175 people out of 1200 said they were left-handed. Suppose that 10% of the population is left-handed. Is the poll result surprising, or within reasonable limits?

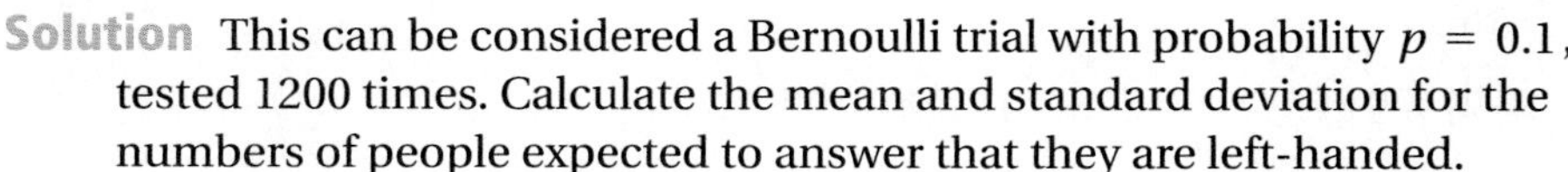

**Solution** This can be considered a Bernoulli trial with probability $p = 0.1$, tested 1200 times. Calculate the mean and standard deviation for the numbers of people expected to answer that they are left-handed.

$$\text{mean } \bar{x} = 1200 \cdot 0.1 = 120$$
$$\text{standard deviation } \sigma = \sqrt{1200 \cdot 0.1 \cdot 0.9} = 6\sqrt{3} \approx 10.39$$

So, most of the time the poll is run, you would expect the result to be within $120 \pm 10.39$ because most of the data will fall within one standard deviation of the mean. The upper bound here is just over 130. But the actual poll result was 175. This is well outside the expected range, so the poll result is very surprising.

One statistic that can be useful to calculate is the **z-score,** the number of standard deviations away from the mean. For Example 2, the $z$-score of the phone poll is approximately

$$\frac{175 - 120}{10.39} \approx 5.29$$

Since most data fall within one standard deviation of the mean, a $z$-score this high is very unusual. It is more than five standard deviations from the mean. This result suggests that the premise that only 10% of people are left-handed might not be correct or that the sample in the poll was not representative of the general population.

> Hypothesis testing is a branch of statistics that deals with these types of claims.

# Exercises Practicing Habits of Mind

## Check Your Understanding

1. For Exercise 8 in Lesson 3.01, you guessed the probability of tossing exactly 120 heads and 120 tails on 240 coin flips.
   **a.** Use the formula given in this lesson to find this probability to four decimal places.
   **b.** How does your answer compare to the guess you made previously?

2. For Exercise 9 in Lesson 3.01, you guessed the probability of rolling exactly 40 ones on 240 number cubes rolls.
   **a.** Use the formula given in this lesson to find this probability to four decimal places.
   **b.** How does your answer compare to the guess you made previously?

3. **a.** Find the mean and standard deviation for the number of sixes you would get when rolling 240 number cubes.
   **b.** If you rolled 240 number cubes and got only 20 sixes, would that be a surprising result or within reasonable limits?

4. In Lesson 3.06, you took a 20-question multiple-choice test by guessing. Each answer had probability $p = 0.2$ of being correct.
   **a.** Explain why the probability of getting all 20 questions correct is $(0.2)^{20}$.
   **b.** Find the probability of getting all 20 questions wrong.
   **c.** Use the formula given in this lesson to find the probability of getting exactly 3 questions out of 20 correct.
   **d.** What percentage of your class actually got exactly 3 questions out of 20 correct?

5. **a.** Write the definition for a function $f$ where the output is the probability of getting exactly $n$ questions correct on the 20-question test from the Getting Started lesson.
   **b.** Copy and complete the table for $n$ from 0 to 10.

| $n$ | $f(n)$ |
|---|---|
| 0 | ■ |
| 1 | ■ |
| 2 | ■ |
| 3 | ■ |
| 4 | ■ |
| 5 | ■ |
| 6 | ■ |
| 7 | ■ |
| 8 | ■ |
| 9 | ■ |
| 10 | ■ |

See the TI-Nspire Handbook on p. 817 for information on how to build the table for Exercise 5.

6. Expand the polynomial $(0.2r + 0.8w)^{20}$. Find the coefficient of the $r^3w^{17}$ term. What is its significance?

7. Show algebraically that $p(1 - p)^2 + p^2(1 - p) = p(1 - p)$.

8. **Take It Further** Consider a Bernoulli trial with probability of success $p$. Build tables similar to the ones on page 95 that show that the mean for the number of successes in two trials is $2p$, and the variance is $2p(1 - p)$.

## On Your Own

**9.** Consider two independent Bernoulli trials. The first has probability of success $p$. The second has probability of success $q$.

**a.** Find the probability that both trials are successful.

**b.** Find the probability that neither trial is successful.

**c.** Find the probability that exactly one trial is successful.

**d.** Take It Further Find the mean and variance for the total number of successes for the two Bernoulli trials.

Here are two carnival games involving number cubes.

**Game 1** Call a number, then roll four number cubes. If the sum from the four number cubes is exactly the number you called, you win.

**Game 2** Call a number, then roll 72 number cubes. If the number of sixes rolled is exactly the number you called, you win.

**10.** Make a quick guess: which game is easier to win, and why?

**11.** What number gives you the best chance to win Game 1? How likely are you to win with this number?

**12.** What number gives you the best chance to win Game 2? How likely are you to win with this number?

**13.** Take It Further Find the mean and standard deviation for each experiment.

**a.** the sum when rolling four number cubes

**b.** the number of sixes when rolling 72 number cubes

Go Online
www.successnetplus.com

**14.** Standardized Test Prep For a Bernoulli trial with probability of success $p$, the variance is $p(1 - p)$. What value of $p$ gives the maximum variance?

**A.** $\frac{1}{4}$ **B.** $\frac{1}{2}$ **C.** $\frac{2}{3}$ **D.** 1

## Maintain Your Skills

**15.** The mean height for an adult woman is 63.5 inches (5 feet $3\frac{1}{2}$ inches), with a standard deviation of 2.5 inches. For each height, calculate the $z$-score.

**a.** 5 feet 6 inches **b.** 5 feet 1 inch **c.** 5 feet 8 inches

**d.** 6 feet **e.** 4 feet 11 inches **f.** 7 feet

**g.** $x$ inches

The $z$-score may be any real number. It can be positive, negative, or zero.

# 3.13 Surveys, Studies, and Experiments

Gathering data for use in statistical analysis is an important task and requires careful attention. This lesson explores several methods of gathering data, including sample surveys, observational studies, and experiments.

The goal of a **sample survey** is to determine information about a population without gathering data from every element of the population. The method used to determine the sample can have a significant impact on the results. Poor methods can prevent the results from being useful for making conjectures about a population.

## In-Class Experiment

On page 260 is a map of an outdoor shopping center — *don't look at it yet!* The map shows 60 stores numbered from 1 to 60.

1. Without talking to your classmates, go to page 260. Take 45 seconds to pick five stores you feel best represent all stores in terms of overall area. Write down the store numbers and their areas (each blue square represents 1000 square feet). Then compute the mean area of your sample.
2. Before sharing your results, predict whether you think all students will get the same sample mean. Explain your reasoning.
3. Use a random number generator to pick five integers from 1 to 60. Using the random numbers as store numbers, write down the area of each store. Then compute the mean area of the random sample.
4. As a class, make two dot plots, one with each student's mean area from his or her first sample, and one with each student's mean area from his or her random sample.

On the TI-Nspire, the command **randInt(1, 60)** will return a random integer between 1 and 60.

## For Discussion

5. Without calculating the actual mean area of all 60 of the stores, which method of sampling do you think does the best job of estimating it? Explain your reasoning.

If the managers of the shopping center wanted to know the average number of customers per hour, they could gather information from a sample of stores. A good sample should be representative of the population. But there are many factors that could bias the results. For example, the sample might include too many stores of a specific type or size. **Random sampling** is a selection method that removes sources of bias. A good random sampling method ensures that all members of the population are equally likely to be chosen.

## Example

The managers of the shopping center invited employees from all stores to attend a workshop intended to help increase sales. The following are the numbers from the map of the stores that participated.

1, 3, 4, 16, 17, 19, 21, 23, 34, 39, 43, 44, 45, 49, 51, 52, 54, 57, 59, 60

Employees from these twenty stores attended the workshop, and the rest did not. After the workshop, the managers of the shopping center recorded the number of customers per hour at all stores. They made the following paired box-and-whisker plot to record their results. (Group A consists of the stores that did not send employees to the workshop. Group B consists of the stores that did send employees to the workshop.)

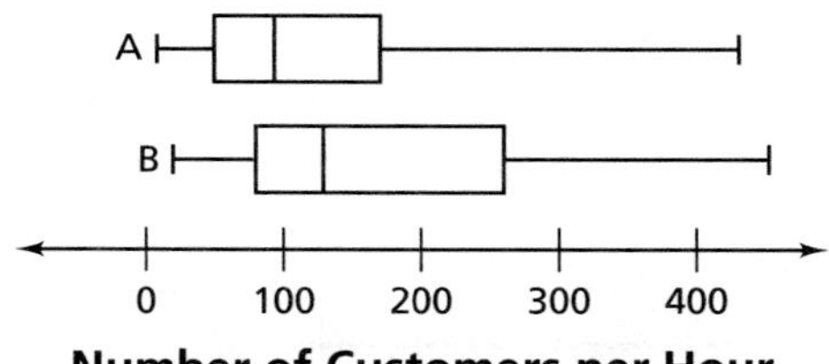


The managers declared that the workshop was a success: "Clearly, the stores that sent employees to the workshop have a greater number of customers per hour."

**Problem** Did the workshop *cause* the difference in customers per hour between the two groups? If not, what else might have caused the difference?

**Solution** There is no way to be certain that the workshop caused the difference in customers per hour. There are many other possible explanations:

- The stores that volunteered for the workshop are larger than the stores that did not volunteer. Larger stores often have more customers than small stores.
- The stores that volunteered are generally located in the south of the shopping center, and which might get more foot traffic.
- The stores that volunteered may already have had a greater number of customers per hour before the workshop was conducted.

For all of these reasons, *it is impossible to know* whether the observed difference in the number of customers per hour is due to the workshop, or due to some other factor or factors.

Can you think of any other possible explanations?

The Example above describes an **observational study.** An observational study gathers information about groups of a population when the groups are not chosen by the people doing the study. In the Example, stores *volunteered* for the workshop and were not chosen by the managers of the shopping center. Because of this, differences between groups may be caused by one or more external factors that cannot be controlled by those doing the study. It is far more difficult for an observational study to prove that the difference between groups was *caused* by a specific change or factor.

You can use randomization in an observational study of a large population by selecting elements of each group to be included. For example, you might choose 200 smokers and 200 non-smokers. Random sampling should be used to reduce potential bias.

## Developing Habits of Mind

**Reason about calculations** When two variables are associated, it does not mean that a change in one *causes* a change in the other. In the observational study, a high number of customers per hour is associated with attending the workshop, but this does not mean that the number of customers is high *because* of the workshop.

Here's a more extreme example. Among countries of the world, there is a positive association between life expectancy and the number of hours spent watching television! This *does not* mean watching more television increases life expectancy. There is often another reason for the correlation.

This is a very common fallacy in statistics, but it is important to remember that **correlation does not imply causation**. To prove causation, you must attempt to eliminate all other possible causes for the association between the variables.

**Remember...**

Two variables are *associated* or *correlated* if a change in one variable is accompanied by a change in the other variable. Variables can be positively or negatively associated.

## For Discussion

6. In a survey of school children, it was determined that height was positively correlated with reading scores. Does being a good reader make you taller? Does being tall make you a better reader? What other variable might be responsible for this correlation?

Unlike an observational study, a statistical **experiment** attempts to create two or more groups that are as similar as possible before treatments are imposed. These treatments then become the only thing fundamentally different between the groups. Any significant difference in the results *must* be due to the treatments.

In the most common form, the experiment creates two groups, with one group called the **treatment group** and the other called the **control group.** The results of the experiment determine whether there is a significant difference between the two groups.

Typically, the control group receives a fake treatment called a *placebo*. Why might a placebo be used?

Avoiding bias in group assignment is critical for an experiment, since bias could significantly impact the results. Well-designed experiments use randomization for group assignment. Every possible group of the same size should have an equal probability of being chosen. Random assignment is crucial in isolating the treatment as the cause of differences between groups. It removes the same biases that can influence surveys and observational studies.

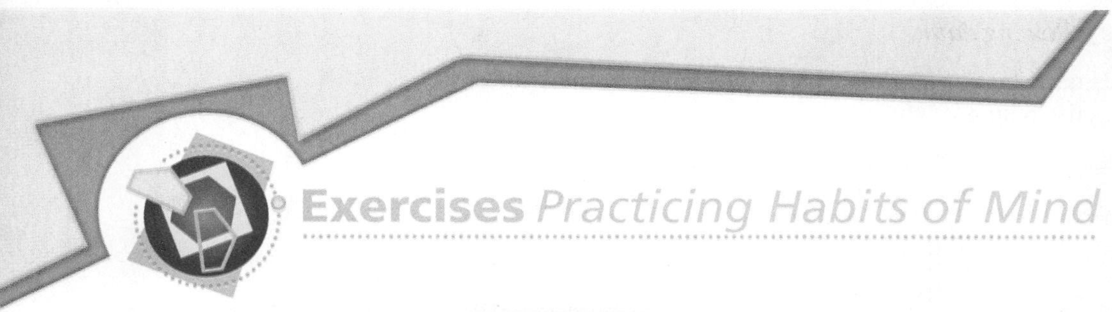

## Exercises *Practicing Habits of Mind*

### Check Your Understanding

1. Describe, in detail, an experiment designed to answer this question for the shopping center: "Does attending a workshop increase sales?" In particular, explain how the experiment differs from the observational study described in the Example.

2. Each country in the world has an average life expectancy of its inhabitants. Each country also has an average number of hours that its inhabitants spend watching television per year. There is a positive association between life expectancy and the number of hours spent watching television. What factors might account for this relationship?

These additional factors are sometimes called *lurking variables.*

3. **a.** Determine the mean area of all 60 stores from the In-Class Experiment.

   **b.** Determine the mean area of the 20 stores that volunteered for the workshop in the Example on page 253.

   **c.** Do the 20 volunteering stores form a representative sample of all 60 stores? Explain.

4. Below are two dot plots with 20 points each, based on the In-Class Experiment. One dot plot is made from the means of twenty random samples, and one is made from the means of twenty "human-chosen" samples. (The numbers represent area in thousands of square feet.)

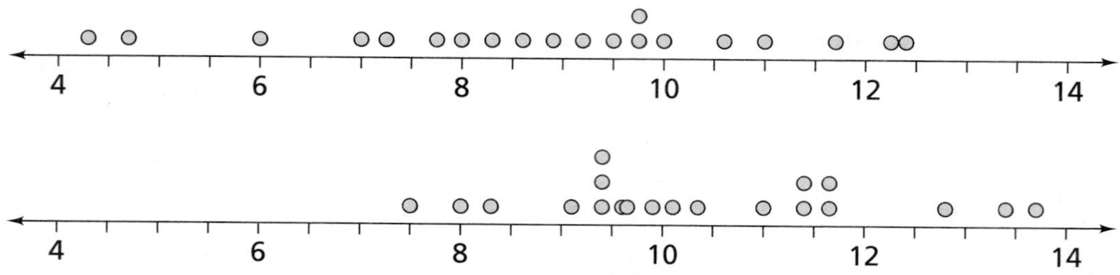


   **a.** Which dot plot do you think is from the "human-chosen" samples? Explain.

   **b.** Describe some biases that might affect human-chosen samples.

*Exercises 5 and 6 use the following data.*

All students in a freshman class of 79 were asked to weigh their backpacks. This histogram shows the results.

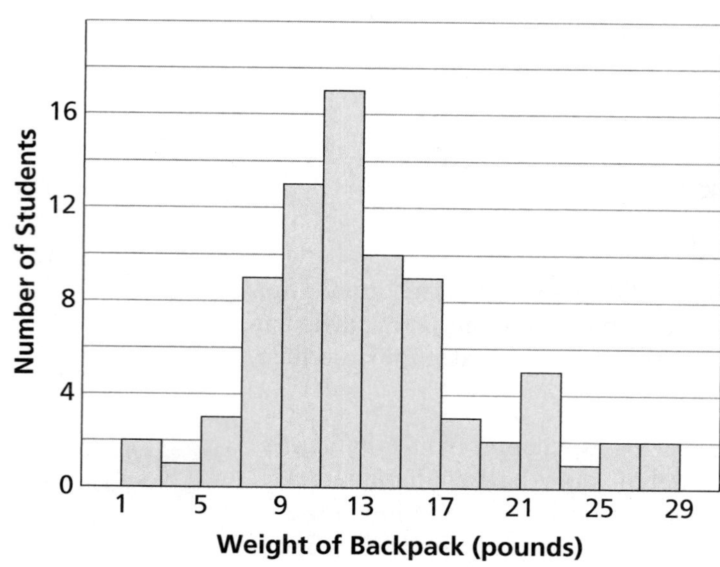


5. Without calculating, estimate the mean, median, and standard deviation of the weights of the 79 backpacks.

6. Six different student groups collected samples of backpack weights from the population of freshmen. Some groups used randomization to select their sample, while others did not. Of these samples, which do you think did not use randomization? What evidence in the dot plots led you to this conclusion?

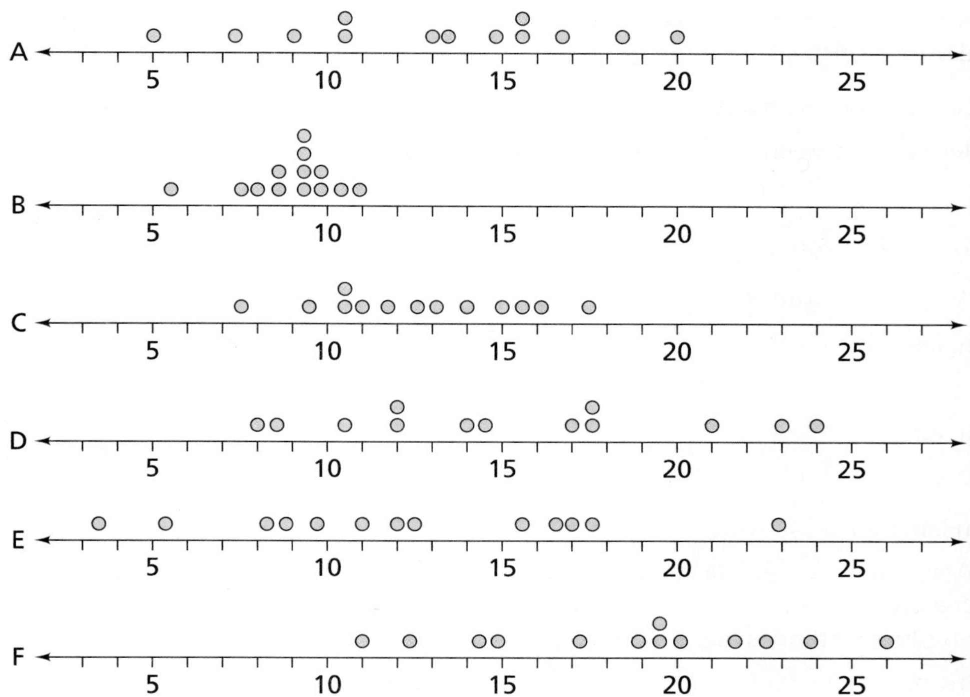

## On Your Own

7. **Write About It** A company wants to estimate the percentage of California drivers who use their cell phones while in the car. Decide whether each of the following methods will find a representative sample of the target population. Explain.

   **a.** Post a billboard inviting people to a website to respond.

   **b.** Play an ad on the radio asking drivers to call and respond.

   **c.** Survey the first 1000 people listed alphabetically in the phone book.

   **d.** Randomly select 1000 names from a list of all California licensed drivers. Contact these 1000 drivers and ask if they use a cell phone while driving.

8. The company in Exercise 7 used a representative sample to poll 1000 drivers. A surprisingly small fraction of drivers said that they had used their cell phone while driving.

   a. Why might the data be biased, even though a representative sample was used?

   b. Describe a way in which the company could more accurately determine the percentage of drivers using cell phones.

9. a. Describe some differences between a survey and an observational study.

   b. Describe some differences between an observational study and an experiment.

*Exercises 10 and 11 refer to this situation.*

From a ball of yarn, 40 pieces of string are cut:

- 20 pieces, each 3 in. long
- 10 pieces, each 6 in. long
- 5 pieces, each 12 in. long
- 5 pieces, each 24 in. long

10. a. Compute the mean length of all 40 strings.

    b. Mariana puts all 40 strings in a cloth bag and mixes them well. She then asks Jordan (who doesn't know what is in the bag) to pull out five strings. Explain why this sampling method is biased.

    c. Jordan guesses at the mean length of all the strings in the bag by calculating the mean length of the five strings he pulls. Would you expect Jordan's estimate to be too low, too high, or pretty close to the mean length of the population of strings?

11. Describe another method for selecting a sample of five strings that reduces the potential for bias. Explain how your method guarantees that all possible groups of five strings are equally likely to be selected.

## Maintain Your Skills

12. 20 men and 40 women volunteered for a study designed to answer this question: "Which exercise, tends to burn more calories in a 60-minute class, spinning or kickboxing?" The volunteers were allowed to choose to participate in the exercise that interested them most. 19 men and 20 women chose kickboxing.

    a. Build a two-way table showing the number of men and women who selected each type of exercise.

**b.** Explain why this study cannot make a valid comparison of the two types of exercise.

**c.** In an experiment, the 20 men and 40 women are assigned equally to the two types of exercise. Build a two-way table showing the number of men and women who should be assigned each type of exercise.

**d.** Describe a specific method for randomly assigning the 60 participants to the two classes.

**e.** Why does randomization help to determine which class tends to burn more calories?

## Historical Perspective
### Political Polling

The largest survey of all time occurred during the 1936 U.S. presidential election. *The Literary Digest* used lists of car and telephone owners along with its own readers to send postcards to over 10 million people, about one-fourth the number of people who voted in the 1932 election. Over 2 million postcards were returned, predicting Alf Landon would win 57% of the vote. This same survey had correctly predicted the winners in 1920, 1924, 1928, and 1932.

But this time, the survey did not match the results at all. Franklin Roosevelt won with over 60% of the popular vote, and won all but two states. How could the survey have gotten things so wrong? It was heavily biased in favor of those who could afford a car, a telephone, or a magazine subscription. And even if it were unbiased, 80% of the postcards sent out were not returned. Only those interested in responding to the survey were counted. The huge size of the sample did not matter.

Conversely, George Gallup polled only 2000 people but chose a *representative* sample of the population. Gallup accurately predicted both the results of the election and the results of the *Literary Digest* survey! Without a representative sample, there is no way the *Literary Digest* poll could be trusted as accurate.

Many polls today suffer from the same issues. When reading a poll, always consider the methods used to conduct the poll. Does the poll uses a representative sample of the population?

*The Literary Digest* never conducted another presidential poll: its last issue was in 1938.

*Use this chart for the In-Class Experiment on page 252.*

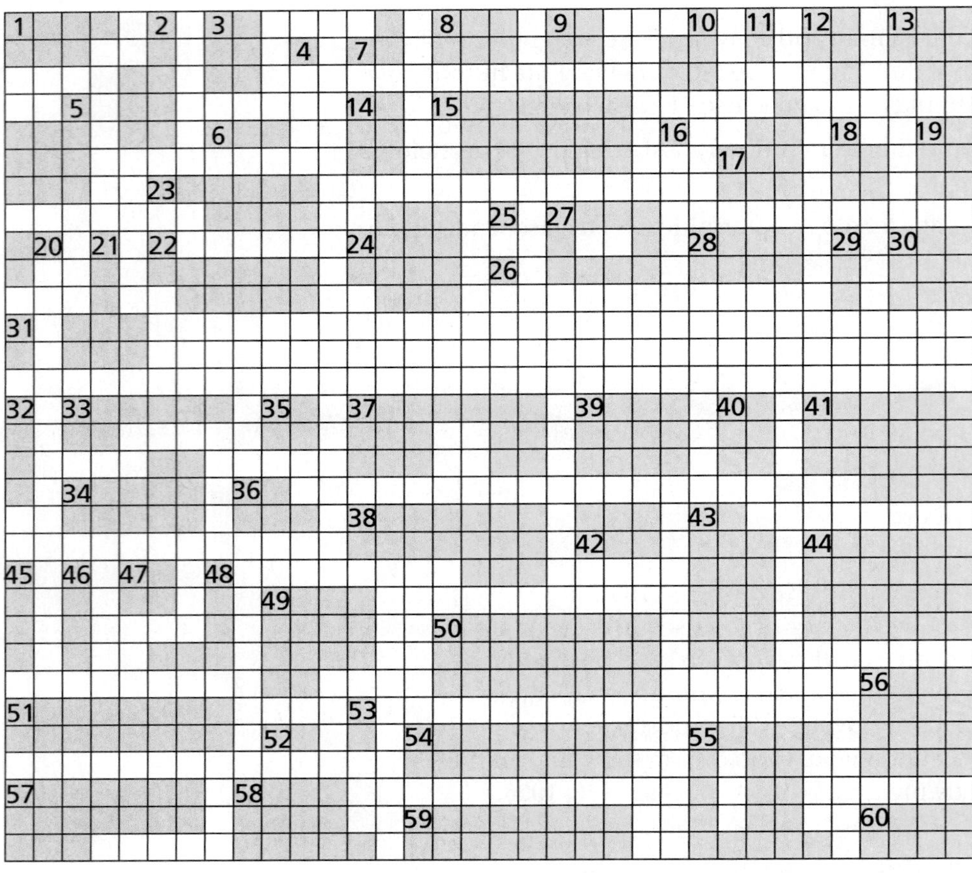

# 3.14 Sampling and Margin of Error

In this Investigation you have learned that experimental probability approaches theoretical probability over a large number of trials. For example, you would not be surprised if you flipped a fair coin 100 times and it came up heads 54% of the time. But if you flip a coin 10,000 times and it comes up heads 54% of the time, you should strongly suspect that the coin is unfair.

When you gather data from a sample survey, the process is reversed. Only the results from the survey are known. You then use these results to make estimates about the population the sample comes from.

## For You to Do

**1.** 100 students at a large school are randomly selected and asked whether they would support a proposal to start and end school 1 hour later. 24% say they would. Estimate an upper and lower bound for the percentage of students in the entire school who would say yes if asked the same question.

The result from a survey like this one is called a **sample statistic.** Sample statistics are used to estimate the **population parameter,** the value you would get if you conducted a census rather than a sample survey. You know that 24% of the sample approves of the proposal. This does *not* mean that 24% of the *population* of students approve. The true value for the population may be smaller or larger. But how much smaller or larger?

This question can be resolved through simulation, using a computer or other tool to run a large number of samples for several population parameters. Here's how:

- Pick a probability $p$, a guess at the population parameter.
- Simulate 100 Bernoulli trials with success rate $p$ and record the fraction of successes. This is called the **sample proportion.**
- Repeat the previous step a large number of times to build a distribution of samples for the probability $p$, displayed as a dot plot or histogram.
- Check to see if 0.24 (24%) is a plausible sample proportion in your distribution.

The numbers 0.24 and 100 came from this particular situation, so those may change, but the process stays the same.

**Remember...**

A Bernoulli trial has two outcomes, success with probability $p$ and failure with probability $1 - p$. If $p = 0.2$, 100 trials probably won't result in exactly 20 successes, but it should be close to it.

## Minds in Action

*Sasha comes in with a printout from a computer, hoping to answer the question about the school survey.*

**Sasha** I chose several values for $p$, then I had the computer run 200 simulations for each value of $p$. Here's what the output looks like.

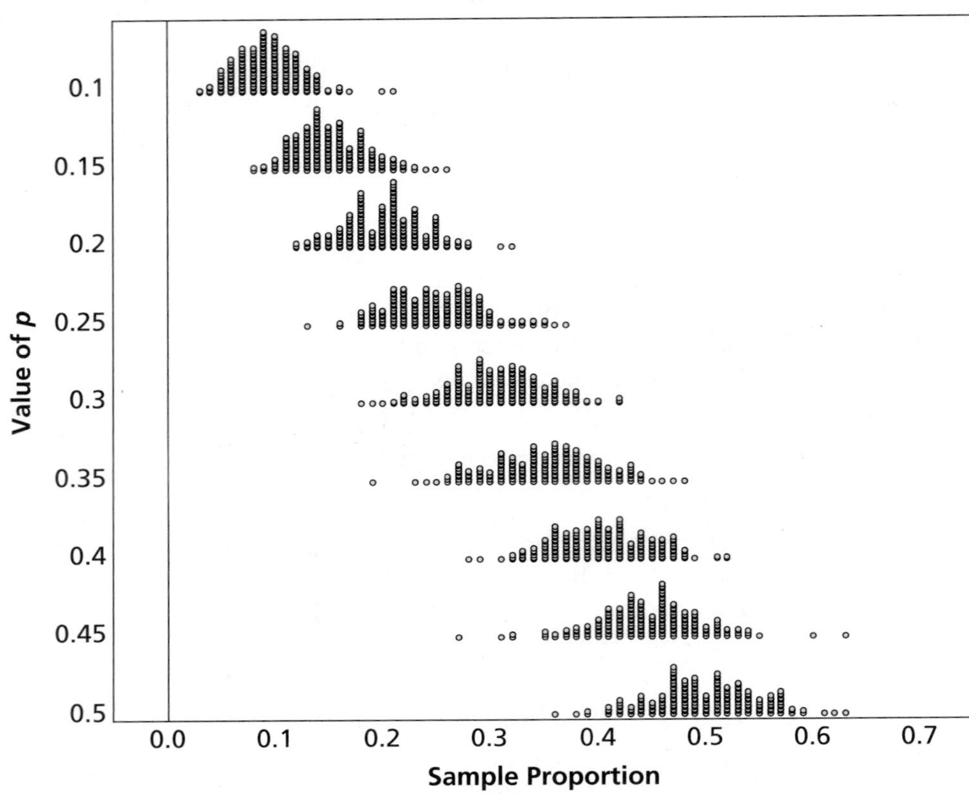


**Tony** What are all these graphs?

**Sasha** Focus on the top one, the one that says "0.1" on the side.

**Tony** It looks kind of like a distribution centered around 0.1. Oh, it's the results of the 200 simulations for $p = 0.1$. Each dot is one simulation, so it looks like a histogram. The horizontal axis shows the proportion of success from each simulation.

**Sasha** Right! And when you increase the value of $p$, the whole distribution moves to the right. It seems to keep roughly the same shape, even though none of them are exactly the same.

**Tony** How do we use this to answer the question about $p$ being equal to 24%?

**Sasha** I'm not really sure. 24% is 0.24, so let's start by finding it on the graph.

*Sasha draws a vertical line through 0.24.*

**Tony** I got it! If that line intersects one of the distributions, it's a reasonable value to choose for $p$. Otherwise, it isn't.

**Sasha** Sounds good. That throws out several of them, like when $p$ is 0.1, and when $p$ is 0.4 or 0.5. The rest are plausible, I'd say.

**Tony** Wait, now I'm not so sure. How many simulations was it for each value of $p$?

**Sasha** 200.

**Tony** Look at the distribution when $p$ is 0.35. It *barely* reaches 0.24. It looks like just four of the 200 simulations reached 24% or below. So, 98% of the time, it doesn't make it.

**Sasha** Hmm. The distribution when $p$ is 0.15 is similar. Now I don't know what to say. Are those plausible or not?

**Tony** It looks like we have to decide between how sure we are and how wide the interval is for plausible values of $p$. If we only want to be 98% sure, we can throw out 0.15 and 0.35. If we want to be closer to 100% sure, we can't.

**Sasha** I'm beginning to think we can never be 100% sure. I only did 200 simulations for each value of $p$. If I did more, maybe some more really rare things would happen.

**Tony** Good point.

## For You to Do

2. A different sample of 100 students was randomly selected, and 31% said they agreed with the proposal. Use Sasha's computer output to estimate a range for the actual proportion of students in the school who agree with the proposal.

31% is the *sample statistic*. You are estimating the *population parameter*.

Often, results from surveys are reported as "70%, plus or minus 4%." This 4% is called the **margin of error.** The margin of error is based on the natural variation expected in a sample statistic. If you took many random samples from a population with a population parameter of 70%, the results from the surveys would not always be exactly 70%. The margin of error estimates how much the sample statistic differs from the population parameter. What influences the margin of error?

## Example

Each day a polling organization asks Americans if they think that economic conditions are getting better or getting worse.

Polls in July 2011 suggested approximately 70% of all Americans felt conditions were getting worse. Suppose that *exactly* 70% of *all* Americans felt this way in July 2011. You can use simulations to estimate the margin of error in a new poll of 1500 randomly selected Americans.

Using population parameter $p = 0.7$, the histogram below shows the results from 4000 simulations of $n = 1500$ Bernoulli trials with success rate 0.7.

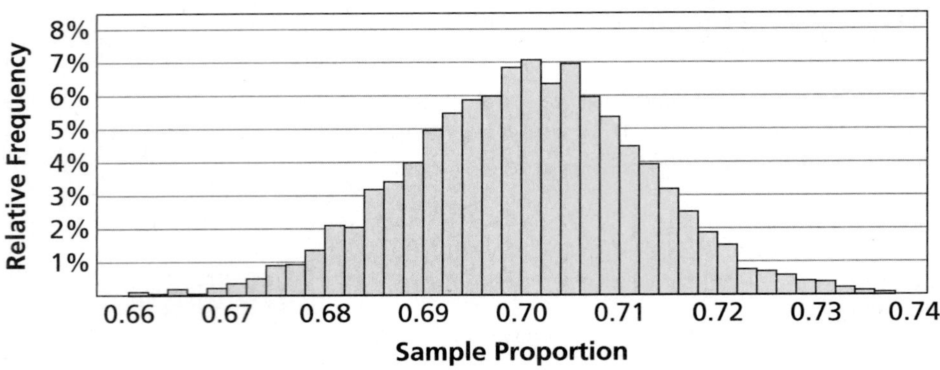


### Problem

a. Use the histogram to give a reasonable margin of error for polls of size 1500.

b. Determine the expected value of the mean and the standard deviation of the number of successes for 1500 Bernoulli trials with success rate $p = 0.7$. Then find the expected value of the mean and the standard deviation for the *proportion* of successes.

c. A poll in August 2011 found that 78% of respondents felt economic conditions were getting worse. Determine an interval likely to contain the true population parameter based on this poll.

### Solution

a. Based on the histogram, a large majority of the sample proportions fall between 0.67 and 0.73, and all fall between 0.66 and 0.74. It is reasonable to say there is a 3% margin of error. A 4% margin of error is wider but provides greater confidence.

b. Each Bernoulli trial has expected value 0.7 and variance $(0.7)(1 - 0.7) = 0.21$. In 1500 trials, the expected value for the mean is $\bar{x} = 1500 \cdot 0.7 = 1050$ and the variance is $\sigma^2 = 1500 \cdot 0.21 = 315$. The standard deviation is $\sqrt{315} \approx 17.75$.

To find the same information for the proportion of successes, divide by the number of trials (1500). The mean is 0.7, and the standard deviation for the proportion is about 0.0118, or 1.18%.

Why does it make sense for the mean to be 0.7?

The 3% margin of error found in part (a) is between 2 and 3 standard deviations from the mean.

**c.** The new sample statistic is 0.78. Like the distributions in the Minds in Action dialogue, the distribution of possible sample proportions for the poll will shift but will keep approximately the same shape. A reasonable interval is between 75% and 81% to reflect the 3% margin of error.

## For Discussion

**3.** Based on the data, do you think that the *actual* percentage of Americans who felt economic conditions were getting worse changed between July and August 2011? How sure are you?

## Developing Habits of Mind

**Generalize from repeated reasoning.** Simulation methods rely on knowing the population parameter. But sample surveys cannot give you that information. The strategy introduced in this lesson is to pick a value for the population parameter, run simulations, then decide if the sample statistic is a plausible estimate for the population parameter. By testing many different values, you can determine which ones are more likely.

At its core, this is the same general principle as the *guess-check-generalize* method for solving algebra word problems. By picking a value for the population parameter and testing it, the question changes from *"What can the population parameter be?"* to *"Can 0.3 be the population parameter?"* This is a much simpler question to answer, and even though it must be answered several times, it provides a method for solving the general question.

Unlike algebra, answering questions in statistics still involves uncertainty. Some samples can be "unlucky" in the sense that they can give you a sample statistic that is very different from the population parameter. It is impossible to determine an exact value for a population parameter without surveying the entire population.

**Remember...**

This assumes the "unlucky" sample was not biased. Be careful! If your sampling method is biased, you cannot make any conclusions, not even ones that are hedged with a degree of uncertainty.

A frequent method of reporting results is to give a confidence interval: "Based on the results of the survey, we are 95% confident that the population parameter is between 0.15 and 0.23."

A greater confidence level requires a wider interval and a greater margin of error. Most studies and polls report at the 95% confidence level.

## Exercises *Practicing Habits of Mind*

### Check Your Understanding

*Exercises 1–5 refer to this information.*

A computer was programmed to simulate shooting many free throws, assuming a success rate of 68%. The program ran 600 simulations each for shooting 80, 160, 320, 640, and 1280 free throws. The computer output below shows the distribution of sample proportions from all 600 runs of each length.

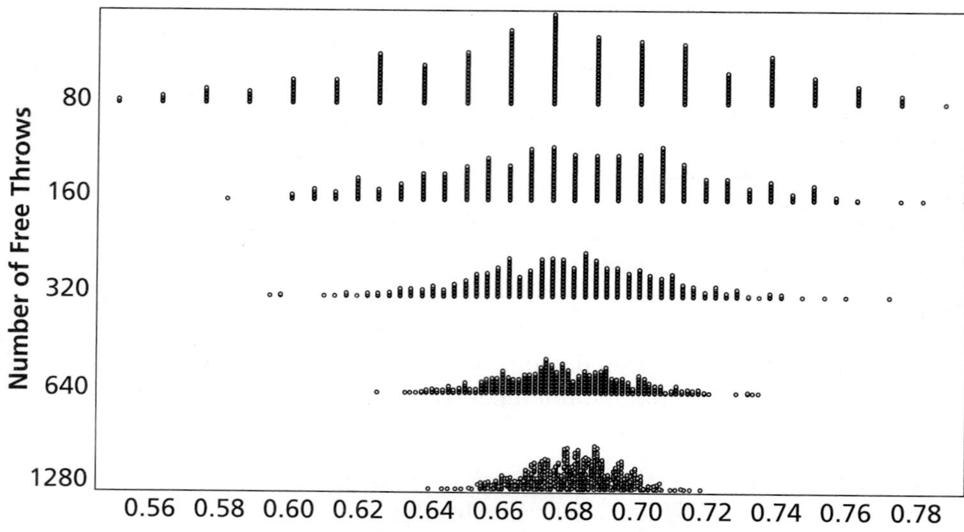


**1.** Which of the following statements are *plausible*, given the results of the simulations?

**a.** In 80 free throws, 75% of the shots went in.

**b.** In 80 free throws, 65% of the shots went in.

**c.** In 80 free throws, 55% of the shots went in.

**d.** In 160 free throws, 75% of the shots went in.

**e.** In 160 free throws, 65% of the shots went in.

**f.** In 160 free throws, 55% of the shots went in.

**g.** In 640 free throws, 75% of the shots went in.

**h.** In 640 free throws, 65% of the shots went in.

**i.** In 640 free throws, 55% of the shots went in.

**j.** In 1280 free throws, 75% of the shots went in.

**k.** In 1280 free throws, 65% of the shots went in.

**l.** In 1280 free throws, 55% of the shots went in.

2. Give a plausible range for the sample proportion for each number of free throws. Remember, in each case the population parameter is assumed to be 0.68.

   a. 80 free throws

   b. 160 free throws

   c. 320 free throws

   d. 640 free throws

   e. 1280 free throws

3. Copy and complete the table.

| $n$ | Center of Distribution | Plausible Range for Population Parameter | Margin of Error for Sample Statistic |
|---|---|---|---|
| 80 | ▨ | ▨ | ▨ |
| 160 | ▨ | ▨ | ▨ |
| 320 | ▨ | ▨ | ▨ |
| 640 | ▨ | ▨ | ▨ |
| 1280 | ▨ | ▨ | ▨ |

4. For each number of free throws, determine the standard deviations for the *number* and the *proportion* of free throws made at a 68% rate.

   a. 80 free throws

   b. 160 free throws

   c. 320 free throws

   d. 640 free throws

   e. 1280 free throws

**Remember...**

This is $n$ Bernoulli trials at a success rate $p = 0.68$, where each $n$ is given in parts (a)–(e).

5. a. Describe a relationship between the sample size and the standard deviation for the number of free throws made.

   b. Describe a relationship between the sample size and the plausible range for the population parameter of free throws made.

   c. Describe a relationship between the sample size and the margin of error.

6. **Write About It** Describe some differences between a sample statistic and a population parameter, and some examples of each.

## On Your Own

7. Suppose you roll ten standard number cubes and add their values.

   a. What are the greatest and least possible sums?

   b. What is the expected value of the sum?

   c. In Lesson 3.07 you determined that the variance for the value of a roll of one number cube is $\frac{35}{12}$. Find the variance for the sum when rolling ten number cubes.

   d. Show that the standard deviation of the sum when rolling ten number cubes is about 5.40.

   e. **Take It Further** Find the probability of getting a sum of 35 when rolling ten number cubes.

8. A computer simulated 400 rolls of ten standard number cubes and reported the sum of the ten numbers from each roll. This histogram shows the results.

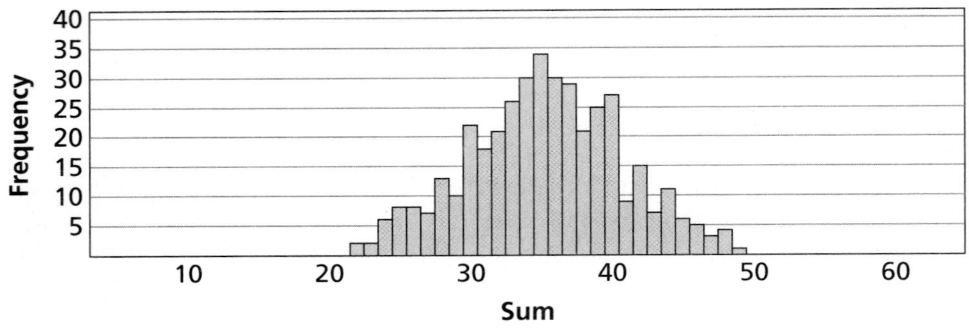


   a. Give a plausible sample statistic and margin of error for the sum when rolling ten number cubes.

   b. In what fraction of these 400 simulations was the sum equal to 35?

   c. In what fraction of these 400 simulations was the sum 50 or larger?

   d. In what fraction of these 400 simulations was the sum 20 or smaller?

9. Complete each statement with plausible values based on the histogram in Exercise 8.

   a. About 50% of the time, the sum of the ten number cubes will be within ____ of the expected value, between ____ and ____.

   b. About 80% of the time, the sum of the ten number cubes will be within ____ of the expected value, between ____ and ____.

   c. About 95% of the time, the sum of the ten number cubes will be within ____ of the expected value, between ____ and ____.

   d. Nearly 100% of the time, the sum of the ten number cubes will be within ____ of the expected value, between ____ and ____.

**10.** Approximately what percentage of the data in the histogram in Exercise 8 falls within each number of standard deviations from the mean?

**a.** 1 standard deviation

**b.** 2 standard deviations

**c.** 3 standard deviations

**11.** Take It Further In the Minds in Action dialogue, Sasha says that the distribution "seems to keep roughly the same shape" as the value of $p$ changes. Do you think this is always true? If so, explain why. If not, describe how the shape of the distribution might change.

**12.** This histogram shows the results of 4000 simulations of 40 coin flips with a fair coin.

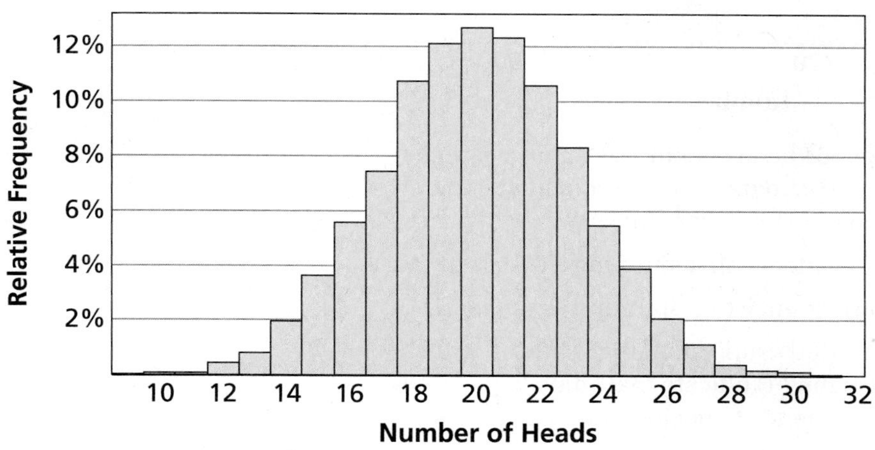


Jamey decided to *spin* a coin instead of flipping it. He got 16 heads out of 40, a sample proportion of 0.4. Using the histogram, which conclusion about Jamey's sample is most plausible? Explain your answer.

**A.** Jamey's sample gives strong evidence that spinning a coin is unfair.

**B.** Jamey's sample gives strong evidence that spinning a coin is fair.

**C.** The difference from the expected proportion might be due to an "unlucky" sample, but it also might indicate that spinning a coin is unfair. There is not enough evidence to decide.

**D.** Jamey's sample is plausible if spinning the coin is fair. There is good reason to believe that spinning a coin is fair.

13. This histogram shows the results of 4000 simulations of 160 coin flips with a fair coin.

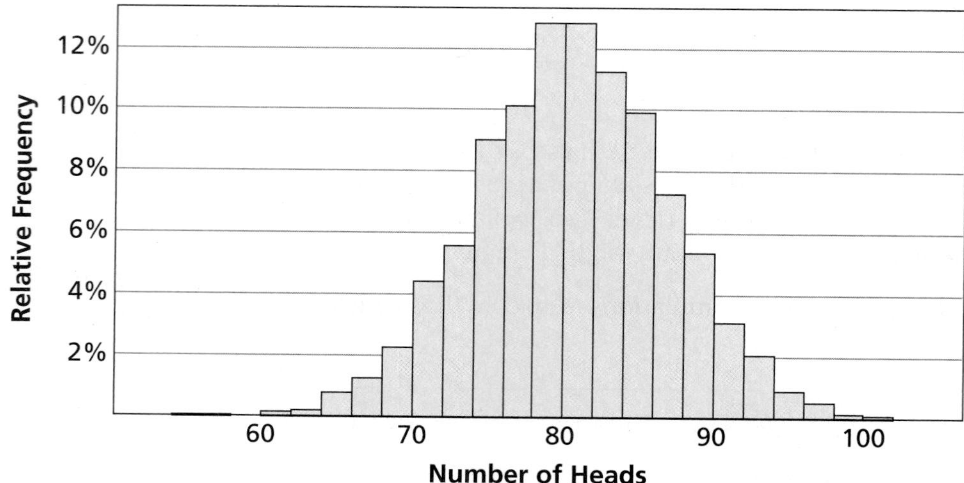


Jamey spun a coin again. He got 64 heads out of 160, again a sample proportion of 0.4. Using the new histogram, which conclusion about Jamey's sample is most plausible? Explain your answer.

**A.** Jamey's sample gives strong evidence that spinning a coin is unfair.

**B.** Jamey's sample gives strong evidence that spinning a coin is fair.

**C.** The difference from the expected proportion might be due to an "unlucky" sample, but it also might indicate that spinning a coin is unfair. There is not enough evidence to decide.

**D.** Jamey's sample is plausible if spinning the coin is fair. There is good reason to believe that spinning a coin is fair.

## Maintain Your Skills

14. For each value of $n$, determine the standard deviation for the *number* and *proportion* of heads when flipping a fair coin $n$ times.

**a.** $n = 10$

**b.** $n = 40$

**c.** $n = 160$

**d.** $n = 640$

15. Suppose you flip a fair coin $n$ times and find that the sample proportion of heads is 0.4. For each value of $n$ below, find the number of standard deviations the sample proportion is from the population parameter 0.5.

**a.** $n = 10$

**b.** $n = 40$

**c.** $n = 160$

**d.** $n = 640$

1. Dan claims his method of teaching is more effective than traditional teaching. Consider the partially completed table below.

| | Passed Exam | Failed Exam | Total |
|---|---|---|---|
| Dan | | | 50 |
| Control | | | 50 |
| Total | 60 | 40 | 100 |

   a. Complete the table if there is *little or no evidence* that Dan's teaching is more effective.

   b. Complete the table if there is *strong evidence* that Dan's teaching is more effective.

2. A 20-question multiple choice test has 3 options in each question. Derman guesses randomly on each question. Find the mean and standard deviation for the number of correct answers Derman will get.

3. In a recent survey conducted by police, 992 of the 1000 people surveyed said they buckle their seatbelt every time they drive. Explain why this data might be biased, and suggest some ways a more accurate percentage could be determined.

4. As the sample size of a simulation grows, what typically happens to the margin of error? Why?

5. How might you decide if a coin is fair or unfair?

6. What are some differences between sample surveys, experiments, and observational studies?

7. 100 fair coins are flipped. What is the mean and standard deviation for the number of coins that come up heads?

## Vocabulary and Notation

In this investigation, you learned these terms. Make sure you understand what each one means and how to use it.

- **Bernoulli trials**
- **control group**
- **experiment**
- **margin of error**
- **observational study**
- **population parameter**
- **random sampling**
- **sample statistic**
- **sample survey**
- **treatment group**
- ***z*-score**

# The Normal Distribution

**In *The Normal Distribution*, you will learn that if you repeat an experiment a large number of times, the graph of the average outcomes is approximately the shape of a bell curve. You will understand Central Limit Theorem, one of the central theorems of statistics.**

**By the end of this investigation, you will be able to answer questions like these.**

1. What is the Central Limit Theorem?
2. Why is the normal distribution so common?
3. What is the probability of rolling 10% or fewer sixes if you roll 1000 number cubes?

**You will learn how to:**

- make a probability histogram
- write an equation for a normal distribution given its mean and standard deviation
- use an appropriate normal distribution to find approximate probabilities

**You will develop these habits and skills:**

- Visualize the effect on a probability histogram of increasing the number of trials.
- Understand the consequences of the Central Limit Theorem and apply it correctly.
- Interpret and solve probability questions using appropriate normal distributions.

By design, the Empire State Building is a lightning rod. It is struck by lightning about 100 times a year. Some years lightning will strike the building fewer times and other years it will strike the building more times. The distribution of the number of lightning strikes to the building per year follows a bell curve.

# 3.15 Getting Started

A **probability histogram** is similar to a regular histogram, except each bar height (and area) is the probability of achieving each result, instead of the frequency of the result. For example, here is the probability histogram for the number of heads when tossing three coins:

The probability of getting 1 head in 3 tosses is $\frac{3}{8} = 0.375$, so that is the height and area of the bar in the histogram. What is the probability of getting at least 1 head in 3 tosses?

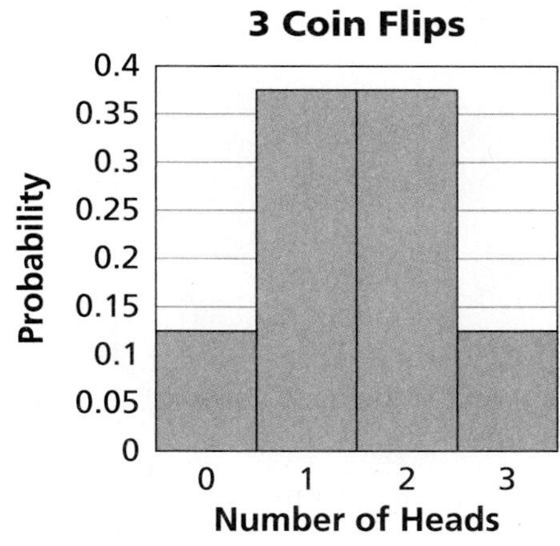


Probability histograms look the same as frequency histograms, but the height of each bar must be between 0 and 1. The sum of all bars' heights (and areas) is exactly 1.

## For You to Explore

1. In Exercise 1 on page 188, you made a frequency histogram for the distribution of sums when rolling four number cubes.

   Copy the diagram below. Make a probability histogram for the distribution of sums when rolling four number cubes. For example, the probability of rolling a sum of exactly 17 is $\frac{104}{1296} \approx 0.0802$.

The least possible sum is 4. The greatest is 24.

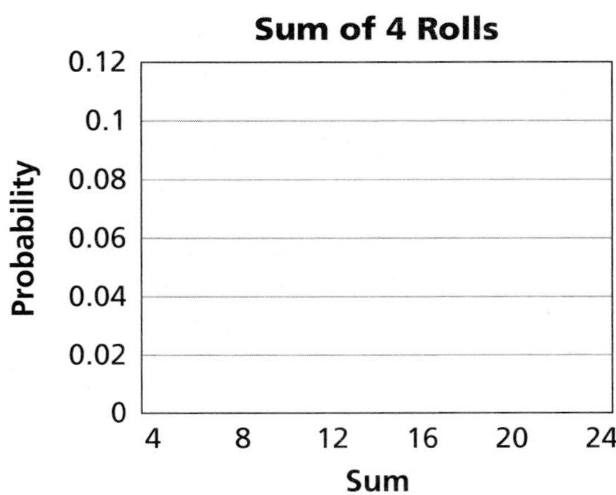

**2.** When flipping 10 coins, there are 1024 possible outcomes.

Copy the diagram below. Make a probability histogram for the distribution of the number of heads when flipping 10 coins. For example, the probability of flipping exactly 2 heads is $\frac{45}{1024} \approx 0.0439$.

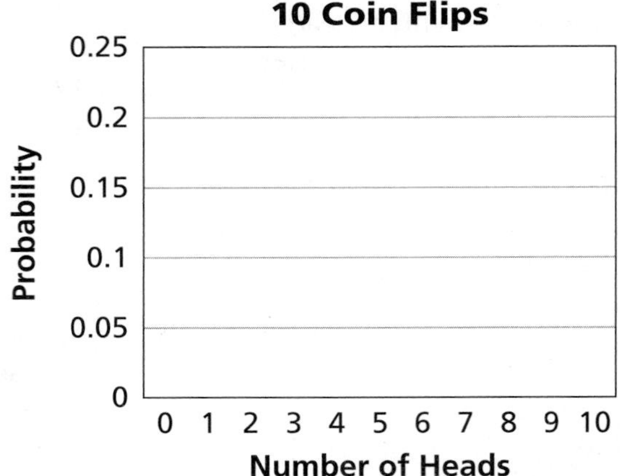


**3.** When the expression $(0.2r + 0.8w)^{20}$ is expanded, what is the coefficient of the $r^2w^{18}$ term? What might this coefficient signify?

**4.** A multiple-choice test has 20 questions, each question with five options. Only one option is correct.

Copy the diagram below. Make a probability histogram for the distribution of the number of questions you would get correct by guessing at random. For example, the probability of getting all 20 questions wrong is about 0.0115.

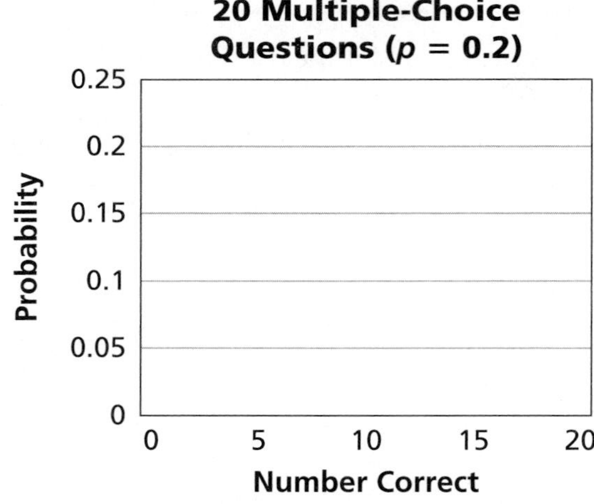

## Exercises *Practicing Habits of Mind*

### On Your Own

**5.** Expand the following polynomial.

$$\left(\frac{1}{6}x + \frac{1}{6}x^2 + \frac{1}{6}x^3 + \frac{1}{6}x^4 + \frac{1}{6}x^5 + \frac{1}{6}x^6\right)^4$$

**a.** Find the coefficient of the $x^{17}$ term to four decimal places.

**b.** What is the sum of all the coefficients?

**6.** Build a probability histogram for the number of heads when flipping

**a.** two coins. **b.** four coins. **c.** five coins.

**7.** Flip ten coins and write down the number of heads that result. Repeat this experiment thirty times and tabulate the results.

Use a cup. Scoop the 10 coins into the cup, and drop them.

| Number of Heads | Frequency |
|---|---|
| 0 | ■ |
| 1 | ■ |
| 2 | ■ |
| 3 | ■ |
| 4 | ■ |
| 5 | ■ |
| 6 | ■ |
| 7 | ■ |
| 8 | ■ |
| 9 | ■ |
| 10 | ■ |

**8. a.** Make a probability histogram for your data from Exercise 7.

**b.** Write About It Compare your probability histogram to the one from Exercise 2. What might explain the differences between the two histograms?

**9.** The probability that Todd makes a free throw is 0.642. In a game, Todd attempts ten free throws. Assuming each free throw is an independent event, find the probability that Todd makes

**a.** exactly 7 out of 10 free throws.

**b.** exactly 8 out of 10 free throws.

**c.** more than 8 out of 10 free throws.

**10.** Copy and complete this table for the function

$$f(n) = \binom{10}{n} \cdot (0.642)^n \cdot (0.358)^{10-n}$$

Give each answer to four decimal places.

| $n$ | $f(n)$ |
|---|---|
| 0 | ■ |
| 1 | ■ |
| 2 | ■ |
| 3 | ■ |
| 4 | ■ |
| 5 | ■ |
| 6 | ■ |
| 7 | ■ |
| 8 | ■ |
| 9 | ■ |
| 10 | ■ |

**11.** When you roll five number cubes, what is the probability of each event?

**a.** All five number cubes show the same number.

**b.** All five number cubes show different numbers.

**c.** Take It Further Exactly four number cubes show the same number.

## Maintain Your Skills

**12.** **a.** When rolling a number cube, there is a 1 in 6 chance of rolling a two. Find the probability, to four decimal places, that you roll the number cube six times and never get a two.

**b.** The spinner in a board game has numbers from 1 through 10, so there is a 1 in 10 chance of spinning a 2. Find the probability, to four decimal places, that you spin this spinner ten times and never get a 2.

**c.** When rolling two number cubes, there is a 1 in 36 chance of rolling a sum of two. Find the probability, to four decimal places, that you roll the pair of number cubes 36 times and never get a sum of two.

**d.** If an experiment with probability of success $\frac{1}{n}$ is run $n$ times, find the probability that none of the $n$ trials will be successful. As $n$ increases, what happens in the long run to this probability?

# 3.16 The Central Limit Theorem

In the Getting Started lesson, you made the probability histogram for several different probability distributions: rolls of a number cube, coin flips, and multiple-choice tests.

A **probability distribution** is a function that assigns a probability to each numeric output of a random variable. For example, if $X$ is the sum of four number cubes, the probability distribution gives $P(X = 17) \approx 0.0802$.

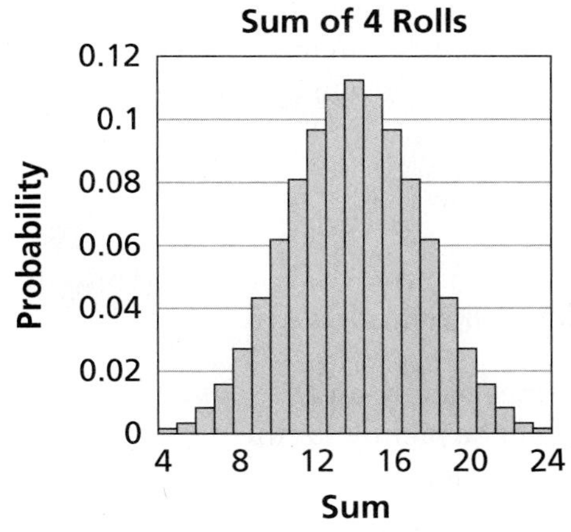


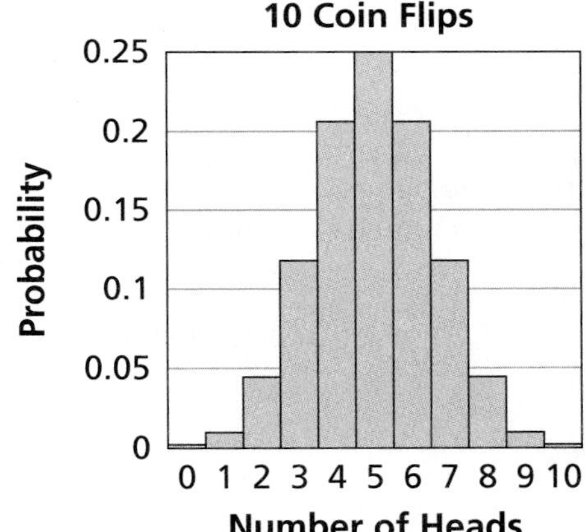


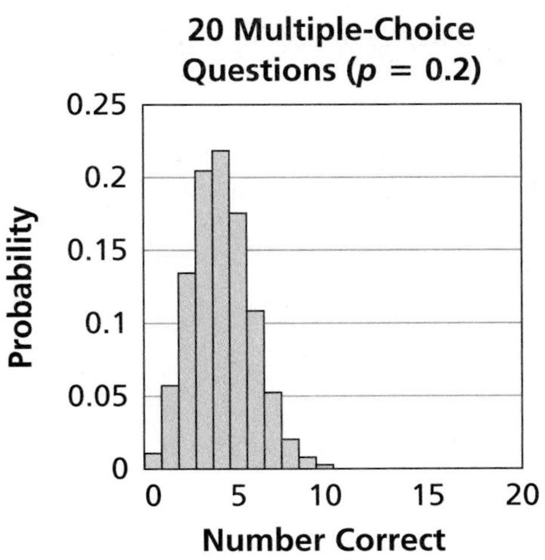


All three are the distributions of sums. The second distribution is the sum of 1's and 0's for the heads and tails of the flips. The third is the sum of 1's and 0's for the right and wrong answers.

## For You to Do

1. Use the first probability histogram on the previous page to estimate the probability of rolling higher than 15 as the sum of four number cubes.

All three histograms show very similar shapes, even though the original experiments are quite different from one another. The same "bell curve" emerges, no matter what you started from. This concept forms the basis of the Central Limit Theorem, which states that the results from repeated trials of an experiment approach a specific distribution: the **normal distribution.**

## Minds in Action

*Derman and Tony are comparing the three histograms shown above.*

**Derman** I don't trust this. Sure, the number cubes picture and the coin picture look similar, but I don't feel like the picture for the multiple-choice questions looks anything like that.

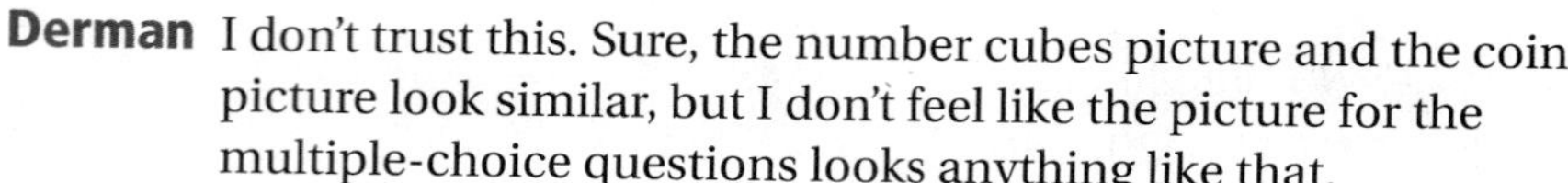

**Tony** Really? It's a little squished to one side, but that's because the questions aren't 50–50.

**Derman** Maybe with more questions?

**Tony** Alright, let's do 50 questions instead of 20.

**Derman** So . . . the probability of getting $n$ questions right on a 50-question test. Each question has a 20% chance of getting it right, 80% chance of getting it wrong.

**Tony** There was a formula for this in Lesson 3.12. For $k$ successes in 50 questions it's going to be

$$\binom{50}{k} \cdot (0.2)^k \cdot (0.8)^{50-k}$$

**Derman** Nice, but I have to keep entering different $k$ values.

**Tony** Then define it as a function on the calculator. For combinations, use "nCr."

See the TI-Nspire Handbook on p. 817 for details on programming this function into your calculator.

**Derman** Oh, very nice!

**Tony** Now I take all these answers and plot them as a histogram. This might take a moment . . .

*After some calculating . . .*

**Tony** Check it out.

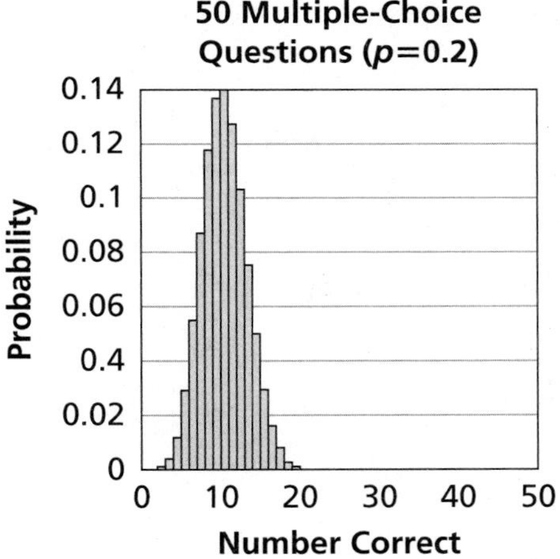


**Tony** I probably should've stopped at 20. Looks like it's really hard to get 20 out of 50 by guessing.

**Derman** And the mean is 10. That looks a lot more like the others. What if I start from something else, like The Wheel of Fish? It's got 1, 2, 3, and 10 on it. That's a mess, there's no way it's going to look like this picture.

**Tony** Use a polynomial. Each number is $\frac{1}{4}$ likely, so the polynomial for one spin is

$$(0.25x + 0.25x^2 + 0.25x^3 + 0.25x^{10})$$

Then raise that to some power. Might need to be a pretty high power to see a curve.

**Derman** Cool, I can get all the percentages for 10 spins by raising that to the 10th power and reading off the coefficients. I'll tell you tomorrow how I did. I'm still totally unconvinced.

**Tony** Good luck.

*The next day . . .*

**Derman** Look at this histogram for the 10 spins!

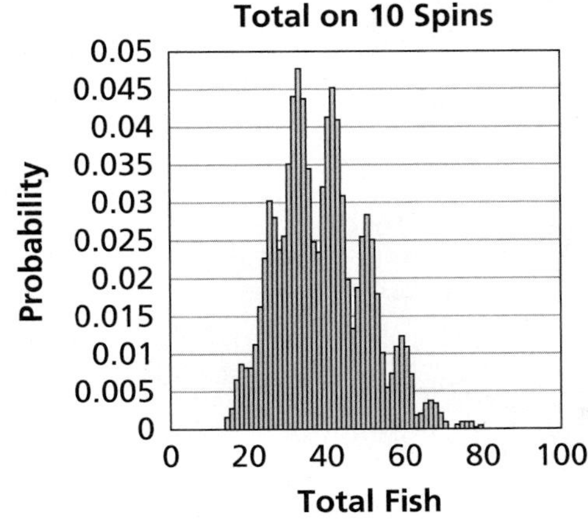


See the TI-Nspire Hand book on p. 817 for details on how Derman might have made this plot.

**Derman** It's like there's one big bell curve with the peaks. Then each peak has its own baby bell curve inside it.

**Tony** Wow, you've really given this a lot of thought.

**Derman** I know! I wasn't convinced about the overall shape for 10 spins, so I did it all again for 25 spins.

**Tony** And?

**Derman** Bam!

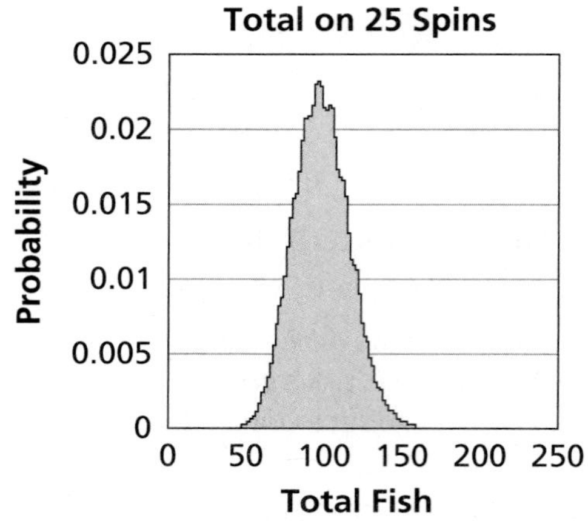


**Derman** And look where the biggest peak is: right at 100! Which is where it should be. The expected value is 4, times 25 spins.

**Tony** Hmm. That seems true for all of these. The coin flip peak is at 5 out of 10, the multiple choice peak is at 10 out of 50 . . . neat.

**Derman** I'm convinced. So when do we learn about this bell curve?

**Habits of Mind**

**Visualize.** The "bars" are much harder to see now, but the height at $n = 97$ is the probability that the sum for 25 spins is exactly 97. The total area of the shape is 1, since that is the total area of all the bars.

## Developing Habits of Mind

**Make a model.** The histograms shown seem to be taking the shape of a bell curve like this one:

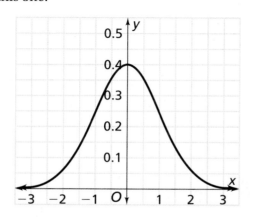

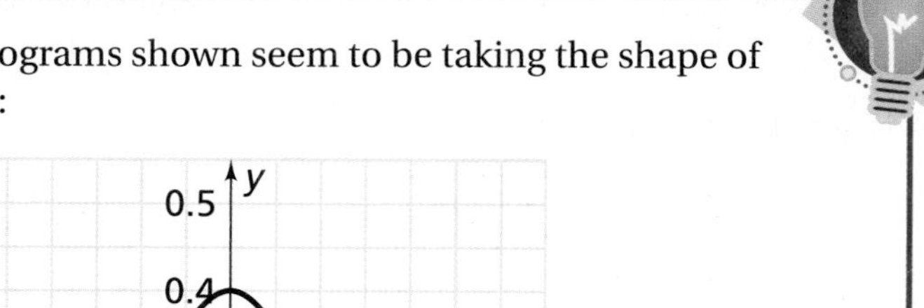

The function that defines this curve is a probability distribution called a *normal distribution.* The graph shows a normal distribution for a random variable with mean 0 and standard deviation 1. By stretching and shifting, you can construct a general normal distribution with any desired mean $\mu$ and any standard deviation $\sigma$. The notation for such a normal distribution is $N(\mu, \sigma)$.

The normal distribution gives you a close approximation for the behavior of repeated experiments. For example, on 25 spins of the spinner from the dialog, the mean is 100 and the standard deviation is $\sqrt{1250}$, or about 35. The behavior of this experiment can be approximated by $N(100, \sqrt{1250})$.

Similarly, the number of heads on 10 coin flips can be approximated by $N\left(5, \frac{\sqrt{10}}{2}\right)$ since those are the mean and standard deviation for the number of heads on 10 coin flips. Here is the probability histogram for the number of heads on 10 coin flips. It is overlaid with the graph of $N\left(5, \frac{\sqrt{10}}{2}\right)$, the corresponding normal distribution.

$P(a \leq X \leq b)$ is the probability that the value of random variable $X$ is between $a$ and $b$, inclusive. This probability equals the area that is under the curve of the distribution function and is between the two vertical lines $x = a$ and $x = b$.

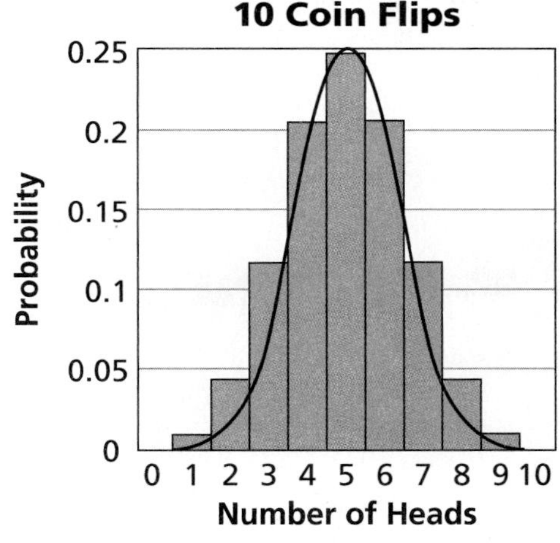


Most calculators have a function for displaying or defining a normal distribution $N(\mu, \sigma)$.

See the TI-NSpire Handbook on p. 817 for details on defining normal distributions.

Note that the normal distribution is an approximation of the probability histogram. The normal distribution is pretty accurate. It becomes even more accurate as the number of trials increases. In the end, the normal distribution is a single powerful tool that you can use to answer many different types of questions.

## For You to Do

2. Find the mean and standard deviation for the sum when rolling four number cubes. Then use a calculator to display the normal distribution that has this mean and standard deviation.

Here is the Central Limit Theorem. A proof of this theorem is beyond the scope of this book. It would be part of an advanced college course in statistics.

### *Theorem 3.3 Central Limit Theorem*

**Let $X$ be a random variable with mean $\mu$ and standard deviation $\sigma$. The distribution for the sum of the outputs of $X$ over $n$ experiments is more and more closely approximated by $N(\mu n, \sigma\sqrt{n})$ as $n$ grows larger.**

Often, people rephrase the Central Limit Theorem in terms of the mean of the results, rather than the sum. The statement is quite similar:

*Let X be a random variable with mean $\mu$ and standard deviation $\sigma$. The distribution for the mean of the outputs of X over n experiments is more and more closely approximated by $N\left(\mu, \frac{\sigma}{\sqrt{n}}\right)$ as n grows larger.*

The statement about the mean is interesting, since the standard deviation drops toward zero as $n$ increases. As you perform an experiment many times and look at the average of the results, the observed mean should get closer and closer to the theoretically expected mean. Try rolling 100 number cubes: the average roll should be close to 3.5. Try rolling 1000 number cubes: the average roll should be even closer to 3.5. The same is true for coin flips, for spins, for any repeated experiment.

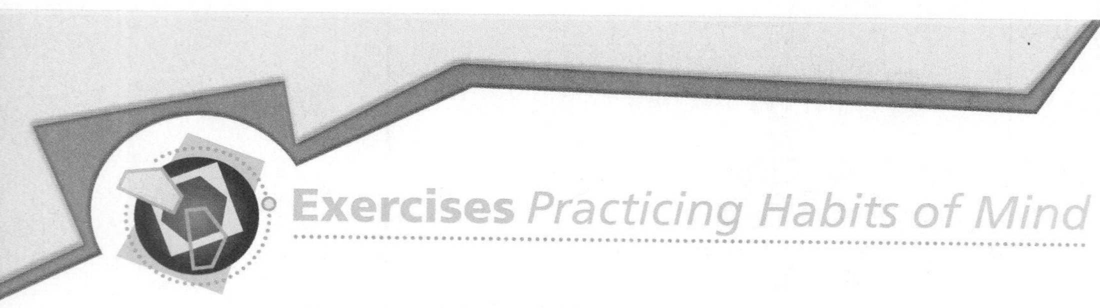

## Exercises *Practicing Habits of Mind*

### Check Your Understanding

1. **a.** As a class, compile the data generated from Exercise 7 from Lesson 3.15. Build a probability histogram for the class data.

   **b.** **Write About It** Compare the probability histogram for the class data to the theoretical distribution given on page 277.

   **c.** **Take It Further** Calculate the mean and standard deviation for the class data. Compare it to the theoretical prediction.

**2.** In this lesson, you learned that the distribution $N\left(5, \frac{\sqrt{10}}{2}\right)$ closely models the distribution for the number of heads when flipping 10 coins.

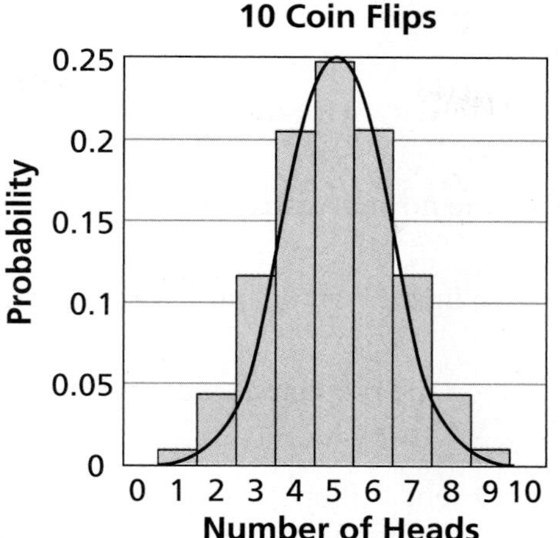


The theoretical distribution has mean 5 and standard deviation $\frac{\sqrt{10}}{2}$.

**a.** Using a calculator, find the value predicted by the distribution for the probability of flipping exactly 4 heads.

**b.** Find the actual probability of flipping exactly 4 heads on 10 coin tosses.

**c.** Find the percent error between the predicted value and the actual probability of flipping 4 heads on 10 coin tosses.

**d.** Find the percent error between the predicted value and the experimental probability that you found for your class in Exercise 1.

On many calculators, this is normpdf $\left(4, 5, \frac{\sqrt{10}}{2}\right)$ See the TI-Nspire Handbook on p. 817 for more information.

## Historical Perspective

The first person to explore the normal distribution was Abraham de Moivre. De Moivre's work is motivated by what he called "Problems of Chance."

> Altho' the Solution of Problems of Chance often require that several Terms of the Binomial $(a + b)^n$ be added together, nevertheless in very high Powers the thing appears so laborious, and of so great a difficulty, that few people have undertaken that Task . . .

De Moivre went on to determine the equation for the normal distribution, and provided some computations. The most well-known of these computations is that for a normal distribution, about 68.3% of data falls within one standard deviation from the mean. He then gives a specific example: 3600 fair "Experiments" (with 50% likelihood).

> Hence $\frac{1}{2}n$ will be 1800, and $\frac{1}{2}\sqrt{n} = 30$, then the Probability of the Event's neither appearing oftner than 1830 times, nor more rarely than 1770, will be 0.682688.

De Moivre goes on to say how his concepts could be used to decide whether a coin was fair: continue flipping it long enough, and the observed probability from its results should come closer and closer to 50–50. If not, the coin must be unfair in some way.

3. a. Find the mean and standard deviation for the number of heads when flipping 100 coins.

   b. Find the value predicted by the normal distribution for the probability of flipping exactly 43 heads.

   c. Use the Binomial Theorem to find the actual probability of flipping exactly 43 heads.

   d. Find the percent error between the predicted value and the actual probability of flipping exactly 43 heads.

4. De Moivre described the experiment of flipping 3600 coins and counting the number of heads. He said that roughly 68% of the time, the actual number of heads will be within one standard deviation of the mean.

   a. Find the mean and standard deviation for the number of heads when flipping 3600 coins.

   b. If the number of coins was doubled to 7200, what would happen to the mean? the standard deviation?

   c. For 7200 coin flips, find an interval that includes roughly 68% of the data.

5. A spinner has the numbers 1, 1, 2, and 4 on its four wedges.

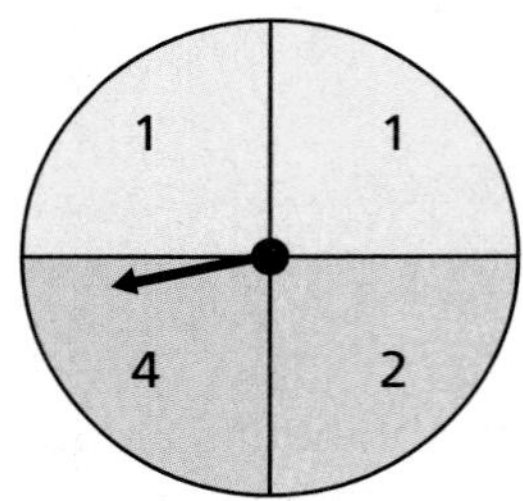


   Build a probability histogram for each experiment.

   a. one spin of the spinner

   b. sum of two spins

   c. the sum of three spins

   d. the sum of four spins

   e. Take It Further the sum of ten spins

**Habits of Mind**

**Represent the situation.** The polynomial $0.25s^4 + 0.25s^2 + 0.5s$ might be helpful in this exercise.

6. The Minds in Action dialog in this lesson refers to 25 spins of the Wheel of Fish with the numbers 1, 2, 3, and 10 on it.

   a. Find the mean and standard deviation for the sum of all 25 spins.

   b. Find a range that includes roughly 68% of the data.

**Remember...**

One spin of the Wheel of Fish has mean 4, variance 12.5, and standard deviation $\sqrt{12.5}$.

7. Suppose you flip 100 coins and count the number of heads.

   a. Using de Moivre's findings, give a range that should include roughly 68% of the data.

   b. Using the Binomial Theorem, find the actual probability that the total number of heads will be in this range.

## On Your Own

**8.** One of de Moivre's other findings is that for experiments that are approximated by a bell curve, roughly 95% of the data falls within two standard deviations of the mean. The range of values within two standard deviations of the mean is the 95% **confidence interval.**

**a.** Find a 95% confidence interval for the number of heads when flipping 3600 coins.

**b.** Find a 95% confidence interval for the number of heads when flipping 100 coins.

**c.** Find a 95% confidence interval for the total in 25 spins of the Wheel of Fish from Exercise 6.

If the mean is 100 and the standard deviation is 20, a 95% confidence interval is from 60 to 140. This assumes and requires that the distribution is close to a bell curve.

**9.** Hannah is a "300 hitter" in softball. She gets a hit on each at-bat with probability $p = 0.3$. Assume each at-bat is an independent Bernoulli trial.

**a.** Find the mean and standard deviation for the numbers of hits Hannah gets in 60 at-bats.

**b.** For 60 at-bats, find a 95% confidence interval for Hannah's batting average, found by dividing the number of hits by the number of at-bats.

**c.** For a full season of 600 at-bats, find a 95% confidence interval for Hannah's batting average.

**Habits of Mind**

**Use a different process.** You could find a confidence interval for the number of hits, then divide by 60.

**10.** **a.** Repeat Exercise 9 for Sally, a "250 hitter" who gets a hit with probability $p = 0.25$.

**b.** Write About It Describe how your results show that Sally could outhit Hannah over a short time period, but is much less likely to do so for an entire season.

**11.** Todd makes free throws with probability of success $p = 0.642$.

**a.** Find the mean and standard deviation for the number of successes in 100 free throws.

**b.** Find a 95% confidence interval for the number of free throws Todd will make in 100 tries.

**c.** Use a normal approximation to estimate, to six decimal places, the probability that Todd makes exactly 70 out of 100 free throws.

**d.** Use the Binomial Theorem to find, accurate to six decimal places, the probability that Todd makes exactly 70 out of 100 free throws.



On a calculator, you might do this using normpdf (70, $\mu$, $\sigma$) where $\mu$ and $\sigma$ are the mean and standard deviation you found in part (a).

**12.** **Take It Further** Use the Binomial Theorem to find the probability that Todd makes between $x$ and $y$ free throws in 100 tries, where $x$ and $y$ are the ends of the confidence interval you found in Exercise 11.

**13.** **What's Wrong Here?** Andrea said she got an unexpected result when thinking about the Central Limit Theorem.

Andrea: It says it should work for just about anything, so I picked a spinner that has 1 through 10 on it. I made a table for two spins and built the probability histogram.

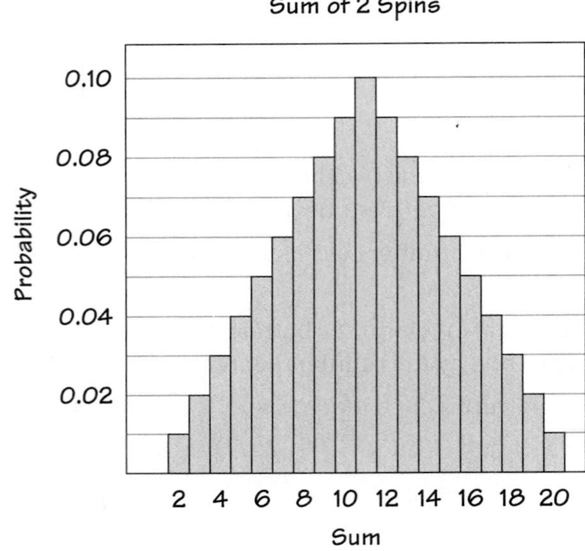


But it's a triangle shape. The lesson says this is supposed to look like a bell curve, but to me it doesn't look anything like that.

What would you say to Andrea in this situation to help?

**14.** **Standardized Test Prep** A spinner with 12 has the numbers 1–12 in equal wedges. What is the probability that the sum of two spins is 13?

**A.** $\frac{1}{18}$ **B.** $\frac{1}{13}$ **C.** $\frac{1}{12}$ **D.** $\frac{1}{8}$

## Maintain Your Skills

**15.** A number cube has 1, 2, 3, 4, 5, and 5 on its faces. Build a probability histogram for the sum of the number for each of the following experiments.

**a.** two rolls

**b.** three rolls

**c.** four rolls

**Remember...**

You can use a polynomial power to help calculate the results.

# 3.17 The Normal Distribution

In Lesson 3.16, you saw the importance of the normal distribution. The heights, weights, and life expectancies of people are (typically) normally distributed. This lesson explores the graphs and properties of the normal distribution.

Each normal distribution is characterized by its mean $\mu$ and standard deviation $\sigma$. The notation for the distribution is $N(\mu, \sigma)$. The **unit normal distribution** has mean 0 and standard deviation 1.

$$N(0, 1) = \frac{1}{\sqrt{2\pi}} e^{\frac{-x^2}{2}}$$

The number e ≈2.71828 has some very important applications. You'll learn more about e in Chapter 8.

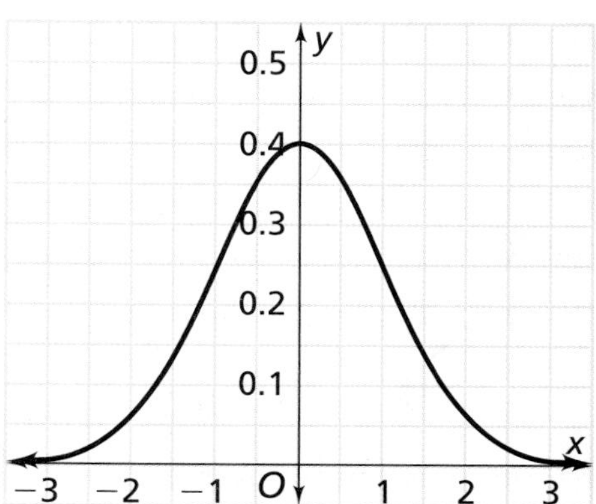


The equation for the normal distribution has the property that the total area between the curve and the $x$-axis is 1. This is very similar to the probability histograms in the Getting Started lesson where the total area of all the bars is exactly 1. It may help to picture many small-width bars on the above graph, between the curve and the $x$-axis.

Since the total area under the curve is 1, the unit normal distribution measures probability. Other normal distributions are shifted in ways that preserve this total area, so that they too are useful in answering questions about probability.

Consider a normal distribution with mean 0 and standard deviation $\sigma$.

$$N(0, \sigma) = \frac{1}{\sigma} \cdot \frac{1}{\sqrt{2\pi}} e^{\frac{-\left(\frac{x}{\sigma}\right)^2}{2}}$$

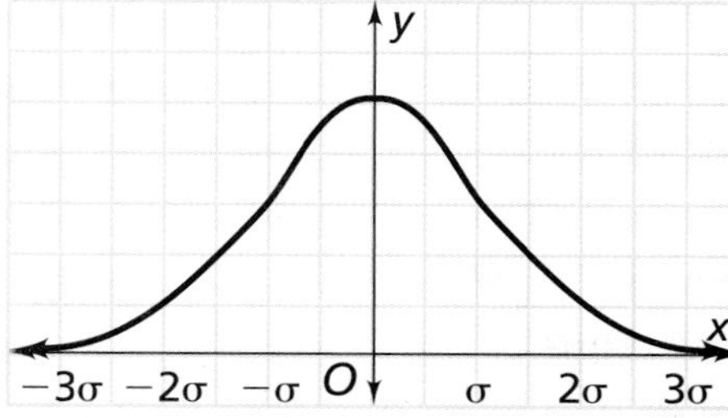


Note that this graph is $\sigma$ times as wide as the unit normal distribution and $x$ has been replaced by $\frac{x}{\sigma}$. This results in a horizontal stretch (for $\sigma < 1$). But the total area under this curve must still be equal to 1 if it is going to serve as a measure of probability. That means that a corresponding vertical shrink (also by a factor of $\sigma$) is done. The factor of $\frac{1}{\sigma}$ in front has this result. So by stretching the curve in the $x$ direction and shrinking it in the $y$ direction, the graph of $N(0, \sigma)$ still has a total area of 1 between its curve and the $x$-axis.

A horizontal shift of $\mu$ units to the right will center this graph at the mean. You can make an equation that has this kind of graph by replacing $x$ in the previous equation by $x - \mu$. This gives you the equation for $N(\mu, \sigma)$, the normal distribution with mean $\mu$ and standard deviation $\sigma$:

$$N(\mu, \sigma) = \frac{1}{\sigma} \cdot \frac{1}{\sqrt{2\pi}} e^{\frac{-\left(\frac{x-\mu}{\sigma}\right)^2}{2}}$$

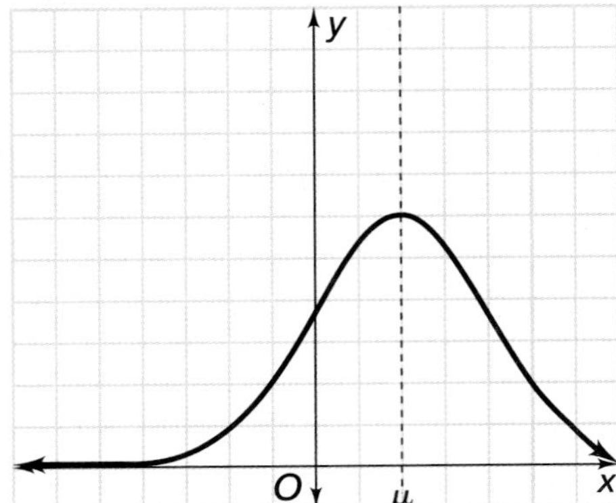


Note that the graph has shifted along the horizontal axis, but the overall shape of the bell curve has not changed.

It is possible to find the area between any two $x$-values under a normal curve. This graphic shows several important percents:

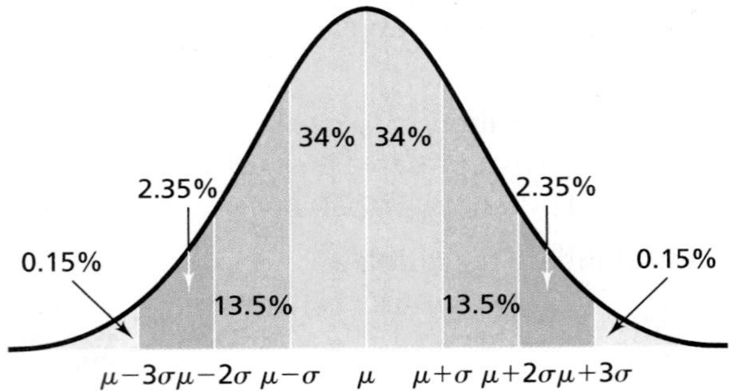


Adding these percents gives the following facts about normal distributions.

## Facts and Notation

**For a normal distribution, approximately**

- **68% of the data lie within one standard deviation of the mean.**
- **95% of the data lie within two standard deviations of the mean.**
- **99.7% of the data lie within three standard deviations of the mean.**

## For You to Do

Adult women's heights are normally distributed, with a mean of 63.5 inches and a standard deviation of 2.5 inches.

1. Approximately what percent of women have height between 61 inches and 66 inches?

2. Give a range in which approximately 99.7% of all women's heights should lie.

You can use a calculator to find the area under a normal distribution. On many calculators, the name for the function is normCdf. Its four inputs are the lower and upper boundaries, then the mean and standard deviation of the distribution. The output is a decimal between 0 and 1, giving the area under the curve.

See the TI-Nspire Handbook p. 817 Appendix for more information.

normCdf $(-2, 2, 0, 1) = 0.9545$
(the 95% rule)

normCdf $(60, 72, 63.5, 2.5) = 0.9189$
(the percent of women with height between 5 feet and 6 feet)

## Developing Habits of Mind

**Explore relationships.** There are two functions for working with normal distributions: normPdf and normCdf. Each has a different use.

Use the PDF, short for **probability density function,** when approximating values in a matching histogram. The approximate percentage of women with height 5 feet 5 inches is given by

normPdf $(65, 63.5, 2.5) = 0.13329$

Approximately 13.3% of adult women have a height of 5 feet, 5 inches.

Think of this one as the height of the histogram bar at 65 inches. The normal distribution gives an approximation for what the real bar's height should be.

Use the CDF, short for **cumulative density function** to find the area under the normal curve between two values. It gives the percentage of values that fall within a range.

normCdf $(60, 65, 63.5, 2.5) = 0.64499$

Approximately 64.5% of adult women have heights between 5 feet and 5 feet 5 inches.

Think of this one as the total area of all the bars between 60 and 65 inches The normal distribution's CDF gives the total area under the curve in this range, which should be close to the total area of the bars in that range.

You will see more about finding the area under a curve in later courses. This concept, called the *integral,* is one of the foundations of calculus. The CDF is the integral of the PDF.

## Example

**Problem** An experiment consists of tossing a coin 10,000 times.

**a.** What is the probability of getting *exactly* 5000 heads and 5000 tails?

**b.** What is the probability of getting between 4900 and 5100 heads?

**Solution**

**a.** According to the Binomial Theorem, the result should be

$$\binom{10000}{5000}(0.5)^{5000}(0.5)^{5000}$$

Most calculators cannot find the result for the binomial. It is too large a number to hold. So, approximate by using a normal curve. For one coin flip, the mean for the number of heads is $\frac{1}{2}$. The variance is $\frac{1}{4}$. For 10,000 coin flips, the mean is $10{,}000 \cdot \frac{1}{2} = 5000$ and the variance is $10{,}000 \cdot \frac{1}{4} = 2500$. The standard deviation is the square root of the variance, or 50. The 10,000 coin flips are approximated by $N(5000, 50)$.

> You could also use the formulas given in Lesson 3.12.

Use the normPdf function to approximate the probability of getting exactly 5000 heads:

normPdf(5000, 5000, 50) $=$ 0.007979

You have about a 0.8% chance of getting exactly 5000 heads when you flip 10,000 coins.

> The actual value is about 0.00797865, while the normal approximation gives 0.00797885. Extremely close!

**b.** Using the standard deviation of 50, 4900 and 5100 are exactly two standard deviations away from the mean of 5000. Apply the 68-95-99.7 rule: you have about a 95% chance of getting between 4900 and 5100 heads when you flip 10,000 coins.

Or you could use normCdf.

normCdf(4900, 5100, 5000, 50) $=$ 0.9545

## Exercises *Practicing Habits of Mind*

### Check Your Understanding

Go Online
www.successnetplus.com

1. The Intelligence Quotient, or IQ, is a score given as the result of an intelligence test. Adult IQ is normally distributed with mean 100 and standard deviation 15.
   **a.** About what percentage of adults have IQ between 85 and 115?
   **b.** About what percentage of adults have IQ between 70 and 130?
   **c.** About what percentage of adults have IQ above 130?

2. Adult men's heights are normally distributed, with a mean of 69 inches and a standard deviation of 3 inches.
   **a.** Approximately what percent of men have heights between 66 and 72 inches?
   **b.** Give a range in which approximately 99.7% of all men's heights should lie.

3. **a.** Find the mean and standard deviation for the number of heads when tossing 2500 coins.
   **b.** Find the approximate probability of getting 49% or fewer heads when tossing 2500 coins.

4. Use the normal CDF to find the approximate probability of getting 49% or fewer heads when tossing each of the following.
   **a.** 100 coins **b.** 400 coins **c.** 900 coins
   **d.** 2500 coins **e.** 10,000 coins **f.** 40,000 coins
   **g.** 1,000,000 coins

5. Exercise 3 in Lesson 3.12 asked this question:

   > If you rolled 240 number cubes and got only 20 sixes, would that be a surprising result or within reasonable limits?

   Use a normal distribution to approximate the number of sixes when rolling 240 number cubes. Find the approximate probability that the number of sixes recorded is 20 or fewer.

6. **Take It Further** For normally distributed data, the range within two standard deviations of the mean is the 95% confidence interval. However, other confidence intervals can be calculated by changing the number of standard deviations. Determine, to two decimal places, how many standard deviations are needed for each of the following.
   **a.** 50% confidence interval **b.** 68% confidence interval
   **c.** 90% confidence interval **d.** 99% confidence interval

## On Your Own

7. a. Using the values from Exercise 2, find the approximate percent of men with heights between 5 feet and 6 feet.

   b. Find the approximate percent of men with height 5 feet 11 inches.

8. Revisit Exercise 13 from Lesson 3.09.

   > In a new promotion, 100 people will spin the Wheel of Fish for prizes. The manager of the market is hoping that no more than 500 fish will be given away. Is this a likely outcome?

   Use the normal curve's CDF to find the probability that more than 500 fish will be given away by the market.

The Wheel of Fish has the values 1, 2, 3, and 10 on it. One spin has mean 4 and variance 12.5.

9. It is believed that 60% of the population is now in favor of Proposition 1338. Suppose a pollster questions 500 people.

   a. Find the mean and standard deviation for the number of people (out of 500) who will say they are in favor of Proposition 1338.

   b. Find a 95% confidence interval for the percentage of people who will say they are in favor of Proposition 1338.

10. A wider poll of Proposition 1338 involves 2000 people. Find a 95% confidence interval for the percentage of people who will say they are in favor of Proposition 1338.

11. Show that for Bernoulli trials, when the number of trials is multiplied by 4, the 95% confidence interval is twice as wide, but is half as wide if expressing the proportion of observed successes.

Go Online
www.successnetplus.com

12. When tossing 240 coins, find the probability that the number of heads will be between 115 and 125, inclusive.

13. **Standardized Test Prep** In an experiment, you are to toss 100 coins and record the proportion that land heads. What is the standard deviation of the experiment?

    **A.** 0.025 **B.** 0.05 **C.** 0.1 **D.** 0.25

## Maintain Your Skills

14. A number cube has the faces 1, 3, 4, 5, 6, and 8. Build a probability histogram for the sum of the rolls in each experiment.

    **a.** two rolls **b.** three rolls **c.** four rolls

**Remember...**

You can use a polynomial power to help calculate the results.

**In this investigation, you learned about the normal distribution, $N(\mu, \sigma)$, a function that approximates the average outcomes of a large number of repeated experiments. People call it a bell curve because of the shape of its graph. The following questions will help you summarize what you have learned.**

1. Make a probability histogram for the number of heads when flipping eight coins.
2. A number cube has the numbers 1, 2, 2, 3, 3, and 4 on it. Find a 95% confidence interval for the sum when rolling this number cube 132 times.
3. Give some examples of situations where a normal distribution could apply. Give some examples of where a normal distribution could not apply.
4. Approximate the probability of getting between 190 and 210 heads when flipping 400 coins.
5. Todd shoots free throws with a probability of success $p = 0.642$. In a season, Todd shoots 164 free throws. Use the normal approximation to find the probability that Todd makes at least 110 free throws in a season.
6. Approximately what percentage of women's heights are between 5 feet 3 inches and 5 feet 9 inches? Recall the mean of women's heights is 63.5 inches. The standard deviation is 2.5 inches.
7. What is the Central Limit Theorem?
8. Why is the normal distribution so common?
9. What is the probability of rolling 10% or fewer sixes if you roll 1000 number cubes?

## Vocabulary and Notation

In this investigation, you learned these terms and symbols. Make sure you understand what each one means and how to use it.

- **confidence interval**
- **cumulative density function**
- **normal distribution, $N(\mu, \sigma)$**
- **probability density function**
- **probability distribution**
- **probability histogram**
- **unit normal distribution, $N(0, 1)$**

# Review

In **Investigation 3A,** you learned to

- calculate probabilities of simple random events.
- determine a set of equally likely outcomes for a probability experiment.
- find a polynomial to model a probability experiment and interpret expansions of its powers.
- calculate the expected value of a random variable.

*The following questions will help you check your understanding.*

**1.** In a game you are to roll a pair of regular octahedrons each with eight faces numbered 1–8.

**a.** Write out the sample space for this experiment.

**b.** What is the probability of rolling two 5's?

**c.** What is the probability of rolling exactly one 5?

**d.** What is the probability that the sum of the numbers on the faces is 9?

**2.** A game spinner has three colors, red, green, and blue. Each is equally likely. Expand $(r + b + g)^3$ to find the probability of getting two reds and one green when you spin three times.

**3.** A local high school is holding a raffle to raise money for extracurricular activities at the school. They plan to sell 1000 tickets. There will be one prize of \$500, 2 prizes of \$200, and 5 prizes of \$100. What is the expected value of one ticket?

In **Investigation 3B,** you learned to

- calculate expected value, mean absolute deviation, variance, and standard deviation.
- calculate statistics for compound events, including repeated experiments.

*The following questions will help you check your understanding.*

**4.** At a recent family reunion, Carla recorded the ages of the ten children, aged 1–9, who were attending. She built the following table:

| Age, *x* | Frequency |
|---|---|
| 1 | 2 |
| 2 | 1 |
| 4 | 3 |
| 5 | 1 |
| 7 | 2 |
| 9 | 1 |

Calculate each statistic.

**a.** the mean

**b.** the mean absolute deviation

**c.** the variance

**d.** the standard deviation

**5.** Karen and Joe each have a spinner. The numbers on Karen's spinner are 1, 2, 4, and 6. The numbers on Joe's spinner are 3, 5, 7, and 11. They each are to spin and then add the numbers that result. Find the mean, variance, and standard deviation for the 16 possible outcomes.

6. Using Karen's spinner from Exercise 5, find the mean, variance, and standard deviation for the sum of each number of spins.

   a. one spin

   b. four spins

   c. ten spins

   d. 100 spins

7. A local bus company advertises that your bus will be on time 85% of the time. If you are to take the bus 40 days, find the mean, variance, and standard deviation for the number of times the bus will be on time.

---

In **Investigation 3C,** you learned to

- identify Bernoulli trials and compute statistics using the specialized formulas for this case.
- Recognize biased and unbiased samples and sampling techniques.
- Use simulations to approximate a margin of error for how well a sample statistic estimates a population parameter.

*The following questions will help you check your understanding:*

8. The Big Shoes company claims its shoes will help athletes clear a 5-foot high jump bar. Consider the partially completed table below.

| | Cleared Jump | Failed Jump | Total |
|---|---|---|---|
| Big Shoes | | | 30 |
| Control | | | 30 |
| Total | 20 | 40 | 60 |

   a. Complete the table if there is *little or no evidence* that Big Shoes are more effective.

   b. Complete the table if there is *strong evidence* that Big Shoes are more effective.

9. What is the probability of getting exactly three sixes when 15 dice are rolled?

10. Todd normally makes 64.2% of his free throws. One day he makes 80 out of 100 free throws.

   a. Find the mean and standard deviation for the number of free throws Todd should make out of 100 trials.

   b. Does it seem plausible for Todd's improved result to have happened by chance? Explain.

---

In **Investigation 3D,** you learned to

- make a probability histogram.
- write an equation for a normal distribution given its mean and standard deviation.
- use an appropriate normal distribution to find approximate probabilities.

*The following questions will help you check your understanding.*

11. Consider this experiment: Place four balls labeled with the numbers 1, 1, 2, and 3 in a bag. Draw one ball, record its number and replace it. Draw again, record the number of the ball. Add the two numbers. Make a probability histogram for the sum of the two numbers.

12. Use the container and numbered balls from Exercise 11. Make 10 draws from the container, recording the number, and replacing the ball after each draw. Find a 95% confidence interval for the sum of the 10 numbers.

13. In each at-bat, Jon has a 26% chance of getting a hit. This year, he will have approximately 180 at-bats. Use the normal approximation to find the probability that Jon will have 50 or more hits.

Chapter 3

# Test

Go Online
www.successnetplus.com

## Multiple Choice

**1.** If you are to toss a coin five times, what is the expected value for the number of tails flipped?

**A.** 2 **B.** 2.5

**C.** 3 **D.** 3.5

**2.** Consider the following two spinners with five equal spaces.

Spinner A: 1, 3, 5, 6, 7
Spinner B: 2, 4, 5, 7, 8

What is the expected value for the sum when you spin the two spinners?

**A.** 10.2 **B.** 8

**C.** 5 **D.** 9.6

**3.** The probability a batter gets a hit is $p = 0.3$. What is the probability that in eight at-bats the batter will get exactly four hits? Round to two decimal places.

**A.** 0.14 **B.** 0.31

**C.** 0.01 **D.** 0.25

**4.** At a local dealership, the average selling prices of new cars are normally distributed. On average a new car sells for $23,000 with a standard deviation of $3500. What percent of cars sell between $25,000 and $30,000? Round to four decimal places.

**A.** 0.1023 **B.** 0.2157

**C.** 0.4772 **D.** 0.2615

**5.** A number cube has the numbers 2, 3, 5, 7, 8, and 11 on its faces. Calculate the mean $\mu$ and standard deviation $\sigma$ for one roll, to three decimal places.

**A.** $\mu = 7; \sigma = 4.021$

**B.** $\mu = 6; \sigma = 3.055$

**C.** $\mu = 7; \sigma = 3.282$

**D.** $\mu = 6; \sigma = 3.155$

**6.** A multiple-choice test has 28 questions each with four choices. If you randomly guess, what is the average number of questions you expect to get correct?

**A.** 4 **B.** 14 **C.** 7 **D.** 10

**7.** Find a 95% confidence interval for the number of tails when you flip a coin 400 times.

**A.** (180, 220) **B.** (190, 210)

**C.** (195, 205) **D.** (200, 220)

**8.** A spinner contains the numbers 1, 1, 2, 2, 4, and 6 in equal wedges. Which polynomial models the sum of three spins?

**A.** $(x^1 + x^2 + x^4 + x^6)^3$

**B.** $(2x^1 + 2x^2 + x^4 + x^6)^3$

**C.** $(x^1 + x^2 + 2x^4 + 2x^6)^3$

**D.** $(3x^1 + 3x^2 + 3x^4 + 3x^6)^3$

## Open Response

**9.** You play a game where you roll a number cube ten times. Each time you roll a six you win. Round off answers to two decimal places.

**a.** What is the probability that you never win?

**b.** What is the probability that you win exactly twice?

**c.** What is the average number of wins in ten rolls?

**10.** A game involves rolling a standard number cube and spinning a spinner with the numbers 2, 3, and 5 in equal wedges. Then sum the two results.

**a.** How many equally-likely outcomes are in this sample space?

**b.** What is the probability of getting a sum of 7?

**c.** What is the probability of getting a sum of 12?

11. You have two decks of eight cards. The cards in each deck are labeled one through eight. You pick a card from each deck and find their sum.

a. Find a polynomial to model the sum.

b. What is the probability of getting a sum of exactly six?

c. What is the probability of getting a sum greater than or equal to twelve?

d. Which sum is most likely to occur?

12. To play a certain lottery, a player chooses five numbers from the numbers 1–50 and then chooses a bonus number from the numbers 1–30.

a. How many different tickets are possible?

b. How many ways can a player match three numbers plus the bonus number?

c. How many ways can a player match two numbers, but not the bonus number?

13. A spinner has the numbers 1, 3, 5, and 7.

a. Build a probability histogram for the sum of two spins.

b. In two spins, what sum is most likely?

c. Build a probability histogram for the sum of four spins.

d. In four spins, what sum is most likely?

14. In a hockey shootout the probability a player will score a goal is $p = 0.25$. If the player takes 80 shots, find the following.

a. the mean for the number of goals

b. the standard deviation for the number of goals scored

c. the probability that the player will score exactly 16 goals

15. Test scores from an 11th grade class are normally distributed with a mean of 77 and a standard deviation of 3.2.

a. Approximately what percentage of students received a grade between 80 and 85?

b. What percent of students received a grade less than 70?

c. Give a range of scores in which approximately 99.7% of all students' scores should lie.

16. A friend tells you that his password is a five-digit number containing the digits 1, 2, 4, 5, and 8. He then asks you to guess his password.

a. How many possible passwords are there?

b. What is the probability that your guess has none of the digits in the correct place?

c. What is the probability that two of the digits are in the correct place?

d. What is the probability that you correctly guess his password?

17. A lottery is played by choosing six numbers from the set 1–42, with payouts as shown.

| Matches | Frequency | Prize |
|---|---|---|
| 0 correct | ■ | $0 |
| 1 correct | ■ | $0 |
| 2 correct | ■ | $2 |
| 3 correct | ■ | $10 |
| 4 correct | ■ | $50 |
| 5 correct | ■ | $20,000 |
| 6 correct | ■ | $1,000,000 |

a. Copy and complete the table.

b. What is the probability of matching exactly four numbers?

c. What is the probability of winning the million dollar prize?

d. Find the expected value of one ticket.

## Investigations at a Glance

# Trigonometry

Trigonometry, at first glance, seems to be about triangles. With further study, you will see that it is also about waves and oscillations. When you graph $y = \sin x$ on your calculator and look at the function for $-720° \leq x \leq 720°$ and $-2 \leq y \leq 2$, you see a wave. This wave has properties in common with many natural systems such as a weight on a spring, a swinging pendulum, or a vibrating string on a musical instrument. You can use the sine function to describe movement in these systems.

In fact, Joseph Fourier, a French engineer, found a method for writing virtually any periodic function as a combination of sine and cosine functions. The entire graph of a periodic function consists of copies of one portion of the graph laid end to end. Light, sound, and even molecules in a solid move as waves. Trigonometry is at the heart of such diverse sciences as acoustics, optics, chemistry, seismology, meteorology, and electrical engineering.

## Vocabulary and Notation

- cosine, $\cos\theta$
- discontinuity
- Heronian triangle
- Law of Cosines
- Law of Sines
- period
- periodic function
- sine, $\sin\theta$
- standard position
- tangent, $\tan\theta$
- trigonometric equation

# 4.0 Right Triangle Trigonometry

In previous courses, you learned about similarity and the AA Theorem: Two triangles are similar if two pairs of corresponding angles have the same measure.

If two triangles have two pairs of corresponding angles with the same measure, the third pair of angles also has the same measure, because the sum of the measures of the angles in a triangle is 180°.

If two right triangles have one pair of acute angles with the same measure, then they are similar. The ratio of any two side lengths in one of the triangles is the same as the ratio of the corresponding side lengths in the other triangle.

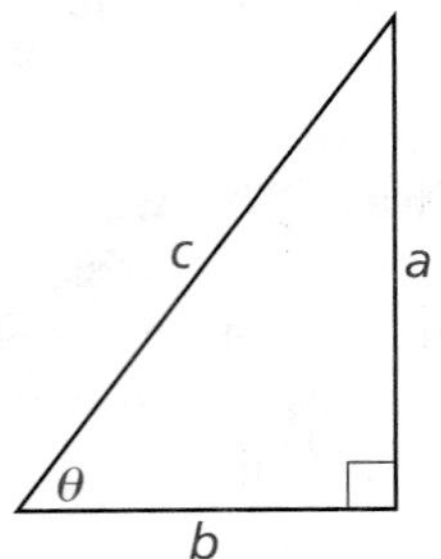


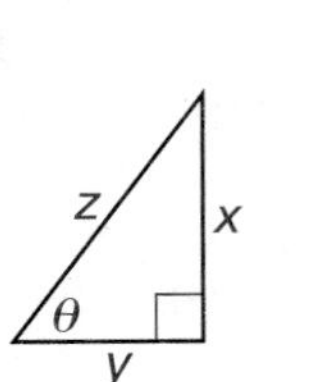


$$\frac{a}{c} = \frac{x}{z}$$

$$\frac{b}{c} = \frac{y}{z}$$

$$\frac{a}{b} = \frac{x}{y}$$

These ratios are determined by the marked angle in the triangle. In other words, each ratio is a function of the given angle. It helps to refer to the three sides of the triangle in terms of their position from the perspective of this angle. There are the leg opposite the angle, the leg adjacent to the angle, and the hypotenuse.

Which side is which depends on which angle you are talking about. The side opposite one acute angle is adjacent to the other. The hypotenuse does not change.

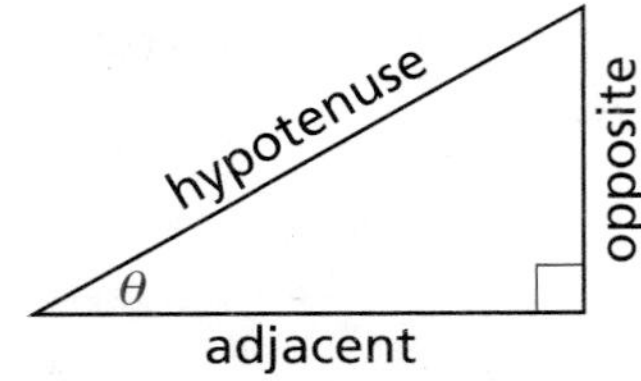


The three ratios are functions of the angle $\theta$. Since they are helpful in many problems, they have standard names.

## Definitions

**The sine of an acute angle $\theta$ is the ratio of the opposite side to the hypotenuse in any right triangle that has $\theta$ as an acute angle. It is denoted by sin $\theta$.**

**The cosine of an acute angle $\theta$ is the ratio of the adjacent side to the hypotenuse. It is denoted by cos $\theta$.**

**The tangent of an acute angle $\theta$ is the ratio of the opposite side to the adjacent side. It is denoted by tan $\theta$.**

Here are those ratios again, written in the form of equations.

$$\sin\theta = \frac{\text{opposite}}{\text{hypotenuse}}$$

$$\cos\theta = \frac{\text{adjacent}}{\text{hypotenuse}}$$

$$\tan\theta = \frac{\text{opposite}}{\text{adjacent}}$$

Calculators have keys for all three of these functions. They also have keys for their inverse functions, which allow you to calculate an angle if you know its sine, cosine, or tangent.

## Example 1

**Problem** A wheelchair ramp should not incline at an angle steeper than 5°. You are building a ramp next to a staircase that rises a total of 2 feet. How long will the ramp be if the angle is 5°?

**Solution** The picture below shows what the ramp would look like.

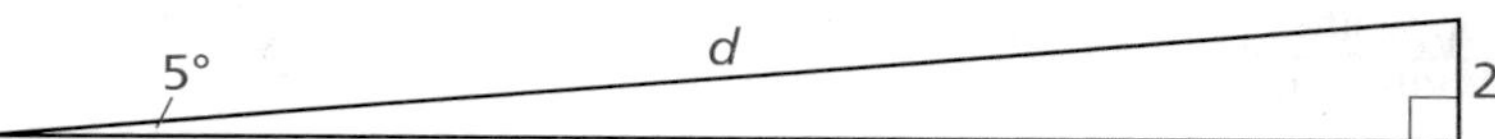


The hypotenuse and the side opposite the 5° angle are involved, so it is simplest to use the sine function. You know the angle measure, and that the length of the opposite side is 2. The hypotenuse is the unknown $d$.

$$\sin 5^\circ = \frac{2}{d}$$

Solve for $d$: $d = \frac{2}{\sin 5^\circ}$. You can use a calculator to find that $d \approx 23$ feet.

A 5° angle is quite small. How does the length of the ramp compare with the horizontal distance from the end of the ramp to the building?

## For You to Do

1. For safety, a ladder manufacturer recommends that you should place a ladder's base a minimum distance from the wall.This distance is at least one foot for every 6 feet of ladder length. How high on the wall can a 20-foot ladder reach if the base is at the minimum distance from the wall?

## Example 2

**Problem** For some angle $\theta$, $\cos\theta = \frac{3}{5}$. Find $\sin\theta$ and $\tan\theta$.

**Solution**

**Method 1** You can use any right triangle with this angle $\theta$, so pick one that has convenient side lengths. Since the ratio given is $\frac{3}{5}$, set up a right triangle with a side of length 3 adjacent to angle $\theta$ and a hypotenuse of length 5.

Method 1 gives exact answers.

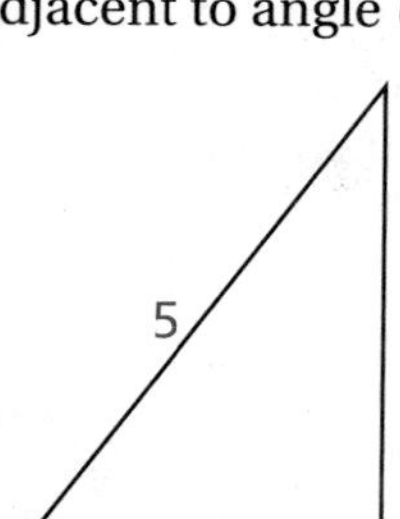


You can find the length of the remaining side with the Pythagorean Theorem or by recognizing the famous 3-4-5 right triangle. Since the third side's length is 4, you know the other ratios.

$$\sin\theta = \frac{\text{opposite}}{\text{hypotenuse}} = \frac{4}{5}$$

$$\tan\theta = \frac{\text{opposite}}{\text{adjacent}} = \frac{4}{3}$$

**Method 2** Use the inverse function to find the angle $\theta$.

Method 2 gives approximate answers.

$$\cos\theta = \frac{3}{5} \Rightarrow \theta = \cos^{-1}\left(\frac{3}{5}\right)$$

The angle $\theta$ is approximately 53.130°. Once you know $\theta$, you can find the other ratios with your calculator.

$$\sin 53.130° \approx 0.8000$$

$$\tan 53.130° \approx 1.3333$$

These values are very close to the exact fractions $\frac{4}{5}$ and $\frac{4}{3}$ you found using Method 1.

## For Discussion

2. For this example, it seems that Method 1 gives more accurate answers, more quickly. Can you think of a situation in which Method 2 might be necessary?

## Developing Habits of Mind

**Look for relationships.** You can express the Pythagorean Theorem using sine and cosine. Consider the triangle drawn at the right. The Pythagorean Theorem tells you that for this triangle,

$$a^2 + b^2 = c^2$$

Divide each side by $c^2$.

$$\frac{a^2}{c^2} + \frac{b^2}{c^2} = 1$$

The trigonometric functions define $\cos\theta$ as $\frac{a}{c}$ and $\sin\theta$ as $\frac{b}{c}$. So,

$$(\cos\theta)^2 + (\sin\theta)^2 = 1$$

The parentheses can get in the way. The exponent is frequently moved to appear next to the function name.

$$\cos^2\theta + \sin^2\theta = 1$$

You read this equation as "cosine squared theta plus sine squared theta equals 1." It is one of the most fundamental relationships in trigonometry.

How far is the point $(\cos\theta, \sin\theta)$ from the origin?

## Exercises *Practicing Habits of Mind*

### Check Your Understanding

1. A right triangle has a 40° angle and hypotenuse of length 10. Find the triangle's perimeter to two decimal places.
2. A right triangle has legs of lengths 20 and 21.
   a. What is the area of this triangle?
   b. How long is the hypotenuse?
   c. Draw an accurate picture of this triangle. Estimate the acute angle measures.
   d. Using a calculator, find the measure of each acute angle to the nearest degree.
3. In a right triangle, the value of $\cos\theta$ is $\frac{8}{17}$. Find the values of $\sin\theta$ and $\tan\theta$ exactly (without decimal approximations).

4. Show that for any angle measure $\theta$ such that $0° < \theta < 90°$,

$$\tan \theta = \frac{\sin \theta}{\cos \theta}$$

5. For some angle $\theta$, $\sin \theta$ is exactly $\frac{1}{4}$. Find the exact value of $\cos \theta$ for this angle by drawing a right triangle.

6. **Take It Further** A right triangle has a 30° angle and one side length that is 12. Find all possible values for the area of the triangle.

## On Your Own

7. A right triangle has an angle $\theta$ and a hypotenuse of length 1. Find the lengths of the other two sides in terms of $\theta$.

8. Explain why it is true that for any angle $\theta$, $0° < \theta < 90°$,

$$\sin \theta = \cos (90° - \theta)$$

**Remember...**

Angles with measure $\theta$ and $90° - \theta$ are complementary. Hence the name cosine.

9. Use this triangle to find the exact values of sine, cosine, and tangent for 30° and 60°.

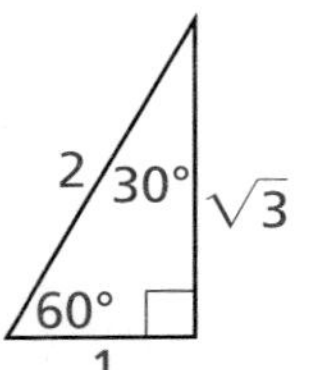


| $\theta$ | $\sin \theta$ | $\cos \theta$ | $\tan \theta$ |
|---|---|---|---|
| 30° | ■ | ■ | ■ |
| 60° | ■ | ■ | ■ |

10. Use this triangle to find the exact values of sine, cosine, and tangent for 45°.

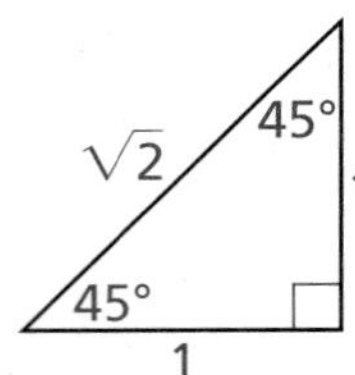


| $\theta$ | $\sin \theta$ | $\cos \theta$ | $\tan \theta$ |
|---|---|---|---|
| 45° | ■ | ■ | ■ |

11. Derman wants to extend the domain of sine and cosine so that he can give a value for sin 90° and cos 90°. What are good values for Derman to pick? Explain.

12. **a.** What are the largest and smallest possible values for $\sin \theta$? Explain.
    **b.** What are the largest and smallest possible values for $\cos \theta$? Explain.
    **c.** What are the largest and smallest possible values for $\tan \theta$? Explain.

For Exercise 12, assume $0° < \theta < 90°$.

**13.** For each triangle, find $\sin\theta$, $\cos\theta$, and $\tan\theta$.

**a.**

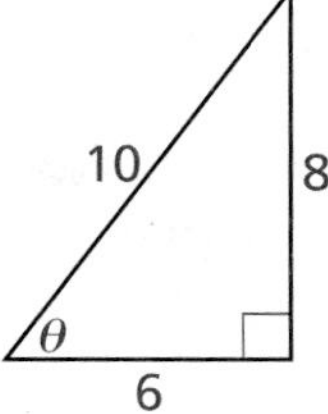


**b.**

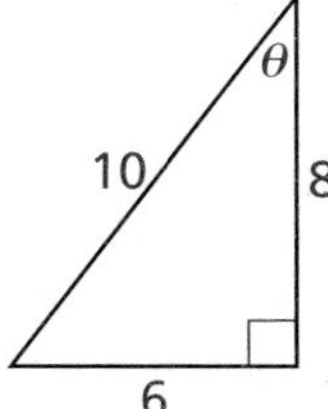


**c.**

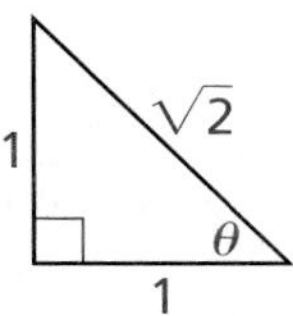


**d.**

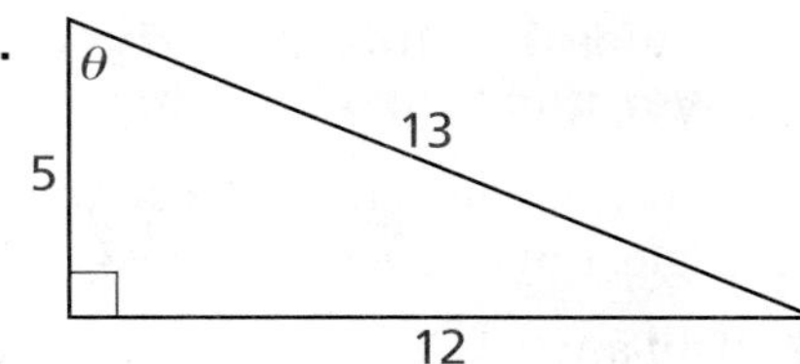


**14.** **What's Wrong Here?** Trent sees $\triangle TRI$.

Trent says, "So side $TI$ is 10 and angle $T$ is 70°, that means I can find side $RI$ by using sine of 70°. So I know $\sin 70° = \frac{RI}{10}$."

What is wrong with Trent's reasoning?

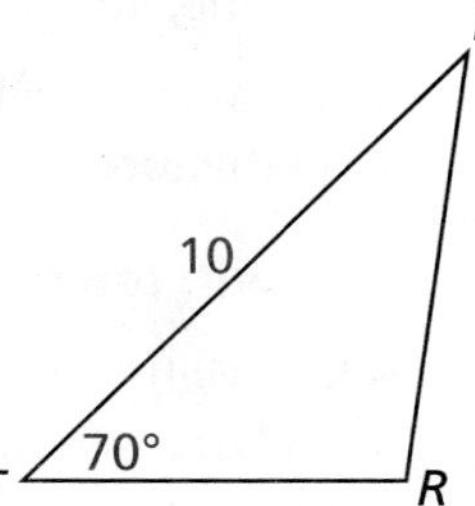


**15.** **Take It Further** Prove that for any angle $\theta$ such that $0° < \theta < 90°$, $\tan(90° - \theta) = \frac{1}{\tan\theta}$.

## Maintain Your Skills

**16.** Copy the following table. Use a calculator to complete it for the sine, cosine, and tangent of angles in increments of 10°. Find each value to three decimal places.

| $\theta$ | $\sin\theta$ | $\cos\theta$ | $\tan\theta$ |
|---|---|---|---|
| 10° | ■ | ■ | ■ |
| 20° | ■ | ■ | ■ |
| 30° | ■ | ■ | ■ |
| 40° | ■ | ■ | ■ |
| 50° | ■ | ■ | ■ |
| 60° | ■ | ■ | ■ |
| 70° | ■ | ■ | ■ |
| 80° | ■ | ■ | ■ |

**Habits of Mind**

**Look for relationships.** Review Exercise 8.

**17.** Explain why $\sin 10°$ and $\cos 80°$ are equal.

# Trigonometric Functions

**In *Trigonometric Functions*, you will explore the relationships between points on a circle with radius 1 centered at the origin and angles with vertex at the origin. You will learn how to find the sine, cosine, and tangent of angles of any measure.**

**By the end of this investigation, you will be able to answer questions like these.**

1. How can you extend the definitions of sine, cosine, and tangent to any angle, not just acute angles?
2. If an angle is in Quadrant IV, what can you say about the sign of its sine, cosine, and tangent?
3. What is the relationship between the equation of the unit circle and the Pythagorean Identity?

**You will learn how to**

- use right triangle trigonometry to find the coordinates of a person walking on the unit circle, given an angle through which an observer has turned
- evaluate the sine, cosine, and tangent functions for any angle
- solve equations involving trigonometric functions

**You will develop these habits and skills:**

- Visualize relationships between coordinates of a point on the unit circle and the angle that an observer at the origin must turn through to look at that point.
- Extend the sine, cosine, and tangent functions carefully, in order to preserve key properties.
- Use logical reasoning to find all possible solutions of a trigonometric equation.

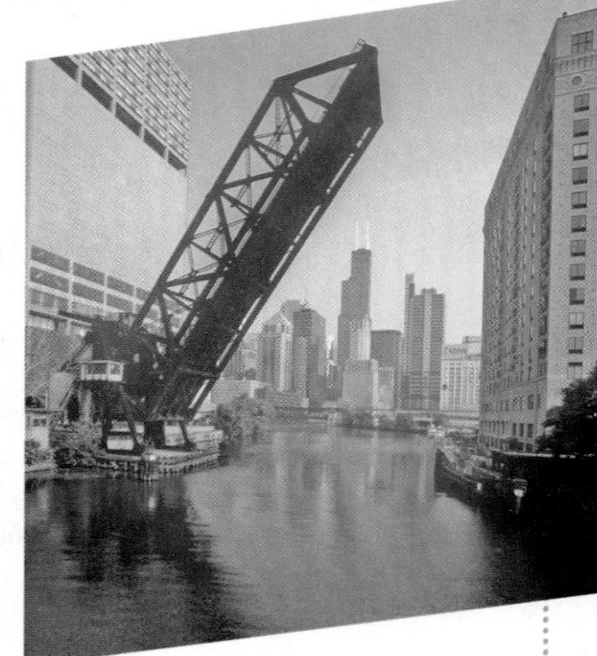

As this drawbridge rises, the angle it forms with the river increases. The right end traces part of a circle.

## 4.01 Getting Started

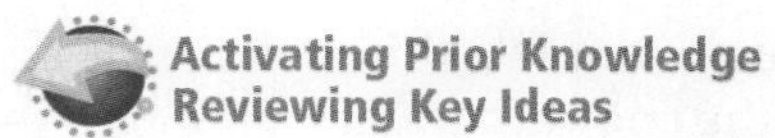


The values of trigonometric functions are related to the coordinates of points on a circle with radius 1 centered at the origin.

### For You to Explore

Olivia watches Paul walk around a circle. The circle's radius is 1 meter. Olivia stands at the center, and Paul begins walking counterclockwise. Consider a coordinate grid, with Olivia standing at the origin and Paul starting at the point (1, 0).

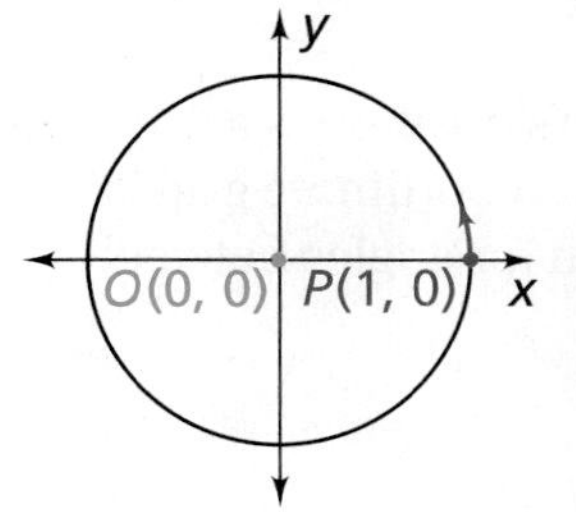


**Remember...**

This circle, with center (0, 0) and radius 1, is the unit circle.

As Paul walks, Olivia watches Paul and keeps track of the angle she has turned. For example, when Olivia has turned 70°, the situation looks like this.

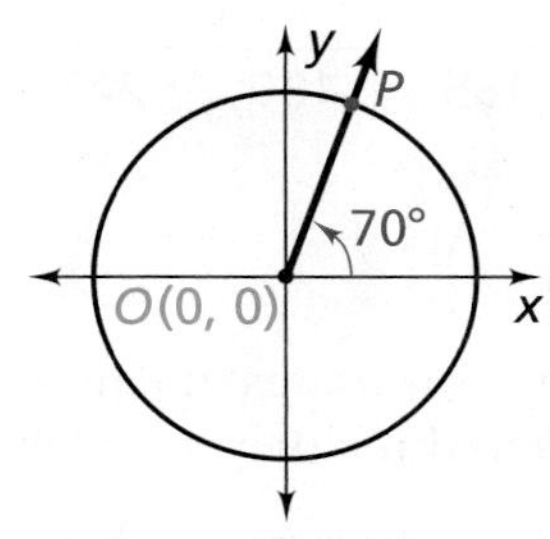


1. **a.** Explain why the distance between Olivia and Paul is always 1.

   **b.** Suppose Paul is at a point with coordinates $(x, y)$. Write an equation in $x$ and $y$ to express the fact that Paul is 1 unit away from (0, 0).

2. Find the coordinates of Paul's location when Olivia has turned 70°. Round to three decimal places.

3. Find the lengths of the other two sides of this triangle.

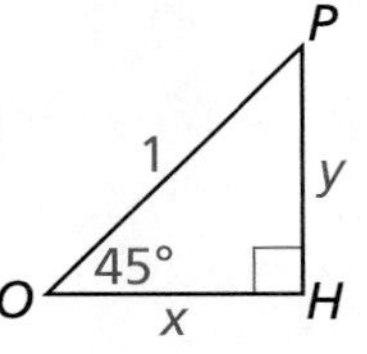


4. Find the coordinates of Paul's location when Olivia has turned 45°.

   (*Hint:* Your work in Problem 3 should be helpful here.)

5. Find the coordinates of Paul's location when Olivia has turned 90°.

Draw a diagram. You do not need to use triangles this time.

6. **a.** Explain why Paul will pass through the point $\left(\frac{3}{5}, \frac{4}{5}\right)$.

   **b.** When Paul is at $\left(\frac{3}{5}, \frac{4}{5}\right)$, find the angle Olivia has turned to the nearest degree.

7. **Write About It** Describe how the $y$-coordinate of Paul's location changes as Olivia's angle increases.

**8.** Copy and complete this table, giving the coordinates of Paul's location when Olivia has turned each angle.

| Angle | Coordinates | Angle | Coordinates |
|---|---|---|---|
| 0° | (1, 0) | 270° | ■ |
| 45° | ■ | 315° | ■ |
| 90° | ■ | 360° | ■ |
| 135° | ■ | 405° | ■ |
| 180° | (−1, 0) | 450° | ■ |
| 225° | ■ | | |

**9.** The $y$-coordinate of Paul's position is a function of the angle through which Olivia has turned. Make a coordinate grid labeled like the one below. Draw the graph of the function for angles between 0° and 360°.

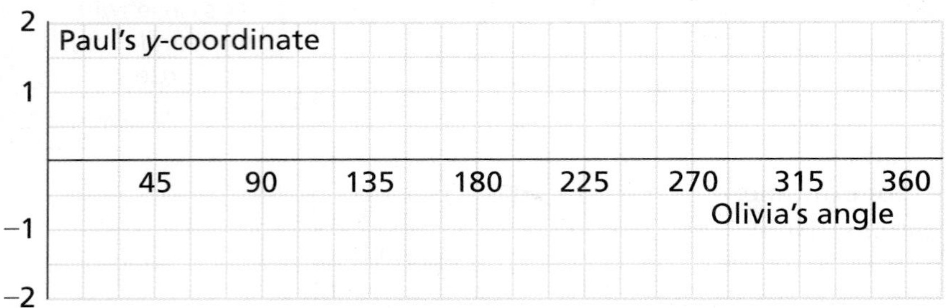


**10.** **Take It Further** Find the coordinates of Paul's location when Olivia has turned 10,000°. Calculate to three decimal places.

## On Your Own

**11.** Copy and complete this table, giving the coordinates of Paul's location when Olivia has turned through each angle. Find each answer to three decimal places.

| Angle | Coordinates | Angle | Coordinates |
|---|---|---|---|
| 0° | (1, 0) | 50° | ■ |
| 10° | ■ | 60° | ■ |
| 20° | ■ | 70° | ■ |
| 30° | ■ | 80° | ■ |
| 40° | ■ | 90° | (0, 1) |

**12.** Which of these points is on the unit circle $x^2 + y^2 = 1$?

**A.** $\left(\frac{1}{2}, -\frac{1}{2}\right)$ **B.** $(1, -1)$

**C.** $\left(-\frac{5}{13}, \frac{12}{13}\right)$ **D.** $\left(\frac{2}{3}, -\frac{4}{5}\right)$

**13. a.** Find the coordinates of Paul's location to three decimal places when Olivia has turned 130°.

**b.** Find the coordinates of Paul's location to three decimal places when Olivia has turned 230°.

**14.** Describe how the $x$-coordinate of Paul's location varies as Olivia's angle increases.

**15.** In Problem 9, you graphed Paul's $y$-coordinate as a function of the angle Olivia had turned. Now graph Paul's $x$-coordinate as a function of the angle Olivia has turned.

Include the points (0, 1) and (180, −1).

**16.** Find the coordinates of Paul's location to three decimal places when Olivia has turned 430°.

## Maintain Your Skills

**17.** Draw the graphs of each pair of equations on the same axes. Find the number of intersections of the two graphs.

**a.** $x^2 + y^2 = 1$, $x = 0.5$

**b.** $x^2 + y^2 = 1$, $x = 0.9$

**c.** $x^2 + y^2 = 1$, $x = 1$

**d.** $x^2 + y^2 = 1$, $x = 1.3$

Go Online
Video Tutor
www.successnetplus.com

**18.** Draw the graphs of each pair of equations on the same axes. Find the number of intersections of the two graphs.

**a.** $x^2 + y^2 = 1$, $y = 0.5$

**b.** $x^2 + y^2 = 1$, $y = -0.5$

**c.** $x^2 + y^2 = 1$, $y = -0.9$

**d.** $x^2 + y^2 = 1$, $y = -1$

# 4.02 Extending the Domain, Part 1—0° to 360°

Right now, you can only find the sine, cosine, or tangent of an angle if the angle has measure between $0^\circ$ and $90^\circ$, since these functions have been defined as ratios of sides in a right triangle. By following Olivia and Paul around their circle, you can extend the domain of these trigonometric functions to include all angles from $0^\circ$ to $360^\circ$. Here is how.

Consider the situation in Lesson 4.01. Suppose Paul has moved along the circle, and Olivia has turned through an angle of $70^\circ$.

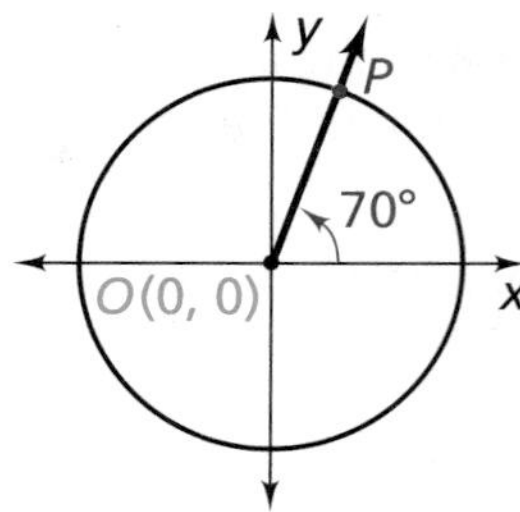


The $70^\circ$ angle Olivia has turned is part of a right triangle with vertices at $O$ and $P$. You complete the triangle by dropping an altitude from point $P$ to the $x$-axis.

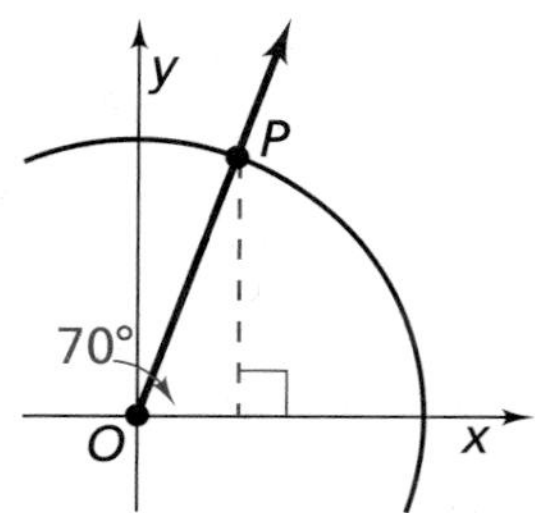


The position of the hammer at the moment of release is related to the angle the athlete has rotated.

The hypotenuse of this right triangle has length 1, so the horizontal leg has length $\cos 70^\circ$ and the vertical leg has length $\sin 70^\circ$. The coordinates of point $P$ are $(\cos 70^\circ, \sin 70^\circ)$.

In fact, this works for any angle in Quadrant I. Angles with measures between $0^\circ$ and $90^\circ$ are in Quadrant I. If the angle at the origin is $\theta$, the coordinates of point $P$ are $(\cos\theta, \sin\theta)$.

In the other quadrants, you can draw right triangles to find Paul's coordinates, but one or both of the coordinates will be negative.

You can find the approximate values of $\cos 70^\circ$ and $\sin 70^\circ$ on a calculator. Note that calculators typically have more than one way to measure angles. Refer to the TI-Nspire™ Handbook on p. 817 to see how to check that your calculator is in degree mode.

## Example

**Problem** Find Paul's coordinates when Olivia has turned 210°.

**Solution** First, draw a diagram for the situation. The angle is in Quadrant III, so both coordinates will be negative. To find the exact coordinates, draw an altitude from $P$ to the $x$-axis.

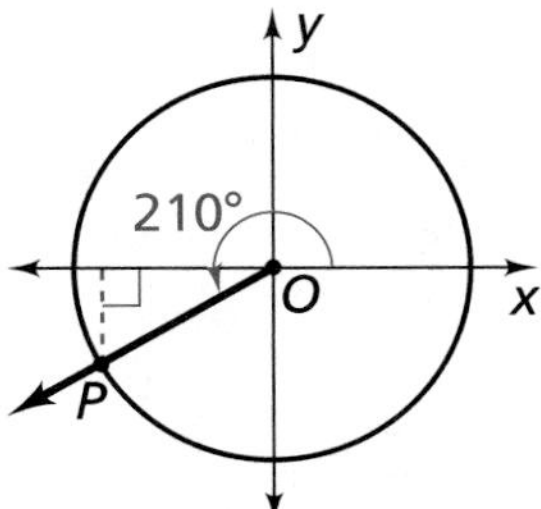


You can use cosine and sine to find the side lengths in this triangle. The triangle has a 30° angle at the origin, so it is a 30-60-90 triangle with hypotenuse length 1. Because this is a special right triangle, you can write exact expressions for its side lengths without using a calculator.

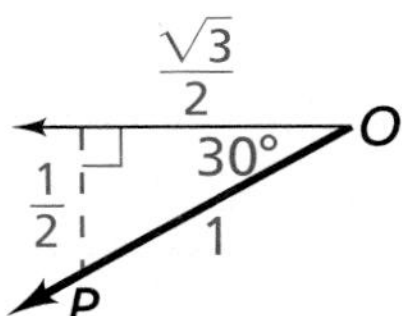


The side opposite the 30° angle has length $\frac{1}{2}$, and the side opposite the 60° angle has length $\frac{\sqrt{3}}{2}$.

To determine the coordinates of point $P$, use the side lengths of the triangle. Note that both coordinates are negative, since $P$ is in Quadrant III. The coordinates of point $P$ are $\left(-\frac{\sqrt{3}}{2}, -\frac{1}{2}\right)$.

**Remember...**

The values $\frac{1}{2}$ and $\frac{\sqrt{3}}{2}$ come up often in trigonometry.

## For Discussion

1. Why does the hypotenuse of the triangle in the Example have length 1?
2. Find another angle in Quadrant III where you can find the coordinates of point $P$ exactly without including a trigonometric function or using a calculator.

**Habits of Mind**

**Give an exact answer.** Finding coordinates exactly means to use a rational number written as a fraction or an expression involving rational numbers and square roots. For example, $\cos 45° = \frac{\sqrt{2}}{2}$ is exact. But 0.707107 is an approximation of $\frac{\sqrt{2}}{2}$.

The unit circle gives you a way to extend the domain of cosine and sine.

### *Definitions*

**Let $\theta$ be an angle centered at the origin and measured counter-clockwise from the positive $x$-axis. The left side of $\theta$ intersects the graph of $x^2 + y^2 = 1$ (the unit circle) in exactly one point.**

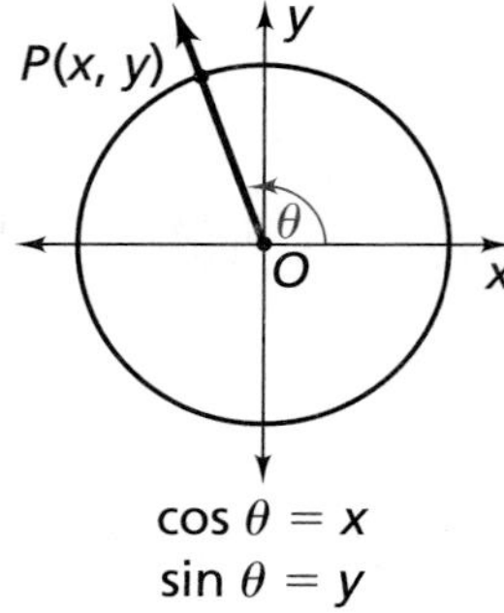


$\cos \theta = x$
$\sin \theta = y$

**The cosine of angle $\theta$ is the $x$-coordinate of this intersection.**

**The sine of angle $\theta$ is the $y$-coordinate of this intersection.**

This is the same as the situation with Olivia and Paul.

**Remember...**

The coordinates of a point P on the unit circle are $(\cos \theta, \sin \theta)$.

This definition is the one calculators use. For example, a calculator gives $\cos 180° = -1$.

## For You to Do

**3.** Is $\sin 280°$ positive or negative? Answer without using a calculator.

**4.** In which quadrants is cosine negative?

For acute angles $\theta$, one of the properties of the tangent function is that

$$\tan \theta = \frac{\sin \theta}{\cos \theta}$$

Since you now have a definition for the sine and cosine of any angle, you can use the above formula to extend the domain of the tangent function to any angle, as well. For example, you can say that

$$\tan 120° = \frac{\sin 120°}{\cos 120°} = \frac{\frac{\sqrt{3}}{2}}{-\frac{1}{2}} = -\sqrt{3}$$

Now you have a tentative definition. If $\theta$ is any angle, define $\tan \theta$ by the rule

$$\tan \theta = \frac{\sin \theta}{\cos \theta}$$

## Developing Habits of Mind

**Check your definition.** Why is this definition only tentative? The formula $\tan\theta = \frac{\sin\theta}{\cos\theta}$ is valid only for $0 \le \theta < 90$, but is often used to define $\tan\theta$ for any angle.

In mathematics, it often happens that you can have a functional equation $\left(\text{in this case, } \tan\theta = \frac{\sin\theta}{\cos\theta}\right)$ that is valid for certain values (in this case, for $0 \le \theta < 90$). Sometimes the right side of the equation makes sense for many more values, so you define the left side for those additional values.

When you do this, you have to be careful. In the case of $\tan\theta = \frac{\sin\theta}{\cos\theta}$, you have to check two things:

- Does the right side make sense for all angles $\theta$? Clearly, the numerator and denominator do, but does the fraction?
- You originally defined the left side of the equation to be "opposite over adjacent" for acute angles $\theta$. Does this still make sense for angles with measure greater than 90°?

## For Discussion

5. As a class, discuss the two bullet points above and make a more precise definition of the tangent function.

**Habits of Mind**

**Represent a function.** To define a function, you have to give its domain.

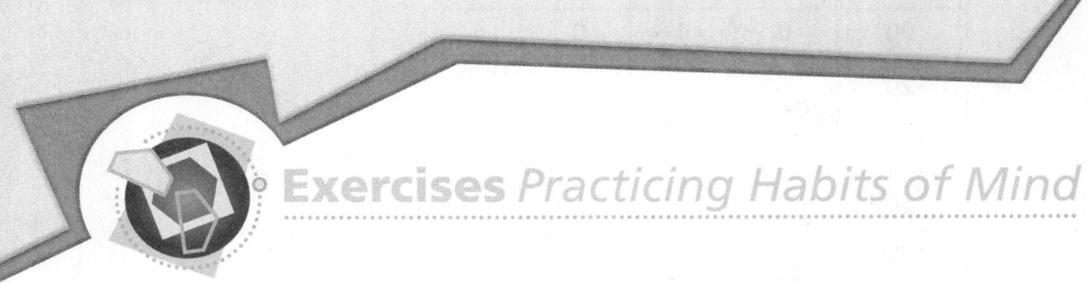

## Exercises *Practicing Habits of Mind*

### Check Your Understanding

1. **What's Wrong Here?** Jo says that sin 45° should be $\frac{1}{2}$. Jo explains, "Well, sin 0° = 0 and sin 90° = 1. The same is true for cosine, except reversed. Halfway between, they should both be $\frac{1}{2}$." Use the unit circle to explain what is wrong with Jo's reasoning.

2. **Write About It** Write an identity that gives the relationship between the two expressions.

   **a.** $\cos\theta$ and $\cos(\theta + 180^\circ)$

   **b.** $\sin\theta$ and $\sin(\theta + 180^\circ)$

   **c.** $\tan\theta$ and $\tan(\theta + 180^\circ)$

3. Find each value.

   **a.** $(\cos 150^\circ)^2 + (\sin 150^\circ)^2$

   **b.** $(\cos 52.696^\circ)^2 + (\sin 52.696^\circ)^2$

4. **a.** Find a formula for all values of $\theta$ such that $\sin\theta = 0$.

   **b.** Find a formula for all values of $\theta$ such that $\cos\theta = 0$.

   **c.** Find a formula for all values of $\theta$ such that $\tan\theta = 0$.

5. For each angle in the table, find the cosine, sine, cosine squared, and sine squared. Look for rules and relationships that allow you to find the results more quickly.

| $\theta$ | $\cos\theta$ | $\sin\theta$ | $\cos^2\theta$ | $\sin^2\theta$ |
|---|---|---|---|---|
| 0° | ■ | 0 | ■ | 0 |
| 30° | $\frac{\sqrt{3}}{2}$ | ■ | $\frac{3}{4}$ | ■ |
| 45° | ■ | $\frac{\sqrt{2}}{2}$ | ■ | $\frac{1}{2}$ |
| 60° | ■ | ■ | ■ | ■ |
| 90° | 0 | 1 | 0 | 1 |
| 120° | ■ | ■ | ■ | ■ |
| 135° | ■ | ■ | ■ | ■ |
| 150° | ■ | $\frac{1}{2}$ | ■ | $\frac{1}{4}$ |
| 180° | ■ | ■ | ■ | ■ |
| 210° | ■ | ■ | ■ | ■ |
| 225° | $-\frac{\sqrt{2}}{2}$ | ■ | ■ | $\frac{1}{2}$ |
| 240° | ■ | ■ | ■ | ■ |
| 270° | 0 | ■ | ■ | ■ |
| 300° | ■ | ■ | ■ | ■ |
| 315° | ■ | ■ | ■ | ■ |
| 330° | ■ | ■ | ■ | ■ |
| 360° | 1 | ■ | ■ | ■ |

**Remember...**

The notation $\cos^2 x$ means $(\cos x)^2$. You use this notation primarily for ease of reading. You read $\cos^2 x$ as "cosine squared of $x$."

## On Your Own

6. For each angle, draw the angle in standard position. Find the sine, cosine, and tangent of the angle.

   a. $210^\circ$

   b. $330^\circ$

   c. $40^\circ$

   d. $320^\circ$

   e. $360^\circ$

7. Standardized Test Prep If $\sin\theta = 0.57358$ and $\tan\theta = 0.70021$, what is $\cos\theta$?

   a. 0.40163 b. 0.81915 c. 1.22077 d. 1.27379

8. Explain why $\sin 310^\circ = -\sin 50^\circ$.

9. Let $\theta = 150^\circ$. Find each value.

   a. $\sin 2\theta$

   b. $2 \cdot \sin\theta \cdot \cos\theta$

**Remember...**

An angle is in **standard position** when its vertex is at the origin and one of its sides lies along the positive *x*-axis. The angle opens counterclockwise from this fixed side.

## Maintain Your Skills

10. Find a formula for all values of $\theta$ such that the given equation is true.

    a. $\sin\theta = 1$

    b. $\cos\theta = 1$

    c. $\tan\theta = 1$

# 4.03 Extending the Domain, Part 2—All Real Numbers

In the last lesson, you learned the meaning of cosine, sine, and tangent for values from 0° to 360°. This lesson extends the definitions to all real numbers.

## For You to Do

1. Using a calculator, find $\cos 20°$, $\cos 380°$, and $\cos 1100°$. Find another angle that produces the same value for the cosine.

The table in Exercise 10 from Lesson 4.02 only goes from 0° to 360°. The reason is that turning through any angle larger than 360° returns you to an angle between 0° and 360°. The coordinates after turning through a 20° angle are the same as the coordinates after turning $360° + 20° = 380°$ or $720° + 20° = 740°$. It makes sense, then, to define the cosine of 740° to be the same as the cosine of 20°.

Two numbers that differ by a multiple of 360 are *congruent modulo 360. Modulo* means "except for." The numbers 20 and 380 are the same, except for 360.

The same goes for negative angle measures: An angle of −35° puts you at the same place on the unit circle as an angle of 325°. So it makes sense to say that $\sin(-35°) = \sin 325°$.

With this extension, you can find the sine or cosine for any angle measure from the set of real numbers. For an angle $\theta$ with measure outside of $0° < \theta < 360°$, simply find another angle that is between 0° and 360° but has the same coordinates on the unit circle. You can use almost exactly the same definition as the one in Lesson 4.02 to extend the definition to any angle measure.

**Habits of Mind**

**Experiment.** Will the tangent of any angle be the same as the tangent of an angle between 0° and 360°?

### *Definitions*

**Let $\theta$ be an angle centered at the origin and measured from the positive $x$-axis. The terminal side of $\theta$ intersects the graph of $x^2 + y^2 = 1$ (the unit circle) in exactly one point.**

**The cosine of angle $\theta$ is the $x$-coordinate of this intersection.**

**The sine of angle $\theta$ is the $y$-coordinate of this intersection.**

**The tangent of angle $\theta$ is $\frac{\sin\theta}{\cos\theta}$, whenever $\cos\theta \neq 0$.**

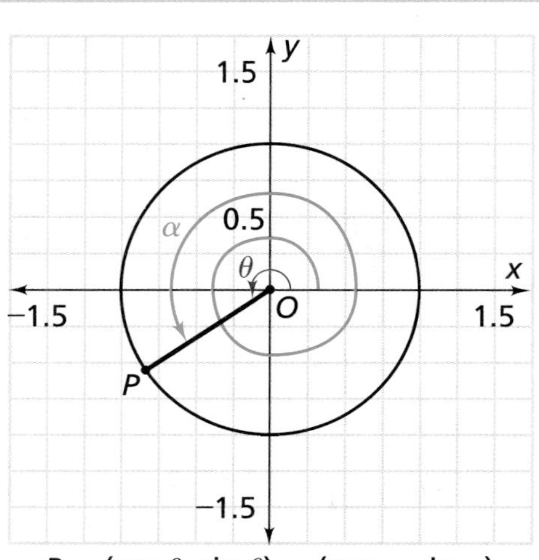

$P = (\cos\theta, \sin\theta) = (\cos\alpha, \sin\alpha)$

One side of $\theta$ passes through (1, 0). This is its initial side. The other side is the terminal side. When are these two sides the same ray?

## For You to Do

**2.** Using a calculator, find cos 20°, cos 160°, cos 200°, and cos 340°.

### *Theorem 4.1*

**If $n$ is an integer and $x$ is an angle in degrees,**

- $\cos(x + 360n) = \cos x$
- $\sin(x + 360n) = \sin x$

## For Discussion

**3.** The functions sine and cosine are periodic with period 360°. What does this mean? Is the tangent function a **periodic function**?

## Developing Habits of Mind

**Visualize.** If you know the cosine and sine of an angle, you can use the symmetry of the circle to determine the cosine and sine of several other angles. Each quadrant has a related angle with coordinates that are the same, except for a sign.

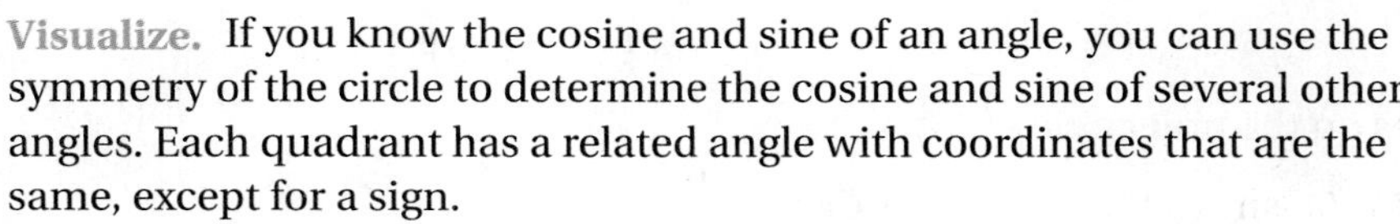

For example, if you know the cosine and sine of a 20° angle, you automatically know the cosine and sine of a 160° angle, as well as a 200° angle and a 340° angle, and many other angles.

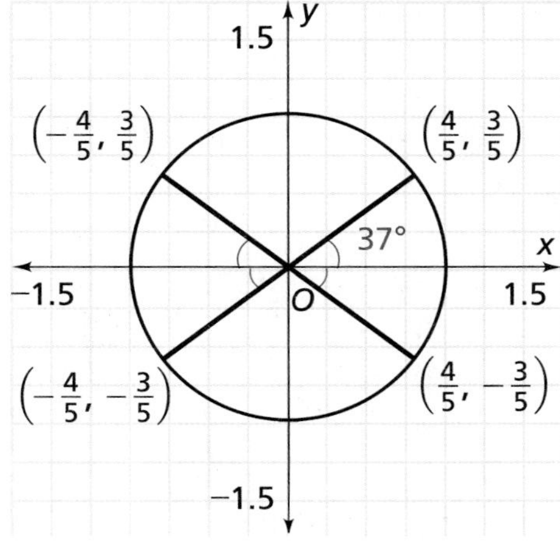


**Habits of Mind**

**Look for relationships.** Equations like $\cos x = -\cos(180° - x)$ express a symmetry of the cosine function.

Knowing about the signs of the coordinates in each quadrant will help you decide quickly about whether the cosine, sine, or tangent of an angle is positive or negative. For example, in Quadrant I, cosine is positive and sine is positive. Therefore, tangent is positive.

**Habits of Mind**

**Look for relationships.** If you are familiar with angles in Quadrant I, then you can handle any other angle using these relationships.

## For You to Do

Find the sign of the sine, cosine, and tangent for angles in each quadrant.

**4.** Quadrant II

**5.** Quadrant III

**6.** Quadrant IV

## Example

**Problem** Express each value as the value of the sine or cosine of an acute angle.

**a.** cos 150°

**b.** sin 460°

**c.** sin 290°

**Solution** It helps to draw the angles on the unit circle:

**a.** The coordinates of $P$ are (cos 150°, sin 150°). That means that $m\angle POC = 30°$. Imagine $\triangle QOD \cong \triangle POC$ in the first quadrant, oriented as in the graph. Then $m\angle DOQ = 30°$, so $OD = \cos 30°$. But $OC = OD$, and the $x$-coordinate of $P$ is the opposite of $OD$. In other words, $\cos 150° = -\cos 30°$. Since $\cos 30° = \frac{\sqrt{3}}{2}$, $\cos 150° = -\frac{\sqrt{3}}{2}$.

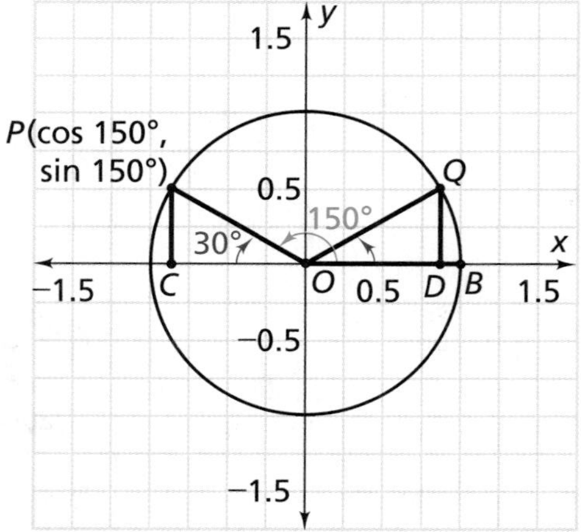


**b.** Note that sin 460° is the same as sin 100°, since traveling around the circle 460° is the same as making one complete revolution (360°) with an additional 100°. Now draw a graph like the one above and convince yourself that sin 100° = sin 80°.

c. The graph shows that $\sin 290° = -\sin 70°$.

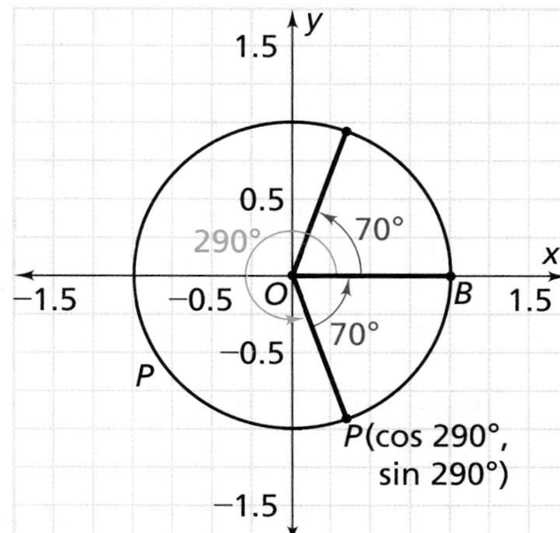


> **Habits of Mind**
>
> **Generalize.** Convince yourself that $\sin(-x) = -\sin x$ for any angle measure $x$.

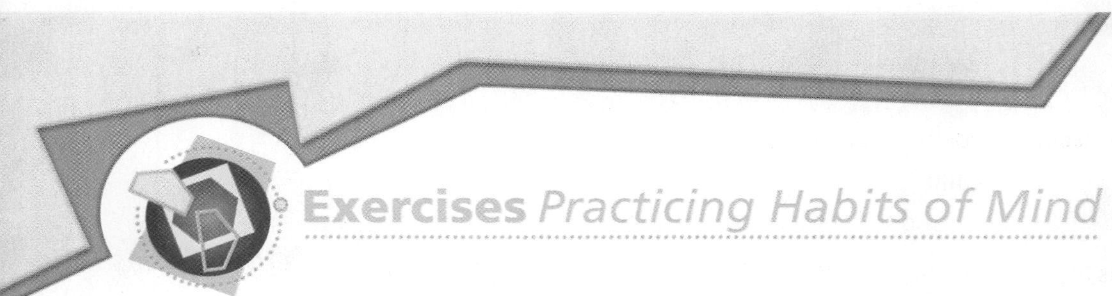

## Exercises *Practicing Habits of Mind*

### Check Your Understanding

1. **Write About It** Explain why $\sin 160° = \sin 20°$ but $\cos 160° = -\cos 20°$.
2. Suppose $\sin \theta = \frac{20}{29}$ for some angle $\theta$.
   a. In what quadrants can $\theta$ be located?
   b. Find both possible values for $\cos \theta$.
   c. Find both possible values for $\tan \theta$.
3. Find an angle $\theta$ for which $\tan \theta > 100$, or explain why no such angle exists.
4. **What's Wrong Here?** Herb wants to calculate $\cos(-60°)$. He says, "I know that $\cos 60°$ is $\frac{1}{2}$. So $\cos(-60°)$ should just be the negative. The answer is $-\frac{1}{2}$."
   What is wrong with Herb's reasoning? What is the correct value of $\cos(-60°)$?
5. List the following values in order from least to greatest.
   $\tan 70°$ $\sin 120°$ $\cos 120°$ $\cos 720°$ $\tan 110°$ $\sin 210°$
6. Find the two angles between 0° and 360° for which $\sin \theta + \sin(180° - \theta) = 1$.

7. Given that $\sin 50° \approx 0.7660$ and $\cos 50° \approx 0.6428$, find each value to four decimal places.

You do not need a calculator for any of the parts of this exercise.

**a.** $\sin 130°$ **b.** $\cos 130°$

**c.** $\cos 230°$ **d.** $\sin 310°$

**e.** $\cos^2 230° + \sin^2 230°$ **f.** $\sin 40°$

8. **a.** There is a relationship between $\tan^2 \theta$ and $\frac{1}{\cos^2 \theta}$. Find the relationship by calculating each expression for several angles.

**b.** **Take It Further** Prove that this relationship holds for any angle $\theta$, as long as $\tan \theta$ is defined.

## On Your Own

9. Find the values of $\cos(-30°)$, $\sin(-30°)$, and $\tan(-30°)$.

10. Express each value as a sine or cosine of an acute angle.

**a.** $\sin 400°$ **b.** $\cos 400°$ **c.** $\cos 300°$

**d.** $\sin 315°$ **e.** $\sin(-100°)$

11. Express each value as a sine or cosine of $\theta$.

**a.** $\sin(180° - \theta)$ **b.** $\cos(180° - \theta)$ **c.** $\sin(180° + \theta)$

**d.** $\cos(180° + \theta)$ **e.** $\sin(270° - \theta)$ **f.** $\cos(270° - \theta)$

**g.** $\sin(270° + \theta)$ **h.** $\cos(270° + \theta)$

**Habits of Mind**

**Use what you know.** There is no need to memorize these identities. You can reconstruct them by looking at the unit circle.

12. Is this statement true or false? Explain.

For any two angles $a$ and $b$, $\sin(a + b) = \sin a + \sin b$ and $\cos(a + b) = \cos a + \cos b$.

This statement says that addition is distributive over the sine and cosine functions. But maybe it is not!

13. Suppose an angle $\theta$ is unknown, but it is between 300° and 350°. Determine whether each expression is positive or negative.

**a.** $\cos \theta$ **b.** $\sin \theta$ **c.** $\tan \theta$

**d.** $\cos^2 \theta + \sin^2 \theta$ **e.** $\tan^3 \theta$

14. **Standardized Test Prep** What is the value of $\cos 120° + \sin 120°$?

**A.** 0 **B.** $\frac{\sqrt{3} - 1}{2}$ **C.** 1 **D.** $\frac{\sqrt{3} + 1}{2}$

15. Find this sum: $\sin 60^\circ + \sin 120^\circ + \sin 180^\circ + \cdots + \sin 360^\circ$.

The missing terms all follow the arithmetic sequence set up by 60, 120, and 180.

16. For which angles between 0° and 360° can you find the sine and cosine exactly without using a calculator or an approximation?

17. Suppose $\theta$ is an angle in Quadrant II with $\sin \theta = \frac{35}{37}$.

a. Find the value of $\cos \theta$.

b. Find the value of $\tan \theta$.

c. Suppose $\theta$ is between 0° and 360°. Find $\theta$ to the nearest degree.

18. a. There is a relationship between $\frac{1}{\tan^2 \theta}$ and $\frac{1}{\sin^2 \theta}$. Find the relationship by calculating each expression for several angles.

b. **Take It Further** Prove that this relationship holds for any angle $\theta$, as long as $\tan \theta$ is defined and $\tan \theta$ and $\sin \theta$ are not equal to 0.

19. **Standardized Test Prep** Lindsay has a four-function calculator (+, −, ×, ÷). She also has a printed table showing values of $\sin \theta$ for values of $\theta$ from 0° to 90° in increments of 1°. Which formula will allow her to use this table and her calculator to compute the values of $\cos \theta$ for several different angles between 0° and 90°?

A. $\cos \theta = 1 - \sin \theta$ B. $\cos \theta = \sin (90 - \theta)$ C. $\cos \theta = -\sin \theta$

D. No relation exists between $\cos \theta$ and $\sin \theta$ for values of $\theta$ between 0° and 90°.

Go Online
www.successnetplus.com

## Maintain Your Skills

20. Find an angle $\theta$, not equal to 30°, that satisfies each equation.

a. $\cos \theta = \cos 30^\circ$ b. $\sin \theta = \sin 30^\circ$ c. $\tan \theta = \tan 30^\circ$

d. Describe how you can find ten other angles $\theta$ such that $\cos \theta = \cos 30^\circ$.

## 4.04 The Pythagorean Identity

While solving Exercise 5 in Lesson 4.02, you may have noticed the following equation is true for all angles between 0° and 360°.

$$\cos^2 \theta + \sin^2 \theta = 1$$

Since then, you have extended the domain for cosine and sine to include all angles. Does the identity still hold? Happily, it does.

### *Theorem 4.2 The Pythagorean Identity*

**If $\alpha$ is any angle, then**

$$\cos^2 \alpha + \sin^2 \alpha = 1$$

The symbol $\alpha$ is the Greek letter alpha. You pronounce it AL fuh.

**Proof** For any angle $\alpha$, $\cos \alpha$ and $\sin \alpha$ are the coordinates of the point $P$ on the unit circle, where the left side of $\alpha$ intersects the unit circle.

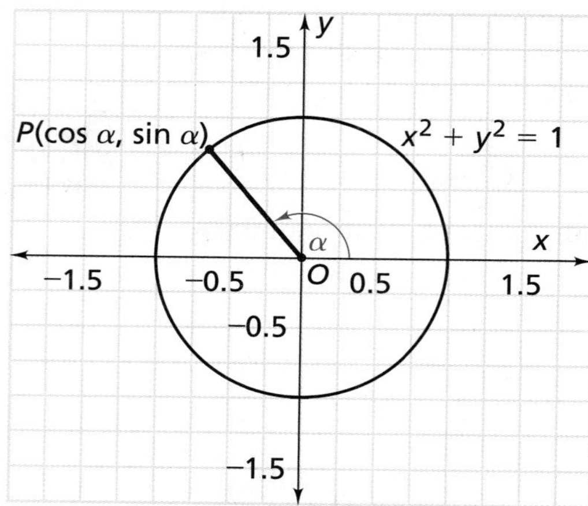


There are several ways to see that the sum of the squares of the coordinates of $P$ is 1.

**Method 1** The equation of the unit circle is $x^2 + y^2 = 1$, and the coordinates of $P$ satisfy this equation.

**Method 2** The distance from $P$ to the origin is 1.

**Method 3** Drop a perpendicular from $P$ to the $x$-axis and use the Pythagorean Theorem.

## For You to Do

1. Pick one of the methods above (or one of your own) and finish the proof of Theorem 4.2.

## Example

**Problem** If $\sin\gamma = \frac{1}{2}$, find $\cos\gamma$.

**Solution** Think of $(\cos\gamma, \sin\gamma)$ as a point $P$ on the unit circle. Then $\sin\gamma$ is the $y$-coordinate of $P$. How many points have a $y$-coordinate of $\frac{1}{2}$ on the unit circle?

In Exercise 20a from Lesson 4.01, you saw that there are two points on the unit circle with $y$-coordinate $\frac{1}{2}$. The $x$-coordinates of these two points are precisely the values of $\cos\gamma$ for which $\sin\gamma = \frac{1}{2}$.

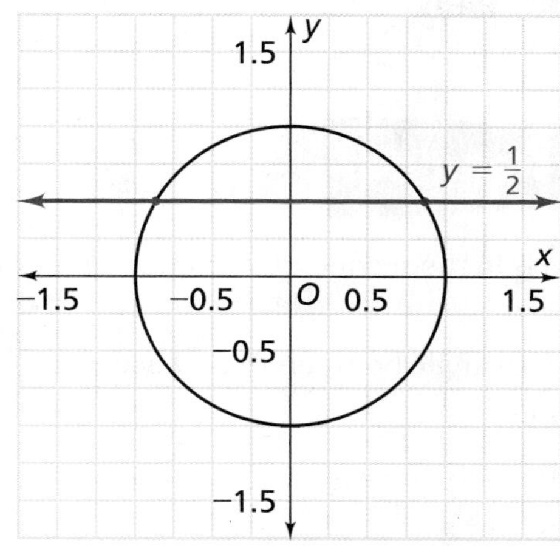


To find the two intersection points, you can do one of two equivalent things.

**Method 1** In the equation $x^2 + y^2 = 1$, substitute $y = \frac{1}{2}$ and solve for $x$.

$$x^2 + \left(\frac{1}{2}\right)^2 = 1$$

$$x^2 + \frac{1}{4} = 1$$

$$x^2 = \frac{3}{4}$$

$$x = \pm\sqrt{\frac{3}{4}} = \pm\frac{\sqrt{3}}{2}$$

**Method 2** Use the Pythagorean Identity.

$$\cos^2\gamma + \sin^2\gamma = 1$$

Substitute $\sin\gamma = \frac{1}{2}$.

$$\cos^2\gamma + \left(\frac{1}{2}\right)^2 = 1$$

$$\cos^2\gamma + \frac{1}{4} = 1$$

$$\cos^2\gamma = \frac{3}{4}$$

$$\cos\gamma = \pm\sqrt{\frac{3}{4}} = \pm\frac{\sqrt{3}}{2}$$

The symbol $\gamma$ is the Greek letter gamma. You pronounce it GAM uh.

Methods 1 and 2 really are the same. On the unit circle, if $(x, y)$ is the point where a radius that forms an angle $\gamma$ with the $x$-axis intersects the circle, then $\cos\gamma = x$ and $\sin\gamma = y$.

## For You to Do

**2.** Solve $\sin\gamma = \frac{1}{2}$ for $\gamma$.

### Habits of Mind

**Consider more than one solution.** If you ask your calculator for $\sin^{-1}(0.5)$, it will probably return 30°. It is true that $\sin 30° = 0.5$, but is that the only solution for $\gamma$? The calculator picks its values for $\sin^{-1}$ from a restricted sine domain.

# Exercises Practicing Habits of Mind

## Check Your Understanding

**1.** Suppose $\sin q = 0.72$ and $q$ is in the second quadrant. Find the approximate value of $\cos q$. Then find the measure of angle $q$ to the nearest degree.

**2.** Suppose $\cos x = \frac{1}{2}$ and $x$ is an angle between $0°$ and $360°$.

**a.** Find all possible values of $x$.

**b.** Find all possible values of $\sin x$.

**c.** Find all possible values of $\sin^2 x$.

**3.** Graph both equations on the same axes.

$$x^2 + y^2 = 1$$

$$y = 0.6$$

**4.** Find all solutions to the system of equations in Exercise 3.

**5.** Suppose $\cos x = 0.6$ and $x$ is an angle between $0°$ and $360°$.

**a.** Find all possible values of $x$.

**b.** Find all possible values of $\sin x$.

**c.** Find all possible values of $\sin^2 x$.

Approximate to one decimal place if necessary.

## On Your Own

**6.** Solve each equation or system for $0 \leq x \leq 360°$.

**a.** $\sin x = \frac{\sqrt{2}}{2}$

**b.** $\begin{cases} \sin x = \frac{\sqrt{2}}{2} \\ \cos x > 0 \end{cases}$

**c.** $\begin{cases} \sin x = \frac{\sqrt{2}}{2} \\ \cos x < 0 \end{cases}$

**d.** $\begin{cases} \sin x = -\frac{\sqrt{2}}{2} \\ \cos x < 0 \end{cases}$

7. Find ten pairs of rational numbers $(a, b)$ such that $a^2 + b^2 = 1$.

8. **Write About It** The Pythagorean Identity says that, if $\theta$ is any angle, $\cos^2\theta + \sin^2\theta = 1$.

   Suppose you have numbers $a$ and $b$ such that $a^2 + b^2 = 1$. Is there an angle $\theta$ such that $\sin\theta = a$ and $\cos\theta = b$? Explain.

Alpha is the first letter of the Greek alphabet. The alpha wolf is the leader of the pack.

9. **a.** Show that
   $$\tan^2 30° = \frac{1}{\cos^2 30°} - 1.$$
   **b.** If $\alpha$ is any angle, is the equation below true? Explain.
   $$\tan^2\alpha = \frac{1}{\cos^2\alpha} - 1$$

10. **a.** Calculate $\cos^2 30° - \sin^2 30°$.
    **b.** Calculate $\cos^4 30° - \sin^4 30°$.
    **c.** Verify that $\cos^2\theta - \sin^2\theta = \cos^4\theta - \sin^4\theta$ for a new choice of $\theta$.
    **d.** Prove that for any angle $\theta$, it must be true that
    $$\cos^2\theta - \sin^2\theta = \cos^4\theta - \sin^4\theta.$$

Pick a $\theta$, any $\theta$.

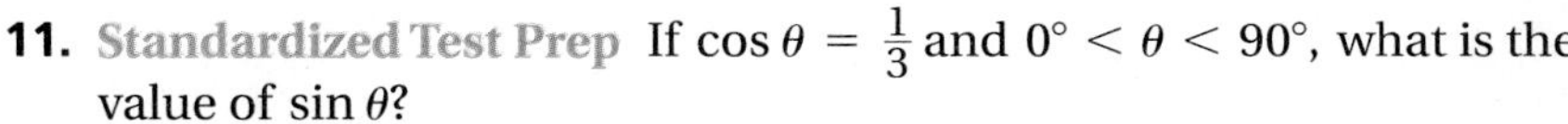

11. **Standardized Test Prep** If $\cos\theta = \frac{1}{3}$ and $0° < \theta < 90°$, what is the value of $\sin\theta$?

    **A.** $\frac{2}{3}$ **B.** $\frac{4}{9}$
    **C.** $\frac{2\sqrt{2}}{3}$ **D.** $\frac{8}{9}$

Go Online
www.successnetplus.com

## Maintain Your Skills

**12.** Copy and complete the table without using a calculator.

| $\theta$ | $\cos\theta$ | $\sin\theta$ | $\tan\theta$ |
|---|---|---|---|
| **0°** | ■ | 0 | ■ |
| 30° | $\frac{\sqrt{3}}{2}$ | ■ | $\frac{1}{\sqrt{3}}$ |
| 45° | ■ | $\frac{\sqrt{2}}{2}$ | 1 |
| 60° | ■ | ■ | ■ |
| **90°** | 0 | 1 | ■ |
| 120° | ■ | ■ | ■ |
| 135° | ■ | ■ | ■ |
| 150° | ■ | $-\frac{1}{2}$ | ■ |
| **180°** | ■ | ■ | ■ |
| 210° | ■ | ■ | ■ |
| 225° | $-\frac{\sqrt{2}}{2}$ | ■ | ■ |
| 240° | ■ | ■ | ■ |
| **270°** | 0 | ■ | ■ |
| 300° | ■ | ■ | ■ |
| 315° | ■ | ■ | ■ |
| 330° | ■ | ■ | ■ |
| **360°** | 1 | ■ | ■ |

You have done much of the work for this table before.

# 4.05 Solving Trigonometric Equations

You solve equations with trigonometric functions in much the same way you solve other equations.

## Minds in Action

*Tony and Sasha are trying to solve the equation $5 \cos x + 6 = 9$ for $x$ between $0°$ and $360°$.*

**Tony** I'm not sure what to do with the $\cos x$.

**Sasha** It's like in Chapter 1, when we chunked things.

*Sasha goes to the board and covers up the $\cos x$ with her hand.*

5 co✋x + 6 = 9

**Sasha** See? Now it looks like it's saying "5 times something plus 6 is 9."

So, let $z$ stand for $\cos x$, for the time being, and solve

$$5z + 6 = 9$$

**Tony** I know how to do that. You get $z = \frac{3}{5} = 0.6$.

**Sasha** But $z$ is just an alias for $\cos x$, so our equation is $\cos x = 0.6$.

Sasha replaces $z$ with $\cos x$ in the equation $z = 0.6$.

**Tony** And I know how to do that, too. In fact, we have already done it in Exercise 5 in the last lesson. You just use the inverse cosine button and get 53.13°. That's an approximation, I know.

**Sasha** Yes, but that's not the only answer. Look:

*Sasha draws on the board.*

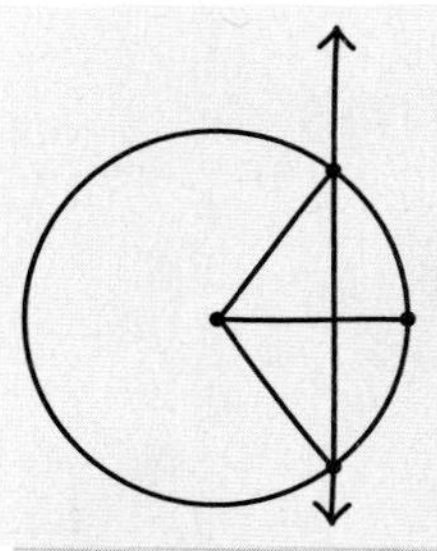

**Sasha** See? Cosine is the $x$-coordinate, and there are two points on the unit circle with $x$-coordinate 0.6. One has a central angle of about 53.13°.

**Tony** And the other is $-53.13°$.

**Sasha** Or, if you want your angles to measure between 0° and 360°, the second angle is about 306.87°.

**Habits of Mind**

**Make strategic choices.** What happens when you allow angles with measure greater than 360°?

## For You to Do

1. Solve $5 \sin x + 3 = 7$ for $x$ between 0° and 360°.

## Developing Habits of Mind

**Look for patterns.** The chunking idea is often used to solve trigonometric equations that look like ordinary algebraic equations.

For example, the trigonometric equation below is a quadratic equation in $\sin x$.

$$10 \sin^2 x - 3 \sin x = 4$$

That is, if you let $z = \sin x$, the equation becomes

$$10z^2 - 3z = 4$$

You can solve this with the methods of Chapter 1. When you find two values for $z$, replace $z$ with $\sin x$. Then solve for $x$.

A **trigonometric equation** is an equation that involves trigonometric functions.

## For You to Do

2. Solve the equation $10 \sin^2 x - 3 \sin x = 4$ for $x$, where $0° \leq x \leq 360°$.

# Exercises *Practicing Habits of Mind*

## Check Your Understanding

1. Suppose $\sin x = \sin 50°$. Find all possible values of $x$.
2. a. Find, to the nearest degree, the two angles between 0° and 360° that make $\sin x = 0.6$.

   b. Find, to the nearest degree, the two angles between 0° and 360° that make $\sin x = -0.6$.

3. a. Find, to the nearest degree, all angles between 0° and 360° that make $\cos x = 0.8$.

   b. Find, to the nearest degree, all angles between 0° and 360° that make $\cos x = -1.2$.

4. Find all solutions to each equation for $0° \le x \le 360°$.

   a. $3 \cos x + 4 = 0$
   b. $6 \sin x - 1 = 3$
   c. $4 \sin^2 x = 1$
   d. $4 \sin^2 x = 4 \sin x + 3$

5. a. Find, to the nearest degree, all angles between 0° and 360° that make $\sin x = \cos x$.

   b. Find, to the nearest degree, all angles between 0° and 360° that make $\sin x = -\cos x$.

   c. Take It Further Find, to the nearest degree, all angles between 0° and 360° that make $\sin x = \tan x$.

6. Solve the equation $6 \cos^2 x + \sin x - 5 = 0$ for $x$, where $0° \le x \le 360°$. (*Hint:* $\cos^2 x + \sin^2 x = 1$)

7. In the isosceles triangle below, $OA = OB = 1$ and $m\angle O = 36°$. Show that $z = 2 \cos 72°$.

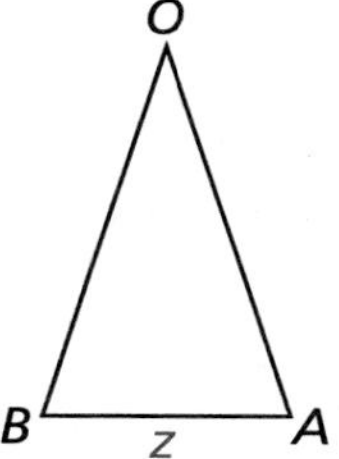


**Habits of Mind**

**Detect the key characteristics.** What is special about the parallelogram that has vertices $0$, $z$, $z + \bar{z}$, and $\bar{z}$?

## On Your Own

8. Find all solutions to each equation for $0° \le x \le 360°$.

   a. $5 \cos x + 4 = 0$
   b. $\sqrt{2} \sin x - 1 = 3$
   c. $4 \cos^2 x = 1$
   d. $4 \cos^2 x = 4 \cos x + 3$

9. Find all solutions to each equation for $0° \le x \le 360°$.

   a. $2 \cos x + 1 = 0$
   b. $\tan x - 1 = 0$
   c. $1 - 3 \sin x + 2 \sin^2 x = 0$
   d. $2 \cos^2 x - 5 \cos x = 2$

10. For what values of $\alpha$ between 0° and 360° is the following equation true?

$$2 \sin^2 \alpha + 5 \cos \alpha = 2$$

**11.** Find or approximate the complex number on the unit circle that has each argument. Write your in $a + bi$ form.

**a.** 20° **b.** 330° **c.** −30° **d.** 100° **e.** 227° **f.** 75°

**12.** Solve the equation $2\sin^3 x - \sin^2 x - 2\sin x + 1 = 0$ for $x$, where $0° \leq x \leq 360°$.

**13.** In the isosceles triangle below, $OA = OB = 1$ and $m\angle O = 36°$. $\overline{BC}$ bisects $\angle OBA$.

See Exercise 8.

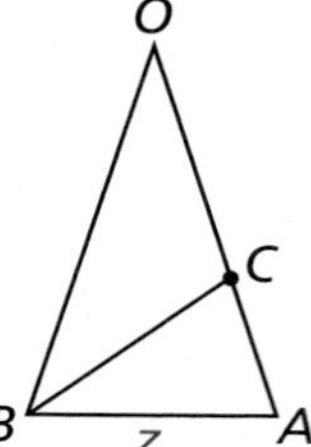


**Habits of Mind**

**Look for relationships.** There are similar triangles in the figure.

**a.** Show that $1 - z^2 = z$.

**b.** Use the result of part (a) to find an exact value for $z$.

**c.** Use parts (a) and (b) and the result of Exercise 8 to find an exact value for cos 72°.

**d.** **Take It Further** Find an exact value for sin 72°.

**14.** **Take It Further** Solve the equation $5\cos 2x + 6 = 9$, where $0° \leq x \leq 360°$.

**15.** **Standardized Test Prep** Solve, to the nearest hundredth of a degree, $\tan x - 10 = -\tan x$ for $-90° < x < 90°$.

**A.** −80° **B.** 1.37° **C.** 78.69° **D.** 84.29°

## Maintain Your Skills

**16.** Here is a graph of the unit circle with a line $\ell$ that intersects the circle at the points $A(0, -1)$ and $P(a, b)$.

Find the coordinates of $P$ for each slope of $\ell$.

**a.** 1 **b.** 2 **c.** $\frac{3}{2}$

**d.** 4 **e.** $\frac{6}{5}$

**f.** **Take It Further** $\frac{r}{s}$

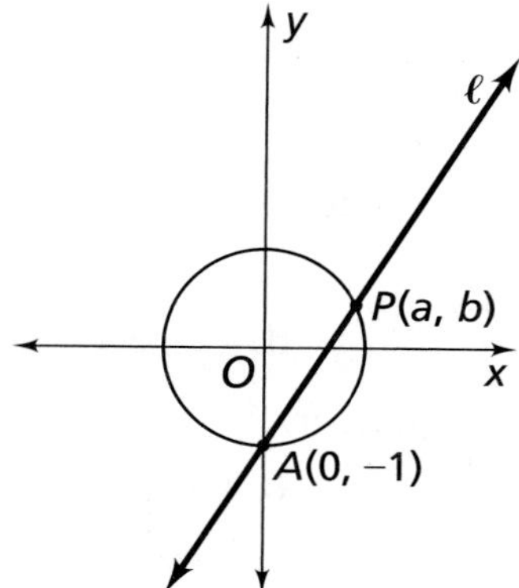

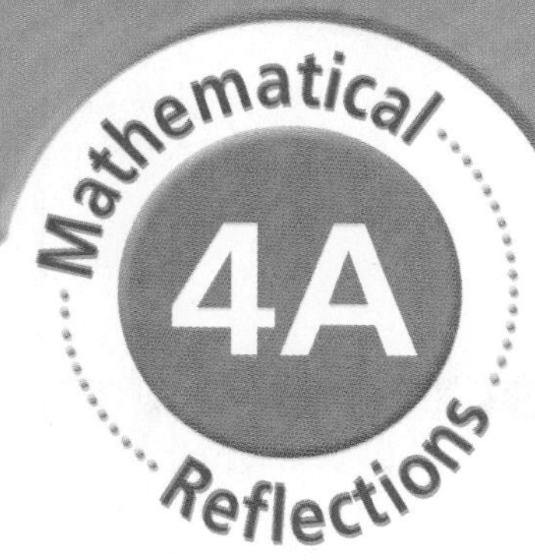


**In this investigation, you learned how to evaluate the sine, cosine, and tangent functions for any angle and to solve equations involving trigonometric equations. These questions will help you summarize what you have learned.**

1. A line through the origin forms a 30° angle with the $x$-axis. What are the coordinates of the points where this line intersects the graph of the unit circle?
2. Sketch each angle in standard position. Find its sine, cosine, and tangent.

   **a.** 150° **b.** 315° **c.** 240°
3. Find five solutions to the equation $\sin x = -1$.
4. For some angle $\theta$, $\sin \theta = \frac{12}{13}$.

   **a.** Find all possible values for $\cos \theta$.

   **b.** Find all possible values for $\tan \theta$.

   **c.** Find a possible $\theta$ between 0° and 360° to the nearest tenth of a degree.
5. Solve the following equation for $\alpha$ between 0° and 360°.

$$10 \cos^2 \alpha + \cos \alpha - 3 = 0$$

6. How can you extend the definitions of sine, cosine, and tangent to any angle, not just acute angles?
7. If an angle is in Quadrant IV, what can you say about the sign of its sine, cosine, and tangent?
8. What is the relationship between the equation of the unit circle and the Pythagorean Identity?

## Vocabulary and Notation

In this investigation, you learned these terms and symbols. Make sure you understand what each one means and how to use it.

- **cosine, cos $\theta$**
- **periodic function**
- **sine, sin $\theta$**
- **standard position**
- **tangent, tan $\theta$**
- **trigonometric equation**

The tip of the wiper moves along a circle as the wiper rotates.

# Graphs of Trigonometric Functions

In *Graphs of Trigonometric Functions*, you will sketch the graphs of the sine, cosine, and tangent functions. You can use these graphs to explore trigonometric identities.

**By the end of this investigation, you will be able to answer questions like these.**

1. What do the graphs of the sine and cosine functions look like?
2. Why does the tangent function have a period of $180°$?
3. What is a simple rule for finding the value of $\cos(90° + \theta)$?

**You will learn how to**

- sketch graphs of the sine, cosine, and tangent functions
- use the graphs of trigonometric functions to solve problems
- prove and use trigonometric identities

**You will develop these habits and skills:**

- Visualize relationships between graphs of trigonometric functions.
- Choose the appropriate representation—graph or unit circle—to understand and develop trigonometric identities.
- Reason logically to prove trigonometric identities.

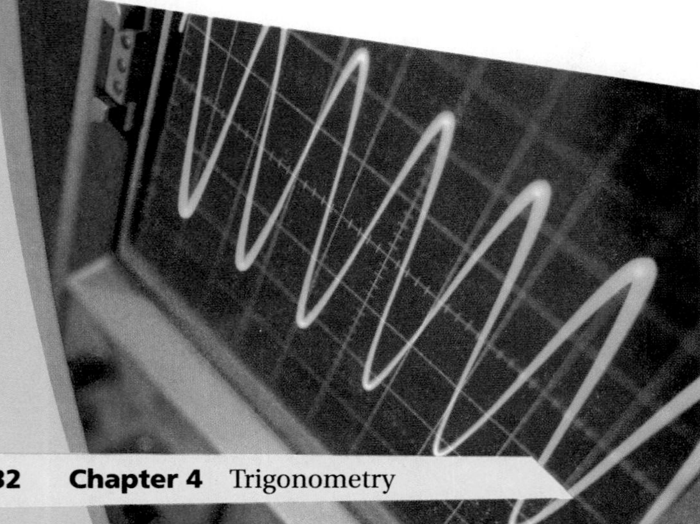

An oscilloscope displays voltage as a function of time. The graph is a sine wave.

# 4.06 Getting Started

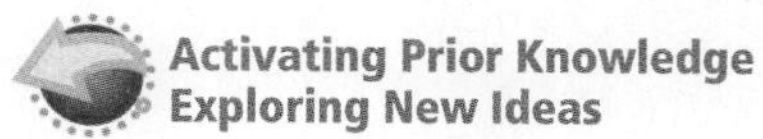


The graphs of the sine, cosine, and tangent functions show the periodic nature of these functions.

## For You to Explore

An exact value for a trigonometric function is an expression that may include square roots. If you use your calculator, it may return a decimal approximation and not an exact value.

**1.** Find the exact values of $\cos 30°$ and $\sin 30°$.

**2.** Find the exact values of $\cos 45°$ and $\sin 45°$.

**3.** Calculate each value.

**a.** $\cos^2 30°$ **b.** $\sin^2 30°$

**c.** $\cos^2 45°$ **d.** $\sin^2 45°$

**e.** $\cos^2 30° + \sin^2 30°$ **f.** $\cos^2 45° + \sin^2 45°$

**4.** Describe how the cosine and sine of 60° are related to the cosine and sine of 30°.

**5.** Describe how the cosine and sine of 150° are related to the cosine and sine of 30°.

## Exercises *Practicing Habits of Mind*

### On Your Own

**6.** Use the information from Exercise 12 in Lesson 4.04 to draw a graph of $y = \cos x$ for $0° \le x \le 360°$.

**7.** Use the graph of $y = \cos x$ to answer this question: Is $\cos 230°$ greater or less than $\cos 190°$?

**8.** Use the information from Exercise 12 in Lesson 4.04 to draw a graph of the function $y = \sin x$ for $0° \le x \le 360°$.

9. Use the graph of $y = \sin x$ to answer this question: Is $\sin 230°$ greater or less than $\sin 190°$?

10. Find and describe a relationship between $\sin \theta$ and $\sin (180° + \theta)$.

11. **Take It Further** Which is greater, $\tan 190°$ or $\tan 230°$? Determine the answer without a calculator. Justify your answer.

## Maintain Your Skills

12. Here is the table you completed in Lesson 4.04, Exercise 12. What patterns can you find in each column?

| $\theta$ | $\cos\theta$ | $\sin\theta$ | $\tan\theta$ |
|---|---|---|---|
| 0° | 1 | 0 | 0 |
| 30° | $\frac{\sqrt{3}}{2}$ | $\frac{1}{2}$ | $\frac{1}{\sqrt{3}}$ |
| 45° | $\frac{\sqrt{2}}{2}$ | $\frac{\sqrt{2}}{2}$ | 1 |
| 60° | $\frac{1}{2}$ | $\frac{\sqrt{3}}{2}$ | $\sqrt{3}$ |
| 90° | 0 | 1 | undefined |
| 120° | $-\frac{1}{2}$ | $\frac{\sqrt{3}}{2}$ | $-\sqrt{3}$ |
| 135° | $-\frac{\sqrt{2}}{2}$ | $\frac{\sqrt{2}}{2}$ | $-1$ |
| 150° | $-\frac{\sqrt{3}}{2}$ | $\frac{1}{2}$ | $-\frac{1}{\sqrt{3}}$ |
| 180° | $-1$ | 0 | 0 |
| 210° | $-\frac{\sqrt{3}}{2}$ | $-\frac{1}{2}$ | $\frac{1}{\sqrt{3}}$ |
| 225° | $-\frac{\sqrt{2}}{2}$ | $-\frac{\sqrt{2}}{2}$ | 1 |
| 240° | $-\frac{1}{2}$ | $-\frac{\sqrt{3}}{2}$ | $\sqrt{3}$ |
| 270° | 0 | $-1$ | undefined |
| 300° | $\frac{1}{2}$ | $-\frac{\sqrt{3}}{2}$ | $-\sqrt{3}$ |
| 315° | $\frac{\sqrt{2}}{2}$ | $-\frac{\sqrt{2}}{2}$ | $-1$ |
| 330° | $\frac{\sqrt{3}}{2}$ | $-\frac{1}{2}$ | $-\frac{1}{\sqrt{3}}$ |
| 360° | 1 | 0 | 0 |

# 4.07 Graphing Cosine and Sine

In Lesson 4.03, you extended the domain of sine and cosine to all of ℝ. This means that you can graph $\sin x$ or $\cos x$ against $x$ on a Cartesian graph. One way to do this is to use the completed table on the facing page.

**Remember...**

ℝ is the set of real numbers.

Consider the sine function first. Notice that the second column in the table starts at 0, climbs to 1, then retreats backs to 0, plunges to $-1$, and then climbs back up to 0.

## For You to Do

1. To get a feeling for the relative sizes, rewrite the sine values as decimal approximations.

Once you get the decimal approximations, you can plot points. If you use your calculator to get decimal approximations for even more sines, you will end up with a graph that looks like this.

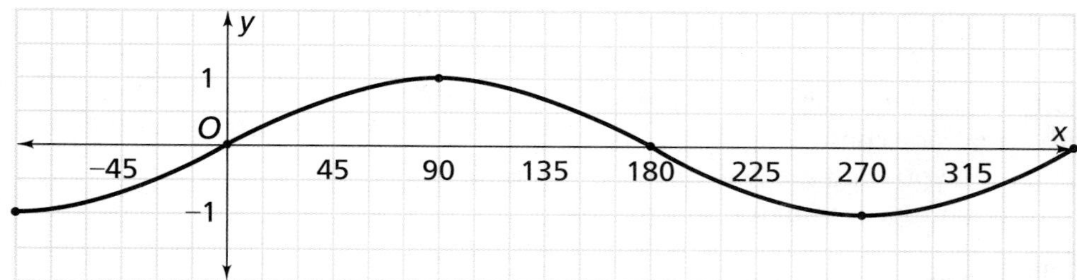


## For Discussion

2. Use the fact that sine is periodic to extend the graph to $-360° \leq x \leq 720°$.

## For You to Do

3. Sketch the graph of $y = \cos x$ for $-360° \leq x \leq 720°$. Describe how the graph of $y = \cos x$ is related to the graph of $y = \sin x$.

**Habits of Mind**

**Visualize.** Because of the symmetry of the graphs, there are many ways to describe this relationship.

Along with the unit circle, the graphs of sine and cosine give you a toolkit that will help you think about the properties of the trigonometric functions.

## Example

**Problem** For how many values of $\alpha$ between $0°$ and $360°$ is $\cos \alpha = -0.4$? What are they, approximately?

**Solution** There are two ways to think about this.

**Method 1** Use the graph of the function $\cos x = y$. Just as on the graph of any function, the output at $x$ is the $y$-height above or below $x$ on the graph. So, to find $\alpha$ such that $\cos \alpha = -0.4$, find the intersections of the graphs of $y = -0.4$ and $y = \cos x$.

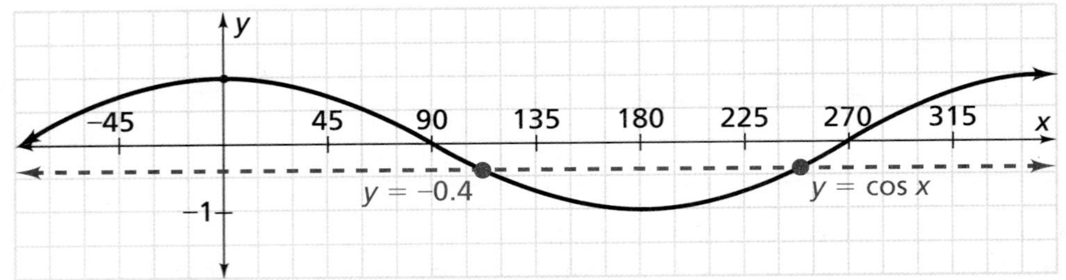


There are two such intersections in the interval $0° \leq x \leq 360°$. And it looks as if the intersections occur at $x \approx 110°$ and $x \approx 250°$. So, $\cos \alpha = -0.4$ for $\alpha \approx 110°$ and $\alpha \approx 250°$.

**Method 2** Use the unit circle. On the unit circle, an angle of measure $\alpha$ with vertex at the origin and with initial side containing $(1, 0)$ cuts the circle with its terminal side at $(\cos \alpha, \sin \alpha)$. If you want $\cos \alpha$ to be $-0.4$, you want to look on the unit circle for points with $x$-coordinate equal to $-0.4$.

Once again, we see that there are two such angles between $0°$ and $360°$. They are approximately $110°$ and $250°$.

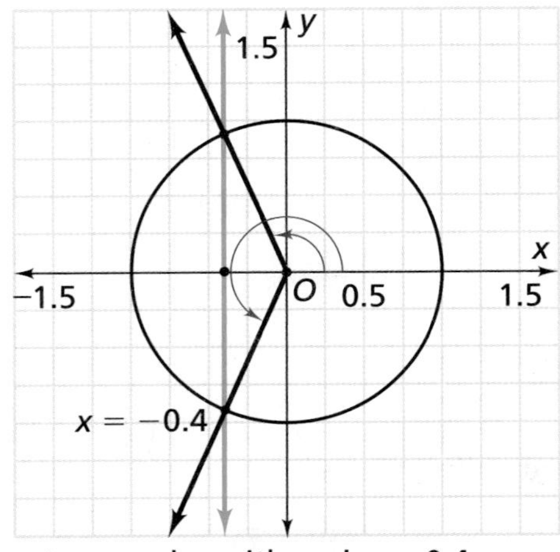


two angles with cosine −0.4

**Go Online**
www.successnetplus.com

## For You to Do

4. Use your calculator's $\cos^{-1}$ key to get better approximations of the angles with cosine $-0.4$. Round to three decimal places.

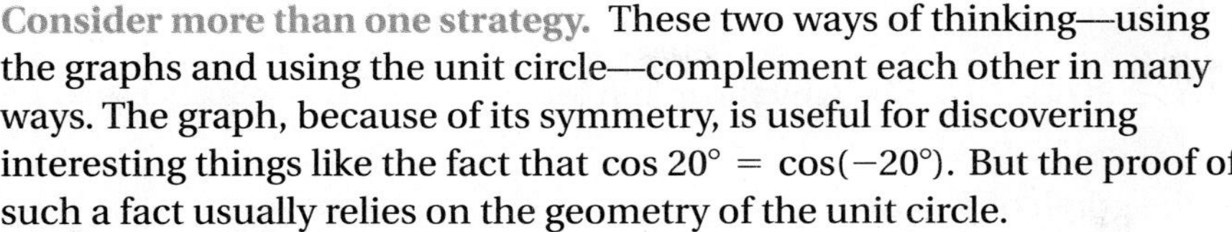

## Developing Habits of Mind

**Consider more than one strategy.** These two ways of thinking—using the graphs and using the unit circle—complement each other in many ways. The graph, because of its symmetry, is useful for discovering interesting things like the fact that $\cos 20° = \cos(-20°)$. But the proof of such a fact usually relies on the geometry of the unit circle.

The unit circle is ideal for figuring out exact values for things like $\sin 240°$, because you can use what you know from geometry. The graph is ideal for finding qualitative facts, such as the number of solutions to $\sin x = 0.7$.

## For You to Do

**5.** Explain why $\cos 20° = \cos(-20°)$. Is it always true that $\cos x = \cos(-x)$?

## For Discussion

For each question, decide whether it is a good idea to use the unit circle, the graph, or both. Then answer each question.

**6.** How many solutions are there to $|\sin x| = 1$ for $-360° \leq x \leq 360°$?

**7.** Find the solutions to $|\sin x| = 1$ for $-360° \leq x \leq 360°$.

**8.** Find a formula for all solutions of $|\sin x| = 1$.

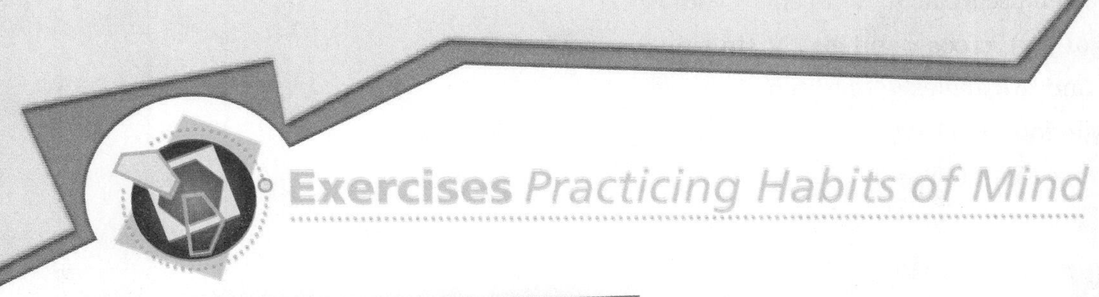

## Exercises *Practicing Habits of Mind*

### Check Your Understanding

**1.** The values of $\sin 50°$ and $\sin(-50°)$ are related.

**a.** Use the unit circle to describe and illustrate this relationship.

**b.** Use the graph of $y = \sin x$ to describe and illustrate this relationship.

**2.** **What's Wrong Here?** Derman uses his graphing calculator to sketch the graph of $y = \sin x$. As is his custom, he sets the window so that $x$ and $y$ go from $-10$ to 10. He is surprised by what he sees. Describe what Derman sees. How can he fix the problem?

To help Derman, see the TI-Nspire Handbook, p. 817.

3. Sketch the graph of $f(x) = \cos(x + 360°)$. Describe why the graph looks the way it does.

4. a. How many $x$-intercepts does the graph of $y = \cos x$ have?

   b. Explain why the cosine function cannot be a polynomial function.

   c. Where is the tangent function undefined? Explain.

Consider the entire graph, not just a small section.

5. Sketch the graph of $f(x) = \sin(30° + x) + \sin(30° - x)$.

6. Sketch the graph of $g(x) = \cos(x - 90°)$.

7. Here are the graphs of $y = \sin x$ and $y = 0.6$ on the same axes.

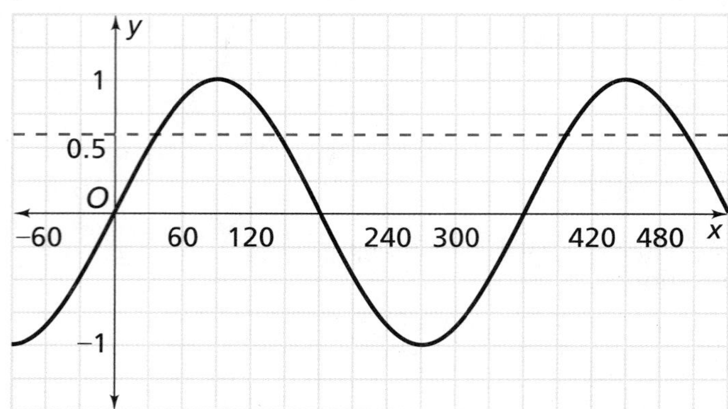


The least positive value of $x$ that solves $\sin x = 0.6$ is about 37°. Find the next two values of $x$, to the nearest degree, that solve the equation.

8. **Take It Further** Sketch the graph of $k(x) = \cos 2x$ without the aid of a graphing calculator. Then use a calculator to check your work.

9. a. Sketch the graphs of $f(x) = \cos x$ and $g(x) = \sin x$ on the same axes.

   b. Use the graphs to find two angles $\theta$ for which $\sin\theta = \cos\theta$.

10. a. For each angle $\theta$ you found in Exercise 9, find $\tan\theta$.

    b. If $\sin\theta = \cos\theta$, prove that $\tan\theta = 1$.

## On Your Own

**Habits of Mind**

**Make strategic choices.** For Exercises 11 and 12, should you draw a unit circle or a graph? You decide.

11. Draw a picture to explain why $\cos(-\theta) = \cos\theta$.

12. Draw a picture to explain why $\sin(-\theta) = -\sin\theta$.

13. Sketch the graph of $s(x) = \cos^2 x + \sin^2 x$.

14. **Standardized Test Prep** Which function has the same graph as $y = \sin x$?

    **A.** $y = \cos(x + 180°)$ **B.** $y = -\sin x$

    **C.** $y = \sin(x + 360°)$ **D.** $y = 2\sin x$

15. Below are the graphs of $y = \cos x$ and $y = 0.8$ on the same axes. The least positive value of $x$ that solves $\cos x = 0.8$ is about 37°. Find the next two values of $x$ that solve the equation, to the nearest degree.

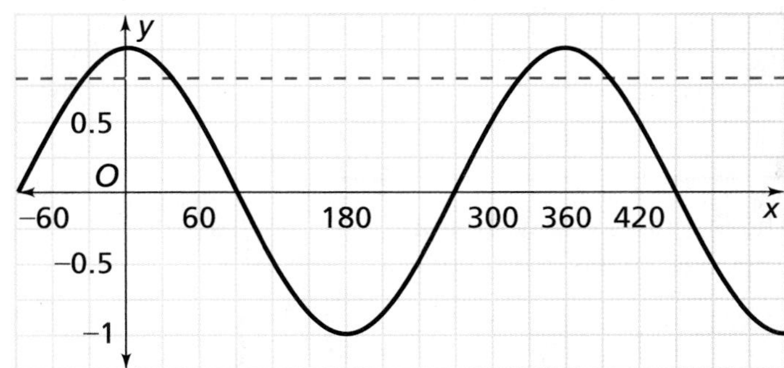


16. Use the unit circle or graphs to illustrate that each identity is true for all $\theta$.

a. $\sin(180° - \theta) = \sin\theta$
b. $\cos(180° - \theta) = -\cos\theta$
c. $\sin(180° + \theta) = -\sin\theta$
d. $\cos(360° - \theta) = \cos\theta$
e. $\sin\theta = \cos(\theta - 90°)$
f. $\cos\theta = -\sin(\theta - 90°)$

17. Sketch the graph of $h(x) = -\sin x$ for at least two periods.

18. Describe the graph of $h(x) = -\sin x$ as a translation of the graph of $g(x) = \sin x$.

19. Sketch an accurate graph of each function.

a. $j(x) = \cos^2 x - \sin^2 x$
b. $r(x) = \cos 2x$
c. $k(x) = \cos^4 x - \sin^4 x$

**Go Online**
www.successnetplus.com

A **period** is a full cycle of the wave: up, down, and back again. It is the smallest piece that you can repeat over and over to produce the entire graph.

## Maintain Your Skills

20. The graph below in black shows a portion of the graph of $y = \cos x$. Find the coordinates of each marked point.

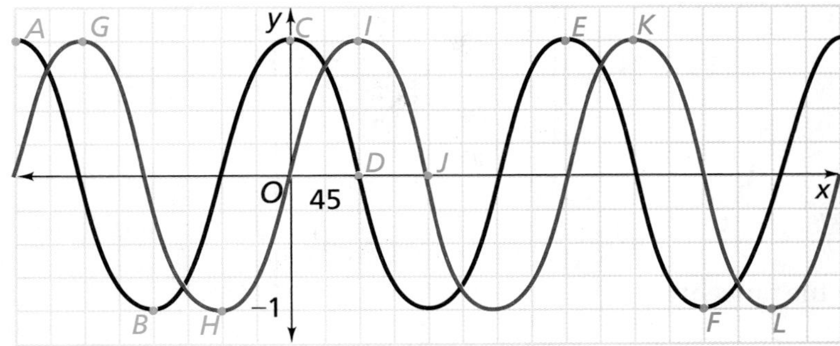


21. The graph above in red shows a portion of the graph of $y = \sin x$. Find the coordinates of each marked point.

# 4.08 Graphing the Tangent Function

You have extended the definition of tangent to $\tan x = \frac{\sin x}{\cos x}$, whenever $\cos x \neq 0$. In other words, tangent is defined for all real numbers except odd multiples of 90°. In this lesson, you will build the graph of $y = \tan x$. First, however, note this interesting way to picture the tangent.

## Developing Habits of Mind

**Visualize.** Why do you call it *tangent*? The diagrams below show a tangent to the unit circle at (1, 0). The angle $x$ is shown in each of the four quadrants.

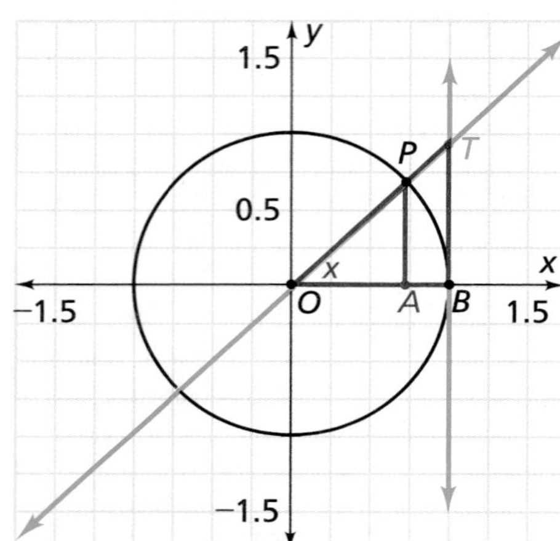


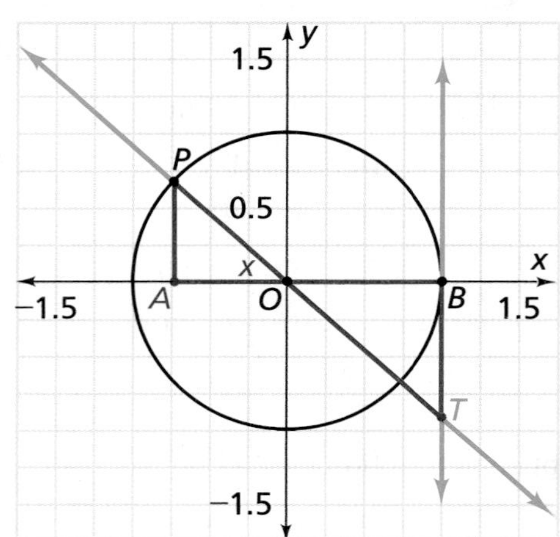


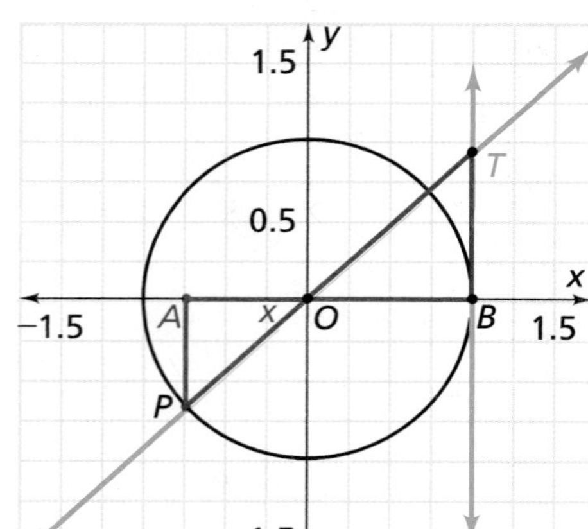


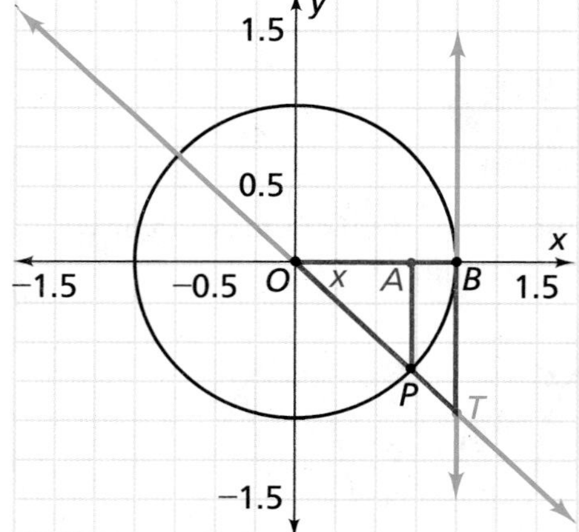


In each case, $\triangle POA \sim \triangle TOB$, so $\frac{TB}{OB} = \frac{PA}{OA}$.

But $OB = 1$, so $TB =$ the length of the tangent $= \frac{PA}{OA}$.

You can use this to show that the coordinates of $T$ are $(1, \tan x)$. So you measure $\tan x$ along the tangent.

## For Discussion

1. Finish the argument above by showing that the coordinates of $T$ are $(1, \tan x)$.
2. What happens when the angle is 90° or 270°?

Check the signs.

## For You to Do

3. What happens to $\tan x$ for values of $x$ close to, but slightly less than, 90°?
4. What happens to $\tan x$ for values of $x$ close to, but slightly greater than, 90°?

Along with the definition of the tangent function, some other information may help you think about the shape of the graph of $y = \tan x$.

The familiar completed table below shows some values of $\tan \theta$.

| $\theta$ | $\cos \theta$ | $\sin \theta$ | $\tan \theta$ |
|---|---|---|---|
| **0°** | 1 | 0 | 0 |
| 30° | $\frac{\sqrt{3}}{2}$ | $\frac{1}{2}$ | $\frac{1}{\sqrt{3}}$ |
| 45° | $\frac{\sqrt{2}}{2}$ | $\frac{\sqrt{2}}{2}$ | 1 |
| 60° | $\frac{1}{2}$ | $\frac{\sqrt{3}}{2}$ | $\sqrt{3}$ |
| **90°** | 0 | 1 | undefined |
| 120° | $-\frac{1}{2}$ | $\frac{\sqrt{3}}{2}$ | $-\sqrt{3}$ |
| 135° | $-\frac{\sqrt{2}}{2}$ | $\frac{\sqrt{2}}{2}$ | $-1$ |
| 150° | $-\frac{\sqrt{3}}{2}$ | $\frac{1}{2}$ | $-\frac{1}{\sqrt{3}}$ |
| **180°** | $-1$ | 0 | 0 |
| 210° | $-\frac{\sqrt{3}}{2}$ | $-\frac{1}{2}$ | $\frac{1}{\sqrt{3}}$ |
| 225° | $-\frac{\sqrt{2}}{2}$ | $-\frac{\sqrt{2}}{2}$ | 1 |
| 240° | $-\frac{1}{2}$ | $-\frac{\sqrt{3}}{2}$ | $\sqrt{3}$ |
| **270°** | 0 | $-1$ | undefined |
| 300° | $\frac{1}{2}$ | $-\frac{\sqrt{3}}{2}$ | $-\sqrt{3}$ |
| 315° | $\frac{\sqrt{2}}{2}$ | $-\frac{\sqrt{2}}{2}$ | $-1$ |
| 330° | $\frac{\sqrt{3}}{2}$ | $-\frac{1}{2}$ | $-\frac{1}{\sqrt{3}}$ |
| **360°** | 1 | 0 | 0 |

**Habits of Mind**

**Detect the key characterisitics.** Notice that the tangent function is undefined for some angles. This happens when you try to divide by 0. Look at what happens close to these points of **discontinuity.**

The discussion and graphs in Developing Habits of Mind show that $\tan x$ is the coordinate of a point related to $x$.

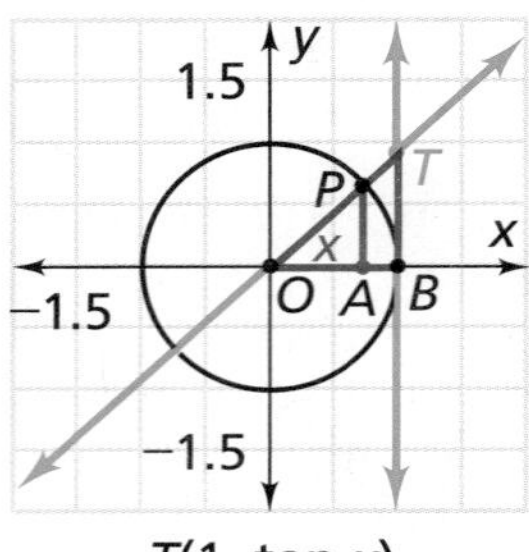


$T(1, \tan x)$

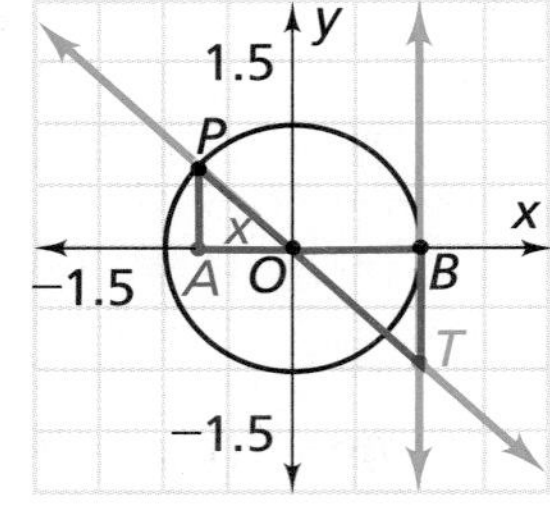


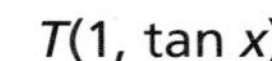

$T(1, \tan x)$

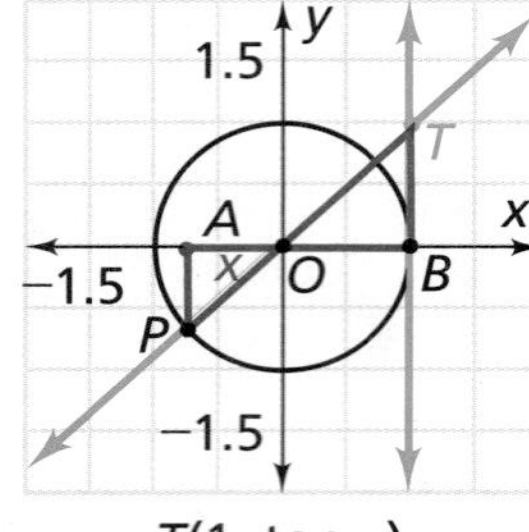


$T(1, \tan x)$

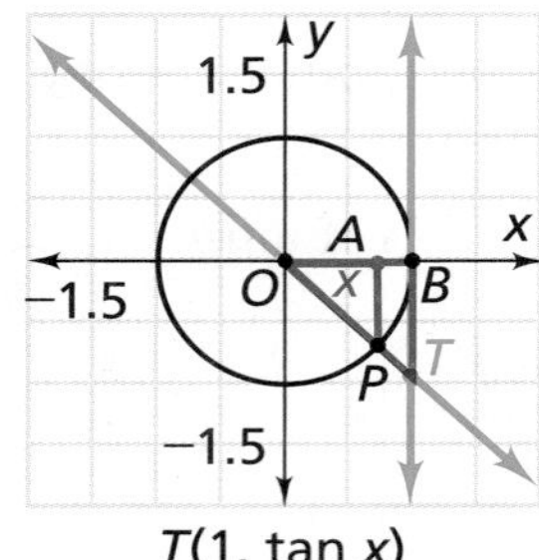


$T(1, \tan x)$

## In-Class Experiment

**5.** Use these ideas or any other information you have to carefully draw the graph of $y = \tan x$. Label the coordinates of all points you plot.

## For Discussion

**6.** Explain why the tangent function is periodic. What is its period?

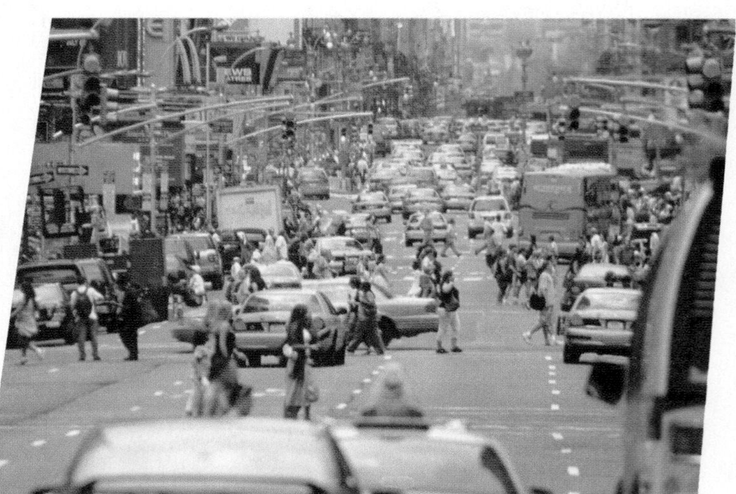

The periods of the traffic lights are set to manage the flow of traffic.

# Exercises *Practicing Habits of Mind*

## Check Your Understanding

**1. a.** Explain why $\cos(180° + \theta) = -\cos\theta$.

**b.** Explain why $\sin(180° + \theta) = -\sin\theta$.

**2.** Use the results from Exercise 1 to explain why $\tan(180° + \theta) = \tan\theta$.

**3.** Suppose $\theta$ is in Quadrant I and $\tan\theta = \frac{2}{3}$.

**a.** Draw a right triangle in the unit circle to indicate the location of $\theta$.

**b.** Find the exact values of $\sin\theta$ and $\cos\theta$.

**4.** Suppose $\theta$ is in Quadrant I and $\tan\theta = \frac{2}{3}$.

**a.** Find the value of $\tan(90° + \theta)$ in terms oftan $\theta$.

**b.** Suppose that $\ell$ is a line. Show that the slope of $\ell$ is the tangent of the angle $\ell$ makes with the positive $x$-axis.

**c.** Show that two lines are perpendicular if and only if their slopes are negative reciprocals.

**5.** As stated at the beginning of this lesson, cosine is equal to 0 for odd multiples of 90°. Explain why this is true.

**6.** Find each angle to the nearest degree.

**a.** $\theta$ is in Quadrant I, and $\tan\theta = \frac{1}{4}$.

**b.** $\theta$ is in Quadrant I, and $\tan\theta = \frac{8}{15}$.

**c.** $\theta$ is in Quadrant II, and $\tan\theta = -4$.

**d.** $\theta$ is in Quadrant III, and $\tan\theta = \frac{8}{15}$.

## On Your Own

7. Write About It Give two different explanations for why $\tan \theta$ is positive when $\theta$ is in Quadrant III but negative when $\theta$ is in Quadrant II.

8. **a.** What is the domain of the tangent function? Give a complete answer, not just one for angles from $0°$ to $360°$.

   **b.** What is the range of the tangent function?

This graph of $y = \tan x$ may be helpful for Exercises 9–11.

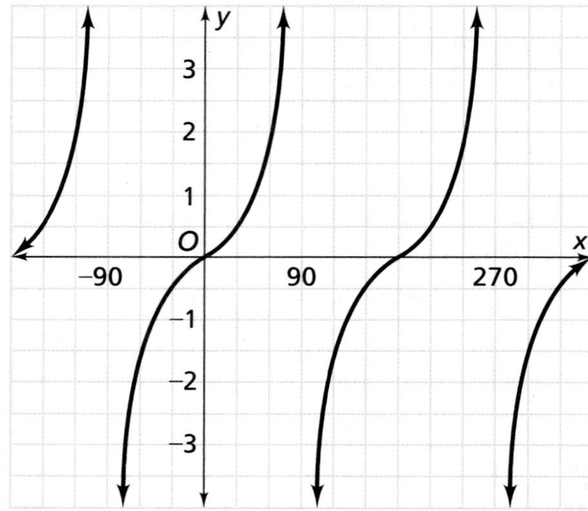


9. **a.** Approximate the solutions to the equation $\tan x = 2$.

   **b.** Approximate the solutions to the equation $\tan x = -2$.

10. Explain how the graph of the tangent function suggests that $\tan (180° + x) = \tan x$.

11. Take It Further Use the graph of $y = \tan x$ to sketch an accurate graph of the function $y = \frac{1}{\tan x}$.

12. Standardized Test Prep Use the equation $\tan (A + B) = \frac{\tan A + \tan B}{1 - (\tan A)(\tan B)}$. What is the value of $\tan 2\theta$ if $\tan \theta = \frac{1}{2}$?

    **A.** $\frac{3}{4}$ **B.** 1 **C.** $\frac{4}{3}$ **D.** 2

**Habits of Mind**

**Experiment.** Where is tangent undefined?

## Maintain Your Skills

13. For each angle $\theta$, calculate $\sin (120° + \theta)$.

    **a.** $\theta = 0°$ **b.** $\theta = 30°$ **c.** $\theta = 60°$ **d.** $\theta = 90°$

    **e.** Suppose $\sin (120° + \theta) = A \cos \theta + B \sin \theta$. Find the values of $A$ and $B$.

# 4.09 The Angle-Sum Identities

If you look back at the results of some of the problems you have solved in this chapter, you can see a thread that has woven its way through many of them. For example, Exercise 16 from Lesson 4.07 and Exercises 1 and 2 from Lesson 4.08 give some interesting identities.

For all $x$:

- $\sin(180° - x) = \sin x$
- $\cos(180° - x) = -\cos x$
- $\cos(360° - x) = \cos x$
- $\sin x = \cos(x - 90°)$
- $\cos x = -\sin(x - 90°)$
- $\cos(180° + x) = -\cos x$
- $\sin(180° + x) = -\sin x$
- $\tan(180° + x) = \tan x$

All of these identities have the same form. They give an alternate expression for $f(a + b)$, where $f$ is a trigonometric function and $a$ and $b$ are numbers. Usually when you see a collection of identities with the same form, there are a few general identities lurking in the background that tie all the special identities together.

**Habits of Mind**

**Look for relationships.** For example, $25 - 9 = (5 + 3)(5 - 3)$, $49 - 25 = (7 + 5)(7 - 5)$, and $x^2 - 1 = (x - 1)(x + 1)$ are all special cases of the general identity $a^2 - b^2 = (a + b)(a - b)$. An important part of algebra is looking for general identities that yield many special ones.

## For You to Do

Derman says, "I bet $\sin(\alpha + \beta) = \sin\alpha + \sin\beta$ for all numbers $\alpha$ and $\beta$."

1. Help Derman see that this is not an identity.
2. Do any values of $\alpha$ and $\beta$ make Derman's equation work? If so, find them.
3. Is $\cos(\alpha + \beta) = \cos\alpha + \cos\beta$ an identity for all $\alpha$ and $\beta$? Explain.

Can you find a function $f$ such that $f(a + b) = f(a) + f(b)$ for all numbers $a$ and $b$?

So, Derman's try at a formula for $\sin(\alpha + \beta)$, while simple, is not correct. The purpose of this lesson is to come up with formulas for $\sin(\alpha + \beta)$ and $\cos(\alpha + \beta)$ that are true for all values of $\alpha$ and $\beta$. The main result is the following theorem.

## *Theorem 4.3 Angle-Sum Identities*

For all $\alpha$ and $\beta$,

- $\cos(\alpha + \beta) = \cos\alpha\cos\beta - \sin\alpha\sin\beta$
- $\sin(\alpha + \beta) = \sin\alpha\cos\beta + \cos\alpha\sin\beta$

Identities that involve functions, such as $\cos(\alpha + \beta) = \cos\alpha\cos\beta - \sin\alpha\sin\beta$ or $\sqrt{(ab)} = \sqrt{(a)} \cdot \sqrt{(b)}$ are functional equations.

### Pick a Proof

This time, you will find the formula and build the proof. In this section, there are two sketches of a derivation for the formulas you want. Your job is to pick a method, study it, and write it up in your own words. You will fill in all the missing steps and explain all the statements.

**Proof 1 (Rotated Triangles)** This derivation uses the unit circle definitions of sine and cosine. Here you will look at sine. (You can look at cosine on your own.) In the graph below, $AD = \sin\alpha$ and $BK = \sin\beta$.

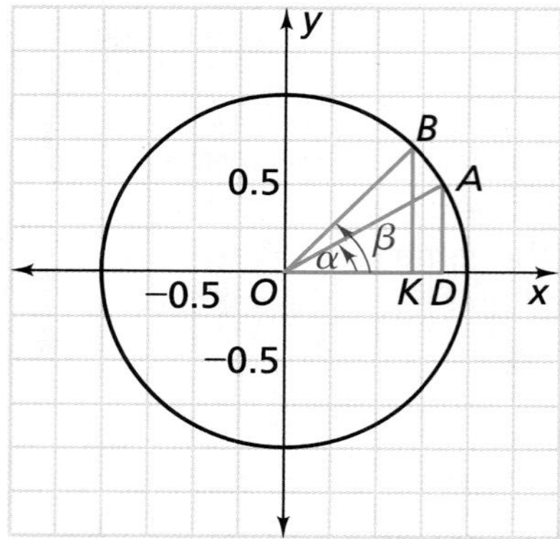


**Habits of Mind**

**Work like a mathematician.** An important part of learning mathematics is learning to read mathematics and to fill in the gaps for yourself.

You want a picture of $\sin(\alpha + \beta)$. To get an $\alpha + \beta$ in the picture, rotate $\triangle OBK$ upward through an angle of $\alpha$.

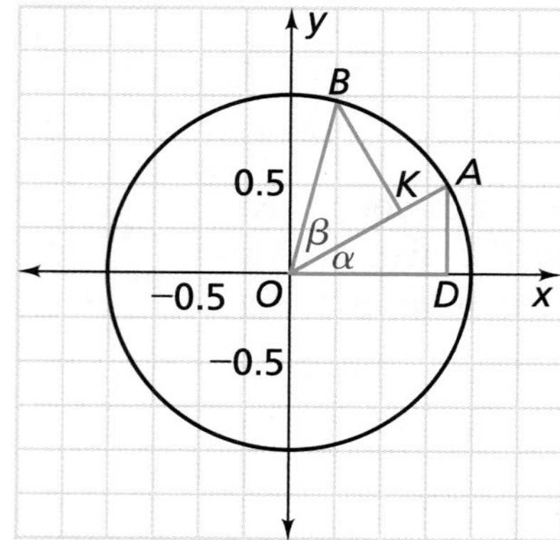

The sine of $\alpha + \beta$ is the $y$-height of $B$—the length of the perpendicular from $B$ to the $x$-axis. Copy the diagram below. Make sure the segments are parallel and perpendicular to the appropriate axes.

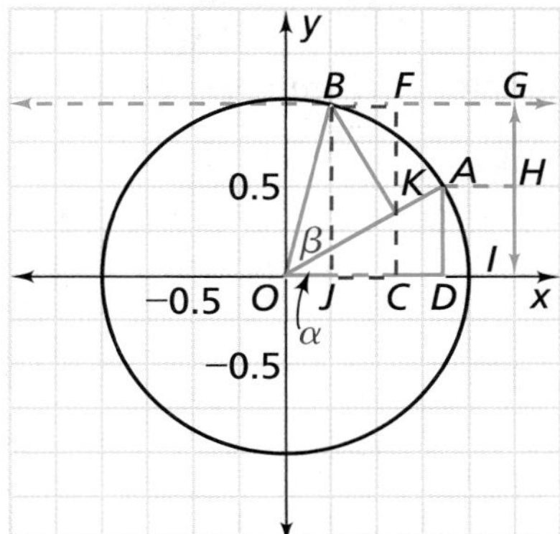


Here is where the work really starts. You need to justify these basic steps.

**Step 1** $BJ = \sin(\alpha + \beta)$, $BK = \sin\beta$, and $AD = \sin\alpha$.

**Step 2** Also, $KO = \cos\beta$ and $DO = \cos\alpha$.

**Step 3** $\sin(\alpha + \beta) = IH + HG$

**Step 4** $IH = KC$

**Step 5** Now, to get $KC$, prove that $\triangle KCO \sim \triangle ADO$, so

$$\frac{KC}{KO} = \frac{AD}{AO}$$

**Step 6** Use Steps 1 and 2 to conclude that

$$\frac{KC}{\cos\beta} = \frac{\sin\alpha}{1}$$

So, $KC = \sin\alpha\cos\beta$.

**Step 7** Next, show $GH = FK$.

**Step 8** To get $FK$, prove that $\triangle FKB \sim \triangle DOA$, so

$$\frac{FK}{BK} = \frac{DO}{AO}$$

**Step 9** Use Steps 1 and 2 to conclude that

$$\frac{FK}{\sin\beta} = \frac{\cos\alpha}{1}$$

So $FK = \sin\beta\cos\alpha$.

**Step 10** Now comes the grand finale. Combine Steps 3, 6, and 9 to conclude that

$$\sin(\alpha + \beta) = \sin\alpha\cos\beta + \cos\alpha\sin\beta$$

**Step 11** To complete your proof, use the same diagram to prove that

$$\cos(\alpha + \beta) = \cos\alpha\cos\beta - \sin\alpha\sin\beta$$

In your description, you might want to explain why the same formulas work if $\alpha$ and $\beta$ are in other quadrants. You can also show how some of the facts from the beginning of the lesson follow from your formulas.

**Proof 2 (Coordinate Geometry)** This derivation uses ideas from basic algebra (slope) and geometry (coordinates and vectors).

The setup is in the graph below. In this picture of the unit circle, $(r, s) = (\cos\alpha, \sin\alpha)$, and $(a, b) = (\cos\beta, \sin\beta)$.

The segment $\overline{HO}$ is perpendicular to $\overline{AO}$. The coordinates of $H$ are $(-s, r)$.

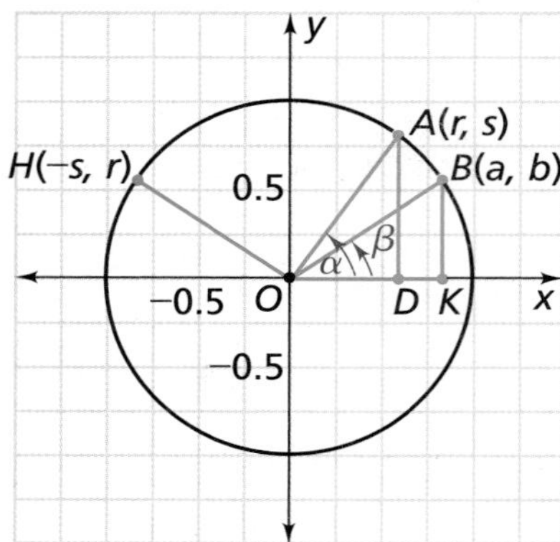


**Step 1** Explain why the coordinates of $H$ are $(-s, r)$.

Copy the graph. Now draw in some lines. Pick $Q$ along $\overline{HO}$ such that $QO = BK$. Pick $R$ along $\overline{AO}$ such that $RO = KO$. Then draw a line through $Q$ parallel to $\overline{OA}$ and a line through $R$ parallel to $\overline{OH}$. These segments intersect at $S$.

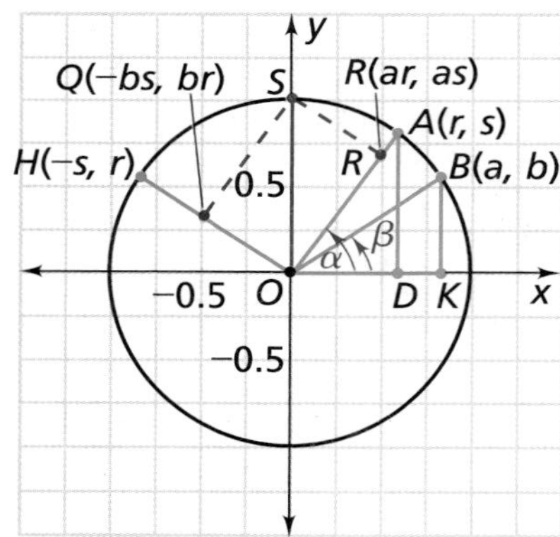


**Step 2** Show that $Q = (-bs, br)$ and $R = (ar, as)$.

**Step 3** Show that $S = (ar - bs, as + br)$.

**Step 4** Show that $S$ is on the circle by showing that it is 1 unit from $O$.

**Step 5** Show that $\triangle OSR \cong \triangle OBK$. Then $m\angle SOR = \beta$ and $m\angle SOK = \alpha + \beta$.

**Step 6** So, the coordinates of $S$ are $(\cos(\alpha + b), \sin(\alpha + b))$.

**Step 7** Combine steps 3 and 6 to get your formulas.

In your description, you might want to explain why the same formulas work if $\alpha$ and $\beta$ are in other quadrants. You can also show how some of the facts from the beginning of the lesson follow from your formulas.

**Remember...**

You can use the distance formula.

# Exercises *Practicing Habits of Mind*

## Check Your Understanding

**1.** One identity for cosine is

$$\cos(a - b) = \cos a \cos b + \sin a \sin b$$

**a.** Use Exercises 11 and 12 from Lesson 4.07 to derive this formula.

**b.** What happens in this identity if $a = b$? Evaluate the left and right sides separately.

**c.** Use this identity to find an exact value for $\cos 15°$.

$45 - 30 = 15$

**2.** Prove each identity by making appropriate substitutions into the angle-sum identities.

**a.** $\cos 2x = \cos^2 x - \sin^2 x$

**b.** $\sin 2x = 2 \sin x \cos x$

**c.** $\cos 2x = 2\cos^2 x - 1$

**Habits of Mind**

**Visualize.** Check your results from Exercise 18 in Lesson 4.07.

**3.** From the identity in Exercise 2c, you know $\cos 30° = 2\cos^2 15° - 1$. Also, $\cos 30° = \frac{\sqrt{3}}{2}$. So if you let $z = \cos 15°$, this equation becomes

$$\frac{\sqrt{3}}{2} = 2z^2 - 1$$

**a.** Use this equation to find an exact value for $\cos 15°$.

**b.** Compare your answer with the answer to Exercise 1c. Are they equal? Explain.

**4.** **Take It Further** Use the angle-sum identities to develop formulas for $\cos 3x$ and $\sin 3x$ in terms of $\cos x$ and $\sin x$.

**5.** Here is an interesting fact about the sine function.

$$\sin 10° + \sin 50° = \sin 70°$$

**a.** Find the values of $\sin 10°$, $\sin 50°$, and $\sin 70°$ to four decimal places. Then verify that the above equation is approximately true.

**b.** For some acute angle $x$, $\sin 20° + \sin 40° = \sin x$. Find $x$.

**c.** For some acute angle $x$, $\sin 5° + \sin 55° = \sin x$. Find $x$.

**6.** **Take It Further** Find a general result from the examples in Exercise 5. Prove it using angle-sum identities.

## On Your Own

Go Online
www.successnetplus.com

**7.** Which expression is equal to $\cos(90° - \theta)$?

**A.** $\cos\theta$ **B.** $-\cos\theta$ **C.** $\sin\theta$ **D.** $-\sin\theta$

**8.** Derive a formula for $\sin(\alpha - \beta)$ in terms of sine and cosine of $\alpha$ and $\beta$.

**9.** Use the angle-sum identities to prove the following identities.

$$\cos(180° + \theta) = -\cos\theta$$

$$\sin(180° + \theta) = -\sin\theta$$

**10.** Simplify each expression.

**a.** $\sin(360° + x)$ **b.** $\sin(90° + x)$ **c.** $\cos(90° + x)$

**d.** $\sin(90° - x)$ **e.** $\sin(180° - x)$

**11.** Use the angle-sum identities to find another expression for $\tan(45° + x)$.

**12.** Use the angle-sum identities to find a rule for $\tan(x + y)$ in terms of $\tan x$ and $\tan y$.

**13.** Take It Further Use your derivation of the formulas in Theorem 4.3, adjusting the diagrams if necessary, to justify the formulas for $\cos(a - b)$ and $\sin(a - b)$.

**14.** Standardized Test Prep If $\cos 2A = \frac{5}{8}$, what is the value of $\frac{1}{(\cos^2 A) - (\sin^2 A)}$?

**A.** $-4.57$ **B.** $0.31$ **C.** $1.6$ **D.** $4$

## Maintain Your Skills

**15.** Rewrite each expression in the form $A\cos\theta + B\sin\theta$.

**a.** $\sin(30° + \theta)$ **b.** $\sin(45° + \theta)$ **c.** $\sin(60° + \theta)$

**d.** $\sin(120° + \theta)$ **e.** $\sin(150° + \theta)$

**In this investigation, you learned how to use the graphs of trigonometric functions to solve problems and to prove and use trigonometric identities. These questions will help you summarize what you have learned.**

1. Sketch a graph of $y = \cos x$ for $90^\circ \le x \le 180^\circ$. Label five points on your graph with exact coordinates.
2. For each interval below, state whether $\sin x$ is *positive* or *negative* in the interval and whether its value is increasing or decreasing as $x$ increases through the interval.
   **a.** $0^\circ < x < 90^\circ$
   **b.** $90^\circ < x < 180^\circ$
   **c.** $180^\circ < x < 270^\circ$
   **d.** $270^\circ < x < 360^\circ$
3. Sketch a picture of the unit circle. Use it to locate and label points with coordinates $(\cos 210^\circ, \sin 210^\circ)$ and $(1, \tan 210^\circ)$.
4. Sketch a graph of $y = \tan x$ that shows two periods of the function.
5. Simplify each expression.
   **a.** $\sin(270^\circ - x)$
   **b.** $\cos(180^\circ - x)$
6. What do the graphs of the sine and cosine functions look like?
7. Why does the tangent function have a period of 180°?
8. What is a simple rule for finding the value of $\cos(90^\circ + \theta)$?

## Vocabulary

In this investigation, you learned these terms. Make sure you understand what each one means and how to use it.

- **discontinuity**
- **period**

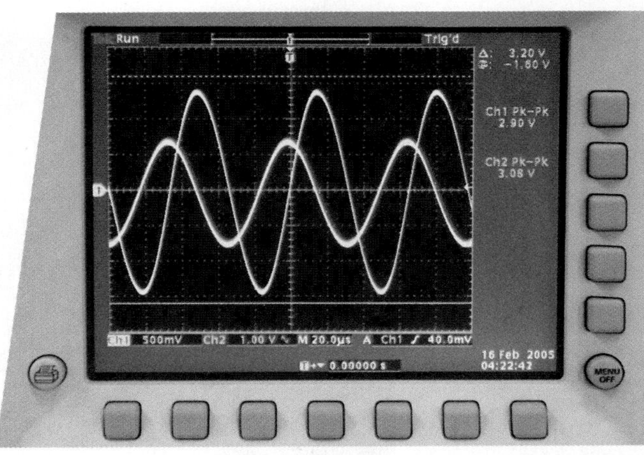


These two sine waves have the same period.

# Applications to Triangles

In *Applications to Triangles*, you will use what you know about trigonometric functions to find the side lengths, angle measures, and areas of triangles.

**By the end of this investigation, you will be able to answer questions like these.**

1. What information do you need to find all of a triangle's side lengths and angle measures?
2. What information do you need to find the area of a triangle?
3. A triangle has sides of length 5, 8, and 10. What is the measure of its largest angle?

**You will learn how to**

- solve a triangle—find all of its side lengths and angle measures—given enough information
- state and use the Law of Sines
- state and use the Law of Cosines
- state and use Heron's Formula

**You will develop these habits and skills:**

- Analyze given information to choose a solution strategy.
- Reason logically to understand and produce a mathematical proof.
- Reason by continuity to examine extreme cases.

You can use triangle relationships to measure the width of the glacier.

# 4.10 Getting Started

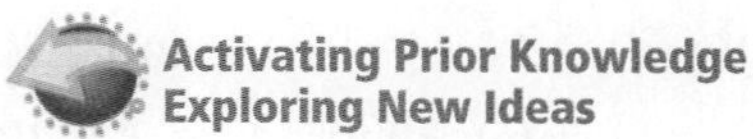


You can use trigonometry to get the information you need to find the area of a triangle.

## For You to Explore

1. **Write About It** Here is a triangle.

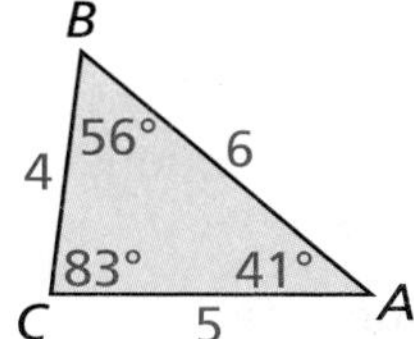


Describe some measurements you could use to find the area of the triangle.

2. In $\triangle ABC$, $AC = 10$, $BC = 12$, and $\angle C$ measures 50°.

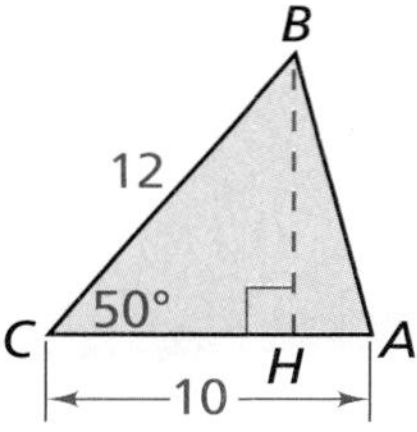


   **a.** Find the length of the altitude $\overline{BH}$.

   **b.** Find the area of $\triangle ABC$.

   **c.** Find the length of side $\overline{AB}$.

3. In $\triangle XYZ$, $XZ = 10$, $YZ = 12$, and $\angle Z$ measures 100°.

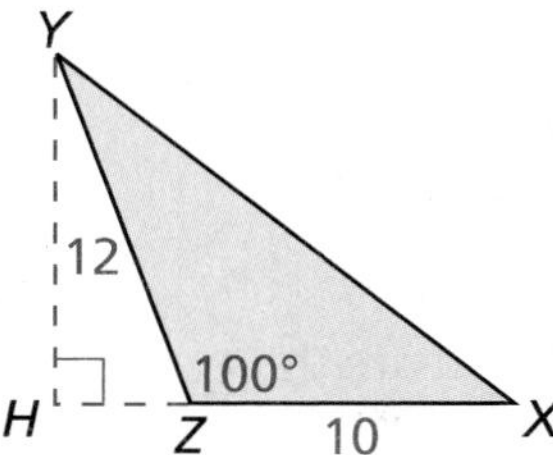


   **a.** Find the length of the altitude $\overline{YH}$.

   **b.** Find the area of $\triangle XYZ$.

   **c.** Find the length of side $\overline{XY}$.

4. In $\triangle PQR$, $PR = 10$, $QR = 12$, and $\angle R$ measures $130°$.

   a. Draw an accurate diagram of $\triangle PQR$. Use your diagram to answer the next two questions.

   b. Which triangle has a greater perimeter, $\triangle PQR$ or $\triangle XYZ$ from Exercise 3?

   c. Which triangle has a larger area, $\triangle PQR$ or $\triangle XYZ$ from Exercise 3?

5. Determine whether each statement is true or false. Justify your answers with a diagram.

   a. The longest side in a triangle is opposite its largest angle.

   b. In $\triangle ABC$, if $\overline{AC}$ and $\overline{BC}$ stay the same length but angle $C$ increases in size, side $\overline{AB}$ increases in length.

   c. In $\triangle ABC$, if $\overline{AC}$ and $\overline{BC}$ stay the same length but $\overline{AB}$ increases in length, the area of $\triangle ABC$ increases.

   d. Two triangles with the same perimeter must have the same area.

6. **Take It Further** Suppose two triangles have the same perimeter and the same area. Must the triangles be congruent? Justify your answer.

**Remember...**

The perimeter of a polygon is the sum of its side lengths.

## On Your Own

7. Suppose $\sin \theta = \sin 50°$ and $\theta$ is between $0°$ and $360°$. What are the possible values of $\theta$?

8. Suppose $\cos \theta = \cos 50°$ and $\theta$ is between $0°$ and $360°$. What are the possible values of $\theta$?

9. Which statement is true?

   **A.** $\cos 70° = \cos 110°$

   **B.** $\sin 70° = \sin 110°$

   **C.** $\tan 70° = \tan 110°$

   **D.** $\sin 70° = -\sin 110°$

**10.** Jan lives 5 miles away from Paul. Paul lives 8 miles away from Dwayne.

**a.** What is the shortest possible distance between Jan's and Dwayne's houses? Draw a diagram to represent this situation.

**b.** What is the longest possible distance between Jan's and Dwayne's houses? Draw a diagram to represent this situation.

**c.** Is it possible for the distance between Jan's and Dwayne's houses to be 10 miles? If so, draw a diagram to represent the situation.

**11.** Consider the labeled diagram below.

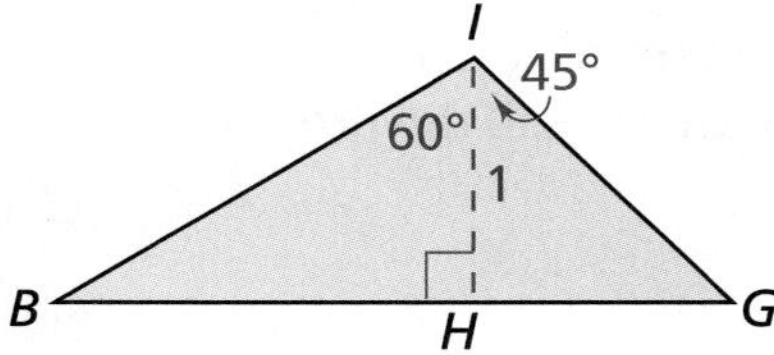


**a.** Find all missing lengths.

**b.** Use any method to find the area of $\triangle BIG$.

**12.** The diagram below gives variables for the side lengths of $\triangle ABC$.

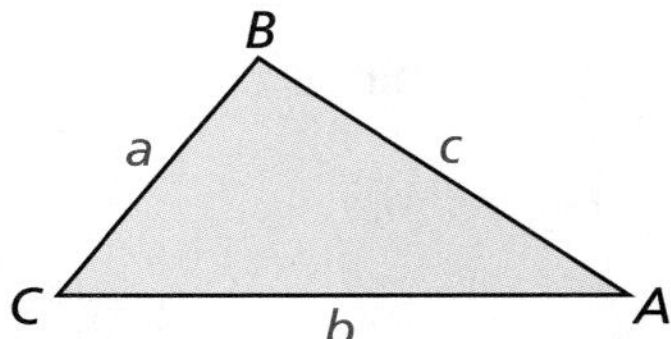


Find at least two different expressions for the area of $\triangle ABC$ in terms of its side lengths and angle measures.

## Maintain Your Skills

**13.** For each set of three lengths, determine whether or not they can be the side lengths of a triangle.

**a.** 8, 6, 10
**b.** 8, 6, 12
**c.** 8, 6, 14
**d.** 8, 6, 16
**e.** 8, 6, 9
**f.** 8, 6, 5
**g.** 8, 6, 3
**h.** 8, 6, 2
**i.** 8, 6, 1

# 4.11 The Area of a Triangle

In previous courses, you learned the area formulas for many shapes, including triangles. For example, a right triangle is half of a rectangle.

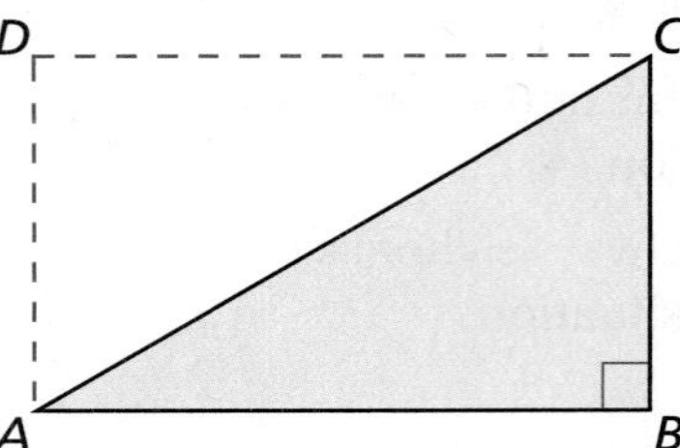


The area of this triangle is $A = \frac{1}{2}bh$, since it is equal to exactly half the rectangle's area. The same applies to any triangle. Its area is half the product of its base and height.

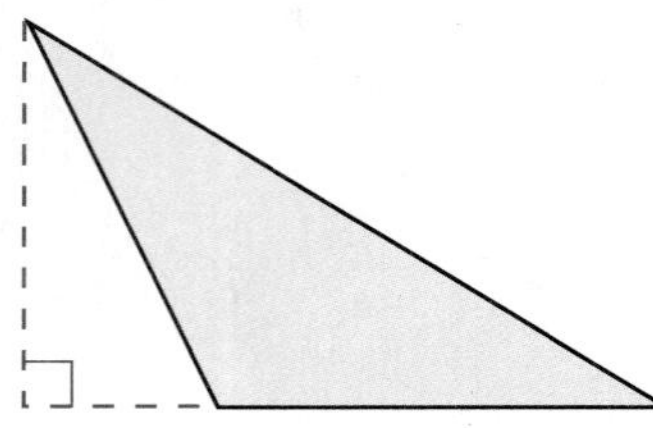

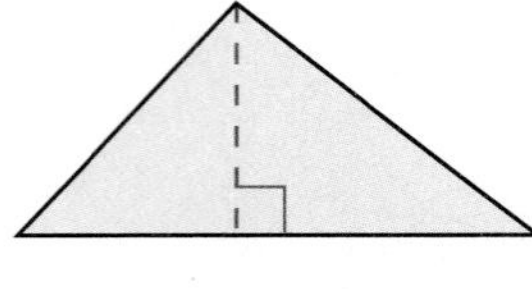

**Remember...**

The height is always measured perpendicular to the base. You can use any side of the triangle as the base.

You can often use trigonometry to find the height of a triangle when it is unknown.

## Example

**Problem** In $\triangle BCU$, $BC = 10$, $UC = 12$, and $\angle C$ measures $50^\circ$. Find an expression for the exact area of this triangle. Then approximate the area to two decimal places.

**Solution** First, sketch the triangle. Here is an accurate sketch of $\triangle BCU$, including the altitude drawn to side $\overline{UC}$.

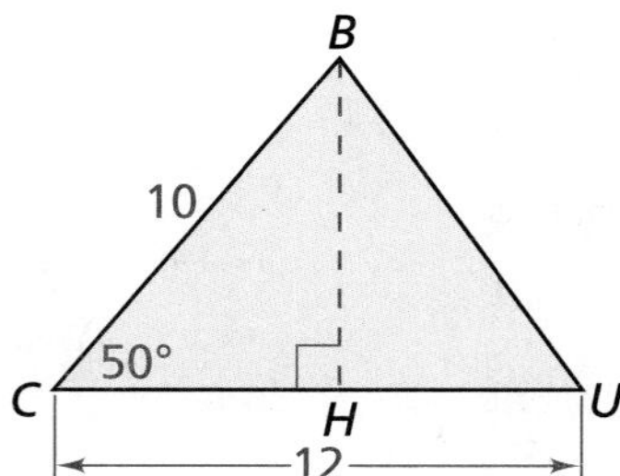

The area is $A = \frac{1}{2}bh$, and the base is 12. So $A = \frac{1}{2} \cdot 12 \cdot h$.

Find $h$ by recognizing the right triangle $BCH$. The missing side $h$ is opposite the $50^\circ$ angle. You know the length of the hypotenuse. Use the sine ratio.

$$\sin 50^\circ = \frac{h}{10}$$

The exact value of $h$ is $10 \sin 50^\circ$. The area is $\frac{1}{2} \cdot 12 \cdot 10 \sin 50^\circ$. This simplifies to $A = 60 \sin 50^\circ$, which is approximately 45.96.

## For You to Do

**1.** Follow the same process as in the Example, but drop the altitude to the side of length 10. What happens?

You can generalize the process in the Example. Consider $\triangle ABC$ with no numbered sides.

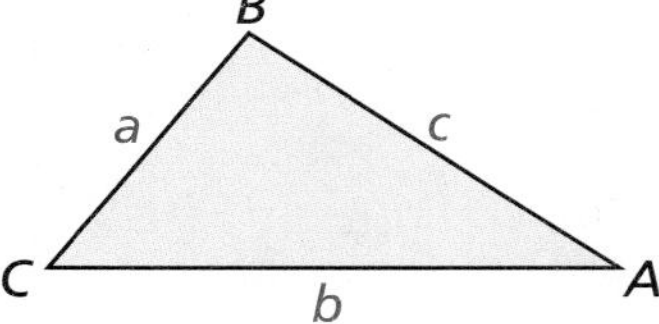


Drop the altitude to the side of length b. One expression for the altitude's length is $a \sin C$. Then the area of the triangle is $\frac{1}{2}ab \sin C$. Since a triangle has three altitudes, there are three possible area formulas.

### *Theorem 4.4* *Area of a Triangle*

**For $\triangle ABC$ with $AB = c$, $AC = b$, and $BC = a$, the area of the triangle is equal to the expressions below.**

$$\frac{1}{2}ab \sin C = \frac{1}{2}bc \sin A = \frac{1}{2}ac \sin B$$

What measurements can you use to calculate the area of this triangular lot?

## Developing Habits of Mind

**Visualize.** Angle $C$ is acute in all the diagrams used to show that the area is $\frac{1}{2}ab \sin C$. But $\angle C$ might not be acute. It could be right or obtuse. What is the area formula then?

If $\angle C$ is a right angle, the triangle looks like this.

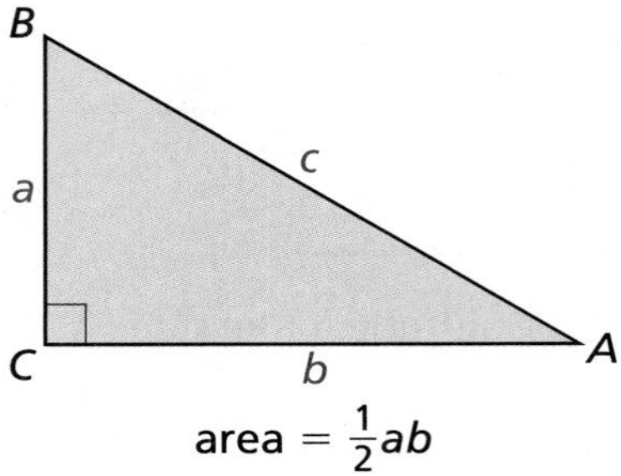


Since this is a right triangle, the area is $\frac{1}{2}ab$. But $\sin 90° = 1$, so this is also equal to $\frac{1}{2}ab \sin C$. The formula covers the case when $\angle C$ is a right angle.

If $\angle C$ is obtuse, the triangle looks like this.

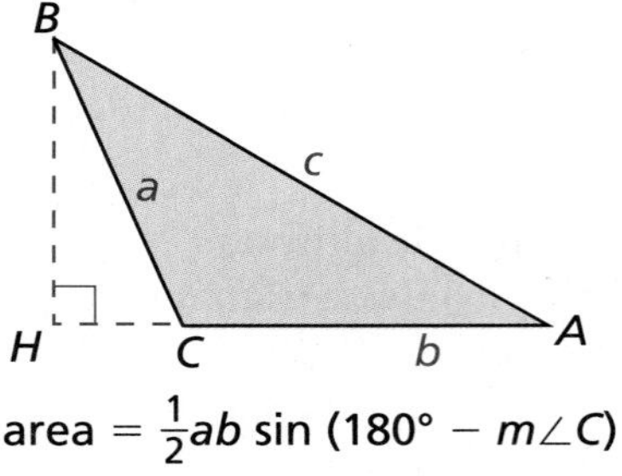


To find the altitude, you use the sine of $\angle BCH$. This angle is the supplement of $\angle ACB$. If $\angle ACB$ measures $\theta$, $\angle BCH$ measures $(180° - \theta)$. Then the altitude is $a \sin(180° - \theta)$.

Earlier, however, you learned that $\sin(180° - \theta) = \sin\theta$. So, the sine of $\angle ACB$ is the same as the sine of $\angle BCH$. The area is $\frac{1}{2}ab \sin C$, even for obtuse triangles.

**Remember...**

See, for example, Exercise 11 from Lesson 4.09.

The formula for the area of the triangle leads to an elegant proof of the formula for $\sin(a + b)$. Consider this diagram.

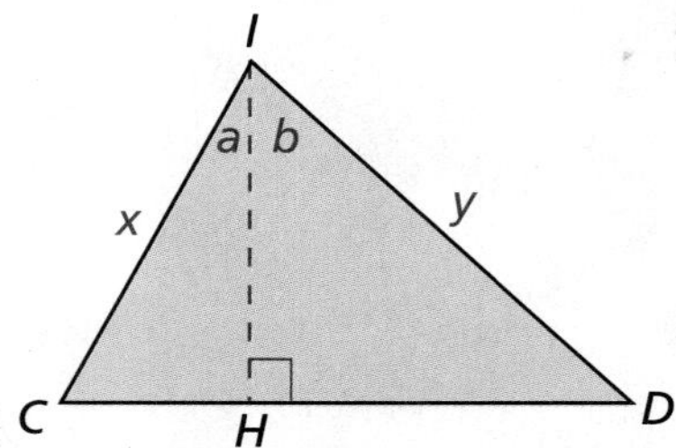

Now, what is the area of $\triangle CID$? There are two ways to find it.

- First, look at $\triangle CID$ as a whole. The area is $\frac{1}{2}xy \sin(a + b)$.
- Second, consider $\triangle CIH$ and $\triangle DIH$ separately. Within $\triangle CIH$, $CH = x \sin a$ and $IH = y \cos b$. The area of $\triangle CIH$ is $\frac{1}{2}(x \sin a)(y \cos b) = \frac{1}{2}xy \sin a \cos b$. Similarly, the area of $\triangle DIH$ is $\frac{1}{2}xy \cos a \sin b$.

The sum of the areas of the two smaller triangles is equal to the area of the larger triangle.

$$\begin{aligned}
\frac{1}{2}xy \sin(a + b) &= \frac{1}{2}xy \sin a \cos b + \frac{1}{2}xy \cos a \sin b \\
\frac{1}{2}xy \sin(a + b) &= \frac{1}{2}xy (\sin a \cos b + \ xy \cos a \sin b) \\
\sin(a + b) &= \sin a \cos b + \cos a \sin b
\end{aligned}$$

This expression for $\sin(a + b)$ is the one you found in Investigation 4B. All the proof uses is the rule for the area of a triangle and the definitions of sine and cosine for right triangles.

## For Discussion

2. When finding the area of $\triangle CIH$, why did you write it as $y \cos b$ and not $x \cos a$? Both are equal, so what purpose is there in using one instead of the other?

## Check Your Understanding

1. Use the diagram of $\triangle EFG$ below.

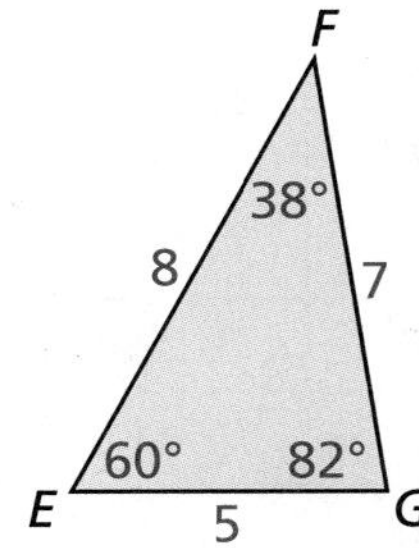


Find at least two different ways to calculate the area of $\triangle EFG$.

2. Use the diagram from Exercise 11 in Lesson 4.10.

   a. Use the formula $A = \frac{1}{2}bh$ to find the exact area of $\triangle BIG$.

   b. Use the formula $A = \frac{1}{2}ab \sin C$ along with the measure of angle $I$ to write another expression for the area of $\triangle BIG$.

   c. Use the two expressions for the area of $\triangle BIG$ to find the exact value of $\sin 105°$.

3. Find the area of a regular pentagon inscribed in a circle of radius 1.

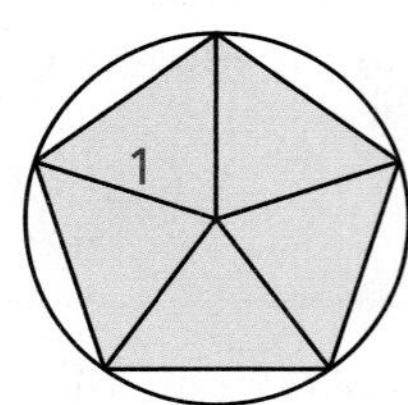


4. Find the exact area and perimeter of a regular hexagon inscribed in a circle of radius 1.

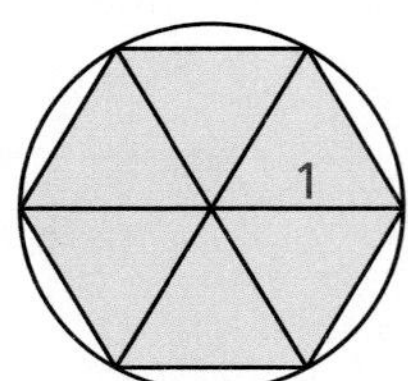


5. Here is a regular decagon (10-sided figure) inscribed in a circle of radius 1.

   a. Approximate the area of the decagon to four decimal places.

   b. **Take It Further** Find an exact value for the area of the decagon that involves no trigonometric functions.

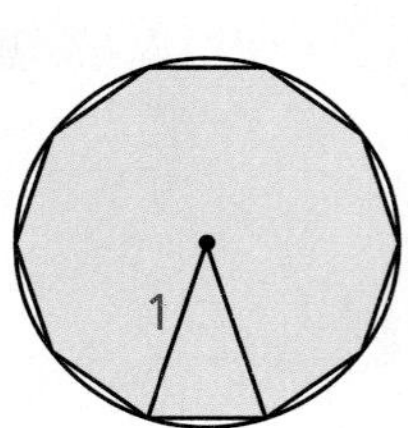


6. a. Write an expression for the area of a regular $n$-gon ($n$-sided figure) inscribed in a circle of radius 1.

   b. Copy and complete this table for the function $A(n)$, the area of the $n$-gon. Find all values to four decimal places.

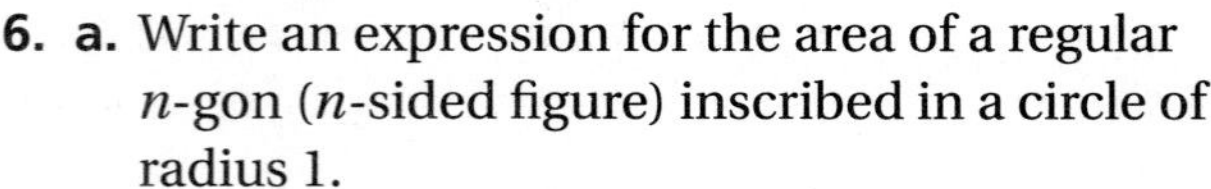

| Sides, $n$ | Area, $A(n)$ |
|---|---|
| 4 | 2 |
| 5 | ■ |
| 6 | ■ |
| 10 | ■ |
| 12 | ■ |
| 20 | ■ |
| 30 | ■ |
| 50 | ■ |
| 100 | ■ |
| 360 | ■ |

**7.** **Write About It** Use your completed table from Exercise 6. Describe what happens to the area of the $n$-gons as the number of sides increases. Explain why this happens.

## On Your Own

**8.** In $\triangle MIB$, $MI = 12$ and $IB = 10$. Find the maximum possible area for this triangle.

**9.** Which statement is true?

**A.** $\cos 20° = \cos 70°$ **B.** $\cos 20° = \cos^2 70°$

**C.** $\cos 20° = \sin^2 70°$ **D.** $\cos 20° = \sin 70°$

**10.** Use this diagram of an isosceles triangle with legs of length 1.

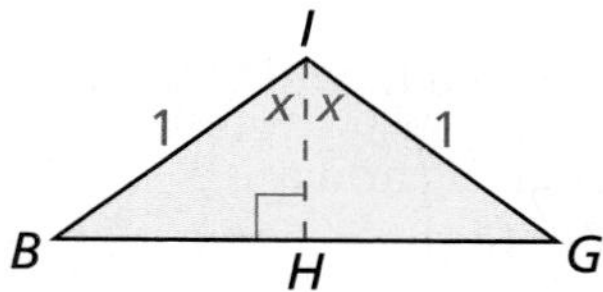


**a.** Find the area of $\triangle BIG$ using the rule $A = \frac{1}{2}bh$.

**b.** Find the area of $\triangle BIG$ using $\angle I$.

**c.** Write a formula for $\sin 2x$ by using the two expressions for the area of $\triangle BIG$.

You will have to find the base and height in terms of $x$ first.

**11.** **a.** Can one side of a triangle be ten times as long as each of the other sides? Explain.

**b.** Can one angle in a triangle be ten times as large as each of the other angles?

**12.** Use this diagram of $\triangle ONE$.

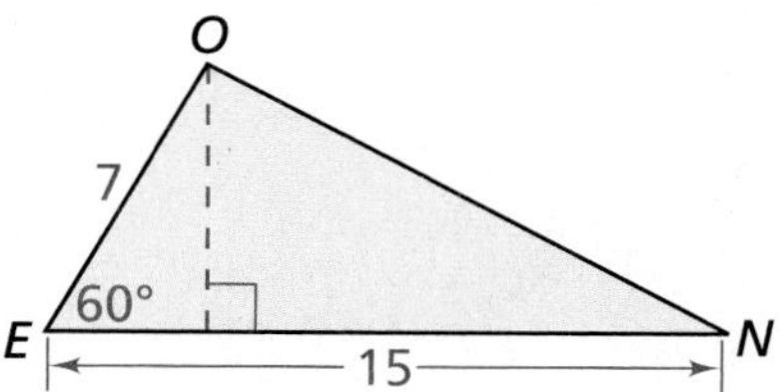


**a.** Explain why there can be only one such $\triangle ONE$.

**b.** Find the length of side $\overline{ON}$.

**Habits of Mind**

**Establish a process.** Keep track of your steps!

**13.** Use what you have learned in this lesson to find area formulas for each figure.

**a.** a parallelogram **b.** a rhombus

**Remember...**

A rhombus is a parallelogram with all four sides equal in length.

**14.** What's Wrong Here? Derman thinks he has found two different formulas for the area of a parallelogram.

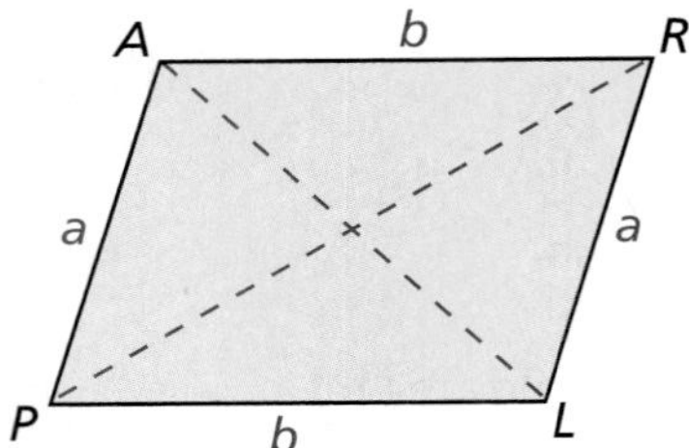


Derman says, "If I cut along one diagonal, I get that the area is $ab \sin P$, but if I cut along the other diagonal, I get that the area is $ab \sin L$. That doesn't seem possible—the areas should be the same. Angle $L$ looks larger than angle $P$, so isn't $\sin L$ greater than $\sin P$?"

What is wrong with Derman's reasoning? Are both area formulas correct?

**15.** A rhombus has perimeter 36. What is the largest possible area it could have?

**16.** Standardized Test Prep A triangle has a side that is 8 cm long and a side that is 12 cm long. The included angle measures 65°. To the nearest hundredth, what is the area of the triangle?

**A.** 24 $cm^2$ **B.** 40.57 $cm^2$ **C.** 43.50 $cm^2$ **D.** 81.14 $cm^2$

## Maintain Your Skills

**17.** Each set of three lengths forms a triangle. Determine whether the triangle is acute, right, or obtuse.

**a.** 8, 6, 10 **b.** 8, 6, 12 **c.** 8, 6, 13 **d.** 8, 6, 9

**e.** 8, 6, 8 **f.** 8, 6, 7 **g.** 8, 6, 6 **h.** 8, 6, 5

# 4.12 The Law of Sines

In the last lesson, you learned to find the area of a triangle using the rule $A = \frac{1}{2}ab \sin C$, where $a$ and $b$ are two side lengths and $C$ is the angle between those sides. This lesson introduces the Law of Sines, which you can prove using that formula. The Law of Sines relates the side lengths in a triangle to their corresponding angle measures.

**Remember...**

You call the angle between two given sides the included angle. Similarly, you call the side between two given angles the included side.

## For Discussion

1. If one angle in a triangle is twice as large as another, is the corresponding side twice as long? Give an example to justify your answer.
2. Can one side of a triangle be ten times as long as each of the other sides? Can one angle in a triangle be ten times as large as each of the other angles? Explain.

There is a correspondence between sides and angles in a triangle, but not a direct one. For example, it is possible for one angle in a triangle to be many times larger than both of the other angles (say, a triangle with angles 10°, 15°, and 165°). But it is not possible for one side of a triangle to be many times larger than both other sides. Still, the longest side in a triangle is opposite the largest angle, so there is a relationship.

That relationship is the **Law of Sines.**

### Theorem 4.5 *Law of Sines*

Given $\triangle ABC$ with corresponding side lengths $a$, $b$, and $c$,

$$\frac{a}{\sin A} = \frac{b}{\sin B} = \frac{c}{\sin C}$$

You can write the Law of Sines with the numerators and denominators switched.

$$\frac{\sin A}{a} = \frac{\sin B}{b} = \frac{\sin C}{c}$$

It is true in either form. Work through Exercise 6 to see why you might want to use the form with $\frac{c}{\sin C}$.

**Proof** Consider $\triangle ABC$.

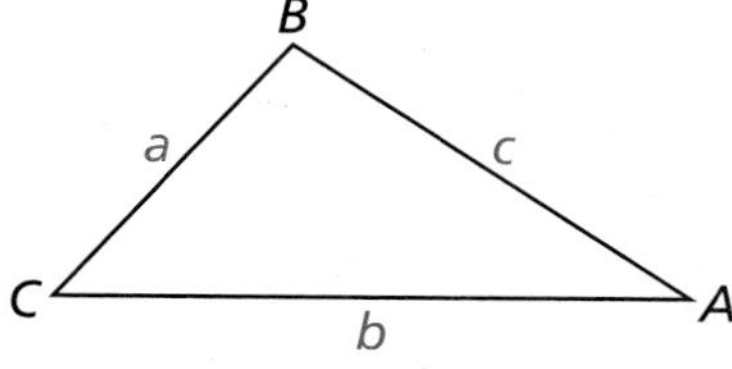


You can write the area of this triangle in three different ways. Choose two.

$$\text{area} = \frac{1}{2}ac \sin B \qquad \text{and} \qquad \text{area} = \frac{1}{2}bc \sin A$$

A triangle cannot have two different areas, so these expressions must be equal.

$$\frac{1}{2}ac \sin B = \frac{1}{2}bc \sin A$$

You can cancel the factors of $\frac{1}{2}$ and $c$ from each side. You know $c \neq 0$ since it is a side length.

$$a \sin B = b \sin A$$

$$\frac{a}{\sin A} = \frac{b}{\sin B}$$

Use the starting point $\frac{1}{2}ac \sin B = \frac{1}{2}ab \sin C$ to obtain the relationship $\frac{b}{\sin B} = \frac{c}{\sin C}$. This completes the proof.

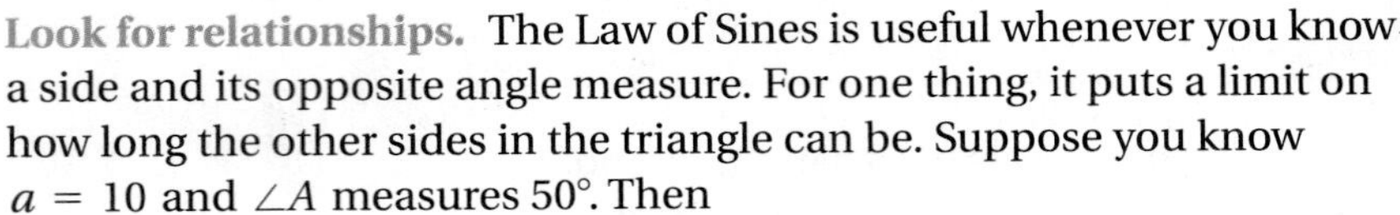

## Developing Habits of Mind

**Look for relationships.** The Law of Sines is useful whenever you know a side and its opposite angle measure. For one thing, it puts a limit on how long the other sides in the triangle can be. Suppose you know $a = 10$ and $\angle A$ measures 50°. Then

$$\frac{a}{\sin A} \approx 13.05$$

The Law of Sines says that this also equals $\frac{b}{\sin B}$. Since $\sin B$ cannot be greater than 1, $b$ cannot be greater than 13.05.

You can rewrite the proportions in the Law of Sines to discover more facts. Here is one way.

$$\frac{a}{b} = \frac{\sin A}{\sin B}$$

This proportion answers the For Discussion problem. If one side of a triangle is twice as long as another side, the sine of the angle opposite the longer side is twice as great.

Note that this does not say that the angle itself is twice as large.

You can see this in a 30-60-90 right triangle.

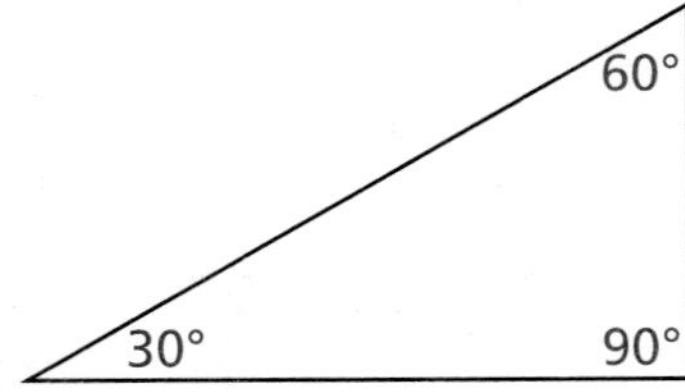


The side opposite the right angle is twice as long as the side opposite the 30° angle. The Law of Sines confirms this: $\sin 90° = 1$ and $\sin 30° = \frac{1}{2}$.

## Example

**Problem** Find all remaining side lengths and angle measures in this triangle.

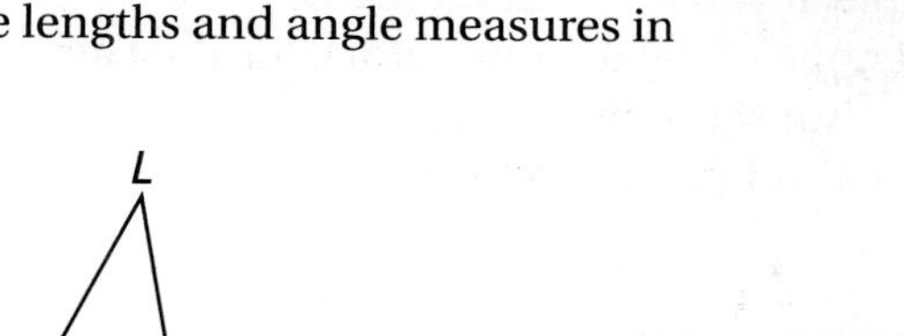

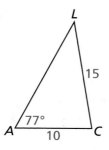

$\triangle LAC$ is not to scale. It could be acute, right, or obtuse.

**Solution** You know the measure of $\angle A$ and the length of its opposite side. Use the Law of Sines.

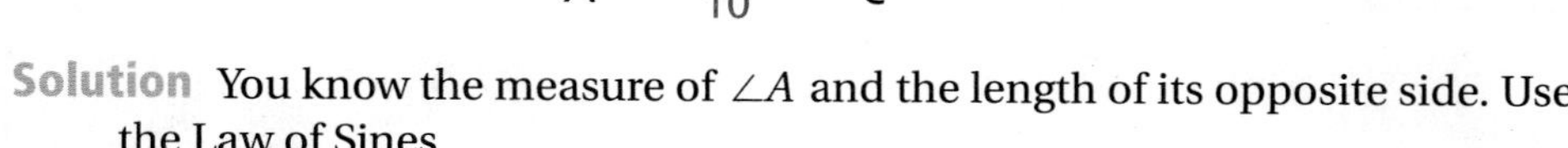

$$\frac{a}{\sin A} = \frac{\ell}{\sin L} = \frac{c}{\sin C}$$

The variables $a$, $\ell$, and $c$ are the side lengths opposite angles $A$, $L$, and $C$. Fill in the known information.

$$\frac{15}{\sin 77^\circ} = \frac{10}{\sin L} = \frac{c}{\sin C}$$

Use the first two equal expressions and solve for $\sin L$.

$$\sin L = \frac{10 \sin 77^\circ}{15} \approx 0.6496$$

A calculator gives $\sin^{-1}(0.6496)$ as approximately 40.5°. Note, though, that this is not the only angle with sine about 0.6496. The other angle is $180^\circ - 40.5^\circ = 139.5^\circ$.

So, are there two possible measures of $\angle L$? No, the 139.5° angle is impossible, since there is a 77° angle in the triangle. The measure of $\angle L$ must be less than 103°.

**Habits of Mind**

**Check your work.** This is an important check. Note that there is no other reason to reject the second angle. If both angles are possible, so be it. There would then be two cases to look at for the rest of the solution.

That means $\angle L$ measures 40.5°, and $\angle C$ measures 62.5°.

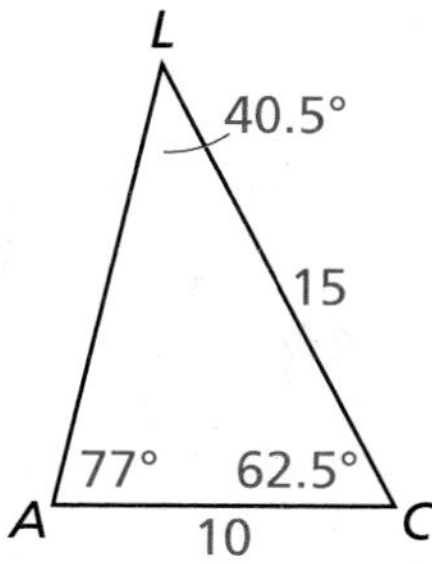


Then use the Law of Sines again to find $c$.

$$\frac{15}{\sin 77^\circ} = \frac{c}{\sin 62.5^\circ}$$

This gives $c \approx 13.66$. Now you know all the side lengths and angle measures.

Note that you need at least three pieces of information about a triangle before you can use the Law of Sines to solve for the rest. And not all groups of three pieces will do. For example, if you only know the three side lengths, you have all the numerators and none of the denominators. So, the Law of Sines helps in solving triangles, but sometimes you need a different method. You will learn another method in the next lesson.

To *solve a triangle* just means to find its side lengths and angle measures. The example's direction line could have been "Solve $\triangle ALC$."

## For You to Do

3. Use the Law of Sines to prove the Side-Angle Inequality Theorem: In a triangle, the longest side is opposite the largest angle and the shortest side is opposite the smallest angle.

# Exercises *Practicing Habits of Mind*

## Check Your Understanding

Figures of triangles in this lesson are not to scale. Do not assume anything about the size of angles or the relative lengths of the sides of a triangle.

1. In $\triangle MIB$, $MI = 12$. This side is opposite a $30^\circ$ angle. Find the maximum possible side length that this triangle can have.

For Exercises 2 and 3, find all the remaining side lengths and angle measures of the triangle. Round answers to one decimal place if necessary.

How can you apply the Law of Sines in Exercise 3? You need a side and an opposite angle.

2. 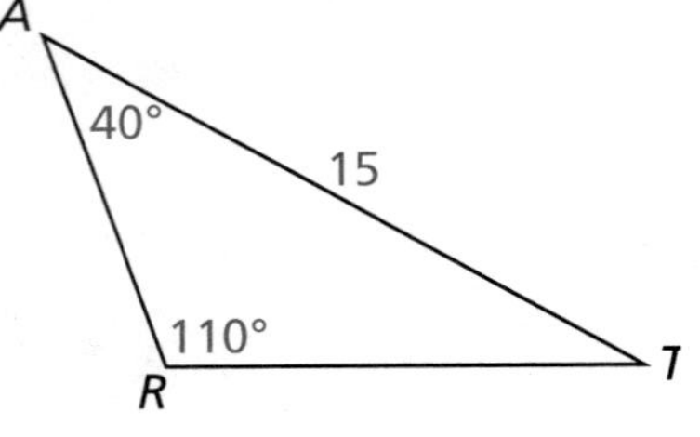


3. 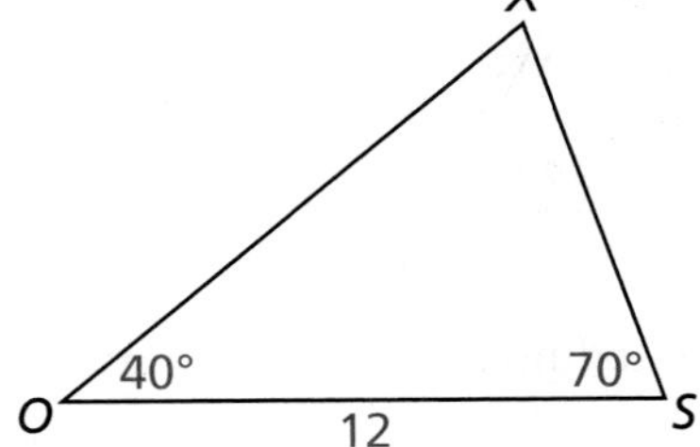

4. Use the triangle below. Find the two possible measures of $\angle K$. Explain why there are two possible answers.

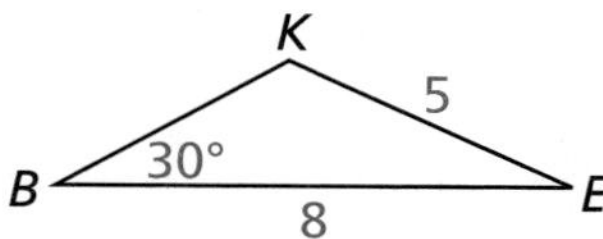


5. **Write About It** What do Exercises 2, 3, and 4 suggest about triangle congruence?

6. You can draw a circle through any three noncollinear points. Draw a circle through the vertices of a triangle such as $\triangle ABC$ below. Draw diameter $\overline{AD}$. Connect points $B$ and $D$.

You can state the result of Exercise 6 as part of the Law of Sines: In a triangle, the ratio of any side to the sine of its opposite angle is the diameter of a circle circumscribing the triangle.

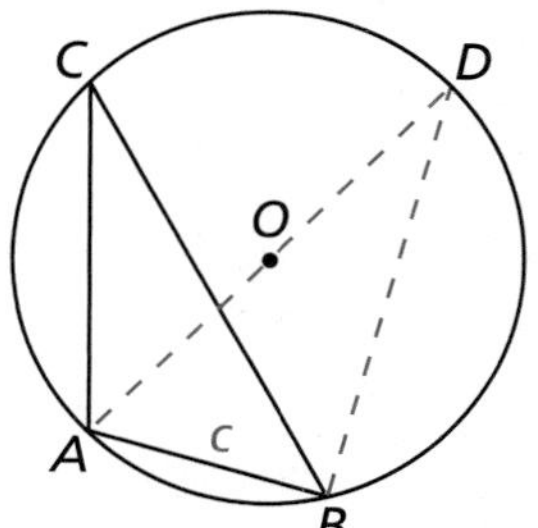


   **a.** Why is $\angle ABD$ a right angle?

   **b.** Explain why $\angle C$ and $\angle D$ are congruent.

   **c.** Explain why $\sin C = \sin D$.

   **d.** Show that the diameter $\overline{AD}$ has length $\frac{c}{\sin C}$.

7. Copy the diagram below. Drop an altitude from any vertex of the triangle. Find two expressions for the length of the altitude. Use these expressions to prove the Law of Sines.

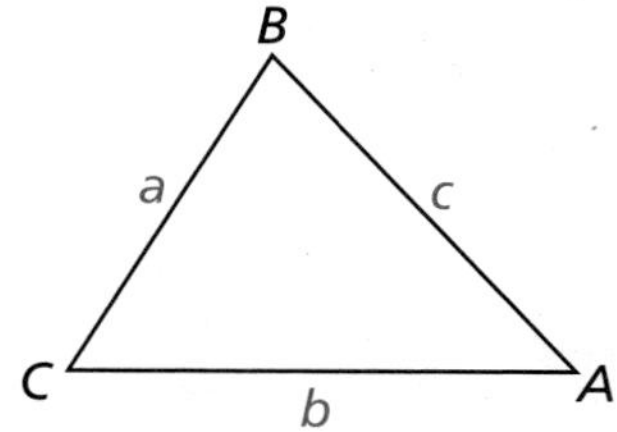

8. Use the diagram of $\triangle TWO$ below. Find the length of $\overline{TW}$. Keep track of your steps!

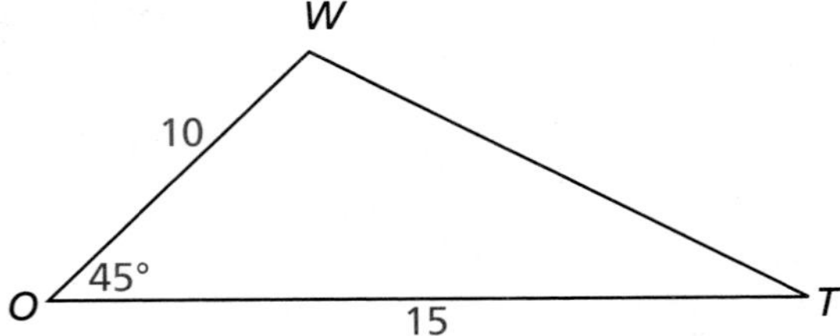


9. **Take It Further** Use the diagram of $\triangle ABC$ below. Find the length of side $\overline{AB}$ in terms of $a$, $b$, and $\angle C$.

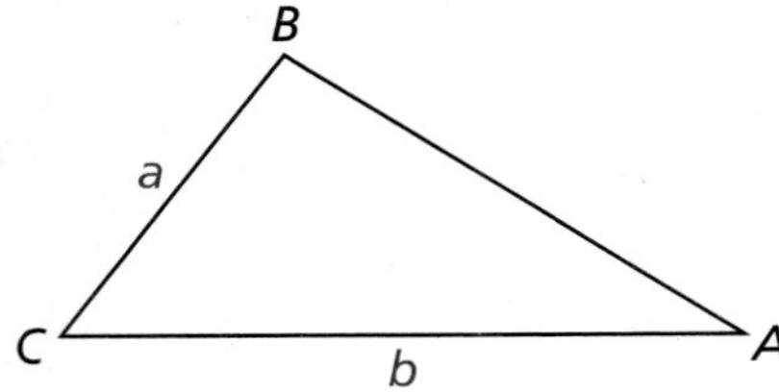


## On Your Own

10. Verify that the Law of Sines is valid for a 30-60-90 right triangle.

11. Verify that the Law of Sines is valid for a 45-45-90 right triangle.

12. In $\triangle ABC$, $AB = 7$, $AC = 15$, and $\angle A$ measures $60^\circ$. What happens if you try to use the Law of Sines to find the other sides and angles in this triangle?

13. **Standardized Test Prep** You are given $\triangle ABC$ with $AB = 14$ cm, $AC = 10$ cm, and $m\angle C = 110^\circ$. What is the length of $\overline{BC}$?

**A.** 4.82 cm

**B.** 5.10 cm

**C.** 6.96 cm

**D.** 7.38 cm

The case in which you know two side lengths and a nonincluded angle measure of a triangle is the "ambiguous case." Exercises 14–18 explore this situation.

**14.** In $\triangle ABC$, $AB = 12$, $AC = 10$, and $\angle B$ measures 40°.

**a.** According to the Law of Sines, what is the value of $\sin C$ to three decimal places?

**b.** Find all possible measures of $\angle C$ to the nearest degree.

**c.** Find all possible measures of $\angle A$ and all possible lengths of side $\overline{BC}$.

**15.** In $\triangle ABC$, $AB = 12$, $AC = 10$, and $\angle C$ measures 40°.

**a.** According to the Law of Sines, what is the value of $\sin B$ to three decimal places?

**b.** Find all possible measures of $\angle B$ to the nearest degree.

**c.** Find all possible measures of $\angle A$ and all possible lengths of side $\overline{BC}$.

**16.** In $\triangle ABC$, $AB = 12$, $AC = 10$, and $\angle B$ measures 70°.

**a.** According to the Law of Sines, what is the value of $\sin C$ to three decimal places?

**b.** Find all possible measures of $\angle C$ to the nearest degree.

**c.** Find all possible measures of $\angle A$ and all possible lengths of side $\overline{BC}$.

**17.** Write About It Tyler says that if the given angle in an ambiguous-case problem is obtuse, then there is exactly one solution. Do you agree? Explain.

**18.** Take It Further For the information given in an ambiguous-case problem, there can be 0, 1, or 2 possible triangles. Determine the conditions on the sides and angle that produce these possible outcomes.

## Maintain Your Skills

**19.** For each set of measurements for $\triangle ABC$, find the remaining side lengths and angle measures.

**a.** $BC = 10$, $\angle A$ measures 30°, and $\angle B$ measures 45°.

**b.** $BC = 20$, $\angle A$ measures 30°, and $\angle B$ measures 45°.

**c.** $AC = 10$, $\angle A$ measures 30°, and $\angle B$ measures 45°.

**d.** $AC = 10$, $\angle A$ measures 30°, and $\angle B$ measures 60°.

**e.** $AC = 10$, $\angle A$ measures 30°, and $\angle B$ measures 120°.

# 4.13 The Law of Cosines

In the last lesson, you learned the Law of Sines. It relates the side lengths of a triangle to their corresponding angle measures. In this lesson, you will learn the **Law of Cosines.** If you know two side lengths of a triangle and the measure of their included angle, the Law of Cosines can help you find the length of the third side. Alternatively, if you know three side lengths of a triangle, you can use the Law of Cosines to figure out the measure of any angle in the triangle.

## Minds in Action

*Derman and Sasha are looking at $\triangle ONE$.*

**Sasha** We need to find the length of side $\overline{ON}$.

**Derman** Can't we just use that $a^2 + b^2 = c^2$ theorem? We know the two sides, so let's just find the length of the third. $(ON)^2 = 7^2 + 15^2$. So $ON$ is about 16.55.

**Sasha** The Pythagorean Theorem only works for right triangles!

**Derman** Oh, right. Well, there are two right triangles in our drawing. Too bad we don't know the height of the dotted line.

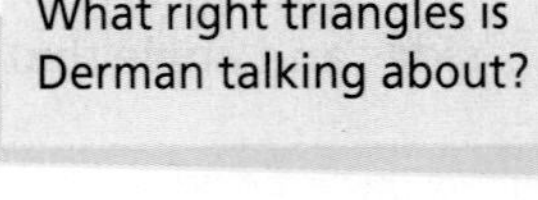


**Sasha** We can figure that out. We can at least figure out the length of the legs of each triangle, using sine and cosine.

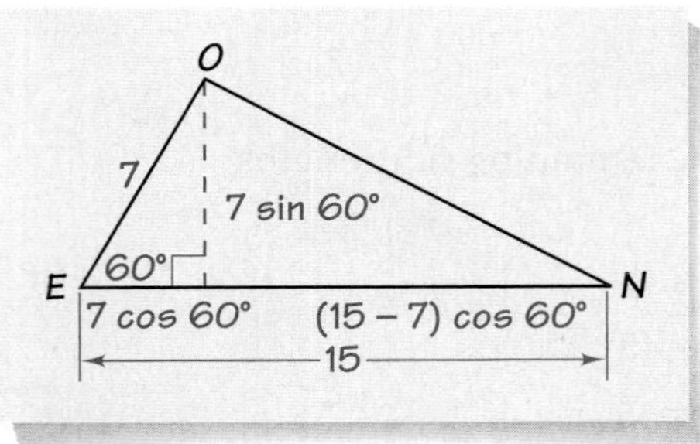


**Derman** Now we can use the Pythagorean Theorem to find $ON$. It looks messy, though.

*They write down their steps.*

$$\begin{aligned}(ON)^2 &= (7 \sin 60°)^2 + (15 - 7 \cos 60°)^2 \\ &= 49 \sin^2 60° + 225 - 2 \cdot 15 \cdot 7 \cos 60° + 49 \cos^2 60°\end{aligned}$$

**Sasha** I wonder if we can simplify this a bit.

**Derman** Hey. There's 49 times sine squared, and 49 times cosine squared, and they're even the same angle. I'm going to combine those and see what happens.

$$(ON)^2 = 49\ (\sin^2 60° + \cos^2 60°) + 225 - 210 \cos 60°$$
$$= 49 + 225 - 210 \cos 60°$$
$$= 274 - 210\left(\frac{1}{2}\right)$$
$$= 169$$

**Derman** Wow! $ON = 13$.

**Sasha** Very smooth.

## For You to Do

1. Find the length of side $\overline{TW}$ in the triangle below.

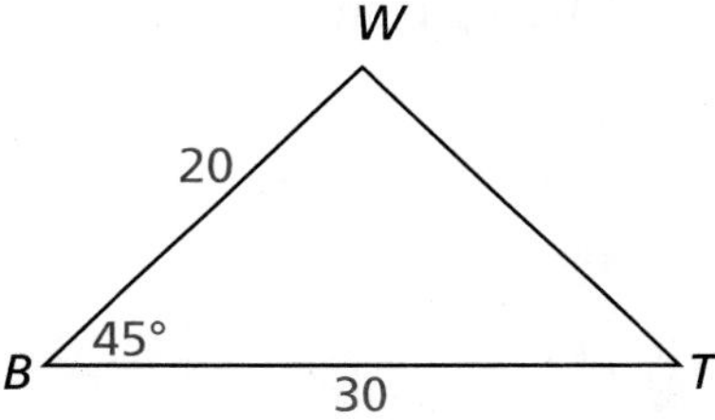


Sasha and Derman found the following equation.

$$c^2 = 49 + 225 - 210 \cos 60°$$

They can rewrite the equation this way.

$$(ON)^2 = 7^2 + 15^2 - 2 \times 7 \times 15 \cos 60°$$

In fact, a similar relationship holds for any triangle with sides of length $a$, $b$, and $c$.

### *Theorem 4.6 The Law of Cosines*

**Given $\triangle ABC$ with corresponding side lengths $a$, $b$, and $c$,**

$$c^2 = a^2 + b^2 - 2ab \cos C$$

The following proof of the Law of Cosines closely follows what Derman and Sasha did in the dialog. There are three possible situations, depending on whether $\angle C$ is acute, right, or obtuse.

**Proof Case 1:** Suppose $\angle C$ is an acute angle. Let $\triangle ABC$ be the triangle below.

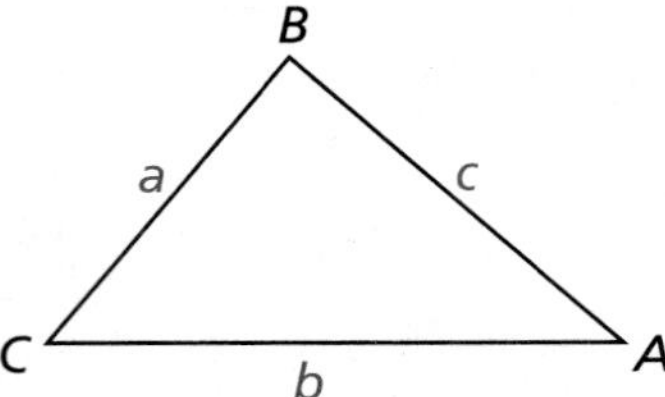


As Sasha did for her triangle, you can write down much more information about this triangle.

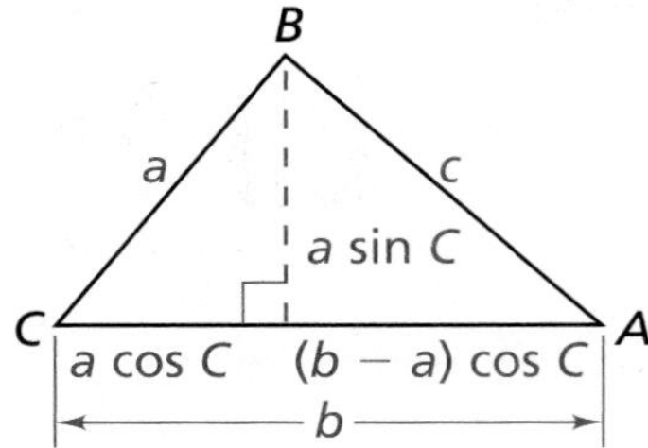


Now find $c^2$ by using the Pythagorean Theorem and the triangle on the right.

$$\begin{aligned} c^2 &= (a \sin C)^2 + (b - a \cos C)^2 \\ &= a^2 \sin^2 C + b^2 - 2\,ab \cos C + a^2 \cos^2 C \\ &= a^2 (\sin^2 C + \cos^2 C) + b^2 - 2\,ab \cos C \\ &= a^2 + b^2 - 2\,ab \cos C \end{aligned}$$

**Case 2:** Suppose $\angle C$ is a right angle. Let $\triangle ABC$ be the triangle below.

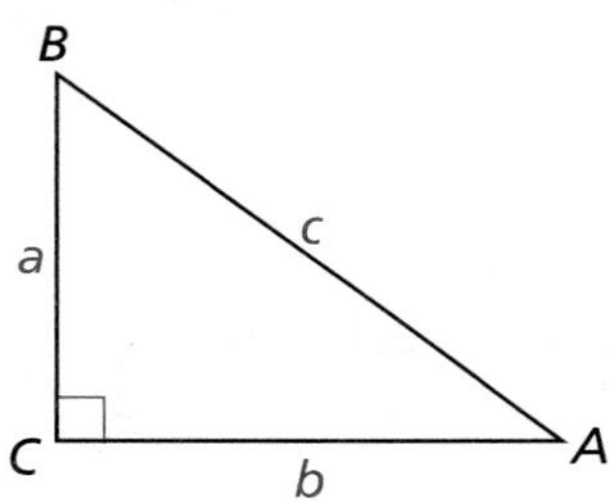


Since $C$ is a right angle, by the Pythagorean Theorem $c^2 = a^2 + b^2$. Also, $\cos C = 0$. So, $c^2 = a^2 + b^2 + (\text{anything}) \cos C$.

In particular, $c^2 = a^2 + b^2 - 2\,ab \cos C$ is true.

**Case 3:** Suppose $\angle C$ is an obtuse angle. Let $\triangle ABC$ be the triangle below.

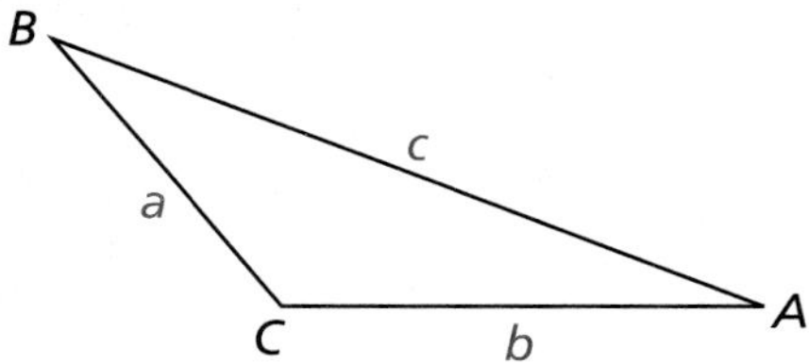


You can extend side $\overline{AC}$ to meet the altitude.

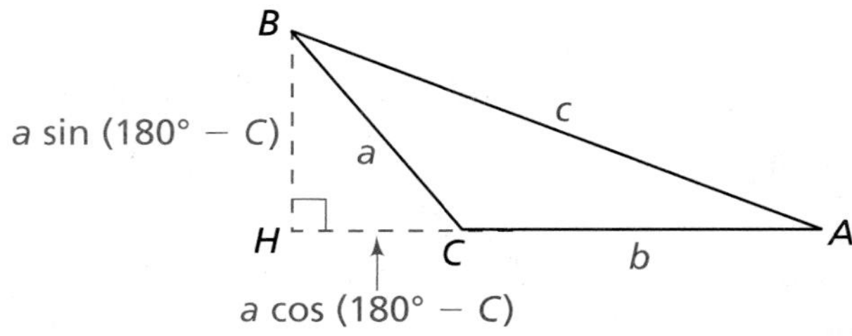


You know that $\sin(180^\circ - C) = \sin C$ and $\cos(180^\circ - C) = -\cos C$. So, you can relabel the diagram to use $\angle C$.

Why is the length of the altitude $a \sin(180^\circ - C)$? Why does $CH = a \cos(180^\circ - C)$?

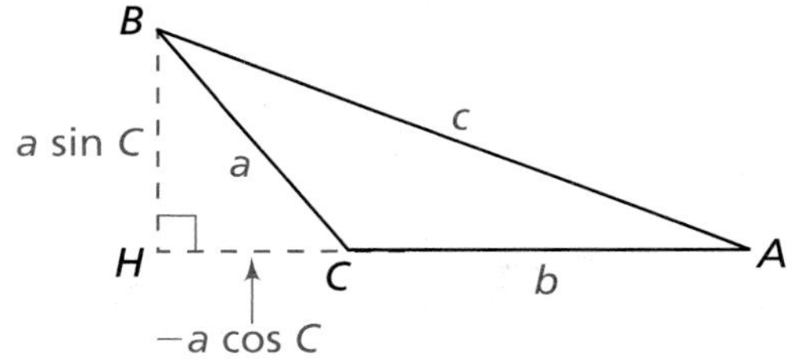


Note that the length $-a \cos C$ is positive, since $\cos C$ is negative. Use the Pythagorean Theorem again. The length along the base is the sum of the two lengths $b$ and $-a \cos C$.

$$\begin{aligned} c^2 &= (a \sin C)^2 + (b + (-a \cos C))^2 \\ &= a^2 \sin^2 C + b^2 - 2ab \cos C + a^2 \cos^2 C \\ &= a^2 (\sin^2 C + \cos^2 C) + b^2 - 2ab \cos C \\ &= a^2 + b^2 - 2ab \cos C \end{aligned}$$

Separating a proof into cases is similar to sorting your laundry into whites and colors.

The Law of Cosines looks very much like the Pythagorean Theorem. The only difference is the little correction of $-2ab \cos C$. This suggests that you can find a different proof using only ideas from geometry.

**Habits of Mind**

**Look for relationships.** You can think of the Law of Cosines as a generalization of the Pythagorean Theorem, since it includes the Pythagorean Theorem as a special case.

**Proof** Suppose you have $\triangle ABC$.

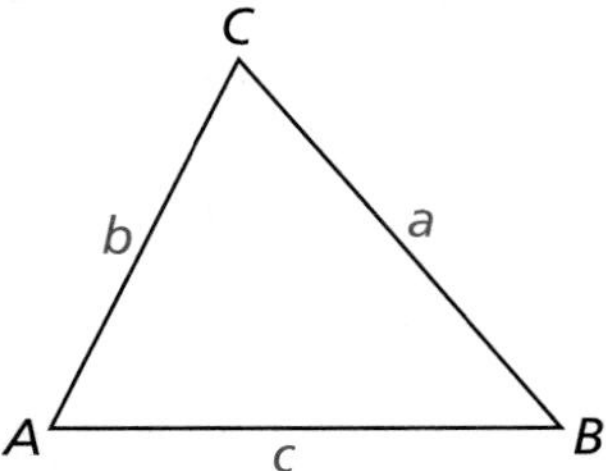


You can draw in squares with areas $a^2$, $b^2$, and $c^2$.

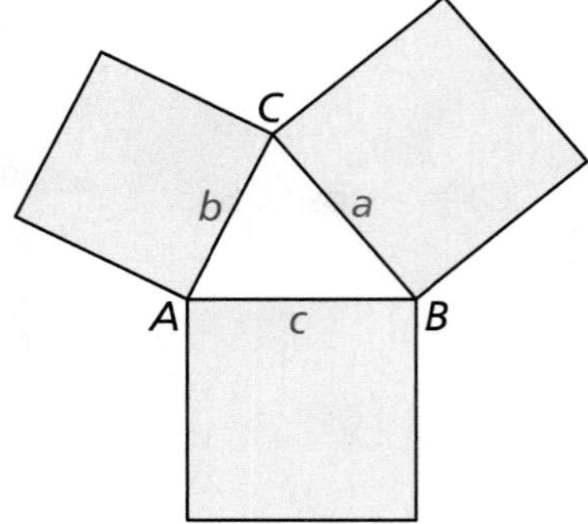


You want to find a way to describe $c^2$ in terms of $a^2$ and $b^2$. The diagram below shows the three altitudes of the triangle.

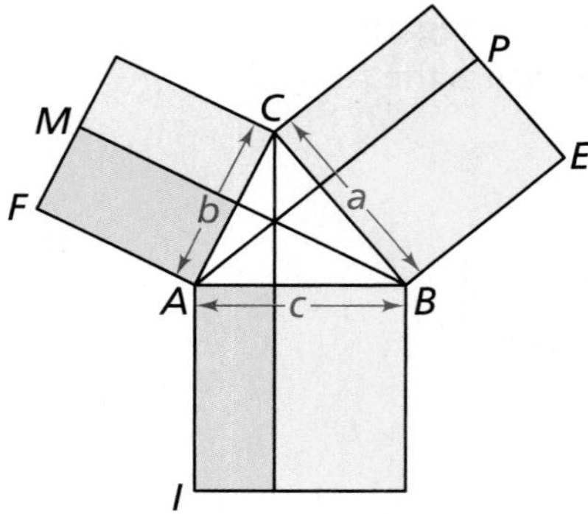


The area of each green rectangle is $ab \cos C$.

If you can show the purple rectangles have the same area and the yellow rectangles have the same area, then

$$c^2 = \text{purple} + \text{yellow} = b^2 - \text{green} + a^2 - \text{green}$$

In other words,

$$c^2 = a^2 + b^2 - 2ab \cos C$$

To show that the purple rectangles have the same area, you have to be a little tricky. Consider the diagram below.

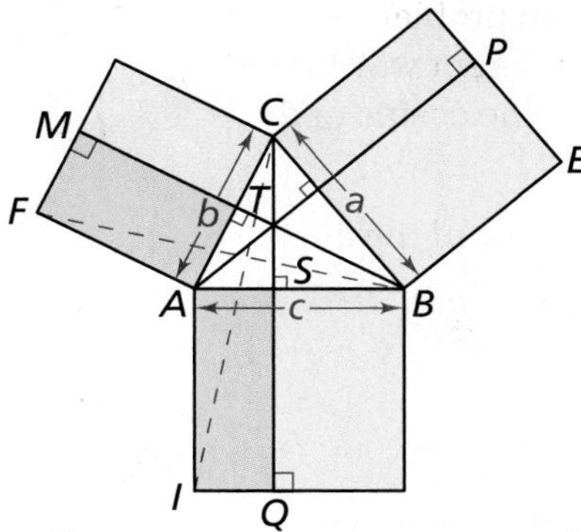


Triangles *CAI* and *FAB* are congruent.

Figure out why $\triangle CAI \cong \triangle FAB$.

The area of rectangle *AIQS* is twice the area of $\triangle CAI$. The area of rectangle *FAMT* is twice the area of $\triangle FAB$.

So rectangles *AIQS* and *FAMT* have the same area.

You can use a similar argument to show that the yellow rectangles have the same area. This proves the result.

## For Discussion

**2.** Use the Law of Cosines to find all the angle measures of this triangle.

## Developing Habits of Mind

**Consider more than one strategy.** The For Discussion problem above required you to use the Law of Cosines in a slightly different way. Since you know the three side lengths, the only unknown is the cosine of the given angle.

You can rewrite the Law of Cosines to solve for the cosine of the angle.

$$c^2 = a^2 + b^2 - 2ab\cos C$$
$$2ab\cos C = a^2 + b^2 - c^2$$
$$\cos C = \frac{a^2 + b^2 - c^2}{2ab}$$

Use this form when you know the three side lengths and need to find the angle measure. You get the cosine of the angle. The $\cos^{-1}$ function on a calculator can give you the angle's approximate measure.

You may recall that the Law of Sines produces two possible angle measures when you know the sine. If $\sin\theta = 0.8$, the angle may be 53° or 127°. This does not happen with the Law of Cosines. If $\cos\theta = 0.8$, the angle is either 37° or 323°. An angle of 323° is impossible in a triangle!

This means that if you are faced with the option of using either the Law of Sines or the Law of Cosines, you might consider using the Law of Cosines. Its answers are always unique.

## For You to Do

**3.** Find the missing side length and angle measures in the triangle below.

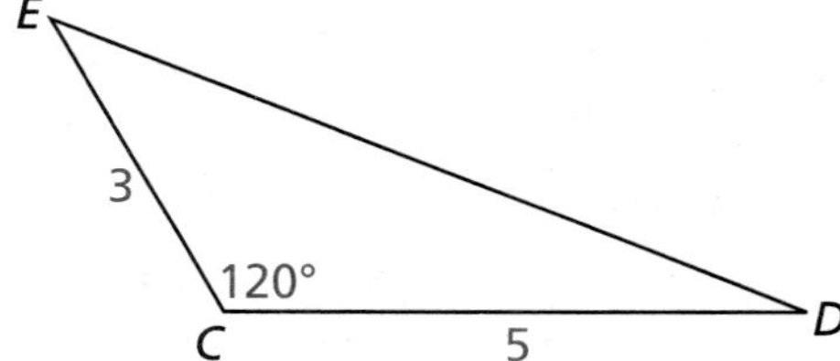


**4.** Find the measures of all three angles in the triangle below.

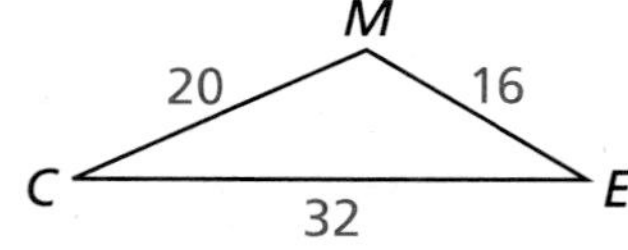


## For Discussion

**5.** You have learned that if you know all three side lengths of a triangle, you can figure out the angle measures. If you have all three angle measures, can you figure out the side lengths? Explain.

## Exercises *Practicing Habits of Mind*

### Check Your Understanding

1. In $\triangle ABC$, $BC = a$ and $AC = b$. Write an expression for the length of side $\overline{AB}$ in terms of $a$, $b$, and the cosine of $\angle C$.
2. For $\triangle ABC$ from Exercise 1, use the properties of the cosine function to find upper and lower bounds on the length of side $\overline{AB}$. Your answers should be expressed in terms of $a$ and $b$.

It is possible to find expressions here that do not involve a square root. Try to figure it out!

3. In $\triangle OBT$, $OB = 3$, $BT = 4$, and $\angle B$ is obtuse. What can you say about the length of side $\overline{OT}$?
4. In $\triangle ACU$, $AC = 3$, $CU = 4$, and $\angle C$ is acute. What can you say about the length of side $\overline{AU}$?
5. **Take It Further** $\triangle FMB$ is acute, with $FM = 12$ and $MB = 5$. Find the range of possible lengths for side $\overline{FB}$.
6. **Write About It** There are six possible combinations of three pieces of information about a triangle. For each combination below, explain how you can find the remaining side lengths and angle measures, or explain why you cannot find them.
   a. SSS (three side lengths)
   b. SAS (two side lengths and the measure of the included angle)
   c. SSA (two side lengths and the measure of a nonincluded angle)
   d. AAS (two angle measures and the length of a nonincluded side)
   e. ASA (two angle measures and the length of the included side)
   f. AAA (three angle measures)
7. A triangle has side lengths 13, 14, and 15.
   a. Find the cosine of each angle in this triangle.
   b. Which is the largest angle, the one with the greatest cosine or the one with the least cosine?
   c. Suppose you draw an altitude to the side of length 14. Find the length of the altitude.
   d. What is the area of this triangle?
8. Suppose all the side lengths of $\triangle ABC$ are integers.
   a. Explain why $\cos C$ must be rational.
   b. **Take It Further** Show that you can write an expression for the area of $\triangle ABC$ in the form $x\sqrt{y}$, where $x$ is rational and $y$ is an integer.

## On Your Own

**9.** In $\triangle MLT$, $ML = 10$, $LT = 3$, and $\angle L$ measures $60°$. Which number is the exact length of side $\overline{MT}$?

**A.** 7 **B.** $\sqrt{79}$ **C.** $\sqrt{139}$ **D.** 13

**10.** In $\triangle ABC$, $BC = 10$ and $AC = 3$. Write an expression for the length of side $\overline{AB}$ in terms of the cosine of $\angle C$.

**11.** For $\triangle ABC$ from Exercise 10, use the properties of the cosine function. Find the upper and lower bounds of the length of side $\overline{AB}$.

**12.** A triangle has sides of length 12, 15, and 10. Find the measure of the smallest angle in the triangle to the nearest degree.

**13.** In $\triangle FOM$, $FO = 12$, $OM = 20$, and $\angle O$ measures $60°$.

**a.** Explain why $\angle O$ cannot be the smallest angle in the triangle.

**b.** Use the Law of Cosines and the Law of Sines to find the measure of the smallest angle in the triangle to the nearest degree.

**14.** Let $\theta$ be an angle between $0°$ and $180°$. Determine whether each statement is true or false.

**a.** $\cos \theta > 0$ **b.** $\sin \theta > 0$

**c.** $\sin^2 \theta = 1 + \cos^2 \theta$ **d.** $\sin \theta = \sqrt{1 - \cos^2 \theta}$

**15.** A triangle has side lengths 7, 10, and 12.

**a.** Find the angles in the triangle to the nearest degree.

**b.** Use the diagram at the right. Find $x$ and $h$.

**c.** Find the area of the triangle.

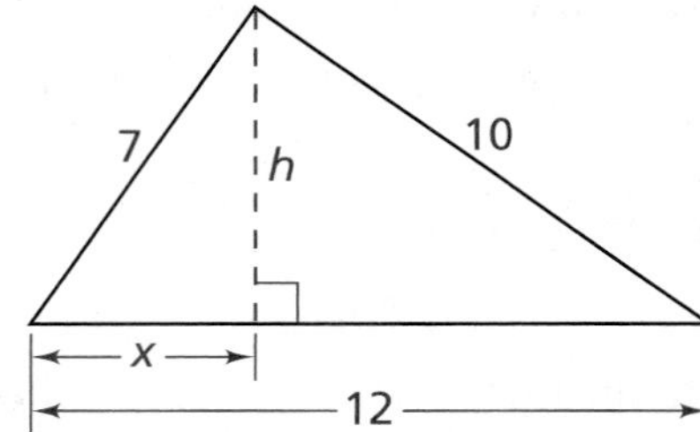


**16.** Take It Further The cosines of two angles of a triangle are $\frac{4}{5}$ and $\frac{5}{13}$. Find the exact cosine of the third angle.

**17.** Standardized Test Prep What is the measure of the smallest angle in a triangle with side lengths 5, 7, and 8 inches?

**A.** $17.19°$ **B.** $34.38°$ **C.** $38.21°$ **D.** $60.00°$

**18.** The diagram below shows $\triangle ABC$ with altitude $\overline{CD}$.

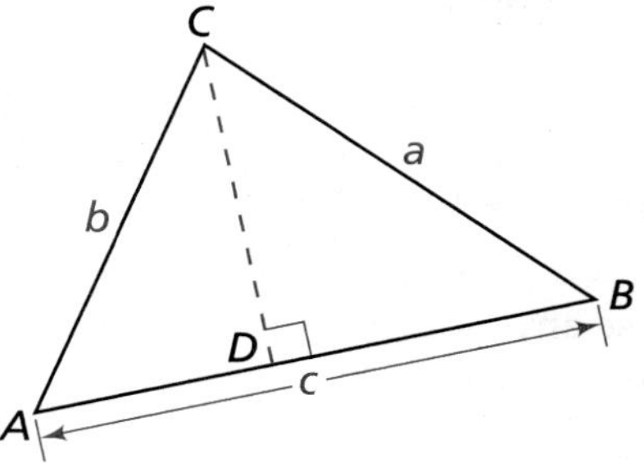


**a.** Show that $b \cos A + a \cos B = c$.

**b.** Use a similar diagram to show that $c \cos A + a \cos C = b$.

**c.** Show that $c \cos B + b \cos C = a$.

**19.** Take It Further Solve the system of equations below for $\begin{pmatrix} \cos A \\ \cos B \\ \cos C \end{pmatrix}$.

$$\begin{pmatrix} b & a & 0 \\ c & 0 & a \\ 0 & c & b \end{pmatrix} \begin{pmatrix} \cos A \\ \cos B \\ \cos C \end{pmatrix} = \begin{pmatrix} c \\ b \\ a \end{pmatrix}$$

This gives you another proof of the Law of Cosines.

This system comes from Exercise 18. For help in finding the inverse of a matrix, see the TI-Nspire Handbook, p. 817.

## Maintain Your Skills

**20.** For each set of measurements for $\triangle ABC$, calculate the length of side $\overline{AB}$ to two decimal places.

**a.** $AC = 13$, $BC = 8$, and $\angle C$ measures $1°$.

**b.** $AC = 13$, $BC = 8$, and $\angle C$ measures $10°$.

**c.** $AC = 13$, $BC = 8$, and $\angle C$ measures $50°$.

**d.** $AC = 13$, $BC = 8$, and $\angle C$ measures $90°$.

**e.** $AC = 13$, $BC = 8$, and $\angle C$ measures $130°$.

**f.** $AC = 13$, $BC = 8$, and $\angle C$ measures $170°$.

**g.** $AC = 13$, $BC = 8$, and $\angle C$ measures $179°$.

**h.** Describe what happens to the length of side $\overline{AB}$ as $\angle C$ increases from $1°$ to $179°$.

# 4.14 Heron's Formula—Using Side Lengths to Find the Area of a Triangle

For any three given side lengths, there is at most one triangle. That means that given the three side lengths, you should be able to find all the angle measures in the triangle, and its area.

The side lengths 10, 50, and 100 cannot form a triangle.

## For You to Do

1. A triangle has side lengths 16, 25, and 31. Use the Law of Cosines to find the angles in this triangle to the nearest degree. Then use any of the angles and the two sides next to the angle to find the area of the triangle.

The Greek mathematician Heron developed a formula for the area of a triangle based only on its side lengths. In this lesson, you will see two proofs of Heron's Formula. The first proof uses algebra. The second proof uses trigonometry. Look for similarities between the proofs.

### *Theorem 4.7 Heron's Formula*

**Given a triangle with side lengths $a$, $b$, and $c$, the area of the triangle is**

$$A = \sqrt{s(s-a)(s-b)(s-c)}$$

**where $s$ is the semiperimeter $\frac{a+b+c}{2}$.**

## For You to Do

2. Use Heron's Formula to find the area of a triangle with side lengths 16, 25, and 31. Find $s$ first. Does the value for the area you get using the formula agree with the answer you got in Problem 1 above?

The two proofs of Heron's Formula rely on the known area formulas for triangles. The diagram for the first proof looks remarkably like the one you used to prove the Law of Cosines.

**Proof 1** Draw a $\triangle ABC$. Label the side lengths. Drop an altitude to side $\overline{AB}$.

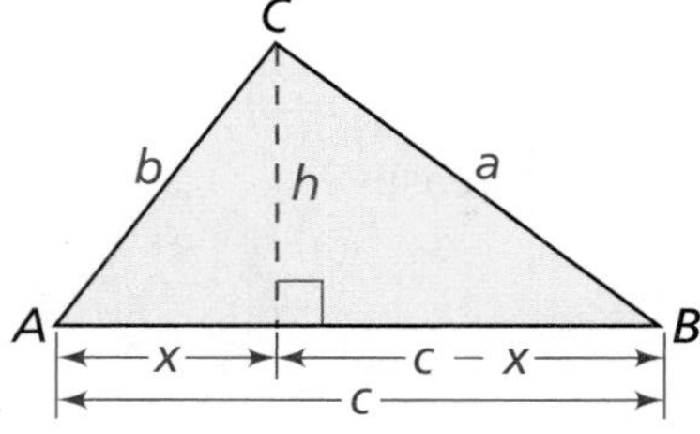

The area of the triangle is $A = \frac{1}{2}ch$. So, the task is to find $h$ in terms of $a$, $b$, and $c$. Apply the Pythagorean Theorem to the right triangles formed by the altitude.

$$h^2 + x^2 = b^2$$
$$h^2 + (c - x)^2 = a^2$$

You can rewrite the second equation as $h^2 + c^2 - 2cx + x^2 = a^2$. Then subtract the first equation from the second to find an expression for $x$.

$$\begin{aligned}(h^2 + c^2 - 2cx + x^2) - (h^2 + x^2) &= a^2 - b^2\\ c^2 - 2cx &= a^2 - b^2\\ c^2 + b^2 - a^2 &= 2cx\\ \frac{c^2 + b^2 - a^2}{2c} &= x\end{aligned}$$

Now that you have a formula for $x$, you can use the first equation to find $h$.

$$\begin{aligned}h^2 &= b^2 - x^2\\ h^2 &= b^2 - \left(\frac{c^2 + b^2 - a^2}{2c}\right)^2\\ h^2 &= \frac{(4b^2c^2 - (c^2 + b^2 - a^2)^2)}{4c^2}\end{aligned}$$

This looks unmanageable, but the key to success is recognizing that the numerator of the right side is a difference of squares.

$$\begin{aligned}h^2 &= \frac{(2bc)^2 - (c^2 + b^2 - a^2)^2}{4c^2}\\ h^2 &= \frac{(2bc + c^2 + b^2 - a^2)(2bc - c^2 - b^2 + a^2)}{4c^2}\\ h^2 &= \frac{((b + c)^2 - a^2)(a^2 - (b - c)^2)}{4c^2}\end{aligned}$$

And there are even *more* differences of squares. You can factor again to find a final formula for $h^2$ and then find $h$.

$$\begin{aligned}h^2 &= \frac{(b + c + a)(b + c - a)(a + b - c)(a - b + c)}{4c^2}\\ h &= \frac{\sqrt{(b + c + a)(b + c - a)(a - b + c)(a + b - c)}}{2c}\end{aligned}$$

The area of the triangle is $A = \frac{1}{2}ch$. Substitute for $h$. You can cancel $c$ in the numerator and denominator.

$$A = \frac{\sqrt{(b + c + a)(b + c - a)(a - b + c)(a + b - c)}}{4}$$

Pushing the 4 inside the square root as a 16 gives Heron's Formula.

$$A = \sqrt{s(s - a)(s - b)(s - c)}$$

You will explain this last step further in the exercises.

The first proof relies primarily on algebra, but some of the work involved closely resembles the Law of Cosines. You can also use the Law of Cosines in a second proof.

**Proof 2** The formula $A = \frac{1}{2}ab \sin C$ gives the area of $\triangle ABC$. A handy formula already exists for the cosine of $C$ in terms of side lengths. Use the Law of Cosines and solve for $\cos C$.

$$\cos C = \frac{a^2 + b^2 - c^2}{2ab}$$

You can use the relationship $\cos^2 \theta + \sin^2 \theta = 1$ here. Exercise 14 in Lesson 4.13 gives the following identity for angles between 0° and 180 °.

$$\sin \theta = \sqrt{1 - \cos^2 \theta}$$

Use this identity to rewrite the formula for the area of the triangle.

$$A = \tfrac{1}{2}ab \sin C = \tfrac{1}{2}ab\sqrt{1 - \cos^2 C}$$

Now swap in the formula for cosine and work inside the square root.

$$\begin{aligned} A &= \tfrac{1}{2}ab\sqrt{1 - \cos^2 C} \\ &= \tfrac{1}{2}ab\sqrt{1 - \left(\frac{a^2 + b^2 - c^2}{2ab}\right)^2} \\ &= \tfrac{1}{2}ab\sqrt{\frac{(2ab)^2 - (a^2 + b^2 - c^2)^2}{(2ab)^2}} \\ &= \tfrac{1}{4}\sqrt{(2ab)^2 - (a^2 + b^2 - c^2)^2} \end{aligned}$$

The remainder of the work under the square root is the same as the work in Proof 1, with a different ordering of the variables. You factor in two steps. Both times you find differences of squares.

If you start with the area as $\frac{1}{2}bc \sin A$, you actually end up with the same ordering of the variables as in Proof 1.

$$\begin{aligned} A &= \tfrac{1}{4}\sqrt{(2ab + a^2 + b^2 - c^2)(2ab - a^2 - b^2 + c^2)} \\ &= \tfrac{1}{4}\sqrt{((a + b)^2 - c^2)(c^2 - (a - b)^2)} \\ &= \tfrac{1}{4}\sqrt{(a + b + c)(a + b - c)(c + a - b)(c - a + b)} \end{aligned}$$

The algebra of the two proofs is quite similar, although the means to get there differs. Since you derived the Law of Cosines using a diagram similar to the one in the first proof, it is not surprising to find similar steps in the two proofs.

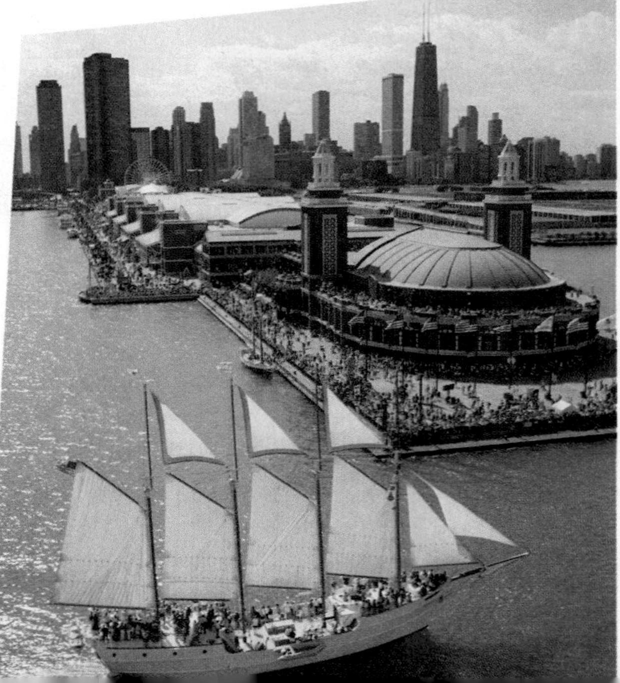

You can use Heron's Formula to find the area of the triangular sails. How can you find the area of the quadrilateral sails?

## Exercises *Practicing Habits of Mind*

### Check Your Understanding

**1.** In $\triangle QED$, $QE = 6$ and $ED = 8$.

**a.** Suppose the remaining side length is $x$. Write a formula for the semiperimeter $s$ in terms of $x$.

**b.** Write a formula for $A(x)$, the area of $\triangle QED$ in terms of $x$.

**c.** Find the zeros of $A(x)$.

**d.** Find the maximum value of $A(x)$ and the value of $x$ that produces it.

**2.** In $\triangle QEU$, $QE = 6$. The triangle's perimeter is 18.

**a.** Suppose $QU = x$. Find the length of $\overline{EU}$ in terms of $x$.

**b.** Write a formula for $A(x)$, the area of $\triangle QEU$ in terms of $x$.

**c.** Find the zeros of $A(x)$.

**d.** Find the maximum value of $A(x)$ and the value of $x$ that produces it.

**3.** Find the area of this quadrilateral.

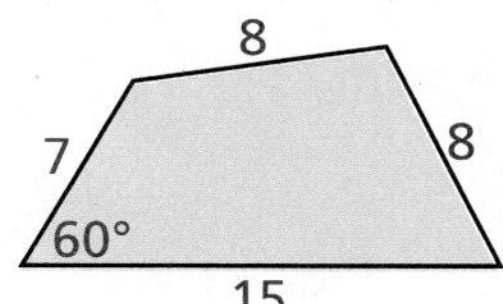


**4.** Peter thinks there is another way to draw the quadrilateral in Exercise 3 given only its marked side lengths and angle measure. He says the quadrilateral might be concave instead.

**a.** What does *concave* mean? Draw an example of a concave quadrilateral.

**b.** Could this quadrilateral be concave? If so, find its area. If not, explain why not.

5. Proof 1 in the lesson gives the formula below.

$$A = \frac{\sqrt{(b+c+a)(b+c-a)(a-b+c)(a+b-c)}}{4}$$

You can rewrite this formula as

$$A = \sqrt{s(s-a)(s-b)(s-c)}$$

where $s = \frac{a+b+c}{2}$.

a. Show that the two expressions below are equal.

$$\frac{\sqrt{(b+c+a)(b+c-a)(a-b+c)(a+b-c)}}{4}$$

$$\sqrt{\frac{b+c+a}{2} \cdot \frac{b+c-a}{2} \cdot \frac{a-b+c}{2} \cdot \frac{a+b-c}{2}}$$

b. Show the remaining steps you need to write the formula in the following form.

$$A = \sqrt{s(s-a)(s-b)(s-c)}$$

## On Your Own

6. **Write About It** What happens when you try to use Heron's Formula to find the area of a triangle with sides of length 12, 25, and 11? Explain.

7. Suppose $\triangle ABT$ is equilateral with $AT = 10$.

a. Find the area of $\triangle ABT$. Use any method.

b. Find the area of $\triangle ABT$ using Heron's Formula.

c. **Take It Further** Use Heron's Formula to show that the formula below gives the area of an equilateral triangle with sides of length $x$.

$$Area = \frac{x^2\sqrt{3}}{4}$$

A **Heronian triangle** is a triangle with integer side lengths and integer area.

8. Which sets of three lengths form a Heronian triangle?

a. 7, 10, 12

b. 6, 8, 9

c. 10, 15, 20

d. 10, 17, 21

9. **Standardized Test Prep** Which set of three lengths does NOT form a Heronian triangle?

A. 10, 13, 13 B. 9, 12, 16 C. 15, 37, 44 D. 5, 29, 30

10. Prove that an equilateral triangle cannot be Heronian.

**Habits of Mind**

**Make strategic choices.** You have seen Heron's Formula in several forms in this lesson. Some forms may be more helpful than others.

**11.** Use the two right triangles below to form a Heronian triangle.

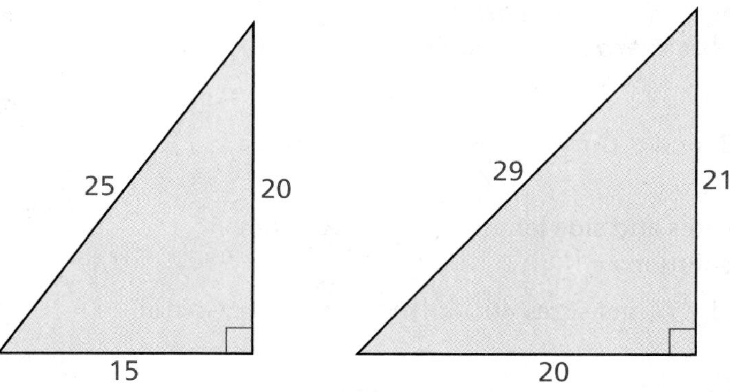


Go Online
www.successnetplus.com

**12.** Take It Further The triangle with side lengths 13, 14, and 15 is Heronian. Its area is 84. Find some more Heronian triangles with side lengths that are consecutive integers.

## Maintain Your Skills

**13.** In a triangle with side lengths 5 and 12, the third side can be any real number between 7 and 17.

**a.** Copy and complete this table for $A(c)$, the area of the triangle with sides 5, 12, and $c$. Find each answer to two decimal places.

| $c$ | $A(c)$ |
|---|---|
| 7 | ■ |
| 8 | ■ |
| 9 | ■ |
| 10 | ■ |
| 11 | ■ |
| 12 | ■ |
| 13 | ■ |
| 14 | ■ |
| 15 | ■ |
| 16 | ■ |
| 17 | ■ |

**b.** What value of $c$ appears to give the maximum area $A(c)$? Explain.

**Habits of Mind**

**Look for relationships.** How do you know that the length of the third side must be between 7 and 17?

**In this investigation, you learned to solve a triangle. You also proved and used the Law of Sines, the Law of Cosines, and Heron's Formula. These questions will help you summarize what you have learned.**

1. In $\triangle DOG$, $DG = 10$, $GO = 8$, and $\angle G$ measures 20°. Find the area of $\triangle DOG$.
2. Find the missing angle measures and side lengths for $\triangle DOG$ from Exercise 1. Give all possible solutions.
3. In $\triangle PIG$, $PI = 7$, $GI = 8$, and $\angle G$ measures 40°. Solve the triangle. Give all possible solutions.
4. In $\triangle CAT$, $CA = 6$, $AT = 4$, and $CT = 8$. Find the angle measures of the triangle.
5. Find the area of $\triangle CAT$ from Exercise 4.
6. What information do you need to find all of a triangle's side lengths and angle measures?
7. What information do you need to find the area of a triangle?
8. A triangle has sides of length 5, 8, and 10. What is the measure of its largest angle?

## Vocabulary

In this investigation, you learned these terms. Make sure you understand what each one means and how to use it.

- **Heronian triangle**
- **Law of Cosines**
- **Law of Sines**

You can use triangle relationships to measure how the glacier changes over time.

# Project: Using Mathematical Habits

## Brahmagupta's Formula

In the 600s, the Indian mathematician Brahmagupta found a generalization of Heron's Formula. It applies to cyclic quadrilaterals. A cyclic quadrilateral is a quadrilateral with four vertices that are all on the same circle. This is not true for most quadrilaterals.

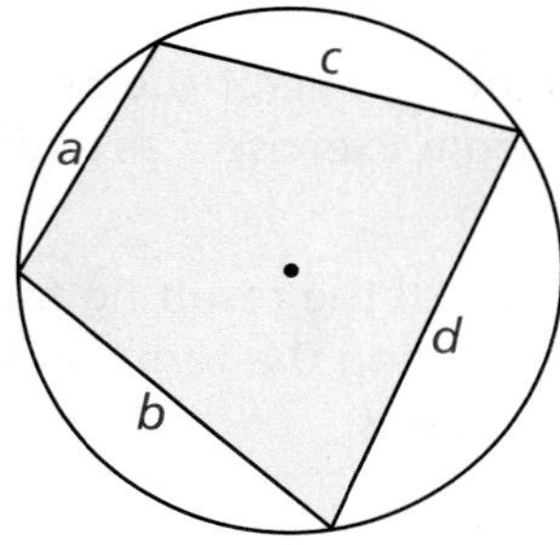


His formula relates the area of the quadrilateral to the lengths of its sides.

### *Theorem 4.8* *Brahmagupta's Formula*

Given a cyclic quadrilateral with side lengths $a$, $b$, $c$, and $d$ the area of the quadrilateral is

$$A = \sqrt{(s - a)(s - b)(s - c)(s - d)}$$

where $s$ is the semiperimeter $s = \frac{a + b + c + d}{2}$.

The goal of this project is for you to work through a proof of the theorem. You will write up the proof in your own words and supply reasons for the major steps.

1. Show that the opposite angles of a cyclic quadrilateral are supplementary. Two angles are supplementary if their measures sum to 180°.

2. Call one of the angles in the cyclic quadrilateral $\alpha$. Let $e$ be the length of the diagonal in the diagram.

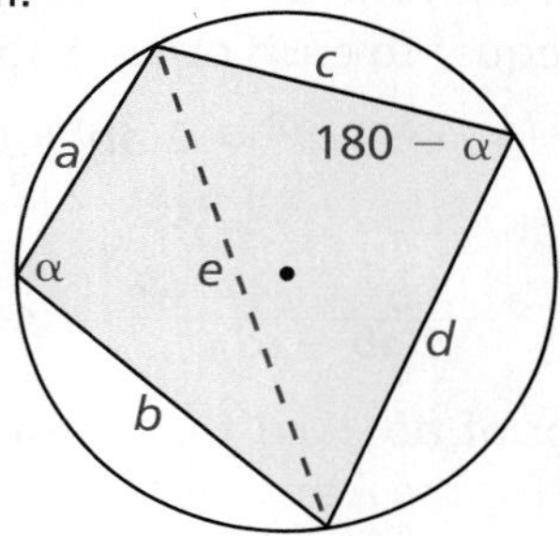


Let $A$ be the area of the quadrilateral. Find expressions for the areas of the two triangles and add them to get a formula for $A$.

$$A = \frac{1}{2}(ab + cd)\sin\alpha$$

You can solve the equation for $\sin\alpha$.

$$\frac{2A}{ab + cd} = \sin\alpha$$

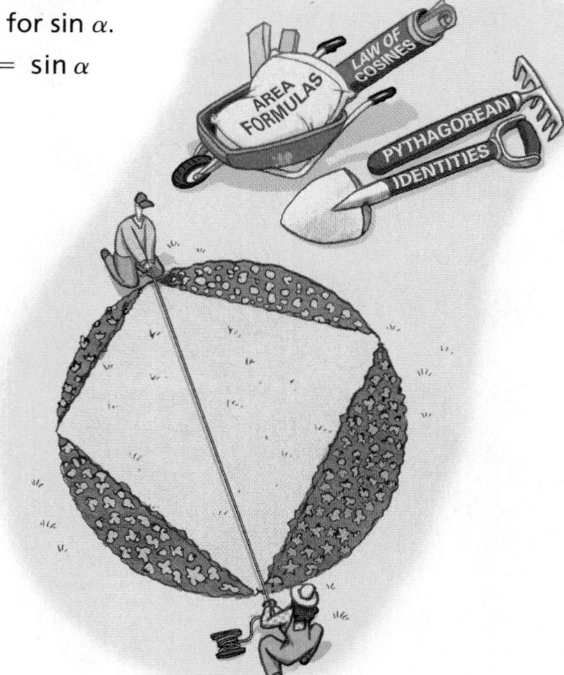

3. Now apply the Law of Cosines to each triangle to find expressions for $e^2$, where $e$ is the length of the diagonal in the diagram. Set these expressions equal to each other. Show that

$$a^2 + b^2 - c^2 - d^2 = 2(ab + cd)\cos\alpha$$

Conclude that

$$\frac{a^2 + b^2 - c^2 - d^2}{2(ab + cd)} = \cos\alpha$$

There is a factor of $ab + cd$ that shows up in both the expression for $\cos\alpha$ and the expression for $\sin\alpha$. This is a good place to use the Pythagorean Identity or at least some form of it. Because the expressions for sine and cosine have so much in common, maybe you can cancel or combine some of the terms in their squares.

4. Use the fact that $\cos^2\alpha = 1 - \sin^2\alpha$ to write the following equation.

$$\left(\frac{a^2 + b^2 - c^2 - d^2}{2(ab + cd)}\right)^2 = 1 - \left(\frac{2A}{ab + cd}\right)^2$$

5. Rearrange the result of Exercise 4 to get the equation below.

$$\frac{4(ab + cd)^2 - (a^2 + b^2 - c^2 - d^2)^2}{4(ab + cd)^2} = \frac{16A^2}{4(ab + cd)^2}$$

So

$$16A^2 = 4(ab + cd)^2 - (a^2 + b^2 - c^2 - d^2)^2$$

6. The rest is factoring. Factor the right side of the equation from Exercise 5 as a difference of two squares.

   Then factor each of the resulting factors some more. Try rearranging the terms so that you see some perfect squares.

7. Now you should have an equation like this.

$$16A^2 = (-a + b + c + d)(a - b + c + d) \cdot (a + b - c + d)(a + b + c - d)$$

   Put it all together to get Brahmagupta's Formula.

8. **Write About It** Explain how you can use Brahmagupta's Formula to prove Heron's Formula.

# Review

In **Investigation 4A,** you learned how to

- use right triangle trigonometry to find the coordinates of a person walking on the unit circle, given an angle through which an observer has turned
- evaluate the sine, cosine, and tangent functions for any angle
- solve equations involving trigonometric equations

*The following questions will help you check your understanding.*

**1.** Paul walks on the unit circle starting at the point (1, 0), in a counterclockwise direction. Olivia is the observer standing at the origin.

**a.** Find the coordinates of Paul's location when Olivia has turned 240°.

**b.** When Paul is at the point $\left(\frac{5}{13}, -\frac{12}{13}\right)$ for the first time, find the angle Olivia has turned to the nearest degree.

**2.** Sketch each angle in standard position. Find its sine, cosine, and tangent.

**a.** 45°

**b.** 90°

**c.** 120°

**d.** 180°

**e.** 210°

**f.** 330°

**3.** Solve each equation for $\alpha$ between 0° and 360°.

**a.** $\sin \alpha - 1 = 0$

**b.** $2 \sin \alpha = \sqrt{2}$

**c.** $4 \cos^2 \alpha - 1 = 0$

**d.** $3 \cos^2 \alpha + 2 \cos \alpha = 1$

In **Investigation 4B,** you learned how to

- sketch the graphs of sine, cosine, and tangent
- use the graphs of trigonometric functions to solve problems
- prove and use trigonometric identities

*The following questions will help you check your understanding.*

**4. a.** Copy and complete the table.

| $x$ | $\sin x$ |
|---|---|
| 0° | ■ |
| 30° | ■ |
| 45° | ■ |
| 90° | ■ |
| 120° | ■ |
| 180° | ■ |
| 210° | ■ |
| 240° | ■ |
| 270° | ■ |
| 315° | ■ |

**b.** Sketch a graph of $y = \sin x$ for $0° \le x \le 360°$. On your graph, label the points that you found for $x = 30°$, $x = 90°$, $x = 120°$, $x = 270°$, and $x = 315°$.

**5. a.** Sketch a graph of $y = \tan x$ for $0° \le x \le 360°$.

**b.** Use the graph of $y = \tan x$ to determine the number of solutions to the equation below for $0° \le x \le 360°$.

$$\tan x = \frac{1}{2}$$

**c.** Use $x = \tan^{-1} \frac{1}{2}$ to find all values of $x$ for $0° \le x \le 360°$ to the nearest degree.

**6.** Use the angle-sum identities to prove each identity.

**a.** $\cos(180° + x) = -\cos x$

**b.** $\sin(180° + x) = -\sin x$

**c.** $\tan(180° + x) = \tan x$

---

In **Investigation 4C** you learned how to

- solve a triangle
- state and use the Law of Sines
- state and use the Law of Cosines
- state and use Heron's Formula

*The following questions will help you check your understanding.*

**7.** In $\triangle ABC$, $AB = 6$, $\angle A = 50°$, and $\angle B = 60°$.

**a.** Find all remaining side lengths and angle measures in this triangle to the nearest tenth.

**b.** Find the area of $\triangle ABC$ to the nearest tenth by drawing the altitude $\overline{CH}$ from $\angle C$ to side $\overline{AB}$.

**8.** In $\triangle DEF$, $DE = 12$, $EF = 10$, and $DF = 9$.

**a.** Find the angle measure of the largest angle of this triangle to the nearest degree.

**b.** Find the area of this triangle using Heron's Formula.

**9.** For each set of equations about $\triangle GHI$, find all possible values for the measure of $\angle G$.

**a.** $GH = 3$, $GI = 8$, and $HI = 7$

**b.** $GI = 8$, $HI = 7$, and $m\angle H = 50°$

**c.** $GI = 18$, $HI = 21$, $m\angle H = 52°$

**d.** $GI = 6$, $HI = 7$, and $m\angle H = 75°$

Chapter 4

# Test

Go Online
www.successnetplus.com

## Multiple Choice

**1.** If $\cos\theta > 0$ and $\sin\theta < 0$, then $\theta$ is in which quadrant?

**A.** I
**B.** II
**C.** III
**D.** IV

**2.** For some angle $\alpha$ in Quadrant II, $\sin\alpha = \frac{15}{17}$. What is $\cos\alpha$?

**A.** $-\frac{15}{17}$
**B.** $-\frac{8}{17}$
**C.** $\frac{8}{17}$
**D.** 1

**3.** For the interval $90° < x < 180°$, is $\sin x$ positive or negative? Is the value of $\sin x$ increasing or decreasing as $x$ increases through the interval?

**A.** positive, increasing
**B.** positive, decreasing
**C.** negative, increasing
**D.** negative, decreasing

**4.** Which is equal to $\cos 200°$?

**A.** $\cos 20°$
**B.** $-\cos 20°$
**C.** $\sin 20°$
**D.** $-\sin 20°$

**5.** In $\triangle ABC$, $AB = 5$, $BC = 9$, and $AC = 8$. What is the area of $\triangle ABC$?

**A.** $\sqrt{22}$
**B.** 11
**C.** $11\sqrt{6}$
**D.** $6\sqrt{11}$

## Open Response

**6.** Sketch each angle in standard position. Find its sine, cosine, and tangent. Give exact values, if possible. Otherwise, round to the nearest hundredth.

**a.** $60°$
**b.** $90°$
**c.** $150°$
**d.** $289°$

**7.** Solve each equation for $0° \leq \theta < 360°$.

**a.** $2\sin\theta + 1 = 0$
**b.** $2\cos^2\theta - 1 = 0$
**c.** $3\cos^2\theta - 5\cos\theta + 2 = 0$

**8.** Simplify each expression.

**a.** $\sin(180° - x)$
**b.** $\cos(180° + x)$
**c.** $\sin(270° + x)$

**9. a.** Sketch a graph of $y = \cos x$ for $0° \leq x \leq 450°$.

**b.** Use your graph to determine the number of solutions to the equation $\cos x = \frac{1}{2}$.

**c.** Find all solutions to $\cos x = \frac{1}{2}$ for $0° \leq x \leq 450°$.

**10.** For each set of information about $\triangle ABC$, find all the missing side lengths to the nearest tenth and angle measures to the nearest degree.

**a.** $AB = 16$, $BC = 12$, and $AC = 8$
**b.** $m\angle A = 34°$, $BC = 5$, and $AC = 7$

**11.** What information do you need about a triangle to find its area?

Chapter
5
Investigations at a Glance
5A The Cosine and Sine Functions
5B Sinusoidal Functions and Their Graphs

# Analyzing Trigonometric Functions

As you know, trigonometry describes the relationships between the angles and sides of triangles. When some of the angles and distances between three locations are known, you use trigonometry to calculate the unknown angles and distances.

But its usefulness is even more wide-ranging. It also describes cyclical behavior such as the height of a seat on a Ferris wheel, the heights of the tides, or the monthly sales of sunscreen over a year. To begin, you look at radians, a more natural way to express the domain of the trigonometric functions. Then you use trigonometric functions to model periodic behavior.

In this chapter, you will develop useful tools. These will prepare you for the study of complex numbers, continuity, limits, and vectors.

## Vocabulary

- amplitude
- arc
- central angle
- decreasing
- increasing
- phase shift
- Pythagorean identity
- radian
- secant line
- sinusoidal function
- turning point
- vertical displacement

# Investigation 5A The Cosine and Sine Functions

In *The Cosine and Sine Functions,* you will learn how to measure in radians. You will learn how to think of cosine and sine as functions of radian measure. You will solve equations involving these trigonometric functions.

**By the end of this investigation, you will be able to answer questions like these.**

1. Where are the turning points of the cosine and sine functions?
2. What is a radian?
3. How can you use a graph of $y = \sin x$ to estimate solutions to the equation $\sin x = -0.6$?

**You will learn how to**

- understand the relationship between degree and radian measure as the length of an arc on the unit circle subtended by a central angle
- relate the motion of an object around a circle to the graphs of the cosine and sine functions
- solve equations that involve cosine and sine (such as $3 \cos x + 2 = 1$)

**You will develop these habits and skills:**

- Calculate cosine and sine using radians directly without converting to degrees.
- Visualize periodic functions, and identify their period.
- Understand how to "undo" cosine or sine to solve equations.
- Compare the cosine and sine functions through their relation to the unit circle and through their graphs.

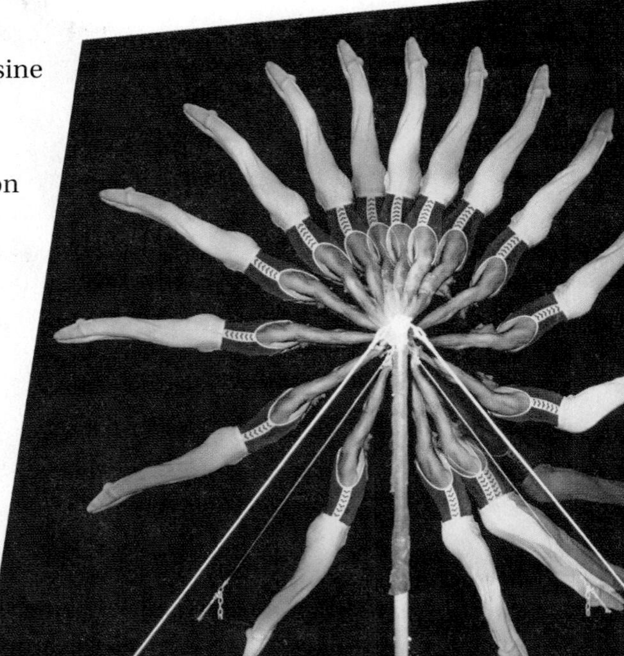

The gymnast traces a circle as he rotates about a fixed point.

## 5.01 Getting Started

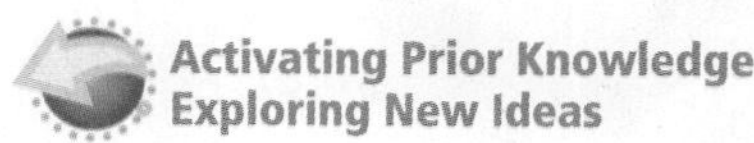


Olivia watches Paul walk around a circle. The circle's radius is 1 meter. Olivia stands at the center, and Paul begins walking counterclockwise. Consider a coordinate grid, with Olivia standing at the origin and Paul starting at the point $(1, 0)$.

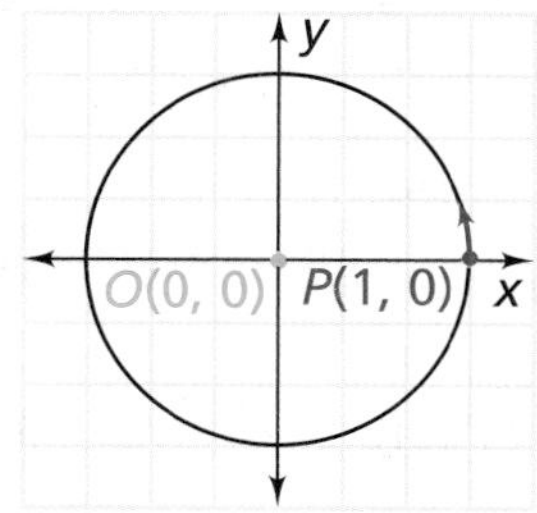


As Paul walks an increasing distance around the circle, he passes through many points. The questions in this Getting Started ask about Paul's location after he has walked a specific distance.

**Remember...**

The equation of the unit circle is $x^2 + y^2 = 1$.

### For You to Explore

1. How far will Paul walk before returning to the point $(1, 0)$?
2. Draw the unit circle and plot the point where Paul will be after walking each distance.
   a. exactly $\pi$ meters
   b. exactly $\frac{\pi}{2}$ meters
   c. exactly $3\pi$ meters
   d. exactly 3 meters
3. At some point, Paul has walked exactly $\frac{9\pi}{4}$ meters.
   a. What quadrant is Paul in after this much walking?
   b. Draw a unit circle and plot the point where Paul is after walking $\frac{9\pi}{4}$ meters.
   c. Find two other distances Paul could have walked around the circle to end up at this same point.
4. At some point, Paul has walked exactly $\frac{\pi}{3}$ meters. Find the exact coordinates of Paul's location.
5. **Write About It** At some point, Paul has walked exactly $\frac{\pi}{4}$ meters. Explain why his $x$- and $y$-coordinates must be equal at this point.
6. a. Find the exact coordinates of Paul's location after he walks $\frac{\pi}{4}$ meters.
   b. Find the exact coordinates of Paul's location after he walks $\frac{5\pi}{4}$ meters.
7. **Take It Further** Paul runs 100 meters along the circle. What quadrant is he in at the end of this 100-meter run?

**Habits of Mind**

**Recognize symmetry.** Is there any symmetry to Paul's location?

**Remember...**

*Exact* here means no decimals, just exact fractions or radicals.

# Exercises *Practicing Habits of Mind*

## On Your Own

**8.** How far will Paul walk when he first reaches the point $(0, -1)$?

**9.** Write About It What is the importance of $\pi$ in measuring the distance Paul has walked? In other words, why are so many of the questions about multiples of $\pi$ and not integers?

**10.** Write About It Olivia, standing at $O(0, 0)$, says that Paul's $\frac{\pi}{2}$ behaves like $90^\circ$. Explain Olivia's observation.

**11.** As Paul continues to walk, he will reach $(0, -1)$ again.

**a.** Give another distance Paul could walk to reach $(0, -1)$.

**b.** Describe a method you could use to generate a large number of these distances.

**12. a.** Draw the unit circle and plot the point where Paul will be after walking exactly $\frac{7\pi}{6}$ meters.

**b.** Find the exact coordinates of Paul's location after he walks $\frac{7\pi}{6}$ meters.

**13.** As Paul walks around the circle, is there ever a time when his $y$-coordinate is *exactly* $\frac{2}{3}$? If so, how many times will this happen each time Paul goes around the circle? If not, how do you know it can never happen?

**14.** As Paul walks around the circle, his $x$- and $y$-coordinates reach maximum and minimum values. What are these maximum and minimum values, and at what walking distances do they occur?

## Maintain Your Skills

**15.** Copy and complete this table, giving the coordinates of Paul's location after walking each distance. Look for patterns to help make your work easier.

| Distance | Coordinates |
|---|---|
| $0$ | $(1, 0)$ |
| $\frac{\pi}{4}$ | $\left(\frac{\sqrt{2}}{2}, \frac{\sqrt{2}}{2}\right)$ |
| $\frac{\pi}{2}$ | ■ |
| $\frac{3\pi}{4}$ | ■ |
| $\pi$ | $(-1, 0)$ |
| $\frac{5\pi}{4}$ | ■ |
| $\frac{3\pi}{2}$ | ■ |
| $\frac{7\pi}{4}$ | ■ |
| $2\pi$ | ■ |
| $\frac{9\pi}{4}$ | ■ |
| $\frac{5\pi}{2}$ | ■ |

# 5.02 Trigonometry With Radians

In Lesson 5.01, Paul walked around a unit circle, and you found the coordinates of his stopping point. You may remember that the coordinates of any point on the unit circle are $(\cos\theta, \sin\theta)$, where $\theta$ is the measure of the angle between the positive $x$-axis and a ray drawn from the origin through the point.

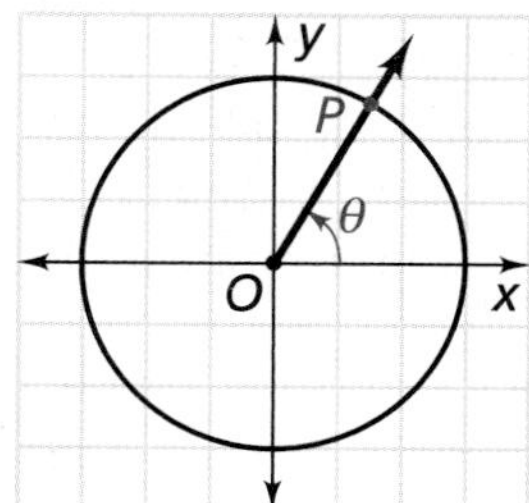


Since the origin is the center of the circle, the angle whose measure is $\theta$ is a **central angle.** The part of the circle that is between the two sides of the angle is an **arc.**

There is a direct correspondence between the length of an arc on the unit circle and the measure of the central angle that defines the arc.

**Remember...**

A central angle for a circle is an angle that has its vertex at the center of the circle.

An arc is a set of points of a circle that lie in the interior of a particular central angle.

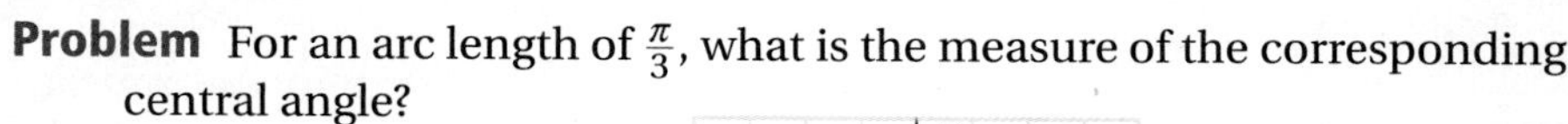

**Problem** For an arc length of $\frac{\pi}{3}$, what is the measure of the corresponding central angle?

**Solution** The circumference of the unit circle is $2\pi$. So the arc with length $\frac{\pi}{3}$ would be $\frac{1}{6}$ of the entire circle (since $\frac{\pi}{3} \cdot 6 = 2\pi$). The central angle is $\frac{\theta}{360^\circ}$ of the full circle. Thus,

$$\frac{1}{6} = \frac{\theta}{360^\circ}$$

so $\theta = 60^\circ$.

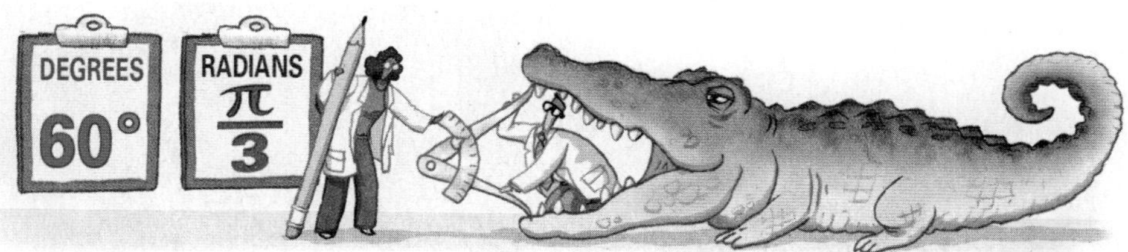

## For You to Do

1. In the unit circle how long is the arc that corresponds to a 135° central angle?

## In-Class Experiment

In this experiment, you will build a model using your graphing calculator or geometry software. You will compare distance traveled around a circle, the corresponding central angle, and the coordinates of the stopping point.

Follow these steps to build your sketch:

**Step 1** Construct a circle of radius of 1 unit on a coordinate grid.

**Step 2** Add a point at $(1, 0)$. Label it $A$.

**Step 3** Construct another point on the circle. Label it $B$.

**Step 4** Have the software display the coordinates of point $B$.

**Step 5** Have the software display the length of $\widehat{AB}$ (counterclockwise).

**Step 6** Have the software display the degree measure of $\angle AOB$.

Drag point $B$ around the circle, and compare the angle measure to the arc length.

See the TI-Nspire™ Handbook on p. 817 on how to make this sketch. Some geometry software will calculate actual length in inches or centimeters, not in relative units.

## For You to Do

2. What is the maximum $y$-coordinate? For what arc length does it occur?
3. What arc length corresponds to $90°$?
4. What angle corresponds to an arc length of $\frac{7\pi}{4}$?

In general, if $R$ is the arc length, and $D$ is the degree measure of the corresponding angle, then

$$\frac{R}{2\pi} = \frac{D}{360°}$$

## For You to Do

Find the measure of the angle (in degrees) for each of the following arc lengths.

5. $\frac{\pi}{4}$
6. $\frac{4\pi}{3}$
7. $4$

At this point, you have defined the functions cosine and sine in terms of degrees. The input is the angle measure in degrees and the output is a real number. When you set the calculator in **radian** mode, it gives you the cosine and sine as a function of the length of an arc along the circle, rather than of the central angle.

Think of a radian as an arc of length 1 unit. So $\pi$ radians would correspond to a central angle of 180°.

Why think of a different way to define the trig functions? With this new definition, you can think of both input and output as lengths or distances—the same type of measurement. You input the arc distance from (1, 0) of a point on a unit circle. The cosine function outputs the distance of that point from the $y$-axis. The sine function outputs the distance from the $x$-axis.

See the TI-Nspire Handbook on p. 817 for details on how to put your calculator in radian mode.

## Example 2

**Problem** Find $\cos \frac{\pi}{3}$ and $\sin \frac{\pi}{3}$.

**Solution** In the previous example, you saw that an arc of $\frac{\pi}{3}$ on the unit circle corresponds to a 60° angle. You might remember cos 60° and sin 60°, since 60° is one of the angles from a 30–60–90 right triangle. So

$$\cos \frac{\pi}{3} = \cos 60^\circ = \frac{1}{2}, \text{ and}$$

$$\sin \frac{\pi}{3} = \sin 60^\circ = \frac{\sqrt{3}}{2}$$

Since your experience now is mostly with degree measure, you may naturally try to convert any radian measure to degrees to find the sine and cosine. With practice, taking this extra step will be unnecessary. Your ultimate goal is to calculate cosine and sine directly from the arc length.

The cosine and sine functions look the same whether you are in degree or radian mode. The only way to be certain which mode is intended is to look at the argument: sin 30° is different from sin 30. When you see sin $x$, you can assume $x$ is radians unless you are told otherwise.

As Paul walked around the circle, you may have noticed a correspondence between the distance he walked (the length of an arc if he walked less than once around the circle) and the coordinates of his stopping point. Using radian mode on your calculator, you can calculate the coordinates of his stopping point directly from the distance he actually traveled, without converting to degrees.

## For You to Do

Find the exact coordinates of Paul's stopping point after walking each distance.

**8.** exactly $\pi$ meters

**9.** exactly $\frac{\pi}{2}$ meters

**10.** exactly $3\pi$ meters

**11.** exactly $\frac{9\pi}{4}$ meters

# Exercises *Practicing Habits of Mind*

## Check Your Understanding

1. Example 2 showed that $\cos\frac{\pi}{3} = \frac{1}{2}$ and $\sin\frac{\pi}{3} = \frac{\sqrt{3}}{2}$.

   a. The value of $\cos\frac{2\pi}{3}$ is negative, while $\sin\frac{2\pi}{3}$ is positive. What are these values?

   b. Find the values of $\cos\frac{4\pi}{3}$ and $\sin\frac{4\pi}{3}$.

   c. Find the values of $\cos\frac{5\pi}{3}$ and $\sin\frac{5\pi}{3}$.

   d. Find the values of $\cos\frac{6\pi}{3}$ and $\sin\frac{6\pi}{3}$.

2. Find the exact values of $\cos\frac{\pi}{4}$ and $\sin\frac{\pi}{4}$.

3. Copy and complete this table with exact values of cosine and sine. It may help to plot the point $(\cos x, \sin x)$ for each value of $x$.

| $x$ | $\cos x$ | $\sin x$ |
|---|---|---|
| $0$ | ■ | ■ |
| $\frac{\pi}{6}$ | $\frac{\sqrt{3}}{2}$ | $\frac{1}{2}$ |
| $\frac{\pi}{4}$ | ■ | ■ |
| $\frac{\pi}{3}$ | $\frac{1}{2}$ | $\frac{\sqrt{3}}{2}$ |
| $\frac{\pi}{2}$ | ■ | ■ |
| $\frac{2\pi}{3}$ | ■ | ■ |
| $\frac{3\pi}{4}$ | $-\frac{\sqrt{2}}{2}$ | $\frac{\sqrt{2}}{2}$ |
| $\frac{5\pi}{6}$ | ■ | ■ |
| $\pi$ | ■ | ■ |
| $\frac{7\pi}{6}$ | ■ | ■ |
| $\frac{5\pi}{4}$ | ■ | $-\frac{\sqrt{2}}{2}$ |
| $\frac{4\pi}{3}$ | ■ | ■ |
| $\frac{3\pi}{2}$ | $0$ | $-1$ |
| $\frac{5\pi}{3}$ | ■ | ■ |
| $\frac{7\pi}{4}$ | ■ | ■ |
| $\frac{11\pi}{6}$ | $\frac{\sqrt{3}}{2}$ | ■ |
| $2\pi$ | ■ | ■ |
| $\frac{13\pi}{6}$ | ■ | ■ |
| $\frac{9\pi}{4}$ | ■ | ■ |
| $\frac{7\pi}{3}$ | ■ | ■ |

**Habits of Mind**

**Simplify the process.** Look for shortcuts to simplify your work.

**Go Online**
www.successnetplus.com

4. For several different values of $x$, calculate the squares of $\cos x$ and of $\sin x$. How do the two values, $\cos^2 x$ and $\sin^2 x$, relate to each other?

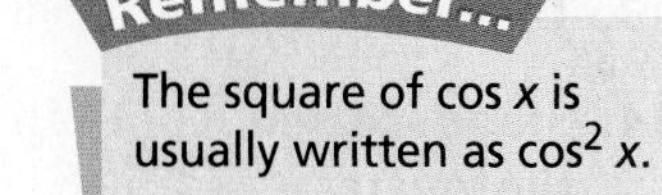


The square of $\cos x$ is usually written as $\cos^2 x$.

5. a. Is there some number $x$ that makes $\cos x = \frac{4}{5}$? Explain.

   b. If $\cos x = \frac{4}{5}$, what could $\sin x$ equal?

6. Which of the following values is greatest?

   A. sin 1  B. sin 2  C. sin 3  D. sin 4

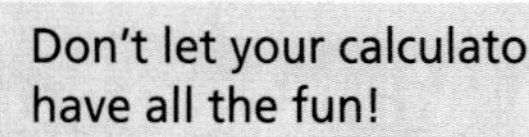

Don't let your calculator have all the fun!

7. Take It Further

   a. Is there an integer $n$ such that $\sin n > 0.999$? Explain.

   b. Is there an integer $n$ such that $\sin n = -1$? Explain.

## On Your Own

8. Locate the point on the unit circle with coordinates $\left(\cos \frac{\pi}{6}, \sin \frac{\pi}{6}\right)$.

9. Explain why $\sin \frac{\pi}{2} = 1$.

10. Simplify the sum $\cos \frac{\pi}{4} + \cos \frac{3\pi}{4} + \cos \frac{5\pi}{4} + \cos \frac{7\pi}{4}$.

11. Suppose $\frac{\pi}{2} < x < \pi$. State whether each of the following is positive or negative.

    a. $\sin x$  b. $\cos x$  c. $\frac{\sin x}{\cos x}$  d. $\cos^2 x + \sin^2 x$

If the length of the arc is between $\frac{\pi}{2}$ and $\pi$, the endpoint will be somewhere in Quadrant II.

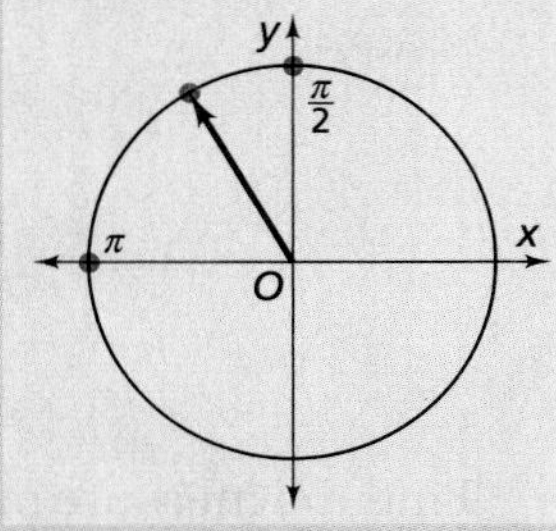


12. What's Wrong Here? Walt can't decide whether sin 5 should be positive or negative.

    Walt says, "I drew a unit circle. Five radians is more than $\pi$, since $\pi$ is just over 3. But 5 is less than $2\pi$. Then 5 radians is somewhere around here:

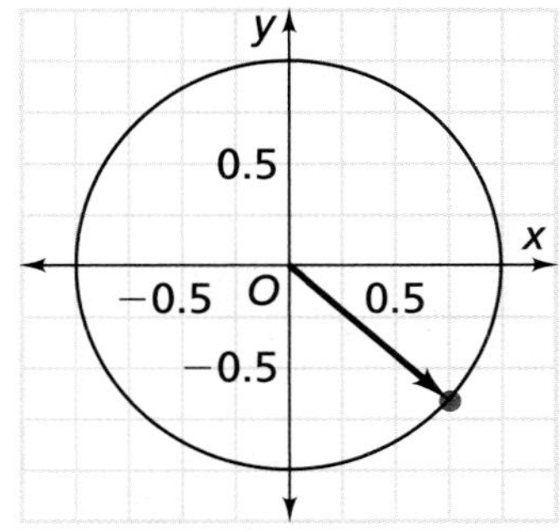


It looks like sin 5 should be negative, but the calculator says that the answer is about 0.087, positive."

Explain what happened. Is Walt right, or is the calculator right?

13. Take It Further Simplify the sum $\cos\frac{2\pi}{5} + \cos\frac{4\pi}{5} + \cos\frac{6\pi}{5} + \cos\frac{8\pi}{5}$.

14. Standardized Test Prep Of the following four cosine values, which is the greatest?

A. $\cos 5.28$ B. $\cos 6.28$ C. $\cos 7.28$ D. $\cos 8.28$

## Maintain Your Skills

15. In the figure below, the angle of the intercepted arc has length equal to the radius.

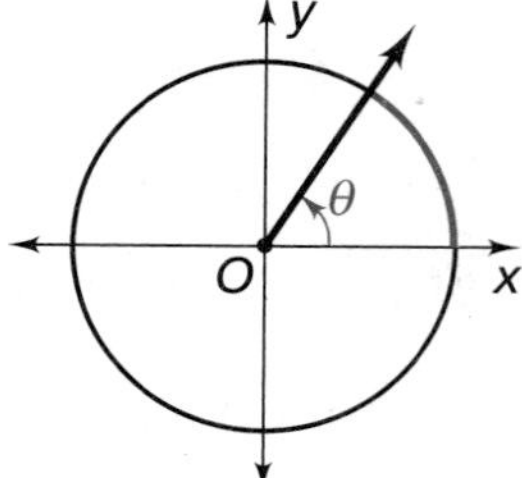


Find the angle to the nearest tenth of a degree.

16. In the figure below, the angle of the intercepted arc has length equal to twice the radius.

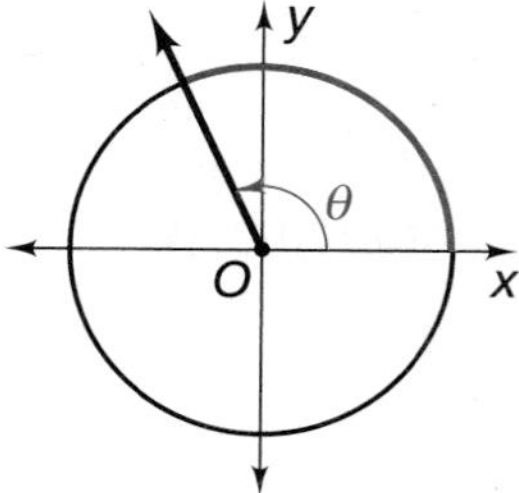


Find the measure of the angle to the nearest tenth of a degree.

# 5.03 Graphing Cosine and Sine Functions

After Paul has moved $\alpha$ meters around his circle of radius 1 meter, he reaches a certain point, $(a, b)$. You can track how $a$ and $b$ change individually as Paul moves around the circle by making a graph.

The following diagram shows a series of arcs of the same unit circle. Each arc starts from the point $(1, 0)$, and ends at some stopping point $(a, b)$. The arc is highlighted, along with the height of the stopping point. That height is, in fact, the same value as the $y$-coordinate of the stopping point, $b$. And $b$ is equal to $\sin \alpha$.

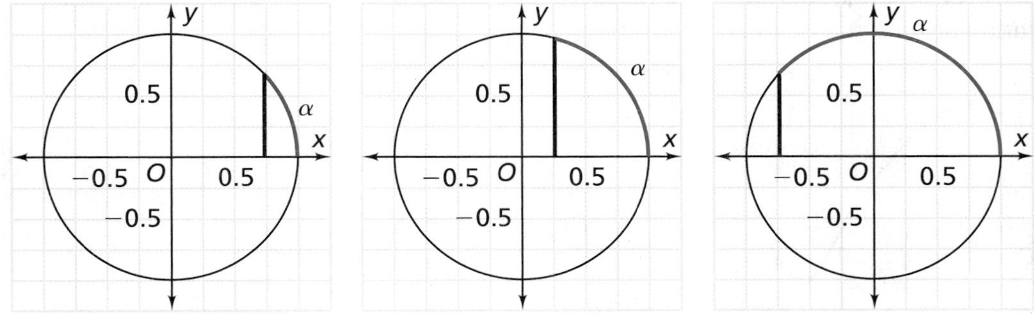


As the value of $\alpha$, the arc length, increases from 0 to $\frac{\pi}{2}$, the $y$-coordinate, or $\sin \alpha$, increases from 0 to 1. Then, as the arc length increases from $\frac{\pi}{2}$ to $\pi$, the sine decreases from 1 to 0. The graph below shows the results for $0 \leq \alpha \leq \pi$.

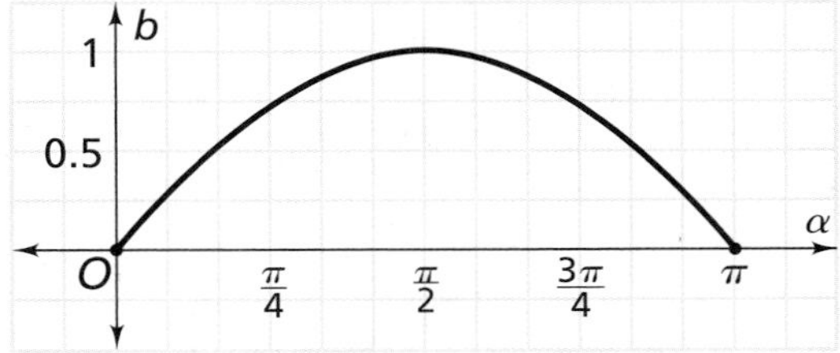

Temporal changes in the height of the sun follow a sine pattern as seen in this time-lapse photograph of the sun's daily cycle from the island of Loppa in Norway, north of the Arctic Circle.

To continue this graph, look at more arcs. As the arc length grows larger than $\pi$, the $y$-coordinate of the stopping point becomes negative.

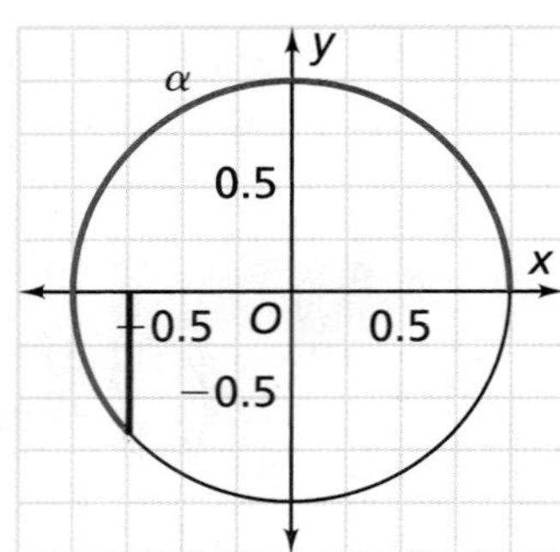


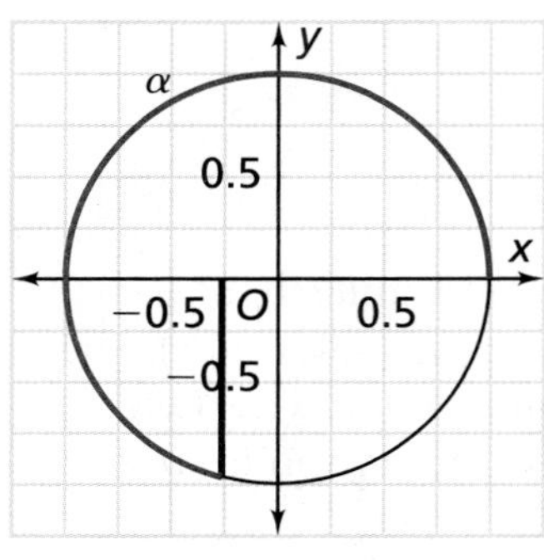


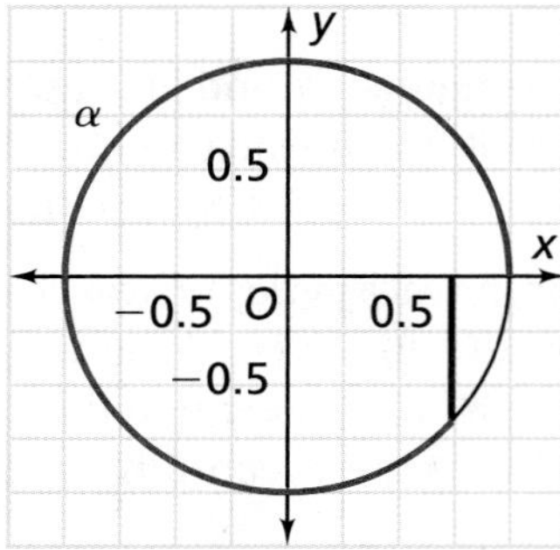


So the sine of arcs that are between $\pi$ and $2\pi$ are all negative. The following graph shows a full rotation around the unit circle.

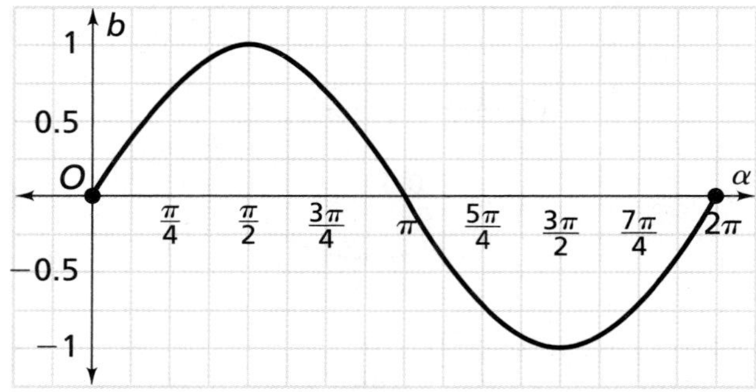


## For You to Do

1. Find all numbers $x$ such that $0 \leq x \leq 2\pi$ and $\sin x = 1$.

After Paul has walked $2\pi$ meters, he has returned to his starting point. If he continues walking, he ends up retracing his earlier steps. For instance, his stopping point is the same when he walks $\frac{\pi}{4}$ meters and when he walks $\frac{9\pi}{4}$ meters.

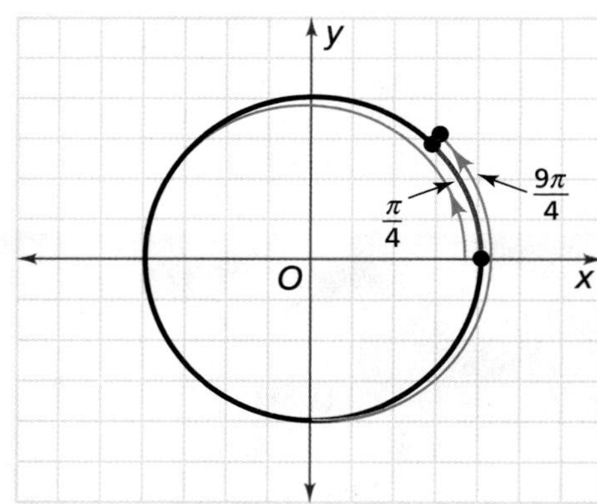

## For You to Do

2. Find 4 values for $x$ such that $\sin x = 1$. Write a general statement in terms of $n$, such that $\sin n\pi = 1$.

The values of $n$ may or may not be integers.

You can generate the graph $a = \cos \alpha$ in a similar manner. As Paul walks from the point $(1, 0)$ to the point $(a, b)$ on his circle, graph the distance he travels $\alpha$ on the horizontal axis and the value of $a$ on the vertical axis. Below is the graph of $a = \cos \alpha$, for domain $0 \leq \alpha \leq 2\pi$.

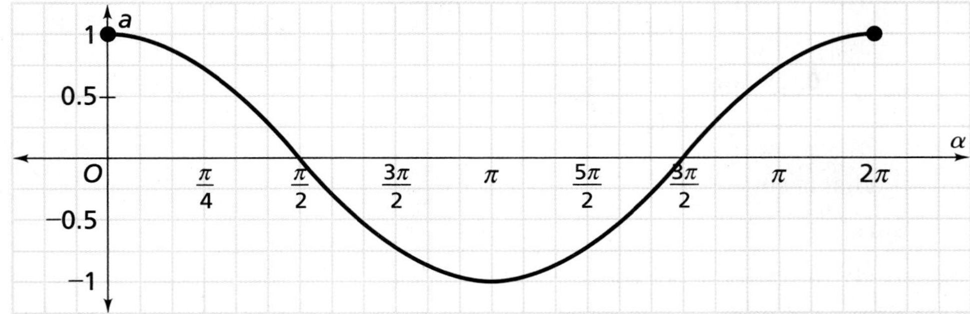


## For Discussion

3. Apply the transformation $x \mapsto x + \frac{\pi}{2}$ to the graph of $y = \cos x$. How does this graph compare to the graph of $y = \sin x$?

You built the graphs for both the cosine and sine functions by observing Paul walking around a circle. Since he only walks around in circles, he will continue to move through the exact same set of points each lap around the circle.

When the outputs of a function, like cosine and sine, repeat in a regular pattern, the function is periodic.

# Exercises Practicing Habits of Mind

## Check Your Understanding

**1.** Starting from standard position, an angle that intercepts an arc of length $\frac{4\pi}{3}$ ends in what quadrant?

**A.** Quadrant I
**B.** Quadrant II
**C.** Quadrant III
**D.** Quadrant IV

**2. a.** If $\cos x = 0.6$, what is $\cos^2 x$? What is $\sin^2 x$?

**b.** Find both possible values of $\sin x$.

**c.** On the unit circle, show the two possible locations where $\cos x = 0.6$.

**3.** On the same axes, sketch the graphs of these two equations.

$$y = \cos x$$
$$y = 0.6$$

Use the graphs to estimate the two solutions to $\cos x = 0.6$ in the interval $0 \le x < 2\pi$.

**4.** You can extend the domain of the cosine and sine functions to include negative values.

For negative values in the domain, think of Paul walking backward, or clockwise, around his circle.

**a.** What should $\cos\left(-\frac{\pi}{2}\right)$ and $\sin\left(-\frac{\pi}{2}\right)$ equal?

**b.** What should $\cos\left(-\frac{\pi}{3}\right)$ and $\sin\left(-\frac{\pi}{3}\right)$ equal?

**5.** Paul and his twin brother Saul follow the instructions from the Getting Started, except Paul moves counterclockwise and Saul moves clockwise. (Assume they walk at the same speed.)

**a.** As Paul and Saul continue, what is the relationship between their $x$-coordinates?

**b.** What is the relationship between Paul and Saul's $y$-coordinates?

**6.** Decide whether each statement is always true. Use what you have learned from Paul and Saul in Exercise 5.

**a.** $\cos(-x) = -\cos x$
**b.** $\cos(-x) = \cos x$
**c.** $\sin(-x) = -\sin x$
**d.** $\sin(-x) = \sin x$

## On Your Own

**7.** Sketch accurate graphs of $y = \cos x$ and $y = \sin x$, where the domain of each is $-2\pi \le x \le 4\pi$.

**Habits of Mind**

**Visualize.** Think about Paul's walk. How many times around the circle would it be from $-2\pi$ to $4\pi$?

8. Paul starts at $(1, 0)$ and walks counterclockwise 24 radians along the unit circle. What quadrant is Paul in?

9. On the unit circle, show the two possible locations where $\sin x = 0.8$.

10. On the same axes, sketch these two graphs.

$$y = \sin x$$
$$y = 0.8$$

Use the graphs to estimate the two solutions to $\sin x = 0.8$ in the interval $0 \le x < 2\pi$.

11. Sketch the graph of the equation.

$$y = \sin\left(x + \frac{\pi}{2}\right)$$

12. Instead of graphing the arc length against the height, Olivia decides to make graphs of Paul's $x$- and $y$-coordinates against time (in seconds).

 a. Suppose Paul walks 1 meter per second. How would Olivia's graph compare to her graph of arc length against the height?

 b. Suppose Paul walks 2 meters per second. How would Olivia's graph compare to the graph from part (a)?

**Go Online**
www.successnetplus.com

13. **Take It Further** Simplify the sum
$\sin \frac{2\pi}{9} + \sin \frac{4\pi}{9} + \sin \frac{\pi}{3} + \cos \frac{\pi}{6} + \cos \frac{13\pi}{18} + \cos \frac{17\pi}{8}$

14. **Standardized Test Prep** Let $x$ be the length of an arc on the unit circle in standard position. In which quadrants can the arc terminate if the product $(\cos x)(\sin x)$ is positive?

 **A.** I and II  **B.** I and III  **C.** I and IV  **D.** II and IV

## Maintain Your Skills

15. Find the corresponding radian measure for each of the following degree values.

 **a.** 30°  **b.** 150°  **c.** 210°  **d.** 330°  **e.** 390°

16. Find the corresponding measure in degrees for each of the following radian values.

 **a.** $\frac{\pi}{3}$ radians  **b.** $\frac{2\pi}{3}$ radians  **c.** $\frac{4\pi}{3}$ radians

 **d.** $\frac{5\pi}{3}$ radians  **e.** $\frac{7\pi}{3}$ radians

**Remember...**

The radian measure is the length of the arc on a unit circle cut by a central angle.

# 5.04 Solving Cosine and Sine Equations

To solve an equation involving a trigonometric function, you begin the same way you begin with an ordinary equation.

## Minds in Action

*Tony and Sasha are trying to solve the equation* $4 \sin x + 5 = 7$, *with x in radians.*

**Tony** I know we want to solve for $x$, but what do we do with $\sin x$?

**Sasha** Let's use the chunking-together technique.

*Sasha goes to the board and covers up the* $\sin x$ *with her hand.*

$$4 \sin x + 5 = 7$$

**Sasha** See? It now looks like it's saying "4 times something plus 5 is 7." That sounds like a simple equation. So, if we let $H$ stand for $\sin x$, we can write the equation as

$$4H + 5 = 7$$

**Tony** I know how to solve that ... $H = \frac{1}{2}$.

**Sasha** Right. And remember, $H$ was just an alias for $\sin x$. So just replace $H$ with $\sin x$ to get the new equation $\sin x = \frac{1}{2}$.

**Tony** And I know how to solve that, too. You just use the $\sin^{-1}$ function and get about 0.52.

Tony typed $\sin^{-1}(0.5)$ into his calculator. His calculator was in radian mode.

**Sasha** We can find the exact answer. Remember, $\frac{1}{2}$ is one of the ratios from a 30–60–90 triangle: $\sin 30^\circ = \frac{1}{2}$.

**Tony** And $30^\circ$ corresponds to $\frac{\pi}{6}$ radians, and $\frac{\pi}{6}$ is about 0.52, the number I got before. So that's it, we're done!

**Sasha** Well, um, no. Look at this:

*Sasha draws on the board.*

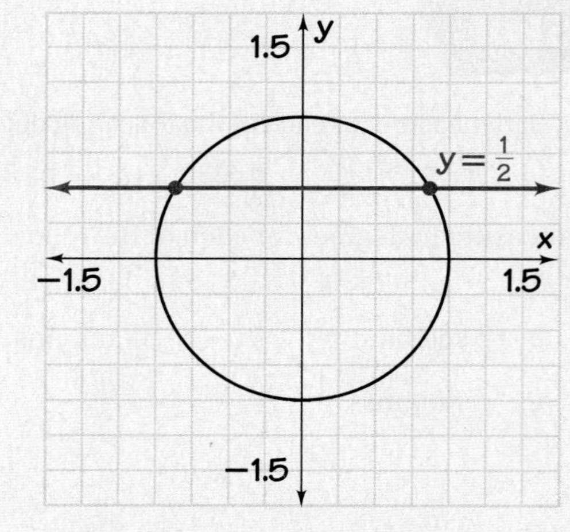

**Sasha** See? Sine is the $y$-coordinate, and there are *two* points on the unit circle whose $y$-coordinate is $\frac{1}{2}$.

**Tony** The point in the first quadrant is the solution we already got, $\frac{\pi}{6}$.

**Sasha** And the other solution is in the second quadrant. It's $\pi - \frac{\pi}{6} = \frac{5\pi}{6}$, which is about 2.62.

**Tony** Okay, so there are two answers. I wonder why the calculator only gave me one. Anyway, is that all?

By the end of this chapter, you will see why the calculator only gave Tony one answer.

**Sasha** That's all we'd find on the unit circle. So we can say at least that that's all between 0 and $2\pi$.

## For You to Do

**1.** Solve $-8 \cos x + 5 = 11$ for $x$ between 0 and $2\pi$ radians.

## Developing Habits of Mind

**Extend the process.** The unit circle makes it clear how many solutions there are between 0 and $2\pi$. But if you lift that restriction, you will find infinitely many solutions to Tony and Sasha's equation.

Since the sine function is periodic, every trip around the circle will uncover two more solutions. Since each trip around the circle adds $2\pi$ to the value of $x$, the new solutions are $\frac{\pi}{6} + 2\pi$ and $\frac{5\pi}{6} + 2\pi$, then $\frac{\pi}{6} + 4\pi$ and $\frac{5\pi}{6} + 4\pi$, and so forth. You can also get solutions going clockwise around the circle: $\frac{\pi}{6} - 2\pi$ and $\frac{5\pi}{6} - 2\pi$ are also solutions.

In the end, there are infinitely many solutions. They are of the form $\frac{\pi}{6} + 2\pi n$ and $\frac{5\pi}{6} + 2\pi n$ for all integer values of $n$.

## For Discussion

**2.** Plot the equations $y = \sin x$ and $y = \frac{1}{2}$ on the same axes. How can you use your graphs to show all the solutions to $\sin x = \frac{1}{2}$?

Your may not actually *see* every solution, but your graph definitely suggests all the solutions.

## Developing Habits of Mind

**Simplify complicated problems.** Use the chunking idea that Sasha used to solve trigonometric equations that look like ordinary algebraic equations. For example, the equation

$$10 \sin^2 x - 3 \sin x = 4$$

is a quadratic equation in $\sin x$. That is, if you let $H = \sin x$, the equation becomes

$$10H^2 - 3H = 4$$

You can solve this equation like any other quadratic. When you find two values for $H$, replace $H$ by $\sin x$ and then solve for $x$.

## For You to Do

**3.** Solve the equation for all $x$, where $0 \leq x < 2\pi$.

$$10 \sin^2 x - 3 \sin x = 4$$

Some trigonometry problems are not explicit equations, but ask you to relate cosine and sine for the same angle.

## Example

**Problem** If $\sin \alpha = 0.4$, find all possible values of $\cos \alpha$.

**Solution** It might help to start with a picture. The figure below shows the two possible points where $\sin \alpha = 0.4$. So the possible values for $\cos \alpha$ will be the $x$-coordinates of those two points, which seem to be about $\pm 0.9$.

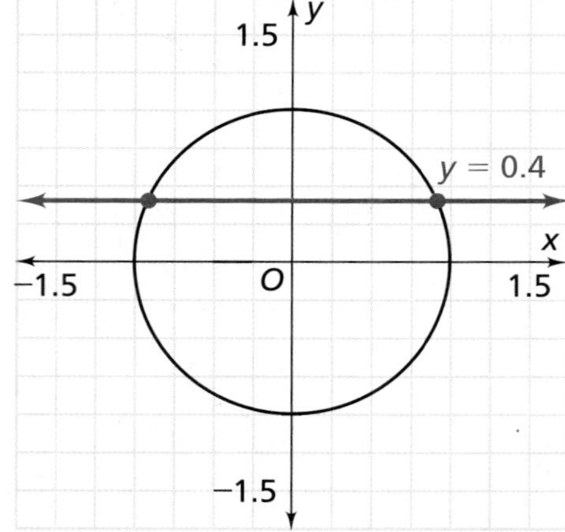


But how do you find the exact answers? You may recall the Pythagorean identity

$$\cos^2 \alpha + \sin^2 \alpha = 1$$

You can use this identity to find the exact answers. Since $\sin x = 0.4$, you have

$$\cos^2 x + (0.4)^2 = 1$$
$$\cos^2 x + 0.16 = 1$$
$$\cos^2 x = 0.84$$
$$\cos x = \pm\sqrt{0.84} = \pm\frac{\sqrt{21}}{5}$$

And $\frac{\sqrt{21}}{5} \approx 0.917$, which is close to the estimate from the graph.

## For You to Do

**4.** If $3\cos x + 4 = 2$, find all possible values of $\sin x$.

## Developing Habits of Mind

**Look for relationships.** When you first saw the identity $\cos^2\theta + \sin^2\theta = 1$, you probably related it to a right triangle.

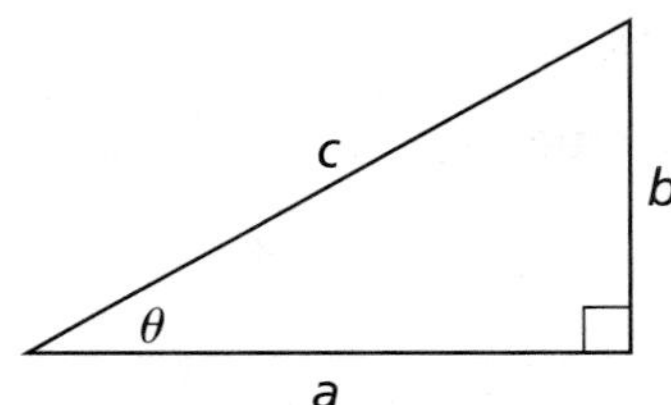


By the Pythagorean Theorem, you know that $a^2 + b^2 = c^2$. You can divide through by $c^2$ to get

$$\left(\frac{a}{c}\right)^2 + \left(\frac{b}{c}\right)^2 = 1$$

If $\theta$ is the angle opposite the side $a$, then $\cos\theta = \frac{a}{c}$ and $\sin\theta = \frac{b}{c}$. Substitution gives you the identity.

Another way to see the identity is to think about the unit circle. An equation for the unit circle is $x^2 + y^2 = 1$. But remember that any point on the circle is $(\cos\theta, \sin\theta)$. Substitute $\cos\theta$ for $x$ and $\sin\theta$ for $y$ and, you get the identity again.

# Exercises Practicing Habits of Mind

## Check Your Understanding

1. If $0 \le x < 2\pi$, find the two possible values of $x$ such that $\sin x = -\frac{1}{2}$.

2. Find all possible values of $x$ so that $\sin x = -\frac{1}{2}$.

3. Suppose $x$ is the length of an arc intercepted by an angle in Quadrant III and $\cos x = -0.65$. Find $\sin x$ to four decimal places.

4. If $\theta$ is degree measure, and $\sin\theta = \sin 50°$, what are all possible values of $\theta$?

5. If $x$ is the length of an arc intercepted by an angle in Quadrant I, and $\sin x = 0.62$, find $\frac{\sin x}{\cos x}$ to two decimal places.

6. Let $0 \le x < 2\pi$. Find a trigonometric equation in $x$ with the given number of solutions.

   **a.** one solution
   **b.** two solutions
   **c.** 0 solutions
   **d.** four solutions
   **e.** six solutions

7. **Take It Further** Find all solutions to this system of equations, if $0 \le \theta \le \pi$ and $0 \le \alpha \le \pi$.

$$4\sin\theta + \cos\alpha = 3$$
$$2\sin\theta + 4\cos\alpha = 5$$

8. **Take It Further** Suppose $\sin x = 2\cos x - 1$.
   Find the two possible values of $\sin x$ if $0 \le x \le 2\pi$.

## On Your Own

9. Find all solutions to the equation.

$$3\sin x + 4 = 0$$

10. **a.** Show, using a unit circle, that $\sin 20° = \sin 160°$.
    **b.** What is the relationship between $\cos 20°$ and $\cos 160°$?

11. If $\theta$ is a degree measure, and $\cos\theta = \cos 50°$, what are all possible values of $\theta$?

12. If $\cos x = \frac{1}{3}$, find both possible values of $\sin x$.

13. If $\cos x = \frac{1}{3}$, find the two possible values of $x$ between 0 and $2\pi$.

14. The value of $\sin 56.3° = 0.832$ to three decimal places.

a. Find all possible angle measures $\theta$, in degrees, for which $\sin \theta = 0.832$.

b. **Take It Further** Find all possible angle measures $\theta$, in degrees, for which $\cos \theta = 0.832$.

15. Find all solutions if $0 \le x < 2\pi$.

$$2 \cos^2 x = \cos x$$

16. **Take It Further** Find all solutions.

$$\cos^2 x + \sin x = 1.$$

17. **Standardized Test Prep** If $\cos x = \frac{5}{13}$, which of the following could be the value of $\sin x$?

A. $\frac{5}{12}$ B. $\frac{5}{13}$ C. $\frac{12}{13}$ D. $\frac{13}{5}$

## Maintain Your Skills

18. Solve each equation if $0 \le x < 2\pi$.

a. $\sin x = \frac{1}{2}$

b. $\sin x = \frac{2}{3}$

c. $\sin x = \frac{5}{3}$

d. $5 \sin x = 4$

e. $3 \sin x + 2 = 0$

f. $3 \sin x - 5 = 0$

g. $(3 \sin x + 2)(3 \sin x - 5) = 0$

The surface of the water intersects the circular paddlewheel in two places. A cross-section view would look similar to the graph of the Example on page 410.

19. Solve each equation if $0 \le x < 2\pi$.

a. $\cos x = \frac{1}{2}$

b. $\cos x = \frac{2}{3}$

c. $\cos x = \frac{5}{3}$

d. $5 \cos x = 4$

e. $3 \cos x + 2 = 0$

f. $3 \cos x - 5 = 0$

g. $(3 \cos x + 2)(3 \cos x - 5) = 0$

# 5.05 Analyzing Graphs—The Sine and Cosine Functions

When you draw the graphs of linear functions, an important property of the graph is the slope of the line. And the most important property of a line is that it has constant slope: pick any two points on the line and calculate the slope between them, and you will always get the same value.

Only lines have constant slope. But you can think about slope for non-linear functions: you can pick any two points on the graph of any function and calculate the slope between them. But those two points can be anywhere on the graph, so the only information you will get is that comparing several calculations of these slopes can tell you that a function is not linear.

To analyze a graph, it is most useful to think of the slope of a curve at a single point. But how do you calculate slope if you are only considering one point?

## In-Class Experiment

In this experiment, you will use your graphing calculator or geometry software to analyze the graph of $y = \sin x$.

Make a figure following these steps.

**Step 1** Draw the graph of $y = \sin x$.

**Step 2** Put two points on the graph. Label them $A$ and $B$. Test to make sure the points are on your graph by dragging them around. You should not be able to move them off of your graph.

**Step 3** Construct the line through points $A$ and $B$.

**Step 4** Measure the slope of $\overleftrightarrow{AB}$.

See the TI–Nspire Handbook on p. 817 for details on how to make this construction.

A line that contains two points of a graph is called a secant line.

Keep point $A$ constant—that will be the point you are analyzing. Move point $B$ slowly toward $A$, observing the slope. Your goal is to estimate the slope of the line when the two points are as close as the software allows you to make them. In some cases, you may get the two points to coincide, making the line and slope disappear. If that happens, move point $B$ off until the line reappears, and record that slope value as your estimate.

## For You to Do

1. Copy and complete the following table by estimating the slope at each value of $x$ to three decimal places. You can use the symmetry of the graph of $f(x) = \sin x$ to help make this task less daunting.

| $x$ | $\sin x$ | Slope |
|---|---|---|
| 0 | 0 | |
| $\frac{\pi}{6}$ | $\frac{1}{2}$ | |
| $\frac{\pi}{4}$ | | |
| $\frac{\pi}{3}$ | $\frac{\sqrt{3}}{2}$ | |
| $\frac{\pi}{2}$ | 1 | |
| $\frac{2\pi}{3}$ | | |
| $\frac{3\pi}{4}$ | $\frac{\sqrt{2}}{2}$ | |
| $\frac{5\pi}{6}$ | | |
| $\pi$ | | |
| $\frac{7\pi}{6}$ | | |
| $\frac{5\pi}{4}$ | $-\frac{\sqrt{2}}{2}$ | |
| $\frac{4\pi}{3}$ | | |
| $\frac{3\pi}{2}$ | $-1$ | |
| $\frac{5\pi}{3}$ | | |
| $\frac{7\pi}{4}$ | | |
| $\frac{11\pi}{6}$ | $-\frac{1}{2}$ | |
| $2\pi$ | 0 | |

When analyzing the graph of $f(x) = \sin x$ or $g(x) = \cos x$, start with inputs like $x = \frac{\pi}{4}$ or $x = \frac{2\pi}{3}$.

As the experiment suggests, you can find the slope of a curve at a particular point $A$ by finding the limit of the slope of a secant $\overleftrightarrow{AB}$, where $B$ is also on the curve, as $B$ gets close to $A$.

A formal definition requires some ideas of calculus that you will see in Chapter 7.

# Exercises Practicing Habits of Mind

## Check Your Understanding

1. When the graph of the sine function reaches a maximum or minimum value, what happens to the slope of its graph there?

2. What are the maximum and minimum values of the slope of the graph of $y = \sin x$, and where does each occur? Could you answer this question by looking at a graph of the sine function?

3. **a.** Zoom in on the graph of $y = \sin x$ near $x = 0$. What specific line does the graph begin to look like?

   **b.** What is the slope of the graph of $\sin x$ at $x = 0$?

4. **a.** By plotting points, sketch the graph of function $s$, where $s(x)$ is the slope of $y = \sin x$ at input $x$.

   **b.** What function most closely matches the values of $s$?

5. **a.** Sketch the graphs of the following two functions on the same axes.

$$d(x) = \cos^2 x - \sin^2 x$$
$$e(x) = \cos^4 x - \sin^4 x$$

   **b.** Take It Further Explain how the functions $d$ and $e$ relate.

## On Your Own

6. **a.** For what value of $x$, where $0 \leq x < 2\pi$, is the function $f(x) = \cos x$ a maximum?

   **b.** For what value of $x$, where $0 \leq x < 2\pi$, is the function $f(x) = \cos x$ a minimum?

   **c.** How do these values compare to the maximums and minimums of the sine function?

7. **a.** For what inputs is the sine function increasing?

   **b.** For what inputs is the sine function decreasing?

   **c.** For what inputs is the cosine function increasing?

A function $f$ is **increasing** on an interval if, for any two values in the interval $a$ and $b$, $a < b$ implies $f(a) < f(b)$.

A function $f$ is **decreasing** on an interval if, for any two values in the interval $a$ and $b$, $a < b$ implies $f(a) > f(b)$.

**8.** A **turning point** for a function is an input $x$ where the function changes from increasing to decreasing, or from decreasing to increasing.

Sometimes the phrase turning point refers instead to the actual coordinates $(x, f(x))$ of the point where this change occurs.

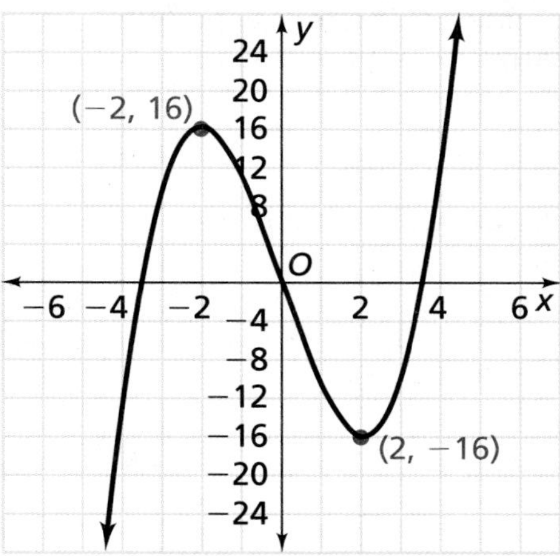


The turning points of $f(x) = x^3 - 12x$ are 2 and −2.

**a.** What inputs are turning points for the sine function?

**b.** What inputs are turning points for the cosine function?

**9.** Repeat the In-Class Experiment on page 414 and Problem 1 on page 415 for the function $g(x) = \cos x$. Then sketch the graph of the function $r$, where $r(x)$ is the slope of $g$ at input $x$. What function matches the table for $r$?

**Go Online**
www.successnetplus.com

**10.** Sketch the graphs of the two functions $a(x) = \cos^2 x$ and $b(x) = \sin^2 x$ on the same axes.

**11.** Without graphing, describe the shape of the graph of $c(x) = a(x) + b(x)$, where $a(x)$ and $b(x)$ are the functions in Exercise 10.

**12.** Take it Further Sketch a reasonably accurate graph of $k(x) = 2^{\sin x}$.

**13.** Standardized Test Prep Given $0 < a < b < 17$, which of the following is the maximum value of $a \sin x + b$?

**A.** $a + b$ **B.** $b - a$ **C.** $-(a + b)$ **D.** 17

## Maintain Your Skills

**14.** Sketch the graph of each equation on the interval $0 \le x \le 2\pi$ and find the maximum and minimum.

The **maximum** of a graph is the highest value achieved on the vertical axis. The **minimum** of a graph is the lowest.

**a.** $y = 5 \sin x$

**b.** $y = 5 \sin x + 7$

**c.** $y = 5 \sin x - 7$

**d.** $y = 10 \sin x + 5$

**e.** $y = A \sin x + B$

**In this investigation, you learned what radians are and how they relate to degrees. You graphed the cosine and sine functions. You solved equations involving these trigonometric functions. The following questions will help you summarize what you have learned.**

1. a. What angle measure corresponds to $\frac{9\pi}{2}$ radians?
   b. For what value of $x$, where $0 \le x < 2\pi$, will both $\cos x = \cos \frac{9\pi}{2}$ and $\sin x = \sin \frac{9\pi}{2}$?
2. a. On a unit circle, locate approximately the point with coordinates $(\cos 3, \sin 3)$.
   b. Estimate the values of $\cos 3$ and $\sin 3$.
   c. Use a calculator to find the values of $\cos 3$ and $\sin 3$ to four decimal places.
3. a. Using a unit circle, identify the places where cosine and sine are equal.
   b. Find all angle measures $\theta$, where $0 \le \theta < 2\pi$, such that $\cos \theta = \sin \theta$.
4. Using the graphs of cosine and sine on the interval $0 \le x < 2\pi$, find all values of $x$ such that $\cos x = \sin x$.
5. Find all solutions if $0 \le x < 2\pi$.
$$\sin x \cos x - 2 \sin x = \sin x$$
6. Where are the turning points of the cosine and sine functions?
7. What is a radian?
8. How can you use a graph of $y = \sin x$ to estimate solutions to the equation $\sin x = -0.6$?

## Vocabulary

In this investigation, you learned these terms. Make sure you understand what each one means and how to use it.

- **arc**
- **central angle**
- **decreasing**
- **increasing**
- **Pythagorean identity**
- **radian**
- **secant line**
- **turning point**

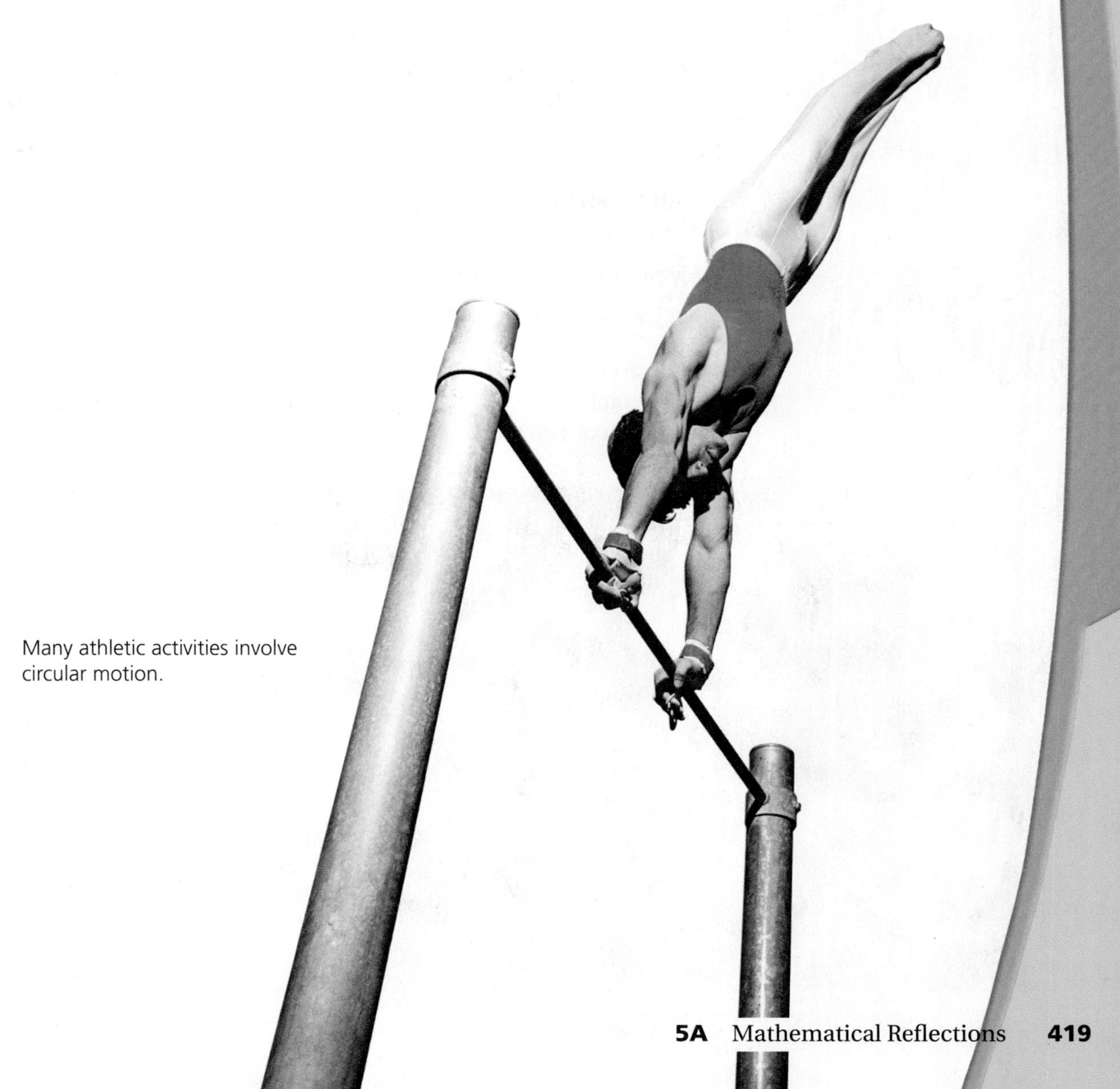

Many athletic activities involve circular motion.

# Sinusoidal Functions and Their Graphs

In *Sinusoidal Functions and Their Graphs*, you will graph translations and dilations of the cosine and sine functions. You will learn how to relate the graphs to the parameters in the sinusoidal forms $A\cos(ax + b) + B$ and $A\sin(ax + b) + B$. You will relate these functions to everyday periodic behavior.

**By the end of this investigation, you will be able to answer questions like these.**

1. Given the maximum and minimum values of a cosine or sine function, how do you find the amplitude and vertical displacement?
2. How can you make a sinusoidal function that has a specific period?
3. How can you use sinusoidal functions to model periodic phenomena?

**You will learn how to**

- make sense of sinusoidal functions in the context of previous experience
- understand the geometry of sinusoidal functions
- model with sinusoidal functions

**You will develop these habits and skills:**

- See the graph of $y = A\sin(ax + b) + B$ is simply a transformation of the basic graph of $y = \sin x$.

The minimum value of a sinusoidal curve that models the height of the tide represents the height of low tide.

# 5.06 Getting Started

As you work though these problems, make sure to write down any conjectures you have about trigonometric functions and their graphs.

## For You to Explore

1. Suppose $f(x) = \sin x$. For each function below, sketch its graph and the graph of $y = f(x)$ on the interval $-\pi \leq x \leq 2\pi$. Describe how the two graphs relate to each other.

   a. $f(2x) = \sin 2x$
   b. $f(3x) = \sin 3x$
   c. $f(4x) = \sin 4x$
   d. $f(10x) = \sin 10x$

See the TI-Nspire Handbook on p. 817 for ideas about how to graph each function.

2. Let $f(x) = \sin x$ as in Problem 1. For each function below, sketch its graph and the graph of $y = f(x)$ on the interval $-\pi \leq x \leq 2\pi$. Describe how the two graphs relate to each other.

   a. $2f(x) = 2 \sin x$
   b. $5f(x) = 5 \sin x$
   c. $\frac{1}{3}f(x) = \frac{1}{3} \sin x$
   d. $-3f(x) = -3 \sin x$

3. Let $g(x) = \cos x$. Sketch the graph of $g(x)$ on the interval $-\pi \leq x \leq 2\pi$ along with the graph of each of these functions. Describe how the two graphs relate to each other.

   a. $g(x) + 1 = \cos x + 1$
   b. $g(x) - 2 = \cos x - 2$
   c. $g(x + 1) = \cos(x + 1)$
   d. $g(x - 2) = \cos(x - 2)$

Note the change in order of operations. Add 1, then take the cosine of the result. As usual, use radians unless the degree symbol is present.

4. Sketch the graph of each function.

   a. $A(x) = 3\cos x$
   b. $B(x) = 3\cos x - 2$
   c. $C(x) = 3\cos(x - 2)$
   d. $D(x) = 2\sin(x + 1) + 2$

5. Find two functions that have graphs that pass through the point $\left(\frac{\pi}{2}, 4\right)$.

6. The function $f(x) = \sin x$ has period $2\pi$. Find a function in the form $h(x) = \sin ax$ with the following period.

   a. period $\pi$
   b. period $\frac{\pi}{2}$
   c. period $4\pi$
   d. period 2
   e. period 1
   f. period 17

**Remember...**

The *period* of a periodic function is the least positive number $p$ so that $f(x + p) = f(x)$ always. On a graph, it is where the function begins to repeat itself.

7. **Take It Further** Determine the number of intersections of the graphs of the following two equations.

$$y = \sin x$$

$$y = \frac{x}{10}$$

## Exercises Practicing Habits of Mind

### On Your Own

**8.** Find a solution to this equation.

$$6\cos(\pi(x-1)) + 2 = 5$$

Exercises 9 through 12 refer to the graph and function below.

$$H(t) = 36\cos\left(\frac{2\pi}{60}t\right) + 39$$

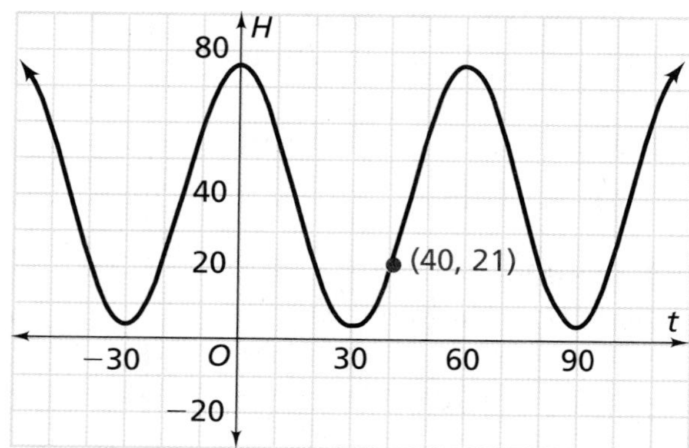


**9.** Use the graph of $H$ to answer these questions.

**a.** What is the maximum possible output of $H$?

**b.** What is the minimum possible output of $H$?

**c.** What is the period of $H$?

**10. a.** What appears to be the average value of $H$?

**b.** How far is it from the average value of $H$ to the maximum?

**c.** How far is it from the average value of $H$ to the minimum?

**11.** According to the graph, $H(40) = 21$.

**a.** Using the symmetry of the graph, find the one positive value of $t < 40$ with $H(t) = 21$.

**b.** Use the period of this function to find the next two values of $t$ with $H(t) = 21$.

**12. a.** Find a value of $t$, that makes $H(t) = 55$. In other words, find a solution to the equation

$$55 = 36 \cos\left(\frac{2\pi}{60}t\right) + 39$$

Round your answer to two decimal places.

**b.** Find the next two larger values of $t$ with $H(t) = 55$.

## Maintain Your Skills

**13.** Copy and complete this table. Each column is a new instance of the variables $D$ and $A$.

| $D + A$ | | | 23 | 46 | 100 | 75 | −10 | $x$ |
|---|---|---|---|---|---|---|---|---|
| $D$ | 7 | −5 | 10 | 20 | | | | |
| $A$ | 3 | 7 | | | | | | |
| $D - A$ | | | | | 40 | 3 | −32 | $y$ |

Sinusoidal patterns are common in the natural world.

# 5.07 Sinusoidal Functions—Amplitude, Period, Phase Shift

Unlike polynomials, trigonometric functions are periodic. For example, cosine and sine are periodic with period $2\pi$. For any real number $x$

$$\cos(x + 2\pi) = \cos x \quad \text{and} \quad \sin(x + 2\pi) = \sin x$$

Because they are periodic, you can use them to model many periodic phenomena like the height of a rider as a Ferris wheel turns or the heights of the tides in the ocean as the day progresses. Actually, you can not model physical situations well directly simply by using cosine and sine. You need a wider class of functions that you could call *sinusoidal.*

**Habits of Mind**

**Recognize periodicity.** This is a direct consequence of the definition of cosine and sine and the way you extended the definition from acute angles to any angle and then from angles to radians. Look back at the definitions in Investigation 5A.

### Definition

A **sinusoidal function** is a function that is defined by a formula of the form

$$f(x) = A\cos(ax + b) + B \text{ or } f(x) = A\sin(ax + b) + B$$

where $A$, $B$, $a$, and $b$ are real numbers.

As you will see in this investigation, if you model a function with one of these formulas, you can also model the function with the other formula.

Look at an example.

## Example

**Problem** Let

$$H(x) = 36\cos\left(2x - \frac{\pi}{3}\right) + 39$$

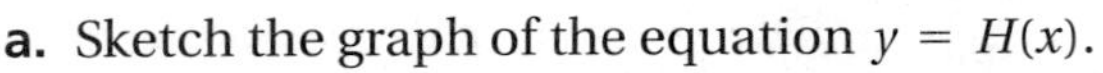

**a.** Sketch the graph of the equation $y = H(x)$.

**b.** What appears to be the average value of $H$?

**c.** How far is it from the average value of $H$ to the maximum?

**d.** How far is it from the average value of $H$ to the minimum?

**e.** What is the period of $H$?

**Solution**

**a.** First, rewrite the equation

$$y = 36\cos\left(2x - \frac{\pi}{3}\right) + 39$$

as

$$\frac{y - 39}{36} = \cos\left(2x - \frac{\pi}{3}\right)$$

Then let

$$M = 2x - \frac{\pi}{3} \text{ and } N = \frac{y - 39}{36}$$

Upon making these substitutions, you have

$$N = \cos M$$

Its graph appears below.

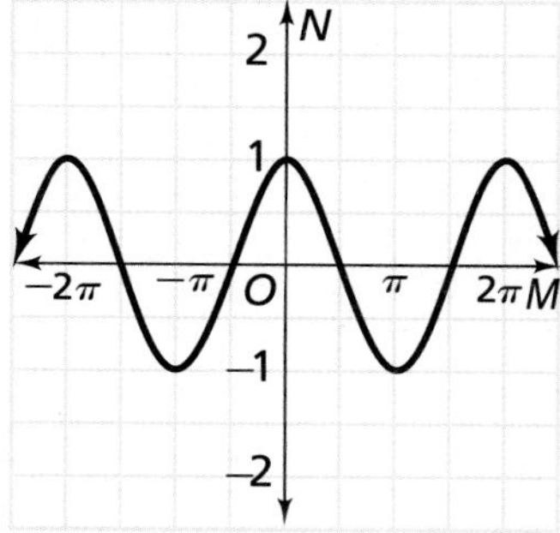


Since

$$M = 2x - \frac{\pi}{3}$$

$$= 2\left(x - \frac{\pi}{6}\right)$$

you have

$$x = \frac{M}{2} + \frac{\pi}{6}$$

And below is a pair of number lines depicting the relationship between $M$ and $x$.

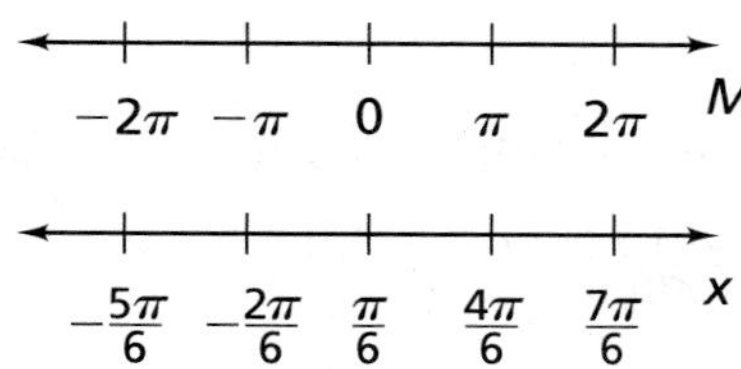


Likewise, $N = \frac{y - 39}{36}$ implies

$$y = 36N + 39$$

which gives the following pair of number lines relating $N$ and $y$.

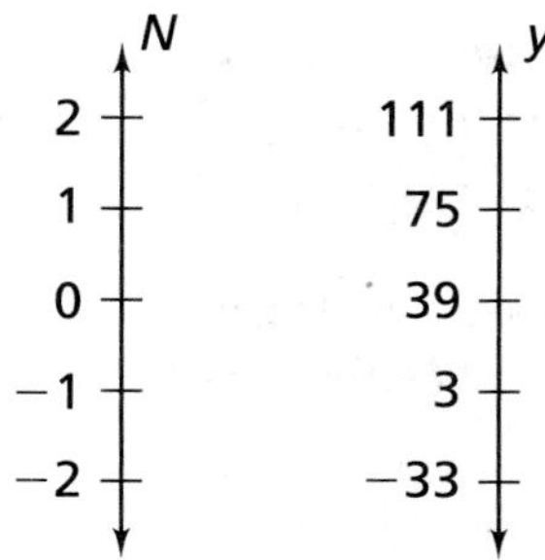


Finally, take the graph of $N = \cos M$ and

- replace the $M$-axis with the $x$-axis.
- replace the $N$-axis with the $y$-axis.

The resulting graph appears below.

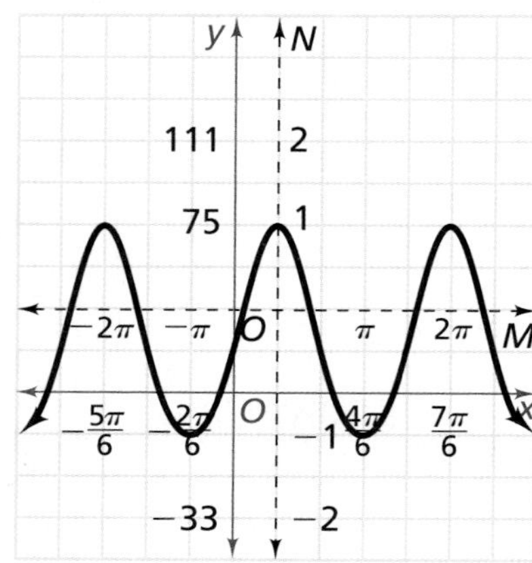


**b.** The horizontal dotted line, which is the graph of the equation $y = 39$, tells you that the average value of $H$ is 39.

**c.** The maximum value of $H$ occurs when $\cos M = 1$. The maximum is

$$36 \cdot 1 + 39 = 75$$

Thus, the distance from the average value to the maximum is

$$75 - 39 = 36$$

**d.** The minimum value of $H$ occurs where $\cos M = -1$.
The minimum is 3. Thus, the distance from the average value to the minimum is

$$39 - 3 = 36$$

You could also use the graph of $H$ to see the values of the maximum and minimum.

**e.** Pick the point $\left(\frac{\pi}{6}, 75\right)$ as a reference point. The graph of $y = H(x)$ starts to repeat itself at $\left(\frac{7\pi}{6}, 75\right)$. Thus, the period of $H$ is

$$\frac{7\pi}{6} - \frac{\pi}{6} = \pi$$

Note that the average value is equidistant to the maximum and the minimum.

**Remember...**

You can find the period by looking for where the graph begins to repeat itself.

The following definitions introduce some new terms that describe the characteristics of the graph of a sinusoidal function.

## Definitions

**Let $f$ be a sinusoidal function.**

**The vertical displacement of $f$ is its average value. More precisely, it is the average of the maximum and the minimum values of $f$.**

**The amplitude of $f$ is the distance from its average value to the maximum or the minimum value.**

Note that the amplitude is always positive.

## For You to Do

1. Find the amplitude and the vertical displacement of

$$H(x) = 36\cos\left(2x - \frac{\pi}{3}\right) + 39$$

2. Find the amplitude and the vertical displacement of

$$g(x) = 5\sin 2x - 7$$

3. Find the amplitude and the vertical displacement of

$$f(x) = A\cos(ax + b) + B$$

The amplitude and the vertical displacement of

$$f(x) = A\cos(ax + b) + B \text{ or } f(x) = A\sin(ax + b) + B$$

describe how the graph of $f$ relates to the graph of $N = \sin M$. More specifically, they describe how you transform the graph of $N = \sin M$ vertically to obtain the graph of $y = f(x)$. The next two concepts deal with how you transform the graph of $N = \sin M$ horizontally to obtain the graph of a sinusoidal function.

## Minds in Action

*Derman and Tony are working on Exercise 6 on page 421.*

**Derman** Okay, we need a function $h(x) = \sin ax$ with period $\pi$.

**Tony** Well, $f(x) = \sin x$ has period $2\pi$ and the graph of $y = f(2x)$ is the same as the graph of $y = f(x)$, except it's shrunk horizontally by the factor $\frac{1}{2}$.

**Derman** So the period of $f(2x) = \sin 2x$ is half of $2\pi$, which is $\pi$.

**Tony** Right. How about a function $h(x) = \sin ax$ with period 2?

**Derman** We'd want it to shrink by the factor of , I think, 1 over $\pi$?

**Tony** That looks good. I guess it would be $f(\pi x) = \sin \pi x$.

**Derman** Fine, but what about this period 17? That seems tougher.

**Tony** It is. But I think you can use the one with period 2. So we could scale it by $\frac{1}{\pi}$ then adjust the coefficient to become 17.

**Derman** What?

**Tony** Instead of scaling by $\frac{1}{\pi}$, we could scale by $\frac{17}{2\pi}$.

$$f\left(\frac{2\pi}{17}x\right) = \sin\frac{2\pi}{17}x$$

**Derman** I put that in the calculator and it worked great! I bet we could do this for any period $P$ by replacing the 17.

**Tony** Yes. I think that works. We want to scale the graph of $y = f(x)$ horizontally by a factor of $\frac{P}{2\pi}$. So the function would be

$$f\left(\frac{2\pi}{P}x\right) = \sin\frac{2\pi}{P}x$$

**Derman** And that has period $P$.

## For Discussion

**4.** In terms of $a$, find the period of the sinusoidal function

$$f(x) = \sin ax$$

**5.** Find the period of the sinusoidal function

$$f(x) = A\sin(ax + b) + B$$

**6.** Find a sinusoidal function with period 3.

Finally, compare the graphs of

$$y = \cos x \text{ and } y = \cos\left(x - \frac{\pi}{6}\right)$$

which appears below.

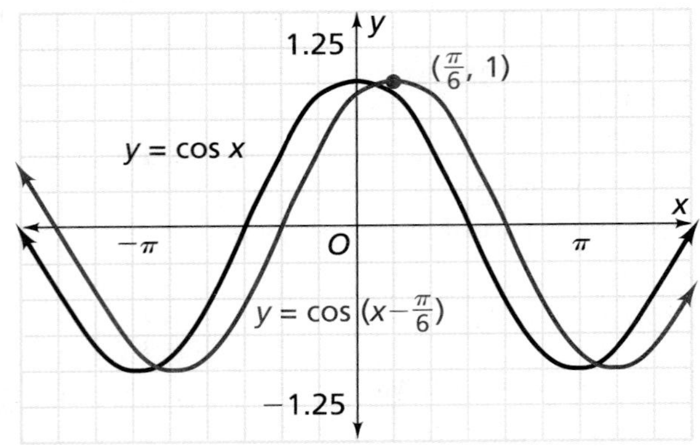


To obtain the graph of $y = \cos\left(x - \frac{\pi}{6}\right)$, shift the graph of $y = \cos x$ to the right by $\frac{\pi}{6}$ units. Thus, the function $y = \cos\left(x - \frac{\pi}{6}\right)$ has a phase shift of $\frac{\pi}{6}$. Here is the precise definition.

> Phase shift is positive because you shifted the graph of $y = \cos x$ to the right.

### *Definition*

**Let**

$$f(x) = A\cos(ax + b) + B \text{ or } f(x) = A\sin(ax + b) + B$$

**be a sinusoidal function. The phase shift of $f$ is the amount of horizontal translation required to obtain the graph of $y = f(x)$ from the graph of**

$$y = A\cos ax \text{ or } y = A\sin ax$$

## For You to Do

**7.** Consider again the function

$$H(x) = 36 \cos\left(2x - \frac{\pi}{3}\right) + 39$$

What is its phase shift? Explain your reasoning.

## Exercises Practicing Habits of Mind

### Check Your Understanding

**1.** Here is the graph of a sinusoidal function $f$.

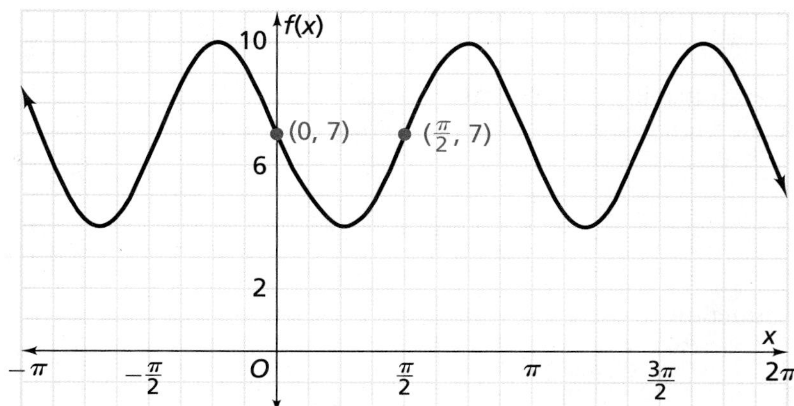


**a.** Find the amplitude and vertical displacement of $f$.

**b.** Find the period of $f$.

**c.** If you write $f$ as a cosine, find a value for the phase shift. (There is more than one possible answer.)

**d.** Write $f$ in the form

$$f(x) = A \cos(ax + b) + B$$

that could generate this graph.

Some of the values of $A$, $B$, $a$, and $b$ might be negative.

**2.** Find a function in the form

$$f(x) = A \sin(ax + b) + B$$

that generates the graph in Exercise 1.

3. **Take It Further** It is possible to write a function that generates the graph in Exercise 1 with no phase shift. How?

4. **a.** Find one solution to the equation $4 \cos 2x + 3 = 5$.

   **b.** Sketch the graph of $y = 4 \cos 2x + 3$. Show how you could use this graph to locate solutions to the equation $4 \cos 2x + 3 = 5$.

   **c.** Find all solutions to the equation $4 \cos 2x + 3 = 5$.

See TI-Nspire Handbook on p. 817 for ideas about how to use a CAS to solve equations like this.

5. Consider the function

$$g(x) = 13 \sin (4x - \pi) + 10$$

   **a.** Show that $\left(\frac{\pi}{4}, 10\right)$ must be on the graph of $g$.

   **b.** Find the amplitude and vertical displacement of $g$.

   **c.** Find the maximum and minimum of $g$.

   **d.** Find the period of $g$.

   **e.** Sketch the graph of $y = g(x)$.

6. **a.** Sketch the graph of $h(x) = \cos^2 x$.

   **b.** Assume this function is sinusoidal. Find its amplitude, vertical displacement, and period.

You will probably have to enter this as $(\cos x)^2$ on the calculator.

7. The graph of $h(x) = \cos^2 x$ appears sinusoidal. Use your results from Exercise 6 to write another expression for $\cos^2 x$ in the form $A \cos ax + B$.

## On Your Own

8. Here is the graph of a sinusoidal function.

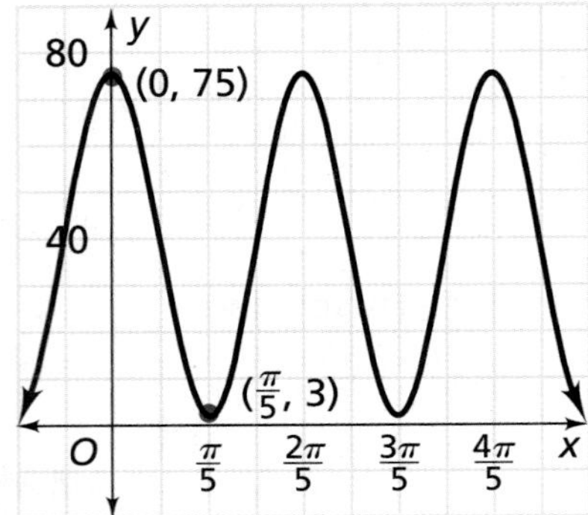


   **a.** Find the amplitude and vertical displacement of this function.

   **b.** Find the period of this function.

   **c.** Explain why you can write this function as a cosine with no phase shift.

   **d.** Write a function in the form $f(x) = A \cos ax + B$ that could generate this graph.

9. **a.** Show that for all numbers $x$, $\sin\left(x + \frac{\pi}{2}\right) = \cos x$

**b.** Graph the equations $y = \sin\left(x + \frac{\pi}{2}\right)$ and $y = \cos x$ on the same axes.

10. Here is the graph of $g(x) = \cos x \sin x$, the product of the cosine and sine functions.

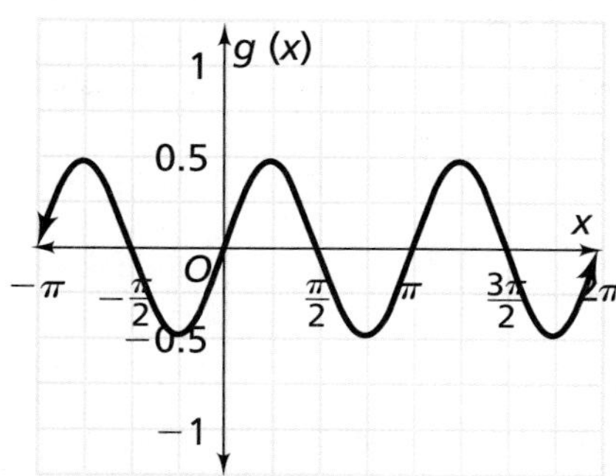

Assume that $g$ is sinusoidal. Find its amplitude, vertical displacement, and period.

11. The graph of $g(x) = \cos x \sin x$ appears sinusoidal. Use your results from Exercise 10 to write another expression for $\cos x \sin x$ in the form

$$\cos x \sin x = A \sin ax + B$$

12. What is the period of the sinusoidal function $f(x) = A \sin(ax + b) + B$?

13. Consider the function

$$h(x) = 20 \cos\left(\frac{2\pi}{7}(x - 4)\right) + 26$$

Evaluate each of these.

**a.** $h(4)$ **b.** $h(11)$ **c.** $h(18)$ **d.** $h(-3)$

**e.** Function $h$ is periodic. What is its period?

14. Write an equation for a sinusoidal function with period 5.

15. **Standardized Test Prep** Which of the following represents the average value of the function $f(x) = A\cos(B(x - C)) + D$?

**A.** $A$ **B.** $B$ **C.** $C$ **D.** $D$

## Maintain Your Skills

16. Write an equation for a sinusoidal function with each given period.

**a.** $\pi$ **b.** $4\pi$

**c.** $10\pi$ **d.** $n\pi$, $n \neq 0$

# 5.08 Applying Trigonometric Functions

In this lesson, you will study some applications of sinusoidal functions. Sinusoidal functions model many phenomena in the world, such as the Ferris wheel, the heights of tides, and lengths of days over the course of a year.

## For Discussion

1. Suppose $f(t)$ describes the height of a person on a Ferris wheel after some time $t$. Based on what you know about how cosine and sine functions are defined using the unit circle, explain why $f(t)$ must be a sinusoidal function.

Remember Paul and Saul from Investigation 5A? Well, their younger brother Gaul also walks around a circle, but a much larger one with a radius of 36 feet. Gaul starts at the point $(36, 0)$ and walks counterclockwise. He takes only 60 seconds to travel one lap around the circle.

The center of the circle is at the origin.

## Example 1

**Problem**

**a.** Find an equation for the function $h(t)$ that describes Gaul's $x$-coordinate after $t$ seconds.

**b.** Suppose instead that the center of the circle is at the point $(39, 0)$. Find an equation for $h(t)$ and sketch its graph.

**Solution**

**a.** Since Gaul's circle is the unit circle scaled by a factor of 36, the definition of the cosine function implies

$$h(t) = 36 \cos (at)$$

for some parameter $a$. You saw in the last lesson that

$$a = \frac{2\pi}{P}$$

where $P$ is the period of $h$. Since it takes Gaul 60 seconds to make one revolution, you have $P = 60$. Therefore, $a = \frac{2\pi}{60}$ and you have

$$h(t) = 36 \cos \left( \frac{2\pi}{60} t \right)$$

Given a real number $t$, locate the point on the unit circle that is at an angle $t$ radians (measured counter-clockwise from the positive $x$-axis). By definition, this point has coordinates $(\cos t, \sin t)$.

**b.** If you were to locate the center of the circle at (39, 0). Gaul's $x$-coordinate simply increases by 39 units at every point on his path. Therefore, you have

What happens to his $y$-coordinates?

$$h(t) = 36 \cos\left(\frac{2\pi}{60} t\right) + 39$$

Its graph appears below.

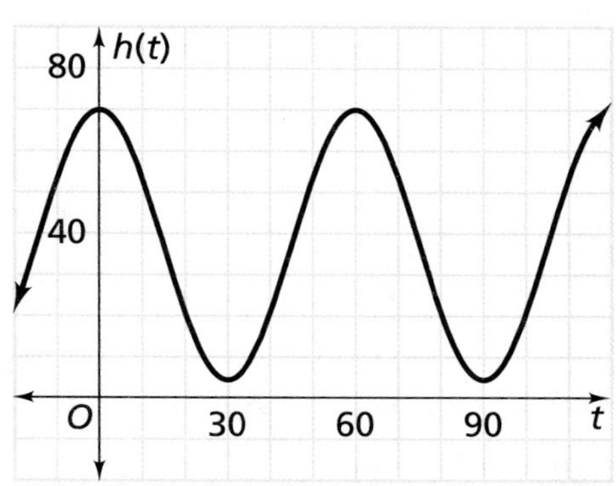


Now consider a Ferris wheel with the following specifications.

- It makes a full revolution every 60 seconds.
- Its maximum height is 75 feet.
- Its minimum height is 3 feet.

Then the center of the Ferris wheel must be at the average of the maximum and the minimum heights.

$$\frac{1}{2}(75 + 3) = 39$$

or 39 feet. The radius of the wheel must be the difference of the maximum height and the average value.

$$75 - 39 = 36$$

Or $39 - 3 = 36$ feet.

or 36 feet. Let $H(t)$ denote the height of a person on this Ferris wheel $t$ seconds after he or she is at the highest point of the wheel.

## For Discussion

**2.** Explain why

$$H(t) = 36 \cos\left(\frac{2\pi}{60} t\right) + 39$$

In other words, explain why $H(t)$ equals the function describing Gaul's $x$-coordinate when his circle has center at (39, 0).

## Developing Habits of Mind

**Think about it another way.** You took a rather rigorous approach to finding an equation for $H(t)$, starting from the unit circle definition of the cosine function. In practice, you often skip these steps and conclude that the height of a person on a Ferris wheel must be sinusoidal because moving around the wheel is like moving around the unit circle.

So, you could write

$$H(t) = A\cos(at + b) + B$$

and proceed to find the parameters $A$, $B$, $a$, and $b$. From the analysis of the Ferris wheel, you can deduce the following

- The amplitude of $H(t)$ equals the radius of the wheel, and thus $A = 36$.
- The vertical displacement of $H(t)$ is the height of the center of the wheel. Therefore $B = 39$.
- The period of $H(t)$ is 60 and so $a = \frac{2\pi}{60}$.
- $H(t)$ assumes its maximum value when $t = 0$. And since you are modeling $H(t)$ using a cosine function, which also assumes its maximum value at $t = 0$, there is no need for horizontal translation. Thus, the phase shift is zero and so $b = 0$.

Therefore, conclude that

$$H(t) = 36\cos\left(\frac{2\pi}{60}t\right) + 39$$

Note that although you could have chosen a sine wave instead, there would be a phase shift involved. Knowing the behavior of the function can help you decide whether to choose a cosine or sine form.

The model comes directly from the geometry of the situation. Here, the person riding the Ferris wheel is moving around a circle, so the definition of cosine and sine dictate that their height over time should be modeled by a sinusoidal function.

**Remember...**

Circular behavior is often the underlying cause of a sinusoidal function.

You could have also written $H(t) = A\sin(at + b) + B$.

Recall that $t = 0$ when the person is at the peak of the wheel.

## For You to Do

3. Consider again the Ferris wheel from the discussion above, but this time, suppose you model it with a sine function—in other words, write

$$H(t) = A\sin(at + b) + B.$$

Find the values of the parameters $A$, $B$, $a$, and $b$.

You can model many phenomena occurring in nature with sinusoidal functions. For example, consider the example of the tide, the periodic rise and fall of the sea level caused by the gravitational pull of the moon. Observations show that when you graph the height of the tide as a function of time, the resulting graph is approximately a sinusoidal curve.

## Example 2

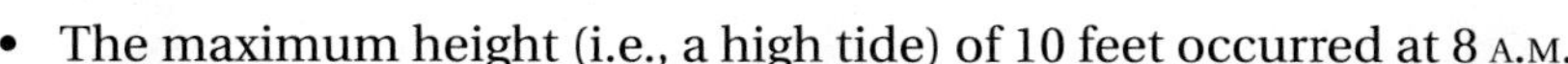

**Problem** Suppose you have the following information about the height of the tide in a particular region.

- The maximum height (i.e., a high tide) of 10 feet occurred at 8 A.M.
- The minimum height (i.e., a low tide) measured 6 feet.
- On average, high tides occur about every 12.4 hours (i.e., 12 hours and 24 minutes).

Assuming that the height of the tide is a sinusoidal function, find the equation for $H(t)$, the height of the tide $t$ hours after midnight.

> The period of the tide depends mostly on the earth's rotation and the moon's orbit around the earth. If the moon never moved, the period of the tide would be 12 hours, but the moon moves in its orbit a little over that time. Note that it is an underlying circular motion that is responsible for the sinusoidal tide.

**Solution** Since you are assuming that $H$ is a sinusoidal function, write

$$H(t) = A\cos(at + b) + B$$

and proceed to find the parameters $A$, $B$, $a$, and $b$.

The average height of the tide is

$$\frac{1}{2}(10 + 6) = 8$$

or 8 feet, and thus the vertical displacement of $H$ is $B = 8$. Moreover, the amplitude of $H$ is

$$10 - 8 = 2$$

> Or $8 - 6 = 2$.

That is, $A = 2$. Since $H$ has period $P = 12.4$, you have

$$a = \frac{2\pi}{12.4}$$

Now consider the function

$$f(t) = 2\cos\left(\frac{2\pi}{12.4}t\right) + 8$$

whose graph appears below.

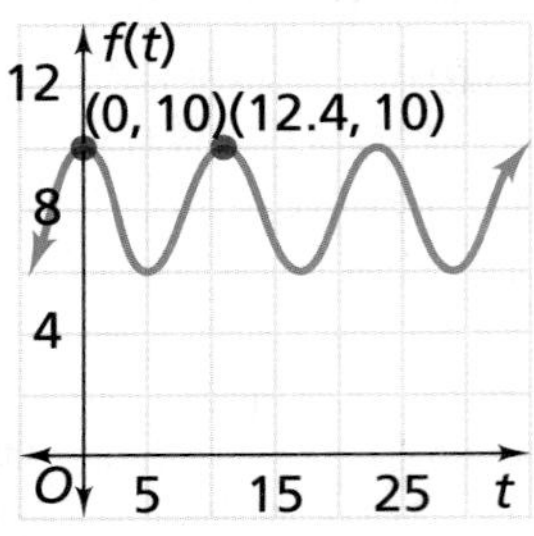


To obtain the graph of $H$, you need to shift the graph of $f$ to the right by 8 units, reflecting the fact that the high tide occurs at 8 A.M. In other words, $H$ has a phase shift of 8 and thus

$$H(t) = 2\cos\left(\frac{2\pi}{12.4}(t - 8)\right) + 8.$$

Here is the graph of $y = H(t)$.

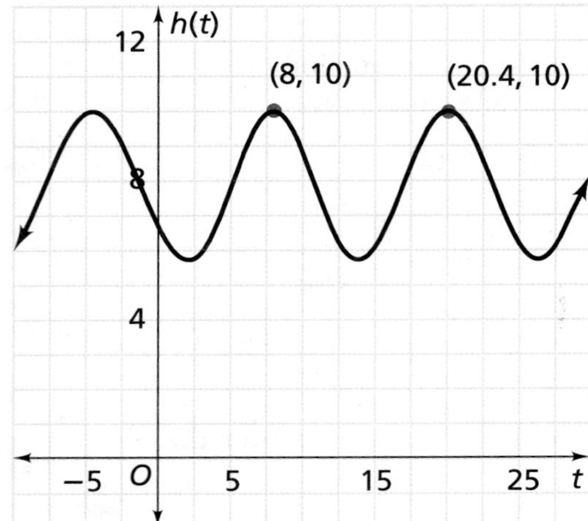


So, $b = -\frac{16\pi}{12.4}$.

## For Discussion

**4.** Explain why, in the above example, you can also obtain the graph of $H$ by translating the graph of $f$ to the left by 4.4 units. What would be the corresponding phase shift and equation for $H$? And how does this equation relate to the equation

$$H(t) = 2\cos\left(\frac{2\pi}{12.4}(t - 8)\right) + 8$$

that you obtained in the above example?

# Exercises Practicing Habits of Mind

## Check Your Understanding

1. The first ever Ferris wheel had a radius of 125 feet, and a maximum height of 264 feet.

This Ferris wheel made a full revolution every 9 minutes. Write a rule for $H(t)$, the height of a person on this wheel $t$ minutes after they are at the peak of the wheel.

Remember, you will need the amplitude, period, phase shift, and vertical displacement. One of them is zero, probably not the period!

2. Sketch an accurate graph of $H$ from Exercise 1 on the domain $-9 \leq t \leq 9$.

3. **a.** Find, to the nearest second, the elapsed time for a person on the Ferris wheel in Exercise 1 to go from the top of the wheel to a height of exactly 200 feet.

   **b.** Use the graph of $H$ from Exercise 2 to locate, approximately, the second time that person will be at a height of exactly 200 feet.

   **c.** Use the symmetry of the graph of $H$ to give an answer to part(b) that is accurate to the nearest second.

What equation do you need to solve here? How can backtracking help?

4. On average, high tides occur about every 12 hours and 24 minutes. Suppose a high tide occurred at 8 A.M. this morning.

   **a.** What time would you predict for the next high tide, and the one after that?

   **b.** What time would you predict for the next low tide? the next low tide after that?

   **c.** Sketch, approximately, the graph of the tide's height for 30 hours, starting at 8 A.M. today.

5. A reporting station records a high tide of 9 feet at 8 A.M., then a low tide of 2 feet at about 2:12 P.M. Assuming the height of the tide is a sinusoidal function with period 12.4 hours, find an equation for $H(t)$, the height of the tide $t$ hours after midnight.

6. Sketch the graph of the function you found in Exercise 5.

7. Use the equation you found in Exercise 5 to answer these questions.

   a. What is the predicted tide height at noon? at midnight?

   b. What is the height of the tide at 11:06 A.M.?

   c. Find another time when the tide is the same as it is at 11:06 A.M.

   d. Find a time, to the nearest minute, when the tide is 6 feet high.

8. Consider the Ferris wheel on page 433. The wheel has a radius of 36 feet. You travel around it once per 60 seconds.

   a. Find your speed as you move around the Ferris wheel, in feet per second. Drawing a picture of the situation may help.

   b. How fast are you traveling in miles per hour?

   c. **Take It Further** Consider the graph of $H$, vertical height on this Ferris wheel. At what times $t$ is $H(t)$ changing the fastest? Use a graphing calculator to determine the maximum change in $H$ as a slope, in feet per second.

## On Your Own

9. Sketch the graph of this function over two periods.

$$f(x) = 20\cos\left(\frac{2\pi}{7}(x - 4)\right) + 26$$

10. Which of these is the period of $g(t) = 5\sin 100\pi t + 3$?

    **A.** $\frac{1}{100}$ **B.** $\frac{1}{50}$ **C.** 50 **D.** 100

11. **Write About It** The equation for the Ferris wheel on page 433 is

$$H(t) = 36\cos\left(\frac{2\pi}{60}t\right) + 39$$

You can simplify the fraction $\frac{2\pi}{60}$ to $\frac{\pi}{30}$. Why does it make sense not to simplify this fraction?

**12.** Suppose you get on at the bottom of the Ferris wheel described on page 433. Then you start keeping track of time immediately as it moves.

**a.** Copy and complete this table for your height on the wheel after $t$ seconds.

Assume the Ferris wheel moves at its full speed immediately. Its period is still 60 seconds.

| Time $t$ (seconds) | Height $H(t)$ (feet) |
|---|---|
| 0 | 3 |
| 15 | ■ |
| 30 | ■ |
| 45 | ■ |
| 60 | ■ |
| 75 | ■ |
| 90 | ■ |

**b.** Sketch the graph of height against time for this situation.

**c.** Write an equation for $H(t)$, the height after $t$ seconds, for this situation.

There is more than one possible answer here.

**13.** Would you move faster if you sat on the Ferris wheel from page 433 or the Ferris wheel from Exercise 1? One completes its rotation more quickly but is smaller in radius.

**14.** Tide tables report the times and depths of high tides, and the times and depths of low tides. For example, here is part of a tide from Salem, Massachusetts, dated September 19, 2006.

| | | |
|---|---|---|
| 10:14 A.M. | 8.14 feet | High Tide |
| 4:05 P.M. | 1.27 feet | Low Tide |
| 10:24 P.M. | 8.97 feet | High Tide |

These tables do not report the tide heights in between. However, there is a guideline called the Rule of Twelfths that you can use to predict the tide each hour (for six hours) between a high and low tide:

Divide the amount the tide changes from high to low (or from low to high) into 12 equal parts. The first hour's gain (or loss) is 1 part (or, $\frac{1}{12}$ of the total change), the second hour is 2 parts, then 3, 3, 2, and 1.

**a.** Show that the predicted tide at 11:14 A.M. should be about 7.57 feet.

**b.** Find the predicted tide for 2:14 P.M. using the Rule of Twelfths.

**c.** Find the predicted tide for 6:05 P.M.

**d.** Draw a plot that includes the predicted tides from 10:14 A.M. to 10:24 P.M.

**15.** Write About It Describe how the Rule of Twelfths is related to sinusoidal behavior. Why does the rule group the equal parts the way it does?

16. **Take It Further** The function $f(x) = \cos x + \sin x$ is sinusoidal.

a. Using the unit circle, show that the maximum possible value of $f$ is $\sqrt{2}$. For what $x$ does the maximum occur?

b. Show that the minimum possible value of $f$ is $-\sqrt{2}$. Find where it occurs.

c. Write an equation for $f$ based on amplitude and phase shift.

17. **Standardized Test Prep** A Ferris wheel has a radius of 20 feet. The center is 35 feet above the ground and the wheel is rotating counterclockwise at a rate of 1 revolution every $\pi$ minutes. Which of the following is a function giving the height of a rider in feet at time $t$ minutes if the rider passes location $S$ (35 feet above the ground) at time $t = 0$?

A. $35 \sin \left(2\left(t - \frac{\pi}{2}\right)\right) + 20$

B. $20 \sin 2t + 35$

C. $2 \sin 20t + 35$

D. $20 \sin (t - 35) + 2$

## Maintain Your Skills

18. Consider the function

$$H(t) = 36 \cos \left(\frac{2\pi}{60}(t - 15)\right) + 39$$

a. Sketch a graph of $H$ on the interval $0 \le t \le 120$.

b. Find a value of $t$ for which $H(t) = 21$.

c. Use the graph of $H$ to find the three other values of $t$ between 0 and 120 that make $H(t) = 21$.

How might it help to draw a line on top of the graph of $H$?

19. Find all the values of $t$ between 0 and 120 that are solutions to the equation

$$36 \cos \left(\frac{2\pi}{60}(t - 5)\right) + 39 = 12$$

to two decimal places.

**In this investigation, you studied graphs, properties, and applications of sinusoidal functions. The following questions will help you summarize what you have learned.**

1. Suppose a Ferris wheel has a radius of 78 feet and a minimum height of 10 feet. It makes a full revolution every 6 minutes. Let $H(t)$ denote the height of a person on this wheel $t$ minutes after they are at the highest point of the wheel.
   **a.** Sketch the graph of $H$ on the domain $-6 \leq t \leq 6$.
   **b.** Find an equation for $H(t)$.
2. Find the amplitude, vertical displacement, period, and phase shift of the sinusoidal function $f(x) = 21 \cos\left(\frac{2\pi}{3}(x - 5)\right) - 14$.
3. Sketch the graph of the function $f(x) = 10 \sin\left(\frac{4\pi}{5}(x + 2)\right) + 3$ over two periods.
4. Find, to two decimal places, a solution to the equation $8 = 10 \sin\left(\frac{4\pi}{5}(x + 2)\right) + 3$.
5. Suppose $f(x) = \sin x$. For each function below, sketch the graph and the graph of $y = f(x)$ on the interval $-\pi \leq x \leq 2\pi$. Describe how the two graphs relate.
   **a.** $f(2x) = \sin 2x$ **b.** $2f(x) = 2 \sin x$ **c.** $f(x) + 1 = \sin x + 1$
6. Given the maximum and minimum values of a cosine or sine function, how do you find the amplitude and vertical displacement?
7. How can you make a sinusoidal function that has a specific period?
8. How can you use sinusoidal functions to model periodic phenomena?

## Vocabulary

In this investigation, you learned these terms. Make sure you understand what each one means and how to use it.

- **amplitude**
- **phase shift**
- **sinusoidal function**
- **vertical displacement**

The differences in high and low tidal levels can often be dramatic.

# Project: Using Mathematical Habits

## "Trigonometry" of the Unit Square

The unit circle was the basis for the work in this chapter. You can measure cosine and sine by looking at the coordinates of someone walking $\alpha$ units counterclockwise around the unit circle.

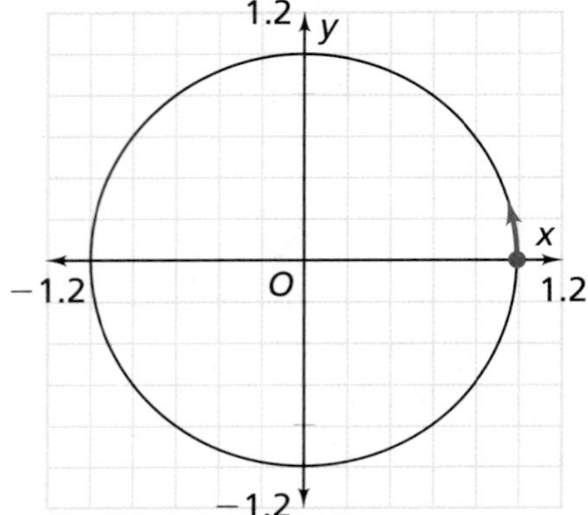


What would happen if everything stayed the same, but you replaced the circle by a square with side length 2?

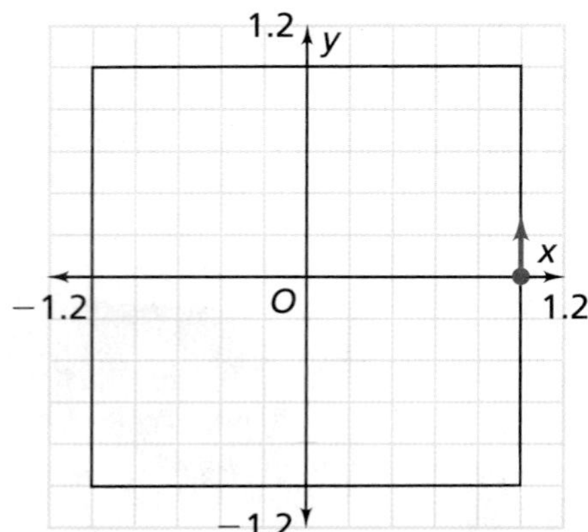


1. Paul walks $2\pi$ units around the unit circle. How far does he walk when he goes completely around the square once?
2. Copy and complete this table. Give the coordinates of Paul's location after walking each distance around a square with side length 2.

| Distance | Coordinates |
|---|---|
| 0 | (1, 0) |
| $\frac{1}{2}$ | $\left(1, \frac{1}{2}\right)$ |
| 1 | ■ |
| $1\frac{1}{2}$ | ■ |
| 2 | (0, 1) |
| 3 | ■ |
| 4 | ■ |
| 5 | ■ |
| 6 | ■ |
| 7 | ■ |
| 8 | ■ |
| 9 | ■ |
| 10 | ■ |

3. After walking around the square for 3 units, Paul is at the point $(-1, 1)$. If he continues walking, how far has he walked once he reaches these coordinates again? Find a rule that generates all the answers to this question.

4. Determine where an exhausted Paul would be after walking 739 units on the square.

On the unit circle, define the sine function by using the distance walked as the input, and the $y$-coordinate as the output.

For the unit square, let $SSIN(t)$ be the $y$-coordinate on the square after walking distance $t$. Let $SCOS(t)$ be the $x$-coordinate on the square after walking distance $t$.

5. Find each value.

   a. $SSIN(5)$
   b. $SSIN(21)$
   c. $SSIN(3.6)$
   d. $SCOS(3.6)$
   e. $SCOS(0)$
   f. $SCOS(2) + SCOS(6)$
   g. $SCOS(3) + SCOS(7)$

6. Two examples above suggest that $SCOS(t) + SCOS(t + 4) = 0$. Is this true for all values of $t$? What is the corresponding identity for the unit circle?

7. Sketch a graph of the $SSIN$ function on the domain $0 \leq t \leq 16$. Consider the proper range before laying out the axes of your sketch.

8. On the same axes used for the $SSIN$ function, sketch the $SCOS$ function on the domain $0 \leq t \leq 16$.

9. Here are some questions for further study.

   - On the unit circle, $\cos^2 t + \sin^2 t = 1$ for all values of $t$. Is there any relationship like this on the unit square? What does the graph of $f(t) = SCOS^2(t) + SSIN^2(t)$ look like?
   - What would cosine and sine look like for someone walking around a different polygon with center (0, 0) and one vertex at (1, 0)? Consider an equilateral triangle, a regular hexagon, a rectangle, and other shapes.
   - What does the graph of the tangent function *STAN* look like for the unit square? Here, define the tangent in any of the ways used for the circle. Will each option for the definition of tangent give the same result?
   - What do the graphs of the reciprocal trigonometric functions look like for the unit square?
   - Is it possible to model the *SSIN* and *SCOS* functions on a graphing calculator?

Let the square base of the Transamerica Pyramid be the unit square. If you walked around the base, how far would you walk?

# Chapter 5 Review

In **Investigation 5A,** you learned how to ...

- understand the relationship between degree and radian measure as the length of an arc on the unit circle subtended by a central angle.
- relate the motion of an object around a circle to the graphs of the cosine, sine, and tangent functions.
- solve equations that involve cosine and sine (such as $3 \cos x + 2 = 1$).

*The following questions will help you check your understanding.*

**1.** Draw the unit circle. A toy car is driving along this circle in the clockwise direction, starting from the point $(0, -1)$. After exactly $\frac{\pi}{2}$ meters, the car will be at which point?

**A.** $(1, 0)$ **B.** $(-1, 0)$

**C.** $(0, 1)$ **D.** $(0, -1)$

**2.** Evaluate the expression below.

$$\sin 30^\circ + \cos \pi - 3 \cos 60^\circ$$

**3.** How many radians corresponds to an angle with degree measure $160^\circ$?

**A.** $\frac{8\pi}{9}$ **B.** $\frac{3\pi}{4}$

**C.** $3\pi$ **D.** $\frac{5\pi}{6}$

**4.** Solve the following system of equations if $0 \leq x \leq \frac{\pi}{2}$.

$$y = 4 \sin x + 1$$
$$y = 3$$

In **Investigation 5B,** you learned how to ...

- make sense of sinusoidal functions in the context of real-world applications.
- understand the geometry of sinusoidal functions.
- model with sinusoidal functions.

*The following questions will help you check your understanding.*

**5.** Give two examples of sinusoidal functions that have period $\frac{\pi}{4}$.

**6.** Sketch the graph of the function.

$$S(x) = 3 \cos (x + 2) + 1$$

# Test

Go Online
www.successnetplus.com

## Multiple Choice

**1.** What is the value of the following expression?

$$\sin \frac{\pi}{2} + 2 \sin \pi - 3 \sin \frac{3\pi}{2}$$

**A.** 4 **B.** $-2$ **C.** $-3$ **D.** 3

**2.** Which of the following radian measures corresponds to 90°?

**A.** $\pi$ **B.** $\frac{\pi}{4}$ **C.** $\frac{\pi}{2}$ **D.** $\frac{3\pi}{2}$

**3.** Which function has the graph below?

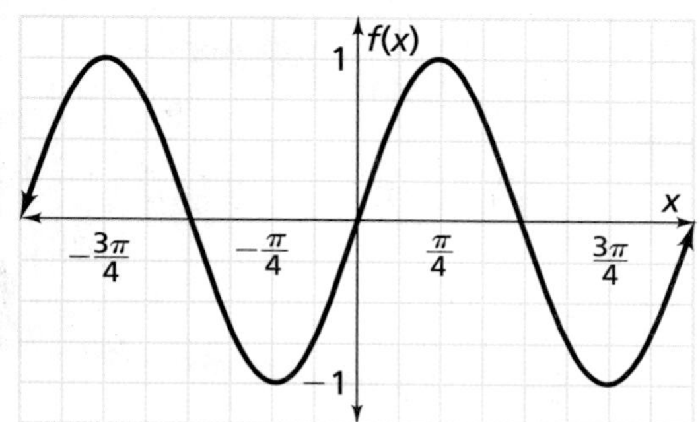


**A.** $f(x) = \sin x$ **B.** $f(x) = 2 \sin x$

**C.** $f(x) = 2 \cos x$ **D.** $f(x) = \sin 2x$

**4.** What is the period of the function below?

$$h(t) = \cos 3t$$

**A.** $\pi$ **B.** $3\pi$ **C.** $\frac{1}{3}$ **D.** $\frac{2\pi}{3}$

**5.** What is the value of the following expression, where $\alpha$ is some real number?

$$\sin(\alpha + \pi) \cdot \sin\left(\frac{\pi}{2} - \alpha\right) + \cos\left(\frac{\pi}{2} - \alpha\right) \cdot \cos \alpha$$

**A.** 0 **B.** 2

**C.** $2 \sin \alpha \cdot \cos \alpha$ **D.** $2(\sin \alpha + \cos \alpha)$

## Open Response

**6.** Answer the following questions. Explain your reasoning.

**a.** For what values of $\alpha$ is $\sin \alpha > 1$?

**b.** For what values of $\alpha$ is $\cos \alpha < -1$?

**7.** Evaluate the expression below, where $a$ and $b$ are real numbers.

$$a^2 \cos 2\pi - 2ab \cos \pi + b^2 \sin \frac{\pi}{2}$$

**8.** Solve the following equation.

$$4 \cos^2 x - 1 = 0$$

**9.** The sea level at a given point on the coast changes sinusoidally as a function of the time $t$. The following function gives the height $x$ (in meters) of the water.

$$x = 6 + 5 \sin \frac{1}{6}\pi(t - 2)$$

**a.** What is the maximum height of the water. What is its minimum height?

**b.** If you start measuring the height at 10 A.M., at what time does the high tide occur?

**c.** How many hours are there between successive high tides?

## Challenge Problem

**10.** Find all the solutions of the following equation.

$$\sqrt{3} \sin x - \cos x = 1$$

Chapter
6
Investigations at a Glance
6A
Graphing Complex Numbers
6B
De Moivre's Theorem

# Complex Numbers and Polynomials

What do complex numbers have to do with trigonometry? As it turns out, a whole lot!

You may have thought about how trigonometry could be used to rewrite complex numbers. In this chapter, you will first learn how to plot complex numbers on the complex plane. Next, you will discover how to transform any complex number $a + bi$ to a new polar form.

Scientists and engineers use complex numbers to model electrical circuits and water flow, to process digital signals, and to study nuclear phenomena. But artists use these same numbers to animate fractal domains in virtual reality scenarios, to visualize stunning works of art, and to compose audacious new soundscapes.

## Vocabulary and Notation

- algebraic numbers
- argument, $\arg(z)$
- complex numbers
- conjugate, $\overline{z}$
- magnitude, $|z|$
- norm, $N(z)$
- polar coordinates
- polar form for complex numbers
- primitive $n$th root of unity
- rectangular coordinates
- rectangular form for complex numbers
- roots of unity

# Graphing Complex Numbers

In *Graphing Complex Numbers*, you will view complex numbers as points in a plane. You will learn two coordinate representations for each complex number.

**By the end of this investigation, you will be able to answer questions like these.**

1. How can you write a complex number using trigonometry?
2. What are the magnitude and argument of a complex number, and how do you find them?
3. How do you use geometry to calculate $(1 - i\sqrt{3}) \cdot (-3\sqrt{3} + 3i)$?

**You will learn how to**

- represent complex numbers using both rectangular coordinates and polar coordinates
- determine the magnitude and argument of any complex number
- decide when it is best to use either rectangular or polar coordinates to represent complex numbers

**You will develop these habits and skills:**

- Graph complex numbers in the complex plane.
- Use geometry to explain arithmetic facts of complex numbers.
- Multiply two complex numbers of the form $r(\cos\theta + i\sin\theta)$.

The famous Mandelbrot set exists in the complex plane as the graph of a complex quadratic polynomial. Its (literally) infinite self-similar features include structures referred to as hooks and antennas, islands and valleys, and seahorses and satellites. You may be able to identify some of these in this detail.

# 6.01 Getting Started

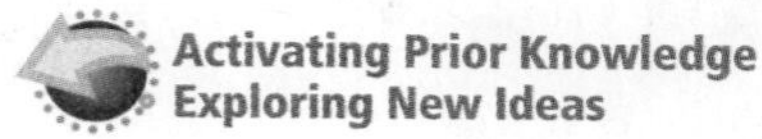


In previous courses, you learned about the complex numbers. A complex number is a number that is written in the form $x + yi$, where $x$ and $y$ are real numbers, and $i$ is the imaginary unit, a number that has a square of $-1$. These Getting Started problems will give you an opportunity to refresh your memory about the arithmetic of complex numbers ($\mathbb{C}$).

## For You to Explore

For Problems 1 and 2, calculate each expression. Write each result in the form $x + yi$ with real numbers $x$ and $y$.

**1.** **a.** $(3 + i) + (2 + i)$ **b.** $(3 + i) - (2 + i)$

**c.** $(3 + i)(2 + i)$ **d.** $(3 + i)^2$

**e.** $(3 + i)^2 \cdot (2 + i)^2$ **f.** $(3 + i)^4 \cdot (2 + i)^4$

The results from part (c) can help you answer parts (e) and (f).

**2.** **a.** $(3 + 5i) + (3 - 5i)$ **b.** $(3 + 5i)(3 - 5i)$

**c.** $(-7 + 2i) + (-7 - 2i)$ **d.** $(-7 + 2i)(-7 - 2i)$

**e.** $(12 + 5i) + (12 - 5i)$ **f.** $(12 + 5i)(12 - 5i)$

**3.** Let $z = x + yi$. The complex number $\bar{z} = x - yi$ is the **conjugate** of $z$.

**a.** What is the conjugate of $12 + 5i$?

**b.** What is the conjugate of $12 - 5i$?

**c.** If $z = x + yi$, show that $z + \bar{z} = 2x$.

**d.** If $z = x + yi$, show that the product $z\bar{z} = x^2 + y^2$.

The real part stays the same. The imaginary part switches its sign. The conjugate of $z = 3 + 5i$ is $\bar{z} = 3 - 5i$.

**4.** For each point $A$, find the coordinates of the point $A'$ by rotating $A$ 90° counterclockwise about the origin.

**a.** $A = (1, 0)$ **b.** $A = (0, -1)$

**c.** $A = (3, 5)$ **d.** $A = (6, -1)$

**5.** Multiply each complex number $z$ by $i$.

**a.** $z = 1$ **b.** $z = -i$ **c.** $z = 3 + 5i$ **d.** $z = 6 - i$

**6.** Let $z = x + yi$.

**a.** Calculate $z^2$.

**b.** What is the real part of $z^2$?

**c.** What is the imaginary part of $z^2$?

**7.** Show that the following equation is true for all $x$ and $y$.

$$(x^2 - y^2)^2 + (2xy)^2 = (x^2 + y^2)^2$$

# Exercises Practicing Habits of Mind

## On Your Own

**8.** Define $f(x) = x^2 - 2x + 2$.

**a.** Show that $f(x) = (x - 1)^2 + 1$.

**b.** Explain why the graph of $f$ does not have any $x$ intercepts.

**c.** Show that $f(1 + i) = 0$.

**d.** Find one other nonreal number for which $f(x) = 0$.

**9.** Find the exact length of each line segment with the given endpoints.

**a.** (0, 0) and (4, 1) **b.** (0, 0) and (2, 1) **c.** (0, 0) and (7, 6) **d.** (0, 0) and (3, 4)

**e.** (0, 0) and (6, 8) **f.** (0, 0) and $(1, \sqrt{3})$ **g.** (0, 0) and $(x, y)$

**10.** Compute each of these products.

**a.** $(4 + i)(4 - i)$ **b.** $(2 + i)(2 - i)$ **c.** $(7 + 6i)(7 - 6i)$

**d.** $(3 + 4i)(3 - 4i)$ **e.** $(6 + 8i)(6 - 8i)$ **f.** $(1 + i\sqrt{3})(1 - i\sqrt{3})$

**11. a.** Let $x = 3$ and $y = 2$ in the equation from Problem 7. Calculate the values of $x^2 - y^2$, $2xy$, and $x^2 + y^2$.

**b.** Copy and complete the table at the right.

| $x$ | $y$ | $x^2 - y^2$ | $2xy$ | $x^2 + y^2$ |
|---|---|---|---|---|
| 3 | 2 | ■ | ■ | ■ |
| 2 | 1 | ■ | ■ | ■ |
| 3 | 1 | ■ | ■ | ■ |
| 4 | 3 | ■ | ■ | ■ |
| 4 | 1 | ■ | ■ | ■ |
| 5 | 2 | ■ | ■ | ■ |

**12. a.** Sketch the graph of $f(x) = \cos^2 x - \sin^2 x$.

**b.** Find the amplitude and period of $f$.

**c.** Sketch the graph of $g(x) = \cos 2x$ on the same axes.

**d.** Compare the graphs of $f$ and $g$.

**13. a.** If $z = x + yi$, find the real part of $z^3$.

**b.** Sketch the graph of $h(x) = \cos^3 x - 3 \cos x \sin^2 x$.

**c.** Sketch the graph of $j(x) = \cos 3x$ on the same axes.

**d.** Compare the graphs of $h$ and $j$.

## Maintain Your Skills

**14.** Expand each of these expressions.

**a.** $(a + b)(a - b)$ **b.** $(a + b\sqrt{2})(a - b\sqrt{2})$ **c.** $(a + b\sqrt{3})(a - b\sqrt{3})$

**d.** $(a + b\sqrt{c})(a - b\sqrt{c})$ **e.** $(x + yi)(x - yi)$

# 6.02 The Complex Plane

Any complex number is made up of two parts, the real part, and the imaginary part. Two complex numbers are equal if and only if their real and imaginary parts are equal. In 1806, Jean-Robert Argand, a Parisian, published his ideas about a geometric representation of complex numbers. He used the $x$-axis to represent the real part, and the $y$-axis to represent the imaginary part.

Another name for the complex plane is the *Argand plane.* Gauss and Caspar Wessel described the complex plane in much the same way around the same time.

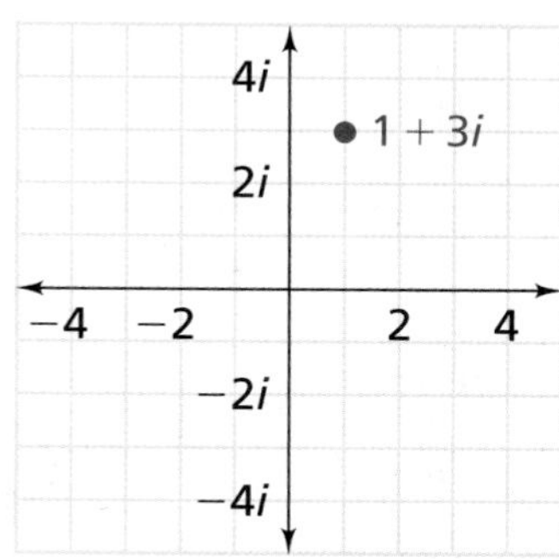

In the complex plane, the horizontal axis is the real axis, and the vertical axis is the imaginary axis.

## For You to Do

1. Identify the complex number represented by each point.

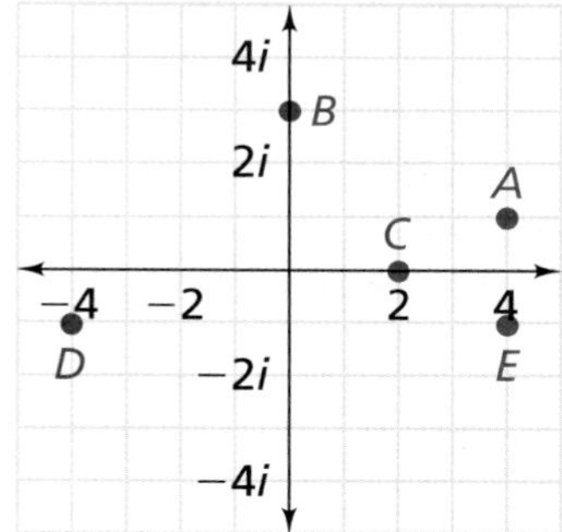


2. Which two of the five points are conjugates of one another?

In previous courses, you saw that the absolute value of a number $x$ is its distance from 0 on the number line. In the same way, the absolute value $|z|$ of a complex number is also the distance from 0 on the complex plane.

### *Definition*

**The magnitude of a complex number $z$, denoted by $|z|$, is the distance between the complex number and 0 in the complex plane.**

Some older texts call the magnitude of a complex number the *modulus*.

If $z = x + yi$, $|z|$ is the length of the line segment connecting 0 and $x + yi$ in the complex plane, or (0, 0) and $(x, y)$ in the coordinate plane.

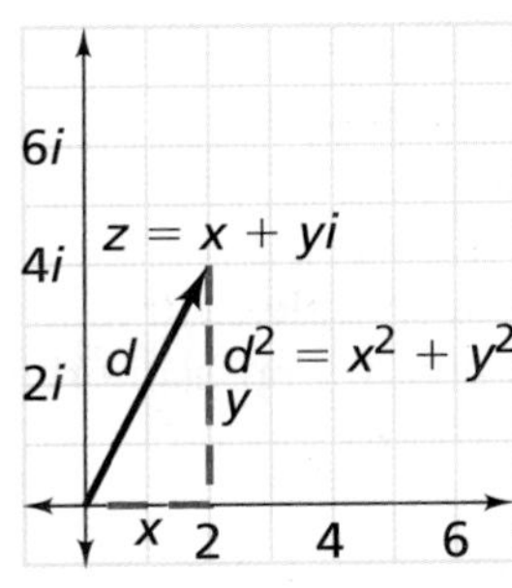


If $d^2 = x^2 + y^2$, then $d = \sqrt{x^2 + y^2}$, so $|x + yi| = \sqrt{x^2 + y^2}$.

## For You to Do

**3.** Find $|-2 + 7i|$.

**4.** Find a complex number in Quadrant IV with magnitude 13.

See TI-Nspire™ Handbook on p. 817 for advice on calculating magnitude.

You may recall another attribute of a complex number, the *norm.*

### *Definition*

**The norm of a complex number $z$, written $N(z)$, is the product of the complex number and its conjugate, $z\bar{z}$.**

The norm and absolute value of a complex number are similar, as the following theorem suggests.

### *Theorem 6.1*

**The absolute value of a complex number is equal to the square root of its norm.**

$$|z| = \sqrt{N(z)}$$

## For You to Do

**5.** Prove Theorem 6.1.

You can think of a real number $x$ as having a size $|x|$, and a positive or negative sign. The absolute value denotes the magnitude of $x$, and the sign is the direction from 0. So the number 3 is 3 units in the positive direction from 0, and $-3$ is 3 units in the negative direction from 0.

The complex plane gives a convenient way to think of the direction of a complex number.

## *Definition*

**The argument of a complex number $z$, written arg($z$), is the measure of the angle in standard position with $z$ on the terminal side.**

The argument arg ($z$) of a complex number is also its direction.

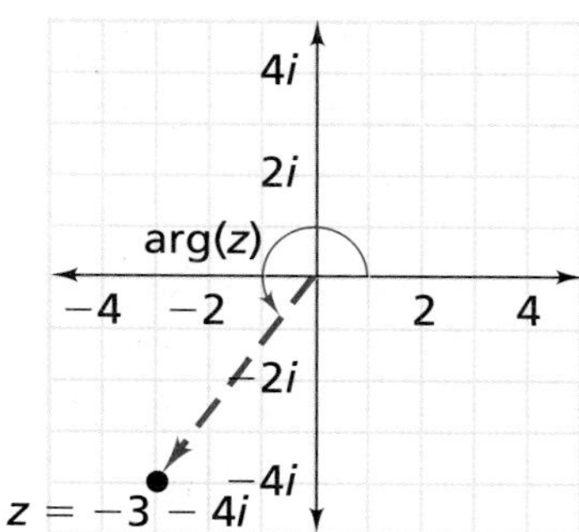


The value arg($z$) is expressed in either degrees or radians. To find the argument, you need to use trigonometry.

A good way to think of a complex number and its attributes is to think of it as a vector. Instead of a ray as described in this definition, you could think of the vector **$z$**.

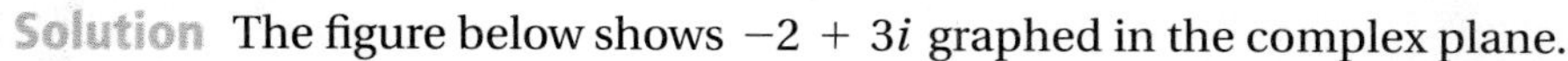

## Example

**Problem** Find the magnitude and argument of $-2 + 3i$.

**Solution** The figure below shows $-2 + 3i$ graphed in the complex plane.

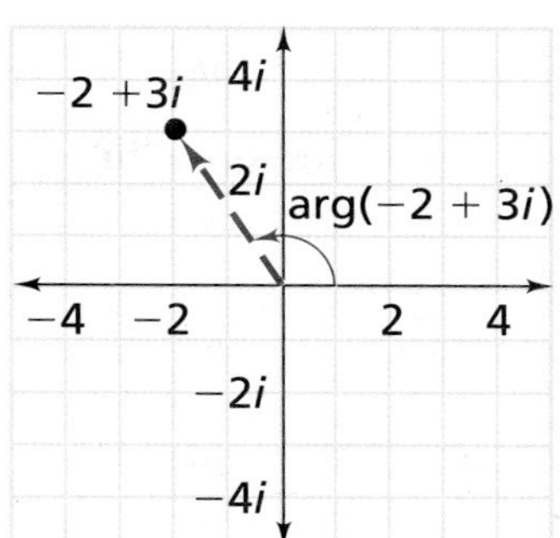


Use the formula $|x + yi| = \sqrt{x^2 + y^2}$ to find the magnitude.

$$|-2 + 3i| = \sqrt{(-2)^2 + (3)^2} = \sqrt{4 + 9} = \sqrt{13}$$

In Chapter 4, you saw that the slope of a line through the origin was equal to the tangent of the angle from the positive $x$-axis to the line. The slope of the line through the origin and the complex number $z$ is $\frac{3 - 0}{(-2) - 0} = -\frac{3}{2}$. You can find the argument by using inverse trigonometric functions. However, you might need to adjust the result from a calculator to find an angle in the correct quadrant.

Your calculator will say that $\tan^{-1}\left(-\frac{3}{2}\right) \approx -0.9828$, which corresponds to an angle in the fourth quadrant. $-2 + 3i$ is in the second quadrant, so

$$\arg(z) \approx \pi - 0.9828 \approx 2.1588$$

## For You to Do

6. Graph and label each of these complex numbers in the same complex plane. For each number, find its magnitude and argument (in degrees between 0° and 360°).

   a. $4 + 3i$ b. $4 - 3i$ c. $-4 + 3i$ d. $-4 - 3i$

# Exercises Practicing Habits of Mind

## Check Your Understanding

Unless otherwise specified, write the argument using radians.

1. For each complex number, find its exact magnitude.

   a. $4 + i$ b. $2 + i$ c. $3 - 2i$ d. $6 + 5i$

2. Compute each product. Compare the result to the magnitudes found in Exercise 1.

   a. $(4 + i)(4 - i)$ b. $(2 + i)(2 - i)$

   c. $(3 - 2i)(3 + 2i)$ d. $(6 + 5i)(6 - 5i)$

3. For each complex number $z$, graph $z$ and $i \cdot z$ as vectors in the same complex plane. Estimate $\arg(z)$ and $\arg(iz)$.

   a. $z = 3 + 2i$ b. $z = -1 + 4i$

   c. $z = -1 - 3i$ d. $z = 2 - 3i$

4. Find the exact magnitude and argument of each complex number.

   a. $2 + 2i$ b. $2 - 2i$ c. $-2 + 2i$ d. $-2 - 2i$

5. Let $z$ be a complex number. For each of the expressions below, describe how its magnitude and argument compare to $|z|$ and $\arg(z)$.

   a. $iz$ b. $i^2z$ c. $(-i)z$ d. $2z$ e. $\frac{1}{z}$

## On Your Own

6. Suppose you triple a complex number $z$. How do $|3z|$ and $\arg(3z)$ compare to $|z|$ and $\arg(z)$?

7. Write About It Suppose you multiply a complex number $z$ by a real number $c$. How do $|cz|$ and $\arg(cz)$ compare to $|z|$ and $\arg(z)$?

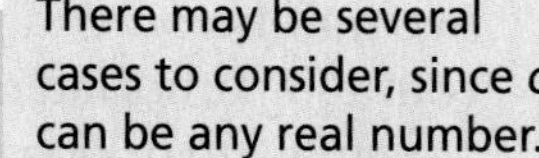

There may be several cases to consider, since $c$ can be any real number.

8. Let $z = x + yi$, where $x$ and $y$ are positive real numbers.

   a. Graph what $z$ and $\overline{z}$ might look like in the same complex plane.

   b. Graph $z + \overline{z}$.

   c. Show that the four complex numbers $0$, $z$, $\overline{z}$, and $z + \overline{z}$ are the vertices of a parallelogram when plotted in the complex plane.

9. Let $z = \cos t + i \sin t$.

   a. Calculate $z^2$.

   b. What is the imaginary part of $z^2$?

10. Find the vertices of a square in the complex plane.

11. Find the four solutions to the equation $x^4 - 16 = 0$. Plot them in the complex plane.

Two of the solutions are real numbers, and two are not.

12. For each complex number, find the exact magnitude. Also, approximate to two decimal places the argument in degrees.

   a. $(3 + 2i)^0$

   b. $(3 + 2i)^1$

   c. $(3 + 2i)^2$

   d. $(3 + 2i)^3$

   e. $(3 + 2i)^4$

13. For each complex number, find the exact magnitude.

   a. $(1 + i)^2$

   b. $(2 + i)^2$

   c. $(3 + i)^2$

   d. $(7 + i)^2$

   e. $(2 + 3i)^2$

   f. Find a complex number $x + yi$ with a magnitude of 29, where $x \neq 0$ and $y \neq 0$.

14. Find the magnitude and argument of each solution to each equation.

   a. $x^2 - 1 = 0$

   b. $x^3 - 1 = 0$

   c. $x^4 - 1 = 0$

15. Establish the identity $(ac - bd)^2 + (bc + ad)^2 = (a^2 + b^2)(c^2 + d^2)$.

16. Standardized Test Prep Which of the following is the product of $-1 + i$ and its complex conjugate?

   A. 0

   B. $-1.1$

   C. $-0.9$

   D. 2

## Maintain Your Skills

17. Let $\omega = \frac{1 + i\sqrt{3}}{2}$. Plot each of the following in the same complex plane.

   a. $\omega$

   b. $\omega^2$

   c. $\omega^3$

   d. $\omega^4$

   e. $\omega^5$

   f. $\omega^6$

   g. $\omega^7$

   h. $\omega^{12}$

$\omega$ is the Greek letter *omega*.

# 6.03 Another Form for Complex Numbers—*r cis θ*

Coordinates are a perfectly good way to describe a point in the plane. The two numbers $x$ and $y$ identify a unique location. You start at the origin. You count $|x|$ units left or right (depending on the sign of $x$). Then you count $|y|$ units up or down (depending on the sign of $y$).

Suppose you are walking from the origin to the point $(x, y)$. Regardless of how you define your axes, you could move $x$ units in some direction, then turn $90^\circ$ clockwise or counterclockwise before moving $y$ units. The key idea is that your second movement would be perpendicular to the first.

But think, for instance, how you would actually move from one point to another. Suppose you were in an open field. You would likely walk in a straight line directly from one point to the other. You would first turn in the proper direction, then walk the proper distance.

This idea, and your work in the previous lesson, suggest another way to identify points in the plane. To get from the origin to the point $(x, y)$, instead of walking two separate distances, you can move just one distance, providing you are heading in the right direction. So if you have two numbers, a direction (given by an angle measurement) and a distance, you can find your point.

Is it easier for you to desribe this fan in terms of polar coordinates or rectangular coordinates?

### Facts and Notation

**You can locate a point *P* in the plane in two ways.**

**Rectangular coordinates: $(x, y)$ denotes distances along two axes that are perpendicular.**

**Polar coordinates: $(r, \theta)$ denotes a direction (an angle $\theta$ counterclockwise from the positive real axis) and distance $r$.**

## For Discussion

Let $P_1$ and $P_2$ be two points in the plane. If $P_1 = (x_1, y_2)$ and $P_2 = (x_2, y_2)$, it is a true statement that

$$P_1 = P_2 \Leftrightarrow x_1 = x_2 \text{ and } y_1 = y_2$$

Can you make the same statement about polar coordinates? Decide if the following statement is true: if $P_1 = (r_1, \theta_1)$ and $P_2 = (r_2, \theta_2)$

$$P_1 = P_2 \Leftrightarrow r_1 = r_2 \text{ and } \theta_1 = \theta_2$$

Consider these questions.

1. Is the statement true for either direction $\Leftrightarrow$?
2. If either implication is not always true, modify the statement to make both implications always true.

Complex numbers of the form $x + yi$ correspond directly to rectangular coordinates of the point $(x, y)$. You can find a complex number if you are given polar coordinates $(r, \theta)$.

## Example

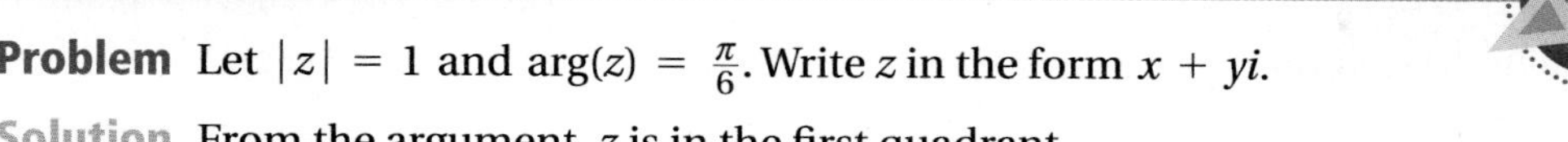

**Problem** Let $|z| = 1$ and $\arg(z) = \frac{\pi}{6}$. Write $z$ in the form $x + yi$.

**Solution** From the argument, $z$ is in the first quadrant.

Since $|z| = 1$, $z$ is on the unit circle. So $x \cos\frac{\pi}{6} = \frac{\sqrt{3}}{2}$ and $y$ is $\sin\frac{\pi}{6} = \frac{1}{2}$. Thus, you can write $z = \cos\frac{\pi}{6} + i\sin\frac{\pi}{6} = \frac{\sqrt{3}}{2} + \frac{1}{2}i$.

Notice that the convention is to write "$i\sin\frac{\pi}{6}$." If you wrote "$\sin\frac{\pi}{6}i$" to match the "$yi$," it would be unclear whether you mean $\sin\left(\frac{\pi}{6}i\right)$ or $\left(\sin\frac{\pi}{6}\right)i$. Of course, parentheses make the intent clear, but the convention is to avoid parentheses whenever possible.

## For You to Do

For each absolute value and argument, write $z$ in the form $x + yi$.

**3.** $|z| = 2$ and $\arg(z) = \frac{\pi}{6}$.

**4.** $|z| = 4$ and $\arg(z) = 135°$.

Just as you can express a point in the coordinate plane in two ways, you can express a complex number in two ways.

**Rectangular Form:** $x + yi$, where $x$ and $y$ are real numbers.

**Polar Form:** $r(\cos\theta + i\sin\theta)$, where $r$ is a nonnegative real number and $\theta$ is a measurement in either degrees or radians.

By convention, $r$ is not negative. You could express a complex number using $r < 0$, but if $r$ is nonnegative, it will be equal to the magnitude of the complex number.

### *Facts and Notation*

**To identify the complex number $\cos\theta + i\sin\theta$, you can use the abbreviation $\text{cis}\,\theta$.**

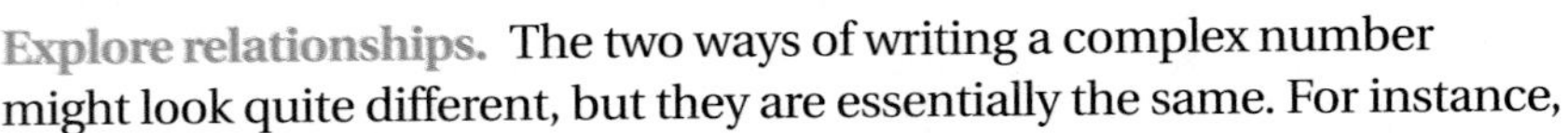

## Developing Habits of Mind

**Explore relationships.** The two ways of writing a complex number might look quite different, but they are essentially the same. For instance,

$$1 + i\sqrt{3} = 2 \operatorname{cis} \frac{\pi}{3}$$

is a true statement. To see why, look at the right side.

$$\begin{aligned} 2 \operatorname{cis} \frac{\pi}{3} &= 2\left(\cos \frac{\pi}{3} + i \sin \frac{\pi}{3}\right) \\ &= 2\left(\frac{1}{2} + i\frac{\sqrt{3}}{2}\right) \\ &= 1 + i\sqrt{3} \end{aligned}$$

Either way you write it, you can see that the complex number has a real part and an imaginary part.

In general, you can write a complex number of the form $r \operatorname{cis} \theta$ as $x + yi$ by realizing that

$$x = r\cos\theta, \text{ and}$$
$$y = r\sin\theta$$

Also, if $z = r \operatorname{cis} \theta$, then you know that

$$|z| = r, \text{ and}$$
$$\arg(z) = \theta$$

So, for any complex number $z$, you can say

$$z = |z| \operatorname{cis} (\arg(z)).$$

## Exercises *Practicing Habits of Mind*

### Check Your Understanding

**1.** Find the magnitude and argument of each complex number.

**a.** $z = 5 \operatorname{cis} 60^\circ$ **b.** $w = \frac{1}{5} \operatorname{cis} 300^\circ$

**2.** Consider the complex numbers $z$ and $w$ from Exercise 1.

**a.** Find the magnitude and argument of $z^2$.

**b.** Find the magnitude and argument of $z^3$.

**c.** Find the magnitude and argument of $zw$.

3. a. In the complex plane, plot (as points) four different numbers with argument $210°$.

   b. Plot the set of all points with argument $210°$.

   c. What complex number has magnitude 10 and argument $210°$?

4. Suppose $q$ is a complex number with $|q| = 4$ and $\arg(q) = \frac{2\pi}{3}$.

   a. Write $q$ using trigonometric functions.

   b. Write $q$ without using trigonometric functions.

5. Let $a$ and $b$ be complex numbers, with $|a| = 5$, $\arg(a) = 60°$, $|b| = 3$, and $\arg(b) = 30°$.

   a. Write $a$ and $b$ in any form.

   b. Calculate the product $ab$. Find its magnitude and argument.

6. Suppose $z = 3 \text{ cis } \theta$ for some value of $\theta$.

   a. Pick seven different values of $\theta$. For each, plot $z$ as a point in the complex plane.

   b. **Write About It** What does the graph of all possible such points look like? Explain.

7. a. Show that, for any value of $\theta$, $|\text{cis } \theta| = 1$.

   b. Show that, for any value of $r$ and $\theta$, $|r \text{ cis } \theta| = |r|$.

## On Your Own

8. Find the magnitude and argument of each complex number.

   a. $5\sqrt{3} - 5i$

   b. $10 \text{ cis } 330°$

   c. $4\sqrt{2} \text{ cis } \frac{5\pi}{4}$

   d. $-4 - 4i$

9. Consider the complex number $z = \text{cis } \frac{\pi}{2}$.

   a. Calculate $z^2$.

   b. Describe the effect in the complex plane of multiplying a complex number by $z$.

10. Suppose $z = 5 \text{ cis } 160°$ and $w = 2 \text{ cis } 110°$. Find $|zw|$ and $\arg(zw)$.

11. Complex number $w$ has magnitude 1 and argument $\alpha$. Complex number $z$ has magnitude 1 and argument $\beta$.

    a. Write expressions for $z$ and $w$.

    b. Write an expression for the product $zw$ in the form $x + yi$, where $x$ and $y$ are in the set $\mathbb{R}$.

**12.** For each pair of complex numbers, find the magnitude and direction of $z$ and $w$. Then find the magnitude and direction of the product $zw$.

**a.** $z = 2 + i$ and $w = 3 + i$

**b.** $z = 2 + i$ and $w = 3 + 2i$

**c.** $z = 5i$ and $w = 3i$

**d.** $z = 2 + i$ and $w = \frac{2 - i}{5}$

**Remember...**

$|z|$ is the magnitude of the complex number $z$.

**13. a.** Based on the results in Exercise 12, describe a relationship between $|z|$, $|w|$, and $|zw|$.

**b.** Describe a relationship between $\arg(z)$, $\arg(w)$, and $\arg(zw)$.

**c.** Let $z = x + yi$ and $w = c + di$. Show that the relationship you found between $|z|$, $|w|$, and $|zw|$ holds for any choice of $z$ and $w$.

**14.** Standardized Test Prep In polar coordinates, which of the following is the same as $(1, \frac{\pi}{3})$?

**A.** $\left(-1, \frac{4\pi}{3}\right)$ **B.** $\left(1, \frac{4\pi}{3}\right)$ **C.** $\left(-1, \frac{\pi}{3}\right)$ **D.** $\left(\frac{\pi}{3}, 1\right)$

**Go Online**
www.successnetplus.com

## Maintain Your Skills

**15.** The complex number $z = \sqrt{3} + i$ has magnitude 2 and direction $\frac{\pi}{6}$ (or 30°). For each complex number $w$ listed below, find its magnitude and argument. Then find the magnitude and argument of $zw$.

**a.** $w = 1 + i\sqrt{3}$

**b.** $w = 5i$

**c.** $w = 10$

**d.** $w = 1 + i$

**e.** $w = -2 + i$

# 6.04 The Multiplication Law

There are two ways to represent a complex number graphically, as a point and as a vector (a directed distance). Both methods are useful, just as it is useful on the number line to present numbers as both points and arrows.

- Thinking of complex numbers as points allows you to apply all the machinery of geometry to questions about complex numbers. This representation helps you do some very algebraic jobs, including equation solving.
- Thinking of complex numbers as vectors allows you to picture operations like adding two vectors or multiplying by $i$. Using vectors also allows you to think about the relative size of complex numbers, since a vector has a length.

Throughout this lesson, the representation of complex numbers will alternate between points and vectors. What is most important is that you become comfortable with both representations and that you develop a knack for when to "think point" and when to "think vector."

Throughout this investigation, you have worked on arithmetic of complex numbers. You may have found the following ways of representing complex arithmetic geometrically.

- You can add two complex numbers by completing a parallelogram. The first two sides are vectors that represent the two numbers.

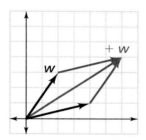

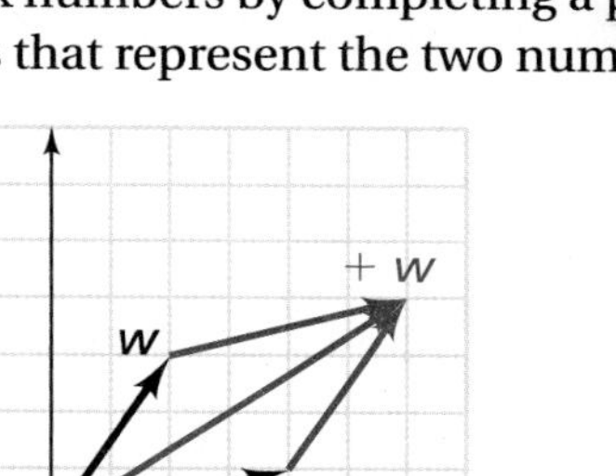


- You can multiply a complex number and a real number $k$ by stretching the vector for the complex number by a factor of $k$.

If $k > 0$, the head of the vector is $k$ times as far from the origin in the same direction. If $k < 0$, the head of the vector is $|k|$ times as far from the origin in the opposite direction.

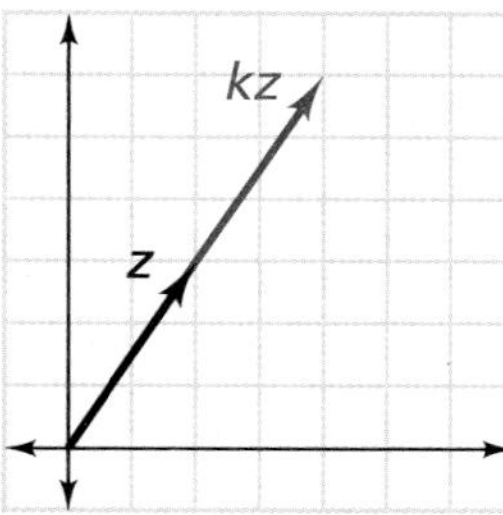


- You can multiply a complex number by $i$ by rotating the vector for the complex number 90 degrees counterclockwise.

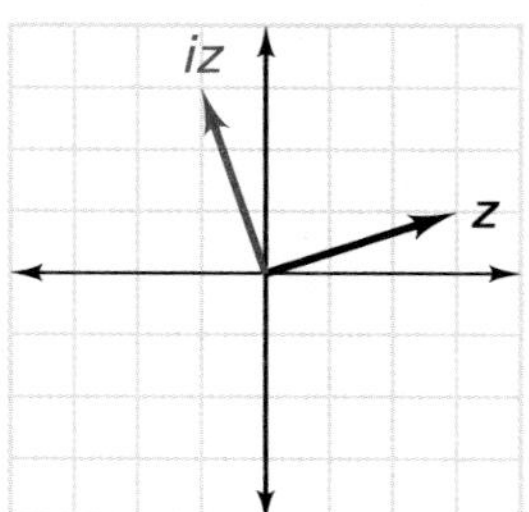

You can also represent the multiplication of two complex numbers geometrically.

## Example

**Problem** Let $z = 3 + 2i$ and $w = 4 + i$. Describe how to find the product $zw$ geometrically.

**Solution** You already know how to multiply two complex numbers.

$$\begin{aligned}(3 + 2i)(4 + i) &= 3(4 + i) + 2i(4 + i)\\ &= (12 + 3i) + (-2 + 8i)\\ &= (12 - 2) + (3 + 8)i\\ &= 10 + 11i\end{aligned}$$

Just graphing the three vectors does not help much.

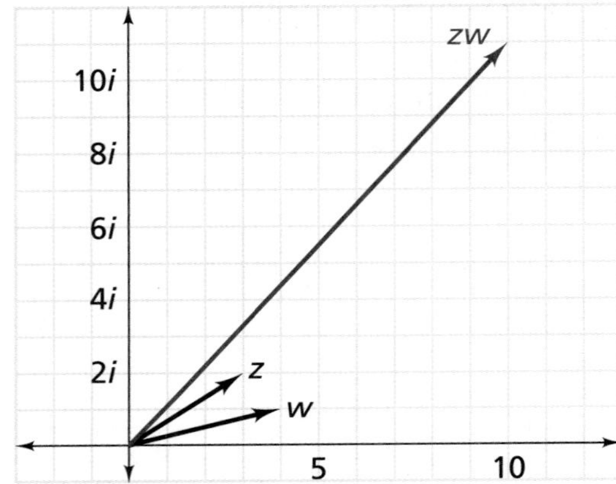


To see the geometry of the multiplication, you need to add a few more lines. Take a look at the first step in the calculation above.

$$(3 + 2i)(4 + i) = 3(4 + i) + 2i(4 + i)$$

On the right side, you have two arithmetic expressions that you know how to represent geometrically.

- $3(4 + i)$ is the product of a real number and a complex number. To show the product geometrically, you stretch the vector $4 + i$ by a factor of 3.

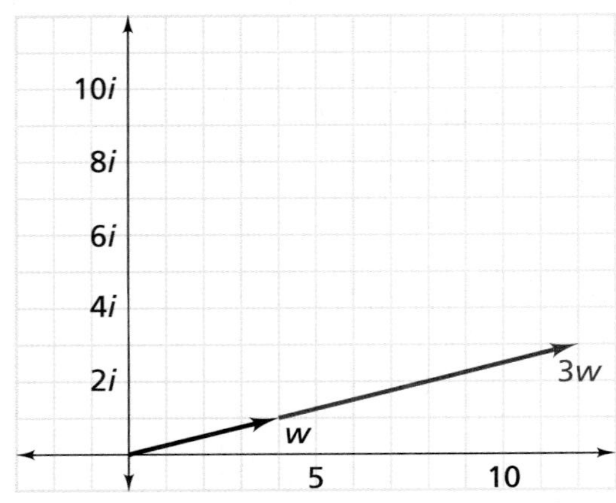

- $2i(4 + i)$ involves two steps. First, you can show the product $i(4 + i)$ by rotating $4 + i$ by 90 degrees counterclockwise.

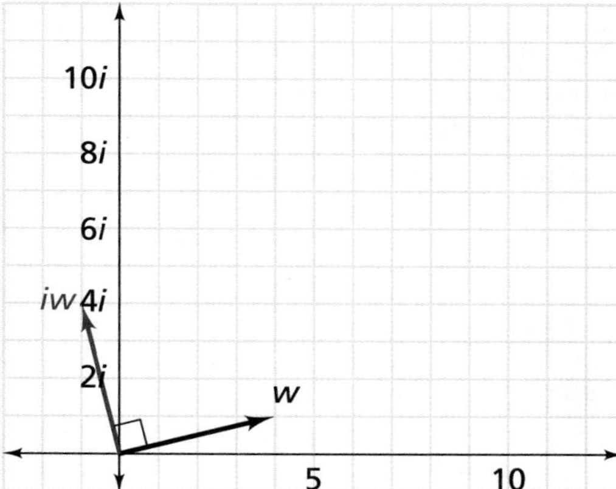


You can show the product of that resulting vector, $-1 + 4i$, and 2 by stretching the vector by a factor of 2.

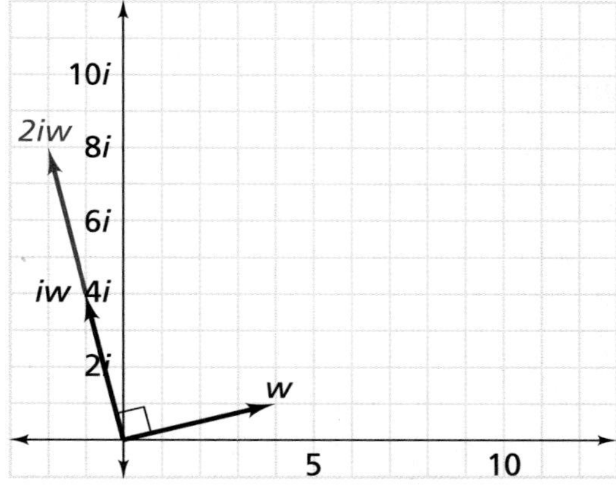


- Finally, add the two vectors by completing the parallelogram.

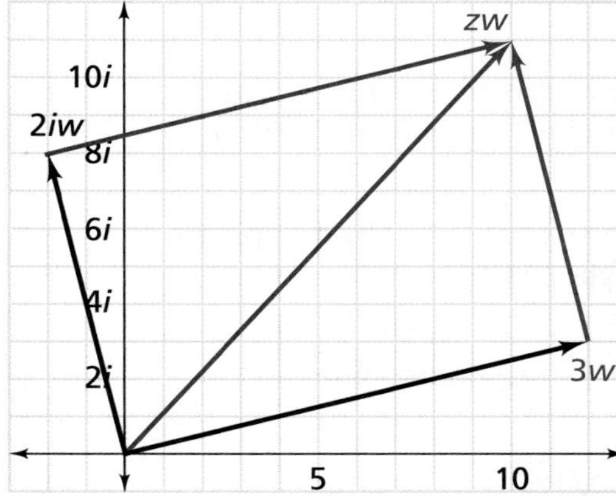


The parallelogram is actually a rectangle, because of the right angle.

The Example shows how to construct the product. But you may find it more difficult to follow the construction steps when finding the product of complex numbers written in cis notation, like $5 \text{ cis } \frac{\pi}{6}$ and $2 \text{ cis } \frac{\pi}{2}$.

To multiply complex numbers written this way, you can use certain properties of absolute value and argument, some of which you may have picked up in the exercises throughout this investigation. Your results from those exercises suggest the following theorem about the magnitude and argument of products.

### Theorem 6.2 The Multiplication Law

Given complex numbers $z = a \text{cis} \alpha$ and $w = b \text{cis} \beta$,

$$zw = (a \text{cis} \alpha)(b \text{cis} \beta) = ab \text{cis}(\alpha + \beta)$$

In other words,

- $|zw| = |z| \cdot |w|$
- $\arg(zw) = \arg(z) + \arg(w)$.

You can use $z = 3 + 2i$ and $w = 4 + i$ from the Example to demonstrate both parts of the theorem. Consider this figure.

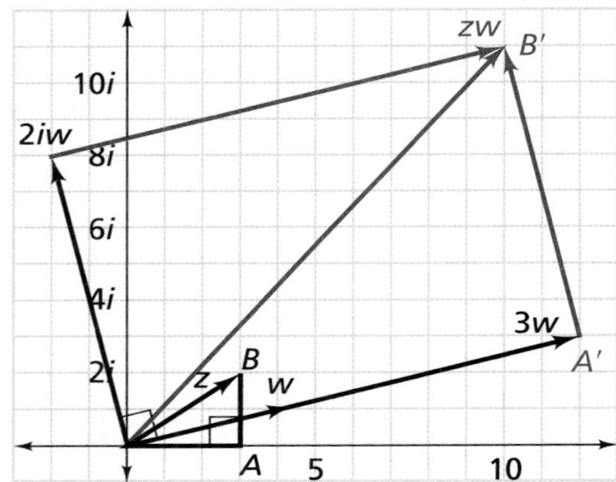


The smaller triangle is made from dropping a perpendicular from $B$ to the real axis. The larger triangle is made from the construction from the examples. The two triangles are similar.

- Both are right triangles: the smaller because you made it by dropping a perpendicular, the larger because the angle at $A'$ is part of a rectangle.
- Two pairs of sides are proportional: since $z = 3 + 2i$, you know that $OA = 3$ and $AB = 2$, so $\frac{OA}{AB} = \frac{3}{2}$. For the corresponding sides on the larger triangle, you have

$$\begin{aligned} OA' &= |3(4 + i)| = |12 + 3i| = \sqrt{12^2 + 3^2} = \sqrt{144 + 9} \\ &= \sqrt{153} = 3\sqrt{17} \end{aligned}$$

and

$$\begin{aligned} A'B' &= \sqrt{(10 - 12)^2 + (11 - 3)^2} = \sqrt{(-2)^2 + 8^2} = \sqrt{4 + 64} \\ &= \sqrt{68} = 2\sqrt{17} \end{aligned}$$

Thus

$$\frac{OA'}{A'B'} = \frac{3\sqrt{17}}{2\sqrt{17}} = \frac{3}{2}$$

Since the ratios are the same, the two pairs of sides are proportional.

Thus, by the SAS Theorem for similar triangles, the two triangles are similar. Now that you know the two triangles are similar, you can show both parts of the theorem.

- Corresponding sides in similar triangles are proportional. Every side in the larger triangle is $\sqrt{17}$ times as long as every side in the smaller triangle, and $\sqrt{17} = |w|$.

  The length of the hypotenuse of the smaller triangle is $|z| = \sqrt{3^2 + 2^2} = \sqrt{13}$. Thus, the length of the hypotenuse of the larger triangle is $\sqrt{13} \cdot \sqrt{17} = |zw|$. Thus, $|z| \cdot |w| = |zw|$.

- Corresponding angles in similar triangles are congruent. Thus, $\angle AOB \cong \angle A'OB'$. By definition, $\arg(z) = m\angle AOB$, $\arg(w) = m\angle AOA'$, and $\arg(zw) = m\angle AOB'$. Notice, though, that

$$\begin{aligned}\arg(zw) &= m\angle AOB' \\ &= m\angle AOA' + m\angle A'OB' \\ &= m\angle AOA' + m\angle AOB \\ &= \arg(z) + \arg(w)\end{aligned}$$

You can double check:
$$\begin{aligned}|zw| &= \sqrt{10^2 + 11^2} \\ &= \sqrt{100 + 121} \\ &= \sqrt{221} \\ &= \sqrt{13} \cdot \sqrt{17}\end{aligned}$$

## For Discussion

1. Using algebra, prove for any two complex numbers $z = a + bi$ and $w = c + di$ that

$$|z| \cdot |w| = |zw|$$

## Developing Habits of Mind

**Visualize.** Another way to envision what is happening with the geometry of complex multiplication is to look at what happens to $z$. You rotate it by $\arg(w)$, and then dilate it by $|w|$.

So, to multiply any complex number by $1 + i$, rotate it 45°, (since $45° = \arg(1 + i)$). Then scale by $\sqrt{2}$ (since $\sqrt{2} = |1 + i|$). To multiply by $i$, rotate it 90° and scale by 1.

It might help to think of the transformation of $z$ by seeing how it transforms as part of the triangle *AOB*.

## For You to Do

2. Describe multiplication of $z$ by each of these numbers in terms of the rotation and scaling of $z$.

   **a.** $\sqrt{3} + i$ **b.** $-i$ **c.** $-1$

# Exercises Practicing Habits of Mind

## Check Your Understanding

1. Suppose $z = 3 \text{ cis } 120°$.

   a. Find the magnitude and argument of $z^2$.

   b. Explain why $z^3 = 27$.

2. Write About It If you know the magnitude and argument of $z$, describe (in words) how to find the magnitude and argument of $z^2$, $z^3$, and in general, $z^n$.

3. Suppose the complex number $z^3$ has magnitude 27 and argument 120°. Decide whether each statement about $z$ could be true. Explain.

   a. $z$ has magnitude 9 and argument 40°.

   b. $z$ has magnitude 3 and argument 40°.

   c. $z$ has magnitude 3 and argument 120°.

   d. $z$ has magnitude 3 and argument 160°.

4. Here are two complex numbers $z$ and $w$ drawn in the complex plane. Estimate the magnitude and argument of $zw$.

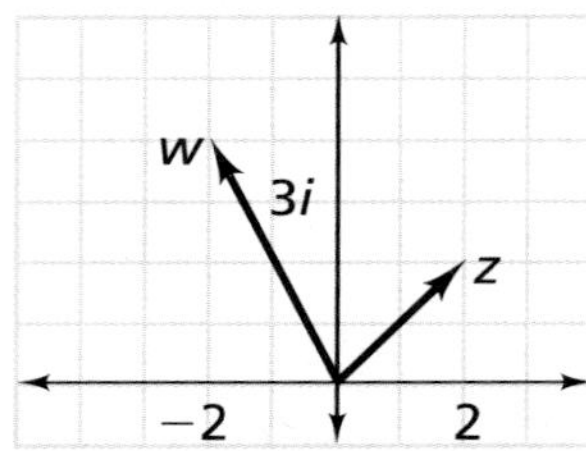


5. Write About It Two complex numbers have arguments that add up to more than 360°. Describe how to find the magnitude and argument of their product.

6. For each $z$, plot the first few powers of $z$ (that is, $z^0, z^1, z^2, \ldots$). If you take higher powers of $z$, describe and explain the pattern you see.

   a. $z = i$

   b. $z = -i$

   c. $z = 1 + i$

   d. $z = 1 - i$

   e. $z = 2 + i$

   f. $z = 2 - i$

## On Your Own

7. Suppose $z$ and $w$ are complex numbers with magnitude 1. For each complex number, decide whether it must also have magnitude 1.

   a. $zw$ b. $z + w$ c. $\overline{w}$

   d. $\frac{1}{z}$ e. $z^2$ f. $2z$

8. a. In the complex plane, plot the triangle with vertices $2 + 3i$, $4 + 6i$, and $7 - i$.

   b. Plot the triangle that results if you multiply each vertex by $i$.

   c. Plot the triangle that results if you multiply each vertex by $1 + i$.

9. The product of two complex numbers is $10i$. Neither is a real number.

   a. Find one possible pair of numbers that works.

   b. **Take It Further** Given any nonzero complex number $z$, explain how to find $w$ so that $zw = 10i$.

10. Here are two complex numbers $z$ and $w$ drawn in the complex plane. Estimate the magnitude and argument of $zw$.

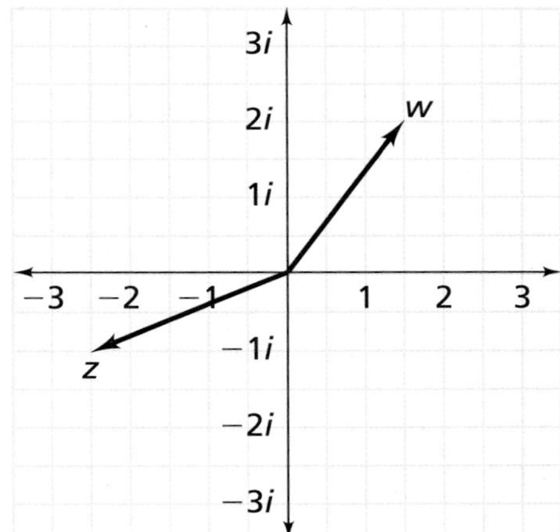


11. Consider the complex numbers $z = 3 - 2i$ and $w = 1 + 3i$.

    a. Plot $z$ and $w$ as vectors. Determine the magnitude and argument of each.

    b. In what quadrant is $zw$? Explain how you know.

    c. Find the magnitude and argument of $zw$.

12. This lesson explains how to find the magnitude and argument of the product of two complex numbers, but what about the quotient? Consider the complex numbers $z = 4 + 2i$ and $w = 3 + i$.

a. Write $\frac{z}{w}$ as $a + bi$ where $a$ and $b$ are real numbers.

b. Find the magnitude and argument of $\frac{z}{w}$.

c. Find a relationship between the magnitudes of $z$, $w$, and $\frac{z}{w}$. Also find a relationship between their arguments.

13. **Take It Further** Plot the set of all complex numbers that satisfy each equation. Make a new graph for each part.

a. $|z| = 3$ b. $|z| = 1$ c. $|z| < 1$ d. $|z| > 1$

e. $|z| = |\frac{1}{z}|$ f. $z^2 = z$ g. $|z|^2 = |z|$

14. **Standardized Test Prep** Which of the following is equivalent to multiplying a complex number $z$ by the number $i$?

A. reflection of $z$ over the $x$-axis

B. reflection of $z$ over the $y$-axis

C. rotation 90° counterclockwise

D. rotation 90° clockwise

## Maintain Your Skills

15. Simplify each expression. Write the result in the form $x + yi$ where $x$ and $y$ are real numbers.

a. $1 + i + i^2$

b. $1 + i + i^2 + i^3$

c. $1 + i + i^2 + i^3 + i^4$

d. $1 + i + i^2 + i^3 + i^4 + i^5$

e. $1 + i + i^2 + i^3 + i^4 + i^5 + i^6$

f. $1 + i + i^2 + i^3 + i^4 + i^5 + i^6 + i^7 + \cdots + i^{67}$

16. **Take It Further** Let $\omega = \frac{-1 + i\sqrt{3}}{2}$.

Simplify each expression. Write the result in the form $x + yi$ where $x$ and $y$ are real numbers.

a. $1 + \omega + \omega^2$

b. $1 + \omega + \omega^2 + \omega^3$

c. $1 + \omega + \omega^2 + \omega^3 + \omega^4$

d. $1 + \omega + \omega^2 + \omega^3 + \omega^4 + \omega^5$

e. $1 + \omega + \omega^2 + \omega^3 + \omega^4 + \omega^5 + \omega^6$

f. $1 + \omega + \omega^2 + \omega^3 + \omega^4 + \omega^5 + \omega^6 + \omega^7 + \cdots + \omega^{67}$

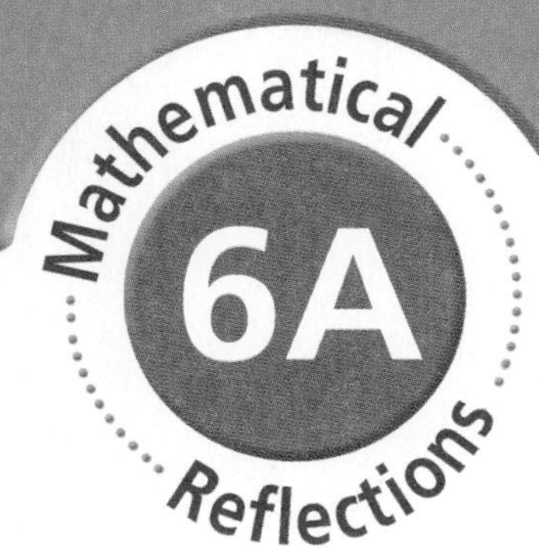


**In this investigation, you described complex numbers as points in a plane using both rectangular and polar coordinates. You learned geometric interpretations of addition and multiplication of complex numbers. The following questions will help you summarize what you have learned.**

1. Describe the effect of multiplying a complex number by $2i$ in terms of scaling and rotation.
2. Graph all complex numbers having magnitude 2.
3. Name three complex numbers that have argument $120^\circ$.
4. If $z$ is any complex number, show that $z\overline{z} = |z|^2$.
5. Use the result from Exercise 4 to show that $\frac{1}{z} = \frac{\overline{z}}{|z^2|}$ for any nonzero complex number $z$.
6. How can you write a complex number using trigonometry?
7. What are the magnitude and argument of a complex number, and how do you find them?
8. How do you use geometry to calculate $(1 - i\sqrt{3}) \cdot (-3\sqrt{3} + 3i)$?

## Vocabulary and Notation

In this investigation, you learned these terms. Make sure you understand what each one means and how to use it.

- **argument, arg($z$)**
- **cis($\theta$)**
- **conjugate, $\overline{z}$**
- **magnitude, $|z|$**
- **norm, $N(z)$**
- **polar coordinates**
- **polar form for complex numbers**
- **rectangular coordinates**
- **rectangular form for complex numbers**

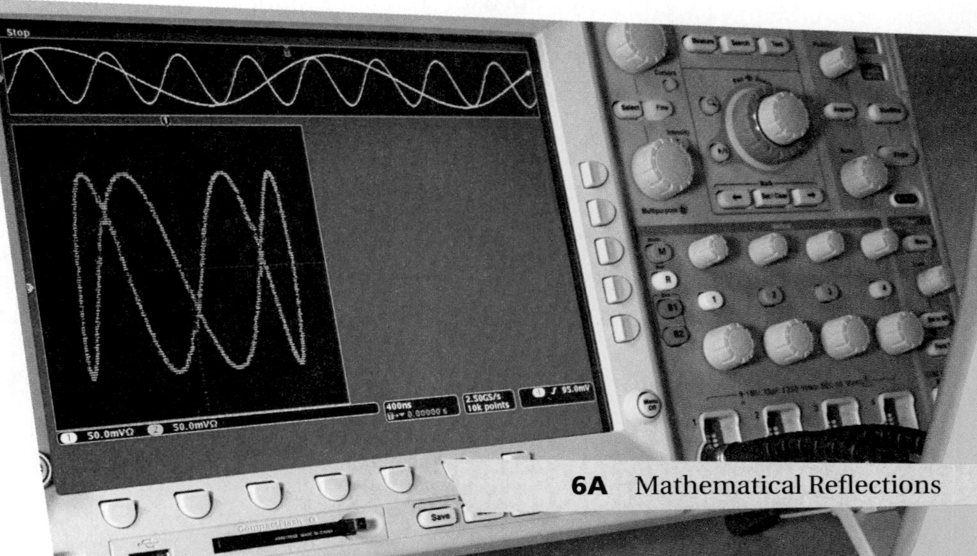

Lissajous figures are the graphs of equations containing cosine and sine functions. You can best observe their lively display on an oscilloscope.

# De Moivre's Theorem

**Complex numbers are rooted in algebra, but once mathematicians like Gauss and Argand had the insight to represent complex numbers geometrically, the floodgates opened. Complex numbers permeated every part of mathematics. One of the most striking applications of complex numbers is to geometry. You have already seen how beautifully the addition and multiplication of complex numbers work on the complex plane, but that is just the beginning.**

**In *De Moivre's Theorem,* you will peek at one of the deepest connections between geometry and algebra. It is the connection between the roots of certain equations (equations of the form $x^n - 1 = 0$, where $n$ is a positive integer) and regular polygons. This connection is sometimes called cyclotomy ("circle division") because regular polygons divide a circle into congruent pieces.**

**By the end of this investigation, you will be able to answer questions like these.**

1. How do you use De Moivre's Theorem to write a rule for $\cos 3x$?
2. How can you connect roots of unity to regular polygons?
3. For what values of $\cos x$ does $\cos 3x = 0$?

**You will learn how to**

- calculate powers of complex numbers using De Moivre's Theorem
- understand the geometry of roots of unity, and the connection to roots of equations of the form $x^n - 1 = 0$
- find exact algebraic expressions for certain trigonometric values

**You will develop these habits and skills:**

- Calculate with complex numbers.
- Visualize complex numbers and their arithmetic.

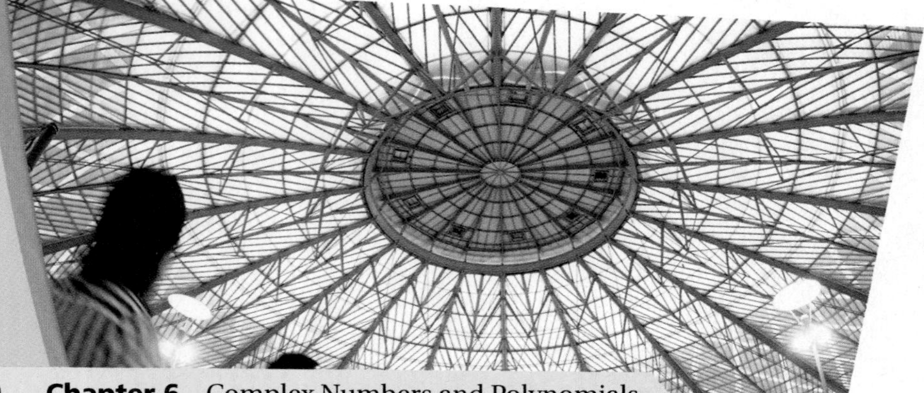

The design of this skylight reflects the connection between the 18 roots of unity and a regular 18-gon.

# 6.05 Getting Started

There are $n$ complex numbers that satisfy the equation $x^n - 1 = 0$. Each is known as an **nth root of unity.** To work with roots of unity, you will have to know how to find powers of complex numbers. The following problems will help you get started.

## For You to Explore

**1.** Play the Factor Game! It is a game for two players.

The board is all the integers from 1 to 30.

| 1 | 2 | 3 | 4 | 5 |
|---|---|---|---|---|
| 6 | 7 | 8 | 9 | 10 |
| 11 | 12 | 13 | 14 | 15 |
| 16 | 17 | 18 | 19 | 20 |
| 21 | 22 | 23 | 24 | 25 |
| 26 | 27 | 28 | 29 | 30 |

Here are the rules.

- Player 1 picks any available number on the board.
- Player 2 identifies all the remaining proper factors of that number.
- If there are no proper factors remaining on the board, Player 1 loses a turn and no points are scored.
- Remove from the board all numbers used in a turn.

For example, the proper factors of 18 are 1, 2, 3, 6, and 9.

In successive rounds, players alternate between picking the number and finding the factors.

*Scoring.*

- Player 1 scores points equal to the value of the number picked.
- For each proper factor identified, Player 2 scores points equal to the value of that factor.
- If there are no factors remaining on the board, Player 1 scores 0.
- **Bonus Points.** If Player 1 finds a factor that Player 2 missed, Player 1 scores points equal to the value of that factor.

If the first pick is 18, that player earns 18 points while the opponent earns $1 + 2 + 3 + 6 + 9 =$ 21 points. Not a great first pick!

**a.** Play the game a few times.

**b.** Describe some of the strategies a player could use in this game.

**2.** Find the 4 complex numbers that are solutions to the equation $x^4 - 1 = 0$. Plot them as points in the complex plane.

3. Plot the first 10 powers of each complex number as points in the complex plane, starting with $z^0 = 1$.

   a. $z = i$
   b. $z = \frac{1}{2} + \frac{\sqrt{3}}{2}i$
   c. $z = \frac{3}{5} + \frac{4}{5}i$
   d. $z = \text{cis } 36°$
   e. $z = 1 + i$
   f. $z = \frac{1}{2} \text{ cis } \frac{\pi}{4}$

4. Describe the picture you get when you plot the powers of a complex number $z$ (starting with $z^0$) given each condition.

   a. $|z| = 1$
   b. $|z| > 1$
   c. $|z| < 1$

5. Calculate the sum

$$\sum_{k=0}^{3} \cos \frac{2\pi k}{4}$$

6. Find the 3 complex numbers that are solutions to the equation $x^3 - 1 = 0$. Plot them as points in the complex plane.

7. Calculate the sum

$$\sum_{k=0}^{2} \sin \frac{2\pi k}{3}$$

8. Calculate the sum

$$\sum_{k=1}^{6} \cos \frac{2\pi k}{7}$$

**Remember...**

You can use summation notation to describe the sum of terms. The general form is

$$\sum_{k=0}^{n} a_k = a_0 + a_1 + a_2 + \cdots + a_n$$

where $k$ is the index variable, 0 is the starting value, and $n$ is the final value.

## Exercises Practicing Habits of Mind

### On Your Own

9. For $z = \text{cis } 72°$, find each of the following.

   a. $\arg(z^2)$
   b. $\arg(z^3)$
   c. $\arg(z^4)$
   d. $\arg(z^5)$
   e. $\arg(z^{10})$
   f. $\arg(z^n)$

10. For each expression, write an equivalent expression that includes only $\cos x$ and $\sin x$.

a. $\cos (x + 90°)$

b. $\cos (x + x)$

c. Write $\cos 4x$ in terms of powers of $\cos x$ and $\sin x$.

d. Write $\cos 4x$ in terms of powers of $\cos x$ only.

The identity $\sin 2x = 2 \sin x \cos x$ might be helpful here.

11. The factorization of $x^6 - 1$ over $\mathbb{Z}$ is

$$x^6 - 1 = (x - 1)(x + 1)(x^2 - x + 1)(x^2 + x + 1)$$

a. Is $x^2 - 1$ a factor of $x^6 - 1$? Explain.

b. Is $x^3 - 1$ a factor of $x^6 - 1$? Explain.

c. Is $x^4 - 1$ a factor of $x^6 - 1$? Explain.

12. Find the two solutions to the equation $x^2 - 8x + 15 = 0$. Then find their sum and product.

13. Find the two solutions to the equation $x^2 - 8x + 17 = 0$. Then find their sum and product.

14. Find the five complex numbers that are solutions to the equation $x^5 - 1 = 0$. Approximate any decimal answers to four decimal places.

See TI-Nspire Handbook on p. 817 for an example of how to solve using your calculator.

15. Plot the five complex numbers from Exercise 14 as points in the same complex plane. Compare the results to your results for Problems 2 and 6.

16. a. Approximate the value of $\cos 72°$ to four decimal places.

b. Approximate the value of $\cos \frac{4\pi}{5}$ to four decimal places.

c. Approximate the value of $\cos \frac{6\pi}{5}$ to four decimal places.

## Maintain Your Skills

17. Calculate each sum.

a. $\sum_{k=0}^{3} \sin \frac{2\pi k}{4}$

b. $\sum_{k=0}^{5} \sin \frac{2\pi k}{6}$

c. $\sum_{k=0}^{5} \cos \frac{2\pi k}{6}$

d. $\sum_{k=0}^{7} \sin (45k)°$

e. $\sum_{k=0}^{7} \cos \frac{2\pi k}{8}$

## 6.06 Powers of Complex Numbers

In Lesson 6.04, you proved a theorem for the multiplication of complex numbers. A direct consequence to Theorem 6.2 lets you find a simpler way to take powers of complex numbers.

### For Discussion

In Exercise 9 of Lesson 6.05, you looked at powers of $z = \text{cis } 72^\circ$. One pattern you may have noticed is that the argument of each successive power was $72^\circ$ greater than the argument of the argument of the previous one.

**1.** Use Theorem 6.2 to explain why $\arg(z^n) = n(\arg(z))$ for any $n \in \mathbb{Z}^+$.

"For any $n \in \mathbb{Z}^+$" means "for any number $n$ contained in the positive integers."

When $|z| = 1$, you can use the statement above to determine exactly where $z^n$ is in the complex plane. Since $|z| = 1$, $|z^n| = 1$, too. So,

$$z^n = \text{cis } \theta$$

Now the only question is, what is $\theta$? The result stated in the discussion above suggests that $\theta = n(\arg(z))$. Theorem 6.3, first published by Abraham de Moivre (1667–1754), summarizes these ideas.

### *Theorem 6.3 De Moivre's Theorem*

**For all real $\theta$, $(\text{cis } \theta)^n = \text{cis } n\theta$.**

The argument outlined above should help you see why De Moivre's Theorem is true, but is not a solid proof.

You can use these ideas here to make a proof by induction.

**Proof** The proof is a repeated application of Theorem 6.2. As a first step, Theorem 6.2 states that

$$(\text{cis } \theta)(\text{cis } \alpha) = \text{cis } (\theta + \alpha)$$

So,

$$\begin{aligned}(\text{cis } \theta)^2 &= (\text{cis } \theta)(\text{cis } \theta) \\ &= \text{cis } (\theta + \theta) \\ &= \text{cis } 2\theta\end{aligned}$$

Similarly,

$$\begin{aligned}(\text{cis } \theta)^3 &= (\text{cis } \theta)(\text{cis } \theta)^2 \\ &= (\text{cis } \theta)(\text{cis } 2\theta) \\ &= \text{cis } (\theta + 2\theta) \\ &= \text{cis } 3\theta\end{aligned}$$

If you keep doing this for $n$ steps, you have

$$\begin{aligned}(\text{cis } \theta)^n &= (\text{cis } \theta)(\text{cis } \theta)^{n-1} \\ &= (\text{cis } \theta)(\text{cis } (n-1)\,\theta) \\ &= \text{cis } (\theta + (n-1)\,\theta) \\ &= \text{cis } n\theta\end{aligned}$$

De Moivre's Theorem as stated here applies only to complex numbers that fall on the unit circle. But you can generalize the theorem to include any complex number.

### Corollary 6.3.1

For all real $\theta$, $(r \text{ cis}\theta)^n = r^n \text{cis} n\theta$.

## For You to Do

**2.** Prove Corollary 6.3.1.

You can use De Moivre's Theorem and Corollary 6.3.1 to solve equations that involve complex numbers.

## Example

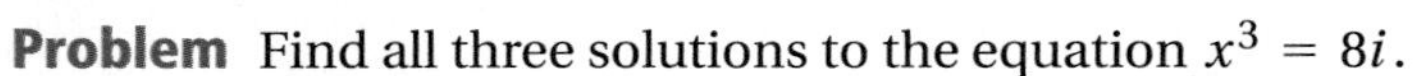

**Problem** Find all three solutions to the equation $x^3 = 8i$.

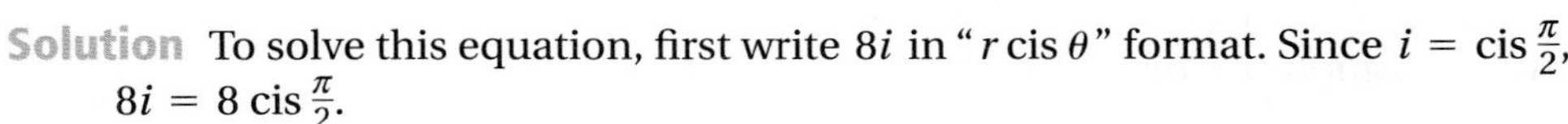

**Solution** To solve this equation, first write $8i$ in "$r \text{ cis } \theta$" format. Since $i = \text{cis } \frac{\pi}{2}$, $8i = 8 \text{ cis } \frac{\pi}{2}$.

Now, suppose $x = a \text{ cis } \alpha$. Then you have $(a \text{ cis } \alpha)^3 = 8 \text{ cis } \frac{\pi}{2}$. By Corollary 6.3.1, $a^3 \text{ cis } 3\alpha = 8 \text{ cis } \frac{\pi}{2}$.

From there, you can say that $a^3 = 8$, so $a = 2$ since $a$ must be a real number.

Also, you have $3\alpha = \frac{\pi}{2}$. So $\alpha = \frac{\pi}{6}$.

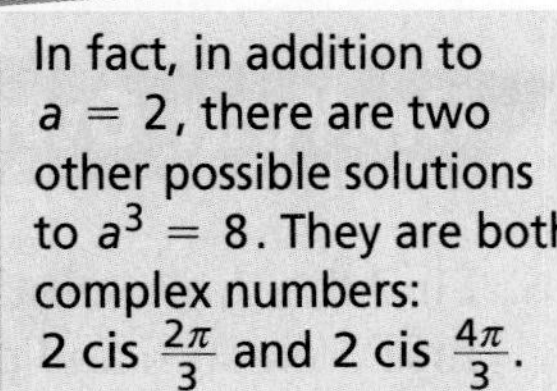

In fact, in addition to $a = 2$, there are two other possible solutions to $a^3 = 8$. They are both complex numbers: $2 \text{ cis } \frac{2\pi}{3}$ and $2 \text{ cis } \frac{4\pi}{3}$.

But recall that when you are solving for radians, you also have to consider $3\alpha = \frac{\pi}{2} + 2\pi k$ for integer values of $k$.

$$3\alpha = \frac{\pi}{2} + 2\pi k$$

$$\alpha = \frac{\pi}{6} + \frac{2\pi}{3} k$$

For $k = 0$, 1, and 2, you get $\alpha = \frac{\pi}{6}, \frac{5\pi}{6}$, and $\frac{3\pi}{2}$, respectively. Any other value for $k$ gives an $\alpha$ value that differs from one of these three by a multiple of $2\pi$. Since $\text{cis } (\alpha + 2\pi) = \text{cis } \alpha$, the three solutions of the equation are $x = 2 \text{ cis } \frac{\pi}{6}$, $x = 2 \text{ cis } \frac{5\pi}{6}$, and $x = 2 \text{ cis } \frac{3\pi}{2}$.

## For You to Do

**3.** Find all four solutions to the equation $x^4 = -16$.

# Exercises Practicing Habits of Mind

## Check Your Understanding

1. Let $z$ be a complex number where $|z| = 3$ and $\arg(z) = \frac{\pi}{3}$. Find the magnitude and argument of each of the following expressions.

   a. $z^2$
   b. $z^3$
   c. $z^5$
   d. $10z$
   e. $z^0$
   f. $z^{-1}$

2. Suppose $z = 3 \text{ cis } \frac{\pi}{3}$ as in Exercise 1. If $a^2 = z$, what possible value(s) can $a$ have?

3. Given each $z$, find $|z^3|$ and $\arg(z^3)$.

   a. $z = 4$
   b. $z = 4 \text{ cis } 120°$
   c. $|z| = 2$ and $\arg(z) = \frac{\pi}{6}$
   d. $z = -2i$

4. In the Example, you found three solutions to the equation $x^3 = 8i$. Find their sum and product.

5. Suppose $a$ is a solution to the equation $x^{11} = 1$.

   a. Show that $a^2$ is also a solution to this equation.
   b. Show that if $k$ is any integer, then $a^k$ is also a solution to this equation.

## On Your Own

6. Find the three solutions to the equation $x^3 + 2x^2 - 80x - 160 = 0$. Then find their sum and product.

> One way to find the solutions is to look at the graph of $f(x) = x^3 + 2x^2 - 80x - 160$. What points on the graph correspond to solutions to the equation?

7. Expand $(\cos\theta + i\sin\theta)^2$. Use the result to generate rules for $\cos 2\theta$ and $\sin 2\theta$.

8. Find a formula for $\cos 5x$ in terms of $\cos x$ and $\sin x$.

9. Describe how to use De Moivre's Theorem to prove this fact about powers of $-1$.

   For integer $n$, $(-1)^n = -1$ if $n$ is odd and $(-1)^n = 1$ if $n$ is even.

10. **Write About It** Describe how to use De Moivre's Theorem to figure out whether a power of $i$ equals $i$, $-i$, 1, or $-1$.

> What are $|i|$ and $\arg(i)$?

11. Given the equation $x^5 - 1 = 0$, one possible solution is $x = 1$.

    a. Show that $x = \text{cis } \frac{2\pi}{5}$ is also a solution to the equation $x^5 - 1 = 0$.
    b. Find all five solutions to $x^5 - 1 = 0$.

**12.** **a.** Sketch the graph of $f(x) = 4\cos^3 x - 3\cos x$ on $0 \le x < 2\pi$.

**b.** Suppose $g(x) = \cos 3x$. Show that $f = g$.

**13.** **a.** Suppose $\cos 3x = 0$. What are the three possible values of $\cos x$?

**b.** Find all angles on $0 \le x < 2\pi$ with $\cos 3x = 0$.

**14.** Find the exact value of $\cos \frac{\pi}{12}$.

**15.** Standardized Test Prep Which of the following is a solution to the equation $x^2 = i$?

**A.** $\text{cis}\left(\frac{\pi}{6}\right)$ **B.** $\text{cis}\left(\frac{\pi}{4}\right)$ **C.** $\text{cis}\left(\frac{\pi}{3}\right)$ **D.** $\text{cis}\left(\frac{\pi}{2}\right)$

## Maintain Your Skills

**16.** Solve each equation. Write the complete set of solutions in the form cis $\theta$.

**a.** $x^2 - 1 = 0$ **b.** $x^3 - 1 = 0$ **c.** $x^4 - 1 = 0$

**d.** $x^5 - 1 = 0$ **e.** $x^6 - 1 = 0$ **f.** $x^7 - 1 = 0$

**17.** Approximate each sum to four decimal places.

**a.** $\sum_{k=0}^{6} \sin \frac{2\pi k}{7}$ **b.** $\sum_{k=0}^{6} \cos \frac{2\pi k}{7}$ **c.** $\sum_{k=0}^{6} \cos \frac{4\pi k}{7}$

**d.** $\sum_{k=0}^{8} \sin \frac{2\pi k}{9}$ **e.** $\sum_{k=0}^{8} \cos (40k)^\circ$ **f.** $\sum_{k=0}^{10} \cos \frac{2\pi k}{12}$

## Historical Perspective

Mathematicians now recognize Abraham de Moivre (1667–1754) as a genius, but this was not always the case. Despite de Moivre's mathematical talent, he did not enjoy the fame he deserved during his lifetime.

When he was 18, de Moivre moved to England because of civil and religious unrest in France. Although he had studied mathematics extensively in France, he was unable to get a job in an English university due to his status as a foreigner.

For most of his life, de Moivre's main source of income was tutoring mathematics. In his later years, he earned money by solving math puzzles in local coffee shops. He is remembered for predicting the day of his own death. He noticed he was sleeping 15 minutes longer each night and calculated he would die on the day he slept 24 hours. He was correct!

# 6.07 Roots of Unity

In Lesson 6.05, you played the Factor Game. Now, it is time to play the Polynomial Factor Game!

## In-Class Experiment

**The Polynomial Factor Game.** This game is also for two players. The rules are similar to those of the Factor Game. Decide who goes first.

- Player 1 picks any available polynomial on the board.
- Player 2 identifies all polynomials on the board that are factors of that polynomial.
- If there are no factors of that polynomial remaining on the board, Player 1 loses a turn and no points are scored.
- All polynomials used in a turn are removed from the board.

For each successive round, players alternate between picking the polynomial and finding the factors.

*Scoring.*

- Player 1 scores points equal to the degree of the polynomial picked.
- For each factor identified, Player 2 scores points equal to the degree of that factor.
- **Bonus Points.** If Player 1 finds a factor that Player 2 missed, Player 1 scores points equal to the degree of that factor.

For example, $x - 1$ is a factor of $x^2 - 1$. So if the first pick was $x^2 - 1$, that player earns 2 points while the other player earns 1.

The board is polynomials of the form $x^n - 1$ for all integer values from 1 to a set maximum. 20 is a good maximum for this game.

For a longer game, you could use 30 as you did in the Factor Game.

| $x - 1$ | $x^2 - 1$ | $x^3 - 1$ | $x^4 - 1$ | $x^5 - 1$ |
|---|---|---|---|---|
| $x^6 - 1$ | $x^7 - 1$ | $x^8 - 1$ | $x^9 - 1$ | $x^{10} - 1$ |
| $x^{11} - 1$ | $x^{12} - 1$ | $x^{13} - 1$ | $x^{14} - 1$ | $x^{15} - 1$ |
| $x^{16} - 1$ | $x^{17} - 1$ | $x^{18} - 1$ | $x^{19} - 1$ | $x^{20} - 1$ |

Play the game a few times.

1. Describe some of the strategies a player could use in this game.
2. Compare strategies in this game with those from the Factor Game you played in Lesson 6.05.

In Chapter 1, you learned an important theorem regarding factors of polynomials.

### *Theorem 6.4 The Factor Theorem*

**Suppose $f(x)$ is a polynomial. Then $x - a$ is a factor of $f(x)$ if and only if the number $a$ is a root of the equation $f(x) = 0$.**

One strategy for finding factors in the Polynomial Factor Game is to find polynomials that have the same roots as the polynomial that the other player picked. That is, $x^n - 1$ is a factor of $x^m - 1$ if and only if every root of $x^n - 1 = 0$ is also a root of $x^m - 1 = 0$.

But what are the roots of those polynomials? You can use De Moivre's Theorem to find them. You can use geometry to get a visual idea of where those roots lie on the complex plane.

## For You to Do

**3.** Find and plot the three roots of the equation $x^3 - 1 = 0$.

**4.** Find and plot the six roots of the equation $x^6 - 1 = 0$.

## For Discussion

**5.** Explain how the results from Problems 3 and 4 show that $x^3 - 1$ is a factor of $x^6 - 1$.

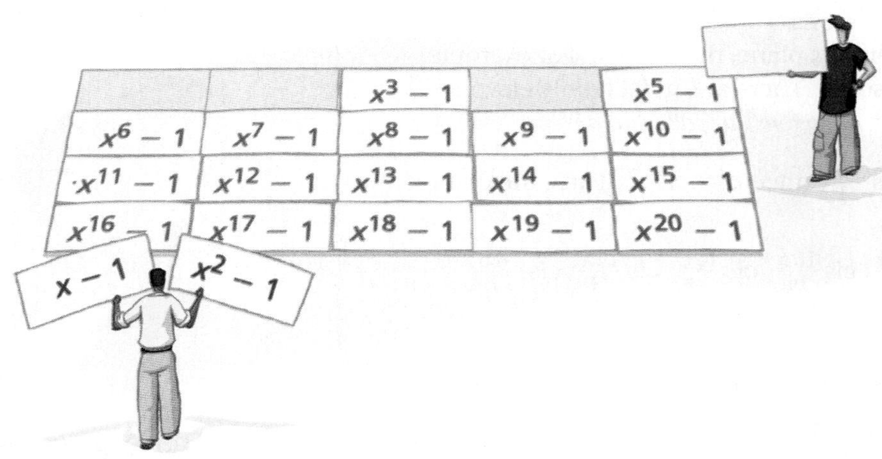

## Developing Habits of Mind

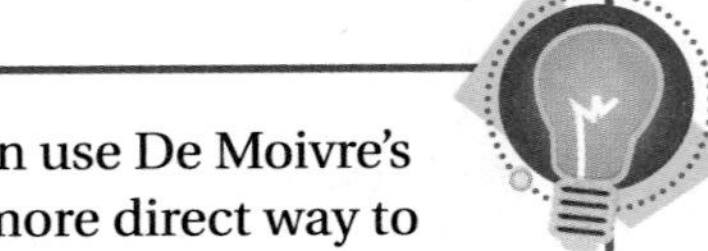

**Find another way.** As you saw in Lesson 6.06, you can use De Moivre's Theorem to find the roots of an equation. There is a more direct way to find all of the roots to equations of the form $x^n - 1 = 0$.

For instance, in Exercise 5 from Lesson 6.06, you supposed $a$ was a solution of $x^{11} - 1 = 0$, and showed that $a^2$ was also a solution.

This fact can help you find all of the solutions to $x^{11} - 1 = 0$.

- One solution is $x = 1$, since $1^{11} = 1$.
- $x^{11} - 1 = 0 \Rightarrow x^{11} = 1$. You can find a second solution by letting $x = r \operatorname{cis} \theta$. Since $1 = \operatorname{cis} 2\pi$ you have

$$\begin{aligned} (r \operatorname{cis} \theta)^{11} &= 1 \operatorname{cis} 2\pi \\ r^{11} \operatorname{cis} 11\theta &= 1 \operatorname{cis} 2\pi \\ r^{11} = 1 \quad \text{and} \quad 11\theta &= 2\pi \\ r = 1 \quad \text{and} \quad \theta &= \frac{2\pi}{11} \end{aligned}$$

  So $\operatorname{cis} \frac{2\pi}{11}$ is also a solution.

- You know that if $a$ is a solution, then $a^2$ is also a solution. Therefore $\left(\operatorname{cis} \frac{2\pi}{11}\right)^2$ is a solution. By De Moivre's Theorem,

$$\left(\operatorname{cis} \frac{2\pi}{11}\right)^2 = \operatorname{cis}\left(2 \cdot \frac{2\pi}{11}\right) = \operatorname{cis} \frac{4\pi}{11}$$

- In fact, any power of $a$ is a solution because

$$(a^k)^{11} = (a^{11})^k = 1^k = 1$$

So, if $a = \operatorname{cis} \frac{2\pi}{11}$, then all of the following are solutions to $x^{11} - 1 = 0$.

$$1, a, a^2, a^3, a^4, a^5, a^6, a^7, a^8, a^9, a^{10}, a^{11}, a^{12}, a^{13}, \ldots$$

It looks like there are too many solutions. There should only be eleven. But if you plot all these on the complex plane, they repeat. For example, $a^{11} = 1, a^{12} = a, a^{13} = a^2$, and so on. There are, in fact, only eleven solutions. They are $1, a, a^2, a^3, a^4, a^5, a^6, a^7, a^8, a^9$, and $a^{10}$.

By De Moivre's Theorem, $a^k = \operatorname{cis} \frac{2k\pi}{11}$, since $a = \operatorname{cis} \frac{2\pi}{11}$. Thus, the complete solution set is

$$\left\{1, \operatorname{cis} \frac{2\pi}{11}, \operatorname{cis} \frac{4\pi}{11}, \operatorname{cis} \frac{6\pi}{11}, \operatorname{cis} \frac{8\pi}{11}, \operatorname{cis} \frac{10\pi}{11}, \operatorname{cis} \frac{12\pi}{11}, \operatorname{cis} \frac{14\pi}{11}, \operatorname{cis} \frac{16\pi}{11}, \operatorname{cis} \frac{18\pi}{11}, \operatorname{cis} \frac{20\pi}{11}\right\}$$

**Habits of Mind**

**Draw a diagram.** As you work through these roots, plot each one on the complex plane.

**Remember...**

*A* $\Rightarrow$ *B* means "*A* implies *B*": if *A* is true then *B* is true.

The solutions to $x^n = 1$ are called roots of unity, so named since solving the equation involves taking a root of 1.

- A square root of unity is a root of the equation $x^2 - 1 = 0$.
- A cube root of unity is a root of the equation $x^3 - 1 = 0$.
- In general, an $n$th root of unity is a root of the equation $x^n - 1 = 0$.

So, 1 is considered "unity." And in $\mathbb{C}$, there are 2 second roots of unity, 3 third roots of unity, 4 fourth roots of unity, and in general, *n* *n*th roots of unity.

# Exercises *Practicing Habits of Mind*

## Check Your Understanding

1. Let $\omega$ be the fifth root of unity marked in this diagram.

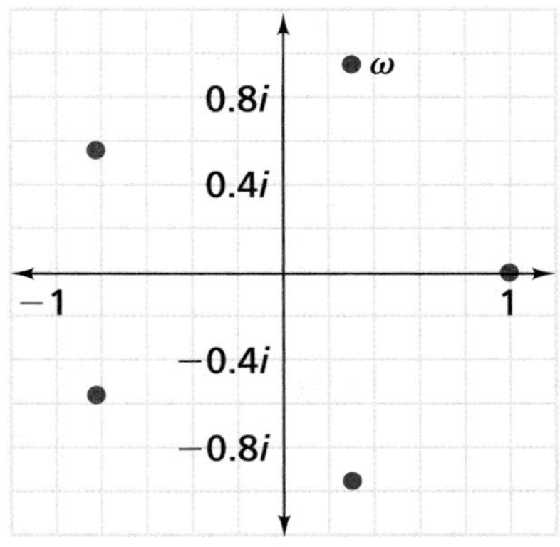


   a. Copy the diagram. Label $\omega^2, \omega^3, \omega^4, \omega^5, \omega^6$, and $\omega^{13}$.

   b. The product of all five fifth roots of unity is $1 \cdot \omega \cdot \omega^2 \cdot \omega^3 \cdot \omega^4$. Simplify this product as much as possible.

2. a. Calculate the sum of the sixth roots of unity.

   b. Evaluate the sum.

$$\sum_{k=0}^{5} \sin \frac{2\pi k}{6}$$

   c. How are the results from parts (a) and (b) related?

3. Plot all 12 solutions to the equation $x^{12} - 1 = 0$ on the complex plane.

4. a. Plot all 6 solutions to the equation $x^6 - 1 = 0$ on the complex plane.

   b. Show that these 6 solutions are also solutions to the equation $x^{12} - 1 = 0$

   c. Show that $x^6 - 1$ is a factor of $x^{12} - 1$.

Your work in Exercise 3 may be helpful here.

5. The fifth roots of unity appear in the diagram for Exercise 1. Find a value of $n$, with $n \neq 5$, such that every fifth root of unity is also an $n$th root of unity.

6. Find the smallest positive integer $n$ such that $w = \frac{1}{2} - \frac{\sqrt{3}}{2}i$ is an $n$th root of unity.

7. Suppose $z = \operatorname{cis} 310°$. Can $z$ be a root of unity? If so, find the smallest $n$ such that $z$ is an $n$th root of unity. If not, explain why $z$ can never be a root of unity.

8. **Take It Further** Suppose $z$ is a fifth root of unity and $w$ is a third root of unity, as pictured.

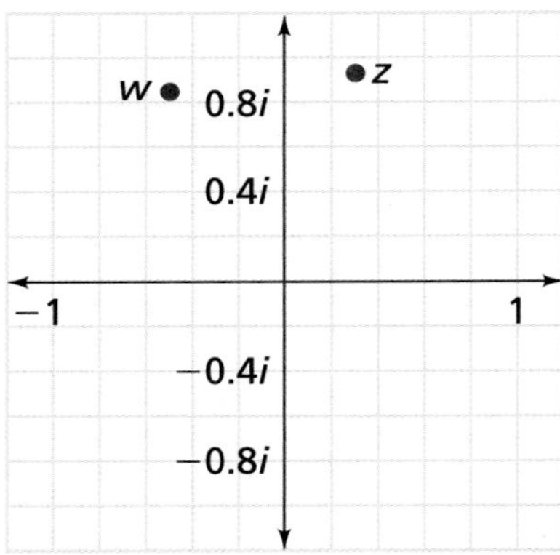


a. Find a root of unity $x$ that lies between $z$ and $w$ on the unit circle.

b. Find a root of unity $y$ that lies between $z$ and $x$.

c. Given any two distinct roots of unity (of any order), can you always find another root of unity between them?

The answer might be a sixth root of unity, or seventh, or eighth. . . .

## On Your Own

9. On the same axes, plot all the fifth roots of unity. Also, plot all the eighth roots of unity. Show how plotting these roots explains why $x^5 - 1$ is not a factor of $x^8 - 1$.

10. a. Find the product of all the sixth roots of unity.

b. Find the product of all the seventh roots of unity.

c. What are all possible values of the product of all the $n$th roots of unity? For what $n$ do each of these results occur?

**Habits of Mind**

**Look for a pattern.** More examples may be helpful.

11. Describe how you can use the roots of $x^6 - 1 = 0$ to find the solutions to these equations.

a. $x^6 - 64 = 0$

b. $x^6 + 64 = 0$

**12.** **a.** Calculate the sum of the eighth roots of unity.

**b.** Find the value of

$$\sum_{k=0}^{7} \cos \frac{2\pi k}{8}$$

**c.** How are the results from parts (a) and (b) related?

**13.** Complex number $z$ is a ninth root of unity. Find all possible values for the magnitude and argument of $z$.

**14.** **Write About It** Roots of unity must lie on the unit circle. That is, they must be complex numbers with magnitude 1. Is every complex number with magnitude 1 a root of unity? Explain.

**15.** Suppose $z$ is an $n$th root of unity.

**a.** Show that $\frac{1}{z} = \overline{z}$.

**b.** Show that $\overline{z}$ is also an $n$th root of unity.

**16.** **Take It Further** Consider the sixth roots of unity as labeled in this diagram.

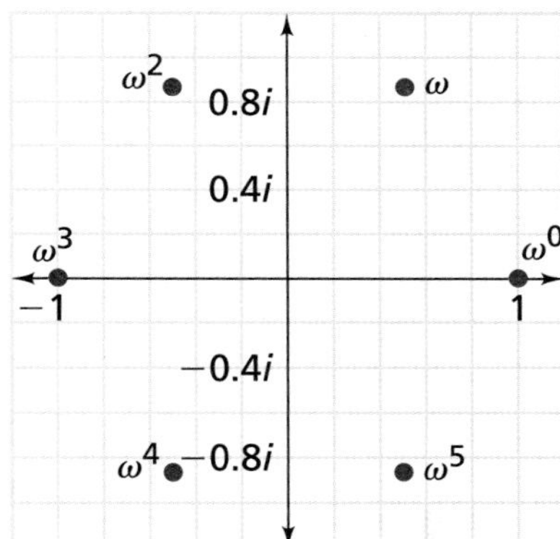


The product of all these roots is $-1$, but the product of the first three roots is 1.

$$\omega \cdot \omega^2 \cdot \omega^3 = \omega^6 = 1$$

**a.** Find another situation where the product of the first $k$ $n$th roots of unity is 1, with $k$ less than $n - 1$.

**b.** For what values of $n$ will this situation occur? In other words, for what $n$ is there a $k$ such that the product of the first $k$ $n$th roots of unity is 1 (with $k < n - 1$)?

17. Take It Further Suppose that $a$ is an $n$th root of unity, and $n$ is odd.

a. Prove that one of the roots of $x^2 - a = 0$ is an $n$th root of unity.

b. Why is this false when $n$ is even?

18. Some roots of unity are repeats. For example, the cube roots of unity (solutions to $x^3 - 1 = 0$) are also sixth roots of unity (solutions to $x^6 - 1 = 0$). And $x = 1$ is always an $n$th root of unity, for any $n$. But some roots of unity are "new" for that power. For example, $i$ and $-i$ are solutions to $x^4 - 1 = 0$, but not $x^3 - 1 = 0$, $x^2 - 1 = 0$, or $x^1 - 1 = 0$.

a. Copy and complete this table with the number of new roots of unity for each equation. It may help to think of the solutions in terms of their argument.

| Equation | # New Roots |
|---|---|
| $x - 1 = 0$ | 1 |
| $x^2 - 1 = 0$ | 1 |
| $x^3 - 1 = 0$ | 2 |
| $x^4 - 1 = 0$ | 2 |
| $x^5 - 1 = 0$ | ■ |
| $x^6 - 1 = 0$ | ■ |
| $x^7 - 1 = 0$ | ■ |
| $x^8 - 1 = 0$ | ■ |
| $x^9 - 1 = 0$ | ■ |
| $x^{10} - 1 = 0$ | ■ |

b. Describe any relationships you notice in the table. State a rule for the number of new roots of unity in terms of $n$.

19. Standardized Test Prep Which of the following is a factor of $x^5 - 1$?

A. $x^4 + x^3 + x^2 + x + 1$ B. $x - 5$

C. $x + 1$ D. $x^4 - 1$

Go Online
www.successnetplus.com

## Maintain Your Skills

20. Evalute each sum based on what you know about roots of unity.

a. $\sum_{k=0}^{2} \sin \frac{2\pi k}{4}$ b. $\sum_{k=0}^{4} \cos \frac{2\pi k}{6}$ c. $\sum_{k=0}^{4} \sin \frac{2\pi k}{6}$ d. $\sum_{k=1}^{4} \cos \frac{2\pi k}{5}$

# 6.08 Geometry of Roots of Unity

Your work in previous lessons revealed interesting geometric patterns generated by powers of complex numbers. For instance, suppose $z = \text{cis}\,\frac{2\pi}{3}$. If you plot $z^0$, $z^1$, and $z^2$, you get the following picture.

You may recognize these numbers. They are the third roots of unity.

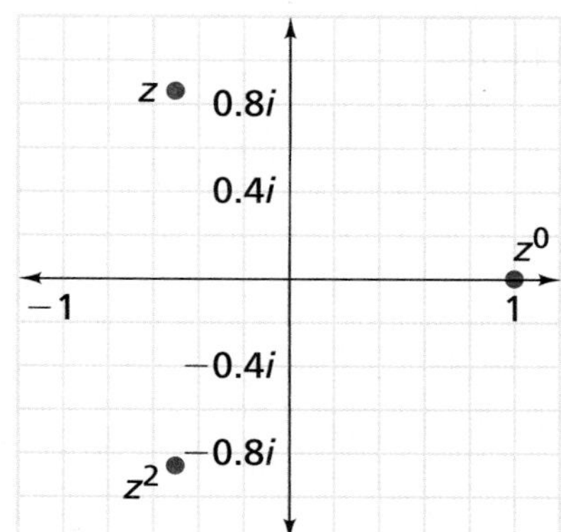


## For You to Do

1. Prove that the three roots of $x^3 - 1 = 0$ form the vertices of an equilateral triangle.

The roots of $x^3 - 1 = 0$ and the equilateral triangle they form exemplify the remarkable connection between the algebra of $\mathbb{C}$ and the geometry of regular polygons. The following theorem generalizes this fact. It also summarizes much of the work so far in this investigation.

### *Theorem 6.5*

**If $n$ is a positive integer, the roots of the equation**

$$x^n - 1 = 0$$

**are**

$$1, z, z^2, z^3, \ldots, z^{n-1}$$

**where**

$$z = \text{cis}\,\frac{2\pi}{n}$$

**If $n \geq 3$, these roots lie on the vertices of a regular $n$-gon inscribed in the unit circle in the complex plane.**

One vertex of this polygon is at 1.

## For You to Do

**2.** Prove Theorem 6.5.

You can use the theorem in two ways. If you know a simple form for the vertices of a regular $n$-gon in the complex plane, you can solve the equation $x^n - 1 = 0$. Conversely, if you can solve the equation, you have a simple form for the vertices of the polygon in the complex plane.

Carl Friedrich Gauss (1777–1855) was one of the greatest mathematicians of all time. He was so proud of his regular 17-sided polygon construction that he wanted it to appear on his tombstone!

In the case $n = 5$, Theorem 6.5 says that the roots of $x^5 - 1 = 0$ are

$$1, z, z^2, z^3, z^4$$

where

$$z = \text{cis}\,\frac{2\pi}{5}$$

These roots lie on the vertices of a regular pentagon inscribed in the unit circle on the complex plane.

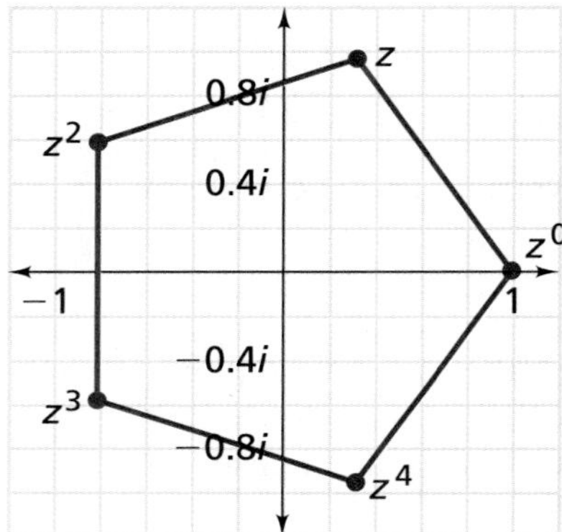

## Exercises *Practicing Habits of Mind*

### Check Your Understanding

**1.** Suppose $w = \text{cis } 20^\circ$. The powers of $w$ form the vertices of a regular polygon in the complex plane. What is the smallest number of sides that this polygon can have?

**2.** The graph below shows the plot of the powers (from 0 to 20) of $z = \text{cis } 17^\circ$.

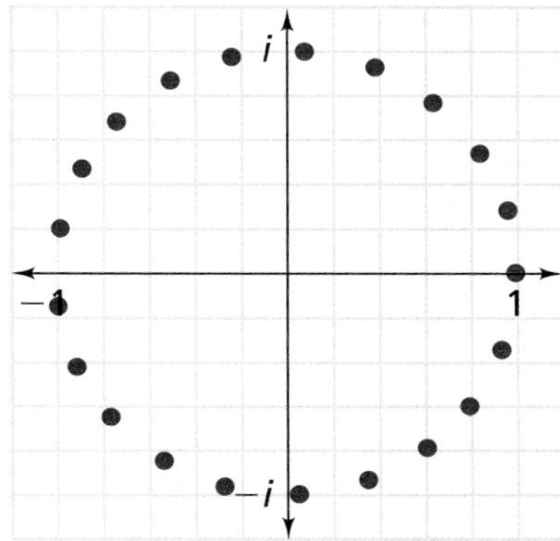


**a.** Why are these powers of $z$ not vertices of a regular polygon?

**b.** Will the powers of $z$ ever come back to 1? If so, how many times around the unit circle will it take? If not, why not?

> $z^{21}$ does not quite make it all the way around.
>
> $z^{22}$ would be back in the first quadrant.

**c.** Describe all the values of $\theta$ for which the powers of $z = \text{cis } \theta$ are vertices of a regular polygon.

For Exercises 3–7, let $z = \operatorname{cis}\frac{2\pi}{5}$, one of the roots of $x^5 - 1 = 0$.

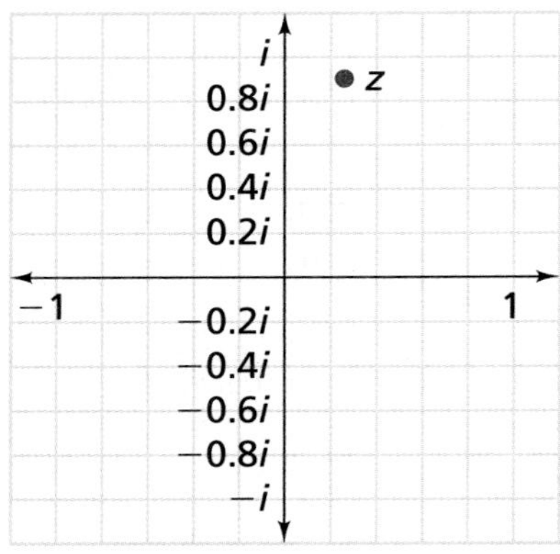


**3.** **a.** Show that $z^4 = \operatorname{cis}\left(-\frac{2\pi}{5}\right)$.

**b.** Show that $z + z^4 = 2\cos\frac{2\pi}{5}$.

**4.** **a.** Factor the expression $x^5 - 1$ into two terms.

**b.** Show that $z^4 + z^3 + z^2 + z = -1$.

**Remember...**

*z* is the fifth root of unity in Quadrant I.

**5.** Let $a = z + z^4$ and $b = z^2 + z^3$.

**a.** Explain why *a* is a positive real number, and *b* is a negative real number.

**b.** Show that $a + b = -1$ using the result from Exercise 4b.

**c.** Write the product *ab* in terms of *z*.

**d.** Show that $ab = -1$.

**6.** In Exercise 5 you showed that *a* and *b* are two numbers that have a sum of $-1$ and a product of $-1$. Find exact values for *a* and *b*, given that *a* is positive and *b* is negative.

**7.** In Exercise 3, you found that $z + z^4 = 2\cos\frac{2\pi}{5}$.

**a.** Find an exact expression for $\cos\frac{2\pi}{5}$ that does not use trigonometric functions.

**b.** **Take It Further** Find an exact expression for $\sin\frac{2\pi}{5}$.

**c.** **Take It Further** Write algebraic expressions for each of the roots of $x^5 - 1 = 0$ that do not involve cosine and sine.

**8.** **Take It Further** Let $\phi = \frac{1 + \sqrt{5}}{2}$. Show that the polynomial $x^5 - 1$ factors over $\mathbb{R}$ as

$$x^5 - 1 = (x - 1)(x^2 + \phi x + 1)\left(x^2 - \frac{1}{\phi}x + 1\right)$$

**Remember...**

The number $\phi = \frac{1 + \sqrt{5}}{2}$ is the *golden ratio.* ($\phi$ is the Greek letter *phi,* pronounced "fie" or "fee.)"

## On Your Own

**9.** Let $w = \text{cis}\,12°$. The powers of $w$ form the vertices of a regular polygon in the complex plane. How many sides does this polygon have?

Exercises 10–13 refer to this isosceles triangle, with each base angle measuring 72°.

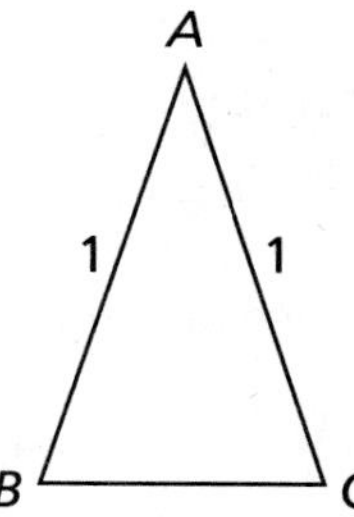


The congruent sides of the triangle have length 1.

**10.** Show that the third side length is $q = 2\cos 72°$.

**11.** Draw $\overline{BD}$ bisecting angle $ABC$.

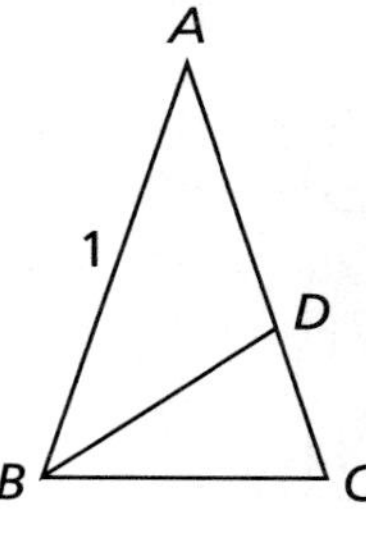

Show that triangle $ABC$ is similar to triangle $BCD$.

**12.** Use the result from Exercise 11 to show the following.

**a.** $CD = q^2$ **b.** $CD = 1 - q$

**13. a.** Use the results from Exercise 12 to find the exact value of $q$ without using trigonometric functions.

**b.** In Exercise 10 you found that $q = 2\cos 72°$. Find the exact value of $\cos 72°$.

**14.** Find the exact value of $\cos 144°$.

**15.** Take It Further Prove the following statement.

In a regular pentagon, any diagonal drawn is exactly $\phi$ times as long as a side of the pentagon, where $\phi$ is the golden ratio $\frac{1 + \sqrt{5}}{2}$.

**16.** Standardized Test Prep The powers of $\text{cis}\left(\frac{3\pi}{7}\right)$ form the vertices of a regular polygon. How many sides does the polygon have?

**A.** 3 **B.** 7 **C.** 14 **D.** 21

## Maintain Your Skills

**17.** Let $\cos\theta = 0.8$. Find the exact value of each of the following.

**a.** $\cos 2\theta$

**b.** $\cos 3\theta$

**c.** $\cos 4\theta$

**d.** $\cos 5\theta$

**18.** Let $z = 0.8 + 0.6i$. Calculate each of these powers of $z$.

**a.** $z^2$

**b.** $z^3$

**c.** $z^4$

**d.** $z^5$

**19.** Let $P(n, x)$ be a sequence of polynomial functions defined as follows.

$$P(n, x) = \begin{cases} 1 & \text{if } n = 0 \\ x & \text{if } n = 1 \\ 2x \cdot P(n-1, x) - P(n-2, x) & \text{if } n > 1 \end{cases}$$

See TI-Nspire Handbook on p. 817 for help in defining this function on your calculator.

**a.** Show that $P(0, x) = 1$ and $P(1, x) = x$.

**b.** Show that $P(2, x) = 2x^2 - 1$.

**c.** Show that $P(3, x) = 4x^3 - 3x$.

**d.** Find $P(4, x)$ and $P(5, x)$.

**e.** Let $x = 0.8$. Find $P(2, x)$, $P(3, x)$, $P(4, x)$, and $P(5, x)$.

Compare these slices of okra to the figure on p. 483. If you pay attention to detail, you will find that symmetrical patterns are common in the natural world.

# 6.09 Arithmetic With Roots of Unity—Regular Polygons

When you perform arithmetic with complex numbers, you likely treat expressions like $3 + 5i$ as "polynomials in $i$." You calculate with them using the basic rules of algebra. Then, you use one more simplification rule: you replace $i^2$ by $-1$. For example, you can reduce expressions like $3 + 2i + 4i^2 - i^3$ to something of the form $x + yi$ where $x$ and $y$ are real numbers.

## For You to Do

1. Write $3 + 2i + 4i^2 - i^3$ in the form $x + yi$, where $x$ and $y$ are real numbers.

In fact, you can define the set of complex numbers by thinking of them as polynomials in $i$.

### *Definition*

**The set of complex numbers $\mathbb{C}$ consists of all expressions in the form $a + bi$ where:**

- **$a$ and $b$ are real numbers**
- **$i^2 = -1$**
- **Perform addition and multiplication as if $a + bi$ were a polynomial in $i$, using the new rule $i^2 = -1$.**

## Developing Habits of Mind

**Recognize a similar process.** When working on any new algebraic system, you often experiment with calculations by following the rules and practicing with examples. Eventually, the calculations begin to feel familiar, ultimately behaving like something you already know.

Working with complex numbers, they start to feel like polynomials with additional simplification rules. In fact, many algebraic systems work this way. In this lesson, you will look at examples where the new objects are expressions that involve roots of unity.

In Exercise 7 from Lesson 6.08, you found the exact value for $\cos \frac{2\pi}{5}$ by looking at the fifth roots of unity (roots of $x^5 - 1 = 0$). First, you grouped the nonreal roots into pairs, then you built a quadratic equation with one solution, $2 \cos \frac{2\pi}{5}$. Following a similar technique, you can find exact values for cosines of other numbers using roots of unity. The equations will not be quadratic, but they will be polynomials.

Consider $\cos \frac{2\pi}{7}$. Does it satisfy an equation with real coefficients? You know from the last lesson that the regular 7-gon is lurking in the background. In fact, here are the roots of $x^7 - 1 = 0$ in the complex plane.

Maybe it even satisfies an equation with rational coefficients. Such numbers are called *algebraic numbers*.

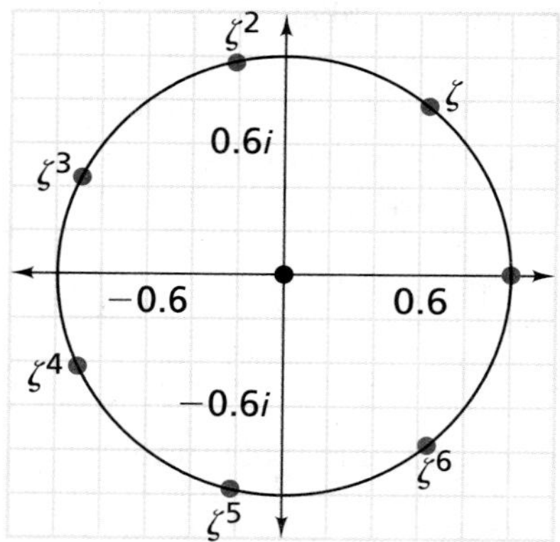

Recall Exercises 3–7 of Lesson 6.08. You know that $\zeta + \zeta^6 = 2 \cos \frac{2\pi}{7}$. If you find an algebraic expression for $\zeta + \zeta^6$, you can find an algebraic expression for $\cos \frac{2\pi}{7}$. ($\zeta$ is the Greek letter *zeta*.)

There are two other pairs of seventh roots of unity that add to real numbers.

## For You to Do

**2.** Show that

$$\zeta^2 + \zeta^5 = 2 \cos \frac{4\pi}{7}$$

$$\zeta^3 + \zeta^4 = 2 \cos \frac{6\pi}{7}$$

**Habits of Mind**

**Develop your understanding.** Recognize that you can evaluate trigonometric functions as sums of roots of unity and know which sums produce real results. Each pair here is a number plus its conjugate. Use the geometry of the *n*-gon to help with this.

You now have three pairs of roots that add to real numbers.

$$\alpha = \zeta + \zeta^6 = 2 \cos \frac{2\pi}{7}$$

$$\beta = \zeta^2 + \zeta^5 = 2 \cos \frac{4\pi}{7}$$

$$\gamma = \zeta^3 + \zeta^4 = 2 \cos \frac{6\pi}{7}$$

You can find a polynomial with roots $\alpha$, $\beta$, and $\gamma$. Those roots satisfy this cubic equation.

$$(x - \alpha)(x - \beta)(x - \gamma) = x^3 - (\alpha + \beta + \gamma)x^2 + (\alpha\beta + \alpha\gamma + \beta\gamma)x - \alpha\beta\gamma = 0 \quad (1)$$

But are the coefficients real?

## Example

### Problem

**a.** Find the value of $\alpha + \beta + \gamma$.

**b.** Find the value of $\alpha\beta + \alpha\gamma + \beta\gamma$.

### Solution

**a.** To find $\alpha + \beta + \gamma$, replace the three real numbers by their definitions to get

$$\alpha + \beta + \gamma = (\zeta + \zeta^6) + (\zeta^2 + \zeta^5) + (\zeta^3 + \zeta^4)$$

This sum includes six of the seven vertices of the 7-gon—all except for the "anchor point" 1. You worked through this sum, approximating each of the terms, using your calculator in Problem 8 of Lesson 6.05. You can also figure out the sum exactly. Try it before continuing.

You know that $\zeta$ is a root of $x^7 - 1 = 0$. The factorization

$$x^7 - 1 = (x - 1)(x^6 + x^5 + x^4 + x^3 + x^2 + 1)$$

means that $\zeta$ is a root of one of the factors on the right-hand side. But it is not a root of the first factor (why?), so it must be true that

$$\zeta^6 + \zeta^5 + \zeta^4 + \zeta^3 + \zeta^2 + \zeta + 1 = 0 \qquad (2)$$

From this identity, you can say that

$$\zeta^6 + \zeta^5 + \zeta^4 + \zeta^3 + \zeta^2 + \zeta = -1$$

But the left-hand side is just $\alpha + \beta + \gamma$, so

$$\alpha + \beta + \gamma = -1$$

**b.** To find $\alpha\beta + \alpha\gamma + \beta\gamma$, again replace each of the numbers by its definition.

$$\alpha\beta + \alpha\gamma + \beta\gamma = (\zeta + \zeta^6)(\zeta^2 + \zeta^5) + (\zeta + \zeta^6)(\zeta^3 + \zeta^4) + (\zeta^2 + \zeta^5)(\zeta^3 + \zeta^4)$$

Expand each product of binomials to get

$$\zeta^3 + \zeta^4 + 2\zeta^5 + 2\zeta^6 + 2\zeta^8 + 2\zeta^9 + \zeta^{10} + \zeta^{11}$$

Finally, replace $\zeta^7$ by 1 and simplify to get

$$2\zeta + 2\zeta^2 + 2\zeta^3 + 2\zeta^4 + 2\zeta^5 + 2\zeta^6 = 2(\zeta + \zeta^2 + \zeta^3 + \zeta^4 + \zeta^5 + \zeta^6)$$

From above, you know that $\zeta + \zeta^2 + \zeta^3 + \zeta^4 + \zeta^5 + \zeta^6 = -1$, so the value of $\alpha\beta + \alpha\gamma + \beta\gamma$ is $-2$.

**Habits of Mind**

**Make connections.** To calculate expressions with $\zeta$, treat them like polynomials in $\zeta$ and use the basic rules of algebra. Then, as a last step, reduce higher powers of $\zeta$ by using the relation $\zeta^7 = 1$.

## For You to Do

**3.** Show that $\alpha\beta\gamma = 1$.

So, the three coefficients are, in fact, real:

$$\alpha + \beta + \gamma = -1,$$
$$\alpha\beta + \alpha\gamma + \beta\gamma = -2, \quad \text{and}$$
$$\alpha\beta\gamma = 1$$

Thus, the three real numbers $2\cos\frac{2\pi}{7}$, $2\cos\frac{4\pi}{7}$, and $2\cos\frac{6\pi}{7}$ are roots of the nice cubic equation (going back to equation (1))

$$x^3 + x^2 - 2x - 1 = 0 \quad (3)$$

From here, you could try to find an exact value of $\cos\frac{2\pi}{7}$ like you did for $\cos\frac{2\pi}{5}$. Just solve the above equation.

For the pentagon in Lesson 6.08, the resulting equation was quadratic, and the quadratic formula helps you solve quadratics easily. To solve equation (3), you need a "cubic formula." Unfortunately, the cubic formula is not very useful for numerical calculations—the resulting solutions involve cube roots of complex numbers.

## For You to Do

**4.** Find approximate solutions to equation (3). Verify that these approximations agree with the value of $2\cos\frac{2\pi}{7}$, $2\cos\frac{4\pi}{7}$, and $2\cos\frac{6\pi}{7}$.

## Developing Habits of Mind

**Establish a process.** When you were expanding the product

$$\alpha\beta + \alpha\gamma + \beta\gamma$$
$$= (\zeta + \zeta^6)(\zeta^2 + \zeta^5) + (\zeta + \zeta^6)(\zeta^3 + \zeta^4) + (\zeta^2 + \zeta^5)(\zeta^3 + \zeta^4)$$

did it not feel as if you were just expanding this polynomial

$$(x + x^6)(x^2 + x^5) + (x + x^6)(x^3 + x^4) + (x^2 + x^5)(x^3 + x^4)$$

to find its normal form?

You could have just entered the above expression in your CAS getting

$$x^3 + x^4 + 2x^5 + 2x^6 + 2x^8 + 2x^9 + x^{10} + x^{11}$$

replacing $x$ by $\zeta$ in the result. Then you replaced high powers of $\zeta$ (powers 8, 9, 10, and 11) by lower ones, using the relation $\zeta^7 = 1$.

But there is an even better idea here. Suppose you take the above polynomial and divide it by $x^7 - 1$. You get:

$$x^3 + x^4 + 2x^5 + 2x^6 + 2x^8 + 2x^9 + x^{10} + x^{11}$$
$$= (x^7 - 1)(2x + 2x^2 + x^3 + x^4) + 2x + 2x^2 + 2x^3 + 2x^4 + 2x^5 + 2x^6$$

Now replace $x$ by $\zeta$ on both sides. Since $\zeta^7 - 1 = 0$, you get

$$\begin{aligned}&\zeta^3 + \zeta^4 + 2\zeta^5 + 2\zeta^6 + 2\zeta^8 + 2\zeta^9 + \zeta^{10} + \zeta^{11}\\ &= (\zeta^7 - 1)(2\zeta + 2\zeta^2 + \zeta^3 + \zeta^4) + 2\zeta + 2\zeta^2 + 2\zeta^3 + 2\zeta^4 + 2\zeta^5 + 2\zeta^6\\ &= 2\zeta + 2\zeta^2 + 2\zeta^3 + 2\zeta^4 + 2\zeta^5 + 2\zeta^6\end{aligned}$$

From here, proceed as before.

If you think about it, this process amounts to

- divide the expression

$$x^3 + x^4 + 2x^5 + 2x^6 + 2x^8 + 2x^9 + x^{10} + x^{11}$$

  by $x^7 - 1$,
- take the remainder,
- replace $x$ by $\zeta$ in this remainder, and
- simplify the result.

Most CAS systems allow you to get the remainder directly with a built in function.

See TI-Nspire Handbook on p. 817 for more about finding the remainder in polynomial division with a CAS.

## For Discussion

**5.** Use a CAS. Find the remainder when you divide
$(x^3 + x^4)(x^2 + x^5) + (x^3 + x^4)(x^1 + x^6) + (x^2 + x^5)(x + x^6)$
by $x^6 + x^5 + x^4 + x^3 + x^2 + x + 1$.
Interpret the reuslt in the context of this lesson.

## Exercises *Practicing Habits of Mind*

### Check Your Understanding

**1.** For each of the following values of $\zeta$, find the sum

$$\sum_{k=0}^{6} \zeta^{5k}$$

**a.** $\zeta = \text{cis}\,\frac{2\pi}{7}$ **b.** $\zeta = \text{cis}\,\frac{2\pi}{5}$ **c.** $\zeta = \text{cis}\,\frac{2\pi}{10}$

**2.** Suppose $\alpha = \text{cis}\,\frac{2\pi}{6}$. Evaluate each sum.

**a.** $\sum_{k=0}^{5} \alpha^k$ **b.** $1 + \alpha^3$ **c.** $\alpha^2 + \alpha^4$

**3.** Suppose $\alpha = \text{cis}\,\frac{2\pi}{5}$. Define a function $f$ on nonnegative integers by

$$f(n) = \sum_{k=0}^{4} \alpha^{kn}$$

Tabulate $f$ and find a simpler way to define it.

**4.** Suppose $z = \text{cis}\,\frac{2\pi}{5}$.

**a.** Find $\sum_{k=0}^{4} z^k$ **b.** Find $\prod_{k=0}^{4} z^k$ **c.** Find $\prod_{k=1}^{4} (1 - z^k)$

The Greek letter $\prod$ (pi) means to form a product. The following product ranges from $k = 0$ to 4:

$$\prod_{k=0}^{4} z^k = z^0 \cdot z^1 \cdot z^2 \cdot z^3 \cdot z^4$$

**5.** Suppose $z = \text{cis}\,\frac{2\pi}{5}$. Find the value of

$$(z - z^2 - z^3 + z^4)^2$$

**6.** Suppose $z = \text{cis}\,\frac{2\pi}{12}$.

**a.** Find the value of $z + z^5 + z^7 + z^{11}$.

**b.** Find the value of

$$\cos\frac{\pi}{6} + \cos\frac{5\pi}{6} + \cos\frac{7\pi}{6} + \cos\frac{11\pi}{6}$$

**7. a.** A *primitive* n*th root of unity* is a solution to $x^n - 1 = 0$ that is not a solution of any equation $x^m - 1 = 0$ where $m < n$. Find all the primitive 12th roots of unity. Graph the corresponding 12-gon on the complex plane.

**b.** Factor $x^{12} - 1$ into irreducible polynomials over $\mathbb{Z}$. Let $\zeta = \text{cis}\,\frac{2\pi}{12}$. Label each vertex of the 12-gon in two ways

- as a power of $\zeta$
- with the factor of $x^{12} - 1$ that it makes zero when you substitute it for $x$.

## On Your Own

**8.** Take It Further Suppose $\alpha = \text{cis}\,\frac{2\pi}{6}$. Define a function $f$ on nonnegative integers by

$$f(n) = \sum_{k=0}^{5} \alpha^{kn}$$

Tabulate $f$ and find a simpler way to define it.

9. Suppose $z = \text{cis}\,\frac{2\pi}{7}$. Find the value of

$$(z + z^2 - z^3 + z^4 - z^5 - z^6)^2$$

10. Suppose $z = \text{cis}\,\frac{2\pi}{11}$. Let

$$\alpha_1 = z + z^3 + z^4 + z^5 + z^9 \quad \text{and}$$
$$\alpha_2 = z^2 + z^6 + z^7 + z^8 + z^{10}$$

Find a quadratic equation satisfied by $\alpha_1$ and $\alpha_2$.

11. Factor $x^5 - 1$ over each of the following sets.

**a.** over $\mathbb{Z}$ **b.** over $\mathbb{R}$ **c.** over $\mathbb{C}$

See TI-Nspire Handbook on p. 817 to learn how to use your CAS to factor over $\mathbb{Z}$, $\mathbb{R}$, and $\mathbb{C}$.

12. Suppose that $\zeta = \text{cis}\,\frac{2\pi}{n}$. Show that $\zeta$ is a primitive $n$th root of unity.

13. Suppose that $\zeta = \text{cis}\,\frac{2\pi}{n}$. Show that if $\zeta^t = 1$ for some integer $t$, then $n$ is a factor of $t$.

14. Suppose that $\zeta = \text{cis}\,\frac{2\pi}{n}$. Show that if $z = \zeta^r$ for some integer $r$ that has no common factor with $n$, then $z$ is a primitive $n$th root of unity.

15. **a.** Find all the primitive ninth roots of unity. Graph the corresponding 9-gon on the complex plane.

**b.** Factor $x^9 - 1$ into irreducible polynomials over $\mathbb{Z}$.
Let $\zeta = \text{cis}\,\frac{2\pi}{9}$. Label each vertex of the 9-gon in two ways

- as a power of $\zeta$
- with the factor of $x^9 - 1$ that it makes zero when you substitute it for $x$.

16. Show that if $z$ is an $n$th root of unity that is not primitive, $z^q = 1$ for some factor $q$ of $n$.

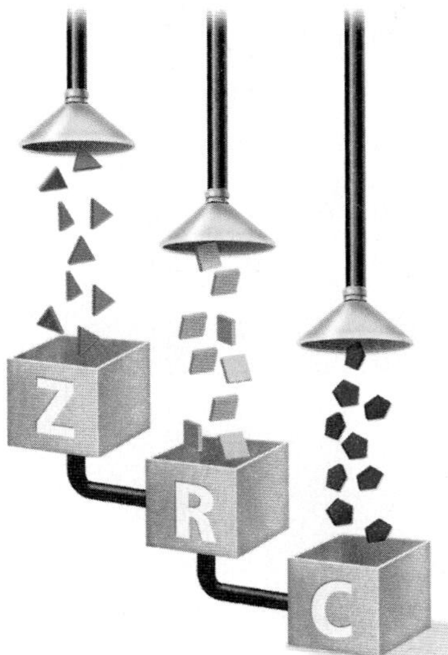

**17.** The polynomial that has the primitive $n$th roots of unity as solutions is usually denoted by $\psi_n(x)$. ($\psi$ is the Greek letter *psi*.) Show that

$$\psi_1(x) = x - 1$$
$$\psi_2(x) = x + 1$$
$$\psi_3(x) = x^2 + x + 1$$
$$\psi_4(x) = x^2 + 1$$

**18.** Find $\psi_m(x)$ for $m = 5, 6, 7, 8, 9, 10, 11$, and 12.

| $m$ | $\psi_m(x)$ |
|---|---|
| 5 | $x^4 + x^3 + x^2 + x + 1$ |
| 6 | ■ |
| 7 | ■ |
| 8 | ■ |
| 9 | ■ |
| 10 | ■ |
| 11 | ■ |
| 12 | ■ |

**19.** Show that $x^{12} - 1$ factors as

$$x^{12} - 1 = \psi_1(x)\psi_2(x)\psi_3(x)\psi_4(x)\psi_6(x)\psi_{12}(x)$$

**Take It Further** In Exercises 20–22, $\zeta = \text{cis}\,\frac{2\pi}{17}$.

- Let $P_0 = \zeta + \zeta^9 + \zeta^{13} + \zeta^{15} + \zeta^{16} + \zeta^8 + \zeta^4 + \zeta^2$ and
  $P_1 = \zeta^3 + \zeta^{10} + \zeta^5 + \zeta^{11} + \zeta^{14} + \zeta^7 + \zeta^{12} + \zeta^6$
- Let
  $$Q_0 = \zeta + \zeta^{13} + \zeta^{16} + \zeta^4,$$
  $$Q_1 = \zeta^3 + \zeta^5 + \zeta^{14} + \zeta^{12},$$
  $$Q_2 = \zeta^9 + \zeta^{15} + \zeta^8 + \zeta^2, \text{ and}$$
  $$Q_3 = \zeta^{10} + \zeta^{11} + \zeta^7 + \zeta^6$$
- And let
  $$r_0 = \zeta + \zeta^{16},$$
  $$r_1 = \zeta^3 + \zeta^{14},$$
  $$r_2 = \zeta^9 + \zeta^8,$$
  $$r_3 = \zeta^{10} + \zeta^7,$$
  $$r_4 = \zeta^{13} + \zeta^4,$$
  $$r_5 = \zeta^5 + \zeta^{12},$$
  $$r_6 = \zeta^{15} + \zeta^2, \text{ and}$$
  $$r_7 = \zeta^{11} + \zeta^6$$

20. Show that each of the $P$'s, $Q$'s, and $r$'s are real numbers.

21. a. Show that

$$P_0 + P_1 = -1 \quad \text{and}$$
$$P_0 P_1 = -4$$

Find $P_0$ and $P_1$.

b. Show that

$$Q_0 + Q_2 = P_0 \quad \text{and}$$
$$Q_0 Q_2 = -1$$

Find $Q_0$ and $Q_2$.

c. Show that

$$Q_1 + Q_3 = P_1 \quad \text{and}$$
$$Q_1 Q_3 = -1$$

Find $Q_1$ and $Q_3$.

Go Online
www.successnetplus.com

22. a. Show that

$$r_0 + r_4 = Q_0 \quad \text{and}$$
$$r_0 r_4 = -1$$

Find $r_0$ and $r_4$.

b. Find an exact formula for $\cos \frac{2\pi}{17}$, using only square roots and the four operations of arithmetic.

23. Standardized Test Prep Which of the following is the sum of the fourth roots of $-1$?

A. 0　　B. $-1$　　C. $-\frac{\sqrt{2}}{2}$　　D. $-\frac{\sqrt{3}}{2}$

## Maintain Your Skills

24. Find all primitive $n$th roots of unity if

a. $n = 3$　　b. $n = 4$　　c. $n = 5$　　d. $n = 7$

e. $n = 10$　　f. $n = 11$　　g. $n = 24$

25. Take It Further In terms of $n$, how many primitive $n$th roots of unity are there?

**In this investigation, you learned De Moivre's Theorem for calculating powers of complex numbers. You saw how this connected to roots of unity and regular polygons in the complex plane. The following questions will help you summarize what you have learned.**

**1.** Find all the roots of each equation.

**a.** $x^6 - 1 = 0$

**b.** $x^8 = 1$

**c.** $x^8 = 256$

**2.** Find the exact value of the following.

**a.** $\cos \frac{\pi}{12}$

**b.** $\cos \frac{\pi}{8}$

**c.** Take It Further $\cos \frac{3\pi}{8}$

**3.** Find the exact value of the following sums.

**a.** $\sum_{k=0}^{6} \sin \frac{2\pi k}{7}$

**b.** $\sum_{k=1}^{6} \cos \frac{2\pi k}{7}$

**c.** $\sum_{k=0}^{6} \cos \frac{(7 - 4k)\pi}{14}$

4. How do you use De Moivre's Theorem to write a rule for $\cos 3x$?

5. How can you connect roots of unity to regular polygons?

6. For what values of $\cos x$ does $\cos 3x = 0$?

## Vocabulary and Notation

In this investigation, you learned these terms. Make sure you understand what each one means and how to use it.

- **algebraic numbers**
- **complex numbers**
- **primitive *n*th root of unity**
- **roots of unity**

Symmetry about the center is a familiar and attractive design element in architecture.

Chapter 6

# Review

Go Online
www.successnetplus.com

In **Investigation 6A,** you learned to

- represent complex numbers using both rectangular coordinates and trigonometry.
- determine the magnitude and argument of any complex number.
- decide when it is best to use rectangular or polar coordinates to represent complex numbers.

*The following questions will help you check your understanding.*

**1. a.** Represent $-3 + 3i$ in polar form.

**b.** Represent $2 \text{ cis } \frac{5\pi}{3}$ in rectangular form.

**2.** Find the magnitude and argument of each complex number $z$.

**a.** $z = 1 - \sqrt{3}i$

**b.** $z = 4$

**c.** $z = -2i$

**d.** $z = -1 - 3i$

**e.** $z = 5 \text{ cis } \frac{\pi}{6}$

**f.** $z = 2 \text{ cis } 35°$

**3.** Let $z$ and $w$ have the following values.

$$z = 2 - 2i$$
$$w = -4i$$

**a.** Find $zw$.

**b.** Copy and complete the following table.

| | Magnitude | Argument |
|---|---|---|
| z | ■ | ■ |
| w | ■ | ■ |
| zw | ■ | ■ |
| $z^2$ | ■ | ■ |
| $w^3$ | ■ | ■ |

**c.** Find the magnitude of $z^5$.

**d.** Find the argument of $w^6$

In **Investigation 6B,** you learned to

- calculate powers of complex numbers using De Moivre's Theorem.
- understand the geometry of roots of unity, and the connection to roots of equations of the form $x^n - 1 = 0$.
- find exact algebraic expressions for certain trigonometric values.

*The following questions will help you check your understanding.*

**4.** Let $z$ and $w$ have the following values.

$$z = 2 \text{ cis } 40°$$
$$w = -2 + 2i$$

Find each of the following.

**a.** $z^2$

**b.** $z^{10}$

**c.** $w^2$

**d.** $w^4$

**5. a.** Find all the roots of

$$x^9 - 1 = 0$$

**b.** Graph the roots of $x^9 - 1 = 0$ on the complex plane.

**c.** Find the exact value of

$$\sum_{k=0}^{8} \sin \frac{2\pi k}{9}$$

**6.** Find the exact value of $\sin \frac{5\pi}{12}$.

# Test

## Multiple Choice

**1.** Find $2 \text{ cis } \frac{3\pi}{4}$ in rectangular form.

**A.** $-1 + i$ **B.** $-\sqrt{2} + i\sqrt{2}$

**C.** $\sqrt{2} - i\sqrt{2}$ **D.** $\frac{\sqrt{2}}{2} - \frac{\sqrt{2}}{2}i$

**2.** Let $z$ and $w$ have the following values.

$$z = 3 \text{ cis } \frac{\pi}{6}$$

$$w = 5 \text{ cis } \frac{2\pi}{3}$$

Find $\arg(zw)$.

**A.** 8 **B.** 15 **C.** $\frac{5\pi}{6}$ **D.** $\frac{\pi}{9}$

**3.** Let $z$ be a complex number where $|z| = 4$ and $\arg(z) = \frac{\pi}{6}$. What is the magnitude of $z^3$?

**A.** $\frac{\pi}{2}$ **B.** $\frac{\pi}{18}$ **C.** 12 **D.** 64

**4.** Evaluate the sum.

$$\sum_{k=0}^{4} \sin \frac{2k\pi}{5}$$

**A.** $-1$ **B.** 0 **C.** 1 **D.** $2\pi$

## Open Response

**5.** Find $|z^4|$ and $\arg(z^4)$.

**a.** $z = 3$ **b.** $z = 3 \text{ cis } 50°$

**c.** $z = -5i$ **d.** $z = \sqrt{3} - i$

**6. a.** Find all the roots of $x^6 - 1 = 0$.

**b.** Graph the roots of $x^6 - 1 = 0$ on the complex plane.

**7.** How can complex numbers be used to find formulas for $\cos 2x$ and $\sin 2x$?

**8.** Let $z$ and $w$ have the following values.

$$z = -2 - 2i$$

$$w = 2\sqrt{3} + 2i$$

Copy and complete the following table.

| | Magnitude | Argument |
|---|---|---|
| $z$ | ■ | ■ |
| $w$ | ■ | ■ |
| $zw$ | ■ | ■ |
| $z^2$ | ■ | ■ |
| $w^3$ | ■ | ■ |

Chapter
7
Investigations at a Glance
7A Polynomial Functions
7B Rational Functions
7C More About Recursive Models

# Polynomial and Rational Functions

The world is full of phenomena that seem to involve an abrupt change from one state to another. A balloon is whole one moment, and the next moment it has burst. A bug is sitting quietly on a branch, and an instant later a predator has eaten it. However, high-speed photography reveals that such phenomena actually involve gradual change over a period of time, albeit a very short one. The balloon that appears to burst all at once in fact tears open, with one or more rips that start out small and grow rapidly larger.

Gottfried Leibniz (1646–1716) grasped this fact, even before the invention of photography. "Nature makes no leaps," he declared, calling this the Law of Continuity. In this chapter, you will learn how to analyze continuous functions, and especially how to describe their rates of change. For instance, you will learn what it means to say that the rip in a balloon grows at a rate of about fifty feet per second. You will also learn about discontinuous functions, which (Leibniz's Law of Continuity notwithstanding) are sometimes useful for modeling real-world phenomena.

## Vocabulary and Notation

- average rate of change
- continuous
- hole
- infinite discontinuity
- instantaneous speed
- power function
- rational function
- reciprocal function
- removable discontinuity
- secant line
- tangent line
- Taylor expansion

# Polynomial Functions

In *Polynomial Functions*, you will study the graphs of polynomial functions from various viewpoints. For each graph, you will learn the connection between the rates of change of the function and the graph's secant and tangent lines.

**By the end of this investigation, you will be able to answer questions like these.**

1. How can you graph a polynomial function given its factored form?
2. How can you determine a polynomial's behavior at very large or very small inputs?
3. How can you use long division to find equations of secant or tangent lines to the graph of a polynomial function?

**You will learn how to**

- state the Change of Sign Theorem and the Intermediate Value Theorem for Polynomials, and to use them to analyze the graphs of polynomial functions
- find the equation of a line secant to a polynomial function and the average rate of change of a function between two points
- write the Taylor expansion for a polynomial function about a point
- find the equation of the tangent to a polynomial curve at a point

**You will develop these habits and skills:**

- Visualize the graph of a polynomial function from its factored form.
- Use the continuity of a polynomial function to draw conclusions about the function's behavior at extreme values or about lines tangent to the graph of the function.
- Relate quotients in polynomial long division to Taylor expansions and to equations of tangent lines.

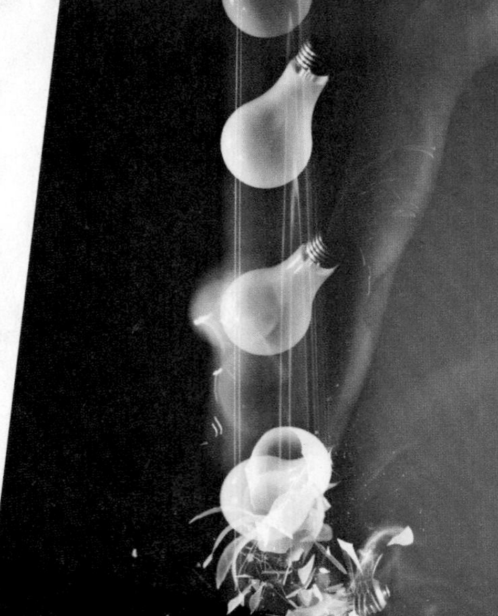

A polynomial function can describe the height, over time, of a falling object.

## 7.01 Getting Started

Polynomial functions can have all kinds of interesting graphs. Here are a few favorites:

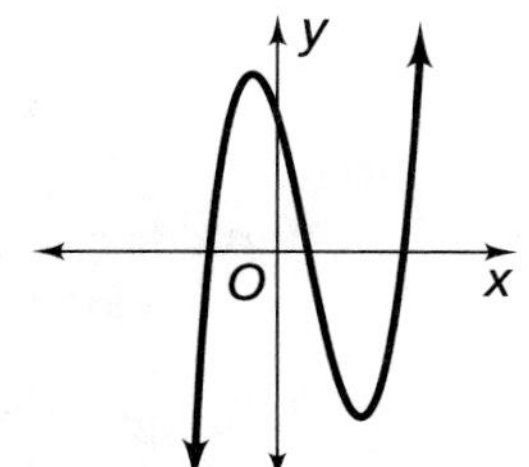


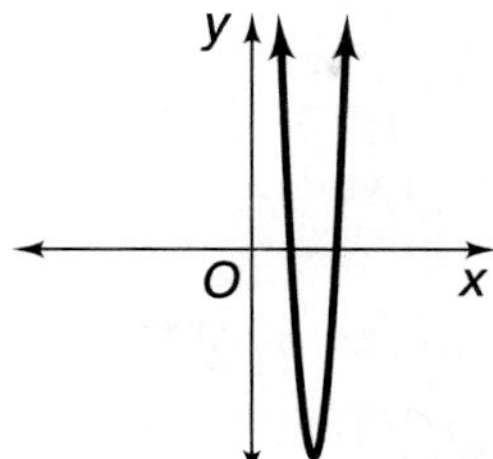


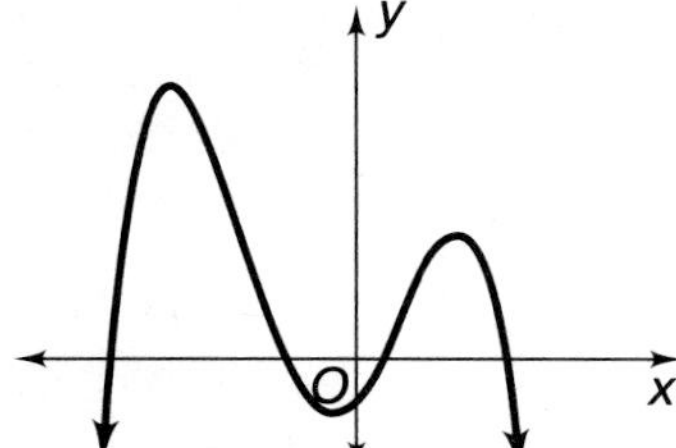


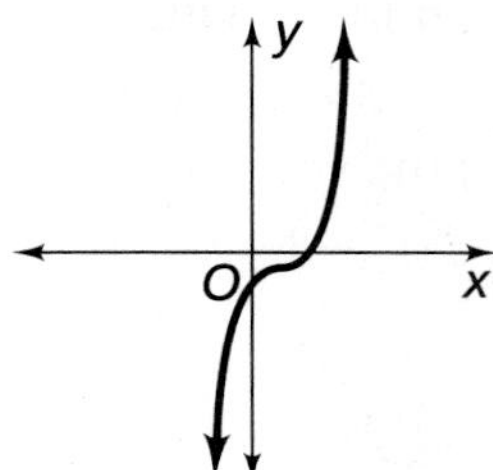


## For You to Explore

1. What shapes can the graph of a cubic polynomial function have? Here are some functions to consider.
   - $f(x) = x^3 - 3x^2 - 6x - 3$
   - $g(x) = x^3 - 3x^2 + 3x + 4$

   Try other examples, too.

For example, the first graph shown above rises, falls, and then rises again, increasing without bound. What other shapes are possible?

2. Find, if possible, a cubic polynomial function with a graph that satisfies these conditions.
   - The graph crosses the $x$-axis at $(-5, 0)$, $(-1, 0)$, and somewhere on the positive $x$-axis.
   - From left to right, the graph rises, falls, and rises.
   - The graph crosses the $y$-axis at $(0, -7)$.

   Explain your work.

3. Find, if possible, a cubic polynomial function with a graph that satisfies these conditions.
   - The graph crosses the line with equation $y = 3$ at $(-5, 3)$, $(-1, 3)$, and somewhere with a positive $x$-coordinate.
   - From left to right, the graph rises, falls, and rises.
   - The graph crosses the $y$-axis at $(0, -4)$.

   Explain your work.

4. Here are some expressions that define a function $f$.

**Expression 1:** $f(x) = (x - 1)(x - 6)(x - 7)$

**Expression 2:** $f(x) = 24 - 2(x - 3) - 5(x - 3)^2 + (x - 3)^3$

**Expression 3:** $f(x) = x^3 - 14x^2 + 55x - 42$

**Expression 4:** $f(x) = -360 + 166(x + 3) - 23(x + 3)^2 + (x + 3)^3$

**Expression 5:** $f(x) = x^3\left(1 - \frac{14}{x} + \frac{55}{x^2} - \frac{42}{x^3}\right)$

a. Show that definitions 1–4 are equivalent and that definition 5 is equivalent to the others except at $x = 0$.

b. Which form is best for finding the zeros of $f$? What are the zeros of $f$?

c. Which form is best for finding $f(-3)$? What is $f(-3)$?

d. Which form is best for deciding how $f(x)$ behaves if $x$ is a large positive number? If $x$ is a large negative number (such as $-1000$)?

e. Which form is best for estimating the outputs of $f$ for very small inputs? Estimate (without a calculator) the value of $f(0.00001)$. Explain your estimate.

f. Sketch the graph of $y = f(x)$.

Try adding a statement for the case $x = 0$ to make the last definition fully equivalent to the others. Could you model this two-part definition in your function-modeling language (FML)?

5. Sketch the graph of each function.

a. $f(x) = (x + 3)(x - 1)(x - 3)$

b. $h(x) = (x + 3)(x - 1.5)(x - 2.5)$

c. $k(x) = (x + 3)(x - 1.99)(x - 2.01)$

d. $g(x) = (x + 3)(x - 2)^2$

**Habits of Mind**

**Make connections.** The idea in Problem 5 is for you to connect what is happening with the equations to what is happening with the graphs. Use your calculator to check your sketches, but try to imagine the graphs before you use the technology.

6. Let $f$ be the function from Problem 4. How close do you have to make $a$ to 5 in order to be sure that the following conditions are met?

a. $|f(a) - f(5)| < 0.1$?

b. $|f(a) - f(5)| < 0.01$?

c. $|f(a) - f(5)| < 0.001$?

d. $|f(a) - f(5)| < 0.0001$?

7. The graph of the function $h$ is at the right.

Which of these could be an equation for $h(x)$?

A. $h(x) = (x + 4)(x + 1)(x - 6)$

B. $h(x) = -(x + 4)(x + 1)(x - 6)$

C. $h(x) = (x + 1)(x - 4)(x - 6)$

D. $h(x) = -(x + 1)(x - 4)(x - 6)$

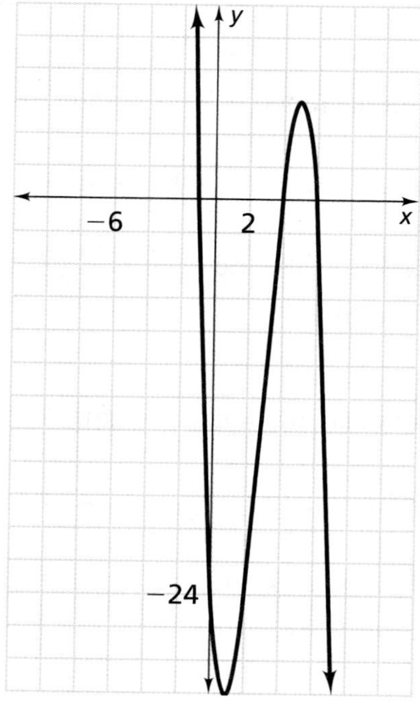

# Exercises *Practicing Habits of Mind*

## On Your Own

**8.** Find, if possible, a cubic polynomial function with a graph that satisfies these conditions:

- The graph crosses the $x$-axis at $(-9, 0)$, $(-5, 0)$, and somewhere on the positive $x$-axis.
- From left to right, the graph falls, rises, and falls.
- The graph passes through the point $(-4, -5)$.

Explain your work.

**9.** Sketch the graph of a function that could not possibly be a polynomial function. Explain why it could not be the graph of a polynomial.

**10.** **Write About It** Make your own polynomial function graph gallery.

- Sketch or generate 10 particularly interesting polynomial function graphs.
- Give the polynomial function for each graph.
- Describe what you find interesting about each graph.

Make believe you are preparing a guided tour in an art museum, except the pictures are graphs of polynomial functions.

**11.** Draw sketches of each of these functions. A calculator should not be necessary.

**a.** $f_1(x) = (x - 2)(x - 4)(x - 7)$ **b.** $f_2(x) = (x - 2)(x - 4)(x - 5)$

**c.** $f_3(x) = (x - 2)(x - 4)(x - 4.5)$ **d.** $f_4(x) = (x - 2)(x - 4)(x - 4.1)$

**e.** $f_5(x) = (x - 2)(x - 4)^2$

Do not worry about being very accurate. Is $f_1(0)$ positive or negative?

**12.** Suppose $f(x) = 3x^3 - 14x^2 + 15x + 9$. Find numbers $A$, $B$, $C$, and $D$ if another way to write $f(x)$ is

$$f(x) = A(x - 2)^3 + B(x - 2)^2 + C(x - 2) + D$$

## Maintain Your Skills

**13.** Sketch the graph of each of these functions.

**a.** $f(x) = (x - 3)^2$ **b.** $g(x) = (x + 4)^2$

**c.** $h(x) = -(x + 2)^2$ **d.** $j(x) = (x - 5)^3$

**e.** $k(x) = -(x - 5)^3$ **f.** $m(x) = x^4$

# 7.02 Continuity of Polynomial Functions

Graphs of polynomial functions have no breaks in them. This means that domain values that are close to each other will always have range values that are close to each other.

## In-Class Experiment

Suppose $f(x) = x^3 - 2x^2 + 7$, so that $f(5) = 82$. How close must $x$ be to 5 to meet the following conditions?

1. $|f(x) - f(5)| < 0.1$
2. $|f(x) - f(5)| < 0.01$
3. $|f(x) - f(5)| < 0.001$
4. $|f(x) - f(5)| < 10^{-6}$

In the In-Class Experiment, you saw that you could make $f(x)$ as close as you wanted to $f(5)$ by making $x$ close enough to 5. How does the graph of $y = f(x)$ reflect this fact?

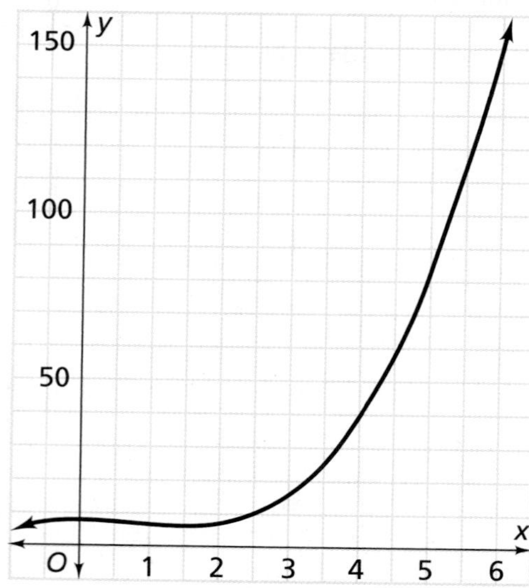


## For Discussion

5. Using the graph of $y = f(x)$, explain why you can make $f(x)$ arbitrarily close to $f(5)$ by making $x$ close enough to 5.

## Definition

**A function $f$ is continuous at an input $a$ if you can make $f(x)$ as close as you want to $f(a)$ by making $x$ close enough to $a$.**

You will learn a more precise definition when you take calculus.

You have seen that $f(x) = x^3 - 2x^2 + 7$ is continuous at $a = 5$. In fact, there was nothing special about the input 5. The function $f$ is continuous at every real number. In this case, you say that $f$ is continuous on $\mathbb{R}$, or simply that $f$ is continuous.

To understand continuous functions, it helps to study functions that are not continuous. Consider a function $f$ with the graph shown below.

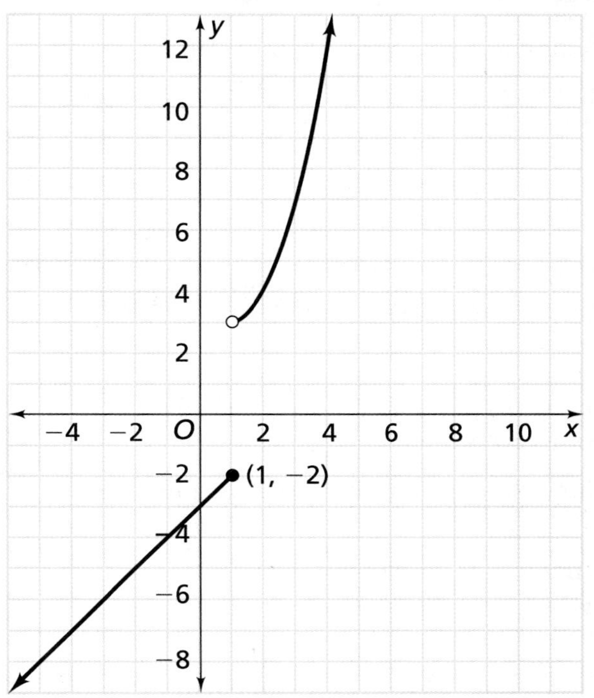


**Habits of Mind**

**Represent a function.** Model $f$ in your FML and graph it.

The graph shows that $f(1) = -2$. However, the graph also shows that the values

$$f(1.01), f(1.001), f(1.0001), f(1.00001), \ldots$$

approach 3. In other words, no matter how close you bring $x$ to 1 (with $x > 1$), the distance between $f(x)$ and $f(1)$ will never be less than 5. Thus, $f$ is not continuous at $x = 1$.

On the other hand, the values

$$f(0.99), f(0.999), f(0.9999), f(0.99999), \ldots$$

do approach $-2$. So you can make $f(x)$ as close as you want to $f(1)$ by making $x$ close enough to 1 with the added restriction that $x < 1$. But to say that $f$ is continuous at 1, you must be able to make $f(x)$ close to $f(1)$ from both sides of $x = 1$. In other words, you need to show it for $x > 1$ and $x < 1$.

You could say, however, that $f$ is continuous at 1 from the left.

## For You to Do

6. Name and sketch the graphs of three functions that are continuous.
7. Sketch the graphs of two functions that are not continuous.

Roughly speaking, a function is continuous if its graph has no breaks. You could trace the entire curve without picking up your pencil. Your experience tells you that polynomial functions are continuous.

## Minds in Action

*Tony and Sasha are trying to show algebraically that* $f(x) = 4x - 3$ *is continuous at* $x = 2$.

**Tony** The graph of $y = 4x - 3$ is a straight line. So it obviously has no breaks, and it must be continuous everywhere.

**Sasha** True, but we're supposed to show this algebraically—so no graphs allowed.

**Tony** Okay, then let's go back to the definition. We need to show that we can make $f(x)$ as close as we want to $f(2)$ by making $x$ close enough to 2.

**Sasha** Well, $f(2) = 5$. And let's say we want to make $f(x)$ be within 0.01 of $f(2)$.

**Tony** So we want,

$$|f(x) - f(2)| < 0.01$$

**Sasha** Looks good. We can substitute for $f(x)$ and $f(2)$, too. So we have

$$|(4x - 3) - 5| < 0.01$$

or, simplifying a bit,

$$\begin{aligned} |4x - 8| &< 0.01 \\ 4 \cdot |x - 2| &< 0.01 \\ |x - 2| &< 0.0025 \end{aligned}$$

So if $x$ is within 0.0025 of 2, then we're guaranteed that $f(x)$ is within 0.01 of $f(2)$.

**Tony** But what if we have to make $f(x)$ within 0.001 of $f(2)$? Do we have to go through this all over again?

**Sasha** No, you don't need to do any extra work. There was nothing special about the value 0.01 in the above calculation. So if we have to make $f(x)$ within any distance $d$ from $f(2)$, just replace 0.01 with $d$ and go through the same steps!

## For You to Do

**8.** Explain what Sasha meant by saying there was nothing special about the value 0.01. Let $d$ be any positive number. How close must $x$ be to $a = 2$ to ensure that $f(x)$ is no more than a distance $d$ away from $f(2)$?

A nice result of the fact that polynomial functions are continuous is that their graphs cannot get from one side of a horizontal line (such as the $x$-axis) to the other without crossing that line.

### *Theorem 7.1 The Change of Sign Theorem*

**Suppose $f$ is a polynomial function and there are two numbers $a$ and $b$ such that $f(a) < 0$ and $f(b) > 0$. Then $f(c) = 0$ for some number $c$ between $a$ and $b$.**

This theorem is easy to believe but not so easy to prove. You will see its proof when you take calculus. The theorem is actually true for all continuous functions, not just polynomial functions.

The Change of Sign Theorem says that if a polynomial changes sign between inputs $a$ and $b$, it must equal zero for some input between $a$ and $b$. The number that makes it zero is a root of the equation $f(x) = 0$. The theorem says nothing about how to find the root. It just says the root exists somewhere between $a$ and $b$.

A more general result, which also follows from the continuity of polynomials, is the following theorem.

### *Theorem 7.2 The Intermediate Value Theorem for Polynomials*

**Suppose $f$ is a polynomial function and $a$ and $b$ are two numbers such that $f(a) < f(b)$. Then for any number $c$ between $f(a)$ and $f(b)$, there is at least one number $d$ between $a$ and $b$ such that $f(d) = c$.**

## For Discussion

**9.** Show that Theorem 7.1 implies Theorem 7.2.

**10.** Show that Theorem 7.2 implies Theorem 7.1.

Have you noticed that some polynomials have real roots while others do not? How can you tell which ones do and which ones do not? The Change of Sign Theorem tells you that if the graph starts out on one side of the $x$-axis and ends up on the other, there must be a real root.

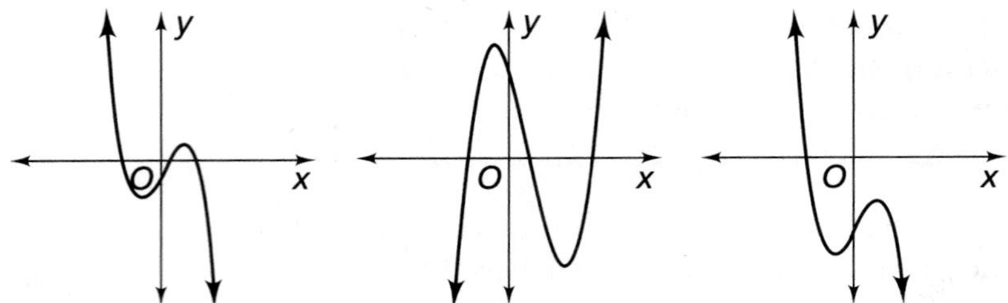


Also, the graph of a polynomial can start and end positive, or start and end negative, and still cross the $x$-axis.

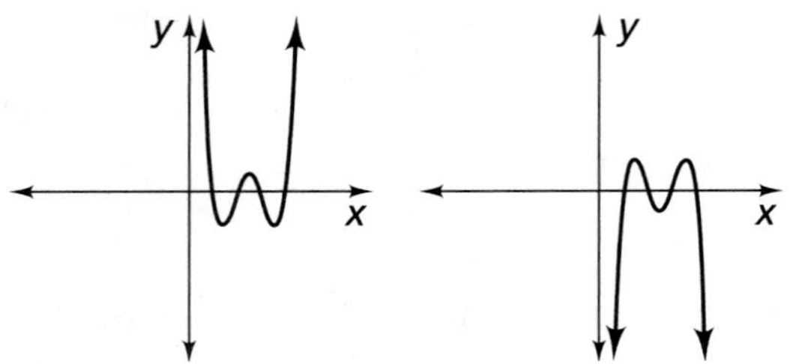


But it does not have to cross.

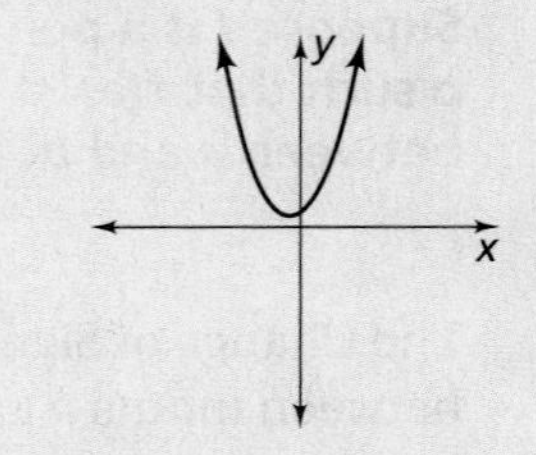


## For Discussion

**11.** Polynomial functions with only one term, like $f(x) = 4x^3$ or $g(x) = -5x^8$, are called **power functions.** Which power functions have graphs that start on one side of the $x$-axis and end on the other?

## For You to Do

**12.** Look at your polynomial function graph gallery (see Exercise 10 of Lesson 7.01). State a conjecture about how you can tell if a polynomial changes sign by looking at its degree. Give evidence to support your conjecture, even if you do not completely prove it.

## Developing Habits of Mind

**Make strategic choices.** Since they only have one term, power functions can be easier to analyze than other polynomial functions. For instance, it is clear that the function $f(x) = x^3$ increases quite quickly as $x$ increases. But consider the polynomial

$$g(x) = x^3 - 14x^2 - 55x - 42$$

Is it equally clear what happens to the function $g$ as $x$ increases?

For $x \neq 0$, you can rewrite $g(x)$ like this:

$$g(x) = x^3\left(1 - \frac{14}{x} - \frac{55}{x^2} - \frac{42}{x^3}\right)$$

As $|x|$ gets large, $\frac{14}{x}$, $\frac{55}{x^2}$, and $\frac{42}{x^3}$ all get closer and closer to 0, so the values inside the parentheses get closer to 1. So when $|x|$ is large,

for example $x = 10^6$ or $x = -10^6$

- $g(x) \approx x^3 =$ a large positive number, when $x > 0$.
- $g(x) \approx x^3 =$ a large negative number, when $x < 0$.

In other words, the graph of $g$ starts out negative and ends positive, just as the graph of $f$ does.

## Exercises *Practicing Habits of Mind*

### Check Your Understanding

**1.** Was there ever a time in your life when your weight in pounds was exactly equal to your height in inches? Justify your answer.

**2.** Consider $a(x) = 2(x - 5)(x + 3)(x - 1) = 2x^3 - 6x^2 - 26x + 30$. Give estimates for each of these values.

An answer like "it's a really big negative number" is fine here.

**a.** $a(5)$ **b.** $a(5.001)$ **c.** $a(0)$
**d.** $a(0.001)$ **e.** $a(1000)$ **f.** $a(0.999)$
**g.** $a(-1000)$

**3. a.** Find a polynomial function $g$ with $g(3) = g(-7) = 0$.

**b.** Find a polynomial function $h$ with $h(5) = h(-3) = 0$ and $h(0) = 10$.

**c.** Find a polynomial function $j$ with $j(5) = j(-3) = 2$ and $j(0) = 12$.

4. Suppose $f(x) = 3x + 2$. How close must $x$ be to 5 to meet the following conditions?

   a. $|f(x) - f(5)| < 0.1$

   b. $|f(x) - f(5)| < 0.01$

   c. $|f(x) - f(5)| < 0.001$

   d. $|f(x) - f(5)| < 10^{-6}$

5. Suppose $g$ is a cubic polynomial and $\ell$ is any line in the plane. What are the maximum and minimum numbers of intersections that $\ell$ can have with the graph of $g$? Explain.

6. What shape can the graph of a fourth degree polynomial function have? Here are some functions to try:

   - $f(x) = x^4 - 3x^3 - 2x^2 + 2x + 4$
   - $g(x) = x^4 - 3x^3 - 2x^2 - 3x + 6$
   - $t(x) = x^4 + 2$

7. **Take It Further** Let $f$ and $g$ be arbitrary cubic polynomial functions.

   a. Must there be three real numbers $x$ that make $f(x) = 0$? Explain.

   b. Let $h$ be the polynomial defined as $h = f \cdot g$ (the product). Must there be a real number $x$ for which $h(x) = 0$? Explain.

   c. Let $j$ be the polynomial defined as $j = f^2$ (the square of function $f$). Must there be a real number $x$ for which $j(x) = 0$? Explain.

   d. Let $k$ be the polynomial defined as $k = f + g$. Must there be a real number $x$ for which $k(x) = 0$? Explain.

   e. Let $m$ be the polynomial defined as $m = f \circ g$. Must there be a real number $x$ for which $m(x) = 0$? Explain.

## On Your Own

**8.** Toby drives exactly 200 miles from San Jose to Morro Bay, CA. The trip takes exactly four hours. Show that at some point in the trip, Toby's speedometer indicates a speed of exactly 50 miles per hour.

**9.** Consider $b(x) = (x - 2)(x + 5)(x - 3) = x^3 - 19x + 30$. Give estimates for each of these values.

**a.** $b(-5)$ **b.** $b(-5.001)$ **c.** $b(0)$

**d.** $b(0.001)$ **e.** $b(-0.001)$ **f.** $b(1000)$

**g.** $b(-1000)$

An answer like "it's a little bit more than 10" is fine. Try to give quick answers without use of paper or calculator.

**10.** Write About It Use the Change of Sign Theorem to explain why the Odd-Degree Root Theorem is true.

### Theorem 7.3 The Odd-Degree Root Theorem

**A polynomial function of odd degree has at least one real root.**

**11.** Suppose $f(x) = x^2$. How close must $x$ be to 5 to meet the following conditions?

**a.** $|f(x) - f(5)| < 0.6$ **b.** $|f(x) - f(5)| < 0.06$

**c.** $|f(x) - f(5)| < 0.006$ **d.** $|f(x) - f(5)| < 6 \cdot 10^{-6}$

**12.** Find, if possible, a fourth degree polynomial function the graph of which satisfies these conditions:

- The graph crosses the $x$-axis at $(-5, 0)$, $(-1, 0)$, and intersects it somewhere on the positive $x$-axis.
- From left to right, the graph rises, falls, rises, and falls.
- The graph crosses the $y$-axis at $(0, -7)$.

Explain your work.

**13.** Suppose $h$ is a degree four polynomial and $\ell$ is any line in the plane.

**a.** What are the maximum and minimum numbers of intersections that $\ell$ can have with the graph of $h$?

**b.** Can $\ell$ ever intersect the graph at an odd number of points? Explain.

**14.** Suppose $g$ is a monic cubic polynomial.

**a.** What can you say about $g(x)$ as $x$ takes on large positive values?

**b.** What can you say about $g(x)$ as $x$ takes on large negative values?

**c.** Sketch an example of what the graph of $g$ could be.

**15. What's Wrong Here** Derman thinks there is a problem with the Odd-Degree Root Theorem.

> Derman says, "What about $\frac{1}{x}$? I can write that as $x^{-1}$, which has an odd exponent. And $\frac{1}{x}$ is positive if $x$ is positive, and it's negative when $x$ is negative, but you'll never find a number that makes $\frac{1}{x}$ equal zero."

Why can you not apply the reasoning in this lesson to a function like $f(x) = \frac{1}{x}$?

**Explore the possibilities.** A degree-4 polynomial has four roots in the complex numbers (some may show up more than once in the factorization into linear factors).

**16. a.** What are the maximum and minimum number of real roots that a degree-4 polynomial can have? Illustrate with graphs.

**b.** Can a fourth degree polynomial have exactly two real roots? Explain.

**17. Take It Further** Let $g(x) = x^3 - 3$. Show that $g$ changes sign. Is there any rational number $x$ such that $g(x) = 0$?

**18.** Is there a polynomial that fits each description? If so, find one. If not, explain why none exists.

**a.** even degree, no real roots

**b.** odd degree, one real root

**c.** odd degree, three real roots

**d.** odd degree, two real roots

**e.** fourth degree, exactly three real roots

**19.** Supose that $f$ is a polynomial function such that $f(a)$ and $f(b)$ have opposite sign for some numbers $a$ and $b$. Can there be more than one value $c$ between $a$ and $b$ with $f(c) = 0$? Give examples to support what you say.

**20.** Let $g_c(x) = x^3 - 7x^2 + 14x + c$. Find, if possible, a value of $c$ such that $g_c(x) = 0$ has

**a.** exactly one real solution

**b.** exactly two real solutions

**c.** exactly three real solutions

**d.** no real solutions

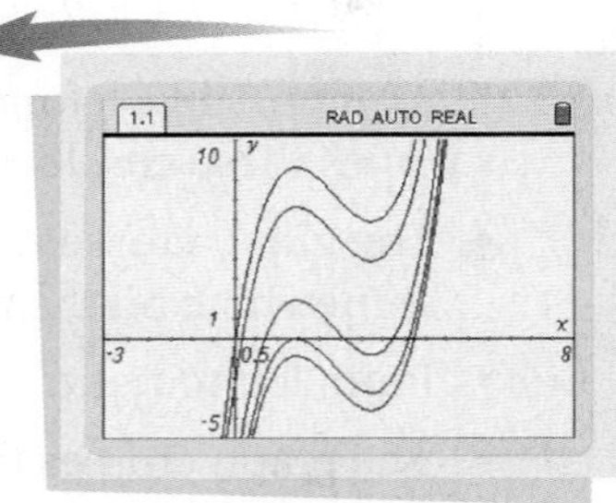


**21. Take It Further** Pick any two points on the graph of $g(x) = x^3 - x$. The coordinates will be

$$(a, g(a)) \text{ and } (b, g(b))$$

**a.** Write an expression for the slope of the line connecting these two points as a polynomial in $a$ and $b$.

**b.** Let $a = 2$ and $b = 2.01$. Calculate the slope using the new expression.

**c.** Suppose $a$ and $b$ are very close together. Write a new expression, using only one variable, that would do a good job of approximating the slope of the line connecting these points.

If $a$ and $b$ are very close to each other, you can approximate the value of the expression by assuming $a = b$.

22. Standardized Test Prep Which of the following functions is continuous?

A. $f(x) = -\sin\left(-\frac{x}{999}\right)$ B. $f(x) = \tan \frac{x}{16}$

C. $f(x) = \frac{1}{\cos x}$ D. $f(x) = \frac{\sin 16x}{x}$

## Maintain Your Skills

If you divide $x^4 - 5x^3 + 3x - 1$ by $x - 3$, the quotient is $x^3 - 2x^2 - 6x - 15$ and the remainder is $-46$.

$$
\begin{array}{r}
x^3 - 2x^2 - 6x - 15 \\
x - 3 \overline{) x^4 - 5x^3 \qquad + 3x - 1} \\
x^4 - 3x^3 \qquad\qquad\qquad \\
\hline
-2x^3 \qquad + 3x - 1 \\
-2x^3 + 6x^2 \qquad\qquad \\
\hline
-6x^2 + 3x - 1 \\
-6x^2 + 18x \qquad \\
\hline
-15x - 1 \\
-15x + 45 \\
\hline
-46
\end{array}
$$

In short,

$$x^4 - 5x^3 + 3x - 1 = (x - 3)(x^3 - 2x^2 - 6x - 15) - 46$$

**Habits of Mind**

**Reason logically.** So $f(3) = -46$. Why?

23. **a.** Find a number $c$ such that

$$x^3 - 2x^2 - 6x - 15 = (x - 3)(x^2 + x - 3) + c$$

**b.** Find a number $d$ such that

$$x^2 + x - 3 = (x - 3)(x + 4) + d$$

To finish the pattern, note that $x + 4 = (x - 3) \cdot 1 + 7$.

**c.** Find numbers $A$, $B$, $C$, $D$, and $E$ such that

$$x^4 - 5x^3 + 3x - 1 = A + B(x - 3) + C(x - 3)^2 + D(x - 3)^3 + E(x - 3)^4$$

# 7.03 Graphs and Secant Lines

At any moment of time, you are moving at a certain speed (which could be 0). Over an interval of time, your average speed is the distance you cover divided by the time you take to do it.

## In-Class Experiment

1. Below is a graph that shows how far Jerry has walked in 40 seconds. Determine his average speed between $t = 10$ and $t = 30$.

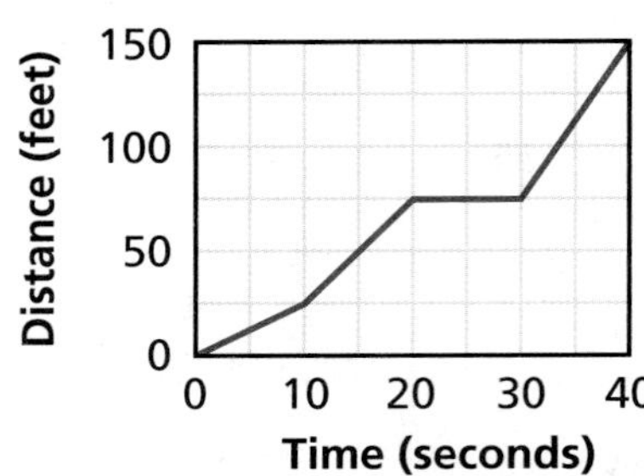


Recall that the average rate of change on a distance-time graph between two events $A$ and $B$ (points on the graph) is the slope $m(A, B)$ between these two points. For example, in the In-Class Experiment, the two points are $A = (10, 25)$ and $B = (30, 75)$, which give the slope

$$m(A, B) = \frac{75 - 25}{30 - 10} = \frac{5}{2}.$$

Thus, Jerry walks with an average speed of $\frac{5}{2}$ feet per second between $t = 10$ and $t = 30$.

More generally, let $f$ be any function and let $A$ and $B$ be points on the graph of $y = f(x)$. The slope $m(A, B)$ is the **average rate of change** of $f(x)$ with respect to $x$ between $A$ and $B$. The line through $A$ and $B$ is so important that it deserves a special name.

### Definition

**Let $f$ be a function and suppose $A$ and $B$ are distinct points on the graph of $y = f(x)$. The line passing through $A$ and $B$ is called a secant to the graph of $y = f(x)$. Its slope is the average rate of change of $f(x)$ with respect to $x$ between $A$ and $B$.**

**Habits of Mind**

**Make a connection.** This use of the word *secant* is the same as in plane geometry, except that there the curve is generally a circle.

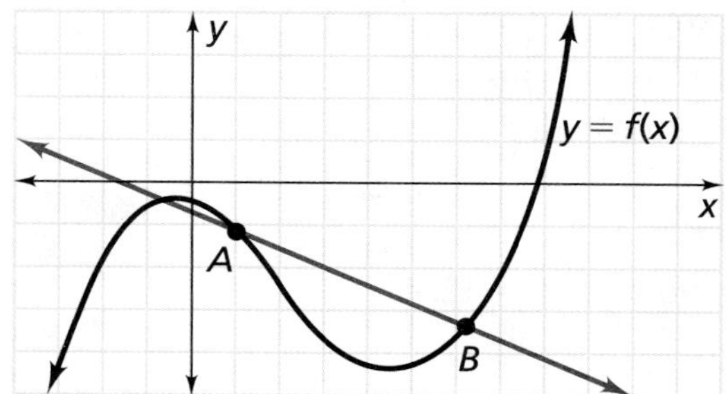

The secant to the graph between $A$ and $B$

Here are three methods for finding or approximating the equations of secants to graphs of polynomial functions.

## Method 1: Use Your Calculator

Some calculators can find the equation of the line through any two points on the $xy$-plane. If you choose your two points to be on the graph of some function, it will then find the equation of the secant to the graph between these points.

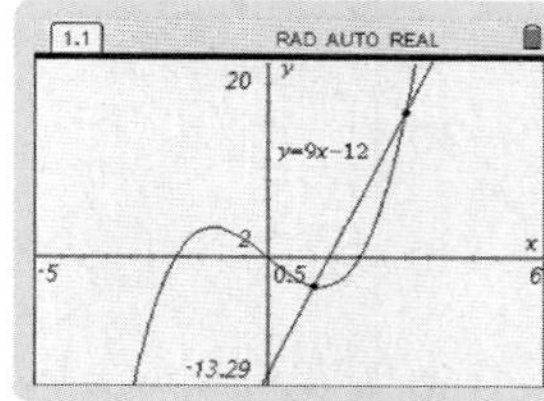


See the TI-Nspire™ Handbook on p. 817 for details about how to set up this sketch.

## Method 2: Use the Definition of Slope

If $(a, f(a))$ and $(b, f(b))$ are points on the graph of $y = f(x)$, then the slope of the secant between them is

$$\frac{f(b) - f(a)}{b - a}$$

From here you can find the equation.

## Example 1

**Problem** Suppose $f(x) = x^3 - 4x$.

**a.** Find the average rate of change of $y$ with respect to $x$ between $x = 1$ and $x = 3$.

**b.** Find the equation of the secant between $(1, f(1))$ and $(3, f(3))$.

**c.** Find all intersections of the graph of $y = f(x)$ and the secant you found in part (b).

**Solution**

**a.** To find the average rate of change, find the slope between the points $(1, f(1))$ and $(3, f(3))$.

$$\frac{f(3) - f(1)}{3 - 1} = \frac{15 - (-3)}{3 - 1} = 9$$

**b.** The secant has slope 9. To find its equation, take the base point to be either $A = (1, f(1)) = (1, -3)$ or $B = (3, f(3)) = (3, 15)$.

Suppose you pick $A$. Then an equation of the secant is

$$\frac{y - (-3)}{x - 1} = 9 \quad \text{or} \quad 9x - y = 12$$

Compare this with the answer you get when you use a calculator to find the equation of the secant.

**c.** Shown below are the graphs of $y = f(x)$ and $9x - y = 12$.

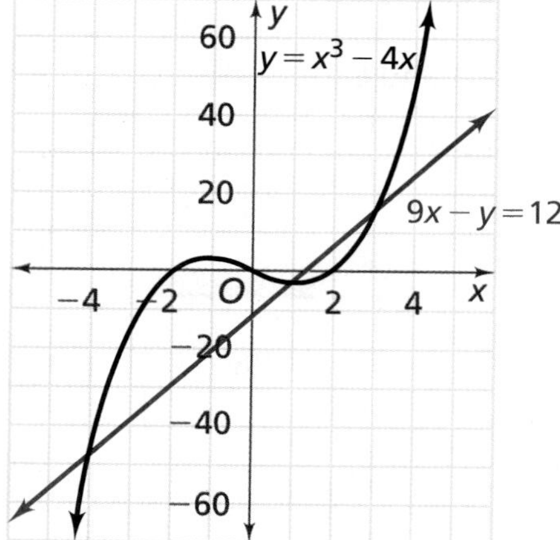


The graphs intersect at three points. You already know two of them, namely $A = (1, -3)$ and $B = (3, 15)$. To find the third, solve $9x - y = 12$ for $y$ and set $y$ equal to $f(x)$. Thus,

$$x^3 - 4x = 9x - 12$$

or equivalently,

$$x^3 - 13x + 12 = 0$$

Since 1 is a root of this equation, $x - 1$ is one of the factors of the cubic polynomial on the left side. Long division and factoring gives

$$\begin{aligned} x^3 - 13x + 12 &= (x - 1)(x^2 + x - 12) \\ &= (x - 1)(x - 3)(x + 4) \end{aligned}$$

So the three roots are 1, 3, and $-4$. The third intersection point is $C = (-4, -48)$.

### Method 3: Use the Remainder Theorem

The Remainder Theorem says that if $a$ is any real number,

$$f(x) = (x - a)q(x) + f(a)$$

where you can find $q(x)$ and $f(a)$ by long division. You can rewrite the equation as

$$\frac{f(x) - f(a)}{x - a} = q(x)$$

This is an identity, so it is true when $x = b$.

$$\frac{f(b) - f(a)}{b - a} = q(b)$$

So $q(b)$ is the slope of the secant between $(a, f(a))$ and $(b, f(b))$. From here you can find the equation.

## Example 2

**Problem** Suppose $f(x) = x^3 - 4x$ again. Using the Remainder Theorem method, find the equation of the secant between $(1, f(1))$ and $(3, f(3))$.

**Solution** Long division gives

$$\begin{array}{r|l} & x^2 + x - 3 \\ \hline x - 1 & x^3 \qquad - 4x \\ & x^3 - x^2 \\ \hline & x^2 - 4x \\ & x^2 - x \\ \hline & -3x \\ & -3x + 3 \\ \hline & -3 \end{array}$$

Write this as

$$f(x) = (x - 1)(x^2 + x - 3) - 3 = (x - 1)(x^2 + x - 3) + f(1)$$

and then as

$$\frac{f(x) - f(1)}{x - 1} = x^2 + x - 3$$

Now substitute $x = 3$ to find the slope of the secant,

$$\frac{f(3) - f(1)}{3 - 1} = 3^2 + 3 - 3 = 9$$

and proceed as in part (b) of Example 1.

This approach may not seem like a time saver, but it is more general than the calculator- and definition-based methods. You can use $x^2 + x - 3$ to find the slope of the secant between $(1, f(1))$ and any point $(b, f(b))$ on the graph.

## For You to Do

Let $f(x) = x^3 - 4x$.

**2.** By long division, you found that

$$f(x) = (x - 1)(x^2 + x - 3) - 3$$

Using this equation, explain why $f(1) = -3$.

**3.** Note that

$$f(x) + 3 = (x - 1)(x^2 + x - 3)$$

Since $x - 1$ is a factor of the right side, it must be a factor of the left side, which equals $x^3 - 4x + 3$. Find the other factor.

Try long division.

**4.** Find the slope of the secant through $(1, f(x))$ and $(3, f(x))$ again, but use $(3, f(3))$ as the base point. In other words, start by dividing $x^3 - 4x$ by $x - 3$ to obtain the quotient $q(x)$. Then write

$$f(x) = (x - 3)q(x) + f(3)$$

Later in this chapter, you will see another way to use long division to find equations of secants. If $f(x) = (x - a)(x - b)q(x) + r(x)$, then $r(x)$ is linear and agrees with $f$ at $x = a$ and $x = b$.

## Exercises *Practicing Habits of Mind*

### Check Your Understanding

**1.** Consider $f(x) = x^2$.

**a.** Let $a = 2$ and $b = 5$. Find the average rate of change of $f(x)$ between $x = a$ and $x = b$.

**b.** Let $a = -3$ and $b = 11$. Find the equation of the secant line through $(a, f(a))$ and $(b, f(b))$.

**c.** Write $m$ as a polynomial in $a$ and $b$ using the equation

$$m = \frac{f(b) - f(a)}{b - a}$$

2. Let $f(x) = x^3 - 2x + 1$.

a. Find the equation of the secant through the points $(2, f(2))$ and $(2.01, f(2.01))$.

b. Calculate, in terms of $b$, the equation of the secant between the points $(2, f(2))$ and $(b, f(b))$.

c. Use geometry software to draw the graph of $f$. Plot the point $A(2, f(2))$. Place a moveable point $B$ on the graph of $f$. Move $B$ closer to $A$. What happens to the slope between $A$ and $B$?

See the TI-Nspire Handbook on p. 817 for details on how set up this sketch.

3. Consider $f(x) = x^3 - 2x + 1$.

a. Use geometry software to draw the graph of $f$. Plot the point $A(1, f(1))$. Place a moveable point $B$ on the graph of $f$.

b. Construct the secant line through $A$ and $B$. Find the equation of this line.

c. Let $b$ be the $x$-coordinate of $B$. Write $m(A, B)$ as a polynomial in $b$, using the formula

$$m(A, B) = \frac{f(b) - f(1)}{b - 1}$$

d. Move $B$ closer to $A$. What happens to the slope of the secant line?

You denote the *limiting value* of the slope as $b$ approaches 1 in Exercise 3d by

$$\lim_{b \to 1} \frac{f(b) - 0}{b - 1}$$

Where does the 0 come from?

4. Consider $f(x) = x^3 - 7x^2 + 3x - 2$.

a. Use geometry software to draw the graph of $f$. Plot the point $A(0, f(0))$. Place a moveable point $B$ on the graph of $f$.

b. Construct the secant line through $A$ and $B$. Find the equation of this line.

c. Let $b$ be the $x$-coordinate of $B$. Write $m(A, B)$ as a polynomial in $b$, using the formula

$$m(A, B) = \frac{f(b) - f(0)}{b - 0}$$

d. Move $B$ closer to $A$. What happens to the slope of the secant line?

5. Let $f(x) = 3x^2 + 5x - 7$. Find an expression in terms of $a$ and $b$ for the slope of the secant connecting $(a, f(a))$ and $(b, f(b))$.

6. Consider $f(x) = x^2$.

a. Let $a = 2$ and $b = 5$. Find the $y$-intercept of the secant line connecting $(a, f(a))$ and $(b, f(b))$.

b. Repeat for part (a) $a = -3$ and $b = 11$.

c. Find and prove a general result based on parts (a) and (b).

7. **Take It Further** Show algebraically that the slope of any secant line on the graph of $y = x^3$ must be positive.

8. John leaves home at 8:00 A.M. riding his mountain bike. He pedals at a constant rate of 15 ft/s.

   a. How far has John ridden at 8:10 A.M.?

   b. How far has John ridden at 8:20 A.M.?

   c. How far has John ridden at 8:45 A.M.?

   d. Write an expression for how far John has ridden $t$ minutes after 8:00 A.M.

9. Pete, John's older brother, leaves 10 minutes after John, heading down the same trail. He rides at 20 ft/s.

   a. How far has Pete ridden at 8:10 A.M.? Has Pete caught John?

   b. How far has Pete ridden at 8:20 A.M.? Has Pete caught John?

   c. How far has Pete ridden at 8:45 A.M.? Has Pete caught John?

   d. Write an expression for how far Pete has ridden at $t$ minutes after 8:00 A.M.

   e. How can you find the exact time Pete caught John?

A speed of 20 feet per second is equivalent to about 13.6 miles per hour.

## On Your Own

**10.** Sketch each graph.

**a.** $y = x^3$ **b.** $y = x^3 - 1$

**c.** $y = (x + 4)^3$ **d.** $y = (x + 4)^3 - 1$

**11.** Sketch the graph of each polynomial function.

**a.** $a(x) = (x - 5)^3$ **b.** $b(x) = (x - 5)^3(x + 2)$

**c.** $c(x) = x^3 - 4x$ **d.** $d(x) = (x - 4.9)(x - 5)(x - 5.1)$

**e.** $e(x) = (x + 3)^{100}$

**Think it through.** Try sketching the graphs first, without a calculator.

**12.** The graph of $g(x) = x^3 - x$ passes through the point (2, 6).

**a.** Use geometry software to draw the graph of $f$. Plot the point $A(2, f(2))$. Place a moveable point $B$ on the graph of $f$.

**b.** Let $b$ be the $x$-coordinate of $B$. The slope of the line through $A$ and $B$ is

$$m(A, B) = \frac{f(b) - f(2)}{b - 2}$$

Describe what happens to this slope as you move $B$ closer to $A$.

**13.** Take It Further Consider a line secant to the graph of $y = x^2$, through (3, 9) and a point very close to (3, 9).

**a.** Approximate the slope of this line.

**b.** Write an equation for a line that has the slope you found in part (a) and passes through (3, 9).

**14.** The graph of $f(x) = x^3 - 3x$ passes through the point $(-1, 2)$.

**a.** Use geometry software to draw the graph of $f$. Plot the point $A(-1, f(-1))$. Place a moveable point $B$ on the graph of $f$.

**b.** Construct the secant line through $A$ and $B$. Find the equation of this line.

**c.** Let $b$ be the $x$-coordinate of $B$. Write $m(A, B)$ as a polynomial in $b$, using the formula

$$m(A, B) = \frac{f(b) - f(-1)}{b - (-1)}$$

**d.** Move $B$ closer to $A$. What happens to the slope of the secant line?

Go Online
www.successnetplus.com

15. Use graphs and your work from Exercise 14 to determine when $f(x) = x^3 - 3x$ is increasing.

16. **Take It Further** Let $g(x) = Ax^2 + Bx + C$. What is the slope of the secant line between $(p, g(p))$ and $(q, g(q))$?

**Remember...**

The slope equals the change in *y* divided by the change in *x*. You can also look back at Exercise 4 for an example using specific values of *A*, *B*, and *C*.

17. On the same axes, sketch the graph of each equation. Where do the graphs intersect?

**a.** $y = x + (4x + 1)$ and $y = 4x + 1$

**b.** $y = x^2 + (4x + 1)$ and $y = 4x + 1$

18. On the same axes, sketch the graph of each equation. Where do the graphs intersect?

**a.** $y = (x - 5) + (2x - 6)$ and $y = 2x - 6$

**b.** $y = (x - 5)^2 + (2x - 6)$ and $y = 2x - 6$

19. **Standardized Test Prep** What is the average rate of change of $f(x) = \frac{3}{x^2}$ as $x$ goes from 1 to 3?

**A.** $-\frac{1}{3}$ **B.** $-\frac{3}{2}$ **C.** $-\frac{3}{4}$ **D.** $-\frac{4}{3}$

## Maintain Your Skills

20. Find a polynomial function that satisfies the conditions.

**a.** $a(0) = 0$ and $a(1) = 1$

**b.** $b(0) = b(1) = 0$ and $b(2) = 1$

**c.** $c(0) = c(1) = c(2) = 0$ and $c(3) = 1$

**d.** $d(0) = d(1) = d(2) = d(3) = 0$ and $d(4) = 1$

**e.** **Take It Further** $f(0) - 0, f(1) = 7, f(2) = 10, f(3) = 20$, and $f(4) = 52$

21. Copy and complete this table for $f(x) = x^2 - 4x + 1$.

| $x$ | $f(x)$ | Slope of secant through $(x, f(x))$ and a point near it |
|---|---|---|
| −1 | 6 | ■ |
| 0 | ■ | ■ |
| 1 | −2 | ■ |
| 2 | ■ | 0 |
| 3 | ■ | ■ |

"Near $(x, f(x))$" might mean that the $x$-value for the point is "within 0.01 of $x$."

# 7.04 Polynomials in Powers of $x - a$

You have a lot of experience writing expressions in different forms. Now you will learn how to write a polynomial in a form that will help you find the rate at which it is changing.

## For You to Do

**1.** Show that

$$2(x-3)^3 + 5(x-3)^2 - 7(x-3) + 14 = 2x^3 - 13x^2 + 17x + 26$$

Given a polynomial written in powers of $x - 3$, you can rewrite it as a polynomial in $x$, expanding it by hand or by using your calculator. The goal in this lesson, however, is to start with a polynomial in $x$ such as

$$f(x) = 2x^3 - 13x^2 + 17x + 26$$

and rewrite it as a polynomial in powers of $x - 3$ or, in general, $x - a$.

There are at least three different methods for doing this.

## Example

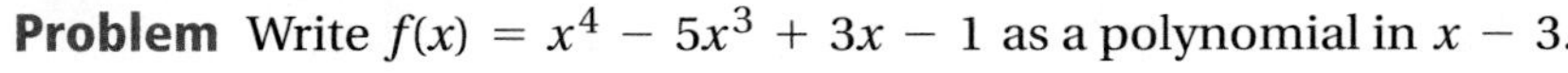

**Problem** Write $f(x) = x^4 - 5x^3 + 3x - 1$ as a polynomial in $x - 3$.

**Solution** Here is the first method.

### Method 1: Iterated Long Division

Start with the calculation in the Maintain Your Skills section on page 519.

$$\begin{array}{r|l}
 & x^3 - 2x^2 - 6x - 15 \\ \hline
x - 3 & x^4 - 5x^3 \qquad\quad + 3x - 1 \\
 & x^4 - 3x^3 \\ \hline
 & -2x^3 \qquad\quad + 3x - 1 \\
 & -2x^3 + 6x^2 \\ \hline
 & -6x^2 + 3x - 1 \\
 & -6x^2 + 18x \\ \hline
 & -15x - 1 \\
 & -15x + 45 \\ \hline
 & -46
\end{array}$$

This says that

$$f(x) = -46 + (x-3)\underbrace{(x^3 - 2x^2 - 6x - 15)}_{q_1(x)}$$

Let $x = 3$ to find that $f(3) = -46$.

Now work with the quotient $q_1(x) = x^3 - 2x^2 - 6x - 15$.

$$\begin{array}{r} x^2 + \phantom{0}x - \phantom{0}3 \\ x-3 \overline{\big) x^3 - 2x^2 - 6x - 15} \\ \underline{x^3 - 3x^2 \phantom{- 6x - 15}} \\ x^2 - 6x - 15 \\ \underline{x^2 - 3x \phantom{- 15}} \\ -3x - 15 \\ \underline{-3x + \phantom{0}9} \\ -24 \end{array}$$

This says that

$$q_1(x) = -24 + (x - 3)\underbrace{(x^2 + x - 3)}_{q_2(x)}$$

Now work with the quotient $q_2(x) = x^2 + x - 3$.

$$\begin{array}{r} x + \phantom{0}4 \\ x-3 \overline{\big) x^2 + \phantom{0}x - \phantom{0}3} \\ \underline{x^2 - 3x \phantom{- 00}} \\ 4x - \phantom{0}3 \\ \underline{4x - 12} \\ 9 \end{array}$$

This says that

$$q_2(x) = 9 + (x - 3)\underbrace{(x + 4)}_{q_3(x)}$$

Now work with the quotient $q_3(x) = x + 4$.

$$\begin{array}{r} 1 \\ x-3 \overline{\big) x + 4} \\ \underline{x - 3} \\ 7 \end{array}$$

This says that

$$q_3(x) = 7 + (x - 3)\underbrace{(\ 1\ )}_{q_4(x)}$$

Now put it all together.

$$\begin{aligned} f(x) &= -46 + (x - 3)\underbrace{(x^3 - 2x^2 - 6x - 15)}_{q_1(x)} \\ &= -46 + (x - 3)(-24 + (x - 3)(x^2 + x - 3)) \\ &= -46 - 24(x - 3) + (x - 3)^2\underbrace{(x^2 + x - 3)}_{q_2(x)} \\ &= -46 - 24(x - 3) + (x - 3)^2(9 + (x - 3)(x + 4)) \\ &= -46 - 24(x - 3) + 9(x - 3)^2 + (x - 3)^3\underbrace{(x + 4)}_{q_3(x)} \\ &= -46 - 24(x - 3) + 9(x - 3)^2 + (x - 3)^3(7 + (x - 3)) \\ &= -46 - 24(x - 3) + 9(x - 3)^2 + 7(x - 3)^3 + (x - 3)^4 \end{aligned}$$

The expression of $f(x)$ in terms of powers of $x - 3$ is the **Taylor expansion** for $f$ about 3. The tools of calculus make it possible to write Taylor expansions for non-polynomial functions, as well.

## For Discussion

Some older math books describe an elegant shorthand for doing polynomial division. Follow the instructions to find $(x^4 - 5x^3 + 3x - 1) \div (x - 3)$.

For a divisor $x - a$, put $a$ in the L-shaped bracket on the left. After the bracket, write the coefficients of the dividend polynomial in descending order of degree. Leave a space, draw a line, and bring down the leading coefficient.

Put in a zero if there is no term with a particular degree.

$$\begin{array}{r|rrrrr} 3 & 1 & -5 & 0 & 3 & -1 \\ & & & & & \\ \hline & 1 & & & & \end{array}$$

Multiply the number you just wrote under the line by the number in the bracket. Put the product under the next coefficient, and add down.

$$\begin{array}{r|rrrrr} 3 & 1 & -5 & 0 & 3 & -1 \\ & & 3 & & & \\ \hline & 1 & -2 & & & \end{array}$$

Repeat the previous step until you reach the end.

$$\begin{array}{r|rrrrr} 3 & 1 & -5 & 0 & 3 & -1 \\ & & 3 & -6 & -18 & -45 \\ \hline & 1 & -2 & -6 & -15 & \boxed{-46} \end{array}$$

Now you have completed the first division. Look back at your long division result on page 530. You can read off the coefficients of the quotient and remainder from this shorthand. You can do repeated divisions to get the complete Taylor expansion.

$$\begin{array}{r|rrrrr} 3 & 1 & -5 & 0 & 3 & -1 \\ & & 3 & -6 & -18 & -45 \\ \hline & 1 & -2 & -6 & -15 & \boxed{-46} \\ & & 3 & 3 & -9 & \\ \hline & 1 & 1 & -3 & \boxed{-24} & \\ & & 3 & 12 & & \\ \hline & 1 & 4 & \boxed{9} & & \\ & & 3 & & & \\ \hline & \boxed{1} & \boxed{7} & & & \end{array}$$

This gives you $(x - 3)^4 + 7(x - 3)^3 + 9(x - 3)^2 - 24(x - 3) - 46$.

**2.** Use this algorithm to expand $2x^3 + 5x^2 + x - 1$ as a polynomial in $x - 2$.

**3.** **Take It Further** Why does this algorithm work?

Here is a second method for writing a polynomial in powers of $x - 3$.

## Method 2: Undetermined Coefficients

Suppose

$$f(x) = x^4 - 5x^3 + 3x - 1 = A + B(x - 3) + C(x - 3)^2 + D(x - 3)^3 + E(x - 3)^4 \quad (1)$$

Why do you only need to go up to $(x - 3)^4$?

You need to find $A$, $B$, $C$, $D$, and $E$.

- Substitute $x = 3$ into (1) to find that $A = f(3) = -46$. Subtract $-46$ from each side of (1) to get

$$x^4 - 5x^3 + 3x + 45 = B(x - 3) + C(x - 3)^2 + D(x - 3)^3 + E(x - 3)^4 \quad (2)$$

The right side of (2) has $x - 3$ as a factor, and the left side does, too. You can check this by noting that

$$3^4 - 5 \cdot 3^3 + 3 \cdot 3 + 45 = 0$$

That is, $x = 3$ is a zero of the left side of (2). The left side of (2) factors as

$$(x - 3)(x^3 - 2x^2 - 6x - 15)$$

- So you can write (2) as

$$(x - 3)(x^3 - 2x^2 - 6x - 15) = B(x - 3) + C(x - 3)^2 + D(x - 3)^3 + E(x - 3)^4$$

Divide each side by $x - 3$ to get

$$x^3 - 2x^2 - 6x - 15 = B + C(x - 3) + D(x - 3)^2 + E(x - 3)^3 \quad (3)$$

Since the left and right sides are equal for $x \neq 3$, they must be equal for $x = 3$, as well.

What property of polynomials justifies this statement?

- Substitute $x = 3$ into (3) to find that $B = -24$. Subtract $-24$ from each side of (3) to get

$$x^3 - 2x^2 - 6x + 9 = C(x - 3) + D(x - 3)^2 + E(x - 3)^3 \quad (4)$$

The right side of (4) has $x - 3$ as a factor, and thus so does the left side. Again, note that $x = 3$ is a zero of the left side, which factors as

$$(x - 3)(x^2 + x - 3)$$

- So (4) becomes

$$(x - 3)(x^2 + x - 3) = C(x - 3) + D(x - 3)^2 + E(x - 3)^3$$

Divide by $x - 3$ to get

$$x^2 + x - 3 = C + D(x - 3) + E(x - 3)^2 \quad (5)$$

Again, the equation holds both for $x \neq 3$ and for $x = 3$.

**Habits of Mind**

**Use a consistent process.** Get into the rhythm of the calculations.

- Substitute $x = 3$ into (5) to find that $C = 9$. Subtract 9 from each side of (5) to get

$$x^2 + x - 12 = D(x - 3) + E(x - 3)^2 \quad (6)$$

The right side of (6) has $x - 3$ as a factor, and so does the left side. Note that $x = 3$ is a zero of the left side, which factors as

$$(x - 3)(x + 4)$$

- So write (6) as $(x - 3)(x + 4) = D(x - 3) + E(x - 3)^2$.

Divide by $x - 3$ to get

$$x + 4 = D + E(x - 3) \tag{7}$$

- Finally, substitute $x = 3$ into (7) to find $D = 7$, and then $E = 1$.

Here is a third method for writing a polynomial in powers of $x - 3$.

### Method 3: Use Your CAS

Your CAS has a built-in function that carries out the calculations you have been doing by hand. It allows you to expand a polynomial in terms of powers of $x - a$ for any number $a$. The function has different names in different systems, but they all work basically the same way.

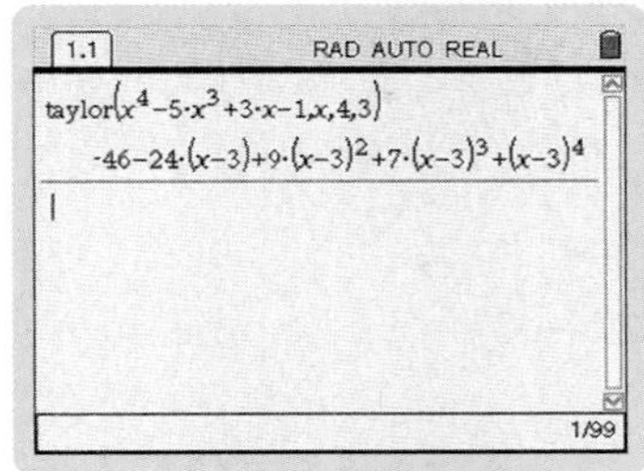

1.1
RAD AUTO REAL
taylor(x^4-5·x^3+3·x-1,x,4,3)
-46-24·(x-3)+9·(x-3)^2+7·(x-3)^3+(x-3)^4
1/99


This says, "Give me the expansion of $x^4 = 5x^3 + 3x - 1$. The variable is $x$, give me terms up to degree is 4, and I want it in terms of $x - 3$."

See the TI-Nspire Handbook on p. 817 for more information about the taylor function.

| taylor ($x^4 - 5x^3 + 3x - 1$, | $x$, | 4, | 3) |
|---|---|---|---|
| ↓ | ↓ | ↓ | ↓ |
| polynomial | variable | degree | in terms of $(x - 3)$ |

## For You to Do

**4.** Using whatever method you prefer, write

$$f(x) = 2x^3 + 5x^2 + x + 3$$

as a polynomial in $x - 1$.

## Exercises *Practicing Habits of Mind*

### Check Your Understanding

**1.** Suppose that $f(x) = 2x^3 + 5x^2 + x - 1$ and $g(x) = x^2 + 2x - 3$. Expand the following in powers of $x - 3$.

**a.** $f(x)$ **b.** $g(x)$ **c.** $f(x) + g(x)$

**d.** $4f(x)$ **e.** $4f(x) - g(x)$

2. Suppose that $f(x) = 2x^3 + 5x^2 + x - 1$ and $g(x) = x^2 + 2x - 3$. Expand the following in powers of $x - 2$.

   a. $f(x)$ b. $g(x)$

   c. $f(x) + g(x)$ d. $3f(x)$

   e. $f(x) \cdot g(x)$

3. Suppose that $g(x) = x^2 + 2x - 3$ and $a$ is some number. Expand $g(x)$ in powers of $x - a$ as

$$g(x) = A + B(x - a) + C(x - a)^2$$

where $A$, $B$, and $C$ are expressions in $a$.

4. Expand each polynomial in powers of $x - 3$.

   a. $x^3$ b. $x^2$ c. $x$ d. 1

*Sasha is thinking about Exercise 4.*

**Sasha** I see an easy way to get the expansion for $f(x) = 2x^3 + 5x^2 + x - 1$ from Exercise 1 in powers of $x - 3$.

**Tony** How?

**Sasha** I use what we got from Exercise 4.

First, we know the expansion for $x^3$. Since $f(x)$ starts out with $2x^3$, I multiply all the coefficients in the expansion for $x^3$ by 2.

Next, we know the expansion for $x^2$. Since $f(x)$ has a $5x^2$ term, I multiply all the coefficients in the expansion for $x^2$ by 5.

**Tony** And you multiply the expansion of $x$ by 1 and the expansion of 1 by $-1$, right?

Where did Tony get the 1 and $-1$?

**Sasha** Right, and then I add all these expressions together, making believe that the variable is $x - 3$. This will work for any cubic—I just need to know the expansions about 3 for the powers of $x$.

**Tony** Nice, but how do we know it works?

**Sasha** There's only one way to find out.

5. **Write About It** Does Sasha's method work for $f(x) = 2x^3 + 5x^2 + x - 1$? Does it work for any cubic polynomial? Justify your answers.

## On Your Own

6. Suppose that $f(x) = 2x^3 + 5x^2 + x - 1$ and $g(x) = x^2 + 2x - 3$. Expand the following in powers of $x - 5$.

   a. $f(x)$ b. $g(x)$ c. $3f(x) - 2g(x)$ d. $f(x) \cdot f(x)$

7. Suppose that $g(x) = rx^2 + sx + t$. Expand $g(x)$ in powers of $x - 3$

$$g(x) = A + B(x - 3) + C(x - 3)^2$$

where, $A$, $B$, and $C$ are in terms of $r$, $s$, and $t$.

8. Suppose that $g(x) = rx^2 + sx + t$ and $a$ is a number. Expand $g(x)$ in powers of $x - a$ as

$$g(x) = A + B(x - a) + C(x - a)^2$$

where, $A$, $B$, and $C$ are in terms of $r$, $s$, $t$, and $a$.

9. Until now, you have been dividing polynomials by a linear term. But the divisor can have any degree.

a. Find the missing numbers in this long division.

$$\begin{array}{r}
x + __ \\
x^2 - 7x + 10 \overline{\big) x^3 - 4x^2 - 10x + 31} \\
x^3 - 7x^2 + __x \phantom{{}+31} \\
\hline
3x^2 + __x + 31 \\
__x^2 + __x + __ \\
\hline
__x + __
\end{array}$$

b. How can you tell when the long division is complete?

c. Write the result as

$$x^3 - 4x^2 - 10x + 31 = (x^2 - 7x + 10)q(x) + r(x)$$

where $q$ and $r$ are polynomials in $x$.

10. Find the remainder when you divide $x^3 - 4x^2 - 10x + 31$ by

a. $x$     b. $x^2$     c. $x^3$

11. *Derman is still reviewing his notes.*

**Derman** I really like the way you can write $f(x)$ in powers of $x + 3$.

$$\begin{aligned} f(x) &= x^3 - 14x^2 + 55x - 42 \\ &= -360 + 166(x + 3) - 23(x + 3)^2 + (x + 3)^3 \end{aligned}$$

**Tony** Why?

**Derman** It lets me find the remainders when I divide $f(x)$ by any power of $x + 3$.

**Tony** Derman, sometimes you can be so deep.

Use Derman's idea to find the remainder when you divide $f(x)$ by

a. $x + 3$     b. $(x + 3)^2$     c. $(x + 3)^3$     d. $(x + 3)^8$

12. In Exercise 6, you expanded combinations of $f(x) = 2x^3 + 5x^2 + x - 1$ and $g(x) = x^2 + 2x - 3$ in powers of $x - 5$. That should make filling in this table a snap. Copy and complete the table.

| | Remainder when divided by | | | | | |
|---|---|---|---|---|---|---|
| | $x - 5$ | $(x - 5)^2$ | $(x - 5)^3$ | $(x - 5)^4$ | $(x - 5)^5$ | $(x - 5)^6$ |
| $f(x)$ | ■ | ■ | ■ | ■ | ■ | ■ |
| $g(x)$ | ■ | ■ | ■ | ■ | ■ | ■ |
| $3f(x) - 2g(x)$ | ■ | ■ | ■ | ■ | ■ | ■ |
| $f(x) \cdot f(x)$ | ■ | ■ | ■ | ■ | ■ | ■ |

13. Write each polynomial in the form $A + B(x - 1) + C(x)(x - 1)^2$ where $C(x)$ is a polynomial in $x$.

**a.** $x^2$ **b.** $x^3$ **c.** $x^4$ **d.** $x^5$ **e.** $x^6$

**f.** $x^n$ (where $n$ is a positive integer)

While you are at it, you might as well expand 1 and $x$, too.

14. **Take It Further** Use the identity $x^n = ((x - 1) + 1)^n$ and the Binomial Theorem to write each polynomial in powers of $x - 1$.

**a.** $x^2$ **b.** $x^3$ **c.** $x^5$ **d.** $x^n$ ($n$ a positive integer)

15. Suppose $f(x) = x^3 - 5x^2 - 2x + 1$. Graph each of the following.

**a.** $f$ **b.** $x \mapsto \text{taylor}(f(x), x, 1, 2)$

**c.** $x \mapsto \text{taylor}(f(x), x, 2, 2)$ **d.** $x \mapsto \text{taylor}(f(x), x, 3, 2)$

The taylor function on your CAS might look a bit different.

16. **Standardized Test Prep** What is the remainder when you divide $P(x) = 3x^5 - 5x^4 + 2x^3 - 4x^2 + x - 1$ by $x - 1$?

**A.** 2 **B.** $-3$ **C.** 4 **D.** $-4$

## Maintain Your Skills

17. For each polynomial $f(x)$,

- Find the remainder $r(x)$ when you divide $f(x)$ by $(x - 3)^2$.
- Sketch the graphs of $f$ and $r$ on the same axes.

**a.** $f(x) = x^3 - 5x + 6$ **b.** $f(x) = (x - 1)(x - 5)$

**c.** $f(x) = x^3$ **d.** $f(x) = x^3 + 3x^2 - 2x + 1$

**e.** $f(x) = (x - 1)^3$ **f.** $f(x) = (x - 3)^3$

# 7.05 Secants and Tangents

You know how to find the average rate of change between two points in time. This lesson will help you find the rate of change at a particular instant in time.

## In-Class Experiment

Let $d = t^2$ denote the distance $d$ (in feet) that Jerry has walked in $t$ seconds. The graph of this function is shown below.

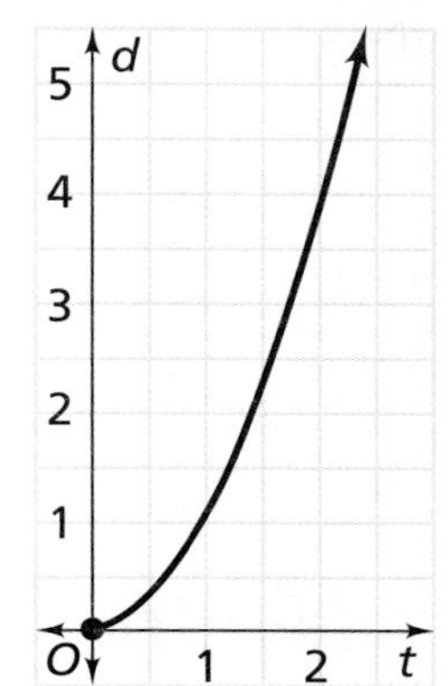


This function does not make sense as a model when $t$ is large, but it is plausible if $t$ is small.

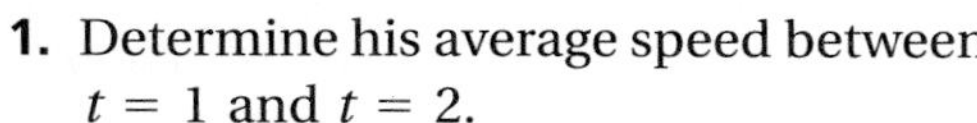

1. Determine his average speed between $t = 1$ and $t = 2$.

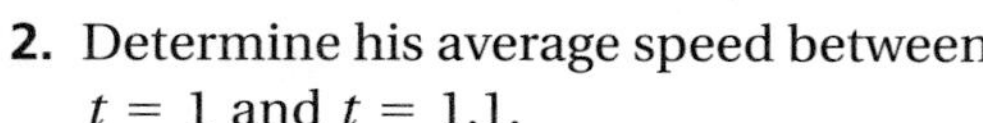

2. Determine his average speed between $t = 1$ and $t = 1.1$.
3. Determine his average speed between $t = 1$ and $t = 1.01$.

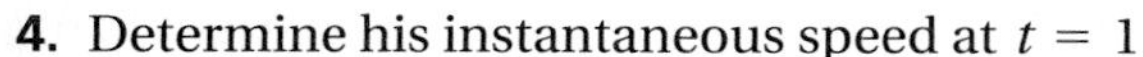

4. Determine his instantaneous speed at $t = 1$.

To find Jerry's **instantaneous speed** at $t = 1$, you need to find the slope of the tangent to the graph of $d = t^2$ at the point $(1, 1)$.

## For You to Do

5. Use geometry software to make a sketch with the graph of $y = x^2$ and a movable point $(a, a^2)$ on the graph. Construct the tangent to the curve at the point $(a, a^2)$.

See the TI-Nspire Handbook on p. 817 for details on how to draw tangent lines.

6. Copy the table below. Move the point along the graph and record the slope of the corresponding tangents in your table.

| $x$ | $y = x^2$ | Slope of the tangent at $(x, x^2)$ |
|---|---|---|
| −1 | ■ | ■ |
| 0 | ■ | ■ |
| 1 | ■ | ■ |
| 2 | ■ | ■ |
| 3 | ■ | ■ |
| 4 | ■ | ■ |
| 10 | ■ | ■ |
| 100 | ■ | ■ |

Given a function $f$ and a point $A = (a, f(a))$ on the graph of $y = f(x)$, you can think of the **tangent line** at $A$ as the secant between $A$ and itself.

You began learning about limits in Lesson 2.12, but more precisely, recall Exercise 2 from Lesson 7.03, where you let $f(x) = x^3 - 2x + 1$ and used geometry software to sketch the graph of $f$, the base point $A = (2, f(2))$ on the graph, and a movable point $B = (b, f(b))$ on the graph.

As $B$ moves closer to $A$, the secant through $A$ and $B$ approaches the tangent at $A$. The slope of the tangent at $A$ is the "limiting value" of the slope of the secant as $b$ approaches 2. The usual way to write this is

$$\lim_{b \to 2} \frac{f(b) - f(2)}{b - 2}$$

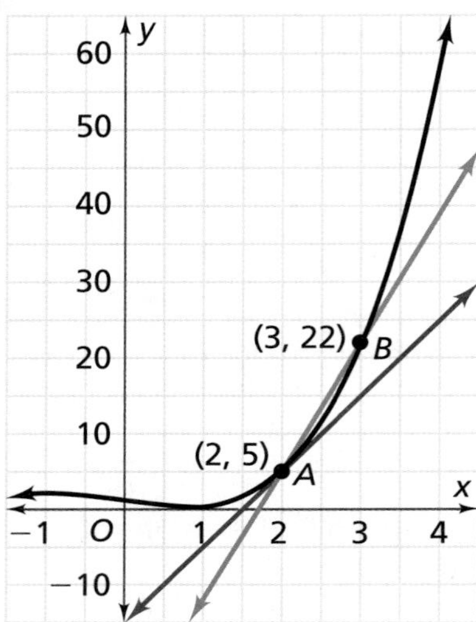


## Computing the Tangent

To find the equation of a tangent line algebraically, go back to secants for a moment. Let $f(x) = x^3 - 2x + 1$. Divide $f(x)$ by $(x - 2)(x - 3) = x^2 - 5x + 6$. Using long division, you get

$$\begin{array}{r|l} & \quad\quad\quad\quad\; x + 5 \\ x^2 - 5x + 6 & x^3 \quad\quad\;\; - 2x + 1 \\ & \underline{x^3 - 5x^2 + 6x} \\ & \quad\;\; 5x^2 - 8x + 1 \\ & \quad\;\; \underline{5x^2 - 25x + 30} \\ & \quad\quad\quad\;\; 17x - 29 \end{array}$$

so you have

$$f(x) = x^3 - 2x + 1 = (x - 2)(x - 3)q(x) + r(x)$$

where $q(x) = x + 5$ and $r(x) = 17x - 29$. Substituting $x = 2$ shows that $f(2) = r(2)$. Likewise, $f(3) = r(3)$. In other words, $r$ is a linear function that agrees with $f$ at $x = 2$ and $x = 3$. So the graph of $y = r(x)$ must be the secant to the graph of $y = f(x)$ through the points $(2, f(2))$ and $(3, f(3))$.

Here is the generalization.

### Theorem 7.4

**Let $f(x)$ be a polynomial and $a, b \in \mathbb{R}$. Write**

$$f(x) = (x - a)(x - b)q(x) + r(x)$$

**where $r(x)$ is a linear function. Then the graph of $y = r(x)$ is the secant to the graph of $y = f(x)$ through $(a, f(a))$ and $(b, f(b))$.**

In the above theorem, all you are really interested in is the remainder $r(x)$. In other words, you do not need to know what $q(x)$ is. A CAS can find this remainder easily and quickly.

See the TI-Nspire Handbook on p. 817 for details on how to use the polyremainder function to find the remainder $r(x)$ when you divide one polynomial by another.

How about the tangent? Let $f(x) = x^3 - 2x + 1$ again. Suppose you want to find the tangent to its graph at $A = (2, f(2))$. Consider a movable point $B = (b, f(b))$ on the graph. The secant between $A$ and $B$ is given by the remainder when you divide $f(x)$ by $(x - 2)(x - b)$. As point $B$ approaches point $A$, the corresponding division by $(x - 2)(x - b)$ becomes division by $(x - 2)^2$.

This type of argument works because polynomial functions are continuous.

The following theorem summarizes this result.

### Theorem 7.5

**Let $f(x)$ be a polynomial and $a \in \mathbb{R}$. Write**

$$f(x) = (x - a)^2 q(x) + r(x)$$

**where $r(x)$ is a linear function. Then the graph of $y = r(x)$ is the tangent to the graph of $y = f(x)$ at $(a, f(a))$.**

## Example 1

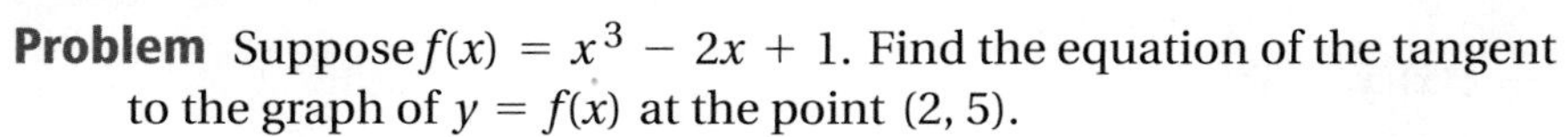

**Problem** Suppose $f(x) = x^3 - 2x + 1$. Find the equation of the tangent to the graph of $y = f(x)$ at the point $(2, 5)$.

**Solution** By Theorem 7.5, the equation of the tangent is the linear function $r(x)$ where

$$f(x) = (x - 2)^2 q(x) + r(x)$$

In other words, $r(x)$ is the remainder when you divide $f(x)$ by $(x - 2)^2 = x^2 - 4x + 4$. A CAS shows that

$$r(x) = 10x - 15$$

So far, you have seen two ways to find the remainder $r(x)$:

- Using long division.
- Using a CAS.

The following technique uses methods from Lesson 7.04.

## Example 2

**Problem** Let $f(x) = 2x^2 + 3x + 1$. Find the equation of the tangent to the graph of $y = f(x)$ at the point $(3, f(3))$.

**Solution** First, write $f(x)$ in powers of $x - 3$.

$$f(x) = 2x^2 + 3x + 1 = m + n(x - 3) + p(x)(x - 3)^2 \quad (1)$$

You can read off the remainder when you divide $f(x)$ by $(x - 3)^2$—it is $m + n(x - 3)$.

See Exercise 11 from Lesson 7.04.

With $r(x) = m + n(x - 3)$, the graph of $r(x)$ is the desired tangent. So you need to solve for $m$ and $n$. Substitute $x = 3$ in (1) to get

$$m = f(3) = 2 \cdot 3^2 + 3 \cdot 3 + 1 = 28$$

So

$$2x^2 + 3x + 1 = 28 + n(x - 3) + p(x)(x - 3)^2 \quad (2)$$

Subtracting 28 from both sides of (2) gives

$$2x^2 + 3x - 27 = n(x - 3) + p(x)(x - 3)^2$$

The right side says that $x - 3$ is a factor of the left side. This makes factoring the left side easy:

$$(x - 3)(2x + 9) = n(x - 3) + p(x)(x - 3)^2$$

Dividing by $x - 3$ gives

$$2x + 9 = n + p(x)(x - 3) \quad (3)$$

Substituting $x = 3$ into (3) gives $n = 15$. So the equation of the tangent is

$$r(x) = 28 + 15(x - 3) = 15x - 17.$$

## For You to Do

**7.** Let $f(x) = 2x^2 + 3x + 1$ again. Using the method in Example 2, find the equation of the tangent to the graph of $y = f(x)$ at the point $(a, f(a))$. (Your equation will be in terms of $a$.)

## Exercises *Practicing Habits of Mind*

### Check Your Understanding

1. Find the equation of the line tangent to the graph of $y = x^2$ at the point $(5, 25)$.

2. Consider $f(x) = x^3 - 7x^2 + 3x - 2$. Write an equation for the line tangent to the graph of $f$ at $(0, -2)$.

3. Generalize the result in Exercise 1 by finding the equation of the line tangent to the graph of $y = x^2$ at the point $(a, a^2)$.

4. Copy and complete this table for $f(x) = x^2 + 1$.

| $x$ | $f(x)$ | Slope of tangent at $(x, f(x))$ |
|---|---|---|
| −1 | ■ | ■ |
| 0 | ■ | ■ |
| 1 | ■ | ■ |
| 2 | ■ | ■ |
| 3 | ■ | ■ |
| 4 | ■ | ■ |
| 10 | ■ | ■ |
| 100 | ■ | ■ |

5. Copy and complete this table for $f(x) = x^2 + x$.

| $x$ | $f(x)$ | Slope of tangent at $(x, f(x))$ |
|---|---|---|
| −1 | ■ | ■ |
| 0 | ■ | ■ |
| 1 | ■ | ■ |
| 2 | ■ | ■ |
| 3 | ■ | ■ |
| 4 | ■ | ■ |
| 10 | ■ | ■ |
| 100 | ■ | ■ |

6. Find the equation of the line tangent to the graph of each polynomial at $(1, 1)$.

   a. $f(x) = x^2$ b. $f(x) = x^3$ c. $f(x) = x^4$
   d. $f(x) = x^5$ e. $f(x) = x^6$ f. $f(x) = x$

7. Find, in terms of $n$, a formula for the equation of the tangent to the graph of $y = x^n$ (where $n$ is a positive integer) at $(1, 1)$.

## On Your Own

8. Find the slope and equation of the line tangent to the graph of $f(x) = x^3 - x$ at the point $(-1, 2)$.

9. Copy and complete this table for $f(x) = x^3$.

| x | f(x) | Slope of tangent at (x, f(x)) |
|---|---|---|
| −1 | ■ | ■ |
| 0 | ■ | ■ |
| 1 | ■ | ■ |
| 2 | ■ | ■ |
| 3 | ■ | ■ |
| 4 | ■ | ■ |
| 10 | ■ | ■ |
| 100 | ■ | ■ |

10. Find, in terms of $a$, the equation of the line tangent to the graph of each polynomial at $(a, f(a))$.

    a. $f(x) = x^2$ b. $f(x) = x^3$ c. $f(x) = x^4$
    d. $f(x) = x^5$ e. $f(x) = x^6$ f. $f(x) = x$

11. Find, in terms of $n$ and $a$, a formula for the equation of the tangent to the graph of $f(x) = x^n$ (where $n$ is a positive integer) at $(a, f(a))$.

12. **Take It Further** Find the equation of the line tangent to the graph of $y = \sqrt{x}$ at $(1, 1)$.

13. **Standardized Test Prep** If a function $f$ has a well-defined slope over its entire domain, which of the following expressions gives the slope of $f(x)$ at $x = 0$?

    A. $\lim_{x \to a} \frac{f(a) - f(0)}{x - a}$ B. $\lim_{a \to b} \frac{f(b) - f(a)}{b - a}$ C. $\lim_{b \to 0} \frac{f(b) - f(0)}{b}$ D. $\lim_{x \to 0} \frac{f(a) - f(0)}{x}$

## Maintain Your Skills

14. Find the remainder when you divide $f(x) = x^3 - 2x + 1$ by each of these linear factors.

    a. $(x + 1)$ b. $x$ c. $(x - 1)$ d. $(x - 2)$
    e. $(x - 3)$ f. $(x - 4)$ g. $(x - 10)$ h. $(x - 100)$

Go Online
www.successnetplus.com

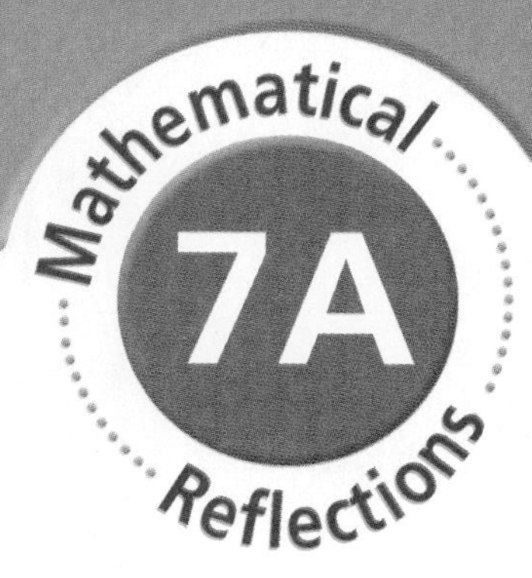

In this investigation, you found slopes of lines secant or tangent to the graph of a polynomial function. You learned that these slopes represent, respectively, average and instantaneous rates of change of the function. The following questions will help you summarize what you have learned.

1. Here are three expressions that each define the function $f$.

   **Expression 1:** $f(x) = x^4 - 5x^3 - x^2 + 17x + 12$

   **Expression 2:** $f(x) = (x + 1)^2(x - 3)(x - 4)$

   **Expression 3:** $f(x) = (x - 1)^4 - (x - 1)^3 - 10(x - 1)^2 + 4(x - 1) + 24$

   a. Which expression would be the most useful for sketching the graph of the function? Choose an expression, use it to sketch the graph of the function, and explain how the form of the expression was helpful.

   b. Which expression is the most useful for finding the equation of the line tangent to the graph at the point $(1, 24)$? Choose an expression, use it to find the equation of the tangent, and explain how the form of the expression was helpful.

2. For each of the following numbers, sketch the graph of a third-degree polynomial which has the indicated number of $x$-intercepts, or explain why such a graph does not exist.

   a. 0 b. 1 c. 2 d. 3 e. 4

3. Let $f(x) = x^3 + 8x^2 + 5x - 50$.

   a. Expand the function $f(x)$ in powers of $x + 4$.

   b. Use your expansion to find the equation of the tangent to the graph of $f(x)$ at the point $(-4, f(-4))$.

4. How can you graph a polynomial function given its factored form?

5. How can you determine a polynomial's behavior at very large or very small inputs?

6. How can you use long division to find equations of secant or tangent lines to the graph of a polynomial function?

## Vocabulary

In this investigation, you learned these terms. Make sure you understand what each one means and how to use it.

- **average rate of change**
- **continuous**
- **instantaneous speed**
- **power function**
- **secant line**
- **tangent line**
- **Taylor expansion**

# Rational Functions

In *Rational Functions,* you will graph functions $f(x)$ that are quotients of polynomials. You will have to pay particular attention to values of $x$ for which the denominator polynomial has value 0.

**By the end of this investigation, you will be able to answer questions like these.**

1. What happens to $f(x) = \frac{3x^2 + 2x - 1}{5x^2 - 3x + 10}$ as $x$ gets larger and larger?
2. Why do the graphs of $g(x) = \frac{x^2 - 15}{x - 4}$ and $h(x) = \frac{x^2 - 16}{x - 4}$ look so different from each other?
3. How can you find tangent lines to rational functions?

**You will learn how to**

- sketch the graph of a rational function, including asymptotes and holes
- evaluate limits of rational expressions
- find the equation of the tangent to the graph of a rational function at a point

**You will develop these habits and skills:**

- Visualize different types of discontinuities, relating equations and their graphs.
- Reason logically to find limits at infinity.
- Extend the methods of Investigation 7A to find the equation of the tangent to the graph of a rational function.

Holes and vertical asymptotes represent discontinuities in the graph of a rational function.

# 7.06 Getting Started

Earlier in this course, you learned to calculate with rational expressions, expressions of the form $\frac{p}{q}$ where $p$ and $q$ are polynomials. The emphasis there was on the formal algebraic properties of these expressions. In this investigation, you will study **rational functions.** A rational function is a function of the form $x \mapsto \frac{p(x)}{q(x)}$, where $p$ and $q$ are polynomial functions of $x$. Rational functions have all kinds of interesting graphs. Here are some examples.

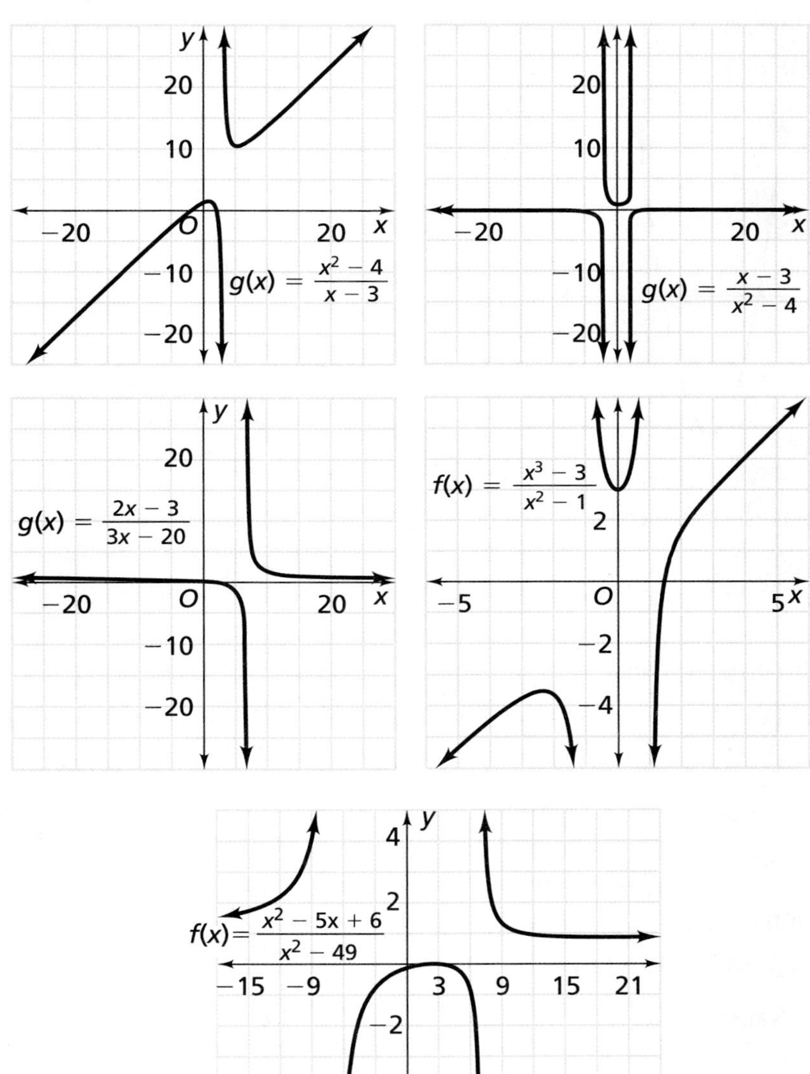

## For You to Explore

1. Suppose $f$ and $g$ are functions with the property that $g(x) = \frac{1}{f(x)}$ for any $x$ in the domain of both functions.

   a. Give an example of two functions $f$ and $g$ that are reciprocal functions.

   b. Suppose $f(a) = 3$. What is the value of $g(a)$?

   c. If $f(b)$ is very large, what can you say about $g(b)$?

   d. If $f(c) = 0$, what can you say about $g(c)$?

   e. If $f(5) = k$ and $g(5) = k$, what are the possible values of $k$?

Functions $f$ and $g$ are called **reciprocal functions.** They are not inverse functions.

2. Suppose $f$ and $g$ are functions with $g(x) = \frac{1}{f(x)}$ for any $x$ in the domain of both functions. Here is the graph of $f$:

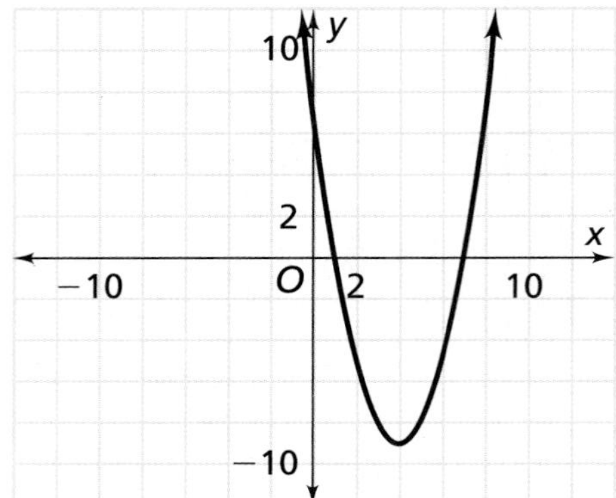


   Copy the graph and, on the same axes, sketch the graph of $g$.

3. a. Find the domain of $g(x) = \frac{1}{x^2 - 8x + 7}$.

   b. Sketch the graph of $f(x) = x^2 - 8x + 12$.

   c. Use the graph of $f(x) = x^2 - 8x + 12$ to sketch the graph of $g(x) = \frac{1}{x^2 - 8x + 12}$.

   d. Find the domain of $g(x) = \frac{1}{x^2 - 8x + 12}$.

4. Let

$$f(x) = \frac{x-2}{x^2-9} \quad \text{and} \quad g(x) = \frac{x-3}{x^2-9}$$

   a. Find the domain of each function.

   b. Describe the behavior of the graphs of $f$ and $g$ near $x = 3$.

5. Give an example of a function that satisfies each condition.

   a. $f(3) = f(5) = 0$.

   b. The function $g$ is undefined at 3 and 5.

   c. As $x$ gets larger, $h(x)$ approaches 0.

   d. As $x$ gets larger, $j(x)$ approaches 3.

6. Write About It Make your own rational function graph gallery.
   - Sketch or generate 10 particularly interesting rational function graphs.
   - Give the rational function for each graph.
   - Describe what you find interesting about each graph.

7. a. Make an accurate sketch of

$$h(x) = \frac{|x|}{x}$$

   b. What can you say about $\lim_{x \to 0} h(x)$?

$\lim_{x \to 0} h(x)$ means the limit of $h(x)$ as $x$ approaches 0.

8. Consider $j(x) = x + \frac{1}{x}$.
   a. Give estimates for $j(100)$ and $j(0.01)$.
   b. What positive value of $x$ makes $j(x)$ as small as possible?
   c. Take It Further Show algebraically that if $x > 0$, then $j(x) \geq 2$.

## Exercises Practicing Habits of Mind

### On Your Own

9. If $f(x) = \frac{x + 3}{2x - 1}$ and $g(x) = \frac{x + 1}{x - 1}$, find all values of $a$ such that $f(a) = g(a) - \frac{4}{3}$.

10. Give an example of a function that satisfies each condition.
   a. $f(3) = 0$ and $f$ has no other zeros.
   b. The domain of $g$ is all real numbers except for 5, and $g$ has no zeros.
   c. The domain of $h$ is all real numbers except for 5, and $h(3) = 0$.
   d. As $x$ gets larger, the graph of $j$ gets closer and closer to the graph of $y = x$.

11. Here is the graph of $f(x) = \sin x$. Use it to sketch the graph of $g(x) = \frac{1}{\sin x}$.

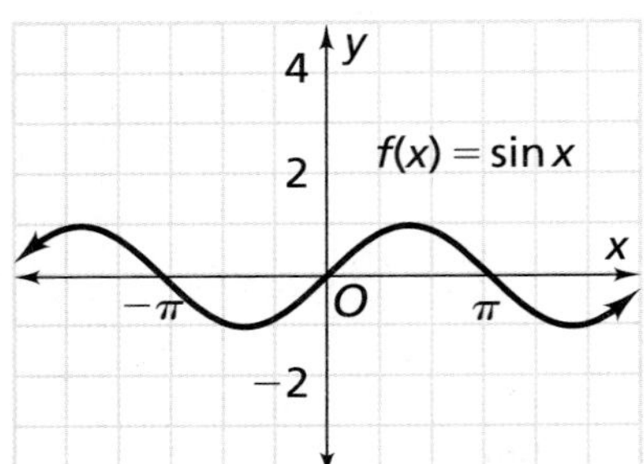


The *cosecant* function is defined as $\csc x = \frac{1}{\sin x}$.

12. Let $k(x) = \frac{x^2 - x - 6}{x - 3}$.

a. Copy and complete this table for $k(x)$.

| $x$ | $k(x)$ |
|---|---|
| 0 | 2 |
| 1 | ■ |
| 2 | ■ |
| 3 | ■ |
| 4 | ■ |

b. Use factoring to simplify the expression $\frac{x^2 - x - 6}{x - 3}$. Assume that $x \neq 3$.

c. Explain why $k$ is not the same function as $m(x) = x + 2$.

d. **Write About It** In what way does the graph of $k$ look different from the graph of $m$?

13. Find a rational function $k$ that is identical to $m(x) = x - 1$, except that $k$ is undefined when $x = 4$.

14. Sketch the graphs of these three functions on the same axes.

$$f_1(x) = x$$

$$f_2(x) = \frac{1}{x}$$

$$f_3(x) = x + \frac{1}{x}$$

You should already be able to graph $f_1$ and $f_2$ without a calculator. Try graphing $f_3$ without a calculator, too.

## Maintain Your Skills

15. Sketch the graph of each function.

a. $f(x) = \frac{1}{x}$

b. $f(x) = \frac{1}{x + 3}$

c. $f(x) = \frac{1}{x + 3} + 5$

d. $f(x) = \frac{1}{x^2}$

e. $f(x) = \frac{1}{(x - 4)^2}$

f. $f(x) = \frac{(x - 3)(x + 5)}{(x - 3)(x + 5)}$

16. Sketch the graph of each function.

a. $f(x) = \frac{1}{x}$

b. $f(x) = \frac{1}{x - 4}$

c. $f(x) = \frac{1}{2x - 4}$

d. $f(x) = \frac{x}{2x - 4}$

e. $f(x) = \frac{x - 3}{2x - 4}$

f. $f(x) = \frac{x - 3}{2x - 4} + 5$

# 7.07 Graphing Rational Functions

Subtle differences in functions can make their graphs look very different.

Consider the rational functions $f$ and $g$ from Problem 4 in Lesson 7.06:

$$f(x) = \frac{x-2}{x^2-9} \quad \text{and} \quad g(x) = \frac{x-3}{x^2-9}$$

Both have denominator $x^2 - 9 = (x+3)(x-3)$, so they are both undefined at $x = 3$. Their graphs, however, look very different. The graph of $f$ has a vertical asymptote at $x = 3$, while the graph of $g$ looks practically flat at $x = 3$. Why the difference?

Of course, they are also undefined at $x = -3$.

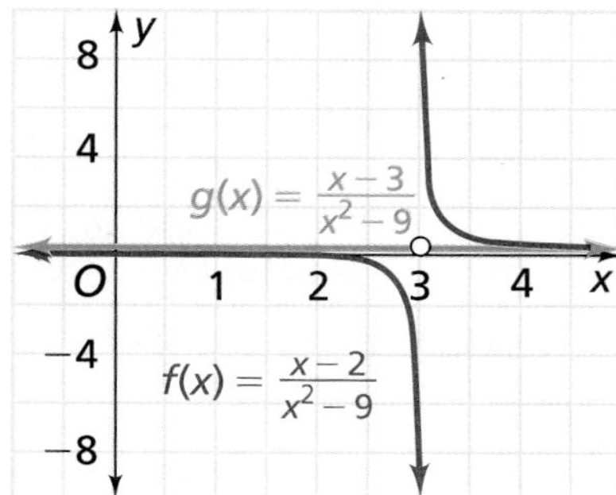


Start with $f$. Since $f(x) = \frac{x-2}{x^2-9}$, you can write it as

$$f(x) = m(x) \cdot \frac{1}{x-3}$$

where $m(x) = \frac{x-2}{x+3}$. Thus,

$$m(3) = \frac{3-2}{3+3} = \frac{1}{6}$$

So near $x = 3$, $f$ behaves like the function

$$x \mapsto \frac{1}{6} \cdot \frac{1}{x-3}$$

the graph of which has a vertical asymptote at $x = 3$.

**Remember...**

A vertical asymptote is a line that the graph of a function approaches, but does not intersect.

Now consider $g(x) = \frac{x-3}{x^2-9}$. For any $a \neq 3$,

$$g(a) = \frac{a-3}{(a+3)(a-3)} = \frac{1}{a+3}$$

Since $a - 3 \neq 0$, you can cancel the term $a - 3$ from the numerator and denominator. So,

$$g(x) = \begin{cases} \frac{1}{x+3} & \text{if } x \neq 3 \\ \text{undefined} & \text{if } x = 3 \end{cases}$$

The graph of $g$ looks just like the graph of $y = \frac{1}{x+3}$, except with a *hole* at $x = 3$.

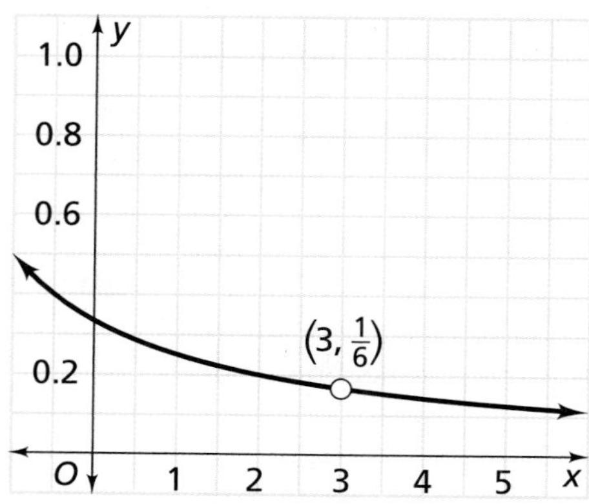


## Example 1

**Problem** For each function below, describe the behavior of its graph near $x = 3$.

**a.** $f(x) = \frac{(x-3)^2}{(x-3)^6}$

**b.** $g(x) = \frac{(x-3)^6}{(x-3)^2}$

**Solution**

**a.** For any $a \neq 3$,

$$f(a) = \frac{(a-3)^2}{(a-3)^6} = \frac{1}{(a-3)^4}$$

Again, you can cancel here because $a - 3 \neq 0$.

Thus, as functions, the maps

$$x \mapsto f(x) \quad \text{and} \quad x \mapsto \frac{1}{(x-3)^4}$$

are equal because neither is defined at $x = 3$ and they agree on all $x \neq 3$. Their graphs are the same and so the graph of $f$ has a vertical asymptote at $x = 3$.

**b.** For any $a \neq 3$,

$$g(a) = \frac{(a-3)^6}{(a-3)^2} = (a-3)^4.$$

Thus, the graph of $g$ looks just like the graph of $y = (x-3)^4$, except with a hole at $x = 3$.

The previous example leads to the following definitions and theorem.

## *Definitions*

Let $h(x) = \frac{f(x)}{g(x)}$ be a rational function such that

- $f(x) = (x - a)^m \cdot p(x)$
- $g(x) = (x - a)^n \cdot q(x)$

where $p(a), q(a) \neq 0$.

1. $h$ has an **infinite discontinuity** at $x = a$ if $n > m \geq 0$.
2. $h$ has a **removable discontinuity** at $x = a$ if $m \geq n > 0$.

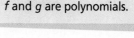

$f$ and $g$ are polynomials.

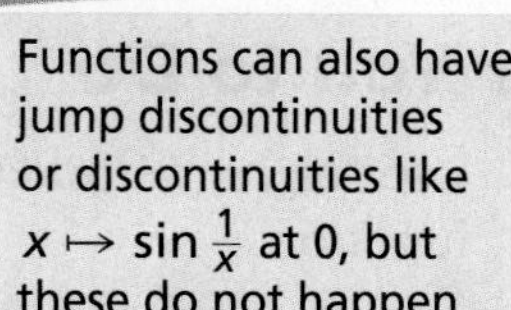
Functions can also have jump discontinuities or discontinuities like $x \mapsto \sin \frac{1}{x}$ at 0, but these do not happen with rational functions.

## *Theorem 7.6*

Let $h$ be a rational function.

1. If $h$ has an infinite discontinuity at $x = a$, then the graph of $h$ has $x = a$ as a vertical asymptote.
2. If $h$ has a removable discontinuity at $x = a$, then the graph of $h$ has a **hole** at $x = a$.

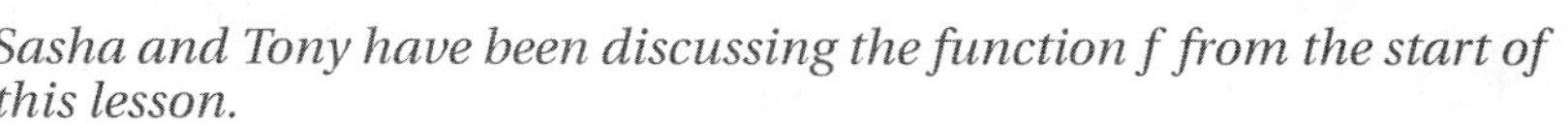

## Minds in Action

*Sasha and Tony have been discussing the function f from the start of this lesson.*

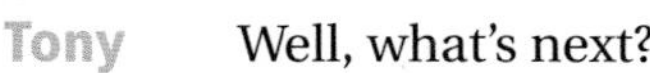

**Tony** Well, what's next?

**Sasha** We know that the graph of $f(x) = \frac{x-2}{x^2-9}$ has vertical asymptotes at $x = 3$ and $x = -3$, but I wonder if it has a horizontal asymptote.

**Tony** I was looking ahead at Exercise 13 in this lesson. How about dividing every term by the highest degree?

**Sasha** What do you mean?

**Tony** Here, like this:

$$f(x) = \frac{x-2}{x^2-9} \cdot \frac{\frac{1}{x^2}}{\frac{1}{x^2}} = \frac{\frac{1}{x} - \frac{2}{x^2}}{1 - \frac{9}{x^2}}.$$

**Sasha** Wait, what if $x = 0$?

**Tony** Then this new expression for $f$ doesn't work. But I'm using it to figure out what happens when $x$ is really big.

**Sasha** Got it. And when $x$ is big, the terms $\frac{1}{x}$, $\frac{2}{x^2}$, and $\frac{9}{x^2}$ are close to zero, and only the 1 is left.

**Tony** Exactly! So if $x$ is really big, we get

$$f(x) \approx \frac{0}{1}$$

And that means the horizontal asymptote is $y = 0$.

## For You to Do

1. Use Tony's method to find the horizontal asymptote of the graph of each function.

   **a.** $g(x) = \dfrac{x-3}{x^2-9}$ **b.** $h(x) = \dfrac{9x^3+5x+1}{4x^3-7}$

2. Explain how Tony's method offers an explanation for why the same method works when $x$ is a large positive or negative number.

**Remember...**

A large negative number is something like $-1$ million. Here, *large* refers to absolute value.

Consider $f(x) = \frac{x-2}{x^2-9}$ again. Sasha and Tony showed that $f(x) \approx 0$ if $x$ is a big number. In other words, you can make $f(x)$ as close to 0 as you want by making $x$ large enough. To express this fact, write

$$\lim_{x\to\infty} f(x) = 0$$

You will see a more precise definition when you take a course in calculus.

As another example, you saw in the For You to Do above that

$$\lim_{x\to\infty} \frac{9x^3+5x+1}{4x^3-7} = \frac{9}{4}$$

In fact, this limit is the same even if $x$ becomes a large negative number. You express this fact by writing

$$\lim_{x\to-\infty} \frac{9x^3+5x+1}{4x^3-7} = \frac{9}{4}$$

### Theorem 7.7

**Let $h(x) = \frac{f(x)}{g(x)}$ be a rational function with deg $f = m$ and deg $g = n$.**

1. **If $m < n$, then $\lim_{x\to\infty} h(x) = 0$.**
2. **If $m = n$, then $\lim_{x\to\infty} h(x)$ is the ratio of the leading coefficients of $f$ and $g$.**

**Moreover, the graph of $h$ has a horizontal asymptote with equation $y = L$ where $L = \lim_{x\to\infty} h(x)$.**

deg $f$ means the degree of the polynomial $f$.

You may be wondering what happens when deg $f >$ deg $g$. Take a look at the following example.

## Example 2

**Problem** Let

$$h(x) = \frac{x^3 - 4x}{x - 1}$$

Describe the behavior of $h$ for large values of $x$.

**Solution** Using long division as shown in Method 3 from Lesson 7.03, you have

$$x^3 - 4x = (x - 1)(x^2 + x - 3) - 3$$

so that

$$h(x) = q(x) + \frac{-3}{x - 1}$$

where $q(x) = x^2 + x - 3$. Thus you can make $h(x)$ as large as you want by making $x$ large enough. In other words,

$$\lim_{x \to \infty} h(x) = \infty$$

This limit statement says that as $x$ increases without bound, so does $h(x)$.

Furthermore,

$$\lim_{x \to \infty}(h(x) - q(x)) = \lim_{x \to \infty} \frac{-3}{x - 1} = 0$$

so that the outputs of $h$ become arbitrarily close to the outputs of $q$ for large positive and negative values of $x$. Thus, the graph of $h$ has a nonhorizontal asymptote, namely the graph of the polynomial $q$.

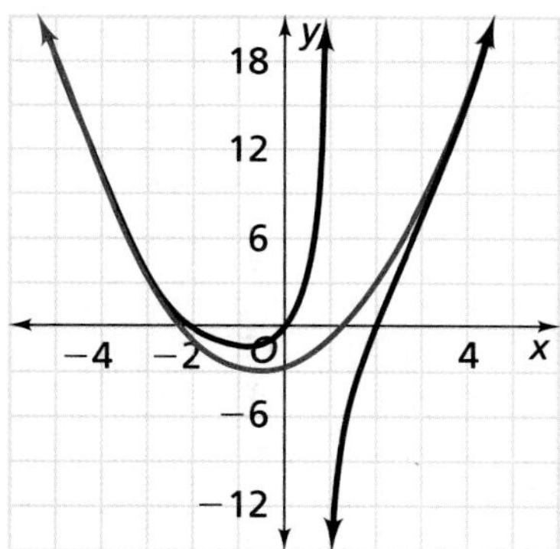

## For You to Do

Let

$$k(x) = \frac{x^2 + x - 1}{3 - x}$$

**3.** Find $\lim_{k \to \infty} k(x)$.

**4.** Find all asymptotes of the graph of $k$.

### Theorem 7.8

Let $h(x) = \frac{f(x)}{g(x)}$ be a rational function with deg $f >$ deg $g$. Then $\lim_{x \to \infty} h(x) = \infty$ or $-\infty$. Moreover, if you write

$$\frac{f(x)}{g(x)} = q(x) + \frac{r(x)}{g(x)}$$

where $q$ and $r$ are polynomials with deg $r <$ deg $g$, then the graph of $q$ is a nonhorizontal asymptote of the graph of $h$.

## Exercises *Practicing Habits of Mind*

### Check Your Understanding

**1.** Calculate each limit.

**a.** $\lim_{x \to \infty} \frac{x - 4}{x^2 - 4}$ **b.** $\lim_{x \to \infty} \frac{x^2 - 4}{x - 4}$ **c.** $\lim_{x \to -\infty} \frac{x - 4}{x^2 - 4}$ **d.** $\lim_{x \to -\infty} \frac{x^2 - 4}{x - 4}$

**2.** Calculate each limit.

**a.** $\lim_{x \to \infty} \frac{3x^2 - 1}{5x^2 + 3}$ **b.** $\lim_{x \to \infty} \frac{10x^3 - 7}{3x^3 + 5}$ **c.** $\lim_{x \to -\infty} \frac{10 + 5x^4}{2x^4 - 2}$

**d.** $\lim_{x \to -\infty} \frac{7x - 6x^5}{3x^5 - 17x}$ **e.** $\lim_{x \to \infty} \frac{10x^3 - 5}{4x^2 + 3x}$ **f.** $\lim_{x \to \infty} \frac{x^2 + 1}{3x^3 - 10}$

**3.** Consider $f(x) = \frac{x^2 - 3x - 4}{x^2 - 2x - 8}$.

**a.** The graph of $f$ has a horizontal asymptote. What is its equation?

**b.** The graph of $f$ has a vertical asymptote. What is its equation?

**c.** The graph of $f$ has a hole at what point?

**4.** Let $f$ be a rational function.

**a.** Give an example of a function $f$ the graph of which has a horizontal asymptote with equation $y = 4$.

**b.** Give an example of a function $f$ that is undefined at $x = 2$ and $x = 5$.

**c.** Give an example of a function $f$ the graph of which has $x = -3$ as a vertical asymptote and has a hole at $x = 2$.

**d.** Give an example of a function $f$ with $f(2) = 0$, $f(1)$ undefined, and a graph with no horizontal asymptote.

**5.** The function $h(x) = \frac{x - 3}{x^2 - 9}$ has a removable discontinuity at $x = 3$. Define function $j$ as

$$j(x) = \begin{cases} h(x) & \text{if } x \neq 3 \\ K & \text{if } x = 3 \end{cases}$$

What value of $K$ would make $j(x)$ continuous at $x = 3$?

What value of $K$ would "plug" the hole left by $h$ at $x = 3$?

**6.** Consider the function $f(x) = \frac{x^2 + 1}{x}$.

**a.** Calculate $f(10)$ and $f(100)$.

**b.** What does the graph of $f(x)$ look like as $x$ gets large?

**c.** Calculate $f(0.1)$ and $f(0.01)$.

**d.** What does the graph of $f(x)$ look like as $x$ approaches zero?

**e.** Sketch the graph of $f$.

**7.** The graph of $y = \frac{x^3 + 1}{x^2 - x^4 + 1}$ looks like which of these when $x > 4$?

**A.** $y = x$ **B.** $y = -x$ **C.** $y = \frac{1}{x}$ **D.** $y = -\frac{1}{x}$

**8. a.** Sketch the graphs of $f(x) = (x - 1)(x + 3)$ and $g(x) = \frac{1}{(x - 1)(x + 3)}$ on the same axes.

**b.** Find the exact values of all $x$ such that $f(x) = g(x)$.

**9.** Take It Further Let $d(x)$ be defined for nonnegative real numbers as the decimal part of $x$. For example, $d(10.63)$ is 0.63, and $d(\pi)$ starts out 0.14159… .

**a.** Let $x = \frac{7}{4}$. Calculate $d(x)$, $d(2x)$, $d(3x)$, and $d(4x)$.

**b.** Sketch a graph of $d$ on $0 \leq x \leq 10$.

**c.** Sketch a graph of $r(x) = \frac{1}{d(x)}$ on $0 \leq x \leq 10$. Describe the domain and range of $r$.

## On Your Own

**10.** Consider $g(x) = \frac{2x^2 - 5x + 2}{x^2 + x - 6}$.

**a.** The graph of $g$ has a horizontal asymptote. What is its equation?

**b.** The graph of $g$ has a vertical asymptote. What is its equation?

**c.** The graph of $g$ has a hole at what point?

**11.** What is the domain of

**a.** $x \mapsto \frac{x - 4}{x^2 - 4}$? **b.** $x \mapsto \frac{x - 2}{x^2 - 4}$?

**12.** Calculate each limit.

**a.** $\lim_{x\to\infty} \dfrac{1 + \frac{1}{x}}{2 + \frac{1}{x}}$  **b.** $\lim_{x\to\infty} \dfrac{x + 1}{2x + 1}$  **c.** $\lim_{x\to\infty} \dfrac{\frac{3}{x} - \frac{4}{x^2}}{1 - \frac{5}{x} + \frac{6}{x^2}}$

**d.** $\lim_{x\to\infty} \dfrac{3x - 4}{x^2 - 5x + 6}$  **e.** $\lim_{x\to\infty} \dfrac{x^2 - 5x + 6}{3x - 4}$

**13. a.** Sketch the graphs of these three functions on the same axes with $x \geq 0$.

$$f_1(x) = \frac{1}{x},\ f_2(x) = \frac{\sin x}{x},\ f_3(x) = -\frac{1}{x}$$

**b.** Use the graphs to find the value of $\lim_{x\to\infty} \frac{\sin x}{x}$.

**14.** Write About It Describe how you can determine the horizontal asymptote, if any, of a given rational function. Include in your explanation an example of a rational function with a horizontal asymptote $y = 0$, one with a horizontal asymptote $y = c$ (where $c$ is a nonzero real number), and one with no horizontal asymptote at all.

**15.** The graphs of these two functions look identical on a graphing calculator.

$$f(x) = \frac{x + 11}{x^2 + 14x + 33}$$

$$g(x) = \frac{1}{x + 3}$$

**a.** Explain why they are not the same function.

**b.** Explain why their graphs look identical on the calculator.

**16. a.** Show that this equation is an identity.

$$\frac{1}{x + 2} - \frac{1}{x + 3} = \frac{1}{x^2 + 5x + 6}$$

**b.** Without using a calculator, sketch the graphs of $f(x) = \frac{1}{x + 2}$ and $g(x) = -\frac{1}{x + 3}$ on the same axes.

**c.** Use the graphs of $f$ and $g$ to make a rough sketch of $h(x) = \frac{1}{x^2 + 5x + 6}$. Check your work using a graphing calculator.

**17. a.** Find constants $A$ and $B$ that make this equation true.

$$\frac{x + 9}{x^2 - 2x - 3} = \frac{A}{x + 1} + \frac{B}{x - 3}$$

**b.** For the values of $A$ and $B$ you found, sketch the graphs of $f(x) = \frac{A}{x + 1}$ and $g(x) = \frac{B}{x - 3}$ on the same axes.

**c.** Use the graphs of $f$ and $g$ to make a rough sketch of $h(x) = \frac{x + 9}{x^2 - 2x - 3}$. Check your work using a graphing calculator.

**18.** Standardized Test Prep Let $P(x) = \dfrac{x^5}{36x^4 - 13x^2 + 1}$. If $h$ is the number of horizontal asymptotes and $v$ is the number of vertical asymptotes of the graph of $P$, what is the value of the product $hv$?

**A.** 0 **B.** 2 **C.** 4 **D.** 8

## Maintain Your Skills

**19.** Sketch the graph of each function.

**a.** $a(x) = \dfrac{x - 2}{x - 3}$

**b.** $b(x) = \dfrac{2x - 5}{x - 3}$

**c.** $c(x) = \dfrac{3x - 8}{x - 3}$

**d.** $d(x) = \dfrac{4x - 11}{x - 3}$

**20.** For each equation, find the value of $a$ that makes the equation true.

**a.** $\dfrac{2x - 5}{x - 3} = a + \dfrac{1}{x - 3}$

**b.** $\dfrac{3x - 8}{x - 3} = a + \dfrac{1}{x - 3}$

**c.** $\dfrac{4x - 11}{x - 3} = a + \dfrac{1}{x - 3}$

**21.** Find each value of $K$ so the function has no removable discontinuity.

What value of $K$ plugs the hole in the graph?

**a.** $f(x) = \begin{cases} \dfrac{x}{x^2 - 3x} & \text{if } x \neq 0 \\ K & \text{if } x = 0 \end{cases}$

**b.** $g(x) = \begin{cases} \dfrac{x^3 - 6x^2 + 11x - 6}{x - 2} & \text{if } x \neq 2 \\ K & \text{if } x = 2 \end{cases}$

**c.** $h(x) = \begin{cases} \dfrac{(x + 1)(x - 4)}{(x - 4)(x + 10)} & \text{if } x \neq 4 \\ K & \text{if } x = 4 \end{cases}$

**d.** $j(x) = \begin{cases} \dfrac{(x + 2)^2(x - 3)}{x^2 - 3x - 10} & \text{if } x \neq -2 \\ K & \text{if } x = -2 \end{cases}$

**22.** Sketch the graph of each function.

**a.** $a(x) = \dfrac{x - 3}{(x + 1)^2}$

**b.** $b(x) = \dfrac{x^2 - 4}{x^2 - 1}$

**c.** $c(x) = \dfrac{x^2 - 6x + 5}{x^2 - 6x + 8}$

**d.** $d(x) = \dfrac{(x - 1)^2}{(x + 2)^2}$

**e.** $e(x) = \dfrac{(x - 1)^2}{(x + 2)^3}$

# 7.08 Revisiting Secants and Tangents

In Lesson 7.05, you saw two theorems (Theorem 7.4 and Theorem 7.5) that provided a method for finding the equations of secants and tangents to graphs of polynomial functions. In this lesson, you will see that the same method works even if $f$ is a rational function.

Of course, you can talk about the tangent at $(a, f(a))$ only if $f$ is continuous at $x = a$.

## Example 1

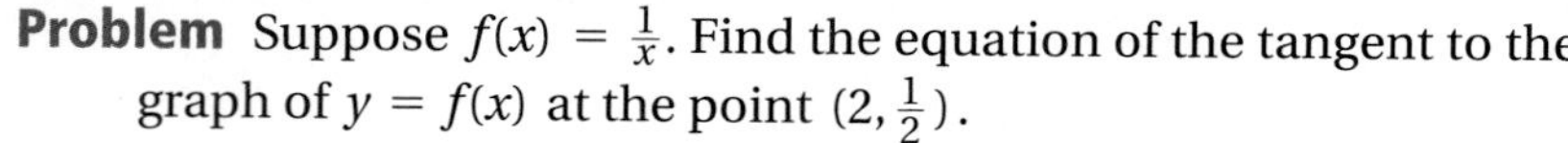

**Problem** Suppose $f(x) = \frac{1}{x}$. Find the equation of the tangent to the graph of $y = f(x)$ at the point $(2, \frac{1}{2})$.

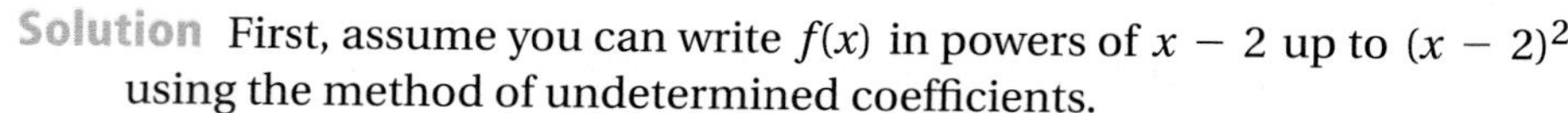

**Solution** First, assume you can write $f(x)$ in powers of $x - 2$ up to $(x - 2)^2$ using the method of undetermined coefficients.

$$f(x) = \frac{1}{x} = m + n(x-2) + p(x)(x-2)^2 \qquad (1)$$

Then the polynomial method indicates that the equation of the line tangent to the graph of $f(x)$ at $(2, f(2))$ is $y = m + n(x - 2)$.

Substitute $x = 2$ in (1) to get

$$m = f(2) = \frac{1}{2}$$

$$\frac{1}{x} = \frac{1}{2} + n(x-2) + p(x)(x-2)^2 \qquad (2)$$

Subtract $\frac{1}{2}$ from each side of (2)

$$\frac{1}{x} - \frac{1}{2} = n(x-2) + p(x)(x-2)^2$$

Rewrite this as

$$\frac{-(x-2)}{2x} = n(x-2) + p(x)(x-2)^2$$

Divide by $x - 2$ to get

$$\frac{-1}{2x} = n + p(x)(x-2) \qquad (3)$$

Now suppose $p$ is defined and continuous at $x = 2$. Since the left and right sides of (3) are equal for $x \neq 2$, they must be equal for $x = 2$, as well. Substitute $x = 2$ in (3) to get $n = -\frac{1}{4}$.

$$\frac{1}{x} = \frac{1}{2} - \frac{1}{4}(x-2) + p(x)(x-2)^2$$

for some function $p(x)$. This means that the equation of the tangent at $x = 2$ is

$$r(x) = m + n(x-2) = \frac{1}{2} - \frac{1}{4}(x-2)$$

## For You to Do

1. Find $p(x)$ if

$$\frac{1}{x} = \frac{1}{2} - \frac{1}{4}(x - 2) + p(x)(x - 2)^2$$

2. For $f(x) = \frac{1}{x}$, find an equation of the tangent to the graph of $y = f(x)$ at the point $(a, f(a))$.

$a \neq 0$, of course.

## Minds in Action

*Sasha and Derman are looking at the above example.*

**Sasha** I'm not completely sure about this method.

**Derman** What could be wrong? I write

$$\frac{1}{x} = \frac{1}{2} - \frac{1}{4}(x - 2) + p(x)(x - 2)^2$$

for some function $p$. Then I think about the secant becoming the tangent. The algebra says that the remainder when I divide by $(x - 2)^2$ is the equation of the tangent. The remainder when I divide the right side is $\frac{1}{2} - \frac{1}{4}(x - 2)$, so that's it.

**Sasha** I'm worried about the assumption that $p$ is continuous at $x = 2$. $p$ is now a rational function. If its denominator had turned out to have some power of $x - 2$ as a factor, that would invalidate the reasoning by which we found $p$ in the first place.

**Derman** Well, $p$ came out the way we needed it to in Example 1. Let's try another example and see if the same thing happens.

At the moment of takeoff, a ski jumper's skis are essentially tangent to the curve of the ramp.

## Example 2

**Problem** Let

$$f(x) = \frac{x + 2}{2x^2 + 3x + 1}.$$

Find an equation of the tangent to the graph of $y = f(x)$ at the point $(3, f(3))$.

**Solution**

Write $f$ in powers of $x - 3$.

$$f(x) = \frac{x + 2}{2x^2 + 3x + 1} = m + n(x - 3) + p(x)(x - 3)^2 \quad (4)$$

If $r(x) = m + n(x - 3)$, then the graph of $r$ will be the tangent.
So you need to solve for $m$ and $n$. Substitute $x = 3$ in (4) and you get

$$m = f(3) = \frac{5}{28}$$

So,

$$\frac{x + 2}{2x^2 + 3x + 1} = \frac{5}{28} + n(x - 3) + p(x)(x - 3)^2 \quad (5)$$

Subtract $\frac{5}{28}$ from each side of (5).

$$\frac{x + 2}{2x^2 + 3x + 1} - \frac{5}{28} = n(x - 3) + p(x)(x - 3)^2$$

Rewrite this as

$$\frac{-10x^2 + 13x + 51}{28(2x^2 + 3x + 1)} = n(x - 3) + p(x)(x - 3)^2$$

The right side of this equation implies that its left side has a factor of $x - 3$.
Use this fact to factor the numerator of the left side.

$$\frac{-(x - 3)(10x + 17)}{28(2x^2 + 3x + 1)} = n(x - 3) + p(x)(x - 3)^2$$

Divide each side by $x - 3$.

$$\frac{-(10x + 17)}{28(2x^2 + 3x + 1)} = n + p(x)(x - 3) \quad (6)$$

Substitute $x = 3$ into (6) to get $n = -\frac{47}{28^2}$. The equation of the tangent at $x = 3$ is

$$r(x) = \frac{5}{28} - \frac{47}{28^2}(x - 3)$$

## For You to Do

**3.** Find $p(x)$ if

$$\frac{x+2}{2x^2+3x+1} = \frac{5}{28} - \frac{47}{28^2}(x-3) + p(x)(x-3)^2$$

**4.** Let

$$f(x) = \frac{2x+5}{x+3}$$

Find an equation of the tangent to the graph of $y = f(x)$ at the point $(1, f(1))$.

## Minds in Action

*Tony, Sasha, and Derman are talking some more about the mysterious $p(x)$.*

**Derman** Look, in both cases we've tried, $p(x)$ had almost the same denominator as the original function.

**Tony** In fact, it was a perfect square times the denominator of the original.

**Sasha** It looks too good to be true. But two examples don't make a theorem.

**Tony** Here's what I think. Suppose the rational function you start with is defined at a number, say 2, and you make believe that $p(x)$ is also defined and continuous at 2. If you plow ahead and find $p(x)$ by first finding $m$ and then $n$ and then solving for $p(x)$, you'll see in the end that $p(x)$ is continuous at 2. I bet it's true.

**Sasha** Here's what worries me. Take the $\frac{1}{x}$ example. We figured out that

$$\frac{1}{x} = \frac{1}{2} - \frac{1}{4}(x-2) + \frac{1}{4x}(x-2)^2$$

If I wanted to, I could write

$$\frac{1}{x} = 3 - 17(x-2) + p(x)(x-2)^2$$

and solve for a different $p(x)$. And I bet that one would not be continuous at 2.

The $\frac{1}{4x}$ comes from Problem 1 on page 559.

**Tony** Right, but I'm finding $m$ and $n$ in by a special method—our method of undetermined coefficients. Replace $x$ by 2, find $m$, divide by $x - 2$, and so on.

**Derman** Try another?

**Tony** Or do it in general, once and for all.

**Sasha** I feel some algebra coming on.

### *Theorem 7.9*

**Suppose that $f$ is a rational function for which the denominator is not zero at $x = r$. Suppose also that you use the method of undetermined coefficients to write**

$$f(x) = m + n(x - r) + p(x)(x - r)^2$$

**finding first the number $m$ and then the number $n$. Then $p$ is a rational function that is defined at $x = r$.**

**Remember...**

**The Method of Undetermined Coefficients:** Replace $x$ by $r$, find $m$, subtract $m$ from both sides, divide by $x - r$, find $n$, subtract $n$ from both sides, divide by $x - r$. . . . When finding $m$ and $n$, assume that $p(x)$ is defined and continuous at $x = r$. In the end, your assumption will be correct.

## For Discussion

**5.** Develop a proof or a plausible argument for Theorem 7.9.

## Developing Habits of Mind

**Use a different process to get the same result.** The Taylor expansion command in your CAS works with rational functions as well. It produces results that agree with the method of undetermined coefficients. For example, to find $m$ and $n$ such that

$$\frac{1}{x} = m + n(x - 2) + p(x)(x - 2)^2$$

tell the system to expand $\frac{1}{x}$ about $x = 2$ up to terms of degree 1.

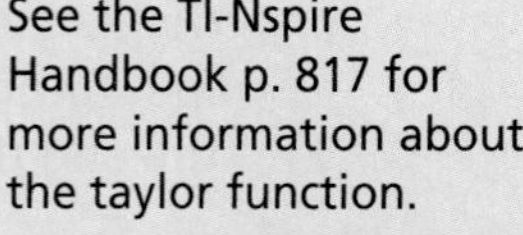

See the TI-Nspire Handbook p. 817 for more information about the taylor function.

## Exercises *Practicing Habits of Mind*

### Check Your Understanding

**1.** Let $g(x) = -\frac{1}{x}$. Find an equation of the tangent to the graph of $g$ at the point $(2, g(2))$.

**2.** In Example 1 on page 558, you saw that the tangent to the graph of $f(x) = \frac{1}{x}$ at $(2, f(2))$ has the equation

$$y = \frac{1}{2} - \frac{1}{4}(x - 2)$$

How does this compare to the tangent of $g$ you found in Exercise 1? Explain your answer.

**3.** Let $h(x) = \frac{1}{x^2}$. Find an equation of the tangent to the graph of $y = h(x)$ at the point $(a, h(a))$.

**4.** Copy and complete this table by finding the slope of the tangent to the graphs of $f(x) = \frac{1}{x}$ and $h(x) = \frac{1}{x^2}$ at each value of $x$. Explain the results using the graphs of $f$ and $h$.

| $x$ | Slope of tangent to $f$ | Slope of tangent to $h$ |
|---|---|---|
| $\frac{1}{10}$ | ■ | ■ |
| $\frac{1}{4}$ | ■ | ■ |
| $\frac{1}{2}$ | ■ | ■ |
| 1 | ■ | ■ |
| 2 | $-\frac{1}{4}$ | $-\frac{1}{4}$ |
| 4 | ■ | ■ |
| 10 | ■ | ■ |

**5.** Let

$$h(x) = \frac{2x - 3}{x^2 + 4x + 5}$$

Find an equation of the tangent to the graph of $h$ at $x = -2$.

**6.** Find $A$ and $B$ so that

$$\frac{4x - 26}{x^2 - 7x + 10} = \frac{A}{x - 2} + \frac{B}{x - 5}$$

7. Let $f(x) = \frac{A}{x-2}$ and $g(x) = \frac{B}{x-5}$ where $A$ and $B$ are the values you found in Exercise 6.

   a. Graph $f$. Find the slope of the line tangent to $f$ at $x = 4$.

   b. Graph $g$. Find the slope of the line tangent to $g$ at $x = 4$.

   c. Graph $h(x) = \frac{4x-26}{x^2-7x+10}$. Find the slope of the line tangent to $h$ at $x = 4$.

## On Your Own

8. **Write About It** The function $f(x) = \frac{1}{x}$ is "decreasing everywhere." What does this mean? Give other examples of functions that are increasing everywhere, functions that are decreasing everywhere, and functions that are neither.

9. Let

$$g(x) = \frac{2x+7}{5x-2}$$

Find an equation of the tangent to the graph of $g$ at $(3, g(3))$.

10. Copy and complete this table with the slope of the tangent to $f(x) = \frac{1}{x}$ and $g(x) = x + \frac{1}{x}$ at each value of $x$. Explain your answer.

| $x$ | Slope of tangent to $f$ | Slope of tangent to $g$ |
|---|---|---|
| $-2$ | ■ | ■ |
| $-1$ | ■ | ■ |
| $-\frac{1}{2}$ | ■ | ■ |
| 0 | undefined | undefined |
| $\frac{1}{2}$ | ■ | ■ |
| 1 | ■ | ■ |
| 2 | ■ | ■ |
| 3 | ■ | ■ |

**11.** Consider the function $j(x) = \frac{1}{x^2 + 1}$.

**a.** Find the slope of the tangent to $j$ at $x = 2$.

**b.** Find the slope of the tangent to $j$ at $x = -2$.

**c.** How are the answers in (a) and (b) related? Explain.

**12.** Let

$$f(x) = \frac{ax + b}{cx + d}$$

Find an equation of the tangent to the graph of $f$ at $x = 0$.

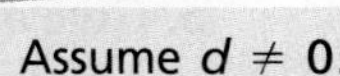

Assume $d \neq 0$.

**13. Take It Further** Let $f(x) = \frac{ax + b}{cx + d}$ again, with $d \neq 0$. Write $f$ as a power series

$$f(x) = \alpha_0 + \alpha_1 x + \alpha_2 x^2 + \alpha_3 x^3 + \alpha_4 x^4 + \cdots$$

You saw in Exercise 12 that

$$\alpha_0 = \frac{b}{d} \text{ and } \alpha_1 = \frac{ad - bc}{d^2}$$

Find $\alpha_n$ for $n \geq 2$.

It might help to use a letter such as $\Delta$ to replace the constant value of $ad - bc$. If you do this, you can get simpler expressions, like $\alpha_1 = \frac{\Delta}{d^2}$.

**14. Standardized Test Prep** What is the slope of the tangent to the graph of $f(x) = \frac{4}{x}$ at $(3, f(3))$?

**A.** $-\frac{9}{4}$ **B.** $-\frac{4}{9}$ **C.** $-\frac{4}{3}$ **D.** $-\frac{3}{4}$

## Maintain Your Skills

**15.** Sketch the graphs of all four functions on the same axes. A graphing calculator may be helpful.

**a.** $a(x) = 1 + x$

**b.** $b(x) = 1 + x + \frac{x^2}{2}$

**c.** $c(x) = 1 + x + \frac{x^2}{2} + \frac{x^3}{6}$

**d.** $d(x) = 1 + x + \frac{x^2}{2!} + \frac{x^3}{3!} + \frac{x^4}{4!}$

**16.** For each of functions in Exercise 15, find the slope of the tangent line through the point $(0, 1)$.

**17. a.** Write out the first six lines of Pascal's Triangle.

**b.** What is the value of $\binom{7}{3}$?

**In this investigation, you learned about removable continuities and infinite discontinuities. You learned the effects of these discontinuities on graphs of functions. You graphed rational functions using their horizontal and vertical asymptotes. You also found equations of lines tangent to these graphs. The following questions will help you summarize what you have learned.**

1. **a.** Give an example of a rational function the graph of which has a hole at $x = 3$. Sketch its graph.
   **b.** Give an example of a rational function the graph of which has a vertical asymptote at $x = 3$. Sketch its graph.
2. **a.** Give an example of a rational function the graph of which has a horizontal asymptote at $y = 0$. Sketch its graph.
   **b.** Give an example of a rational function the graph of which has a horizontal asymptote at $y = 2$. Sketch its graph.
3. Let $f(x) = \frac{3x^2 + 10x + 8}{x - 3}$.
   **a.** Find all $x$- and $y$-intercepts of the graph of $f$.
   **b.** Find all asymptotes of the graph of $f$.
   **c.** Sketch the graph of $f$.
4. Find an equation for the tangent to the graph of $g(x) = \frac{4x + 1}{x - 3}$ at $(0, g(0))$.
5. Let $h(x) = \frac{x - 1}{x}$.
   **a.** Find an equation for the tangent to the graph of $h$ at $(a, h(a))$ for $a \neq 0$.
   **b.** Use your answer to part (a) to find all values of $x$ where the function $h$ is increasing. Explain your answer.

6. What happens to $f(x) = \frac{3x^2 + 2x - 1}{5x^2 - 3x + 10}$ as $x$ gets larger and larger?

7. Why do the graphs of $g(x) = \frac{x^2 - 15}{x - 4}$ and $h(x) = \frac{x^2 - 16}{x - 4}$ look so different from each other?

8. How can you find tangent lines to rational functions?

## Vocabulary and Notation

In this investigation, you learned these terms. Make sure you understand what each one means and how to use it.

- **hole**
- **infinite discontinuity**
- **rational function**
- **reciprocal function**
- **removable discontinuity**

# More About Recursive Models

**In *More About Recursive Models,* you will analyze the following question.**

**How does a bank figure out the monthly payment on a loan?**

**You will answer this question with a recursively defined function that calculates the balance you owe in any month of a car loan.**

**You will also see a function that has no simple closed form—its recursive model is its primary definition. This is the factorial function. Its value at $n$ is the product of all integers between 1 and $n$.**

$$f(n) = 1 \cdot 2 \cdot 3 \cdot \cdots \cdot n$$

## By the end of this investigation, you will be able to answer questions like these.

1. What is a recursive definition of a function? When is this type of definition useful?
2. What is the recursive definition of the factorial function?
3. What is the monthly payment on a loan of \$10,000 for 36 months with an interest rate of 5%?

## You will learn how to

- find the monthly payment on a loan given the interest rate, term, and amount you borrow
- understand how the monthly payment on a loan changes with the amount you borrow
- build a recursively defined function that agrees with a table
- use the recursive model for the factorial function

## You will develop these habits and skills*:*

- Build and modify recursive definitions for functions.
- Search for hidden regularity in tables of numbers.
- Reason about algebraic forms.
- Build models for recursively defined functions in your function-modeling language.

You have to set the table. There are $3 \cdot 2 \cdot 1$, or 6, possible arrangements of three utensils.

## 7.09 Getting Started

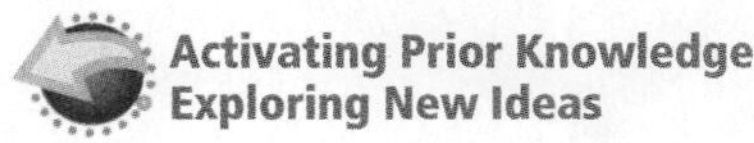


You can use a table to help you rewrite a recursive definition for a function as a closed-form definition.

### For You to Explore

For Exercises 1–5, make a table of the function values for inputs between 0 and 10. Then find a closed-form definition that agrees with the table. Use your closed-form definition to find the outputs at 103, 104, and 245.

**1.** $g(n) = \begin{cases} 5 & \text{if } n = 0 \\ g(n-1) + 7 & \text{if } n > 0 \end{cases}$

You can build models of the functions in your function-modeling language.

**2.** $t(n) = \begin{cases} 1 & \text{if } n = 0 \\ 2 \cdot t(n-1) & \text{if } n > 0 \end{cases}$

**3.** $j(n) = \begin{cases} 0 & \text{if } n = 0 \\ j(n-1) + 2n - 1 & \text{if } n > 0 \end{cases}$

**4.** $k(n) = \begin{cases} 0 & \text{if } n = 0 \\ k(n-1) + 2n & \text{if } n > 0 \end{cases}$

**5.** $\ell(n) = \begin{cases} 0 & \text{if } n = 0 \\ \ell(n-1) + n & \text{if } n > 0 \end{cases}$

For Exercises 6–8, find a recursively defined function that agrees with each table. Make a table of the function values for inputs from 0 to 10.

**6.**

| Input | Output |
|---|---|
| 0 | 6 |
| 1 | 9 |
| 2 | 12 |
| 3 | 15 |
| 4 | 18 |
| 5 | 21 |

**7.**

| Input | Output |
|---|---|
| 0 | 7 |
| 1 | 11 |
| 2 | 15 |
| 3 | 19 |
| 4 | 23 |
| 5 | 27 |

**8.**

| Input | Output |
|---|---|
| 0 | 7 |
| 1 | 18 |
| 2 | 33 |
| 3 | 52 |
| 4 | 75 |
| 5 | 102 |

## Exercises Practicing Habits of Mind

### On Your Own

For Exercises 9–12, make a table of the function values for inputs between 0 and 10. Then find a closed-form definition that agrees with the table. Use your closed-form definition to find the outputs at 103, 104, and 245.

**9.** $g(n) = \begin{cases} 0 & \text{if } n = 0 \\ g(n-1) + 1 & \text{if } n > 0 \end{cases}$

You can build models of the functions in your function language.

**10.** $t(n) = \begin{cases} 1 & \text{if } n = 0 \\ 3 \cdot t(n-1) & \text{if } n > 0 \end{cases}$

**11.** $j(n) = \begin{cases} 1 & \text{if } n = 0 \\ j(n-1) + 2n + 1 & \text{if } n > 0 \end{cases}$

**12.** $k(n) = \begin{cases} 0 & \text{if } n = 0 \\ k(n-1) + \dfrac{n(n-1)}{2} & \text{if } n > 0 \end{cases}$

**13.** Find a recursively defined function that agrees with the table below. Make a table of the function values for inputs from 0 to 10.

| Input | Output |
|---|---|
| 0 | 1 |
| 1 | 1 |
| 2 | 2 |
| 3 | 6 |
| 4 | 24 |
| 5 | 120 |

**14.** Make a table of the function $f$ defined below for inputs from 0 to 10.

$$f(n) = \begin{cases} 1 & \text{if } n = 0 \\ 1 & \text{if } n = 1 \\ f(n-1) + f(n-2) & \text{if } n > 1 \end{cases}$$

For advice on modeling recursive functions, see the TI-Nspire Handbook, p. 817.

15. **a.** Use your function-modeling language to model the function $b$ defined below. For what value of $n$ is $b(n)$ closest to 0?

$$b(n) = \begin{cases} 10{,}000 & \text{if } n = 0 \\ \frac{12.05}{12} \cdot b(n-1) - 438.71 & \text{if } n > 0 \end{cases}$$

**b.** Find the value of $x$ that makes $b(36)$ closest to 0 for the definition of $b$ below.

$$b(n) = \begin{cases} 10{,}000 & \text{if } n = 0 \\ \frac{12.02}{12} \cdot b(n-1) - x & \text{if } n > 0 \end{cases}$$

## Maintain Your Skills

16. How many ways are there to arrange the letters in each word?

**a.** TO

**b.** MOP

**c.** FORM

**d.** SHOWN

**e.** CLOSED

17. How many ways are there to arrange the letters in "ABCDEFHIJ"?

18. Show that the following identity is true.

$$\frac{n(n+1)}{2} - \frac{(n-1)n}{2} = n$$

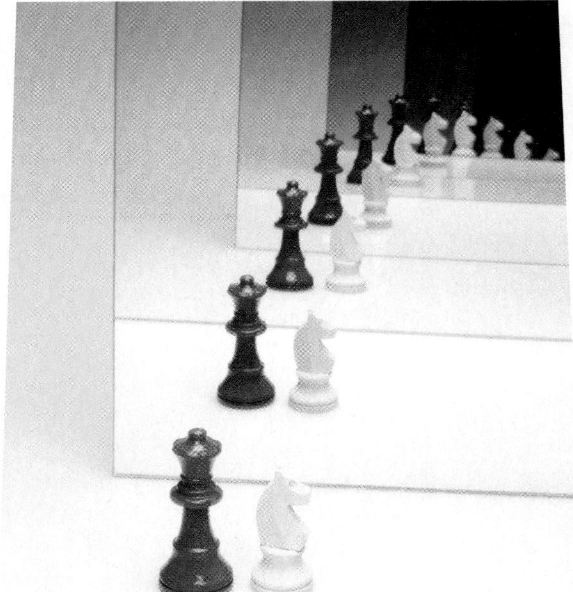

Recursion Using Mirrors

## 7.10 Monthly Payments

Suppose you want to buy a car. You can put \$1000 down and pay \$250 per month. The interest rate is 5%, and the dealer wants the loan paid off in three years. How much can you afford to spend on the car?

A recursive approach lets you experiment using your function modeling language. Can you afford a \$10,000 car? Well, after you pay \$1000 down, you can borrow \$9000. At the end of 36 months, you want the balance to be 0.

Begin with a simpler model, one that would hold in an ideal world where you did not have to pay any interest.

Every now and then, car dealers offer a 0% interest rate.

- At the end of Month 0, you owe \$9000 (that is how much you borrowed, and Month 0 is when the loan starts).
- For any month after Month 0, you owe \$250 less than the month before (because you paid \$250).

If $b(n)$ is the balance in dollars at the end of the $n$th month, then

$$b(n) = \begin{cases} 9000 & \text{if } n = 0 \\ b(n-1) - 250 & \text{if } n > 0 \end{cases}$$

### For You to Do

For Problems 1–4, find how much you owe after each time span.

1. 1 month
2. 2 months
3. 6 months
4. 1 year
5. Can you pay off your car in 36 months? If not, how much do you still owe?

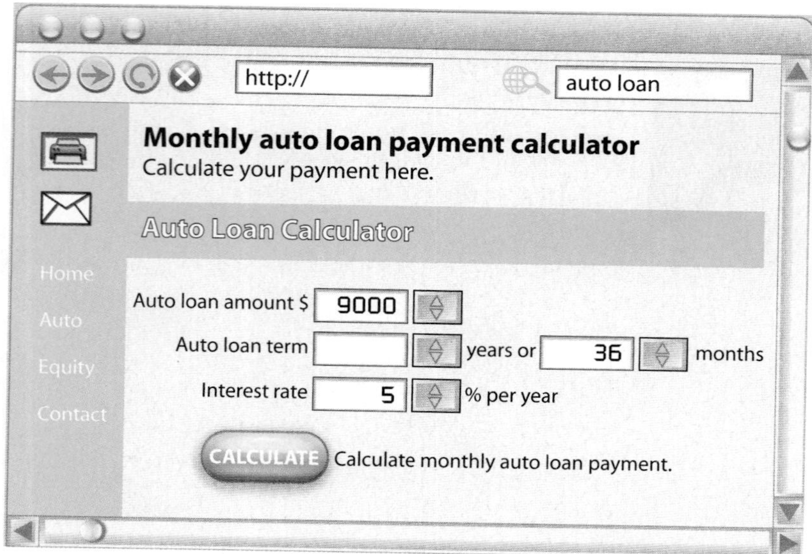


Go Online
www.successnetplus.com

## For Discussion

6. Find a closed form for the function $b$ on the previous page.

What happens when you take the 5% interest into account?

- Month 0 is when the loan starts. At the end of Month 0, you owe \$9000. That amount is how much you borrowed.
- For any month after Month 0, you owe the balance from the previous month, plus the interest on that balance, minus \$250.

The interest for one month is one twelfth the interest for a whole year. The interest for a year is 5%, so the interest for a month is $\frac{0.05}{12}$ times the balance for that month.

You can now refine the definition of $b$.

$$b(n) = \begin{cases} \$9000 & \text{if } n = 0 \\ b(n-1) + \frac{0.05}{12} \cdot b(n-1) - \$250 & \text{if } n > 0 \end{cases}$$

At the end of the first month you owe

- \$9000 (what you owed at the beginning of the month)
- plus $\frac{0.05}{12} \cdot \$9000$ (which is \$45.83)
- minus \$250 (your monthly payment)

$$\$9000 + \left(\frac{0.05}{12} \cdot \$9000\right) - \$250 = \$8787.50$$

Banks use the following rule: What you owe at the end of the month is what you owed at the start of the month, plus $\frac{1}{12}$ of the yearly interest on that amount, minus the monthly payment.

## For You to Do

7. What do you owe at the end of Month 2?
8. What do you owe at the end of Month 3?

### The Memory Error

When you model the new recursive definition for $b$, your system can quickly run out of memory. Why?

Your calculator may return a message such as "Recursion too deep."

How does a computer find $b(4)$ using this definition? You tell it that $n = 4$, and, as it scans the definition, it notes what it needs to do. It sees two places where it will need to compute $b(3)$.

$$b(4) = b(3) + \frac{0.05}{12} \cdot b(3) - 250$$

$$b(2) + \frac{0.05}{12} \cdot b(2) - 250 \qquad b(2) + \frac{0.05}{12} \cdot b(2) - 250$$

? ? ? ?

In each of these 2 computations of $b(3)$, the computer needs to compute $b(2)$ twice, for a total of 4 times. Continuing, it computes $b(1)$ 8 times, and the base case $b(0)$ 16 times. Then it feeds this information back through three layers of computation to do 1 last calculation to get $b(4)$.

Adding the number of evaluations of $b$, you have

$$1 + 2 + 4 + 8 + 16 = 31 = 2^{(4+1)} - 1$$

That is how many computations the computer needs to compute $b(4)$. In general, calculating $b(n)$ requires tracking $2^{(n+1)} - 1$ evaluations of $b$. No wonder your calculator or computer runs into trouble quickly.

**Habits of Mind**

**Estimate.** Estimating shows that $2^{10} \approx 1000$ and $2^{20} \approx 1{,}000{,}000$.

But where your calculator sees two calculations to be done separately, a person would notice that they are the same—both $b(n-1)$. You can figure it out once and then plug it in both places.

$$b(4) = b(3) + \frac{0.05}{12} \cdot b(3) - 250$$

$$b(2) + \frac{0.05}{12} \cdot b(2) - 250$$

You can force the computer to do the calculation the smart way as well. If you take the expression $b(n-1) + \frac{0.05}{12} \cdot b(n-1)$ and factor out $b(n-1)$, you get the following expression.

$$\begin{aligned} b(n-1) + \frac{0.05}{12} \cdot b(n-1) &= 1 \cdot b(n-1) + \frac{0.05}{12} \cdot b(n-1) \\ &= b(n-1)\left(1 + \frac{0.05}{12}\right) \end{aligned}$$

Now the computer only needs to track $n + 1$ evaluations of $b$ in order to find $b(n)$. This change makes the computation manageable.

Smart calculation does not guarantee you will never get the memory error, just that you will not get it as soon!

## For You to Do

**9.** Build a model in your function-modeling language for the function $b$ below.

$$b(n) = \begin{cases} 9000 & \text{if } n = 0 \\ \left(1 + \frac{0.05}{12}\right) \cdot b(n-1) - 250 & \text{if } n > 0 \end{cases}$$

**10.** How much do you owe after 6 months? How long does it take you to pay the loan down to \$8000?

You can add extra inputs that will let you change the monthly payment, the amount of the loan, or the interest rate on the loan. See the TI-Nspire Handbook, p. 817.

## Exercises *Practicing Habits of Mind*

### Check Your Understanding

For Exercises 1–3, suppose you take a $9000 loan at 5% interest with a $250 monthly payment.

1. How much do you owe at the end of one year?
2. Can you pay off the loan in 36 months?
3. What monthly payment will let you pay off the loan in each amount of time?

   **a.** 36 months  **b.** 39 months  **c.** 48 months
4. If you can only afford to pay $250 per month, and you must pay your loan off in 36 months at 5% interest, how much money can you borrow?
5. What does the interest rate have to be so that you can afford a $12,000 car with $1000 down and payments of $310 per month for 36 months?

### On Your Own

6. Suppose you want to pay off a car loan in 36 months. Pick an interest rate and keep it constant. Investigate how the monthly payment changes with the cost of the car.

   Make sure you state what interest rate you are using. You can find a rate in a newspaper car ad.

   **a.** Make a table like the one below and complete it.

| Cost of Car (thousands of dollars) | Monthly Payment |
|---|---|
| 10 | ■ |
| 11 | ■ |
| 12 | ■ |
| 13 | ■ |
| 14 | ■ |
| 15 | ■ |
| 16 | ■ |
| ⋮ | ⋮ |



   **b.** Find either a closed-form or a recursive definition for a function that agrees with your table. Build a model of your function.

   If this function works for all inputs, you can use it to calculate the monthly payment in terms of the cost of the car.

   **c.** Use your model to find the monthly payment on a $26,000 car.

**7.** A local car dealer has an ad each week that offers two deals on its cars.

- You can get a \$2000 rebate on the list price of the car. You then pay off the rest in 36 months at 5% interest.
- Instead of the rebate, you can get a low 0.9% interest rate and then pay off the full list price of the car in 36 months.

Cars on the lot sell at prices between \$20,000 and \$40,000. For which cars is it better to take the rebate? For which cars is it better to take the low interest rate? For what price are the deals the same?

**8.** Standardized Test Prep Suppose you take a \$10,000 loan at 5% interest. How much do you owe after three monthly payments of \$500?

**A.** \$1500.00 **B.** \$8500.00 **C.** \$8619.27 **D.** \$8925.00

**Habits of Mind**

**Organize what you know.** Make a table for prices between \$20,000 and \$40,000 in increments of \$1000. Figure out the monthly payment for each price. You can use your function-modeling language and a spreadsheet.

## Maintain Your Skills

**9.** Evaluate each sum.

**a.** $1 + 2$

**b.** $1 + 2 + 2^2$

**c.** $1 + 2 + 2^2 + 2^3$

**d.** $1 + 2 + 2^2 + 2^3 + 2^4$

**e.** $1 + 2 + 2^2 + 2^3 + 2^4 + 2^5$

**f.** $1 + 2 + 2^2 + 2^3 + 2^4 + 2^5 + \cdots + 2^9$

**10.** Use the description of $s$ below.

$$s(n) = 1 + 2 + 2^2 + 2^3 + \cdots + 2^n$$

**a.** Find a recursive definition for $s$.

**b.** Find a closed form for $s$.

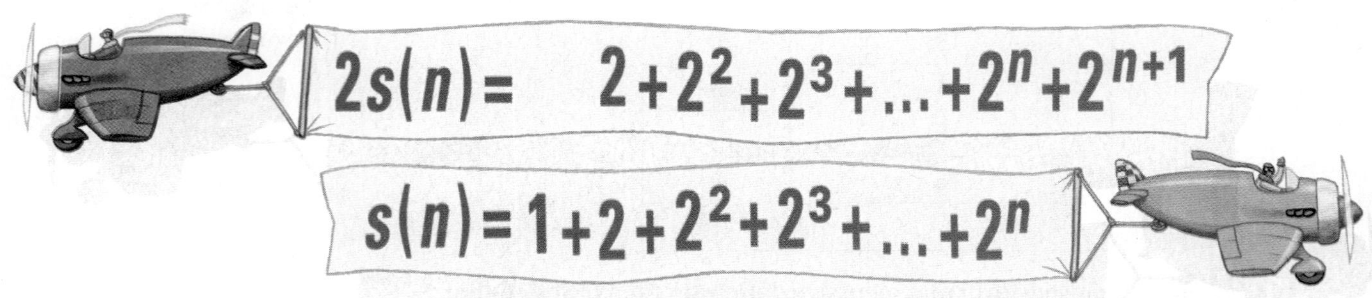

# 7.11 The Factorial Function

Not all useful functions have both closed forms and recursive models. In this lesson, you will study a very useful function that has no simple closed form.

Suppose you have three books, labeled A, B, and C. In how many ways can you arrange them on a shelf? Well, you could make a systematic list.

A B C
A C D
B A C
B C A
C A B
C B A

So there are six arrangements. But what if you have 5 books? Or 8 books? Making a list of all possible arrangements would take a long time.

## Developing Habits of Mind

**Establish a process.** One way to think about the arrangement problem is to model it with a function. Let

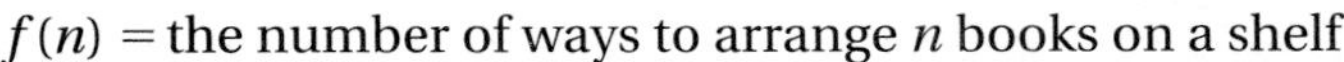

$f(n)$ = the number of ways to arrange $n$ books on a shelf

> This is an example of a counting problem. In many counting problems, recursive definitions are easier to find than closed forms.

You can think about $f$ and try to get a closed-form or recursive definition for it. For example, since there is one way to arrange a single book, two ways to arrange 2 books, and six ways to arrange 3 books, you have the start of a table for $f$.

| $n$ | $f(n)$ |
|---|---|
| 1 | 1 |
| 2 | 2 |
| 3 | 6 |

There are many functions that agree with $f$ for inputs 1, 2, and 3. You want one that counts arrangements of any number of books.

Look for a recursive relation. Can you use the fact that there are six ways to arrange 3 books to find how many ways there are to arrange 4 books? Consider the following steps.

**Step 1** Suppose your books are labeled A, B, C, and D. First place D. There are four places to do that. Pick one.

**Step 2** Now you have three books left and three spots in which you can place them. But you have already solved that problem. There are $f(3)$, or 6, ways to arrange 3 books.

**Step 3** So, for each of your four choices for Book D, there are $f(3)$, or 6, ways to arrange the rest of the books. There must be $4 \cdot f(3) = 24$ ways to arrange the four books.

## For You to Do

1. Write out the 24 arrangements of four books in a list. Start by placing D, and then fill out the shelf with all six arrangements of A, B, and C.

## For Discussion

2. Come up with an argument to show that $f(n) = n \cdot f(n - 1)$ for $n > 1$.

This leads to the definition of a function that appears throughout mathematics.

### *Definition*

**The recursive rule below defines the factorial function.**

$$f(n) = \begin{cases} 1 & \text{if } n = 0 \\ n \cdot f(n - 1) & \text{if } n > 0 \end{cases}$$

In how many ways can you arrange 0 books on a shelf?

## For Discussion

3. Build a model for $f$ in your function-modeling language. Make a table of $f$ for inputs between 1 and 6.

Is there a closed form for $f$? Look at $f(5)$.

$$\begin{aligned} f(5) &= 5 \cdot f(4) && \text{But } f(4) = 4 \cdot f(3). \\ &= 5 \cdot 4 \cdot f(3) && \text{But } f(3) = 3 \cdot f(2). \\ &= 5 \cdot 4 \cdot 3 \cdot f(2) && \text{But } f(2) = 2 \cdot f(1). \\ &= 5 \cdot 4 \cdot 3 \cdot 2 \cdot f(1) && \text{You know } f(1) = 1. \\ &= 5 \cdot 4 \cdot 3 \cdot 2 \cdot 1 && \text{Now you can compute.} \\ &= 120 \end{aligned}$$

You can work out $f(n)$ for other positive integers $n$. You will see that $f(n)$ is the product of all the integers from 1 to $n$.

## Developing Habits of Mind

**Detect the key characteristics.** So, is $f(n) = 1 \cdot 2 \cdot 3 \cdot \cdots \cdot n$ a closed-form definition for the factorial function?

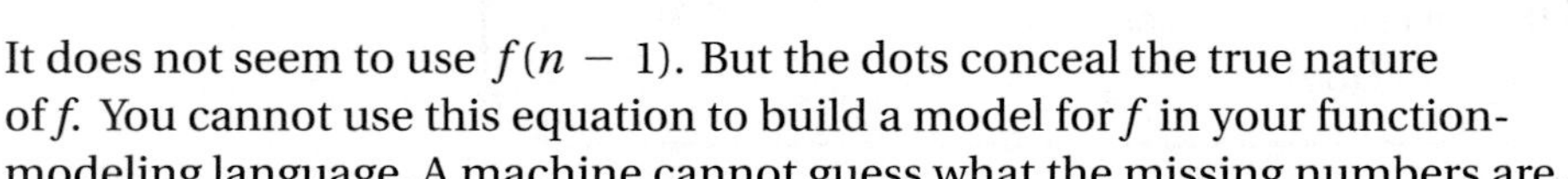

It does not seem to use $f(n - 1)$. But the dots conceal the true nature of $f$. You cannot use this equation to build a model for $f$ in your function-modeling language. A machine cannot guess what the missing numbers are.

Can you write a closed-form definition for the factorial function? The answer is no. In a closed-form definition, you can calculate the output of the function at $n$ by a fixed number of operations regardless of the value of $n$. But computing the factorial function requires more operations for larger values of the input. The factorial function has no simple closed form.

Computer scientists use this distinction between closed-form and recursive definitions.

The factorial function is so useful that it has a formal notation. You represent the factorial of $n$ as $n!$. So, $n!$ is the product of all the integers from 1 to $n$.

## For You to Do

Find the numerical value of each expression.

**4.** $5!$ **5.** $7!$ **6.** $\frac{7!}{5!}$ **7.** $\frac{100!}{98!}$

Your calculator has a model of the factorial function built in. Or you can use your own recursive model.

## Exercises *Practicing Habits of Mind*

### Check Your Understanding

**1.** Use the definition of $g$ below.

$$g(n) = \frac{n!}{(n-1)!}$$

Make a table for $g$ with inputs from 2 to 10. Find a closed form for $g$.

**2.** Use the definition of $h$ below.

$$h(n) = \frac{n!}{(n-2)!}$$

Make a table for $h$ with inputs from 3 to 10. Find a closed form for $h$.

**3.** Express $k(n) = n(n-1)(n-2)(n-3)$ in terms of factorials.

**4.** Express $q(n)$ below in terms of $n!$.

$$q(n) = \begin{cases} 1 & \text{if } n = 0 \\ n^2 \cdot q(n-1) & \text{if } n > 0 \end{cases}$$

**5.** Without computing the numbers exactly, find how many zeros are at the end of each number.

**a.** $5!$ **b.** $10!$ **c.** $20!$

## On Your Own

6. Solve each equation for $n$.

   a. $\frac{n!}{(n-2)!} = 56$ b. $\frac{(n-1)!}{(n-3)!} = 56$ c. $\frac{(n+1)!}{(n-1)!} = 56$ d. $\frac{(n+1)!}{n!} = 56$

7. Find a recursively defined function that agrees with the table at the right.

| Input | Output |
|---|---|
| 1 | 2 |
| 2 | 4 |
| 3 | 12 |
| 4 | 48 |
| 5 | 240 |
| 6 | 1440 |

Is there a closed form?

8. **Standardized Test Prep** The formula for the number of possible ways to choose $r$ objects from a set of $n$ objects is $\frac{n!}{r!(n-r)!}$. How many different ways can you choose a group of 3 students from a group of 8 students?

   **A.** 24 **B.** 56

   **C.** 120 **D.** 336

9. How many zeros are at the end of 150!?

**Go Online**
www.successnetplus.com

For each function in Exercises 10–13, do parts (a)–(c).

**a.** Make an input-output table for whole-number inputs from 1 to 5.

**b.** Find a recursive model for the function.

**c.** Decide whether there is a closed form. Explain.

10. $r(n) = 1 + 2 + \ldots + n$
11. $s(n) = 1 + 3 + 5 + \ldots + (2n + 1)$
12. $t(n) = 1 \cdot 3 \cdot 5 \cdot \ldots \cdot (2n + 1)$
13. $r(n) = 1 + 3 + 3^2 + \ldots + 3^n$
14. **Take It Further** Are there any values of $n$ such that $n! > 100^n$?

*Hint*: If $S$ is the sum of the powers of 3 from 1 to $3^n$, then what is $3S$?

## Maintain Your Skills

For the expanded form of each expression, find the coefficient of the second-highest power of $x$ and the constant term.

15. $(x - 1)(x - 2)$
16. $(x - 1)(x - 2)(x - 3)$
17. $(x - 1)(x - 2)(x - 3)(x - 4)$
18. $(x - 1)(x - 2)(x - 3)(x - 4)(x - 5)(x - 6)(x - 7)(x - 8)$

**In this investigation, you learned to evaluate recursive functions, including the factorial function. You calculated the balance on a loan and solved for an unknown variable in a monthly payment situation. These questions will help you summarize what you have learned.**

**1.** Find a closed form for the following function.

$$k(n) = \begin{cases} 0 & \text{if } n = 0 \\ k(n-1) + 4n & \text{if } n > 0 \end{cases}$$

For Exercises 2 and 3, find a recursively defined function that agrees with each table. Make a table of the function for inputs from 1 to 10.

**2.**

| Input | Output |
|---|---|
| 0 | 3 |
| 1 | 8 |
| 2 | 13 |
| 3 | 18 |
| 4 | 23 |
| 5 | 28 |

**3.**

| Input | Output |
|---|---|
| 0 | 3 |
| 1 | 11 |
| 2 | 24 |
| 3 | 42 |
| 4 | 65 |
| 5 | 93 |

There are 4!, or 24, possible arrangements of four utensils.

**4.** Make a table for the function $b$ below with inputs from 1 to 10.

$$b(n) = \begin{cases} 12{,}000 & \text{if } n = 0 \\ \frac{12.06}{12} \cdot b(n-1) - 400 & \text{if } n > 0 \end{cases}$$

**a.** Suppose $b(n)$ is a model for the balance on a loan at the end of month $n$. What is the amount of the loan? What is the interest rate?

**b.** For what value of $n$ is $b(n)$ closest to 0?

**5.** What is a recursive definition of a function? When is this type of definition useful?

**6.** What is the recursive definition of the factorial function?

**7.** What is the monthly payment on a loan of $10,000 for 36 months with an interest rate of 5%?

## Vocabulary and Notation

In this investigation, you learned this term and symbol. Make sure you understand what each one means and how to use it.

- **factorial function, $n!$**

# Review

Go Online
www.successnetplus.com

In **Investigation 7A,** you learned to

- state the Change of Sign Theorem and the Intermediate Value Theorem for Polynomials, and to use them to analyze the graphs of polynomial functions
- find the equation of a line secant to a polynomial function and the average rate of change of a function between two points
- write the Taylor expansion for a polynomial function about a point
- find the equation of the tangent to a polynomial curve at a point

*The following questions will help you check your understanding.*

**1. a.** Find, if possible, a third-degree polynomial function $f$ with a graph that satisfies the following conditions.

- The graph of $f$ crosses the $x$-axis at $(-4, 0)$ and $(-1, 0)$, and intersects it somewhere on the positive $x$-axis.
- From left to right, the graph of $f$ rises, falls, and rises.
- The graph of $f$ crosses the $y$-axis at $(0, -3)$.

**b.** Can you find a polynomial that satisfies the first two conditions but crosses the $y$-axis at $(0, 3)$ instead of $(0, -3)$? Explain.

**2.** Suppose $f(x) = x^4 - x^3 - 2x^2 - 1$.

**a.** Find the average rate of change of $y$ with respect to $x$ as $x$ goes from $-1$ to $1$.

**b.** Find the equation of the secant line between $(-1, f(-1))$ and $(1, f(1))$.

**c.** Find all intersections of the graph of $y = f(x)$ and the secant you just found. Give coordinates to the nearest thousandth.

**3.** Suppose that $f(x) = 4x^3 + x^2 - 3x + 5$.

**a.** Expand $f(x)$ in powers of $x + 1$.

**b.** Find the equation of the line tangent to the graph of $f(x)$ at the point $(-1, 5)$.

In **Investigation 7B,** you learned to

- sketch the graph of a rational function, including asymptotes and holes
- evaluate limits of rational expressions
- find the equation of the tangent to the graph of a rational function at a point

*The following questions will help you check your understanding.*

**4.** For the graph of each rational function, find, if possible,

- the $x$- and $y$-intercepts
- the equation of each vertical asymptote
- the equation of each horizontal asymptote
- the coordinates of any holes

Then sketch the graph.

**a.** $f(x) = \dfrac{x + 1}{x^2 - 1}$

**b.** $g(x) = \dfrac{x - 3}{4x^2 - 9}$

**c.** $h(x) = \dfrac{2x^2 - 5x - 12}{6x^2 + 11x + 3}$

**d.** $j(x) = \dfrac{x^2 + 5x + 6}{x - 1}$

**5.** Find each limit.

**a.** $\lim\limits_{x \to \infty} \dfrac{3x + 1}{2x + 3}$

**b.** $\lim\limits_{x \to \infty} \dfrac{4x - 5}{3x^2 - x - 2}$

**c.** $\lim\limits_{x \to \infty} \dfrac{x^2 - 2x + 1}{x - 2}$

**6.** Find an equation of the line tangent to the graph of $f(x) = \frac{x - 3}{x^2 + 3x - 4}$ at the point $(2, f(2))$.

---

In **Investigation 7C,** you learned how to

- define, identify, and evaluate recursive functions including the factorial function
- calculate the balance on a loan given a loan amount, interest rate, length, and monthly payment
- solve for an unknown variable in a monthly payment situation

The following questions will help you check your understanding.

**7.** Make a table of the function

$g(n) = \frac{n!}{(n - 2)!2!}$ with inputs from 3 to 10.

**8.** Find recursive and closed-form functions that agree with your table from Exercise 7.

**9.** Suppose that you can afford to pay $1000 down and $300 per month. You can get a 36-month loan at 3%. What is the maximum price of a car that you can buy in this situation?

**10.** The car Maya wants to buy costs $12,000. The dealer offers her a choice of loans. She can get a $1000 rebate that she can use as her down payment. She can then take out a loan at 5% interest for 36 months to pay off the loan. Or, she can choose a zero down payment option with a 0.9% interest rate for 36 months. Which loan has the lower monthly payment?

Chapter 7

# Test

## Multiple Choice

**1.** Here is a graph of function $g$.

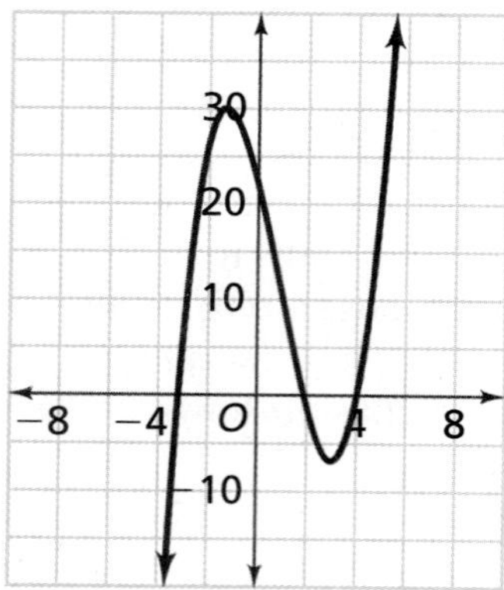


Which of these could be the equation of $g$?

**A.** $g(x) = (x + 4)(x + 2)(x - 3)$

**B.** $g(x) = -(x + 4)(x + 2)(x - 3)$

**C.** $g(x) = -(x - 4)(x - 2)(x + 3)$

**D.** $g(x) = (x - 4)(x - 2)(x + 3)$

**2.** Consider $f(x) = 2x^2 - 5x + 6$. What is the $y$-intercept of the line tangent to the graph of $f$ at the point $(2, f(2))$?

**A.** $-2$ **B.** 2 **C.** 3 **D.** 4

**3.** Suppose $h(x) = x^3 - 4x^2 + 8x + 11 = A + B(x - 3) + C(x - 3)^2 + D(x - 3)^3$. Find $C$.

**A.** $-13$ **B.** $-1$ **C.** 5 **D.** 11

**4.** What is the equation of the horizontal asymptote of the function $f(x) = \frac{x - 1}{x^2 - x - 6}$?

**A.** $x = 0$ **B.** $y = 0$

**C.** $y = -2$ **D.** $x = 3$

**5.** Which of the following is an $x$-intercept of the function $f(x) = \frac{2x^2 - 2}{x^2 - 4}$?

**A.** $-2$ **B.** $\frac{1}{2}$

**C.** 1 **D.** 2

**6.** Let $h(x) = \frac{3x - 7}{x - 2}$. Find $\lim_{x \to \infty} h(x)$.

**A.** $\infty$ **B.** 3

**C.** 2 **D.** $-\infty$

**7.** Solve the equation below for $n$.

$$\frac{(n + 1)!}{(n - 1)!} = 72$$

**A.** $n = 7$ **B.** $n = 8$

**C.** $n = 9$ **D.** $n = 10$

## Open Response

**8.** Consider $f(x) = -(x - 4)(x + 2)(x + 3)$.

**a.** Sketch the graph of $f$.

**b.** Identify all intercepts of the graph.

**c.** Find the average rate of change of $y$ with respect to $x$ as $x$ goes from 1 to 3.

**d.** Write the equation of the secant between $(1, f(1))$ and $(3, f(3))$.

**9.** Suppose that $h(x) = x^3 - 3x^2 + 3x + 1$.

**a.** Expand $h(x)$ into powers of $x - 1$.

**b.** Divide the result by $x - 1$.

**c.** Simplify $\frac{h(x)}{x - 1}$.

**d.** What conclusion can you draw from your answers to parts (b) and (c)?

**10.** Let $p(x) = \frac{2x^3 - 3x^2 - 5x - 12}{x - 3}$.

**a.** Copy and complete this table for $p(x)$.

| x | p(x) |
|---|---|
| 0 | ■ |
| | ■ |
| | ■ |
| | ■ |
| | ■ |

**b.** Simplify the expression $\frac{2x^3 - 3x^2 - 5x - 12}{x - 3}$.

**c.** Let $q(x) = 2x^2 + 3x + 4$. Find $\lim_{x\to 3} p(x)$ and $\lim_{x\to 3} q(x)$.

**d.** Explain why the graph of $p$ is not the same as $q$.

**11.** Find the limit.

**a.** $\lim_{x\to\infty} \frac{x + 2}{3x + 2}$ **b.** $\lim_{x\to\infty} \frac{\cos x}{x}$

**12.** Let $f(x) = \frac{5x - 1}{x^2 - 2x - 15}$, $g(x) = \frac{A}{x + 3}$, and $h(x) = \frac{B}{x - 5}$, where $A$ and $B$ are constants.

**a.** Find $A$ and $B$ so that $f(x) = g(x) + h(x)$.

**b.** Find the slope of the line tangent to $g$ at $x = 4$.

**c.** Find the slope of the line tangent to $h$ at $x = 4$.

**d.** Find the slope of the line tangent to $f$ at $x = 4$.

**13.** Find the polynomial function that has the following characteristics:

- Leading coefficient 2
- Degree 3
- Zeros $-2, 1$, and 4
- From left to right, its graph rises, falls, and rises.

**14.** Shawn can put \$1200 down and pay \$300 a month on a loan. He can get a 36-month loan at 5% interest. How much can Shawn afford to pay for a car?

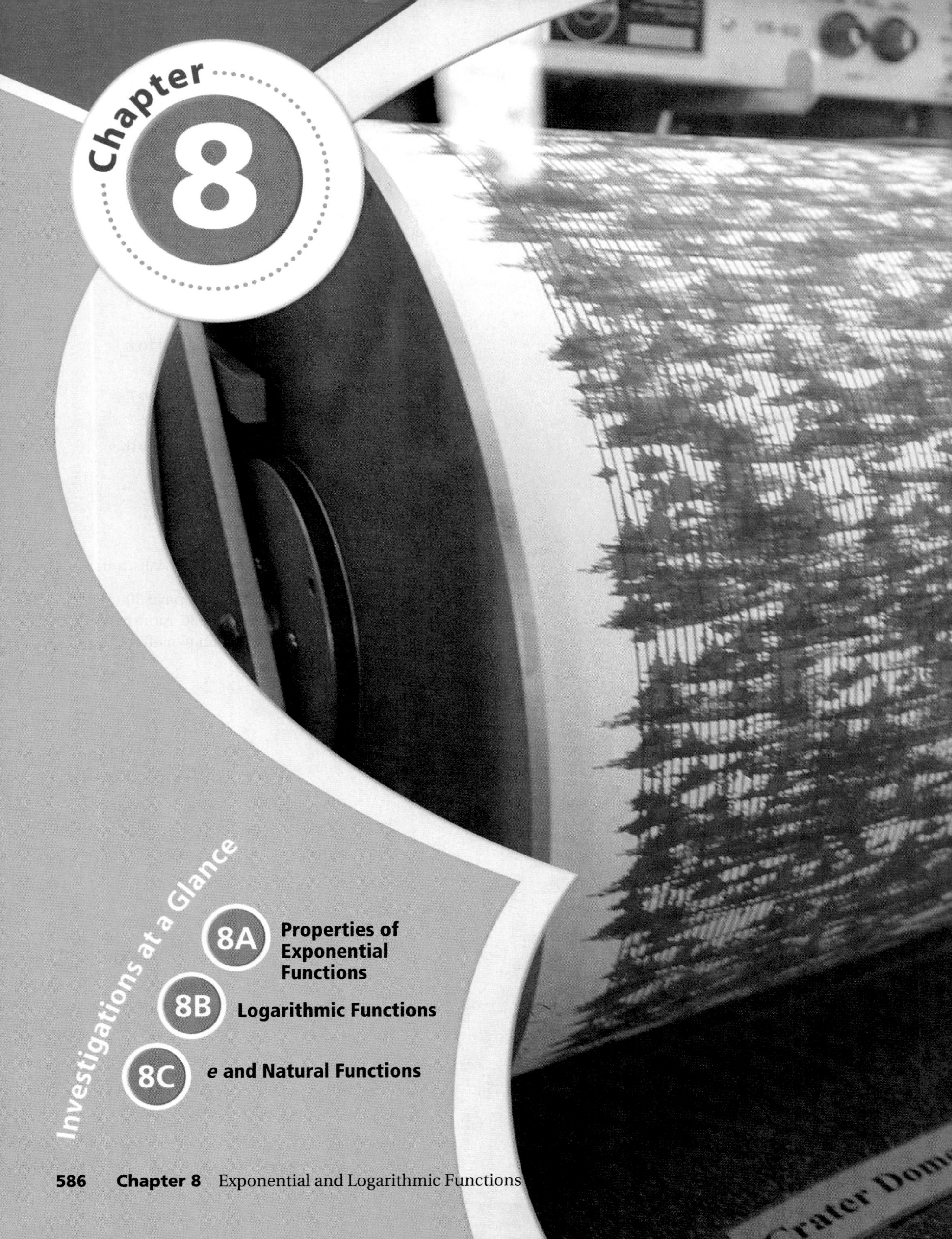
Chapter
8
Investigations at a Glance
8A Properties of Exponential Functions
8B Logarithmic Functions
8C e and Natural Functions
Crater Dome

# Exponential and Logarithmic Functions

In the 1930s, Charles Richter developed the Richter scale at the California Institute of Technology. The Richter scale measures the magnitude of earthquakes. Earthquake magnitudes vary widely, from tiny microearthquakes that only sensitive seismographs can detect to catastrophic events that cause widespread destruction.

The wide variation of magnitude led Richter and his colleagues to use the base-10 logarithm in their formula. This limits the possible values of the magnitude to a more manageable and understandable range.

To calculate the magnitude $M_L$ of an earthquake, you measure the maximum amplitude $A$ of the wave pattern that your seismograph records. Richter used the formula $M_L = \log_{10} A - \log_{10} A_0$, where $A_0$ is a correction value based on the seismograph's distance from the earthquake and local conditions.

A small earthquake can have a negative magnitude. The largest magnitude ever recorded was 9.5, during the Great Chilean Earthquake on May 22, 1960. Instruments detect over a million earthquakes every year. Humans can only feel about one third of these.

## Vocabulary and Notation

- base
- common logarithm, $\log x$
- continuously compounded interest
- $e$
- exponential decay
- exponential function
- exponential growth
- functional equation
- linear scale
- logarithmic function, $x \to \log_b x$
- logarithmic scale
- monotonic
- natural logarithm, $\ln x$
- strictly decreasing
- strictly increasing

# Properties of Exponential Functions

**In *Properties of Exponential Functions,* you will use the laws of exponents to explore exponential functions. You will sketch the graphs of exponential functions and write exponential function rules from tables and points on graphs. You will also explore the properties of the inverse of the function $y = b^x$.**

**By the end of this investigation, you will be able to answer questions like these.**

1. For $f(x) = b^x$, why is it true that $f(m) \cdot f(n) = f(m + n)$?
2. Why must an exponential function have an inverse function?
3. If you invest \$1000 in an account at 6% interest, compounded annually, how much money will you have after 30 years?

**You will learn how to**

- graph an exponential function and determine the equation of an exponential function given two points on its graph
- identify an exponential function from the table it generates and use the table to create a closed-form or recursive definition of the function
- evaluate the inverse of the function $y = b^x$ either exactly or by approximation

**You will develop these habits and skills:**

- Reason by continuity to extend the definition of exponent to include all real numbers.
- Visualize exponential growth by examining graphs and tables of exponential functions.
- Draw logical conclusions from the laws of exponents and properties of exponential functions to solve problems and prove conjectures.

Archaeologists use exponential functions that model radioactive decay to determine the age of objects.

# 8.01 Getting Started

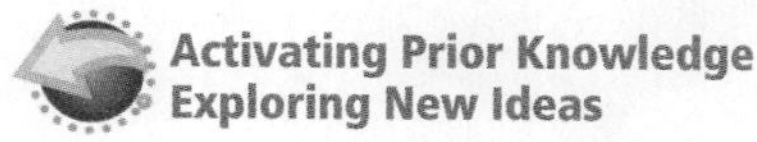


A difference table can help you find a function rule that fits a table. For some tables, a ratio table will help you find a rule that fits the table.

## For You to Explore

For each function in Problems 1–5, make a difference table. Show the outputs for the inputs 0 through 5 and the differences between terms.

| Input | Output | Δ |
|---|---|---|
| 0 | ■ | ■ |
| 1 | ■ | ■ |
| 2 | ■ | ■ |
| 3 | ■ | ■ |
| 4 | ■ | ■ |
| 5 | ■ | |

1. $a(x) = 3x + 1$
2. $b(x) = x^2 - x + 1$
3. $c(x) = 3^x$
4. $d(x) = 3 \cdot 5^x$
5. $f(x) = \left(\frac{1}{2}\right)^x$
6. Find a function $g(x)$ for which the difference column is equal to the output column.

Note that $d(x)$ is not equal to $15^x$, since only the 5 is raised to the $x$th power.

Instead of calculating the difference between one term and the next, it sometimes makes sense to calculate the ratio of one term to the next.

7. a. Copy and complete this ratio table for $a(x) = 3x + 1$. Round to the nearest hundredth.

   b. What happens to the numbers in the ratio column if you continue the table for larger inputs? Explain.

| Input | Output | ÷ |
|---|---|---|
| 0 | 1 | 4 |
| 1 | 4 | ■ |
| 2 | 7 | ■ |
| 3 | 10 | 1.3 |
| 4 | 13 | ■ |
| 5 | 16 | |

8. For each function from Problems 2–5, build a ratio table with the inputs from 0 to 5.
9. **Write About It** Suppose you have an input-output function table with integer inputs from 0 to 5.

   a. Describe how to find a rule that fits the table if the table has constant differences.

   b. Describe how to find a rule that fits the table if the table has constant ratios.
10. **Take It Further** Find a function $h(x)$ for which the ratio column is equal to the output column.

# Exercises Practicing Habits of Mind

## On Your Own

**11.** Solve each equation any way you choose. Then, decide which equation was the most difficult for you to solve. Explain.

**a.** $5 = x^2$

**b.** $5 = 2^x$

**c.** $x = 5^2$

**d.** $8 = 2^x$

**12.** Sketch the graph of $c(x) = 3^x$.

You will need more input-output pairs than the ones you found in Problem 3.

The expression $3^{\sqrt{2}}$ is undefined so far, since you cannot write $\sqrt{2}$ as a rational number.

**13.** Use your graph of $c(x) = 3^x$ to explain why $3^{\sqrt{2}}$ should be between 3 and 9.

**14.** **Write About It** Describe how you can make a more accurate estimate of $3^{\sqrt{2}}$.

**15.** Copy and complete the table of values for each exponential function.

**a.** $f(a) = 3 \cdot 2^a$

| Input, *a* | Output, *f*(*a*) |
|---|---|
| −2 | ■ |
| −1 | ■ |
| 0 | ■ |
| 1 | ■ |
| 2 | ■ |

**b.** $g(a) = 30 \cdot 2^a$

| Input, *a* | Output, *g*(*a*) |
|---|---|
| −2 | ■ |
| −1 | ■ |
| 0 | ■ |
| 1 | ■ |
| 2 | ■ |

**c.** $h(a) = \frac{1}{5} \cdot 5^a$

| Input, *a* | Output, *h*(*a*) |
|---|---|
| 0 | ■ |
| 1 | ■ |
| 2 | ■ |
| 3 | ■ |
| 4 | ■ |

**d.** $j(a) = 27 \cdot \left(\frac{1}{3}\right)^a$

| Input, *a* | Output, *j*(*a*) |
|---|---|
| −1 | ■ |
| 0 | ■ |
| 1 | ■ |
| 2 | ■ |
| 3 | ■ |

16. Find an exponential function that agrees with each table.

a.

| Input, $a$ | Output, $k(a)$ |
|---|---|
| 0 | 4 |
| 1 | 12 |
| 2 | 36 |
| 3 | 108 |
| 4 | 324 |

b.

| Input, $h$ | Output, $L(h)$ |
|---|---|
| 0 | 100 |
| 1 | 50 |
| 2 | 25 |
| 3 | 12.5 |
| 4 | 6.25 |

c.

| Input, $x$ | Output, $p(x)$ |
|---|---|
| 0 | 2 |
| 1 | $\frac{1}{2}$ |
| 2 | $\frac{1}{8}$ |
| 3 | $\frac{1}{32}$ |
| 4 | $\frac{1}{128}$ |

d.

| Input, $n$ | Output, $Q(n)$ |
|---|---|
| 0 | 8 |
| 1 | 12 |
| 2 | 18 |
| 3 | 27 |
| 4 | 40.5 |

An *exponential function* is a function that you can write in the form $f(x) = a \cdot b^x$.

17. Copy and complete this input-output table for $f(x) = 2^x$. Round to three decimal places.

| $x$ | $f(x) = 2^x$ |
|---|---|
| 0 | 1 |
| 1 | ■ |
| 1.4 | ■ |
| 1.41 | ■ |
| 1.414 | ■ |
| 1.4142 | ■ |
| 1.41421 | ■ |
| 1.414213 | ■ |

18. **a.** Explain why there are no integers $a$ and $b$ other than $a = b = 0$ that satisfy the equation $2^a = 5^b$.

**b.** Determine whether there are integers $c$ and $d$ other than $c = d = 0$ that satisfy the equation $4^c = 8^d$. If so, what are $c$ and $d$?

## Maintain Your Skills

19. Consider the function $f(x) = 2^x$. State whether you believe each value is a rational number. Find each rational value exactly, without using a calculator.

**a.** $f(0)$ **b.** $f\left(\frac{1}{2}\right)$ **c.** $f(\pi)$ **d.** $f(f(2))$

**e.** all values of $a$ such that $f(a) = \frac{1}{8}$

**f.** all values of $a$ such that $f(a) = 7$

**g.** all values of $a$ such that $f(a) = -1$

# 8.02 Graphs of Exponential Functions

Several of the functions in the Getting Started lesson of this investigation are *exponential functions.*

## Definitions

An **exponential function** is a function $f$ that you can write in the form $f(x) = a \cdot b^x$, where $a \neq 0$, $b > 0$, and $b \neq 1$. The number $b$ is the **base.**

The function $d(x) = 3 \cdot 5^x$ is exponential. What is its domain?

## For Discussion

**1.** What happens if $a = 0$? What happens if $b = 1$?

Here are the graphs of $f(x) = 2^x$ and $g(x) = 5^x$.

Both graphs have their $y$-intercept at (0, 1). Both graphs pass through Quadrants I and II. Both functions are increasing. The greater $x$ is, the greater the corresponding $y$ is.

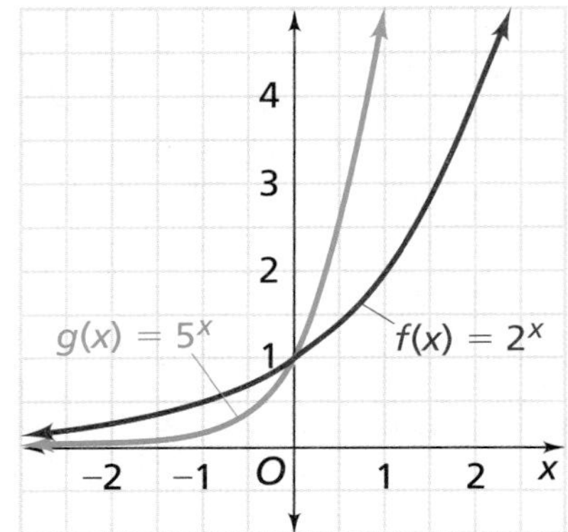


**Habits of Mind**

**Establish a process.** How can you decide whether the point (−3.5, 0.1) is on the graph of $f(x)$?

## For You to Do

**2.** According to the graphs, for what values of $x$ is $2^x > 5^x$?

Here are the graphs of $h(x) = \left(\frac{1}{2}\right)^x$ and $j(x) = \left(\frac{1}{5}\right)^x$.

Both graphs have their $y$-intercept at (0, 1). Both graphs pass through Quadrants I and II. Both functions are decreasing. The greater $x$ is, the less the corresponding $y$ is.

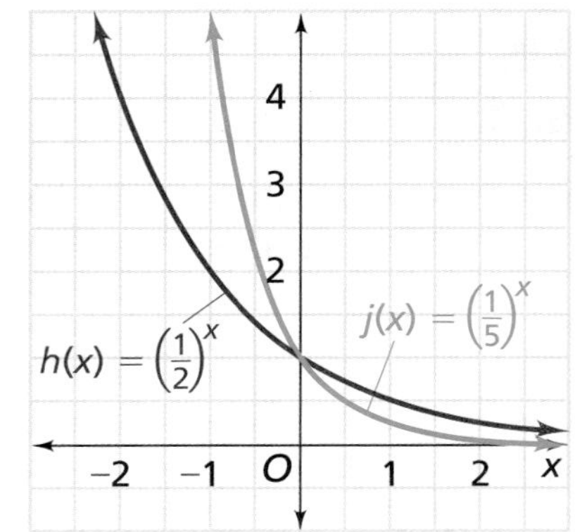


**Habits of Mind**

**Establish a process.** How can you decide whether the point (3.5, 0.1) is on the graph of $h(x)$?

## In-Class Experiment

3. Graph $f(x) = 2^x$ and $k(x) = 3 \cdot 2^x$. How are the graphs related?
4. Graph $k(x) = 3 \cdot 2^x$ and $m(x) = -3 \cdot 2^x$. How are the graphs related?
5. Graph $f(x) = 2^x$ and $h(x) = \left(\frac{1}{2}\right)^x$. How are the graphs related?

## Monotonic Functions

As you have seen, the graph of $f(x) = 2^x$ seems to indicate that this function is **strictly increasing.** In other words, if $s > t$, then $f(s) > f(t)$. You will now verify this observation.

### Lemma 8.1

**Let $b > 1$ and let $x$ be a positive rational number. Then $b^x > 1$.**

**Proof** Since $x$ is positive and rational, you can write $x = \frac{p}{q}$ for some positive integers $p$ and $q$. First, use the following fact about power functions.

Let $g(x) = x^n$, where $n$ is a positive integer. Then $g(x)$ is strictly increasing on nonnegative inputs. In other words, if $s$ and $t$ are nonnegative, then $s^n > t^n$ if and only if $s > t$.

Now, let $s = b^{\frac{1}{q}}$, $t = 1$, and $n = q$. By the above fact,

$$(b^{\frac{1}{q}})^q > 1^q \Leftrightarrow b^{\frac{1}{q}} > 1$$

But $(b^{\frac{1}{q}})^q = b$, so

$$b > 1 \Leftrightarrow b^{\frac{1}{q}} > 1$$

Since $b > 1$ is given, then $b^{\frac{1}{q}} > 1$.

Now use the above fact again, with $n = p$.

$$(b^{\frac{1}{q}})^p > 1^p \Leftrightarrow (b)^{\frac{1}{q}} > 1$$

Therefore $b^{\frac{p}{q}} > 1$ for any positive integers $p$ and $q$.

So $b^x > 1$, as desired.

**Remember...**

A function of the form $y = x^n$ is a polynomial function and not an exponential function.

### Theorem 8.1

**If $b > 1$, then the function $f(x) = b^x$ is strictly increasing on rational-number inputs. In other words, if $s$ and $t$ are rational numbers such that $s > t$, then $f(s) > f(t)$.**

**Proof** Suppose $s$ and $t$ are rational numbers such that $s > t$. Then $s - t > 0$, so that gives

$$b^{s-t} > 1$$

You know $b^t$ is positive. You can multiply each side of the inequality by $b^t$.

$$b^{s-t} \cdot b^t > 1 \cdot b^t$$

$$b^{s-t+t} > b^t$$

$$b^s > b^t$$

$$f(s) > f(t)$$

This is the desired result.

Similarly, you have observed from its graph that the function $h(x) = \left(\frac{1}{2}\right)^x$ is **strictly decreasing.** In general, if $0 < b < 1$, the function $g(x) = b^x$ is strictly decreasing on rational number inputs. See Exercise 4 for the proof.

## Domain and Range

You can draw the graph of $f(x) = 2^x$ without any gaps. This suggests that its domain should be the set of all real numbers, $\mathbb{R}$. The real numbers include irrational numbers such as $\sqrt{2}$ and $\pi$. How should you define $2^{\sqrt{2}}$?

You want to define $2^{\sqrt{2}}$ in such a way that the function $f(x) = 2^x$ is increasing on all real-number inputs. For example, since

$$1 < \sqrt{2} < 2$$

you must have

$$2^1 < 2^{\sqrt{2}} < 2^2$$

Thus, you must define $2^{\sqrt{2}}$ to be a number between 2 and 4. In fact, the graph suggests $2^{\sqrt{2}}$ should be between 2 and 3.

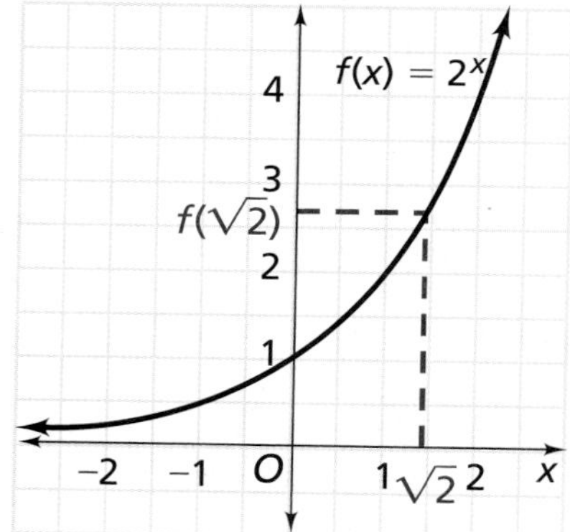


The key to defining irrational exponents is that, even though $\sqrt{2}$ is irrational, you can pick rational numbers that are as close to $\sqrt{2}$ as desired. As the rational numbers on either side get closer to $\sqrt{2}$, the outputs of $f(x) = 2^x$ get closer to a specific real number. You use this number for $2^{\sqrt{2}}$.

**Habits of Mind**

**Extend what you know.** This type of reasoning is *extension by continuity*. You can often use it to take things that work for integers or rational numbers and apply them to real numbers.

## Developing Habits of Mind

**Establish a process.** Evaluate $2^{\sqrt{2}}$ by approximating it with nearby rational exponents. Terminating decimals work well, since they are all rational numbers. Since $\sqrt{2} \approx 1.41421356$, you can get a good estimate for $2^{\sqrt{2}}$ by finding $2^{1.41}$ and $2^{1.42}$.

$$2^{1.41} < 2^{\sqrt{2}} < 2^{1.42}$$

You can do even better using better approximations.

$$2^{1.414} < 2^{\sqrt{2}} < 2^{2.415}$$

This table shows how you can approximate $2^{\sqrt{2}}$ by using decimals close to $\sqrt{2}$ as inputs to the function $f(x) = 2^x$, with outputs rounded to five decimal places.

| Input, $x$ | Output, $f(x) = 2^x$ |
|---|---|
| 1.41 | 2.65737 |
| 1.414 | 2.66475 |
| 1.4142 | 2.66512 |
| 1.41421 | 2.66514 |
| 1.414213 | 2.66514 |
| 1.4142135 | 2.66514 |

The value of $2^{\sqrt{2}}$ to five decimal places is 2.66514. As the inputs get closer to $\sqrt{2}$, the outputs get closer to a number, and you take that number as the value of $2^{\sqrt{2}}$. It is possible to approximate any irrational number with rational numbers. Therefore, it is possible to define $f(x) = 2^x$ for any real number $x$. So, the domain of $f$ is the set of all real numbers.

This limiting process only works for positive bases. Therefore, you cannot define expressions like $(-2)^{\sqrt{2}}$ in a reasonable way.

**Habits of Mind**

**Make strategic choices.** In Chapter 2, you explored this concept of calculating a result as a limit of other results.

Based on this extension, the domain of an exponential function is the set of all real numbers. The range of $f(x) = b^x$ is restricted to positive numbers as long as $b > 0$ (see Exercise 20). Then the value of $a$ determines whether the range of $f(x) = a \cdot b^x$ is all positive numbers or all negative numbers.

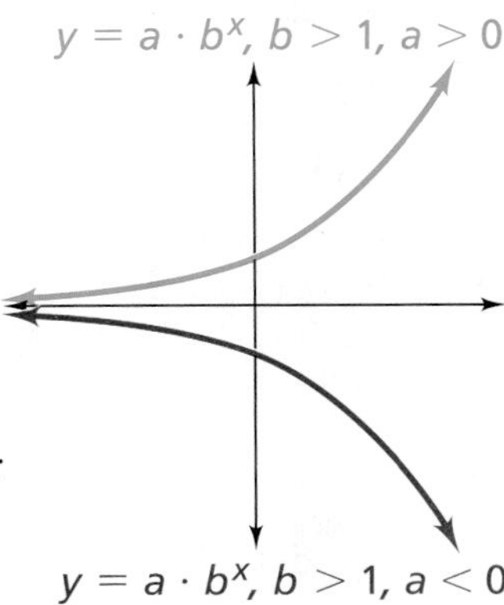


As the input $x$ becomes more negative, the corresponding output $y$ approaches but never reaches 0. This behavior—approaching but not reaching $f(x) = 0$—is very different from the behavior of any polynomial function.

## *Summary* Properties of Exponential Functions

**An exponential function $f : \mathbb{R} \mapsto \mathbb{R}$ is defined as $f(x) = a \cdot b^x$.**

- **The value of $a$ cannot be zero, and $b$ must be positive and not 1.**
- **The domain of $f$ is $\mathbb{R}$.**
- **The range of $f$ is all positive real numbers if $a > 0$, and all negative real numbers if $a < 0$.**
- **The graph of $y = f(x)$ has one $y$-intercept at $(0, a)$ and no $x$-intercepts.**
- **If $a > 0$, the graph of $y = f(x)$ is strictly increasing when $b > 1$ and strictly decreasing when $0 < b < 1$.**

## Exercises *Practicing Habits of Mind*

### Check Your Understanding

**1.** Match each graph with its equation.

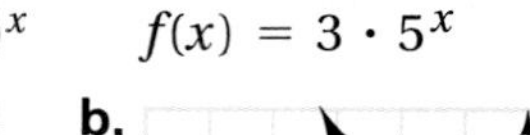

$f(x) = 3 \cdot 2^x$ $\quad f(x) = 3 \cdot \left(\frac{1}{2}\right)^x$ $\quad f(x) = 3 \cdot 5^x$ $\quad f(x) = -3 \cdot 2^x$

**a.**

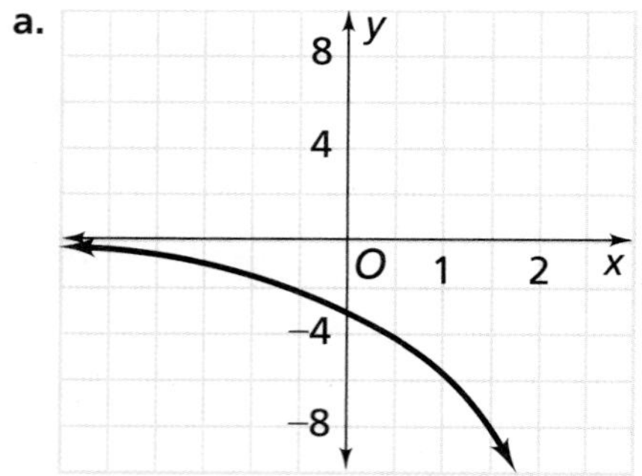


**b.**

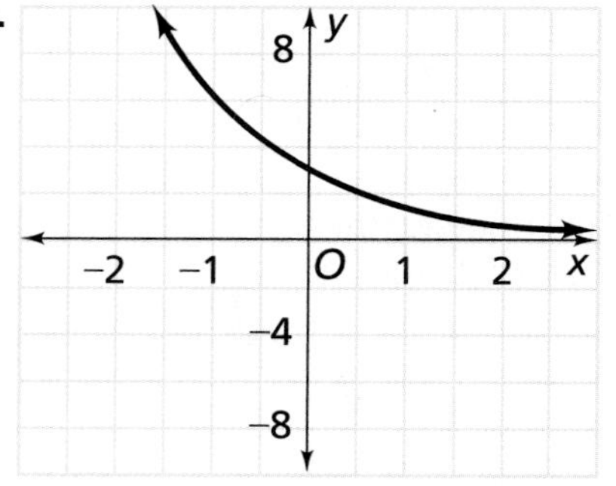


**c.**

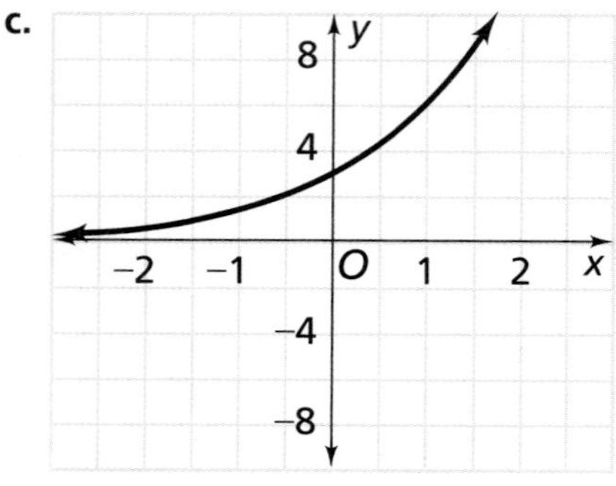


**d.**

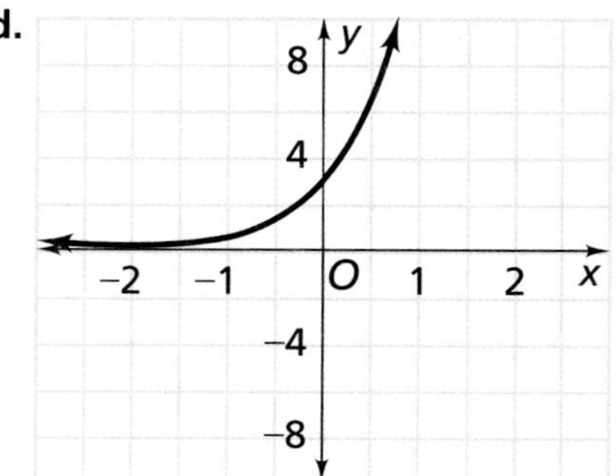

2. a. The graph of an exponential function contains the points (0, 12) and (2, 3). Find its equation.

b. The graph of an exponential function contains the points (2, 12) and (4, 3). Find its equation.

3. a. Write the equations for at least two exponential functions with graphs that contain the point (2, 72).

b. **Take It Further** Write the general form for any exponential function with a graph that contains the point (2, 72).

4. Prove the following lemma and theorem.

### Lemma 8.2

**Let $0 < b < 1$ and let $x$ be a positive rational number. Then $b^x < 1$.**

### Theorem 8.2

**Let $0 < b < 1$. Then the function $f(x) = b^x$ is strictly decreasing on rational-number inputs.**

5. The graphs of $f(x) = 2^x$ and $g(x) = \left(\frac{1}{2}\right)^x$ are reflections of each other in the $y$-axis.

Explain why this reflection property makes sense, using the definition of a negative exponent.

$$b^{-x} = \frac{1}{b^x}$$

If $f(x) = 2^x$ is increasing and $g(x) = \left(\frac{1}{2}\right)^x$ is its reflection over the $y$-axis, what can you say about $g(x)$?

For Exercises 6 and 7, estimate the solution to each equation.

6. $2^x = 7$

7. $2^x = \frac{1}{7} \cdot 4^x$

8. a. Sketch the graph of each function for $-10 \leq x \leq 10$ and $-10 \leq y \leq 10$.

$$f(x) = 5 \cdot (1.07)^x$$

$$g(x) = (1.12)^x$$

Do the graphs intersect in this window?

b. Determine the total number of intersections of the two graphs.

For advice on how to find an intersection point, see the TI-Nspire™ Handbook, p. 817.

9. In the lesson, you learned that $2^{\sqrt{2}}$ is a number $a \approx 2.66514$.

a. Calculate $a^{\sqrt{2}}$.

b. Is there a way to directly calculate $(2^{\sqrt{2}})^{\sqrt{2}}$? Explain.

10. Try to use the method in the Developing Habits of Mind section to define $(-2)^{\sqrt{2}}$. What happens?

## On Your Own

Go Online
www.successnetplus.com

11. Explain why the $y$-intercept of the graph of $f(x) = a \cdot b^x$ is $(0, a)$.

12. **Standardized Test Prep** Which of these points is on the graph of $f(x) = -3 \cdot 2^x$?

    A. $(0, 1)$  B. $(-1, 6)$

    C. $(-2, -0.75)$  D. $(2, 36)$

13. Due to inflation, the cost of a Big Burger grows by 3% every year. This year a Big Burger costs \$3.99.

    a. How much will a Big Burger cost next year and the year after that?

    b. How can you find the cost of a Big Burger ten years from now?

    c. Will a Big Burger ever cost more than \$20? Explain.

    d. Find a rule for the function $C(n)$, with an output that is the cost of a Big Burger $n$ years from now.

14. **What's Wrong Here?** Cody says, "The graph of $y = 2^x$ can't get to *every* positive number if it doesn't make it to zero. It has to stop somewhere. I'll bet it never gets below one millionth."

    Show that Cody is mistaken by finding a number $x$ such that $2^x$ is positive but less than $\frac{1}{1{,}000{,}000}$.

15. Explain why $3^{\sqrt{6}}$ must be greater than 9 and less than 27.

16. Dorris claims the solution $x$ in Exercise 6 must be an irrational number. She says, "If $2^x = 7$ is solved by a fraction, then it looks like $2^{\frac{p}{q}} = 7$. Then I raise both sides to a power of $q$.

$$2^{\frac{p}{q}} = 7$$
$$\left(2^{\frac{p}{q}}\right)^q = 7^q$$
$$2^p = 7^q$$

"And $p$ and $q$ have to be integers. I'm pretty sure that can't happen unless $p$ and $q$ are both zero."

Is it possible for $2^p = 7^q$ if $p$ and $q$ are nonzero integers? Explain.

17. Dorris's explanation above shows that the solution to $2^x = 7$ must be irrational. How does her argument break down if you try to apply it to the equation $2^x = 8$?

18. **a.** Copy and complete this table for $f(x) = (-2)^x$.

**b.** What happens if you try to make a smooth graph for $f(x) = (-2)^x$?

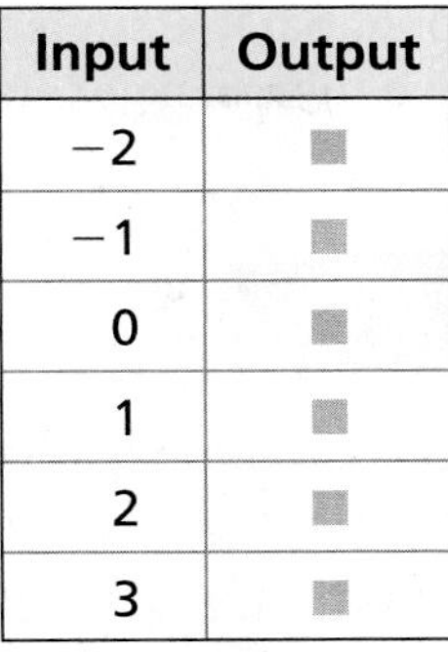

| Input | Output |
|---|---|
| −2 | ■ |
| −1 | ■ |
| 0 | ■ |
| 1 | ■ |
| 2 | ■ |
| 3 | ■ |

19. **Take It Further** The equation

$$a \cdot b^x = c \cdot d^x$$

may have a different number of solutions, depending on the values of $a$, $b$, $c$, and $d$. Describe the conditions on these parameters that make the equation have each number of solutions.

- exactly one
- none
- more than one

20. **a.** If $b > 0$ and $x$ is an integer, explain why $b^x$ must be positive.

**b.** If $b > 0$ and $x$ is rational, use the definition of rational exponent to explain why $b^x$ must be positive.

## Maintain Your Skills

21. Simplify each expression.

**a.** $\left(3^{\sqrt{2}}\right)^{\sqrt{2}}$ **b.** $\left(3^{\sqrt{2}}\right)^{2}$ **c.** $\left(3^{-\sqrt{2}}\right)^{-1}$

**d.** $\left(3^{\sqrt{8}}\right)^{\sqrt{2}}$ **e.** $3^{\sqrt{2}} \cdot 3^{-\sqrt{2}}$ **f.** $\left(3^{-\sqrt{2}}\right)^{-\sqrt{2}}$

**g.** $3^{\sqrt{2}} \cdot 5^{\sqrt{2}}$ **h.** $\left(3^{\sqrt[3]{2}}\right)^{\sqrt[3]{2}}$ **i.** $\left(3^{\sqrt[3]{2}}\right)^{\sqrt[3]{4}}$

Decide for yourself what *simplify* means, but your answer cannot be identical to the given expression.

22. Graph each function on the same set of axes. Let $-10 \le x \le 10$ and let $0 \le y \le 10$.

- $a(x) = 3^x$
- $b(x) = 3 \cdot 3^x$
- $c(x) = 9 \cdot 3^x$
- $d(x) = 27 \cdot 3^x$
- $f(x) = 81 \cdot 3^x$

How are these graphs related?

The logarithmic spiral is the graph of $r = ae^{b\theta}$ in polar coordinates. The arrangement of seeds in a sunflower approximates the logarithmic spiral.

# 8.03 Tables of Exponential Functions

This lesson focuses on exponential functions from a tabular perspective. It also focuses on how recursive rules can generate exponential functions.

## In-Class Experiment

Consider this function defined on nonnegative integers.

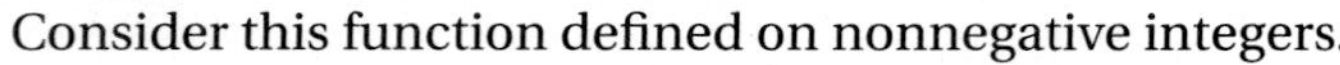

$$B(n) = \begin{cases} 500 & \text{if } n = 0 \\ 1.06 \cdot B(n-1) & \text{if } n > 0 \end{cases}$$

This recursive function can be modeled. See the TI-Nspire Handbook, p. 817.

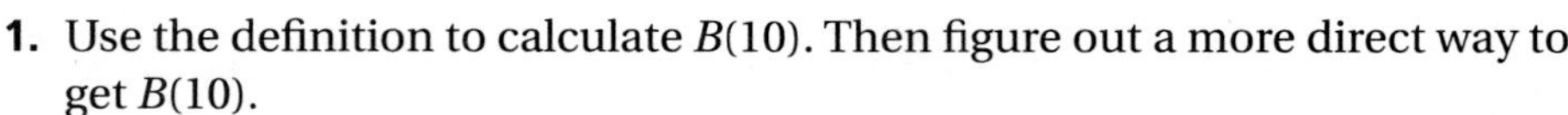

1. Use the definition to calculate $B(10)$. Then figure out a more direct way to get $B(10)$.
2. Calculate $B(50)$.
3. Find the smallest integer $n$ such that $B(n) > 4000$.

The exponential function $L(h) = 100 \cdot \left(\frac{1}{2}\right)^h$ is decreasing. If $h = 0,\ L = 100$.

If the base $b$ is between 0 and 1, it is an **exponential decay** function. If the base is greater than 1, it is an **exponential growth** function.

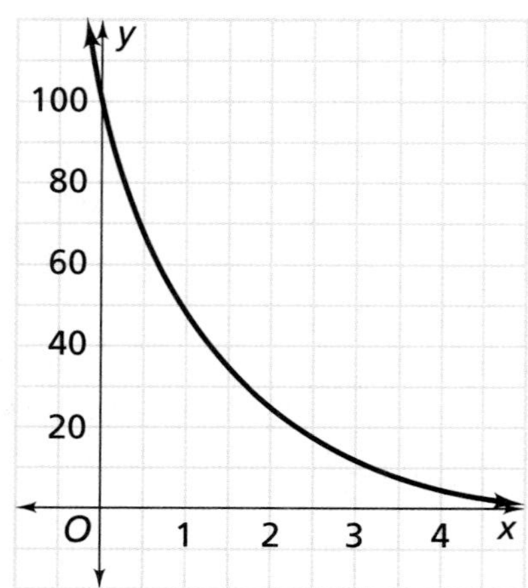


Here is a table for $L(h)$ for integer values of $h$ from 0 to 4.

| *h* | *L(h)* |
|---|---|
| 0 | 100 |
| 1 | 50 |
| 2 | 25 |
| 3 | 12.5 |
| 4 | 6.25 |

## Minds in Action

*Tony thinks he can start with the table and find an exponential function rule.*

**Tony** If you just gave me that table, I could find an exponential function that matches it. There's an exponential that matches the table, since it has a constant ratio between any pair of successive terms. Here's a ratio table.

| h | L(h) | ÷ |
|---|---|---|
| 0 | 100 | $\frac{1}{2}$ |
| 1 | 50 | $\frac{1}{2}$ |
| 2 | 25 | $\frac{1}{2}$ |
| 3 | 12.5 | $\frac{1}{2}$ |
| 4 | 6.25 | |

You calculate the ÷ column by computing ratios of successive terms.

$$\frac{50}{100} = \frac{1}{2}$$

And I know $L(0) = 100$, so $L(h)$ is 100 times one half to the $h$. Now, that's not the only function that matches the table, but it's probably the simplest one. And I can describe $L(h)$ term by term. Start with 100 and divide by 2 each time the input increases by 1.

## For You to Do

**4.** Find a rule that fits this table.

| $x$ | $f(x)$ |
|---|---|
| 0 | 12 |
| 1 | 18 |
| 2 | 27 |

## Developing Habits of Mind

**Make strategic choices.** Tony describes $L(h)$ using a recursive rule: Start with $L(0) = 100$ and divide by 2 each time. You can describe any exponential function $f(x) = a \cdot b^x$ in this way. In this case, the value of $a$ is 100 and the base $b$ is $\frac{1}{2}$, since dividing by 2 is the same as multiplying by one half.

Exponential functions arise naturally in situations like the following.

- the number of teams in an elimination tournament (Half of the teams move on to the next round.)
- the growth of money in a bank account (with 6% interest compounded annually)
- the growth of a population over time (The population doubles every 50 years.)

The function $L$ is connected to the concept of a half-life in biology. Specifically, $L(h)$ outputs the percentage remaining of an element after $h$ half-lives.

The recursive definition for $L(h)$ looks like this.

$$L(h) = \begin{cases} 100 & \text{if } h = 0 \\ 0.5 \cdot L(h-1) & \text{if } h > 0 \end{cases}$$

There is an important concern about domain here. The recursive rule for $L(h)$ limits its domain to nonnegative integers, since it fails to give a value for something like $L(1.5)$ or $L(-2)$. In some situations, it may make sense to use only nonnegative integers as inputs. However, remember that there is a difference between this version of $L(h)$ and the closed-form definition $L(h) = 100 \cdot \left(\frac{1}{2}\right)^h$, which has all real numbers as its domain.

**Habits of Mind**

**Experiment.** Build a model for $L$ in your function-modeling language.

If you have a table for an exponential function, but the inputs do not start at 0 or they have gaps, you can still find the function using algebra if you know at least two input-output pairs.

## Example

**Problem** An exponential function $P$ defined as $P(x) = a \cdot b^x$ has this table of inputs and outputs. Find the values of $a$ and $b$.

| $x$ | $P(x)$ |
|---|---|
| −2 | 108 |
| −1 | 36 |
| 2 | $\frac{4}{3}$ |

The outputs are positive and decreasing, so it must be exponential decay. The base $b$ must be between 0 and 1.

**Solution**

**Method 1** When two terms have inputs that differ by 1, you can calculate the base $b$ directly as the ratio between these successive terms.

$$b = \frac{36}{108} = \frac{1}{3}$$

Then $P(x) = a \cdot \left(\frac{1}{3}\right)^x$. You can find $a$ using any of the input-output pairs. Use $(-1, 36)$.

$$\begin{aligned} P(x) &= a \cdot \left(\tfrac{1}{3}\right)^x \\ 36 &= a \cdot \left(\tfrac{1}{3}\right)^{-1} \\ 36 &= a \cdot 3 \\ 12 &= a \end{aligned}$$

The function is $P(x) = 12 \cdot \left(\frac{1}{3}\right)^x$.

**Method 2** Pick any two points and set up the equation $P(x) = a \cdot b^x$ for each. For example, take $(-1, 36)$ and $\left(2, \frac{4}{3}\right)$.

$$\begin{aligned} 36 &= a \cdot b^{-1} \\ \tfrac{4}{3} &= a \cdot b^2 \end{aligned}$$

Then divide to build an equation for $b$.

$$\begin{aligned} \frac{36}{\frac{4}{3}} &= \frac{a \cdot b^{-1}}{a \cdot b^2} \\ 27 &= b^{-3} \end{aligned}$$

Solve for $b$. If $b^{-3} = 27$, then $b^3 = \frac{1}{27}$ and $b = \frac{1}{3}$. Then find $a$.

## For You to Do

**5.** Find the exponential function with a graph that contains the points $(1, 36)$ and $(2, 108)$.

## Minds in Action

*Tony has another way to think about finding an exponential function from two points on its graph.*

**Tony** I guess the example does the same thing, but I like to think of it as how far apart the points are in a geometric sequence. Say the points are $(-3, 10)$ and $(2, 20)$. The $x$-values have a difference of 5, so it's a geometric sequences with five steps from 10 to 20.

10, ■, ■, ■, ■, 20

So whatever the base is, the output doubles from 10 to 20 in five terms. That means the base has to solve the equation $b^5 = 2$. And once you find $b$, you can use either point to find $a$.

# Exercises Practicing Habits of Mind

## Check Your Understanding

1. For each table, find the exponential function that matches the table or explain how you know that an exponential function cannot fit the table.

a.

| $n$ | $A(n)$ |
|---|---|
| 0 | 18 |
| 1 | 6 |
| 2 | 2 |
| 3 | $\frac{2}{3}$ |

b.

| $x$ | $B(x)$ |
|---|---|
| 0 | −2 |
| 1 | −8 |
| 2 | −32 |
| 3 | −128 |

c.

| $t$ | $C(t)$ |
|---|---|
| 0 | 4 |
| 1 | 6 |
| 2 | 9 |
| 3 | 12 |

d.

| $z$ | $D(z)$ |
|---|---|
| 1 | 2 |
| 2 | 12 |
| 3 | 72 |
| 4 | 432 |

2. For each exponential function in Exercise 1, build a recursive model in your function-modeling language.

3. Suppose $q$ is an exponential function with $q(3) = 100$ and $q(5) = 4$. Find $q(x)$.

4. **What's Wrong Here?** George says there are two possible values of the base $b$ for the exponential function in Exercise 3.

   George says, "The function goes from 100 to 4 in two steps, which means dividing by 25. So $b^2 = \frac{1}{25}$. But then there are two possible values of $b$. It could be either $\frac{1}{5}$ or $\frac{-1}{5}$. Either could be right."

   Do you agree or disagree with George's statement? Explain.

5. Find two functions for which $f(-3) = 10$ and $f(2) = 20$.

The function $f(x)$ does not need to be an exponential function.

6. $T$ is an exponential function with this table.

   a. If $T(x) = a \cdot b^x$, find $a$ and $b$.

   b. Copy and complete the table.

| $x$ | $T(x)$ | ÷ |
|---|---|---|
| 0 | 100 | ■ |
| 1 | ■ | ■ |
| 2 | ■ | ■ |
| 3 | ■ | ■ |
| 4 | ■ | ■ |
| 5 | 300 | |

7. Suppose a new car that costs \$20,000 depreciates in value about 20% each year.

   a. How much will the car be worth after 1 year? After 2 years? After 3 years?

   b. Find a rule for $V(n)$, the value of the car after $n$ years of driving.

   c. Will the car ever be worth less than \$1000? Explain.

Most cars actually depreciate more than 20% the first year.

8. **Take It Further** The graph of an exponential function passes through the points $(x_1, y_1)$ and $(x_2, y_2)$. Find the function in terms of these coordinates.

**Habits of Mind**

**Generalize.** Exercise 8 is a generalization of the type of problem found in Exercises 3 and 12.

## On Your Own

9. **Standardized Test Prep** Suppose $f$ is an exponential function $f(x) = a \cdot b^x$ with $f(0) = 4$ and $f(2) = 25$. What are the values of $a$ and $b$?

   A. $a = 1, b = 5$
   B. $a = 1, b = 10$
   C. $a = 4, b = 2.5$
   D. $a = 4, b = 5$

10. The ratio column of this table is filled in.

| $n$ | $M(n)$ | ÷ |
|---|---|---|
| 0 | 16 | 1.5 |
| 1 | ■ | 1.5 |
| 2 | ■ | 1.5 |
| 3 | ■ | 1.5 |
| 4 | ■ | |

Copy and complete the table. Define $M(n)$ with both a closed-form rule and a recursive rule.

Go Online
www.successnetplus.com

**11.** This table has the first output and the ratio column filled in.

| $n$ | $F(n)$ | ÷ |
|---|---|---|
| 0 | 1 | 1 |
| 1 | | 2 |
| 2 | | 3 |
| 3 | | 4 |
| 4 | | 5 |
| 5 | | 6 |
| 6 | | |

**a.** Copy and complete the table.

**b.** Is $F$ an exponential function? Explain.

**c.** Describe how to calculate $F(10)$ if the pattern in the ratio column continues.

**12.** Here are the graphs of three exponential functions. Find a closed-form rule that defines each function.

**a.**

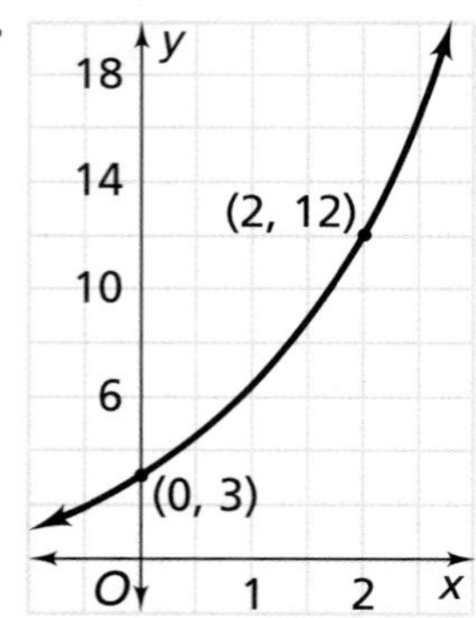


**b.**

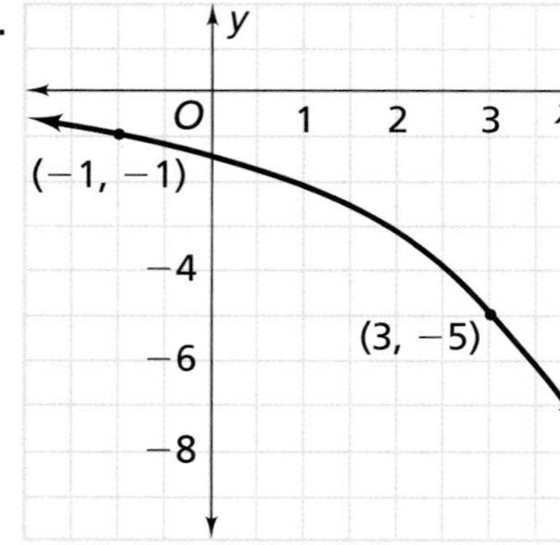


**c.**

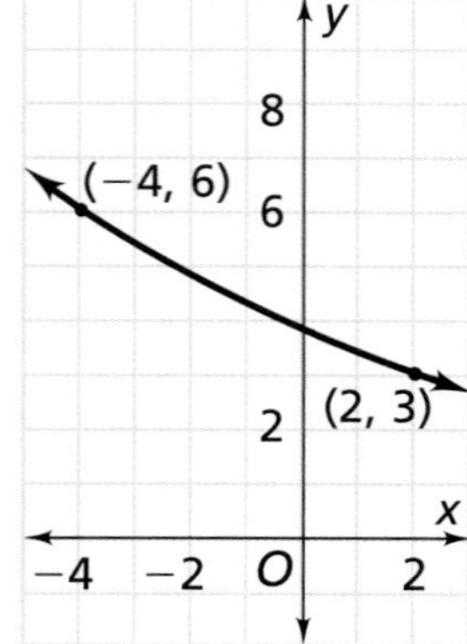

13. Money in a savings account typically grows by about 3% per year. Kara's savings account has \$1000 in it.

a. Find the amount of money in Kara's account after 1 year, 2 years, and 3 years.

b. Find the amount of money in Kara's account after 20 years.

So, Kara will earn \$30 (3% of \$1000) interest during the first year. Why will she earn more than \$30 interest during the second year?

14. Some credit cards offer 0% interest on their balance for 12 months, as long as you make a required monthly payment of at least 2% of the balance. Suppose you owe \$2000 on one of these cards and make only the minimum payment each month.

a. Find the balance after 1 month, 2 months, and 3 months.

b. Find a rule for $B(n)$, the balance after $n$ months.

c. What is the domain of $B(n)$? Explain.

15. Suppose you have the credit card in Exercise 14, but want to be sure to pay off half the total balance by the end of the first year. If you plan to pay the same percentage of the remaining balance each month, about what percent of the balance do you need to pay?

16. **Write About It** Use the two function definitions below.

$$f(x) = 5 \cdot 2^x$$

$$g(x) = \begin{cases} 5 & \text{if } x = 0 \\ 2 \cdot g(x-1) & \text{if } x > 0 \end{cases}$$

Explain why the graphs of these functions do not look the same.

## Maintain Your Skills

17. Suppose $b(x) = 3^x$. Calculate each value.

a. $b(5)$ b. $b(3) \cdot b(2)$ c. $b(1)$

d. $\dfrac{b(3)}{b(2)}$ e. $b(6)$ f. $(b(2))^3$

18. Suppose $f(x) = b^x$ for $b > 0$ with $f(3) = p$ and $f(5) = q$. Find each value in terms of $p$ and $q$.

a. $f(0)$ b. $f(-3)$ c. $f(8)$

d. $f(6)$ e. $f(15)$

**Habits of Mind**

**Look for relationships.** How is $f(8)$ related to $f(3)$ and $f(5)$? Use the fact that $f(x) = b^x$.

# 8.04 Properties of Exponential Functions

This lesson explores several properties of exponential functions that are dictated by the laws of exponents.

## In-Class Experiment

1. Sketch the graph of $f(x) = 2^x$. Then sketch the graphs of each pair of functions.
   - $f(x+1)$ and $2 \cdot f(x)$
   - $f(x-2)$ and $\frac{f(x)}{4}$
2. How are the graphs of each pair related?

You can now apply the laws of exponents to any real-number exponent.

### *Laws of Exponents*

**Let base $b > 0$ and let $x$ and $y$ be real numbers.**

*The Fundamental Law of Exponents*

- $b^{x+y} = b^x \cdot b^y$

*Corollaries*

- $b^{x-y} = \frac{b^x}{b^y}$
- $b^{xy} = (b^x)^y$

See the discussion on how you extend exponents from rational numbers to real numbers in the Developing Habits of Mind section in Lesson 8.02.

The graphs for each pair of functions in the In-Class Experiment were identical. A similar example is the graph of $f(x) = 3^x$. The graphs of $f(x+1)$ and $3 \cdot f(x)$ are identical.

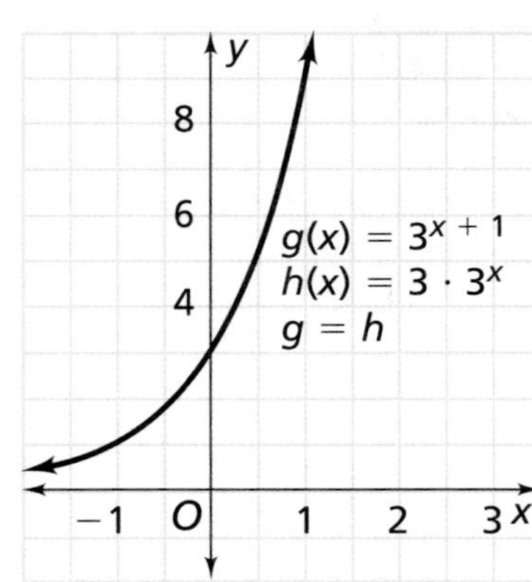


This is not a coincidence. It is a consequence of the Fundamental Law of Exponents. If $f(x) = 3^x$, then

$$f(x+1) = 3^{x+1} = 3^x \cdot 3^1 = 3 \cdot 3^x = 3f(x)$$

You can rewrite the laws of exponents using function notation. It is important to note that none of the results below is new. They are just written using the language of functions.

### *Laws of Exponents* *Function Version*

Let $f(x) = b^x$ with $b > 0$ and domain $\mathbb{R}$.

*The Fundamental Law of Exponents*

- $f(x + y) = f(x) \cdot f(y)$

*Corollaries*

- $f(x - y) = \frac{f(x)}{f(y)}$
- $f(xy) = (f(x))^y$

The definitions for zero and negative exponents give these equations.

- $f(0) = 1$
- $f(-x) = \frac{1}{f(x)}$

A **functional equation** is an equation that relates some values of a function to other values of the function. For example, $g(n) = g(n - 1) + 3$ is a functional equation for a linear function with a slope of 3. This list of functional equations relates values of the function $f(x) = b^x$.

## For Discussion

**3.** Let $f(x) = b^x$ with $b > 0$. Prove that $f(x + y) = f(x) \cdot f(y)$.

The statement that $f(x + 1) = 3 \cdot f(x)$ for $f(x) = 3^x$ is the Fundamental Law of Exponents, with 1 replacing $y$.

## Example

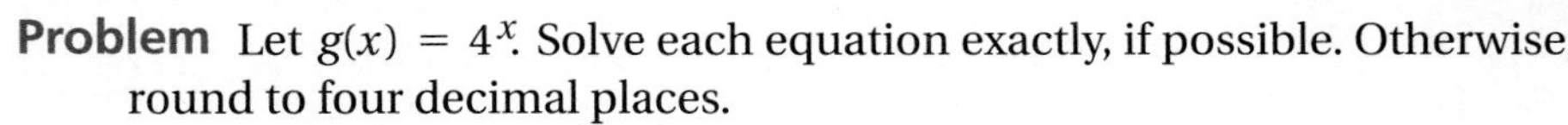

**Problem** Let $g(x) = 4^x$. Solve each equation exactly, if possible. Otherwise, round to four decimal places.

**a.** $g(a) = 5$ **b.** $g(b) = 8$ **c.** $g(c) = 40$

**Solution**

**a.** You cannot find the solution $g(a) = 5$ exactly as an integer or as a fraction. The exact solution to $4^x = 5$ is irrational. Approximate the solution by successive guesses at $a$. Use the fact that $g(x) = 4^x$ is increasing.

| Guess, $a$ | $g(a) = 4^a$ | The next guess should be . . . |
|---|---|---|
| 1 | 4 | Higher |
| 1.2 | 5.2780 | Lower |
| 1.15 | 4.9246 | Higher |
| 1.16 | 4.9933 | Higher (close!) |

Successive approximations give the value $a \approx 1.1610$ to four decimal places.

If the solution is rational, then $4^{\frac{p}{q}} = 5$, and $4^p = 5^q$. This is impossible if $p$ and $q$ are nonzero integers.

**b.** The solution to $g(b) = 8$ is exactly $\frac{3}{2}$. Both 8 and 4 are powers of 2, so you can solve $4^b = 8$ by rewriting each number as a power of 2.

$$(2^2)^b = 2^3$$

Then $2b = 3$ and $b = \frac{3}{2}$.

**c.** The solution to $g(c) = 40$ is irrational, since you cannot write 40 as a rational power of 2. Approximate the solution by successive guesses at $c$.

| Guess, $c$ | $g(c) = 4^c$ | The next guess should be . . . |
|---|---|---|
| 2 | 16 | Higher |
| 2.5 | 32 | Higher |
| 2.7 | 42.2243 | Lower |
| 2.65 | 39.3966 | Higher |
| 2.66 | 39.9466 | Higher (close!) |

Successive approximations give the value $c \approx 2.6610$ to four decimal places.

You can find the value of $c$ more quickly by using the Fundamental Law of Exponents. It says that the following equation is true for any choices of $a$ and $b$.

$$g(a + b) = g(a) \cdot g(b)$$

If $g(a) = 5$ and $g(b) = 8$, then $g(a + b) = 40$, which is exactly what you need for this problem. Then $c = a + b \approx 2.6610$ is the solution.

## For You to Do

Use the information that $g(1.1610) \approx 5$ and $g(1.5) = 8$ to solve each equation.

4. $g(m) = 25$
5. $g(n) = 1.6$
6. $g(p) = 200$
7. $g(q) = 0.2$
8. $g(r) = 1$

In the next lesson, you will look at another important property of exponential functions: They are one-to-one, and therefore have inverse functions. An inverse function for something like $g(x) = 4^x$ is very useful, since it allows you to solve equations such as $g(x) = 5$ more quickly.

$$g(x) = 5$$

$$g^{-1}(g(x)) = g^{-1}(5)$$

$$x = g^{-1}(5)$$

For now, that inverse function is unknown, but you will study its properties in the next investigation.

Exponential functions are one-to-one because they are **monotonic**. This means these functions are either increasing for all inputs or decreasing for all inputs.

## Exercises *Practicing Habits of Mind*

### Check Your Understanding

For Exercises 1–4, use the equation $C = a \cdot b^x$. This equation has four variables. If you know three of them, you can find the fourth.

1. Describe how to find $C$ if you know $a$, $b$, and $x$.
2. Describe how to find $a$ if you know $C$, $b$, and $x$.
3. Describe how to find $b$ if you know $C$, $a$, and $x$.
4. Describe how to find $x$ if you know $C$, $a$, and $b$.
5. Let $f(x) = 2^x$. The solution of $f(a) = 3$ is approximately 1.5850. The solution to $f(b) = 5$ is approximately 2.3219.

   a. You can use the information above and the properties of exponents to find all but one of this table's missing entries. Copy and complete the table, except for that entry. Give all answers to four decimal places.

   b. Find the last missing entry by approximating it to four decimal places.

| $x$ | $f(x) = 2^x$ |
|---|---|
| 0 | 1 |
| 1 | 2 |
| 1.5850 | 3 |
| ■ | 4 |
| 2.3219 | 5 |
| ■ | 6 |
| ■ | 7 |
| ■ | 8 |
| ■ | 9 |
| ■ | 10 |

6. The function versions of the laws of exponents work only for functions in the form $f(x) = b^x$. Other exponential functions have the form $f(x) = a \cdot b^x$. How do the rules change if $f(x) = a \cdot b^x$ instead? For example, is it still true that $f(x + y) = f(x) \cdot f(y)$? If not, what adjustments can you make?

7. Binh tells you that by investing, he expects to have ten times as much money in 30 years as he has now. He expects his investment to grow by about the same percentage every year. He says he can break the 30 years into 15-year halves, where each half has the same proportional growth.

**Earnings per Dollar Invested**

| Years Invested | Earnings | ÷ |
|---|---|---|
| 0 | \$1 | $k$ |
| 15 | ■ | $k$ |
| 30 | \$10 | |

a. Find $k$ to three decimal places.

b. Find the exact value of $k$ using a radical or rational exponent.

c. If Binh invests \$1500, how much money does he expect to have after 15 years?

8. Binh goes on to explain that he can also break the 30 years of investing into three groups of 10 years each.

**Earnings per Dollar Invested**

| Years Invested | Earnings | ÷ |
|---|---|---|
| 0 | \$1 | $j$ |
| 10 | ■ | $j$ |
| 20 | ■ | $j$ |
| 30 | \$10 | |

Financial analysts use exponential functions to model the growth of investments.

a. Find $j$ to three decimal places.

b. Find the exact value of $j$ using a radical or rational exponent.

c. If Binh invests \$1500, how much money does he expect to have after 20 years?

9. **Take It Further** Find all real numbers $x$ and $y$ for which $x^y = 1$.

## On Your Own

10. Using $g(x) = 5^x$, solve each equation for $x$.

a. $g(x) = 25$ b. $g(x) = 5^{-11}$ c. $g(x) = 25^3$ d. $g(x) = 0$

11. Let $f(x) = 10^x$. Give examples to verify the function version of each law of exponents for this particular function.

12. Sophie has made a deal with her father. She can deposit any amount of money with him, and he will guarantee her 6% interest per year. She deposits \$100. The amount of money she can withdraw from the Bank of Dad after $x$ years is given by the exponential function $f(x) = 100(1.06)^x$.

    a. How long will it take for Sophie's money to double in value?

    b. How long will it take for Sophie's money to triple in value?

    c. How long will it take for Sophie's money to sextuple in value, or in other words, for her original deposit to be worth \$600?

13. Sketch the graph of each function.

    - $a(x) = 3^x$
    - $b(x) = 3 \cdot 3^x$
    - $c(x) = 9 \cdot 3^x$
    - $d(x) = 27 \cdot 3^x$
    - $f(x) = 81 \cdot 3^x$

    How are these graphs related? Explain.

See Exercise 22 in Lesson 8.02.

14. The table in Exercise 5 stops when the output is 10. Give three other examples of outputs $N$ for which you can solve $f(x) = N$ by using the solutions to $f(a) = 3$ and $f(b) = 5$.

15. If $x$ is an integer, $f(x) = i^x$ is a function that calculates the powers of the imaginary unit $i = \sqrt{-1}$.

    a. Calculate $f(2)$, $f(3)$, and $f(5)$. Is it true that $f(2) \cdot f(3) = f(5)$?

    b. Do all the laws of exponents work for this function $f$?

16. Alicia gets her first full-time job with a starting salary of \$25,000. She is offered two compensation plans for the future.

    Plan 1: Alicia will earn a raise of \$3000 every year.

    Plan 2: Alicia will earn an 8% raise every year.

    Determine how many years it will take for Alicia's salary to reach each amount under the two plans.

    a. at least \$30,000

    b. at least \$40,000

    c. at least \$50,000

    d. at least \$100,000

**17.** **What's Wrong Here?** Stacy says the function versions of the laws of exponents do not always work. "Here's one example. I take an exponential function $f(x) = x^3$. It says $f(x)$ times $f(y)$ equals $f(x + y)$, but that doesn't work. Take $x = 1$ and $y = 2$, for example: $f(x)$ times $f(y)$ is 8, but $f(x + y)$ is 27. I've got plenty of these."

What is wrong with Stacy's reasoning?

**18.** **Take It Further** Suppose a one-to-one function $L(x)$ has $L(2) = 1$ and follows the rule below for any positive numbers $a$ and $b$.

$$L(a) + L(b) = L(ab)$$

**a.** Show that $L(4) = 2$ and $L(1) = 0$.

**b.** Find $x$ if $L(x) = 6$.

**c.** Show that if $n$ is an integer, then $L(a^n) = n \cdot L(a)$.

**d.** Find $x$ if $L(x) = \frac{1}{2}$.

**19.** **Standardized Test Prep** Suppose a restaurant's sales increase 15% each year for 8 years. Use the approximations $(1.15)^3 \approx 1.521$ and $(1.15)^8 \approx 3.059$. What is the ratio of the restaurant's sales in the sixth year to the restaurant's sales in the first year?

**A.** 1.538 **B.** 2.011 **C.** 2.136 **D.** 4.580

## Maintain Your Skills

**20.** Solve each equation. Round to three decimal places.

**a.** $2^x = 7$ **b.** $4^x = 7$

**c.** $8^x = 7$ **d.** $16^x = 7$

**e.** $1024^x = 7$

**Go Online**
**Video Tutor**
www.successnetplus.com

**21.** Solve each equation. Round to three decimal places.

**a.** $6^x = 35$ **b.** $35^x = 6$

**c.** $3^x = 28$ **d.** $28^x = 3$

**e.** $9^x = 28$ **f.** $28^x = 9$

# 8.05 Exponential Functions, One-to-One

Consider the equation $8^x = 32$. You can solve this equation by writing 8 and 32 as powers of 2.

$$8^x = 32$$
$$(2^3)^x = 2^5$$
$$2^{3x} = 2^5$$
$$3x = 5$$
$$x = \frac{5}{3}$$

The step that removes the exponent is an interesting one. If $2^x = 2^y$, is it always true that $x = y$? This has been an assumption throughout the chapter. This lesson provides a proof, as well as some initial exploration of the inverse functions of exponential functions.

Recall the definition of *one-to-one*: A function is one-to-one if there is a unique input that produces a given output. Algebraically, a function $f$ is one-to-one if $f(a) = f(b)$ only when $a = b$.

The graph of a function can suggest whether it is one-to-one. For example, $f(x) = x^3 - 4x$ is not one-to-one. You can see this from its graph.

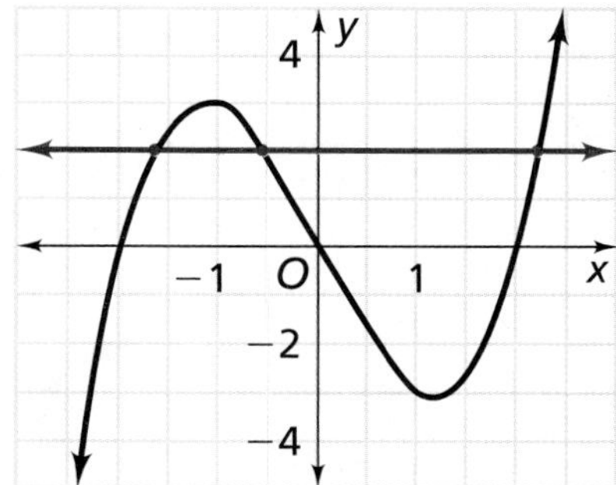


This function cannot be one-to-one since there is more than one input that gives the output $y = 2$. However, the graph of $f(x) = 2^x$ suggests that this function is one-to-one.

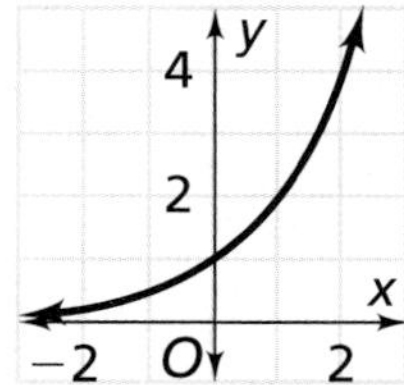


**Remember...**

Since you use a horizontal line to find such counterexamples, this is the horizontal-line test. A function is not one-to-one if a horizontal line intersects the graph more than once.

You can state the fact that all exponential functions are one-to-one as a theorem.

### *Theorem 8.3 One-to-One Property for Exponential Functions*

**If $f$ is an exponential function, then $f$ is one-to-one.**

**Proof** Suppose that $f(a) = f(b)$, where $a$ and $b$ are real numbers. Recall from Lesson 8.02 that an exponential function is either strictly increasing or strictly decreasing. Assume that $f$ is strictly increasing. If $a < b$, you have $f(a) < f(b)$, which contradicts the assumption that $f(a) = f(b)$. You get a similar contradiction if $a > b$. Thus, $a = b$. The proof is almost identical for the case in which $f$ is strictly decreasing.

You must show that $a = b$.

## For Discussion

1. Complete the missing cases in the proof.

The fact that exponential functions are one-to-one provides an algebraic corollary. The algebraic step of "undoing the exponent" is valid as long as the base is positive and not equal to 1.

### *Corollary 8.3.1*

**If $b > 0$, $b \neq 1$, and $b^x = b^y$, then $x = y$.**

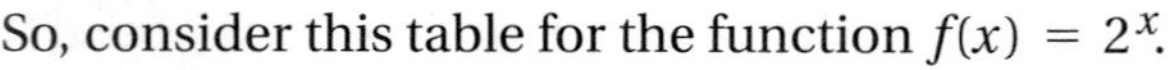

## Developing Habits of Mind

**Detect the key characteristics.** One other important property of a one-to-one function is that it has an inverse function. That means that any exponential function has an inverse function.

So, consider this table for the function $f(x) = 2^x$.

| $x$ | $f(x)$ |
|---|---|
| −1 | $\frac{1}{2}$ |
| 0 | 1 |
| 1 | 2 |
| 2 | 4 |
| 3 | 8 |
| 4 | 16 |

There is another function, which you can call $L_2(x)$, that is the inverse function. So its table would include these input-output pairs.

| $x$ | $L_2(x)$ |
|---|---|
| $\frac{1}{2}$ | −1 |
| 1 | 0 |
| 2 | 1 |
| 4 | 2 |
| 8 | 3 |
| 16 | 4 |

The use of the subscript 2 helps remind you that the original function had base 2. So, you could give the inverse function of $f(x) = 10^x$ the name $L_{10}(x)$. You will learn the more standard notation for this function in Investigation 8B.

Note that these are the same pairs listed for $f(x) = 2^x$ with the inputs and outputs switched.

But what can you do for other inputs to $L_2(x)$? For example, what is $L_2(3)$? The value of $L_2(3)$ is the number that solves $2^x = 3$, since 3 would appear as the output in the $2^x$ table. That value is an irrational number, about 1.5850 (see Exercise 5 in Lesson 8.04). So $L_2(3)$ is about 1.5850, which seems reasonable, given the table. You expect it to be somewhere between 1 and 2.

## For You to Do

**2.** What two integers is $L_2(9)$ between? Find its value to three decimal places.

Any one-to-one function has an inverse function. If the point $(x, y)$ is on the graph of the function $f$, then the point $(y, x)$ is on the graph of the inverse $f^{-1}$. You can draw the graph of the inverse by reflecting the graph of the function across the line $y = x$.

As in Chapter 1, the −1 in the notation $f^{-1}(x)$ means "inverse with respect to function composition."

Here are the graphs of $f(x) = 2^x$ and its inverse function, which you will temporarily call $L_2(x)$.

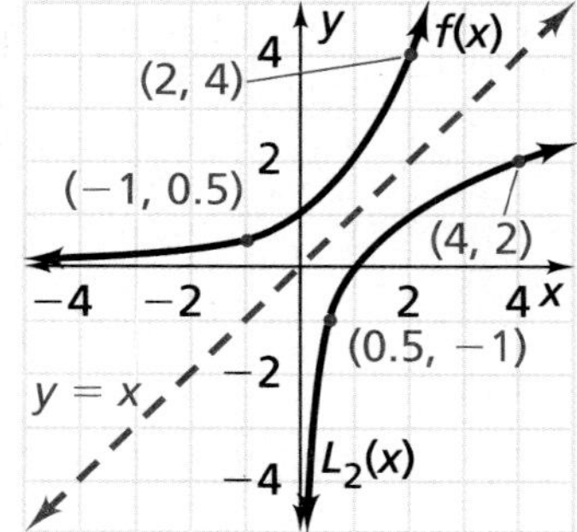


The next investigation focuses on functions such as $L_2(x)$, their properties, and how they are used to solve equations in algebra.

# Exercises Practicing Habits of Mind

## Check Your Understanding

Throughout these exercises, $L_b(x)$ refers to the inverse of $f(x) = b^x$.

**1.** Based on what you know about $f(x) = 2^x$, find the domain and range of the inverse function $L_2(x)$.

**2.** Find each value. Each result is an integer.

**a.** $L_5(25)$ **b.** $L_7(1)$ **c.** $L_{11}(11^6)$

**d.** $L_{0.1}(0.001)$ **e.** $L_3(\frac{1}{9})$

**3.** Find each value, either exactly or to four decimal places.

**a.** $L_4(5)$ **b.** $L_4(8)$ **c.** $L_4(40)$ **d.** $L_4(\frac{8}{5})$

**4.** Copy the graph below of $f(x) = (0.5)^x$. Sketch the graph of the inverse function.

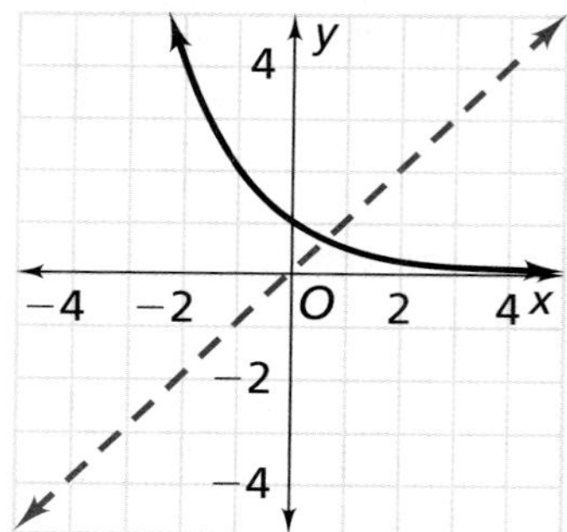


**5.** Let $f(x) = 2^x$. Determine which value in each pair is greater. (*Hint:* Use the graph of $f(x) = 2^x$.)

**a.** the mean of $f(3)$ and $f(5)$ $f(4)$

**b.** the mean of $f(5)$ and $f(7)$ $f(6)$

**c.** the mean of $f(-4)$ and $f(-2)$ $f(-3)$

**d.** the mean of $f(x)$ and $f(y)$ $f(\frac{x+y}{2})$

**6. a.** Sketch the graphs of $y = 2^x$ and $y = x^2$.

**b.** How many numbers $x$ satisfy $2^x = x^2$?

**7.** As $x$ increases, $2^x$ becomes greater than $x^2$. Consider the values of $1.06^x$. Use the graphs of $y = x^2$ and $y = 1.06^x$.

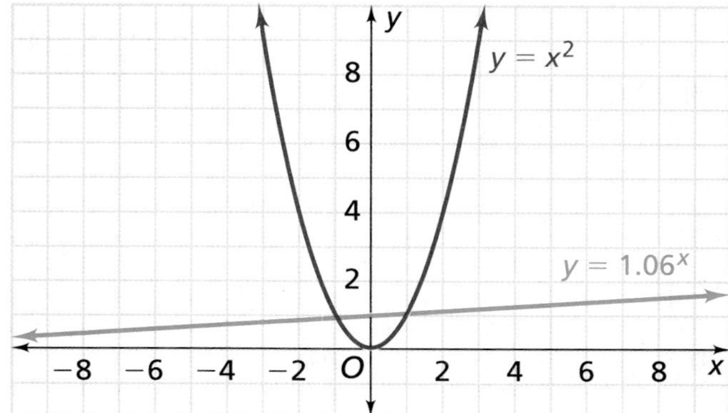


As $x$ increases, will $x^2$ always be greater than $1.06^x$?

**8.** As $x$ increases, $2^x$ becomes greater than $x^2$. Consider the values of $x^{10}$. Use the graphs of $y = x^{10}$ and $y = 2^x$.

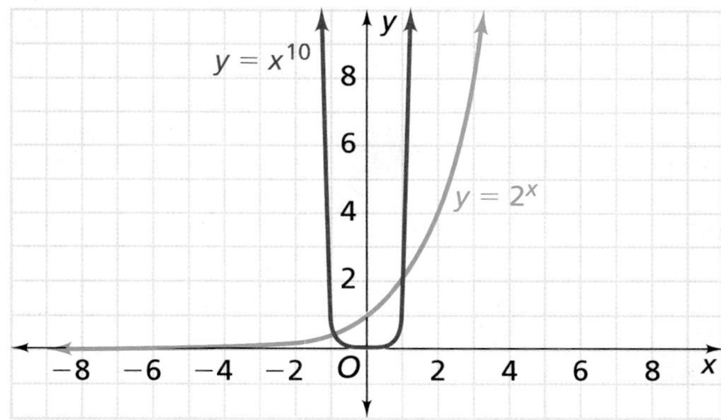


**a.** As $x$ increases, will $x^{10}$ always be greater than $2^x$?

**b.** As $x$ increases, will $x^{10}$ always be greater than $1.06^x$?

**c.** As $x$ increases, will $2^x$ always be greater than $1.06^x$?

**9.** **Take It Further** The graph of $y = 2^x$ does not intersect the graph of $y = x$. The graph of $y = 1.06^x$ intersects the graph of $y = x$ in two places. Approximate the greatest number $b$ such that the graph of $y = b^x$ intersects the graph of $y = x$. Approximate the coordinates of the one point at which $y = b^x$ intersects $y = x$.

## On Your Own

**10.** Is $L_2(x)$ a one-to-one function? Explain.

**11.** **Standardized Test Prep** The value of $L_3(28)$ is between what two integers?

**A.** 1 and 2 **B.** 2 and 3 **C.** 3 and 4 **D.** 4 and 5

**12.** Copy and complete this table for $L_2(x)$. Give approximations to four decimal places.

| $x$ | $L_2(x)$ |
|---|---|
| 1 | 0 |
| 2 | 1 |
| 3 | 1.5850 |
| 4 | ■ |
| 5 | ■ |
| 6 | ■ |
| 7 | ■ |
| 8 | ■ |
| 9 | ■ |

**13.** **a.** Explain why $L_8(8) = 1$.

**b.** Explain why $L_8(2) = \frac{1}{3}$.

**c.** Copy and complete this table for $L_8(x)$. Give approximations to four decimal places.

| $x$ | $L_8(x)$ |
|---|---|
| 1 | 0 |
| 2 | 0.3333 |
| 3 | 0.5283 |
| 4 | ■ |
| 5 | ■ |
| 6 | ■ |
| 7 | ■ |
| 8 | 1 |
| 9 | ■ |

**14.** **Take It Further** Prove that $L_2(x) = 3 \cdot L_8(x)$ for any positive real number $x$.

**15.** Ariela puts $500 in an investment account. She earns 9% interest per year. After how many years will she be closest to doubling her starting investment?

16. Ariela wonders what will happen with higher or lower interest rates. Copy the table at the right. For each interest rate, find out after how many years Ariela will be closest to doubling her starting $500 investment.

**Doubling Time**

| APR | Years to Double |
|---|---|
| 3% | ■ |
| 4% | ■ |
| 5% | ■ |
| 6% | 12 |
| 7% | ■ |
| 8% | ■ |
| 9% | ■ |
| 10% | ■ |
| 11% | ■ |
| 12% | ■ |

Any APR will show exponential growth. See the TI-Nspire Handbook, p. 817.

APR stands for "annual percentage rate."

17. Many financial advisors use the Rule of 72 when offering advice about long-term investments.

**Rule of 72** To find the number of years it takes to double an investment's value, divide 72 by the annual percentage rate.

**a.** Recopy the table from Exercise 16 and use the Rule of 72 to complete it. How do your results using the Rule of 72 compare to the results you found in Exercise 16?

**b.** According to the Rule of 72, how long will it take a credit card balance to double if the interest rate is 18% APR?

**c.** If Ariela invests $500 in an account at 9% APR for 40 years, how many times will her money double in value? How much money does the Rule of 72 suggest she will have after 40 years?

**Go Online**
www.successnetplus.com

## Maintain Your Skills

In Exercises 18 and 19, find each value to four decimal places.

**18.** **a.** $L_5(3)$ **b.** $L_5(9)$ **c.** $L_5(27)$ **d.** $L_5(81)$

**19.** **a.** $L_2(7)$ **b.** $L_4(7)$ **c.** $L_8(7)$ **d.** $L_{16}(7)$ **e.** $L_{1024}(7)$

**In this investigation, you graphed exponential functions. You wrote rules for exponential functions, given a table of inputs and outputs or two points on the graph of the function. These exercises will help you summarize what you have learned.**

**1.** Give the definition of *exponential function*. Pay special attention to any restrictions on the variables in your definition. Give an example of an exponential function and describe its domain and range. Describe where your function is increasing and where it is decreasing.

**2.** Use this table for the exponential function $g(x)$.

| $x$ | $g(x)$ |
|---|---|
| 0 | −5 |
| 1 | −10 |
| 2 | −20 |
| 3 | −40 |
| 4 | −80 |

**a.** Write a recursive definition for $g(x)$.

**b.** Write a closed-form definition for $g(x)$.

**c.** Do your answers for parts (a) and (b) define the same function? Explain.

**3. a.** Copy and complete this ratio table for $h(x)$.

| $x$ | $h(x)$ | ÷ |
|---|---|---|
| 0 | ■ | $\frac{2}{3}$ |
| 1 | 6 | $\frac{2}{3}$ |
| 2 | ■ | $\frac{2}{3}$ |
| 3 | ■ | $\frac{2}{3}$ |
| 4 | ■ | |

**b.** Find $h(23)$ to four decimal places.

**c.** Could $h(x)$ be an exponential function? Explain.

**4.** Find the exact values of $x$ that solve each equation.

**a.** $12 = 3x^2$

**b.** $x = 5 \cdot 4^{-\frac{1}{2}}$

**c.** $16 = 4 \cdot 32^x$

**d.** $-5 = x \cdot 27^{\frac{2}{3}}$

5. $L_3(x)$ is the inverse of the function $f(x) = 3^x$.

   a. Find $L_3(1)$.

   b. Find $L_3(81)$.

   c. If $L_3(2) \approx 0.6309$, find $L_3(4)$ and $L_3(8)$.

   d. Approximate $L_3(5)$ to four decimal places.

6. For $f(x) = b^x$, why is it true that $f(m) \cdot f(n) = f(m + n)$?

7. Why must an exponential function have an inverse function?

8. If you invest \$1000 in an account at 6% interest, compounded annually, how much money will you have in 30 years?

## Vocabulary

In this investigation, you learned these terms. Make sure you understand what each one means and how to use it.

- **base**
- **exponential decay**
- **exponential function**
- **exponential growth**
- **functional equation**
- **monotonic**
- **strictly decreasing**
- **strictly increasing**

# Logarithmic Functions

In *Logarithmic Functions,* you will learn that logarithms are the inverses of exponential functions. You will use logarithms to solve exponential equations.

**By the end of this investigation, you will be able to answer questions like these.**

1. What are some reasons to use logarithms?
2. What is a logarithmic scale and when do you use it?
3. If you invest \$1000 at 6% interest, compounded annually, how many years will it take until your money grows to \$10,000?

**You will learn how to**

- evaluate logarithms of any base using a calculator
- use logarithms to solve exponential equations
- graph logarithmic functions

**You will develop these habits and skills:**

- Reason logically from the definition of a logarithmic function and the laws of exponents to develop the laws of logarithms.
- Visualize the graph of a logarithmic function from the graph of the corresponding exponential function.
- Convert flexibly and strategically between logarithmic form and exponential form, and choose the best form to solve problems.

The Krumbein scale is a logarithmic scale used to classify the size of particles. A boulder with diameter 256 mm or greater has a scale value of −8 or less.

# 8.06 Getting Started

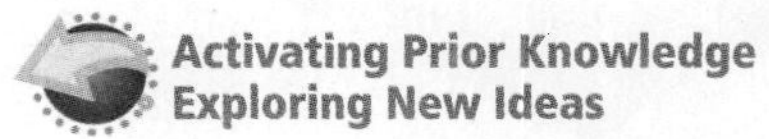


In this lesson, you will investigate a function on your calculator called LOG. There may be a LOG key on your calculator. If there is not, look in your calculator's function library. You use the notation $\log x$ for this function.

Although you use parentheses in $f(x)$ function notation, the parentheses are optional for the log function. You can write $\log(x)$ or $\log x$. You still must use parentheses when needed to avoid confusion, for example in expressions such as $\log(x + 1)$.

## For You to Explore

1. Use your calculator to find the output when you use the LOG key for each integer input from 0 to 10. Copy and complete the table below. Record each output to four decimal places.

| $x$ | $\log x$ |
|---|---|
| 0 | ■ |
| 1 | ■ |
| 2 | ■ |
| 3 | ■ |
| 4 | ■ |
| 5 | ■ |
| 6 | ■ |
| 7 | ■ |
| 8 | ■ |
| 9 | ■ |
| 10 | ■ |

2. Find the value of $\log 2 + \log 3$ to four decimal places.
3. **a.** Calculate $\log 2 + \log 6$.

   **b.** Calculate $\log 3 + \log 4$.

   **c.** Calculate $\log 3 + \log 2 + \log 2$.

   **d.** Find the number $x$ such that $\log x = \log 2 + \log 6$.
4. Estimate each result using the table from Problem 1 and any patterns you have seen so far. Then use a calculator to confirm the answer.

   **a.** $\log 15$ **b.** $\log 24$ **c.** $\log 36$ **d.** $\log 63$
5. Find a rule for calculating $\log MN$ in terms of $\log M$ and $\log N$. (*Hint:* Refer to the results from Problem 4.)
6. Estimate each result using the table from Problem 1 and any patterns you have seen so far. Then use a calculator to confirm the answer.

   **a.** $\log 16$ **b.** $\log 32$ **c.** $\log 64$ **d.** $\log 2^{10}$ **e.** $\log 3^5$
7. Find a rule for calculating $\log M^p$ in terms of $p$ and $\log M$. (*Hint:* Refer to the results from Problem 6.)
8. **Write About It** Explain how you can use the result from Problem 7 and the table from Problem 1 to estimate $\log \frac{1}{8}$.
9. Determine the domain and range of the function $x \mapsto \log x$.
10. **Take It Further** Use the rules that govern the function $x \mapsto \log x$ to find the solution to the following equation.

$$2^x = 5$$

## Exercises Practicing Habits of Mind

### On Your Own

**11.** You have seen that $\log 10 = 1$. Now calculate each of the following values.

**a.** $\log 10^2$ **b.** $\log 10^3$ **c.** $\log 10^6$
**d.** $\log 10^{10}$ **e.** $\log 10^{-3}$

Try evaluating these expressions without using a calculator.

**12.** Calculate each value.

**a.** $10^{\log 2}$ **b.** $10^{\log 3}$ **c.** $10^{\log 6}$
**d.** $10^{\log 10}$ **e.** $10^{\log -3}$

**13.** Describe the relationship between the functions $x \mapsto \log x$ and $x \mapsto 10^x$. Give examples.

**14.** Solve each equation for $x$.

**a.** $\log \frac{5}{4} + \log 4 = \log x$ **b.** $\log \frac{7}{3} + \log 3 = \log x$
**c.** $\log \frac{6}{17} + \log 17 = \log x$ **d.** $\log x + \log 2 = \log 5$
**e.** $\log x + \log 7 = \log 3$ **f.** $\log x = \log 11 - \log 4$

**15.** Find a rule for calculating $\log \frac{M}{N}$ in terms of $\log M$ and $\log N$.

Refer to the results from Exercise 14.

**16.** On the same axes, sketch the graphs of $f(x) = 3^x$ and its inverse function.

**17.** On the same axes, sketch the graphs of $f(x) = \log x$ and its inverse function.

**18.** Suppose $\log(A) = 1.6$ and $\log(B) = 2.7$. Find each value.

**a.** $\log AB$ **b.** $\log A^2$ **c.** $\log \frac{1}{A}$
**d.** $\log \frac{B}{A}$ **e.** $\log AB^2$ **f.** $\log \sqrt{A}$

### Maintain Your Skills

**19.** Find a pair of consecutive integers $j$ and $k$ that satisfy each inequality.

- $j < \log 7 < k$
- $j < \log 70 < k$
- $j < \log 7000 < k$
- $j < \log 143{,}265 < k$

# 8.07 Defining Logarithms

Until now, you had to solve an equation such as $2^x = 5$ by trial and error. Knowledge that the graph of $y = 2^x$ is increasing can help, but you can only closely approximate the solution by making many guesses. This lesson introduces logarithms, including their definition. It gives an example of how you can use logarithms to solve equations, such as $2^x = 5$, where the variable is in the exponent.

In the last investigation, you learned that exponential functions such as $g(x) = 2^x$ are one-to-one, and therefore have inverse functions. The inverse function of an exponential function is a *logarithmic function.*

## Definition

The **logarithmic function** $x \mapsto \log_b x$ is the inverse function of the exponential function $x \mapsto b^x$.

In the last investigation, you used the notation $L_b(x)$ for logarithmic functions. So, you have actually already seen them. This is just a version of the standard notation.

The logarithmic function is often called the logarithm.

The output $\log_b M$ is the exponent $k$ that solves $b^k = M$. In other words, $\log_b M$ is the power to which you have to raise $b$ in order to get $M$. So these two statements are equivalent.

$$b^k = M \Leftrightarrow \log_b M = k$$

The base $b$ must be positive and cannot equal 1 in order for $x \mapsto b^x$ to be an exponential function. Therefore, the same restriction applies to logarithmic functions. The base of a logarithm must be positive and cannot equal 1.

Exponential and logarithmic functions are closely related. You can see this by looking at tables and graphs. Consider the function $f(x) = \log_3 x$ and its inverse function $g(x) = 3^x$. The tables for the functions show reversed pairs of values. This is true for any function and its inverse.

| $x$ | $g(x) = 3^x$ | $x$ | $f(x) = \log_3 x$ |
|---|---|---|---|
| $-1$ | $\frac{1}{3}$ | $\frac{1}{3}$ | $-1$ |
| 0 | 1 | 1 | 0 |
| 1 | 3 | 3 | 1 |
| 2 | 9 | 9 | 2 |
| 3 | 27 | 27 | 3 |

The two graphs are reflections of each other over the line with equation $y = x$.

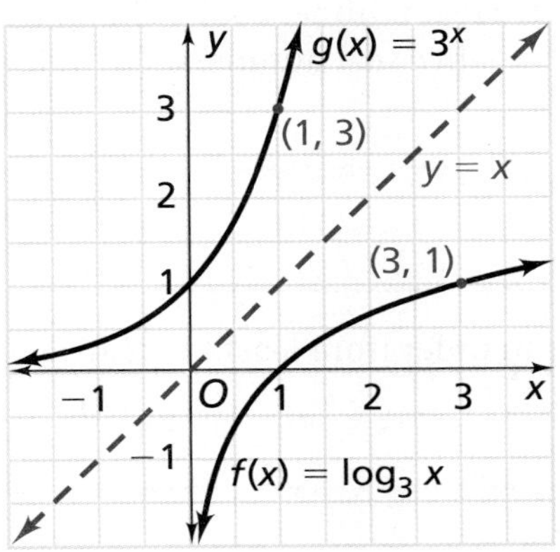

## For You to Do

1. Explain why $\log_3 9 = 2$. Find $\log_3 \frac{1}{9}$ and $\log_3 81$.

### *Facts and Notation*

**The expression log *x* without a base generally refers to base 10. This is the common logarithm. In this course, if the base is not given for a logarithm, assume the base is 10.**

Not all books or software use log *x* to mean base 10.

## Example

**Problem** Find the exact value of each expression, if possible. Otherwise, give an approximation.

**a.** $\log_5 26$ **b.** $\log \frac{1}{10}$ **c.** $\log_4 32$ **d.** $\log_3 -1$

**Solution** For each expression, write an equivalent expression involving an exponent.

**a.** If $\log_5 26 = x$, then $5^x = 26$. You cannot find the value of $\log_5 26$ exactly. It is a little greater than 2, since $5^2 = 25$.

**b.** If $\log \frac{1}{10} = x$, then $10^x = \frac{1}{10}$. You can solve the equation exactly, since $\frac{1}{10}$ is an exact power of 10. The value of $\log \frac{1}{10}$ is exactly $-1$.

**c.** If $\log_4 32 = x$, then $4^x = 32$. Both 4 and 32 are powers of 2, so you can find $x$ exactly.

$$\begin{aligned} 4^x &= 32 \\ (2^2)^x &= 2^5 \\ 2^{2x} &= 2^5 \\ 2x &= 5 \\ x &= \frac{5}{2} \end{aligned}$$

The value of $\log_4 32$ is exactly $\frac{5}{2}$.

**d.** If $\log_3 -1 = x$, then $3^x = -1$. This is impossible, since the range of the function $g(x) = 3^x$ is positive real numbers only. That means that the domain of $f(x) = \log_3 x$ is positive real numbers. The value of $\log_3 -1$ does not exist.

**Remember...**

In this course, if no base is given for a logarithm, assume the base is 10.

Look at the graphs of $f(x) = \log_3 x$ and $g(x) = 3^x$ on the previous page. You can use either graph to show that $\log_3 -1$ does not exist.

## For You to Do

2. Put the following numbers in order from least to greatest.

$$\log_{11} 10,\ \log_7 8,\ \log_5 1,\ \log_3 10,\ \log_2 \frac{1}{4}$$

## Developing Habits of Mind

**Establish a process.** Now you can write the solution to $2^x = 5$ using logarithms.

$$\text{If } 2^x = 5, \text{ then } x = \log_2 5.$$

This is useful because it gives an expression for the exact value of $x$, just as $\sqrt{5}$ is one of the exact solutions of $x^2 = 5$. This process happens frequently in mathematics. You have a useful function, such as the inverse of $x \mapsto 2^x$, that you cannot express in terms of the standard functions at your disposal. So, you invent a new name for this function, in this case $\log_2$. You incorporate it into the toolkit of standard functions. You study its behavior, build it into calculators and computers, and use it until it becomes as familiar as $x \mapsto \sqrt{x}$.

You can find an approximate value for an expression such as $\log_2 5$ by finding other nearby logarithmic outputs with exact values you know. For example, $\log_2 4 = 2$, so $\log_2 5$ must be a bit more than 2.

But this does not help find the value of $\log_2 5$ accurately. Calculators can work with logarithms, but many can only use those with base 10. What can you do? You can argue as follows: Suppose $\log 2 = c$ and $\log 5 = d$. Then

$$10^c = 2 \text{ and } 10^d = 5$$

If $\log_2 5 = x$, then $2^x = 5$ and

$$(10^c)^x = 10^d$$

or

$$10^{cx} = 10^d$$

But then, since exponential functions are one-to-one, you have

$$cx = d$$
$$x = \frac{d}{c} = \frac{\log 5}{\log 2}$$

This is another way to write $x = \log_2 5$. This is a way that calculators can calculate the value of $x$.

$$x = \log_2 5 = \frac{\log 5}{\log 2} \approx \frac{0.6990}{0.3010} \approx 2.322$$

By using logarithms, you can quickly solve equations that were once unsolvable to any degree of accuracy except by trial and error.

Use the logarithm template to work in any positive base. See the TI-Nspire Handbook, p. 817.

If you carry out the steps above in general for any base, you end up with a useful theorem.

### Theorem 8.4 Change-of-Base Rule

If $b, x, y > 0$, and $b, x \neq 1$. then

$$\log_x y = \frac{\log_b y}{\log_b x}$$

You will prove this theorem in the next lesson. The Developing Habits of Mind section on the previous page gives the proof for a specific case.

When working with a calculator, the choice $b = 10$ is often the most practical. The change-of-base rule is the reason why every calculator does not need to have a way to work with logarithms of other bases.

### Summary Properties of Logarithmic functions

A logarithmic function $f: \mathbb{R}^+ \to \mathbb{R}$ is defined as $f(x) = \log_b x$.

- The base $b$ must be positive and not 1.
- The domain of $f$ is $\mathbb{R}^+$, positive real numbers.
- The range of $f$ is all real numbers.
- The graph of $y = f(x)$ has one $x$-intercept at (1, 0) and no $y$-intercepts.
- The graph of $y = f(x)$ is increasing when $b > 1$ and decreasing when $0 < b < 1$.

## Exercises Practicing Habits of Mind

### Check Your Understanding

**1. a.** Sketch the graphs of $f(x) = \log_2 x$ and its inverse on the same axes.

**b.** What is the inverse of $f(x) = \log_2 x$?

**2.** Which of these statements is true?

**A.** $\log_2 9 = 3$ **B.** $\log_{16} 4 = 2$

**C.** $\log_5 10 > \log_5 9$ **D.** $\log_4 0 = 1$

**3.** Find each value.

**a.** $\log_4 2$ **b.** $\log_4 2 + \log_4 32$ **c.** $\log_4 64$

**d.** $\log_9 27$ **e.** $\log_9 27 + \log_9 3$ **f.** $\log_9 81$

Go Online
www.successnetplus.com

4. **Write About It** Explain why $\log_b 0$ does not exist, no matter what the base is.

5. Put these expressions in order from least to greatest.

$$\log_4 18, \log 99, \log_2 0.1, \log_{100} 10, \log_{73} 1, \log_5 \tfrac{1}{5}, \log_2 18$$

6. Suppose $\log_b 9 = 4$ for some base $b$.
   a. Write an equation involving $b$ that does not include a logarithm.
   b. Find the exact value of $b$.

7. Find the value of $3^{\log_3 75}$.

8. Suppose $\log_b 2 = 1.35$ and $\log_b 3 = 2.14$, to two decimal places. Evaluate each expression without finding the value of $b$.
   a. $b^{1.35}$
   b. $b^{2.14}$
   c. $b^{3.49}$
   d. $b^{6.42}$
   e. $\log_b 6$
   f. $\log_b 27$

9. Use the method from the Developing Habits of Mind section to find the solution to $4^x = 25$ to three decimal places.

10. **Take It Further** The value of log 20,000 to four decimal places is 4.3010. Traditionally, the value 4.3010 is considered as two pieces—the characteristic 4, which is the greatest integer less than the number, and the mantissa .3010, which is the decimal part of the number. Experiment to figure out how to interpret these two pieces. For example, if a number $M$ has $\log M = 3.6435$, what does the characteristic 3 tell you about $M$? What does the mantissa .6435 tell you about $M$?

Sometimes, people write the mantissa without the decimal point.

## On Your Own

11. Explain why $\log_b b = 1$ for any base $b$.

12. Explain why $\log_b 1 = 0$ for any base $b$.

13. Suppose $b^x = M$.
   a. If $b^y = M^2$, what is the relationship between $y$ and $x$?
   b. Find the missing exponent in the equation below.

$$b^{(\blacksquare)} = M^{10}$$

   c. Explain why this statement is true.

$$\log_b M^2 = 2 \log_b M$$

14. **Standardized Test Prep** Which of these points is on the graph of $f(x) = \log x$?
   A. (0, 1)
   B. (100, 2)
   C. (100, 10)
   D. (2, 0.3)

The equation $\log_2 \frac{a}{b} = n$ relates the frequencies $a$ and $b$ of two notes that are $n$ octaves apart.

15. a. Sketch the graph of $f(x) = \log x$. Include the coordinates of three points on the graph.

b. Sketch the graph of the inverse function $f^{-1}$ on the same axes.

c. Find the domain and range of $f$ and the domain and range of $f^{-1}$.

d. What is the inverse function of $f(x) = \log x$?

Go Online
www.successnetplus.com

16. Use the change-of-base rule and the LOG key on your calculator to find each value to three decimal places.

a. $\log_4 18$ b. $\log_2 0.1$ c. $\log_{73} 1$

d. $\log_1 9$ e. $\log_3 7$ f. $\log_9 49$

17. Find each value.

Try to do this without using a calculator!

a. $\log_2 \frac{1}{8}$ b. $\log_2 8$ c. $\log_4 16$

d. $\log_4 \frac{1}{16}$ e. $\log_{\frac{1}{2}} 8$ f. $\log_{\frac{1}{4}} \frac{1}{16}$

18. Prove each statement using the definition of logarithm.

a. If $\log_b M = k$, then $\log_b \frac{1}{M} = -k$.

b. $\log_b M = \log_{\frac{1}{b}} \frac{1}{M}$ for any valid base $b$ and $M > 0$.

19. **Take It Further** Exercise 16 suggests that $\log_3 7 = \log_9 49$. Generalize this fact. Then prove it using the definition of logarithm.

20. **What's Wrong Here?** Sharon says there should be two solutions for $b$ in Exercise 6. Sharon explains, "I rewrote the log equation as $b^4 = 9$. Since it's an even exponent, there are two real numbers $b$ that make it true: $b$ is close to plus or minus 1.73. Actually, now that I think about it, I don't need a decimal, it's $\sqrt{3}$ that works. So $b = \pm\sqrt{3}$."

There is only one correct value of $b$. Explain.

## Maintain Your Skills

21. Find each value.

a. $\log_4 2$ b. $\log_2 4$ c. $\log_9 27$

d. $\log_{27} 9$ e. $\log_2 32$ f. $\log_{32} 2$

g. A calculator gives the value of $\log_{10} 2$ as approximately 0.3010. Use this to approximate the value of $\log_2 10$.

22. Find each number to three decimal places.

a. $\log 7.3$ b. $\log 73$

c. $\log 730$ d. $\log (7.3 \times 10^6)$

e. Find $\log 300{,}000$ to four decimal places using the table from Exercise 1 of Lesson 8.06.

# 8.08 Laws of Logarithms

Review the laws of exponents.

### *Laws of Exponents*

**Let base $b > 0$, $b \neq 1$, and $x$ and $y$ be real numbers.**

*The Fundamental Law of Exponents*

- $b^{x+y} = b^x \cdot b^y$

*Corollaries*

- $b^{x-y} = \frac{b^x}{b^y}$
- $b^{xy} = (b^x)^y$

In this lesson you will learn the laws of logarithms, which are restatements of the laws of exponents.

## For You to Do

Let $b^x = M$ and $b^y = N$.

1. Find $b^{x+y}$ in terms of $M$ and $N$.
2. Find $b^{x-y}$ in terms of $M$ and $N$.
3. Find $b^{px}$ in terms of $M$ and $p$.

The results from Problems 1–3 follow from the laws of exponents. For example,

$$\text{If } b^x = M \text{ and } b^y = N\text{, then } b^{x+y} = MN.$$

You can rewrite each of the three equations in the above statement, using the definition of logarithm.

$$\text{If } \log_b M = x \text{ and } \log_b N = y\text{, then } \log_b MN = x + y.$$

Add the first two statements.

$$\log_b M + \log_b N = x + y$$

Now you have two expressions for $x + y$, so they must be equal.

$$\log_b M + \log_b N = \log_b MN$$

You can restate each of the three laws of exponents in terms of logarithms. This gives you the laws of logarithms.

## *Laws of Logarithms*

**Let base $b > 0$, $b \neq 1$ and $M$ and $N$ be positive real numbers.**

***The Fundamental Law of Logarithms***

- $\log_b MN = \log_b M + \log_b N$

***Corollaries***

- $\log_b \frac{M}{N} = \log_b M - \log_b N$
- $\log_b M^p = p \log_b M$

In other words, a logarithm $g(x) = \log_b x$ satisfies the functional equation $g(xy) = g(x) + g(y)$.

You can prove the laws of logarithms with arguments like the one above, or a set of statements like this proof of the third law.

**Proof** Let $\log_b M = x$. Then

| | |
|---|---|
| $b^x = M$ | Convert the form. |
| $(b^x)^p = M^p$ | Build $M^p$. |
| $b^{px} = M^p$ | Use a law of exponents. |
| $\log_b M^p = px$ | Convert the form. |
| $\log_b M^p = p \log_b M$ | Substitute for $x$. |

*Convert the form* means to change from exponent notation to logarithm notation, or vice versa.

The three laws of logarithms provide the means to solve many equations that you previously had to solve by trial and error.

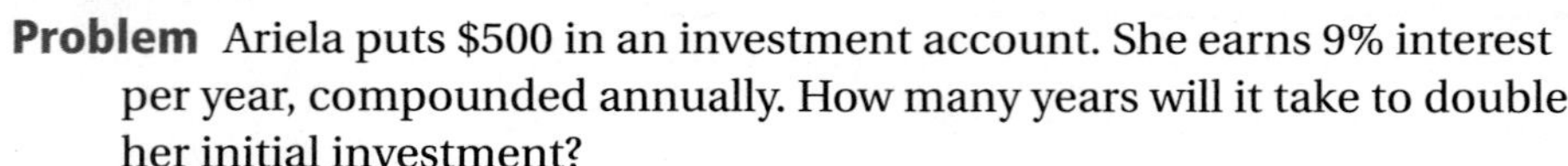

## Example 1

**Problem** Ariela puts \$500 in an investment account. She earns 9% interest per year, compounded annually. How many years will it take to double her initial investment?

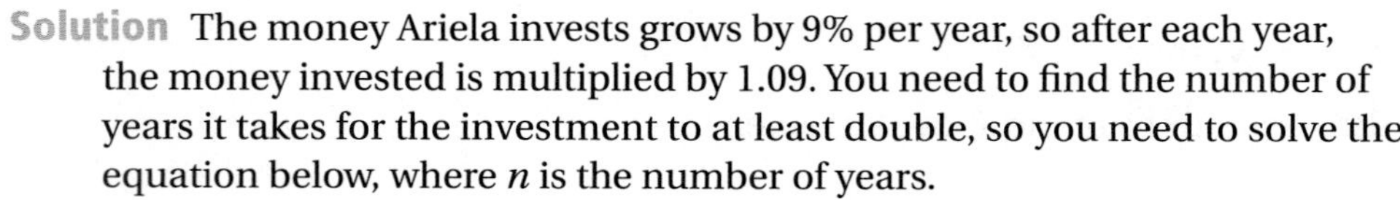

**Solution** The money Ariela invests grows by 9% per year, so after each year, the money invested is multiplied by 1.09. You need to find the number of years it takes for the investment to at least double, so you need to solve the equation below, where $n$ is the number of years.

$$1000 = 500 \cdot 1.09^n$$

Apply the laws of logarithms to find $n$.

**Method 1** Divide through by 500. Then find the base-10 logarithm of each side.

$$\begin{aligned} 1000 &= 500 \cdot 1.09^n \\ 2 &= 1.09^n \\ \log 2 &= \log 1.09^n \\ \log 2 &= n \log 1.09 \\ \frac{\log 2}{\log 1.09} &= n \\ 8.043 &\approx n \end{aligned}$$

Why do you find the base-10 logarithm, and not some other base?

**Method 2** Apply the base-10 logarithm first. Then apply the laws of logarithms.

$$\begin{aligned}
1000 &= 500 \cdot 1.09^n \\
\log 1000 &= \log (500 \cdot 1.09^n) \\
\log 1000 &= \log 500 + \log 1.09^n \\
\log 1000 &= \log 500 + n \log 1.09 \\
\log 1000 - \log 500 &= n \log 1.09 \\
\frac{\log 1000 - \log 500}{\log 1.09} &= n \\
8.043 &\approx n
\end{aligned}$$

Either equation produces the solution $n \approx 8.043$, but this is not the correct answer. Ariela's account compounds annually, so after the end of the eighth year, there is no further interest paid until the ninth year is complete. It will take 9 years to at least double her initial investment, even though the account is very close to \$1000 after 8 years.

The balance at the end of 8 years is $500 \cdot 1.09^8 \approx 996.28$. That is not quite enough.

## For Discussion

**4.** The two methods generate two different expressions for $n$.

Method 1 $n = \dfrac{\log 2}{\log 1.09}$ Method 2 $n = \dfrac{\log 1000 - \log 500}{\log 1.09}$

Is there a way to show these are equivalent using the laws of logarithms? Explain.

## Developing Habits of Mind

**Use a different process to get the same answer.** Method 1 above solves the equation $2 = 1.09^n$ to get $n = \frac{\log 2}{\log 1.09}$. But the definition of logarithms gives another solution: $n = \log_{1.09} 2$. So, you can write the following equation.

$$\log_{1.09} 2 = \frac{\log 2}{\log 1.09}$$

This is an example of the change-of-base rule.

$$\log_x y = \frac{\log_b y}{\log_b x}$$

Here is a quick proof of the change-of-base rule. Let $\log_x y = k$. Then $x^k = y$. Find the base-$b$ logarithm of each side.

$$\begin{aligned}
x^k &= y \\
\log_b x^k &= \log_b y \\
k \log_b x &= \log_b y \\
k &= \frac{\log_b y}{\log_b x}
\end{aligned}$$

Then, since you also know $\log_x y = k$, the proof is complete.

**Habits of Mind**

**Look for relationships.** Note that these are the same steps you use to solve a problem involving actual numbers. So your work with numbers basically provides the proof.

Fractions such as $\frac{\log 2}{\log 1.09}$ lead to one of the most common mistakes made with logarithms. It is tempting to look at the corollary

$$\log_b \frac{M}{N} = \log_b M - \log_b N$$

and say that it applies to a fraction like $\frac{\log 2}{\log 1.09}$, so that

$$\frac{\log 2}{\log 1.09} = \log 2 - \log 1.09$$

This is incorrect reasoning. It is also incorrect to cancel the word *log* from the top and bottom of a fraction. It is generally not true that $\frac{\log M}{\log N}$ is equal to $\frac{M}{N}$.

When you solve equations that involve logarithms, it is important to check the solutions for validity. The logarithmic function is only defined for positive real numbers.

## Example 2

**Problem** Find all values of $x$ that solve the equation

$$\log(x + 7) + \log(x + 22) = 2$$

**Solution** First, rewrite 2 using a logarithm. The base is not given, so by convention it is 10. Since $10^2 = 100$, you have $\log 100 = 2$.

$$\log(x + 7) + \log(x + 22) = \log 100$$

Then use one of the laws of logarithms.

$$\begin{aligned} \log(x + 7) + \log(x + 22) &= \log 100 \\ \log((x + 7)(x + 22)) &= \log 100 \\ (x + 7)(x + 22) &= 100 \end{aligned}$$

Now solve by factoring or using the quadratic formula.

$$\begin{aligned} (x + 7)(x + 22) &= 100 \\ x^2 + 29x + 154 &= 100 \\ x^2 + 29x + 54 &= 0 \\ (x + 2)(x + 27) &= 0 \end{aligned}$$

This equation has two solutions, $x = -2$ and $x = -27$. However, consider the domain of the logarithmic function. It can only accept positive inputs. Letting $x = -27$ in the original equation gives the result

$$\log -20 + \log -5 = 2$$

This makes no sense. Neither $\log -20$ nor $\log -5$ exists. So you reject the solution $x = -27$. The solution $x = -2$ is still valid. It gives the result

$$\log 5 + \log 20 = 2$$

All the inputs to the logarithmic function are positive.

Note that $x$ may still be negative. It is the inputs to the logarithmic function that must be positive. Reject any solutions that result in negative inputs to a logarithm.

## *Laws and Properties of Logarithms*

**Let base $b > 0$, $b \neq 1$ and $M$ and $N$ be positive real numbers.**

*The Fundamental Law of Logarithms*

- $\log_b MN = \log_b M + \log_b N$

*Corollaries*

- $\log_b \frac{M}{N} = \log_b M - \log_b N$
- $\log_b M^p = p \log_b M$

*Other Properties*

- change-of-base rule: $\log_M N = \frac{\log_b N}{\log_b M}$, if $M \neq 1$
- $\log_b 1 = 0$ and $\log_b b = 1$
- $\log_b \frac{1}{N} = -\log_b N$
- $\log_b M = \log_b N \Leftrightarrow M = N$, since the logarithm function is one-to-one.
- $\log_b(b^x) = x = b^{\log_b x}$, since the logarithm and the exponential are inverse functions.

## Exercises *Practicing Habits of Mind*

### Check Your Understanding

1. Let $\log_b M = 2$ and $\log_b N = 5$. Calculate each value.

   **a.** $\log_b M^2$ **b.** $\log_b MN$ **c.** $\log_b \frac{M^3}{N}$

   **d.** $\log_b (MN)^3$ **e.** $\log_b \sqrt{MN}$

2. Find the value of this product.

$$\log_2 3 \cdot \log_3 4 \cdot \log_5 6 \cdot \log_6 25$$

See if you can do this one without a calculator.

3. **What's Wrong Here?** Explain what is wrong with the reasoning in the calculation below. Then determine the correct value.

$$\frac{\log_2 32}{\log_2 8} = \log_2 32 - \log_2 8 = 5 - 3 = 2$$

4. Prove the second law of logarithms in two ways.

$$\log_b \frac{M}{N} = \log_b M - \log_b N$$

a. Use the definition.

$$b^x = M \Leftrightarrow \log_b M = x$$

b. Use the Fundamental Law of Logarithms.

$$\log_b MN = \log_b M + \log_b N$$

5. Prove each statement.

a. $\log_b 1 = 0$ b. $\log_b b = 1$ c. $\log_b \frac{1}{N} = -\log_b N$

6. Due to inflation, the cost of a Big Burger grows by 3% every year. This year a Big Burger costs $3.99.

a. Write a rule for the function $C(n)$, where $C(n)$ is the cost of a Big Burger $n$ years from now.

b. Using logarithms, find how long, to the nearest year, it will take for the cost of a Big Burger to reach $20.

7. Find the solution to this equation.

$$2 \cdot 5^x = 7$$

Give an exact answer. Then approximate the answer to three decimal places.

The solutions to the next few exercises will include the logarithmic function in some way.

8. Find the solution to this equation in terms of the constants $a$, $b$, and $c$.

$$a \cdot b^x = c$$

9. Find the solution to this equation.

$$2 \cdot 5^x = 7 \cdot 3^x$$

Give an exact answer. Then approximate the answer to three decimal places.

10. In terms of the constants $a$, $b$, $c$, and $d$, find the solution to this equation.

$$a \cdot b^x = c \cdot d^x$$

11. In Exercise 21 in Lesson 8.04, you saw that the solution to the equation $6^x = 35$ is the reciprocal of the solution to $35^x = 6$. Use logarithms to explain why this makes sense.

Can you explain it without using logarithms?

12. Find all solutions of each equation.

a. $\log x + \log (x + 1) = \log 6$

b. $\log (x^2 + x) = \log 6$

c. $\log 2x - \log x = \log 2$

d. $\log_2 (x - 3) + \log_2 (x + 3) = 4$

e. $\log_2 (x - 3) - \log_2 (x + 3) = 4$

13. Take It Further Suppose $\log 2 = 0.3$ exactly and $\log 3 = 0.5$ exactly. Assume both of these equations are true and prove that $0 = 1$.

14. Take It Further Recall the Rule of 72 from Lesson 8.05, Exercise 17.

**Rule of 72** To find the number of years it takes to double an investment's value, divide 72 by the annual percentage interest rate.

Explain why the Rule of 72 gives fairly accurate results for relatively low interest rates (for example, from 6% to 12%).

## On Your Own

15. Which is greater, $\log_5 135$ or $\log_7 300$? Explain completely without relying on a calculator answer.

16. Copy and complete this table for $f(x) = \log_3 x$. Use a calculator and the change-of-base rule. Give any approximate answers to four decimal places.

Even if your calculator can work with a base-3 logarithm, use the change-of-base rule here.

| $x$ | $\log_3 x$ |
|---|---|
| 1 | 0 |
| 2 | 0.6309 |
| 3 | ■ |
| 4 | ■ |
| 5 | ■ |
| 6 | ■ |
| 7 | ■ |
| 8 | ■ |
| 9 | ■ |

17. The value of $\log_3 7 + \log_9 81$ is between which two integers?

Try this one without a calculator.

**A.** 0 and 1
**B.** 1 and 2
**C.** 2 and 3
**D.** 3 and 4

18. Suppose $\log_b 297{,}736 = 7$. Find the base $b$.

19. Let $a = \log 2$ and $b = \log 3$. Find each value in terms of a and $b$.

a. $\log 6$
b. $\log 1.5$
c. $\log 27$
d. $\log 200$
e. $\log \sqrt{3}$

20. Each value below is between 1 and 2. Put them in order from least to greatest.

$$\log_3 7, \log_9 50, \log 60, \log_8 40, \log_{12} 83, \log_2 3.44$$

Be sure to do this exercise with a calculator.

21. **What's Wrong Here?** Explain what is wrong with the reasoning in the calculation below. Then determine the correct value.

$$\log 100 + \log_2 8 = \log 800 \approx 2.903$$

22. Use logarithms to find the solution to the equation $2^x = \frac{1}{1{,}000{,}000}$ to three decimal places.

23. Let $L(h) = 100 \cdot 0.5^h$.

   a. If $L(h) = 50$, find $h$.

   b. If $L(h) = 20$, find $h$.

   c. If $L(h) = 10$, find $h$. How is the answer here related to your answers in parts (a) and (b)?

   d. If $L(h) = c$, find $h$ in terms of $c$.

   e. If $L(h) = 1$, find $h$. How is the answer here related to your answer in part (d)?

24. **Write About It** Is $(\log x)^2$ the same as $\log x^2$? Explain.

25. Find all solutions to each equation.

   a. $\log_2 x^2 - 5 \log_2 x + 6 = 0$

   b. $(\log_2 x)^2 - 5 \log_2 x + 6 = 0$

   c. **Take It Further** $\log x = 1 + \frac{6}{\log x}$

26. Show that the result $\log_b \frac{1}{N} = -\log_b N$ follows from the second law of logarithms.

27. **Take It Further** The Developing Habits of Mind section, earlier in this lesson, says that it is generally not true that $\frac{\log M}{\log N}$ equals $\frac{M}{N}$. When is it true? Explain.

## Maintain Your Skills

28. **Standardized Test Prep** Which of the following expressions is equal to $\log \frac{xy^2}{z}$?

   A. $\log x + 2 \log y + \log z$

   B. $\log x + 2 \log y - \log z$

   C. $\log z - \log x - 2 \log y$

   D. $2 \log xy - \log z$

29. The government of Justinia reports that the current population is 10 million. The population is growing at 2.5% per year. Experts report the population will keep growing at this rate. Give the number of years it will take for the population to reach each milestone. Round to two decimal places.

**a.** 20 million
**b.** 30 million
**c.** 40 million
**d.** 60 million
**e.** 120 million
**f.** 240 million

So, a sample answer is 16.43 years.

## Historical Perspective

Logarithms used to play a much larger role in second-year algebra courses, because you can use them for arithmetic calculation. Consider the Fundamental Law of Logarithms.

$$\log_b MN = \log_b M + \log_b N$$

You can use it to transform a multiplication problem into an addition problem. To multiply two numbers $M$ and $N$, you can use base-10 logarithms.

This may seem like a much more complicated way to multiply two numbers, but suppose $M$ and $N$ both have five digits. Adding five-digit numbers by hand is much faster than multiplying five-digit numbers by hand. The other laws of logarithms allow you to reduce division to subtraction and exponentiation to multiplication, which you can then reduce further to addition.

For example, here is how to calculate $\frac{6.453}{2.179}$ using logarithms.

- Call the numerator $M = 6.453$ and the denominator $N = 2.179$.
- Calculate $\log M \approx 0.8098$ and $\log N \approx 0.3383$.
- Subtract: $\log M - \log N \approx 0.4715$.
- This is $\log \frac{M}{N}$, so undo the logarithm: $10^{0.4715} \approx 2.961$.

The result at each step has four significant figures, so the answer is correct to four significant figures. Compare that to the task of dividing these decimals by hand. You reduce the division step to subtraction by using the laws of logarithms.

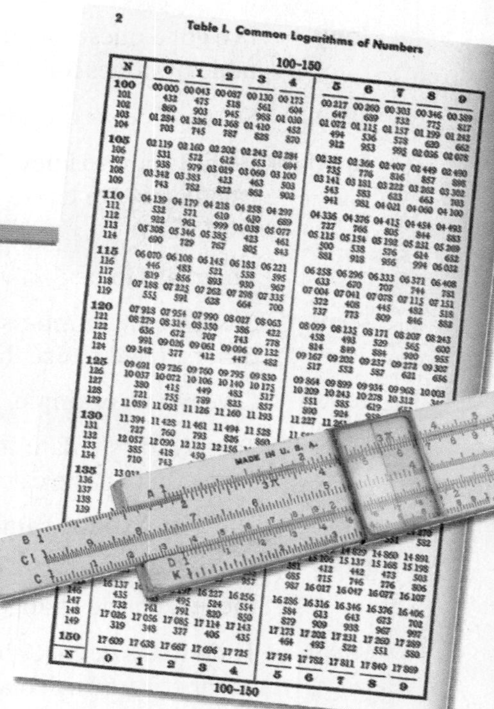


Before the development of pocket calculators, people used logarithm tables and slide rules for complicated arithmetic calculations.

# 8.09 Graphing Logarithmic Functions

This lesson focuses on some properties of the graphs of logarithmic functions. It includes a method for graphing a logarithm for any given base.

## Minds in Action

*Tony wants to know how to graph a logarithmic function.*

**Tony** I've got a question. Exercise 16 in Lesson 8.08 asked us to make a table of values for $f(x) = \log_3 x$. And I can do that.

**Sasha** So what's your question?

**Tony** What I want to know is, how do I graph $y = \log_3 x$ on the graphing calculator? Do I have to just enter all these points as data and live with that?

Assume that Tony's calculator can work with base-10 logarithms only.

**Sasha** There has to be a way. How did you make the table?

**Tony** Some of the numbers I can just fill in, like $\log_3 9 = 2$. For the others, I had to use the change-of-base rule.

**Sasha** Give me an example.

**Tony** Take 7. To calculate $\log_3 7$, I split it so it's $\log 7$ divided by $\log 3$. I type that on the calculator and I get 1.7712.

**Sasha** Did you do it the same way each time?

**Tony** Yes, except the ones that I did in my head. But I could even do those with the change-of-base rule.

**Sasha** Then that's it. That's how you make the graph. Just take your number $x$ and calculate $\log x$ divided by $\log 3$. That works for any number.

**Tony** And I can type that in as a function on the calculator! The function is

$$f(x) = \frac{\log x}{\log 3}$$

You can program this version of Tony's $f(x)$ into your function-modeling language. Define $f(x) = \frac{\log x}{\log 3}$.

*Sasha types in the equation.*

**Sasha** Hey, that fraction worked! And the graph goes through the point (9, 2).

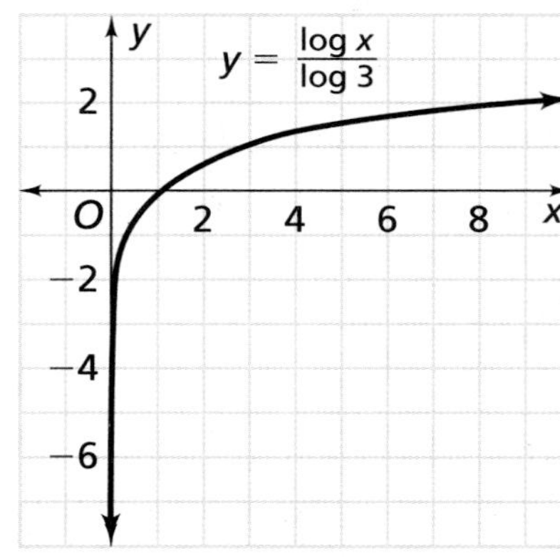

You can graph the logarithm for any base by using the relationship $\log_b x = \frac{\log x}{\log b}$. One interesting consequence of this fact is that the graphs of all logarithmic functions are related to each other by a vertical stretch.

Every one of these functions has the same domain and range. The domain is all positive reals. The range is all real numbers.

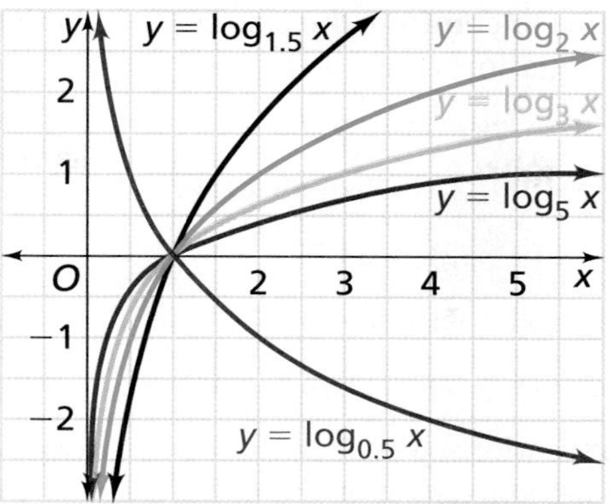


## For You to Do

1. Find and graph a function $f(x) = \log_b x$ with a graph that contains the point $(2, 5)$.

*Hint:* If $y = \log_b x$ contains the point (2, 5), what equation must $b$ solve?

You can use graphs to find the number of solutions of some equations that involve logarithms.

## Example

### Problem

a. How many solutions are there to the equation $\log_3 (x - 2) + \log_3 x = \log_3 63$?

b. Find all values of $x$ that make $\log_3 (x - 2) + \log_3 x = \log_3 63$ true.

### Solution

a. Graph each side of the equation. You can use the equation $y_1 = \frac{\log (x - 2)}{\log 3} + \frac{\log x}{\log 3}$ to graph the left side. The right side is the horizontal line $y_2 = \frac{\log 63}{\log 3}$.

Plot the two graphs on the same axes.

Each solution to the original equation corresponds to an intersection between the two graphs. The graphs intersect once, so there is one solution.

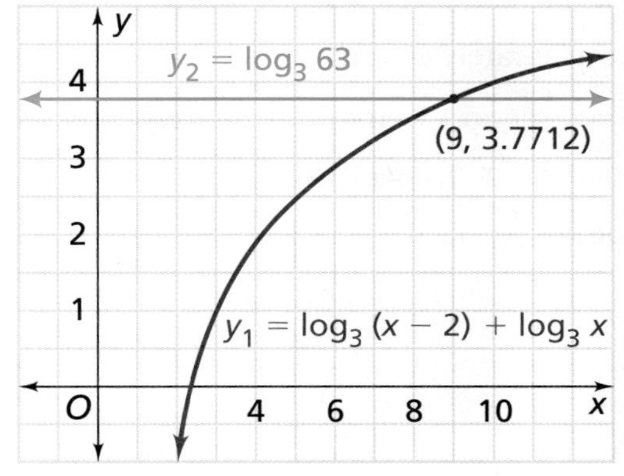


Why is the graph of $y_2 = \frac{\log 63}{\log 3}$ a horizontal line?

**b.** Use the laws of logarithms to combine the expressions on the left side. Then build a quadratic equation.

$$\begin{aligned}
\log_3(x-2) + \log_3 x &= \log_3 63 \\
\log_3(x(x-2)) &= \log_3 63 \\
x(x-2) &= 63 \\
x^2 - 2x - 63 &= 0 \\
(x-9)(x+7) &= 0
\end{aligned}$$

The equation gives two solutions, $x = 9$ and $x = -7$. However, the solution $x = -7$ is invalid, since it leads to negative inputs for the logarithms in the original equation. The only solution is $x = 9$.

## Exercises Practicing Habits of Mind

### Check Your Understanding

**1.** Find all solutions to this equation.

$$\log_2(3x+1) - \log_2(2x-3) = 2$$

**2.** The **LN** key on a calculator also performs logarithms, but not to base 10. So, $\ln x = \log_b x$ for some unknown base $b$.

**a.** Without using a calculator, determine what $\ln 1$ and $\ln 0$ should be. Then verify your results with a calculator.

**b.** Determine the base $b$ as accurately as you can.

**3. a.** Sketch the graphs of $y = \sqrt{x}$ and $y = \log_2 x$ accurately.

**b.** How many numbers $x$ make $\sqrt{x} = \log_2 x$ true?

**4.** As $x$ increases, $\log_2 x$ becomes less than $\sqrt{x}$. Consider the values of $\log_{1.06} x$. Use the graphs of $y = \sqrt{x}$ and $y = \log_{1.06} x$. As $x$ increases, will $\sqrt{x}$ always be less than $\log_{1.06} x$?

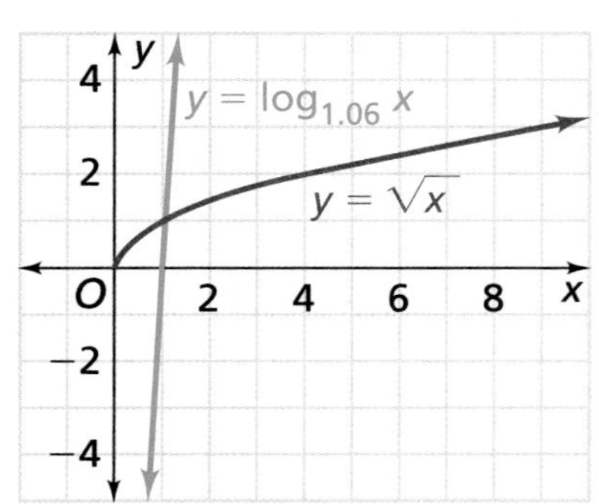


You can locate intersection points on a graph. See the TI-Nspire Handbook, p. 817.

5. As $x$ increases, $\log_2 x$ becomes less than $\sqrt{x}$. Consider the values of $\sqrt[10]{x}$. Use the graphs of $y = \sqrt[10]{x}$ and $y = \log_2 x$.

a. As $x$ increases, will $\sqrt[10]{x}$ always be less than $\log_2 x$?

b. As $x$ increases, will $\sqrt[10]{x}$ always be less than $\log_{1.06} x$?

c. As $x$ increases, will $\log_2 x$ always be less than $\log_{1.06} x$?

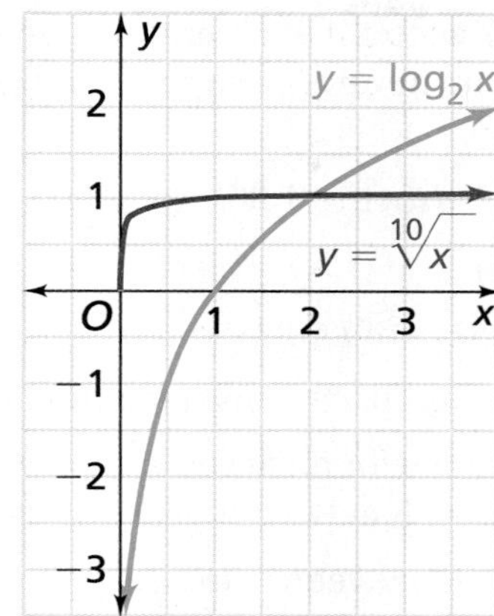


6. Find the number of solutions to each equation.

a. $\log x^2 = 1$

b. $2 \log x = 1$

c. $\log_3 x = \sqrt{x} - 1$

d. $\log_2 x = 2^x$

e. $\log_{1.4} x = 1.4^x$

7. **Take It Further** The graphs of $y = \log_2 x$ and $y = 2^x$ do not intersect, but the graphs of $y = \log_{1.4} x$ and $y = 1.4^x$ do. For some base $b$ such that $b > 1$, the graphs of $y = \log_b x$ and $y = b^x$ intersect exactly once. Find such a value of $b$ and the intersection point of the two graphs as accurately as you can.

## On Your Own

8. Use this detail of the graph of $x \mapsto \log_2 x$ with $x$ between 1.3 and 1.4.

a. Approximate $\log_2 1.383$.

b. Approximate the solution to the equation $\log_2 x = 0.4$.

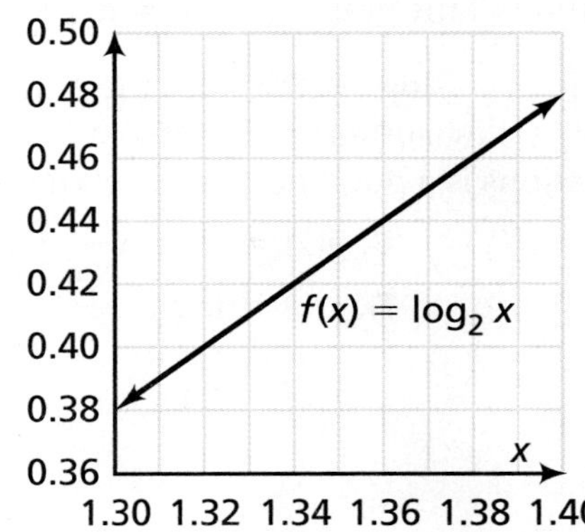


9. Asako says, "According to one of the laws of logarithms, $\log x^2 = 2 \log x$. So the graphs of $f(x) = \log x^2$ and $g(x) = 2 \log x$ should look exactly the same."

Do you agree or disagree with Asako's statement? Explain.

Go Online
www.successnetplus.com

**10.** If you put money in a bank account at 6% interest per year, the function below outputs the factor the money in the account has grown by after $n$ years.

$$D(n) = 1.06^n$$

**a.** Sketch the graph of $D(n)$.

**b.** What is the inverse function of $D(n)$?

**c.** On a graphing calculator, graph the inverse function of $D(n)$.

**d.** How many years does it take for an amount of money to grow to 10 times its initial value if you invest it at 6% per year?

**11.** Let $f(x) = \log_b x$ with base $b$ between 0 and 1.

**a.** Graph an example of one such function.

**b.** Explain why all such functions are decreasing.

**12.** Show that $f(x) = \log_2 x$ is exactly three times greater than $g(x) = \log_8 x$.

**13. a.** Sketch the graph of $y = \log 10^x$. Give another name for a function that is equivalent to $f(x) = \log 10^x$. Explain your reasoning.

**b.** Sketch the graph of $y = 10^{\log x}$. Explain why this graph is not the same as the graph of $y = \log 10^x$.

**14.** Take It Further

**a.** For $a > 0$, show that the graph of $f(x) = a \cdot 3^x$ is a translation of the graph of $g(x) = 3^x$.

Compare with Exercise 22 from Lesson 8.02.

**b.** For numbers $a$ and $b$ such that $a > 0$ and $b > 0$, show that the graph of $f(x) = a \cdot b^x$ is a translation of the graph of $g(x) = b^x$. Assume $b \neq 1$.

**15.** Standardized Test Prep Let $f(x) = \log_4 x$. Suppose the graph of $g(x)$ is a translation of the graph of $f(x)$ two units to the left and one unit down. Which of the following equations is a possible rule for $g(x)$?

**A.** $g(x) = \log_4 (x - 2) + 1$

**B.** $g(x) = \log_4 (x - 2) - 1$

**C.** $g(x) = \log_4 (x + 2) - 1$

**D.** $g(x) = \log_4 (x - 1) - 2$

## Maintain Your Skills

**16.** Sketch each graph on the same axes.

**a.** $y = \log_3 x$ **b.** $y = \log_3 (x - 3)$ **c.** $y = \log_3 (x + 4)$

**d.** $y = \log_3 x - 3$ **e.** $y = \log_3 x + 4$

**f.** Explain why the graph of $y = \log_3 (x - 3)$ is not the same as the graph of $y = \log_3 x - 3$.

## Historical Perspective

In 1938, physicist Frank Benford published a paper describing something he had noticed in scientific data: Numbers started with the digit 1 much more frequently than 2 or 3, and far more frequently than 9. He compiled numeric information from many sources. He found that, on average, just over 30% of numbers started with the digit 1, while fewer than 5% started with the digit 9.

This numeric phenomenon is known as Benford's Law. It works for many sources of data, but not all. For example, it does not work for ZIP codes or telephone numbers, which are assigned to produce an even distribution of initial digits.

So, how do you find the expected frequencies? You use logarithms.

For example, take a number $n$ with a first digit 4. The decimal part of $\log n$ must be between 0.6020 and 0.6990. If Benford's Law is true, then about 9.70% of the numbers observed should start with 4. And this is what actually happens with many sources of data. Numbers starting with 4 are less than one third as common as numbers starting with 1, which occur 30.1% of the time. The diagram at the right shows the relative frequency with which each digit occurs.

Accountants often use Benford's Law in investigating financial fraud. If the data in a financial report do not come close to the frequencies predicted by Benford's Law, they may be dishonest data.

# 8.10 The Logarithmic Scale

You can use different scales for the axes of a graph.

## In-Class Experiment

1. Your teacher will give you four pieces of graph paper with the scales on the axes already marked. On the piece with the standard scales, plot the following graphs. On each other piece, plot only the graphs that are straight lines on that set of axes. (*Hint:* The graphs of nonlinear equations can be straight lines when you plot them on axes with different scales. Try to predict which graphs will be straight lines on each piece of graph paper.)

   **a.** $y = x$
   **b.** $y = x^2$
   **c.** $y = x^3$
   **d.** $y = 2^x$
   **e.** $y = 2 \cdot 3^x$
   **f.** $y = 8 \cdot 0.5^x$
   **g.** $y = \log x$
   **h.** $y = \log_2 x$

When you measure with a ruler, you use a **linear scale** to keep track of the number of inches, centimeters, yards, or other units you measure. You count by adding: 1 inch, 2 inches, 3 inches . . .

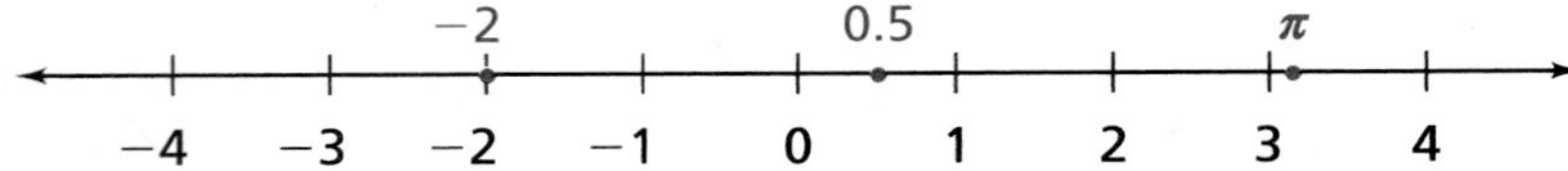


The linear scale is not the only choice. You can also use a **logarithmic scale.** You count by multiplying: 1 unit, 10 units, 100 units, 1000 units . . .

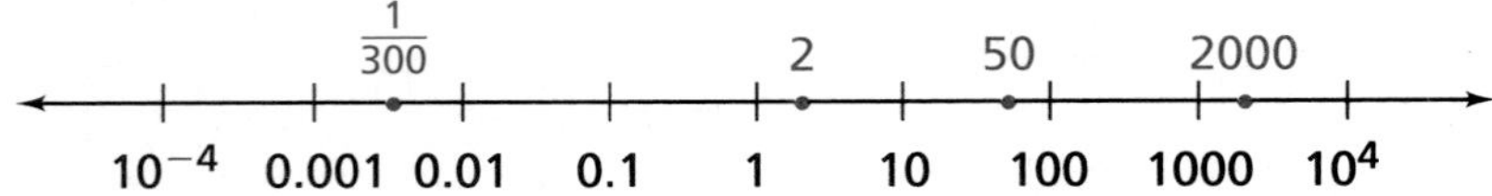


Note that zero and negative numbers do not appear on the logarithmic scale.

You can use a logarithmic scale when working with data that have widely varying values or when relative change is more important than absolute change. Well-known and frequently used logarithmic scales include the pH scale for acidity and the Richter scale for earthquakes.

So, you might consider using a logarithmic scale if a change from 1 to 2 is just as important as a change from 100 to 200. The scale for Benford's Law is logarithmic.

Logarithmic scales are so named because the logarithm outputs of the numbers on the axis increase linearly. For example, the numbers 1, 10, 100, and 1000 are equally spaced. The base-10 logarithms of these numbers are 0, 1, 2, and 3.

## Example

**Problem** The U.S. Census has been taken every 10 years since 1790. It counts the number of people living in the United States. Here are two graphs of the data from the census. One uses a linear scale on both axes. The other uses a logarithmic scale on the *y*-axis.

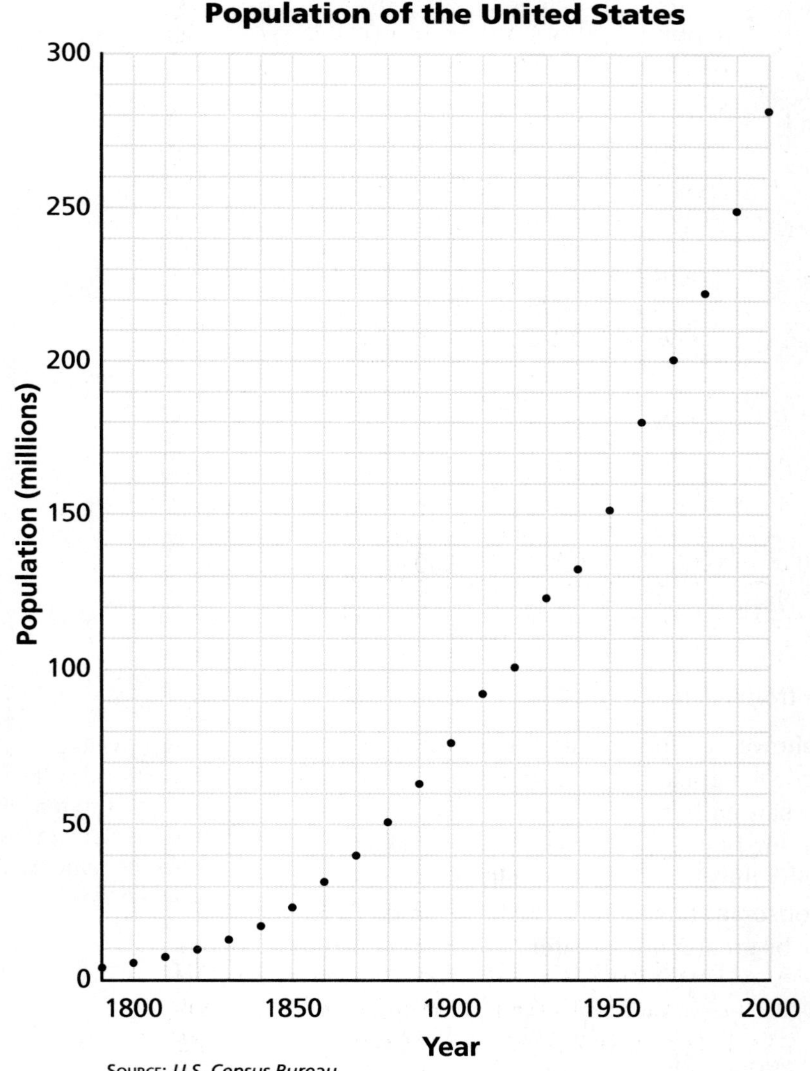

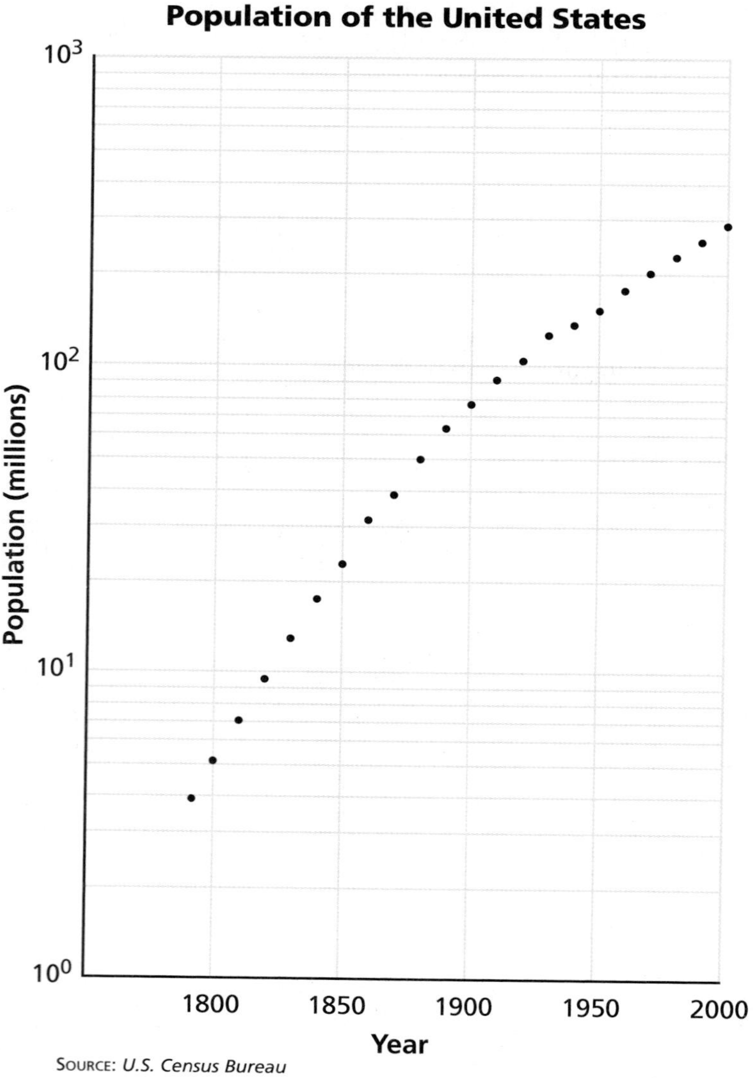


What information can you gather from each graph?

**Solution** The graph on a linear scale shows that the population is growing roughly exponentially, since the graph appears similar to the graphs of exponential growth functions you saw earlier in this chapter. One possible observation is that the population for 1940 appears to be slightly lower than might be expected by following the curve. But generally the curve seems to rise consistently. Other observations include the fact that the U.S. population appears to be growing by greater and greater amounts at each census, at least since 1950.

The graph on a logarithmic scale has two portions that appear to be linear. This means that during these two periods the population increased by the same growth factor every $n$ years. In other words, if you compare two populations $n$ years apart, they will have the same ratio as any other pair of populations $n$ years apart.

**Habits of Mind**

**Detect the key characteristics.** It is important to remember that the two graphs show the same data. Only the way the data are displayed is different.

The noticeable change in the slope occurs at around 1900. The ratio appears to have changed. This suggests that the U.S. population has grown at a slower rate since 1900. Note that this observation is very difficult to make when viewing the data on a linear scale. This is the advantage of working with a logarithmic scale: ratios between successive outputs, whether equal or different, become immediately visible.

You can also use a logarithmic scale on the $x$-axis to show the ratios between successive inputs more clearly.

## For Discussion

2. The linear scale suggests the U.S. population grew by its greatest amount between 1990 and 2000, but the logarithmic scale suggests the population grew more slowly during that decade than in the past. Is this a contradiction? Explain.

You can use a logarithmic scale on the vertical or the horizontal axis, or on both. Some people prefer to say that you are actually graphing the logarithms of the values when you use this scale.

Graph paper with one logarithmic axis is called *semilog* graph paper. Graph paper with two logarithmic axes is *log-log* graph paper.

### Proving the Relationships

The In-Class Experiment and the U.S. Census example both show that when you plot an exponential function using a logarithmic $y$-axis, the function appears linear. For example, this graph is $y = 3 \cdot 2^x$ plotted with a logarithmic scale on the $y$-axis.

$10^2$
$10^1$
(2, 12)
(0, 3)
$10^0$
(−2, 0.75)
$10^{-1}$
$10^{-2}$
−4 −2 0 2 4

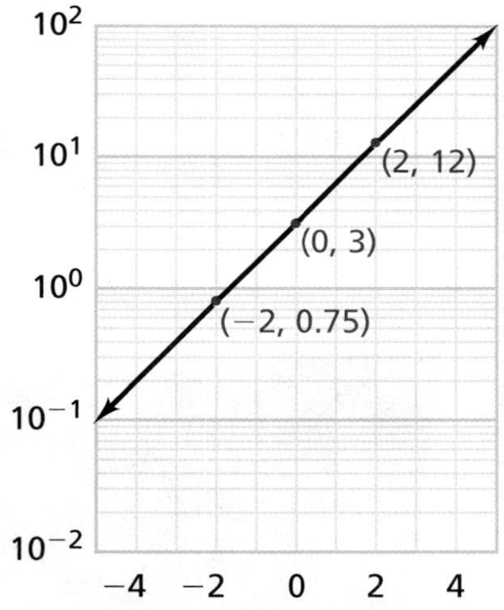

You can prove that the function $y = 3 \cdot 2^x$ should appear as a straight line on a logarithmic scale on the $y$-axis using the laws of logarithms.

## Theorem 8.5

**When you use a logarithmic *y*-axis and a linear *x*-axis, the graph of an exponential function $y = a \cdot b^x$ with $a > 0$ and $b > 0$ appears as a straight line.**

**Proof** Consider any exponential function $y = a \cdot b^x$ with $a > 0$ and $b > 0$. When you use this scale, you display the logarithms of the *y*-values. So, calculate $\log y$ in terms of *b* and *x* using the laws of logarithms.

$$y = a \cdot b^x$$

$$\log y = \log (a \cdot b^x)$$

$$\log y = \log a + \log b^x$$

$$\log y = \log a + x \log b$$

This may not look like much, but remember that $\log a$ and $\log b$ are just numbers. If $\log a = A$ and $\log b = B$, then $\log y = A + Bx$. This is an equation for a line in the plane. The graph of $\log y$ against *x* is linear.

**Remember...**

When making a graph, you choose to graph one thing against another. Here, choosing to graph $\log y$ against *x* gives a different picture than graphing *y* against *x*.

There is an interesting corollary to this theorem. It has to do with two exponential functions graphed on the same set of axes. They appear as lines. Any two lines intersect unless they have the same slope. For example, there is exactly one solution to $2 \cdot 3^x = 8 \cdot 0.5^x$, since they are two lines with different slopes when graphed on this kind of scale. Here is the general statement.

## Corollary 8.5.1

**The graphs of two exponential functions $f_1(x) = a_1 \cdot {b_1}^x$ and $f_2(x) = a_2 \cdot {b_2}^x$, with all $a_i$ and $b_i$ positive, must intersect exactly once unless $b_1 = b_2$.**

This is true no matter what scale you use.

Overall, a logarithmic scale is another way of presenting data, one that stresses proportion instead of magnitude. You can use it to recognize graphically whether a function is exponential or logarithmic, or whether it makes sense to represent a set of data with an exponential or logarithmic function.

The stellar magnitude scale is a logarithmic scale. Brighter stars have lower values on the scale.

## Exercises *Practicing Habits of Mind*

### Check Your Understanding

The following table gives outputs for $\pi(x)$, the number of prime numbers less than or equal to $x$. The third column is a measure of the likelihood of choosing a prime among the integers from 1 to $x$. Out of all the integers from 1 to $x$, one in every $\frac{x}{\pi(x)}$ will be prime.

| $x$ | $\pi(x)$ | $\frac{x}{\pi(x)}$ |
|---|---|---|
| 2 | 1 | 2 |
| 5 | 3 | 1.6667 |
| 10 | 4 | 2.5 |
| 50 | 15 | 3.3333 |
| 100 | 25 | 4 |
| 1000 | 168 | 5.9524 |
| 10,000 | 1229 | 8.1367 |
| 100,000 | 9592 | 10.4254 |
| $10^{10}$ | 455,052,511 | 21.9755 |

For example, $\pi(6) = 3$ for the three primes 2, 3, and 5. This function's name is unrelated to the constant $\pi$ that you know from studying circles. Amazingly, the primes from 1 to 100 million were calculated in the mid 1800s.

1. According to the table, do prime numbers become more or less frequent among larger integers? Explain.
2. Graph $x$ against $\pi(x)$ using logarithmic $x$- and $y$-axes. Is there any observable pattern?
3. Graph $x$ against $\frac{x}{\pi(x)}$ using a logarithmic $x$-axis and a linear $y$-axis. Is there any observable pattern?
4. The graph below shows the closing price of a stock from April 1, 2002, through April 1, 2004. Financial graphs use either linear or logarithmic scales on their vertical axis. Which scale does this graph use? Explain.

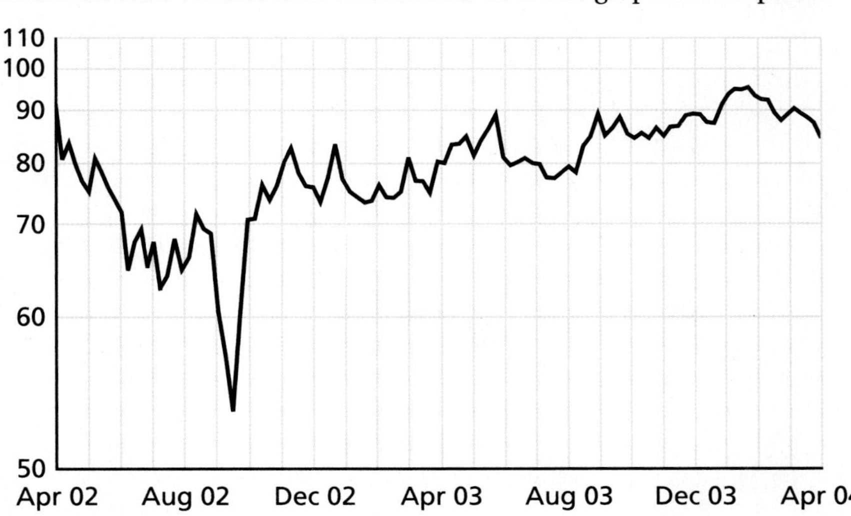

5. a. Use Theorem 8.5 as a model to prove the following result.

   When you use a logarithmic $x$-axis and a linear $y$-axis, the logarithmic function $y = \log_b x$ appears as a straight line.

   b. What is the slope of the line in part (a)? Assume that you use the base-10 logarithm for the $x$-axis.

6. a. Prove the following result.

   When you use a logarithmic $x$-axis and a logarithmic $y$-axis, the power function $y = a \cdot x^b$ appears as a straight line.

   b. What is the slope of the line in part (a)? Assume that you use the base-10 logarithm for both axes.

7. **What's Wrong Here?** Stephanie graphs $y = x^2$ and $y = 10x^2$ on the same piece of graph paper with both axes logarithmic.

   Stephanie says, "Now wait a minute, these look parallel. Parallel lines don't intersect. But I know the graphs of $y = x^2$ and $y = 10x^2$ intersect at the point (0, 0). Shouldn't these intersect too?"

   What happened? Why do the graphs not appear to intersect?

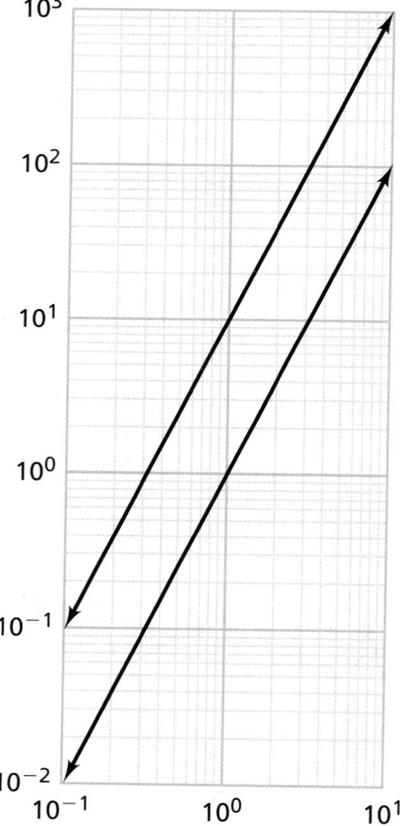

## On Your Own

Go Online
www.successnetplus.com

8. Is $f(x) = \log_2 x$ a one-to-one function? Explain.

9. a. Sketch the graph of $y = x$ on a logarithmic $y$-axis. Describe what the graph looks like.

   b. Sketch the graph of $y = \frac{1}{x}$ on the same axes.

   c. Take It Further Explain how the two graphs are related and why they are related in this way.

10. Find all solutions to each equation.

   a. $\log_3 x = \log_3 7$
   b. $\log_3 x + \log_3 (x + 1) = \log_3 12$
   c. $\log x^2 = 4$
   d. $\log_5 (x + 1) - \log_5 x = 1$

11. Standardized Test Prep Without a calculator, determine which of these four numbers is the greatest.

   A. $\log_4 17$ B. $\log_3 27$ C. $\log_5 117$ D. $\log_2 9$

12. This table includes the frequency for each of the eight A notes on a piano.

| Note | Frequency (Hz) |
|---|---|
| A0 | 27.5 |
| A1 | 55 |
| A2 | 110 |
| A3 | 220 |
| A4 | 440 |
| A5 | 880 |
| A6 | 1760 |
| A7 | 3520 |

Hz (or *hertz*) is a unit measuring cycles per second of a periodic event. In this case, it measures vibrations of a piano string.

Consider the function $F(n)$, where $n$ is the note's octave (0 through 7), and $F(n)$ is the frequency of that note.

   a. Is $F(n)$ an exponential function, a logarithmic function, or neither? Explain.

   b. Graph $F(n)$. Choose the appropriate graph paper to make the graph of $F(n)$ appear as a straight line.

13. Take It Further Find or graph all the solutions to the equation $x^y = y^x$ with $x > 0$, $y > 0$, and $x \neq y$.

## Maintain Your Skills

**14. a.** Copy and complete the following table.

| $x$ | $\log_2 x$ | $\log_8 x$ |
|---|---|---|
| 0 | ■ | ■ |
| 1 | ■ | ■ |
| 2 | ■ | ■ |
| 3 | ■ | ■ |
| 4 | ■ | ■ |
| 5 | ■ | ■ |
| 6 | ■ | ■ |
| 7 | ■ | ■ |
| 8 | ■ | ■ |
| 9 | ■ | ■ |
| 10 | ■ | ■ |

**b.** A calculator gives the value of $\log_8 23$ as approximately 1.5079. Approximate the value of $\log_2 23$.

**15.** Sketch each graph on a linear $x$-axis and logarithmic $y$-axis.

**a.** $y = 2^x$

**b.** $y = 10 \cdot 2^x$

**c.** $y = 1.5^x$

**d.** $y = 10 \cdot 1.5^x$

**16.** Sketch each graph on a logarithmic $x$-axis and logarithmic $y$-axis.

**a.** $y = x^2$

**b.** $y = x^3$

**c.** $y = 10x^2$

**d.** $y = 10x^3$

**In this investigation, you learned to evaluate logarithms of any base, to use logarithms in solving exponential equations, and to graph logarithmic functions. These questions will help you summarize what you have learned.**

1. Solve each equation for $x$.

   a. $\log \frac{5}{6} + \log 6 = \log x$

   b. $\log_3 2 + \log_3 \frac{1}{2} = \log_3 x$

   c. $\log 10 \cdot \log x = \log 30$

   d. $\log_2 4 \cdot \log_2 \frac{1}{2} = \log_2 x$

2. Arrange the following numbers in order from least to greatest.

$$\log_4 \frac{5}{2}, \log_2 \frac{1}{8}, \log 0.3, \log_7 1, \log_{\frac{1}{2}} 4$$

3. Let $N = \log_3 17$.

   a. Find two consecutive integers $j$ and $k$ such that $j < N < k$. Explain how you made your choice.

   b. Show how to use the change-of-base rule to evaluate $N$ on a calculator that can only compute base-10 logarithms.

   c. Express $\log_3 (3 \cdot 17^2)$ in terms of $N$.

4. Find all values of $x$ that are solutions of the equation $\log (x - 20) + \log (x - 50) = 3$.

5. Let $f(x) = \log_b x$, with $b > 0$ and $b \neq 1$.

   a. What do you know about $b$ if the graph of $y = f(x)$ is increasing? If the graph is decreasing?

   b. For what values of $x$ is $f(x) = 0$?

   c. Give the coordinates of one point on the graph of $f(x)$ without using any variables.

   d. How can you use the graph of $f(x)$ to determine the base $b$ of the logarithm?

6. What are some reasons to use logarithms?

7. What is a logarithmic scale and when do you use it?

8. If you invest \$1000 at 6% interest, compounded annually, how many years will it take until your money grows to \$10,000?

Sand particles with diameters between $\frac{1}{4}$ mm and $\frac{1}{2}$ mm have values between 2 and 1 on the Krumbein scale.

## Vocabulary and Notation

In this investigation, you learned these terms and symbols. Make sure you understand what each one means and how to use it.

- **common logarithm, log $x$**
- **linear scale**
- **logarithmic function, $x \mapsto \log_b x$**
- **logarithmic scale**

# *e* and Natural Functions

In earlier math courses you learned to use the constant $\pi$. In *e and Natural Functions*, you will learn about another important constant, e. You will see how it naturally appears in a variety of settings.

**By the end of this investigation, you will be able to answer questions like these.**

1. What happens when interest is compounded more and more frequently?
2. What are some reasons to introduce the number $e$?
3. How can you relate any exponential or logarithmic function to $f(x) = e^x$ and $g(x) = \ln x$?

**You will learn how to**

- state and use the limit and factorial definitions of $e$ and $e^x$
- use the inverse relationship between $e^x$ and $\ln x$ to solve equations
- find an equation for the line tangent to the graph of $y = e^x$ or $y = \ln x$ at a point

**You will develop these habits and skills:**

- Develop a definition of continuously compounded interest.
- Visualize relationships between the graphs of $f(x) = e^x$ and $g(x) = \ln x$ and the slopes of the tangents to these graphs.
- Use functional equations to recognize the ln function as a logarithm.

The same street in Shanghai, before and after several decades of essentially exponential growth.

# 8.11 Getting Started

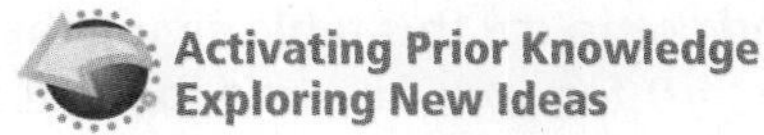


A bank could compound interest every year, half year, quarter year, month, week, day, hour, or second, or over even smaller intervals. The limiting action is to compound interest continuously. For each compounding plan, a wise consumer should know how the interest grows.

## For You to Explore

**1.** A representative of Seventh Fifth Bank offered Danielle an incredible investment, a 100% APR savings account, but only for one year. Danielle went for the offer right away, giving them all the money she had, \$100.

As she left the bank, Danielle realized she forgot to ask how often the interest was compounded. Determine, to the nearest penny, how much money Danielle will have after a year if interest is compounded on each of the following schedules.

**a.** annually (once per year)

**b.** semi-annually (twice per year)

**c.** quarterly (four times per year)

**d.** monthly (12 times per year)

As much as Danielle would like to get 100% interest every time the bank calculates it, the interest is broken up over the year. With semi-annual compounding, Danielle would earn 50% each period. With quarterly compounding, she earns 25% per quarter.

**2.** Danielle, still thinking about her incredible offer, says, "Maybe they'll compound every day, or every minute, or every second! Then I'll really be raking it in."

**a.** Is this true? How much money could Danielle have after a year if interest were compounded more frequently?

**b.** If interest is compounded $n$ times during the year, write a formula for the amount of money Danielle will have at the end of the year (in terms of $n$).

**3.** Sketch the graph of $f(x) = 2^x$.

**a.** Draw a secant line connecting $(0, f(0))$ and $(2, f(2))$. Calculate its slope.

**b.** Draw a secant line connecting $(0, f(0))$ and $(0.5, f(0.5))$. Calculate its slope to two decimal places.

**c.** Give a good estimate for the slope of the tangent line to the graph of $f$ at $x = 0$.

**Habits of Mind**

**Check your results.** Set up a sketch using your geometry software, similar to the sketch described in the first For You to Do section in Lesson 3.05.

**4.** Sketch the graph of $g(x) = 4^x$.

**a.** Draw a secant line connecting $(0, g(0))$ and $(0.25, g(0.25))$. Calculate its slope to two decimal places.

**b.** Give a good estimate for the slope of the tangent line to the graph of $g$ at $x = 0$.

**5.** Copy and complete this table giving the approximate slope of the tangent line at $x = 0$ for each function in the form $f(x) = b^x$.

| Base $b$ | Slope of tangent to $f(x) = b^x$ at $x = 0$ |
|---|---|
| 2 | ■ |
| 3 | ■ |
| 4 | ■ |
| 5 | 1.609 |
| 8 | ■ |
| 10 | ■ |

**6.** By continuity, there must be some base $b$ where the slope of the tangent line to the graph of $f(x) = b^x$ at $x = 0$ is exactly 1.

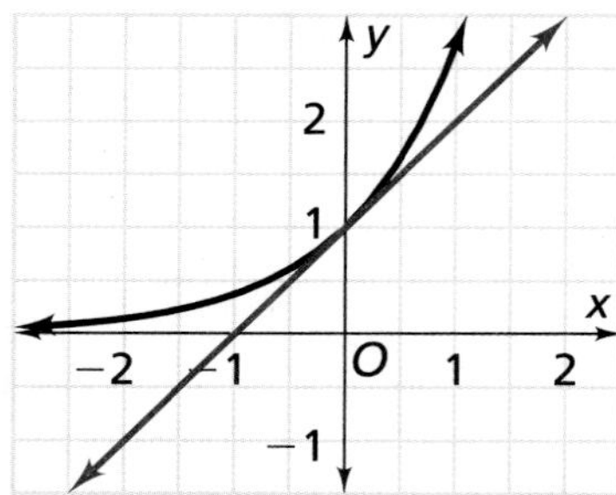


Give a good estimate for this base $b$.

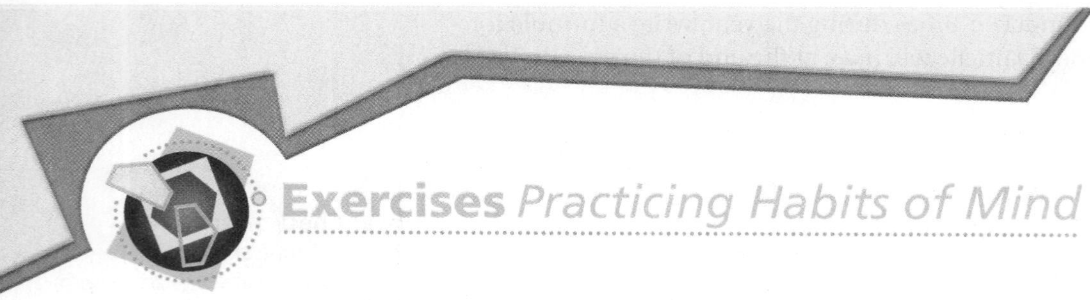


## On Your Own

**7.** Sketch the graph of $f(x) = \log_2 x$.

**a.** Draw a secant line connecting $(1, f(1))$ and $(2, f(2))$. Calculate its slope.

**b.** Draw a secant line connecting $(1, f(1))$ and $(1.2, f(1.2))$. Calculate its slope to two decimal places.

**c.** Give a good estimate for the slope of the line tangent to the graph of $f$ at $x = 1$.

**8.** Sketch the graph of $g(x) = \log_4 x$.

**a.** Draw a secant line connecting $(1, g(1))$ and $(2, g(2))$. Calculate its slope.

**b.** Give a good estimate for the slope of the line tangent to the graph of $g$ at $x = 1$.

**9.** Copy and complete this table giving the approximate slope of the tangent line at $x = 1$ for each function in the form $f(x) = \log_b x$.

| Base $b$ | Slope of tangent to $f(x) = \log_b x$ at $x = 1$ |
|---|---|
| 2 | ■ |
| 3 | ■ |
| 4 | ■ |
| 5 | 0.621 |
| 8 | ■ |
| 10 | ■ |

**10.** By continuity, there must be some base $b$ where the slope of the tangent line to the graph of $f(x) = \log_b x$ at $x = 1$ is exactly 1.

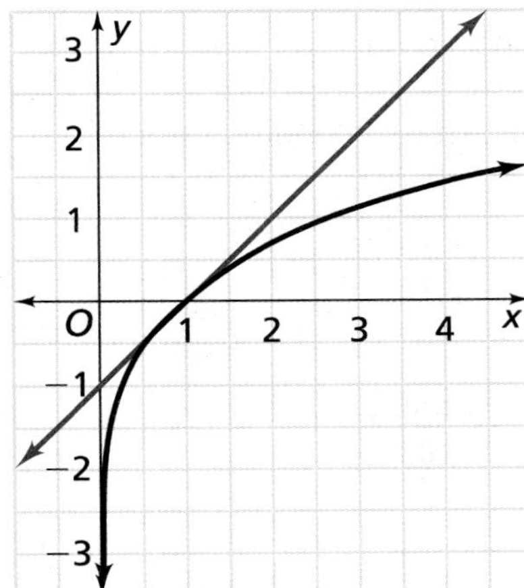


Give a good estimate for this base $b$.

## Maintain Your Skills

**11.** Use the Binomial Theorem to expand each expression.

**a.** $\left(1 + \frac{x}{2}\right)^2$ **b.** $\left(1 + \frac{x}{3}\right)^3$ **c.** $\left(1 + \frac{x}{4}\right)^4$

**12.** Let $f(x, n) = \left(1 + \frac{x}{n}\right)^n$ for any real $x$ and positive integer $n$. Calculate each of the following.

**a.** $f(1, n)$ for $n = 1, 2, 3, 4, 10, 100, 10000$

**b.** $f(2, n)$ for $n = 1, 2, 3, 4, 10, 100, 10000$

**c.** $f(0.05, n)$ for $n = 1, 4, 12, 365, 10000$

# 8.12 Compound Interest; the Number $e$

In Problems 1 and 2 from Lesson 8.11, you helped Danielle figure out how much money she would make on her \$100 investment in a savings account with 100% APR, compounded at different intervals. You can write a function that takes the period as the input and outputs the balance at the end of the year.

Let $F(n)$ denote the amount of money Danielle would have after a year if interest were compounded $n$ times during the year. Then

$$F(n) = 100\left(1 + \frac{1}{n}\right)^n$$

You can evaluate $F(n)$ for large values of $n$, rounded to six decimal places:

$$\begin{aligned} F(100) &= 270.481383 \\ F(1000) &= 271.692393 \\ F(10^4) &= 271.814593 \\ F(10^5) &= 271.826824 \\ F(10^6) &= 271.828047 \\ F(10^7) &= 271.828169 \end{aligned}$$

It seems that $F$ keeps growing as $n$ grows, which makes sense. After all, the more compounding of the interest there is, the more money Danielle earns. But for large values of $n$, the rate of growth of $F$ slows down considerably. For example, it seems unlikely that $F(n)$ will ever surpass 300, no matter how large $n$ is.

The key point here is that

$$f(n) = \left(1 + \frac{1}{n}\right)^n$$

Assume $n > 0$.

is an increasing function, but it also has an upper bound. In fact, the graph of $f$ seems to have a horizontal asymptote at $y \approx 2.7183$.

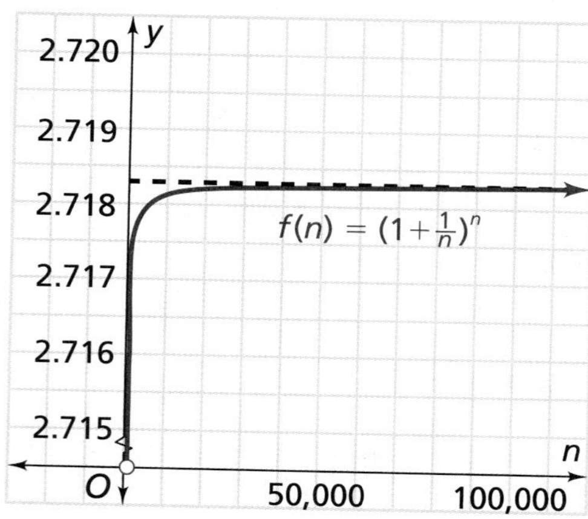


In the context of investing money, the function $f(n)$ only makes sense for positive integers $n$. But you can certainly evaluate $f(n)$ at all real $n > 0$.

Historically, many people felt (as Danielle did) that more frequent compounding could lead to unbounded interest. But in the late 17th century, mathematician Jacob Bernoulli showed that there was an upper limit on the amount of money that you can earn. His proof introduced a new mathematical constant.

### Definition

The number **e** is, by definition,

$$e = \lim_{n\to\infty}\left(1 + \frac{1}{n}\right)^n$$

The value of e is approximately $e \approx 2.71828\ldots$

See the TI-Nspire Handbook on p. 817 for information about how to find e on your calculator.

**Continuously compounded interest** is computed by taking the limit as the frequency of compounding increases. In Danielle's case, this amounts to

$$\begin{aligned}\lim_{n\to\infty} F(n) &= \lim_{n\to\infty} 100\left(1 + \frac{1}{n}\right)^n \\ &= 100 \cdot e \\ &\approx 271.828\end{aligned}$$

So, rounded to the nearest penny, Danielle would have \$271.83 after a year if the interest were compounded continuously.

## Example 1

**Problem** Suppose David invests \$100 at 12% APR. If the interest is compounded quarterly, how much money will he have after five years?

**Solution** The 12% APR means David earns 3% per quarter. Since there are 20 quarters in five years, you can calculate

$$100(1.03)^{20} \approx 180.61$$

to show that David will have \$180.61 at the end of five years.

$3 = 12 \div 4$
$20 = 4 \cdot 5$

Now suppose you invest $P$ dollars at interest rate $r$, compounded $n$ times per year. Let $B(t)$ denote your balance at the end of $t$ years. Then

$$B(t) = P\left(1 + \frac{r}{n}\right)^{nt}$$

- The interest rate in each compounding period is $\frac{r}{n}$.
- There are $nt$ compounding periods in $t$ years.

An interest rate of 12% means $r = 0.12$.

## Example 2

**Problem** Suppose David invests \$100 at 12% APR, but this time the interest is compounded continuously. How much money will he have after five years?

**Solution** Let $n$ be the number of times the interest gets compounded per year so that:

- the interest rate in each compounding period is $\frac{0.12}{n}$.
- there are $5n$ compound periods in five years.

Thus after five years, David will have $100\left(1 + \frac{0.12}{n}\right)^{5n}$ dollars.

As $n$ grows larger and larger, you get

$$\lim_{n\to\infty} 100\left(1 + \frac{0.12}{n}\right)^{5n} \approx 182.212$$

So David has approximately \$182.21.

See the TI-Nspire Handbook on p. 817 to use your CAS to approximate $\lim_{n\to\infty} 100\left(1 + \frac{0.12}{n}\right)^{5n}$.

# Exercises *Practicing Habits of Mind*

## Check Your Understanding

Go Online
www.successnetplus.com

1. Suppose Danielle could invest \$100 with Seventh Fifth Bank at 100% APR for more than just a year.

   a. What would her balance be at the end of two years if compounding were annual? At the end of three years? At the end of $t$ years?

   b. What would her balance be at the end of two years if compounding were quarterly? At the end of three years? At the end of $t$ years?

   c. In terms of the number $e$, what would her balance be at the end of three years of continuous compounding? Find this value to the nearest cent.

2. Jamie says that 100% APR is totally unrealistic. "I've never seen any savings account with more than 5% or 6% interest. So could we please look at something more realistic?"

   a. If Jamie invests \$100 at 6% APR, compounded annually, how much money will she have at the end of one year? At the end of two years? At the end of $t$ years?

   b. If the 6% APR is compounded twice per year, how much money will she have at the end of one year? At the end of two years? At the end of $t$ years?

   c. **Write About It** Danielle says that after three years of monthly compounding at 6% APR, Jamie will have $100(1.005)^{36}$ dollars in the account. Describe in detail where the values 100, 1.005, and 36 come from.

3. Jamie invests $P$ dollars at 5% APR, compounded $n$ times per year for $t$ years. Find a formula for the balance of this account at the end of $t$ years in terms of $P$, $n$, and $t$.

4. Jamie invests \$100 at 5% APR and is looking at what happens as interest is compounded more and more often. To the nearest penny, find the balance of Jamie's account after one year if interest is compounded on each of the following schedules.

   a. quarterly
   b. monthly
   c. daily
   d. hourly

5. Jamie invests \$100 at 5% APR, compounded continuously to earn the maximum interest. Find Jamie's balance, to the nearest penny, after each of the following time periods.

   a. 5 years
   b. 10 years
   c. 20 years
   d. 40 years

6. For each of the values found in Exercise 5, rewrite the result in terms of $e$.

7. This exercise is a proof of the fact that for $x > 0$,

$$\lim_{n\to\infty}\left(1 + \frac{x}{n}\right)^n = e^x$$

using the limit definition of $e$.

a. If $\frac{1}{K} = \frac{x}{n}$, write $n$ in terms of $x$ and $K$.

b. Rewrite the expression

$$\left(1 + \frac{x}{n}\right)^n$$

by making the substitution $\frac{1}{K} = \frac{x}{n}$.

c. Explain why the equation is true.

$$\lim_{n\to\infty}\left(1 + \frac{x}{n}\right)^n = \lim_{K\to\infty}\left(1 + \frac{1}{K}\right)^{Kx}$$

As $n$ grows, what happens to $K$?

d. Show that

$$\lim_{K\to\infty}\left(1 + \frac{1}{K}\right)^{Kx} = e^x$$

using the limit definition of $e$.

8. You have already seen that if you invest $P$ dollars at an APR of $r$, compounded $n$ times per year, your balance at the end of $t$ years is

$$B(t) = P\left(1 + \frac{r}{n}\right)^{nt}$$

Consider the limit of the expression on the right as $n$ gets larger and larger. Show that

$$\lim_{n\to\infty} P\left(1 + \frac{r}{n}\right)^{nt} = Pe^{rt}$$

## On Your Own

9. Find the value of $\sum_{k=0}^{\infty} \frac{1}{k!}$ to five decimal places.

10. Suppose Danielle was able to invest \$1000 instead of \$100 in her Seventh Fifth Bank account.

a. What would be the effect on her balance at the end of the year?

b. What is the maximum amount of money Danielle could have at the end of a year, investing \$1000 this way?

**Remember...**

Danielle's investment was \$100 at 100% APR.

11. Jamie puts \$1000 in a savings account that earns 6% APR, compounded continuously.

    a. How much money will Jamie have after 3 years? After 5 years? After $t$ years?

    b. How long will it take for Jamie's account balance to double?

    c. How long will it take for Jamie's account to be worth \$4000?

12. Which would be a better investment—an account at 6% APR compounded annually, or an account at 5.5% APR compounded continuously?

Try putting the same amount of money into each account for the same time period. What does $e^{0.055}$ have to do with this exercise?

13. Sketch the graphs of these two functions on the same axes.

$$f(t) = 1.06^t, \ g(t) = e^{0.055t}$$

14. The graph of $g(t) = e^{0.055t}$ passes through the point $(0, 1)$. Find the slope of the line tangent to the graph of $g$ at this point. Round your answer to three decimal places.

15. Rewrite $g(t)$ from Exercise 13 in the form $g(t) = b^t$ with base $b$ accurate to four decimal places.

16. **Standardized Test Prep** Jo and Eddie each deposited \$100 in a bank account paying 4% (APR) interest. Jo's bank compounds interest quarterly, while Eddie's bank compounds it continuously. What is the difference between the two account balances after one year?

    A. \$0.02 B. \$0.20 C. \$2.00 D. \$20.00

Go Online
www.successnetplus.com

## Maintain Your Skills

17. Write the first four terms of the expansion of each expression (starting with $1 + x + \cdots$).

    a. $\left(1 + \frac{x}{3}\right)^3$

    b. $\left(1 + \frac{x}{5}\right)^5$

    c. $\left(1 + \frac{x}{10}\right)^{10}$

    d. $\left(1 + \frac{x}{n}\right)^n$

18. Find each limit.

    a. $\lim_{n\to\infty} \frac{\binom{n}{1}}{n}$

    b. $\lim_{n\to\infty} \frac{\binom{n}{2}}{n^2}$

    c. $\lim_{n\to\infty} \frac{\binom{n}{3}}{n^3}$

    d. $\lim_{n\to\infty} \frac{\binom{n}{4}}{n^4}$

    e. $\lim_{n\to\infty} \frac{\binom{n}{5}}{n^5}$

You can use most CAS software to evaluate the binomial coefficient $\binom{n}{2}$ as *nCr*(*n*, 2).

## 8.13 Another Way to Find $e$

In Lesson 8.12, you saw the following definition for the number $e$.

$$e = \lim_{n \to \infty} \left(1 + \frac{1}{n}\right)^n \tag{1}$$

Using this definition, you proved that

$$e^x = \lim_{n \to \infty} \left(1 + \frac{x}{n}\right)^n \tag{2}$$

Actually, you proved this for $x > 0$ only. But (2) holds for all real $x$. See Exercise 12.

Equations (1) and (2) are the limit definitions of $e$ and $e^x$, respectively. You can, however, define $e$ and $e^x$ another way, using the *factorial definition*. These alternatives are equivalent to the limit definitions.

### A Useful Lemma

Recall Exercise 18 from Lesson 8.12. In it, you saw that

$$\begin{aligned}
\lim_{x \to \infty} \frac{\binom{n}{5}}{n^5} &= \lim_{x \to \infty} \frac{n(n-1)(n-2)(n-3)(n-4)}{5!n^5} \\
&= \frac{1}{5!} \lim_{n \to \infty} \left(\frac{n}{n} \cdot \frac{n-1}{n} \cdot \frac{n-2}{n} \cdot \frac{n-3}{n} \cdot \frac{n-4}{n}\right) \\
&= \frac{1}{5!} \lim_{n \to \infty} \left(1 \cdot \left(1 - \frac{1}{n}\right)\left(1 - \frac{2}{n}\right)\left(1 - \frac{3}{n}\right)\left(1 - \frac{4}{n}\right)\right)
\end{aligned}$$

As $n \to \infty$, the terms $\frac{1}{n}$, $\frac{2}{n}$, $\frac{3}{n}$, and $\frac{4}{n}$ all go to zero, and thus

$$\lim_{x \to \infty} \frac{\binom{n}{5}}{n^5} = \frac{1}{5!}$$

You can generalize this result to state the following lemma.

### *Lemma 8.3*

**Let $k \geq 0$ be an integer. Then**

$$\lim_{x \to \infty} \frac{\binom{n}{k}}{n^k} = \frac{1}{k!}$$

It even works for $k = 0$. Remember that $0! = 1$.

### Factorial Definitions of $e$ and $e^x$

Let

$$f(n) = \sum_{k=0}^{n} \frac{1}{k!} = 1 + \frac{1}{1!} + \frac{1}{2!} + \frac{1}{3!} + \cdots + \frac{1}{n!}$$

Compute $f(n)$ for some values of $n$, rounded to five decimal places.

$$\begin{aligned} f(1) &= 2 \\ f(5) &= 2.71667 \\ f(6) &= 2.71806 \\ f(7) &= 2.71825 \\ f(8) &= 2.71828 \\ f(100) &= 2.71828 \end{aligned}$$

Recall Exercise 9 from Lesson 8.12.

It appears that

$$\lim_{n\to\infty} f(n) = e$$

and the series seems to converge to $e$ rather quickly.

To confirm this conclusion, start by expanding

$$\left(1 + \frac{1}{n}\right)^n$$

using the Binomial Theorem.

$$\left(1 + \frac{1}{n}\right)^n = 1 + n\left(\frac{1}{n}\right) + \binom{n}{2}\left(\frac{1}{n}\right)^2 + \binom{n}{3}\left(\frac{1}{n}\right)^3 + \cdots \qquad (3)$$

$$+ \binom{n}{2}\left(\frac{1}{n}\right)^k + \cdots + \binom{n}{n}\left(\frac{1}{n}\right)^n$$

A typical term on the right side of (3) has the form

$$\binom{n}{k}\left(\frac{1}{n}\right)^k = \frac{\binom{n}{k}}{n^k}$$

Using the lemma above,

$$\lim_{n\to\infty} \binom{n}{k}\left(\frac{1}{n}\right)^k = \lim_{n\to\infty} \frac{\binom{n}{k}}{n^k} = \frac{1}{k!}$$

Now let $n$ get large in equation (3). The left side, by the limit definition, approaches $e$. And the right side looks like this:

$$1 + \frac{1}{1!} + \frac{1}{2!} + \frac{1}{3!} + \cdots + \frac{1}{k!} + \cdots$$

"Letting $n$ get large" here is actually a tricky issue involving calculus. But you should get the general gist of what is going on.

You can now state the following theorem.

### Theorem 8.6

$$\lim_{n\to\infty}\left(1 + \frac{1}{n}\right)^n = 1 + \frac{1}{1!} + \frac{1}{2!} + \frac{1}{3!} + \cdots = \sum_{k=0}^{\infty} \frac{1}{k!}$$

Theorem 8.6 states that the following definition of $e$ is equivalent to the limit definition.

### Definition

The factorial definition of e is

$$e = 1 + \frac{1}{1!} + \frac{1}{2!} + \frac{1}{3!} + \cdots = \sum_{k=0}^{\infty} \frac{1}{k!}$$

## For You to Do

1. Using the limit definition of $e^x$,

$$e^x = \lim_{n \to \infty} \left(1 + \frac{x}{n}\right)^n$$

derive the factorial definition of $e^x$:

$$e^x = 1 + x + \frac{x^2}{2!} + \frac{x^3}{3!} + \cdots = \sum_{k=0}^{\infty} \frac{x^k}{k!}$$

Expand $\left(1 + \frac{x}{n}\right)^n$ using the Binomial Theorem, and let $n$ get large.

Using the factorial definition, you can approximate $e^x$ accurately with polynomials. For example, consider the cubic polynomial

$$c(x) = 1 + x + \frac{x^2}{2!} + \frac{x^3}{3!}$$

The graphs of $y = e^x$ and $y = c(x)$ are shown below.

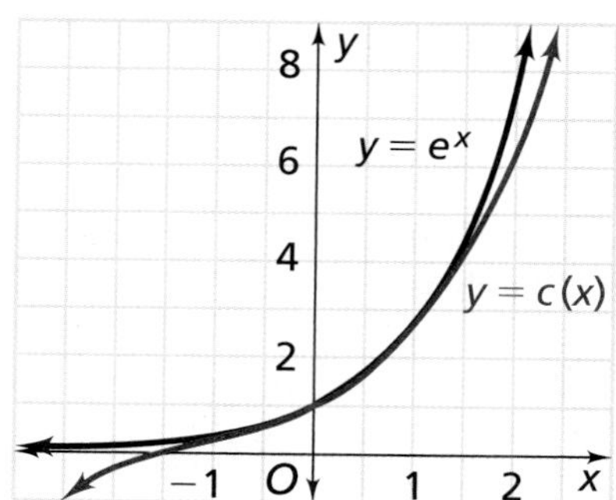


Notice how the two graphs almost agree when $-1 \leq x \leq 1$.

## Developing Habits of Mind

**Make strategic choices.** Why is it useful to have different equivalent definitions of $e$ and $e^x$ based on factorials, when there are already ones using limits? It is useful because you can pick and choose the definition that is most convenient a given context.

For example, here is a proof that the number $e$ is irrational, using its factorial definition. By the factorial definition of $e$,

$$e = 1 + \frac{1}{1!} + \frac{1}{2!} + \frac{1}{3!} + \cdots + \frac{1}{k!} + \frac{1}{(k+1)!} + \frac{1}{(k+2)!} + \cdots \quad (4)$$

Suppose $e$ is a rational number and write $e = \frac{p}{q}$ for some integers $p$ and $q$, with $q > 0$. Choose a positive integer $k$ such that $k > q$. Therefore,

We will come up with a contradiction.

$$k! = k(k-1)(k-2)\cdots q(q-1)(q-2)\cdots 3 \cdot 2 \cdot 1$$

and thus $\frac{k!}{q}$ is an integer. Multiply each side of (4) by $k!$ to get

$$k!e = k!\left(1 + \frac{1}{1!} + \frac{1}{2!} + \frac{1}{3!} + \cdots + \frac{1}{k!}\right) + k!\left(\frac{1}{(k+1)!} + \frac{1}{(k+2)!} + \cdots\right) \quad (5)$$

The left side of (5) equals

$$k!e = \frac{k!}{q} \cdot p$$

which is an integer. On the right side of (5), the term

$$k!\left(1 + \frac{1}{1!} + \frac{1}{2!} + \frac{1}{3!} + \cdots + \frac{1}{k!}\right)$$

is an integer because $m!$ is a divisor of $k!$ for all $m$ such that $0 \le m \le k$. Hence the remaining term on the right side of (5), namely

$$k!\left(\frac{1}{(k+1)!} + \frac{1}{(k+2)!} + \cdots\right)$$

must also be an integer. But

$$\begin{aligned}
k!\left(\frac{1}{(k+1)!} + \frac{1}{(k+2)!} + \cdots\right) &= \frac{1}{k+1} + \frac{1}{(k+2)(k+1)} + \\
&\quad \frac{1}{(k+3)(k+2)(k+1)} + \cdots \\
&< \frac{1}{k+1} + \frac{1}{(k+1)^2} + \frac{1}{(k+1)^3} + \\
&\quad \frac{1}{(k+1)^4} + \cdots \\
&= \frac{1}{k+1}\left(1 + \frac{1}{k+1} + \frac{1}{(k+1)^2} + \right. \\
&\quad \left. \frac{1}{(k+1)^3} + \frac{1}{(k+1)^4} + \cdots\right) \\
&= \frac{1}{k+1}\left(\frac{1}{1 - \frac{1}{k+1}}\right) \\
&= \frac{1}{k} \\
&< 1
\end{aligned}$$

Replace each term in the sum by something greater.

**Remember...**

$\sum_{i=0}^{\infty} r^i = \frac{1}{1-r}$ when $|r| < 1$. Here, $r = \frac{1}{k+1}$.

Therefore

$$k!\left(\frac{1}{(k+1)!} + \frac{1}{(k+2)!} + \cdots\right)$$

is a positive integer which is strictly less than 1, a contradiction. And thus, $e$ must be irrational.

# Exercises Practicing Habits of Mind

## Check Your Understanding

1. **a.** Use the factorial definition of $e$ to find the value of $e$ correctly to 10 decimal places. How many terms are necessary?

   **b.** Calculate $\left(1 + \frac{1}{n}\right)^n$ for $n = 10^7$. How many digits of $e$ does this calculation correctly find?

2. The quadratic function $q(x) = 1 + x + \frac{x^2}{2}$ is a good approximation of $f(x) = e^x$ when $x$ is near 0.

   **a.** Calculate $q(0.05)$ and $e^{0.05}$ to five decimal places. What is the percent error for $q(0.05)$ as an approximation to $e^{0.05}$?

   **b.** Calculate $q(0.5)$ and $e^{0.5}$ to five decimal places and find the percent error.

   **c.** Calculate $q(-1)$ and $e^{-1}$ to five decimal places and find the percent error.

The percent error is $\frac{\text{Estimate} - \text{Actual}}{\text{Actual}} \cdot 100$

3. Find, to three decimal places, the value of $x$ such that $e^x = 2$.

**Habits of Mind**

**Make a connection.** How does the graph of $y = e^x$ suggest that there is a solution to the equation $e^x = 2$?

4. In Lesson 8.11, you learned that the line tangent to the graph of $y = e^x$ at $(0,1)$ has slope 1.

   **a.** The graph of $y = e^x$ gets steeper as $x$ gets larger. At some point $(x, y)$, the tangent line has slope 2. Give a good estimate for the coordinates of this point.

   **b.** At some other point, the tangent line has slope 3. Give a good estimate for the coordinates of this point.

5. **a.** Calculate this value to five decimal places.

$$\sum_{k=0}^{\infty} \frac{(-1)^k}{k!}$$

   **b.** Compare your results with those from Exercise 2c.

See the TI-Nspire Handbook on p. 817 for advice on how to do this on your calculator.

6. Sketch the graph of each function.

   **a.** $f(x) = e^{-x}$  **b.** $g(x) = -e^x$  **c.** $h(x) = \frac{1}{e^x}$

## On Your Own

7. Give a good estimate for $e^{0.03}$ without using a calculator.

8. The cubic function $c(x) = 1 + x + \frac{x^2}{2} + \frac{x^3}{6}$ is a good approximation of $f(x) = e^x$ when $x$ is small.

**a.** Calculate $c(0.1)$ and $f(0.1)$, then calculate the percent error in the approximation.

**b.** Repeat part (a) for $x = 0.2, 0.5, 1, 2$.

**c.** Explain why $c(x)$ is a good approximation to $e^x$ for small values of $x$ but not for large values of $x$.

**d.** For how many values of $x$ does $c(x) = f(x)$ exactly?

Use the graphs of $c$ and $f$ to help.

**9.** Find the exact value of this infinite sum.

$$1 + 2 + \frac{4}{2} + \frac{8}{6} + \frac{16}{24} + \frac{32}{120} + \cdots + \frac{2^k}{k!} + \cdots$$

**10.** Find the solution to each equation to three decimal places.

**a.** $e^k = 3$ **b.** $e^m = 5$ **c.** $e^n = 15$

**d.** $e^p = 45$ **e.** $e^r = -5$

**11.** Let $k$ be the solution to $e^k = 3$, as in Exercise 10a. Sketch the graph of the function

$$f(x) = e^{kx}$$

Is there a simpler formula for $f(x)$?

**12.** Take It Further Use the limit definition of $e$.

**a.** Use a substitution to show that $\lim_{n\to\infty}\left(1 - \frac{1}{n}\right)^n = \frac{1}{e}$.

**b.** Use your result in part (a) to show that $\lim_{n\to\infty}\left(1 + \frac{x}{n}\right)^n = e^x$ for $x \le 0$.

**13.** Standardized Test Prep Which of the following infinite series gives the exact value of $e^5$?

**A.** $\sum_{i=1}^{\infty} \frac{5^i}{i!}$ **B.** $\sum_{i=0}^{\infty} \frac{5^i}{i!}$ **C.** $\sum_{i=0}^{\infty} \frac{e^i}{5!}$ **D.** $\sum_{i=0}^{\infty} \frac{i^5}{5^i}$

## Maintain Your Skills

**14.** Write each of these as fractions in the form $\frac{p}{q}$ where $p$ and $q$ are integers. Then approximate each to four decimal places.

**a.** $1 + \frac{2}{1}$

**b.** $1 + \cfrac{2}{1 + \cfrac{1}{6}}$

**c.** $1 + \cfrac{2}{1 + \cfrac{1}{6 + \cfrac{1}{10}}}$

**d.** $1 + \cfrac{2}{1 + \cfrac{1}{6 + \cfrac{1}{10 + \cfrac{1}{14}}}}$

# 8.14 The Natural Logarithm Function

In this In-Class Experiment, you will investigate a function on your calculator called "ln." One way to investigate a function is to tabulate it and to see if there are any familiar "functional equations" lurking in the background.

## In-Class Experiment

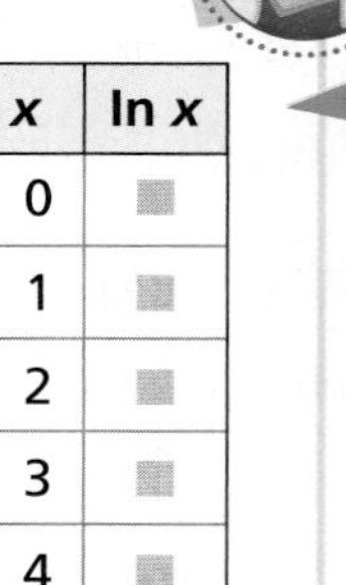

1. Use your calculator to find the output of the ln function for each integer input from 0 to 10. Record each output to five decimal places.
2. Calculate the value of $\ln 2 + \ln 3$ to four decimal places.
3. Calculate the value of $3 \ln 2$ to four decimal places.
4. Find and describe some rules that appear to be true for the ln function.
5. Find $x$, to four decimal places, if $\ln x = 1$.
6. Draw the graph of $y = \ln x$.

| $x$ | $\ln x$ |
|---|---|
| 0 | ■ |
| 1 | ■ |
| 2 | ■ |
| 3 | ■ |
| 4 | ■ |
| 5 | ■ |
| 6 | ■ |
| 7 | ■ |
| 8 | ■ |
| 9 | ■ |
| 10 | ■ |

It is only by convention that $\ln x$, like $\sin x$, is normally written without parentheses. On a calculator, parentheses are usually required.

Your table in the In-Class Experiment should show that

- $\ln 2 + \ln 3 = \ln 6$
- $\ln 2 + \ln 5 = \ln 10$
- $\ln 3 + \ln 3 = \ln 9$

And if you extend the table, you can also see that

- $\ln 3 + \ln 4 = \ln 12$
- $\ln 5 + \ln 7 = \ln 35$
- $\ln 6 + \ln 9 = \ln 54$

and so on. In other words, for $M, N > 0$, the function $g(x) = \ln x$ seems to satisfy the functional equation

$$\ln(MN) = \ln M + \ln N$$

But this is precisely the Fundamental Law of Logarithms.

A functional equation is an equation satisfied by a function.

## For You to Do

Use your table of data from the In-Class Experiment to verify that the ln function has the following properties.

**7.** $\ln \frac{M}{N} = \ln M - \ln N$

**8.** $\ln M^p = p \ln M$

Recall that these are the corollaries to the Fundamental Law of Logarithms.

Why does the function ln behave like a logarithm? Because it is a logarithm! In other words,

$$\ln x = \log_b x$$

for some base $b > 0$. What, then, is the base?

- From the definition of the logarithm, you know that the output of $\log_b M$ is the exponent $k$ such that $b^k = M$, that is

$$b^k = M \Longleftrightarrow \log_b M = k \qquad (1)$$

- $\log_b$ is a one-to-one function.
- It follows from equation (1) that if $\log_b x = 1$, then $x = b$, the base of the logarithm.
- In the In-Class Experiment, you found that $\ln e$ seems to be 1. If that were so, the base of ln would be $e$.

And in fact, the ln function built into your calculator is just the logarithm to the base $e$.

### Definition

The **natural logarithm** function ln is the logarithm to base $e$:

$$\ln x = \log_e x$$

Why "natural" logarithm? You will see why in the next lesson.

## For You to Do

**9.** Copy and complete the following table.

| $x$ | $e^x$ |
|---|---|
| 0 | ■ |
| 0.69315 | ■ |
| 1.09861 | ■ |
| 1.38629 | ■ |
| 1.60944 | ■ |
| 1.79176 | ■ |
| 1.94591 | ■ |
| 2.07944 | ■ |
| 2.19722 | ■ |
| 2.30259 | ■ |

From the two tables of data you have generated so far in this lesson,

- $e^{0.69315} = 2$ and $\ln 2 = 0.69315$
- $e^{1.09861} = 3$ and $\ln 3 = 1.09861$
- $e^{1.38629} = 4$ and $\ln 4 = 1.38629$

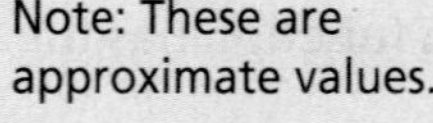

Note: These are approximate values.

and so on. And in general,

$$e^a = b \iff \ln b = a \qquad (2)$$

Statement (2) is another way of saying that the functions $x \mapsto e^x$ and $x \mapsto \ln x$ are inverses of each other. This should come as no surprise, since the logarithmic function

$$x \mapsto \log_b x$$

is the inverse of the exponential function

$$x \mapsto b^x$$

In this case, $b = e$.

## For You to Do

**10.** Sketch the graphs of $x \mapsto e^x$ and $x \mapsto \ln x$ on the same axes.

**11.** Find the domain and range of each function. Do your results make sense? Explain.

**12.** How are the two graphs related?

**13.** Why is the ln function undefined for $x \leq 0$?

## Example

**Problem** Solve the equation

$$e^{x^2} = 27$$

**Solution** Apply the ln function to each side and use a corollary to the Law of Logarithms to proceed.

$$\begin{aligned} \ln e^{x^2} &= \ln 27 \\ x^2 \ln e &= \ln 27 && \ln M^p = p \ln M \\ x^2 &= \ln 27 && \ln e = 1 \\ x^2 &\approx 3.29584 \\ x &\approx \pm 1.81544 \end{aligned}$$

# Exercises Practicing Habits of Mind

## Check Your Understanding

**1.** Using only the table from the In-Class Experiment, find the value of ln 1024 to three decimal places.

**2.** Use the fact that $\ln M^p = p \ln M$.

**a.** Find values for $p$ and $M$ if $\ln 81 = p \ln M$.

**b.** Write $\ln \sqrt[3]{2}$ as a multiple of $\ln 2$.

**c.** Write $\ln \frac{1}{25}$ as a multiple of $\ln 5$.

Indeed, for any number $b > 0$, $\log_b M^p = p \log_b M$.

**3.** Simplify each of the following.

**a.** $\ln e^2$

**b.** $\ln e^{10}$

**c.** $\ln \frac{1}{e}$

**d.** $e^{\ln 5}$

**4.** In Lesson 8.13, you found a number $k$ such that $e^k = 3$.

**a.** If you use a CAS to solve the equation $e^k = 3$, what answer do you get?

**b.** What number $m$ is the solution to $e^m = 5$?

**c.** Show that this statement is true for any real number $x$.

$$e^{x \ln 2} = 2^x$$

**5.** Show that you can write any exponential function $f(x) = a^x$, where $a > 0$ is real, in the form

$$f(x) = e^{kx}$$

for some real number $k$.

**6.** Logarithms are useful in solving equations that involve exponents.

**a.** If $2^x = 7$, show that $x \ln 2 = \ln 7$. Then find $x$ to three decimal places.

**b.** Find $z$ to three decimal places if $5^z = 123$.

**c.** Use logarithms to find the one solution to $2 \cdot 6^x = 0.1$.

**d.** Take It Further In terms of the parameters $a$, $b$, $c$, and $d$, find the solution to

$$a \cdot b^x = c \cdot d^x$$

7. You have seen that $e^a = b$ if and only if $\ln b = a$. Here are the graphs of $y = e^x$ and $y = \ln x$ on the same axes.

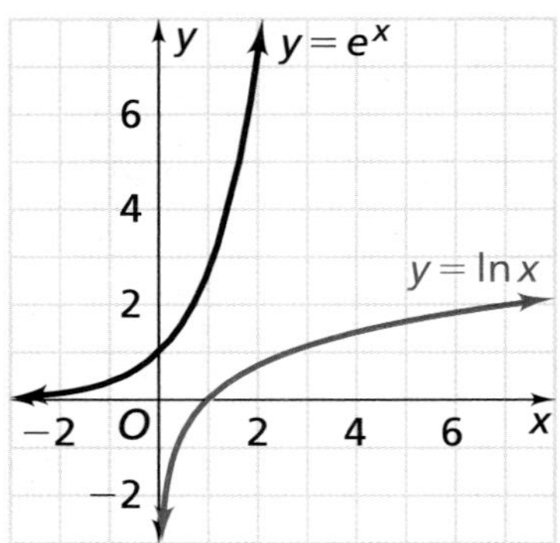


a. Exactly one point on the graph of $y = \ln x$ has $x$-coordinate 3. What are the coordinates of this point?

b. Exactly one point on the graph of $y = e^x$ has $y$-coordinate 3. What are the coordinates of this point?

c. Exactly one point on the graph of $y = e^x$ has $x$-coordinate 2. What are the coordinates of this point?

d. Exactly one point on the graph of $y = \ln x$ has $y$-coordinate 2. What are the coordinates of this point?

e. If the point $(g, 4)$ is on the graph of $y = \ln x$, find $g$.

f. If the point $(p, 4)$ is on the graph of $y = e^x$, find $p$.

## On Your Own

8. Calculate each of the following to three decimal places, if possible.

a. $\ln 3$
b. $\ln 5$
c. $\ln 15$
d. $\ln 45$
e. $\ln \frac{5}{3}$
f. $\ln(-5)$

9. Jamie invests \$100 at 6% APR, compounded continuously. After $t$ years her account balance is

$$B = 100e^{0.06t}$$

a. How much money will Jamie have in this account after 5 years? After 10 years? After 20 years?

b. How long will it take for Jamie's account to grow to exactly \$200?

c. How long will it take for Jamie's account to grow to exactly \$400?

d. Solve the equation $B = 100e^{0.06t}$ for $t$. Use the result to determine how long it will take for Jamie's account to grow to \$1000.

**10.** For each interest rate, compounded continuously, determine how long (in years) it will take for a savings account to double in value.

**a.** 2% APR  **b.** 3% APR  **c.** 4% APR

**d.** 5% APR  **e.** 8% APR  **f.** $p$% APR

**11.** Many financial advisors use the Rule of 72 to estimate the doubling time of an account. To find the number of years it takes to double an investment's value, divide 72 by the percent interest rate.

If the interest rate is 6%, divide by 6.

**a.** How does the Rule of 72 compare to the results of Exercise 10?

**b.** **Take It Further** Ryo jokes that it should have been called the "Rule of ln 2." Why?

**12.** **Standardized Test Prep** On the day Aaron was born, his parents deposited $24,000 into an account paying 8% (APR) interest compounded continuously. How old will Aaron be, to the nearest month, when the account balance is $100,000?

**A.** 17 years, 1 month  **B.** 17 years, 10 months

**C.** 18 years, 3 months  **D.** 18 years, 6 months

## Maintain Your Skills

**13.** Find the slope of the line segment connecting each pair of points.

**a.** (3, 5) and (4, 8)  **b.** (5, 3) and (8, 4)

**c.** (2, 1) and (10, 2)  **d.** (1, 2) and (2, 10)

**e.** (0, 4) and $(a, b)$  **f.** (4, 0) and $(b, a)$

**14.** For parts (a) through (f), find a good estimate for the slope of the line tangent to the graph of $y = \ln x$ at each value of $x$.

**a.** $x = 1$  **b.** $x = 2$  **c.** $x = 3$

**d.** $x = 10$  **e.** $x = \frac{1}{2}$  **f.** $x = \frac{1}{3}$

**g.** What relationship does the slope of the tangent have to $x$?

# 8.15 Analysis of $f(x) = e^x$ and $g(x) = \ln x$

In Exercise 14 from Lesson 8.14, you looked at the slopes of several tangents to the graph of $y = \ln x$. From your results, you might have made a conjecture that describes an interesting property of the ln function. That property is detailed in the following theorem.

### Theorem 8.7

**The tangent to the graph of $y = \ln x$ at the point $(a, \ln a)$ has slope $\frac{1}{a}$.**

The proof of this theorem requires results from calculus. For now, you can assume it is true.

Is there a similar theorem to be found regarding tangents to $y = e^x$? You could repeat the experiment and try to find a pattern. But you can use the fact that $f(x) = e^x$ and $g(x) = \ln x$ are inverses of each other to determine a statement about tangents to $f$.

The figure below shows the graphs of $f$ and $g$ with the point $P = (2, \ln 2)$ on the graph of $g$ and the corresponding point $Q = (\ln 2, 2)$ on the graph of $f$. The figure also shows the tangent to $f$ at $P$, and the tangent to $g$ at $Q$.

From Theorem 8.7, you know that the line tangent to $g$ at $P$ has slope $\frac{1}{2}$. But what is the slope of the line tangent to $f$ at $Q$? From the figure, it looks as though the two tangent lines are also reflections of each other over $y = x$. The next problems help you prove this.

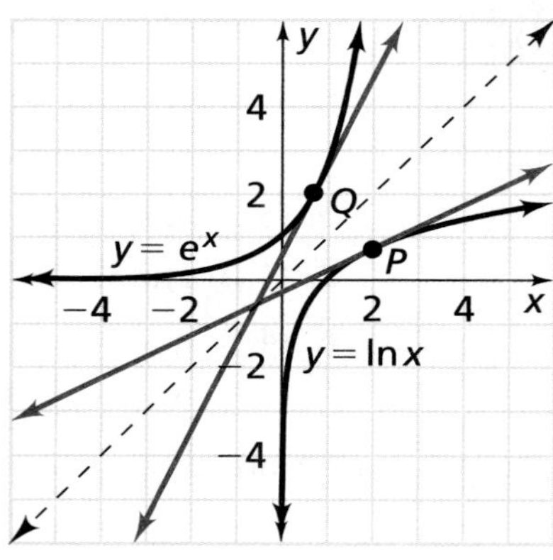


**Remember...**

If $f$ and $g$ are inverse functions, the graph of $f$ is the reflection of the graph of $g$ across the line $y = x$. A point $(a, b)$ is on the graph of $f$ if and only if $(b, a)$ is on the graph of $g$.

## For You to Do

Suppose $h$ and $j$ are inverse functions.

1. Let $R = (a, b)$ and $R' = (c, d)$ be a pair of points on the graph of $h$, and $S = (b, a)$ and $S' = (d, c)$ the corresponding points on the graph of $j$. Show that the slope of the secant between $R$ and $R'$ is the reciprocal of the slope of the secant between $S$ and $S'$.
2. Explain why Problem 1 implies that the slope of the tangent at $R$ is the reciprocal of the slope of the tangent at $S$.

If you let $R'$ approach $R$, what happens to $S'$?

Since the slope of the line tangent to $g$ at $P$ is $\frac{1}{2}$, by Problem 2, the slope of the line tangent to $f$ at $Q$ is its reciprocal. Therefore, the line tangent to the graph of $f(x) = e^x$ at $Q = (\ln 2, 2)$ has slope 2. From this result, you can state the following theorem.

If you cannot see the pattern, think about a point on $f$ such as $(4, e^4)$. What would the slope of the tangent at this point be? The corresponding point on the graph of $g$ would be $(e^4, 4)$, which is $(e^4, \ln e^4)$. The slope of the tangent at that point would be $\frac{1}{e^4}$.

### Theorem 8.8

**The tangent to the graph of $y = e^x$ at the point $(a, e^a)$ has slope $e^a$.**

## For You to Do

**3.** Prove Theorem 8.8.

Once you know how to find the slopes of these tangent lines, you can find their equations.

## Example

**Problem**

**a.** Find the equation $y = j(x)$ of the tangent to the graph of $g(x) = \ln x$ at $(3, \ln 3)$.

**b.** Find the equation $y = k(x)$ of the tangent to the graph of $f(x) = e^x$ at $(\ln 3, 3)$.

**c.** Verify that $j$ and $k$ are inverses of each other.

**Solution**

**a.** From Theorem 8.7, the slope of the tangent is $\frac{1}{3}$. Since the line passes through the point $(3, \ln 3)$, an equation for the line is

$$\frac{1}{3} = \frac{y - \ln 3}{x - 3}$$

and

$$j(x) = \frac{1}{3}(x - 3) + \ln 3$$

**b.** From Theorem 8.8, the slope of the tangent is 3. The line passes through the point $(\ln 3, 3)$, so its equation is

$$3 = \frac{y - 3}{x - \ln 3}$$

and

$$k(x) = 3(x - \ln 3) + 3$$

**c.** You can verify that $j$ and $k$ are inverses by showing that $j(k(x)) = k(j(x)) = x$.

$$\begin{aligned} j(k(x)) &= \tfrac{1}{3}(k(x) - 3) + \ln 3 \\ &= \tfrac{1}{3}([3(x - \ln 3) + 3] - 3) + \ln 3 \\ &= \tfrac{1}{3}(3(x - \ln 3)) + \ln 3 \\ &= (x - \ln 3) + \ln 3 \\ &= x \end{aligned}$$

Likewise, $k(j(x)) = x$. Consequently, the graphs of $j$ and $k$ are reflections of each other across the line $y = x$.

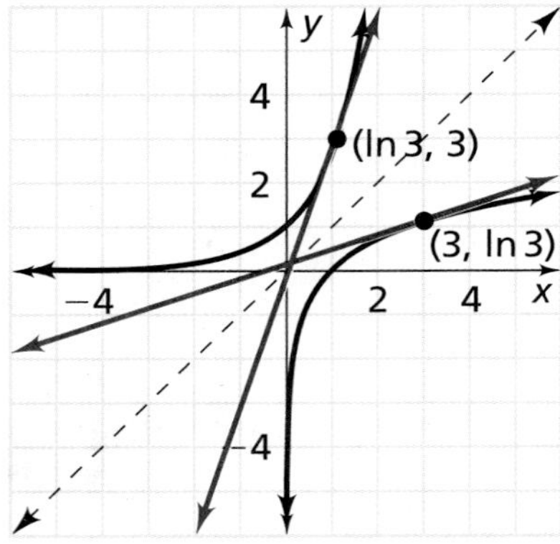


## For You to Do

**4.** Find the equation of the line tangent to $f(x) = e^x$ at the point $\left(\frac{1}{2}, \sqrt{e}\right)$.

## Exercises *Practicing Habits of Mind*

### Check Your Understanding

**1.** In this lesson you learned that $f(x) = e^x$ has an interesting property: the slope of its tangent line at any point $(x, y)$ is the same as the $y$-coordinate of that point. What can you say about the slopes of the following functions?

**a.** $h(x) = 3e^x$

**b.** $j(x) = e^{2x}$

**c.** $k(x) = e^{5x}$

**d.** $m(x) = e^{x \ln 2}$

2. Exercise 4 of Lesson 8.14 asked you to show that $e^{x \ln 2} = 2^x$ for any $x$. Exercise 1 of this lesson asked about the function $m(x) = e^{x \ln 2}$. You can also write this function as $m(x) = 2^x$.

   a. What is the slope of the tangent to the graph of $m(x) = 2^x$ at the point $(0, 1)$?

   b. What is the slope of the tangent to the graph of $m$ at the point $(2, 4)$? Write your answer in terms of a logarithm.

   c. What is the slope of the tangent to the graph of $p(x) = 5^x$ at the point $(1, 5)$? Write your answer in terms of a logarithm. Verify by using a graphing calculator.

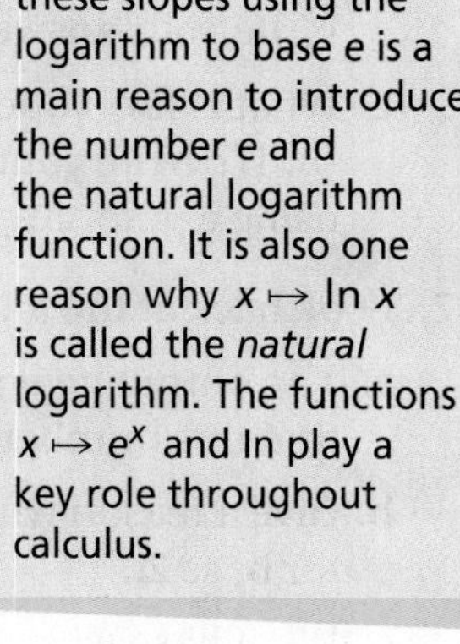

The ability to express these slopes using the logarithm to base e is a main reason to introduce the number e and the natural logarithm function. It is also one reason why $x \mapsto \ln x$ is called the *natural* logarithm. The functions $x \mapsto e^x$ and ln play a key role throughout calculus.

3. Look back at the table from Problem 5 of Lesson 8.11.

   a. The output for base 5 is 1.609. What expression could you use to find this number directly?

   b. Give a reason why the output for base 8 is three times the output for base 2.

   c. What base would make the slope of the tangent exactly 1?

   d. What base would make the slope of the tangent equal to zero?

4. Below is a three-step proof that

$$\log_2 x = \frac{\ln x}{\ln 2}$$

Justify each step.

   a. If $\log_2 x = y$, then $2^y = x$.

   b. If $2^y = x$, then $y \ln 2 = \ln x$.

   c. $\log_2 x = \dfrac{\ln x}{\ln 2}$

5. In this lesson you learned that $g(x) = \ln x$ has an interesting property: the slope of its tangent line at any point $(x, y)$ is the reciprocal of the $x$-coordinate of that point. What can you say about the slopes of the following functions?

   a. $h(x) = 3 \ln x$

   b. $j(x) = \ln 2x$

   c. $k(x) = \dfrac{\ln x}{5}$

   d. $m(x) = \dfrac{\ln x}{\ln 2}$

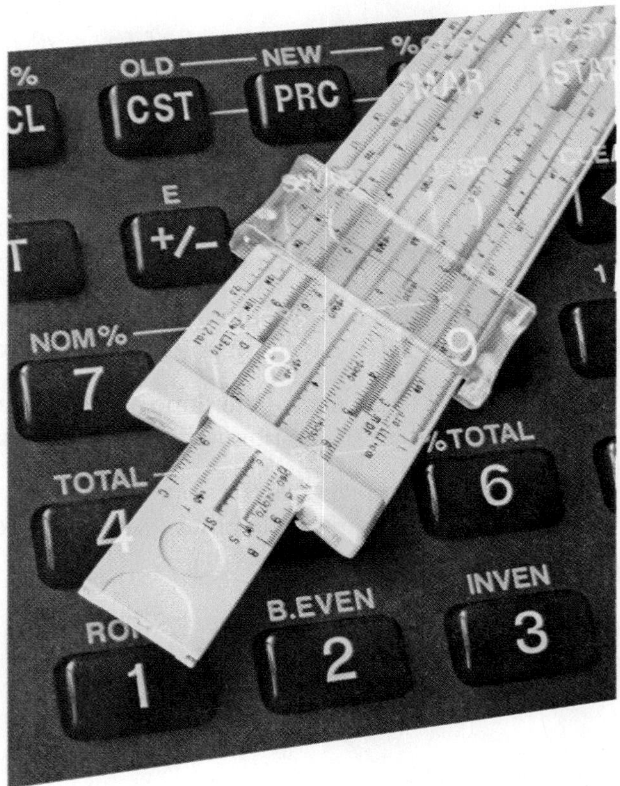


A slide rule uses logarithmic scales to perform multiplication and division by the addition and subtraction of lengths.

6. Exercise 4 asked you to show that $\log_2 x = \frac{\ln x}{\ln 2}$ for $x > 0$. Exercise 5 asked about the function $m(x) = \frac{\ln x}{\ln 2}$, which you can also write as $m(x) = \log_2 x$.
   a. What is the slope of the tangent to the graph of $m(x) = \log_2 x$ at the point $(1, 0)$?
   b. What is the slope of the tangent to the graph of $m$ at the point $(4, 2)$? Write your answer in terms of a logarithm.
   c. What is the slope of the tangent to the graph of $p(x) = \log_5 x$ at the point $(5, 1)$? Write your answer in terms of a logarithm. Verify your answer using a graphing calculator.

7. Look back at the table from Exercise 9 of Lesson 8.11.
   a. The output given for base 5 is $0.621$. What expression could you use to find this number directly?
   b. Give a reason why the output for base 8 is one-third of the output for base 2.
   c. What base would make the slope of the tangent exactly 1?
   d. What base would make the slope of the tangent equal to zero?

Of what significance is the reciprocal of 0.621?

## On Your Own

8. a. At what point does the graph of $f(x) = e^x$ have a tangent line of slope 8?
   b. What is the $y$-intercept of this tangent line? Is it positive or negative?

9. Exactly one line tangent to the graph of $f(x) = e^x$ passes through the origin. What is its equation? At what point is it tangent to the graph of $f$?

10. Find a rule that can give the slope of the line tangent to the graph of $p(x) = Ae^{bx}$ at any given point $(x, p(x))$ on the graph.

This rule generalizes some of the results from Exercise 1.

11. Find a rule that can give the slope of the line tangent to the graph of $q(x) = A \ln Bx$ at any given point $(x, q(x))$ on the graph.

12. Find a rule that can give the slope of the line tangent to the graph of $r(x) = b^x$ at any given point $(x, r(x))$ on the graph.

13. Find a rule that can give the slope of the line tangent to the graph of $s(x) = \log_b x$ at any given point $(x, s(x))$ on the graph.

14. Write About It Compare and contrast the results from Exercises 2 and 6 from this lesson. Why are the answers similar, and in what ways do they differ?

15. Take It Further Using the rules from Exercises 10 and 11, show that if a line tangent to $p(x) = Ae^{bx}$ at $(c, d)$ has slope $m$, then the line tangent to the inverse function $p^{-1}(x)$ at $(d, c)$ has slope $\frac{1}{m}$.

16. Standardized Test Prep Which of the following is an equation of the line tangent to the graph of $f(x) = 5^x$ at $(c, 5^c)$?

A. $y = 5^c(x - c) + 5^c$

B. $y = (\ln c)(x - c) + 5^c$

C. $y = 5^c(x - c) + \ln c$

D. $y = 5^c(\ln 5)(x - c) + 5^c$

## Historical Perspective

Leonhard Euler (1707–1783) was one of the greatest mathematicians of all time. He was an extraordinary algebraist—he loved to calculate with expressions, series, and functions. He was the person who first derived the identity

$$e^x = \sum_{k=0}^{\infty} \frac{x^k}{k!}$$

Euler established hundreds of identities like this, and he found connections among many of them.

Go Online
www.successnetplus.com

**In this investigation, you saw how the constant *e* arises, and you found different ways of computing it. You studied the natural logarithm (base *e*) function and its inverse, $f(x) = e^x$. You used the ln function to solve exponential equations. The following questions will help you summarize what you have learned.**

1. Adam has had \$500 invested at 6% interest, compounded quarterly for 5 years. He was telling Jamie about his account, and Jamie said. "If you'd invested that money at my bank, where they compound continuously, you would have made more money." How much more would Adam have made in 5 years at the same rate of interest?
2. **a.** Approximate $e$ using the first five terms of its factorial definition.
   **b.** What is the percent error in your estimate from part (a)?
   **c.** How large must $n$ be for the expression $\left(1 + \frac{1}{n}\right)^n$ to give just as good an approximation?
3. If you put \$5000 into an account paying 7% interest compounded continuously, when will the value of the account reach \$8000?
4. Find an equation for the tangent to the graph of $y = 3 \ln x$ at the point $(2, 3 \ln 2)$.
5. Rewrite the function $g(x) = 5^x$ in terms of $e$. Find an equation for the tangent to the graph of $g$ at the point $(2, 25)$.
6. What happens when interest is compounded more and more frequently?
7. What are some reasons to introduce the number $e$?
8. How can you relate any exponential or logarithmic function to $f(x) = e^x$ and $g(x) = \ln x$?

## Vocabulary and Notation

In this investigation, you learned these terms. Make sure you understand what each one means and how to use it.

- **continuously compounded interest**
- ***e***
- **natural logarithm, ln *x***

# Chapter 8 Review

In **Investigation 8A,** you learned how to

- graph an exponential function and determine the equation of an exponential function given two points on its graph
- identify an exponential function from the table it generates and use the table to write a closed-form or recursive definition of the function
- evaluate the inverse of the function $y = b^x$, either exactly or by approximation

*The following questions will help you check your understanding.*

**1. a.** Suppose $f$ is an exponential function with $f(2) = \frac{9}{2}$ and $f(3) = \frac{27}{2}$. Find $f(x)$.

**b.** Sketch the graph of $y = f(x)$.

**2.** Copy this table for the exponential function $g(x)$.

| x | g(x) | ÷ |
|---|---|---|
| 0 | −2 | ■ |
| 1 | −20 | ■ |
| 2 | −200 | ■ |
| 3 | −2000 | |

**a.** Complete the ratio column and write a recursive definition for $g(x)$.

**b.** Write a closed-form definition for $g(x)$.

**c.** Find $g(4)$ and $g(6)$.

**3.** Let $L_4(x)$ be the inverse of the function $h(x) = 4^x$.

**a.** Find $L_4(1)$.

**b.** Find $L_4(64)$.

**c.** Find $L_4\left(\frac{1}{16}\right)$.

In **Investigation 8B,** you learned how to

- evaluate logarithms of any base using a calculator
- use logarithms to solve exponential equations
- graph logarithmic functions

*The following questions will help you check your understanding.*

**4.** Arrange the following numbers in order from least to greatest.

$\log_2 16, \log 5, \log_3 8, \log_4 \frac{1}{8}, \log_{\frac{1}{2}} 16$

**5.** Solve each equation. Give decimal answers to three places.

**a.** $\log x - \log 5 = \log 15$

**b.** $\log_2 (x - 1) + \log_2 (x + 1) = 3$

**c.** $5^x = 7$

**d.** $3 \cdot 2^x = 20$

**6.** Let $f(x) = \log_3 x$ and $g(x) = -2x + 3$.

**a.** Graph $f(x)$ and $g(x)$ on the same set of axes.

**b.** From the graph, determine the number of solutions to the equation $\log_3 x = -2x + 3$.

**c.** Use the graph to estimate the solution(s) to $\log_3 x = -2x + 3$.

In **Investigation 8C,** you learned to

- state and use the limit and factorial definitions of $e$ and $e^x$
- use the inverse relationship between $e^x$ and $\ln x$ to solve equations
- find the equation for the line tangent to the graph of $y = e^x$ or $y = \ln x$ at a point

*The following questions will help you check your understanding.*

**7. a.** Give an estimate of $e^{0.08}$ using the first four terms of the factorial definition of $e^x$.

**b.** Give an estimate of $e^{0.08}$ by evaluating $\left(1 + \frac{0.08}{n}\right)^n$ for $n = 10$.

**c.** Use your calculator to find $e^{0.08}$ to five decimal places.

**8.** Jane invests $1000 at 5.5% APR, compounded continuously. After $t$ years, her account balance is

$$B = 1000e^{0.055t}$$

**a.** How much money will Jane have in this account after 5 years? After 10 years?

**b.** How long will it take for Jane's account to grow to $2000? $10,000?

**9.** Let $f(x) = e^x$ and $g(x) = \ln x$.

**a.** Find an equation of the line tangent to the graph of $f$ at the point $(2, f(2))$.

**b.** Find an equation of the line tangent to the graph of $g$ at the point $(2, g(2))$.

**c.** At what point does the graph of $f$ have a tangent line of slope 3?

**d.** At what point does the graph of $g$ have a tangent line of slope $\frac{1}{3}$?

Chapter

# 8 Test

Go Online
www.successnetplus.com

## Multiple Choice

**1.** Which of the following expressions is NOT equal to $\log_2 (60)$?

**A.** $\log_2 10 + \log_2 6$

**B.** $\log_2 120 - \log_2 2$

**C.** $\log_2 30 \cdot \log_2 2$

**D.** $\log_2 12 + \log_2 5$

**2.** Which point is on the graph of $f(x) = \log_3 x$?

**A.** (0, 1)

**B.** (2, 9)

**C.** (9, 2)

**D.** (60, 20)

**3.** Calculate the total value after 6 years of an initial investment of \$2250 that earns 7% interest compounded quarterly.

**A.** \$3412.00 **B.** \$3424.41

**C.** \$3472.16 **D.** \$3472.27

## Open Response

**4.** Copy this table for the exponential function $h(x)$.

| $x$ | $h(x)$ | ÷ |
|---|---|---|
| 0 | 6 | ■ |
| 1 | 3 | ■ |
| 2 | $\frac{3}{2}$ | ■ |
| 3 | $\frac{3}{4}$ | ■ |
| 4 | $\frac{3}{8}$ | |

**a.** Complete the ratio column.

**b.** Find a recursive definition for $h(x)$.

**c.** Find a closed-form definition for $h(x)$.

**d.** Find the exact value of $h(8)$.

**5.** Solve for $x$ to three decimal places.

**a.** $e^x = 5$ **b.** $\ln x = 2$

**6.** At what point does the graph of $f(x) = \ln x$ have a tangent line of slope 5?

**7.** Use the two function definitions below.

$$f(x) = 4^x$$
$$g(x) = \log_4 x$$

**a.** Copy and complete each table.

| $x$ | $f(x)$ |
|---|---|
| −1 | ■ |
| 0 | ■ |
| $\frac{1}{2}$ | ■ |
| 1 | ■ |
| 2 | ■ |

| $x$ | $g(x)$ |
|---|---|
| $\frac{1}{4}$ | ■ |
| 1 | ■ |
| 2 | ■ |
| 4 | ■ |

**b.** On a single set of axes, sketch the graphs of $f$ and $g$.

**c.** Is the graph of $f$ increasing or decreasing?

**d.** Is the graph of $g$ increasing or decreasing?

**8.** Suppose $N = \log_2 28$.

**a.** Find two consecutive integers $j$ and $k$ such that $j < N < k$.

**b.** Express $\log_2 7$ in terms of $N$. (*Hint:* $7 = \frac{28}{4}$)

**c.** Find the value of $N$ to three decimal places.

**9.** If you invest \$10,000 at 5.5% interest, compounded annually, how many years will it take until your money grows to \$15,000?

**10.** Copy and complete the table, using continuous compounding.

| Initial Investment | APR | Time to Double | Amount in 15 years |
|---|---|---|---|
| \$12,500 | 9% | ■ | ■ |
| \$32,500 | 8% | ■ | ■ |
| \$9,500 | ■ | 4 years | ■ |
| \$16,800 | ■ | 6 years | ■ |

# Chapter 9

## Investigations at a Glance

- **9A** **Making the *Least* of a Situation**
- **9B** **Making the *Most* of a Situation**
- **9C** **Conic Sections**

# Optimization and Geometric Modeling

Optimization is a process of evaluating alternatives to determine the best solution to a problem. It is a rich topic because the best solution often depends on many factors. People develop mathematical models to find the best solutions to both theoretical and practical problems. Many topics in math have been developed to answer the optimization questions that follow.

- What is the fastest way?
- What is the shortest way?
- What is the least?
- What is fairest?
- What is the cheapest way?
- What is the longest way?
- What is the largest?

## Vocabulary and Notation

- angle of incidence
- angle of reflection
- apex
- axis
- conic sections
- Dandelin sphere
- directrix
- distance
- double cone, $z^2 = x^2 + y^2$
- eccentricity
- ellipse
- focus, foci
- generator
- hyperbola
- locus
- major axis
- minor axis
- parabola
- path
- perpendicular bisector
- point-tester
- vertex

# 9.0 Equations as Point-Testers

In previous courses, you learned that graphs are point-testers. The graph of an equation is the set of the points on the Cartesian plane that make the equation true. Sometimes you can describe a graph using words, and sometimes by its shape and some key points. If you can write an equation that captures all the characteristics of the graph, that equation will be an equation for the graph.

## For You to Do

1. Find an equation describing the points $(x, y)$ that are 5 units away from $(3, 4)$.
2. Sketch a graph of all points $(x,y)$ in the plane satisfying the equation $|y - 2| = 3$.

## *Facts and Notation*

Here are some useful formulas from previous courses.

- *Distance formula*: The distance between points $A(x_1, y_1)$ and $B(x_2, y_2)$ is

$$d(A, B) = \sqrt{(x_2 - x_1)^2 + (y_2 - y_1)^2}$$

- *Midpoint formula*: The midpoint of the segment between points $A(x_1, y_1)$ and $B(x_2, y_2)$ is

$$M(A, B) = \left(\frac{x_1 + x_2}{2}, \frac{y_1 + y_2}{2}\right)$$

- *Slope formula*: The slope between points $A(x_1, y_1)$ and $B(x_2, y_2)$ is

$$m(A, B) = \frac{y_2 - y_1}{x_2 - x_1}$$

This assumes that $x_1 \neq x_2$. What happens if $x_1 = x_2$?

- *Perpendicular slopes*: Two lines in the plane are perpendicular if the product of their slopes is $-1$, or if one line is vertical and the other is horizontal.

**Remember...**

In previous work, you proved that if the slope of a line $\ell$ is $m$ (with $m \neq 0$), then the slope of any line perpendicular to $\ell$ is $-\frac{1}{m}$.

## Example 1

**Problem** Find an equation for the set of points equidistant from (5, 2) and (11, 0).

**Solution**

**Method 1** Use the distance formula. Consider any point $(x, y)$ on the graph. Its distance from (5, 2) must equal its distance from (11, 0).

$$\text{distance from } (x, y) \text{ to } (5, 2) = \text{distance from } (x, y) \text{ to } (11, 0)$$
$$\sqrt{(x-5)^2 + (y-2)^2} = \sqrt{(x-11)^2 + y^2}$$

This is a valid equation but you can simplify it. Since the expressions under the radicals are nonnegative (why?), squaring both sides will not introduce any new solutions.

$$\begin{aligned} (x-5)^2 + (y-2)^2 &= (x-11)^2 + y^2 \\ x^2 - 10x + 25 + y^2 - 4y + 4 &= x^2 - 22x + 121 + y^2 \\ -10x - 4y + 29 &= -22x + 121 \\ -4y &= -12x + 92 \\ y &= 3x - 23 \end{aligned}$$

**Method 2** Use the geometric observation that the solution will be the equation of the perpendicular bisector of the segment connecting (5, 2) and (11, 0).

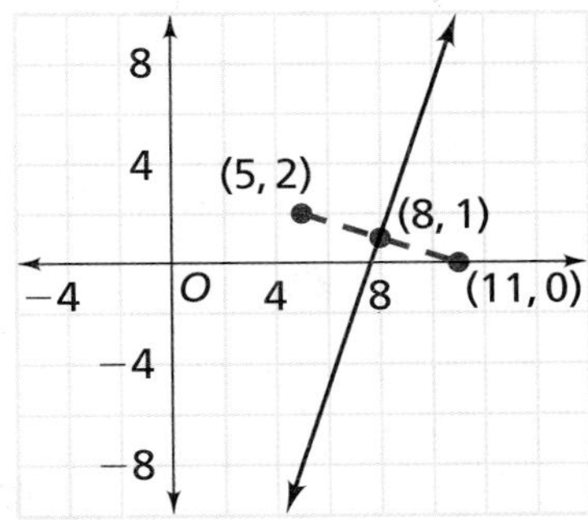


The perpendicular bisector must pass through the midpoint (8, 1) and be perpendicular to the segment. The slope between (5, 2) and (11, 0) is $-\frac{1}{3}$, so the slope of the perpendicular bisector is 3. One equation for the perpendicular bisector is $y - 1 = 3(x - 8)$. This equation is equivalent to $y = 3x - 23$ as found earlier.

**Remember...**

If you write the equation of a line in the form $y - k = m(x - h)$, the line passes through the point $(h, k)$ and has slope $m$.

## Example 2

**Problem** Find an equation for the set of points that are equidistant from the origin and the line with equation $y = 2$.

**Solution** Take an arbitrary point $(x, y)$. Its distance to the origin is $\sqrt{x^2 + y^2}$. Its distance from the line with equation $y = 2$ is $|y - 2|$.

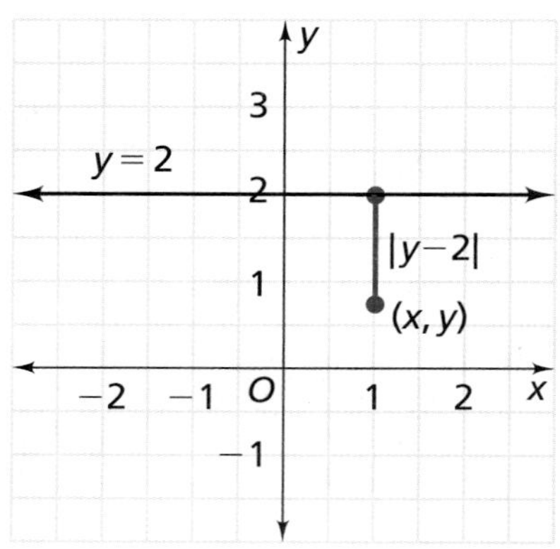


The set of points equidistant from both satisfies the equation $\sqrt{x^2 + y^2} = |y - 2|$. Simplify and solve for $y$.

$$\begin{aligned}\sqrt{x^2 + y^2} &= |y - 2| \\ x^2 + y^2 &= (y - 2)^2 \\ x^2 + y^2 &= y^2 - 4y + 4 \\ x^2 + 4y &= 4 \\ y &= -\tfrac{1}{4}x^2 + 1\end{aligned}$$

The graph of the equation is a downward opening parabola.

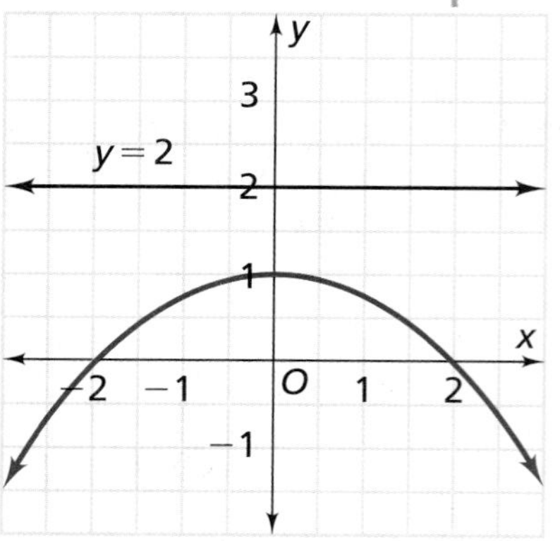


**Habits of Mind**

**Understand the process.** Why is it legal to square both sides?

## Developing Habits of Mind

**Establish a process.** The intersection of the graphs of two equations is the set of points that satisfies both of their equations. Suppose you want to find all intersections of the graphs of the equations $x^2 - y^2 = 9$ and $x + y = 5$. You can solve this algebraically. Note that you can factor $x^2 - y^2$.

$$(x + y)(x - y) = 9$$

But $x + y = 5$ is known, so $x - y$ must equal 1.8. Then a system of equations emerges.

$$\begin{aligned} x + y &= 5 \\ x - y &= 1.8 \end{aligned}$$

You can solve this system of equations by many methods, including adding the two equations together. The solution $x = 3.4$, $y = 1.6$ is the only intersection of the two graphs.

# Exercises Practicing Habits of Mind

## Check Your Understanding

1. **a.** Write a point-tester that is true for any point $(x, y)$ 3 units away from the line with equation $y = 2$.

   **b.** Sketch the graph of all points $(x, y)$ that are 3 units away from the line with equation $y = 2$.

2. Consider the set of all points $(x, y)$ that are the same distance away from $(4, 0)$ as they are from the $y$-axis.

   **a.** Determine whether $(3, 3)$ is in this set of points.

   **b.** Determine whether $(10, 8)$ is in the set.

   **c.** Explain why any point $(a, b)$ with $a < 0$ cannot be in this set of points.

   **d.** Write a point-tester that is true for any point $(x, y)$ equidistant from $(4, 0)$ and the $y$-axis.

3. You have learned that the set of points equidistant from two given points in the plane is a line. But now, consider the set of points that are twice as far away from $(15, 0)$ as they are from $(6, 0)$.

   **a.** Is $(5, 3)$ in this set? Justify your answer.

   **b.** Find the two points on the $x$-axis that are in this set.

   **c.** Write a point-tester equation that you can use to determine whether any point $(x, y)$ is in this set.

   **d.** Sketch the graph of the point-tester equation.

4. A triangle has vertices $A(2, 0)$, $B(6, -2)$, and $C(8, 4)$.

   **a.** Find an equation for the perpendicular bisector of $\overline{AB}$.

   **b.** Find an equation for the perpendicular bisector of $\overline{AC}$.

   **c.** Find the intersection of the two perpendicular bisectors.

5. Point-testers can be useful to find equations in three-dimensional space. Consider the set of points exactly 5 units away from the point $(2, 3, 4)$.

   **a.** Find five points that are in this set.

   **b.** Find five points that are not in this set.

   **c.** Write a point-tester equation that you can use to determine whether any point $(x, y, z)$ is in this set of points.

6. Consider the set of points in space that are the same distance from the origin $(0, 0, 0)$ as they are from the point $(2, 4, 6)$.

   a. In the plane, the set of points equidistant from two points would be a line. What kind of shape should it be in space?

   b. Determine whether or not $(3, 7, -1)$ is in this set of points.

   c. What equation would you use to check to see if $(x, y, z)$ is in this set of points? Simplify the equation as much as possible.

   d. Use the point-tester from part (c) to determine whether or not the point $(15, 4, -3)$ is in this set of points.

   e. Take It Further Sketch the graph of all points in this set.

## On Your Own

7. Exercise 4 looked at the perpendicular bisectors of $\triangle ABC$.

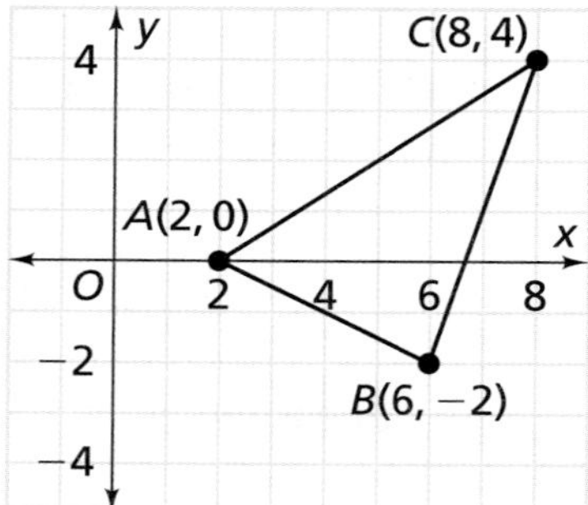


   a. Find an equation for the perpendicular bisector of $\overline{BC}$.

   b. Find an intersection for the perpendicular bisectors of $\overline{AB}$ and $\overline{BC}$.

8. Find equations for the three medians of $\triangle ABC$. Show that the three medians intersect in one point.

9. Consider the equation in three variables

$$z^2 = x^2 + y^2$$

a. Find several points $(x, y, z)$ that are on the graph of this equation.

b. Suppose $z = 5$. Describe the set of $x$ and $y$ values that make the equation true.

c. Suppose $z = 11$. Describe the set of $x$ and $y$ values that make the equation true.

d. Suppose $z = -11$. Describe the set of $x$ and $y$ values that make the equation true.

e. Suppose $z = 0$. Describe the set of $x$ and $y$ values that make the equation true.

f. Sketch the graph of $z^2 = x^2 + y^2$ as accurately as you can.



10. **Take It Further** The graph of $z^2 = x^2 + y^2$ is sometimes called a *double cone.*

a. What kind of figure does slicing the double cone perpendicular to the $z$-axis (say, with the plane with equation $z = 5$) produce?

b. What is the graph that results when the plane with equation $x = 3$ slices the double cone?

c. Find what other shapes might be possible with other slices. Give some examples.

An equation for the plane that contains the point $(0, 0, c)$ is $z = c$. Similarly, an equation for the plane that contains the point $(a, 0, 0)$ is $x = a$.

11. **Standardized Test Prep** Which of the following is an equation for the set of points equidistant from (2, 3) and (6, 1)?

a. $\sqrt{(x-2)^2 + (y-3)^2} = \sqrt{(x-6)^2 + (y-1)^2}$

b. $\frac{y-3}{x-2} = \frac{y-1}{x-6}$

c. $y - 3 = -\frac{1}{2}(x - 2)$

d. $2x + 3y = 6x + y$

## Maintain Your Skills

12. The *centroid* of a triangle is the intersection of its medians. Given the three vertices of $\triangle ABC$, find its centroid.

a. $A(0, 0), B(10, 0), C(2, 9)$

b. $A(0, 0), B(10, 0), C(2, -9)$

c. $A(0, 0), B(100, 0), C(20, 90)$

d. $A(1, 2), B(10, 11), C(19, 5)$

e. $A(0, 0), B(3a, 0), C(3b, 3c)$

f. $A(x_1, y_1), B(x_2, y_2), C(x_3, y_3)$

# Making the *Least* of a Situation

**In *Making the* Least *of a Situation,* you will minimize things. You minimize quantities in architecture, computer programming, economics, engineering, and medicine. This is because real-world optimization often involves making something as small as possible. You can minimize a rate, time, distance, area, volume, or angle measure.**

**By the end of this investigation, you will be able to answer questions like these.**

1. What is the difference between the length of a path from one point to another and the distance between the points?
2. When and how can reflection help you find the shortest path for a situation?
3. In the following figure, $\overline{AS}$ and $\overline{BF}$ are perpendicular to $\overleftrightarrow{AB}$. $AS = 54$ ft, $BF = 27$ ft, and $AB = 84$ ft.

   Describe the location of $P$ on $\overleftrightarrow{AB}$ such that the path from $S$ to $P$ to $F$ is as short as possible.

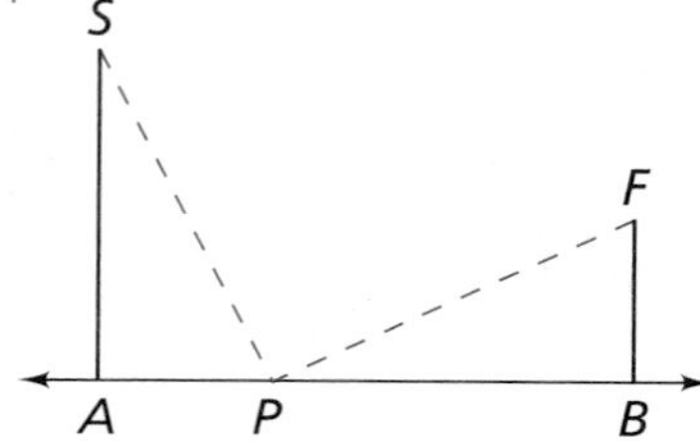


**You will learn how to**

- find the length of a path under given restrictions
- choose points that result in a minimum length for a path
- compute lengths and distances on the coordinate plane

**You will develop these habits and skills:**

- Distinguish between distance and the length of a path.
- Draw conclusions from trends in experimental data.
- Visualize reflections that will help minimize a path.
- Recognize key problem situations and choose techniques based on experience.

In this game, the least number of turns possible for moving one peg across the board is 1.

# 9.01 Getting Started

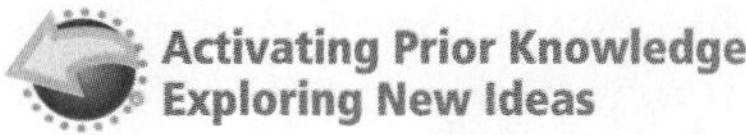


The **distance** between two fixed points is the length of the segment that contains them as endpoints. The distance is fixed. You cannot minimize or maximize it. A **path** between two points can be as long as you would like. A path between two points cannot be shorter than the distance between the points.

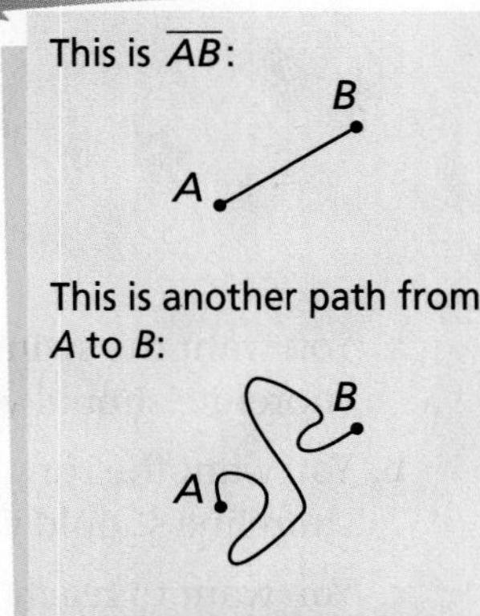

This is $\overline{AB}$:
B
A
This is another path from A to B:
B
A
Which is shorter?


In the real world, the shortest possible path between two points may not be the segment containing them as endpoints. There may be obstacles in the way, or there may be an intermediate destination. In this investigation, you will find the shortest path from one point to another given a set of restrictions.

## For You to Explore

1. Suppose you and a friend are at a corner of a parking lot and it is raining hard. All the spaces are taken and you want to get to your car by the shortest way possible. You can run around the cars or between them. What route minimizes the length of your path to the car? Is there more than one best route to the car?

2. This time, suppose you are standing in a courtyard with regularly spaced columns.

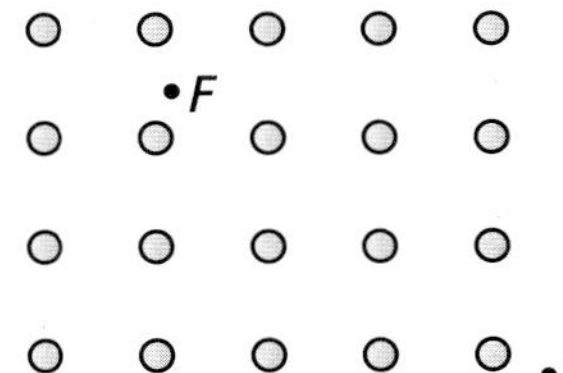


Find the shortest path you can from $S$ to $F$. Did you use a different technique than you did in Problem 1? Explain.

**Habits of Mind**

**Visualize.** Would it be possible to travel along the segment with endpoints at New York and Tokyo?

**3.** You are lounging on the beach at $L$. You want to run to the shoreline and swim out to your friends at $K$.

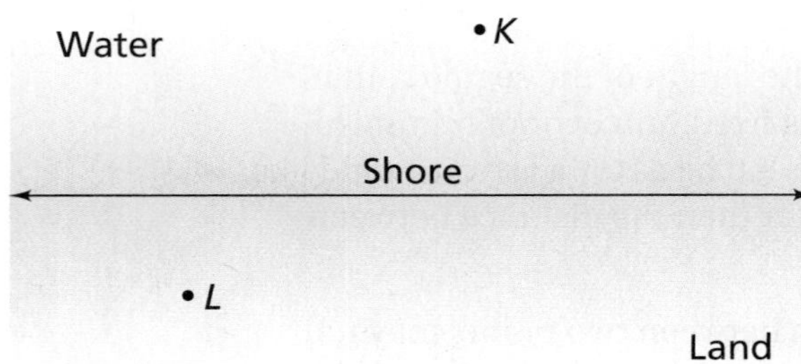


**a.** You want the swim to be as short as possible. To what point on the shoreline should you run to minimize the path you swim? Explain.

**b.** You want the run to be as short as possible. At what point on the shoreline should you enter the water now? Explain.

**c.** You want to reach $K$ in the least possible total distance. Now where should you enter the water? Explain.

**4.** Use the following figure to answer parts (a) and (b).

**a.** Find the distance from $A(-2, 3)$ to $B(5, 7)$.

**b.** Add the restriction that no path from $A$ to $B$ may intersect $\overline{MN}$. Now find the length of the shortest path.

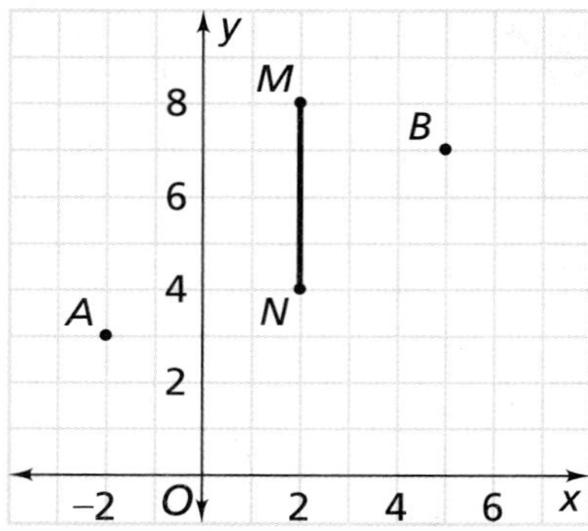


This run-and-swim problem will be referenced later in the chapter.

## Exercises Practicing Habits of Mind

### On Your Own

**5.** How do you measure the distance between two points when you are not in math class? How do you measure the distance between two points on the coordinate plane?

**6.** How do you measure the distance from a point to a line outside of math class? On the coordinate plane? Describe the process you would go through, rather than giving a formula.

For Exercises 7–10, use this new way to think about a coordinate grid. Imagine that the coordinate grid is actually a wire mesh set in a vertical plane, and an ant walks on it. There are wires at each whole-number value for $x$ and $y$. The ant can walk only horizontally or vertically along the wires. The distance between two adjacent horizontal or vertical wires is 1 unit.

**7. a.** Describe the ant's path from $A$ to $B$.

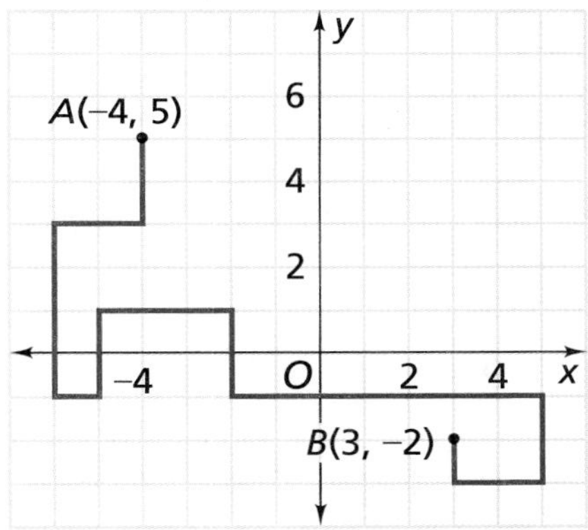


**b.** What is the length of this path?

**c.** Describe three different paths that an ant could take from $A$ to $B$ and give the length for each.

**d.** What is the length of the shortest possible path of an ant from $A$ to $B$? Explain your answer.

**e.** Is the shortest path of an ant from $A$ to $B$ unique? If not, what do all the shortest paths from $A$ to $B$ have in common?

8. Find the distance between each pair of points on the coordinate plane. Then find the length of a shortest path of an ant between them.

   a. $(-1, 3)$ and $(3, -1)$

   b. $(2, 4)$ and $(-1, -5)$

   c. $(4, 0)$ and $(-3, 8)$

9. **Take It Further** Name several pairs of points for which the distance between them is the same as the length of a shortest path of an ant. What relationship must the two points have for this to be true?

10. **Take It Further** Write a formula that gives the length of the shortest path of an ant from $(x_1, y_1)$ to $(x_2, y_2)$. Check that your formula works for points in any quadrant.

## Maintain Your Skills

11. In the following graph, $A$, $B$, $S$, and $F$ are fixed and $P$ can be anywhere along $\overleftrightarrow{AB}$.

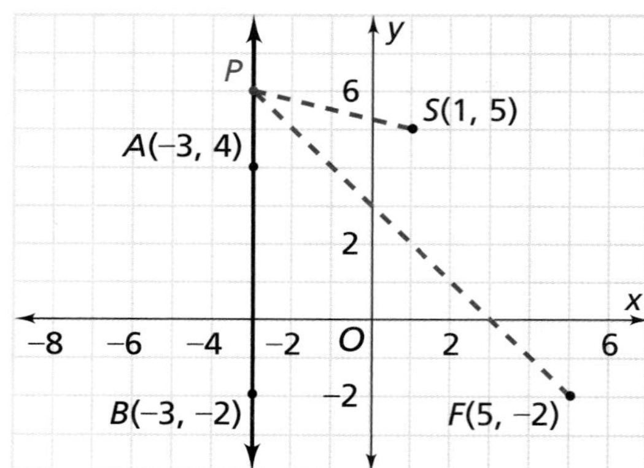


Find the length of the path from $S$ to $P$ to $F$ for the following coordinates of $P$.

   a. $P(-3, 6)$

   b. $P(-3, 4)$

   c. $P(-3, 2)$

   d. $P(-3, 0)$

   e. $P(-3, -2)$

   f. $P(-3, -4)$

12. Refer to the information in Exercise 11.

   a. What is the distance from $S$ to $F$?

   b. What location of $P$ makes the length of the path from $S$ to $P$ to $F$ the shortest possible? Explain.

   c. What is the length of the shortest path from $S$ to $P$ to $F$?

# 9.02 Finding the Shortest Path

As you saw in Lesson 9.01, you cannot always take the shortest path between two points. There may be something in the way, or you may have an intermediate stop.

> **Remember...**
> In the parking lot problem, cars were in the way.

Imagine that you are motorboating on a river and you need fuel. First you must drop a passenger off on one river bank. Then you must refuel at a station on the other river bank.

Below are some pictures of the situation. The boat is at $A$. After you drop the passenger off at $P$, you will refuel at $B$. You can choose the location for $P$ anywhere along the south bank. Because you are low on fuel, you want to minimize the length of the path you travel.

Should you land here?

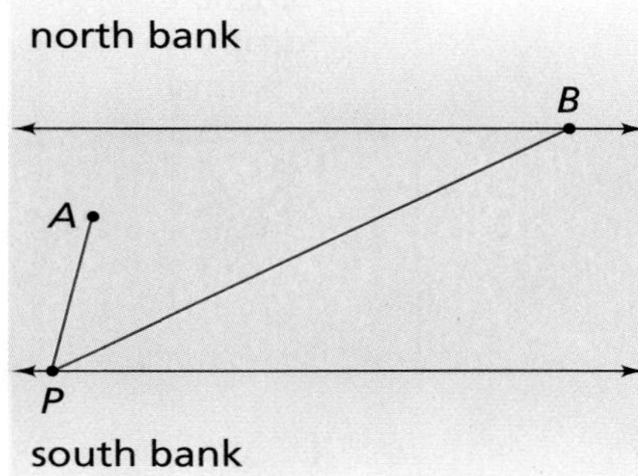


. . . or here?

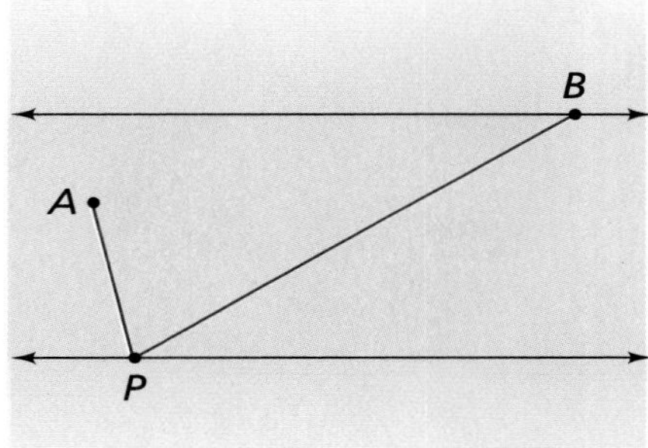


. . . or maybe here?

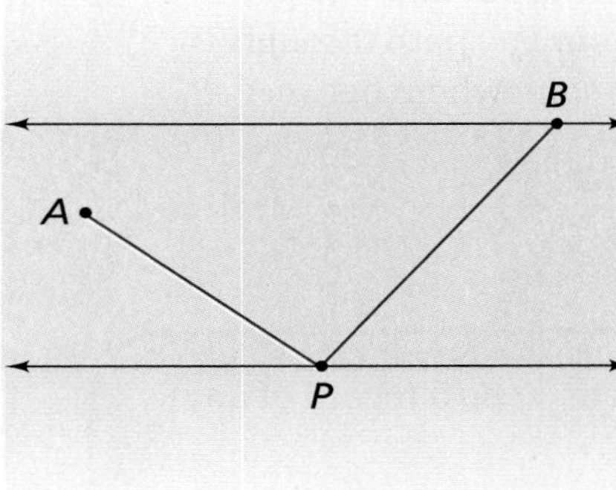

## Minds in Action

*Tony and Sasha think about the refueling problem.*

**Sasha** If you are traveling downstream, there's no way that you'd go back upstream from $A$ to drop off the passenger before refueling.

**Tony** And you'd never go farther downstream than the fuel station at $B$.

**Sasha** So the best solution has to be somewhere downstream from $A$ and upstream from $B$.

**Tony** Let's try some different places for $P$. We can measure to see what happens to the total distance traveled as we move $P$ from left to right.

Possible drop-off points fall between the two vertical lines.

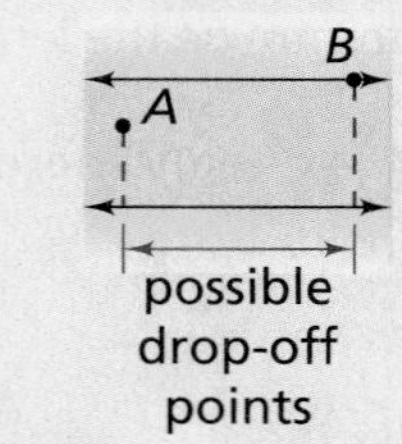


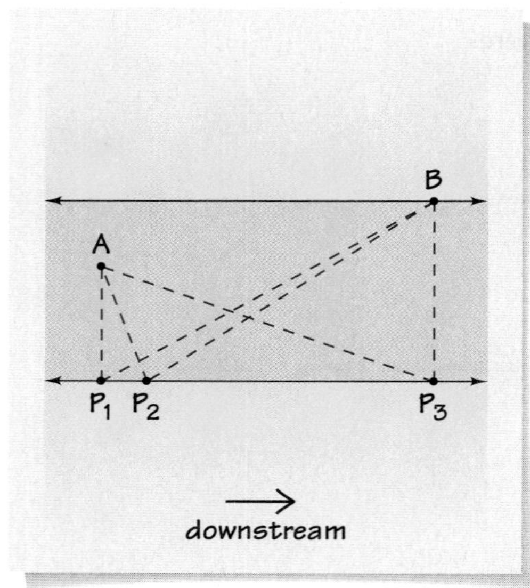


**Sasha** The path through $P_1$ directly below $A$ is about 63 mm. The path through $P_3$ directly below $B$ is about 68 mm. The path through $P_2$ measures 59 mm. The best path has to be somewhere between $P_1$ and $P_3$.

## For You to Do

Here are some questions about the refueling problem. Keep a record of any conjectures you make, and justify your conclusions.

1. What happens to $AP$ as $P$ moves downstream? What happens to $PB$?
2. How does the sum $AP + PB$ change as $P$ moves downstream?
3. Visualize, or draw, a sketch in which you hold $A$ constant, but widen the river and move $B$ farther away. Does the best location for $P$ move to the left or right?

## Developing Habits of Mind

**Visualize.** Here is another way to think about the refueling problem. When you look into a mirror, an object's reflection appears to be the same distance from the mirror as the real object. However, the reflection appears to be on the opposite side of the mirror from the real object. This makes the image and the real object symmetric with respect to the mirror.

Picture a mirror along the south bank of the river. You are standing on the north bank looking across the river.

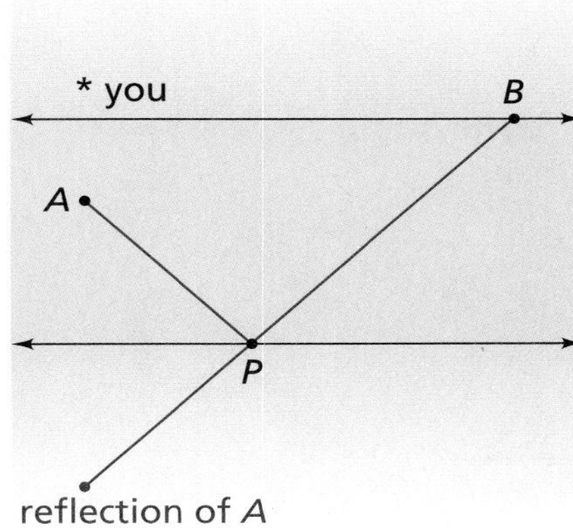


You can make the path from the *reflection of A* to *B* as short as possible by connecting the two points with a line segment. The point where this path crosses the south bank is also the point that minimizes the trip from *A* to *P* to *B*.

**Remember...**

A mirror line is the perpendicular bisector of the segment joining a point and its reflected image.

## For Discussion

4. The length of the path from the *reflection of A* to *P* to *B* is the same as the length of the path from *A* to *P* to *B*. Explain. Make a sketch using reflection to solve the refueling problem. Does it matter whether *A* or *B* is reflected? Explain.

# Exercises Practicing Habits of Mind

## Check Your Understanding

Use the figure below for Exercises 1–3.

You are in a rowboat, docked on the south bank of a river at $D$. You have to drop off a passenger on the north bank and then return the boat at $F$.

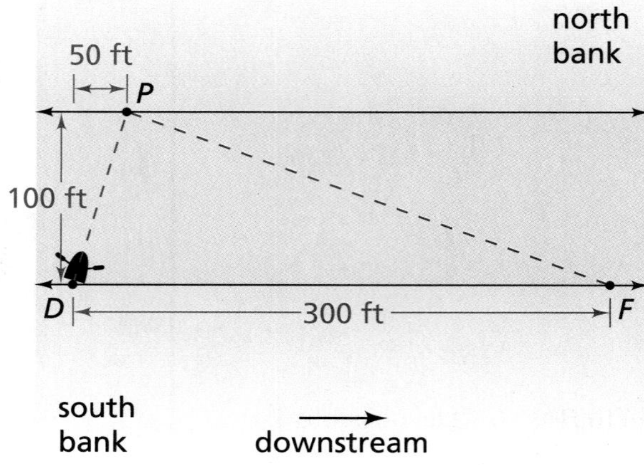


**1.** Find the total distance you have to row if the drop-off point $P$ is 50 feet downstream from $D$. Assume that you can row in a straight line in spite of the river's current.

If $P$ were $x$ feet downstream, what would be the length of the path?

**2.** In the figure above, $P$ is 50 feet downstream from $D$. Describe the location of $Q$ on the north bank if the path from $D$ to $Q$ to $F$ has the same length as the path from $D$ to $P$ to $F$. Explain how you know the length is the same without calculating it. Where would $Q$ be if $P$ were $x$ feet downstream from $D$?

**3.** Refer again to the figure above. Use reflection to find a location on the north bank for $P$ that minimizes the length of the path from $D$ to $P$ to $F$. How far downstream is $P$? Is there another point on the north bank that has a path equal in length to the path from $D$ to $P$ to $F$?

> **Habits of Mind**
>
> **Visualize.** As you move $P$ to the right, what happens to $Q$?

## On Your Own

This "burning-tent" problem will appear later in the text.

4. **Write About It** Returning from picking berries near a campground, you find your tent on fire. Luckily, the river is nearby. You must quickly empty your berry bucket and figure out at which point $P$ you should fill your bucket with water to minimize the distance you travel. Write about methods you could use to find the shortest path from where you are, to the river, and then to the tent.

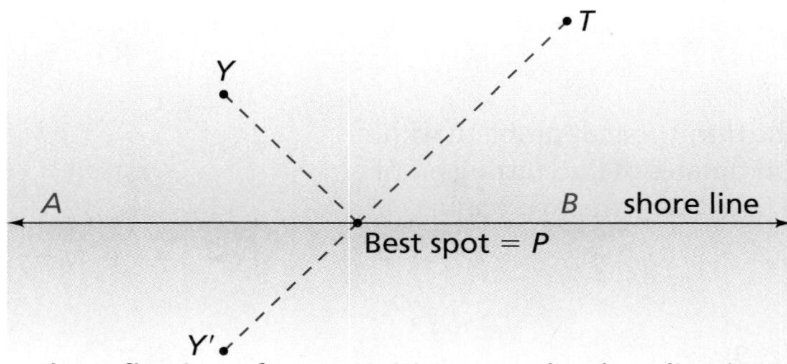


The reflection of your position over the shoreline is $Y'$.

5. Find the shortest path from $A(-4, 3)$ through any point $P$ on the line $3x - 2y = 0$, to $B(4, -1)$.

   a. Sketch a graph of the situation.

   b. What point $P$ on the line $3x - 2y = 0$ should the path go through? Explain.

   c. What is the length of the shortest path?

6. Find the shortest path from $A(-4, 3)$ to any point $P$ on the line $y = 5$, to $B(4, -1)$.

   a. Sketch a graph of the situation.

   b. What point $P$ on the line $y = 5$ should the path go through? Explain.

   c. What is the length of the shortest path?

7. Line $\ell$ has equation $2x - y = 0$. Because $\ell$ can also be written in the form $y = 2x$, points in $\ell$ are of the form $(x, 2x)$. Find a function that will give the distance between $(1, 2)$ and any other point on $\ell$. For what value of $x$ is this function at a minimum?

8. You are at an arbitrary point $M$ in a swimming pool with many sides. Describe the shortest path out of the pool. Is the path to a corner or to a side?

9. Draw a new pool and a position for $M$ such that the shortest path is to a corner.

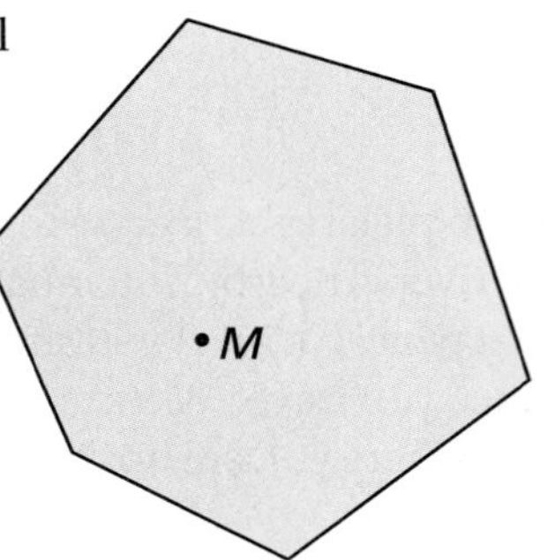


**Habits of Mind**

**Expand your thinking.** How would you describe all the points that are a given distance away from where you are in the pool?

## Maintain Your Skills

In Exercises 10–13, you will examine the burning-tent problem with trigonometry. This figure shows the coordinates of the starting point and the location of the burning tent. The $x$-axis is the riverbank.

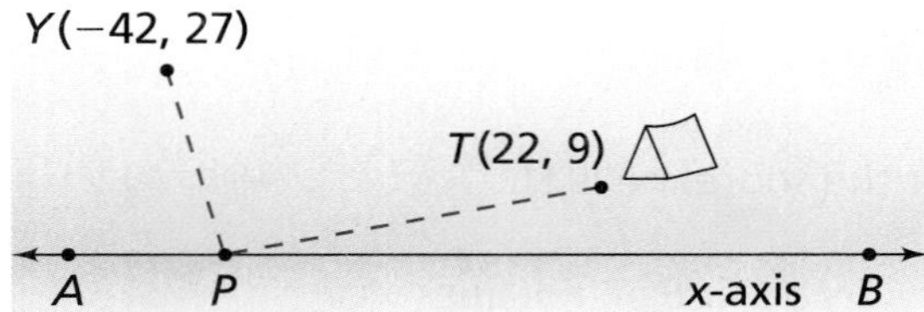


10. For each proposed location of $P$, the place you fill up your bucket, find the total length of the path.

    a. $(-42, 0)$
    b. $(-30, 0)$
    c. $(-15, 0)$
    d. $(-3, 0)$
    e. $(10, 0)$
    f. $(22, 0)$

11. For each proposed location of $P$, find and compare the approximate measures of $\angle YPA$ and $\angle TPB$.

    a. $(-42, 0)$
    b. $(-30, 0)$
    c. $(-15, 0)$
    d. $(-3, 0)$
    e. $(10, 0)$
    f. $(22, 0)$

12. Analyze your data from Exercise 10. The point $P$ with the shortest path falls between which two points? Analyze your data from Exercise 11. What happens to $\angle YPA$ and $\angle TPB$ as you approach this location for $P$?

13. Find the approximate location for the point $P$ with the shortest path. Use your reasoning from Exercise 12.

# 9.03 Reflecting to Find the Shortest Path

When you used reflection in the burning-tent and boating problems, you may have noticed similarities. Think about the angles at which the minimum-length paths intersect the riverbank. The situation is similar to the game of pool. The angle at which a ball hits the bumper is the same as the angle at which it ricochets off the bumper.

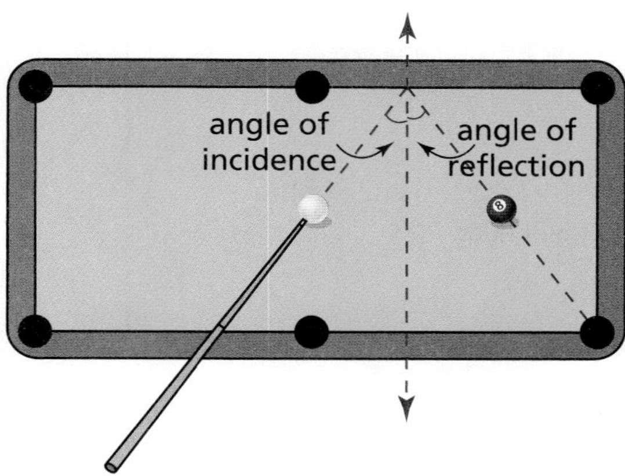


The **angle of incidence** is the angle between the incoming ball and the line perpendicular to the bumper at the collision point. The **angle of reflection** is the angle between the ball and the perpendicular line as the ball leaves the bumper.

## For Discussion

1. Does this relationship hold for the minimum path length in the burning-tent problem? Is the angle at which you approach the river the same as the angle at which you leave the river? Does the reflection method guarantee this result? Explain.

In pool, friction affects the ball, and the ball's collision with the bumper is not perfectly elastic. This means that the measure of its angle of reflection is only approximately equal to the measure of its angle of incidence. In this lesson, imagine an ideal pool table, with no friction and perfectly elastic collisions.

## Example

**Problem** Your goal is to hit the white ball in the figure off the top bumper, the right bumper, and then knock the black ball into the bottom center pocket.

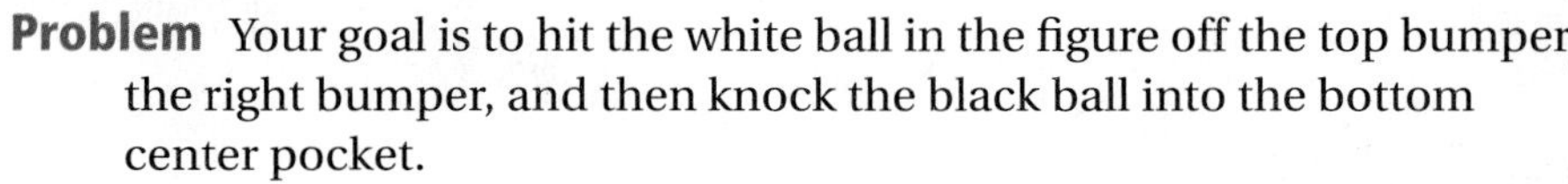

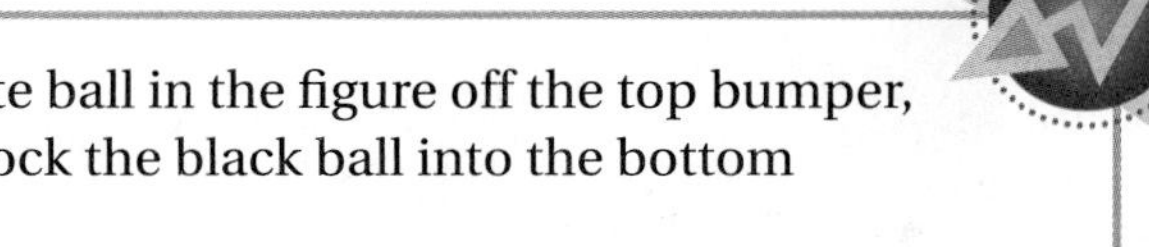

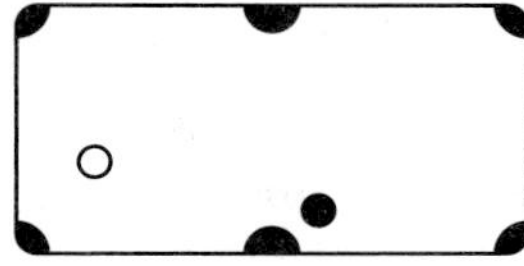

Find the point on the top bumper where the white ball should hit.

**Solution** You want to make a straight line through the top bumper of the table, the right bumper, and the target pocket. Reflect the pool table over its top edge. Reflect it again over its right edge. Now you can draw the straight line you want, as in the figure below. (The word *pool* is in the figure to help you visualize the reflections.)

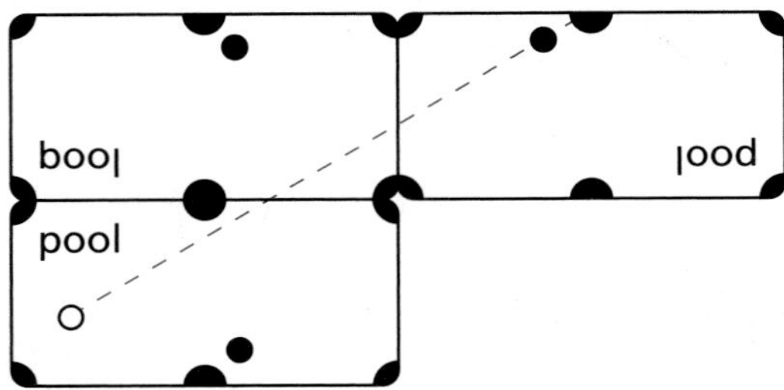


You should aim for the point where this line crosses the top edge of the table. Here is a sketch of the path the white ball will take.

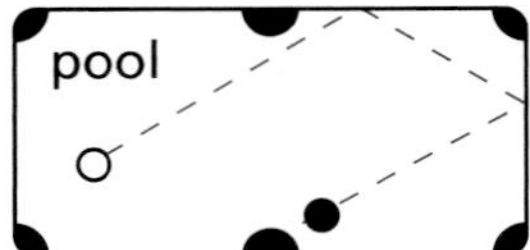


## For You to Do

2. Use the figure from the Example for the starting point of the white ball. This time, you want the white ball to hit the right bumper, the left bumper, and then go into the bottom center pocket. Find the point you should aim for and sketch the path of the ball.

# Exercises Practicing Habits of Mind

## Check Your Understanding

1. Your goal is to hit the white ball off the top bumper, the bottom bumper, and then knock the black ball into the top left corner pocket.

   Locate the point you should aim for and sketch the path you expect the ball to take.

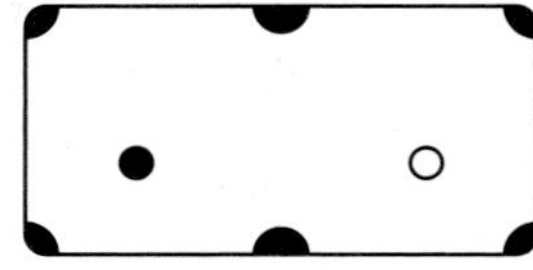

2. Design your own pool-shot problem involving at least two bumpers. Solve the problem yourself. Then give your problem to a classmate and compare your solutions.

3. A canoe is at $R$ in the figure at the right. First, a passenger must be let off on the west bank. Then a passenger must be picked up on the east bank and dropped off at island $S$. Find the drop-off and pickup points that minimize the total distance traveled. Explain your reasoning. Check your answer with a ruler and string, or geometry software.

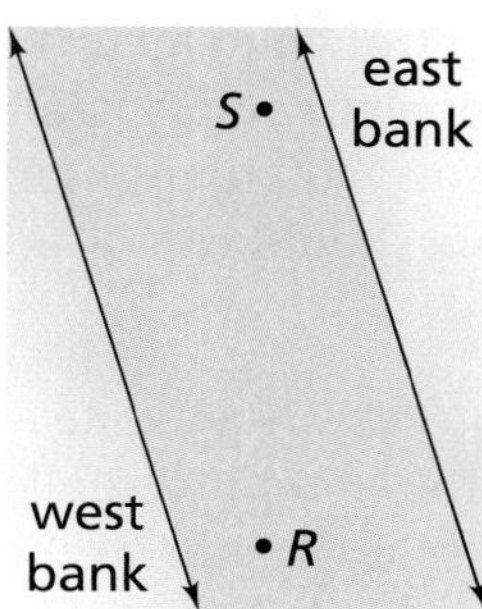


## On Your Own

4. **Write About It** You are given line $\ell$ and two points $S$ and $F$ that are not on the line. Describe a strategy for finding $P$ on $\ell$ that minimizes the length of the path from $S$ to $P$ to $F$.

5. You are in a rectangular swimming pool at $K$, out of reach of the sides of the pool. Before swimming to $L$, you want to swim to a side of the pool to put down your sunglasses.

   Explain how to find the place to put your sunglasses that minimizes the length of the path you swim.

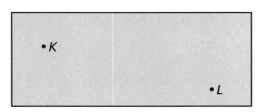

6. A path on the coordinate plane must go from $P(3, -1)$ to point $L$ on line $\ell$ with equation $x = -1$. Then the path goes to point $M$ on line $m$ with equation $x = 7$, and finally to $Q(3, 8)$. Graph the shortest path and find the coordinates of $L$ and $M$.

7. In Exercise 6, $P$ is exactly halfway between lines $\ell$ and $m$.

   a. If $P$ moves closer to line $\ell$ than to line $m$, how does the path from $P$ to $\ell$, to $m$, and then to $Q$ change?

   b. Check your prediction in part (a) by solving the problem again, but with $P(0, -1)$.

8. You are running a race at a July Fourth party. There are water troughs all along the left and right sides of the course.

The goal is to run to the left trough to fill up a pitcher, run to the right trough to empty it, and then cross the finish line. You want to minimize the distance you run. Where should you fill and empty the pitcher?

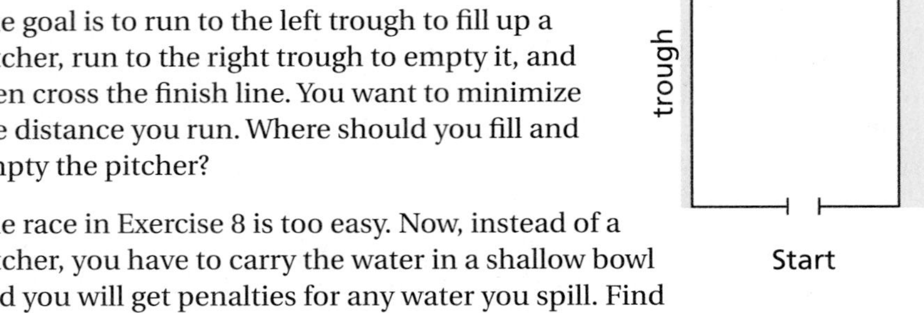

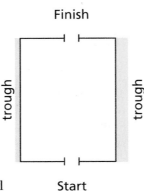

9. The race in Exercise 8 is too easy. Now, instead of a pitcher, you have to carry the water in a shallow bowl and you will get penalties for any water you spill. Find a new route that minimizes the distance you have to carry the water-filled bowl.

10. **Standardized Test Prep** The measure of the angle at which a ray of light hits a mirror is 30°. What is the measure of the angle at which the ray of light reflects off the mirror?

**A.** 30° **B.** 60° **C.** 90° **D.** 150°

## Maintain Your Skills

You have been minimizing lengths of paths that go through only two or three points. In this next series of problems, you will explore situations with more stopping points. In Exercises 11–13, you have $A(-3, -2)$, $B(1, 3)$, and $C(4, -1)$. A path is defined as follows.

- The path must start and end at $A$.
- It must pass through each of the other given points once and only once.
- For two paths to be considered different, one must contain at least one point that is not on the other path.

Answer the following questions for each of the given situations.

**a.** How many different paths meet the requirements?

**b.** Find the length of each path that fits the requirements. Which path is the shortest?

11. A path in this situation is made up of segments having $A$, $B$, and $C$ as endpoints. (A path must pass through $B$ and $C$ once and only once.)

12. Include a fourth point $D(-2, 0)$ in the situation. Now the path consists of segments having $A$, $B$, $C$, and $D$ as endpoints.

13. Include a fifth point $E(0, 5)$ in the situation. Now the path consists of segments having $A$, $B$, $C$, $D$, and $E$ as endpoints.

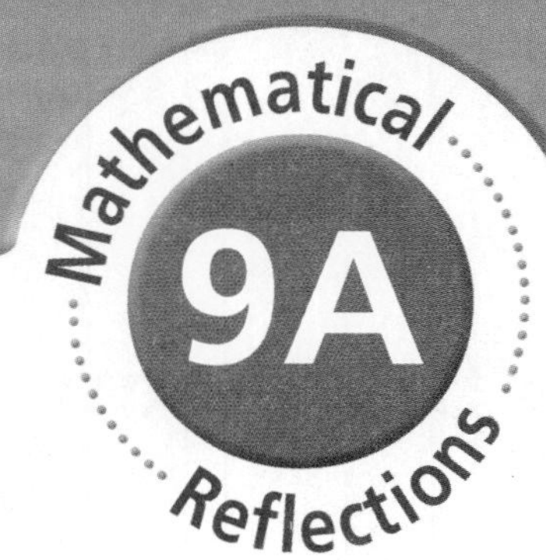


**In this investigation, you learned to distinguish between path and distance, and find the length of a path under given restrictions. These questions will help you summarize what you have learned.**

1. Describe this ant's path from $A$ to $B$ and find the path's length.

   Is this the shortest possible path between $A$ and $B$? Explain your answer.

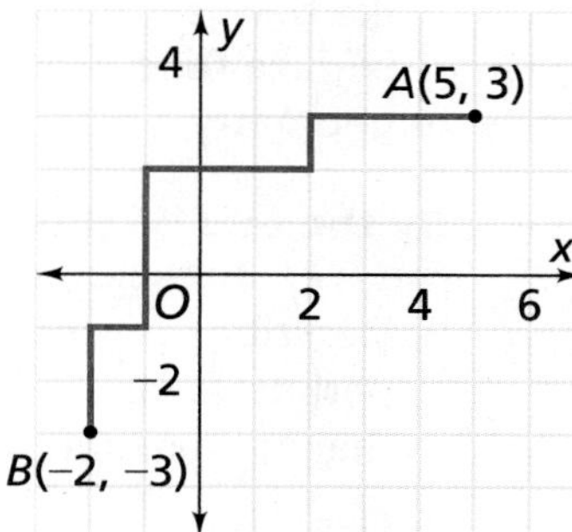


In Exercises 2 and 3, a path must lead from $(-3, 2)$, to the $x$-axis, and then to (5, 2).

2. One path touches the $x$-axis at (2, 0). Find the length of the path.
3. Find a different path that has the same length as the path in Exercise 2.
4. A path must lead from (3, 5), to the line $2x + y = 4$, and then to (1, 1). Where does the shortest path cross the line?
5. Find the path of minimum length that goes from $(-1, 4)$, to the line $y = 5$, to the line $y = -2$, and ends at (2, 2). Your solution should include a graph and the coordinates of any significant points.
6. What is the difference between the length of a path from one point to another and the distance between the points?
7. When and how can reflection help you find the shortest path for a situation?
8. In the figure, $\overline{AS}$ and $\overline{BF}$ are perpendicular to $\overleftrightarrow{AB}$. $AS = 54$ ft, $BF = 27$ ft, and $AB = 84$ ft.

   Describe the location of $P$ on $\overleftrightarrow{AB}$ such that the path from $S$ to $P$ to $F$ is as short as possible.

It's your turn. Can you move one peg across the board?

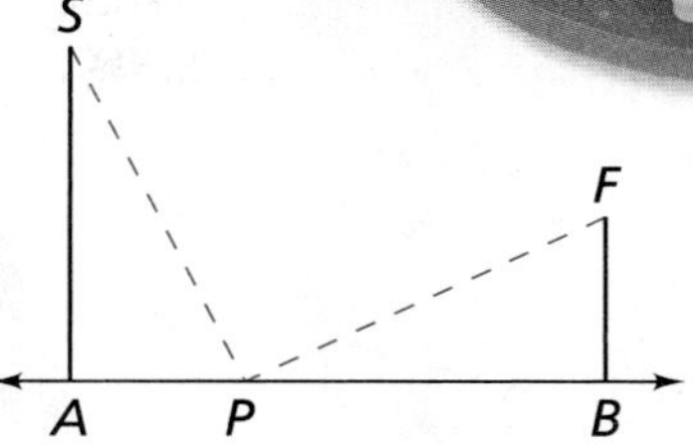


## Vocabulary

In this investigation, you learned these terms. Make sure you understand what each one means and how to use it.

- **angle of incidence**
- **angle of reflection**
- **distance**
- **path**

# Making the *Most* of a Situation

**In *Making the* Most *of a Situation*, you will maximize things—make things as large as possible. In general, people want to maximize food production, profit, gas mileage, fun, or comfort. In geometry, area, angles, and height are often maximized.**

**By the end of this investigation, you will be able to answer questions like these.**

1. Describe some characteristics of a rectangle that has maximum perimeter for a given area. Describe some characteristics of a rectangle that has maximum area for a given perimeter.
2. Describe several situations in which reflection can help you find the maximum area for a figure.
3. You want to build a rectangular garden against one wall of your house. You have 29 feet of border fencing. What are the area and dimensions of the largest possible garden you can build?

**You will learn how to**

- find grid polygons with a given area or perimeter
- maximize area for a triangle or rectangle under given conditions
- find the maximum area for a shape with a given perimeter

**You will develop these habits and skills:**

- Draw conclusions from trends in experimental data.
- Visualize reflections that will help maximize area.
- Reason by continuity to find maximums.

In-car monitors help you get the most miles per gallon.

# 9.04 Getting Started

Area and perimeter seem as though they should be related to each other. For example, if one fence encloses a greater area than another, it seems that the walk around the first fence should be longer. However, it does not always work that way. Here are two fields entirely enclosed by fences. You have to check the fences to see if they are in good repair.

Field A

Field B

Which field has more acreage? Which field has more fence for you to check?

An acre is a unit of area equal to 43,560 square feet.

## For You to Explore

1. Use only the grid lines on a sheet of graph paper. Draw several polygons with area 8 square units. Find the perimeter of each one. What are the greatest and least possible perimeters for grid polygons of this area?
2. Use only the grid lines on a sheet of graph paper. Draw several polygons with perimeter 12 units. Find the area of each one. What are the greatest and least possible areas for grid polygons of this perimeter?
3. Use only $1 \times 1 \times 1$ unit cubes joined face to face. Build and sketch several three-dimensional shapes with volume 8 cubic units. Find the surface area of each structure. What are the greatest and least possible surface areas for cube structures of this volume?
4. Use only $1 \times 1 \times 1$ unit cubes joined face to face. Build and sketch several three-dimensional shapes with surface area 22 square units. Find the volume of each structure. What are the greatest and least possible volumes for cube structures that have this surface area?

### Habits of Mind

**Find another way.** You do not need a formula to find the surface area of your structures. Just count the exposed cube faces on the top, bottom, and sides of your structure. What is the area of each cube face?

# Exercises *Practicing Habits of Mind*

## On Your Own

5. Describe several situations in which maximizing area would help in making food or money, saving time, or providing other benefits.

6. Each of the following grid polygons is changing. One square unit of area will be added to the polygon in the location shown. Find the perimeter and area for both the original and the new polygon.

In part (d), the original figure is not a polygon. The new figure is a polygon. The square with the missing center is included for the sake of completeness.

a. 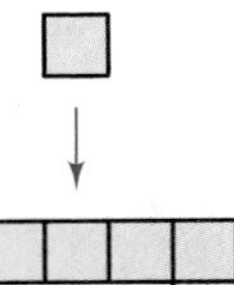

b. 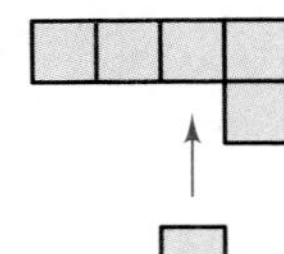

c. 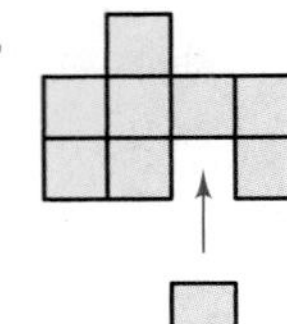

d. 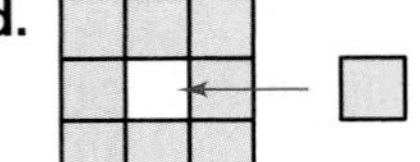

**Habits of Mind**

**Look for patterns.** Are there any cases not included in this exercise? Explain.

7. Change this grid polygon by adding as many square units to the polygon as you can without changing its perimeter. Show each step you take and check that the perimeter is unchanged. What is the greatest area you can get?

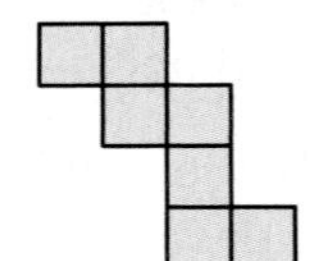

8. Each cube structure is changing. One cubic unit of volume will be added to the structure in the location shown. Find the surface area and volume of both the original and the new structures.

a. 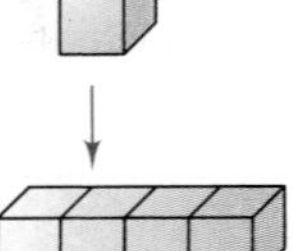

b. 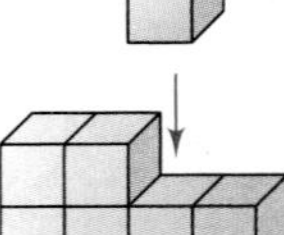

c. 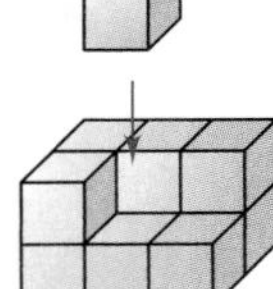

d. 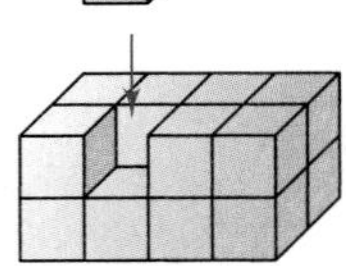

Parts (e) and (f) may be difficult to visualize. Each figure is shown with an exploded view that shows the floors of the structure separately.

**Original Structure**

**e.**

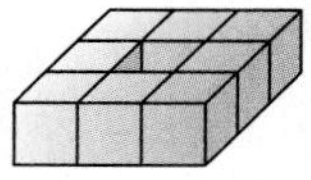

top floor: 8 cubes

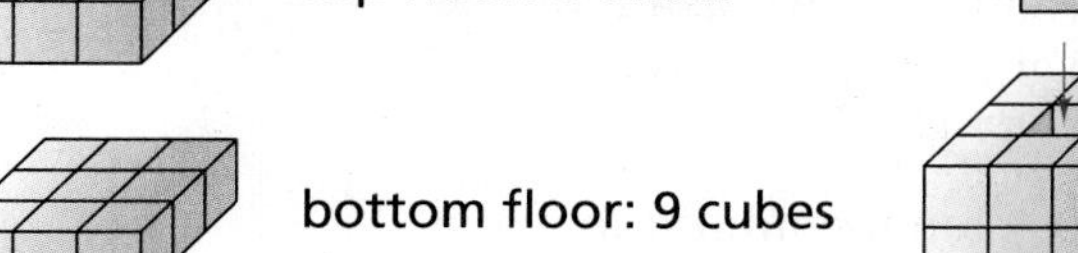

bottom floor: 9 cubes

**f.** Defining the surface area of the original structure is difficult because the structure has a hollow space in the middle. Count any square face that is touched by air as part of the surface area.

**Original Structure**

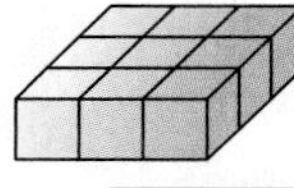

top floor: 9 cubes

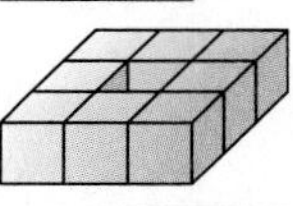

middle floor: 8 cubes

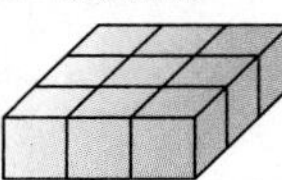

bottom floor: 9 cubes

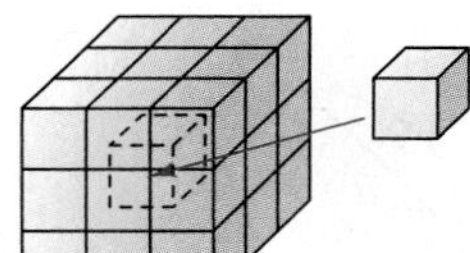
The added cube
fills in the hollow
space.

**9.** Change this cube structure by adding as many cubic units as you can without changing its surface area. Show each step you take and check that the surface area is unchanged. What is the greatest volume you can get?

**10.** **Write About It** Describe the characteristics of grid polygons that have maximum perimeter for a given area. What do they look like? What features *don't* they have?

**11.** **Write About It** Describe the characteristics of grid polygons that have minimum perimeter for a given area. What do they look like? What features *don't* they have?

**12.** Find four polygons with area 12 square units. Each must meet one of the following criteria.

- It is a grid polygon that has maximum perimeter.
- It is a grid polygon that has minimum perimeter.
- It is a polygon of any type that has a greater perimeter than the maximum for grid polygons. (This polygon is not restricted to grid lines on graph paper.)
- It is a polygon of any type that has a perimeter less than the minimum for grid polygons.

## Maintain Your Skills

For Exercises 13–16, the regular polygon is inscribed in a circle of radius 1.

- Find the measure of the central angle $\theta$, which intersects two adjacent vertices of the polygon.
- Find the length of one side of the polygon.
- Find the perimeter of the polygon.

**13.**

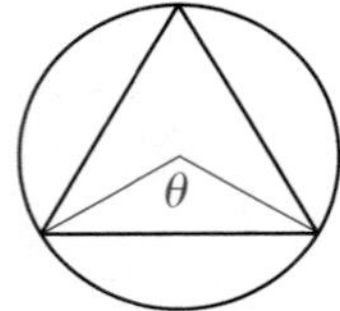


**14.**

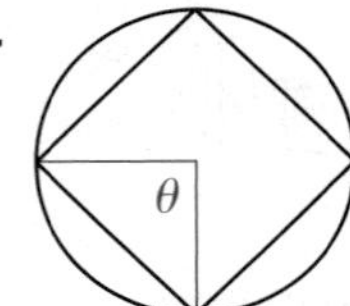


**15.**

**16.**

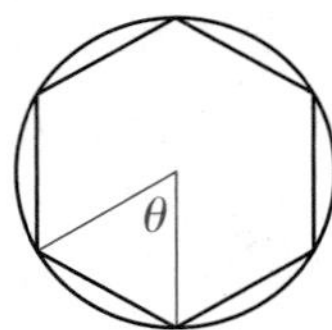


**17.** Look at your results for Exercises 13–16. Describe any patterns that allow you to predict results for inscribed polygons with more sides.

# 9.05 Maximizing Areas, Part 1

In Lesson 9.04, you were able to find maximums by trial and error. You were working in a restricted environment, so you could try each of the possible structures that met the given requirements. Now, you are going to prove some results about maximum area using familiar shapes.

## Minds in Action

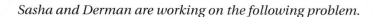

*Sasha and Derman are working on the following problem.*

Suppose you want to build a house with a rectangular base. The most expensive part of the house to frame is the exterior walls. You decide you can afford a house with a base (or floor) that has a total perimeter of 128 feet. What dimensions should you choose for the base if you want to maximize the floor area?

**Derman** After working with the grid polygons, we know it has to be a square. So it's a square with sides 32 feet long.

**Sasha** Well, we *think* it has to be a square. We haven't proven anything yet.

**Derman** Okay, I'll take a stab at it. The $32 \times 32$ square is better than a $40 \times 24$ rectangle. The area of the square is 1024 ft$^2$, while the area of the $40 \times 24$ rectangle is only 960 ft$^2$.

Is this a good example? (What is the perimeter of a $40 \times 24$ rectangle?)

**Sasha** True, but that's just one case. We have to show that the square has a greater area than any rectangle we could choose. Let's draw a picture.

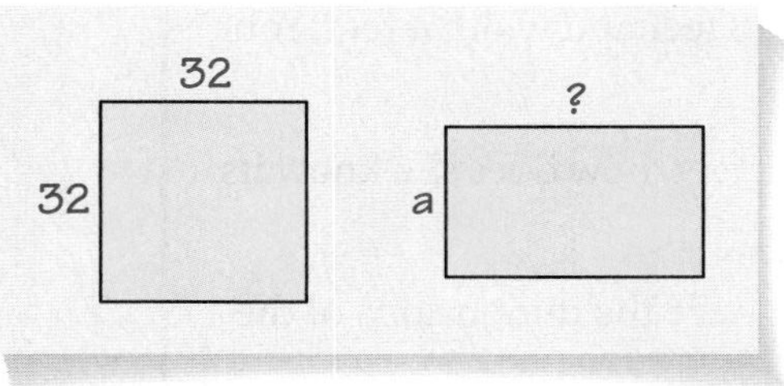


**Derman** Okay, the width of the rectangle is $a$, which is supposed to be less than 32 feet. How can we find the length of the rectangle?

**Habits of Mind**

**Strategize.** Use the perimeter.

**Sasha** We can try a cutting proof. The length of the rectangle has to be greater than 32. Our rectangle has a width $a$ and a length greater than 32 feet, so we can cut off a rectangle $a$ feet by 32 feet.

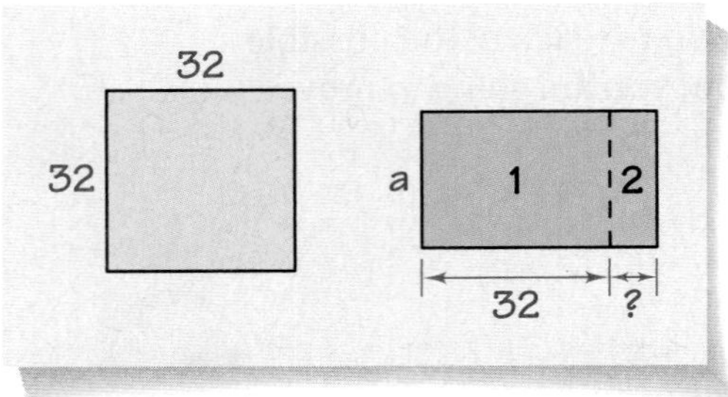


**Derman** Then we can fit both pieces inside the square like this!

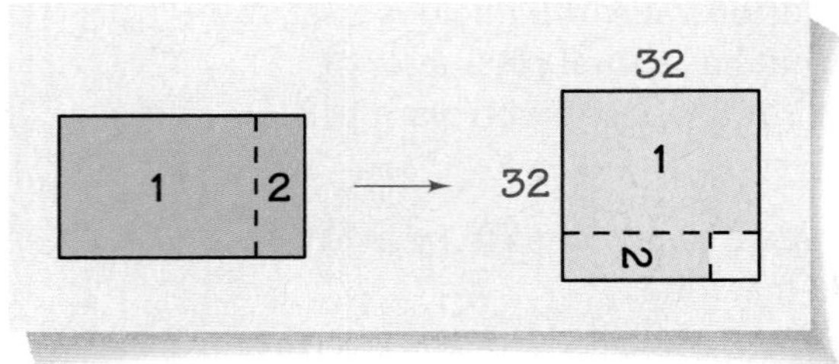


**Sasha** Great. Now you can see that the area of the rectangle is less than the area of the square.

**Habits of Mind**

**Develop your understanding.** What are the dimensions of the rectangle that is left after the cut?

## For You to Do

There are some details missing in the dialog above.

1. Find the length of a rectangle with perimeter 128 feet and width $a$ feet. Your answer should be in terms of $a$.
2. If the width $a$ of Sasha's rectangle is less than 32 feet, how does she know its length is greater than 32 feet?
3. When Sasha cut off the $32 \times a$ rectangle, what were the dimensions of the little rectangle that was left?
4. Do both pieces of the rectangle really fit into the square as Derman said they would? Explain.
5. Write out a proof of Sasha's cutting argument in your own words. Prove that any nonsquare rectangle with a perimeter of 128 feet has less area than a square with the same perimeter.

## Example

**Problem** You want to fence in a rectangular exercise run for your dog. You have 36 feet of fencing material. You decide that to enclose more area, you will use a wall of your house as the fourth side of the run. What are the dimensions of the greatest area you can enclose?

**Solution** This figure shows a run with width $a$ and length $b$.

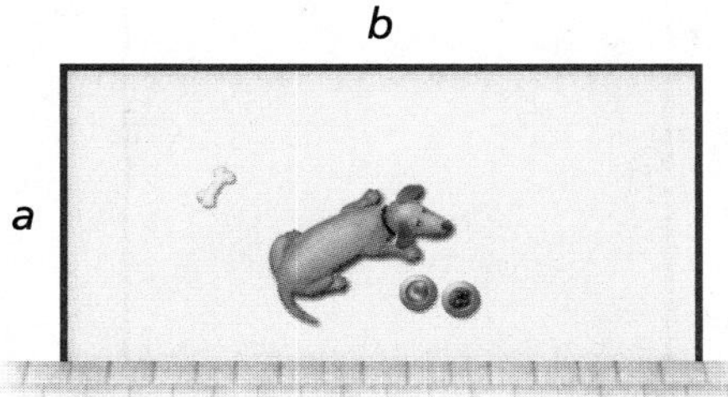


The total amount of fencing is 36 feet, so the perimeter equation is as follows.

$$2a + b = 36$$

You want to maximize $A_{\text{run}}$, which is the area of the run. The formula follows.

$$A_{\text{run}} = ab$$

Rewrite this formula in terms of one variable, say $a$, using the previous perimeter equation.

$$\begin{aligned} A_{\text{run}} &= a(36 - 2a) \\ &= 36a - 2a^2 \end{aligned}$$

Graph $A_{\text{run}}$ as a function of $a$ on a coordinate grid, either by hand or with a graphing calculator.

For help graphing a function, see the TI-Nspire™ Handbook, p. 817.

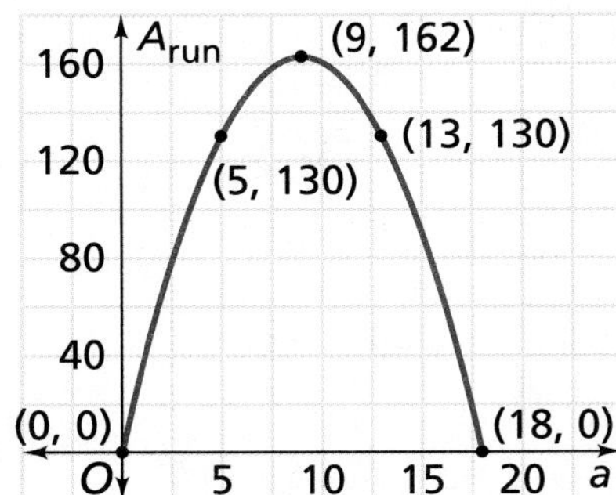


The graph is a parabola opening downward. The maximum value for $A_{\text{run}}$ occurs at $a = 9$ feet. The dimensions of the run with the greatest area are 9 feet by 18 feet. Its area is 162 square feet.

## Developing Habits of Mind

**Use another method.** Another way to approach the rectangular dog run problem is to use reflection. Reflect the dog run over the line of the house wall. Now you have a problem that you know how to solve.

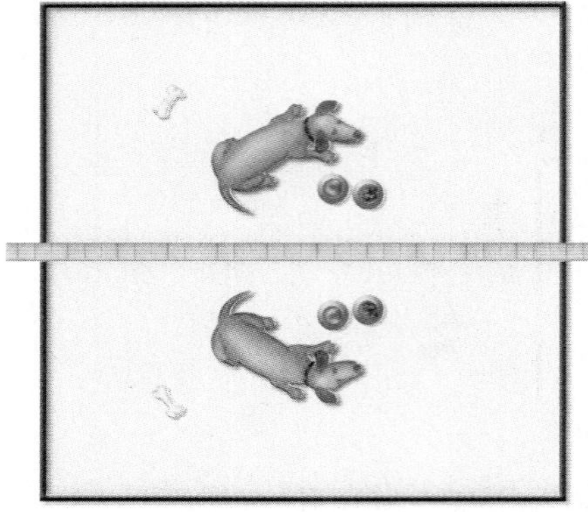

The new rectangle has a perimeter of 72 feet. You want to maximize the area. The maximum area will occur when the rectangle is a square with a side length of 18 feet. The real dog run is half of that square, so it measures 9 feet by 18 feet.

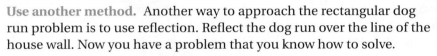

## Exercises *Practicing Habits of Mind*

### Check Your Understanding

1. Find the area of the triangle described in parts (a)–(c). In each case, the triangle is isosceles with a perimeter of 15 inches. Then answer part (d).

   **a.** base = 4 in. **b.** base = 5 in. **c.** base = 6 in.

   **d.** Make a conjecture about which isosceles triangle of a given perimeter will enclose the most area.

2. A triangle has a perimeter of 36 cm, and one side is 10 cm long. What should the lengths of the other two sides be to maximize the area of the triangle? Experiment and make a conjecture about the maximum area for this triangle.

   You will prove your conjecture in Exercise 8.

3. Of all the rectangles with a given perimeter, which one has the greatest area? Explain.

## On Your Own

4. Standardized Test Prep Ned draws a rectangle such that its length is twice its width, and its perimeter is half its area. What is the area of Ned's rectangle?

   **A.** 8 units$^2$ **B.** 18 units$^2$ **C.** 32 units$^2$ **D.** 72 units$^2$

5. Refer back to the cutting method used in this lesson's Minds in Action. Show that an $a \times b$ nonsquare rectangle has less area than a square with the same perimeter. (This is not the same problem as in Minds in Action. Here the perimeter is fixed, but you do not know what it is.)

6. Suppose as in the Example you have 36 ft of fencing. You want to build a rectangular dog run against a barn wall that is 13 ft long. Again, you plan to use the barn as one side of the run. What size rectangle maximizes the area of the run now?

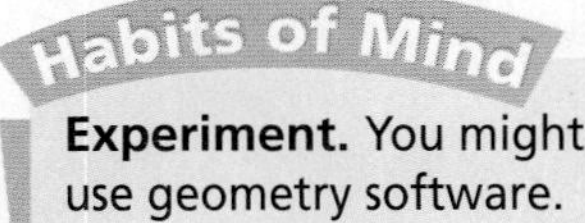


**Experiment.** You might use geometry software.

7. Triangles of many different shapes may have one side of length 5 in. and one of length 6 in. Which of these triangles encloses the most area? Explain.

8. In Exercise 2, you studied triangles with one side 10 cm and perimeter 36 cm. You may have conjectured that the triangle with maximum area is isosceles. It would have two 13-cm sides. The conjecture is true. In this exercise, you will prove it.

   Suppose the height you conjectured is not the maximum. So there is another point that gives a greater height for the triangle. Therefore, the two unknown sides are not equal. One must be greater than 13 cm and one must be less by the same amount. Also, the perpendicular from the third vertex of the triangle does not intersect the 10-cm side at its midpoint. The point of intersection is closer to one side.

   This scenario is shown in the figure.

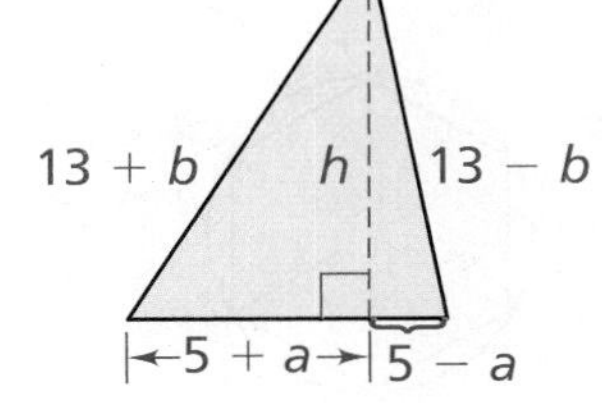


   **a.** Write equations relating $a$, $b$, and $h$ for each of the small right triangles in the figure. Use the Pythagorean Theorem.

   **b.** Expand and simplify each side of the equation. Subtract one equation from the other. Find an expression for $a$ in terms of $b$.

   **c.** Using either of the two equations you wrote in part (a), write an equation for $h$ in terms of $b$.

   **d.** Show that the value of $h$ is greatest when $b = 0$ and the triangle is isosceles.

9. A triangle has one side that measures $s$ cm and a total perimeter of $p$ cm. What lengths for the other two sides will maximize its area?

10. Out of all the triangles with perimeter 18 cm, which has the greatest area? Explain.

11. Find the maximum area for a triangle with perimeter 24 in. Now, find the maximum area for a rectangle with perimeter 24 in. Which is greater?

## Maintain Your Skills

Go Online
Video Tutor
www.successnetplus.com

**12.** Find the area of a regular triangle (an equilateral triangle) with perimeter 60 cm.

**13.** Find the area of a regular quadrilateral (a square) with perimeter 60 cm.

**14.** Take It Further

**a.** This regular pentagon is inscribed in a circle and cut into 5 congruent isosceles triangles.

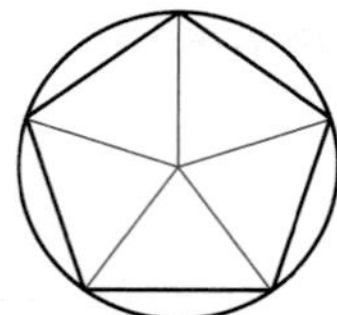

Find the measurements of all three angles in one of the triangles.

**b.** Here is one of the triangles by itself.

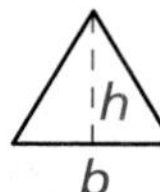


Use the tangent function to find an approximation for $h$ in terms of $b$.

**c.** Find the area of a regular pentagon with perimeter 60 cm.

**15. a.** This regular hexagon is inscribed in a circle and cut into 6 congruent isosceles triangles.

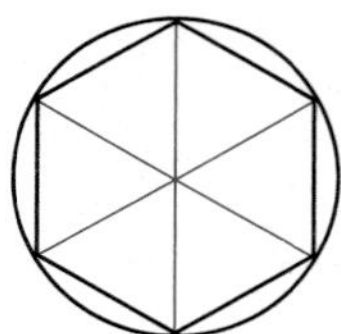

Find the measurements of all three angles in one of the triangles.

**b.** Here is one of the triangles by itself.

Use the tangent function to find an approximation for $h$ in terms of base $b$.

**c.** Find the area of a regular hexagon with perimeter 60 cm.

Go Online
www.successnetplus.com

**16.** Refer to Exercises 12–15. Make some conjectures about what kind of shape will have the maximum area for a given perimeter.

# 9.06 Maximizing Areas, Part 2

In Lesson 9.05, you explored problems in which the perimeter of a polygon is fixed. You discovered that the triangle with the greatest area is equilateral. The rectangle with the greatest area is a square. These two results may have led you to a conjecture similar to the following theorem.

***Theorem 9.1** The Regular Polygon Theorem*

**Of all the polygons having a given perimeter and a given number of sides, the regular polygon has the greatest area.**

You will work toward a proof of this theorem in the exercises for this lesson.

In Exercise 11 of the previous lesson, an equilateral triangle and a square have the same perimeter. The area of the square is greater. Exercises 12–15 support the conjecture that for a fixed perimeter, the more sides a regular polygon has, the greater is its area.

## For Discussion

Suppose for now that Theorem 9.1 is true, even though you have not seen it proven. Also suppose that for a given perimeter, a regular polygon with more sides encloses more area than a polygon with fewer sides. Propose an answer to the following area-maximization problem.

1. For all shapes with the same perimeter, which has the greatest area?

## Check Your Understanding

1. Which polygon has the greater area? Find a way to convince your teacher or someone else that your answer is correct.

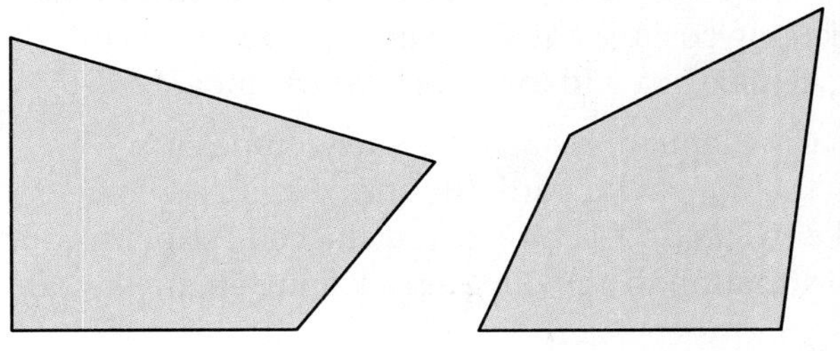

**Habits of Mind**

**Consider more than one strategy.** Could you trace and then cut up the polygons to compare the parts? What else might you do?

2. Consider the polygon at the right. Describe a way to make a polygon with the same side lengths, but with greater area.

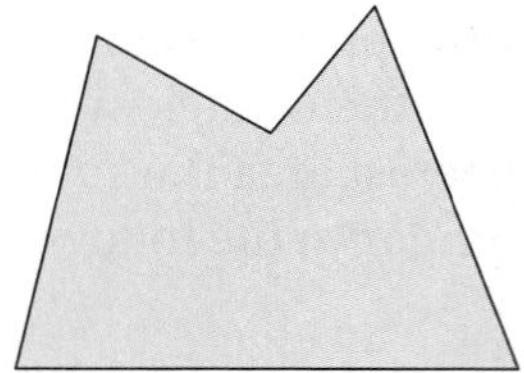

3. Consider all the parallelograms with side lengths 20, 30, 20, and 30. Which one encloses the most area? Explain.

## On Your Own

4. Standardized Test Prep Suppose you have four regular polygons: a triangle, a quadrilateral, a pentagon, and a hexagon. The perimeters of the polygons are the same. Which polygon has the greatest area?

   **A.** triangle **B.** quadrilateral **C.** pentagon **D.** hexagon

5. Consider all the quadrilaterals of a given perimeter. Prove that the one that encloses the most area is a rhombus. You might draw a diagonal that cuts the quadrilateral into two triangles. How can you guarantee that the triangles both have maximum area? What do you find if you draw the other diagonal?

6. Show that the $n$-gon of a given perimeter that encloses the most area must be equilateral. Use your reasoning from Exercise 5.

7. Prove that the rhombus of a given perimeter that encloses the most area is a square.

8. Use Theorem 9.1 to solve the following problem, which is similar to the example in Lesson 9.05.

   Suppose you want to build a four-sided pen that is not necessarily a rectangle. You plan to use a stone wall as one side of the pen. The other three walls will be built with 840 feet of fencing. What shape and dimensions maximize the area of the pen?

9. Explain why the hypotenuse is always the longest side of a right triangle.

**Remember...**

The hypotenuse of a right triangle is the side opposite the right angle.

10. A typical juice box contains about 250 milliliters (mL) of juice. It measures 10.5 cm by 6.5 cm by 4 cm.
    **a.** What is the volume of this box in cubic centimeters?
    **b.** Is this the best box size? Suppose the manufacturer wants to maximize profit by reducing packaging costs. What size rectangular box has the same volume as a typical juice box and uses the least cardboard?
    **c.** Design a container (of any shape) that has the same volume as a typical juice box, using the least cardboard. (Be sure that it can be held comfortably by a child and can be assembled and stacked.) Explain your choice with enough information to convince a packaging engineer that it is the best shape.

**11.** Cut wood is often sold by the cord. A cord is a stack that measures 4 feet × 4 feet × 8 feet. This picture shows one way to stack a cord of 8-foot logs, all with the same diameter.

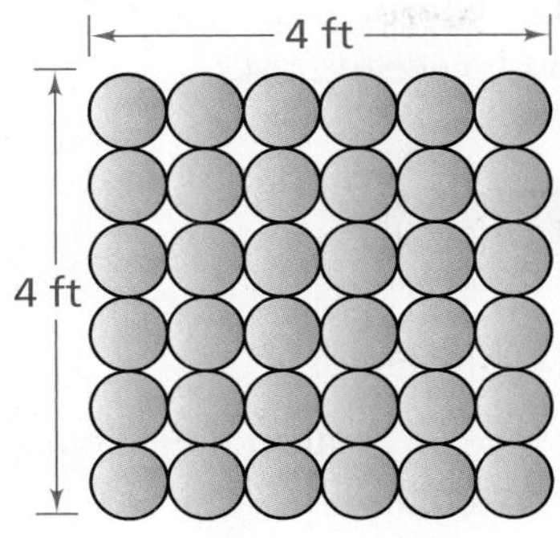


Jamal is ordering a cord of wood stacked this way. Suppose he can choose the diameter of the logs he buys. (In reality, there are many different diameters in a cord of wood.) What diameter should Jamal choose if he wants to maximize the amount of wood in the stack? (He wants to minimize the amount of air he buys.) Should Jamal buy one big log or many small logs?

## Maintain Your Skills

Use the following description for Exercises 12–15.

Danae wants to build a rectangular dog run for her beagle, Bruiser. She has 48 feet of fencing to use. One wall of her house will serve as a side of the run. She wants Bruiser to have the maximum area possible.

**12.** What are the dimensions and area of the run she should build?

**13.** You tell Danae that the rectangular dog run is not the best possible 4-sided run. Instead, her run should be half of a regular hexagon. Give Danae directions (including lengths and angles) and the area of this dog run.

**14.** The wall of Danae's house is only 20 feet long. She cannot build the optimal rectangular run or the optimal half-hexagonal run. Find the new best rectangular run. Find the new best hexagonal run.

**15.** Danae has another problem. If she builds more than 9 feet from the house, she will run into the neighbor's property line. She has two possible solutions. Find the dimensions and the area of the best run of each type described below.

**a.** The run is a 9-foot wide rectangle. The 20-foot wall is part of one side.

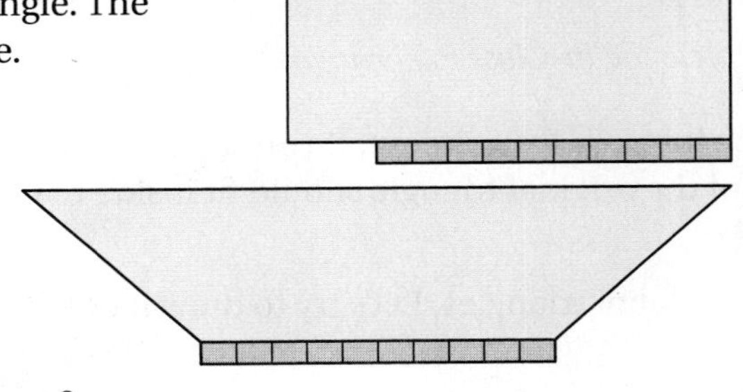

**b.** The run is a 9-foot-wide isosceles trapezoid. The 20-foot wall is one complete base of the trapezoid.

**c.** Which run should Danae choose?

Go Online
www.successnetplus.com

# 9.07 Areas of Similar Polygons

How do the areas of similar polygons compare? Checking simple polygons, such as rectangles, is a good place to start.

## In-Class Experiment

Draw a rectangle. Scale it by the factor 2.

1. How do the dimensions of the original rectangle compare with the dimensions of the scaled rectangle?
2. How many copies of the original rectangle fit into the scaled rectangle?
3. How does the area of the scaled rectangle compare to the area of the original rectangle?

Draw a rectangle. Scale it by the factor $\frac{1}{3}$.

4. How do the dimensions of the two rectangles compare?
5. How many copies of the scaled rectangle fit into the original rectangle?
6. How do the areas of the two rectangles compare?

If two triangles are similar and the scale factor is $r$, you know that the ratio of the lengths of two corresponding sides is $r$. Show that the following statements are true.

7. The ratio of their perimeters is $r$.
8. The ratio of the lengths of two corresponding altitudes is also $r$.
9. The ratio of their areas is $r^2$.

## Minds in Action

*Hannah and Derman complete the In-Class Experiment.*

**Hannah** According to the In-Class Experiment, if you scale a triangle by 4, then 16 copies of the original triangle should fit inside the scaled copy.

**Derman** That sounds like a lot of triangles. Let's try to draw it out.

**Hannah** It's easy! Look, here's a small triangle. And here's a picture showing 16 copies of the small triangle inside the triangle that has been scaled by 4.

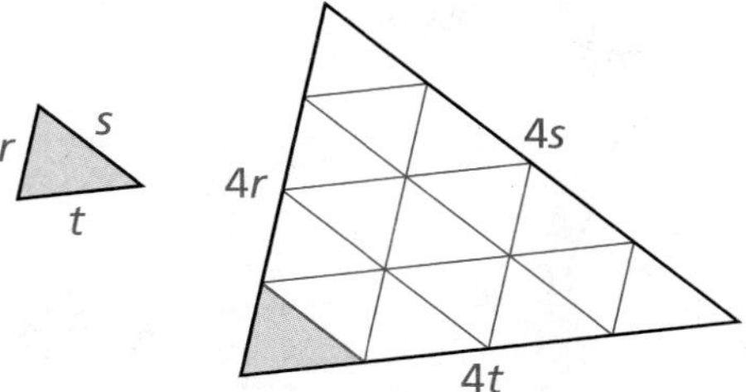


**Derman** Okay, that works. But what if you scale a triangle by $2\frac{1}{2}$? Then there should by $6\frac{1}{4}$ copies of the original triangle inside the scaled one. What would that look like?

## For Discussion

**10.** Draw a figure that answers Derman's question. Show that if you scale a triangle by the factor $2\frac{1}{2}$, then the scaled triangle has $6\frac{1}{4}$ times the area of the original triangle.

Now that you have calculated the areas of similar rectangles and triangles, take a look at similar polygons with any number of sides.

## For You to Do

In the figures below, you scale polygon 1 by the factor *r* to obtain polygon 2. You divide polygon 1 into four triangles with areas *a*, *b*, *c*, and *d*.

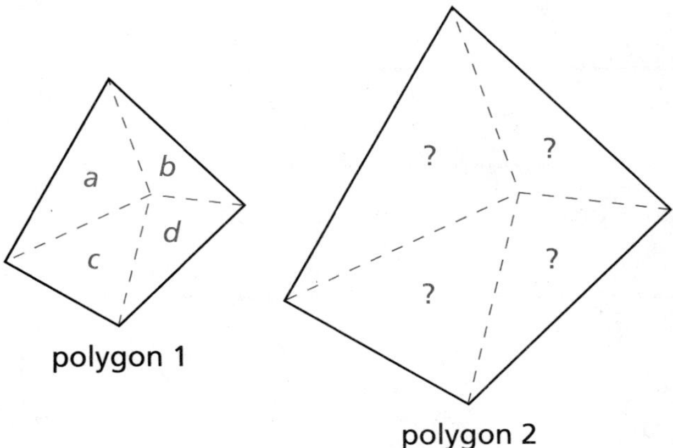


polygon 1

polygon 2

**11.** What are the areas of the corresponding triangles in polygon 2?

**12.** What is the total area of polygon 2?

**13.** What is the total area of polygon 1?

The results of your work lead to the following theorem.

### Theorem 9.2

**If you scale a polygon by some positive number $r$, then the ratio of the area of the scaled copy to the area of the original polygon is $r^2$.**

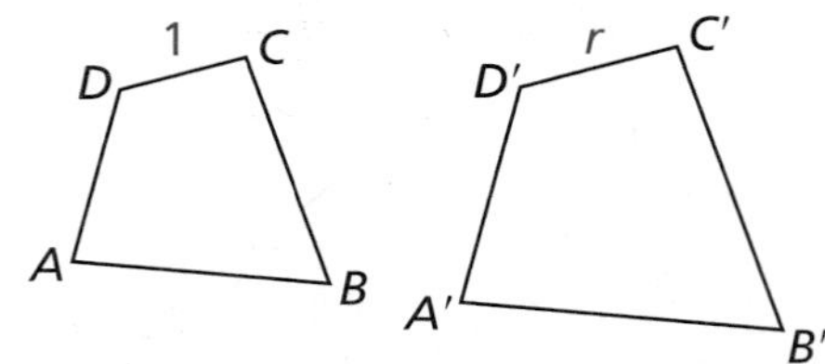


## Developing Habits of Mind

**Prove a special case.** An argument for a special case can suggest how an argument could be made in general. Here's a proof of Theorem 9.2 for a quadrilateral. It suggests how a proof might proceed for any polygon.

Suppose you scale $ABCD$ by $r$ to get $A'B'C'D'$. Pick a point $O$ inside $ABCD$. Connect it to each of the vertices, dividing $ABCD$ into triangles. (There would be four in this case, but in general there would be as many as there are sides.) Let the areas of these triangles be $a$, $b$, $c$, and $d$. Then

$$\text{area}(ABCD) = a + b + c + d$$

If the image of $O$ is $O'$, then the triangle $AOB$ gets scaled by a factor of $r$ to triangle $A'O'B'$, and so on. So, by the results of Problem 9 of the In-Class Experiment, the area of the triangles in $A'B'C'D'$ are $r^2a$, $r^2b$, $r^2c$, and $r^2d$. Then

$$\begin{aligned}\text{area}(A'B'C'D') &= r^2a + r^2b + r^2c + r^2d \\ &= r^2(a + b + c + d) \\ &= r^2 \cdot \text{area}(ABCD)\end{aligned}$$

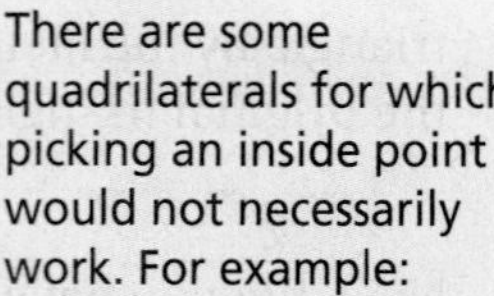

There are some quadrilaterals for which picking an inside point would not necessarily work. For example:

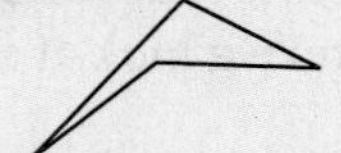

A complete proof would have to cover all possible cases, including ones like these.

## For You to Do

**14.** Draw diagrams to go along with the above proof. Label them to help you understand this proof.

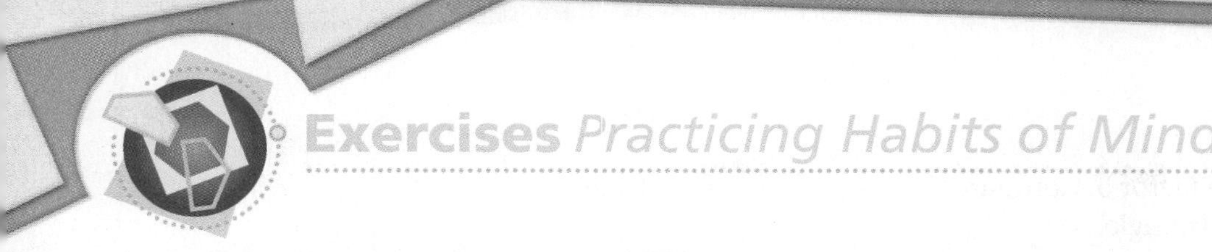

# Exercises *Practicing Habits of Mind*

## Check Your Understanding

1. One side of a triangle has length 10. The altitude to that side has length 12. If you make a new triangle for which all the sides of the original triangle are tripled, what is the area of the new triangle?

2. Jerry wants to plant two cornfields. One measures 400 ft by 600 ft. The other measures 200 ft by 300 ft. Becky, the owner of the seed-and-grain store, says, "The big field will take eight bags of seed. The small field has sides half as big, so you'll need four more bags for that. Will that be cash or charge?" A few days later, Jerry returns to the store very upset. Explain.

3. **a.** Trace this polygon onto a sheet of paper. Estimate its area in square centimeters.

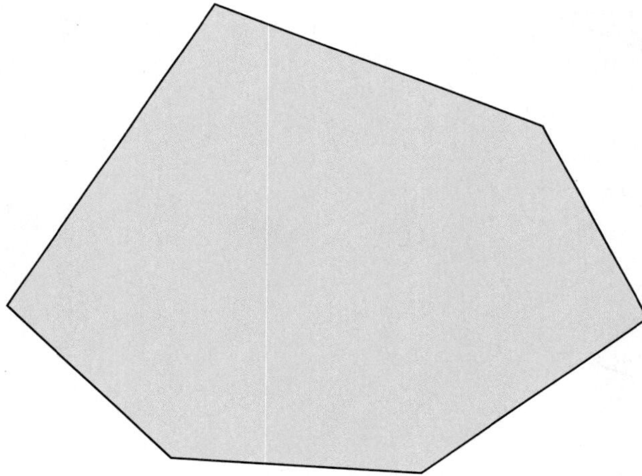

**b.** If you scale the polygon by the factor 1.5, what will be the area of the scaled copy?

**Habits of Mind**

**Recall what you know.** Think about figures for which a ruler can help you find area. Can you see such figures in this polygon?

## On Your Own

4. The area of one square is 12 times the area of another square. Find the ratio of the lengths of the following.

   **a.** their sides

   **b.** their diagonals

5. You scale a rectangle by the factor $\frac{1}{4}$. Compare the area of the scaled rectangle to the area of the original rectangle.

6. You scale a triangle by the factor 5. Compare the area of the scaled triangle to the area of the original triangle.

7. The area of a polygon is 17 square inches. You scale the polygon by the factor 2. What is the area of the new polygon?

8. Standardized Test Prep The area of a regular hexagon with 10-cm sides is about 259.8 $cm^2$. To the nearest square centimeter, what is the area of a regular hexagon with 5-cm sides?

**A.** 130 $cm^2$ **B.** 100 $cm^2$ **C.** 65 $cm^2$ **D.** 52 $cm^2$

## Maintain Your Skills

In Exercises 9–12, find the volume of each figure. Then apply the given scale factor and find the volume of the new figure.

9. scale factor = 3

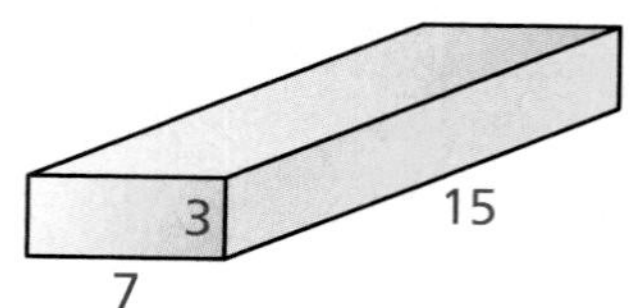

rectangular prism

10. scale factor = 2

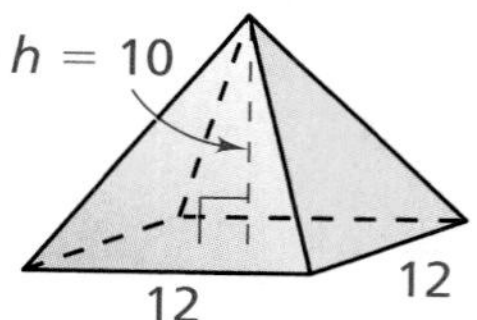

square pyramid

11. scale factor = 5

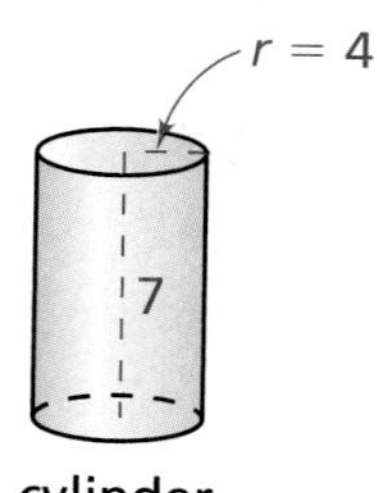

cylinder

12. scale factor = $r$

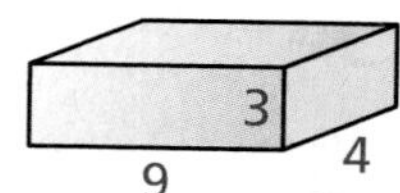

rectangular prism

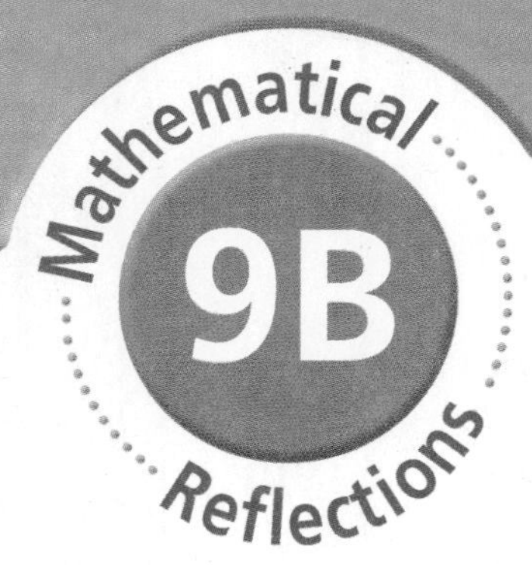


**In this investigation, you learned how to find grid polygons with a given area or perimeter, and to maximize the area for a shape with certain restrictions. These questions will help you summarize what you have learned.**

1. Use only the grid lines on a sheet of graph paper. Find the polygon that has area 8 square units with the maximum perimeter possible.
2. Use only the grid lines on a sheet of graph paper. Find the polygon that has perimeter 12 units with the maximum area possible.
3. Several triangles have one side of length 7 cm and one side of length 5 cm. Which of these triangles encloses the most area? What is its perimeter?
4. Find the maximum possible area for a triangle with perimeter 24 in.
5. Find the maximum possible area for a quadrilateral with perimeter 24 in.
6. Describe some characteristics of a rectangle that has a large perimeter for a given area. Describe some characteristics of a rectangle that has maximum area for a given perimeter.
7. Describe several situations in which reflection can help you find the maximum area for a figure.
8. You want to build a rectangular garden against one wall of your house. You have 29 feet of border fencing. What are the area and dimensions of the largest possible garden you can build?

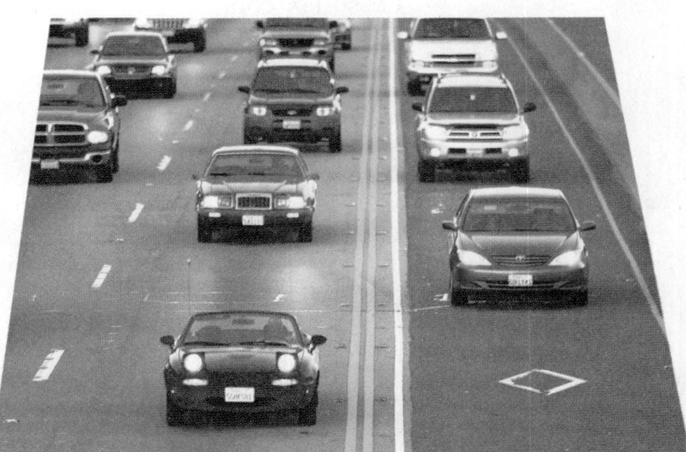

Carpool lanes help move the most people per gallon.

# Conic Sections

**In *Conic Sections*, you will study circles, ellipses, parabolas, and hyperbolas from visual, verbal, geometrical, and analytical viewpoints.**

**By the end of this investigation, you will be able to answer questions like these.**

1. How do you slice an infinite double cone with a plane to get a parabola?
2. What is the locus definition of a hyperbola?
3. What kind of conic section do you get when you graph $x^2 + 16y^2 - 8x + 64y + 64 = 0$? How can you identify the conic section from its equation?

**You will learn how to**

- visualize each of the conic sections as the intersection of a plane with an infinite double cone
- give a locus definition for each of the conic sections
- identify the equations for the graphs of the conic sections, and sketch their graphs

**You will develop these habits and skills:**

- Visualize the effect of different angles of intersection of a plane with an infinite double cone.
- Make connections between the different definitions of each type of conic section.
- Reason by continuity to make connections between the different types of conic section.

Parabolic curves form the surfaces of radio telescopes, freeway overpass arches, field microphones, solar ovens, and these reflectors of a solar electric generating system.

# 9.08 Getting Started

The intersection of a plane and a solid gives you a cross section of the solid. It is a challenging visualization habit to determine what cross section shapes are possible for different solids.

## For You to Explore

1. Consider a cube.

When you take a planar slice through the cube (a smooth cut with a knife), what possible shapes could you make?

> Consider the boundary of the cut as the shape of the slice. One possible shape for the slice is a square, but there are a lot more.

2. Consider a sphere.

When you take a planar slice through the sphere, what possible shapes could you make?

3. Consider a cone that extends forever from its tip.

When you take a planar slice through the cone, what possible shapes could you make?

4. Sketch the graph of each equation.

**a.** $x^2 + y^2 = 16$ **b.** $x^2 - y^2 = 16$

**c.** $4x^2 + y^2 = 16$ **d.** $x^2 + y = 16$

5. Take It Further Find and graph an equation for the set of points $\frac{4}{5}$ times as far from (5, 2) as they are from the line $x = 14$.

## Exercises Practicing Habits of Mind

### On Your Own

6. Find all solutions to the following equation.

$$\sqrt{x - 12} + \sqrt{x - 7} = 5$$

7. Sketch the graph of each equation.
   - a. $x^2 + y^2 = 25$
   - b. $(x - 3)^2 + y^2 = 25$
   - c. $(x + 3)^2 + y^2 = 25$
   - d. $(x - 1)^2 + (y + 4)^2 = 25$
   - e. $\frac{x^2}{5^2} + \frac{y^2}{5^2} = 1$

8. Sketch the graph of each equation.
   - a. $x^2 + y^2 = 1$
   - b. $\frac{x^2}{4^2} + \frac{y^2}{4^2} = 1$
   - c. $\frac{x^2}{3^2} + \frac{y^2}{5^2} = 1$
   - d. $\frac{x^2}{3^2} + \frac{y^2}{2^2} = 1$
   - e. $9x^2 + 25y^2 = 225$

**Remember...**

Equations are point-testers. Find some points that make the equations true.

This whispering gallery is in the Cincinnati Museum Center. To concentrate sound of one point in the hall, architects make use of the reflective properties of one of the conics. As you work through this investigation, can you guess which one?

**9.** You are on a camping trip. As you are returning from a hike in the woods, you see that your tent is on fire. Luckily, you are holding an empty bucket and you are near a river. You plan to run to the river to fill the bucket and then run to the tent.

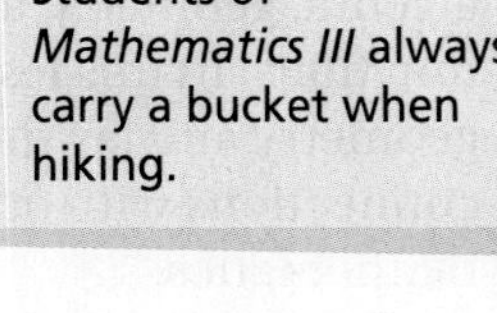


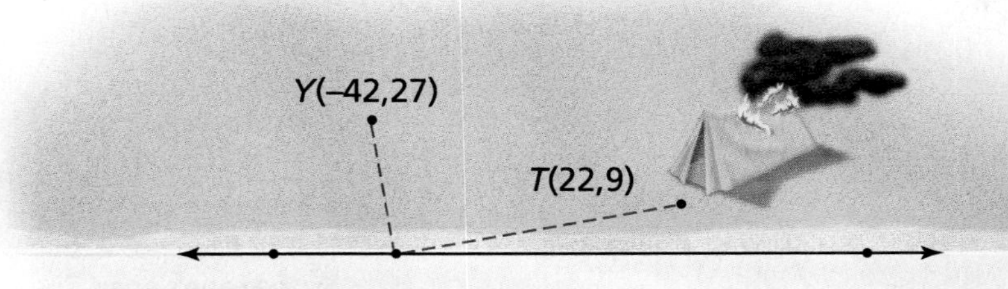


In Investigation 9A, you found the shortest total path by reflecting your position $Y$ over the line of the river's edge and connecting the reflected image $Y'$ to $T$ with a straight line. The intersection of that line and the river's edge is the point $P$ that minimizes the path. Explain why this method produces the shortest path.

## Maintain Your Skills

**10.** Find all solutions to the following equation.

$$\sqrt{x + 10} + \sqrt{x + 31} = 7$$

# 9.09 Slicing Cones

The theory of **conic sections** ties together algebra, geometry, and the analysis of functions. In this lesson, you start with the geometry and lay the foundations for the connections with other parts of mathematics.

Picture a line in space, fixed at one point, while another point on the line moves along a circle.

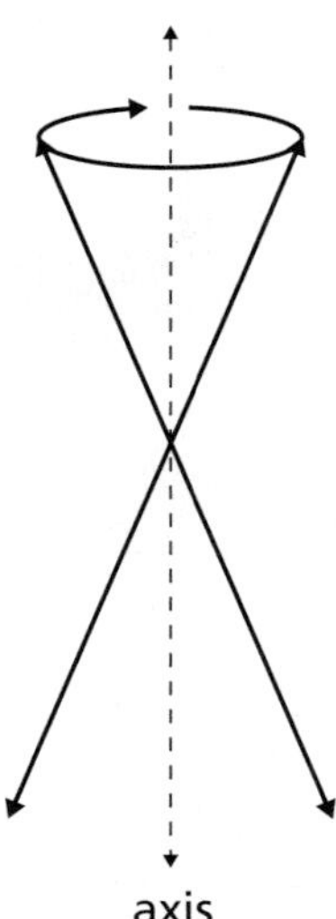


The fixed point is the cone's *apex*. The rotating line is called the *generator* of the cone. The line through the apex perpendicular to the circle is the cone's *axis*.

The surface made by the moving line is an infinite double cone. Now picture a plane passing through the cone.

The plane slices the cone in a curve. That curve is a conic section. You get different kinds of curves depending on how the plane slices the cone.

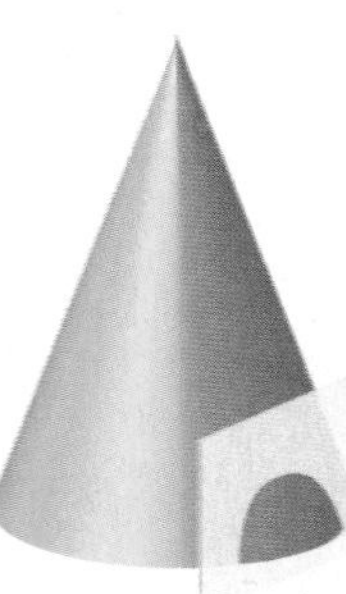

## In-Class Experiment

Draw sketches of the possible intersections of a plane with this infinite double cone. Classify and name your sketches. Discuss their features. Here are some questions you should answer about your intersections.

1. Is the intersection curve closed like a polygon or circle, or open like the graph of $y = x^2$?
2. Does the intersection curve have two branches like the graph of $xy = 1$ or is it a single connected curve?
3. Does the intersection curve have any symmetry?

The intersection curves look like curves you have encountered before in previous work. And it turns out that they are the same curves.

## *Facts and Notation*

- **The curve you get by slicing the cone with a plane that intersects only one branch of the cone is an ellipse.**
- **The curve you get by slicing the cone with a plane that is parallel to its generator is a parabola.**
- **The curve you get by slicing the cone with a plane that intersects both branches of the cone is a hyperbola.**

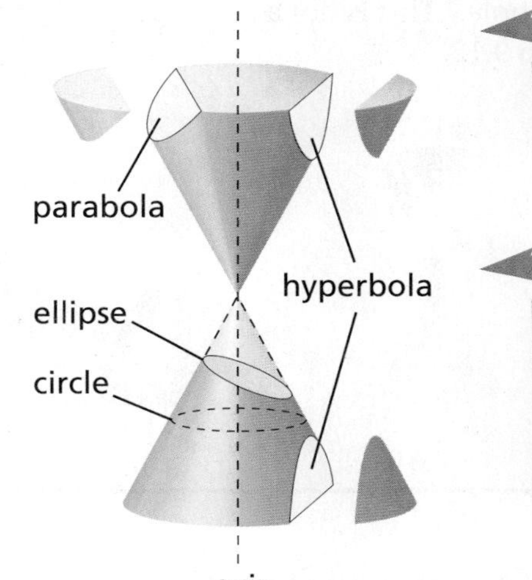


A circle is a special kind of ellipse.

Because the plane is parallel to the generator, it only slices one branch of the cone but it does not produce an ellipse. (Why?)

It should not be obvious to you that the curve you get when you slice a cone parallel to its generator is exactly the same kind curve as the one you get when you graph $y = x^2$. Or that the oval conic section is the same kind of curve as the oval you get when you graph $4x^2 + 9y^2 - 36 = 0$. Or that the conic section called "hyperbola" has the same kind of shape as the graph of $xy = 1$. One purpose of the lessons in this investigation is to see why this is the case.

## Developing Habits of Mind

**Visualize.** Here is an interesting thought experiment: Picture a fixed line $\ell$ in space, outside a cone and between the apex and the base. The line $\ell$ is parallel to the base of the cone. Next imagine a single plane that contains $\ell$ and rotates around $\ell$. The plane starts out perpendicular to the axis of the cone, cutting the cone in a circle. Then it rotates down, creating a family of ellipses (increasing in size) until it is parallel to the generator, producing a parabola. It continues its rotation down, creating hyperbolas until it is parallel to the generator again (now on the opposite side of the cone).

In some sense, these conic sections are all the same. You will look more carefully at this idea in Lesson 9.12.

Where did the names "ellipse," "parabola," and "hyperbola" come from? They bear a striking resemblance to the English language terms "ellipsis," "parable," and "hyperbole." This is not a coincidence—you will see the connections in Lesson 9.12.

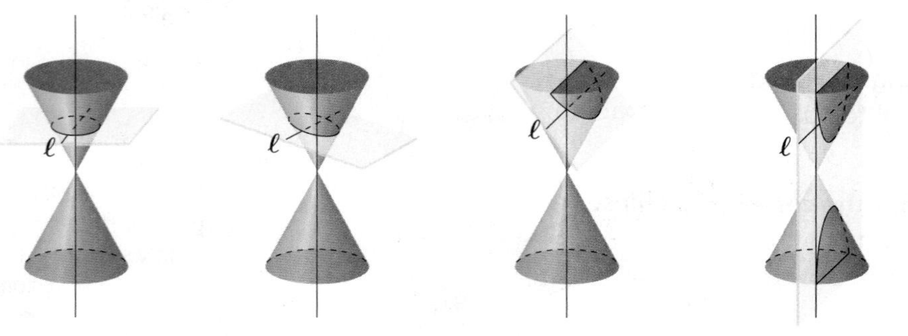


### Locus Definitions for Conics: The Ellipse

In previous work, you defined an ellipse with a pin and string construction. Suppose $F_1$ and $F_2$ are two fixed points—the **foci** of the ellipse—and you have a fixed length, say $s$. Then the ellipse with foci $F_1$ and $F_2$ and string length $s$ is the set (locus) of all points $P$ such that $PF_1 + PF_2 = s$.

The singular of *foci* is *focus*.

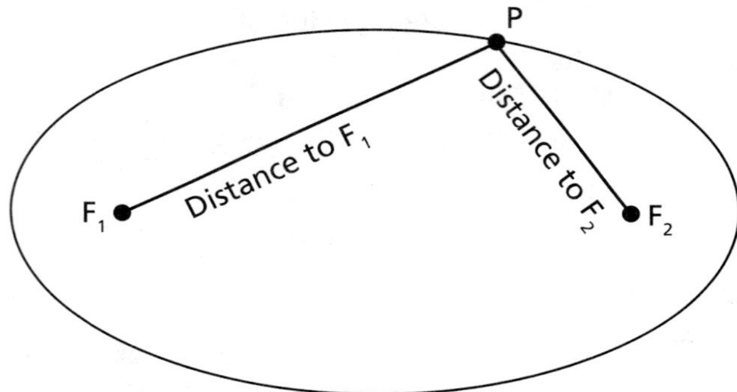


distance to $F_1$ + distance to $F_2$ = a constant

## For You to Do

4. You can draw half of an ellipse by taking a string of length $s$ and pinning its ends to $F_1$ and $F_2$. Then use a pencil to pull the string tight and trace the curve by moving the pencil, keeping tension on the string. Try it. How does the string length affect the size of the ellipse? How does the distance between the foci affect the size of the ellipse?

See the TI-Nspire™ Handbook on p. 817 for instructions about using the pin and string idea to make an ellipse with your geometry software.

You may also have a feeling that a section of a cone sliced by a plane that only cuts one branch of the cone and is not parallel to the generator is an ellipse.

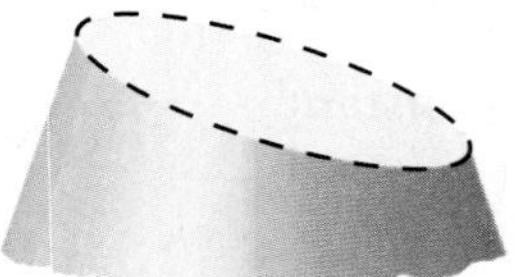

A proof by the French mathematician Germinal Dandelin shows why this is so. Begin with a cone that a plane has passed through. Now imagine placing two spheres in this cone. Put the first one into the top of the cone, big enough so it just touches the sides of the cone and just touches the plane in only one spot—it is tangent to both the cone and the plane. Then put a larger sphere into the cone under the ellipse. Again make this sphere just the right size, so it is tangent to the cone and to the plane of the ellipse.

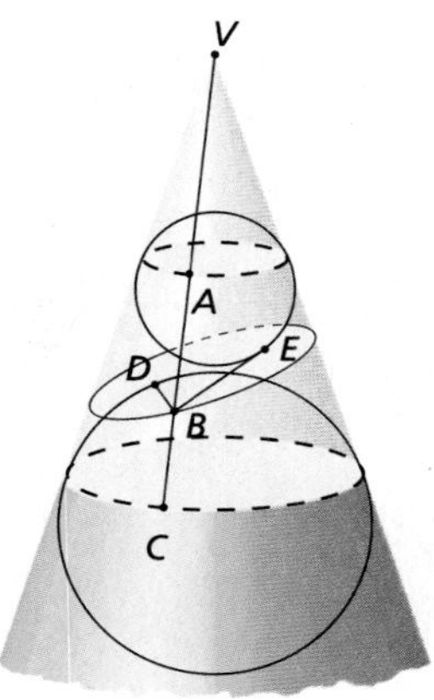


Pass a straight line down the surface of the cone, beginning at the apex *V*. Label the points of intersection with the smaller sphere, the plane, and the larger sphere *A*, *B*, and *C* in the figure above. Point *D* is the point where the larger sphere is tangent to the plane. Point *E* is the point where the smaller sphere is tangent to the plane. $BA = BE$ because $\overrightarrow{BA}$ and $\overrightarrow{BE}$ each emanates from *B* and are tangent to the smaller sphere.

For this same reason $BC = BD$, because both $\overrightarrow{BC}$ and $\overrightarrow{BD}$ are tangent to the larger sphere.

No matter what line you choose to draw from *V*, the lengths *VA* and *VC* are invariant. Note that since this is so, *AC*, the difference between *VA* and *VC*, is also invariant. Also note that $AC = BA + BC$. Since $BA = BE$ and $BC = BD$ then $BA + BC = BD + BE$. $BA + BC$ is constant so this means that $BD + BE$ must also be constant. So an ellipse must be a set of all points in the plane, such that the sum of the distances from two fixed points (*E* and *D*) remains constant.

**Remember...**

Given a circle and a point *P* outside the circle, the two segments from *P* tangent to the circle are equal in length. Rotating this gives a sphere with the same property.

## Locus Definitions for Conics: The Parabola and the Hyperbola

There are similar ways to show that the other two conics have locus properties.

- A hyperbola is the set of points such that the absolute value of the difference of the distances from two fixed points is constant.

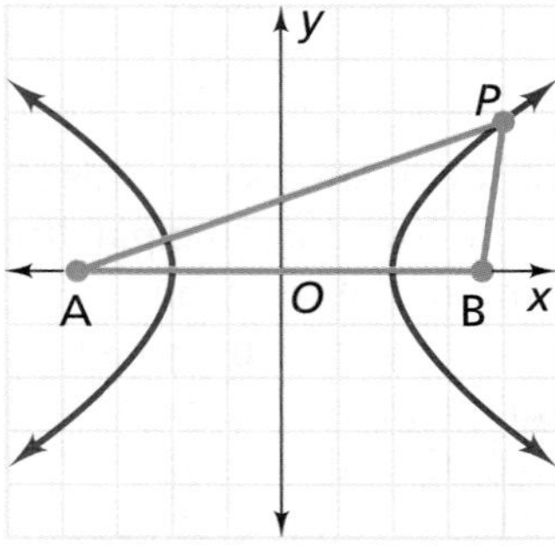


$|PA - PB| = \text{Constant}$

- A parabola is the set of points equidistant from a fixed point and a line.

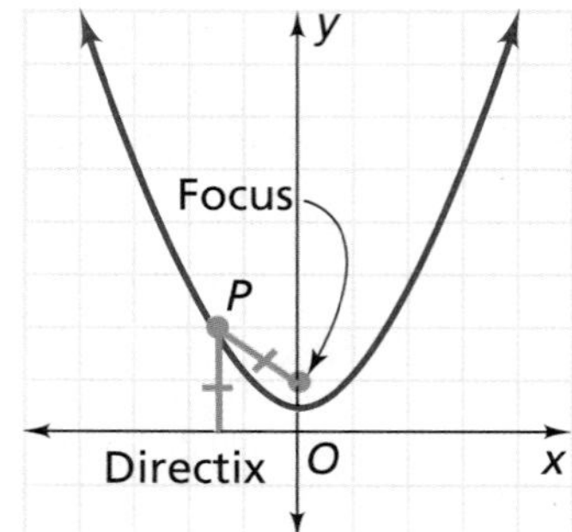


Dandelin showed that the cone slices that you call parabola and hyperbola are the same ones that satisfy the locus descriptions above, using the same idea of putting spheres around the slicing planes. The spheres are now called Dandelin spheres. The arguments are the same in spirit, but they are considerably more complicated.

See the TI-Nspire Handbook on p. 817 for instructions to use the locus definition to draw a hyperbola and a parabola in your dynamic geometry environment.

Why did you not need the absolute value in the definition of the ellipse?

A hyperbola has two foci. A parabola has only one. The fixed line in the parabola definition is called its **directrix.**

# Exercises *Practicing Habits of Mind*

## Check Your Understanding

1. **a.** Using the pin-and-string model, draw an ellipse that closely resembles a circle.

   **b.** Using the same string but different pin locations, draw an ellipse that does not resemble a circle.

   **c.** Where might you place the pins to draw a circle?

   The locus definition of an ellipse uses two points $F_1$ and $F_2$, the foci, and a distance $s$. The ellipse is the set of points $P$ with $PF_1 + PF_2 = s$.

2. Consider foci $F_1(3, 0)$ and $F_2(-3, 0)$, and the distance $s = 10$.

   **a.** Find the two values of $b$ so that $(0, b)$ is on the ellipse.

   **b.** Find the two values of $a$ so that $(a, 0)$ is on the ellipse.

   **c.** Is the point $(2, 3)$ on the ellipse? Explain how you know.

   **d.** Write an equation that you could use to test whether or not any point $(x, y)$ is on the ellipse.

3. The lesson shows what the two Dandelin spheres look like after slicing a double-cone to produce an ellipse. Suppose you slice a double cone to produce a circle. Describe what the two Dandelin spheres look like. Also, describe the points where the Dandelin spheres touch the sliced circle.

4. By its locus definition, a hyperbola is the set of points such that the absolute value of the difference of the distances from two fixed points is constant. Suppose the two points are $F_1 = (3, 0)$ and $F_2 = (-3, 0)$, with the fixed difference $d = 4$.

   **a.** Find five points that are on this hyperbola.

   **b.** Sketch a graph of the hyperbola.

   **c.** **Take It Further** Find an equation for the graph of the hyperbola.

5. **What's Wrong Here?** Joachim decides to make a hyperbola with fixed points $A(3, 0)$ and $B(-3, 0)$, and the fixed difference $d = 10$. But he is having trouble finding points that work. Why?

## On Your Own

6. On the coordinate plane, a parabola has focus $(1, 0)$ and directrix with equation $x = -1$. Which of these points is on the parabola?

   **A.** $(1, 1.5)$ **B.** $(1.5, 2.5)$ **C.** $(2.25, 3)$ **D.** $(9, 36)$

7. Find three points on the parabola with focus $(1, 0)$ and directrix with equation $x = -1$. Do not use points listed in Exercise 6.

8. Find $a$ given each condition.

 **a.** $(1, a)$ is on the parabola with focus $(1, 0)$ and directrix with equation $x = -1$.

 **b.** $(a, 1)$ is on the parabola with focus $(1, 0)$ and directrix with equation $x = -1$.

9. Find an equation of the parabola with focus $(1, 0)$ and directrix with equation $x = -1$.

10. One equation for an ellipse with foci $(3, 0)$ and $(-3, 0)$ and string length $s = 10$ is

$$\sqrt{(x-3)^2 + y^2} + \sqrt{(x+3)^2 + y^2} = 10$$

 **a.** Write another equation that must also be true but only involves a single square root. Proceed as follows. Move one square root to the other side. Square both sides. Simplify the equation as much as possible.

 **b.** Show that you can simplify the equation above to

$$\frac{x^2}{25} + \frac{y^2}{16} = 1$$

**Habits of Mind**

**Represent the situation.** Equations are point testers.

11. Take It Further In Exercise 2 you found an equation for an ellipse with foci $(3, 0)$ and $(-3, 0)$ and string length $s = 10$.

 **a.** Find an equation for the ellipse with the same foci, but leave string length as a variable $s$.

 **b.** If $s = 20$, find several points on the ellipse.

 **c.** Sketch the graph of the ellipse when $s = 20$.

 **d.** Sketch the graph of the ellipse when $s = 8$.

 **e.** Sketch the graph when $s = 6$.

**Go Online**
www.successnetplus.com

12. Standardized Test Prep Which of the following points is on the parabola with focus (3, 4) and directrix $y = 5$?

 **A.** (–3, 4) **B.** (0, 0) **C.** (3, 3) **D.** (5, 4)

## Maintain Your Skills

13. Sketch the graph of each equation.

 **a.** $x^2 + y^2 - 2x + 4y - 4 = 0$

 **b.** $x^2 + y^2 - 2x + 4y = 0$

 **c.** $x^2 + y^2 - 2x + 4y + 4 = 0$

 **d.** $x^2 + y^2 - 2x + 4y + 5 = 0$

 **e.** $x^2 + y^2 - 2x + 4y + 9 = 0$

# 9.10 Conics at the Origin

The words *ellipse, parabola,* and *hyperbola* showed up in your previous courses in another context. You gave these names to graphs of certain equations. In this lesson, you will find general forms for equations for each of the conics when you put them on the coordinate plane. These equations will connect to the curves you already know about.

## Equations for Parabolas

You already found an equation for one parabola in Exercise 9 from the previous lesson. Suppose $c \neq 0$. Consider the parabola with focus $(0, c)$ and directrix with equation $y = -c$.

In the figures that accompany this derivation, $c > 0$. The same derivation works if $c < 0$. Try it.

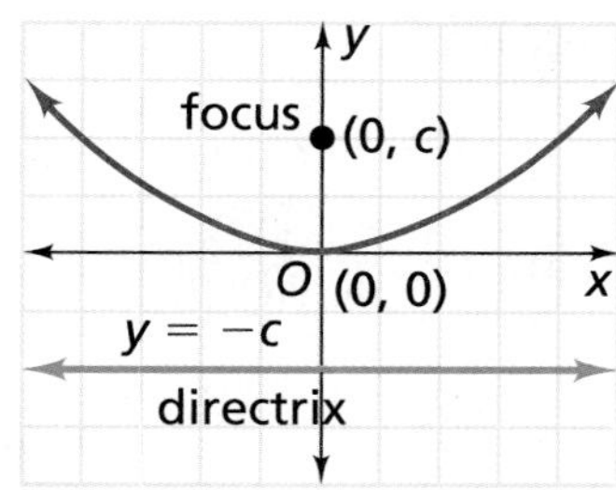


The origin is on this parabola because it is equidistant from the focus and the directrix. In fact, the parabola looks like the graph of a quadratic function with vertex $(0, 0)$.

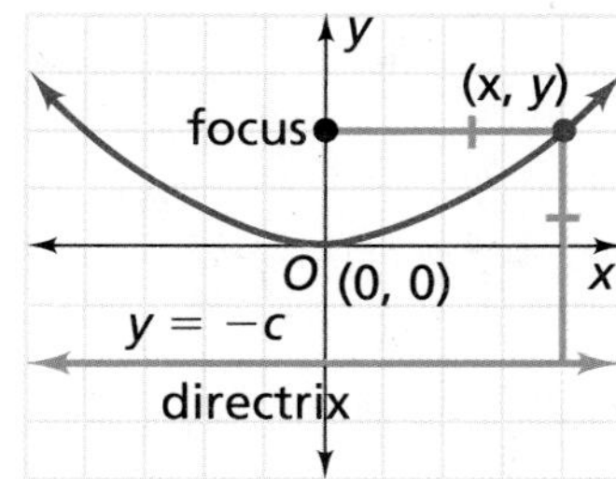


What is the point-tester for this graph? You want the distance from $(x, y)$ to the point $(0, c)$ to be the same as the distance from $(x, y)$ to the line $y = -c$. That gives you

$$\sqrt{x^2 + (y - c)^2} = |y + c|$$

This is fine as a point-tester. For example, $(2c, c)$ is on the graph because

$$\sqrt{(2c)^2 + (c - c)^2} = |c + c|$$

as you can check.

## For You to Do

1. Find all values of $x$ so that $(x, c)$ is on the parabola.

You can simplify the equation in ways that will make it look familiar.

$$\sqrt{x^2 + (y - c)^2} = |y + c| \quad \text{Square both sides.}$$
$$x^2 + (y - c)^2 = (y + c)^2 \quad \text{Expand.}$$
$$x^2 + y^2 - 2cy + c^2 = y^2 + 2cy + c^2 \quad \text{Cancel and simplify.}$$
$$x^2 = 4cy$$

### Theorem 9.3

**An equation for the parabola with focus (0, $c$) and directrix with equation $y = -c$ is**

$$x^2 = 4cy$$

This should look familiar. In earlier courses, you wrote it as

$$y = \frac{1}{4c}x^2$$

So, your parabola is the graph of the quadratic function $f(x) = \frac{1}{4c}x^2$.

## Example

**Problem** A favorite quadratic curve has equation $y = x^2$.

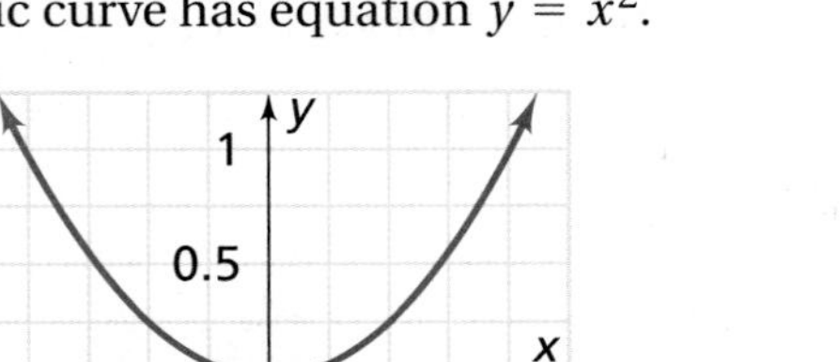

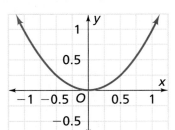

It has a focus and directrix. What are they?

**Solution** You can read the information from the general equation

$$x^2 = 4cy$$

In this equation, $4c = 1$ so $c = \frac{1}{4}$. Hence the focus of the standard parabola is $(0, \frac{1}{4})$ and its directrix has equation $y = -\frac{1}{4}$.

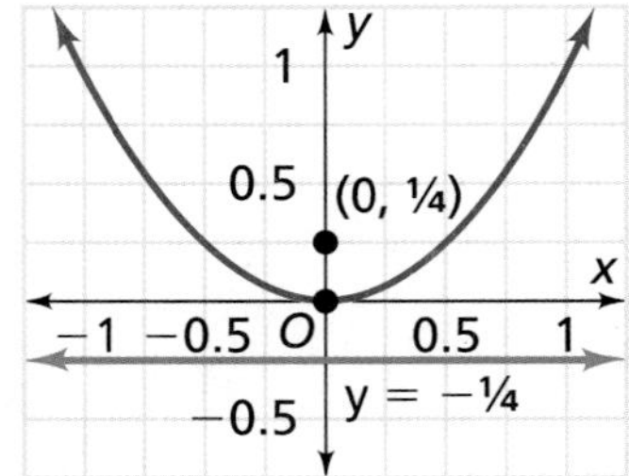

## For Discussion

2. Find the equation of the parabola with focus $(c, 0)$ and directrix with equation $x = -c$.

### Equations for Ellipses

Suppose an ellipse has foci $(c, 0)$ and $(-c, 0)$ and has string length is $s$.

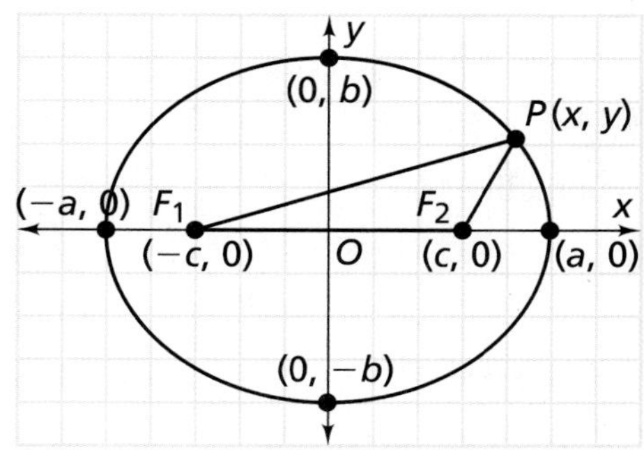


**Remember...**

An ellipse is the set of points such that the sum of the distances to two fixed foci is constant.

### *Facts and Notation*

- **The center of the ellipse is the origin.**
- **The ellipse has two lines of symmetry. They intersect the interior of the ellipse in two segments. The longer segment is called the major axis for the ellipse and the shorter segment is called the minor axis.**
- **The endpoints of the axes for the ellipse are sometimes called the vertices of the ellipse. Label the vertices $(a, 0)$, $(-a, 0)$, $(0, b)$ and $(0, -b)$.**
- **For any point $P$ on the ellipse with foci $F_1$ and $F_2$ and string length $s$, $PF_1 + PF_2 = s$.**

**Habits of Mind**

**Explore the possibilities.** Can an ellipse have major and minor axes of the same length?

What is the point-tester for this ellipse? The "sum of distances is constant" becomes, in this notation

$$\sqrt{(x-c)^2 + y^2} + \sqrt{(x+c)^2 + y^2} = 2a$$

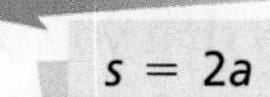

$s = 2a$

This is a perfectly good point-tester, but you can simplify it. Isolate the radicals.

$$\sqrt{(x-c)^2 + y^2} = 2a - \sqrt{(x+c)^2 + y^2}$$

Square both sides.

$$(x-c)^2 + y^2 = 4a^2 - 4a\sqrt{(x+c)^2 + y^2} + (x+c)^2 + y^2$$

Expand a little and isolate again.

$$x^2 - 2cx + c^2 + y^2 = 4a^2 - 4a\sqrt{x^2 + 2cx + c^2 + y^2} + x^2 + 2cx + c^2 + y^2$$

so

$$-4cx - 4a^2 = -4a\sqrt{x^2 + 2cx + c^2 + y^2}$$

or

$$cx + a^2 = a\sqrt{x^2 + 2cx + c^2 + y^2}$$

Now square both sides once more.

$$c^2x^2 + 2a^2cx + a^4 = a^2x^2 + 2a^2cx + a^2c^2 + a^2y^2$$

The $2a^2cx$ cancels. You can rearrange terms to look like this.

$$a^4 - a^2c^2 = (a^2 - c^2)x^2 + a^2y^2$$

or

$$a^2(a^2 - c^2) = (a^2 - c^2)x^2 + a^2y^2$$

But $a^2 = b^2 + c^2$, so $a^2 - c^2 = b^2$. So the equation simplifies to

$$a^2b^2 = b^2x^2 + a^2y^2$$

It is often useful to divide both sides of this equation by $a^2b^2$ to get

$$1 = \frac{x^2}{a^2} + \frac{y^2}{b^2}$$

**Habits of Mind**

**Understand the process.** Each of these steps is reversible (as long as *a* and *c* are not negative). Make sure you understand why.

**Habits of Mind**

**Make connections.** Looking at this equation, you might also recognize it as a scaling of the unit circle by a factor of *a* horizontally and *b* vertically.

### *Theorem 9.4*

**The ellipse with foci $(c, 0)$ and $(-c, 0)$ and string length $2a$ has equation**

$$1 = \frac{x^2}{a^2} + \frac{y^2}{b^2} \quad \text{where} \quad b^2 = a^2 - c^2.$$

## Developing Habits of Mind

**Understand the process.** A careful proof of this theorem would require you to show that you did not gain or lose any points when you went from the raw point-tester to the equation in the theorem. There is some work to do here, because you squared both sides of the equation twice, making it possible for extra solutions to creep in. Make sure every step is reversible.

## For Discussion

**3.** Discuss what happens to the graph of the equation $1 = \frac{x^2}{a^2} + \frac{y^2}{b^2}$ as $a$ gets closer and closer to $b$.

**4.** Find an equation for the ellipse with foci at $(0, c)$ and $(0, -c)$ and string length $2a$.

### Equations for Hyperbolas

Consider a hyperbola with foci $F_1(c, 0)$ and $F_2(-c, 0)$ defined by the condition

$$|PF_1 - PF_2| = s$$

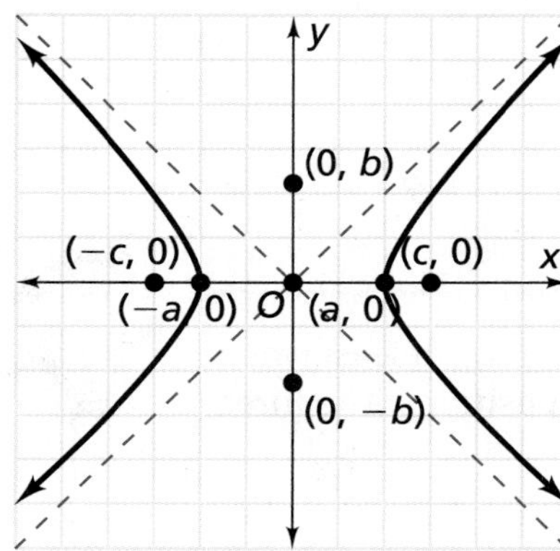


### *Facts and Notation*

- **The points $(a, 0)$ and $(-a, 0)$ are the *vertices* of the hyperbola. Therefore, $s = 2a$. The segment connecting the vertices is the hyperbola's *major axis*.**
- **The constant $b$ is defined by the equation $a^2 + b^2 = c^2$.**

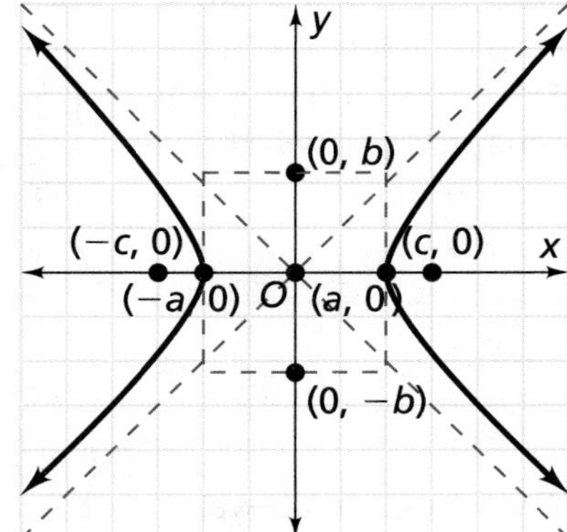


The diagonals of this little rectangle have an interesting relationship to the hyperbola. You will explore that relationship in the exercises.

**You can construct $b$ by creating a rectangle around the origin with sides parallel to the axes, one side of length $2a$, and diagonals of length $2c$. The vertical side of the rectangle is $2b$. The segment connecting $(0, b)$ to $(0, -b)$ is the hyperbola's *minor axis*.**

The point-tester for the hyperbola is $|PF_1 - PF_2| = 2a$. In terms of coordinates, this translates into

$$\left|\sqrt{(x+c)^2 + y^2} - \sqrt{(x-c)^2 + y^2}\right| = 2a$$

This is a perfectly good point-tester. But you can simplify it considerably using exactly the same algebraic technique that you used to derive the equation of the ellipse. You will take care of the details in Exercise 12.

Well, there is one complication that you did not have with the ellipse: the absolute value. But you can avoid this by treating one branch of the hyperbola at a time. In the end, both equations come out the same.

### Theorem 9.5

**The hyperbola with foci $(c, 0)$ and $(-c, 0)$ and constant difference $2a$ has equation**

$$1 = \frac{x^2}{a^2} - \frac{y^2}{b^2}$$

**where $b^2 = c^2 - a^2$.**

## Developing Habits of Mind

**Generalize.** You now have equations for all three conics, at least when they are placed on the coordinate plane in certain positions. The three equations

- $b^2x^2 + a^2y^2 = a^2b^2$,
- $b^2x^2 - a^2y^2 = a^2b^2$, and
- $x^2 = 4cy$

are all special cases of the following general quadratic equation in two variables.

$$rx^2 + sxy + ty^2 + ux + vy + w = 0$$

where $r$, $s$, $t$, $u$, $v$, and $w$ are real numbers. In the next lesson, you will show that if $s = 0$, the equation's graph is a conic with axis parallel to one of the coordinate axes. In fact, a very simple calculation with two numbers will tell you what kind of a conic it is. In the project for this chapter, you will show that even if $s \neq 0$, the graph is a conic, although its axis is not horizontal or vertical.

**Habits of Mind**

**Find relationships.** This predictive power—being able to tell the shape of a graph from a simple calculation—is something that mathematicians prize.

## For You to Do

**5.** Find the values of $r$, $s$, $t$, $u$, $v$, and $w$ in each of the three equations above.

## Exercises Practicing Habits of Mind

### Check Your Understanding

1. Many different ellipses have centers at the origin and pass through the point $(0, 5)$.

   a. Show that the ellipse with equation $25x^2 + 169y^2 = 4225$ passes through $(0, 5)$.

   b. Find four other points on the ellipse from part (a).

   c. Show that the length of the major axis is 26.

   d. The foci of this ellipse are $(c, 0)$ and $(-c, 0)$. Find the value of $c$.

   e. Sketch a graph of this ellipse.

2. The ellipse with equation $25x^2 + 9y^2 = 225$ also has its center at the origin and passes through $(0, 5)$.

   a. Find four other points on this ellipse.

   b. Show that the length of the major axis is 10.

   c. The foci of this ellipse are $(0, c)$ and $(0, -c)$. Find the value of $c$.

   d. Sketch a graph of this ellipse.

3. **Write About It** Describe, as completely as possible, how to find the foci and sketch the graph of

$$1 = \frac{x^2}{a^2} + \frac{y^2}{b^2}$$

   Be careful to describe cases where $a > b$, $a = b$, and $a < b$.

4. The graph of the equation $y^2 - 9x^2 = 36$ is a hyperbola.

   a. Show that the points $(0, 6)$ and $(0, -6)$ are on the hyperbola.

   b. If $x = 1$, find approximate values of $y$ to four decimal places.

   c. If $x = 5$, find approximate values of $y$ to four decimal places.

   d. If $x = 100$, find approximate values of $y$ to four decimal places.

   e. As $x$ grows larger, what relationship is there between the $x$- and $y$-coordinates of points on the hyperbola?

5. In Exercise 4, you worked with the equation

$$y^2 - 9x^2 = 36$$

A slight change to this equation can produce very different results.

a. Sketch the graph of $y^2 - 9x^2 = 9$. How is the graph similar to the one from Exercise 4. How is it different?

b. Sketch the graph of $y^2 - 9x^2 = 1$.

c. Sketch the graph of $y^2 - 9x^2 = 0$.

**Habits of Mind**

**Recall what you know.** What techniques can you use when one side of an equation is set equal to zero?

6. **Take It Further** The following equation gives the distance from a point $(x, y)$ to the line with equation $x + y = 10$.

$$D = \frac{|x + y - 10|}{\sqrt{2}}$$

a. Find an equation for the parabola with focus at the origin and with directrix with equation $x + y = 10$.

b. Find the two points on the graph with $x$-coordinate $-5$.

c. Sketch the graph of this parabola.

**Go Online**
www.successnetplus.com

## On Your Own

7. Find an equation for the parabola with focus $(-2, 0)$ and directrix with equation $x = 2$.

8. The graph of the following equation is a hyperbola.

$$\frac{x^2}{16} - \frac{y^2}{9} = 1$$

a. If $(x, y)$ is on this hyperbola, then so are $(-x, y)$, $(-x, -y)$ and $(x, -y)$. Explain.

b. Copy and complete this table to find the nonnegative value of $y$ for each value of $x$. Approximate your results to four decimal places.

c. As $x$ grows larger, what relationship is there between the $x$- and $y$-coordinates of points on the hyperbola?

| x | y |
|---|---|
| 3 | undefined |
| 4 | 0 |
| 5 | ■ |
| 6 | ■ |
| 8 | ■ |
| 10 | ■ |
| 20 | ■ |
| 40 | ■ |
| 100 | ■ |
| 1000 | ■ |

9. Show that every point on the graph of $y = x^2$ is equidistant from the focus $(0, \frac{1}{4})$ and the directrix with equation $y = -\frac{1}{4}$.

10. Consider the equation $1 = \frac{x^2}{9} + \frac{y^2}{4}$.

    a. Find all values of $x$ if $(x, 0)$ is on the graph of the equation.

    b. Find all values of $y$ if $(0, y)$ is on the graph of the equation.

    c. Sketch the graph of the equation.

    d. Find all values of $x$ if $(x, x)$ is on the graph of the equation.

    e. Find three points that are close to being on the graph but not actually on it.

11. **Take It Further** An ellipse has foci $(8, -6)$ and $(-6, 8)$ and string length 20.

    a. Show that this ellipse passes through the origin.

    b. Find the center of the ellipse.

    c. Find the endpoints of the major axis.

    d. Find an equation of the ellipse.

    e. Sketch the graph of the ellipse.

The major axis contains the foci. It has the same length as the string length.

12. Prove Theorem 9.5, which gives an equation for a hyperbola.

13. **Standardized Test Prep** Which of the following are the foci of the ellipse with equation $\frac{x^2}{25} + \frac{y^2}{9} = 1$?

    A. $(-1, 0)$, $(1, 0)$  B. $(-2, 0)$, $(2, 0)$

    C. $(-3, 0)$, $(3, 0)$  D. $(-4, 0)$, $(4, 0)$

## Maintain Your Skills

14. Each of these is the equation of a parabola. For each, find the coordinates of the focus and an equation of the directrix.

    a. $y = \frac{1}{4}x^2$  b. $x = \frac{1}{4}y^2$  c. $y = -\frac{1}{4}x^2$

    d. $x = -\frac{1}{4}y^2$  e. $y = 2x^2$  f. $x = 2y^2$

# 9.11 Conics Anywhere

In this lesson, you will look at equations for conics where the center (or vertex, for the parabola) is not at the origin.

You looked at various affine transformations of parabolas in previous work. The ideas here are exactly the same. It is easiest to understand the general methods through examples.

## Example 1

**Problem** Find equation of the ellipse $\mathcal{E}$ with foci at (3, 16) and (3, −8) and with string length 26.

**Solution** The situation looks like this.

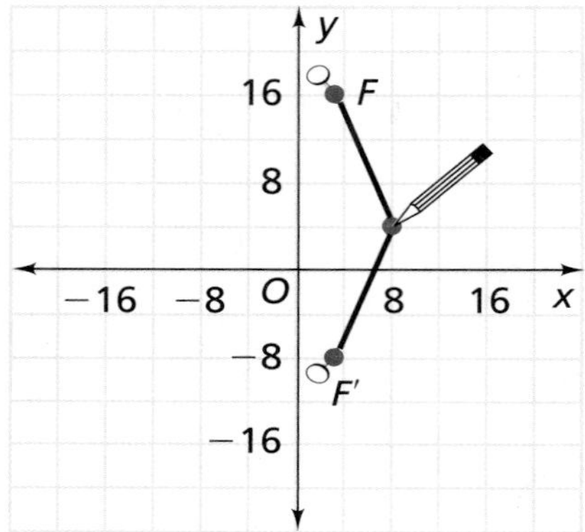


The center of an ellipse is the midpoint of the segment connecting its foci, so the center of this ellipse is (3, 4). The major axis is vertical and the distance from the center to each focus is $c = 12$. Since the string length is 26, $a = 13$ and the vertices are at $(3, 4 + 13) = (3, 17)$ and $(3, 4 - 13) = (3, -9)$.

Since $a^2 = b^2 + c^2$, $b = 5$. So the minor axis connects $(-2, 4)$ to $(8, 4)$.

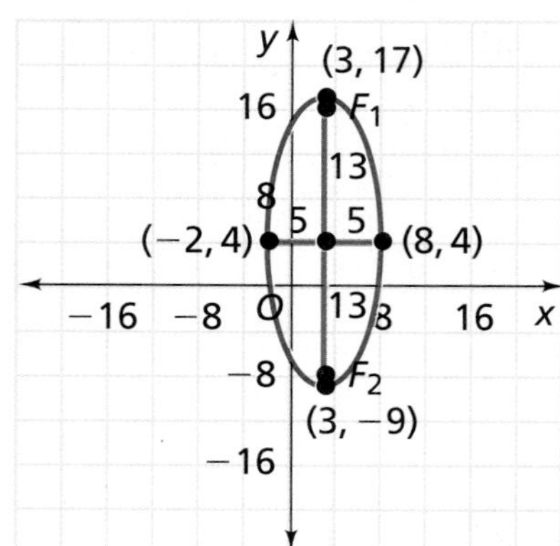

This ellipse $\mathcal{E}$ is a translation of an ellipse $\mathcal{E}'$, centered at the origin with foci located at (0, 12) and (0, −12) and string length 26.

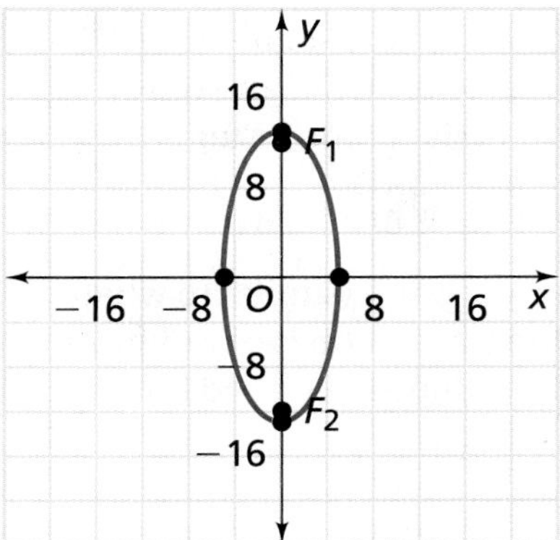


You already know how to find an equation of ellipse centered at the origin. An equation for $\mathcal{E}'$ is

$$\frac{x^2}{25} + \frac{y^2}{169} = 1$$

How can you use this equation to find an equation of the ellipse centered at (3, 4)? Notice that the distance from any point $(x, y)$ to (3, 16) is the same as the distance from $(x - 3, y - 4)$ to $(3 - 3, 16 - 4) = (0, 12)$. (Why?) Similarly, the distance from any point $(x, y)$ to (3, −8) is the same as the distance from $(x - 3, y - 4)$ to $(3 - 3, -8 - 4) = (0, -12)$. So, the sum of the distances from $(x, y)$ to (3, 16) and (3, −8) is the same as the sum of the distances from $(x - 3, y - 4)$ to (0, 12) and (0, −12). In particular, it follows that $(x, y)$ is on $\mathcal{E}$ if and only if $(x - 3, y - 4)$ is on $\mathcal{E}'$.

So, the point-tester for $\mathcal{E}$ is "See if $(x - 3, y - 4)$ is on $\mathcal{E}'$." That is the same as "See if $(x - 3, y - 4)$ satisfies the equation for $\mathcal{E}'$." In other words, check to see if

$$\frac{(x-3)^2}{25} + \frac{(y-4)^2}{169} = 1$$

So this is an equation for the ellipse $\mathcal{E}$.

**Habits of Mind**

**Use what you know.** You have done translations of basic graphs for quite a while now. Conic sections work the same way.

## Developing Habits of Mind

**Simplify complicated problems.** In the above example, you could have gone right to the locus definition. The point $P = (x, y)$ is on $\mathcal{E}$ if and only if the sum of the distances from $P$ to the foci is 26, so the point-tester is

$$\sqrt{(x-3)^2 + (y-16)^2} + \sqrt{(x-3)^2 + (y+8)^2} = 26$$

To simplify this, you would have to face some hefty algebra (similar to what you did in the proof of Theorem 9.4). But using the translation idea reduces the problem to one you have already solved and eliminates the need for the complex calculations.

Of course, some people love to do algebraic calculations. If you are one of them, go ahead and see if you get the same equation as you got in the example.

## For Discussion

1. Suppose $F_1 = (1, 1)$ and $F_2 = (11, 1)$. Find an equation of the hyperbola defined by

$$|PF_1 - PF_2| = 8$$

## Minds in Action

*Tony and Sasha are looking at the example above*

**Sasha** I'm one of those people who loves algebra. I think I'll see what our equation

$$\frac{(x-3)^2}{25} + \frac{(y-4)^2}{169} = 1$$

looks like if I expand everything and put it in normal form.

**Tony** Be my guest.

*Sasha pulls out some chalk and begins to write on the board. A few minutes later, she smiles at her work.*

**Sasha** I get

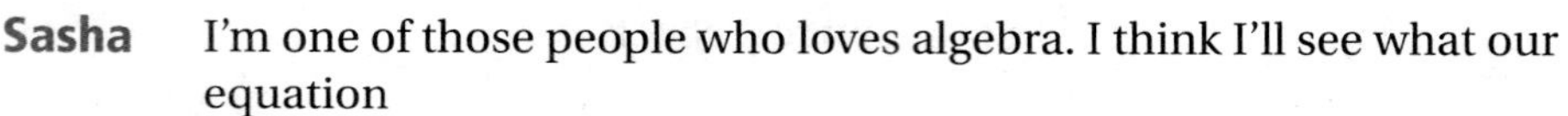


**Tony** I wonder how we could have graphed the ellipse if we had been given this equation.

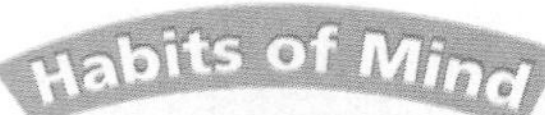


**Find a process.** How would you help Tony answer his question?

## Example 2

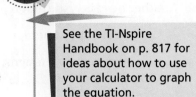

**Problem** Is the graph of

$$9y^2 + 18y - 16x^2 + 64x - 199 = 0$$

a conic? If so, what kind is it?

**Solution** Complete the square in $x$ and $y$ on the left side so that you can write the equation in terms of $x - r$ and $y - s$ for some constants $r$ and $s$.

$$\begin{aligned}
9y^2 + 18y - 16x^2 + 64x - 199 &= 0 \\
9y^2 + 18y - 16x^2 + 64x &= 199 \\
9(y^2 + 2y + ?) - 16(x^2 - 4x + ??) &= 199 + 9 \cdot ? - 16 \cdot ?? \\
9(y^2 + 2y + 1) - 16(x^2 - 4x + 4) &= 199 + 9 \cdot 1 - 16 \cdot 4 \\
9(y + 1)^2 - 16(x - 2)^2 &= 199 + 9 - 64 \\
9(y + 1)^2 - 16(x - 2)^2 &= 144
\end{aligned}$$

So the equation is

$$9(y + 1)^2 - 16(x - 2)^2 = 144$$

Divide both sides by 144 to get

$$\frac{(y + 1)^2}{16} - \frac{(x - 2)^2}{9} = 1$$

The graph is a hyperbola with center $(2, -1)$.

See the TI-Nspire Handbook on p. 817 for ideas about how to use your calculator to graph the equation.

## Developing Habits of Mind

**Generalize.** This method will work on any equation of the form

$$rx^2 + ty^2 + ux + vy + w = 0$$

and the result will tell you what kind of a conic the graph is. When you complete the square on the left side and simplify, you will get an equation of the form

$$r(x - h)^2 + t(x - k)^2 = c$$

for constants $h$, $k$, and $c$.

The graph might be a degenerate conic—a point or a pair of lines, for example. See the Maintain Your Skills exercises from Lesson 9.09.

## For Discussion

Suppose the conic is not degenerate. Discuss each statement.

2. If either $r$ or $t$ is 0, the graph is a parabola.
3. If $r$ and $t$ have the same sign, the graph is an ellipse.
4. If $r$ and $t$ have opposite signs, the graph is a hyperbola.

A little more work produces the following classification theorem.

To a mathematician a classification theorem is truly a thing of beauty.

### *Theorem 9.6*

**The graph of**

$$rx^2 + ty^2 + ux + vy + w = 0$$

**is a (possibly degenerate) conic. In fact, the nature of the conic is determined by the sign of $rt$:**

- **If $rt > 0$, the graph is an ellipse.**
- **If $rt = 0$, the graph is a parabola.**
- **If $rt < 0$, the graph is a hyperbola.**

## For You to Do

5. How can you tell from the equation if the graph is a circle?
6. How can you tell from the equation if the graph is a single point?

Educators and scientists use ripple tanks to discover and demonstrate the additive and subtractive properties of combinations of waves in a shallow basin of water. Here the spreading rings of drops of liquid produce interference patterns. Such patterns are the common conic sections you studied in this chapter.

## Exercises Practicing Habits of Mind

### Check Your Understanding

1. The graph of the following equation is a hyperbola.

$$\frac{(x-3)^2}{16} - \frac{(y-2)^2}{9} = 1$$

The hyperbola is related to the one from Exercise 8 of Lesson 9.10.

**a.** What is the center of the hyperbola?

**b.** Copy and complete this table to find the nonnegative value of $y$ for each value of $x$. Approximate your results to four decimal places.

| $x$ | $y$ |
|---|---|
| 6 | undefined |
| 7 | 2 |
| 8 | ■ |
| 9 | ■ |
| 11 | ■ |
| 13 | ■ |
| 23 | ■ |
| 43 | ■ |
| 103 | ■ |
| 1003 | ■ |

**c.** As $x$ grows larger, what relationship is there between the $x$- and $y$-coordinates of points on the hyperbola?

2. The graph of the equation

$$9(x-3)^2 + 16(y+2)^2 = N$$

depends on the value of $N$.

**a.** Sketch the graph when $N = 144$.

**b.** Does the ellipse you drew in part (a) pass through the origin?

**c.** Sketch the graph when $N = 36$.

**d.** Sketch the graph when $N = 0$.

**e.** Sketch the graph when $N = -144$.

**f.** Find all values of $N$ such that the graph passes through the point $(13, -1)$.

3. a. Is the graph of $25x^2 - 4y^2 + 150x + 32y + 61 = 0$ a conic? If so, what kind is it?

   b. Sketch the graph of the equation.

4. a. Is the graph of $4x^2 + 25y^2 - 16x + 250y + 641 = 0$ a conic? If so, what kind is it?

   b. Sketch the graph of the equation.

5. The graph of $\frac{(x+3)^2}{4} - \frac{(y-2)^2}{16} = 1$ is not the graph of a function, but it can be the union of two function graphs.

   a. Solve the equation above for $(y - 2)^2$.

   b. Why is it not possible to uniquely solve for $y$?

   c. Write $y$ as two functions. Plot each function. Then combine them to sketch the entire hyperbola.

6. Sketch an accurate graph of these two equations on the same axes.

$$\frac{(x-3)^2}{16} - \frac{(y-2)^2}{9} = 1$$

$$\frac{(x-3)^2}{16} - \frac{(y-2)^2}{9} = 0$$

7. **Take It Further** Find an equation of a hyperbola that is the graph of all points $P$ with

$$|PF_1 - PF_2| = 2\sqrt{2}$$

with foci $F_1 = (\sqrt{2}, \sqrt{2})$ and $F_2 = (-\sqrt{2}, -\sqrt{2})$.

## On Your Own

8. Explain why the equation $\frac{(x+5)^2}{16} + \frac{(y-3)^2}{9} = -1$ has no graph, but the equation $\frac{(x+5)^2}{16} - \frac{(y-3)^2}{9} = -1$ does.

9. Consider the equation

$$\frac{(x-11)^2}{36} + \frac{(y+14)^2}{25} = 1$$

   a. What possible values of $x$ could make the equation true? Explain.

   b. What possible values of $y$ could make the equation true?

Try to do this without graphing the ellipse. What must be true about the entire $x$ term?

10. Consider the equation $\frac{(x+9)^2}{49} - \frac{(y-5)^2}{16} = 1$.

a. What possible values of $x$ could make the equation true? Explain.

b. What possible values of $y$ could make the equation true?

11. Find the coordinates of the foci of the ellipse with equation

$$36x^2 + 11y^2 - 288x - 110y + 455 = 0$$

12. **What's Wrong Here?** Pam thought about stretching an ellipse.

Pam: You can stretch these ellipses in any direction, and everything moves along. If you double the length of an axis, I think you'll double the distance between the foci, too.

a. Give an example that shows Pam's conjecture is not correct.

b. Can you stretch an ellipse to double the distance? Explain.

13. An ellipse is centered at (3, 5) and (10, 5) is one of its foci.

a. Find the coordinates of the other focus.

b. If the point (1, 17) is on the ellipse, find the length of the major and minor axes. Find an equation for the ellipse.

14. Show algebraically that the sum of the distances from $(x, y)$ to (3, 16) and (3, −8) is the same as the sum of the distances from $(x - 3, y - 4)$ to (0, 12) and (0, −12).

15. **Standardized Test Prep** Which of the following is a hyperbola with foci at (3, 4) and (3, −4) and vertices 6 units apart?

A. $\frac{(x-3)^2}{9} - \frac{(y-4)^2}{16} = 1$

B. $\frac{(x-3)^2}{9} - \frac{y^2}{7} = 1$

C. $\frac{(y-4)^2}{9} - \frac{x^2}{16} = 1$

D. $\frac{y^2}{9} - \frac{(x-3)^2}{7} = 1$

## Maintain Your Skills

16. An ellipse has center (2, −1) and one vertex is (6, −1).

a. Find the coordinates of the other vertex.

b. Find the foci if (2, 0) is one of the endpoints of the minor axis.

c. Find the foci if (2, 1) is one of the endpoints of the minor axis.

d. Find the foci if (2, 2) is one of the endpoints of the minor axis.

e. Find the foci if (2, 3) is one of the endpoints of the minor axis.

f. Find the foci if (2, 4) is one of the endpoints of the minor axis.

# 9.12 They Are All the Same—A Continuous Family of Curves

In Lesson 9.09, you saw each of the conics as a planar slice of an infinite double cone. The only difference between the different types of conic was the position of the slicing plane. This lesson shows another way to see the conics as in some sense the same. All of them come from a single class of equations.

The locus definition of a parabola is the set of points that are equidistant from a point $F$ (the focus) and a line $d$ (the directrix).

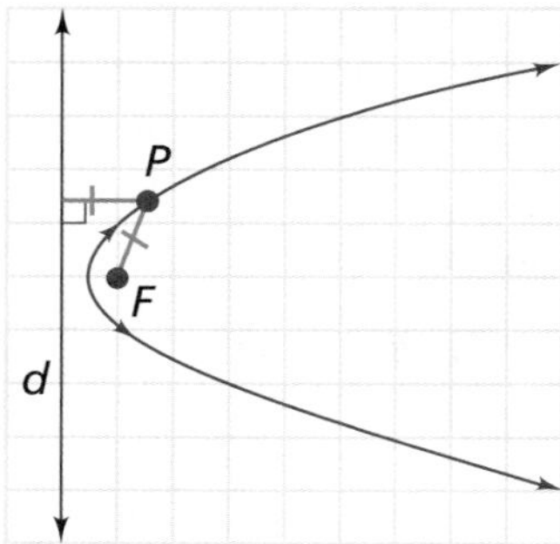


Another way to say that $PF = Pd$ is to say that $\frac{PF}{Pd} = 1$.

*Pd* means the distance from *P* to the line *d*, measured along the perpendicular from *P* to *d*.

## Developing Habits of Mind

**Experiment.** Mathematicians like to tweak definitions. What would the curve look like if $\frac{PF}{Pd}$ were 2 instead of 1? What would it look like if the ratio were $\frac{1}{2}$? Experimenting with definitions like this often leads to new connections.

## In-Class Experiment

You can set up an experiment in your geometry software in which you can control a slider and then produce the set of all points $P$ so that the ratio of $\frac{PF}{Pd}$ is the length of the slider (a nonnegative real number). Here are some snapshots of such an experiment.

See the TI-Nspire Handbook on p. 817 for instructions on how to build the experiment.

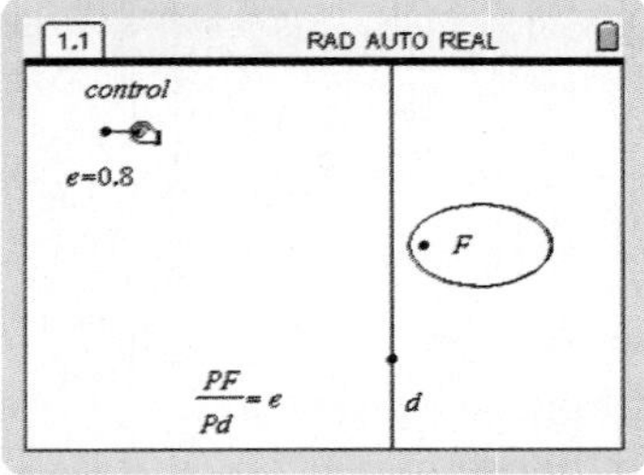


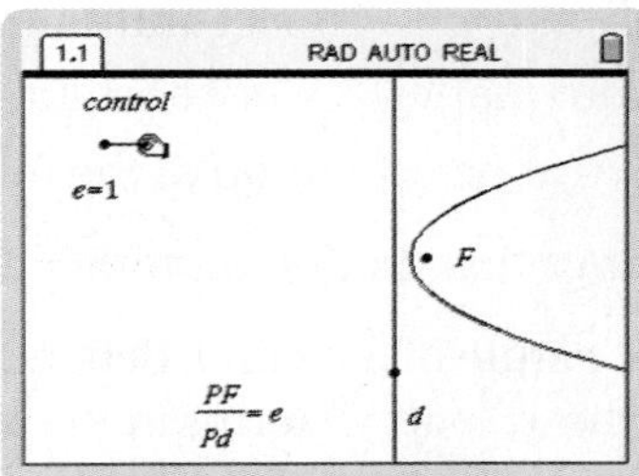


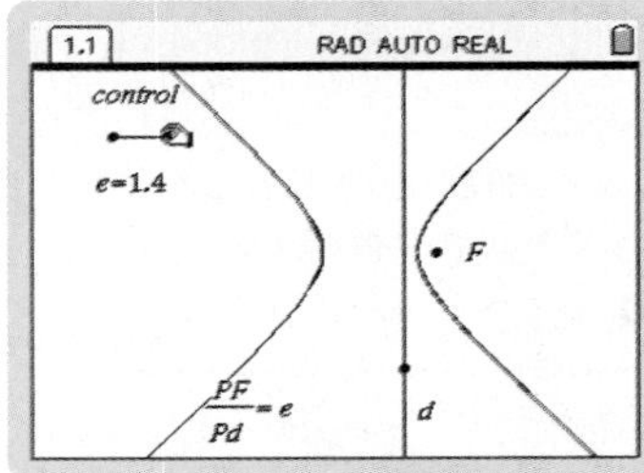


You know that when $e = 1$, the curve is a parabola. (Why?) But it sure looks as if other values of $e$ produce conics, too. Before you see if this is so, experiment some with the sketch.

The letter e is used for the ratio for reasons that will become apparent in the exercises. But this has nothing to do with the constant e from Chapter 8.

**1.** For what values of $e$ do the curves seem to be ellipses? Hyperbolas? Parabolas?

**2.** Experiment with the distance between the directrix and the focus. How does that affect things?

Just because something looks like a conic does not mean that it is a conic. To find out, you can use the algebra. Set up the situation on a coordinate plane. Then translate the locus definition into coordinates.

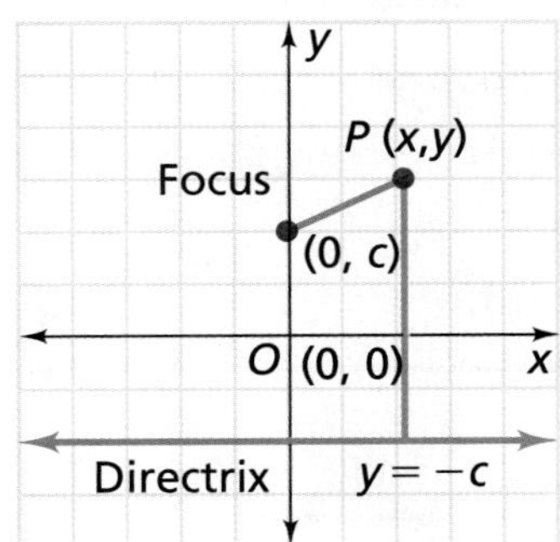


Suppose the focus is $(0, c)$ and the directrix has equation $y = -c$.

What is the point-tester? $P(x, y)$ is on the curve if and only if the distance from $(x, y)$ to $(0, c)$ is $e$ times the distance from $(x, y)$ to the graph of $y = -c$.

$\frac{PF}{Pd} = e$ is the same as $PF = e \cdot Pd$.

But the distance from $(x, y)$ to $(0, c)$ is $\sqrt{x^2 + (y - c)^2}$ and the distance from $(x, y)$ to the graph of $y = -c$ is $|y - (-c)| = |y + c|$.

(Why?) So, the point tester is $\sqrt{x^2 + (y - c)^2} = e|y + c|$.

This is fine as a point-tester. But you can simplify the equation in ways that will make it look familiar. Remember, thanks to Theorem 9.6, if you know that the equation is a polynomial in $x$ and $y$ of degree 2 set equal to 0, you only need the coefficients of $x^2$ and $y^2$ to tell which conic the graph will be.

| | |
|---|---|
| $\sqrt{x^2 + (y - c)^2} = e\lvert y + c \rvert$ | Square both sides. |
| $x^2 + (y - c)^2 = e^2(y + c)^2$ | Expand. |
| $x^2 + y^2 - 2cy + c^2 = e^2y^2 + 2e^2cy + e^2c^2$ | Cancel and simplify. |
| $x^2 + (1 - e^2)y^2 + \text{(things that do not matter)} = \text{a constant}$ | |

So, the set of all points $P$ so that $\frac{PF}{Pd} = e$ has equation of the form

$$x^2 + (1 - e^2)y^2 + \text{(things that do not matter)} = 0$$

You know from Theorem 9.6 that the nature of the curve depends on the sign of the product of the coefficients of the $x^2$ and $y^2$ terms in the equation: $rt = 1 \cdot (1 - e^2) = 1 - e^2$. This leads to the following classification theorem.

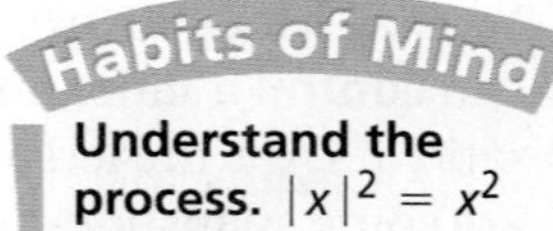


**Understand the process.** $|x|^2 = x^2$ (Why?)

Habits of Mind

**Verify a conjecture.** So, what the experiment suggested was true. The curve defined by $\frac{PF}{Pd} = e$ is always a conic.

### *Theorem 9.7*

**Let $F$ be a fixed point, $d$ be a fixed line, and $e$ be a positive real number. The set of points $P$ such that $\frac{PF}{Pd} = e$ is a (possibly degenerate) conic. It is an ellipse if $e < 1$, a parabola if $e = 1$, and a hyperbola if $e > 1$.**

## Developing Habits of Mind

**Make connections.** Theorem 9.7 is one reason for the names *ellipse, parabola,* and *hyperbola.* If you check a dictionary you will discover that the words *ellipsis, parable,* and *hyperbole* have roughly these meanings in English.

- **ellipsis:** fall short—something is missing
- **parable:** fall beside—usually a story that illustrates a message
- **hyperbole:** fall beyond—an exaggeration

The theorem says that the curve is

- an ellipse if $e$ "falls short" of 1.
- a parabola if $e$ "falls beside" 1.
- a hyperbola $e$ "falls beyond" 1.

In English, the symbol "..." is used to denote that something is missing, usually from a quotation and it is called an *ellipsis.* For example, "Now is the winter of our discontent..." means that the writer has cut this Shakespeare quotation before the end of the sentence.

## For Discussion

3. Give an example of an English sentence that exhibits ellipsis, parable, or hyperbole.

# Exercises Practicing Habits of Mind

## Check Your Understanding

Some ellipses are flatter than others. One way to measure this is the **eccentricity,** the ratio of the distance between the foci, called the focal distance, to the distance between the vertices. Define the eccentricity by the ratio $\frac{c}{a}$.

**1.** Find the eccentricity of the ellipse given by each equation.

**a.** $\frac{x^2}{25} + \frac{y^2}{16} = 1$ **b.** $\frac{x^2}{25} + \frac{y^2}{9} = 1$ **c.** $\frac{x^2}{25} + \frac{y^2}{24} = 1$ **d.** $\frac{x^2}{25} + \frac{y^2}{100} = 1$

**2.** Find an equation of an ellipse with center (8, 0), focus (6, 0), and eccentricity $\frac{1}{2}$.

**3.** The set of points $P$ with the ratio $\frac{PF}{Pd} = \frac{1}{2}$ using focus $F(6, 0)$ and the $y$-axis as directrix forms a conic section. Find its equation. Find its center.

The definition of eccentricity given above also applies to hyperbolas. The eccentricity is still the focal distance divided by the distance between the vertices, also expressed as $\frac{c}{a}$.

**Remember...**

For an ellipse, $a^2 = b^2 + c^2$ where $a$ is half the major axis length, $b$ is half the minor axis length, and $c$ is half the distance between the foci.

**4.** The set of points 1.5 times as far from (3, 5) as they are from the graph of $x = -2$ is a hyperbola.

**a.** Find its center, vertices, and foci.

**b.** Find its eccentricity.

**c.** Sketch the graph of the hyperbola.

**5.** The set of points 3 times as far from $(-3, 4)$ as they are from the graph of $y = -4$ is a hyperbola. Find its eccentricity.

**6.** Take It Further Given focus $F(0, 1)$ and directrix $d$ given by $x = -1$. A conic section is defined by the points $P$ with $\frac{PF}{Pd} = e$.

**a.** If $e = 1$, how do you know that the conic is a parabola?

**b.** If $e < 1$ show that the conic is an ellipse with eccentricity $e$.

**c.** If $e > 1$ show that the conic is a hyperbola with eccentricity $e$.

7. Take It Further Graph the ellipse with a graphing window of $-5 \le x \le 5$, $-5 \le y \le 5$.

$$\frac{x^2}{49} + \frac{(y-100)^2}{10{,}000} = 1$$

a. What do you notice?

b. Find another ellipse that behaves similarly.

## On Your Own

8. What is the eccentricity of a circle? Explain.

9. a. Explain why the eccentricity of an ellipse must always be less than 1.

   b. Explain why the eccentricity of a hyperbola must always be greater than 1.

10. A hyperbola has foci $(5, 5)$ and $(-7, 5)$. One endpoint of the major axis is $(-2, 5)$.

    a. Find an eccentricity of this hyperbola.

    b. Find an equation of the hyperbola.

    c. Sketch the graph of the hyperbola.

11. Which of these is an equation of an ellipse?

    A. $4x^2 + 1 = 9y^2$

    B. $4x + 6y + x^2 - y^2 = 36$

    C. $4x^2 + 9y + 8x - 36 = 0$

    D. $-16x + 8y + 4x^2 + 8y^2 - 25 = 0$

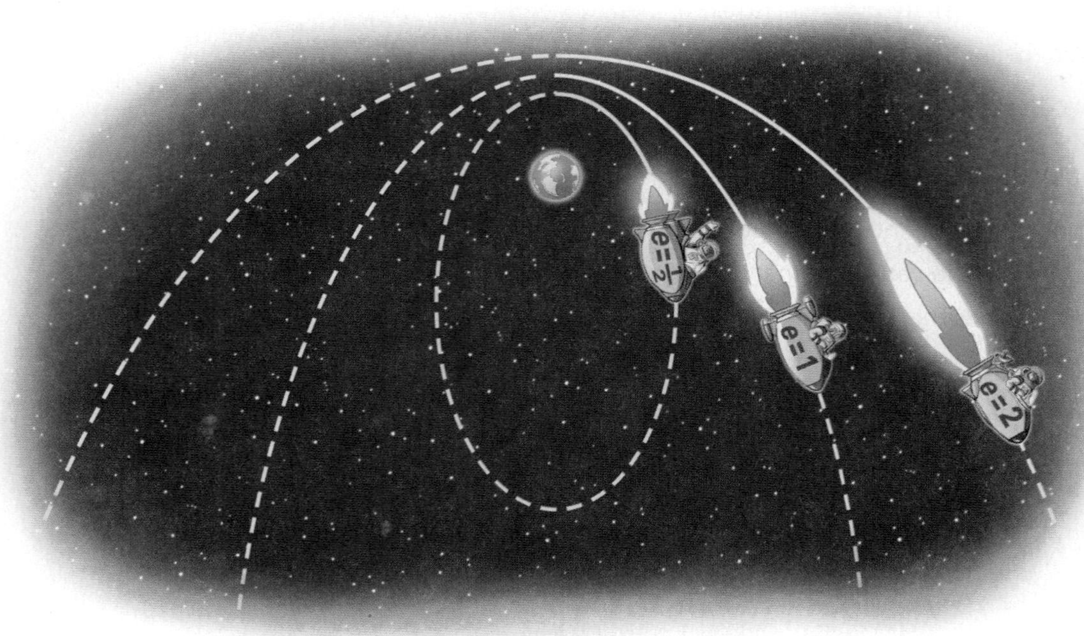

12. The set of points that are twice as far from (3, 7) as they are from the $y$-axis is a hyperbola. Find the other focus of this hyperbola.

13. Take It Further As seen in the lesson, fix focus point $F$ and directrix line $d$, then vary the ratio $\frac{PF}{Pd}$ to produce different conic sections. One focus of the conic stays in place. But ellipses and hyperbolas have two foci: what happens to the other focus?

   a. As the ratio $\frac{PF}{Pd}$ approaches zero, what does the other focus move toward?

   b. As the ratio $\frac{PF}{Pd}$ gets larger toward 1, what does the other focus move toward?

   c. What happens when the ratio equals 1?

   d. As the ratio continues to grow, what does the other focus move toward?

14. Standardized Test Prep Which of the following could be the eccentricity of an ellipse with a focus at (5, 0), vertex at (7, 0), and directrix $x = 12$?

   A. $\frac{2}{5}$ B. $\frac{5}{7}$ C. $\frac{5}{12}$ D. $\frac{7}{12}$

## Maintain Your Skills

15. The orbit of every planet is an ellipse. Each elliptical orbit has the sun as one focus and some eccentricity $e$. This table gives the length of the major axis and the eccentricity for each planet's orbit.

Kepler proved this fact about the planets in the early 17th Century. Orbits of comets may be parabolic or even hyperbolic.

| Planet | Major Axis Length (million km) | Eccentricity e |
|---|---|---|
| Mercury | 115.8 | 0.2056 |
| Venus | 216.4 | 0.0068 |
| Earth | 299.2 | 0.0167 |
| Mars | 455.9 | 0.0934 |
| Jupiter | 1556.8 | 0.0484 |
| Saturn | 2853.5 | 0.0542 |
| Uranus | 5741.9 | 0.0472 |
| Neptune | 8996.5 | 0.0086 |

   a. Which planet's orbit is most like a circle? the least like a circle?

   b. For each planet, determine how far away the sun is from the center of the planet's orbit.

**Remember...**

The sun is a focus of the ellipse. The eccentricity is known.

**In this investigation, you sliced a cone to get a conic section—a circle, an ellipse, a parabola, or a hyperbola. You described each conic section verbally as a locus of points, or algebraically by an equation. Then, given an equation, you described its graph as a conic section. The following questions will help you summarize what you have learned.**

1. Determine an equation (in the form $y = a(x - h)^2 + k$) for the parabola having focus $(1, 2)$ and directrix the $x$-axis.
2. Find the center, foci, and the lengths of the major and minor axes of the ellipse having equation $16x^2 - 64x + 25y^2 + 50y = 311$.
3. We know from Theorem 9.6 that the graph of the equation $rx^2 + ty^2 + ux + vy + w = 0$ is a conic. In order for the conic to be a circle, what must be the relationship between $r$ and $t$?
4. **a.** In order for the graph of the equation $2x^2 + cy^2 + 4x + 4cy + f = 0$ to be an ellipse, what must be true about the value of $c$?
   **b.** In order for the graph of the equation $2x^2 + cy^2 + 4x + 4cy + f = 0$ to be a nondegenerate ellipse, what must be true about the value of $f$?
5. Explain how you know that the graph of the equation $x^2 + y^2 - 2x + 4y + 5 = 0$ is a degenerate conic.
6. How do you slice an infinite double cone with a plane to get a parabola?
7. What is the locus definition of a hyperbola?
8. What kind of conic section do you get when you graph $x^2 + 16y^2 - 8x + 64y + 64 = 0$? How can you identify the conic section from its equation?

## Vocabulary

In this investigation, you learned these terms. Make sure you understand what each one means and how to use it.

- apex
- axis
- conic sections
- Dandelin sphere
- directrix
- eccentricity
- ellipse
- focus, foci
- generator
- hyperbola
- locus
- major axis
- minor axis
- parabola
- vertex

Chapter 9

# Review

Go Online
www.successnetplus.com

In **Investigation 9A** you learned how to

- distinguish between distance and the length of a path
- use reflection to make a straight path from a segmented path
- find the shortest path between two points if you must pass through a third point

*The following questions will help you check your understanding.*

**1.**

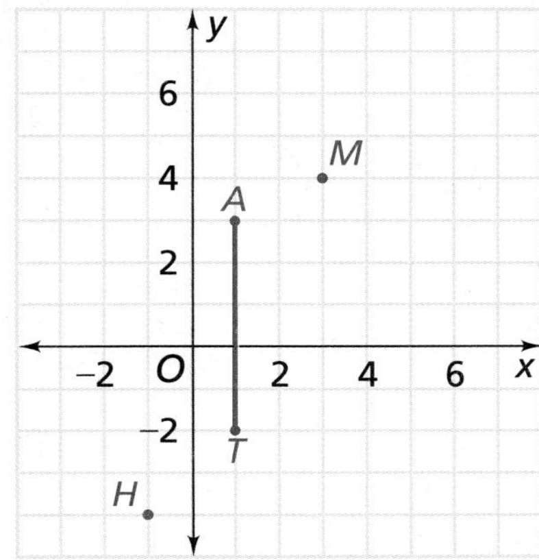


**a.** Find the distance from $M(3, 4)$ to $H(-1, -4)$.

**b.** Now find the shortest path from $M$ to $H$ if your path cannot intersect $\overline{AT}$.

**2.** Let $A$ and $B$ fall on opposite sides of a line. Explain how to find $P$ on the line so that $AP + PB$ is a minimum. Include a sketch.

**3.** Let $X$ and $Y$ be on the same side of a line. Explain how to use reflection to find $P$ on the line so that $XP + PY$ is a minimum. Include a sketch.

In **Investigation 9B** you learned how to

- find grid polygons with a given area or perimeter
- find the triangle or rectangle that maximizes area for a given perimeter
- find the polygon that maximizes area for a given perimeter

*The following questions will help you check your understanding.*

**4.** Use only grid lines on a sheet of graph paper. Find the maximum perimeter possible for a grid polygon with an area of 12 square units.

**5.** Find the maximum area for a triangle with perimeter 36 in.

**6.** The perimeter of a rectangle is 80 cm and its length is 32 cm. What is its area?

**7.** Find the area of each regular polygon, given that its perimeter is 52 in.

**a.** a triangle

**b.** a square

**c.** a hexagon

**d.** a dodecagon

**8.** You want to build a dog kennel along an outer wall of a barn. You have 200 feet of fencing. What is the maximum area of the dog kennel for each number of sides?

**a.** 4 sides

**b.** 5 sides

**c.** 6 sides

In **Investigation 9C,** you learned to

- visualize each of the conic sections as the intersection of a plane with an infinite double cone
- give a locus definition for each of the conic sections
- identify the equations for the graphs of the conic sections, and sketch their graphs

*The following questions will help you check your understanding.*

**9.** A parabola has focus $(0, 2)$ and directrix with equation $y = -2$.

**a.** Find an equation of the parabola.

**b.** Sketch the graph of the parabola. Graph and label the focus and the directrix.

**10.** An ellipse has foci $(-3, 2)$ and $(3, 2)$. One endpoint of the major axis is $(5, 2)$

**a.** Find the eccentricity of the ellipse.

**b.** Find the endpoints of the minor axis.

**c.** Find an equation of the ellipse.

**d.** Sketch the graph of the ellipse.

**11.** Consider the following equations.

- $9x^2 - 4y^2 - 36x - 8y - 4 = 0$
- $9x^2 + y^2 + 54x + 4y + 76 = 0$

**a.** Identify the graph of each equation (circle, parabola, ellipse, or hyperbola).

**b.** Find the coordinates of the center and foci.

**c.** Find the eccentricity.

**d.** Sketch the graph of the equation.

# Test

## Multiple Choice

1. Suppose you want to enclose a rectangular garden with 50 feet of fencing. A stone wall will serve as the back of the garden. What are the dimensions of the rectangle that will maximize the area of the garden?

   A. 15 ft by 20 ft

   B. 17.5 ft by 15 ft

   C. 12.5 ft by 25 ft

   D. 7 ft by 18 ft

2. A company wants to minimize the costs associated with packaging a box of 30 markers. The length of each marker is 6.5 in., and the diameter of each marker is 0.5 in. What are the dimensions of the box that will minimize the costs?

   A. 0.5 in. by 15 in. by 6.5 in.

   B. 1 in. by 7.5 in. by 6.5 in.

   C. 1.5 in. by 5 in. by 6.5 in.

   D. 2.5 in. by 3 in. by 6.5 in.

Suppose you want to find the shortest path from $A(-2, 3)$ to any point $P$ on the line $y = -1$ to $B(1, 2)$.

3. What point $P$ on the line $y = -1$ should the path pass through?

   A. $(0, -1)$

   B. $\left(-\frac{2}{7}, -1\right)$

   C. $\left(-\frac{7}{3}, -1\right)$

   D. $\left(-\frac{5}{3}, -1\right)$

4. What is the length of the shortest path? Round your answer to the nearest hundredth.

   A. 7.62 B. 7.63

   C. 8.03 D. 8.50

5. Find the type of conic given by the equation $12x^2 + 2y^2 - 72x + 20y - 206 = 0$.

   A. circle

   B. ellipse

   C. hyperbola

   D. parabola

## Open Response

6. Which has the greatest area? Explain.
   - an equilateral triangle with perimeter 120 cm
   - a square with perimeter 120 cm
   - a nonsquare rectangle with perimeter 120 cm

7. Consider the equation

$$4x^2 + 9y^2 - 24x + 36y + 36 = 0$$

   a. Determine if this equation represents a conic. If it does, state what kind of conic.

   b. Sketch the graph of the equation.

8. An ellipse has foci $(-5, 2)$ and $(7, 2)$ and string length 20.

   a. Find the center of the ellipse.

   b. Find the coordinates of the vertices.

   c. Write an equation of the ellipse.

9. Consider the equation $\frac{(x-4)^2}{144} - \frac{(y+7)^2}{81} = 1$.

   a. Find what type of conic is given by the graph of this equation.

   b. Find the center and foci.

   c. Sketch the graph of the equation.

10. An ellipse is centered at $(-1, -3)$ with a focus at $(-1, 3)$ and eccentricity $\frac{3}{5}$.

   a. Find the major axis of the ellipse.

   b. Find the coordinates of the other focus.

   c. Find the vertices of the ellipse.

# Honors Appendix

## Investigations at a Glance

A Other Trigonometric Functions

B Trigonometric Identities

# Honors Appendix

## Vocabulary

- asymptote
- identically equal
- identity
- inverse function

# Other Trigonometric Functions

In *Other Trigonometric Functions*, you will study the tangent function and draw its graph. You will define the inverse cosine, sine, and tangent functions. You will also learn about the three other trigonometric functions: secant, cosecant, and cotangent.

**By the end of this investigation, you will be able to answer questions like these.**

1. How are the six trigonometric functions defined?
2. Why does the $\sin^{-1}$ function on a calculator only return results between $-\frac{\pi}{2}$ and $\frac{\pi}{2}$?
3. How many solutions are there to the equation $\cos x = 0.8$?

**You will learn how to**

- understand several relationships between the tangent function and the unit circle
- sketch and describe the graph of the tangent function
- define an inverse of cosine, sine, and tangent
- recognize three other trigonometric functions: secant, cosecant, and cotangent

**You will develop these habits and skills:**

- Use the unit circle to generate the graph of $y = \tan x$.
- Visualize geometrically the tangent and secant functions.
- Restrict the domain of a function to make it one-to-one.
- Solve equations and prove identities using trigonometric functions.

Since the column and its shadow form a right angle, you can use elementary trigonometry to calculate its height.

# H.01 Getting Started

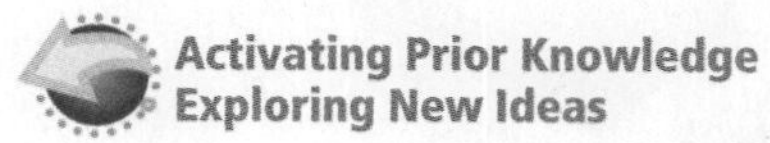


To start this investigation, you will have to work with definitions. You will have to recall how to relate the inverse of a function to the function. You will also have to work with definitions of some new functions.

## For You to Explore

1. Two of these four functions are inverses of each other. Which two?

   **I.** $f(x) = 3x + 5$ **II.** $g(x) = 3x - 5$

   **III.** $h(x) = \frac{1}{3}x + 5$ **IV.** $k(x) = \frac{1}{3}(x + 5)$

   **A.** I and III

   **B.** I and IV

   **C.** II and III

   **D.** II and IV

2. On the same axes, sketch the graphs of the two functions $f$ and $g$ over the domain $-\pi \leq x \leq 2\pi$.

$$f(x) = \sin x$$
$$g(x) = \frac{1}{\sin x}$$

Make sure you leave enough room for the graph of $g$. You might want your $y$-axis to range from $-10$ to $10$.

3. **Write About It** Consider the two functions in Problem 2. Is $g$ the inverse of $f$? Justify your answer.

4. **a.** Sketch the graph of $h(x) = \cos x$ on the domain $-\pi \leq x \leq 2\pi$.

   **b.** Explain why $h(x)$ does not have an inverse function on this domain.

   **c.** Can $h(x)$ have an inverse function on some other domain? If so, give an example. If not, explain why not.

5. **Take It Further** Sketch and describe the graph of the equation

$$j(x) = \sin \frac{1}{x}$$

**Habits of Mind**

**Think it through.** Can you explain why $j(x)$ is not the same as $g(x) = \frac{1}{\sin x}$?

## Exercises *Practicing Habits of Mind*

### On Your Own

In this investigation, you will be using the cosine and sine functions frequently, as well as these four other functions related to them:

$$\tan x = \frac{\sin x}{\cos x} \qquad \textbf{tangent} \text{ of } x$$

$$\sec x = \frac{1}{\cos x} \qquad \textbf{secant} \text{ of } x$$

$$\csc x = \frac{1}{\sin x} \qquad \textbf{cosecant} \text{ of } x$$

$$\cot x = \frac{\cos x}{\sin x} \qquad \textbf{cotangent} \text{ of } x$$

The names tangent and secant have geometric meanings, and you will see how those meanings apply to the unit circle later in this investigation.

**6.** Find the domain and range for the function.

$$g(x) = \csc x$$

Have you sketched the graph of *g* earlier?

**7.** Find each value.

**a.** $\sec \frac{\pi}{3}$ **b.** $\tan \frac{3\pi}{4}$

**c.** $\cot \frac{3\pi}{4}$ **d.** $\sec \frac{\pi}{4} \cdot \cos \frac{\pi}{4}$

**8. a.** Let $x = 1.22$. Which is greater, $\tan x$ or $\sec x$?

**b.** Let $x$ be the length of an arc intercepted by any angle in Quadrant I. Which is greater, $\tan x$ or $\sec x$? Explain.

**Habits of Mind**

**Make a connection.** Think about how to calculate tan *x* and sec *x*. How are they similar? How are they different?

**9. a.** For any value of $x$ where both functions are defined, which is larger: $\tan^2 x$ or $\sec^2 x$?

**b.** Take It Further Justify, with proof, your answer.

### Maintain Your Skills

**10.** Let $PROD(x)$ be the product of the six trigonometric functions.

$$PROD(x) = \cos x \cdot \sin x \cdot \tan x \cdot \sec x \cdot \csc x \cdot \cot x$$

For each $x$, calculate $PROD(x)$.

**a.** $x = \frac{\pi}{4}$ **b.** $x = \frac{\pi}{3}$ **c.** $x = 30°$

**d.** $x = 0$ **e.** $x = 150°$

**11.** Find the domain and range of the *PROD* function given in Exercise 10.

# H.02 The Tangent Function

You first learned the tangent function in earlier work using a right triangle.

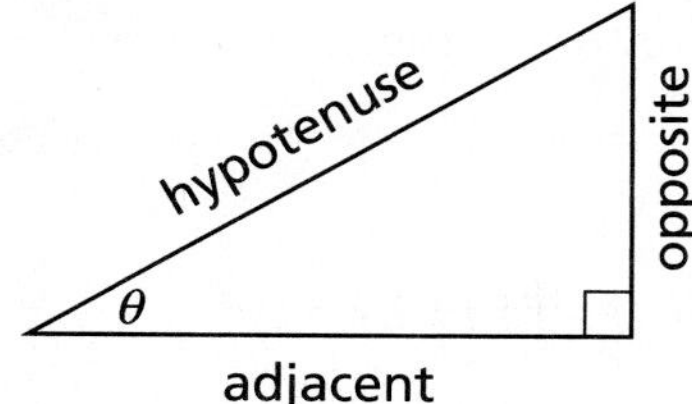


Using that, you defined $\tan\theta$ as

$$\tan\theta = \frac{\text{opposite}}{\text{adjacent}}$$

In Lesson H.01, you defined tangent as

$$\tan\theta = \frac{\sin\theta}{\cos\theta}$$

## For You to Do

**1.** Show how the two definitions will give the same results for $0° < \theta < 90°$.

By using the words *opposite* and *adjacent*, you are referring to sides of a right triangle. Therefore, the definition of tangent in a right triangle is limited to angle inputs from 0° to 90°.

Since $\cos x$ and $\sin x$ are just numbers, and you have definitions of them for any real value of $x$ (with $x$ in either degrees or radians), you can use the relationship $\tan x = \frac{\sin x}{\cos x}$ to extend the definition of tangent as well.

## For Discussion

**2.** The cosine and sine functions have the same domain: all real numbers. What is the domain of the tangent function?

**Remember...**

The *natural domain* of a function $f$ is the set of values $x$ for which $f(x)$ is defined. When you are asked "What is the domain of $f$?" the real question is "What is the natural domain of $f$?"

You can also relate the tangent function to the unit circle.

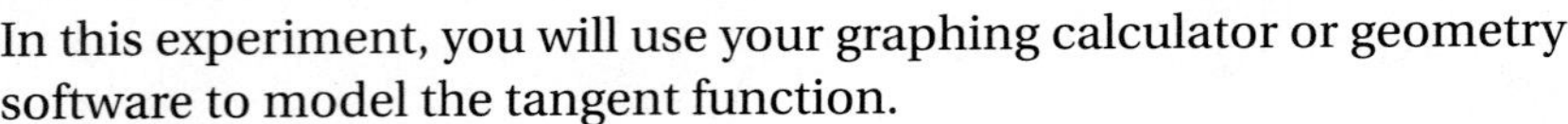

## In-Class Experiment

In this experiment, you will use your graphing calculator or geometry software to model the tangent function.

See the TI-Nspire Handbook on p. 817 for details on how to make this sketch on your calculator.

Follow these steps to build your sketch:

**Step 1** Construct a circle of radius of 1 unit with center at the origin on a coordinate grid.

**Step 2** Add a point at $(1, 0)$, and label it $A$.

**Step 3** Construct the graph of the equation $x = 1$.

**Step 4** Place another point on the circle. Label it $B$.

**Step 5** Construct a line containing the origin $(0, 0)$ and point $B$.

**Step 6** Construct the intersection between this line and the graph of the equation $x = 1$. Label that point $T$.

**Step 7** Have the software display the $y$-coordinate of point $T$.

**Step 8** Have the software display the length of $\widehat{AB}$.

**Step 9** Have the software calculate the tangent of that arc length.

As you drag your point around the circle, compare the $y$-coordinate of point $T$ to the value tan $m\widehat{AB}$.

Your geometry software may not be able to graph equations like $x = 1$. In that case, you need to construct a line perpendicular to the $x$-axis through the point (1, 0).

## For You to Do

**3.** In the experiment, how did the $y$-coordinate of $T$ compare to the tangent calculation?

**4.** What happens when you drag $B$ across $(0, 1)$? Explain.

**5.** What are the coordinates of $B$ if the $y$-coordinate of $T$ is equal to 2? Is there more than one answer? If so, how are the answers related?

As the experiment suggests, the $y$-coordinate of the point $T$ is equal to the tangent of the arc measure $m\widehat{AB}$.

## Exercises *Practicing Habits of Mind*

### Check Your Understanding

**1.** With a unit circle, draw one line that indicates the two possible solutions to each equation in the interval $0 \le x < 2\pi$.

**a.** $\sin x = 0.5$  **b.** $\sin x = -0.7$  **c.** $\cos x = 0.3$

**d.** $\tan x = 2.5$  **e.** $\tan x = -0.4$

**2.** Suppose your calculator could compute only the sine function. Describe how you might calculate tan 0.38.

**3.** Describe how $\tan x$ relates to $\tan\left(\frac{\pi}{2} + x\right)$.

**4.** Write About It Suppose $\widehat{AB}$ is on the unit circle with $A$ at $(1, 0)$. In which two quadrants can $B$ be in if the tangent of $m\widehat{AB}$ negative? Justify your answer in at least two different ways.

**Habits of Mind**

**Represent a function.** Which representation of the tangent function is most helpful here?

**5.** Is it possible for $\tan x$ to be larger than 200? If so, find a number $x$ such that $\tan x > 200$. If not, explain why not.

**6.** Answer the following to prove that $x < \tan x$ for $0 \le x < \frac{\pi}{2}$.

**a.** Find $\tan\frac{\pi}{6}$, $\tan\frac{\pi}{4}$, and $\tan 1$. For these values, is it true that $x < \tan x$? Calculate $\tan x$ for three other values of $x$ between 0 and $\frac{\pi}{2}$ to show that $x < \tan x$ for each value.

**b.** The figure below shows a unit circle and the graph of the equation $x = 1$. $\alpha$ is the length of $\widehat{AB}$. Find the area of $\triangle OAT$ and sector $OAB$.

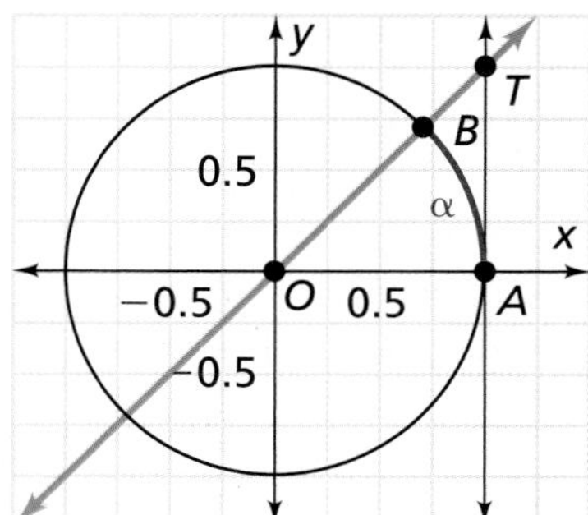


**c.** Use the information from part (b) to prove that $x < \tan x$ for $0 \le x < \frac{\pi}{2}$.

## On Your Own

**7.** Use what you know about cosine and sine to copy and complete this table for $f(x) = \tan x$. Look for shortcuts to simplify your work.

| $x$ | $\tan x$ |
|---|---|
| $0$ | ■ |
| $\frac{\pi}{6}$ | $\frac{\sqrt{3}}{3}$ |
| $\frac{\pi}{4}$ | ■ |
| $\frac{\pi}{3}$ | ■ |
| $\frac{\pi}{2}$ | ■ |
| $\frac{2\pi}{3}$ | ■ |
| $\frac{3\pi}{4}$ | $-1$ |
| $\frac{5\pi}{6}$ | ■ |
| $\pi$ | ■ |
| $\frac{7\pi}{6}$ | ■ |
| $\frac{5\pi}{4}$ | ■ |
| $\frac{4\pi}{3}$ | $\sqrt{3}$ |
| $\frac{3\pi}{2}$ | undefined |
| $\frac{5\pi}{3}$ | ■ |
| $\frac{7\pi}{4}$ | ■ |
| $\frac{11\pi}{6}$ | ■ |
| $2\pi$ | $0$ |
| $\frac{13\pi}{6}$ | ■ |
| $\frac{9\pi}{4}$ | ■ |

**8.** Write About It Explain why $\tan \alpha$ is equal to the slope from the origin $(0, 0)$ to a point on the unit circle at distance $\alpha$.

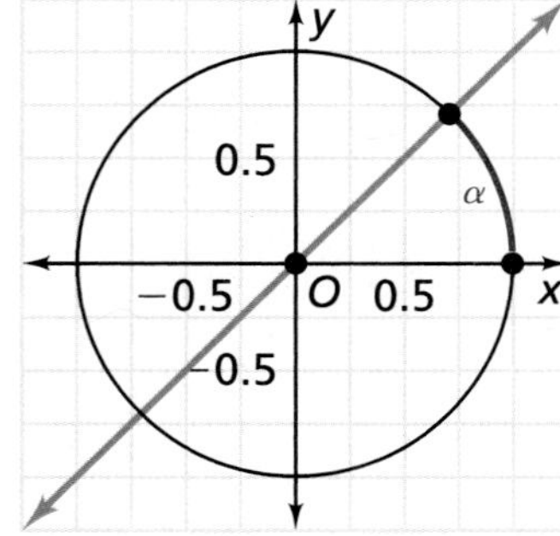

9. For each angle $\theta$ in degrees, calculate $\sin\theta$ and $\cos(90° - \theta)$.

**a.** $\theta = 30°$ **b.** $\theta = 83°$ **c.** $\theta = 90°$ **d.** $\theta = 160°$ **e.** $\theta = -90°$

10. Here are two relationships for cosine and sine.

$$\sin\left(\frac{\pi}{2} - x\right) = \cos x$$

$$\cos\left(\frac{\pi}{2} - x\right) = \sin x$$

What can you say about $\tan\left(\frac{\pi}{2} - x\right)$? How do $\tan\left(\frac{\pi}{2} - x\right)$ and $\tan x$ compare?

11. What is the relationship between $\tan(\pi - x)$ and $\tan x$?

12. What is the relationship between $\tan(\pi + x)$ and $\tan x$?

13. Standardized Test Prep Suppose that the walk on the unit circle from the point (1, 0) to point $B$ has length $\alpha$. Which of the following gives the slope of $OB$?

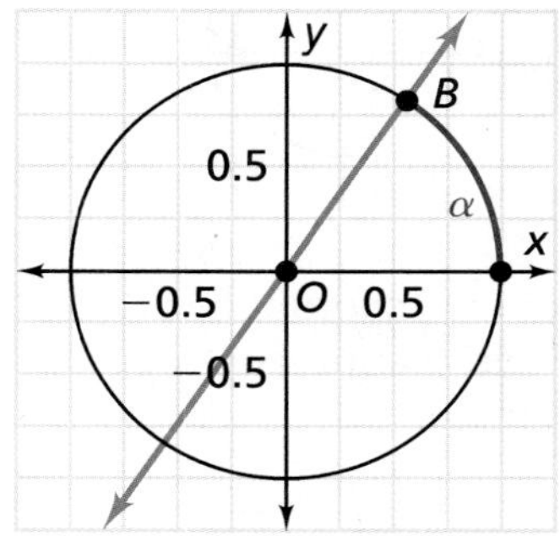


**A.** $\sin\alpha$ **B.** $\cos\alpha$ **C.** $\tan\alpha$ **D.** $\cot\alpha$

## Maintain Your Skills

14. Let $f(x) = 5\sin x + 7$.

**a.** What is the maximum possible value of $f(x)$? Find two values of $x$ that produce this maximum.

**b.** What is the minimum possible value of $f(x)$? Find two values of $x$ that produce this minimum.

**c.** How many solutions are there to the equation $5\sin x + 7 = 0$?

15. For each function, find the maximum and minimum value.

**a.** $g(x) = 10\sin x + 7$ **b.** $h(x) = 20\sin x + 7$

**c.** $j(x) = 20\sin x + 34$ **d.** $k(x) = A\sin x + B$

Go Online
www.successnetplus.com

# H.03 Graphing Periodic Functions—Tangent and Others

In the last lesson, you built a model for seeing the tangent function in relation to the unit circle. As you move your point a distance $\alpha$ around the unit circle, the line connecting the origin and your point intersects the graph of the equation $x = 1$ at the point $(1, b)$. You can track how $b$ changes as the point moves around the circle by making a graph.

The following diagram shows a series of arcs of the same unit circle. Each arc starts from the point $A(1, 0)$, and ends at some stopping point $B$. Draw the line containing the origin $O$ and the point $B$ which intersects the graph of the equation $x = 1$ at point $T$. You can calculate the $y$-coordinate of the point $T$ as $\tan \alpha$.

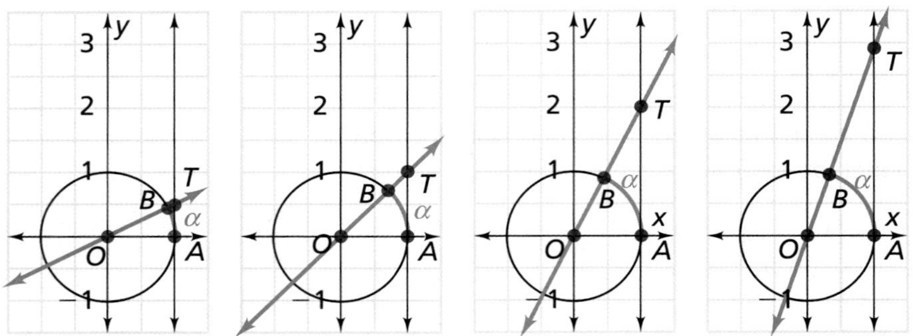


As the value of the arc length $\alpha$ increases from 0 to $\frac{\pi}{2}$, the $y$-coordinate of $T$, or $\tan \alpha$, also increases. As $B$ approaches $(0, 1)$ and $\alpha$ approaches $\frac{\pi}{2}$, the $y$-coordinate of $T$ grows greater and greater.

When $B$ is at $(0, 1)$, $\overleftrightarrow{OB}$ is parallel to the graph of the equation $x = 1$, so there is no intersection point $T$. The graph shows that the values of the tangent function increase without bound as $\alpha$ approaches $\frac{\pi}{2}$.

An **asymptote** is a line that the graph of a function approaches, but does not intersect. The dotted vertical line in this graph is an asymptote.

To continue this graph, look at more arcs. When $B$ is in Quadrant II, $\overleftrightarrow{OB}$ intersects the graph of the equation $x = 1$ in Quadrant IV, so the $y$-coordinate of $T$ is negative.

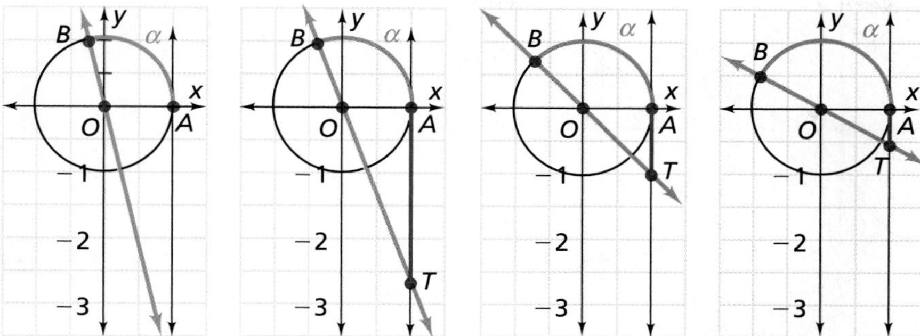


If $\alpha$ is a little less than $\frac{\pi}{2}$, the outputs of the tangent function are large positive numbers. If $\alpha$ is a little more than $\frac{\pi}{2}$, then the outputs of the tangent function are large negative numbers. As $\alpha$ increases from $\frac{\pi}{2}$ to $\pi$, the outputs of the tangent function are negative, but increase toward 0.

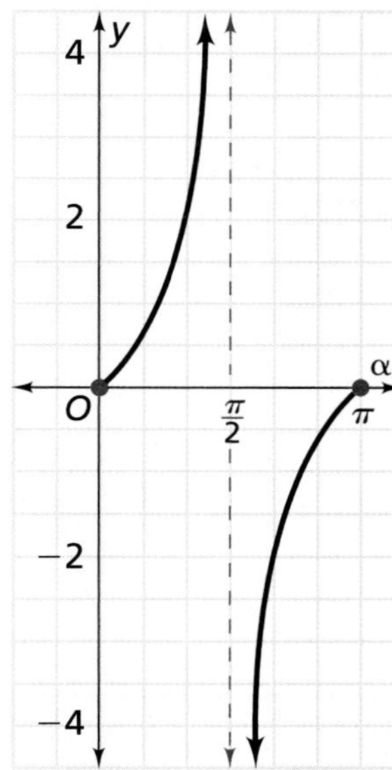

What happens next? As point $B$ moves into Quadrant III, notice what happens to $T$. It follows the same path as it did when $B$ was in Quadrant I.

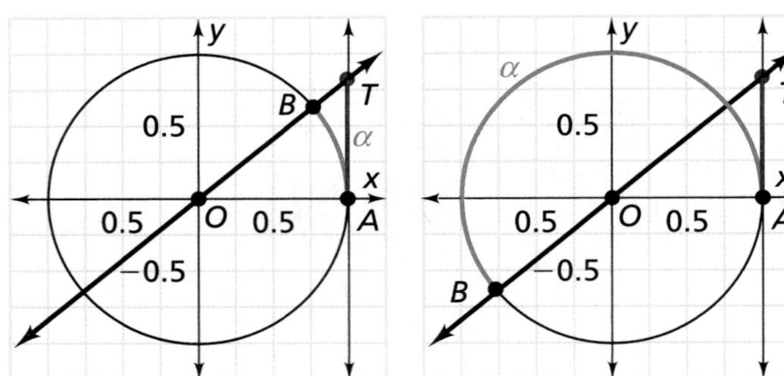


Notice that $T$ is in the same position in both pictures, but $B$ is at opposite ends of a diameter. So $\tan \alpha$ is equal for two different values on the unit circle.

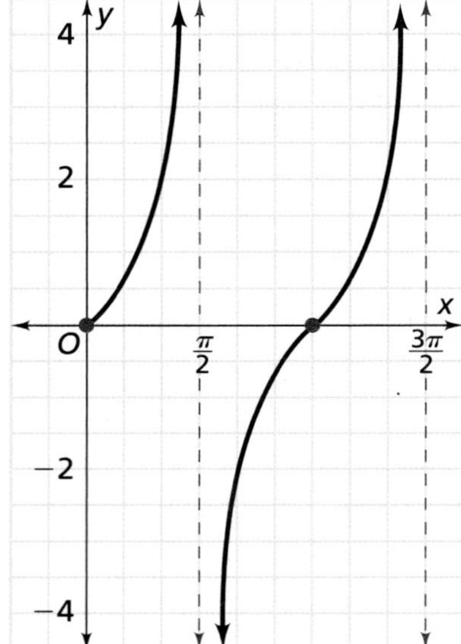


## For You to Do

1. Find all numbers $x$ such that $0 \leq x \leq 2\pi$ and $\tan x = 1$.
2. What is the period of the tangent function?
3. Find all real numbers $x$ such that $\tan x = 1$.

**Remember...**

The period of a periodic function is the least value $p$ such that, for all $x$, $f(x + p) = f(x)$.

## Exercises *Practicing Habits of Mind*

### Check Your Understanding

1. The period of the tangent function is $\pi$.
   a. What is the period of $g(x) = \tan 2x$?
   b. What is the period of $h(x) = \tan \frac{x}{2}$?

2. a. Use the graph of $y = \tan x$ to find the least value of $x$ such that $x > 0$ and $\tan x = 3$.
   b. How many solutions are there to the equation $\tan x = 3$? What are they?

3. a. Sketch the graph of $r(x) = \sin^2 x$.
   b. Find the period of $r$.
   c. Take It Further Prove, using properties of the sine function, that this is the correct period for $r$.

4. Consider the function $t(x) = \sin x + x$.
   a. Sketch a graph of this function on the interval $-2\pi \le x \le 2\pi$.
   b. Is $t$ a periodic function? Justify your answer.

5. a. Find the period of $n(x) = \sin \frac{x}{2}$.
   b. Write About It For a real number $B > 0$, describe how the period of $p(x) = \sin Bx$ relates to the value of $B$. Include examples when $B > 1$ and when $B < 1$.

### On Your Own

6. This lesson showed that this statement is true for every value of $x$.

$$\tan (x + \pi) = \tan x$$

How does $\tan (x + 2\pi)$ relate to $\tan x$?

7. Suppose $f$ is a periodic function with period 10, and $f(3) = 13$. Which of the following must also be true?

   A. $f(10) = 13$
   B. $f(13) = 3$
   C. $f(-13) = 13$
   D. $f(83) = 13$

8. Sketch the graphs of $g(x) = \cos 2x$ and $s(x) = \cos^2 x - \sin^2 x$ on the same axes. How do the graphs of $g$ and $s$ compare?

9. Problem 2 on page 775 asked you to graph

$$g(x) = \frac{1}{\sin x} = \csc x$$

Is $g$ a periodic function? If so, what is its period? If not, explain why.

The notation "csc" is short for "cosecant."

10. In Lesson H.05, you will learn more about three additional trigonometric functions: secant (sec), cosecant (csc), and cotangent (cot). The definitions are as follows.

$$\sec x = \frac{1}{\cos x}, \csc x = \frac{1}{\sin x}, \text{ and } \cot x = \frac{\cos x}{\sin x}$$

For this exercise, consider the function given by the following rule.

$$h(x) = \sin x \cdot \csc x + \cos x \cdot \sec x + \tan x \cdot \cot x$$

**a.** Use a calculator. Find the value of $h(0.5)$ to three decimal places.

**b.** Find $h(1)$ to three decimal places.

**c.** Describe the overall behavior of $h$.

11. **Take It Further** Let $n$ be a positive integer. For what values of $n$ does the function $z(x) = \sin nx$ have a maximum at the point $\left(\frac{\pi}{2}, 1\right)$?

12. **Standardized Test Prep** Which of the following is the period of $f(x) = \tan ax$?

**A.** $a$ **B.** $\frac{2\pi}{a}$ **C.** $2a\pi$ **D.** $\frac{\pi}{a}$

## Maintain Your Skills

13. Find the period of each function.

**a.** $f(x) = 5 \sin x + 7$

**b.** $g(x) = 3 \cos x - 10$

**c.** $h(x) = 2 \tan x + 1$

**d.** $j(x) = 4 \sin 2x - 3$

**e.** $k(x) = 6 \cos 5x + 14$

**f.** $m(x) = A \sin ax + B$

# H.04 Inverse Trigonometric Functions

In Lesson 5.04, you learned how to solve equations that involve trigonometric functions. Tony found the solution by using the $\sin^{-1}$ function on his calculator, the inverse sine.

In earlier work, you learned about inverse functions.

### Definition

**Suppose $f$ is a one-to-one function with domain $A$ and range $B$. The inverse function $f^{-1}$ is a function with these properties.**

- **$f^{-1}$ has domain $B$ and range $A$**
- **$f(f^{-1}(x)) = x$**

You later proved that $f^{-1}(f(x)) = f(f^{-1}(x)) = x$. An important part of this definition and the subsequent theorem is that a function $f$ must be one-to-one in order for the inverse function $f^{-1}$ to exist.

## For Discussion

Recall that a function $f$ is one-to-one if $f(a) = f(b)$ only when $a = b$.

For instance, $f(x) = x^2$ is not one-to-one, because $f(2) = f(-2) = 4$, but $2 \neq -2$.

1. Explain why a periodic function cannot be one-to-one.
2. Explain why a function that is not one-to-one cannot have an inverse function.

Since the cosine, sine, and tangent functions are periodic, they cannot be one-to-one. So how can you define inverse trigonometric functions?

Public transportation schedules are periodic. The period may be an hour, a day, or a week but the plane, train, bus, or ferry will eventually retrace its route.

## Minds in Action

*Tony and Sasha are trying to decide what* $\tan^{-1}$ *means.*

**Tony** I'm lost. If the tangent function is periodic, then it can't be one-to-one, so it can't have an inverse. Then what does the $\tan^{-1}$ mean?

*Sasha jabs at the keys on her calculator.*

**Sasha** Look. I've calculated the inverse tangent of a bunch of numbers. The answers the calculator gives all fall in the range between about $-1.57$ and $-1.57$.

**Tony** That's a weird number. I wonder where it comes from. Wait a second. Let me check.

*Tony hits a few keys on his calculator.*

Yes. It looks like your numbers are all between $-\frac{\pi}{2}$ and $\frac{\pi}{2}$.

**Sasha** Of course, that makes sense. Look. If I draw only one cycle of the graph of $y = \tan x$, between $-\frac{\pi}{2}$ and $\frac{\pi}{2}$, it looks like this.

One *cycle* of the graph of a periodic function $f(x)$ results as $x$ ranges over one fundamental period.

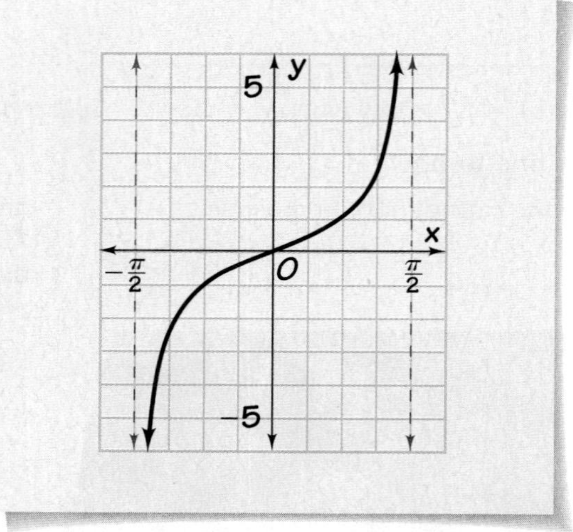


Now it looks one-to-one. Any horizontal line I draw will hit the graph in only one spot.

**Tony** So if we restrict the domain of tangent to include just the interval $-\frac{\pi}{2}$ to $\frac{\pi}{2}$, it's one-to-one, and the range is all real numbers.

**Sasha** And then the domain of the inverse tangent function would be all real numbers, and the range would be $-\frac{\pi}{2}$ to $\frac{\pi}{2}$.

## For You to Do

**3.** Sketch a graph of the equation $y = \tan^{-1} x$. How does it compare to the graph of $y = \tan x$ with domain $-\frac{\pi}{2} < x < \frac{\pi}{2}$?

Just as Tony and Sasha did for the tangent function, you can restrict the domains of the cosine and sine functions to make them one-to-one. The figure below shows the graph of one cycle of $y = \sin x$, for $-\pi \leq x \leq \pi$.

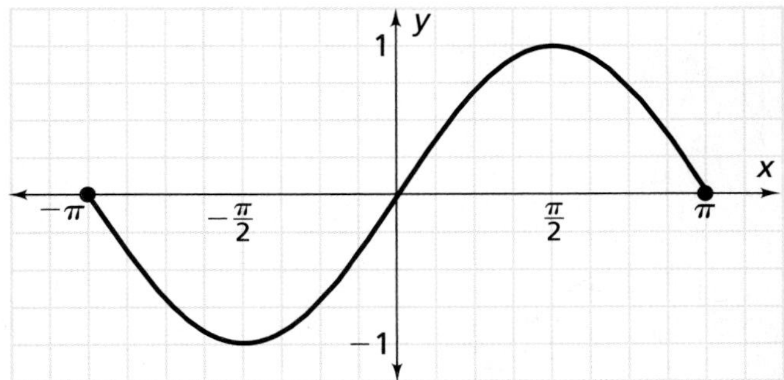


Notice that in most cases, if you draw a horizontal line, it will still hit the graph of $y = \sin x$ in two spots. If you restrict the domain to $-\frac{\pi}{2} \leq x \leq \frac{\pi}{2}$, any horizontal line will intersect the graph in at most one point.

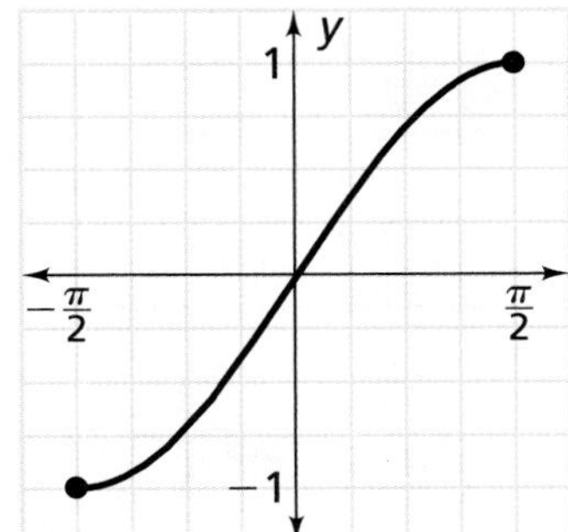


The domain for the inverse sine function is $-1 \leq x \leq 1$, and the range is $-\frac{\pi}{2} \leq x \leq \frac{\pi}{2}$. Its notation is $f(x) = \sin^{-1} x$.

## For You to Do

**4.** Sketch a graph of the equation $y = \sin^{-1} x$.

Restricting the cosine function to a domain between $-\frac{\pi}{2}$ and $\frac{\pi}{2}$ will not work as it did for the tangent and sine functions.

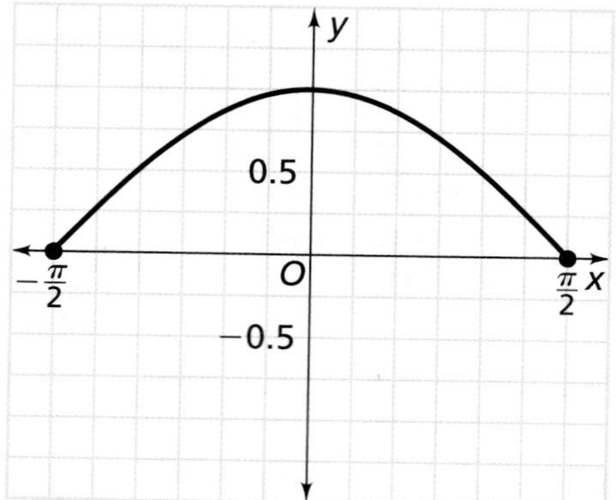


This portion of the cosine graph is not one-to-one, so you must use a different interval. One interval that makes the function one-to-one is $0 \leq x \leq \pi$.

The domain for the inverse cosine function is $-1 \leq x \leq 1$, and the range is $0 \leq y \leq \pi$. Its notation is $f(x) = \cos^{-1} x$.

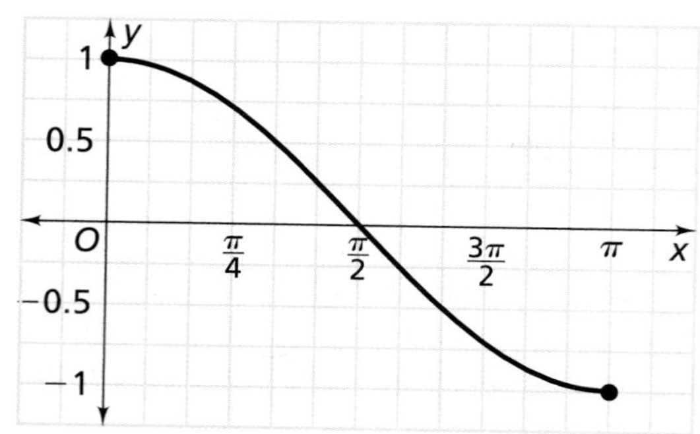


## For You to Do

**5.** Sketch a graph of the equation $y = \cos^{-1} x$.

## Developing Habits of Mind

**Make strategic choices.** Since the cosine, sine, and tangent functions are periodic, you could have chosen to restrict your domain in infinitely many ways. For example, the cosine function is also one-to-one on the interval $-\pi \leq x \leq 0$. So why are these particular intervals important?

The reason goes back to the unit circle, and even the right triangle. Each interval includes lengths of arcs intersected by angles that terminate in Quadrant I, the angles over which you first defined the functions. So it makes sense to include these angles in the restricted domains. The shape of its graph determines the rest of the interval for each function.

# Exercises *Practicing Habits of Mind*

## Check Your Understanding

**1.** Solve each equation, if possible.

**a.** $3 \sin x + 7 = 5$

**b.** $5 \cos x - 12 = 14$

**c.** $2 \tan x + 3 = -10$

**d.** $10 \cos(x + 3) - 7 = 13$

**2.** Consider the equation $\tan x = 0.75$.

**a.** Use a calculator. Find one solution for $x$ to three decimal places.

**b.** Use the graph of the tangent function to show where more solutions lie.

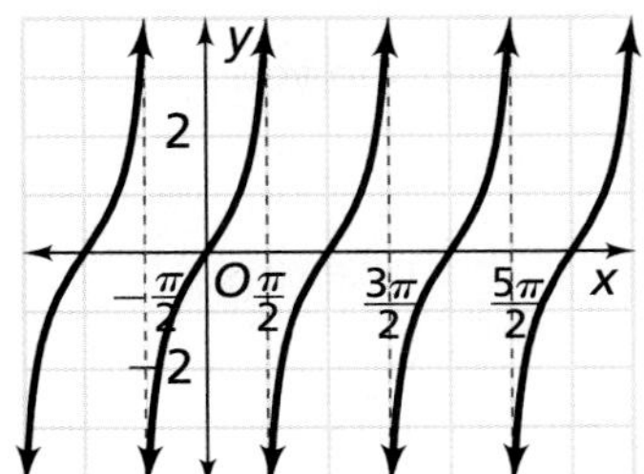


**c.** For $\tan x = 0.75$, find the least solution that is greater than your solution in part (a).

**3.** Consider the equation $\cos x = 0.8$.

**a.** Use a calculator. Find one solution for $x$ to three decimal places.

**b.** Use the graph of the cosine function to show where more solutions lie.

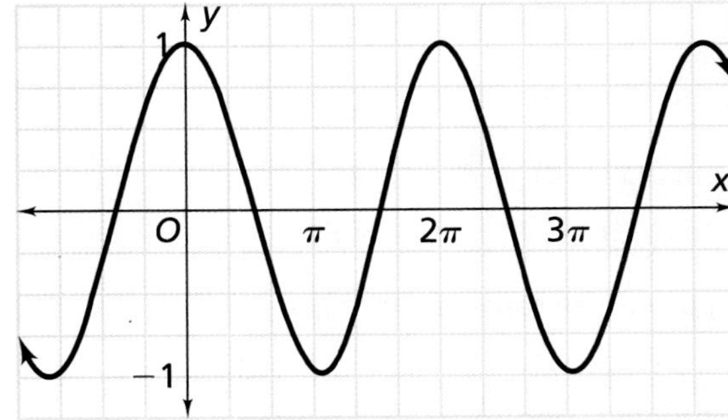


**c.** For $\cos x = 0.8$, find the least solution greater than your solution in part (a).

4. Consider the equation $\sin x = 0.6$.

   a. Use a calculator. Find one solution for $x$ to three decimal places.

   b. Use the graph of the sine function to show where more solutions lie.

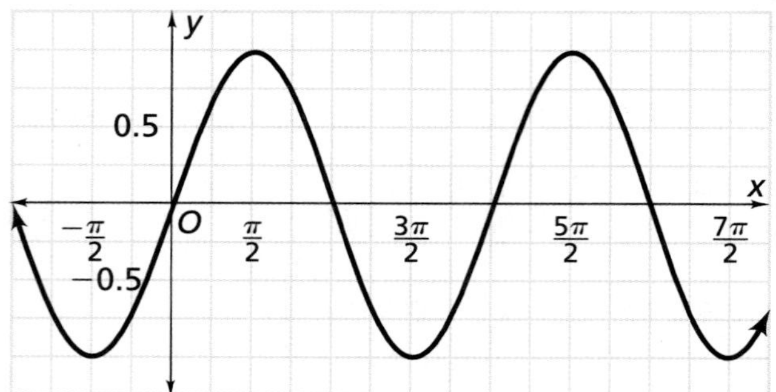


   c. For $\sin x = 0.6$, find the least solution greater than the solution you found in part (a).

5. Determine each value.

   a. $\sin^{-1}\frac{1}{2}$
   b. $\cos^{-1}0$
   c. $\tan^{-1}1$
   d. $\cos^{-1}(\cos 120°)$
   e. $\tan(\tan^{-1}2.14)$
   f. $\cos^{-1}\left(\cos\frac{11\pi}{6}\right)$

Don't let your calculator have all the fun!

6. a. If $x$ is the length of an arc intersected by an angle in Quadrant I and $\sin x = \frac{7}{25}$, find $\cos x$.

   b. Determine the value of $\cos\left(\sin^{-1}\frac{7}{25}\right)$.

## On Your Own

7. Solve each equation, if possible.

   a. $6\sin 2x + 1 = -2$
   b. $12\sin 2(x - 3) + 8 = 22$
   c. $3\sin \pi(x - 5) + 4 = 7$
   d. $36\cos\left(\frac{2\pi}{30}(x - 3)\right) + 39 = 50$

8. Look back at Exercises 2–4. You should have gotten the same answer for part (a) of each exercise.

   a. Draw a triangle that has one angle of measure corresponding to an arc of length $\tan^{-1}0.75$. Find integer lengths for each of the sides of the triangle that satisfy the three statements for $\tan^{-1}0.75$, $\sin^{-1}0.6$, and $\cos^{-1}0.8$. What special triangle is it?

   b. Write About It Explain why the answer you got in part (a) from each exercise was the same, but the answer you got in part (c) was not.

**9.** **a.** Find the value of $\sin^{-1}\frac{1}{2} + \cos^{-1}\frac{1}{2}$.

**b.** Find the value of $\sin^{-1}\frac{\sqrt{3}}{2} + \cos^{-1}\frac{\sqrt{3}}{2}$.

**c.** Find the value of $\sin^{-1}(-1) + \cos^{-1}(-1)$.

**d.** Take It Further Explain why the pattern in these three results occurs.

**10.** Is this statement true for every $x$?

$$\sin^{-1}(\sin x) = x$$

If so, explain why. If not, when is it true and when is it false?

**11.** Find the maximum and minimum values for each function.

**a.** $a(x) = 5 \sin x + 8$

**b.** $b(x) = 10 \sin x + 17$

**c.** $c(x) = 10 \sin x + 3$

**d.** $d(x) = 4 \sin x - 2$

**12.** **a.** Find a function using cosine or sine that has a maximum of 27, and a minimum of 11.

**b.** Find a function using cosine or sine that has a maximum of 75, and a minimum of 3.

**c.** Find a function using cosine or sine that has a maximum of 23, and a minimum of $-15$.

**13.** Standardized Test Prep Which of the following is true?

**A.** $\cos^{-1} x = \frac{1}{\cos x}$

**B.** $\cos^{-1} x = \sin x$

**C.** $\cos^{-1} x = \frac{1}{\sin x}$

**D.** $\cos(\cos^{-1} x) = x$

## Maintain Your Skills

Go Online
www.successnetplus.com

**14.** Find one solution to each equation.

**a.** $4 \cos x + 5 = 7$

**b.** $4 \cos 2x + 5 = 7$

**c.** $4 \cos \frac{x}{2} + 5 = 7$

**d.** $4 \cos \pi x + 5 = 7$

**e.** $4 \cos(\pi(x + 3)) + 5 = 7$

**f.** $4 \cos\left(\frac{2\pi}{10}(x - 3)\right) + 5 = 7$

Taking the output of $f$ as the input for $f^{-1}$ is like flipping a toggle switch twice. In the end, you are back where you started.

# H.05 Reciprocal Trigonometric Functions

There are six possible ratios of side lengths of a right triangle. The three more common trig functions, cosine, sine, and tangent.

$$\cos\theta = \frac{\text{adjacent}}{\text{hypotenuse}} \quad \sin\theta = \frac{\text{opposite}}{\text{hypotenuse}} \quad \tan\theta = \frac{\text{opposite}}{\text{adjacent}}$$

The reciprocal of each of these ratios account for the other three.

$$\sec\theta = \frac{\text{hypotenuse}}{\text{adjacent}} \quad \csc\theta = \frac{\text{hypotenuse}}{\text{opposite}} \quad \cot\theta = \frac{\text{adjacent}}{\text{opposite}}$$

**Go Online**
www.successnetplus.com

You can represent each of these functions on the unit circle as well. Recall in Lesson H.02 you built a model for $\tan\alpha$. You can use that same model to find $\sec\alpha$.

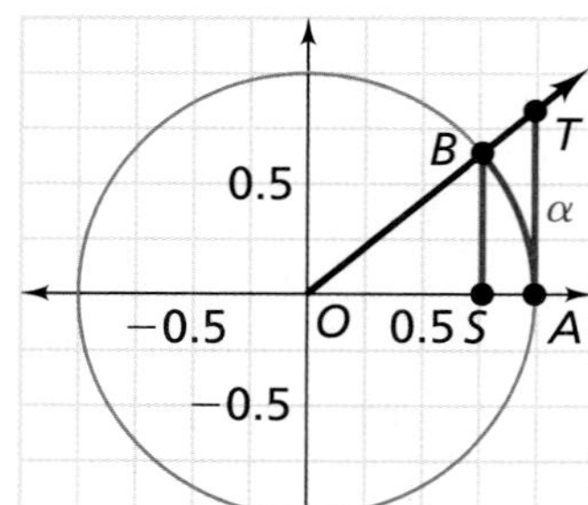


The measure of $\widehat{AB}$ is $\alpha$. $\overline{OA}$ and $\overline{OB}$ are both radii. So they each have length 1. As you saw in Investigation 1A, $\cos\alpha = OS$ and $\sin\alpha = SB$. Earlier in this investigation, you saw that $\tan\alpha = AT$, and $\overline{AT}$ is on a line tangent to the unit circle at $A$.

Recall that a secant line is a line that intersects a curve in at least two points. Notice that $\overline{OT}$ is on a secant line through the center of the unit circle.

## In-Class Experiment

Start with the sketch you made in the In-Class Experiment of Lesson H.02. Follow these steps to add to your sketch.

**Step 1** Label the origin as point $O$.

**Step 2** Construct the line segment $\overline{OT}$.

**Step 3** Have the software display the length of $\overline{OT}$.

**Step 4** Have the software calculate the secant of the radian measure of $\widehat{AB}$.

As you drag point $B$ around the circle, compare the length of segment $\overline{OT}$ to the value of the secant of the radian measure of $\widehat{AB}$.

If your software does not calculate $\sec x$ directly, have it calculate $\frac{1}{\cos x}$.

## For You to Do

1. In the experiment, how did the length of $\overline{OT}$ compare to the secant calculation?
2. What happens to the two values when you drag $B$ across $(0, 1)$? Explain.

## For Discussion

3. Your sketch will display the length of $\overline{OT}$ as positive, since length is a measure of distance, which is always positive. The value of the secant function, however, can be negative. For arcs terminating in which quadrants will the secant of the arc be negative? Explain how your sketch shows where the secant is negative.

You can also define the secant, cosecant, and cotangent functions by their relationships to the cosine and sine functions.

$\sec x = \frac{1}{\cos x}$ $\qquad$ $\csc x = \frac{1}{\sin x}$ $\qquad$ $\cot x = \frac{\cos x}{\sin x}$

The following figures show the graphs of $y = \sec x$, $y = \csc x$ and $y = \cot x$.

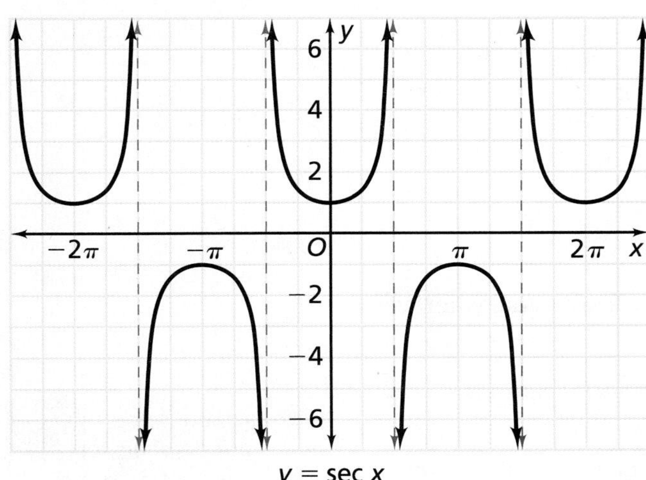


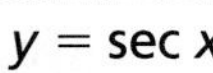
$y = \sec x$

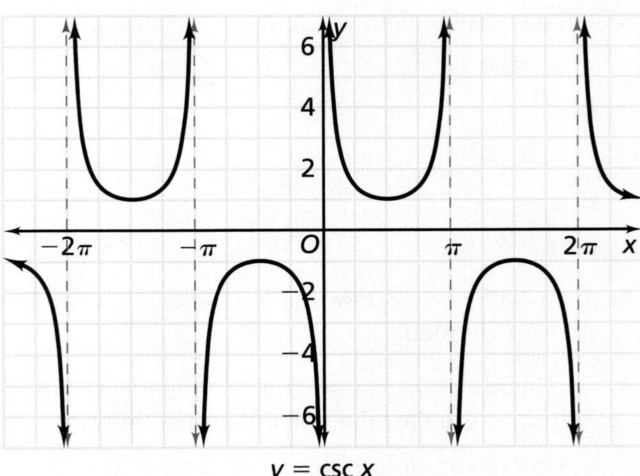


$y = \csc x$

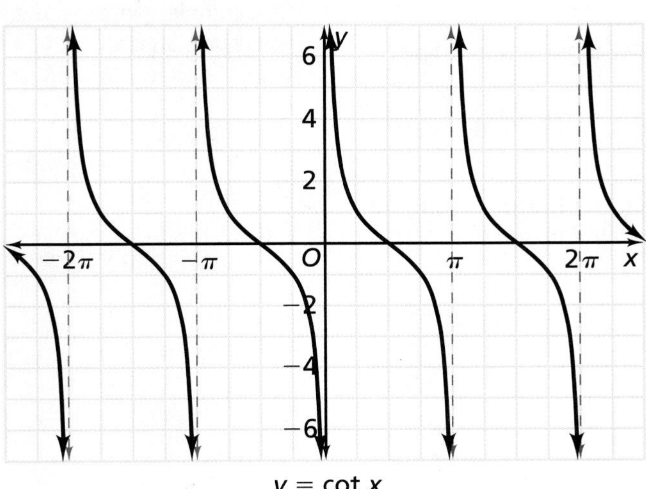


$y = \cot x$

# Exercises *Practicing Habits of Mind*

## Check Your Understanding

**1.** Find all solutions to each equation if $0 \le x \le 2\pi$.

**a.** $\csc x = 2$

**b.** $\cot x = \sqrt{3}$

**c.** $\sec x = 0$

**d.** $\sec^2 x = 1$

**Remember...**

Use radians unless the degree symbol is present.

**2.** Consider the functions $f$ and $g$.

$$f(x) = \sec^2 x + \csc^2 x$$

$$g(x) = \sec^2 x \cdot \csc^2 x$$

For each value below, calculate $f(x)$ and $g(x)$.

**a.** $x = 30°$

**b.** $x = \frac{\pi}{4}$

**c.** $x = 60°$

**d.** $x = 120°$

**e.** $x = 2$

**3.** **Take It Further** Show that $f(x)$ and $g(x)$ from Exercise 2 are equal wherever they are defined.

**4.** The identity $\cos \theta = \sin(90° - \theta)$ is the *co-function identity*. Similar identities exist for the tangent and secant functions.

**a.** Give an example to show that $\cot \theta = \tan(90° - \theta)$ for a particular angle measure $\theta$.

**b.** Give an example to show that $\csc \theta = \sec(90° - \theta)$ for a particular angle measure $\theta$.

**c.** Show that $\cot \theta = \tan(90° - \theta)$ for any angle measure $\theta$ in the domain of the cotangent function.

**d.** Show that $\csc \theta = \sec(90° - \theta)$ for any angle measure $\theta$ in the domain of the cosecant function.

In fact, the co part of *cosine* is short for *complement*. Two angles are complementary if the measures add up to 90°.

5. Consider the following graph of the unit circle and the tangent at $(1, 0)$.

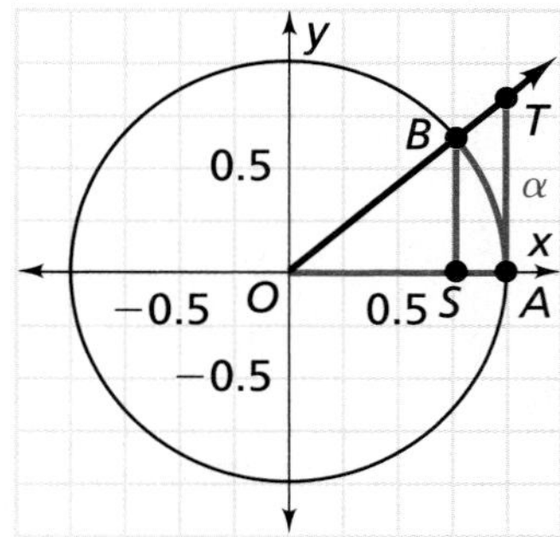


a. Explain why $\triangle OSB \sim \triangle OAT$.

b. Use similar triangles to show that the length of $\overline{OT}$ is $\sec \alpha$.

6. Consider the following geometric series.

$$1 + \sin^2 x + \sin^4 x + \sin^6 x + \cdots$$

As long as $|\sin x| < 1$, this series converges to a specific sum. Which is it?

A. $\cos^2 x$ B. $\tan^2 x$

C. $\cot^2 x$ D. $\sec^2 x$

Recall that if the first term of an infinite geometric series is $a$ and the common ratio is $r$ with $|r| < 1$, the sum is $\frac{a}{1 - r}$.

7. Consider the following geometric series.

$$\sin^2 x + \sin^4 x + \sin^6 x + \sin^8 x + \cdots$$

Assuming $|\sin x| < 1$, which of these is the sum of this series?

A. $\cos^2 x$ B. $\tan^2 x$

C. $\cot^2 x$ D. $\sec^2 x$

## On Your Own

8. Here is the graph of $f(x) = \sec x$ on the interval $-\pi \leq x \leq 2\pi$.

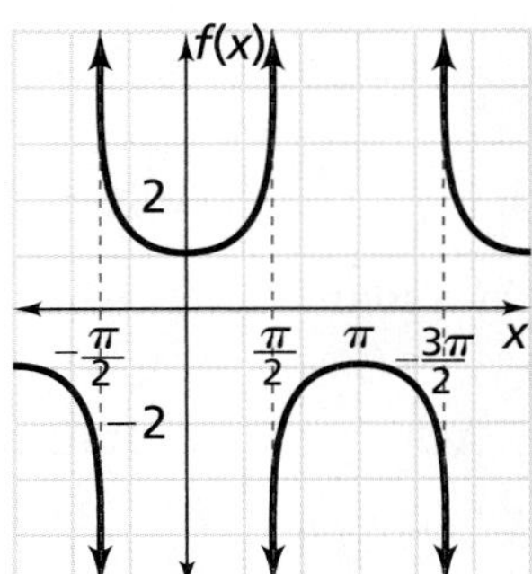


a. Find the domain and range of $f$.

b. Explain why there is a horizontal gap in the graph between the graphs of the equations $y = -1$ and $y = 1$.

9. Show graphically that there are two solutions to the equation

$$\sec x = -2$$

in the interval $0 \le x \le 2\pi$.

10. Use the results from Exercises 6 and 7 to show the following.

$$1 + \tan^2 x = \sec^2 x$$

11. The Pythagorean identity $\cos^2 x + \sin^2 x = 1$ leads to two other major identities.

a. If you divide through each term of $\cos^2 x + \sin^2 x = 1$ by $\cos^2 x$, you will get the following equation.

$$\frac{\cos^2 x}{\cos^2 x} + \frac{\sin^2 x}{\cos^2 x} = \frac{1}{\cos^2 x}$$

You can simplify each of these terms. What do you get after simplifying?

b. Construct a second identity by dividing through by $\sin^2 x$.

12. Use the picture from Exercise 5 to show the following identity.

$$1 + \tan^2 \alpha = \sec^2 \alpha$$

13. **Take It Further** In Investigation 5A, you looked at the slope of lines tangent to the graph of $y = \sin x$. Those slopes approximated the outputs of the function $f(x) = \cos x$. You can apply the same process to $f(x) = \tan x$. Find a function that matches the slopes you find.

14. **Standardized Test Prep** Which of the following is false?

A. $\sin x \cdot \csc x = 1$ for all $x$ in the domain of the cosecant function.

B. $\cos x \cdot \sec x = 1$ for all $x$ in the domain of the secant function.

C. $\tan x \cdot \cot x = 1$ for all $x$ in the domain of both the tangent and cotangent functions.

D. $\cot x = \frac{\sin x}{\cos x}$ for all $x$ in the domain of the cosine function.

## Maintain Your Skills

15. Each of these equations has $x = 30°$ as a solution. Find the other solution in the interval $0 \le x \le 360°$.

a. $2 \sin x = 1$  b. $2 \cos x = \sqrt{3}$  c. $3 \tan x = \sqrt{3}$

d. $\csc x = 2$  e. $\sqrt{3} \sec x = 2$  f. $\sqrt{3} \cot x = 3$

16. Calculate each of these to three decimal places.

a. $\sin 40°$  b. $\sin(180° - 40°)$  c. $\cos 40°$

d. $\cos(360° - 40°)$  e. $\tan 40°$  f. $\tan(180° + 40°)$

Go Online
www.successnetplus.com

**In this investigation, you learned the relationship between the tangent function and lines tangent to the unit circle. You defined inverse cosine, sine, and tangent functions by restricting domains. You graphed all six trigonometric functions, including secant, cosecant, and cotangent. The following questions will help you summarize what you have learned.**

**1.** Suppose $\tan x = 2.4$. Find the two possible exact values of $\sec x$.

**2.** Let $A = (1, 0)$, and let $\widehat{AB}$ be an arc on the unit circle with length $\alpha$. What is the slope of the line $\overleftrightarrow{OB}$, where $O$ is the origin, in terms of $\alpha$?

**3.** Solve the equation $7 \csc 5x - 8 = 6$.

**4.** Each of these equations has $x = \frac{\pi}{3}$ as a solution. Find the other solution in the interval $0 \leq x \leq 2\pi$.

**a.** $2 \cos x = 1$ **b.** $\tan x = \sqrt{3}$ **c.** $\sqrt{3} \csc x = 2$ **d.** $3 \cot x = \sqrt{3}$

**5.** The figure at the right shows the unit circle with three triangles, $\triangle OSB$, $\triangle OAT$, and $\triangle OPQ$. Point $A$ is at $(1, 0)$ and $\overleftrightarrow{AT}$ is perpendicular to the $x$-axis. Point $P$ is at $(0, 1)$ and $\overleftrightarrow{PQ}$ is perpendicular to the $y$-axis. $B$ and $T$ are both on $\overleftrightarrow{OQ}$. You have already seen how $\triangle OSB$ lets you find cosine and sine of $\alpha$, and how $\triangle OAT$ lets you find tangent and secant of $\alpha$.

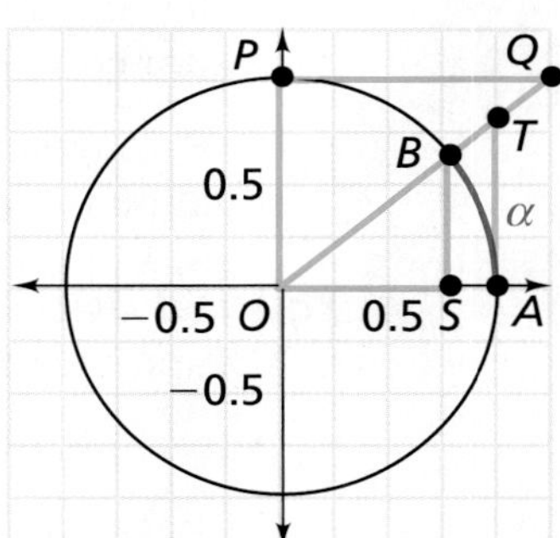


**a.** Show that $\triangle OPQ \sim \triangle TAO$.

**b.** Use similar triangles to show that the length of $\overline{OQ}$ is equal to $\csc \alpha$ and that the length of $\overline{PQ}$ is equal to $\cot \alpha$.

**6.** How are the six trigonometric functions defined?

**7.** Why does the $\sin^{-1}$ function on a calculator in degree mode return only results between $-90$ and 90 degrees?

**8.** Solve the equation $\cos x = 0.8$ for $x$. How many solutions are there?

## Vocabulary

In this investigation, you learned these terms. Make sure you understand what each one means and how to use it.

- **asymptote**
- **inverse function**

# Trigonometric Identities

In *Trigonometric Identities*, you will use complex arithmetic to prove basic trigonometric identities. You will learn techniques to validate other identities.

**By the end of this investigation, you will be able to answer questions like these.**

1. How can you test to see if an equation might be an identity?
2. How can you use complex numbers to find formulas for $\cos 2x$ and $\sin 2x$?
3. How can you use identities to prove other identities?

**You will learn how to**

- test trigonometric equations to predict whether they are identities
- show the basic addition rules for cosine and sine using the Multiplication Law for complex numbers
- use Pythagorean identities and algebra to prove that a trigonometric equation is an identity

**You will develop these habits and skills:**

- Manipulate trigonometric expressions.
- Determine useful test cases and techniques to identify identities.
- Use basic rules to generate more complicated rules.

Much like these multicolored plastic toy bricks, you assemble theorems using mathematical objects. If you don't put the pieces together correctly, the resulting structure may fall apart.

# H.06 Getting Started

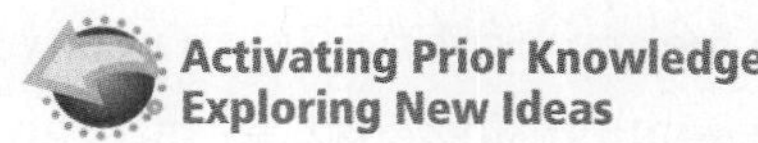


Two expressions are **identically equal** if you can transform one to the other using the basic rules of algebra, and any other proven identities or theorems. An **identity** is any equation that equates two identically equal expressions.

The basic rules of algebra include the commutative, associative, and distributive properties, along with the additive and multiplicative inverses and identities.

To prove an identity, you have to show that the equation is true for all values of the variable for which both expressions are defined. Even before you prove an identity, however, you should convince yourself that the equation is indeed likely an identity.

Here are two ways to gather evidence that an equation is an identity.

**Try some numbers:** The fastest way to prove an equation is not an identity is to provide a counterexample. Treat each side of the equation as a separate function. Choose several numbers to plug into each of the functions.

- If the outputs are different, you know the equation is not an identity.
- If the outputs are the same, you have some evidence that the expressions are identically equal.

**Compare graphs:** Graph each side of the equation as a separate function. If the two graphs look identical, you have good evidence that the equation may be an identity.

## For You to Explore

**1.** For which values of $x$ is the following equation true?

$$\sec^2 x + \csc^2 x = \sec^2 x \cdot \csc^2 x$$

**a.** $x = \frac{3\pi}{4}$ **b.** $x = 115°$

**c.** $x = \frac{2\pi}{7}$ **d.** all of the above

**2.** Find the pairs of expressions that are identically equal.

| | | |
|---|---|---|
| $\cos^4 x - \sin^4 x$ | $\cot^2 x$ | $\sin^3 x + \sin x \cos^2 x$ |
| $\sin(-x)$ | $\cot x$ | $\sec^2 x$ |
| $1 + \tan^2 x$ | $-\sin x$ | $(\csc x + 1)(\csc x - 1)$ |
| $\cos^2 x - \sin^2 x$ | $\frac{\csc x}{\sec x}$ | $\sin x$ |

**3.** Is this statement true? If so, explain why. If not, what changes to the statement will make it an identity? (Your answer should not be of the trivial form $A = A$.)

$$\frac{\cos x + 1}{\sin x} = \frac{\sin x}{\cos x - 1}$$

**4.** Sketch and describe the graph of $f(x) = \cos^3 x + \cos x \sin^2 x$.

**5.** Define the function $g(n) = n^2 + n + 41$ for whole-number values of $n$.

**a.** Calculate $g(0)$ through $g(5)$, $g(10)$, and $g(20)$.

**b.** The values of $g(0)$ through $g(5)$ are prime. Do you think $g(n)$ will be prime for all values of $n$? Explain your answer.

6. a. Sketch the graphs of $f(x) = \sin x \cos x$ and $g(x) = \sin 2x$ on the same axes.

b. Is the equation $\sin x \cos x = \sin 2x$ an identity? Explain your answer.

7. One of these two equations is an identity, and the other is not.

$$(\tan x \sin x)^2 = (\tan x + \sin x)(\tan x - \sin x)$$
$$\sin^2 x + \cos^2 x \csc x = \csc x$$

a. Pick a value for $x$ and test it in each equation.

b. Which equation is the identity?

8. **What's Wrong Here?** Candace thinks the equation $\cos 13x = \cos x$ is an identity.

Candace says, "I decided to test some values. I tried 0 and it worked, I tried $\frac{\pi}{6}$ and it worked, I tried $\frac{\pi}{2}$ and it worked. I even tried $\frac{7\pi}{6}$, and *that* worked! So, I'm convinced, it's an identity."

Help Candace see why this equation is not an identity.

9. a. On the same axes, sketch the graphs of $f(x) = \sin\left(x + \frac{\pi}{3}\right)$ and $g(x) = \cos\left(x - \frac{\pi}{6}\right)$. How do the two graphs compare?

b. Must the equation

$$\sin\left(x + \frac{\pi}{3}\right) = \cos\left(x - \frac{\pi}{6}\right)$$

be an identity, according to these graphs?

10. **Take It Further** Candace found several values of $x$ that make $\cos 13x = \cos x$. Find the total number of values of $x$ with $0 \le x < 2\pi$ that make $\cos 13x = \cos x$.

## Exercises Practicing Habits of Mind

### On Your Own

11. Simplify the following product.

$$(\csc^2 x - 1)(\sec^2 x - 1)$$

a. $\sin x$ b. $\tan^2 x$ c. $\sec^4 x$ d. 1

12. a. Sketch graphs of $f(x) = \sin x$ and $g(x) = \cos x$ on $-2\pi \le x \le 2\pi$.

b. Use the graph of $f$ to demonstrate that $\sin(-x) = -\sin x$.

c. Use the graph of $g$ to demonstrate an identity involving $\cos(-x)$.

**Remember...**

Sine is an odd function. Cosine is an even function.

13. Find the pairs of expressions that are identically equal.

| | | |
|---|---|---|
| $\sin^4 x - \cos^4 x$ | $\tan^2 x$ | $-\cos^3 x - \cos x \sin^2 x$ |
| $\cos(-x)$ | $\tan x$ | $\csc^2 x$ |
| $1 + \cot^2 x$ | $\cos x$ | $(\sec x + 1)(\sec x - 1)$ |
| $\sin^2 x - \cos^2 x$ | $\frac{\sec x}{\csc x}$ | $-\cos x$ |

14. Calculate the product $(\operatorname{cis} x)\left(\operatorname{cis} \frac{\pi}{4}\right)$ to show that

$$\sin\left(x + \frac{\pi}{4}\right) = \frac{\sqrt{2}}{2}(\sin x + \cos x)$$

15. Write this expression as a single trigonometric function of $x$.

$$\frac{\tan x}{(\sec x + 1)(\sec x - 1)}$$

16. One of these equations is an identity, and the other is not. Determine which equation is the identity by testing values for the variables.

$$\sin(x + y) + \sin(x - y) = 2 \sin x \sin y$$
$$\cos(x + y) + \cos(x - y) = 2 \cos x \cos y$$

17. Show that these three expressions are all equivalent.

$$\cos^2 x - \sin^2 x$$
$$2\cos^2 x - 1$$
$$1 - 2\sin^2 x$$

**Remember...**

Two expressions are *equivalent* if you can get from one expression to the other using the basic rules of algebra.

18. Find all values of $x$ on the interval $0 \le x < 2\pi$ with $\cos^2 x - \sin^2 x = \frac{1}{2}$.

19. Find all values of $x$ on the interval $0 \le x < 2\pi$ with $\cos^2 x - \sin^2 x = \sin x$.

20. Determine whether or not the equation, $\cos 5x = 2 \cos x \cos 4x - \cos 3x$, is an identity. Explain your answer.

Do not try to prove it, just decide whether or not you think it is an identity.

## Maintain Your Skills

21. In Exercise 1, you may have found that $\sec^2 x + \csc^2 x = \sec^2 x \cdot \csc^2 x$. It is quite rare for two numbers to have the same sum and product.

    **a.** If $\sec^2 x = 3$, what is $\csc^2 x$?

    **b.** If $\sec^2 x = 4$, what is $\csc^2 x$?

    **c.** If $\sec^2 x = 11$, what is $\csc^2 x$?

    **d.** If $\sec^2 x = A$, find a formula for $\csc^2 x$ in terms of $A$.

    **e.** **Take It Further** What is the smallest possible value of $\sec^2 x + \csc^2 x$? Explain your answer.

22. Simplify $\sin\frac{\pi}{7} + \sin\frac{2\pi}{7} + \sin\frac{3\pi}{7} + \sin\frac{-\pi}{7} + \sin\frac{-2\pi}{7} + \sin\frac{-3\pi}{7}$.

23. Simplify $\cos\frac{\pi}{2} + \cos\frac{\pi}{3} + \cos\frac{\pi}{4} + \cos\frac{-\pi}{4} + \cos\frac{-\pi}{3} + \cos\frac{-\pi}{2}$.

# H.07 Building Formulas and Identities

Recall Theorem 6.2, the Multiplication Law for complex numbers. If $z = r_1 \operatorname{cis} \alpha$ and $w = r_2 \operatorname{cis} \beta$, then

$$zw = (r_1 \operatorname{cis} \alpha)(r_2 \operatorname{cis} \beta) = r_1 r_2 \operatorname{cis} (\alpha + \beta)$$

If both $z$ and $w$ are on the unit circle, then $r_1 = r_2 = 1$ and you get a simpler expression.

$$zw = (\operatorname{cis} \alpha)(\operatorname{cis} \beta) = \operatorname{cis} (\alpha + \beta)$$

In fact, the product of any two complex numbers on the unit circle will also be on the unit circle.

Jacques Hadamard (1865–1963) said, "The shortest path between two truths in the real domain passes through the complex domain."

These facts about complex numbers will help you find many important trigonometric relationships, which involve real numbers only.

## Developing Habits of Mind

**Simplify complicated problems.** There are two ways to go about building and proving identities for trigonometric functions.

- Cosine and sine are real-valued functions. They take a real input (like $\pi$) and they give you a real output (like $\sin \pi = 0$). You can study their relationships entirely in the real numbers without ever thinking about complex numbers at all. But when you try to prove many of these relationships with real numbers, you end up with long, tedious calculations—not exactly elegant mathematics.
- As you have seen in this chapter, you can use cosine and sine to describe coordinates of complex numbers on the unit circle. This relationship lets you use the properties of complex numbers to prove relationships involving cosine and sine. You can write a proof that could be 15 lines long using real numbers alone in only 1 or 2 lines using complex numbers.

Cosine and sine are still real-valued functions. They take a real input (the argument of the complex number) and give real outputs (the $x$- and $y$-coordinates of the complex number).

You can build many identities involving cosines and sines with mathematical elegance by using complex numbers. You may want to try proving some of these identities with real numbers just to appreciate how nice it is to work with the complex numbers.

## Example

**Problem** Write a formula for $\cos\left(x + \frac{\pi}{3}\right)$.

**Solution** From the Multiplication Law, you know that

$$\operatorname{cis}\left(x + \frac{\pi}{3}\right) = (\operatorname{cis} x)\left(\operatorname{cis}\frac{\pi}{3}\right)$$

From there, expand the cis notation.

$$\begin{aligned}(\operatorname{cis} x)\left(\operatorname{cis}\frac{\pi}{3}\right) &= (\cos x + i\sin x)\left(\cos\frac{\pi}{3} + i\sin\frac{\pi}{3}\right)\\ &= (\cos x + i\sin x)\left(\frac{1}{2} + \frac{\sqrt{3}}{2}i\right)\\ &= \left(\frac{1}{2}\cos x - \frac{\sqrt{3}}{2}\sin x\right) + i\left(\frac{1}{2}\sin x + \frac{\sqrt{3}}{2}\cos x\right)\end{aligned}$$

Since

$$\begin{aligned}\cos\left(x + \frac{\pi}{3}\right) + i\sin\left(x + \frac{\pi}{3}\right) &= \left(\frac{1}{2}\cos x - \frac{\sqrt{3}}{2}\sin x\right)\\ &\quad + i\left(\frac{1}{2}\sin x + \frac{\sqrt{3}}{2}\cos x\right)\end{aligned}$$

then the real parts are equal, so

$$\cos\left(x + \frac{\pi}{3}\right) = \frac{1}{2}\cos x - \frac{\sqrt{3}}{2}\sin x$$

Likewise, the imaginary parts are also equal, so

$$\sin\left(x + \frac{\pi}{3}\right) = \frac{1}{2}\sin x + \frac{\sqrt{3}}{2}\cos x$$

## For You to Do

1. Use the Multiplication Law to write a formula for $\sin(x + \pi)$.

The Multiplication Law makes it easy to prove two of the most useful trigonometric identities.

### *Theorem H.1 The Angle-Sum Formulas*

**The following two equations are true for all values of $\alpha$ and $\beta$.**

$$\cos(\alpha + \beta) = \cos\alpha\cos\beta - \sin\alpha\sin\beta$$
$$\sin(\alpha + \beta) = \sin\alpha\cos\beta + \cos\alpha\sin\beta$$

**Proof**

$$\begin{aligned}\operatorname{cis}(\alpha + \beta) &= (\operatorname{cis}\alpha)(\operatorname{cis}\beta)\\ &= (\cos\alpha + i\sin\alpha)(\cos\beta + i\sin\beta)\\ &= (\cos\alpha\cos\beta + i^2\sin\alpha\sin\beta) + (i\sin\alpha\cos\beta + i\cos\alpha\sin\beta)\\ &= (\cos\alpha\cos\beta - \sin\alpha\sin\beta) + i(\sin\alpha\cos\beta + \cos\alpha\sin\beta)\end{aligned}$$

Recall that $a + bi = c + di \Leftrightarrow a = c$ and $b = d$. So if

$$\cos(\alpha + \beta) + i\sin(\alpha + \beta) = (\cos\alpha\cos\beta - \sin\alpha\sin\beta) + i(\sin\alpha\cos\beta + \cos\alpha\sin\beta)$$

then

$$\cos(\alpha + \beta) = \cos\alpha\cos\beta - \sin\alpha\sin\beta$$

and

$$\sin(\alpha + \beta) = \sin\alpha\cos\beta + \cos\alpha\sin\beta$$

The Angle-Sum Formulas lead directly to four more identities.

### *Corollary H.1.1 The Angle-Difference Formulas*

**The following two equations are true for all values of $\alpha$ and $\beta$.**

$$\cos(\alpha - \beta) = \cos\alpha\cos\beta + \sin\alpha\sin\beta$$
$$\sin(\alpha - \beta) = \sin\alpha\cos\beta - \cos\alpha\sin\beta$$

## For You to Do

**2.** Prove the Angle-Difference Formulas.

Use the relationship $\alpha - \beta = \alpha + (-\beta)$.

### *Corollary H.1.2 The Double-Angle Formulas*

**The following two equations are true for all values of $\theta$.**

$$\cos 2\theta = \cos^2\theta - \sin^2\theta$$
$$\sin 2\theta = 2\sin\theta\cos\theta$$

## For Discussion

**3. a.** If $z = \cos\theta + i\sin\theta$, show that

$$z^2 = (\cos^2\theta - \sin^2\theta) + (2\sin\theta\cos\theta)i$$

**b.** Explain how the result from part (a) leads to the Double-Angle Formulas.

## Developing Habits of Mind

**Prove a special case.** Remember that corollaries are typically statements that follow directly from a previous theorem. In this case, the formulas for $\cos(\alpha - \beta)$, $\sin(\alpha - \beta)$, $\cos(2\theta)$, and $\sin(2\theta)$ all follow directly from the Angle-Sum Formulas for cosine and sine. You do not really have to memorize six formulas. You can quickly derive the Angle-Difference Formulas and the Double-Angle Formulas from the Angle-Sum Formulas.

In fact, you do not even need to memorize the Angle-Sum Formulas! The fact that

$$(\cos\alpha + i\sin\alpha)(\cos\beta + i\sin\beta) = \cos(\alpha + \beta) + i\sin(\alpha + \beta)$$

means you can always perform the arithmetic on the left side to rebuild the Angle-Sum Formulas. So here, you get six formulas for the price of one.

## Minds in Action

*Sasha says she has a way of building identities.*

**Sasha** I can build an identity starting with anything I want if I make an expression equal to 0.

**Derman** What? How can you make something zero?

**Sasha** I multiply what I start with by zero, then the product is zero.

**Derman** But if you multiply by zero, there won't be any expression to see! It'll just say "0".

**Sasha** I will show you what I mean. Start with cosecant of $x$ and multiply it by something equal to zero.

$$(\csc x)(\cos^2 x + \sin^2 x - 1) = 0$$

That's an identity. The left side is always zero, right?

**Derman** Well yeah, since $\cos^2 x + \sin^2 x = 1$.

**Sasha** Now expand the left side.

$$\csc x \cos^2 x + \sin x - \csc x = 0$$

That's still an identity. If I know an equation is always true, I can use the basic rules to make new equations that are also always true. I can add $\csc x$ to each side to get another identity.

$$\csc x \cos^2 x + \sin x = \csc x$$

**Derman** Clever. Maybe they used your idea when writing this book.

## For You to Do

**4.** Show how you can build the identity

$$2\cos x - 2\sec x + \sec^2 x = 1 + \tan^2 x - 2\sin x \tan x$$

by starting from the identity

$$(2\cos x - 1)(1 + \tan^2 x - \sec^2 x) = 0$$

## Exercises Practicing Habits of Mind

### Check Your Understanding

1. Find formulas for $\cos 3x$ and $\sin 3x$ in terms of $\cos x$ and $\sin x$.
2. a. Find two "nice" complex numbers that have a product with argument $75^\circ$.
   b. Use the complex numbers you found in part(a) to get exact values for $\cos 75^\circ$ and $\sin 75^\circ$.
   c. Find the value of $2 \sin 75^\circ \cos 75^\circ$.

**Remember...**

Arguments add, so you need to find two complex numbers with "nice" arguments that add to 75°.

3. a. Evaluate the product.
$$\left(\frac{3}{5} + \frac{4}{5}i\right)\left(\frac{12}{13} + \frac{5}{13}i\right)$$
   b. If $\alpha$ and $\beta$ are in Quadrant I and $\cos \alpha = \frac{3}{5}$ and $\sin \beta = \frac{5}{13}$, find the value of $\sin(\alpha + \beta)$.
4. a. Show that this equation is an identity by using the Angle-Sum and Angle-Difference Formulas on the left side.
$$\cos(\alpha + \beta) + \cos(\alpha - \beta) = 2 \cos \alpha \cos \beta$$
   b. Determine a similar identity for $\sin(\alpha + \beta) + \sin(\alpha - \beta)$.
5. **Write About It** Use Sasha's method in episode 4 to write your own identity.
6. Write a formula for $\tan(\alpha + \beta)$ that includes only $\tan \alpha$ and $\tan \beta$.
7. **Take It Further** Determine formulas for $\cos(\alpha + \beta + \gamma)$ and $\sin(\alpha + \beta + \gamma)$. ($\gamma$ is the Greek letter *gamma.*)

### On Your Own

8. a. Find the magnitude and argument of the complex number $\frac{\sqrt{2}}{2} + \frac{\sqrt{2}}{2}i$.
   b. Evaluate the product $(\cos x + i \sin x)\left(\frac{\sqrt{2}}{2} + \frac{\sqrt{2}}{2}i\right)$.
   c. Write a rule for $\cos\left(x + \frac{\pi}{4}\right)$ and for $\sin\left(x + \frac{\pi}{4}\right)$.

**Go Online**
www.successnetplus.com

9. Use the Angle-Sum and Angle-Difference Formulas for cosine and sine to prove each of these identities.
   a. $\cos(x + \pi) = -\cos x$
   b. $\sin\left(\frac{\pi}{2} - x\right) = \cos x$
   c. $\cos\left(x + \frac{\pi}{2}\right) = -\sin x$
   d. $\cos(x + 2\pi) = \cos x$
   e. $\tan\left(x + \frac{\pi}{2}\right) = -\frac{1}{\tan x}$
   f. **Take It Further** Prove $\tan\left(x + \frac{\pi}{4}\right) = \frac{\cos x + \sin x}{\cos x - \sin x}$.

**10.** **a.** What do you get if you use the Angle-Difference Formula to expand the expression $\cos(x - x)$?

**b.** What is the value of $\cos(x - x)$?

**11.** **a.** Write a formula for $\tan 2x$ in terms of $\tan x$.

**b.** Write a formula for $\tan 3x$ in terms of $\tan x$.

**Habits of Mind**

**Use facts you know.** First express $\tan 2x$ and $\tan 3x$ in terms of cosine and sine.

**12.** Is this equation an identity? Justify your answer.

$$\cos 5x + \cos 3x = 2 \cos x \cos 4x$$

**13.** **a.** Calculate this product: $\left(\frac{2}{3} + \frac{\sqrt{5}}{3} i\right)\left(\frac{3}{4} + \frac{\sqrt{7}}{4} i\right)$

**b.** If $\alpha$ and $\beta$ are in Quadrant I and $\cos \alpha = \frac{3}{5}$ and $\sin \beta = \frac{5}{13}$, find the value of $\cos(\alpha + \beta)$.

**14.** Verify the Angle-Difference Formulas by expanding this complex number multiplication.

$$(\cos \alpha + i \sin \alpha)(\cos(-\beta) + i \sin(-\beta))$$

Cosine is an even function, and sine is an odd function.

**15.** Show that this equation is an identity.

$$\sin(\alpha + \beta) \sin(\alpha - \beta) = \sin^2 \alpha - \sin^2 \beta$$

**16.** **Take it Further** The Angle-Sum Formulas for cosine and sine show that, in general,

$$\cos(\alpha + \beta) \neq \cos \alpha + \cos \beta$$

Are the two expressions ever equal? Explain.

**17.** **Standardized Test Prep** Which of the following is equal to $\cos\left(x - \frac{\pi}{2}\right)$?

**A.** $\sin x$ **B.** $-\sin x$ **C.** $\cos^2 x - \sin^2 x$ **D.** $\cos\left(x + \frac{\pi}{2}\right)$

## Maintain Your Skills

**18.** Suppose $\theta$ is the measure of an angle in Quadrant I.

**a.** If $\cos \theta = \cos 40° + \cos 80°$, find $\theta$.

**b.** If $\cos \theta = \cos 50° + \cos 70°$, find $\theta$.

**c.** If $\cos \theta = \cos 55° + \cos 65°$, find $\theta$.

**d.** If $\cos \theta = \cos 57° + \cos 63°$, find $\theta$.

**e.** Write a general rule suggested by the pattern above.

**f.** Use the identities from this lesson to prove your rule.

# H.08 Proving Identities

In Chapter 5, you proved geometrically one of the key trigonometric identities, the Pythagorean identity.

$$\cos^2 x + \sin^2 x = 1$$

Two identities that follow directly from the one above are

$$1 + \tan^2 x = \sec^2 x \quad \text{and} \quad \cot^2 x + 1 = \csc^2 x$$

You proved both of these identities in Chapter 5 as well. How do they relate to $\cos^2 x + \sin^2 x = 1$?

These two identities differ slightly from the first one since there are values of $x$ where their expressions are not defined. But it is true that the two sides are equal wherever the expressions are defined.

One way to build these identities is to start with a known identity and then transform it using the basic rules of algebra. But how would you proceed if you wanted to consider

$$\csc x \cos^2 x + \sin x = \csc x$$

as a possible identity? A first step is to gather evidence to decide whether the equation might indeed be an identity. Lesson H.06 suggested two ways to gather such evidence:

- substituting some values for $x$, and
- comparing graphs.

## Example 1

**Problem** Determine whether $\cos\left(\frac{\pi}{2} - x\right) = \sin x$ is an identity.

**Solution** Gather some evidence.

Start by picking numbers for $x$ that make the calculations easy. But be careful. Some expressions are equal for the "easy" numbers, but equal elsewhere.

- Try some values of $x$

**a.** Let $x = 0$.

$$\cos\left(\frac{\pi}{2} - 0\right) = \cos\frac{\pi}{2} = 0$$

$$\sin 0 = 0$$

The equation is true when $x = 0$.

**b.** Let $x = \frac{\pi}{2}$.

$$\cos\left(\frac{\pi}{2} - \frac{\pi}{2}\right) = \cos 0 = 1$$

$$\sin\frac{\pi}{2} = 1$$

The equation is true when $x = \frac{\pi}{2}$.

**c.** Let $x = \pi$.

$$\cos\left(\frac{\pi}{2} - \pi\right) = \cos\left(-\frac{\pi}{2}\right) = 0$$

$$\sin\pi = 0$$

The equation is true when $x = \pi$.

These results support the idea that the equation is an identity.

- Graph $y = \cos\left(\frac{\pi}{2} - x\right)$ and $y = \sin x$.

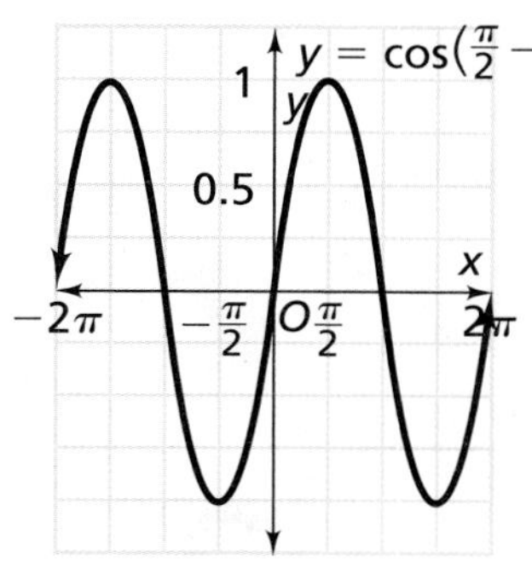


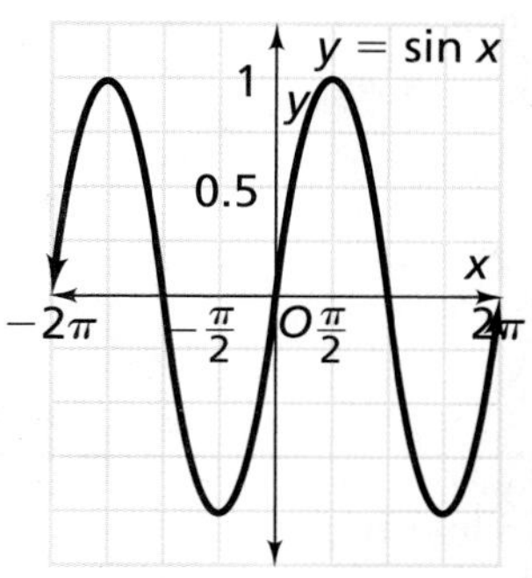


Always have the graphs of cosine and sine handy.

Both graphs look identical. If you graph them on the same axes on your calculator, they look like just one graph. So it is a good bet that the equation is an identity.

Keep in mind that evidence is not proof. Just because the two sides agree on lots of inputs and their graphs look the same, you cannot conclude that you have an identity. This first step can help you decide to try to prove the identity. But it does not constitute a proof.

One way to prove an identity is to use the basic rules of algebra, along with any other theorems you know, to transform one side of the equation into the other.

## Minds in Action

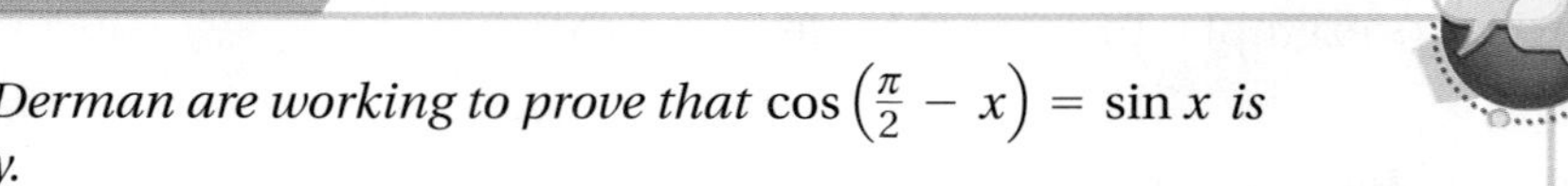
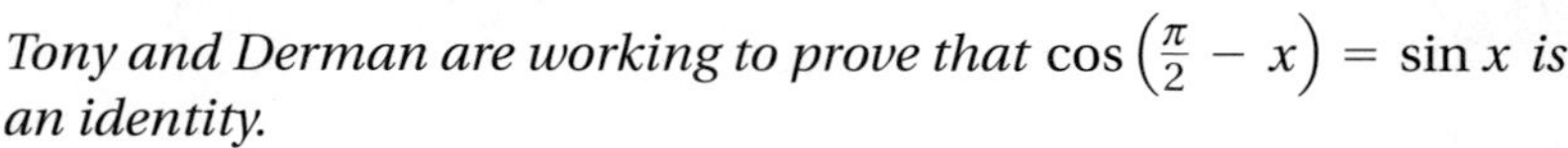

*Tony and Derman are working to prove that* $\cos\left(\frac{\pi}{2} - x\right) = \sin x$ *is an identity.*

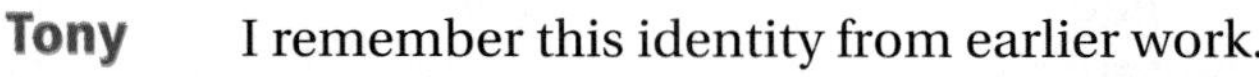

**Tony** I remember this identity from earlier work.

**Derman** Of course, then we were only talking angles in triangles, and we worked with degrees.

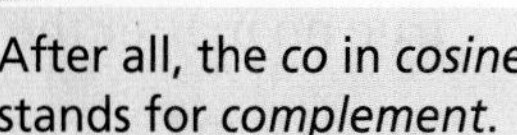

After all, the *co* in *cosine* stands for *complement.*

**Tony** Yeah, it was $\cos(90° - \theta) = \sin\theta$. The sine of an angle is equal to the cosine of its complement.

**Derman** Right, because the leg opposite one angle is the leg adjacent to the other one. But $\theta$ has values between 0° and 90°, and we want to prove the identity for any value of $x$.

**Tony** Well, we can use the Angle-Difference Formulas, right?

**Derman** Great idea.

*Tony writes on his paper.*

$$\cos(A - B) = \cos A \cos B + \sin A \sin B$$
$$\cos\left(\frac{\pi}{2} - x\right) = \cos\frac{\pi}{2}\cos x + \sin\frac{\pi}{2}\sin x$$
$$= 0 \cdot \cos x + 1 \cdot \sin x$$
$$= \sin x$$

**Tony** And there it is!

## For You to Do

**1.** Prove that the following equation is an identity.

$$\sin\left(x + \frac{\pi}{3}\right) = \cos\left(x - \frac{\pi}{6}\right)$$

You graphed the left and right sides of this identity in Exercise 9 of Lesson H.06.

The idea of proving identities is to show that two expressions are identically equal. In other words, you can transform one expression to the other using

- the basic rules of algebra (the commutative, associative, and distributive properties, the additive and multiplicative identities, and additive and multiplicative inverses)
- substitution
- proven theorems

In the Minds in Action above, Tony started with one side of the identity, and showed each step he took to end up with the other side of the identity.

For some identities, like $\csc x \cos^2 x + \sin x = \csc x$, the steps may not be as apparent as in Tony's example. To prove this identity, treat it like an equation.

There are three types of equations: those with one solution, no solution, or those with all real numbers as a solution. Equations with all real numbers as a solution are identities. They are always true no matter the value of the variable.

You saw in Chapter 5 that you can solve trigonometric equations much as you do any other equations. In fact, if you try to solve a trigonometric equation and the resulting statement is always true, then the original equation is an identity.

You may find it easier to prove some trigonometric identities by trying to solve them as you would any equation, looking for an equation that you know is true. Make sure that each step you take is reversible.

There are many routes from Point A to Point B. Some are shorter while others are more scenic. Proving an identity is similar. The important thing is arriving at the goal.

## Example 2

**Problem** Prove that $\csc x \cos^2 x + \sin x = \csc x$ is an identity.

**Solution** One way to prove an identity is to minimize the number of different functions shown. Here, each term has $\sin x$ in it.

$$\frac{1}{\sin x}(1 - \sin^2 x) + \sin x = \frac{1}{\sin x}$$

$$\frac{1 - \sin^2 x}{\sin x} + \frac{\sin^2 x}{\sin x} = \frac{1}{\sin x}$$

$$\frac{(1 - \sin^2 x) + \sin^2 x}{\sin x} = \frac{1}{\sin x}$$

$$\frac{1}{\sin x} = \frac{1}{\sin x} \checkmark$$

You may have recognized this identity. Sasha built it in Lesson H.07. So another way to prove the identity is to reverse Sasha's steps. To show $\csc x \cos^2 x + \sin x = \csc x$, show $\csc x \cos^2 x + \sin x - \csc x = 0$.

You could make some progress by factoring out $\csc x$ from the expression on the left side, but the second term does not have a factor of $\csc x$. But notice that, since $\csc x = \frac{1}{\sin x}$, then $\csc x \sin x = 1$, so you can multiply the second term, $\sin x$, by $\sin x \csc x$.

$$\csc x \cos^2 x + \sin x - \csc x = 0$$

$$\csc x \cos^2 x + \sin x \sin x \csc x - \csc x = 0$$

$$\csc x \cos^2 x + \sin^2 x \csc x - \csc x = 0$$

$$\csc x(\cos^2 x + \sin^2 x - 1) = 0$$

$$\csc x \cdot 0 = 0$$

$$0 = 0 \checkmark$$

In each method, your steps are reversible, so you are done. Notice that the two methods are quite similar. In fact, you could combine ideas from both methods to write a very simple formal proof.

$$\begin{aligned} \csc x \cos^2 x + \sin x &= \csc x \cos^2 x + \sin^2 x \csc x && \text{(since } \sin x \csc x = 1\text{)} \\ &= \csc x(\cos^2 x + \sin^2 x) && \text{(by factoring out } \csc x\text{)} \\ &= \csc x \checkmark && \text{(since } \cos^2 x + \sin^2 x = 1\text{)} \end{aligned}$$

## For You to Do

**2.** Prove that the following equation is an identity.

$$\frac{\sin^2 y}{1 - \cos y} - 1 = \cos y$$

## Exercises Practicing Habits of Mind

### Check Your Understanding

**1.** Prove each of these identities.

**a.** $\tan^2 x \sin^2 x = \tan^2 x - \sin^2 x$ **b.** $\dfrac{\cos x}{1 - \sin x} = \dfrac{1 + \sin x}{\cos x}$

**c.** $\cot^2 x \cos^2 x = \cot^2 x - \cos^2 x$ **d.** $\dfrac{\sin x}{1 - \cos x} = \dfrac{1 + \cos x}{\sin x}$

**2.** Only one of these two equations is an identity. Find and prove the identity.

$$\cos 2x + 1 = \frac{1}{2}\cos^2 x$$

$$\sin 2x + 1 = (\cos x + \sin x)^2$$

Use the identity from Exercise 4a in Lesson H.07.

**3.** Prove this identity.

$$\cos 5x = 2\cos x \cos 4x - \cos 3x$$

**4.** Show that, for any integer $n > 1$,

$$\cos((n + 1)x) = 2\cos x \cos nx - \cos((n - 1)x)$$

Exercise 3 showed a specific case of this identity, with $n = 4$. Perhaps you could use the same method to prove this identity?

**5. a.** Show that this expression is equal to zero.

$$(\sec x \sin x)^2 - (\sec x + 1)(\sec x - 1)$$

**b.** Explain how to use the results from part (a) to justify this identity.

$$(\sec x \sin x)^2 = (\sec x + 1)(\sec x - 1)$$

### On Your Own

**6. a.** Show that you can use the result in Exercise 4 to get a formula for $\cos 2x$.

$$\cos 2x = 2\cos^2 x - 1$$

**b.** Use the result in Exercise 4 to find a formula for $\cos 3x$.

**7.** One of these two equations is an identity. Find and prove the identity.

$$\tan^2 x - \cos^2 x = (\sec x - \sin x)^2$$

$$\tan^2 x - \sin^2 x = (\sec x - \cos x)^2$$

**8.** Provide explicit steps to transform the expression

$$\frac{1 - \tan x}{\sec x} + \frac{\sec x}{\tan x} \text{ into } \frac{1 + \tan x}{\sec x \tan x}$$

**9.** Peter has an idea for proving the identity

$$\frac{\sec x + 1}{\tan x} = \frac{\tan x}{\sec x - 1}$$

Peter says, "The right side of the identity has $\sec x - 1$ in the denominator. Maybe I should try to get $\sec x - 1$ in the denominator of the left side, too. I can do this by multiplying both the numerator and denominator of the left side by $\sec x - 1$, since that's the same thing as multiplying by 1."

**a.** Prove the identity using Peter's idea.

**b.** Use Peter's method to prove this identity.

$$\frac{\cot x}{\csc x - 1} = \frac{\csc x + 1}{\cot x}$$

**10.** Show that each of these equations is an identity.

**a.** $\sin 2x = \dfrac{2 \tan x}{1 + \tan^2 x}$ **b.** $\cos 2x = \dfrac{1 - \tan^2 x}{1 + \tan^2 x}$

**c.** $\tan 2x = \dfrac{2 \tan x}{1 - \tan^2 x}$

It might help to rewrite $1 + \tan^2 x$ using an identity.

**11.** Take It Further Prove each of these identities.

**a.** $\cos^6 x + \sin^6 x = 3 \cos^4 x - 3 \cos^2 x + 1$

**b.** $\dfrac{1 + \cos x}{\sin x} = \dfrac{1 + \cos x + \sin x}{1 - \cos x + \sin x}$

**12.** Standardized Test Prep Which of the following equations is a trigonometric identity?

**A.** $\cos x + \sin x = 1$ **B.** $\sin x = \sin(-x)$

**C.** $\cos x = \cos(-x)$ **D.** $\sin^{-1} x = x$

## Maintain Your Skills

**13.** Consider the identities from Exercise 10.

**a.** Let $\tan x = \frac{1}{2}$. Calculate the exact values of $\sin 2x$, $\cos 2x$, and $\tan 2x$.

**b.** Let $\tan x = \frac{2}{3}$. Calculate $\sin 2x$, $\cos 2x$, and $\tan 2x$.

**c.** Let $\tan x = \frac{1}{4}$. Calculate $\sin 2x$, $\cos 2x$, and $\tan 2x$.

**d.** Let $\tan x = \frac{3}{4}$. Calculate $\sin 2x$, $\cos 2x$, and $\tan 2x$.

**e.** Let $\tan x = \frac{m}{n}$. Calculate $\sin 2x$, $\cos 2x$, and $\tan 2x$ in terms of $m$ and $n$.

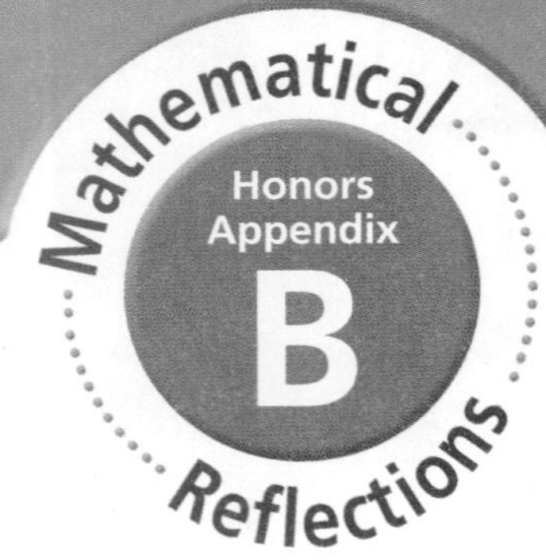


**In this investigation, you used the Multiplication Law to prove the Angle-Sum Formulas. You used known identities to prove new trigonometric identities. The following questions will help you summarize what you have learned.**

**1.** For which values of $x$ is the following equation true?

$$\cos x - \cos^3 x = \cos x \sin^2 x$$

**a.** $x = \frac{\pi}{3}$

**b.** $x = \frac{4\pi}{3}$

**c.** $x = \pi$

**d.** all of the above

**2.** Find the pairs of expressions that are identically equal.

| | |
|---|---|
| $\csc^2 x$ | $\cos x + \tan x \cdot \sin x$ |
| $(1 + \sin x)(1 - \sin x)$ | $\cos^2 x$ |
| $1 + \cos^2 x \cdot \csc^2 x$ | $\sec x$ |

**3. a.** Find the magnitude and argument of the complex number $\frac{1}{2} + \frac{\sqrt{3}}{2}i$.

**b.** Multiply out the product $(\cos x + i \sin x)\left(\frac{1}{2} + \frac{\sqrt{3}}{2}i\right)$.

**c.** Write a rule for $\cos\left(x + \frac{\pi}{3}\right)$ and another for $\sin\left(x + \frac{\pi}{3}\right)$.

**4.** Prove each of these identities.

**a.** $\sin(x + \pi) = -\sin x$

**b.** $\cos\left(\frac{\pi}{2} - x\right) = \sin x$

**c.** $\cos(2\pi - x) = \cos x$

**d.** $\sin(2\pi - x) = -\sin x$

**5.** One of these two equations is an identity and the other is not. Find and prove the identity.

$(\cos x - \sin x)^2 = \cos 2x$ $\qquad$ $(\cos x + \sin x)(\cos x - \sin x) = \cos 2x$

**6.** How can you test to see if an equation might be an identity?

**7.** How can you use complex numbers to find formulas for $\cos 2x$ and $\sin 2x$?

**8.** How can you use identities to prove other identities?

## Vocabulary and Notation

In this investigation, you learned these terms. Make sure you understand what each one means and how to use it.

- **identically equal**
- **identity**

Beginning with the same set of materials, you might construct a car while your friend may build a house. Each is a personal expression. Just as two figures built with the same pieces can look quite dissimilar, two sides of a mathematical identity can look very different.

# .... TI-Nspire™ Technology Handbook ....



Recognizing how to use technology to support your mathematics is an important habit of mind. Although the use of technology in this course is independent of any particular hardware or software, this handbook gives examples of how you can apply the TI-Nspire™ handheld technology.

## Handbook Contents

## Dividing Polynomials, Lesson 1.05

1. Choose **Polynomial Tools** from the **Algebra** menu. Choose **Quotient of Polynomial**.

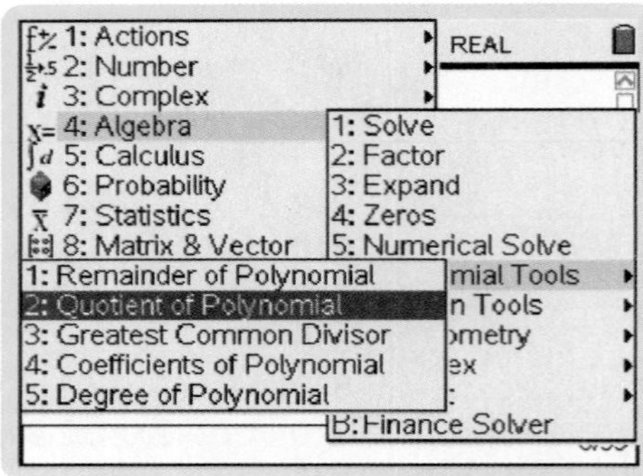


2. Type the polynomial to divide and then ,. Type the polynomial you are dividing by. Press **enter** to show the quotient without remainder.

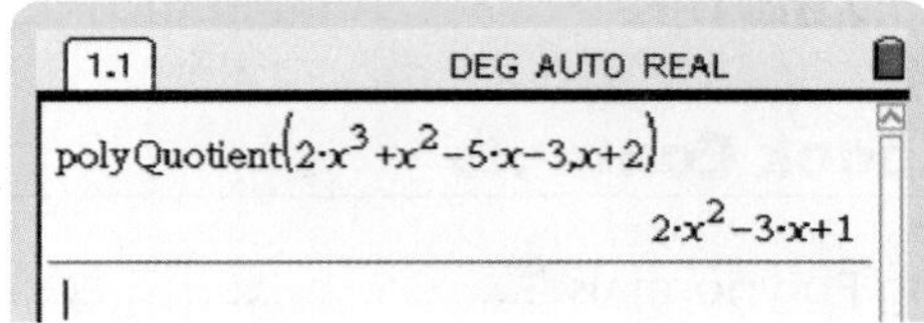


3. Choose **Polynomial Tools** from the **Algebra** menu. Choose **Remainder of Polynomial**.

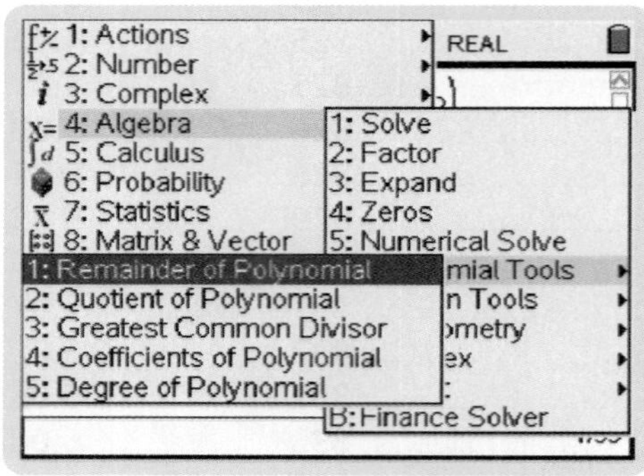


4. Type the polynomial to divide and then ,. Type the polynomial you are dividing by. Press **enter** to find the remainder after dividing the polynomials.

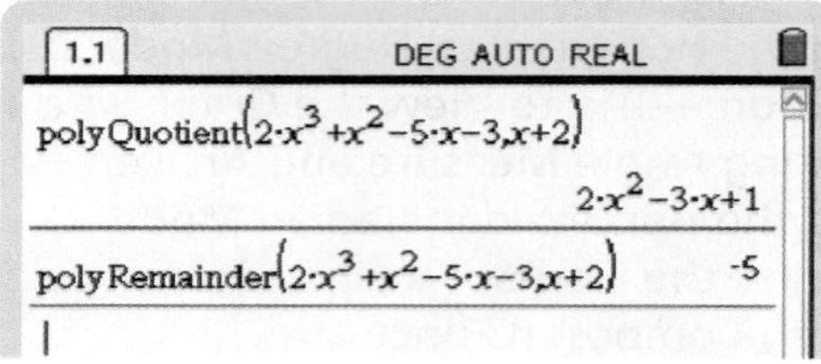


## Factoring a Polynomial, Lesson 1.08

1. Choose **Factor** from the **Algebra** menu.

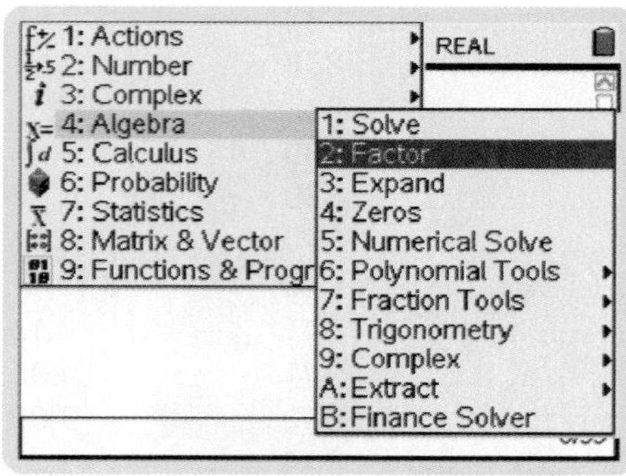


2. Type the polynomial to be factored. Press **enter**.

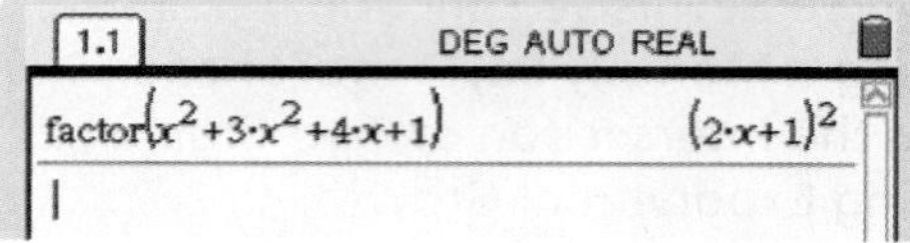

## Modeling a Function, Lesson 2.0

1. Choose **Define** from the **Actions** menu (or type D E F I N E).

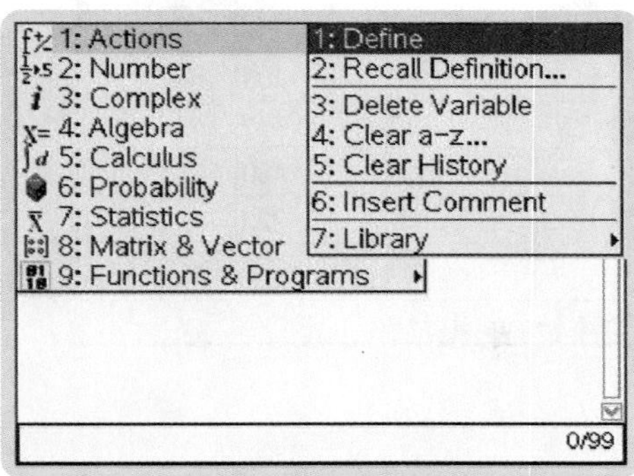


2. Type the function. Press enter.

## Modeling a Recursive Function I, Lesson 2.0

1. Choose **Define** from the **Actions** menu. Name the function by typing B ( N ) =. Press ctrl × to open the Templates palette. Select the piecewise template. Press enter.

2. Enter the function. Press tab to move from box to box. Press enter when done.

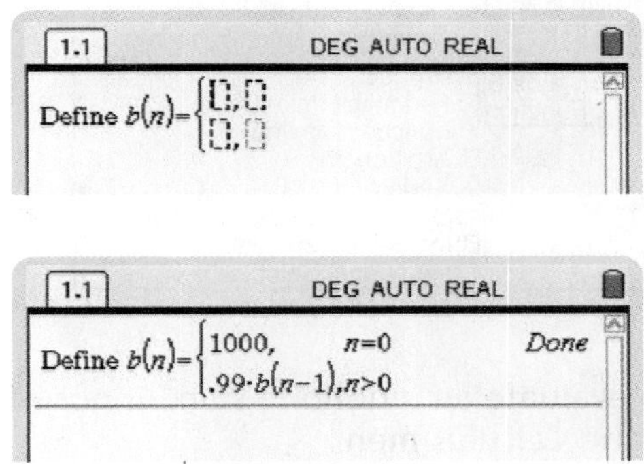


## Using a Spreadsheet to Make a Summation Column, Lesson 2.01, 2.06

1. In column A, make an index column with 1 in the first row, 2 in the second row, and so on. In column B, enter the data to be summed. In cell C1, type = S U M ( B ctrl ( , ctrl " A ctrl " 1 , A 1. Press enter.

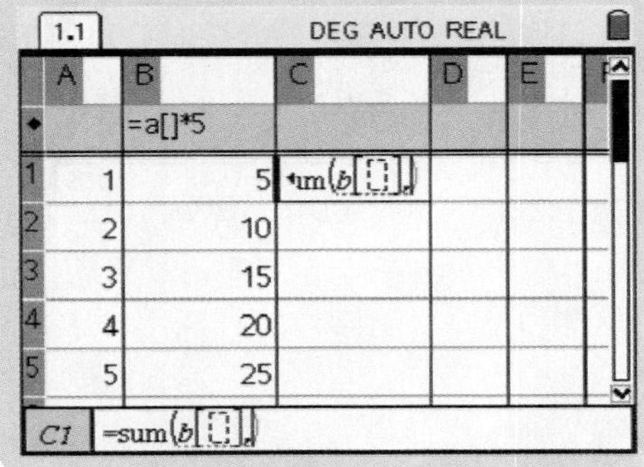


2. Move the cursor back to cell C1. Choose **Fill Down** from the **Data** menu.

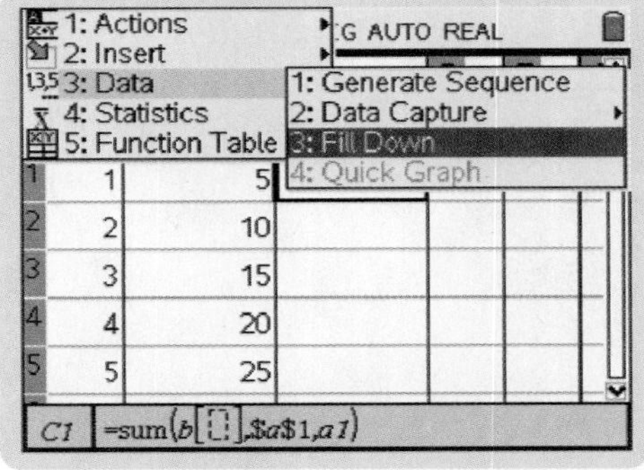

## Using a Spreadsheet to Make a Summation Column (continued)

3. Press ▽ to extend highlighted cells to match the last data cell in column B. Press **enter**.

1.1 DEG AUTO REAL

| | A | B | C | D | E |
|---|---|---|---|---|---|
| ◆ | | =a[]*5 | | | |
| 6 | 6 | 30 | 105 | | |
| 7 | 7 | 35 | 140 | | |
| 8 | 8 | 40 | 180 | | |
| 9 | 9 | 45 | 225 | | |
| 10 | 10 | 50 | 275 | | |

C10 =sum(b[ ],$a$1,a10)

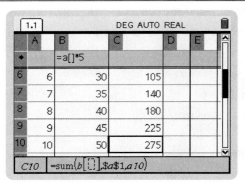

## Using Sigma Notation, Lessons 2.04, 2.07, 2.10

1. Choose **Sum** in the **Calculus** menu.

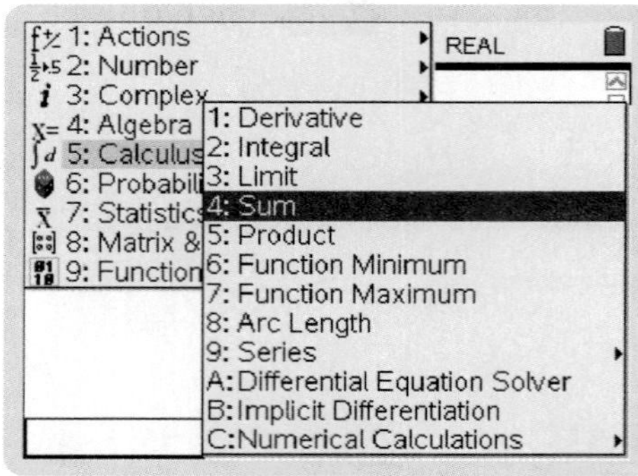


2. Press **tab** to move from box to box. Type the upper limit, the lower limit, and the expression for the sequence. Press **enter**.

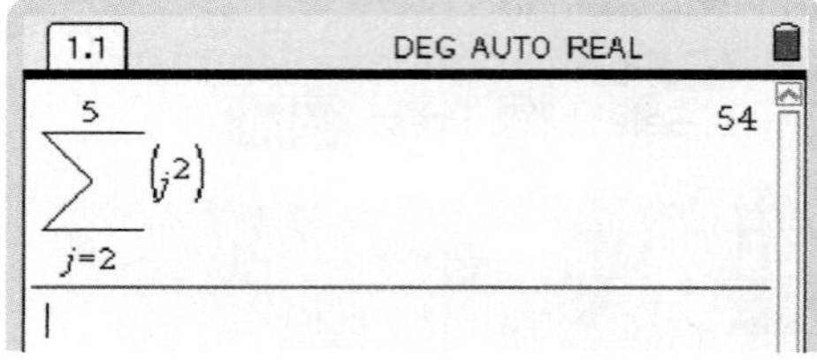


3. To evaluate an indefinite sum, Choose **Sum** in the **Calculus** menu.

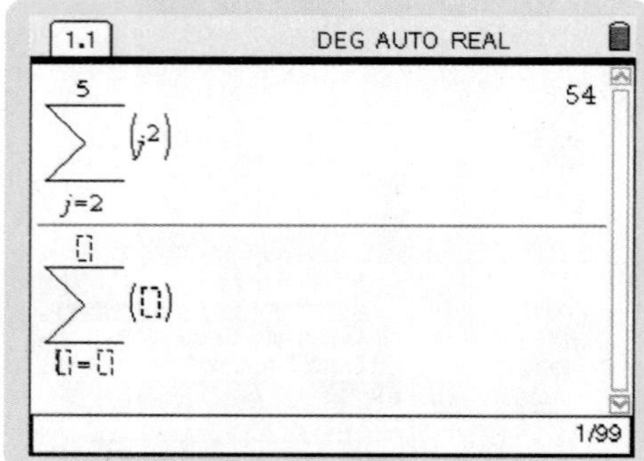


4. Press **tab** to move from box to box. Use a variable for the upper limit, and an integer for the lower limit. Type an expression for the sequence using the upper limit variable. Press **enter** to evaluate the sum.

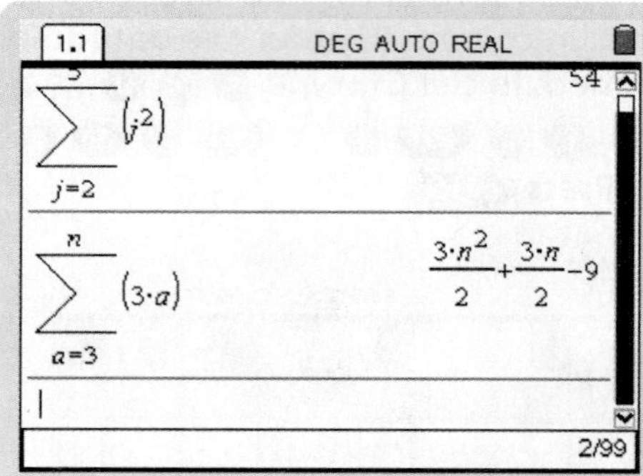

## Expanding Expressions, Lessons 3.01, 3.03

1. Press E X P A N D (. Type an expression. Press **enter**.

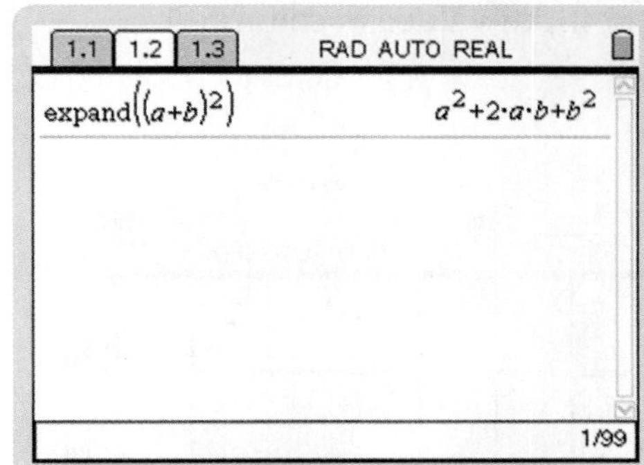


## Calculating Standard Deviation and Variance, Lesson 3.07

1. Choose **List Math** from the **Statistics** menu. Choose **Population Standard Deviation**. Enter a list variable, or manually type a list in curly braces ({ and }) Press **enter**.

1.1 RAD AUTO REAL

Define list1={3,2,6,4,9,12,44} Done

stDevPop(list1) $\frac{\sqrt{9182}}{7}$

2/99

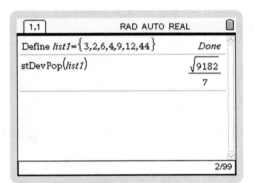

2. Choose **List Math** from the **Statistics** menu. Choose **Population Variance**. Enter a list variable, or manually type a list in curly braces ({ and }). Press **enter**.

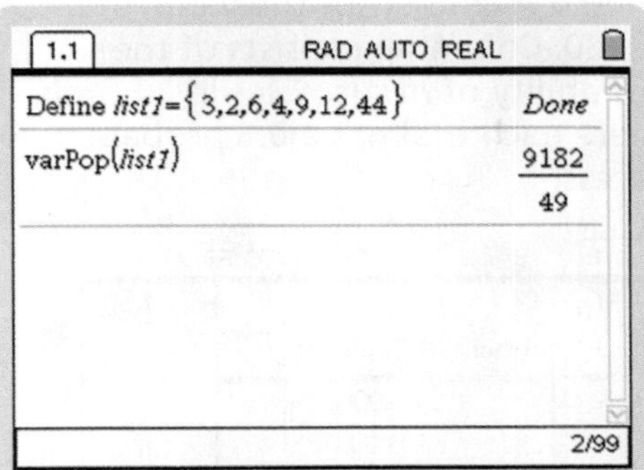


## Making a Function Table, Lesson 3.12

1. Define a function *f*.

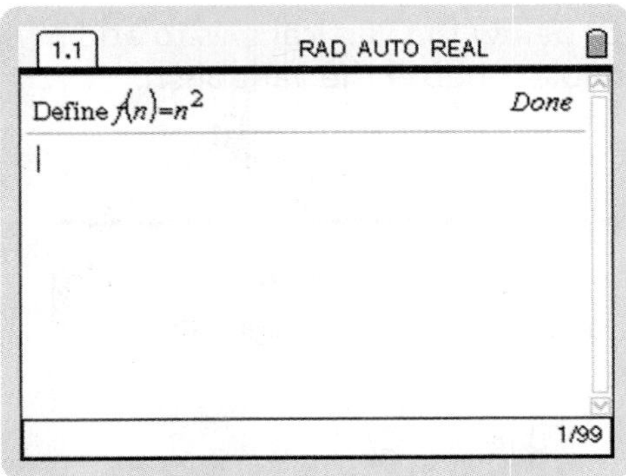


2. Navigate to the Lists & Spreadsheet application. Label the input column *n*.

1.1 1.2 RAD AUTO REAL

| | A n | B | C | D | E | F | G |
|---|---|---|---|---|---|---|---|
| ◆ | | | | | | | |
| 1 | | | | | | | |
| 2 | | | | | | | |
| 3 | | | | | | | |
| 4 | | | | | | | |
| 5 | | | | | | | |

A *n*

## Making a Function Table (continued)

3. Enter input values in column A.

| | A n | B | C | D | E | F | G |
|---|---|---|---|---|---|---|---|
| ◆ | | | | | | | |
| 1 | 0 | | | | | | |
| 2 | 1 | | | | | | |
| 3 | 2 | | | | | | |
| 4 | 3 | | | | | | |
| 5 | 4 | | | | | | |

*A1* 0

4. Navigate to the second row of the column header in column B. Press = F ( ' N ctrl ( enter.

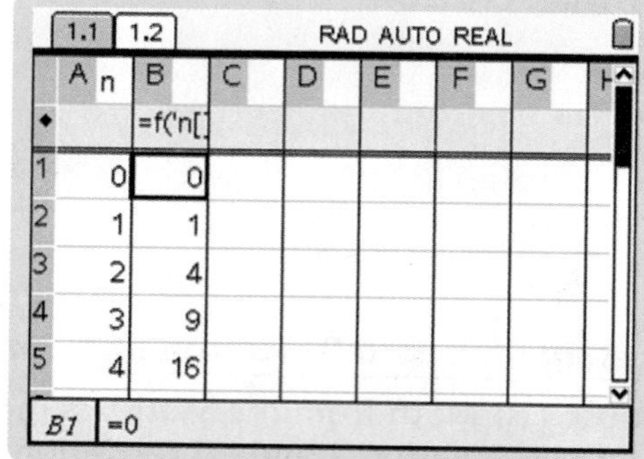


## Making a Scatter Plot, Lesson 3.16

1. Column A consists of the value of *m* from 1 to 20. Column B consists of the probability of *m* successes in 20 trials, where each trial has a 0.5 probability of success.

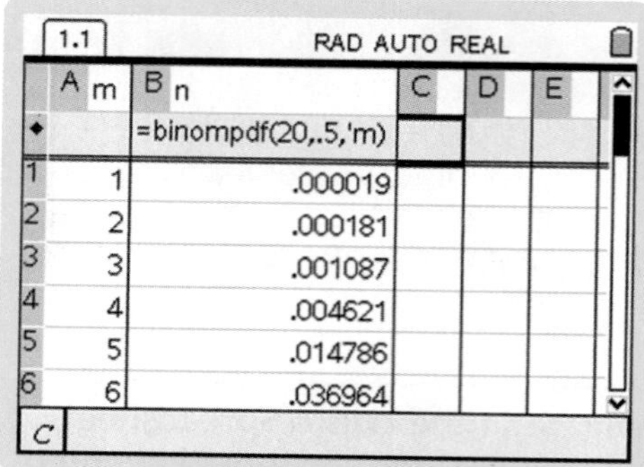


2. Navigate to the Data & Statistics application.

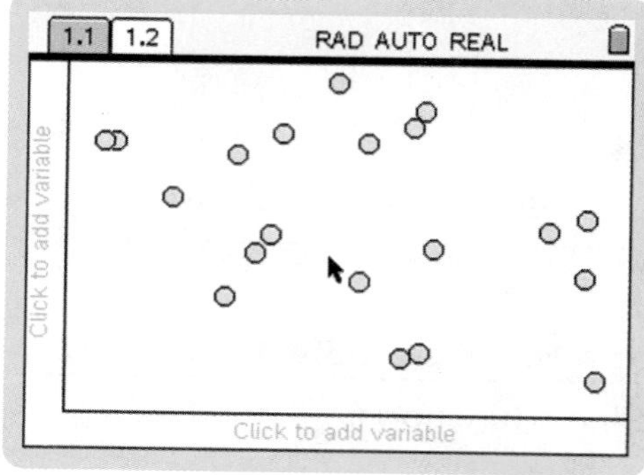


3. Click below the horizontal axis to add a variable. Choose the variable *m*.

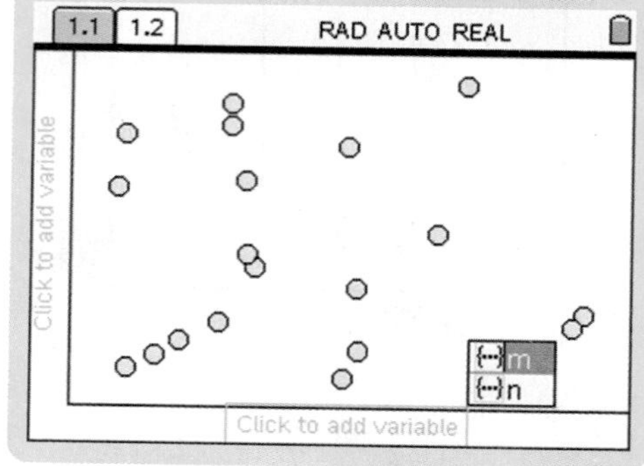


4. Click below the vertical axis to add a variable. Choose the variable *n*.

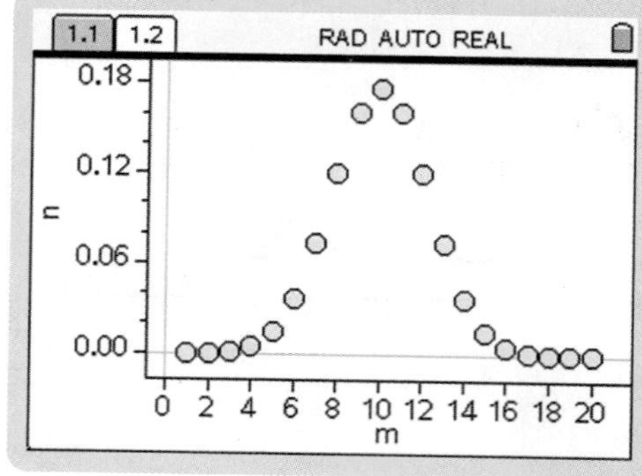

## Defining a Normal Distribution, Lesson 3.16

1. Navigate to the second row of the column header in an empty column.

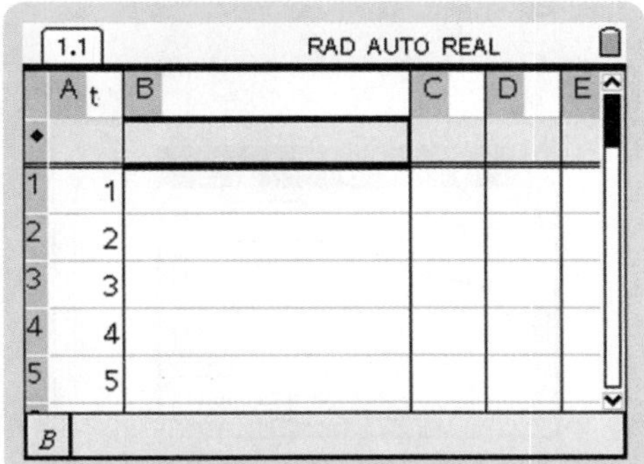


2. Press [menu] Choose **Distributions** from the **Statistics** menu. Choose **Normal Pdf**.

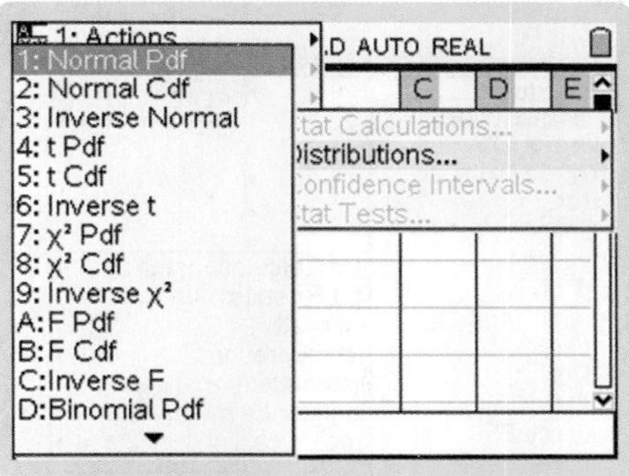


3. Choose *'t* from the drop down menu.

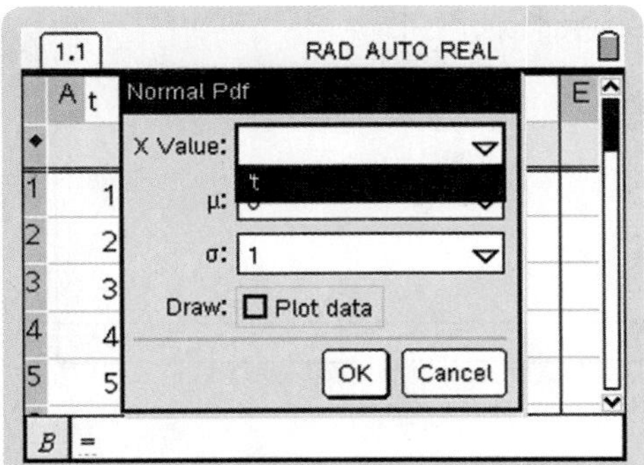


4. Press [tab] to move to the $\mu$ field. Type [M] [E] [A] [N] [(] ['] [T] [)]. Press [enter].

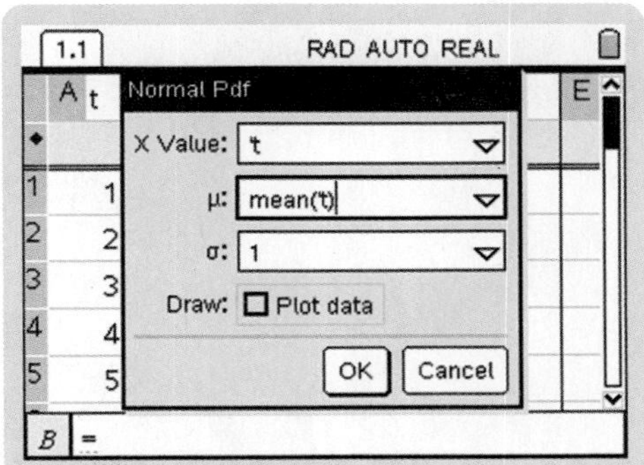


5. Press [tab] the $\sigma$ field. Type [S] [T] [D] [E] [V] [P] [O] [P] [(] ['] [T] [)]. Press [enter] [enter].

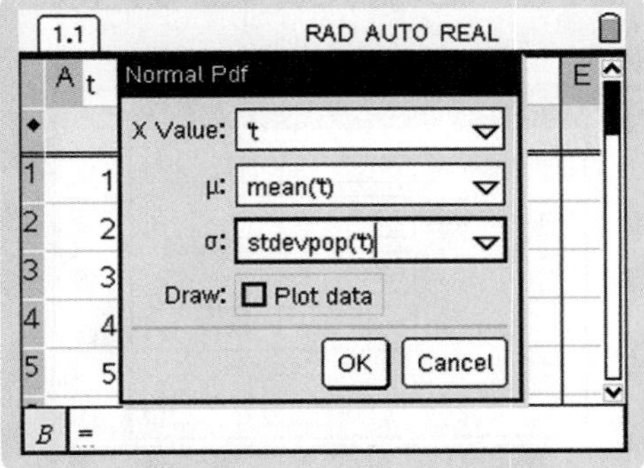


6. Press [enter] to populate the column.

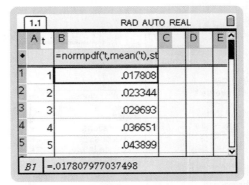

1.1 RAD AUTO REAL

| | A t | B | C | D | E |
|---|---|---|---|---|---|
| ◆ | | =normpdf('t,mean('t),st | | | |
| 1 | 1 | .017808 | | | |
| 2 | 2 | .023344 | | | |
| 3 | 3 | .029693 | | | |
| 4 | 4 | .036651 | | | |
| 5 | 5 | .043899 | | | |

B1 =.017807977037498

## Using the normPdf command, Lesson 3.16

1. Choose **Distributions** from the **Statistics** menu. Choose **Normal Pdf**.

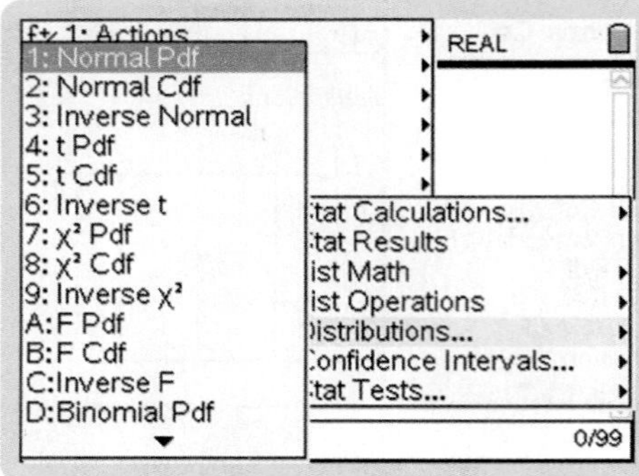


2. Press tab to move between the **X Value**, $\mu$, and $\sigma$ fields. Enter the appropriate values. Press enter enter.

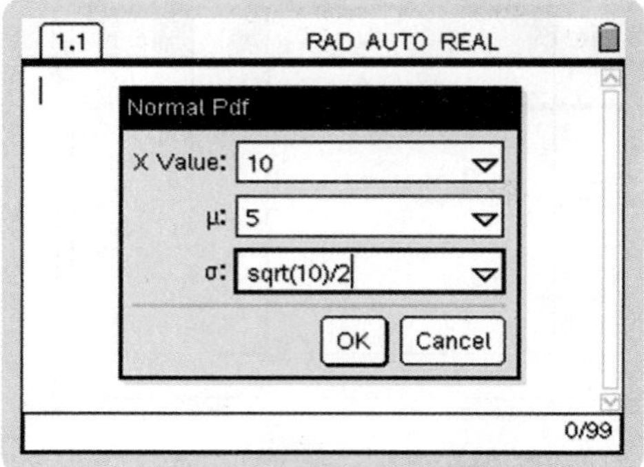


3. Press enter.

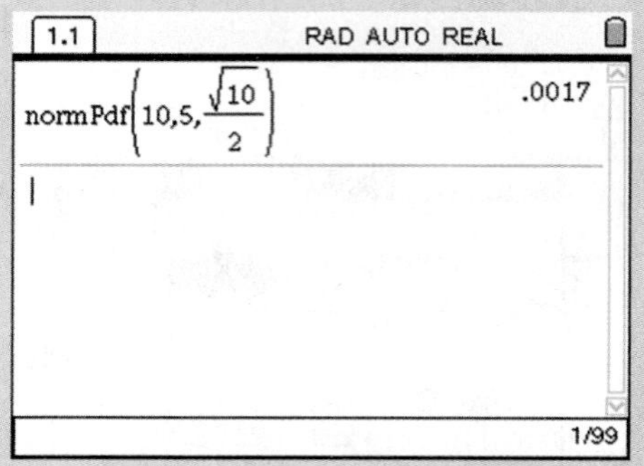


## Using the normCdf Command, Lesson 3.17

1. Choose **Distributions** from the **Statistics** menu. Choose **Normal Cdf**.

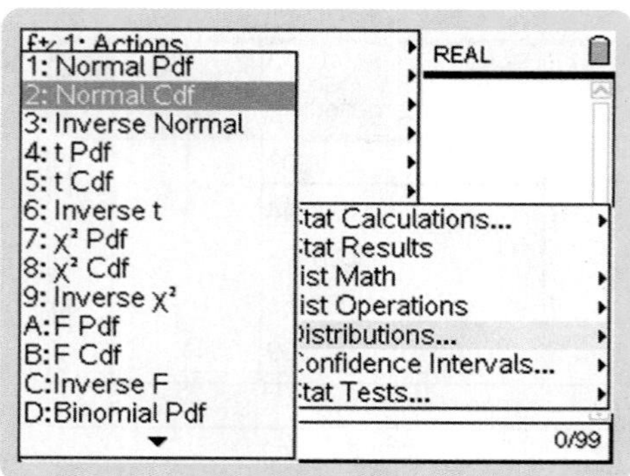


2. Press tab to move between the **Lower Bound, Upper Bound,** $\mu$, and $\sigma$ fields. Enter the appropriate values. Press enter enter.

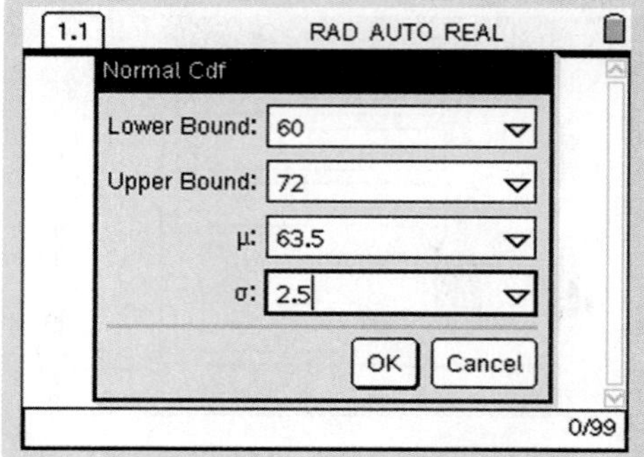

## Using the normCdf command (continued)

3. Press **enter**.

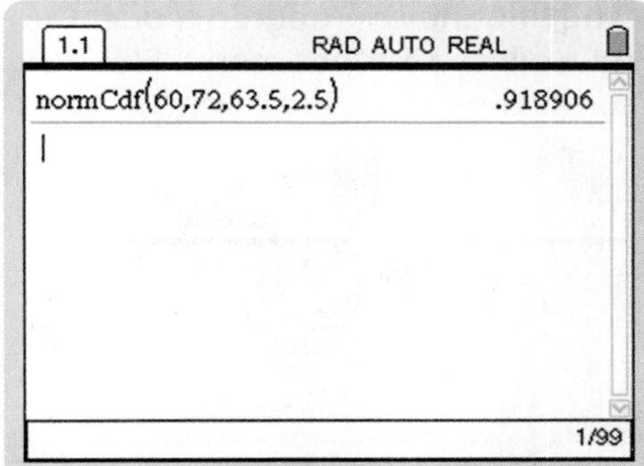


## Setting the Handheld to Degree Mode, Lesson 4.02

1. Press **ctrl** **home**. Choose **File** and then **Document Settings**. Press **enter**.

2. Tab down to the **Angle** menu. Press ▽ until **Degree** is highlighted. Press **enter** **enter**.

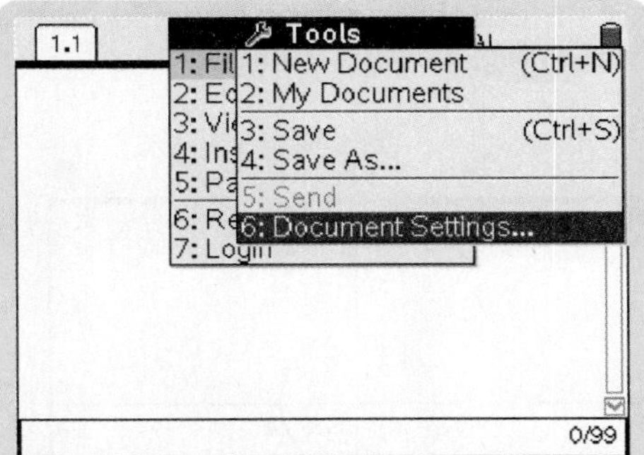


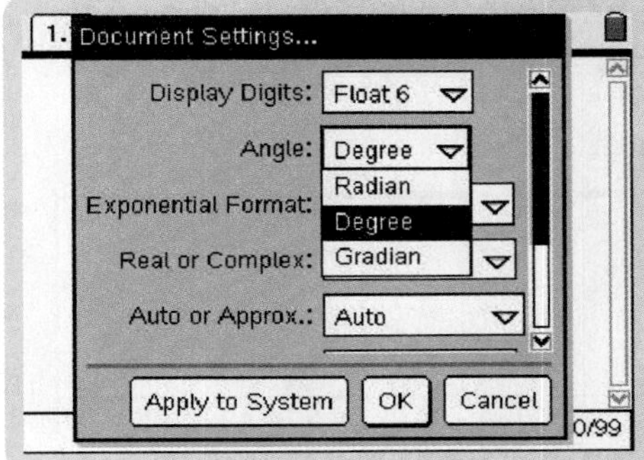


## Using Zoom—Trig to View the Graph of a Trigonometric Function, Lesson 4.07

1. Choose **Zoom–Trig** from the **Window** menu.

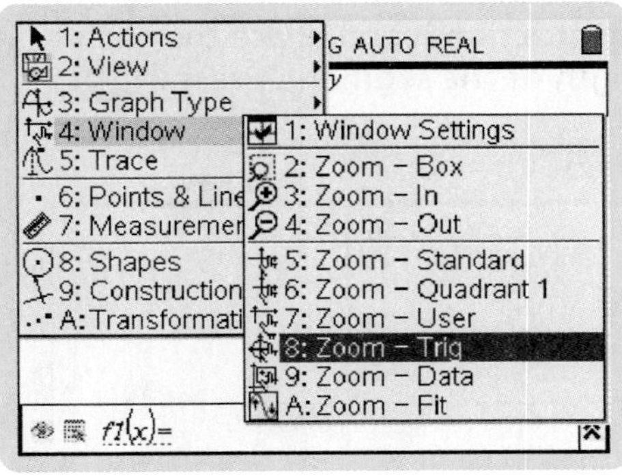


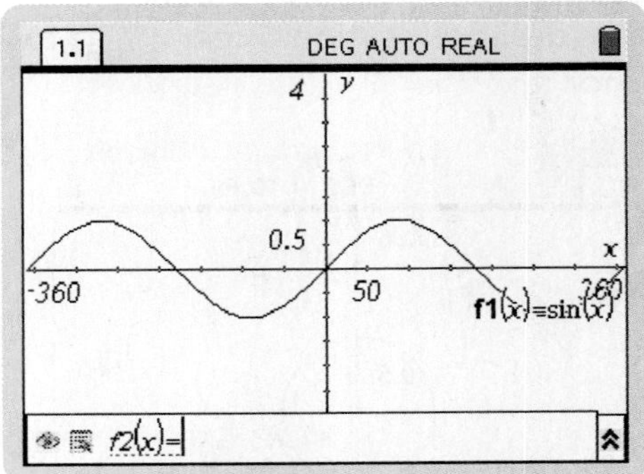

## Comparing Angle Measure and Arc Length, Lesson 5.02

1. Put the handheld in degree mode. Choose **Circle** from the **Shapes** menu. Place the cursor at the origin. Press enter.

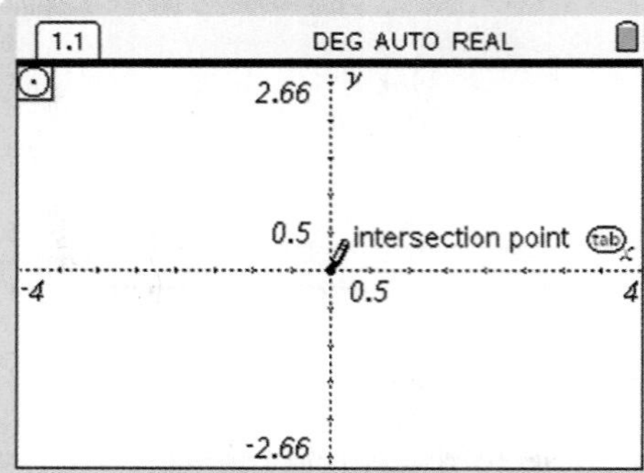


2. Place the cursor close the point (1, 0). The cursor will jump to the point (1, 0). Press enter. Press ⇧ A to label the point.

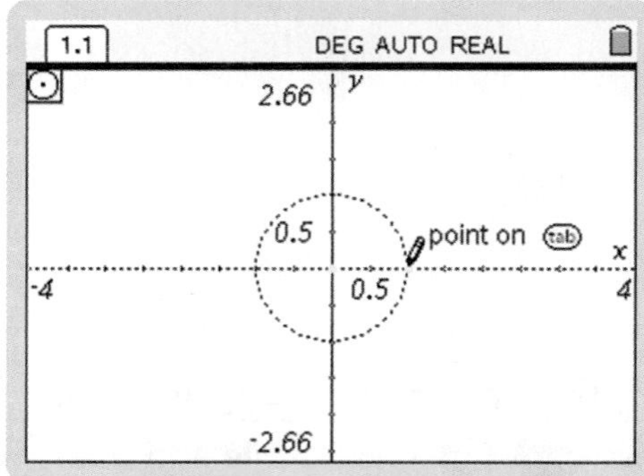


3. Choose **Segment** from the **Points & Lines** menu. Draw a segment on the screen. Press B ' to label the end point.

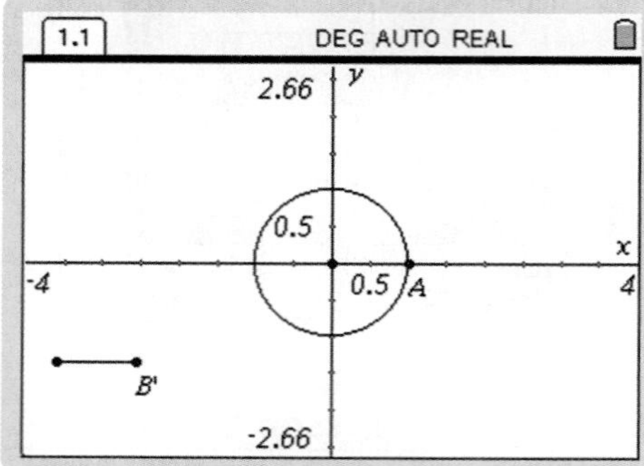


4. Choose **Length** from the **Measurement** menu. Place the cursor on the segment. Press enter.

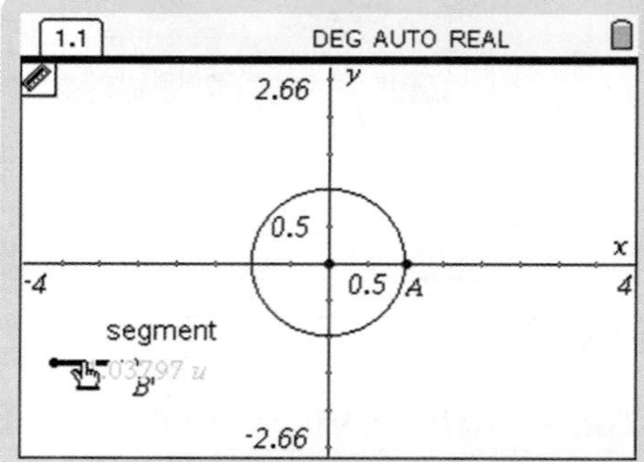


5. Move the cursor to drag the measurement to the desired location. Press enter to anchor it.

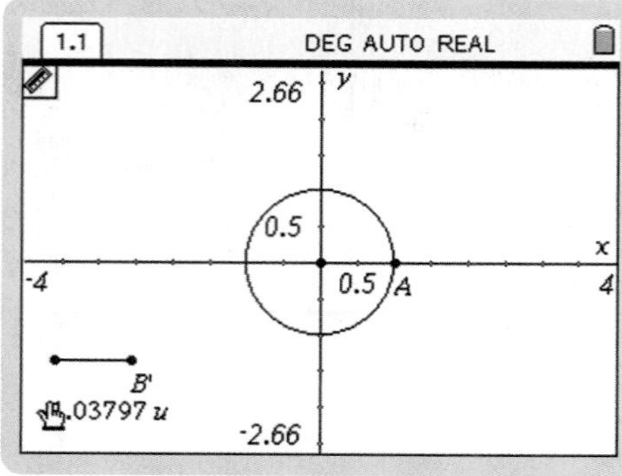


6. Choose **Measurement transfer** from the **Construction** menu. Place the cursor on the length of the segment. Press enter.

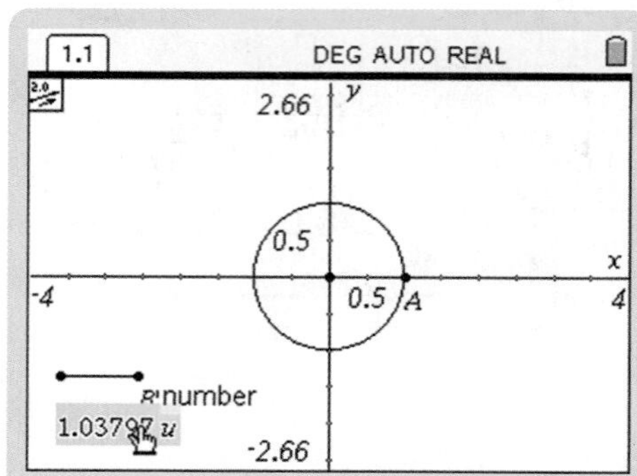

7. Place the cursor on the circle. Press enter.

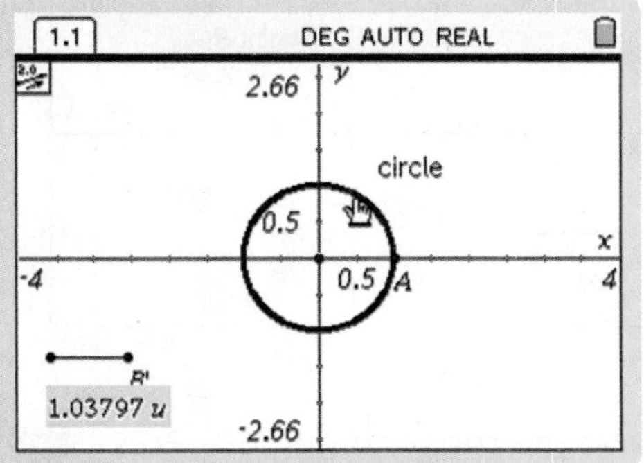


8. Place the cursor on point *A*. Press enter. The length of the arc from *A* to the new point that appears is equal to the length of the segment.

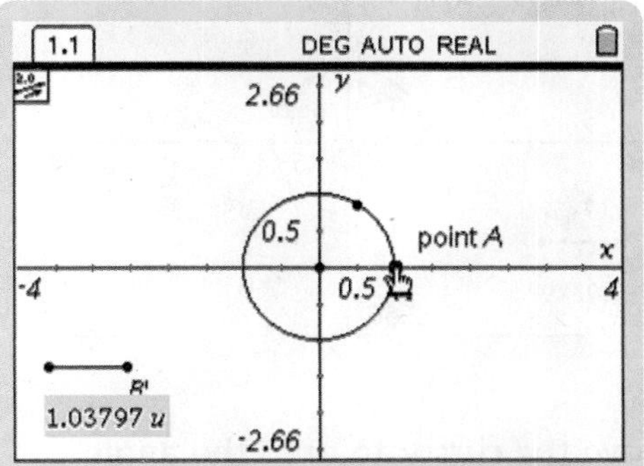


9. Use the **Text** tool from the **Actions** menu to label the new point.

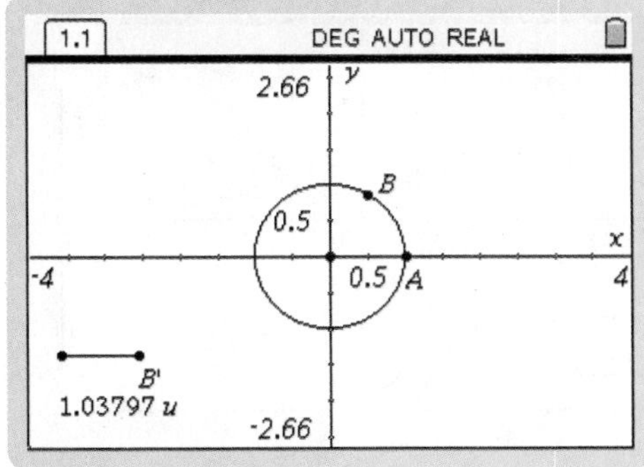


10. Choose **Coordinates and Equations** from the **Actions** menu. Place the cursor on point *B*. Press enter.

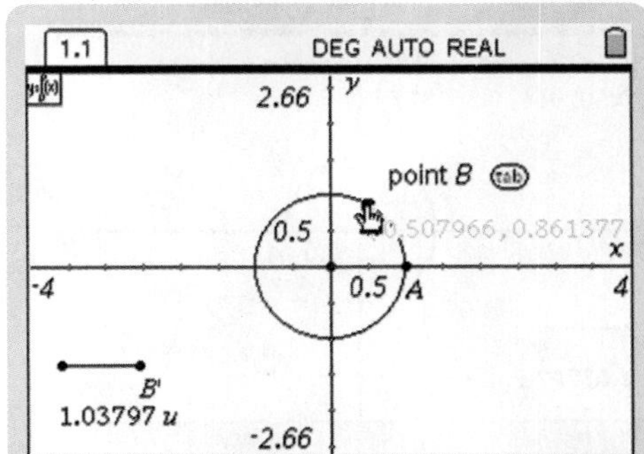


11. Move the cursor to drag the coordinates to the desired location. Press enter to anchor it.

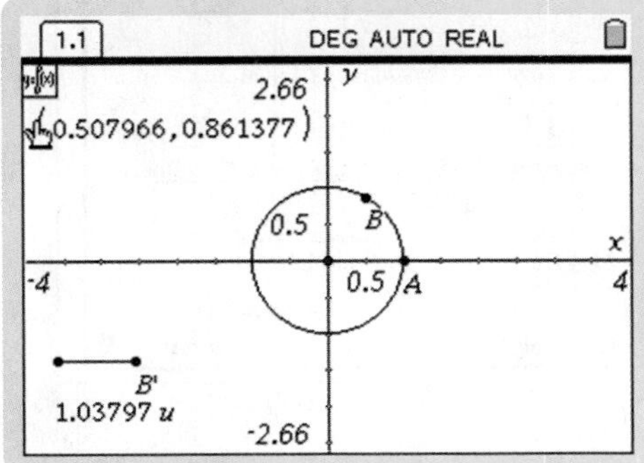


12. Choose **Angle** from the **Measurement** menu. Place the cursor on point *A*. Press enter.

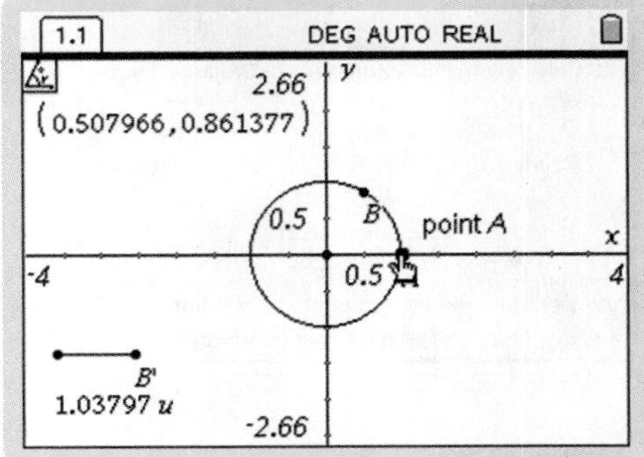

## Comparing Angle Measure and Arc Length (continued)

**13.** Place the cursor on the origin. Press enter.

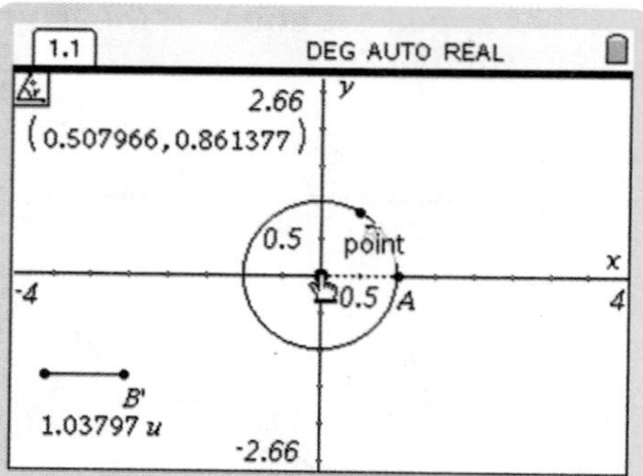


**14.** Place the cursor on point *B*. Press enter.

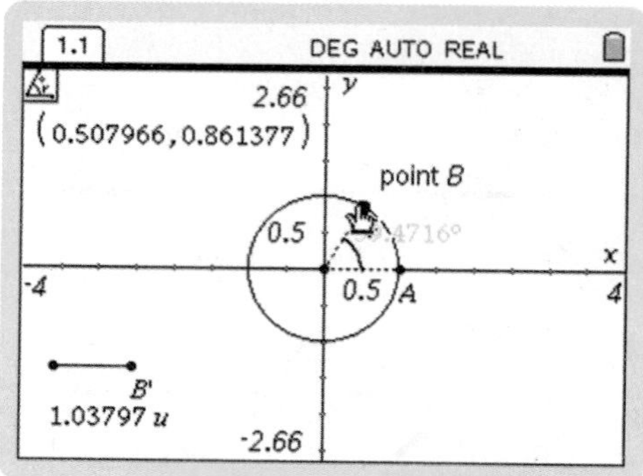


**15.** Move the cursor to drag the angle measurement to the desired location. Press enter to anchor it.

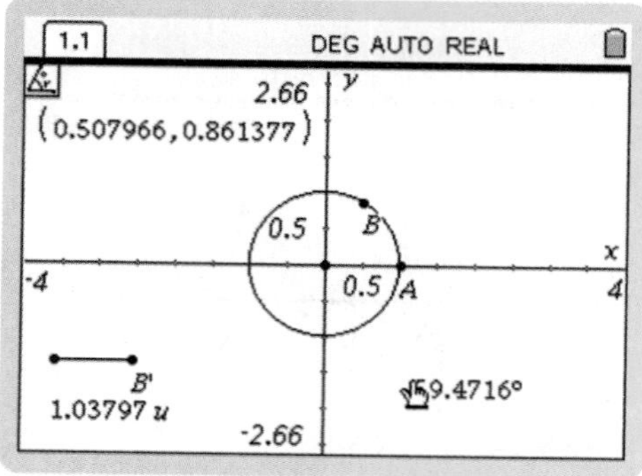


**16.** Move the cursor to point *B'*. Press ctrl to grab the point. Drag the point and observe the relationship between the length of the segment and the angle measurement.

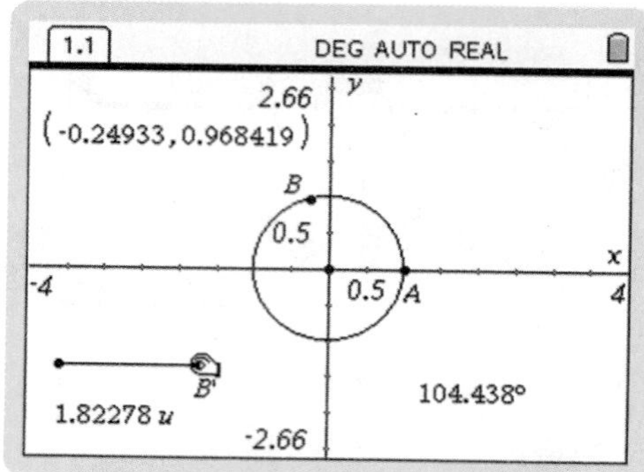


## Putting the Handheld in Radian Mode, Lesson 5.02

1. Press . Choose **System Info.** Press enter.

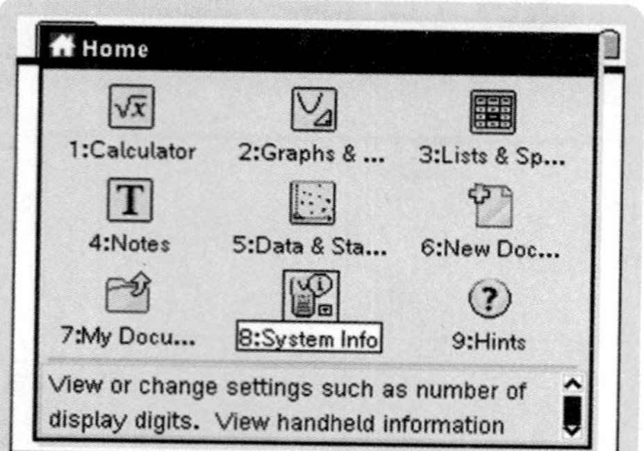


2. Choose **System Settings**. . . . Press enter.

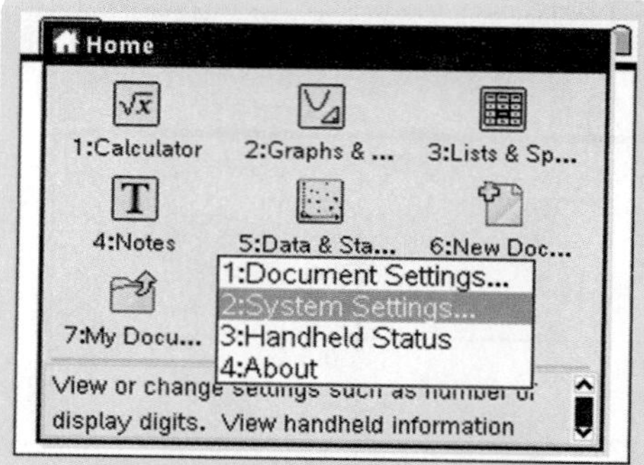

## Putting the Handheld in Radian Mode (continued)

3. Press tab until you reach the **Angle** field. Press ▽ to open the menu. Press ▽ until **Radian** is highlighted. Press enter enter.

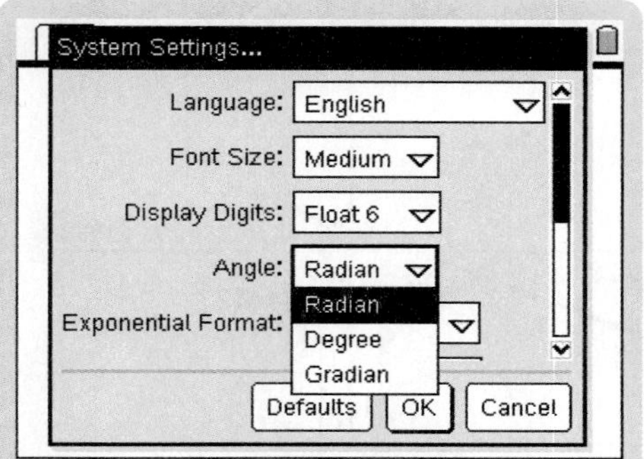


4. Press enter to confirm the change to Radian mode.

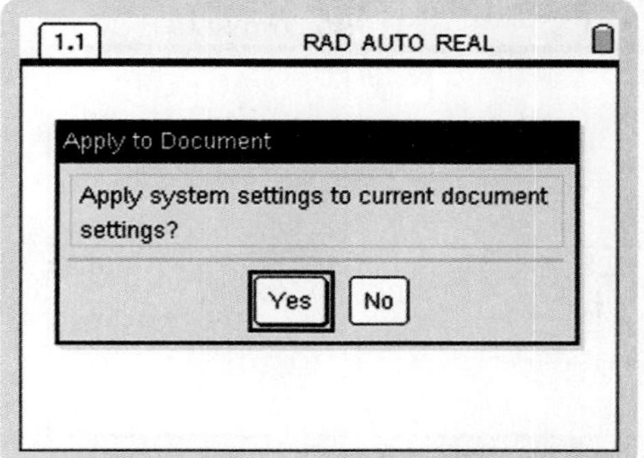


## Measuring the Slope of a Line Secant to a Sine Curve, Lesson 5.05

1. Start with the graph of $y = \sin x$.

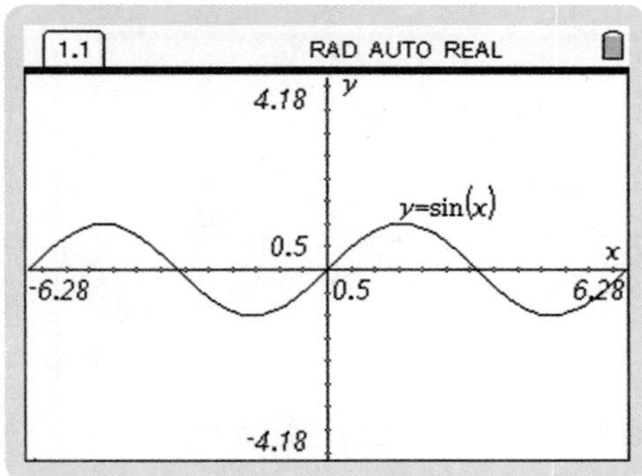


2. Choose **Point On** from the **Points & Lines** menu. Place the cursor on the curve. Press enter.

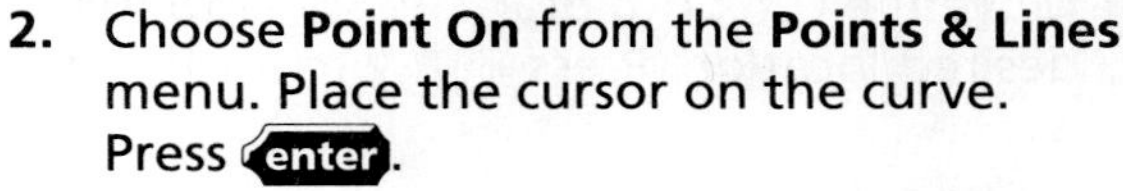

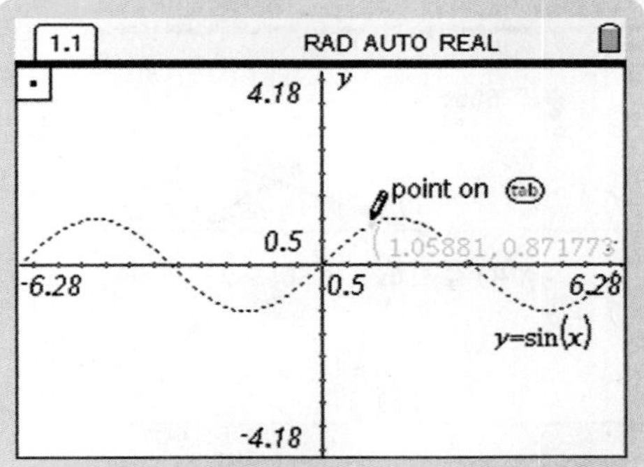


3. Press A to label the point.

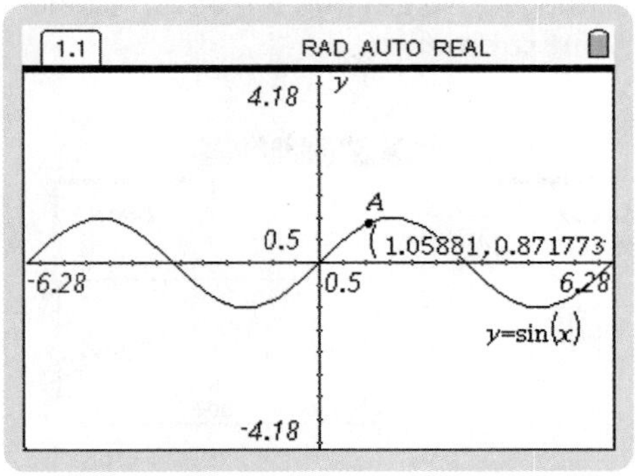

4. Place point *B* on the curve in the same way.

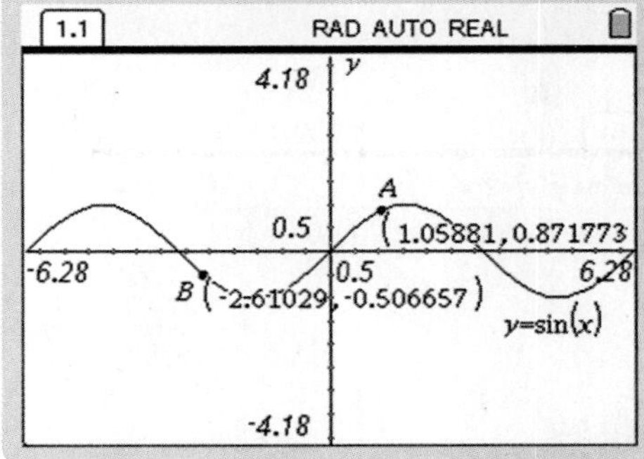

## Measuring the Slope of a Line Secant to a Sine Curve (continued)

5. Choose **Line** from the **Points & Lines** menu. Place the cursor on point *B*. Press enter. Place the cursor on point *A*. Press enter.

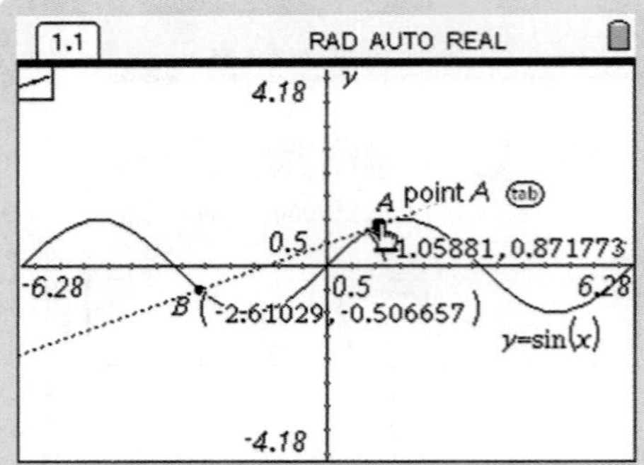


6. Choose **Slope** from the **Measurement** menu. Place the cursor on the line. Press enter.

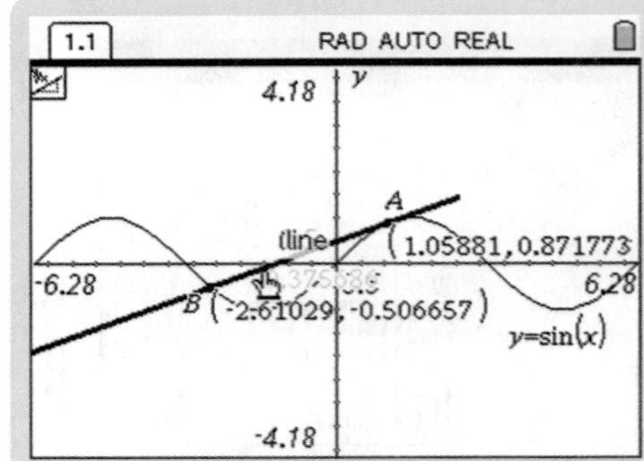


7. Move the cursor to drag the slope to the desired location. Press enter to anchor it.

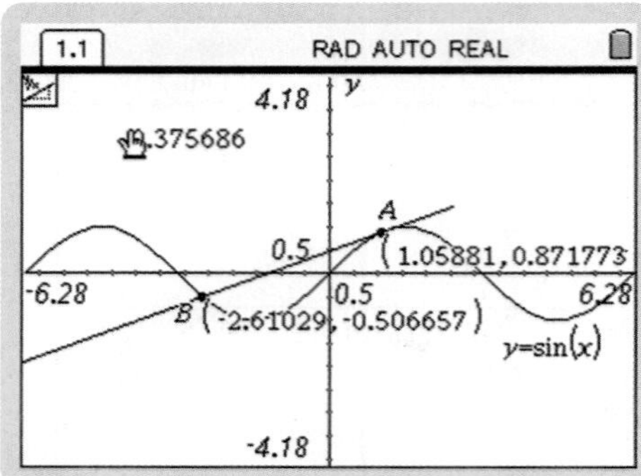


8. Place the cursor on point *B*. Press ctrl to grab it. Drag point *B* along the curve. Observe how the slope changes.

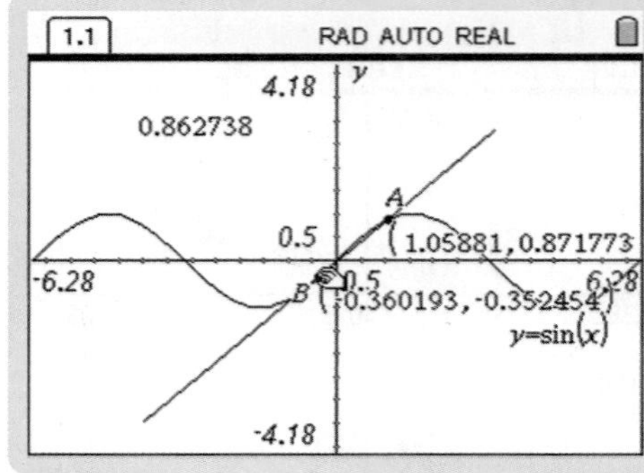


## Graphing Composed Functions, Lesson 5.06

1. Choose **Define** from the **Actions** menu. Define *g* as a function of *x*.

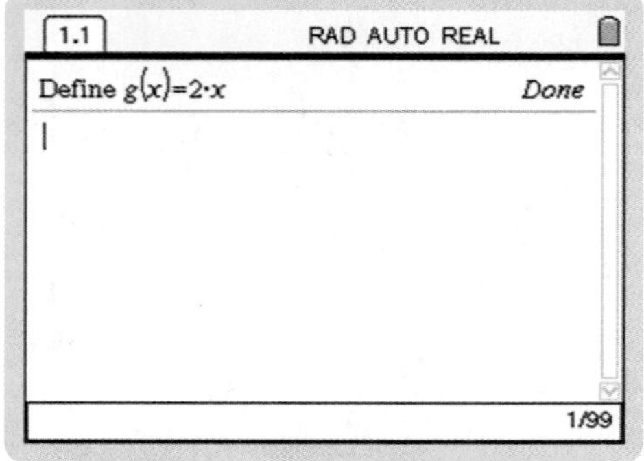


2. Press ctrl home. Choose the **Page Layout** menu. Choose **Layout 3** from the **Select Layout** submenu.

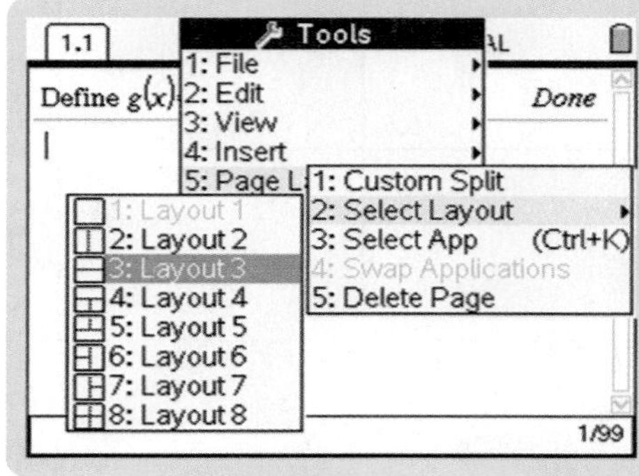

## Graphing Composed Functions (continued)

3. Press ctrl tab to highlight the new window pane.

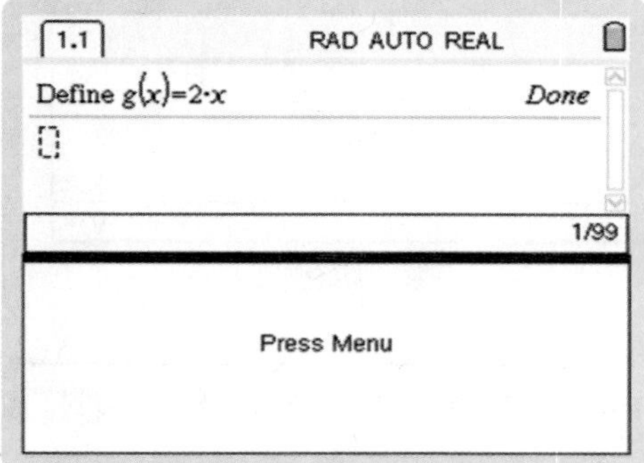


4. Add the Graphs & Geometry application. Choose **Zoom – Trig** from the Window menu. Press ctrl G to hide the function entry line.

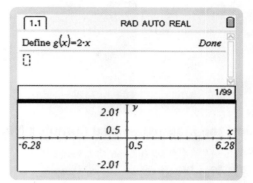

5. Use the **Text** tool in the **Actions** menu to write "$y$ = sin ($g$($x$))" on the screen. Drag the text to the axes to graph the equation.

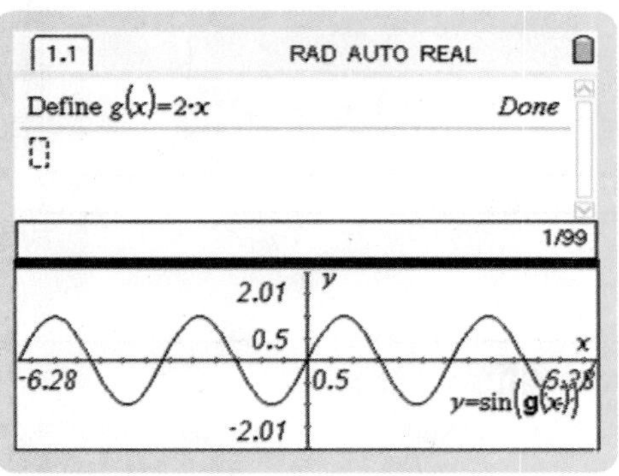


6. Press ctrl tab to switch back to the Calculator application. Redefine the function $g$. Observe the change in the graph of $y$ = sin ($g$($x$)).

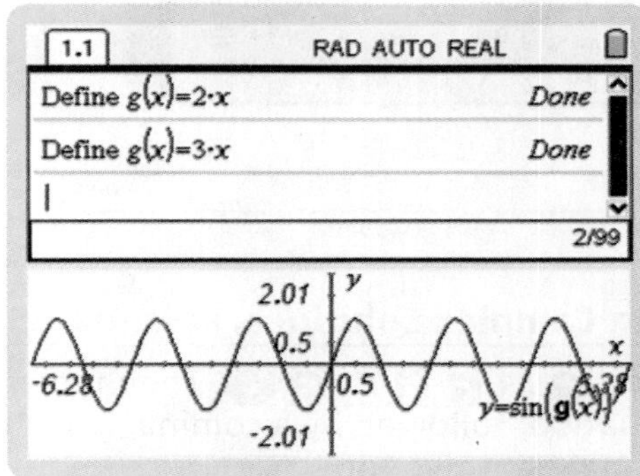


## Solving Trigonometric Equations, Lesson 5.07

1. Choose **Solve** from the **Algebra** menu.

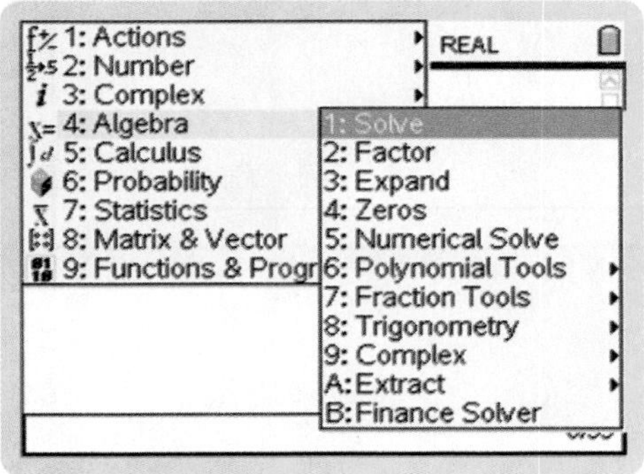


2. Type the equation, followed by a comma, then the variable. Press enter.

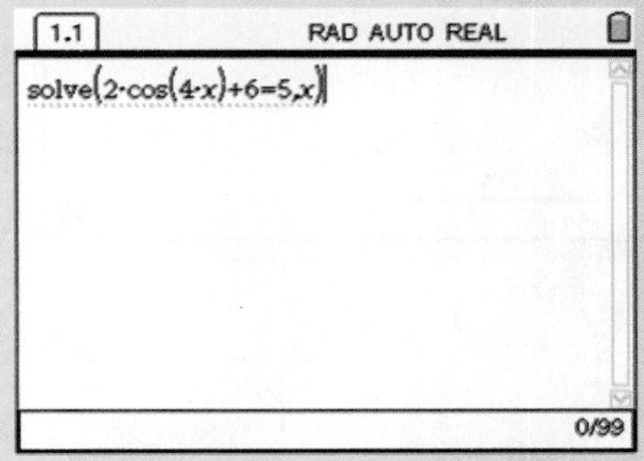

## Solving Trigonometric Equations (continued)

3. The general solution uses the variable ***n1***, which ranges over the integers. (You may also see ***n2***, ***n3***, ***n4***, and so on, as variables that range over the integers.)

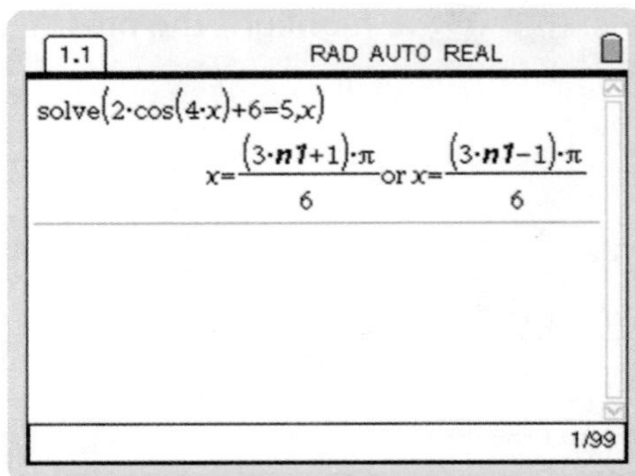

## Finding the Magnitude of a Complex Number, Lesson 6.02

1. Press ctrl ✕ to access the templates palette. Choose |□|.

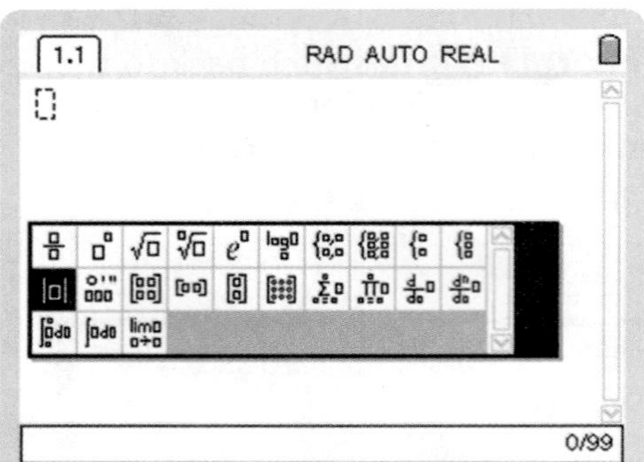

2. Type the complex number. Press enter.

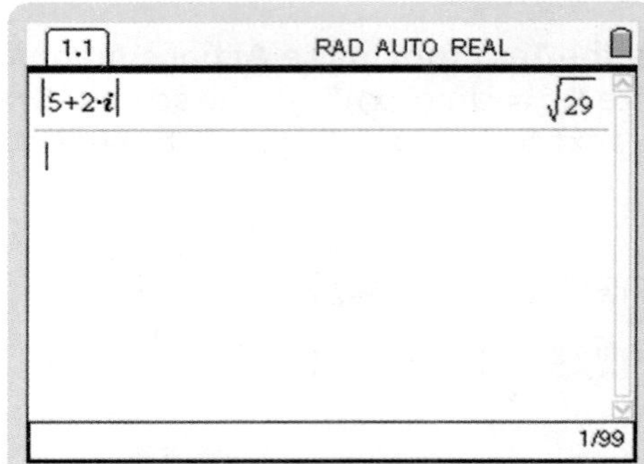

## Finding Complex Solutions, Lesson 6.05

1. Type C S O L V E (. Then type the equation, followed by a comma, and the variable to solve for.

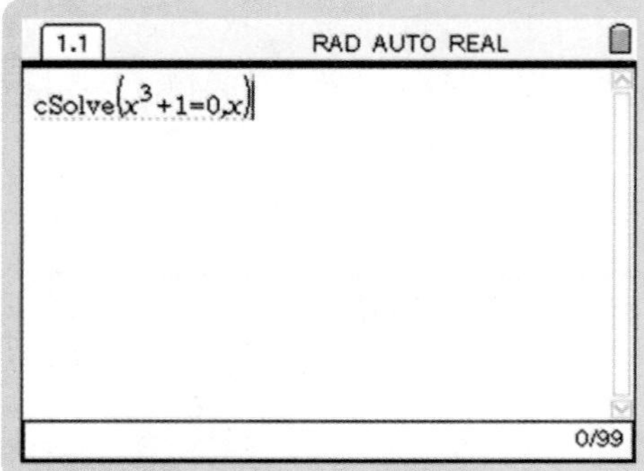

2. Press enter.

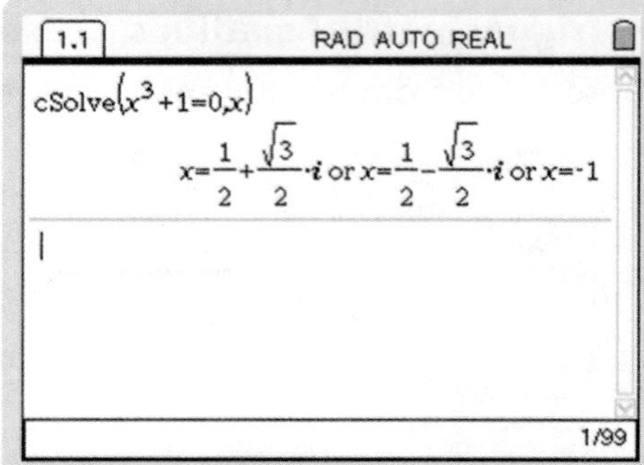

## Modeling a Piecewise Defined Function, Lesson 6.08

1. Choose **Define** from the **Actions** menu. Type P ( N , X ) =. Press ctrl × to access the templates palette. Choose the piecewise template.

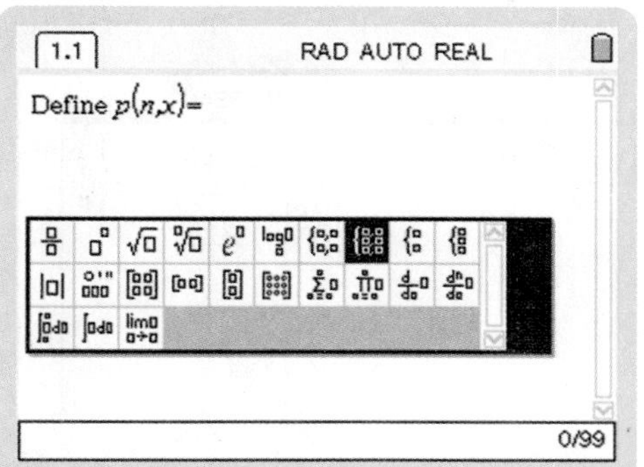


2. Select the correct number of function pieces, 3, in the dialog box. Press enter.

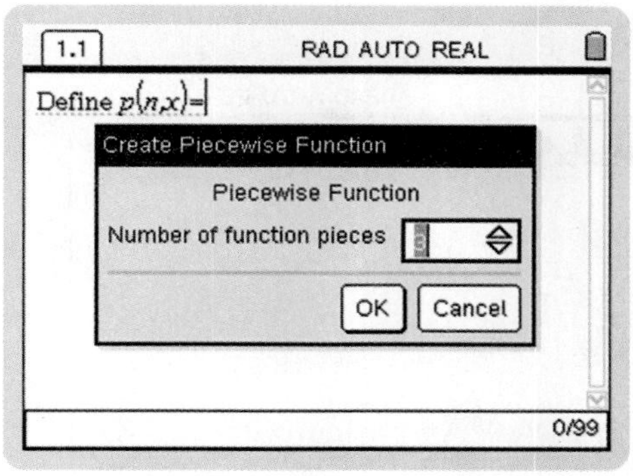

3. Press tab to move from box to box.

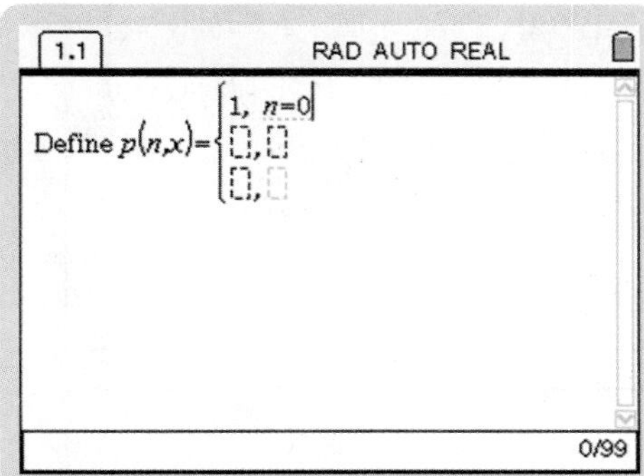


4. Complete the function definition. Press enter.

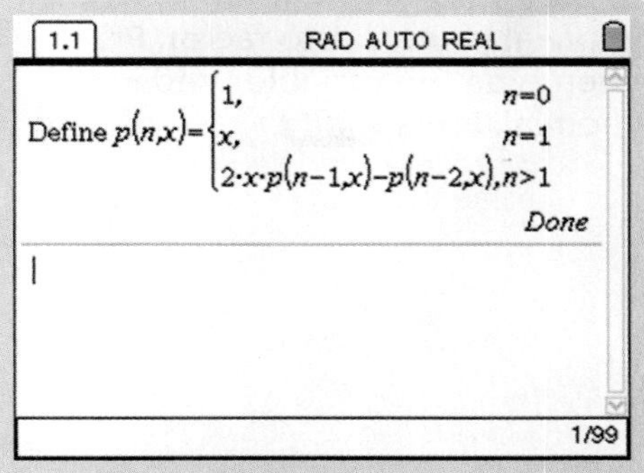


## Using the polyRemainder Function, Lesson 6.09

1. Choose the **Polynomial Tools** submenu from the **Algebra** menu. Choose **Remainder of Polynomial**.

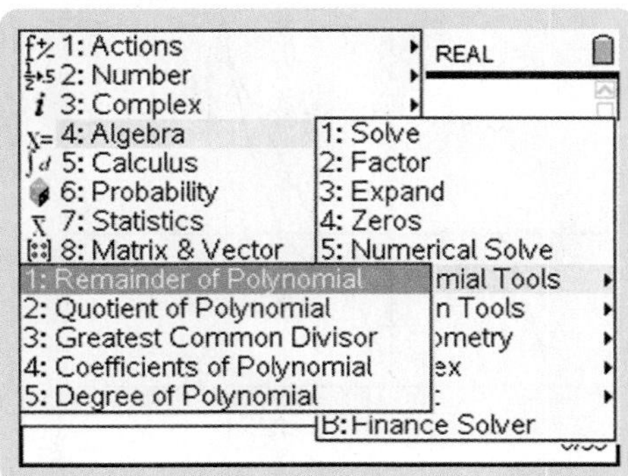


2. Enter two polynomials. The first is divided by the second. Press enter. The result is the remainder of the polynomial division.

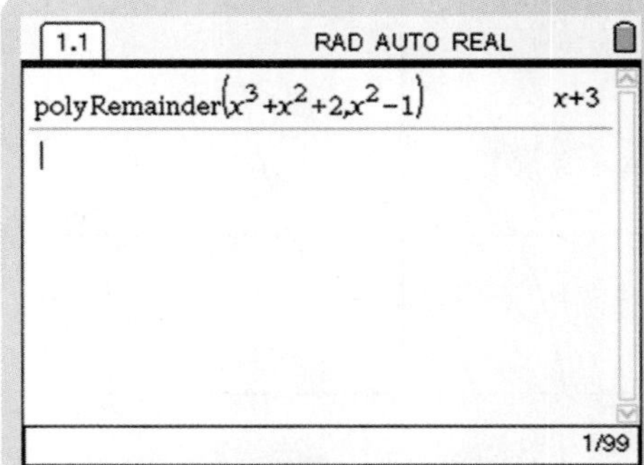

## Factoring a Polynomial Over ℤ, ℝ, and ℂ, Lesson 6.09

1. To factor a polynomial over ℤ, press F A C T O R (, then type the polynomial you want to factor. Press enter.

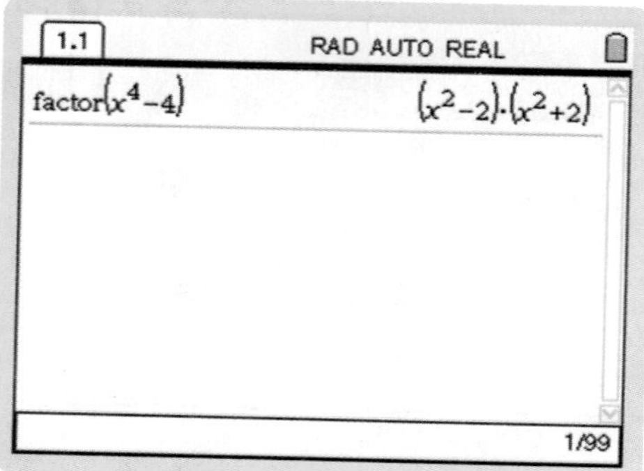


2. To factor a polynomial over ℝ, press F A C T O R (, then type the polynomial you want to factor. Press ,, then type the variable used in the polynomial. Press enter.

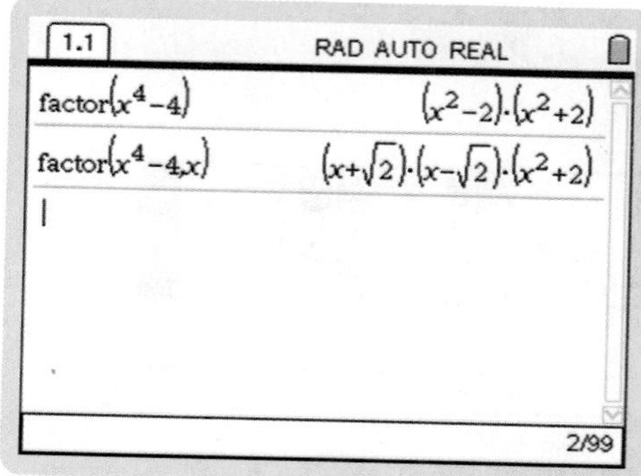


3. To factor a polynomial over ℂ, press C F A C T O R (. Then type the polynomial you want to factor. Press ,, then type the variable used in the polynomial. Press enter.

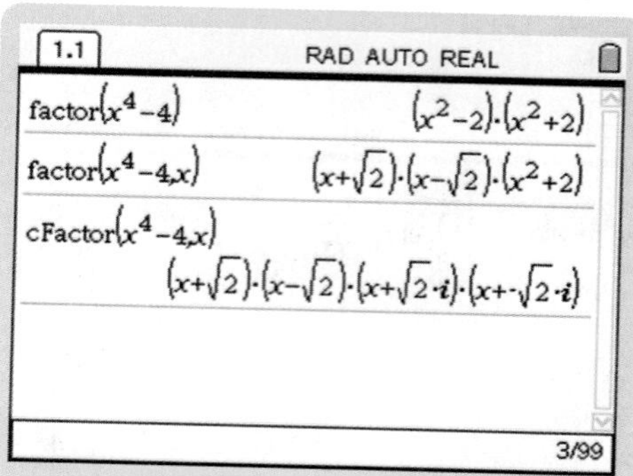


## Finding the Equation of a Secant Line, Lesson 7.03

1. Graph the equation.

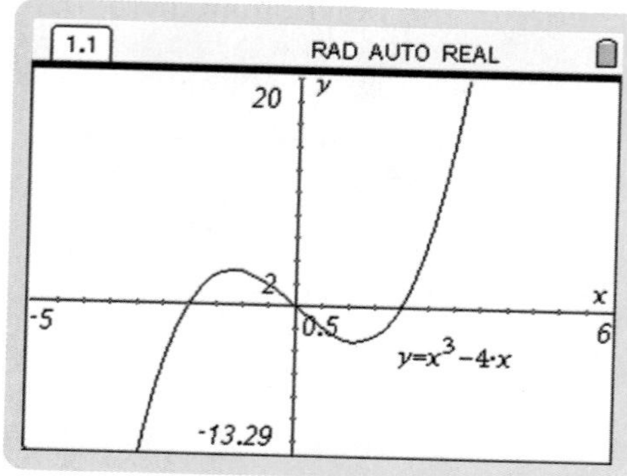


2. Follow steps 2–5 of *Finding the Slope of a Line Secant to a Sine Curve* to construct a secant line.

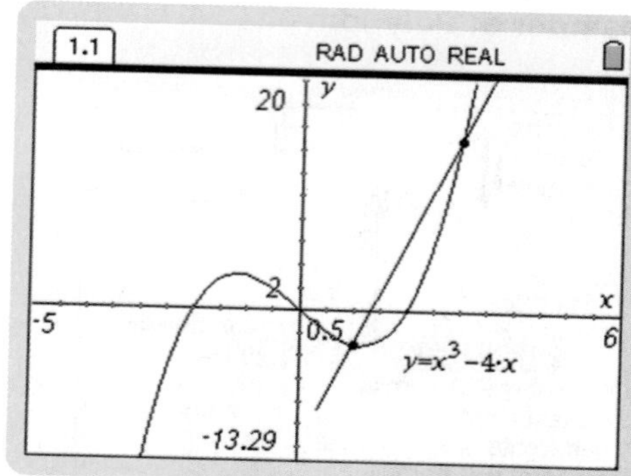

## Finding the Equation of a Secant Line (continued)

3. Choose **Coordinate and Equations** from the **Actions** menu. Place the cursor on the secant line. Press **enter**.

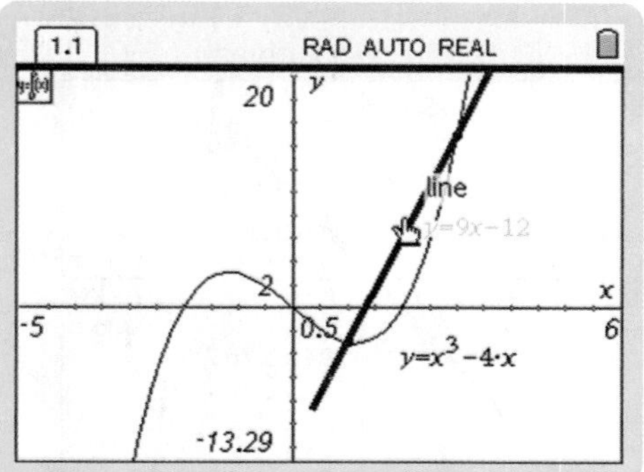


4. Move the cursor to drag the equation to the desired location. Press **enter** to anchor it.

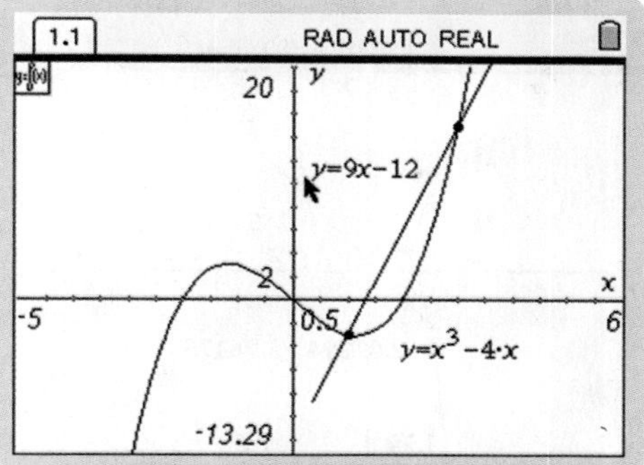


## Finding the Slope of a Secant Line, Lesson 7.03

1. Graph the equation $y = x^3 - 2x + 1$.

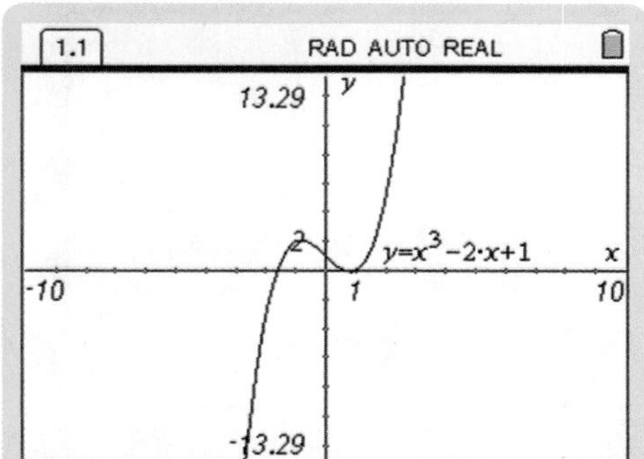


2. Choose **Point On** from the **Points & Lines** menu. Place the cursor on the curve. Press **enter**.

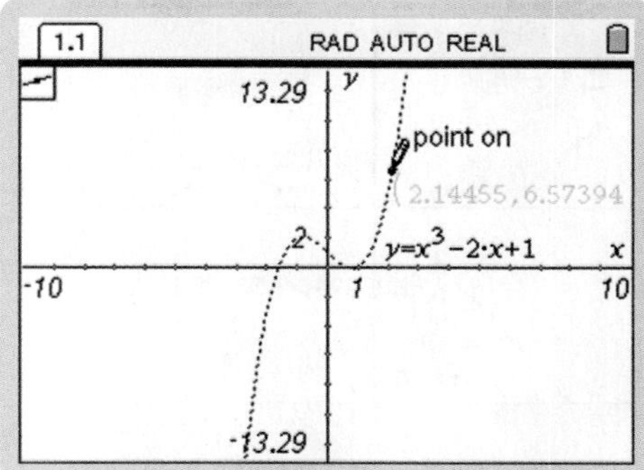


3. Place the cursor on the *x*-coordinate of the new point. Press ⊛ ⊛.

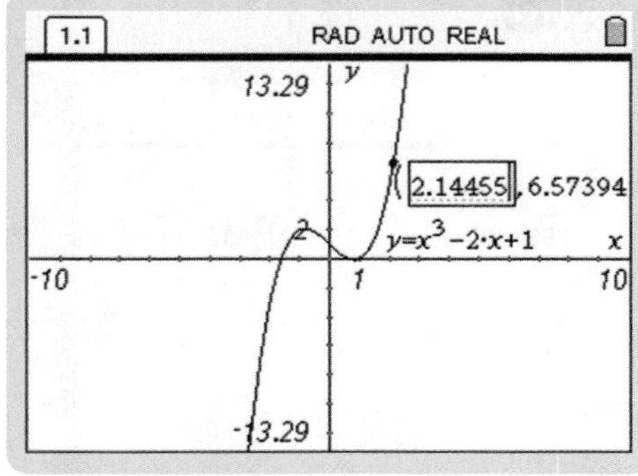


4. Press **ctrl** ⟵ to delete the *x*-coordinate. Press **2** to change the *x*-coordinate to 2. Press **enter**. The point jumps to $(2, f(2))$.

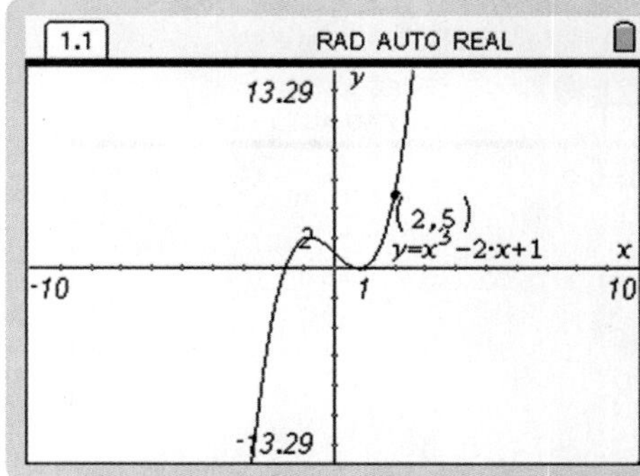

## Finding the Slope of a Secant Line (continued)

5. Construct a secant line through the point (2, 5). Label the other point the secant passes through *B*.

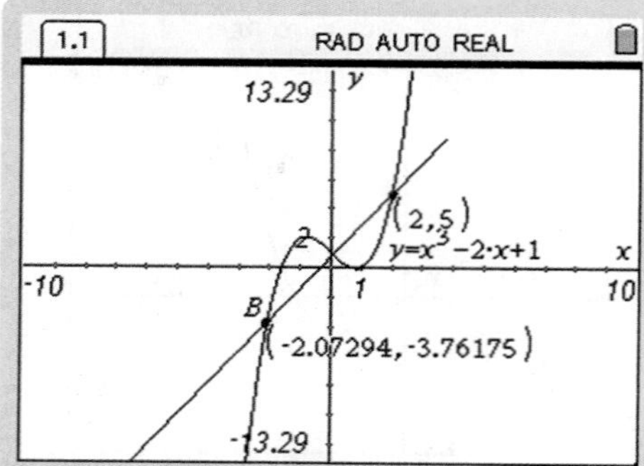


6. Choose **Slope** from the **Measurement** menu. Place the cursor on the secant line. Press enter.

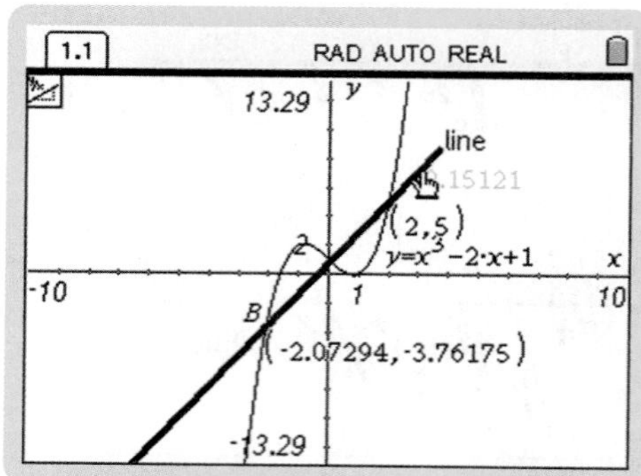


7. Move the cursor to drag the slope to the desired location. Press enter to anchor it.

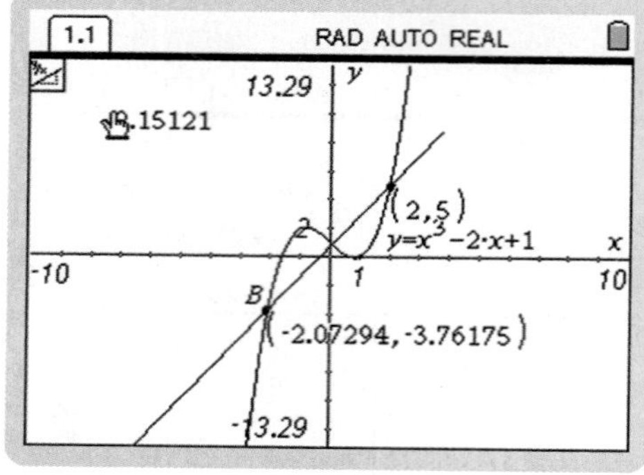


8. Place the cursor on point *B*. Press ctrl to grab it. Drag point *B* and observe how the slope of the secant changes.

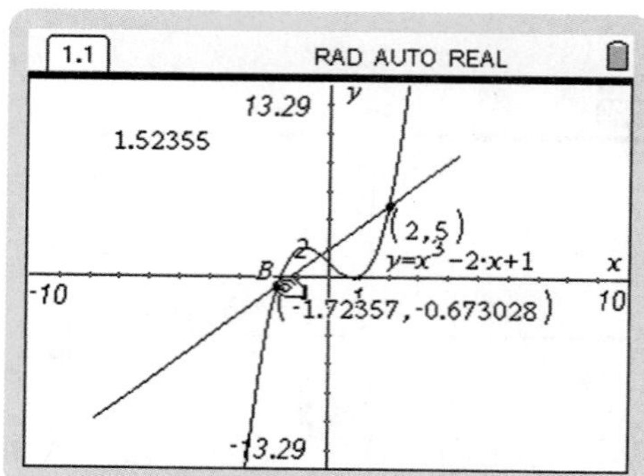


## Finding a Taylor Expansion, Lesson 7.04

1. Press T A Y L O R (.

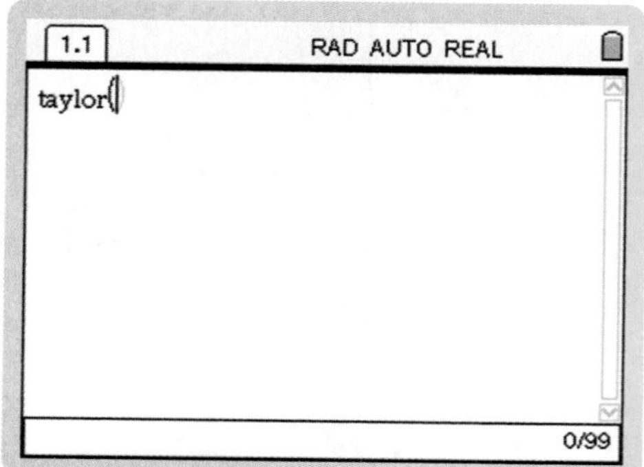


2. Enter the polynomial, the variable of the polynomial, the degree of the Taylor expansion, and the center of the expansion. Separate each with commas. Press enter.

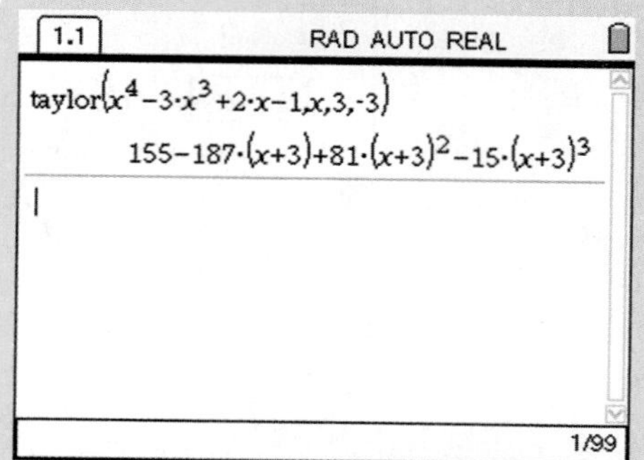

## Constructing a Tangent Line, Lesson 7.05

1. Choose **Point On** from the **Points & Lines** menu. Place the cursor on the curve. Press enter.

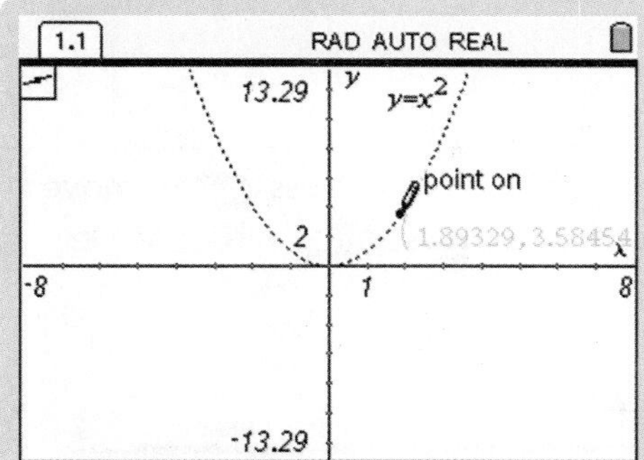


2. Choose **Tangent** from the **Points & Lines** menu. Place the cursor on the point. Press enter.

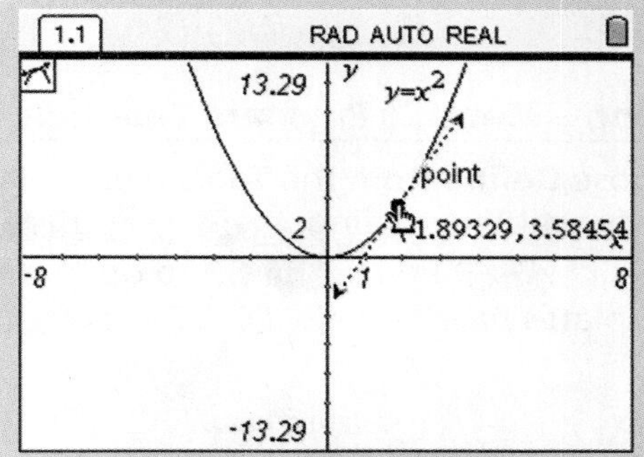


3. Place the cursor on the point. Press ctrl (click) to grab it. Drag the point to the desired location. The line remains tangent to the curve at the point.

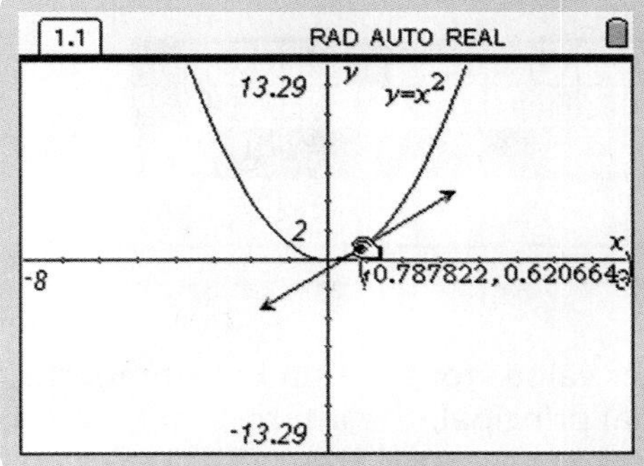


## Modeling a Recursive Function II, Lesson 7.09

1. Choose **Define** from the **Actions** menu. Name the function by typing G ( N ) =. Press ctrl (×) to open the Templates palette. Select (piecewise template). Press enter.

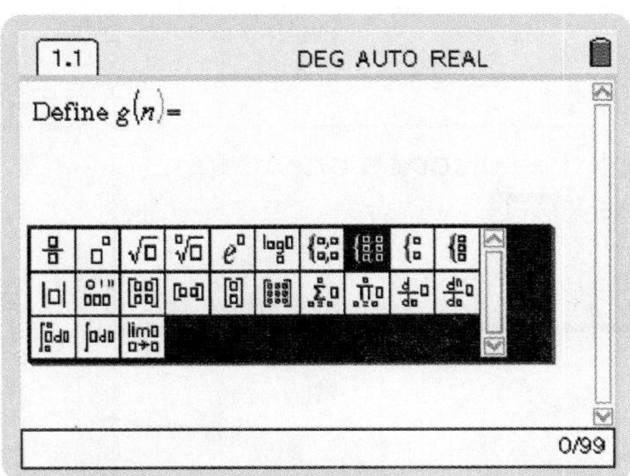


2. Select the number of pieces in the definition. Press enter.

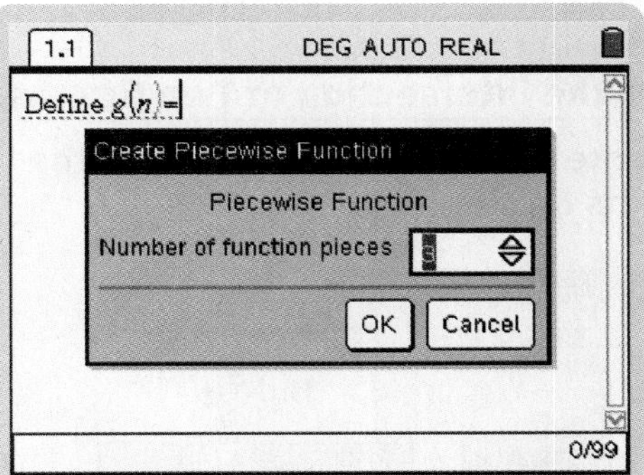

## Modeling a Recursive Function II (continued)

3. Enter the function. Press tab to move from box to box. Press enter when done.

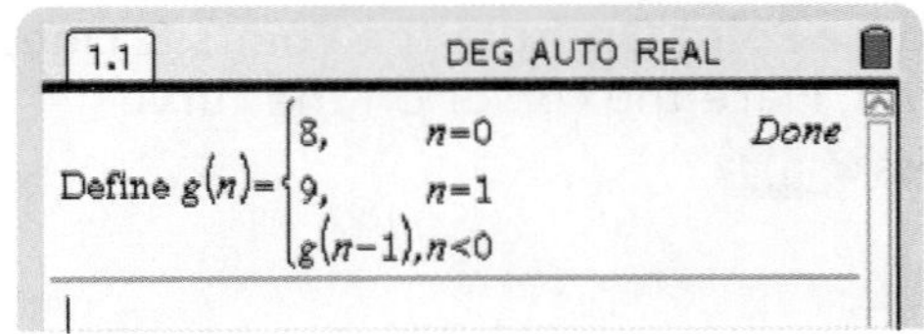


## Modeling a Monthly Payment Function, Lesson 7.10

1. Choose **Define** from the **Tools** menu. Name the function by typing B ( N , C , I , M ) =. Press ctrl × to open the Templates palette. Select [template]. Press enter.

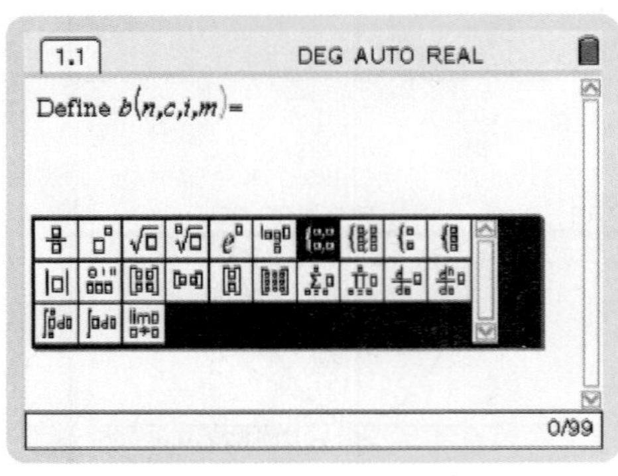


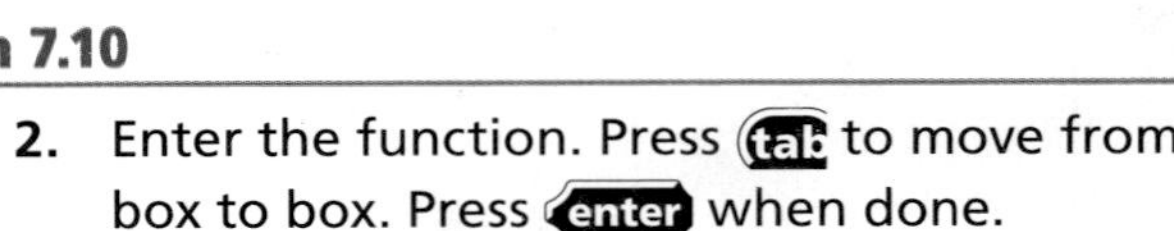

2. Enter the function. Press tab to move from box to box. Press enter when done.

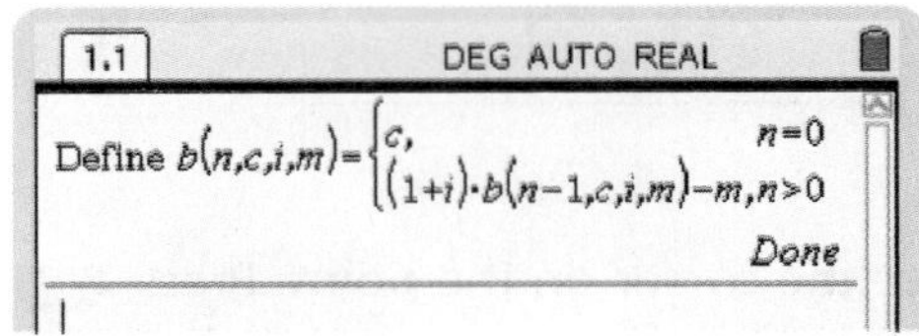


3. Enter values for the number of months, the initial principal, the interest rate, and the monthly payment. Press enter to calculate the current balance.

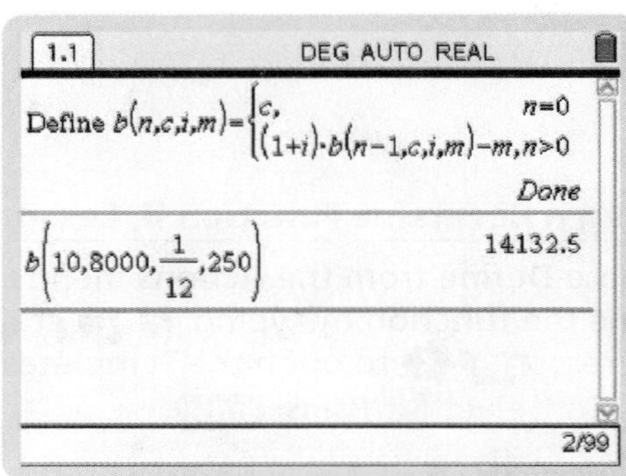


## Finding the Intersection of Two Graphs, Lessons 8.02, 8.09

1. Choose **Intersection Point(s)** from the **Points & Lines** menu.

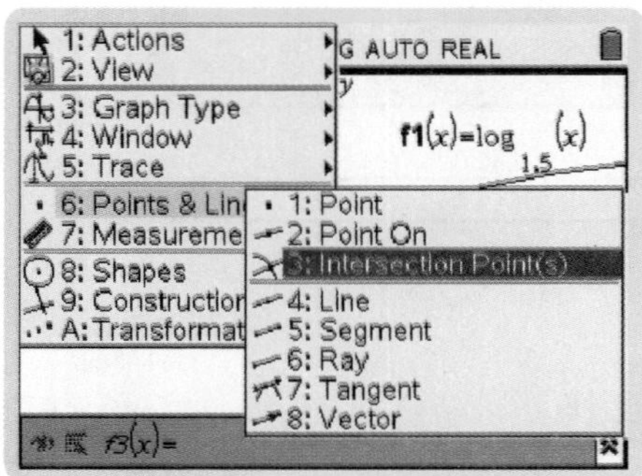


2. Place the cursor on one graph. Press enter.

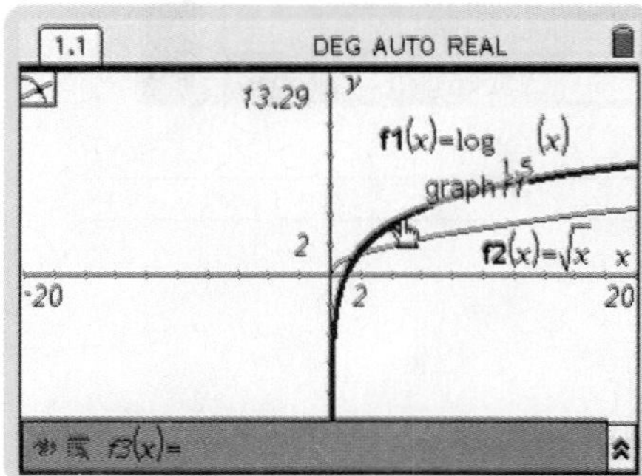

## Finding the Intersection of Two Graphs (continued)

3. Place the cursor on the other graph. Press enter.

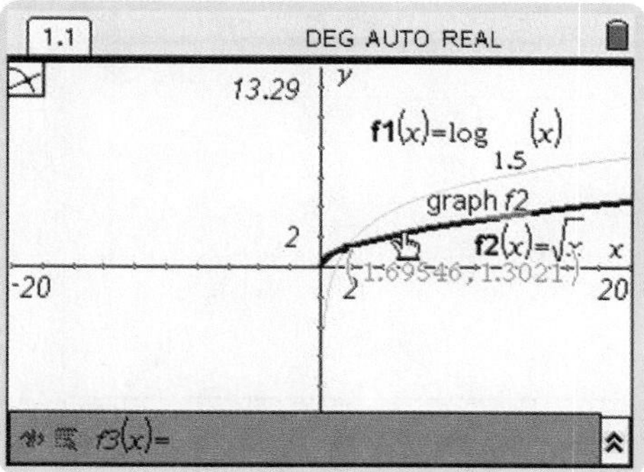

4. Move the cursor to drag the coordinates of the point of intersection. Press enter to anchor the coordinates.

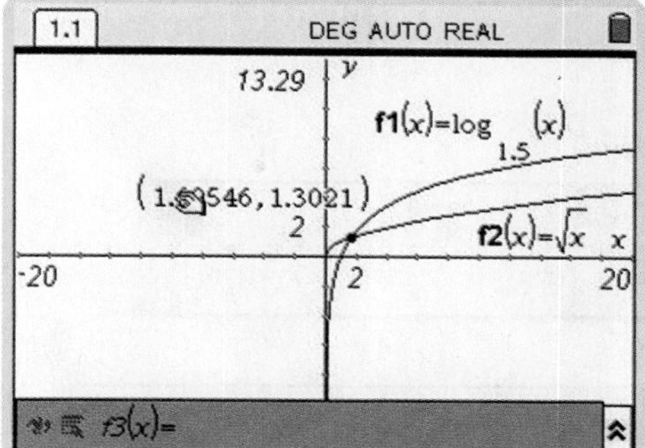

## Modeling Exponential Growth, Lesson 8.05

1. Choose **Solve** from the **Algebra** menu.

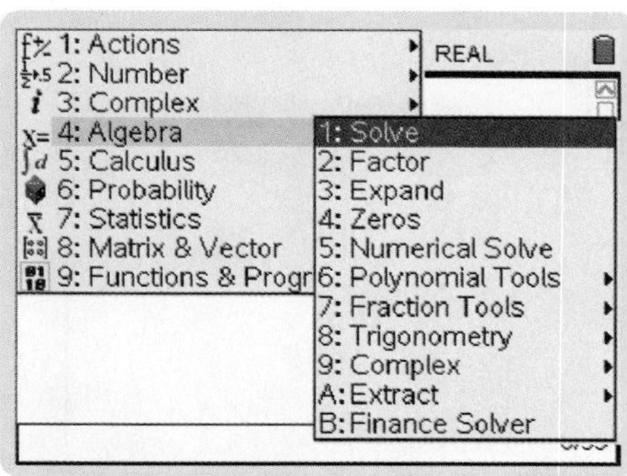

2. Type the equation $1000 = 500(1.03)^n$ to model an initial investment of \$500 growing to \$1000 at an interest rate of 3% per year. Press ·, N, enter to find the number of years needed to reach \$1000.

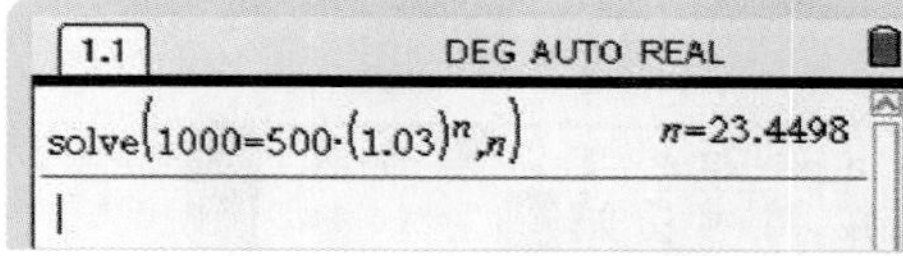

## Using the Logarithm Template, Lesson 8.07

1. Press ctrl × to open the Templates palette. Select $\log_{\square}\square$. Press enter.

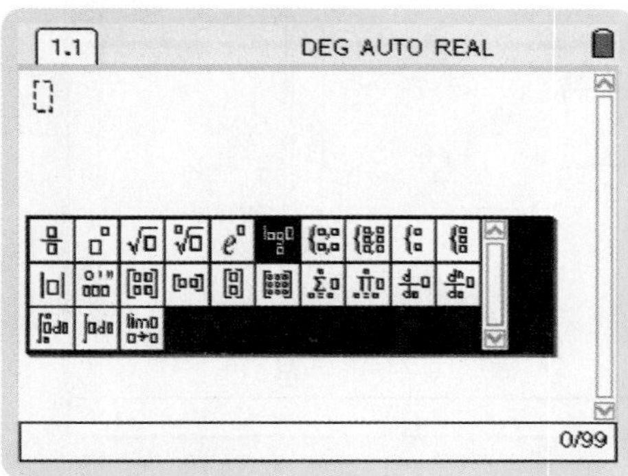

2. Press tab to move from box to box. Press enter when done.

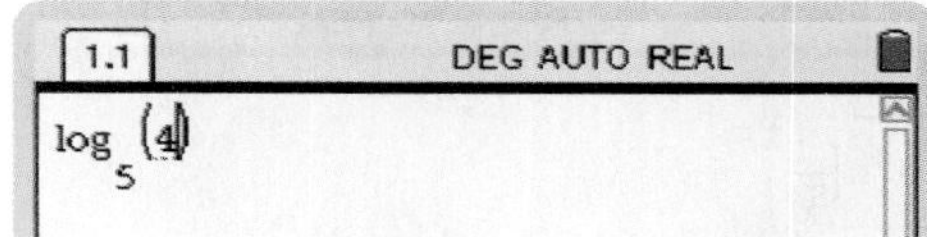

## Using the Number *e*, Lesson 8.12

1. Press ctrl ⊗ to access the templates palette. Choose *e*.

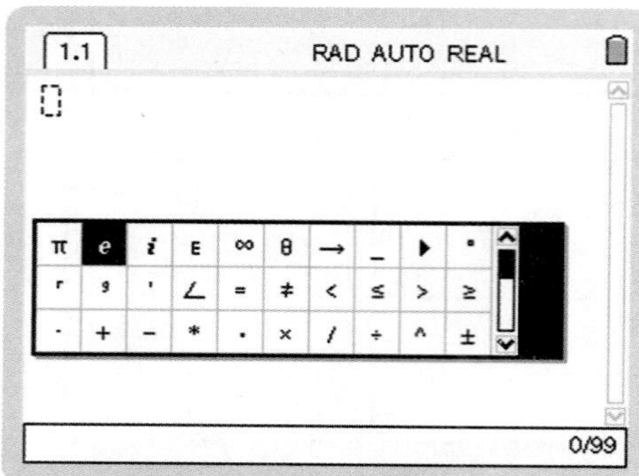


2. Press ctrl enter to find the approximate value of e.

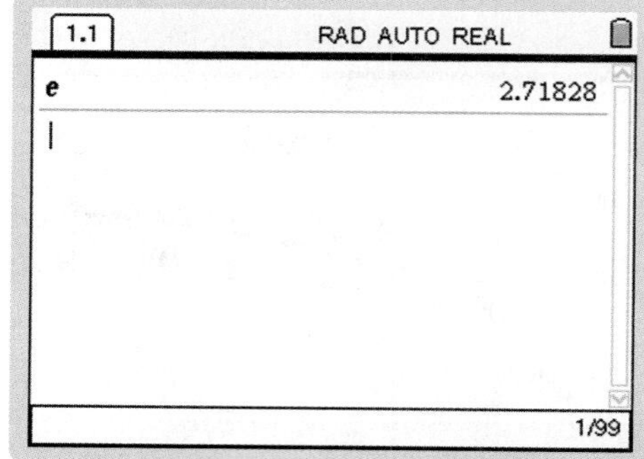


## Evaluating an Infinite Sum, Lessons 8.12, 8.13

1. Press ctrl ⊗ to access the templates palette. Choose Σ.

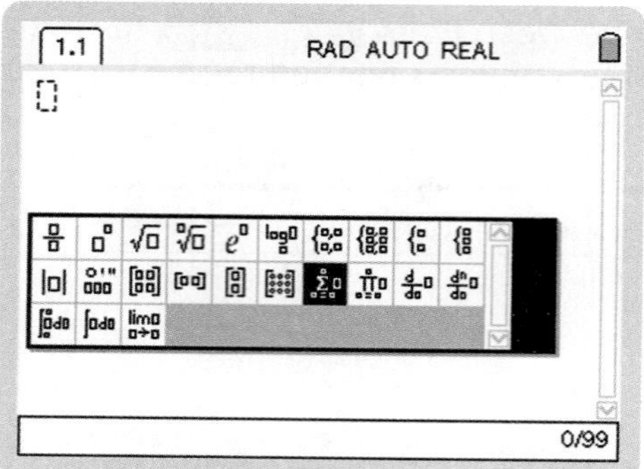


2. Press tab to move from box to box.

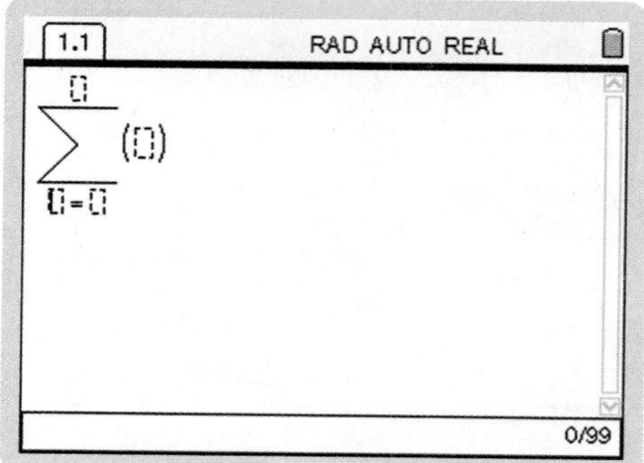


3. To enter ∞, press ctrl i.

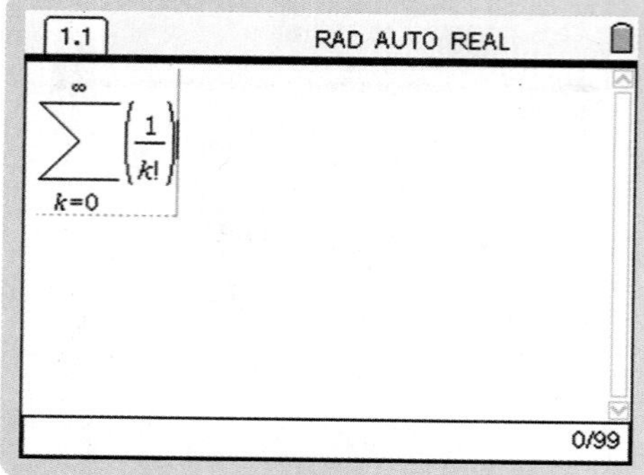


4. Press enter to evaluate the sum.

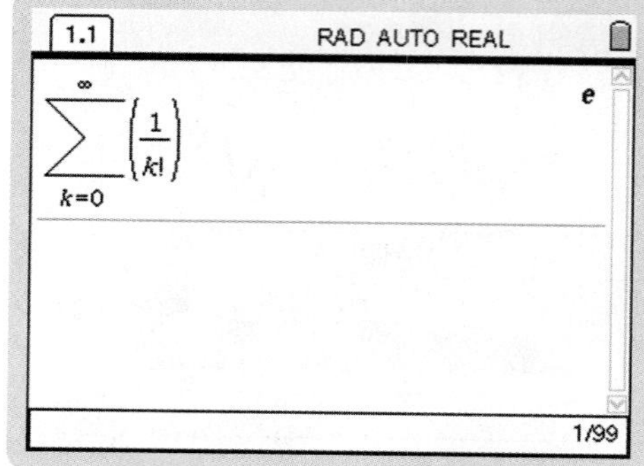

## Evaluating a Limit, Lesson 8.12

1. Press ctrl ⌫ to access the templates palette. Choose [lim template].

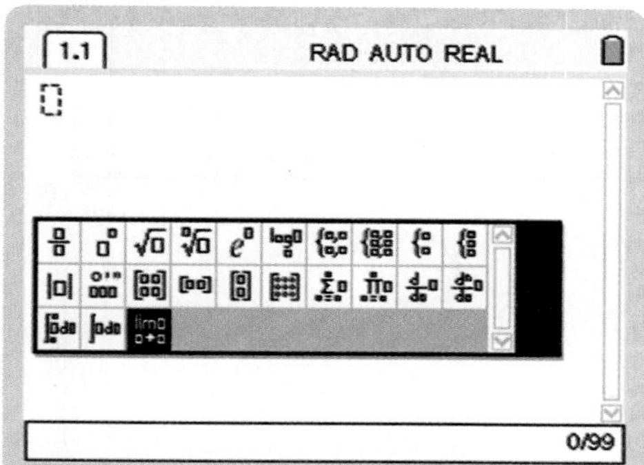


2. Press tab to move from box to box. To enter ∞ Press ctrl i.

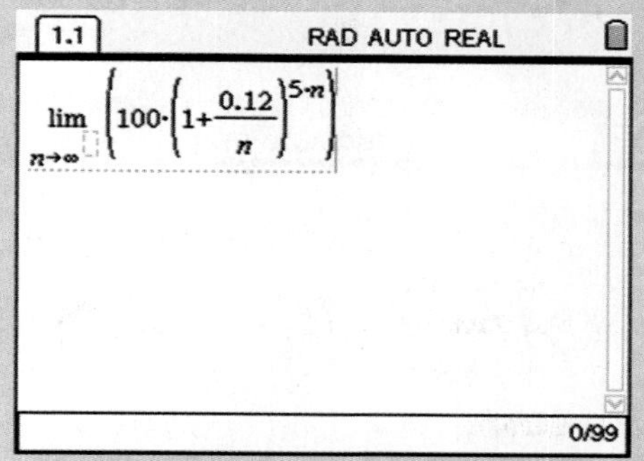


3. Press enter to evaluate the limit.

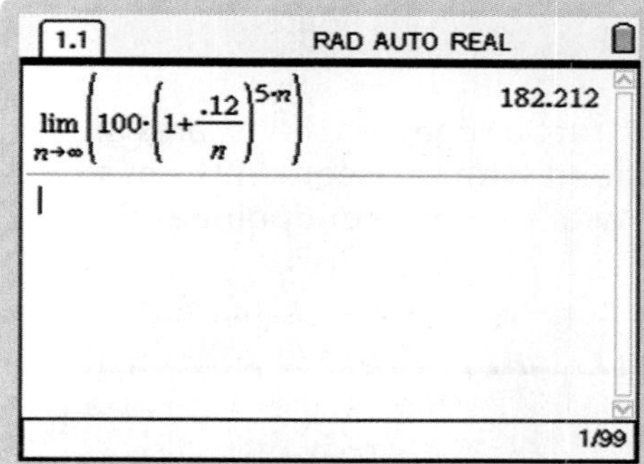


## Graphing a Function (Graphing View Only), Lesson 9.05

1. Tab down to the entry line at the bottom of the screen. Type an expression in *x*.

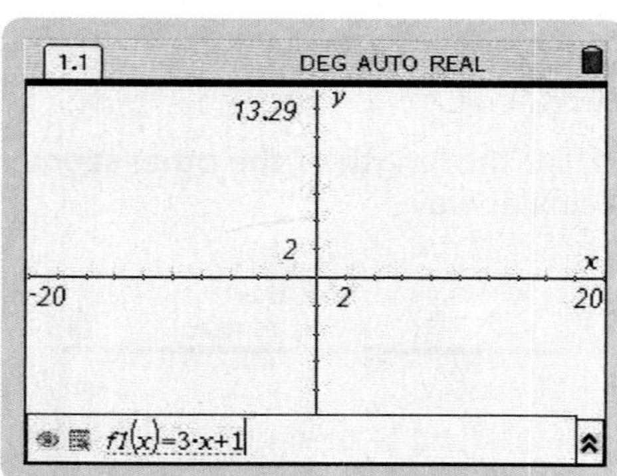


2. Press enter.

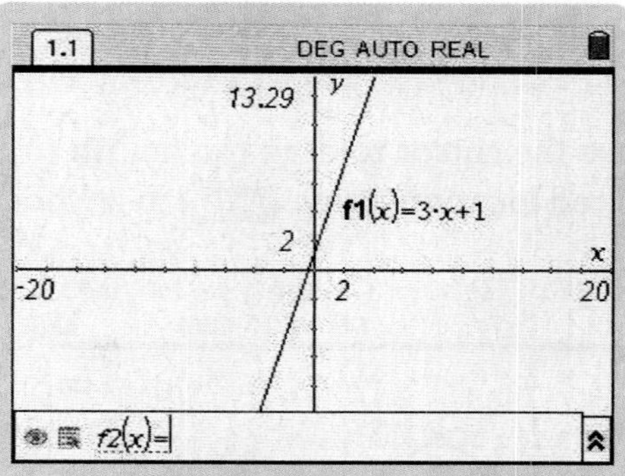


TI-Nspire Handbook

## Constructing an Ellipse, Lesson 9.09

1. Choose **Point** from the **Points & Lines** menu. Press enter to place a point. Construct two points. Label them *F1* and *F2*.

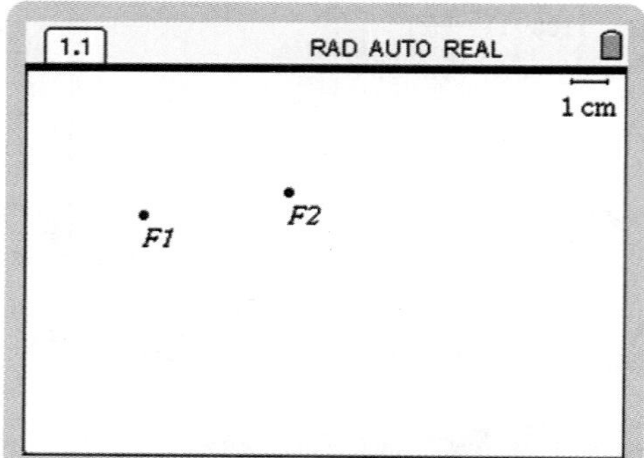


2. Choose **Segment** from the **Points & Lines** menu. Construct a segment with one endpoint at *F1*.

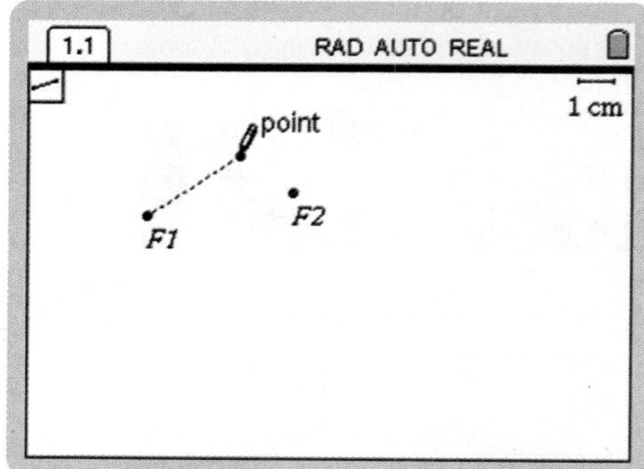


3. Construct a segment that shares an endpoint with the segment from step 2, and with the other endpoint at *F2*.

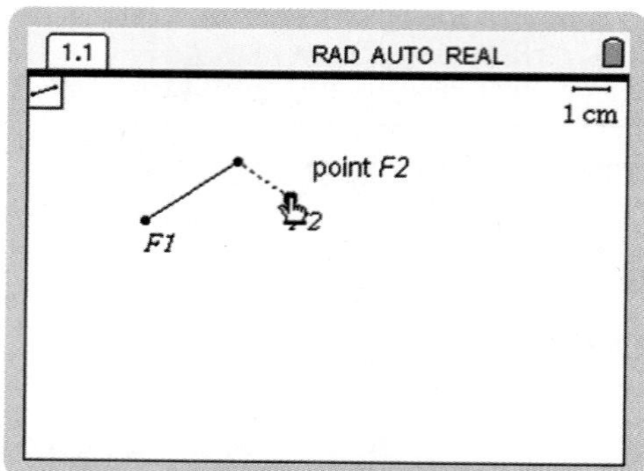


4. Choose **Length** from the **Measurement** menu. Place the cursor on the first segment. Press enter.

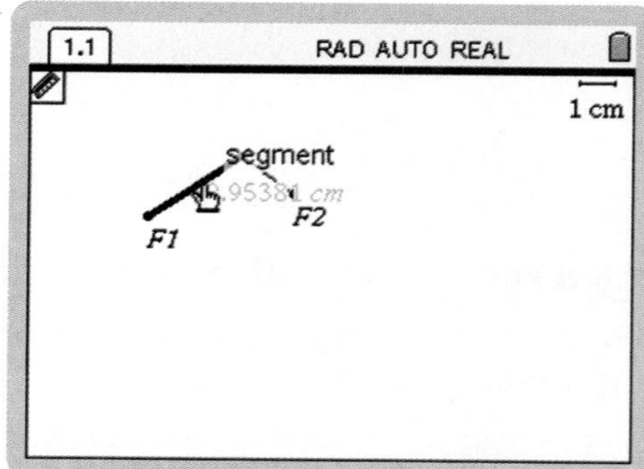


5. Move the cursor to drag the length to the desired location. Press enter to anchor it.

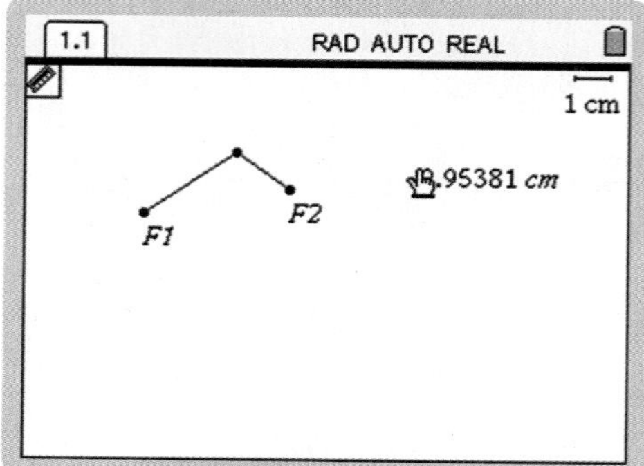


6. Measure the length of the other segment in a similar way.

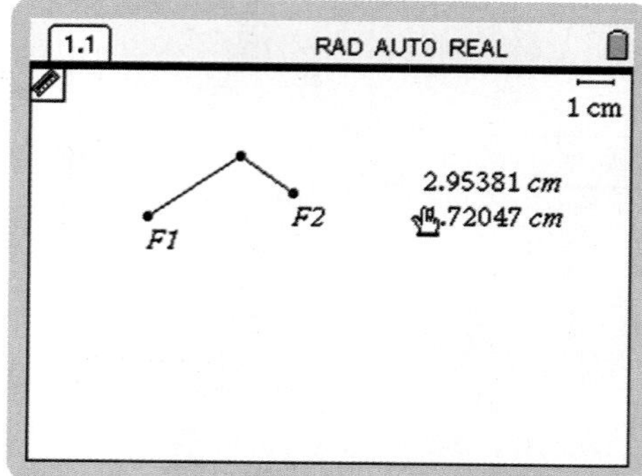

7. Choose **Text** from the **Actions** menu. Press enter on an open area of the screen. Press S 1 + S 2. Press enter.

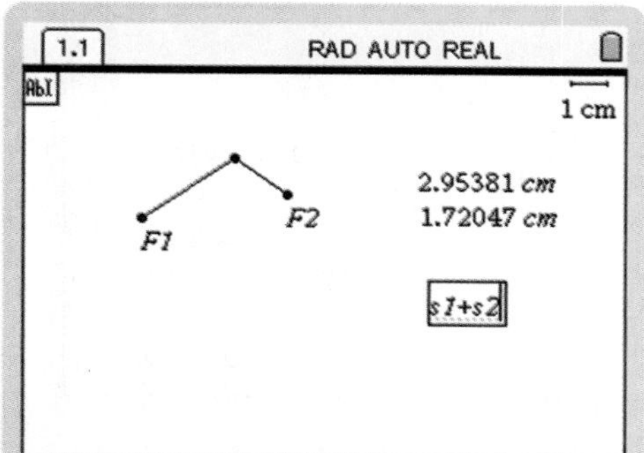


8. Choose **Calculate** from the **Actions** menu. Place the cursor on the expression *s1* + *s2*. Press enter.

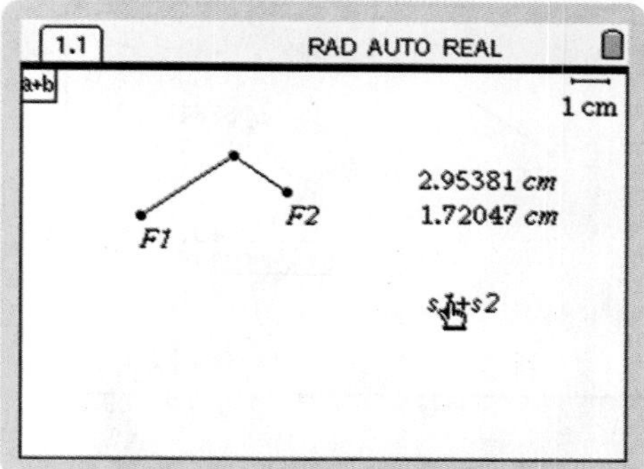


9. Place the cursor on the first segment length. Press enter.

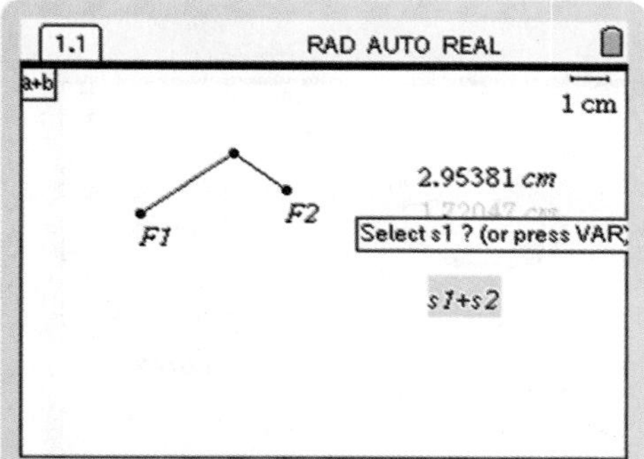


10. Place the cursor on the second segment length. Press enter.

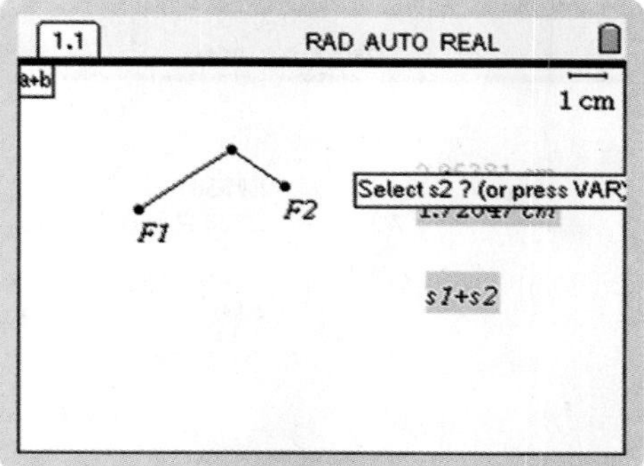


11. Move the cursor to drag the result of the calculation to the desired location. Press enter to anchor it.

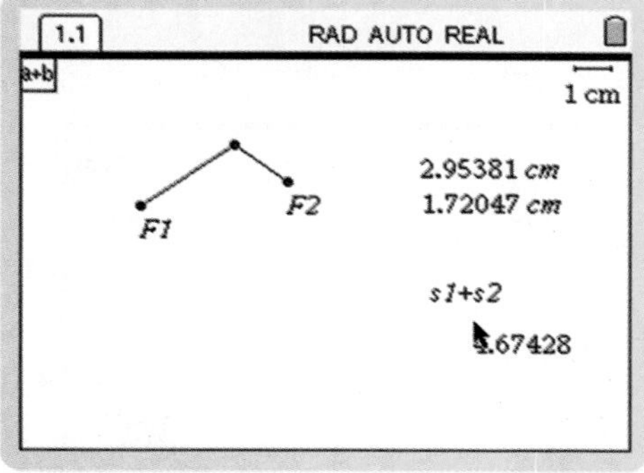


12. Place the cursor on the result of the calculation. Press ctrl menu. Choose **Attributes**.

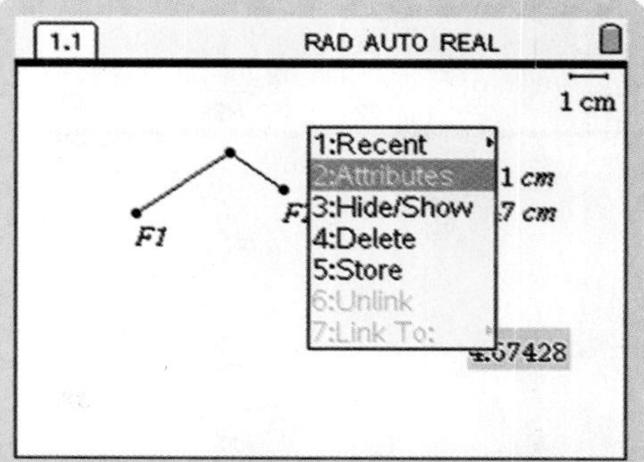

## Constructing an Ellipse (continued)

**13.** Press ▽ to select the Lock/Unlock attribute.

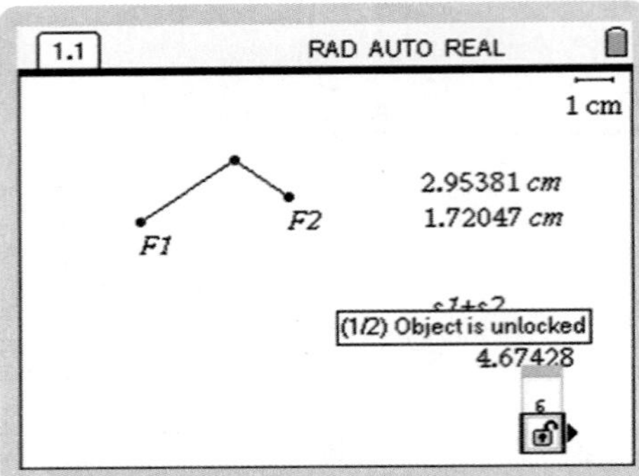


**14.** Press ▷ enter to lock the sum.

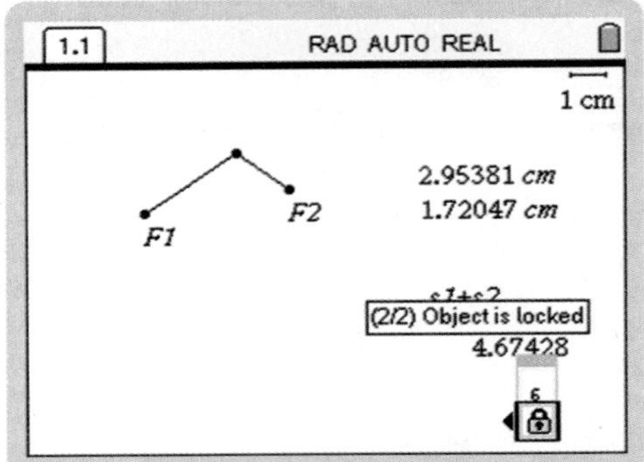


**15.** Choose **Geometry Trace** from the **Trace** menu. Place the cursor on the common endpoint of the two segments. Press enter. Press ctrl ☉ to grab the point.

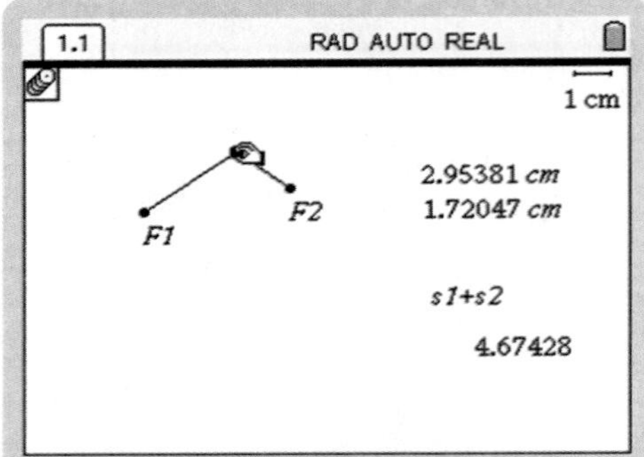


**16.** Drag the point. The sum of the lengths of the two segments remains constant. The point traces the path of an ellipse.

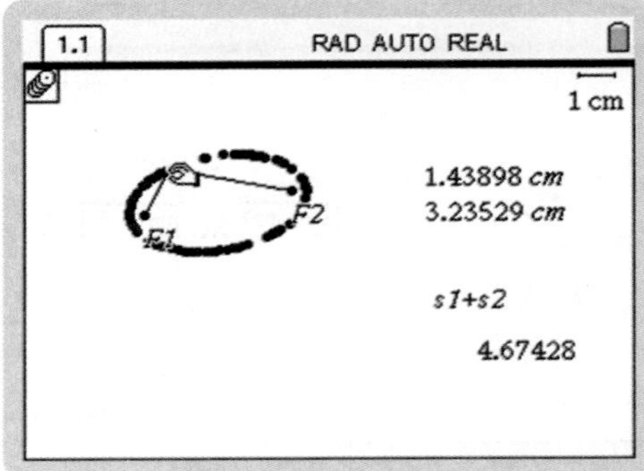


## Constructing a Parabola, Lesson 9.09

**1.** Choose **Line** from the **Points & Lines** menu. Draw the directrix. Label the line *d*.

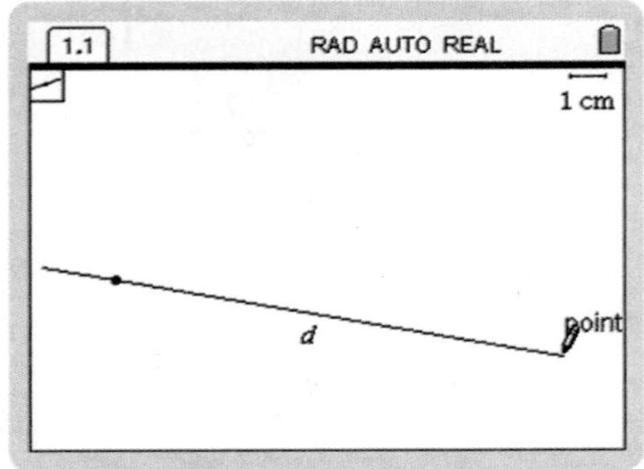


**2.** Choose **Point** from the **Points & Lines** menu. Place the focus on the screen. Label the point *F*.

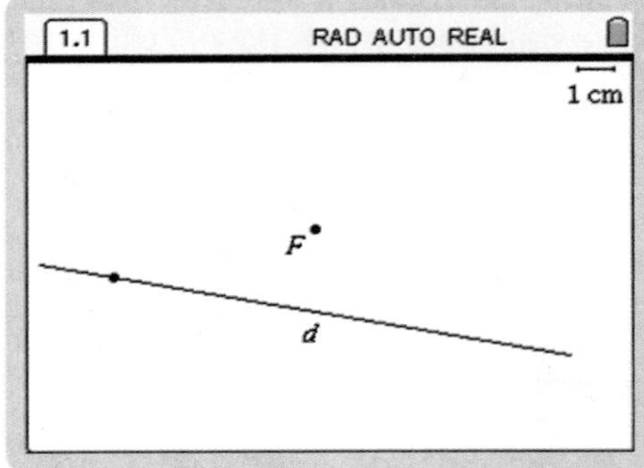

## Constructing a Parabola (continued)

3. Choose **Segment** from the **Points & Lines** menu. Place the cursor on line *d*. Press **enter**. Place the cursor on point *F*. Press **enter**.

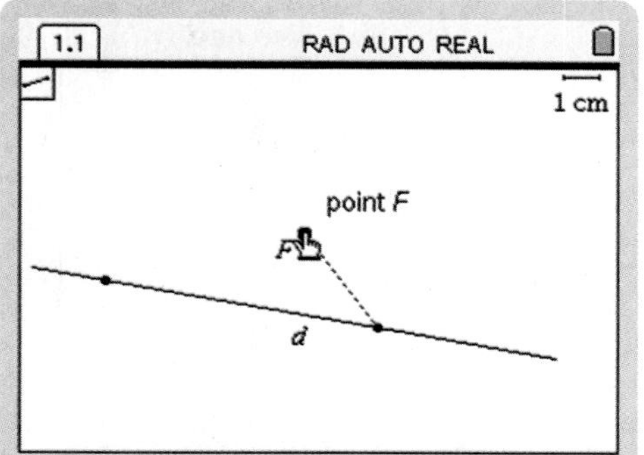


4. Choose **Perpendicular Bisector** from the **Construction** menu. Place the cursor on the segment. Press **enter**.

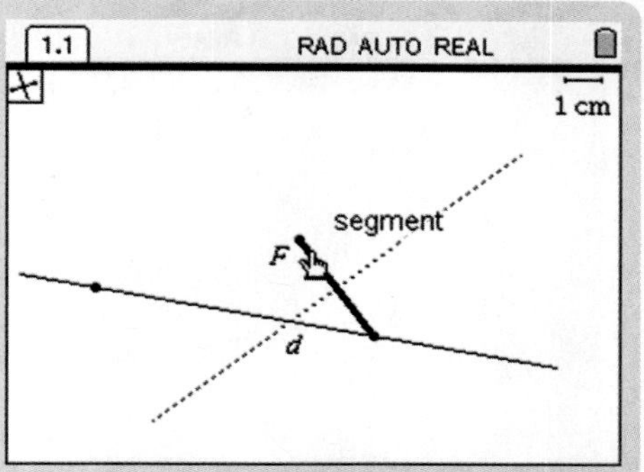


5. Choose **Perpendicular** from the **Construction** menu. Place the cursor on line *d*. Press **enter**. Place the cursor on the intersection of line *d* and the segment. Press **enter**.

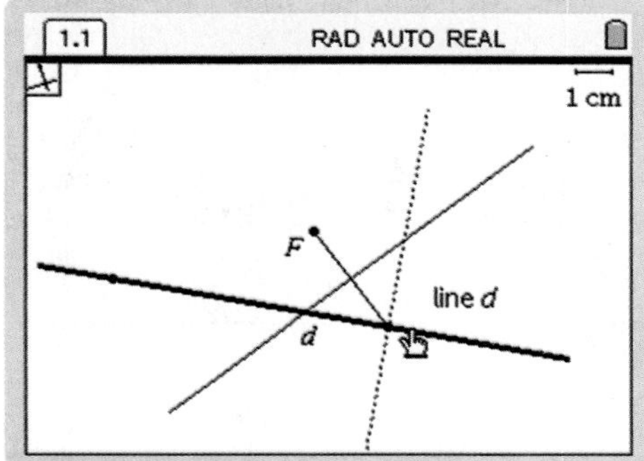


6. Choose **Intersection Point(s)** from the **Points & Lines** menu. Place the cursor on the perpendicular line you constructed in step 5. Press **enter**.

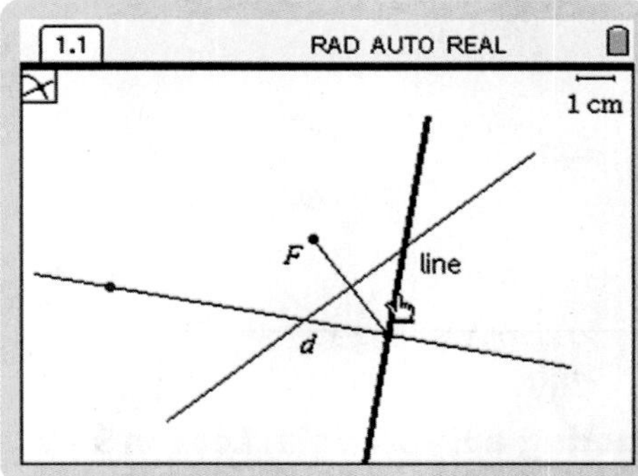


7. Place the cursor on the perpendicular bisector you constructed in step 4. Press **enter**.

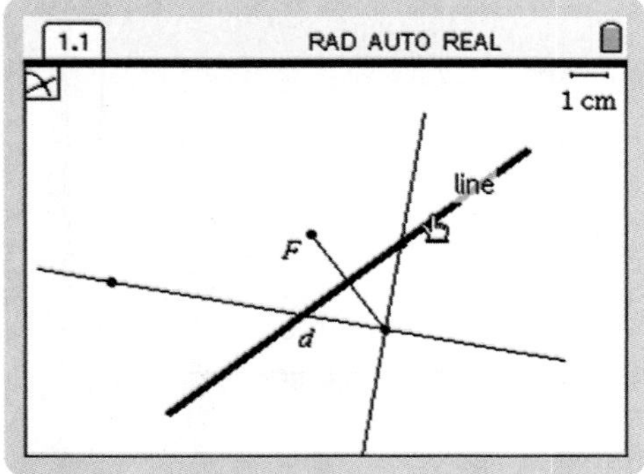


8. Choose **Hide/Show** from the **Actions** menu. Place the cursor on the perpendicular bisector from step 4. Press **enter** to hide the line.

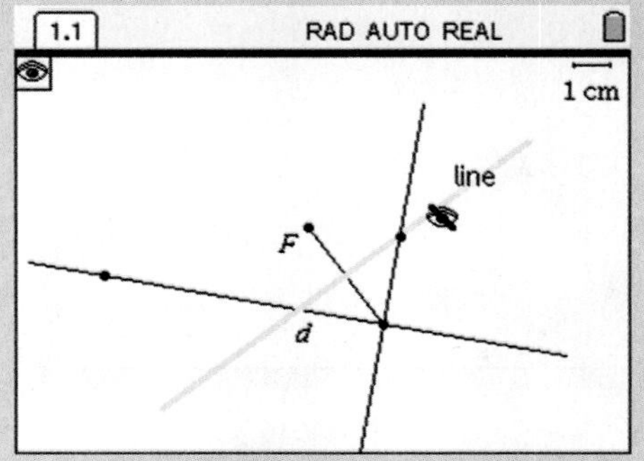

## Constructing a Parabola (continued)

9. Hide the segment and the line perpendicular to the directrix in the same way.

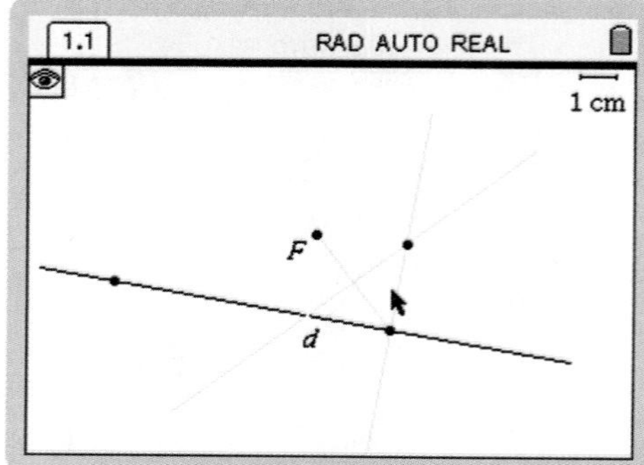


10. Choose **Locus** from the **Construction** menu. Place the cursor on the intersection point you constructed in step 7. Press **enter**.

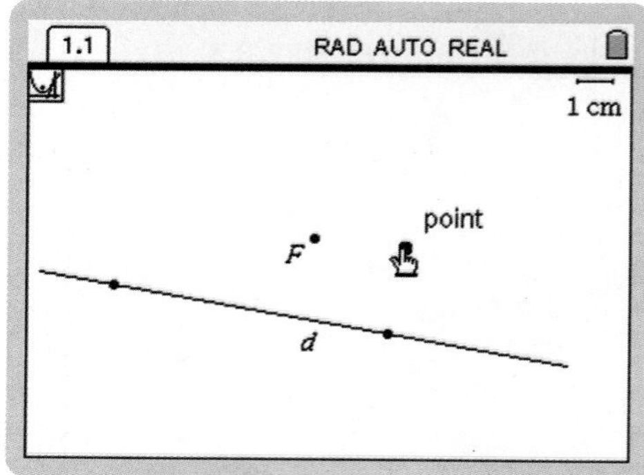


11. Place the cursor on the intersection of the directrix and the segment you constructed in step 3.

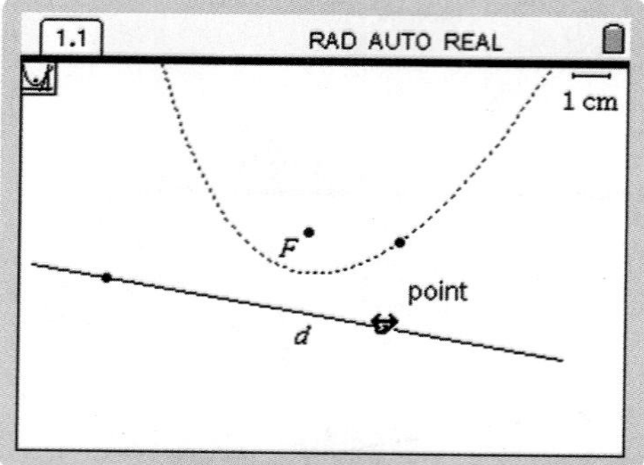


12. Press **enter** to construct the parabola.

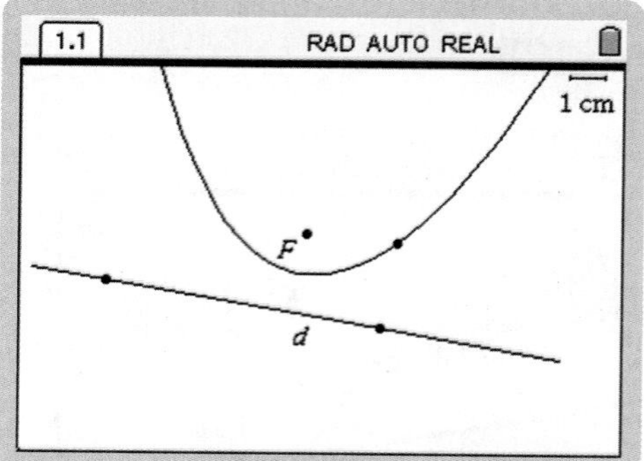


## Constructing a Hyperbola, Lesson 9.09

1. Choose **Point** from the **Points & Lines** menu. Place two points on the screen. Label them *F1* and *F2*.

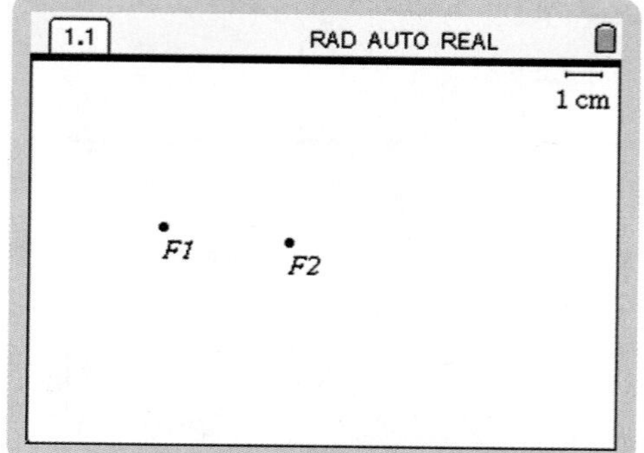


2. Choose **Segment** from the **Points & Lines** menu. Construct two segments with endpoints *F1* and *F2* that have a common endpoint.

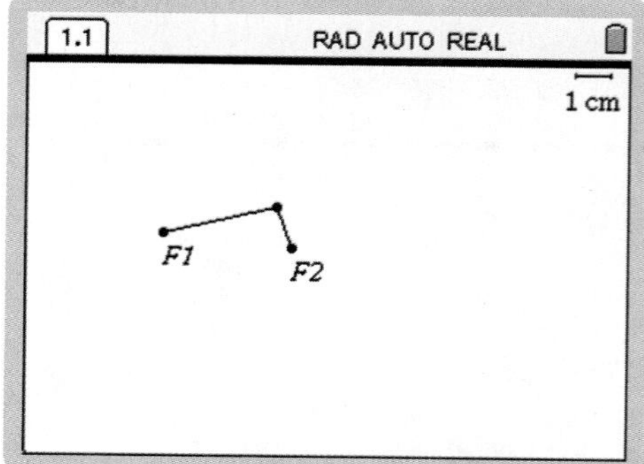

## Constructing a Hyperbola (continued)

3. Choose **Length** from the **Measurement** menu. Place the cursor on the first segment. Press **enter**. Move the cursor to drag the length to the desired location. Press **enter** to anchor it.

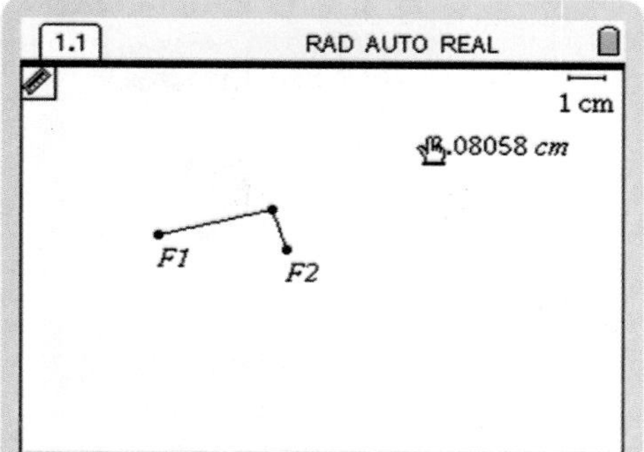


4. Find the length of the second segment in the same way.

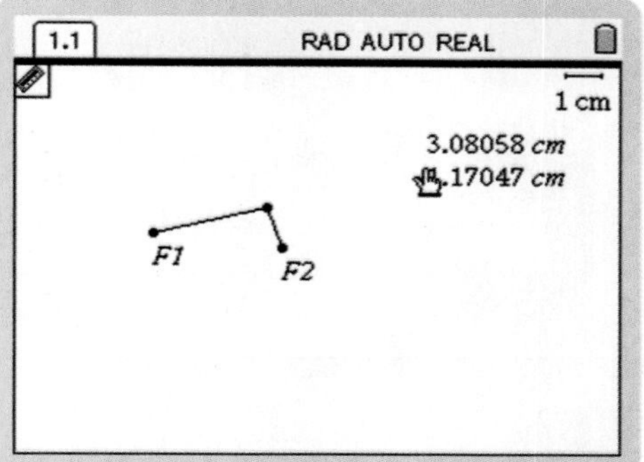


5. Choose **Text** from the **Actions** menu. Click on an open part of the screen. Type **A** **B** **S** **(** **S** **1** **−** **S** **2** **)**. Press **enter**.

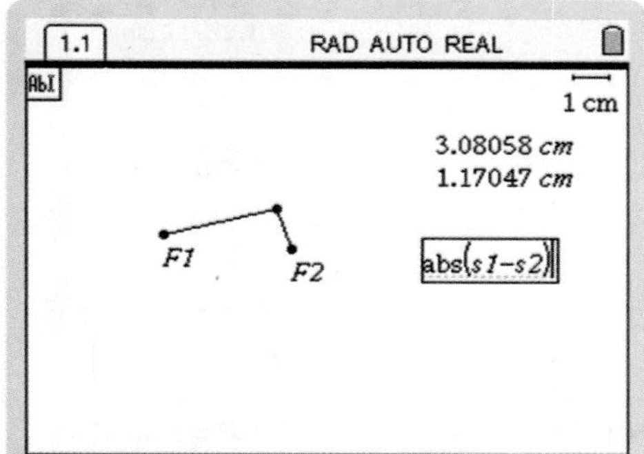


6. Choose **Calculate** from the **Actions** menu. Place the cursor on the text you wrote in step 5. Press **enter**.

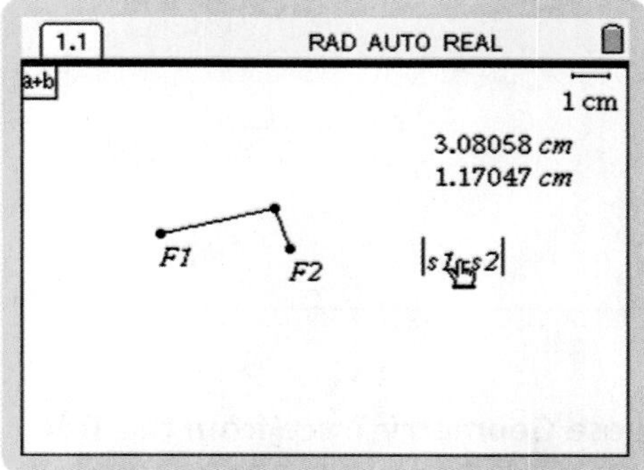


7. Place the cursor on the first length. Press **enter**.

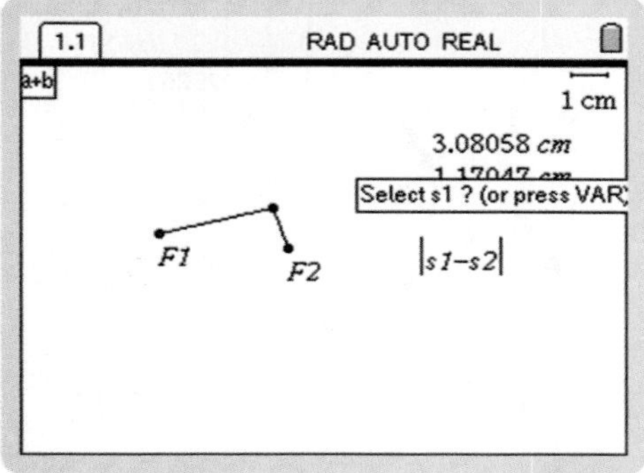


8. Place the cursor on the second length. Press **enter**.

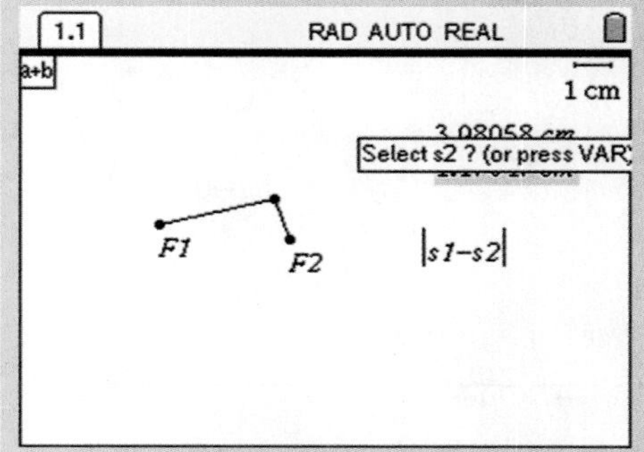

## Constructing a Hyperbola (continued)

9. Move the cursor to drag the result of the calculation to the desired location. Press enter to anchor it.

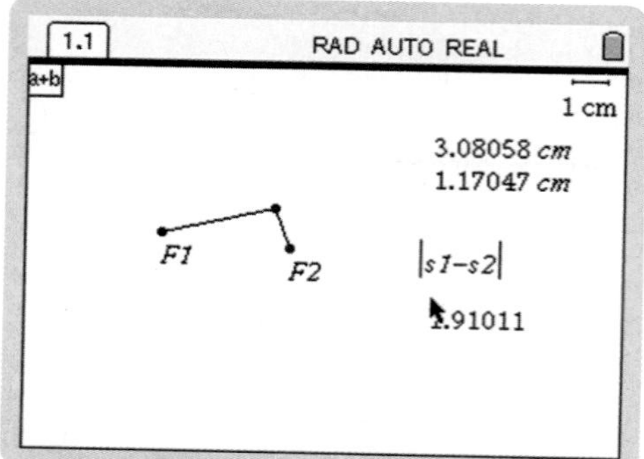


10. Place the cursor on the result of the calculation. Press ctrl menu. Choose **Attributes**.

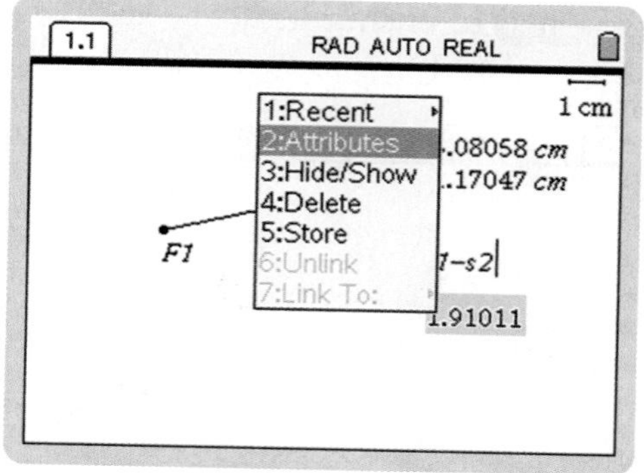


11. Press ▽ to select the Lock/Unlock attribute.

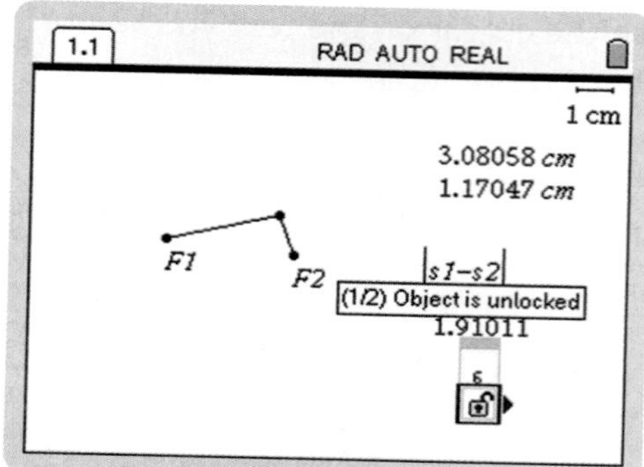


12. Press ▷ enter to lock the value of $|s1 - s2|$.

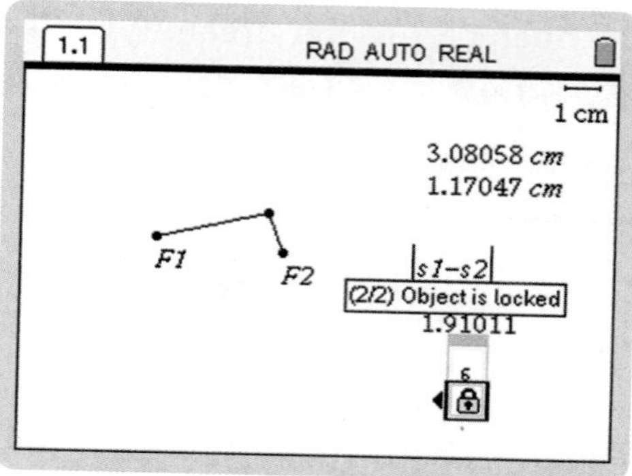


13. Choose **Geometry Trace** from the **Trace** menu. Place the cursor on the common endpoint of the two segments. Press enter. Press ctrl ⊛ to grab the point.

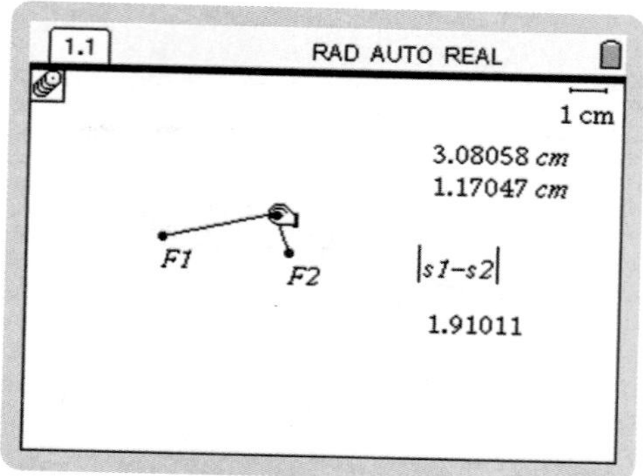


14. Drag the point. The absolute value of the difference of the lengths of the two segments remains constant. The point traces the path of an ellipse.

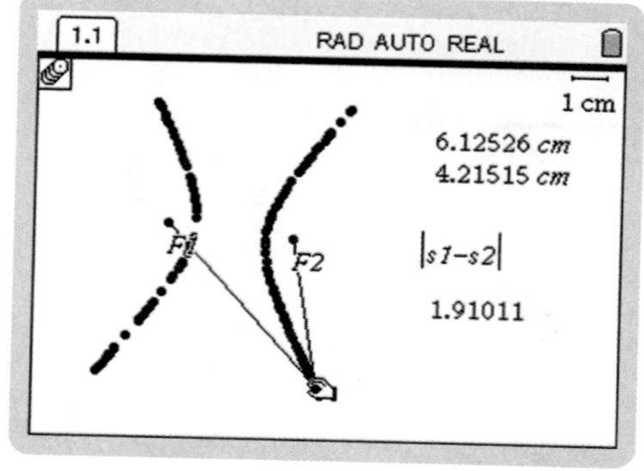

## Constructing Conic Sections Using Eccentricity, Lesson 9.12

1. Draw the directrix and focus. Label them *d* and *F* respectively.

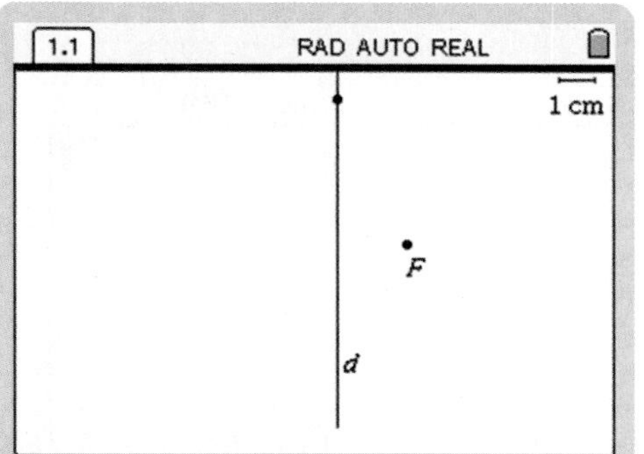


2. Draw two lines.

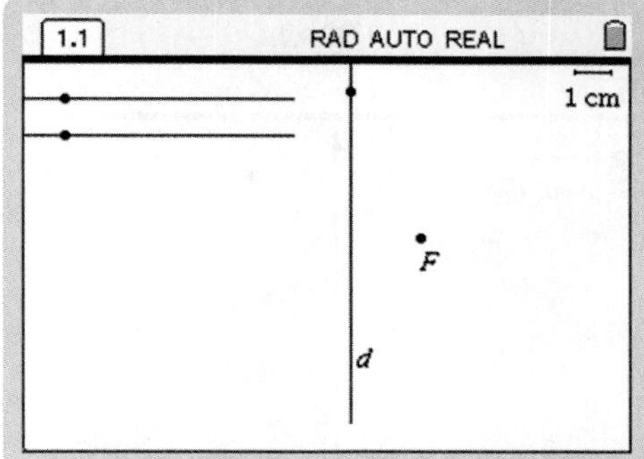


3. Construct a segment on each of the two lines you drew in step 2.

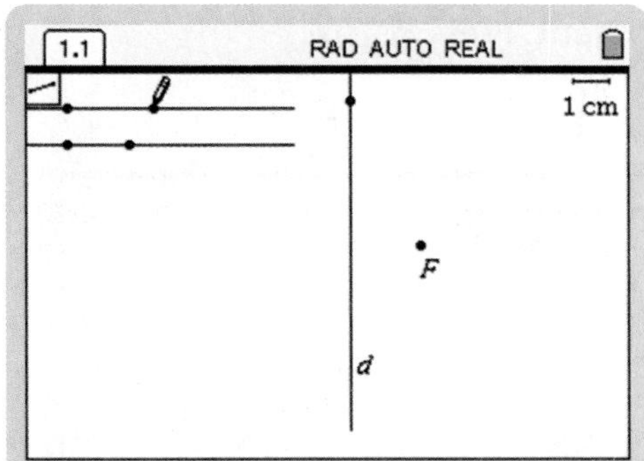


4. Use the **Hide/Show** tool to hide lines so that only the segments are visible.

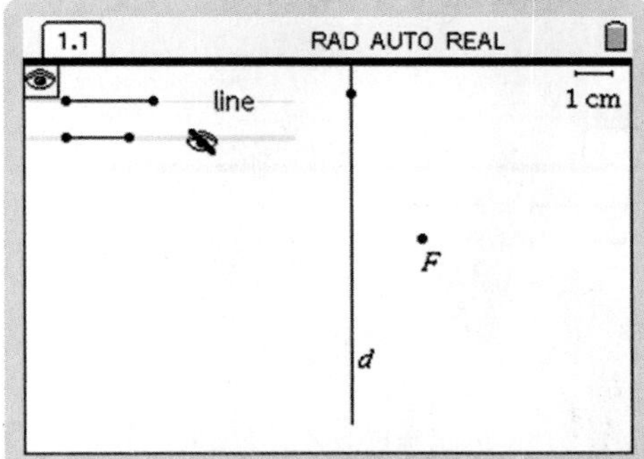


5. Use the **Length** tool from the **Measurment** menu to measure the length of the bottom segment. Drag the length to an open area of the screen.

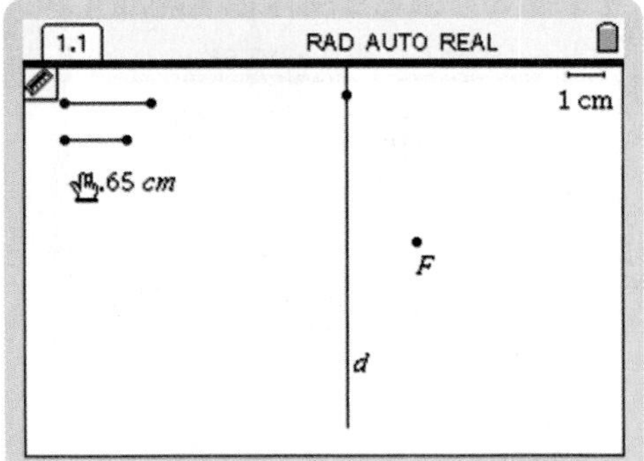


6. Double click on the length measurement. Move the cursor to the beginning of the text box. Press E = enter.

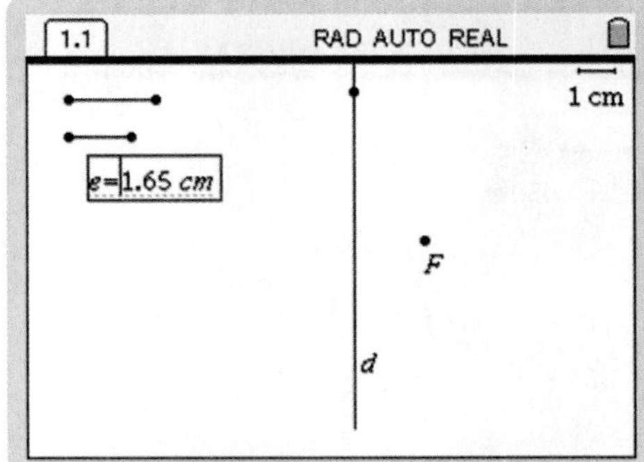

## Constructing Conic Sections Using Eccentricity (continued)

7. Choose **Dilate** from the **Transformation** menu. Place the cursor on the left endpoint of the top segment. Press **enter**.

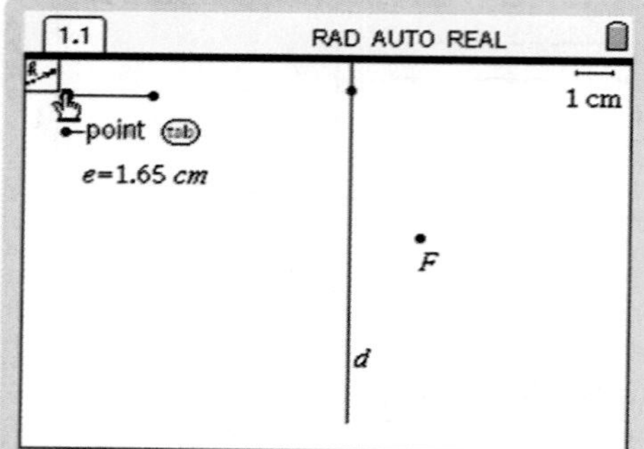


8. Place the cursor on the right endpoint of the top segment. Press **enter**.

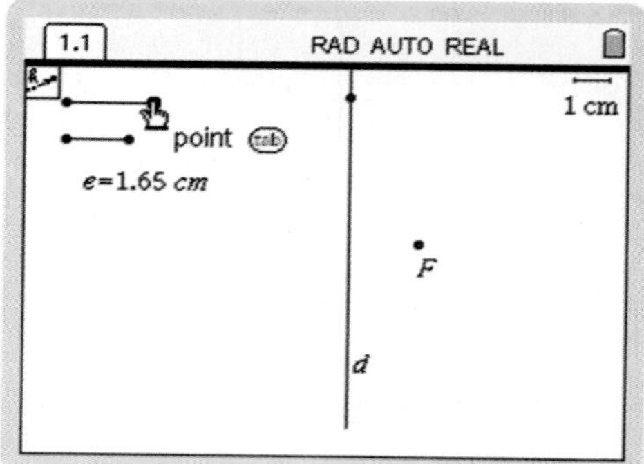


9. Place the cursor on the length measure. Press **enter**. A new point appears.

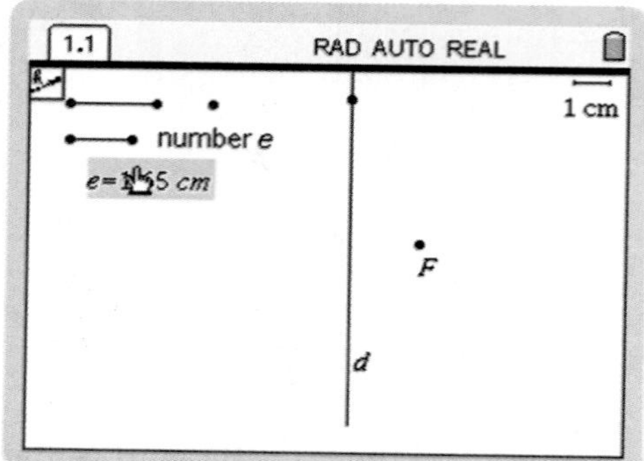


10. Choose **Compass** from the **Construction** menu. Place the cursor on the top segment. Press **enter**.

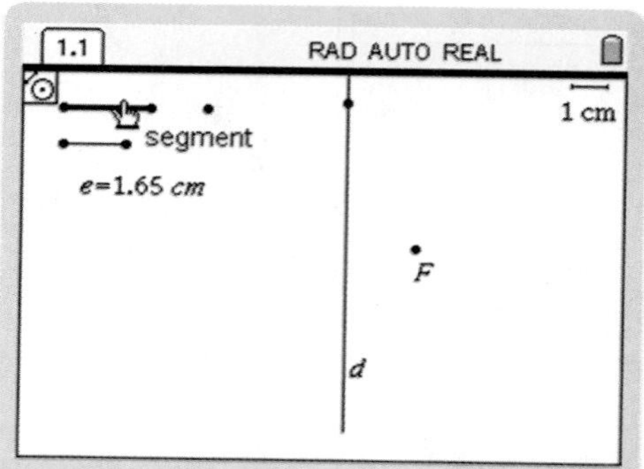


11. Place the cursor on line *d*. Press **enter**.

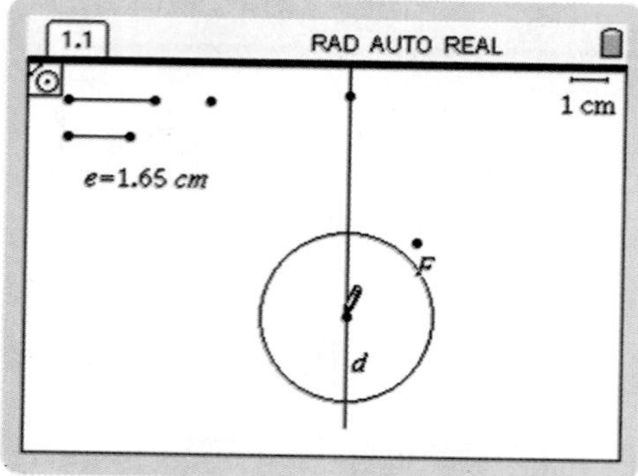


12. Use the **Hide/Show** tool to hide the top segment.

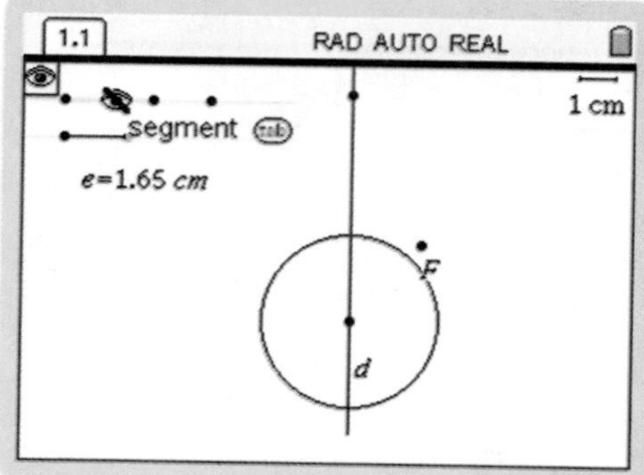

13. Construct a segment with one endpoint at the right endpoint of the segment you hid in step 12, and the other endpoint at the new point from step 9.

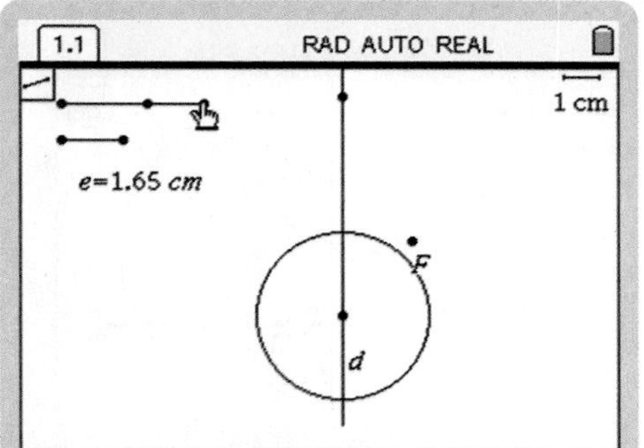


14. Choose **Compass** from the **Construction** menu. Place the cursor on the top segment. Press enter.

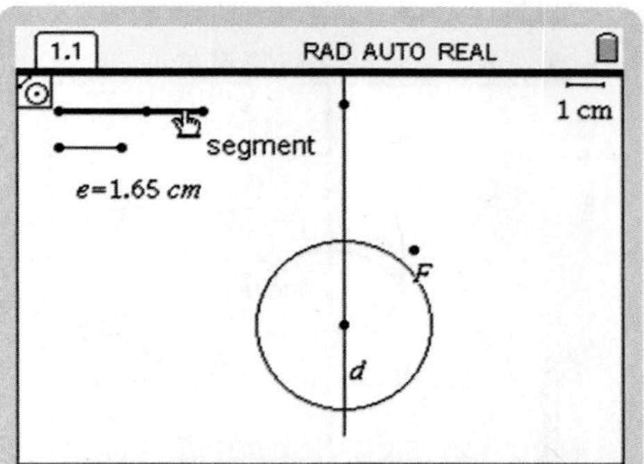


15. Place the cursor on the point *F*. Press enter.

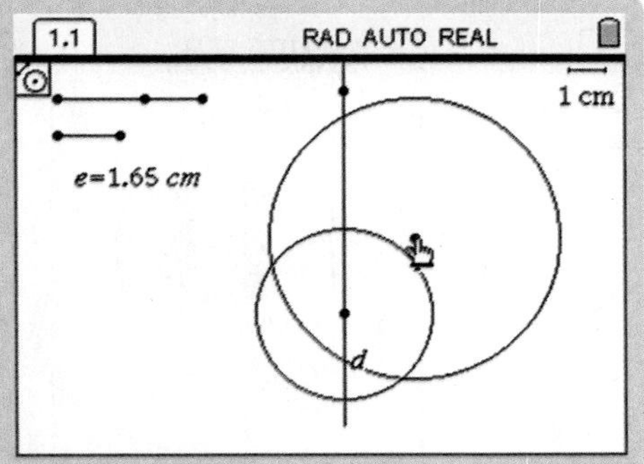


16. Choose **Perpendicular** from the **Construction** menu. Place the cursor on the center of the circle you constructed in step 11. Press enter.

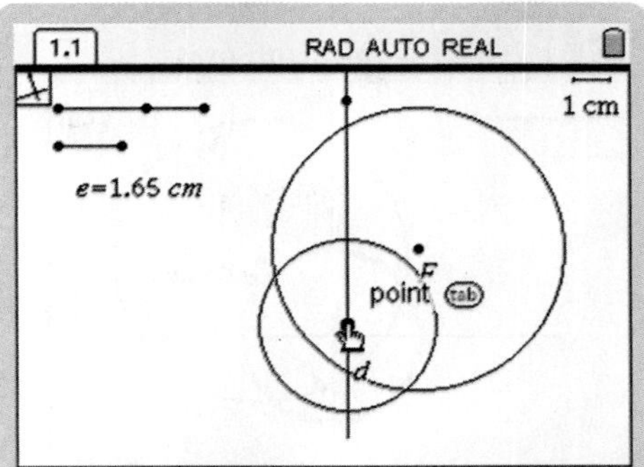

## Constructing Conic Sections Using Eccentricity (continued)

**17.** Place the cursor on the directrix. Press **enter**.

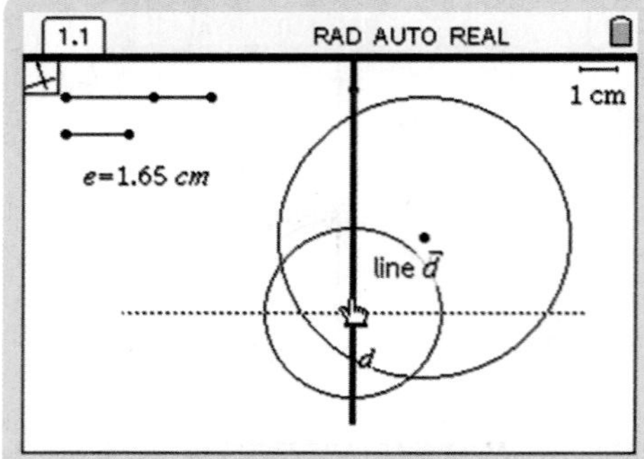


**18.** Choose **Intersection Point(s)** from the **Points & Lines** menu. Place the cursor on the line you constructed in step 17. Press **enter**.

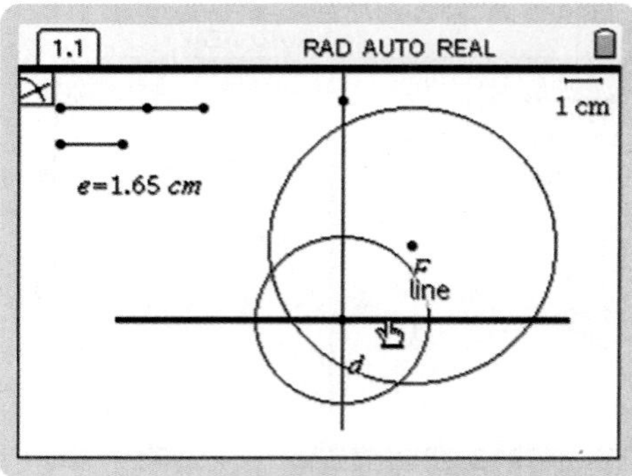


**19.** Place the cursor in the circle with center on the directrix. Press **enter**.

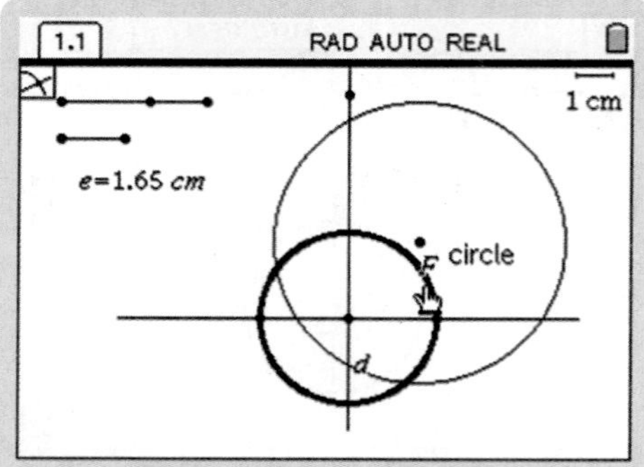


**20.** Construct lines through the resulting intersection points that are perpendicular to the line you constructed in step 17. Press **enter**.

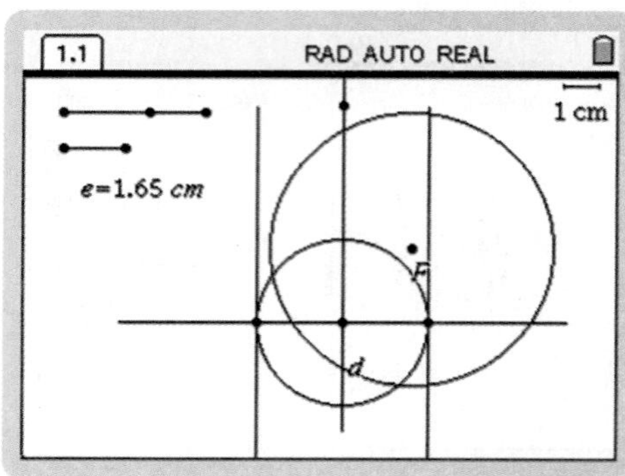


**21.** Choose **Intersection Point(s)** from the **Points & Lines** menu. Place the cursor on one of the lines you constructed in step 20. Press **enter**.

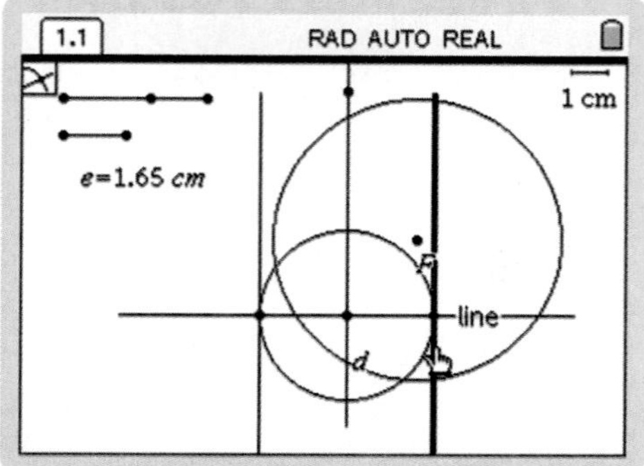


**22.** Place the cursor on the circle with center at *F*. Press **enter**.

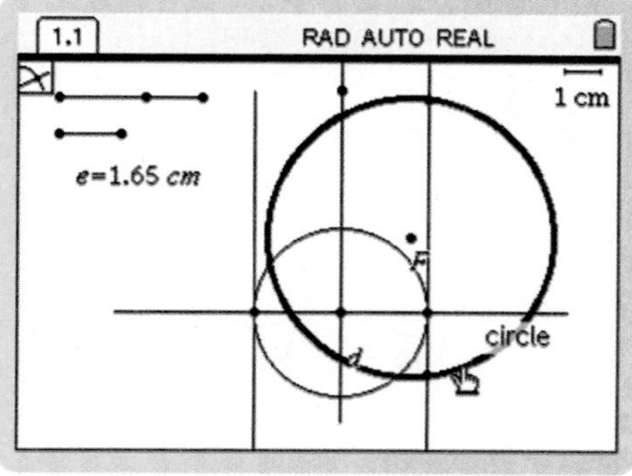

## Constructing Conic Sections Using Eccentricity (continued)

**23.** Place the cursor on the other line you constructed in step 20. Press **enter**.

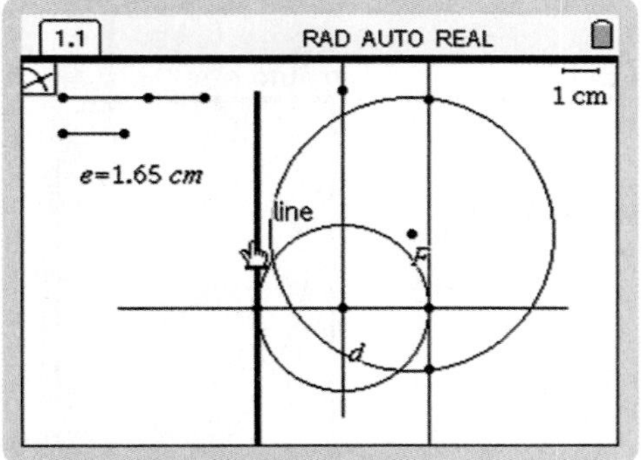


**24.** Place the cursor on the circle with center at *F*. Press **enter**.

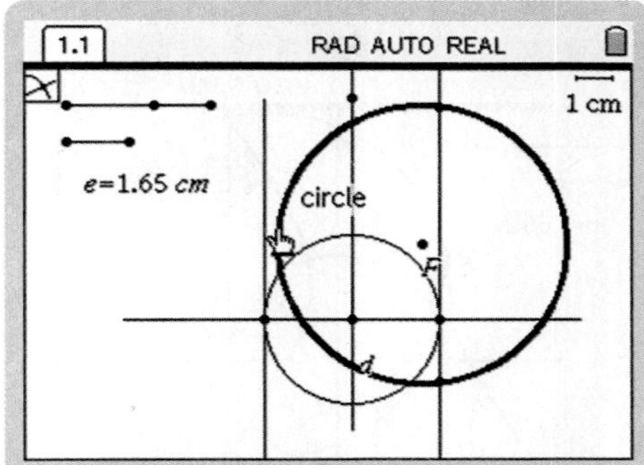


**25.** If there are no intersection points in step 24, drag the middle point in the top segment until intersection points appear.

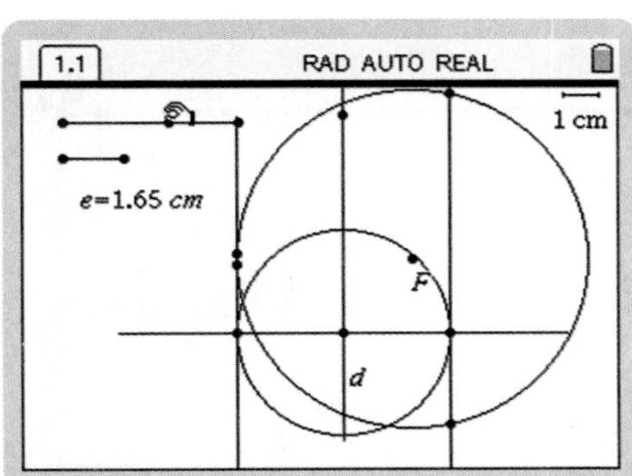


**26.** Choose **Locus** from the **Construction** menu. Place the cursor the middle point in the top segment. Press **enter**.

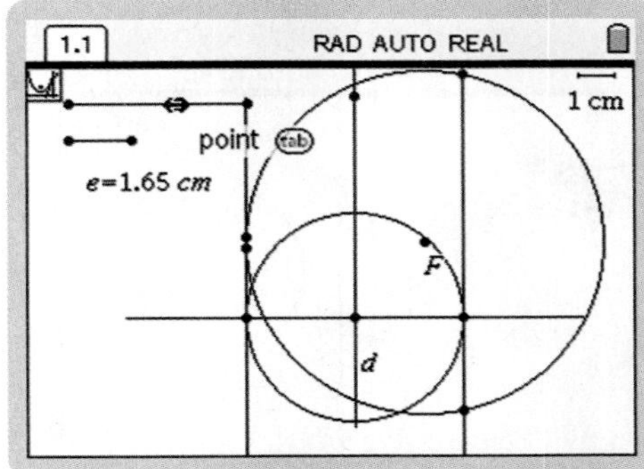


**27.** Place the cursor on one of the intersection points from step 22. Press **enter**.

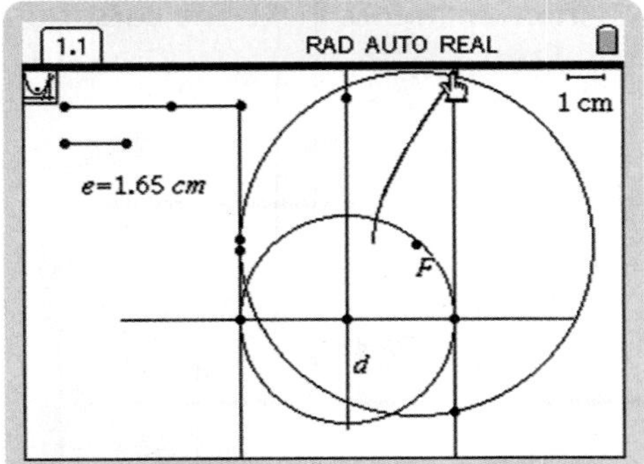


**28.** Construct the locus in the same way for the other intersection point.

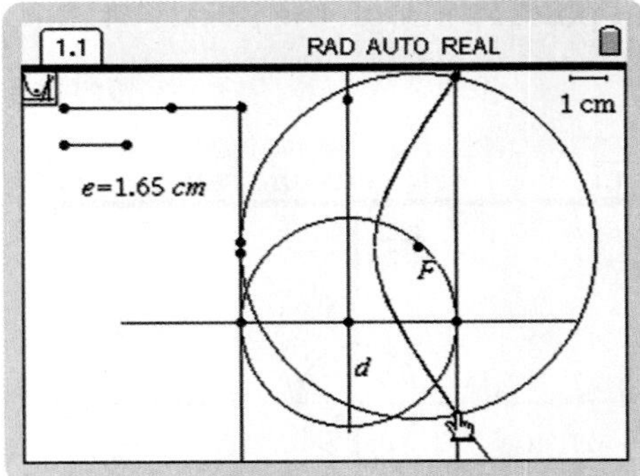


TI-Nspire Handbook

## Constructing Conic Sections Using Eccentricity (continued)

**29.** Construct the loci in the same way for the other pair of intersection points.

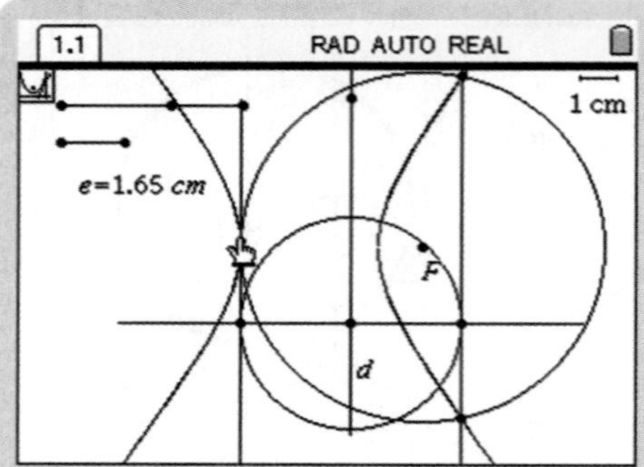


**30.** Use the **Hide/Show** tool from the **Actions** menu to hide the points and lines used in the construction.

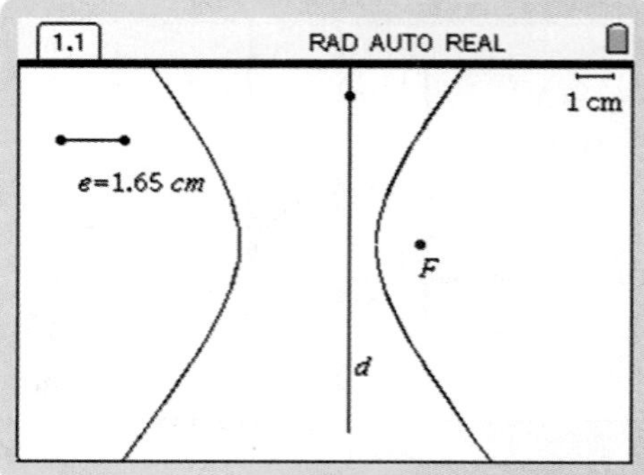


**31.** Drag one endpoint of the segment to change the value of *e*. when *e* = 1, the locus is a parabola.

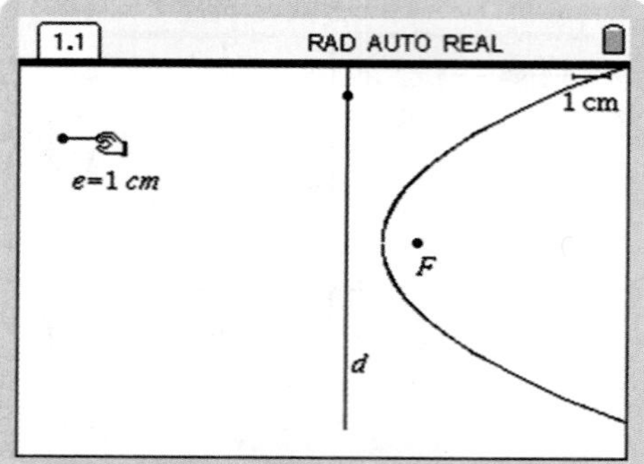


**32.** When *e* < 1, the locus is an ellipse.

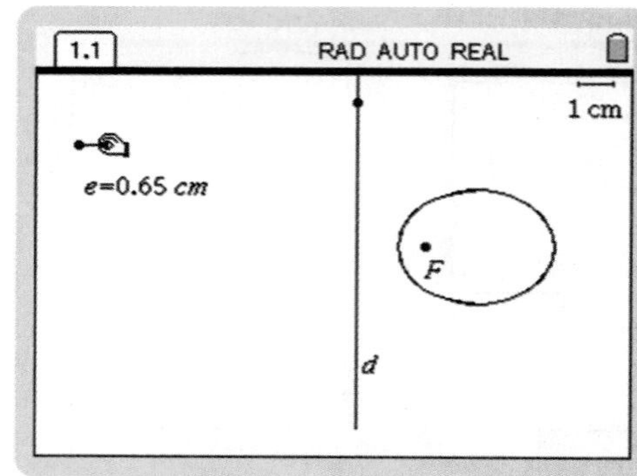


## Modeling the Tangent Function, Lesson H.02

1. Construct a circle with center at the origin that passes through the point *A*(1, 0).

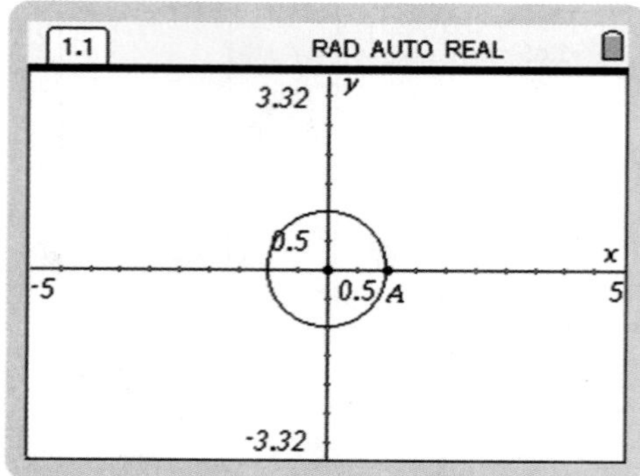


2. Choose **Perpendicular** from the **Construction** menu. Place the cursor on the *x*-axis. Press **enter**.

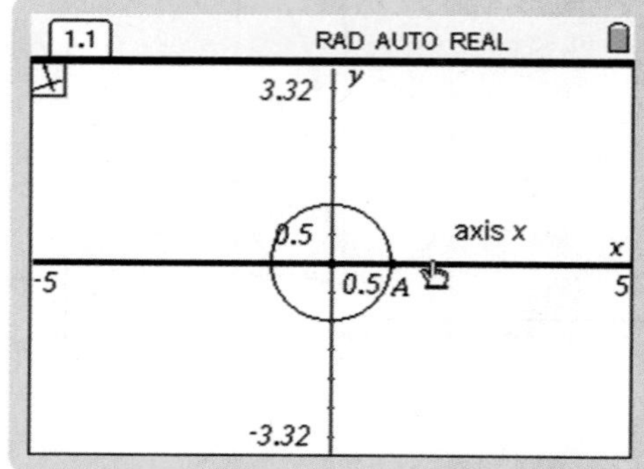

## Modeling the Tangent Function (continued)

3. Place the cursor on point *A*. Press enter to set the line through *A* perpendicular to the *x*-axis.

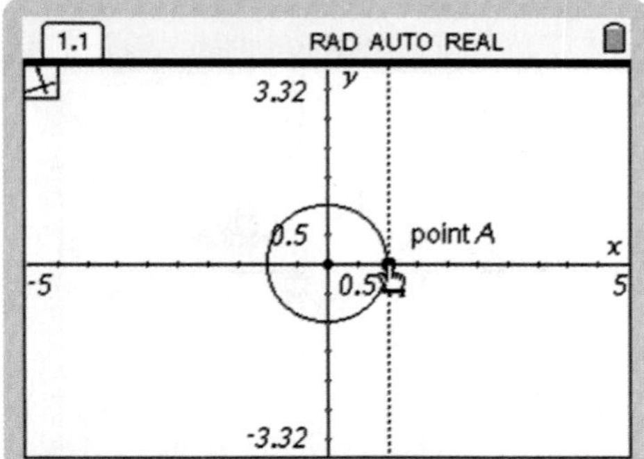


4. Choose **Segment** from the **Points & Lines** menu. Construct a segment in an open area of the screen. After setting the second endpoint, press B ' to label it.

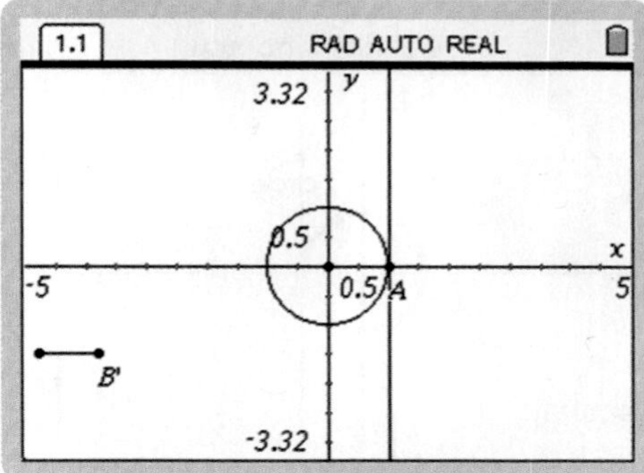


5. Choose **Length** from the **Measurement** menu. Place the cursor on the segment. Press enter to measure the length. Move the cursor to drag the measurement to the desired location. Press enter to anchor it.

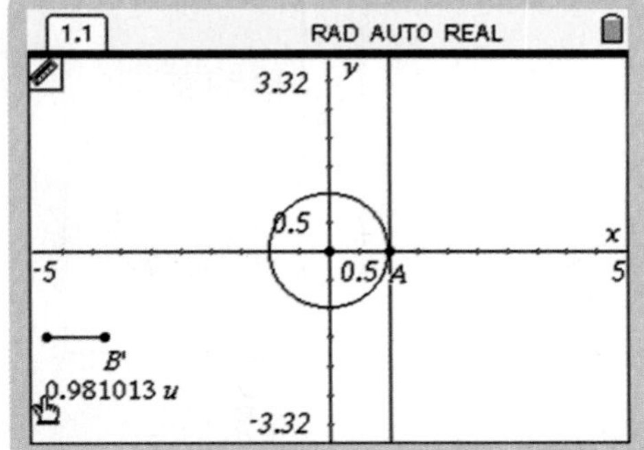


6. Choose **Measurement transfer** from the **Construction** menu. Place the cursor on the length of the segment. Press enter.

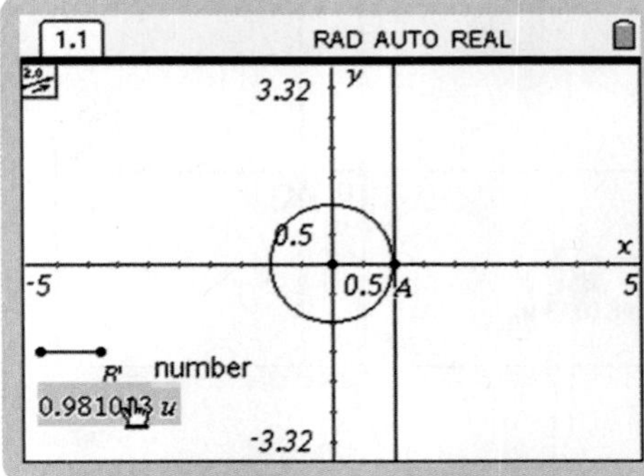

## Modeling the Tangent Function (continued)

7. Place the cursor on the circle. Press enter.

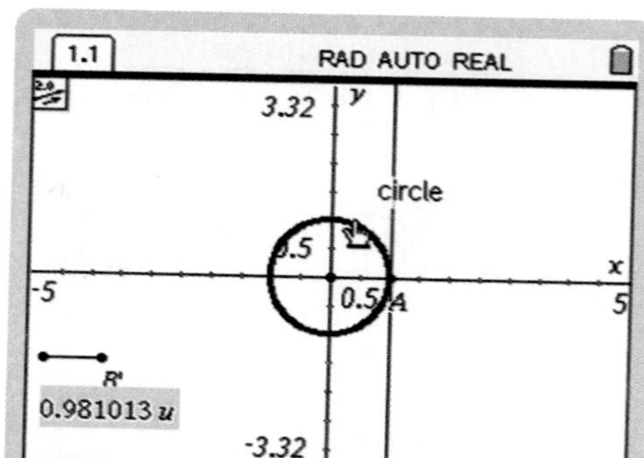


8. Place the cursor on point *A*. Press enter. The length of the arc from *A* to the new point that appears is equal to the length of the segment.

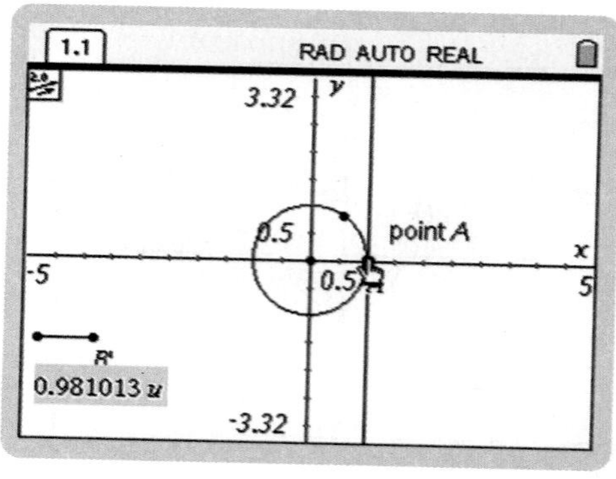


9. Use the **Text** tool in the **Actions** menu to label the new point.

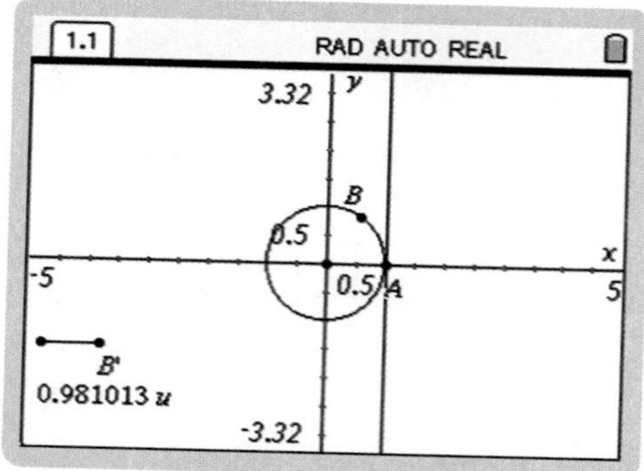


10. Choose **Line** from the **Points & Lines** menu. Place the cursor on the origin. Press enter. Place the cursor on the point *B*. Press enter.

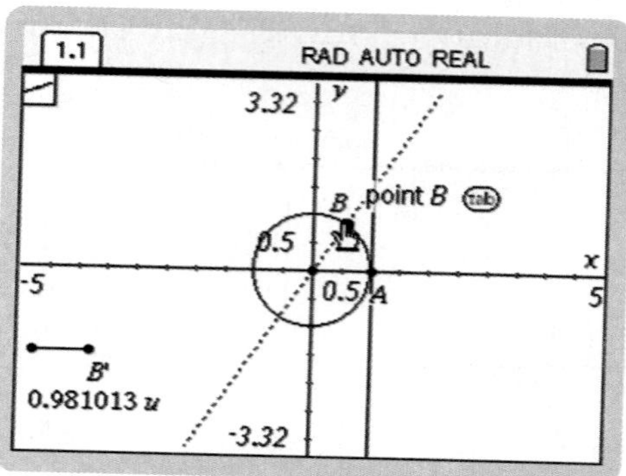


11. Choose **Intersection Point(s)** from the **Points & Lines** menu. Place the cursor on the line through the origin. Press enter.

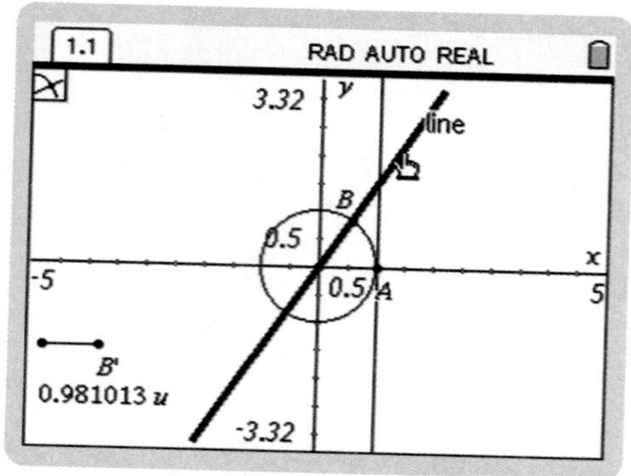


12. Place the cursor on the vertical line through the point *A*. Press enter to construct the intersection of the two lines.

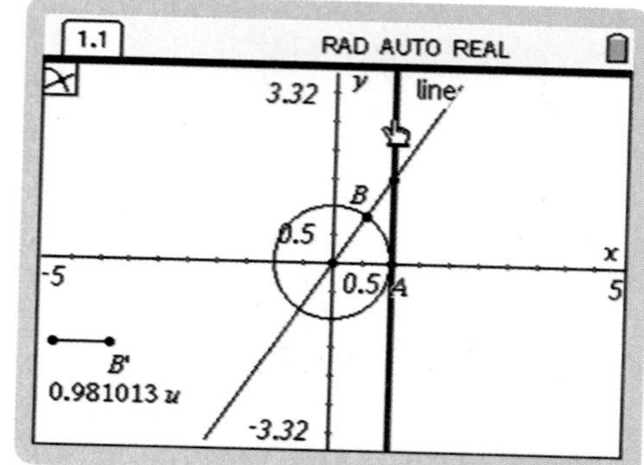

## Modeling the Tangent Function (continued)

**13.** Use the **Text** tool in the **Actions** menu to label the new point.

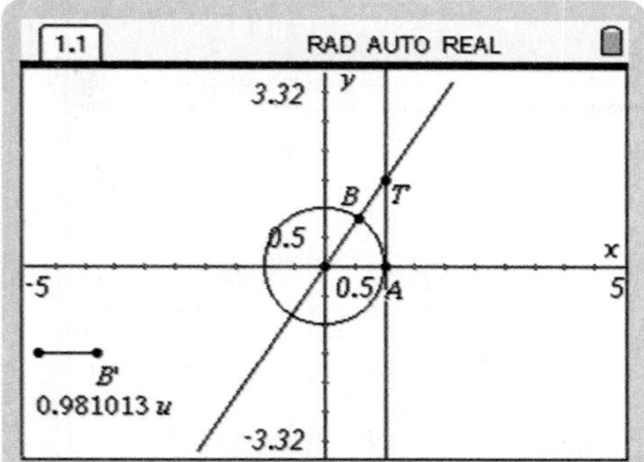


**14.** Choose **Coordinates and Equations** from the **Actions** menu. Place the cursor on point *T*. Press enter.

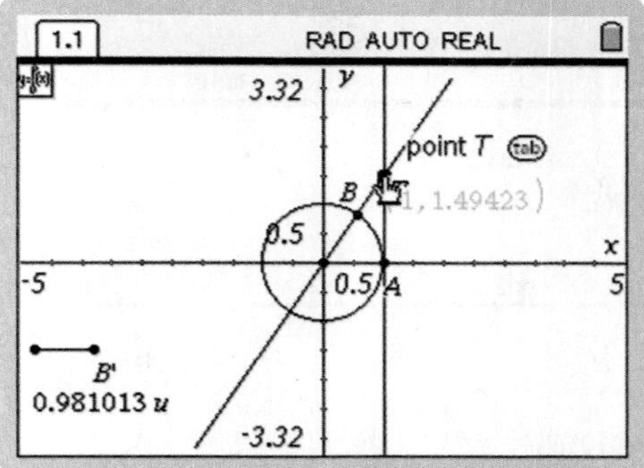


**15.** Move the cursor to drag the coordinates to the desired location. Press enter to anchor it.

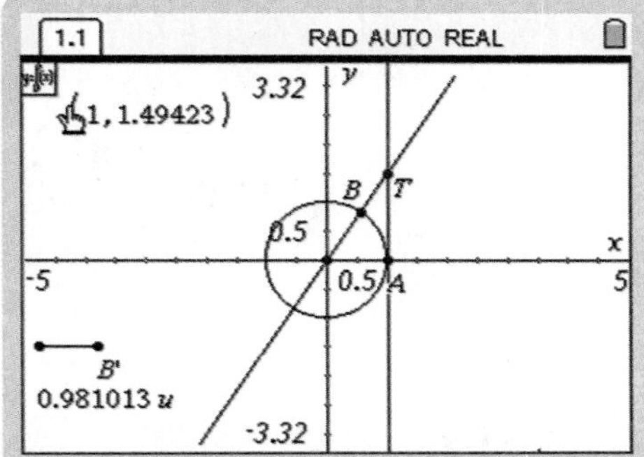


**16.** Choose **Text** from the **Actions** menu. Click on an empty area of the screen. Type T A N ( V. Press enter.

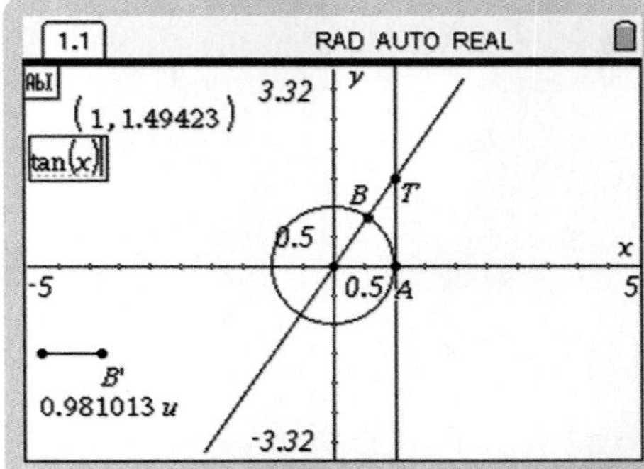


**17.** Choose **Calculate** from the **Actions** menu. Place the cursor on the text you wrote in step 16. Press enter.

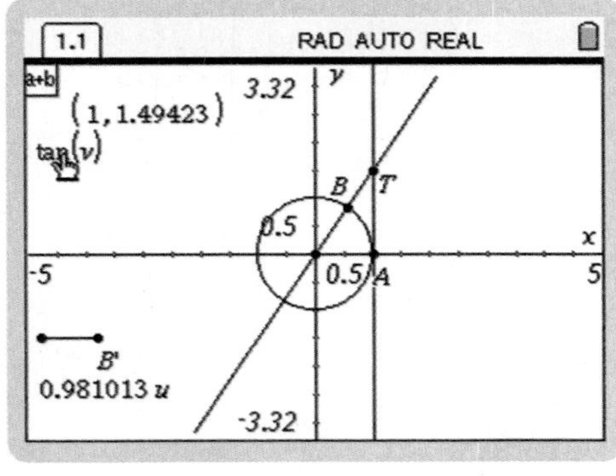


**18.** Place the cursor on the length of the segment. Press enter.

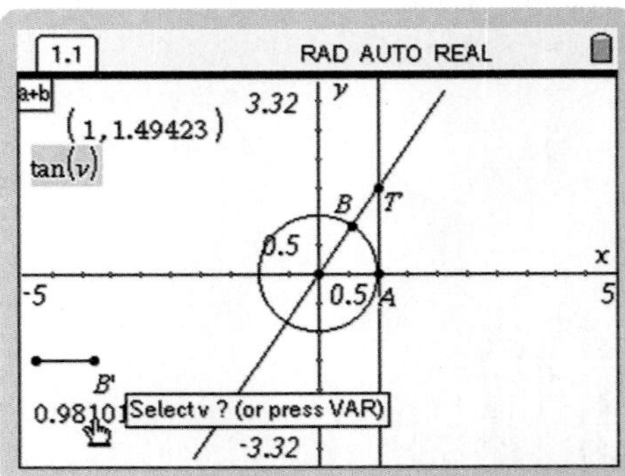

## Modeling the Tangent Function (continued)

19. Move the cursor to drag the result of the calculation to the desired location. Press **enter** to anchor it.

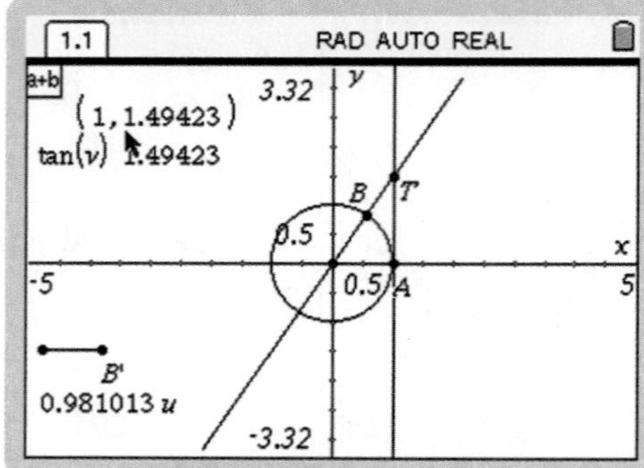


20. Place the cursor on the point $B'$. Press **ctrl** and the click key to grab it. Drag the point and observe the relationship between the coordinates of $T$, and the tangent of $m\widehat{AB}$.

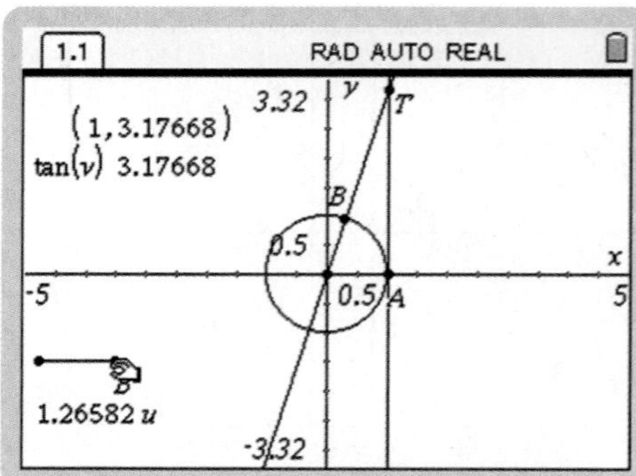

# Tables

## Table 1 Math Symbols

| Symbol | Meaning |
|---|---|
| $\ldots$ | and so on |
| $=$ | is equal to |
| $\approx$ | is approximately equal to |
| $\neq$ | is not equal to |
| $>$ | is greater than |
| $\geq$ | is greater than or equal to |
| $<$ | is less than |
| $\leq$ | is less than or equal to |
| $\cdot$, $\times$ | multiplication |
| $+$ | addition |
| $-$ | subtraction |
| $\pm$ | plus or minus |
| $\mapsto$ | which gives, leads to, maps to |
| $a_n \to r$ | $a_n$ approaches $r$ |
| $n^2$ | $n$ squared |
| $\sqrt{x}$ | nonnegative square root of $x$ |
| $\Delta$ | difference (delta) |
| $\Leftrightarrow$ | if and only if |
| $A$ | point $A$ |
| $A'$ | image of $A$, $A$ prime |
| $\overleftrightarrow{AB}$ | line through $A$ and $B$ |
| $\overline{AB}$ | segment with endpoints $A$ and $B$ |
| $\overrightarrow{AB}$ | ray with endpoint $A$ through $B$ |
| $\overrightarrow{AB}$ | vector with tail $A$ and head $B$ |
| $AB$ | length of $\overline{AB}$ |
| $\parallel$ | is parallel to |
| $\perp$ | is perpendicular to |
| $\cong$ | is congruent to |
| $\sim$ | is similar to |
| $\angle A$ | angle $A$ |
| $\angle ABC$ | angle with sides $\overline{BA}$ and $\overline{BC}$ |
| $m\angle A$ | measure of angle $A$ |
| $^\circ$ | degree(s) |
| $\triangle ABC$ | triangle with vertices $A$, $B$, and $C$ |
| $\square ABCD$ | parallelogram with vertices $A$, $B$, $C$, and $D$ |
| $n$-gon | polygon with $n$ sides |
| $s$ | length of a side |
| $b$ | base length |
| $h$ | height, length of an altitude |
| $a$ | apothem |
| $P$ | perimeter |
| $A$ | area |
| $B$ | area of a base |
| L.A. | lateral surface area |
| S.A. | total surface area |
| $\ell$ | slant height |
| $V$ | volume |
| $d$ | diameter |
| $r$ | radius |
| $C$ | circumference |
| $\pi$ | pi, the ratio of the circumference of a circle to its diameter |
| $\odot A$ | circle with center $A$ |
| $\widehat{AB}$ | arc with endpoints $A$ and $B$ |
| $\widehat{ABC}$ | arc with endpoints $A$ and $C$ and containing $B$ |
| $m\widehat{AB}$ | measure of $\widehat{AB}$ |
| $a : b$, $\frac{a}{b}$ | ratio of $a$ to $b$ |
| $\sin A$ | sine of $\angle A$ |
| $\cos A$ | cosine of $\angle A$ |
| $\tan A$ | tangent of $\angle A$ |
| $\sin^{-1} x$ | inverse sine of $x$ |
| $\Pi(P)$ | power of point $P$ |

## Table 2 Formulas

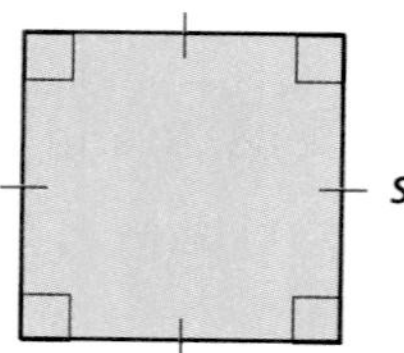


$P = 4s$
$A = s^2$

**Square**

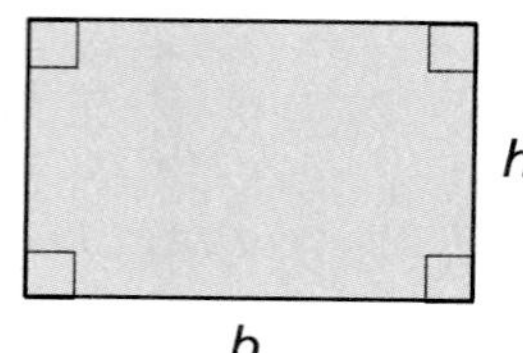


$P = 2b + 2h$
$A = bh$

**Rectangle**

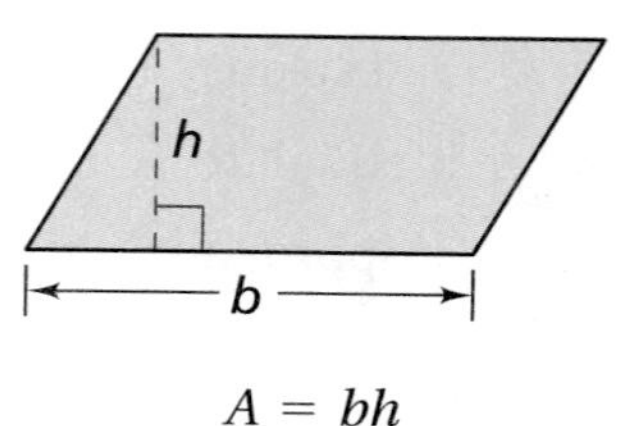


$A = bh$

**Parallelogram**

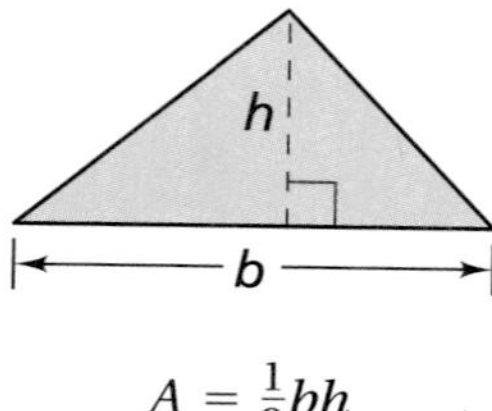


$A = \frac{1}{2}bh$

**Triangle**

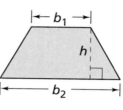

$A = \frac{1}{2}h(b_1 + b_2)$

**Trapezoid**

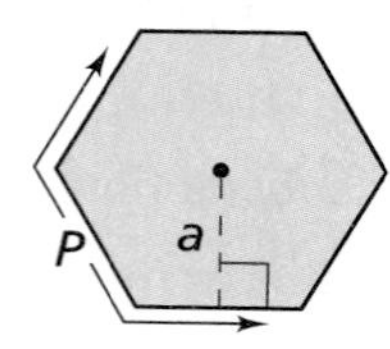


$A = \frac{1}{2}aP$

**Regular Polygon**

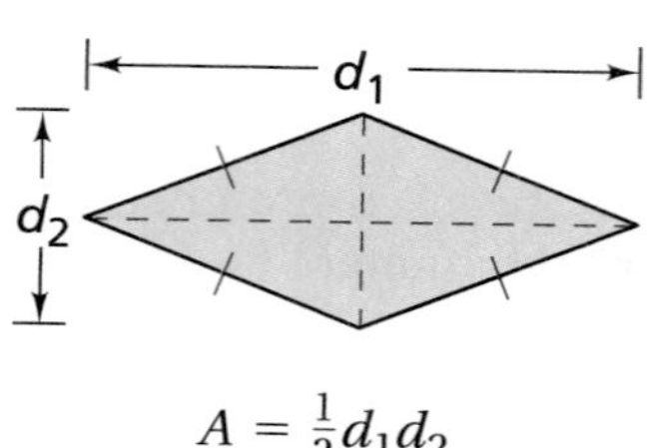


$A = \frac{1}{2}d_1d_2$

**Rhombus**

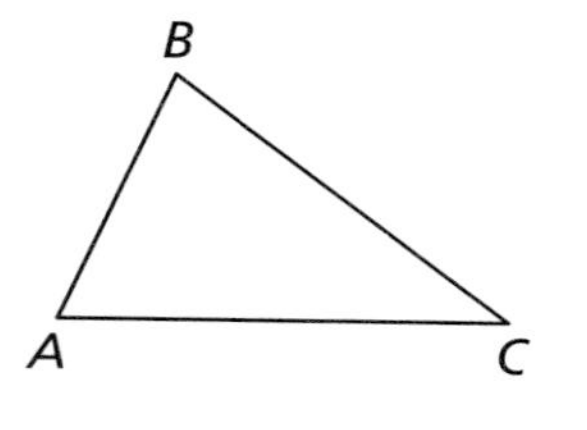


$m\angle A + m\angle B + m\angle C = 180^\circ$

**Triangle Angle Sum**

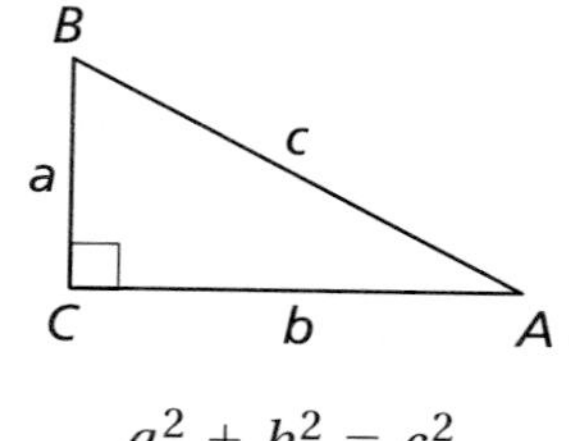


$a^2 + b^2 = c^2$

**Pythagorean Theorem**

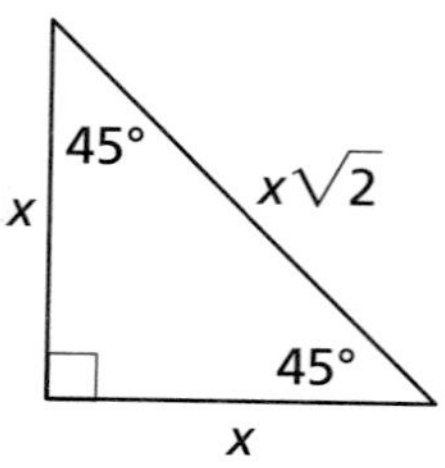


Ratio of sides $= 1 : 1 : \sqrt{2}$

**45°-45°-90° Triangle**

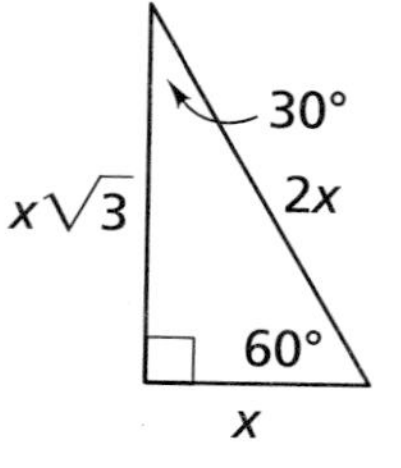


Ratio of sides $= 1 : \sqrt{3} : 2$

**30°-60°-90° Triangle**

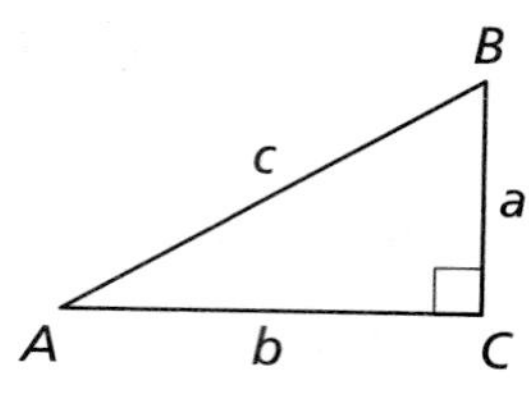


$\tan A = \frac{a}{b}$
$\sin A = \frac{a}{c} \quad \cos A = \frac{b}{c}$

**Trigonometric Ratios**

## Table 2 Formulas (continued)

| | | |
|---|---|---|
| 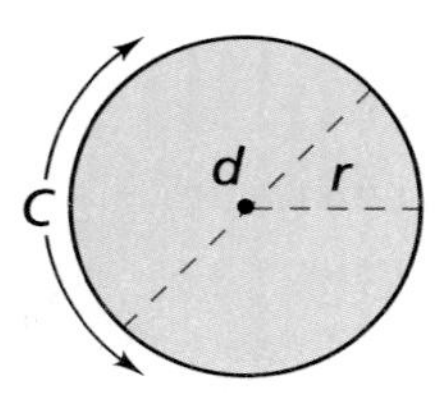  $C = \pi d$ or $C = 2\pi r$<br>$A = \pi r^2$<br>**Circle** | 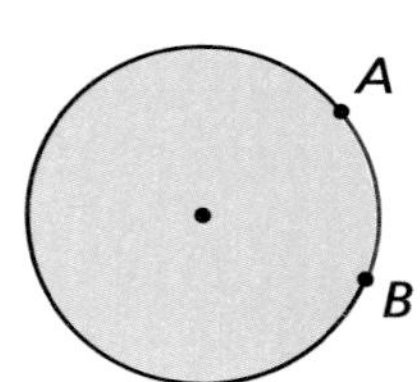  Length of $\widehat{AB} = \frac{m\widehat{AB}}{360} \cdot 2\pi r$<br>**Arc** | 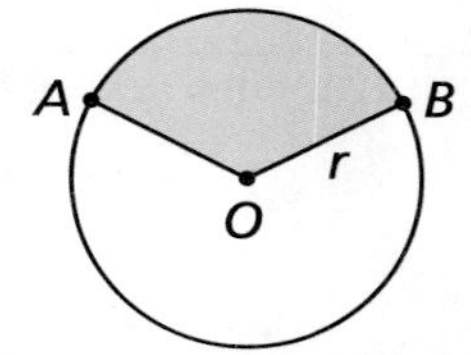  Area of sector $AOB = \frac{m\widehat{AB}}{360} \cdot \pi r^2$<br>**Sector of a Circle** |
| 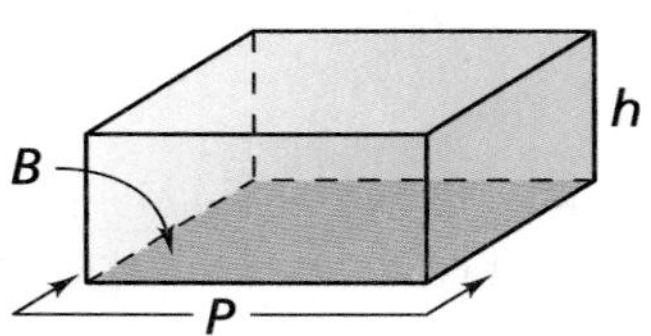  L.A. $= Ph$<br>S.A. $=$ L.A. $+ 2B$<br>$V = Bh$<br>**Right Prism** | 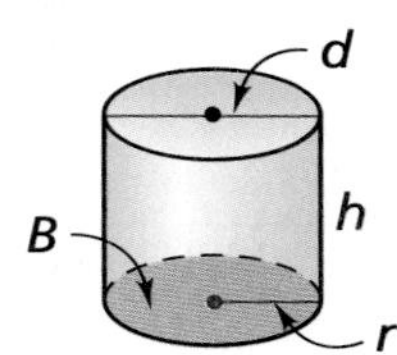  L.A. $= 2\pi rh$ or L.A. $= \pi dh$<br>S.A. $=$ L.A. $+ 2B$<br>$V = Bh$<br>**Right Cylinder** | 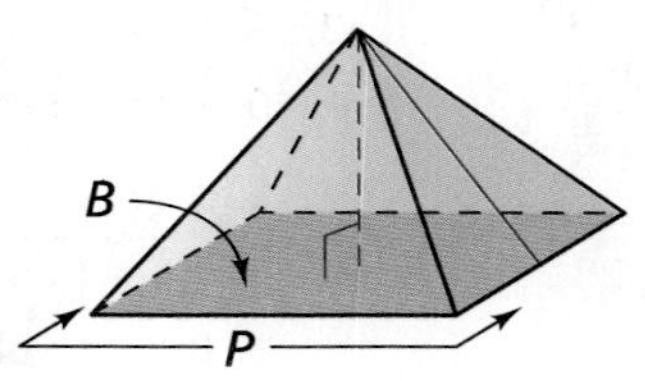  L.A. $= \frac{1}{2}P\ell$<br>S.A. $=$ L.A. $+ B$<br>$V = \frac{1}{3}Bh$<br>**Regular Pyramid** |
| 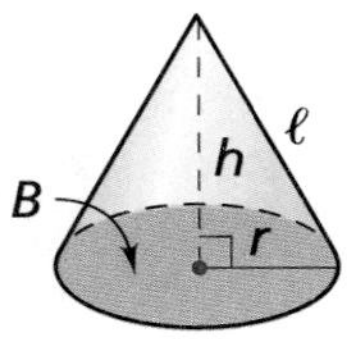  L.A. $= \pi r\ell$<br>S.A. $=$ L.A. $+ B$<br>$V = \frac{1}{3}Bh$ or $V = \frac{1}{3}\pi r^2 h$<br>**Right Cone** | 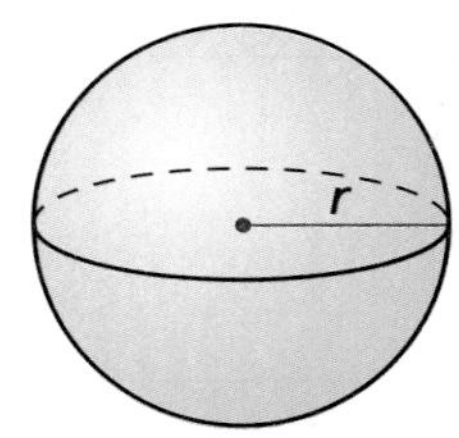  S.A. $= 4\pi r^2$<br>$V = \frac{4}{3}\pi r^3$<br>**Sphere** | 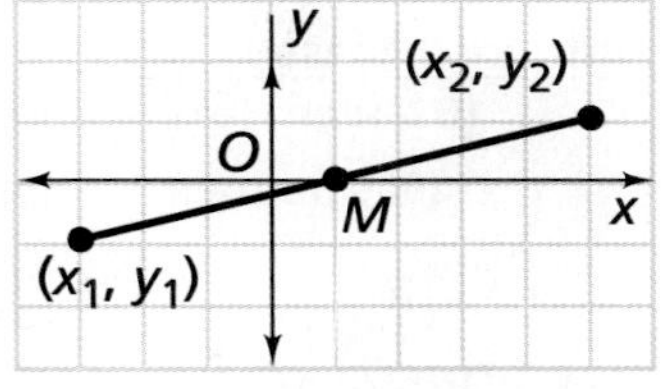  $d = \sqrt{(x_2 - x_1)^2 + (y_2 - y_1)^2}$<br>$M = \left(\frac{x_1 + x_2}{2}, \frac{y_1 + y_2}{2}\right)$<br>**Distance and Midpoint** |
| 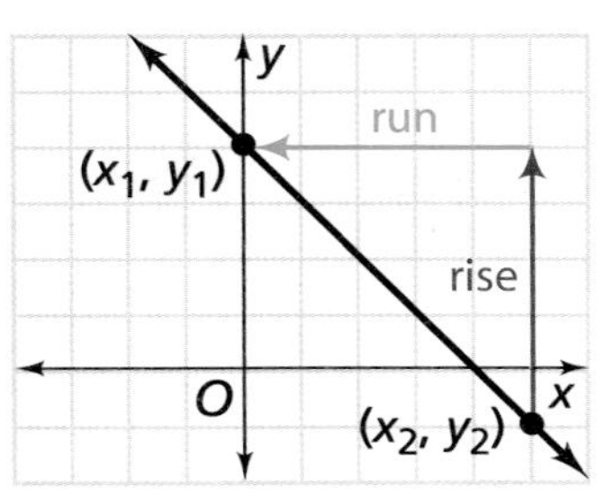  $m = \frac{\text{rise}}{\text{run}} = \frac{y_2 - y_1}{x_2 - x_1}$<br>**Slope** | | |



Tables

## Table 3 Measures

| | United States Customary | Metric |
|---|---|---|
| **Length** | | |
| | 12 inches (in.) = 1 foot (ft) | 10 millimeters (mm) = 1 centimeter (cm) |
| | 36 in. = 1 yard (yd) | 100 cm = 1 meter (m) |
| | 3 ft = 1 yard | 1000 mm = 1 meter |
| | 5280 ft = 1 mile (mi) | 1000 m = 1 kilometer (km) |
| | 1760 yd = 1 mile | |
| **Area** | | |
| | 144 square inches (in.$^2$) = 1 square foot (ft$^2$) | 100 square millimeters (mm$^2$) = 1 square centimeter (cm$^2$) |
| | 9 ft$^2$ = 1 square yard (yd$^2$) | 10,000 cm$^2$ = 1 square meter (m$^2$) |
| | 43,560 ft$^2$ = 1 acre | 10,000 m$^2$ = 1 hectare (ha) |
| | 4840 yd$^2$ = 1 acre | |
| **Volume** | | |
| | 1728 cubic inches (in.$^3$) = 1 cubic foot (ft$^3$) | 1000 cubic millimeters (mm$^3$) = 1 cubic centimeter (cm$^3$) |
| | 27 ft$^3$ = 1 cubic yard (yd$^3$) | 1,000,000 cm$^3$ = 1 cubic meter (m$^3$) |
| **Liquid Capacity** | | |
| | 8 fluid ounces (fl oz) = 1 cup (c) | 1000 milliliters (mL) = 1 liter (L) |
| | 2 c = 1 pint (pt) | 1000 L = 1 kiloliter (kL) |
| | 2 pt = 1 quart (qt) | |
| | 4 qt = 1 gallon (gal) | |
| **Weight and Mass** | | |
| | 16 ounces (oz) = 1 pound (lb) | 1000 milligrams (mg) = 1 gram (g) |
| | 2000 pounds = 1 ton (t) | 1000 g = 1 kilogram (kg) |
| | | 1000 kg = 1 metric ton |
| **Temperature** | | |
| | 32°F = freezing point of water | 0°C = freezing point of water |
| | 98.6°F = normal body temperature | 37°C = normal body temperature |
| | 212°F = boiling point of water | 100°C = boiling point of water |
| **Time** | | |
| | 60 seconds (s) = 1 minute (min) | 365 days = 1 year (yr) |
| | 60 minutes = 1 hour (h) | 52 weeks (approx.) = 1 year |
| | 24 hours = 1 day (d) | 12 months = 1 year |
| | 7 days = 1 week (wk) | 10 years = 1 decade |
| | 4 weeks (approx.) = 1 month (mo) | 100 years = 1 century |

## Table 4 Properties of Real Numbers

Unless otherwise stated, $a$, $b$, $c$, and $d$ are real numbers.

### Identity Properties

| | |
|---|---|
| **Addition** | $a + 0 = a$ and $0 + a = a$ |
| **Multiplication** | $a \cdot 1 = a$ and $1 \cdot a = a$ |

### Commutative Properties

| | |
|---|---|
| **Addition** | $a + b = b + a$ |
| **Multiplication** | $a \cdot b = b \cdot a$ |

### Associative Properties

| | |
|---|---|
| **Addition** | $(a + b) + c = a + (b + c)$ |
| **Multiplication** | $(a \cdot b) \cdot c = a \cdot (b \cdot c)$ |

### Inverse Properties

**Addition**

The sum of a number and its *opposite*, or *additive inverse*, is zero.

$a + (-a) = 0 = -a + a = 0$

**Multiplication**

The reciprocal, or multiplicative inverse, of a rational number $\frac{a}{b}$ is $\frac{b}{a}$ $(a, b \neq 0)$.

$a \cdot \frac{1}{a} = 1$ and $\frac{1}{a} \cdot a = 1$ $(a \neq 0)$

### Distributive Properties

| | |
|---|---|
| $a(b + c) = ab + ac$ | $(b + c)a = ba + ca$ |
| $a(b - c) = ab - ac$ | $(b - c)a = ba - ca$ |

### Properties of Equality

| | |
|---|---|
| **Addition** | If $a = b$, then $a + c = b + c$. |
| **Subtraction** | If $a = b$, then $a - c = b - c$. |
| **Multiplication** | If $a = b$, then $a \cdot c = b \cdot c$. |
| **Division** | If $a = b$ and $c \neq 0$, then $\frac{a}{c} = \frac{b}{c}$. |
| **Substitution** | If $a = b$, then $b$ can replace $a$ in any expression. |
| **Reflexive** | $a = a$ |
| **Symmetric** | If $a = b$, then $b = a$. |
| **Transitive** | If $a = b$ and $b = c$, then $a = c$. |

### Properties of Proportions

$\frac{a}{b} = \frac{c}{d}$ $(a, b, c, d \neq 0$ is equivalent to

(1) $ad = bc$ (2) $\frac{b}{a} = \frac{d}{c}$

(3) $\frac{a}{c} = \frac{b}{d}$ (4) $\frac{a + b}{b} = \frac{c + d}{d}$

### Zero-Product Property

If $ab = 0$, then $a = 0$ or $b = 0$.

### Properties of Inequality

| | |
|---|---|
| **Addition** | If $a > b$ and $c \geq d$, then $a + c > b + d$. |
| **Multiplication** | If $a > b$ and $c > 0$, then $ac > bc$. If $a > b$ and $c < 0$, then $ac < bc$. |
| **Transitive** | If $a > b$ and $b > c$, then $a > c$. |
| **Comparison** | If $a = b + c$ and $c > 0$, then $a > b$. |

### Properties of Exponents

For any nonzero numbers $a$ and $b$, any positive number $c$, and any integers $m$ and $n$,

| | |
|---|---|
| **Zero Exponent** | $a^0 = 1$ |
| **Negative Exponent** | $a^{-n} = \frac{1}{a^n}$ |
| **Product of Powers** | $a^m \cdot a^n = a^{m+n}$ |
| **Quotient of Powers** | $\frac{a^m}{a^n} = a^{m-n}$ |
| **Power to a Power** | $(c^m)^n = c^{mn}$ |
| **Product to a Power** | $(ab)^n = a^n b^n$ |
| **Quotient to a Power** | $\left(\frac{a}{b}\right)^n = \frac{a^n}{b^n}$ |

### Properties of Square Roots

For any nonnegative numbers $a$ and $b$, and any positive number $c$,

| | |
|---|---|
| **Product of Square Roots** | $\sqrt{a} \cdot \sqrt{b} = \sqrt{ab}$ |
| **Quotient of Square Roots** | $\frac{\sqrt{a}}{\sqrt{c}} = \sqrt{\frac{a}{c}}$ |

Tables

# Properties and Theorems

## Chapter 1

**_Euclidean Property,_ p. 36**

Given positive integers $a$ and $b$, there are unique nonnegative integers $q$ (the quotient) and $r$ (the remainder) such that

- $b = a \cdot q + r$
- $0 \le r < a$

**_Euclidean Property for Polynomials,_ p. 36**

Given polynomials $f(x)$ and $g(x)$, there are unique polynomials $q(x)$ (the quotient) and $r(x)$ (the remainder) such that

- $f(x) = g(x) \cdot q(x) + r(x)$
- $\deg(r(x)) < \deg(g(x))$

**Theorem 1.1 _The Remainder Theorem,_ p. 37**

If you divide a polynomial $f(x)$ by $x - a$, where $a$ is a number, the remainder is the number $f(a)$.

**Theorem 1.2 _The Factor Theorem,_ p. 41**

Suppose $f(x)$ is a polynomial. Then the number $a$ is a root of the equation $f(x) = 0$ if and only if $x - a$ is a factor of $f(x)$.

**Corollary 1.2.1, p. 42**

A polynomial of degree $n$ can have at most $n$ distinct real-number zeros.

**Corollary 1.2.2, p. 42**

If two polynomials of degree $n$ agree at $n + 1$ inputs, they are identical.

**Corollary 1.2.3, p. 43**

A polynomial of degree $n$ is completely determined by its output values for $n + 1$ inputs.

**Theorem 1.3, p. 55**

The following identities show the factoring for the difference of cubes and the sum of cubes.

- $x^3 - y^3 = (x - y)(x^2 + xy + y^2)$
- $x^3 + y^3 = (x + y)(x^2 - xy + y^2)$

**Theorem 1.4, p. 60**

The following are identities.

- $(x + y)^3 = x^3 + 3x^2y + 3xy^2 + y^3$
- $(x - y)^3 = x^3 - 3x^2y + 3xy^2 - y^3$

## Chapter 2

**Theorem 2.1, p. 112**

The following are identities.

- Factors come out.

$$\sum_{k=0}^{n} cf(k) = c \times \sum_{k=0}^{n} f(k)$$

where $c$ is any number

- The sigma of a sum is the sum of the sigmas.

$$\sum_{k=0}^{n} (f(k) + g(k)) = \sum_{k=0}^{n} f(k) + \sum_{k=0}^{n} g(k)$$

- Splitting up a sum

$$\sum_{k=0}^{n} f(k) = \sum_{k=0}^{m} f(k) + \sum_{k=m+1}^{n} f(k)$$

where $0 < m < n$

- Add a bunch of ones.

$$\sum_{k=0}^{n} 1 = n + 1 \text{ or } \sum_{k=1}^{n} 1 = n$$

- Think Gauss.

$$\sum_{k=0}^{n} k = \frac{n(n+1)}{2}$$

- Think Euclid.

$$\sum_{k=0}^{n} r^k = \frac{r^{n+1} - 1}{r - 1}$$

**Theorem 2.2 _The Binomial Theorem,_ p. 164**

For $n \ge 0$,

$$(a + b)^n = \binom{n}{0}a^n b^0 + \binom{n}{1}a^{n-1}b^1 + \binom{n}{2}a^{n-2}b^2 + \cdots + \binom{n}{k}a^{n-k}b^k + \cdots + \binom{n}{n-1}a^1 b^{n-1} + \binom{n}{n}a^0 b^n$$

## Chapter 3

**Theorem 3.1 _Vandermonde's Identity,_ p. 200**

Let $r \le n$ be nonnegative integers. Then

$$\binom{n}{r} = \sum_{k=0}^{r} \binom{n}{k} \cdot \binom{n-r}{r-k}$$

**Theorem 3.2, p. 222**

Let $Z$ be the random variable defined by adding the results of independent random variables $X$ and $Y$. Then

- The expected value, or mean, of $Z$ is the sum of the expected values for $X$ and $Y$, and
- The variance, or mean squared deviation, of $Z$ is the sum of the variances $X$ and $Y$.

**Theorem 3.3 _Central Limit Theorem,_ p. 282**

Let $X$ be a random variable with mean $\mu$ and standard deviation $\sigma$. The distribution for the sum of the outputs of $X$ over $n$ experiments is more and more closely approximated by $N(\mu n, \sigma\sqrt{n})$ as $n$ grows larger.

## Chapter 4

### Theorem 4.1, p. 317

If $n$ is an integer and $x$ is an angle in degrees,

- $\cos(x + 360n) = \cos x$
- $\sin(x + 360n) = \sin x$

### Theorem 4.2 *The Pythagorean Identity*, p. 322

If $\alpha$ is any angle, then $\cos^2 \alpha + \sin^2 \alpha = 1$.

### Theorem 4.3 *Angle-Sum Identities*, p. 346

For all $\alpha$ and $\beta$,

- $\cos(\alpha + \beta) = \cos\alpha\cos\beta - \sin\alpha\sin\beta$
- $\sin(\alpha + \beta) = \sin\alpha\cos\beta + \cos\alpha\sin\beta$

### Theorem 4.4 *Area of a Triangle*, p. 357

For $\triangle ABC$ with $AB = c$, $AC = b$, and $BC = a$, the area of the triangle is equal to the expressions below.

$$\frac{1}{2}ab\sin C = \frac{1}{2}bc\sin A = \frac{1}{2}ac\sin B$$

### Theorem 4.5 *Law of Sines*, p. 363

Given $\triangle ABC$ with corresponding side lengths $a$, $b$, and $c$,

$$\frac{a}{\sin A} = \frac{b}{\sin B} = \frac{c}{\sin C}$$

### Theorem 4.6 *The Law of Cosines*, p. 371

Given $\triangle ABC$ with corresponding side lengths $a$, $b$, and $c$,

$$c^2 = a^2 + b^2 - 2ab\cos C$$

### Theorem 4.7 *Heron's Formula*, p. 380

Given a triangle with side lengths $a$, $b$, and $c$, the area of the triangle is

$$A = \sqrt{s(s-a)(s-b)(s-c)}$$

where $s$ is the semiperimeter $\frac{a+b+c}{2}$.

### Theorem 4.8 *Brahmagupta's Formula*, p. 387

Given a cyclic quadrilateral with side lengths $a$, $b$, $c$, and $d$, the area of the quadrilateral is

$$A = \sqrt{(s-a)(s-b)(s-c)(s-d)}$$

where $s$ is the semiperimeter $s = \frac{a+b+c+d}{2}$.

## Chapter 6

### Theorem 6.1, p. 452

The absolute value of a complex number is equal to the square root of its norm.

$$|z| = \sqrt{N(z)}$$

### Theorem 6.2 *The Multiplication Law*, p. 464

Given complex numbers $z = a \text{ cis } \alpha$ and $w = b \text{ cis } \beta$,

$$zw = (a \text{ cis } \alpha)(b \text{ cis } \beta) = ab \text{ cis}(\alpha + \beta)$$

In other words,

- $|zw| = |z| \cdot |w|$
- $\arg(zw) = \arg(z) + \arg(w)$

### Theorem 6.3 *DeMoivre's Theorem*, p. 474

For all real $\theta$, $(\text{cis } \theta)^n = \text{cis } n\theta$.

### Corollary 6.3.1, p. 475

For all real $\theta$, $(r \text{ cis } \theta)^n = r^n \text{ cis } n\theta$.

### Theorem 6.4 *The Factor Theorem*, p. 479

Suppose $f(x)$ is a polynomial. Then $x - a$ is a factor of $f(x)$ if and only if the number $a$ is a root of the equation $f(x) = 0$.

### Theorem 6.5, p. 485

If $n$ is a positive integer, the roots of the equation

$$x^n - 1 = 0$$

are

$$1, z, z^2, \ldots, z^{n-1}$$

where

$$z = \text{cis } \frac{2\pi}{n}$$

If $n \geq 3$, these roots lie on the vertices a regular $n$-gon inscribed in the unit circle in the complex plane.

## Chapter 7

### Theorem 7.1 *The Change of Sign Theorem*, p. 513

Suppose $f$ is a polynomial function and there are two numbers $a$ and $b$ such that $f(a) < 0$ and $f(b) > 0$. Then, $f(c) = 0$ for some number $c$ between $a$ and $b$.

### Theorem 7.2 *The Intermediate Value Theorem for Polynomials*, p. 513

Suppose $f$ is a polynomial function and $a$ and $b$ are two numbers such that $f(a) < f(b)$. Then for any number $c$ between $f(a)$ and $f(b)$ there is at least one number $d$ between $a$ and $b$ such that $f(d) = c$.

### Theorem 7.3 *The Odd Degree Root Theorem*, p. 517

A polynomial function of odd degree has at least one real root.

### Theorem 7.4, p. 539

Let $f(x)$ be a polynomial and $a, b \in \mathbb{R}$. Write

$$f(x) = (x-a)(x-b)q(x) + r(x)$$

where $r(x)$ is a linear function. Then the graph of $y = r(x)$ is the secant to the graph of $y = f(x)$ through $(a, f(a))$ and $(b, f(b))$.

**Theorem 7.5, p. 539**

Let $f(x)$ be a polynomial and $a \in \mathbb{R}$. Write

$$f(x) = (x - a)^2 q(x) + r(x)$$

where $r(x)$ is a linear function. Then the graph of $y = r(x)$ is the tangent to the graph of $y = f(x)$ at $(a, f(a))$.

**Theorem 7.6, p. 551**

Let $h$ be a rational function.

1. If $h$ has an infinite discontinuity at $x = a$, then the graph of $h$ has $x = a$ as a vertical asymptote.
2. If $h$ has a removable discontinuity at $x = a$, then the graph of $h$ has a hole at $x = a$.

**Theorem 7.7, p. 552**

Let $h(x) = \dfrac{f(x)}{g(x)}$ be a rational function with $\deg f = m$ and $\deg g = n$.

1. If $m < n$, then $\lim\limits_{x\to\infty} h(x) = 0$.
2. If $m = n$, then $\lim\limits_{x\to\infty} h(x)$ is the ratio of the leading coefficients of $f$ and $g$.

Moreover, the graph of $h$ has a horizontal asymptote with equation $y = L$ where $L = \lim\limits_{x\to\infty} h(x)$.

**Theorem 7.8, p. 554**

Let $h(x) = \dfrac{f(x)}{g(x)}$ be a rational function with $\deg f > \deg g$. Then

$$\lim_{x\to\infty} h(x) = \infty \text{ or } -\infty.$$

Moreover, if you write

$$\frac{f(x)}{g(x)} = q(x) + \frac{r(x)}{g(x)}$$

where $q$ and $r$ are polynomials with $\deg r < \deg g$, then the graph of $q$ is a nonhorizontal asymptote of the graph of $h$.

**Theorem 7.9, p. 562**

Suppose that $f$ is a rational function for which the denominator is not zero at $x = r$. Suppose also that you use the method of undetermined coefficients to write

$$f(x) = m + n(x - r) + p(x)(x - r)^2$$

finding first the number $m$ and then the number $n$. Then $p$ is a rational function that is defined at $x = r$.

## Chapter 8

**Lemma 8.1, p. 593**

Let $b > 1$ and let $x$ be a positive rational number. Then $b^x > 1$.

**Theorem 8.1, p. 593**

If $b > 1$, then the function $f(x) = b^x$ is strictly increasing on rational-number inputs. In other words, if $s$ and $t$ are rational numbers such that $s > t$, then $f(s) > f(t)$.

**Lemma 8.2, p. 597**

Let $0 < b < 1$ and let $x$ be a positive number. Then $b^x < 1$.

**Theorem 8.2, p. 597**

Let $0 < b < 1$. Then the function $f(x) = b^x$ is strictly decreasing on rational-number inputs.

**Theorem 8.3 *One-to-One Property for Exponential Functions*, p. 616**

If $f$ is an exponential function, then $f$ is one-to-one.

**Corollary 8.3.1, p. 616**

If $b > 0$, $b \neq 1$, and $b^x = b^y$, then $x = y$.

**Theorem 8.4 *Change-of-Base Rule*, p. 630**

If $b, x, y > 0$, and $b, x, y \neq 1$, then

$$\log_x y = \frac{\log_b y}{\log_b x}$$

**Theorem 8.5, p. 652**

When you use a logarithmic $y$-axis and a linear $x$-axis, the graph of an exponential function $y = a \cdot b^x$ with $a > 0$ and $b > 0$ appears as a straight line.

**Corollary 8.5.1, p. 652**

The graphs of two exponential functions $f_1(x) = a \cdot b_1{}^x$ and $f_2(x) = a_2 \cdot b_2{}^x$, with all $a_i$ and $b_i$ positive, must intersect exactly once, unless $b_1 = b_2$.

**Lemma 8.3, p. 668**

Let $k \geq 0$ be an integer. Then

$$\lim_{n\to\infty} \frac{\binom{n}{k}}{n^k} = \frac{1}{k!}$$

**Theorem 8.6, p. 669**

$$\lim_{n\to\infty}(1 + \tfrac{1}{n})^n = 1 + \frac{1}{1!} + \frac{1}{2!} + \frac{1}{3!} + \cdots = \sum_{k=0}^{\infty} \frac{1}{k!}$$

**Theorem 8.7, p. 680**

The tangent to the graph of $y = \ln x$ at the point $(a, \ln a)$ has slope $\frac{1}{a}$.

**Theorem 8.8, p. 681**

The tangent to the graph of $y = e^x$ at the point $(a, e^a)$ has slope $e^a$.

## Chapter 9

**Theorem 9.1 Regular Polygon Theorem, p. 725**

Of all the polygons having a given perimeter and a given number of sides, the regular polygon has the greatest area.

**Theorem 9.2, p. 730**

If you scale a polygon by some positive number $r$, then the ratio of the area of the scaled copy to the area of the original polygon is $r^2$.

**Theorem 9.3, p. 746**

An equation for the parabola with focus $(0, c)$ and directrix with equation $y = -c$ is

$$x^2 = 4cy$$

**Theorem 9.4, p. 748**

The ellipse with foci $(c, 0)$ and $(-c, 0)$ and string length $2a$ has equation

$$1 = \frac{x^2}{a^2} + \frac{y^2}{b^2}$$

where $b^2 = a^2 - c^2$.

**Theorem 9.5, p. 750**

The hyperbola with foci $(c, 0)$ and $(-c, 0)$ and constant difference $2a$ has equation

$$1 = \frac{x^2}{a^2} - \frac{y^2}{b^2}$$

where $b^2 = c^2 - a^2$.

**Theorem 9.6, p. 758**

The graph of

$$rx^2 + ty^2 + ux + vy + w = 0$$

is a (possibly degenerate) conic. In fact, the nature of the conic is determined by the sign of $rt$:

- If $rt > 0$, the graph is an ellipse.
- If $rt = 0$, the graph is a parabola.
- If $rt < 0$, the graph is a hyperbola.

**Theorem 9.7, p. 764**

Let $F$ be a fixed point, $d$ be a fixed line, and $e$ be a positive real number. The set of points $P$ such that $\frac{PF}{Pd} = e$ is a (possibly degenerate) conic. It is an ellipse if $e < 1$, a parabola if $e = 1$, and a hyperbola if $e > 1$.

## Honors Appendix

**Theorem H.1** ***The Angle-Sum Formulas,* p. 805**

The following two equations are true for all values of $\alpha$ and $\beta$.

$$\cos(\alpha + \beta) = \cos\alpha\cos\beta - \sin\alpha\sin\beta$$
$$\sin(\alpha + \beta) = \sin\alpha\cos\beta + \cos\alpha\sin\beta$$

**Corollary H.1.1** ***The Angle-Difference Formulas,* p. 806**

The following two equations are true for all values of $\alpha$ and $\beta$.

$$\cos(\alpha - \beta) = \cos\alpha\cos\beta + \sin\alpha\sin\beta$$
$$\sin(\alpha - \beta) = \sin\alpha\cos\beta - \cos\alpha\sin\beta$$

**Corollary H.1.2** ***The Double-Angle Formulas,* p. 806**

The following two equations are true for all values of $\theta$.

$$\cos 2\theta = \cos^2\theta - \sin^2\theta$$
$$\sin 2\theta = 2\sin\theta\cos\theta$$

# Glossary

## A

**acre (p. 715)** An acre is a unit of area equal to 43,560 $ft^2$.

**algebraic numbers (p. 490)** Algebraic numbers are numbers that satisfy an equation with rational coefficients.

**amplitude (p. 426)** The amplitude of a sinusoidal function $f$ is the distance from its average value to the maximum or minimum.

**angle of incidence (p. 709)** The angle of incidence is the angle between an incoming ray and the line perpendicular to the surface at the point of arrival.

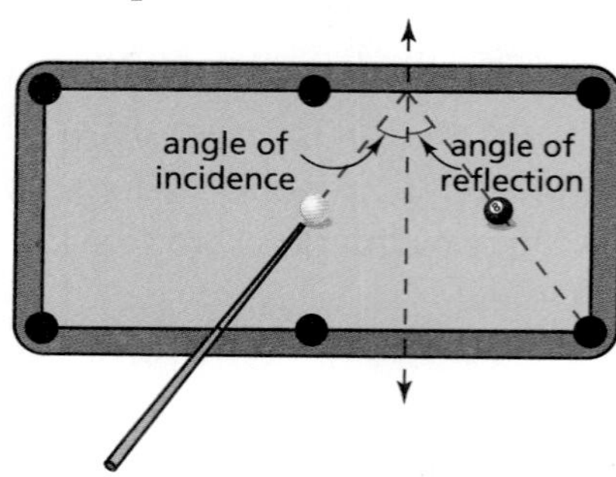


**angle of reflection (p. 709)** The angle of reflection is the angle between a reflected ray and the line perpendicular to the surface at the point of reflection.

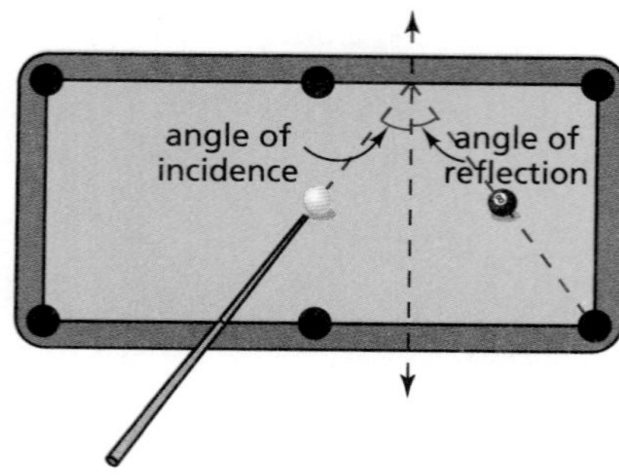


**angle of rotation** *See* **rotation.**

**apex (p. 738)** The apex of an infinite double cone is the fixed point used to generate the cone.

**arc (p. 397)** An arc is a set of points of a circle that lie in the interior of a particular central angle.

**argument (p. 453)** The argument of a complex number $z$, written $\arg(z)$, is the angle measured in a counterclockwise direction from the positive real axis to the ray from the origin through $z$.

**arithmetic mean (p. 134)** The arithmetic mean of any two numbers is their sum divided by two.

**arithmetic sequence (p. 131)** A sequence is an arithmetic sequence if its domain is the set of integers $n \geq 0$, and there is a number $d$, the common difference, for the sequence such that $f(n) = f(n - 1) + d$ for all integers $n > 0$.

**arithmetic series (p. 132)** If the sequence $t$ is an arithmetic sequence with initial term $t(0)$, the associated series $T$ defined on integers $n$, such that $n \geq 0$ by $T(n) = \sum_{k=0}^{n} t(k)$ is an arithmetic series.

**asymptote (p. 783)** An asymptote is a line that the graph of a function approaches, but does not intersect.

**average rate of change (p. 520)** Let $f$ be any function and let $A$ and $B$ be two points on the graph of $y = f(x)$. The average rate of change of $f(x)$ with respect to $x$ between $A$ and $B$ is the slope $m(A, B)$.

**axis (p. 738)** The axis of an infinite double cone is the line through the apex perpendicular to the circle used to make the cone.

## B

**base (p. 592)** In the exponential function $f(x) = a \cdot b^x$, $b$ is the base.

**Bernoulli trial (p. 247)** A Bernoulli trial is an experiment with two outcomes—typically called success and failure.

**Bernoulli's formulas (p. 114)** Bernoulli's formulas give closed-form sums for series associated with the functions $x \mapsto x^m$ for positive integers $m$. For example, $\sum_{k=0}^{n} k = \frac{n(n+1)}{2}$, and $\sum_{k=0}^{n} k^2 = \frac{n(n+1)(2n = 1)}{6}$.

## C

**central angle (p. 397)** A central angle for a circle is an angle that has its vertex at the center of the circle.

**centroid (p. 697)** The centroid of a triangle is the intersection of its medians.

**closed-form definition (p. 79)** A closed-form definition of a function uses direct calculation to find an output for any input.

**coefficient (p. 4)** A coefficient is the number factor in a monomial.

**combination (p. 167)** Any unordered selection of $r$ objects from a set of $n$ objects is a combination. The number of combinations of $n$ objects taken $r$ at a time is ${}_nC_r = \frac{n!}{r!(n-r)!}$ for $0 \le r \le n$.

**common difference (p. 131)** The common difference for a sequence is a number $d$ such that $f(n) = f(n-1) + d$ for all $n > 0$.

**common logarithm (p. 628)** A common logarithm is a logarithm that uses base 10. You can write the common logarithm $\log_{10} y$ as $\log y$.

**common ratio (p. 138)** The common ratio for a sequence is a number $r \neq 0$ such that $f(n) = r \cdot f(n-1)$ for all integers $n > 0$.

**complementary (p. 796)** Two angles are complementary if they add up to 90 degrees.

**complex numbers (p. 491)** The set of complex numbers $\mathbb{C}$ consists of all expressions in the form $a + bi$ where:

- $a$ and $b$ are real numbers
- $i^2 = -1$
- Addition and multiplication are carried out as if $a + bi$ were a polynomial in $i$, together with the new rule $i^2 = -1$.

**confidence interval (p. 285)** A confidence interval is the range of values about the mean for a given percentage.

**conic sections (p. 738)** Conic sections are curves that result from the intersection of infinite double cones and planes.

**conjugate (p. 449)** The conjugate of a complex number $z = x + yi$ is the complex number $x - yi$ and is denoted by $\overline{z}$.

**continuous (p. 511)** A function $f$ is continuous at an input $a$ if you can make $f(x)$ as close as you to $f(a)$ by making $x$ as close as you want to $a$.

**continuously compounded interest (p. 663)** Continuously compounded interest is computed by taking the limit as the frequency of compounding increases.

**control group (p. 255)** The control group is the subject in a statistical experiment that does not receive the treatment.

**converge (p. 147)** When the outputs of an iteration get closer and closer to a number, the iteration converges to that number.

**cosine (pp. 312, 316)** The cosine function, $y = \cos\theta$, matches the measure $\theta$ of an angle in standard position with the $x$-coordinate of a point on the unit circle. This point is where the terminal side of the angle intersects the unit circle.

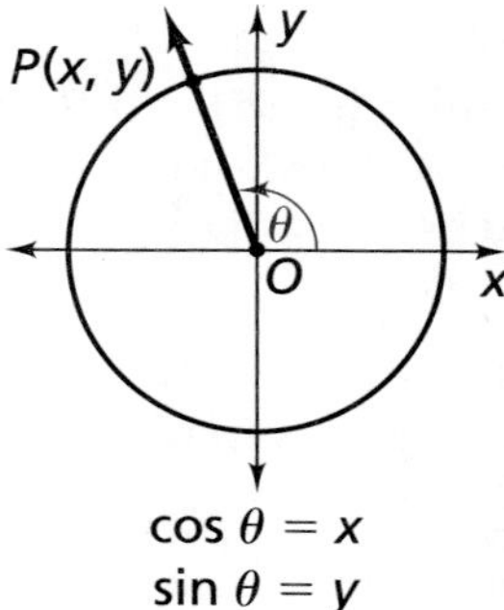


$\cos\theta = x$
$\sin\theta = y$

**cubic polynomial (p. 5)** A cubic polynomial is a polynomial of degree 3.

**cumulative density function (p. 289)** The cumulative density function (CDF) finds the amount of area under the normal curve between two values for a given mean and standard deviation.

**cycle (p. 790)** One cycle of the graph of a periodic function $f$ results as the input $x$ ranges over one fundamental period.

**cyclotomic identity (p. 491)** The identity $\zeta^{n-1} + \zeta^{n-2} + \cdots + \zeta^2 + \zeta + 1 = 0$ where $\zeta$ is a primitive $n$th root of unity is called a cyclotomic identity.

**cyclotomy (p. 470)** Cyclotomy ("circle division") is the connection between the roots of equations of the form $x^n - 1 = 0$, where $n$ is a positive integer, and regular polygons.

**Dandelin sphere (p. 742)** A Dandelin sphere is a sphere inside a double cone that is tangent to both the cone and a plane slicing the cone.

**decreasing (p. 416)** A function $f$ is decreasing on an interval if for any two values in the interval $a$ and $b$, $a < b$, then $f(a) > f(b)$.

**definite sum (p. 108)** A definite sum is a summation with numbers for starting and ending values.

**degree of a monomial (p. 4)** The degree of a monomial is the sum of the exponents of each variable within the monomial.

**degree of a polynomial (p. 5)** The degree of a polynomial is the greatest degree among all the monomials in the polynomial.

**deviation (p. 211)** The deviation of an output value of a random variable is the difference between the output value and the mean of the random variable.

**difference of cubes (p. 55)** A difference of cubes is an expression of the form $x^3 - y^3$. It can be factored as $(x - y)(x^2 + xy + y^2)$.

**difference table (p. 80)** A difference table shows the difference between consecutive outputs. It can help show patterns that lead to recursive definitions.

**directrix (p. 742)** A parabola can be defined by the set of points equidistant from a fixed point and line. The directrix of the parabola is the fixed line.

**discontinuity (p. 341)** A point of discontinuity in a graph occurs whenever the function is undefined at that point.

**distance (p. 699)** The distance between two points is the length of the segment that contains them as endpoints. The distance between a point and a line is the length of the perpendicular segment from the point to the line.

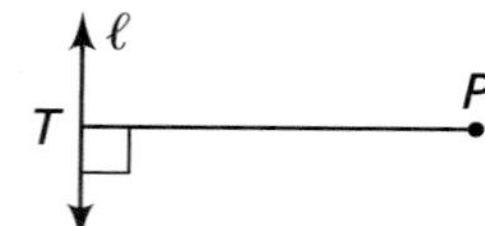


The distance from point *P* to line ℓ is *PT*.

**distance formula (p. 692)** The distance formula between points $A(x_1, y_1)$ and $B(x_2, y_2)$ is
$d(A, B) = \sqrt{(x_2 - x_1)^2 + (y_2 - y_1)^2}$

**double cone (p. 697)** The graph of $z^2 = x^2 + y^2$ is called a double cone.

# E

**e (factorial definition) (p. 670)** The factorial definition of *e* is given by

$$e = 1 + \frac{1}{1!} + \frac{1}{2!} + \frac{1}{3!} + \cdots = \sum_{k=0}^{\infty} \frac{1}{k!}$$

**e (limit definition) (p. 663)** The limit definition of *e* is given by

$$e = \lim_{n \to \infty} \left(1 + \frac{1}{n}\right)^n$$

The value of *e* is approximately 2.17828.

**eccentricity (p. 765)** The eccentricity is the ratio of the distance between the foci to the distance between the vertices.

**ellipse (p. 739)** An ellipse is the curve you get by slicing an infinite double cone with a plane that intersects only one branch of the cone in a closed curve.

**Euclid's method (p. 92)** Euclid's method tells how to find the sum of a sequence with a constant ratio.

**evaluate (p. 79)** To evaluate an expression, substitute numbers for the variables in the expression and follow the order of operations.

**even function (p. 802)** A function *f* is an even function if it satisfies $f(-x) = f(x)$ for all numbers *x* in its domain. If the point $(x, y)$ is on the graph of *f*, the point $(-x, y)$ is also on the graph.

**event (p. 178)** An event is a subset of a sample space, a set of outcomes.

**expected value (p. 194)** The expected value of a random variable *X* is the sum when each value of *X* is multiplied by its probability. The typical notation is

$$E(X) = \sum_i x_i \cdot p_i$$

where the $x_i$ are the values of the random variable, and the $p_i$ are the probabilities of each value. An alternative notation is

$$E(X) = \sum_i s_i \cdot P(X = s_i)$$

where $P(X = s_i)$ is the probability that the random variable *X* takes on the value $s_i$.

**experiment (p. 255)** A statistical experiment attempts to create two or more groups that are as similar as possible before treatments are imposed.

**experimental probability (p. 228)** The experimental probability of an event is equal to the ratio between the number of times the event occurred and the total number of trials of the experiment.

**exponential decay (p. 600)** Given $f(x) = a \cdot b^x$, if $0 < b < 1$, the function shows exponential decay.

**exponential equations (p. 624)** An equation of the form $b^{cx} = a$, where the exponent includes a variable, is an exponential equation. You can solve an exponential equation by taking the logarithm of each side of the equation.

**exponential function (p. 592)** An exponential function is a function $f$ that you can write in the form $f(x) = a \cdot b^x$, where $a \neq 0$, $b > 0$, and $b \neq 1$.

**exponential growth (p. 600)** Given $f(x) = a \cdot b^x$, if $b > 1$, the function $f(x)$ shows exponential growth.

## F

**factorial function (p. 578)** The factorial function is defined by the recursive function

$$f(n) = \begin{cases} 1 & \text{if } n = 0 \\ n \cdot f(n-1) & \text{if } n > 0 \end{cases}$$

**factoring (p. 41)** Factoring is rewriting an expression as the product of its factors.

**figurate numbers (p. 120)** Figurate numbers tell the number of dots needed to make a series of regular geometric shapes of increasing size. Examples of figurate numbers include the triangular, square, and pentagonal numbers.

**frequency (p. 185)** Let $A$ be an event. The frequency of the event $|A|$ is the number of outcomes in $A$.

**focus, foci (p. 740)** The focus of a parabola is the fixed point in the locus definition of a parabola.

The foci of an ellipse are the two fixed points used in the locus definition of an ellipse.

The foci of a hyperbola are the two fixed points used in the locus definition of a hyperbola.

Focus is the singular of foci.

**functional equation (p. 609)** A functional equation is an equation with unknowns that are functions.

## G

**Gauss's method (p. 92)** Gauss's method tells how to find the sum of a sequence with a constant difference.

**generator (p. 738)** The generator of an infinite double cone is the rotating line through the apex used to make the cone.

**geometric sequence (pp. 138)** A sequence is a geometric sequence if its domain is the integers $n \geq 0$, and there is a number $r \neq 0$, called the common ratio, such that $f(n) = r \cdot f(n - 1)$ for all integers $n > 0$.

**geometric series (p. 138)** If a sequence $g$ is a geometric sequence with initial term $g(0)$, the associated series $G(n) = \sum_{k=0}^{n} g(n)$ is a geometric series.

**golden ratio (p. 488)** The golden ratio is the number $\phi = \frac{1 + \sqrt{5}}{2}$.

## H

**Heronian triangle (p. 384)** A Heronian triangle is a triangle with integer side lengths and integer area.

**histogram (p. 190)** A histogram is a graphical representation that shows frequencies as bars.

**hole (p. 551)** A hole in a graph is a point at which a graph of a function is not connected but can be made connected by adding the point.

**hyperbola (p. 739)** A hyperbola is the curve you get by slicing an infinite double cone with a plane that intersects both branches of the cone.

## I

**identically equal (p. 801)** Identically equal expressions are two expressions such that one expression can be transformed to the other using the basic rules of algebra and any other proven identities or theorems.

**identity (p. 109)** An identity is a statement that two expressions that may seem different are actually equivalent under the basic rules of algebra.

**identity (p. 801)** An identity is any equation that equates two identically equal expressions.

**increasing (p. 416)** A function $f$ is increasing on an interval if for any two values in the interval $a$ and $b$, $a < b$, then $f(a) < f(b)$.

**indefinite sum (p. 108)** An indefinite sum is a summation with a variable for the ending value of the index.

**independent (p. 180)** Two events $A$ and $B$ are independent if the result from one event has no effect on the other. If $A$ and $B$ are independent, then $P(A \text{ and } B) = P(A) \cdot P(B)$.

**index (p. 100)** The index of a summation indicates the range of the variable.

**infinite discontinuity (p. 551)** Let $h(x) = \dfrac{f(x)}{g(x)}$ be a rational function such that

- $f(x) = (x - a)^m \cdot p(x)$
- $g(x) = (x - a)^n \cdot q(x)$

where $p(a), q(a) \neq 0$. $h$ has an infinite discontinuity at $x = a$ if $n > m \geq 0$.

**infinite double cone (p. 738)** An infinite double cone is the surface made by rotating a line in space fixed at one point. The line is rotated by moving another point on the line along a circle.

**initial side (of an angle) (p. 316)** When an angle is in standard position, the side along the $x$-axis is the initial side of the angle, and the side not along the $x$-axis is the terminal side of the angle.

**instantaneous speed (p. 537)** Let $d$ be the distance function of time $t$. The instantaneous speed of $d$ at $t = a$ is the slope of the tangent to the graph of $y = d(t)$ at the point $(a, d(a))$.

**interest (p. 572)** Interest is the amount of money paid regularly at a particular rate for the use of money lent.

**inverse function (p. 787)** Suppose a function $f$ is a one-to-one function with domain $A$ and range $B$. The inverse function $f^{-1}$ is a function with these properties.

- $f^{-1}$ has domain $B$ and range $A$
- $f(f^{-1}(x)) = x$

## L

**Lagrange interpolation (p. 21)** Lagrange interpolation is a method of finding a polynomial to fit a data set.

**Law of Cosines (p. 371)** Given $\triangle ABC$ with corresponding side lengths $a$, $b$, and $c$, $c^2 = a^2 + b^2 - 2ab \cos C$.

**Law of Sines (p. 363)** Given $\triangle ABC$ with corresponding side lengths $a$, $b$, and $c$, $\dfrac{a}{\sin A} = \dfrac{b}{\sin B} = \dfrac{c}{\sin C}$.

**limit (p. 145)** A limit is a value a series or summation converges to as the input values increase.

**linear polynomial (p. 5)** A linear polynomial is a polynomial of degree 1.

**linear scale (p. 648)** A linear scale increases by a constant amount.

**locus (p. 740)** A locus is the set of all points that satisfy an equation.

**logarithm (p. 627)** A logarithm of a positive number $y$ to the base $b$ is defined as follows: If $y = b^x$, then $\log_b y = x$. If a base is not given, it is assumed to be 10. The logarithmic function is often called the logarithm.

**logarithmic function (p. 627)** The logarithmic function $x \mapsto \log_b x$ is the inverse function of the exponential function $x \mapsto b^x$.

**logarithmic scale (p. 648)** A logarithmic scale increases by a common multiple.

## M

**machine formula (p. 214)** The machine formula for computing the variance is the mean of the squares minus the square of the mean.

**magnitude (p. 451)** The modulus of a complex number z, denoted by $|z|$, is the distance between the complex number and 0 in the complex plane.

In some older texts, the magnitude of a complex number is called the modulus.

**major axis (p. 747)** The major axis of an ellipse is the longer of the two intersections of the ellipse with the axes of symmetry of the ellipse.

**margin of error (p. 263)** The margin of error estimates how much the sample statistic differs from the population parameter.

**maximize (p. 714)** To maximize a quantity, you make the quantity as great as possible.

**maximum (p. 417)** The maximum of a graph is the highest value achieved on the vertical axis.

**mean absolute value deviation (p. 212)** The mean absolute value deviation is calculated by first finding the absolute value of each deviation and then finding the mean of these numbers.

**mean squared deviation (p. 212)** The mean squared deviation is calculated by first finding the square of each deviation, and then finding the mean of these numbers.

**median (p. 696)** A median of a triangle is a segment connecting a vertex to the midpoint of the opposite side.

**midpoint formula (p. 692)** The midpoint formula of the segment between points $A(x_1, y_1)$ and $B(x_2, y_2)$ is

$$M(A, B) = \left(\frac{x_1 + x_2}{2}, \frac{y_1 + y_2}{2}\right)$$

**minimize (p. 698)** To minimize a quantity, you make the quantity as small as possible.

**minimum (p. 417)** The minimum of a graph is the lowest value achieved on the vertical axis.

**minor axis (p. 747)** The minor axis of an ellipse is the shorter of the two intersections of the ellipse with the axes of symmetry of the ellipse.

**modulus (p. 451)** *See* **magnitude.**

**monomial (p. 4)** A monomial is the product of a number, the *coefficient*, and one or more variables raised to nonnegative integer powers.

**monotonic (p. 610)** A function is monotonic if it either increases or decreases over its domain.

**mutually exclusive (p. 180)** Two events $A$ and $B$ are mutually exclusive if they do not share any outcomes in the same sample space: whenever $P(A \text{ and } B) = 0$. If $A$ and $B$ are mutually exclusive, then $P(A \text{ or } B) = P(A) + P(B)$.

## N

**natural logarithm function (p. 675)** The natural logarithm function ln is the logarithm to the base $e$:

$$\ln x = \log_e x$$

***n* factorial (*n*!) (p. 579)** For any positive integer $n$, $n!$ is the product of all of the integers between $n$ and 1. $0! = 1$.

**norm (p. 452)** The norm of a complex number $z$, written $N(z)$, is the product of the number and its conjugate, $z\bar{z}$.

**normal distribution (p. 281)** A normal distribution $N(\mu, \sigma)$ is a probability distribution determined by the values of the mean $\mu$ and standard deviation $\sigma$.

***n*th root of unity (p. 471)** An $n$th root of unity is each complex number that satisfies the equation $x^n - 1 = 0$.

## O

**observational study (p. 254)** An observational study gathers information about groups of a population when the groups are not chosen by the people doing the study.

**odd function (p. 802)** A function $f$ is an odd function if it satisfies $f(-x) = -f(x)$ for all numbers $x$ in its domain. If the point $(x, y)$ is on the graph of $f$, the point $(-x, -y)$ is also on the graph.

**one-to-one (p. 787)** A function $f$ is one-to-one if $f(a) = f(b)$ only when $a = b$.

**optimization (p. 691)** Optimization is the process of evaluating alternatives to determine the best solutions to a problem.

**outcome (p. 178)** An outcome is an element of a sample space.

## P

**parameter (p. 5)** A parameter is an unknown coefficient.

**Pascal's Triangle (p. 159)** Pascal's triangle is a pattern that can be used to find combinations of $n$ things taken $k$ at a time. Each entry can be labeled $\binom{n}{k}$, where $n$ is the row number and $k$ is the column number.

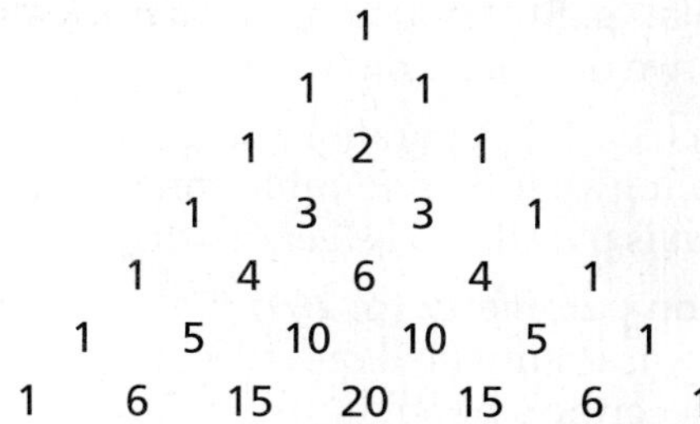


**path (p. 699)** A path is a continuous route from one point to another. A path between two points cannot be shorter than the distance between the points.

**period (p. 339)** A period of a periodic function is one complete pattern of $y$-values.

**period (p. 405)** The period of a periodic function is the smallest value $p$ such that, for all $x$, $f(x + p) = f(x)$.

**periodic (p. 405)** A nonconstant function $f$ is periodic if there exits a real number $p > 0$ such that, for all $x$, $f(x + p) = f(x)$.

**periodic function (p. 317)** A periodic function repeats a pattern of $y$-values at regular intervals

**perpendicular (p. 692)** Two lines in the plane are perpendicular if and only if the product of their slopes is $-1$, or if one line is vertical and the other is horizontal.

**perpendicular bisector (p. 693)** A perpendicular bisector is a line that is perpendicular to a line segment at the segment's midpoint.

**phase shift (p. 428)** The phase shift of a sinusoidal function

$$f(x) = A \sin (ax + b) + B \text{ or}$$
$$f(x) = A \cos (ax + b) + B$$

is the amount of horizontal translation required to obtain the graph of $y = f(x)$ from the graph of $y = A \sin ax$ or $y = A \cos ax$ respectively.

**point-tester (p. 692)** A point-tester is an equation used to determine whether particular points are on a graph.

**polar coordinates (p. 456)** Polar coordinates $(r, \theta)$ denote a direction (an angle $\theta$ counterclockwise from the reference axis) and distance $r$.

**polar form for complex numbers (p. 457)** The polar form for complex numbers is written $r(\cos \theta + i \sin \theta)$, where $r$ is a non-negative real number and $\theta$ is a measurement either in degrees or radians.

**polynomial (p. 5)** A polynomial is a monomial or a sum of two or more monomials.

**parabola (p. 739)** A parabola is the curve you get by slicing an infinite double cone with a plane that is parallel to its generator.

**population parameter (p. 261)** The population parameter is a statistical measure that can be used to describe a population.

**power functions (p. 514)** Power functions are polynomial functions with only one term.

**primitive *n*th root of unity (p. 496)** A primitive $n$th root of unity is a solution to $x^n - 1 = 0$ that is not a solution any equation $x^m - 1 = 0$ where $m < n$.

**probability density function (p. 289)** The probability density function (PDF) finds the height on a normal curve at a value for a given mean and standard deviation to approximate the height in the matching histogram.

**probability distribution (p. 277)** A probability distribution is a function that assigns a probability to each numeric output of a random variable.

**probability histogram (p. 273)** A probability histogram is a histogram where the heights (and areas) of the bars are probabilities instead of frequencies.

**probability of an event (p. 178)** The probability of an event $A$, denoted $P(A)$, is the number of outcomes in $A$, divided by the number of outcomes in the sample space $S$.

$$P(A) = \frac{\text{number of outcomes in } A}{\text{number of outcomes in } S} = \frac{|A|}{|S|}$$

**Pythagorean identity (p. 410)** $\cos^2 x + \sin^2 x = 1$ respectively.

## Q

**$\mathbb{Q}$ (p. 67)** $\mathbb{Q}$ is the set of all rational numbers.

**quadratic formula (p. 55)** A quadratic equation written in standard form $ax^2 + bx + c = 0$, can be solved using the quadratic formula.

$$x = \frac{-b \pm \sqrt{b^2 - 4ac}}{2a}$$

**quadratic polynomial (p. 5)** A quadratic polynomial is a polynomial of degree 2.

**quartic (p. 62)** A quartic polynomial is a fourth-degree polynomial.

**quartic polynomial (p. 5)** A quartic polynomial is a polynomial of degree 4.

**quintic polynomial (p. 5)** A quintic polynomial is a polynomial of degree 5.

**quotient (p. 36)** Given positive integers $a$ and $b$, there are nonnegative integers $q$ (the quotient) and $r$ (the remainder) such that $b = a \cdot q + r$ and $0 \leq r < a$. Given polynomials $f(x)$ and $g(x)$, there are unique polynomials $q(x)$ (the quotient) and $r(x)$ (the remainder) such that $f(x) = g(x) \cdot q(x) + r(x)$ and deg $(r(x)) <$ deg $(g(x))$.

**radian (p. 399)** A radian is an arc of length 1 unit on the unit circle.

**random sampling (p. 253)** Random sampling is a selection method that removes sources of bias.

**random variable (p. 191)** A random variable is function whose inputs are outcomes, and whose outputs are numbers.

**rational expression (p. 70)** A rational expression is a ratio of two expressions.

**rational functions (p. 545)** Rational functions are functions of the form $x \mapsto \frac{p(x)}{q(x)}$, where $p$ and $q$ are polynomial functions of $x$.

**reciprocal functions (p. 546)** Functions $f$ and $g$ are called reciprocal functions if they have the property that $g(x) = \frac{1}{f(x)}$ for any $x$ in the domain of both functions.

**rectangular coordinates (p. 456)** Rectangular coordinates $(x, y)$ denote distances along two axes that are perpendicular.

**rectangular form for complex numbers (p. 457)** The rectangular form for complex numbers is written $x + yi$, where $x$ and $y$ are real numbers.

**recursive definition (p. 79)** A recursive definition of a function $f$ defines most of the outputs of $f$ in terms of other outputs.

**remainder (p. 36)** Given positive integers $a$ and $b$, there are nonnegative integers $q$ (the quotient) and $r$ (the remainder) such that $b = a \cdot q + r$ and $0 \leq r < a$. Given polynomials $f(x)$ and $g(x)$, there are unique polynomials $q(x)$ (the quotient) and $r(x)$ (the remainder) such that $f(x) = g(x) \cdot q(x) + r(x)$ and $\deg(r(x)) < \deg(g(x))$.

**removable discontinuity (p. 551)** Let $h(x) = \frac{f(x)}{g(x)}$ be a rational function such that

**repeating decimal (p. 153)** A repeating decimal is a decimal that has a set of digits that repeat infinitely many times.

**root mean squared deviation (p. 212)** The root mean squared deviation is calculated by finding the square root of the mean squared deviation.

**roots of unity (p. 478)** Roots of unity are solutions to $x^n = 1$.

# S

**sample proportion (p. 261)** The sample proportion is the fraction $x/n$, representing $x$ successes in $n$ Bernoulli trials.

**sample space (p. 178)** The sample space is a set.

**sample statistic (p. 261)** A sample statistic is a result from a sample that can be used to make estimates about the population from which the sample was drawn.

**sample survey (p. 252)** A sample survey is a study that determines information about a population without gathering data from every element of the population.

**secant (p. 520)** Let $f$ be a function and suppose $A$ and $B$ are distinct points on the graph of $y = f(x)$. A line secant to the graph of $y = f(x)$ is the line passing through $A$ and $B$.

**sequence (p. 130)** A sequence is a function with a domain that is the set of nonnegative integers.

**series associated with *f* (p. 109)** Given a function having a domain that contains the nonnegative integers, the series associated with $f$ is the function defined on nonnegative integers by

$$F(n) = \sum_{k=0}^{n} f(k) = f(0) + f(1) + f(2) + \cdots + f(n)$$

**sine (pp. 312, 316)** The sine function, $y = \sin\theta$, matches the measure $\theta$ of an angle in standard position with the $y$-coordinate of a point on the unit circle. This point is where the terminal side of the angle intersects the unit circle.

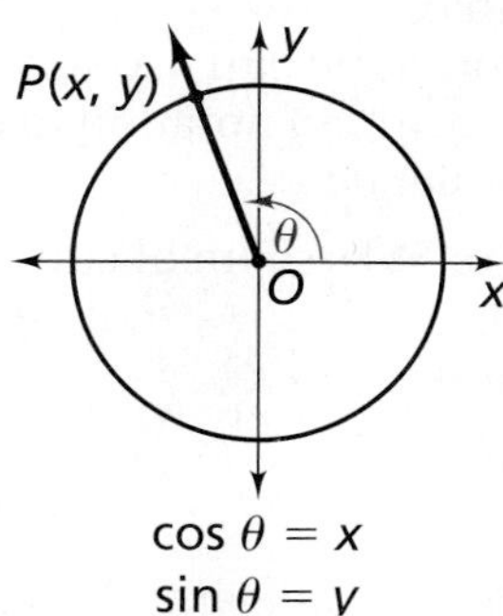


$\cos\theta = x$
$\sin\theta = y$

**sinusoidal function (p. 424)** A sinusoidal function is a function that's defined by a formula of the form

$$f(x) = A\sin(ax + b) + b \text{ or}$$
$$f(x) = A\cos(ax + b) + B$$

$A$, $B$, $a$ or $b$ are real numbers.

**slope (p. 85)** Slope is the ratio of the change in the $y$-coordinates to the change in the $x$-coordinates.

**slope formula (p. 692)** The slope formula between points $A(x_1, y_1)$ and $B(x_2, y_2)$ is

$$m(A, B) = \frac{y_2 - y_1}{x_2 - x_1}$$

**spread (p. 211)** The spread of the output values of a random variable is the difference of the maximum output value and the minimum output value.

**standard deviation (p. 213)** The standard deviation $\sigma$ for a data set $\{x_1, x_2, \ldots, x_n\}$ is given by

$$\sigma = \sqrt{\frac{\sum_i (x_i - \bar{x})^2}{n}}$$

**standard position (of an angle) (p. 314)** An angle is in standard position when its vertex is at the origin and one of its sides lies along the positive $x$-axis. The angle opens counterclockwise from this fixed side.

**strictly decreasing (p. 594)** A function $f$ is strictly decreasing if for any $s$ and $t$ such that $s > t$, then $f(s) < f(t)$.

**strictly increasing (p. 593)** A function $f$ is strictly increasing if for any $s$ and $t$ such that $s > t$, then $f(s) > f(t)$.

**summation notation (p. 100)** The general form of summation notation is

$\sum_{k=0}^{n} f(k) = f(0) + f(1) + \cdots f(n)$, where $k$ is the index variable, 0 is the starting value, and $n$ is the final value. You can use summation notation as a shorthand notation to describe the sum of a sequence.

**sum of cubes (p. 55)** A sum of cubes is an expression of the form $x^3 + y^3$. It factors as $(x + y)(x^2 - xy + y^2)$.

## T

**tangent (p. 316)** The tangent of angle $\theta$ is $\frac{\sin \theta}{\cos \theta}$, whenever $\cos \theta \neq 0$.

**tangent line (p. 538)** Let $f$ be a function and $A$ is a point on the graph of $y = f(x)$. The tangent line to the graph of $y = f(x)$ at $A$ is the line secant between $A$ and itself.

**Taylor expansion (p. 530)** The Taylor expansion for a function $f$ about $c$ is the expression of $f(x)$ in terms of powers of $x - c$.

**terminal side (of an angle) (p. 316)** When an angle is in standard position, the side along the $x$-axis is the initial side of the angle, and the side not along the $x$-axis is the terminal side of the angle.

**term of a sequence (p. 130)** Each number in a sequence is a term.

**theoretical probability (p. 228)** The theoretical probability of an event is equal to the ratio of the number of outcomes that meet the criteria for the event to the total number of possible outcomes.

**treatment group (p. 255)** The treatment group are the subjects in a statistical experiment that receive the treatment.

**triangular numbers (p. 84)** The triangular numbers are numbers determined by how many dots are needed to form a triangle with $n$ dots on a side. The number of dots in a triangular pattern with $n$ dots on a side is the $n$th triangular number.

**trigonometric equation (p. 328)** A trigonometric equation is an equation that involves trigonometric functions.

**trigonometric identities (p. 332)** A trigonometric identity is a trigonometric equation that is true for all values except those for which an expression on either side of the equal sign is undefined.

**turning point (p. 417)** A turning point for a function is an input $x$ where the function changes from increasing to decreasing, or from decreasing to increasing. Sometimes the phrase turning point refers to the actual coordinates $(x, f(x))$ of the point where this change occurs.

## U

**unit cube (p. 715)** A unit cube is a cube with edge length one unit.

**unit normal distribution (p. 287)** The unit normal distribution is a normal distribution that has mean 0 and standard deviation 1. Here are it's equation and graph:

$$N(0, 1) = \frac{1}{\sqrt{2\pi}} e^{\frac{-x^2}{2}}$$

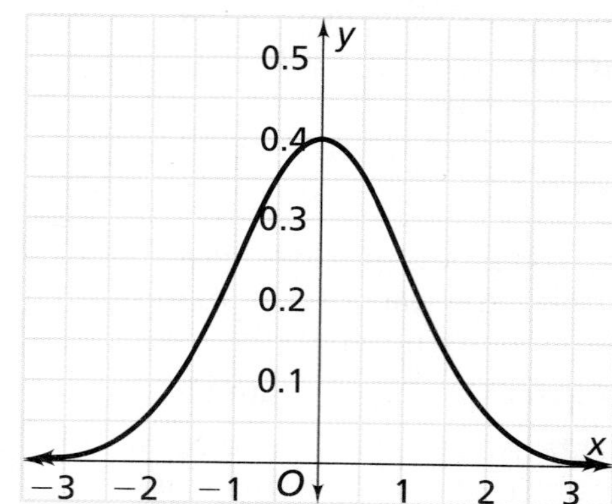

## V

**variance (p. 213)** The variance $\sigma^2$ for a data set $\{x_1, x_2, \ldots, x_n\}$ is given by

$$\sigma^2 = \frac{\sum_i (x_i - \bar{x})^2}{n}$$

where $\bar{x}$ is the mean of the data set.

The variance is the common name for the mean squared deviation.

**vertical displacement (p. 426)** The vertical displacement of a sinusoidal function $f$ is its average value. More precisely, it is the average of the maximum and the minimum values of $f$.

**vertices (p. 747)** The vertices of an ellipse are the endpoints of the major and minor axes of the ellipse.

## Y

***y*-intercept (p. 592)** The point at which a line crosses the $y$-axis (or the $y$-coordinate of that point) is a $y$-intercept.

## Z

**$\mathbb{Z}$ (p. 49)** $\mathbb{Z}$ is the set of all integers.

***z*-score (p. 249)** The $z$-score is the number of standard deviations away from the mean.

# Selected Answers

## Chapter 1

### Lesson 1.0

#### Check Your Understanding

**1. a.** Answers may vary. Sample: $x^3 - 2x + 4$, $2x^3 + x^2 + x - 5$ **b.** Not possible; if the sum has degree 4, the product must have degree 4 or greater. **c.** Answers may vary. Sample: $x^4$, 1 **d.** Not possible; if the sum has degree 2, the product must have degree 2 or greater.
**2.** Answers may vary. Sample: $x^2$, $-x^2 + x$
**3. a–d.** Answers may vary. Samples are given.
**a.** $2x^2 + 4x + 2$, $x^2 + 3x + 2$
**b.** $3x^2 + 6x + 1$, $x + 3$ **c.** $x + 5$, $-x - 1$
**d.** $x + 1$, $x - 1$ **4.** The degree of the squared polynomial is twice the degree of the original; answers may vary. Sample:
$(x + 1)^2 = x^2 + 2x + 1$,
$(x^2 + 2)^2 = x^4 + 4x^2 + 4$,
$(2x^3 + 1)^2 = 4x^6 + 4x^3 + 1$

#### On Your Own

**5.** Answers may vary. Samples are given.
**a.** $x$, $x^5$ **6. b.** $s(x) = x^2 - 4x + 5$ **7.** $a = 2$

### Lesson 1.01

#### On Your Own

**10a.** $A = 6$, $B = -2$, $C = 3$ **12a.** The $f(x)$ values are $-5$, $-2$, 1, 4, 7, 10, 13, and 16; the $g(x)$ values are 499, $-2$, $-55$, 4.7, $-46$, 13, 520. **13a.** Answers may vary. Sample: $g(x) = 5$ (or any polynomial function for which $g(2) = 5$).

### Lesson 1.02

#### Check Your Understanding

**1.** $f(x) = 6x^2 - 22x + 28$
**2.** $f(x) = 9x - 7$ **3.** $f(x) = 4x^2 - 3x + 1$
**4.** $f(x) = x^3 + 3x^2 + 5x - 8$ **5a.** $A = 1$, $B = 21$, $C = 9$, $D = 1$ **b.** yes **6.** Answers may vary. Sample: As in Exercise 18 in Lesson 1.01, when $A = -3$, $B = 1$, and $C = 2$, the final coefficient of $x^2$ was 0 so the equation was linear. Whenever the coefficient of the leading term is 0, the degree will be smaller than expected.

#### On Your Own

**10.** greatest degree: 4; least degree: 0
**11.** Answers may vary. Sample:
$h(x) = (x - 1)(x - 2)(x - 3)(x - 4)$
$= x^4 - 10x^3 + 35x^2 - 50x + 24$

### Lesson 1.03

#### Check Your Understanding

**1.** The graphs intersect at (1, 4), (2, 6), and (3, 8).
**2.** $j(x) = 2x + 2 + T(x - 1)(x - 2)(x - 3)$ where $T$ is a polynomial or a constant.
**3a.** $f(x) = 2x - 1$; the next term is 7.
**b.** Answers may vary. Sample: For the rule $g(x) = 2x - 1 + (x - 1)(x - 2)(x - 3)$, the next term $g(4)$ is 13. **c.** $g(x) = 2x - 1 + 2(x - 1)(x - 2)(x - 3)$ or $g(x) = 2x^3 - 12x^2 + 24x - 13$ **d.** $g(x) = 2x - 1 - (x - 1)(x - 2)(x - 3)$ or $g(x) = -x^3 + 6x^2 - 9x + 5$
**4a.** $f(4) = 8$ if $f(x) = 2x$ **b.** $f(4) = 10$ if $f(x) = 2x + \frac{1}{3}(x - 1)(x - 2)(x - 3)$ or $f(x) = \frac{x^3}{3} - 2x^2 + \frac{17}{3}x - 2$ **c.** $f(4) = 80$ if $f(x) = 2x + 12(x - 1)(x - 2)(x - 3)$ or $f(x) = 12x^3 - 72x^2 + 134x - 72$ **d.** $f(4) = 0$ if $f(x) = 2x + \frac{4}{3}(x - 1)(x - 2)(x - 3)$ or $f(x) = -\frac{4}{3}(x^3 + 8x^2 - \frac{38}{3}x + 8)$ **5a.** 3 points **b.** 6 points **c.** $(n + 1)$ points

#### On Your Own

**8.** Answers may vary. Sample: $p(x) = 4 - x^2 - 3x(x - 1)(x - 2)(x - 3)$ The graphs intersect at (0, 4), (1, 3), (2, 0), and (3, $-5$). **11a.** Yes; a sample is $f(x) = 3(x - 2)^2$.

### Lesson 1.04

#### On Your Own

**8a.** 1 and $-3$ **9.** $x^3 - a^3$

### Lesson 1.05

#### Check Your Understanding

**1a.** quotient: $x^2 - 3$; remainder: 0 **b.** 0 **2.** 3
**3.** $-1$ **4.** 0 **5a.** Answers may vary. Sample: 8
**b.** Answers may vary. Samples: 113 and 218, or any number of the form $8 + 105n$, where $n$ is a nonnegative integer. **6a.** Answers may vary. Sample: $f(x) = 2x^2 - 3x + 7$ **b.** Answers may vary. Sample: any polynomial of the form $g(x) = 2x^2 - 3x + 7 + p(x)(x - 3)(x - 5)(x - 7)$, where $p(x)$ is a polynomial

#### On Your Own

**8a.** 26 **9a.** 11 **10a.** 8

### Lesson 1.06

#### Check Your Understanding

**1.** A polynomial of degree 2 can have at most 2 real roots. **2a.** Checking 5 values, $P(0) = R(0) = -2$, $P(1) = R(1) = -2$, $P(-1) = R(-1) = -2$, $P(\sqrt{2}) = R(\sqrt{2}) = 0$, and $P(-\sqrt{2}) = R(-\sqrt{2}) = 0$. So $P(x) = R(x)$.

**b.** Checking 3 values, $P(1) = R(1) = 0$, $P(0) = R(0) = 0$, $P(-1) = R(-1) = 0$, but $P(2) \neq R(2)$. So $P(x) \neq R(x)$. **c.** Checking three values, $P(-3) = R(-3) = -7$, $P(0) = R(0) = 2$, $P(-2) = R(-2) = -6$. So $P(x) = R(x)$. **3.** $-5$ **4.** $a = 7$, $b = 1$ **5.** $-3, -1, 1, 2$ **6.** Answers may vary. Sample: Checking 3 values, for $x = 1$ both sides are 2; for $x = 3$ both sides are 2, and for $x = 2$ both sides are $-1$. So the expressions are equivalent. **7.** Answers may vary. Sample: Checking 3 values, for $x = 1$ both sides are 20; for $x = 3$ both sides are 12; and for $x = 6$ both sides are 60. So the two expressions are equivalent. **8.** $P(x) = 1$

**On Your Own**

**12a.** $f(2) = 0$, so $(x - 2)$ is a factor of $f(x)$. **b.** $g(x) = \frac{f(x)}{x-2} = 3x^3 - 6x^2 + x - 2$ and $g(2) = 0$, so $x - 2$ is a factor of $g(x)$.

**Lesson 1.07**

**On Your Own**

**5a.** $(x + 1)(x + 5)$ **d.** It doesn't factor; there are no rational numbers with sum 10 and product $-20$. **6a.** $x^3 - 1$ **7c.** $(x - 2)(x^2 + 2x + 4)$ **f.** $(2x + 1)(4x^2 - 2x + 1)$ **i.** $x(x^2 + 3x + 3)$

**Lesson 1.08**

**Check Your Understanding**

**1a.** $(3x + 7)(3x - 1)$ **b.** $(2x - 7)(3x - 5)$ **c.** $(3x - 1)(5x + 7)$ **d.** $(9x - 1)(x + 7)$ **e.** $-(9x + 1)(2x + 7)$ **f.** $-(9x + 1)(2x - 7)$ **g.** $(3x + 1)(3x - 1)(x^2 + 7)$ **h.** $(5 - 2x)(5 + 2x)$ **i.** $x(9x + 1)(2x - 7)$ **2a.** $(3x + 7y)(3x - y)$ **b.** $(2x - 7y)(3x - 5y)$ **c.** $(3x - a)(5x + 7a)$ **d.** $(9x - b)(x + 7b)$ **e.** $-(9x + a)(2x + 7a)$ **f.** $-(9x + y)(2x - 7y)$ **g.** $(5y + 2x)(5y - 2x)$ **h.** $x(9x + y)(2x - 7y)$

**On Your Own**

**3d.** $(2x + 5)(2x + 1)$ **e.** $(2x + 1)(2x - 1)(x^2 - 3)$ **5a.** $z^2 = 2$

**Lesson 1.09**

**Check Your Understanding**

**1.** Expand the left sides: $(x + y)^3 = (x + y)(x^2 + 2xy + y^2) = x^3 + 3x^2y + 3xy^2 + y^3$, and $(x - y)^3 = (x - y)(x^2 - 2xy + y^2) = x^3 - 3x^2y + 3xy^2 - y^3$ **2a.** $(x - 4)(x^2 + 4x + 16)$ **b.** $(x + 4)(x^2 - 4x + 16)$ **c.** $(3x - 4)(9x^2 + 12x + 16)$ **d.** $(3x - 4)(9x^2 - 12x + 16)$ **e.** $(x - 3)(x^2 - 2x + 21)$ **f.** $(2x + 1)(4x^2 - 20x + 37)$ **g.** $(x + 3)(x - 3)(x + 3)$ **h.** $(x + a)(x - a)(x + a)$ **i.** $(-2x - 1)(4x + 1)$ **j.** $(x - y + z)(x + y - z)$ **k.** $(x - 2)(x - 7)(x + 5)$ **l.** $(x - 2y)(x - 7y)(x + 5y)$ **m.** $(x + 1)(x^2 - x + 1)$ **3.** Multiply each term by 25 to get $125x^3 + 75x^2 + 75x - 50$; that can be rewritten as $(5x)^3 + 3(5x)^2 + 15(5x) - 50$, which can be factored as $25(5x - 2)(x^2 + x + 1)$. Divide by 25 to get $(5x - 2)(x^2 + x + 1)$.

**On Your Own**

**4l.** $(x - 2)(x^2 - x + 1)$ **5.** $(x - 4)(x^2 + 4x + 1)$

**Lesson 1.10**

**Check Your Understanding**

**1a.** $(x^2 + 2)(x^2 - 3)$ **b.** $(x - 1)(x^2 + x + 1)(x - 2)(x^2 + 2x + 4)$ **c.** $(x^2 + 4)(x + 2)(x - 2)$ **d.** $(x^2 - 2)(x^4 + 2x^2 + 4)$ **e.** $(x^2 + 4y^2)(x + 2y)(x - 2y)$ **f.** $(x^2 + 2)(x^4 - 2x^2 + 4)$ **g.** $(x^2 + x - 4)(x^2 - x - 4)$ **h.** $(x^2 + x + 1)(x^2 - x + 1)$ **2a.** $(x - 1 - \sqrt{5})(x - 1 + \sqrt{5})$ **b.** $\left(x - 0.5 - \frac{\sqrt{5}}{2}\right)\left(x - 0.5 + \frac{\sqrt{5}}{2}\right)$ **3a.** Answers may vary. Sample: $x^2 - 4x + 1$ **b.** Answers may vary. Sample: $x^2 - 4x + 1$ **c.** $x^4 - 10x^2 + 1 = 0$ **4.** yes; Sample: $x^2 - \frac{1}{4} = (x - \frac{1}{2})(x + \frac{1}{2})$

**On Your Own**

**5e.** $(x^2 - x + 5)(x^2 + x + 5)$ **6a.** 49 **c.** 81

**Lesson 1.11**

**Check Your Understanding**

**1a.** $\frac{3}{x}$ **b.** $x - y$ **c.** $\frac{x-y}{x+y}$ **d.** $\frac{1}{x^2+1}$ **e.** $\frac{2x-3}{3x-2}$ **f.** $\frac{(x+1)(x^2+1)}{x^2+x+1}$ **2.** $f(x) = \frac{(2x-3)(x+2)}{(3x-2)(x+2)}$ and $g(x) = \frac{2x-3}{3x-2}$. The graph of $f(x)$ will have a "hole" at $f(-2)$, or $(-2, 0.875)$, since $f(-2)$ is undefined. The graph of $g(x)$ will not have a hole, since $g(-2)$ is defined. **3a.** 1 **b.** $\frac{1}{(x-a)(x-b)}$ **4a.** $\frac{2x^2-10x+1}{3(x-1)(x-4)}$ **b.** $\frac{-x^2+12x+9}{x(x-3)(x+3)}$ **c.** 0 **5.** $A = -\frac{1}{2}$, $B = \frac{1}{2}$

**On Your Own**

**6c.** $x^3 + 1$ **7a.** $\frac{x^2+1}{x^2-1}$

Selected Answers

## Chapter 2

### Lesson 2.0

### Check Your Understanding

**1.**

| Input, $n$ | Output, $B(n)$ | $\Delta$ |
|---|---|---|
| 0 | 0 | 2 |
| 1 | 2 | 4 |
| 2 | 6 | 6 |
| 3 | 12 | 8 |
| 4 | 20 | |

**2a.** no **b.** no **c.** yes **d.** no **3a.** no **b.** yes **c.** yes **d.** no

**4.**

| Input | Output | $\Delta$ |
|---|---|---|
| 0 | 5 | 6 |
| 1 | 11 | **8** |
| 2 | 19 | 10 |
| 3 | **29** | 15 |
| 4 | **44** | |

**5.**

| Input | Output | $\Delta$ |
|---|---|---|
| 0 | **6** | 3 |
| 1 | **9** | 3 |
| 2 | **12** | 3 |
| 3 | **15** | 3 |
| 4 | 18 | |

**6.**

| Input | Output | $\Delta$ |
|---|---|---|
| 0 | 5 | −3 |
| 1 | **2** | **15** |
| 2 | 17 | **−13** |
| 3 | **4** | −5 |
| 4 | −1 | |

**7a.** $f(1) = 1 \cdot f(0) = 1 \cdot 1 = 1$
$f(2) = 2 \cdot f(1) = 2 \cdot 1 = 2$
$f(3) = 3 \cdot f(2) = 3 \cdot 2 = 6$
$f(4) = 4 \cdot f(3) = 4 \cdot 6 = 24$
$f(5) = 5 \cdot f(4) = 5 \cdot 24 = 120$
$f(6) = 6 \cdot f(5) = 6 \cdot 120 = 720$
**b.** $f(n) = n!$

**8a.**

| Input | Output |
|---|---|
| 0 | 2 |
| 1 | 6 |
| 2 | **10** |
| 3 | **14** |
| 4 | **18** |

**b–c.**

| Input | Output |
|---|---|
| 0 | 2 |
| 1 | 6 |
| 2 | **18** |
| 3 | **54** |
| 4 | **162** |

**d.** see part (a) **9.** Answers may vary. Sample: Tables E, F, and G have a constant difference in the difference table; Tables I, J, and K include an $x^2$ term in the rule.

### On Your Own

**10.**

| Side Length | Number of Dots | $\Delta$ |
|---|---|---|
| 0 | 0 | **1** |
| 1 | 1 | **2** |
| 2 | 3 | **3** |
| 3 | 6 | **4** |
| 4 | 10 | **5** |
| 5 | 15 | |

**11a.** $T(n) = T(n-1) + n$
**12a.** The differences are all $a$.

### Lesson 2.01

### On Your Own

**6a.**

| Roll | Gain | Total |
|---|---|---|
| 1 | 5 | 55 |
| 2 | −2 | 53 |
| 3 | −4 | 49 |
| 4 | 3 | 52 |
| 5 | −6 | 46 |
| 6 | 1 | 47 |
| 7 | −6 | 41 |

**7.**

| $n$ | $t(n)$ | $\Sigma$ |
|---|---|---|
| 0 | 1 | 1 |
| 1 | 9 | 10 |
| 2 | 90 | 100 |
| 3 | 900 | 1000 |
| 4 | 9000 | 10,000 |

$\sum = 10^n$ **12a.** $h(n) = 100n^2$

**Lesson 2.02**
**Check Your Understanding**

**1a.** $S = \frac{n(n+1)}{2}$ **b.** $S = \frac{n(n+1)}{2}$ **c.** $S = \frac{(n-1) \cdot n}{2}$ **2a.** 6 **b.** 30 **c.** 250,500 **3a.** 16 **b.** 49 **c.** 250,000 **4a.** $S = n(n+1)$ **b.** $S = (n+1)^2$ **5a.** 65,504 **b.** 196,512 **c.** $\approx 5.862$ **d.** $1 - \frac{1}{10^{10}} \approx 1$ **e.** $\approx 0.664$ **6a.** Answers may vary. Sample: $1 + 2 + 3 + \cdots + 10 = 55$; $2 + 4 + 6 + \cdots + 22 = 132$; $4 + 7 + 10 + \cdots + 31 = 175$; Gauss's method works when there is a constant difference between successive terms. **b.** Answers may vary. Sample: $2 + 4 + 8 + \cdots + 64 = 126$; $5 + 10 + 20 + 40 + \cdots + 640 = 1275$; $4 + 12 + 36 + \cdots + 4 \cdot 3^{100} = 2 \cdot 3^{101} - 2 \approx 3.09 \cdot 10^{48}$; Euclid's method works when there is a constant ratio between successive terms. **7a.** $S = \frac{r^{n+1} - 1}{r - 1}$ **b.** $S = a \cdot \frac{r^{n+1} - 1}{r - 1}$

**On Your Own**

**8a.** $-10$ **10.** $-19$

**12.**

| $n$ | $f(n)$ |
|---|---|
| 1 | $\frac{1}{2}$ |
| 2 | $\frac{3}{4}$ |
| 3 | $\frac{7}{8}$ |
| 4 | $\frac{15}{16}$ |
| 5 | $\frac{31}{32}$ |
| $n$ | $\frac{2^n - 1}{2^n}$ |

$f(n) = \frac{2^n - 1}{2^n}$

**Lesson 2.03**
**Check Your Understanding**

**1.** Answers may vary. Sample: Cori is correct that the sum is never more than the whole sheet. David is correct that the total area of the rectangles on the desk increases, although by smaller and smaller amounts. **2.** Answers may vary. Sample: The area of the piece of paper in her hand keeps getting smaller and smaller, so the area of the "rest" of the paper gets closer to the starting area of 1. **3a.** 300 **b.** 1596 **c.** 3240 **d.** 7626 **e.** $\frac{n(n+1)}{2}$ **4a.** $1 - r^2$ **b.** $1 - r^3$ **c.** $1 - r^4$ **d.** $1 - r^{n+1}$ **5a.** $\approx 2.92$ **b.** $\approx 1.33$ **c.** 11,111,111,111 **6.** $\frac{1 - r^{n+1}}{1 - r} = \frac{-1}{-1} \cdot \frac{1 - r^{n+1}}{1 - r} = \frac{-1 + r^{n+1}}{-1 + r} = \frac{r^{n+1} - 1}{r - 1}$

**On Your Own**

**8a.**

| $n$ | $s(n)$ | $\Sigma$ |
|---|---|---|
| 0 | 2 | 2 |
| 1 | 5 | 7 |
| 2 | 8 | 15 |
| 3 | 11 | 26 |

**b.** $s(n) = 3n + 2$ **9a.** $\frac{1}{9}$ in hand, $\frac{4}{9}$ in pile 1, $\frac{4}{9}$ in pile 2

**Lesson 2.04**
**Check Your Understanding**

**1a.** 91 **b.** 324 **c.** 10 **d.** 969 **2.** Yes; Answers may vary. Sample: After you substitute values for the placeholder, the placeholder does not appear in the sequence.

**3a.** $\sum_{i=1}^{n} n^2$ **b.** $\sum_{i=1}^{6} 1$ **c.** $\sum_{i=1}^{10} i$ **4a.** $\sum_{i=1}^{10} \frac{1}{2^i}$ **b.** $\sum_{i=1}^{n} \frac{1}{2^i}$ **c.** $\sum_{i=1}^{\infty} \frac{1}{2^i}$ **5.** $\frac{1023}{1024} \approx 0.999023438$

**On Your Own**

**6a.** $\sum_{i=1}^{10} \frac{1}{3^i}$ **7.** $\frac{29,524}{59,049} \approx 0.499991532$

**Lesson 2.05**
**On Your Own**

**3a.** $q(n) = 3n + 5$, which is linear.

**Lesson 2.06**
**Check Your Understanding**

**1a.** yes **b.** yes **c.** no **d.** yes **e.** yes **f.** yes **g.** yes **h.** no **i.** no **j.** yes **k.** yes **2a.** 440; 442 **b.** 4,782,966; 2186 **c.** 182; 332 **3a.** 25 **b.** 100 **c.** 75 **d.** $\sum_{k=1}^{n} (2k - 1) = n^2$ **e.** 1,000,000

### On Your Own

**4.** $\sum_{k=0}^{n}(5k-1) = \frac{(n+1)(5n-2)}{2}$ **7a.** 42
**9a.** 99,999

### Lesson 2.07
### Check Your Understanding

**1.** 6625 **2a.** 374 **b.** 1.99988 **c.** 0.99988 **3a.** 377 **b.** 572 **c.** 1326 **d.** 332

### On Your Own

**4e.** 765 **5a.** 70 **b.** 66 **c.** 70 **d.** 12,207,241
**10b.** 1,039,600 **11a.** $\frac{n(n+1)(n+2)}{3}$ **13a.** 450

### Lesson 2.08
### Check Your Understanding

**1.** $H(n) = \frac{n^2+n+6}{2}$

**2a.** $q(n) = \begin{cases} 32 & \text{if } n = 0 \\ q(n-1) + 2n & \text{if } n > 0 \end{cases}$

**b.** $Q(n) = n(n+1) + 32$ **3.** $S(n) = n^2$

### On Your Own

**5a.**

| $n$ | $s(n)$ | $\Delta$ |
|---|---|---|
| 0 | 7 | 1 |
| 1 | 8 | 4 |
| 2 | 12 | 9 |
| 3 | 21 | |

$s(n) = \begin{cases} 7 & \text{if } n = 0 \\ s(n-1) + n^2 & \text{if } n > 0 \end{cases}$

**6a.** $t(n) = \sum_{k=0}^{n} 2^k$

**10a.** $p(n) = \begin{cases} 1 & \text{if } n = 1 \\ p(n-1) + (3n-2) & \text{if } n > 1 \end{cases}$

**b.** $P(n) = \frac{3n^2-n}{2}$

### Lesson 2.09
### On Your Own

**5a.** A.M.: $h(n) = 3n$; P.M.: $g(n) = 3n + 5$
**7.** $708

### Lesson 2.10
### Check Your Understanding

**1.** $\frac{4}{n-1}$ **2.** Yes; $\frac{1}{6}, \frac{1}{3}, \frac{1}{2}, \frac{2}{3}, \frac{5}{6}$, 1, . . . **3.** Yes; 1, 3, $\pi$; Any multiple of the difference between 3 and $\pi$ cannot equal a multiple of the difference between 1 and 3.

**4a.**

| $n$ | $q(n)$ | $\Sigma$ |
|---|---|---|
| 0 | 9 | 9 |
| 1 | 15 | 24 |
| 2 | 21 | 45 |
| 3 | 27 | 72 |
| 4 | 33 | 105 |

$q(n) = 6n + 9$;
$Q(n) = 3n^2 + 2n + 9$

**b.**

| $n$ | $p(n)$ | $\Sigma$ |
|---|---|---|
| 0 | 12 | 12 |
| 1 | 7 | 19 |
| 2 | 2 | 21 |
| 3 | −3 | 18 |
| 4 | −8 | 10 |

$p(n) = 12 - 5n$ ; $P(n) = -\frac{5}{2}n^2 + \frac{19}{2}n + 12$

**5.** 8, 10, 12, 14, 16, . . . ; there is no other arithmetic sequence with the same 0th and 2nd terms. **6a.** 2, 5, 8, 11, 14, . . . **b.** 2, 7, 15, 26, 40, . . . **c.** $g(n) = 2 + 3n$; $G(n) = \frac{3}{2}n^2 + \frac{7}{2}n + 2$

**7a.**

| $n$ | $t(n)$ | $\Sigma$ |
|---|---|---|
| 0 | 5 | 5 |
| 1 | 14 | 19 |
| 2 | 23 | 42 |
| 3 | 32 | 74 |
| 4 | 41 | 115 |

$t(n) = 5 + 9n$; $T(n) = \frac{9}{2}n^2 + \frac{19}{2}n + 5$

**b.**

| $n$ | $h(n)$ | $\Sigma$ |
|---|---|---|
| 0 | 7 | 7 |
| 1 | 3 | 10 |
| 2 | −1 | 9 |
| 3 | −5 | 4 |
| 4 | −9 | −5 |

$h(n) = 7 - 4n$; $H(n) = -2n^2 + 5n + 7$

**c.**

| $n$ | $t(n)$ | $\sum$ |
|---|---|---|
| 0 | 6 | 6 |
| 1 | 6.5 | 12.5 |
| 2 | 7 | 19.5 |
| 3 | 7.5 | 27 |
| 4 | 8 | 35 |

$t(n) = 6 + \frac{1}{2}n$; $T(n) = \frac{1}{4}n^2 + \frac{25}{4}n + 6$

**8a.**

| $n$ | $f(n)$ | $\sum$ |
|---|---|---|
| 0 | $a$ | $a$ |
| 1 | $a + d$ | $2a + d$ |
| 2 | $a + 2d$ | $3a + 3d$ |
| 3 | $a + 3d$ | $4a + 6d$ |
| 4 | $a + 4d$ | $5a + 10d$ |
| 5 | $a + 5d$ | $6a + 15d$ |

**b.** $F(n) = \frac{1}{2}(n + 1)(2a + nd)$

### On Your Own

**11.** If the integers are $n$, $n + 1$, and $n + 2$, then the average is $\frac{n + (n + 1) + (n + 2)}{3} = \frac{3n + 3}{3} = n + 1$, which is the middle number. **13a.** 1, 5, 14, 30, 55 **15.** 1, 6, 11, 21, ... or 7, 10, 13, 16, 19, ... **16.** Answers may vary. Sample: for the sequence 1, 4, 9, 16, 25, 36, ..., the $\Delta$ values are 3, 5, 7, 9, 11, ..., which is an arithmetic sequence. A closed form is $f(n) = n^2$.

## Lesson 2.11

### Check Your Understanding

**1a.** 320 **b.** 320 **c.** 5 **d.** $\frac{5}{64}$ **e.** 4.5 **f.** 75 **g.** $\pm 18$ **h.** 18 **2.** Yes; Any constant sequence such as 3, 3, 3, 3, ... has a constant difference (0) and a constant ratio (1), so it is both arithmetic and geometric. **3.** Answers may vary. Sample: $a_1 = 2, 4, 6, 8, \ldots$ and $g_1 = 2, 4, 8, 16, 32, \ldots$, the common difference is greater than 1 and the terms of the sequence increase, the common ratio is greater than 1, if the first term is positive the terms will increase, if the first term is negative the terms will decrease; $a_2 = 1, 2, 3, 4, 5, \ldots$ and $g_2 = 1, 1, 1, 1, 1, \ldots$, the common difference is 1 and the terms of the sequence increase, the common ratio is 1 and the terms of the sequence remain constant; $a_3 = 6, 5, 4, 3, 2, \ldots$ and $g_3 = 6, -6, 6, -6, 6, \ldots$ the common difference is negative 1 and the terms of the sequence decrease, the common ratio is $-1$, the terms will alternate between positive and negative values with the same absolute value; $a_4 = 5, 2, -1, -4, -7, \ldots$ and $g_4 = 5, -15, 45, -135, 405, \ldots$ the common difference is less than $-1$ and the terms of the sequence decrease, the common ratio is less than $-1$, the terms will alternate between positive and negative values; $a_5 = 10, 9.5, 9, 8.5, 8, 7.5, \ldots$ and $g_5 = 10, 5, \frac{5}{2}, \frac{5}{4}, \frac{5}{8}, \ldots$, the common difference is between 0 and 1, and the terms of the sequence decrease, the common ratio is between 0 and 1, if the first term is positive the terms will decrease towards zero, if the first term is negative the terms will increase towards zero

**4a.** $\sum_{i=0}^{n} 5 \cdot \left(\frac{1}{2}\right)^n = -10\left[\left(\frac{1}{2}\right)^{n+1} - 1\right]$ or $\sum_{i=0}^{n} 5 \cdot \left(\frac{1}{2}\right)^n = 10\left[1 - \left(\frac{1}{2}\right)^{n+1}\right]$ **b.** $\approx 9.999847$

### On Your Own

**5a.** $g(n) = 5 \cdot 2^{n-1}$ **e.** $g(n) = 576 \cdot \left(\frac{1}{2}\right)^n$

**7.**

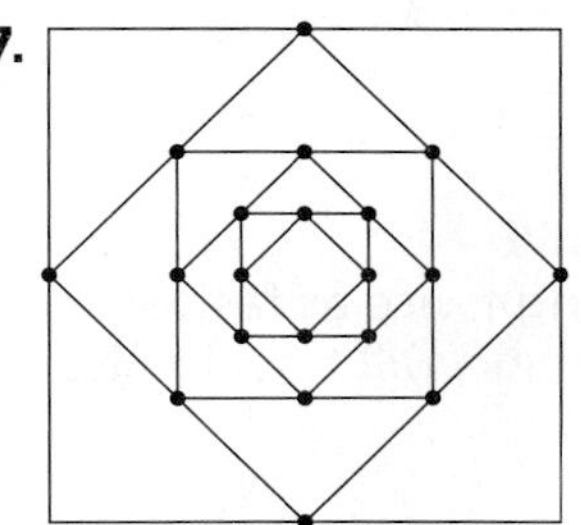

**a.** $\frac{\sqrt{2}}{2}; \frac{1}{2}$ **b.** Yes, the first term is 1 and the common ratio is $\frac{\sqrt{2}}{2}$. **9a.** $2^{63} \approx 9.22 \cdot 10^{18}$ **11a.** at least 5.5 mi

## Lesson 2.12

### Check Your Understanding

**1a.**

| $n$ | $t(n)$ | $T(n)$ |
|---|---|---|
| 1 | 7 | 7 |
| 2 | $7 \cdot \left(\frac{2}{9}\right) = \frac{14}{9}$ | $8\frac{5}{9}$ |
| 3 | $7 \cdot \left(\frac{2}{9}\right)^2 = \frac{28}{81}$ | $8\frac{73}{81}$ |
| 4 | $7 \cdot \left(\frac{2}{9}\right)^3 = \frac{56}{729}$ | $8\frac{713}{729}$ |

$T(n)$ has a limit, which is 9.

Selected Answers

**b.**

| $n$ | $t(n)$ | $T(n)$ |
|---|---|---|
| 1 | 100 | 100 |
| 2 | $100 \cdot \frac{1}{2} = 50$ | 150 |
| 3 | $100 \cdot \left(\frac{1}{2}\right)^2 = 25$ | 175 |
| 4 | $100 \cdot \left(\frac{1}{2}\right)^3 = 12.5$ | 187.5 |

$T(n)$ has a limit, which is 200.

**c.**

| $n$ | $t(n)$ | $T(n)$ |
|---|---|---|
| 1 | $\frac{3}{4}$ | $\frac{3}{4}$ |
| 2 | $\frac{3}{4} \cdot 2 = \frac{3}{2}$ | $2\frac{1}{4}$ |
| 3 | $\frac{3}{4} \cdot 2^2 = 3$ | $5\frac{1}{4}$ |
| 4 | $\frac{3}{4} \cdot 2^3 = 6$ | $11\frac{1}{4}$ |

$T(n)$ does not have a limit.

**d.**

| $n$ | $t(n)$ | $T(n)$ |
|---|---|---|
| 1 | 1 | 1 |
| 2 | 1 | 2 |
| 3 | 1 | 3 |
| 4 | 1 | 4 |

$T(n)$ does not have a limit.
**2.** 2 miles (she is traveling twice as fast, so in the same time period she will travel twice as far).

**On Your Own**
**3a.**

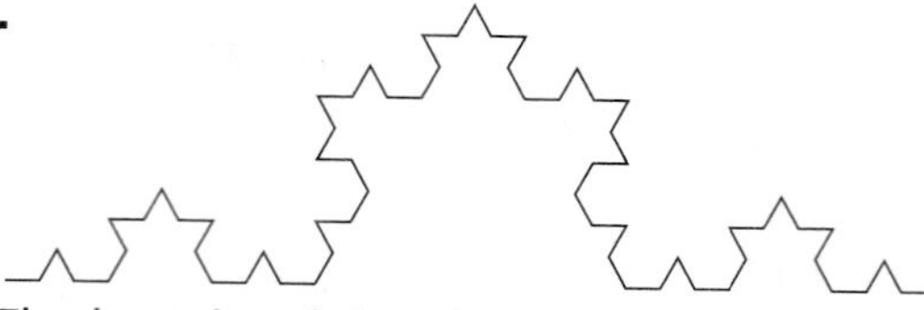

**b.** The lengths of the ends of Stages 0, 1, 2, and 3 are 1, $\frac{4}{3}$, $\frac{16}{9}$, and $\frac{64}{27}$, respectively.
**5a.** $\frac{9}{5}$ square units

**Lesson 2.13**
**Check Your Understanding**
**1a.** $a = 0.123$ **b.** $r = 0.001$ **c.** $\frac{123}{999}$ $\left(\text{or } \frac{41}{333}\right)$
**2a.** $\frac{12}{99}$ $\left(\text{or } \frac{4}{33}\right)$ **b.** $\frac{807}{999}$ $\left(\text{or } \frac{269}{333}\right)$ **c.** $\frac{123}{9990}$ $\left(\text{or } \frac{41}{3330}\right)$
**d.** $\frac{75,048}{999,000}$ $\left(\text{or } \frac{3127}{41,625}\right)$

**On Your Own**
**4.** The series $1 + 2 + 3 + 4 + \ldots$ does not have a finite value, so it was not possible to "call it $x$."

**Lesson 2.14**
**On Your Own**
**6a.** $(a + b)^2 = a^2 + 2ab + b^2$
**b.** $(a + b)^3 = a^3 + 3a^2b + 3ab^2 + b^3$
**8a.** $\frac{1}{16}r^2 + \frac{3}{8}rs + \frac{9}{16}s^2$ **b.** $\frac{1}{64}r^3 + \frac{9}{64}r^2s + \frac{27}{64}rs^2 + \frac{27}{64}s^3$

**Lesson 2.15**
**Check Your Understanding**
**1a.** 32 or $2^5$ **b.** 64 or $2^6$ **c.** 128 or $2^7$ **d.** $2^n$
**2.** Answers may vary. Sample: Each element in row $(n - 1)$ contributes twice to row $n$, so the sum of entries in row $n$ is twice the sum of entries in row $(n - 1)$.

**Lesson 2.16**
**Check Your Understanding**
**1a.** $(x + y)^7 = x^7 + 7x^6y + 21x^5y^2 + 35x^4y^3 + 35x^3y^4 + 21x^2y^5 + 7xy^6 + y^7$
**b.** $(x + 2y)^5 = x^5 + 10x^4y + 40x^3y^2 + 80x^2y^3 + 80xy^4 + 32y^5$ **2a.** 56 **b.** $a^5b^3$
**c.** entry $\binom{8}{4}$ **3a.** 120 **b.** 10 **c.** 252

**On Your Own**
**4.** 0; 0; 0

## Chapter 3
**Lesson 3.01**
**On Your Own**
**7. b.** $\frac{19}{25}$ **d.** $\frac{35}{49}$ **8. a.** 120

**Lesson 3.02**
**Check Your Understanding**
**1. a.** $\frac{1}{2}$ **b.** $\frac{1}{4}$ **c.** $\frac{1}{2}$ **d.** $\frac{1}{2}$ **e.** 0 **f.** $\frac{1}{36}$ **g.** $\frac{35}{36}$
**2.** The results are not equally likely because there are 5 ways to roll a sum of 8 on two dice out of 36 outcomes; $\frac{5}{36}$ **3.** 15; HHTTTT, HTHTTT, HTTHTT, HTTTHT, HTTTTH, THHTTT, THTHTT, THTTHT, THTTTH, TTHHTT, TTHTHT, TTHTTH, TTTHHT, TTTHTH, TTTTHH
**4.** $\binom{6}{2} = 15$; this represents 15 ways to pick two items from a group of six. **5.** 20; this is the coefficient of the $t^3h^3$ term; $(t + h)^6 = t^6 + 6t^5h + 15t^4h^2 + 20t^3h^3 + 15t^2h^4 + 6th^5 + t^6$ **6.** $\frac{21}{216}$

**On Your Own**
**9.** $\frac{84}{512}$ **10. a.** $\frac{1}{6}$ **11. a.** 36

**Lesson 3.03**
**Check Your Understanding**

**1. a.**

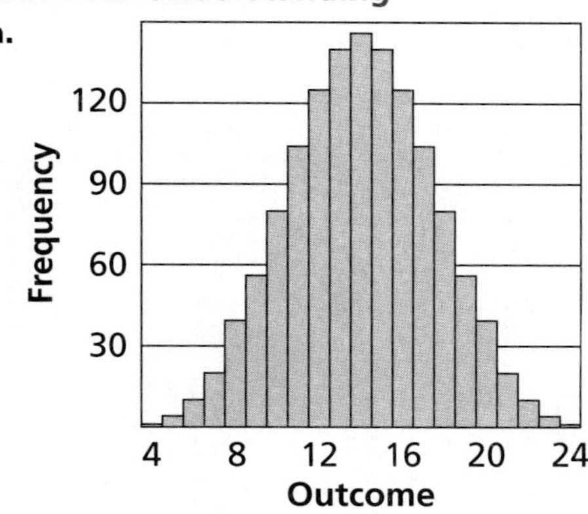


**b.** To roll a 5, the only possible roll is the four variations of 1-1-1-2. To roll a 23, the only possible roll is the four variations of 6-6-6-5. Also, the frequencies appear symmetric on either side of 14. **2.** $\frac{1}{2}$ **3. a.** $x^2 + x^3 + x^4 + x^5 + x^6 + x^{10}$ **b.** 20; $\frac{95}{1296}$ **4. a.** Answers may vary. Sample: $2x^5$ represents the two faces with 5 on them, while the other exponents indicate single faces with 1 through 4 on them. **b.** 13; $\frac{164}{1296}$ **5. a.** $q(x) = 4x^{10} + 4x^9 + 5x^8 + 6x^7 + 7x^6 + 4x^5 + 3x^4 + 2x^3 + x^2$; this represents the frequencies of the sums when the 1-2-3-4-5-5 number cube is rolled twice. **b.** 36 **c.** 4 **d.** 4 **6. a.** $\frac{3}{50}$ or 0.06 **b.** $\frac{425}{1000}$ or 0.425 **c.** $\frac{7760}{10,000}$ or 0.776

**On Your Own**

**7. a.** $1 + x + 2x^2 + x^7$ **b.** $\frac{72}{625}$ **8. a.** 0.2; 0.2 **b.** $(0.2)^6 = 0.000064$

**Lesson 3.04**
**Check Your Understanding**

**1. a.** $\frac{1}{24}$ **b.** $\frac{3}{8}$ **2.** 1 **3.** $5719.53 **4.** There is nothing wrong with Daisuke's calculation. His mistake was in the interpretation of his r esults. Expected value is not a probability and can be greater than 1. $\frac{12}{8}$ represents the number of heads expected when you toss 3 coins. **5. a.** $(0.2r + 0.8w)^6 = 0.000064r^6 + 0.001536r^5w + 0.01536r^4w^2 + 0.08192r^3w^3 + 0.24576r^2w^4 + 0.39322rw^5 + 0.26214w^6$; each term is the probability of getting a specific number of questions correct. **b.** 1.2 **6. a.** $(x^1 + x^2 + x^3 + x^{10})^3 = x^{30} + 3x^{23} + 3x^{22} + 3x^{21} + 3x^{16} + 6x^{15} + 9x^{14} + 6x^{13} + 3x^{12} + x^9 + 3x^8 + 6x^7 + 7x^6 + 6x^5 + 3x^4 + x^3$ **b.** $\frac{27}{64}$ **7.** 16

**On Your Own**

**8. b.** $14,925.80 **10. a.** 7 **b.** 10.5 **13.** 0

**Lesson 3.05**
**Check Your Understanding**

**1.**

| Matches | Frequency |
|---|---|
| 0 correct | 2,118,760 |
| 1 correct | 1,151,500 |
| 2 correct | 196,000 |
| 3 correct | 12,250 |
| 4 correct | 250 |
| 5 correct | 1 |

**2.** $\frac{5}{11}$ **3.** $\frac{44,800,030}{146,107,962} \approx 0.30662$

**4. a.** $\frac{1,000,000m + 28,800,030}{146,107,962} = 0.006844m + 0.197115$, where $m$ is the number of millions **b.** 0.88154 **c.** greater than $117,308,932

**5.**

| Ticket Type | Frequency | Payout |
|---|---|---|
| 5 balls + bonus | 1 | Jackpot |
| 5 balls + no bonus | 45 | $250,000 |
| 4 balls + bonus | 255 | $10,000 |
| 4 balls + no bonus | 11,475 | $150 |
| 3 balls + bonus | 12,750 | $150 |
| 3 balls + no bonus | 573,750 | $7 |
| 2 balls + bonus | 208,250 | $10 |
| 1 ball + bonus | 1,249,500 | $3 |
| Bonus only | 2,349,060 | $2 |
| Losing ticket | 171,306,450 | $0 |
| **Total outcomes** | **175,711,536** | |

0.25029 **6.** $10.64.

**On Your Own**

**7.** $\frac{6}{7}$ **8. a.** $\frac{1,110,353,500}{65,530,000} \approx 16.9468$ **b.** $200,046,500 **11. a.** 720

**Lesson 3.06**
**On Your Own**

**4. a.** higher **d.** higher **e.** Bill should go higher for $n \leq 53$ and lower for $n \geq 54$.

**Lesson 3.07**
**Check Your Understanding**

**1. a.** 4.5 **b.** 1.5 **c.** 2.917 **d.** 1.708 **2. a.** 7 **b.** 3 **c.** 11.667 **d.** 3.4156 **3. a.** 3.3333 **b.** 1.3333 **c.** 2.2222 **d.** 1.4907 **4. a.** 3 **b.** 0 **c.** 0 **d.** 0 **5. a.** The mean increases by c, but the mean absolute deviation, variance, and standard deviation are unchanged. Answers may vary. Sample: Compare the data set 1, 2, 3, 4, 5, 6 with the data set from Exercise 1. The mean increased by 1, but the other values are the same.

**b.** The mean, mean absolute deviation, and standard deviation are multiplied by k, and the variance is multiplied by $k^2$. Answers may vary. Sample: Compare the data set 1, 2, 3, 4, 5, 6 with the data from Exercise 2. The mean, mean absolute deviation, and standard deviation were multiplied by 2. The variance was multiplied by 4. **6.** 3.96; 1.8018
**7.** Let the original data be $\{x_1, x_2, \ldots, x_n\}$ with mean $\bar{x}$. **a.** The new data is $\{(x_1 + c), (x_2 + c), \ldots, (x_n + c)\}$. The mean of the data $\frac{x_1 + c + x_2 + c + \ldots x_n + c}{n} = \frac{x_1 + x_2 + \ldots + x_n + n \cdot c}{n} = \frac{x_1 + x_2 + \ldots + x_n}{n} + c = \bar{x} + c$ Each deviation is $(x_i + c) - (\bar{x} + c)$; the value of c cancels. **b.** The new data is $\{kx_1, kx_2, \ldots, kx_n\}$. The mean of the data is $\frac{kx_1 + kx_2 + \ldots + kx_n}{n} = k \cdot \frac{x_1 + x_2 + \ldots + x_n}{n} = k\bar{x}$. Each deviation is $kx_i - k\bar{x} = k(x_i - \bar{x})$; each deviation is k times larger. The variance will be $k^2$ times larger since each deviation is the variance squared. **8.** 7; $\frac{35}{18}$; $\frac{35}{6}$; 2.415; the mean and variance are doubled and the standard deviation is $\sqrt{2}$ times as large. The mean absolute deviation is larger by factor of $\frac{35}{27}$ which doesn't seem to be part of the pattern.

### On Your Own

**9. a.** $\frac{1}{2}$ **b.** $\frac{1}{2}$ and $-\frac{1}{2}$ **10. b.** 1, 0, 0, −1
**12. b.** $\frac{9}{2}$; 25

## Lesson 3.08

### Check Your Understanding

**1. a.**

| Sum | Frequency |
|---|---|
| 3 | 1 |
| 4 | 3 |
| 5 | 6 |
| 6 | 10 |
| 7 | 15 |
| 8 | 21 |
| 9 | 25 |
| 10 | 27 |
| 11 | 27 |
| 12 | 25 |
| 13 | 21 |
| 14 | 15 |
| 15 | 10 |
| 16 | 6 |
| 17 | 3 |
| 18 | 1 |

**b.** 10.5 **c.** $\frac{35}{4}$; $\frac{\sqrt{35}}{2}$ **d.** 3 times **e.** $\sqrt{3}$ times
**2. a.** 7; 25; 5 **b.** 16; 144; 12 **c.** 18; 256; 16
**3. a.**

| + | 1 | 7 | 13 | 25 | 34 |
|---|---|---|---|---|---|
| 2 | 3 | 9 | 15 | 27 | 36 |
| 12 | 13 | 19 | 25 | 37 | 46 |

**b.** 23; 169; 13
**4. a.**

| Y | 1 | 7 | 13 | 25 | 34 |
|---|---|---|---|---|---|
| 10 | 11 | 17 | 23 | 35 | 44 |
| 10 | 11 | 17 | 23 | 35 | 44 |
| 10 | 11 | 17 | 23 | 35 | 44 |
| 10 | 11 | 17 | 23 | 35 | 44 |
| 50 | 51 | 57 | 63 | 75 | 84 |

**b.** 34; 400; 20 **5.** 17 **6. a.** Spinner A: 5; Spinner B: 10.8; Spinner C: 12.8 **b.** 11.2 **c.** 16.32 **d.** Answers may vary. Sample: There is not an obvious pattern in the relationships of the mean absolute deviation of the combined spinners. **7.** Answers may vary. Sample: If the original standard deviations are *a* and *b*, and the new standard deviation is *c*. The numbers for the standard deviation are in the relationship, $a^2 + b^2 = c^2$.

### On Your Own

**8. a.** $\frac{5}{2}$; $\frac{11}{12}$; $\frac{\sqrt{33}}{6}$ **12. b.** −6.25 cents; yes, the game will make money over time. **13. a.** 25; 5

## Lesson 3.09

### Check Your Understanding

**1.** $\frac{1}{5}$; 0.16; 0.4 **2. a.** $\frac{1}{25}$; $\frac{8}{25}$; $\frac{16}{25}$ **b.** 0.4; 0.32; $\sqrt{0.32} \approx 0.566$ **3.** 0.6; 0.48; $\sqrt{0.48} \approx 0.693$
**4.** 4; 3.2; $\sqrt{3.2} \approx 1.789$ **5. a.** $\frac{1}{4}$; $\frac{1}{2}$ **b.** $\frac{1}{2}$; $\sqrt{0.5} \approx 0.707$ **c.** 1; 1 **d.** $\frac{9}{4}$; $\frac{3}{2}$ **e.** 25; 5 **6. a.** 3
**b.** Answers may vary. Sample: Yes, it is unusual most results should be in the range 18 ± 3, between 15 and 21. Only 10 head is far outside this range.
**c.** 0.003699 or 0.37% **7. a.** $p$; $p(1 - p)$; $\sqrt{p(1 - p)}$ **b.** $np$; $np(1 - p)$; $\sqrt{np(1 - p)}$

### On Your Own

**8. a.** 781.25; 27.95 **c.** 3125; 55.90 **9. e.** $\frac{5n}{36}$; $\frac{\sqrt{5n}}{6}$

## Lesson 3.12

### Check Your Understanding

**1. a.** 0.0514 **2. a.** 0.0690 **3. a.** 40; 5.7735 **b.** Answers may vary. Sample: This is an unusual result. Most of the results should be from 40 ± 5.7735. This is roughly from 34 to 46. Getting only 20 sixes is far outside this range. **4. a.** Each question has $p = 0.2$ probability of getting a correct answer. They are independent of one another, so the probability of getting *n* consecutive questions right is $0.2^n$.

**b.** 0.0115 or 1.15% **c.** 0.2054 or 20.54%

**5. a.** $f(n) = \binom{20}{n}(0.20)^n(0.8)^{(20-n)}$

**b.**

| $n$ | $f(n)$ |
|---|---|
| 0 | 0.0115 |
| 1 | 0.0576 |
| 2 | 0.1369 |
| 3 | 0.2054 |
| 4 | 0.2182 |
| 5 | 0.1746 |
| 6 | 0.1091 |
| 7 | 0.0545 |
| 8 | 0.0222 |
| 9 | 0.0074 |
| 10 | 0.0020 |

**6.** 0.2054; the coefficient is the probability of getting 3 correct and 17 wrong answers.

**7.**
$$\begin{aligned} p(1-p)^2 + p^2(1-p) &= p(1-p) \\ &= p(1-2p+p^2) + p^2 - p^3 \\ &= p - 2p^2 + p^3 + p^2 - p^3 \\ &= p - p^2 \\ &= p(1-p) \end{aligned}$$

**8.**

| Number of Successes | Probability | Product |
|---|---|---|
| 2 | $p^2$ | $2p^2$ |
| 1 | $2p(1-p)$ | $2p(1-p)$ |
| 0 | $(1-p)^2$ | 0 |
| Total | | $2p$ |

| Success | Deviation | Deviation² | Probability | Product |
|---|---|---|---|---|
| 2 | $2-2p$ | $(2-2p)^2$ | $p^2$ | $(2-2p)^2 \cdot p^2$ |
| 1 | $1-2p$ | $(1-2p)^2$ | $2p(1-p)$ | $(1-2p)^2 \cdot 2p(1-p)$ |
| 0 | $-2p$ | $(-2p)^2$ | $(1-p)^2$ | $(-2p)^2 \cdot (1-p)^2$ |
| Total | | | | $2p(1-p)$ |

### On Your Own

**9. a.** $pq$ **b.** $(1-p)(1-q)$ **c.** $p + q - 2pq$

**11.** 14; $\frac{146}{1296} \approx 0.1127 \approx 11.27\%$

## Lesson 3.15
### On Your Own

**5. a.** $\frac{13}{162} \approx 0.0802$ **b.** 1 **9. a.** 0.2475 **c.** 0.0782

## Lesson 3.16
### Check Your Understanding

**2. a.** 0.2066; **b.** 0.2051 **c.** 0.73% **3. a.** 50; 5 **b.** 0.2995 **c.** 0.0301 **d.** 0.41% **4. a.** 1800; 900 **b.** mean doubles to 3600; standard deviation is multiplied by $\sqrt{2}$ to 42.43 **c.** 3558 to 3642

**5. a.**

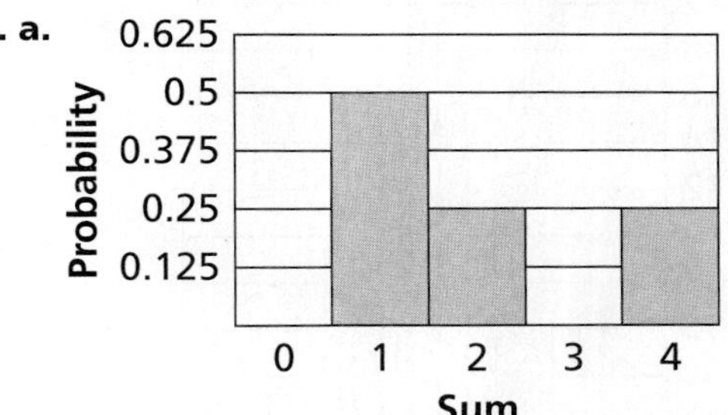


**b.**

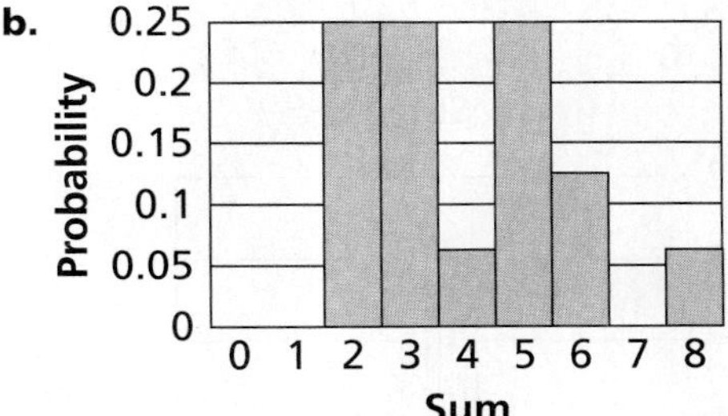

c.

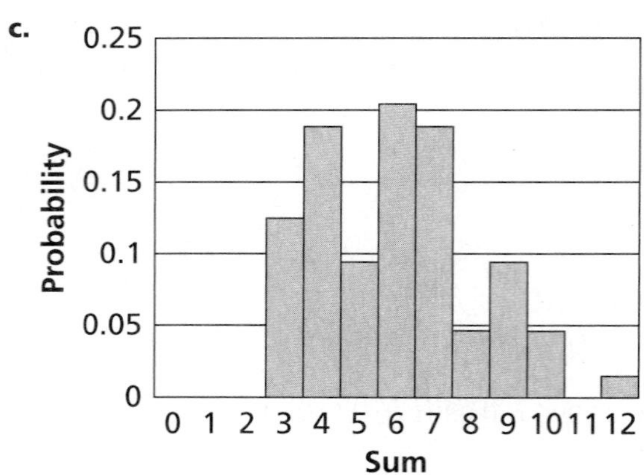


d.

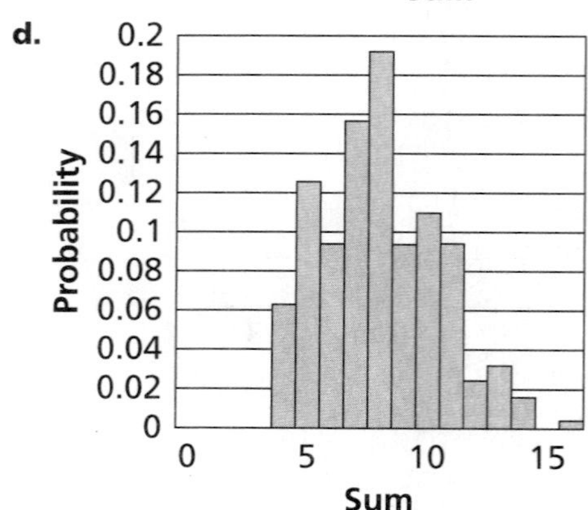


e.

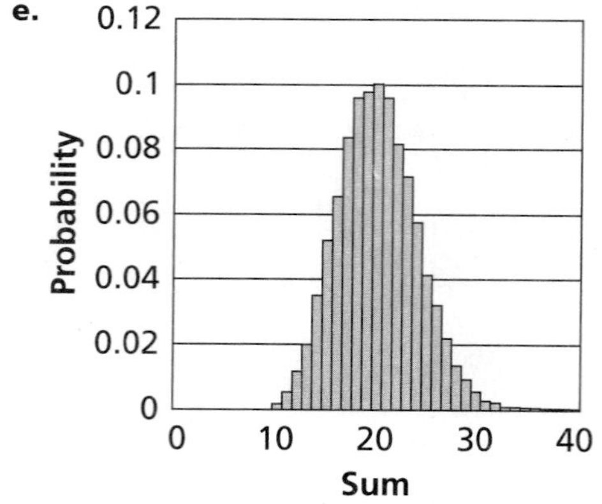


**6. a.** 100; 17.68 **b.** 82 to 118 **7. a.** 45 to 55 heads

**b.** $\sum_{k=45}^{55} \binom{100}{k} \cdot 0.5^k \cdot 0.5^{100-k} \approx 0.7287$

**On Your Own**

**8. a.** 1740 to 1860 heads **9. a.** 18; 3.55 **b.** 0.183 to 0.417 **12. c.** 0.040029 **d.** 0.040915

**Lesson 3.17**

**Check Your Understanding**

**1. a.** 68% **b.** 95% **c.** 2.5% **2. a.** 68% **b.** 60 to 78 inches **3. a.** 1250; 25 **b.** 16% **4. a.** 0.42074 **b.** 0.344578 **c.** 0.274253 **d.** 0.158655 **e.** 0.022750 **f.** 0.000032 **g.** 0 **5.** using the binomial theorem: 0.00013475, using the normal CDF: 0.00026605 **6. a.** .675 **b.** 1 **c.** 1.65 **d.** 2.58

**On Your Own**

**7. a.** 84% **b.** 10.6% **8.** 0.21% **12.** 52.2%

## Chapter 4

### Lesson 4.0

**Check Your Understanding**

**1.** 24.09 **2a.** 210 **b.** 29

**c.**

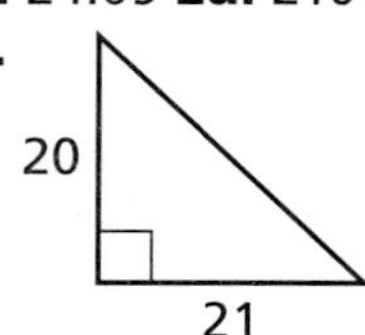


Each angle measures about 45°. **d.** 46°, 44° **3.** $\sin\theta = \frac{15}{17}$, $\tan\theta = \frac{15}{8}$ **4.** $\sin\theta = \frac{\text{opp}}{\text{hyp}}$ and $\cos\theta = \frac{\text{adj}}{\text{hyp}}$, so $\frac{\sin\theta}{\cos\theta} = \frac{\frac{\text{opp}}{\text{hyp}}}{\frac{\text{adj}}{\text{hyp}}} = \frac{\text{opp}}{\text{adj}} = \tan\theta$.

**5.** $\frac{\sqrt{15}}{4}$ **6.** $72\sqrt{3} \approx 124.71$, $24\sqrt{3} \approx 41.57$, or $18\sqrt{3} \approx 31.2$

**On Your Own**

**9.**

| $\theta$ | $\sin\theta$ | $\cos\theta$ | $\tan\theta$ |
|---|---|---|---|
| 30° | $\frac{1}{2}$ | $\frac{\sqrt{3}}{2}$ | $\frac{\sqrt{3}}{3}$ |
| 60° | $\frac{\sqrt{3}}{2}$ | $\frac{1}{2}$ | $\sqrt{3}$ |

**12a.** The largest value is 1 and the smallest is 0. As $\theta$ gets close to 90°, sin $\theta$ gets close to 1, and as $\theta$ gets close to 0, sin $\theta$ gets close to 0. **13a.** $\sin\theta = \frac{4}{5}$, $\cos\theta = \frac{3}{5}$, $\tan\theta = \frac{4}{3}$ **14.** You do not know that $\triangle TRI$ is a right triangle.

### Lesson 4.01

**On Your Own**

**11.**

| Angle | Coordinates |
|---|---|
| 0° | (1, 0) |
| 10° | **(0.985, 0.174)** |
| 20° | **(0.940, 0.342)** |
| 30° | **(0.866, 0.5)** |
| 40° | **(0.766, 0.643)** |
| 50° | **(0.643, 0.766)** |
| 60° | **(0.5, 0.866)** |
| 70° | **(0.342, 0.940)** |
| 80° | **(0.174, 0.985)** |
| 90° | (0, 1) |

**12a.** magnitude 5, argument ≈ 53°

**15.** Answers may vary. Sample: The *x*-coordinate starts at 1 when Olivia's angle is 0°, decreases to 0 as her angle increases to

90°, decreases to −1 as her angle increases to 180°, increases to 0 as her angle increases to 270°, and increases to 1 as her angle increases to 360°. This pattern will repeat from 360° to 720°, from 720° to 1080°, and so on.
**18.** $a = -1, b = \sqrt{3}$

### Lesson 4.02

#### Check Your Understanding

**1.** Answers may vary. Sample: If Jo's reasoning were correct, then the point $\left(\frac{1}{2}, \frac{1}{2}\right)$ should be on the unit circle and satisfy the equation $x^2 + y^2 = 1$. However, $\left(\frac{1}{2}\right)^2 + \left(\frac{1}{2}\right)^2 \neq 1$, so the point $\left(\frac{1}{2}, \frac{1}{2}\right)$ is not on the circle. **2.** $a = 0.342, b = 0.940$ **3.** $-\frac{\sqrt{3}}{2} - \frac{1}{2}i \approx -0.866 - 0.5i$ **4a.** $\cos\theta = -\cos(\theta + 180°)$
**b.** $\sin\theta = -\sin(\theta + 180°)$
**c.** $\tan\theta = \tan(\theta + 180°)$ **5a.** 1 **b.** 1 **6.** If the magnitude of a complex number is 1, such as $i$ or $-i$, then it must lie on the unit circle.
**7a.** $\theta = 0°$ or $180°$, or $\theta = 180° \cdot k$, where $k$ is an integer. **b.** $\theta = 90°$ or $270°$, or $\theta = 90° + 180° \cdot k$, where $k$ is an integer.
**c.** $\theta = 0°$ or $180°$, or $\theta = 180° \cdot k$, where $k$ is an integer.

#### On Your Own

**8a.**

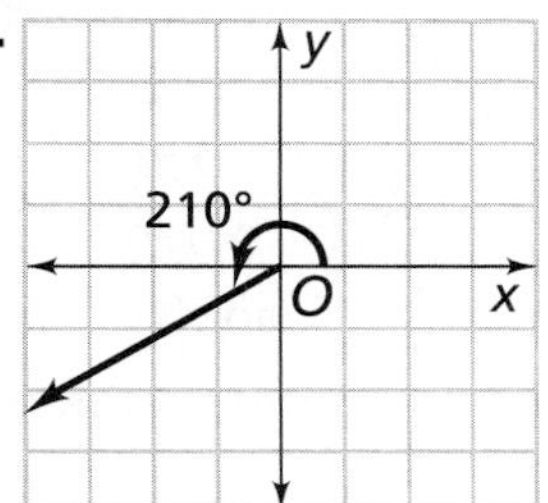


$\sin 210° = -\frac{\sqrt{3}}{2}$, $\cos 210° = -\frac{1}{2}$, $\tan 210° = \frac{\sqrt{3}}{3}$ **11.** Answers may vary. Sample: Since 310° is the same as −50° on the unit circle, we know that $\sin 310° = \sin(-50°)$. And because −50° is in Quadrant IV, where sine is negative, $\sin(-50°) = -\sin 50°$. So, $\sin 310° = -\sin 50°$.
**12a.** $-\frac{\sqrt{3}}{2}$

### Lesson 4.03

#### Check Your Understanding

**1.** Answers may vary. Sample: 160° is in Quadrant II and 20° is in Quadrant I. Since $\sin\theta$ is positive in both quadrants, $\sin 160° = \sin 20°$. Since $\cos\theta$ is positive in Quadrant I and negative in Quadrant II, then $\cos 160° = -\cos 20°$. **2a.** I or II **b.** $\cos\theta = \pm\frac{21}{29}$
**c.** $\tan\theta = \pm\frac{20}{21}$ **3.** Answers may vary. Sample: $\theta \approx 89.5°$ **4.** Answers may vary. Sample: Since −60° intersects the unit circle in Quadrant IV, the cosine will be positive. In general, $\cos(-\theta) = \cos\theta$. So $\cos(-60°) = \cos 60° = \frac{1}{2}$.
**5.** $\tan 110°$; $\cos 120° = \sin 210°$; $\sin 120°$; $\cos 720°$; $\tan 70°$ **6.** 30°, 150° **7a.** 0.7660
**b.** −0.6428 **c.** −0.6428 **d.** −0.7660 **e.** 1
**f.** 0.6428 **8a.** $\tan^2\theta = \frac{1}{\cos^2\theta} - 1$ or $\tan^2\theta + 1 = \frac{1}{\cos^2\theta}$ **b.** $\tan^2\theta + 1 = \frac{\sin^2\theta}{\cos^2\theta} + 1 = \frac{\sin^2\theta}{\cos^2\theta} + \frac{\cos^2\theta}{\cos^2\theta} = \frac{\sin^2\theta + \cos^2\theta}{\cos^2\theta} = \frac{1}{\cos^2\theta}$.
So, $\tan^2\theta = \frac{1}{\cos^2\theta} - 1$ or $\tan^2\theta + 1 = \frac{1}{\cos^2\theta}$.

#### On Your Own

**9.** $\cos(-30°) = \frac{\sqrt{3}}{2}$, $\sin(-30°) = -\frac{1}{2}$, $\tan(-30°) = -\frac{\sqrt{3}}{3}$ **10a.** $\sin 40°$ **d.** $-\sin 45°$
**11a.** $\sin\theta$ **f.** $-\sin\theta$ **13a.** positive **c.** negative
**17a.** $-\frac{12}{37}$

### Lesson 4.04

#### Check Your Understanding

**1.** $\cos q \approx -0.69$; $m\angle q \approx 134°$
**2a.** 60°, 300° **b.** $\pm\frac{\sqrt{3}}{2}$ **c.** $\frac{3}{4}$
**3.**

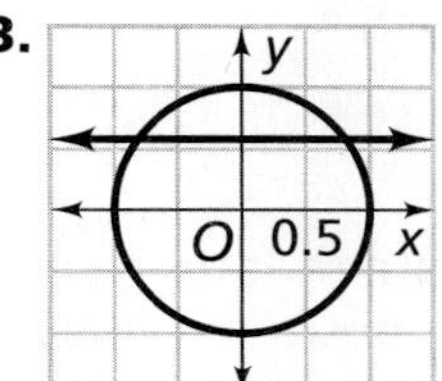


**4.** (0.8, 0.6), (−0.8, 0.6) **5a.** 53.1°, 306.9°
**b.** ±0.8 **c.** 0.64 **6.** Answers may vary. Sample:
$\frac{1}{z} = \frac{1}{\cos 30° + i\sin 30°} = \frac{1}{\frac{\sqrt{3}}{2} + \frac{1}{2}i} = \frac{1}{\frac{\sqrt{3}}{2} + \frac{1}{2}i} \cdot \frac{\frac{\sqrt{3}}{2} - \frac{1}{2}i}{\frac{\sqrt{3}}{2} - \frac{1}{2}i} = \frac{\frac{\sqrt{3}}{2} - \frac{1}{2}i}{\frac{3}{4} + \frac{1}{4}} = \frac{\sqrt{3}}{2} - \frac{1}{2}i = \bar{z}$

#### On Your Own

**8a.** 45°, 135° **11a.** Answers may vary. Sample: $\tan 30° = \frac{\sqrt{3}}{3}$ and $\cos 30° = \frac{\sqrt{3}}{2}$, so $\frac{1}{\cos^2 30°} - 1 = \frac{1}{\left(\frac{\sqrt{3}}{2}\right)^2} - 1 = \frac{1}{\frac{3}{4}} - 1 = \frac{4}{3} - \frac{3}{3} = \frac{1}{3} = \frac{3}{9} = \left(\frac{\sqrt{3}}{3}\right)^2 = \tan^2 30°$. **12a.** $\frac{1}{2}$

### Lesson 4.05

#### Check Your Understanding

**1.** $x = 50° + 360° \cdot k$, where $k$ is an integer.
**2a.** 37°, 143° **b.** 217°, 323° **3a.** 37°, 323°
**b.** no solution **4a.** no solution **b.** 41.8°, 138.2°
**c.** 30°, 150°, 210°, 330° **d.** 210°, 330° **5a.** 45°, 225° **b.** 135°, 315° **c.** 0°, 180°, 360° **6.** 30°, 150°, 199.47°, 340.53° **7.** Using the

Parallelogram Law, you find the vertices of the parallelogram formed by $z$ and $\overline{z}$ are (0, 0), ($a$, $b$), ($a$, $-b$), and ($2a$, 0). So $z + \overline{z} = 2a$. Also, if $\arg z = \theta$, then $\cos\theta = \frac{a}{|z|}$ (because $a$ is the value of the $x$-coordinate and $|z|$ is the distance from the origin to $z$). So $a = |z|\cos\theta$ and $2a = 2|z|\cos\theta$. **8.** Drop a perpendicular from $O$ to $\overline{AB}$ to form two congruent right triangles with acute angles 18° and 72°, legs $\frac{z}{2}$ and $\frac{z\sqrt{3}}{2}$, and hypotenuse 1. Then $\cos 72° = \frac{\text{adjacent}}{\text{hypotenuse}} = \frac{z}{2}$, so $z = 2 \cdot \cos 72°$.

**On Your Own**

**10b.** 45°, 225° **12a.** $0.940 + 0.342i$ **e.** $-0.682 - 0.731i$ **13a.** 36.87°

**Lesson 4.06**

**On Your Own**

**6.**

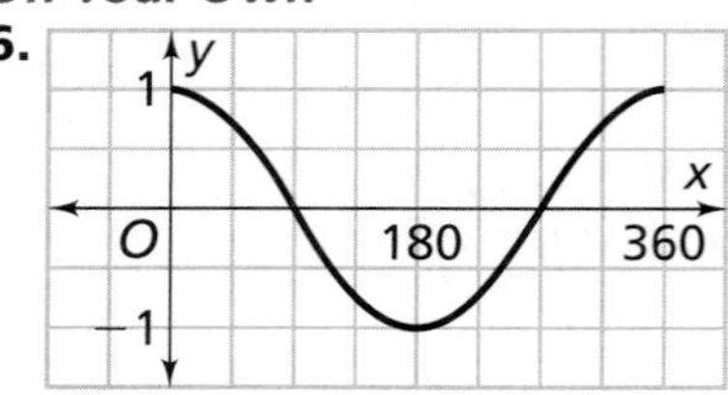


**7.** cos 230° > cos 190°

**Lesson 4.07**

**Check Your Understanding**

**1a.** The points on the unit circle that represent sin 50° and sin (−50°) have opposite $y$-values. So, sin 50° = −sin (−50°). **b.** The $y$-values for $x = 50°$ and $x = -50°$ on the graph of $y = \sin x$ are opposites. So, sin 50° = −sin (−50°). **2.** Answers may vary. Sample: Derman sees only a portion of $y = \sin x$, and all the $y$-values are close to the $x$-axis. He should reset his window so that $-360 \le x \le 360$ and $-2 \le y \le 2$.

**3.**

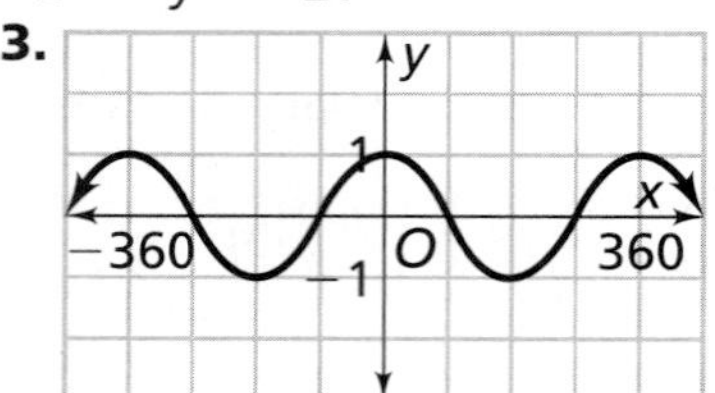


The graph looks like $y = \cos x$ because $\cos(x + 360°) = \cos x$. **4a.** There are infinitely many $x$-intercepts of $y = \cos x$. **b.** A polynomial function must have a finite degree and a finite number of $x$-intercepts, so the cosine function cannot be written as a polynomial function. **c.** The tangent function, $\frac{\sin\theta}{\cos\theta}$, is undefined when $\cos\theta = 0$, that is when $\theta = 90° + k \cdot 180°$, where $k$ is an integer.

**5.**

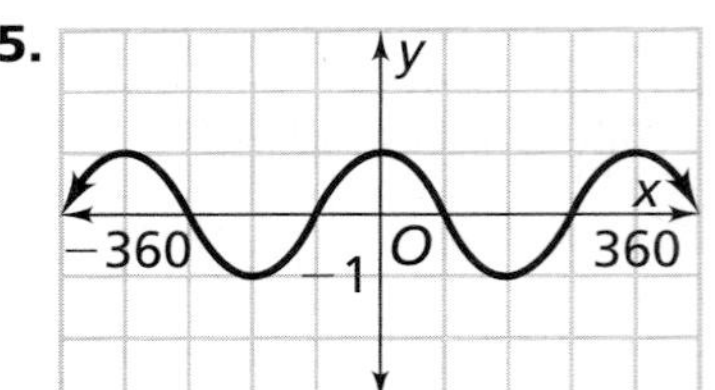


**6.**

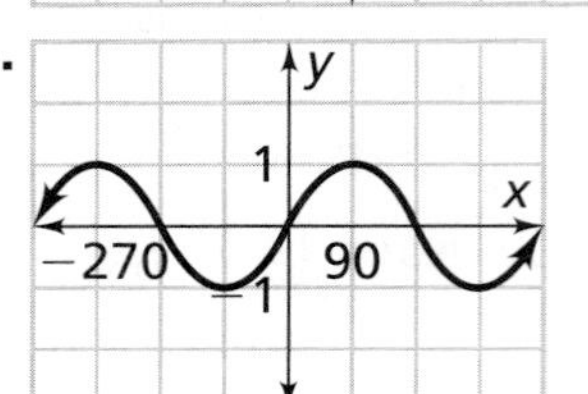


**7.** 143°, 397°

**8.**

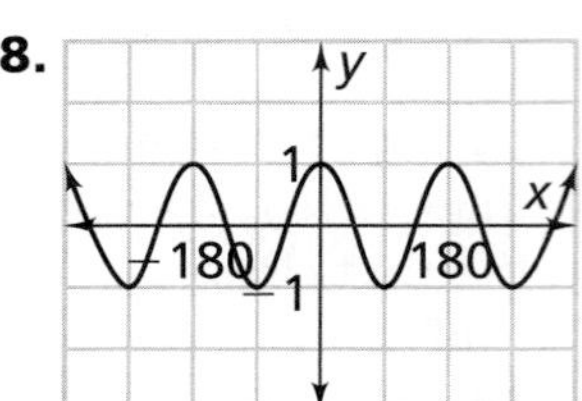


**9a.**

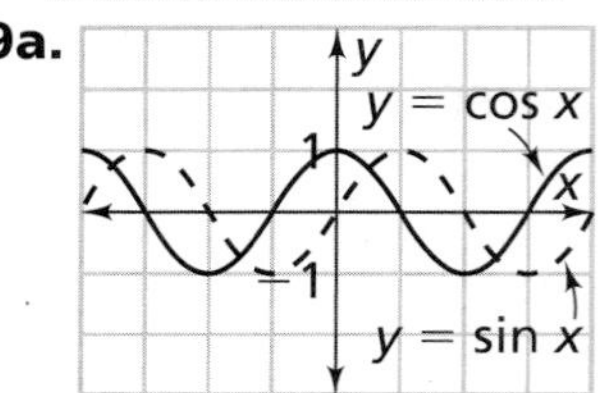


**b.** Answers may vary. Sample: 45°, 225°. Any angle of the form $45° + k \cdot 180°$, where $k$ is an integer. **10a.** 1 **b.** $\tan\theta = \frac{\sin\theta}{\cos\theta}$ and if $\sin\theta = \cos\theta$, then the tangent must be 1.

**On Your Own**

**11.** Answers may vary. Sample:

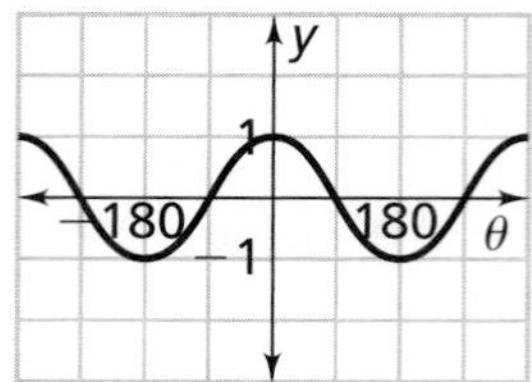


The graph of $y = \cos\theta$ is symmetric about the $y$-axis, so $\cos(-\theta) = \cos\theta$. **16.** Answers may vary. Samples:

**a.**

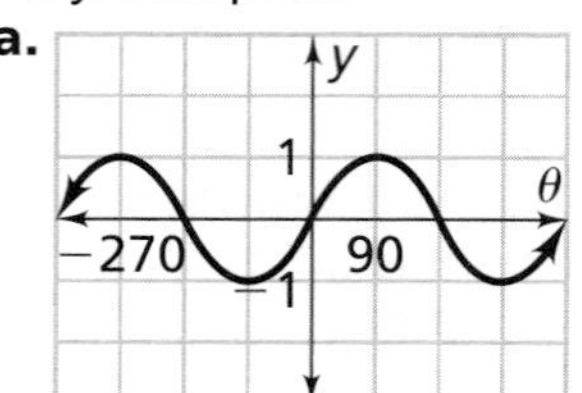

From the graph, $\sin x$ and $\sin(180° - x)$ are equal for any given $x$, so $\sin(180° - x) = \sin x$.
**17.** Answers may vary. Sample:

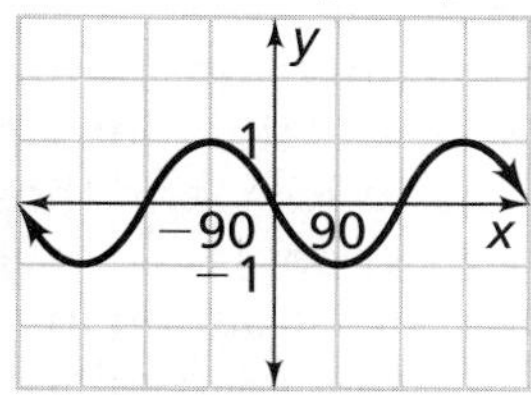


**Lesson 4.08**
**Check Your Understanding**
**1a.**

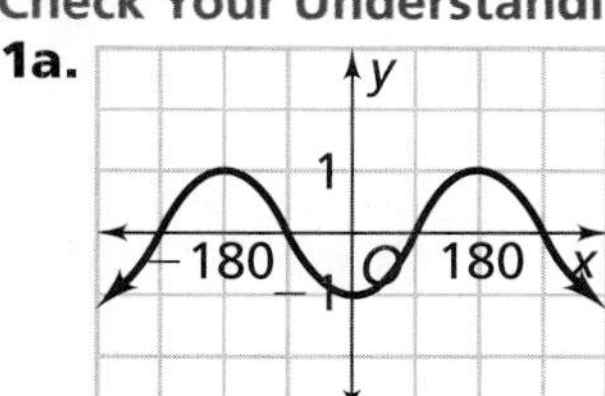


From the graph, $\cos(180° + x)$ and $-\cos x$ are equal for any given $x$, so $\cos(180° + x) = -\cos x$.
**b.**

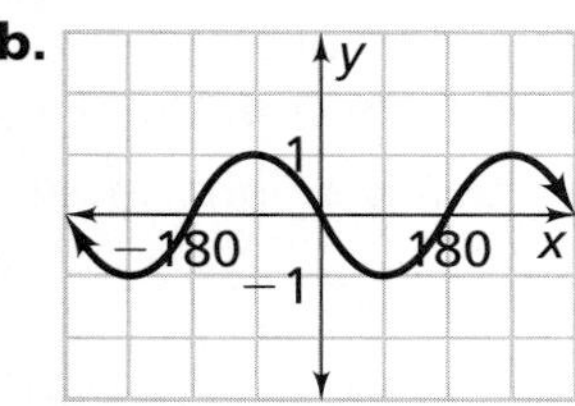


From the graph, $\sin(180° + x)$ and $-\sin x$ are equal for any given $x$, so $\sin(180° + x) = -\sin x$.
**2.** $\tan(180° + x) = \frac{\sin(180° + x)}{\cos(180° + x)} = \frac{-\sin x}{-\cos x} = \tan x$
**3a.**

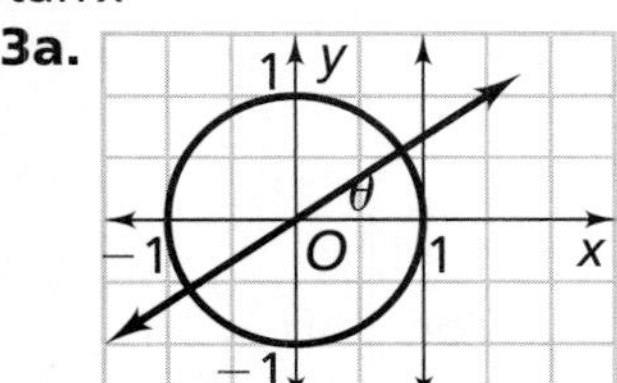


**b.** $\sin\theta = \frac{2\sqrt{13}}{13}$, $\cos\theta = \frac{3\sqrt{13}}{13}$
**4a.** $\tan(90° + \theta) = -\frac{3}{2} = -\frac{1}{\tan\theta}$ **b.** Answers may vary. Sample: The slope of the line is $\frac{y}{x}$, which is the same as the tangent of the angle formed by the line and the positive $x$-axis.
**c.** Answers may vary. Sample: If two perpendicular lines intersect at the origin and are not the $x$- and $y$-axes, and if $(a, b)$ is a point on one line, then $(-b, a)$ is a point on the other line. So the slopes are $\frac{b}{a}$ and $-\frac{a}{b}$, which are negative reciprocals. Now suppose two lines have slopes that are negative reciprocals $\frac{b}{a}$ and $-\frac{a}{b}$. Using the results of Exercise 4a, $\tan(90° + \theta) = -\frac{1}{\tan\theta}$. If the line through $(a, b)$ forms an angle of $\theta$ with the positive $x$-axis, then the line through $(-b, a)$ forms an angle of $(\theta + 90°)$, so the two lines are perpendicular. **5.** Answers may vary. Sample: $\cos\theta$ is 0 for $\theta = 90° + k \cdot 180°$, where $k$ is an integer. We can rewrite $90 + 180k$ as $90(1 + 2k)$. The values $2k + 1$ are the odd integers, so the values $90°(1 + 2k)$ are the odd multiples of 90°. **6a.** 14° **b.** 28° **c.** 104° **d.** 208°
**7a.** 14° **b.** 28° **c.** 104° **d.** 208°
**8a.** $(x^2 - y^2) + (2xy)i$ **b.** $\frac{2xy}{x^2 - y^2}$

**On Your Own**
**10a.** All real numbers except $90° + k \cdot 180°$, where $k$ is an integer **11a.** $x \approx 65° + k \cdot 180°$, where $k$ is an integer.

**Lesson 4.09**
**Check Your Understanding**
**1a.** $\cos(-x) = \cos x$ and $\sin(-x) = -\sin x$. So, $\cos(a - b) = \cos(a + (-b)) = \cos a \cos(-b) - \sin a \sin(-b) = \cos a \cos b - (\sin a)(-\sin b) = \cos a \cos b + \sin a \sin b$. **b.** If $a = b$, then $\cos(a - b) = \cos 0° = 1$ and $\cos a \cos b + \sin a \sin b = \cos^2 a + \sin^2 a = 1$.
**c.** $\frac{\sqrt{2} + \sqrt{6}}{4}$ **2a.** $\cos(2x) = \cos(x + x) = \cos x \cos x - \sin x \sin x = \cos^2 x - \sin^2 x$
**b.** $\sin(2x) = \sin(x + x) = \sin x \cos x + \cos x \sin x = 2\sin x \cos x$ **c.** $\cos 2x = \cos^2 x - \sin^2 x = \cos^2 x - (1 - \cos^2 x) = \cos^2 x - 1 + \cos^2 x = 2\cos^2 x - 1$ **3a.** $\frac{\sqrt{2 + \sqrt{3}}}{2}$
**b.** Yes; if $A = \frac{\sqrt{2 + \sqrt{3}}}{2}$, then $4A = 2\sqrt{2 + \sqrt{3}}$ and $(4A)^2 = (4)(2 + \sqrt{3}) = 8 + 4\sqrt{3}$. If $B = \frac{\sqrt{2} + \sqrt{6}}{4}$, then $4B = \sqrt{6} + \sqrt{2}$ and $(4B)^2 = 6 + 2\sqrt{12} + 2 = 8 + 2\sqrt{4} \cdot \sqrt{3} = 8 + 4\sqrt{3}$. So, $\frac{\sqrt{2 + \sqrt{3}}}{2} = \frac{\sqrt{2} + \sqrt{6}}{4}$.
**4.** $\cos 3x = \cos^3 x - 3\sin^2 x \cos x$, $\sin 3x = 3\sin x \cos^2 x - \sin^3 x$ **5.** $\frac{\sqrt{3}}{2} + \frac{1}{2}i$
**5a.** $\sin 10° = 0.1736$, $\sin 50° = 0.7660$, and $\sin 70° = 0.9397$; $\sin 10° + \sin 50° = 0.1736 + 0.7660 = 0.9396$, which is about 0.9397. **b.** 80° **c.** 65°
**6.** $\sin x + \sin(60° - x) = \sin(60° + x)$; to prove that result, the left side is $\sin x +$

Selected Answers

$\sin(60° - x) = \sin x + (\sin 60°)(\cos x) - (\cos 60°)(\sin x) = \sin x + \left(\frac{\sqrt{3}}{2}\right)(\cos x) - \left(\frac{1}{2}\right)(\sin x) = \left(\frac{1}{2}\right)(\sin x) + \left(\frac{\sqrt{3}}{2}\right)(\cos x)$. The right side is $(\sin 60°)(\cos x) + (\cos 60°)(\sin x) = \left(\frac{\sqrt{3}}{2}\right)(\cos x) + \left(\frac{1}{2}\right)(\sin x)$. The two sides are equal, so $\sin x + \sin(60° - x) = \sin(60° + x)$.

**On Your Own**

**7.** C **11.** $x \mapsto 2^x$ matches $f(a + b) = f(a) \cdot f(b)$.

**Lesson 4.10**

**On Your Own**

**7.** 50°, 130° **9.** B

**10a.** 3 miles; 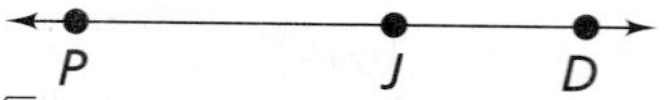


**11a.** $BH = \sqrt{3}$, $BI = 2$, $HG = 1$, $IG = \sqrt{2}$, $BG = 1 + \sqrt{3}$

**Lesson 4.11**

**Check Your Understanding**

**1.** Answers may vary. Sample: You can use $\frac{1}{2}(8)(5 \sin 60°)$ or $\frac{1}{2}(5)(7 \sin 82°)$ to find the area. **2a.** $\frac{\sqrt{3} + 1}{2}$ **b.** $\sqrt{2} \sin 105°$ **c.** $\frac{\sqrt{6} + \sqrt{2}}{4}$

**3.** $\frac{5}{2} \sin 72° \approx 2.38$ **4.** $A = \frac{3\sqrt{3}}{2}$, $P = 6$

**5a.** 2.9389 **b.** $\frac{5\sqrt{10 - 2\sqrt{5}}}{4}$ **6a.** $\frac{n}{2} \cdot \sin\left(\frac{360°}{n}\right)$

**b.**

| Sides $n$ | Area $A(n)$ |
|---|---|
| 4 | 2 |
| 5 | 2.3776 |
| 6 | 2.5981 |
| 10 | 2.9389 |
| 12 | 3 |
| 20 | 3.0902 |
| 30 | 3.1187 |
| 50 | 3.1333 |
| 100 | 3.1395 |
| 360 | 3.1414 |

**7.** As $n$ increases, the polygon approaches a circle with radius 1, so the area approaches $\pi$.

**On Your Own**

**8.** 60 **10a.** $\sin x \cos x$ **11a.** No; the sides cannot have lengths $x$, $x$, and $10x$ because $x + x < 10x$, and the sum of any two sides of a triangle must be greater than the third side. **12a.** Any other triangle with the same SAS would be congruent by SAS.

**Lesson 4.12**

**Check Your Understanding**

**1.** 24 **2.** $m\angle S = 30°$, $RS = 10.3$, $AR = 8.0$ **3.** $m\angle W = 70°$, $WS = 8.2$, $WO = 12$ **4.** $m\angle K = 53.1°$ or $126.9°$; there are two solutions for $\sin K = 0.8$. **5.** The situations in Exercises 2 and 3 are AAS and ASA, and those situations result in a unique triangle, so they are congruence theorems. The situation in Exercise 4 is SSA, and that situation results in two triangles, so it is not a congruence theorem.

**6.**

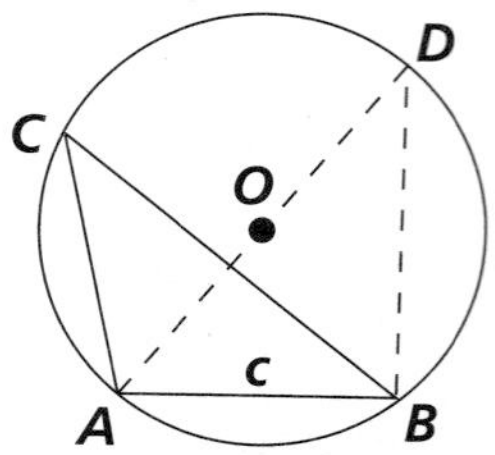


**a.** $\angle ABD$ is inscribed in a semicircle, so it is a right angle. **b.** $\angle C$ and $\angle D$ intercept the same arc, $\overset{\frown}{AB}$, so they are congruent. **c.** $m\angle C = m\angle D$, so $\sin C = \sin D$ **d.** We know $\frac{c}{\sin C} = \frac{AD}{\sin \angle ABD}$. $\angle ABD$ is a right angle, so $\sin \angle ABD = 1$. Thus $AD = \frac{c}{\sin C}$.

**7.**

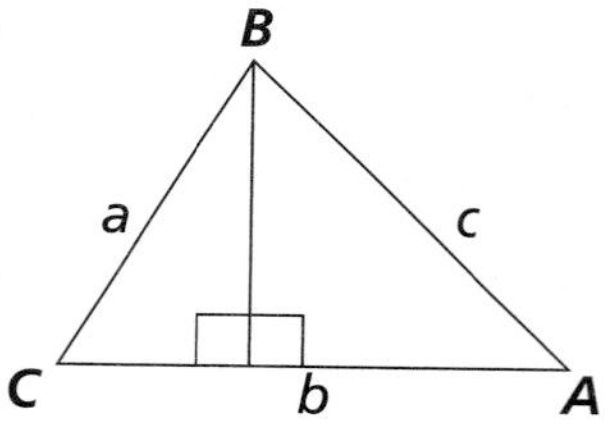


The length of the altitude from vertex $B$ is $a \sin C$ or $c \sin A$. Therefore the area of the triangle is $\frac{1}{2} a \sin C \cdot c$ or $\frac{1}{2} c \sin A \cdot c$. The expressions are equal, so $\frac{1}{2} a \sin C \cdot c = \frac{1}{2} c \sin A \cdot c$, and $a \sin C = c \sin A$. Then $\frac{a}{\sin A} = \frac{c}{\sin C}$. By using a different altitude you can make a similar argument to prove $\frac{a}{\sin A} = \frac{b}{\sin B}$. Therefore $\frac{a}{\sin A} = \frac{b}{\sin B} = \frac{c}{\sin C}$.

**8.** $TW = \sqrt{325 - 150\sqrt{2}}$

**9.** $AB = \sqrt{a^2 + b^2 - 2ab \cos C}$

**On Your Own**

**10.** Answers may vary. Sample: The sides 1, $\sqrt{3}$, and 2 are opposite the angles with measures 30°, 60°, and 90°, so $\frac{1}{\sin 30°} = 2$, $\frac{\sqrt{3}}{\sin 60°} = 2$, $\frac{2}{\sin 90°} = 2$. **12.** To use the Law of Sines, you need to know a side and the angle opposite that side. There is not enough information for this exercise, so you cannot use the Law of Sines. **14a.** $\sin C = 0.771$ **b.** 50°, 130° **c.** $m\angle A = 90°$ or 10°; $BC = 15.6$ or 2.7

### Lesson 4.13
### Check Your Understanding

**1.** $\sqrt{a^2 + b^2 - 2ab\cos C}$
**2.** $|a - b| < AB < a + b$ **3.** $5 < OT < 7$
**4.** $1 < AU < 5$ **5.** $\sqrt{119} < FB < 13$
**6a.** Use the Law of Cosines to find one angle. Then use the Law of Cosines or the Law of Sines to find a second angle. Subtract the sum of the angles from 180° to find the third angle. **b.** Use the Law of Cosines to find the third side. Then use the Law of Cosines or the Law of Sines to find a second angle. Subtract the sum of the angles from 180° to find the third angle. **c.** Use the Law of Sines to find the angle opposite the other given side (there may be 0, 1, or 2 values). Subtract the sum of the angles from 180° to find the third angle. Use the Law of Sines or the Law of Cosines to find the third side length. **d.** Subtract the sum of the angles from 180° to find the third angle. Use the Law of Sines to find a second side. Use the Law of Sines or the Law of Cosines to find the length of the third side. **e.** Subtract the sum of the angles from 180° to find the third angle. Use the Law of Sines to find a second side. Use the Law of Sines or the Law of Cosines to find the length of the third side. **f.** This cannot be solved. The triangle will not be unique because you are not given the length of a side. **7a.** The cosines opposite the sides of length 13, 14, and 15 are 0.6, 0.5077, and 0.3846, respectively. **b.** The largest angle has the smallest cosine. **c.** 12 **d.** 84 **8a.** $\cos C = \frac{a^2 + b^2 - c^2}{2ab}$, and the numerator and denominator must be integers, so $\cos C$ must be rational. **b.** The area of a triangle can be written as $\frac{1}{2}ab\sin C$. We know that $ab$ is an integer, and part a showed that $\cos C$ is rational. So $\frac{1 - \cos^2 C}{4} = \frac{\sin^2 C}{4}$ is rational. Therefore $\sqrt{\frac{\sin^2 C}{4}} = \frac{1}{2}\sin C$ is the square root of a rational number. So the area of a triangle, $\frac{1}{2}ab\sin C$ or $ab \cdot \frac{1}{2}\sin C$, is the product of an integer times the square root of a rational number.

### On Your Own

**12.** 42° **13a.** If $\angle O$ is the smallest angle, the measures of angles $F$ and $M$ would be greater than 60°. But the sum of the angles in a triangle cannot be greater than 180°. So $\angle O$ cannot be the smallest angle. **14a.** false **15a.** The angles opposite the sides of length 7, 10, and 12 are 36°, 56°, and 88°, respectively.

### Lesson 4.14
### Check Your Understanding

**1a.** $s = \frac{x + 14}{2}$ **b.** $A(x) = \frac{1}{4}\sqrt{(x + 14)(-x + 14)(x - 2)(x + 2)}$ **c.** 2, 14 **d.** The maximum of $A(x)$ is 24 when $x = 10$.
**2a.** $12 - x$ **b.** $A(x) = \sqrt{27(9 - x)(-3 + x)}$ **c.** 3, 9 **d.** The maximum of $A(x) \approx 15.6$ when $x = 6$. **3.** 75.8
**4a.**

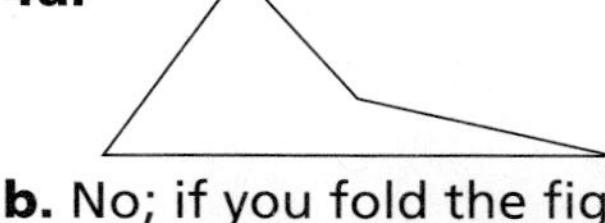

**b.** No; if you fold the figure on its diagonal, you do not get a concave quadrilateral. **5a.** The denominator 4 is outside the radical. You can move the denominator into the radical and change it to 16, which can be expressed as a denominator 2 for each of the four factors. **b.** If $a + b + c = 2s$, then $b + c - a = 2s - 2a$; $a - b + c = 2s - 2b$; $a + b - c = 2s - 2c$. Therefore $\frac{a + b + c}{2} = s$, $\frac{b + c - a}{2} = s - a$, $\frac{a + c - b}{2} = s - b$, and $\frac{a + b - c}{2} = s - c$. Then substitute each expression above into the second expression in part (a) to get the expression $\sqrt{s(s - a)(s - b)(s - c)}$.

### On Your Own

**7a.** $25\sqrt{3}$ **8.** D

## Chapter 5
### Lesson 5.01
### On Your Own

**11. b.** Start with $\frac{3\pi}{2}$ and add $2\pi$ repeatedly.
**14.** The maximum and minimum values for the $x$-coordinates are 1 and $-1$, respectively, and likewise for the $y$-coordinates. For one trip around the circle, the maximum value of the $x$-coordinates occurs when the distance walked is 0 m and $2\pi$ m, and the minimum value occurs when the distance walked is $\pi$ m. The maximum value of the $y$-coordinates occurs when the distance walked is $\frac{\pi}{2}$ m, and the minimum value occurs when the distance walked is $\frac{3\pi}{2}$ m.

## Lesson 5.02

### Check Your Understanding

**1. a.** $\cos\frac{2\pi}{3} = -\frac{1}{2}$, $\sin\frac{2\pi}{3} = \frac{\sqrt{3}}{2}$ **b.** $\cos\frac{4\pi}{3} = -\frac{1}{2}$, $\sin\frac{4\pi}{3} = -\frac{\sqrt{3}}{2}$ **c.** $\cos\frac{5\pi}{3} = \frac{1}{2}$, $\sin\frac{5\pi}{3} = -\frac{\sqrt{3}}{2}$ **d.** $\cos\frac{6\pi}{3} = 1$, $\sin\frac{6\pi}{3} = 0$ **2.** $\cos\frac{\pi}{4} = \sin\frac{\pi}{4} = \frac{\sqrt{2}}{2}$

**3.**

| $x$ | $\cos x$ | $\sin x$ |
|---|---|---|
| 0 | 1 | 0 |
| $\frac{\pi}{6}$ | $\frac{\sqrt{3}}{2}$ | $\frac{1}{2}$ |
| $\frac{\pi}{4}$ | $\frac{\sqrt{2}}{2}$ | $\frac{\sqrt{2}}{2}$ |
| $\frac{\pi}{3}$ | $\frac{1}{2}$ | $\frac{\sqrt{3}}{2}$ |
| $\frac{\pi}{2}$ | 0 | 1 |
| $\frac{2\pi}{3}$ | $-\frac{1}{2}$ | $\frac{\sqrt{3}}{2}$ |
| $\frac{3\pi}{4}$ | $-\frac{\sqrt{2}}{2}$ | $\frac{\sqrt{2}}{2}$ |
| $\frac{5\pi}{6}$ | $-\frac{\sqrt{3}}{2}$ | $\frac{1}{2}$ |
| $\pi$ | $-1$ | 0 |
| $\frac{7\pi}{6}$ | $-\frac{\sqrt{3}}{2}$ | $-\frac{1}{2}$ |
| $\frac{5\pi}{4}$ | $-\frac{\sqrt{2}}{2}$ | $-\frac{\sqrt{2}}{2}$ |
| $\frac{4\pi}{3}$ | $-\frac{1}{2}$ | $-\frac{\sqrt{3}}{2}$ |
| $\frac{3\pi}{2}$ | 0 | $-1$ |
| $\frac{5\pi}{3}$ | $\frac{1}{2}$ | $-\frac{\sqrt{3}}{2}$ |
| $\frac{7\pi}{4}$ | $\frac{\sqrt{2}}{2}$ | $-\frac{\sqrt{2}}{2}$ |
| $\frac{11\pi}{6}$ | $\frac{\sqrt{3}}{2}$ | $-\frac{1}{2}$ |
| $2\pi$ | 1 | 0 |
| $\frac{13\pi}{6}$ | $\frac{\sqrt{3}}{2}$ | $\frac{1}{2}$ |
| $\frac{9\pi}{4}$ | $\frac{\sqrt{2}}{2}$ | $\frac{\sqrt{2}}{2}$ |
| $\frac{7\pi}{3}$ | $\frac{1}{2}$ | $\frac{\sqrt{3}}{2}$ |

**4.** $\cos^2 x + \sin^2 x = 1$ **5. a.** Yes; the vertical line through $\left(\frac{4}{5}, 0\right)$ intersects the unit circle in two points. **b.** $\pm\frac{3}{5}$ **6.** B **7. a.** Yes; answers may vary. Sample: $\sin 33 \approx 0.999912$ **b.** No; if $\sin x = -1$, then $x$ must be a number of the form $\frac{3\pi}{2} + n(2\pi)$, where $n$ is an integer.

### On Your Own

**8.** $\left(\frac{\sqrt{3}}{2}, \frac{1}{2}\right)$ **11. b.** negative **14.** $-1$

## Lesson 5.03

### Check Your Understanding

**1.** A **2. a.** 0.36; 0.64 **b.** $\pm 0.8$

**c.**

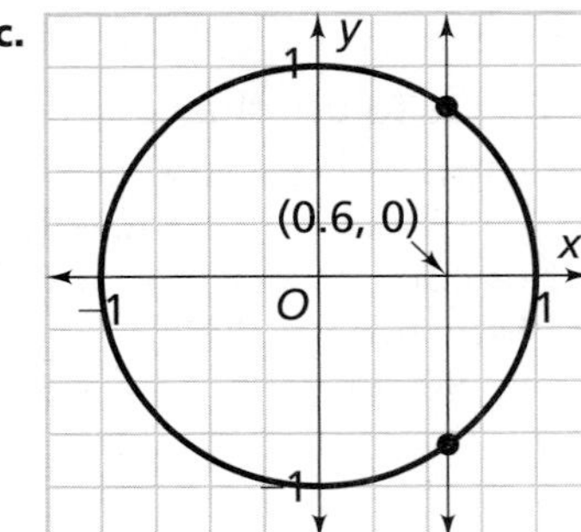


**3.** The solutions are approximately 0.9 and 5.4.

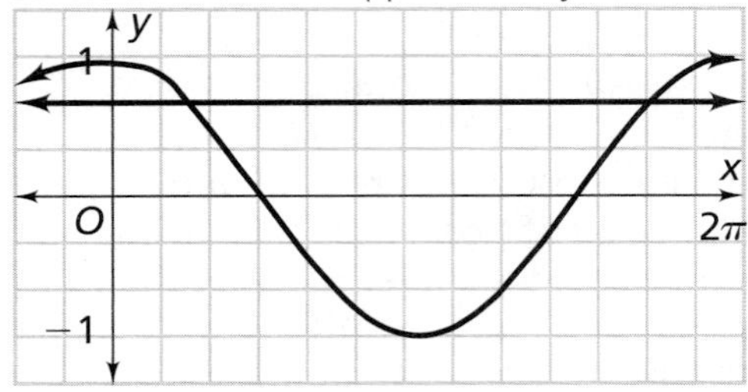


**4. a.** $\cos\left(-\frac{\pi}{2}\right) = 0$, $\sin\left(-\frac{\pi}{2}\right) = -1$

**b.** $\cos\left(-\frac{\pi}{3}\right) = \frac{1}{2}$, $\sin\left(-\frac{\pi}{3}\right) = -\frac{\sqrt{3}}{2}$

**5. a.** They are equal. **b.** They are opposites.

**6. a.** not always **b.** always **c.** always **d.** not always

### On Your Own

**7.**

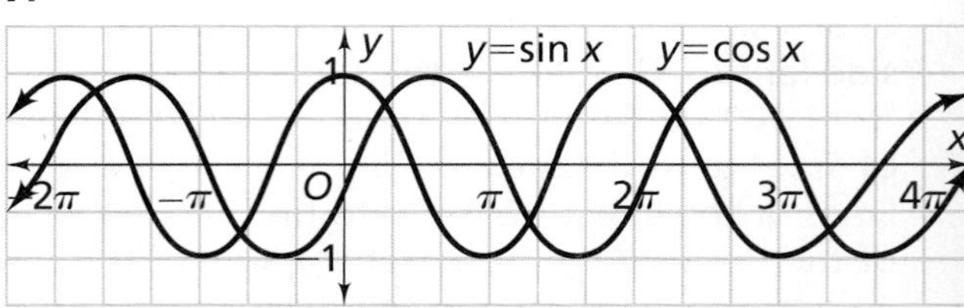


**8.** Quadrant IV **12. b.** The period of the new graph will be half the period of the graph in part (a).

## Lesson 5.04

### Check Your Understanding

**1.** $\frac{7\pi}{6}$ and $\frac{11\pi}{6}$ **2.** all numbers of the forms $\frac{7\pi}{6} + 2\pi n$ and $\frac{11\pi}{6} + 2\pi n$, where $n$ is an integer **3.** $-0.7599$ **4.** all measures of the forms $50° + 360°n$ and $130° + 360°n$, where $n$ is an integer **5.** 0.79 **6. a–e.** Answers may vary. Samples are given. **a.** $\sin x = 1$ **b.** $\sin x = \frac{1}{2}$ **c.** $\cos x = 2$ **d.** $\sin 2x = \frac{1}{2}$ **e.** $\sin 3x = \frac{1}{2}$ **7.** $\alpha = 0$, $\theta = \frac{\pi}{6}$ or $\alpha = 0$, $\theta = \frac{5\pi}{6}$

### On Your Own

**8.** $-1$ and $\frac{3}{5}$ **10. b.** $\cos 160° = -\cos 20°$ **14. a.** $\theta \approx 56.3° + 360°n$ and $\theta \approx 123.7° + 360°n$, where $n$ is an integer **15.** $\frac{\pi}{3}, \frac{\pi}{2}, \frac{3\pi}{2}, \frac{5\pi}{3}$

## Lesson 5.05

### Check Your Understanding

**1.** The slope is 0. **2.** The maximum slope is 1, and it occurs where $x = 2\pi n$ ($n$ an integer). The minimum slope is $-1$, and it occurs where $x = (2n + 1)\pi$ ($n$ an integer). You can estimate these maximum and minimum slopes by examining the graph of $y = \sin x$. **3. a.** $y = x$ **b.** 1 **4. a.** The graph should look the same as the graph of $y = \cos x$. **b.** the cosine function

**5. a.**

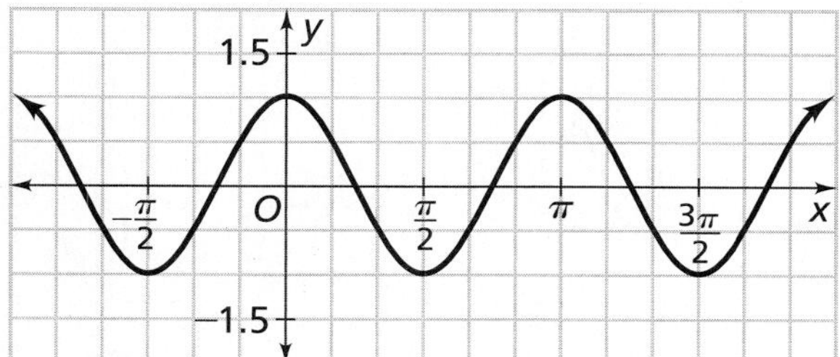

**b.** The functions have the same value for each value of x since $\cos^4 x - \sin^4 x = (\cos^2 x + \sin^2 x)(\cos^2 x - \sin^2 x) = 1 \cdot (\cos^2 x - \sin^2 x) = \cos^2 x - \sin^2 x$.

**On Your Own**

**6. c.** The values of $x$ where the maximum and minimum of $y = \sin x$ occur are, respectively, $\frac{\pi}{2}$ units greater than those for $y = \cos x$. **7. a.** in intervals of the form $\left[-\frac{\pi}{2} + 2\pi n, \frac{\pi}{2} + 2\pi n\right]$, where $n$ is an integer **11.** The graph of $c(x)$ is the same as the graph of $y = 1$.

**Lesson 5.06**

**On Your Own**

**8.** Answers may vary. Sample: $\frac{4}{3}$ **9. a.** 75 **11. a.** 20

**Lesson 5.07**

**Check Your Understanding**

**1. a.** amplitude = 3, vertical displacement = 7 **b.** $\pi$ **c.** Answers may vary. Sample: $\frac{\pi}{2}$ **d.** Answers may vary. Sample: $f(x) = -3\cos 2\left(x - \frac{\pi}{4}\right) + 7$

**2.** $f(x) = -3\sin 2x + 7$ **3.** $f(x) = -3\sin 2x + 7$

**4. a.** Answers may vary. Sample: $\frac{\pi}{6}$

**b.**

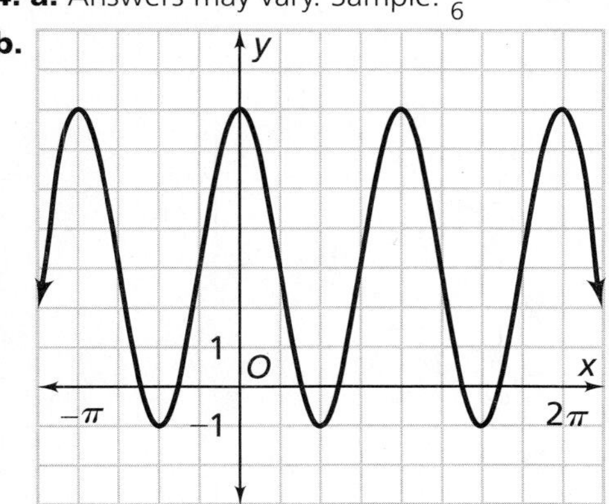

Graph $y = 4\cos 2x + 3$ and $y = 5$ on the same axes. Find the $x$-coordinates of the points of intersection of the graphs.

**c.** $\frac{\pi}{6} + n\pi$ and $\frac{5\pi}{6} + n\pi$ ($n$ an integer)

**5. a.** $g(x) = 13\sin\left(4 \cdot \frac{\pi}{4} - \pi\right) + 10 = 13\sin 0 + 10 = 10$ **b.** amplitude = 13, vertical displacement = 10 **c.** maximum = 23, minimum = $-3$ **d.** $\frac{\pi}{2}$

**e.**

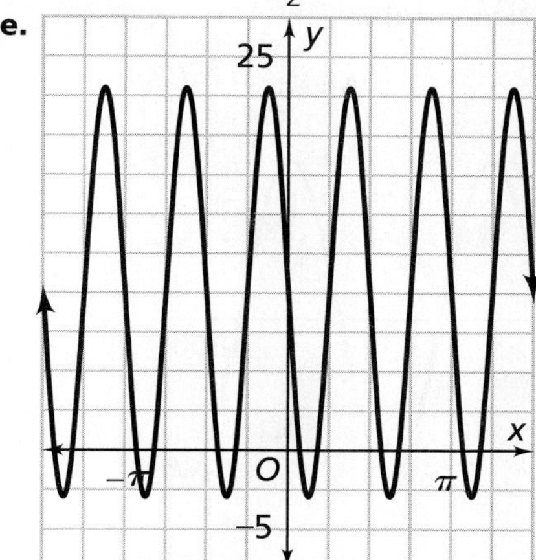

**6. a.**

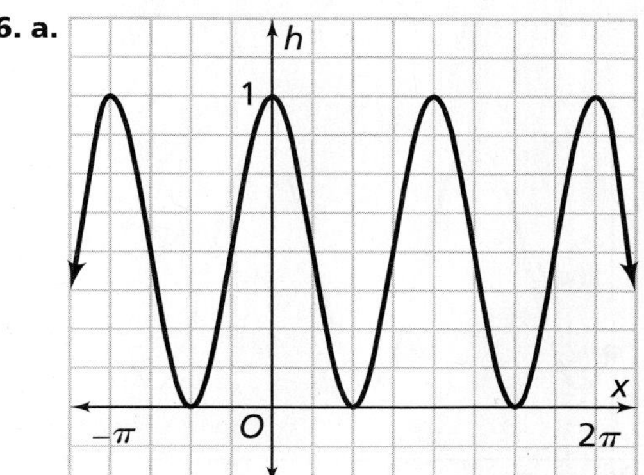

**b.** amplitude = $\frac{1}{2}$, vertical displacement = $\frac{1}{2}$, period = $\pi$ **7.** $\frac{1}{2}\cos 2x + \frac{1}{2}$

**On Your Own**

**8. b.** $\frac{2\pi}{5}$ **11.** $\frac{1}{2}\sin 2x$ **14.** Answers may vary. Sample: $f(x) = \sin\frac{2\pi}{5}x$

**Lesson 5.08**

**Check Your Understanding**

**1.** $H(t) = 125\cos\frac{2\pi}{9}t + 139$

**2.**

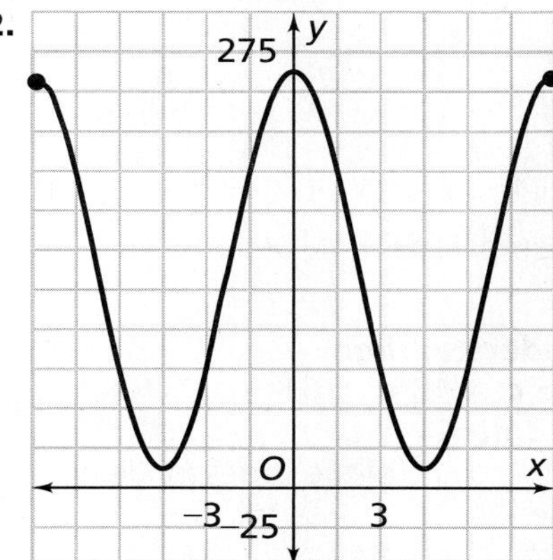

**3. a.** 1 min 31 s **b.** about $7\frac{1}{2}$ min **c.** 7 min 29 s

**4. a.** 8:24 P.M., 8:48 A.M. (next day) **b.** 2:12 P.M.; 2:36 A.M. (next day)
**c.** The numbers along the horizontal axis represent minutes.

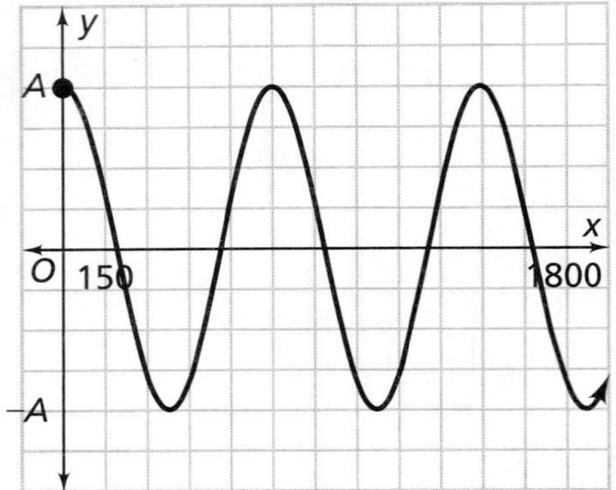


**5.** $H(t) = 3.5 \cos \frac{2\pi}{12.4}(t - 8) + 5.5$

**6.**

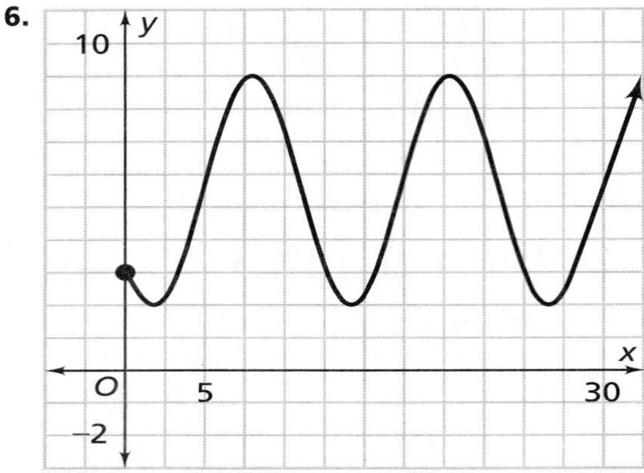


**7. a.** about 4 ft; about 4.6 ft **b.** about 5.5 ft
**c.** Answers may vary. Sample: about 11:30 P.M.
**d.** Answers may vary. Sample: about 10:49 A.M.
**8. a.** about 3.77 ft/s **b.** about 2.57 mph
**c.** The first two times are $t = 15$ s and $t = 45$ s.

### On Your Own

**10.** B **13.** the Ferris wheel with radius 36 ft

**14. b.** about 2.99 ft

## Chapter 6

### Lesson 6.01

### On Your Own

**8. c.** $f(1 + i) = (1 + i - 1)^2 + 1 = i^2 + 1 = 0$

**10. d.** 25 **12. b.** amplitude = 1, period = $\pi$

### Lesson 6.02

### Check Your Understanding

**1. a.** $\sqrt{17}$ **b.** $\sqrt{5}$ **c.** $\sqrt{13}$ **d.** $\sqrt{61}$
**2. a.** 17 **b.** 5 **c.** 13 **d.** 61
Each product is the square of the corresponding answer in Exercise 1.

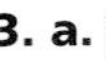

**3. a.**

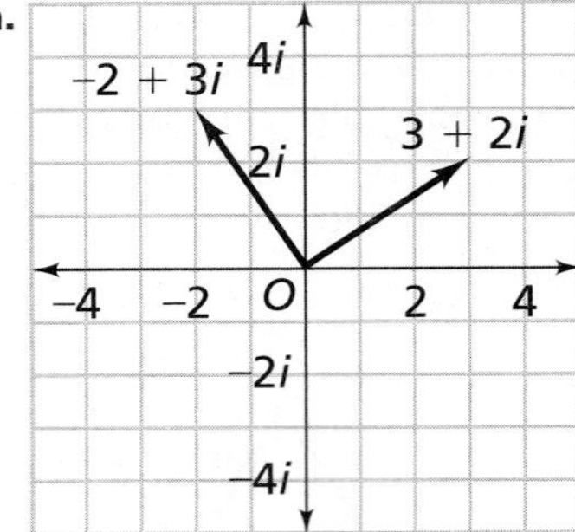


$\arg(z) \approx 0.588$, $\arg(i \cdot z) \approx 2.159$

**b.**

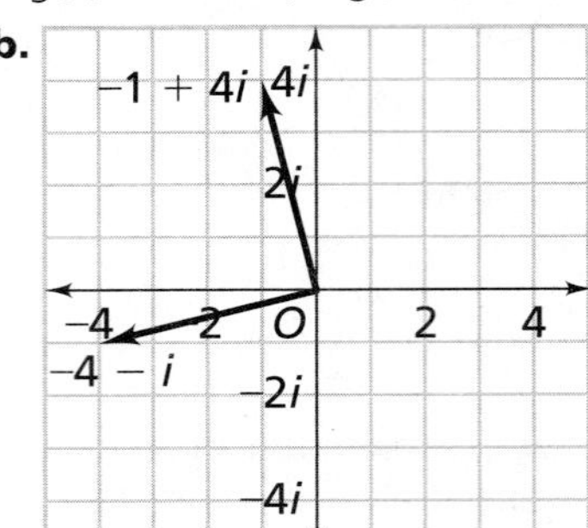


$\arg(z) \approx 1.816$, $\arg(i \cdot z) \approx 3.387$

**c.**

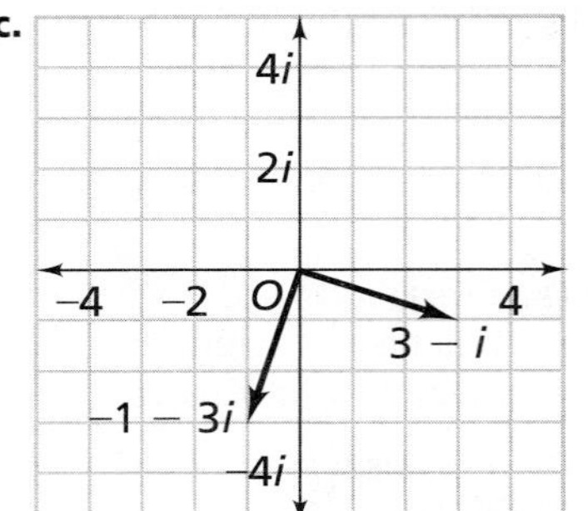


$\arg(z) \approx 4.391$, $\arg(i \cdot z) \approx 5.961$

**d.**

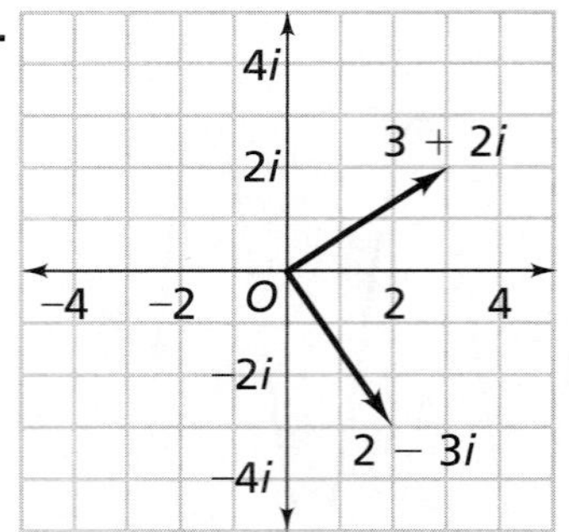


$\arg(z) \approx 5.300$, $\arg(i \cdot z) \approx 0.588$

**4. a.** magnitude $= 2\sqrt{2}$, argument $= \frac{\pi}{4}$
**b.** magnitude $= 2\sqrt{2}$, argument $= \frac{7\pi}{4}$
**c.** magnitude $= 2\sqrt{2}$, argument $= \frac{3\pi}{4}$
**d.** magnitude $= 2\sqrt{2}$, argument $= \frac{5\pi}{4}$

**5. a.** $|iz| = |z|$, $\arg(iz) = \arg(z) + \frac{\pi}{2}$
**b.** $|i^2z| = |z|$, $\arg(i^2z) = \arg(z) + \pi$
**c.** $|(-i)z| = |z|$, $\arg((-i)z) = \arg(z) + \frac{3\pi}{2}$
**d.** $|2z| = 2|z|$, $\arg(2z) = \arg(z)$
**e.** $\left|\frac{1}{z}\right| = \frac{1}{|z|}$, $\arg\left(\frac{1}{z}\right) = 2\pi - \arg(z)$

### On Your Own

**6.** $|3z| = 3|z|$ and $\arg(3z) = \arg(z)$
**9. a.** $(\cos^2 t - \sin^2 t) + (2 \sin t \cos t)i$ **13. c.** 10

## Lesson 6.03

### Check Your Understanding

**1. a.** magnitude = 5, argument = 60°
**b.** magnitude = $\frac{1}{5}$, argument = 300°

**2. a.** magnitude = 25, argument = 120°
**b.** magnitude = 125, argument = 180°
**c.** magnitude = 1, argument = 0° (or 360°)

**3. a.**

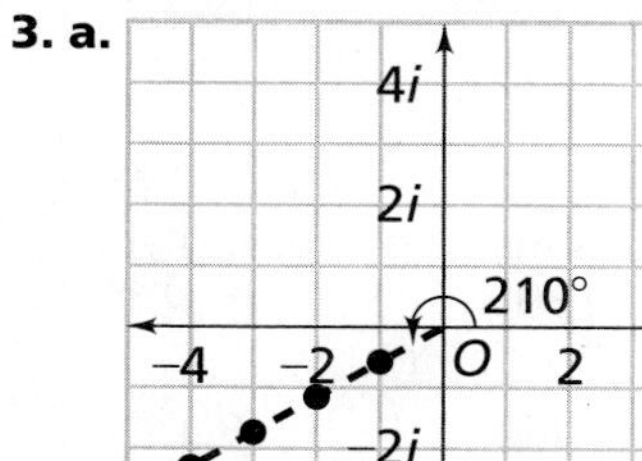


**b.**

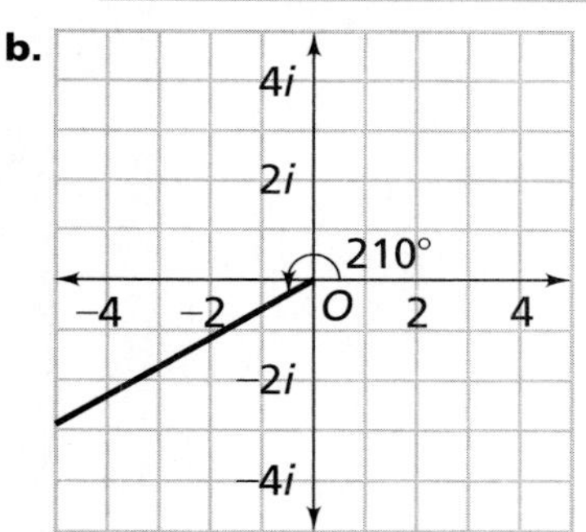


**c.** $-5\sqrt{3} - 5i$ **4. a.** $4 \cos \frac{2\pi}{3} + 4i \sin \frac{2\pi}{3}$
**b.** $-2 + 2i\sqrt{3}$ **5. a.** Answers may vary. Samples: $a = 5 \text{ cis } 60°$ or $a = \frac{5}{2} + \frac{5\sqrt{3}}{2}i$, $b = 3 \text{ cis } 30°$ or $b = \frac{3\sqrt{3}}{2} + \frac{3}{2}i$ **b.** $15i$; magnitude = 15, argument = 90° **6. a.** Check students' work. The values of $\theta$ will vary, but for each value of $\theta$ that is selected, the number $z$ should be on the ray that has endpoint $O$ and makes an angle of measure $\theta$ with the positive $x$-axis, and $z$ should be 3 units from $O$.
**b.** The circle with center $O$ and radius 3; $|z| = 3$ since $z = 3 \text{ cis } \theta$. Since there are no restrictions on $\theta$, all points 3 units from $O$ are included.

**7. a.** $|\text{cis } \theta| = |\cos \theta + i \sin \theta| = \sqrt{\cos^2 \theta + \sin^2 \theta} = 1$ **b.** $|r \text{ cis } \theta| = |r| \cdot |\text{cis } \theta| = |r| \cdot 1 = |r|$

### On Your Own

**8. b.** magnitude = 10, argument = 330°

**11. b.** $(\cos \alpha \cos \beta - \sin \alpha \sin \beta) + (\cos \alpha \sin \beta + \sin \alpha \cos \beta)i$

## Lesson 6.04

### Check Your Understanding

**1. a.** $|z^2| = 9$, $\arg(z^2) = 240°$ **b.** Answers may vary. Sample: $z^3 = 3^3 \text{ cis } 3(120°) = 27(\cos 360° + i \sin 360°) = 27(1 + i \cdot 0) = 27$
**2.** To find $|z^2|$, square $|z|$; to find $\arg(z^2)$, multiply $\arg(z)$ by 2. To find $|z^3|$, cube $|z|$; to find $\arg(z^3)$, multiply $\arg(z)$ by 3. In general, if $n$ is a nonnegative integer, to find $|z^n|$, raise $|z|$ to the $n$th power; to find $\arg(z^n)$, multiply $\arg(z)$ by $n$. **3. a.** false
**b.** true; $3^3 = 27$ and $3 \cdot 40° = 120°$ **c.** false
**d.** true; $3^3 = 27$ and $3 \cdot 160° = 480°$ and $480° - 360° = 120°$ **4.** Answers may vary. Sample: $|zw| \approx 13$, $\arg(zw) \approx 160°$ **5.** To find the magnitude of the product, multiply the magnitudes of the two numbers. To find the argument of the product, use the sum modulo 360° of the arguments of the numbers.

**6. a.**

Since $|i| = 1$, all the powers have magnitude 1. Multiplying a number by $i$ rotates the number around $O$ counterclockwise by 90°. Since 360° is evenly divisible by 90°, the set of powers consists of just 4 numbers.

**b.**

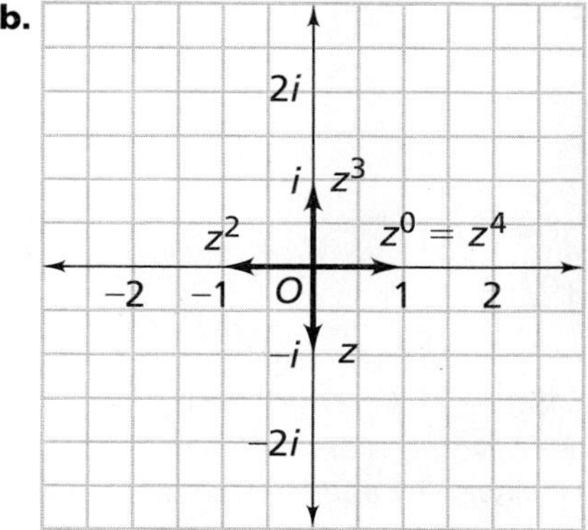


Since $|-i| = 1$, all the powers have magnitude 1. Because of the minus sign, multiplying by $-i$ rotates the other number not counterclockwise but clockwise around $O$ by 90°. Since 360° is evenly divisible by 90°, the set of powers consists of just 4 numbers.

**c.**

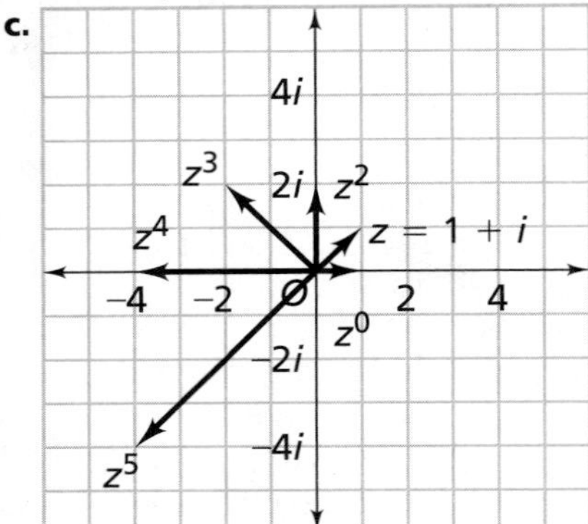


$|z| = \sqrt{2}$ and $\arg(z) = 45°$, so for each nonnegative integer $n$, you can obtain $z^{n+1}$ if you rotate $z^n$ counterclockwise 45° and then scale by $\sqrt{2}$.

**d.**

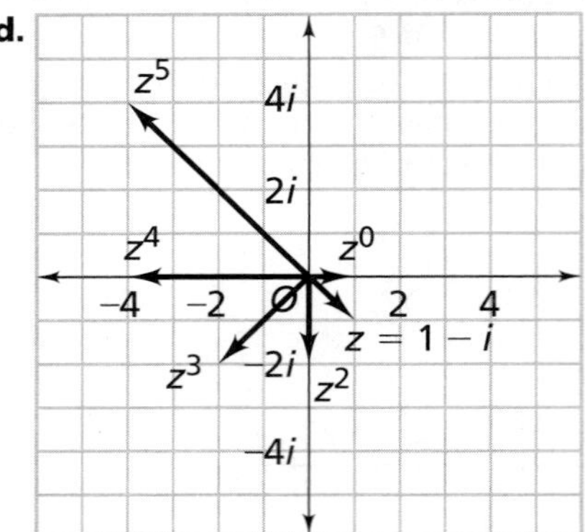


$|z| = \sqrt{2}$ and $\arg(z) = 315°$, so for each nonnegative integer $n$, you can obtain $z^{n+1}$ if you rotate $z^n$ clockwise 45° and then scale by $\sqrt{2}$.

**e.**

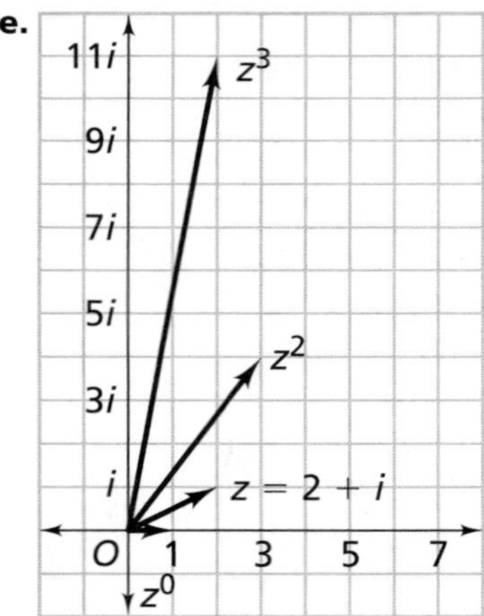


$|z| = \sqrt{5}$ and $\arg(z) \approx 26.6°$, so for each nonnegative integer $n$, you can obtain $z^{n+1}$ if you rotate $z^n$ counterclockwise by about 26.6° and then scale by $\sqrt{5}$.

**f.**

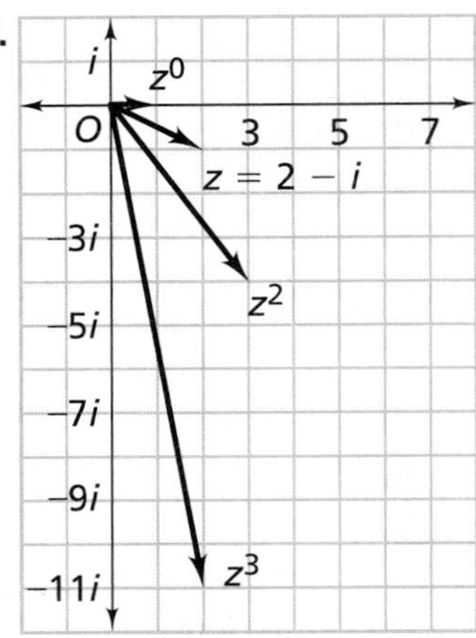


$|z| = \sqrt{5}$ and $\arg(z) \approx 333.4349°$, so for each nonnegative integer $n$, you can obtain $z^{n+1}$ if you rotate $z^n$ clockwise by about 26.6° and then scale by $\sqrt{5}$.

### On Your Own

**9. a.** Answers may vary. Sample: $1 + i$ and $5 + 5i$ **11. b.** Quadrant I; $\arg(zw)$ is the sum of $\arg(z)$ and $\arg(w)$, or about 398°. Since $398° - 360° = 38°$, the vector for $zw$ will be in Quadrant I.

**12. b.** $\left|\frac{z}{w}\right| = \sqrt{2}$, $\arg\left(\frac{z}{w}\right) = \tan^{-1}\left(\frac{1}{7}\right) \approx 8.13°$

## Lesson 6.05

### On Your Own

**9. c.** 288° **13.** $4 + i$ and $4 - i$; sum $= 8$, product $= 17$

## Lesson 6.06

### Check Your Understanding

**1. a.** $|z^2| = 9$, $\arg(z^2) = \frac{2\pi}{3}$

**b.** $|z^3| = 27$, $\arg(z^3) = \pi$

**c.** $|z^5| = 243$, $\arg(z^5) = \frac{5\pi}{3}$

**d.** $|10z| = 30$, $\arg(10z) = \frac{\pi}{3}$

**e.** $|z^0| = 1$, $\arg(z^0) = 0$

**f.** $|z^{-1}| = \frac{1}{3}$, $\arg(z^{-1}) = \frac{5\pi}{3}$

**2.** $\sqrt{3}\ \text{cis}\ \frac{\pi}{6}$, $\sqrt{3}\ \text{cis}\ \frac{7\pi}{6}$

**3. a.** $|z^3| = 64$, $\arg(z^3) = 0$

**b.** $|z^3| = 64$, $\arg(z^3) = 0°$

**c.** $|z^3| = 8$, $\arg(z^3) = \frac{\pi}{2}$

**d.** $|z^3| = 8$, $\arg(z^3) = \frac{\pi}{2}$

**4.** sum $= 0$, product $= 8i$ **5. a.** $a^2$ is a solution of $x^{11} = 1$ if and only if $(a^2)^{11} = 1$. Since $(a^2)^{11} = (a^{11})^2 = 1^2 = 1$, $a^2$ is a solution.
**b.** The proof is the same as in part (a), but with 2 replaced by $k$.

## On Your Own

**6.** The solutions are $-2$ and $\pm 4\sqrt{5}$; their sum is $-2$, and their product is 160. **11. b.** cis 0, cis $\frac{2\pi}{5}$, cis $\frac{4\pi}{5}$, cis $\frac{6\pi}{5}$, and cis $\frac{8\pi}{5}$ **14.** $\frac{\sqrt{2} + \sqrt{6}}{4}$

## Lesson 6.07

### Check Your Understanding

**1. a.** The solution in Quadrant I should be labeled $\omega$, $\omega^6$, the solution in Quadrant II should be labeled $\omega^2$, the solution in Quadrant III should be labeled $\omega^3$, $\omega^{13}$, the solution in Quadrant IV should be labeled $\omega^4$, and the solution on the positive part of the real axis should be labeled $\omega^5$. **b.** 1 **2. a.** 0 **b.** 0 **c.** The sum in part (b) is the sum of the imaginary parts of the six roots of $x^6 = 1$, and this sum must be 0 since the sum of the roots is 0.

**3.**

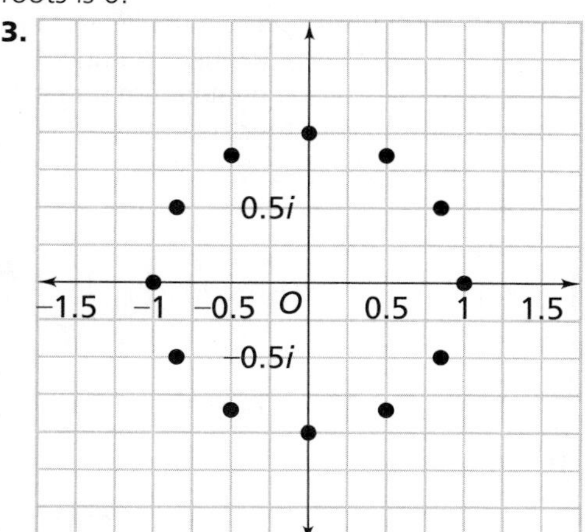


**4. a.**

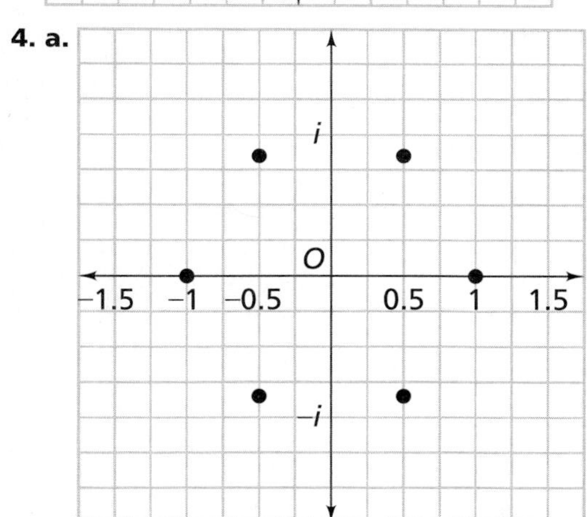


**b.** The plot in part (a) is part of the plot from Exercise 3, so this illustrates graphically that the solutions of $x^6 - 1 = 0$ are solutions of $x^{12} - 1 = 0$. Algebraically, the solutions of $x^6 - 1 = 0$ are the numbers cis$\frac{2\pi}{6}k$ where $k$ goes from 0 to 5. The solutions of $x^{12} - 1 = 0$ are the numbers cis$\frac{2\pi}{6}n$ where $n$ goes from 0 to 11. **c.** This result follows immediately from part (b). **5.** Every multiple of 5 greater than 5 will work. **6.** 6 **7.** Yes; $n = 36$

**8. a.** Answers may vary. Sample: $i$ **b.** Answers may vary. Sample: cis $\left(\frac{4\pi}{9}\right)$ **c.** yes

### On Your Own

**10. a.** $-1$ **12. b.** 0 **15. a.** Suppose $z = x + yi$ and that $z$ is a root of unity. Then $\frac{1}{z} = \frac{1}{x + yi} = \frac{x - yi}{x^2 + y^2}$. But $x^2 + y^2 = 1$ since $z$ is a root of unity. So $\frac{1}{z} = x - yi = \bar{z}$.

## Lesson 6.08

### Check Your Understanding

**1.** 18 **2. a.** $z^{21} = \text{cis } 357°$ **b.** Yes; 360 times **c.** all rational values of $\theta$ **3. a.** $z^4 = \left(\text{cis } \frac{2\pi}{5}\right)^4 = \text{cis } \frac{8\pi}{5} = \text{cis}\left(-\frac{2\pi}{5}\right)$ **b.** Use the result from part (a). $z + z^4 = \text{cis } \frac{2\pi}{5} + \text{cis}\left(-\frac{2\pi}{5}\right) = 2 \cos \frac{2\pi}{5}$

**4. a.** $(x - 1)(x^4 + x^3 + x^2 + x + 1)$ **b.** $z$ is a root of $(z - 1)(z^4 + z^3 + z^2 + z + 1) = 0$, and since $z \neq 1$, the value of $z^4 + z^3 + z^2 + z + 1$ must be 0. It follows that $z^4 + z^3 + z^2 + z = -1$.

**5. a.** From Exercise 3(b), we know that $z + z^4$ is positive, since $2 \cos\frac{2\pi}{5}$ is positive. (We know this is so because $0 < \frac{2\pi}{5} < \frac{\pi}{2}$.) By Exercise 4(b), $z^2 + z^3 = -1 - (z + z^4)$, and subtracting a positive number from $-1$ results in a negative number.
**b.** This result follows immediately from Exercise 4(b).
**c.** $z^3 + z^4 + z^6 + z^7$, or $z + z^2 + z^3 + z^4$ (since $z^6 = z$ and $z^7 = z^2$) **d.** $ab = -1$ follows directly from part (c) and Exercise 4(b).

**6.** $a = \frac{-1 + \sqrt{5}}{2}$, $b = -\frac{1 + \sqrt{5}}{2}$

**7. a.** Use the result from Exercise 6, the fact that $a = z + z^4$, and Exercise 3(b) to obtain $2 \cos 72° = \frac{-1 + \sqrt{5}}{2}$. This last equation gives $\cos 72° = \frac{-1 + \sqrt{5}}{4}$.

**b.** $\sin 72° = \frac{\sqrt{10 + 2\sqrt{5}}}{4}$

**c.** $z^0 = 1$, $z = \frac{-1 + \sqrt{5}}{4} + \frac{\sqrt{10 + 2\sqrt{5}}}{4}i$,

$z^2 = -\frac{1 + \sqrt{5}}{4} + \frac{\sqrt{10 - 2\sqrt{5}}}{4}i$,

$z^3 = -\frac{1 + \sqrt{5}}{4} - \frac{\sqrt{10 - 2\sqrt{5}}}{4}i$,

$z^4 = \frac{-1 + \sqrt{5}}{4} - \frac{\sqrt{10 + 2\sqrt{5}}}{4}i$

**8.** $x^5 - 1 = (x - 1)(x^4 + x^3 + x^2 + x + 1)$, so the given factorization is correct if $x^4 + x^3 + x^2 + x + 1$ equals $(x^2 + \Phi x + 1)\left(x^2 - \frac{1}{\Phi}x + 1\right)$. Expand this last expression and collect like terms to obtain $x^4 + \left(\Phi - \frac{1}{\Phi}\right)x^3 + x^2 + \left(\Phi - \frac{1}{\Phi}\right)x + 1$. Use $\Phi = \frac{1 + \sqrt{5}}{2}$ to show that $\Phi - \frac{1}{\Phi} = 1$. It follows that $x^4 + x^3 + x^2 + x + 1 = (x^2 + \Phi x + 1)\left(x^2 - \frac{1}{\Phi}x + 1\right)$.

### On Your Own

**9.** 30 sides **10.** Let $\overline{AM}$ be the altitude to the base $\overline{BC}$ of isosceles $\triangle ABC$. Right triangle trigonometry tells you that $\cos \angle B = \cos 72° = \frac{BM}{1} = BM$. Likewise, $CM = \cos 72°$. **14.** $-\frac{\sqrt{5}+1}{4}$

### Lesson 6.09

### Check Your Understanding

**1. a.** 0 **b.** 7 **c.** 1 **2. a.** 0 **b.** 0 **c.** $-1$ **3.** $f(n) = 5$ if $n$ is a multiple of 5, otherwise $f(n) = 0$ **4. a.** 0 **b.** 1 **c.** 5 **5.** 5 **6. a.** 0 **b.** 0 **7. a.** $\text{cis}\left(\frac{2\pi}{12} \cdot 1\right)$, $\text{cis}\left(\frac{2\pi}{12} \cdot 5\right)$, $\text{cis}\left(\frac{2\pi}{12} \cdot 7\right)$, $\text{cis}\left(\frac{2\pi}{12} \cdot 11\right)$ **b.** $x^{12} - 1 = (x-1) \cdot (x+1)(x^2+1)(x^2+x+1)(x^2-x+1) \cdot (x^4-x^2+1)$

The table shows which powers of $\zeta$ make which factors equal to 0.

| Factor | Powers of $\zeta$ |
|---|---|
| $x-1$ | $\zeta^0$ |
| $x+1$ | $\zeta^6$ |
| $x^2+1$ | $\zeta^3, \zeta^9$ |
| $x^2+x+1$ | $\zeta^4, \zeta^8$ |
| $x^2-x+1$ | $\zeta^2, \zeta^{10}$ |
| $x^4-x^2+1$ | $\zeta, \zeta^5, \zeta^7, \zeta^{11}$ |

### On Your Own

**9.** $-7$ **11. c.** $(x-1)(x-\zeta)(x-\zeta^2)(x-\zeta^3) \cdot (x-\zeta^4)$, where $\zeta = \text{cis}\,\frac{2\pi}{5} = \frac{-1+\sqrt{5}}{4} + \frac{\sqrt{10+2\sqrt{5}}}{4}i$ **15. a.** If $\zeta = \text{cis}\,\frac{2\pi}{9}$, then the primitive 9th roots of unity are $\zeta, \zeta^2, \zeta^4, \zeta^5, \zeta^7$, and $\zeta^8$.

## Chapter 7

### Lesson 7.01

### On Your Own

**8.** Not possible. For the graph to meet the first and third conditions, it would have to change directions more than just twice, as described in the second condition.

**9.** Answers may vary. Sample:
$f(x) = |x+3| - 2$

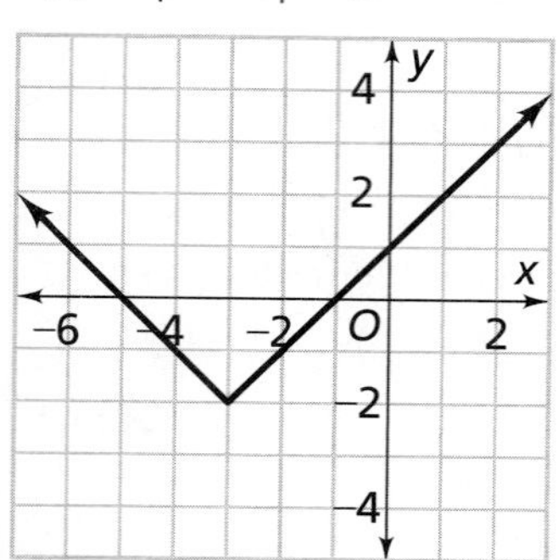


### Lesson 7.02

### Check Your Understanding

**1.** At birth, height in inches is larger; later in life, weight in pounds is larger. Since both change continuously, there must be at least one intersection. **2. a.** $a(5) = 0$ **b.** $a(5.001)$ is a very small positive number. **c.** $a(0) = 30$ **d.** $a(0.001)$ is approximately 30. **e.** $a(1000)$ is a very large positive number. **f.** $a(0.999)$ is a very small positive number. **g.** $a(-1000)$ is a very large negative number. **3. a.** Answers may vary. Sample: $g(x) = x^2 + 4x - 21$ **b.** Answers may vary. Sample: $h(x) = -\frac{2}{3}x^2 + \frac{4}{3}x + 10$ **c.** Answers may vary. Sample: $j(x) = -\frac{2}{3}x^2 + \frac{4}{3}x + 12$ **4. a.** $x$ must be within 0.033 of 5. **b.** $x$ must be within 0.0033 of 5. **c.** $x$ must be within 0.00033 of 5. **d.** $x$ must be within $0.00000033 = 3.3 \cdot 10^{-7}$ of 5. **5.** The maximum number of intersections is 3 and the minimum number of intersections is 1. **6.** Consider fourth degree polynomials with a positive leading coefficient. Some possible shapes are:

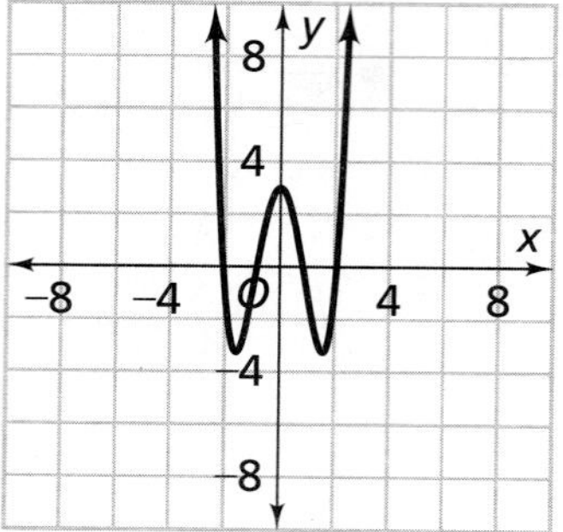


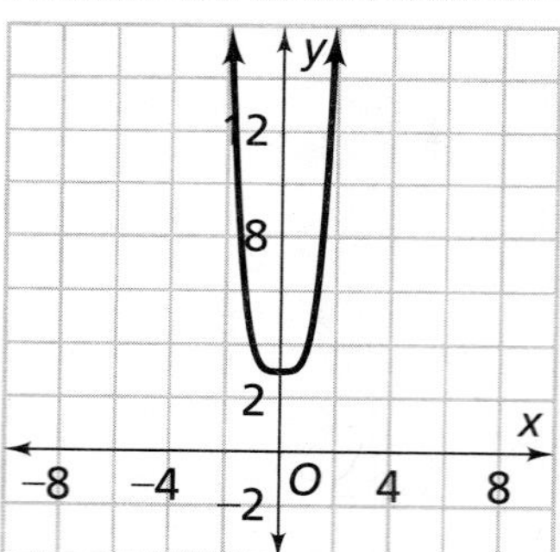


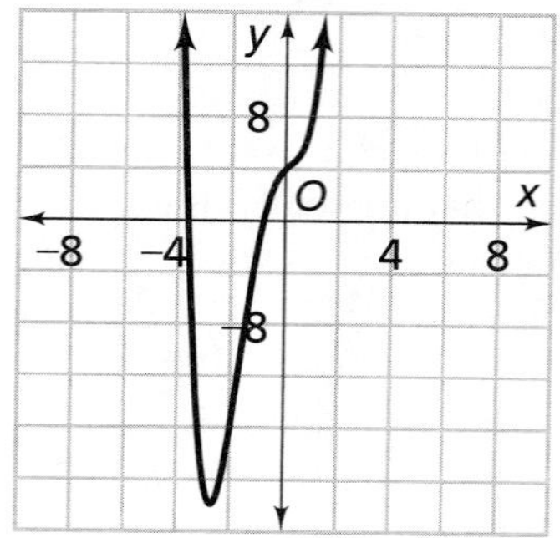

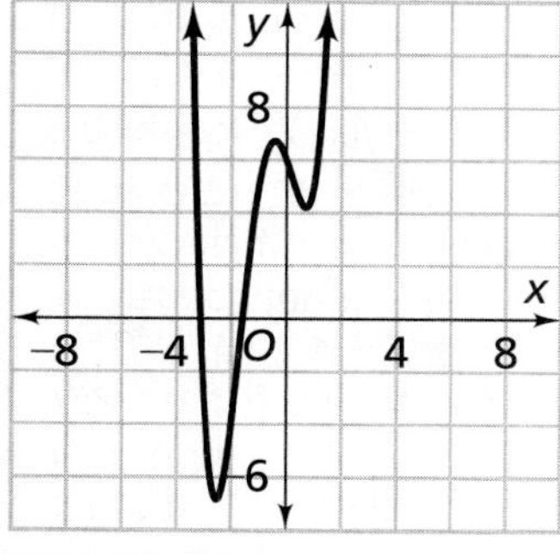


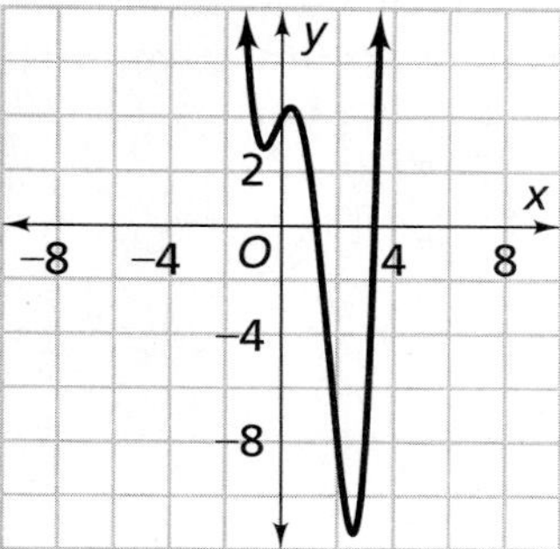


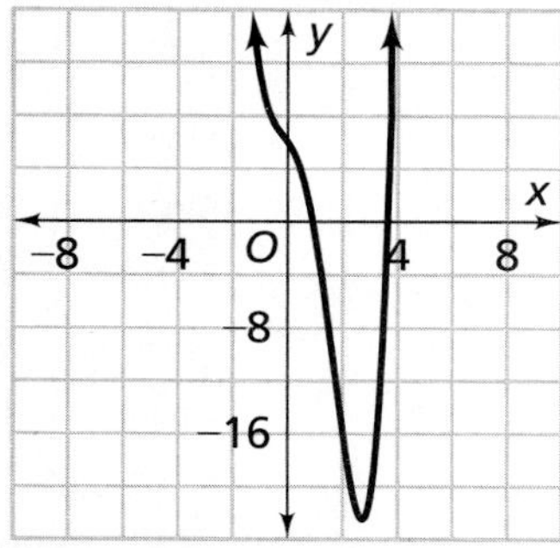


Each of these can be turned upside-down if the leading coefficient is negative.

**7. a.** No. For example, $f(x) = x^3$ has only one real zero. **b.** Yes. Since $f$ has at least one real zero, $f \cdot g$ will have at least one real zero. **c.** Yes. Every zero of $f$ is also a zero of $f^2$. Since $f$ has at least one real zero, so does $f^2$. **d.** No. For example, $f(x) = x^3 + x^2$ and $g(x) = -x^3 + 4$ each have real zeros, but $k(x) = f(x) + g(x) = x^2 + 4$ does not. **e.** Yes. The composition of two cubic functions is a polynomial function of degree 9, and it must have at least one real zero.

### On Your Own

**9. a.** $b(-5) = 0$ since one of the factors is zero. **b.** $b(-5.001)$ is a little bit less than 0. **c.** $b(0) = 30$ **d.** $b(0.001)$ is a little bit less than 30. **g.** $b(-1000)$ is a very large negative number. **11. a.** $x$ must be within 0.059 of 5. **b.** $x$ must be within 0.0059 of 5.

**12.** If the fourth degree polynomial rises, falls, rises, and falls and crosses the $x$-axis at $(-5,0)$, $(-1,0)$, and intersects it somewhere on the positive $x$-axis, it is of the form $f(x) = A(x + 5)(x + 1)(x - b)^2$ where $A < 0$ and $b > 0$. Choose some positive value for $b$, say $b = 1$. Then

$$f(x) = A(x + 5)(x + 1)(x - 1)^2$$
$$= A(x^4 + 4x^3 - 6x^2 - 4x + 5)$$

To find $A$, use the fact that $f(0) = -7$:

$$f(0) = A(5) = -7 \Rightarrow A = -\frac{7}{5}$$

A polynomial that satisfies the conditions is

$$f(x) = -\frac{7}{5}(x^4 + 4x^3 - 6x^2 - 4x + 5)$$
$$= -\frac{7}{5}x^4 - \frac{28}{5}x^3 + \frac{42}{5}x^2 + \frac{28}{5}x - 7$$

**14. a.** $g(x)$ takes on large positive values.
**b.** $g(x)$ takes on large negative values.

**18.** Answers may vary. **a.** Yes; sample: $f(x) = x^4 + 1$.
**b.** Yes; sample: $f(x) = x^3 + 8$. **c.** Yes; sample:

$$f(x) = (x - 1)(x - 2)(x - 3)$$
$$= x^3 - 6x^2 + 11x - 6$$

**19.** Yes; sample: let $g(x) = x^3 - 4x + 1$. If $a = -3$, then $g(-3) = -14$ and if $b = 3$, $g(3) = 16$, but $g(x) = 0$ three times between $a = -3$ and $b = 3$. $g(x) = 0$ between $x = -3$ and $x = -2$, between $x = 0$ and $x = 1$ and between $x = 1$ and $x = 2$.

## Lesson 7.03

### Check Your Understanding

**1. a.** The average rate of change is 7.
**b.** The equation of the secant is $8x - y = -33$.
**c.** $m = a + b$

**2. a.** The equation of the secant is

$$\frac{y - 5}{x - 2} = 10.0601 \text{ or } 10.0601x - y = 15.1202.$$

**b.** The equation of the secant is

$$\frac{y - 5}{x - 2} = b^2 + 2b + 2 \text{ or } (b^2 + 2b + 2)x - y = 2b^2 + 4b - 1.$$

**c.**

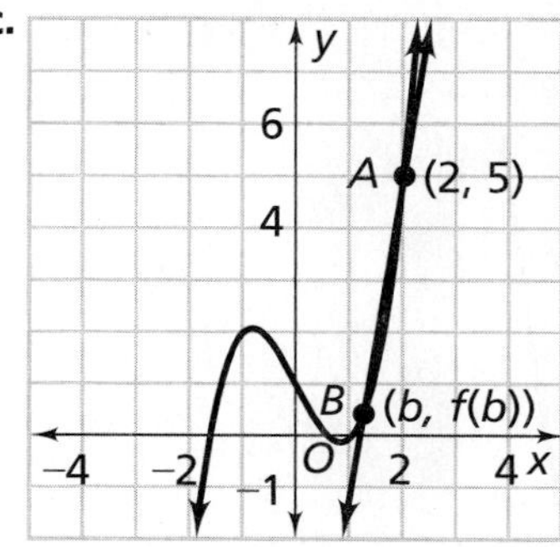


As $b$ moves closer to 2, the slope gets closer to 10.

**3. a.** Answers may vary. Sample:

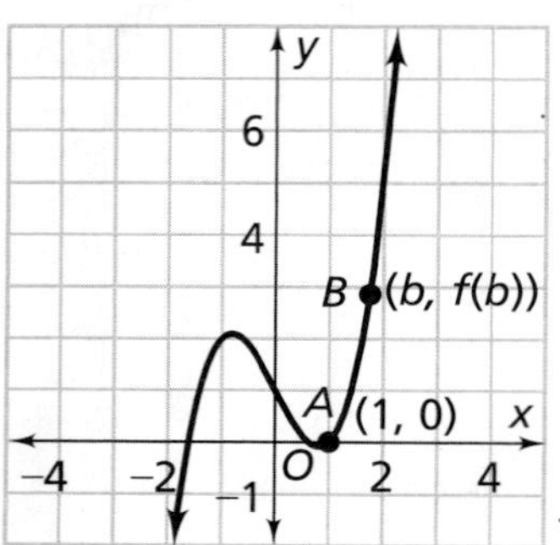


**b.** Answers may vary. Sample:

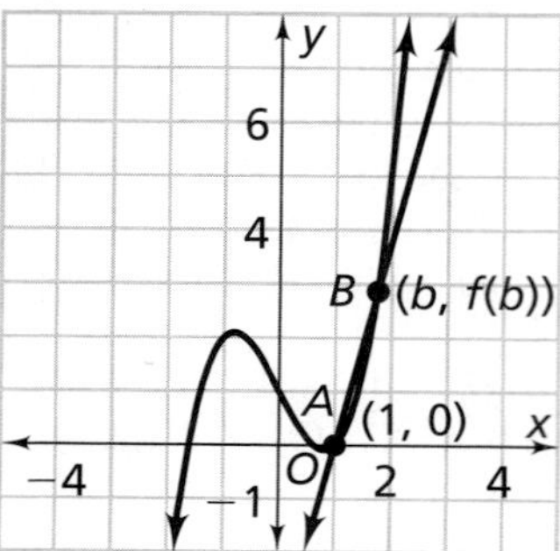


**c.** $m = b^2 + b - 1$ **d.** As $b$ gets closer to 1, the slope gets closer to $1^2 + 1 - 1 = 1$.

**4. a.** Answers may vary. Sample:

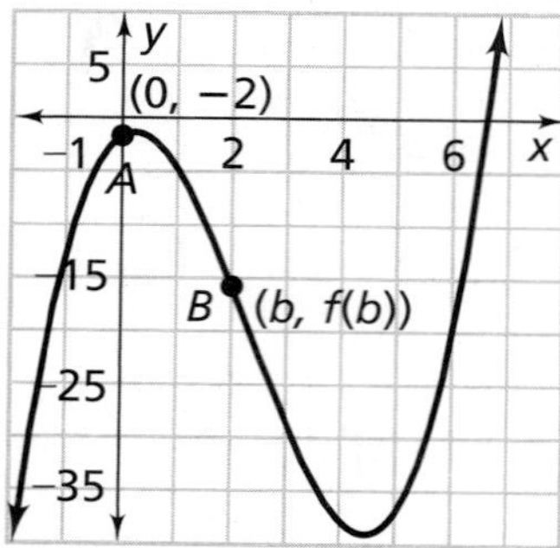


**b.** Answers may vary. Sample:

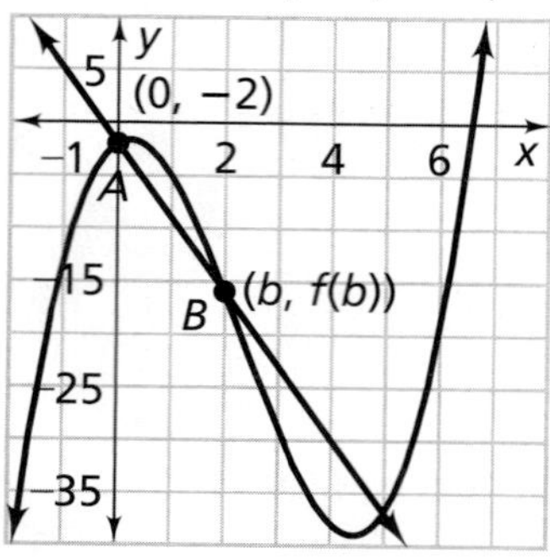


**c.** $m = \dfrac{f(b) - (-2)}{b}$

$= \dfrac{b^3 - 7b^2 + 3b - 2 + 2}{b}$

$= \dfrac{(b)(b^2 - 7b + 3)}{b} = b^2 - 7b + 3$

**d.** As $b$ gets closer to 0, the slope gets closer to $0^2 - 7(0) + 3 = 3$. **5.** $m = 3a + 3b + 5$ **6. a.** (0, −10) **b.** (0, 33) **c.** $(0, -ab)$ **7.** The slope is $a^2 + ab + b^2 = (a - b)^2 + 3ab = (a + b)^2 - ab$. Either the second or third expression must always be positive unless $a = b = 0$, which cannot happen since $a \neq b$. **8. a.** 9000 ft or approx. 1.7 mi **b.** 18,000 ft or approx. 3.4 mi **c.** 40,500 ft or approx. 7.7 mi **d.** $900t$ ft **9. a.** 0 ft; Pete has not caught John yet. **b.** 12,000 ft, or about $2\frac{1}{4}$ mi; Pete has not caught John yet. **c.** 42,000 ft, or about 8 mi; Pete has passed John. **d.** $1200(t - 10)$, where $t \geq 10$ **e.** Solve $900t = 1200(t - 10)$. **10. a.** Yakov **b.** 2 s **c.** 20 ft **d.** Yakov: 10 ft/s; Demitri: 5 ft/s **e.** $y = 10x$ **f.** $y = 5x + 10$ **g.** $10x = 5x + 10$

**On Your Own**

**11. a.**

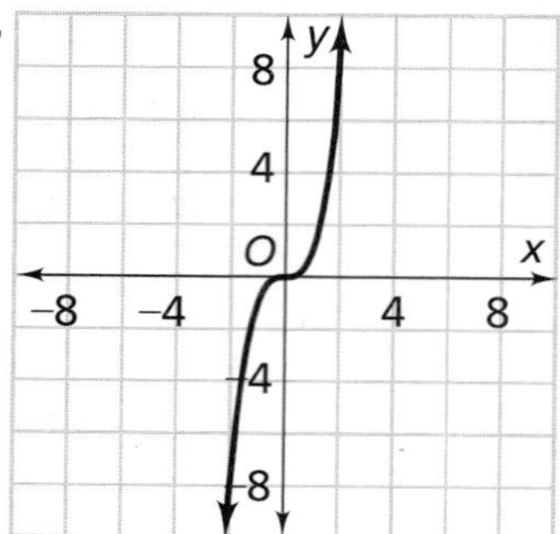


**d.**

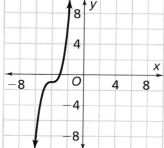

**12. a.**

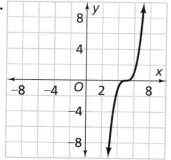

**b.**

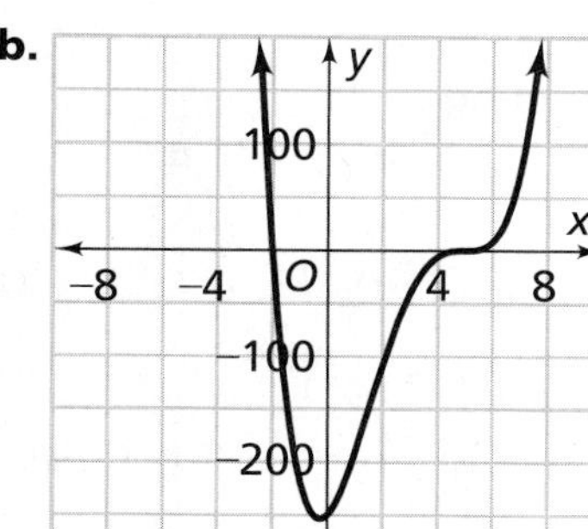


**c.**

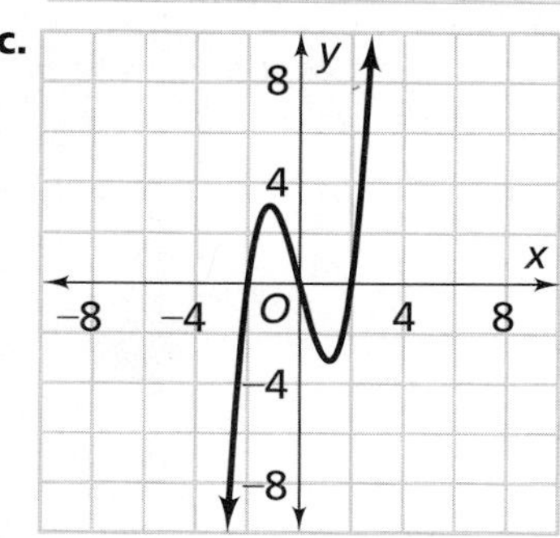


**18. a.** The graphs intersect at (0, 1).

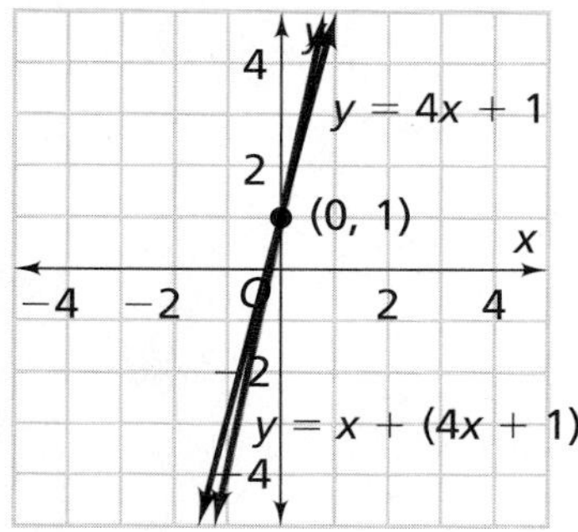


**19. a.** The graphs intersect at (5, 4).

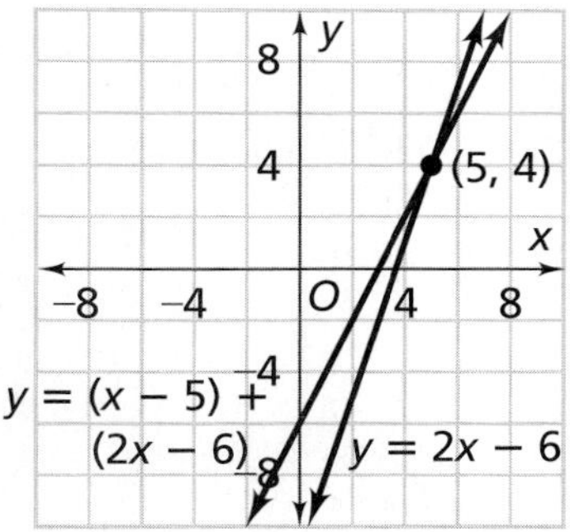


### Lesson 7.04

#### Check Your Understanding

**1. a.** The expansion is $2x^3 + 5x^2 + x - 1 = 101 + 85(x - 3) + 23(x - 3)^2 + 2(x - 3)^3$. **b.** The expansion is $x^2 + 2x - 3 = 12 + 8(x - 3) + (x - 3)^2$. **c.** The expansion is $2x^3 + 5x^2 + x - 1 = 113 + 93(x - 3) + 24(x - 3)^2 + 2(x - 3)^3$. **d.** The expansion is $8x^3 + 20x^2 + 4x - 4 = 404 + 340(x - 3) + 92(x - 3)^2 + 8(x - 3)^3$. **e.** The expansion is $8x^3 + 19x^2 + 2x - 1 = 392 + 332(x - 3) + 91(x - 3)^2 + 8(x - 3)^3$. **2. a.** The expansion is $2x^3 + 5x^2 + x - 1 = 37 + 45(x - 2) + 17(x - 2)^2 + 2(x - 2)^3$. **b.** The expansion is $x^2 + 2x - 3 = 5 + 6(x - 2) + (x - 2)^2$. **c.** The expansion is $2x^3 + 6x^2 + 3x - 4 = 42 + 51(x - 2) + 18(x - 2)^2 + 2(x - 2)^3$. **d.** The expansion is $6x^3 + 15x^2 + 3x - 3 = 111 + 135(x - 2) + 51(x - 2)^2 + 6(x - 2)^3$. **e.** The expansion is $2x^5 + 9x^4 + 5x^3 - 14x^2 - 5x + 3 = 185 + 447(x - 2) + 392(x - 2)^2 + 157(x - 2)^3 + 29(x - 2)^4 + 2(x - 2)^5$. **3.** $x^2 + 2x - 3 = a^2 + 2a - 3 + (2a + 2)(x - a) + (x - a)^2$ **4. a.** $27 + 27(x - 3) + 9(x - 3)^2 + (x - 3)^3$ **b.** $9 + 6(x - 3) + (x - 3)^2$ **c.** $3 + (x - 3)$ **d.** $1 + 0(x - 3)$ **5.** Yes, it works for $f(x) = 2x^3 + 5x^2 + x - 1$. It will work for any cubic.

#### On Your Own

**6. a.** $379 + 201(x - 5) + 35(x - 5)^2 + 2(x - 5)^3$ **b.** $32 + 12(x - 5) + (x - 5)^2$ **c.** $1073 + 579(x - 5) + 103(x - 5)^2 + 6(x - 5)^3$ **d.** $143{,}641 + 152{,}358(x - 5) + 66{,}931(x - 5)^2 + 15{,}586(x - 5)^3 + 2029(x - 5)^4 + 140(x - 5)^5 + 4(x - 5)^6$ **7.** The expansion is $rx^2 + sx + t = 9r + 3s + t + (6r + s)(x - 3) + r(x - 3)^2$. **8.** The expansion is $rx^2 + sx + t = a^2r + as + t + (2ar + s)(x - a) + r(x - a)^2$. **10. a.** 31 **b.** $-10x + 31$ **c.** $-4x^2 - 10x + 31$ **13. a.** $x^2 = 1 + 2(x - 1) + (x - 1)^2$ **b.** $x^3 = 1 + 3(x - 1) + (x + 2)(x - 1)^2$

**f.** $x^n = 1 + n(x - 1) + (x - 1)^2 \sum_{k=1}^{n-1} (k \cdot x^{n-k-1})$

for positive integer $n$.

### Lesson 7.05

#### Check Your Understanding

**1.** $y = 10x - 25$ **2.** $y = 3x - 2$ **3.** $y = 2ax - a^2$

**4.**

| $x$ | $f(x)$ | Slope of tangent at $(x, f(x))$ |
|---|---|---|
| −1 | 2 | −2 |
| 0 | 1 | 0 |
| 1 | 2 | 2 |
| 2 | 5 | 4 |
| 3 | 10 | 6 |
| 4 | 17 | 8 |
| 10 | 101 | 20 |
| 100 | 10,001 | 200 |

Selected Answers

**5.**

| $x$ | $f(x)$ | Slope of the tangent at $(x, f(x))$ |
|---|---|---|
| −1 | 0 | −1 |
| 0 | 0 | 1 |
| 1 | 2 | 3 |
| 2 | 6 | 5 |
| 3 | 12 | 7 |
| 4 | 20 | 9 |
| 10 | 110 | 21 |
| 100 | 10,100 | 201 |

**6. a.** $y = 2(x - 1) + 1 = 2x - 1$
**b.** $y = 3(x - 1) + 1 = 3x - 2$
**c.** $y = 4(x - 1) + 1 = 4x - 3$
**d.** $y = 5(x - 1) + 1 = 5x - 4$
**e.** $y = 6(x - 1) + 1 = 6x - 5$
**f.** $y = (x - 1) + 1 = x$
**7.** Using the results of Exercise 6, the tangent will be $y = n(x - 1) + 1$.

**On Your Own**

**8.** The equation of the tangent is $y = 2x + 2$; the slope of the tangent line is 2.
**10. a.** $y = 2a(x - a) + a^2 = 2ax - a^2$
**b.** $y = 3a^2(x - a) + a^3 = 3a^2x - 2a^3$
**c.** $y = 4a^3(x - a) + a^4 = 4a^3x - 3a^4$
**11.** Use your solution to Exercise 10. The equation of the tangent will be $y = na^{n-1}(x - a) + a^n = na^{n-1}x - (n - 1)a^n$.

### Lesson 7.06

**On Your Own**

**9.** $x = -\frac{1}{5}$ or $x = 2$ **10. a.** Answers may vary. Sample: $f(x) = \frac{x - 3}{x^2}$ **b.** Answers may vary. Sample: $f(x) = \frac{1}{x - 5}$ **c.** Answers may vary. Sample: $f(x) = \frac{x - 3}{x - 5}$ **d.** Answers may vary. Sample: $f(x) = \frac{x^2 - 5x + 1}{x - 5}$

**12. a.**

| $x$ | $k(x)$ |
|---|---|
| 0 | 2 |
| 1 | 3 |
| 2 | 4 |
| 3 | not defined |
| 4 | 6 |

**b.** $\frac{(x - 3)(x + 2)}{x - 3} = x + 2$ **c.** $k(x)$ is *not* the same function as $m(x) = x + 2$, because the domain of $m(x)$ is $\mathbb{R}$, while the domain of $k(x)$ is $\{x \mid x \neq 3\}$.

### Lesson 7.07

**Check Your Understanding**

**1. a.** 0 **b.** $\infty$ **c.** 0 **d.** $-\infty$ **2. a.** $\frac{3}{5}$ **b.** $\frac{10}{3}$ **c.** $\frac{5}{2}$ **d.** −2 **e.** $\infty$ **f.** 0 **3. a.** $y = 1$ **b.** $x = -2$ **c.** $\left(4, \frac{5}{6}\right)$
**4.** Answers may vary. **a.** $f(x) = \frac{4x}{x - 5}$ **b.** $f(x) = \frac{x}{(x - 2)(x - 5)}$ **c.** $f(x) = \frac{x - 2}{(x - 2)(x + 3)}$ **d.** $f(x) = \frac{x(x - 2)}{x - 1}$ **5.** $K = \frac{1}{6}$ **6. a.** $f(10) = 10.1$ and $f(100) = 100.01$. **b.** The graph approaches the line $y = x$. **c.** $f(0.1) = 10.1$ and $f(0.01) = 100.01$. **d.** The graph of $f(x)$ as $x$ approaches zero goes to $\infty$; the function has a vertical asymptote $x = 0$.
**e.**

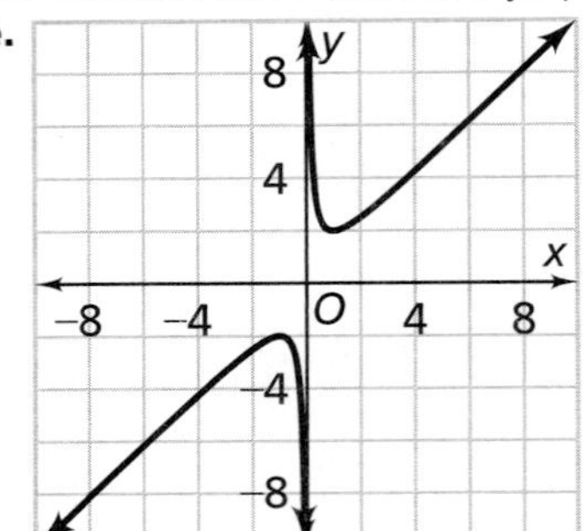


**7.** D
**8. a.**

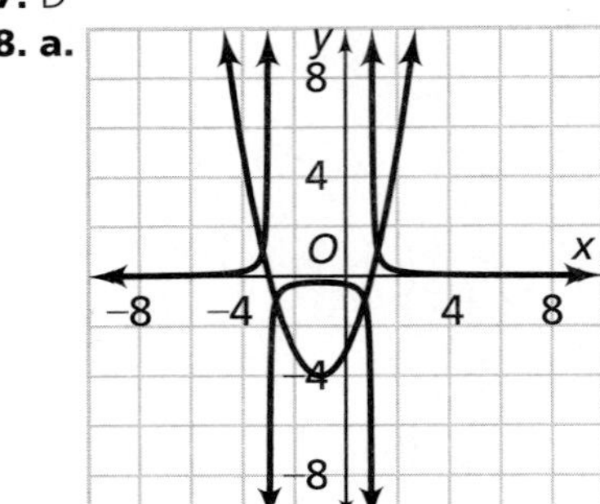


**b.** $-1 + \sqrt{3}$; $-1 - \sqrt{3}$; $-1 + \sqrt{5}$; $-1 - \sqrt{5}$
**9. a.** $d(x) = 0.75$; $d(2x) = 0.5$; $d(3x) = 0.25$; $d(4x) = 0$
**b.**

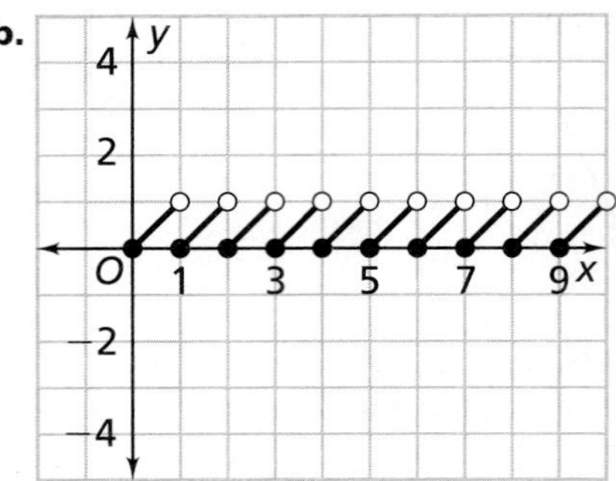

c.

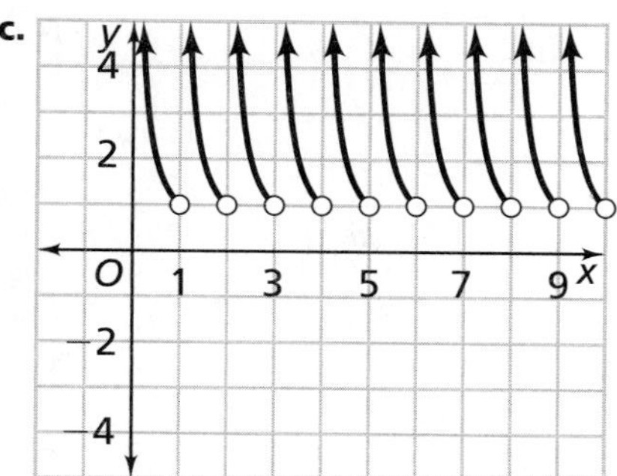

The domain of $r(x)$ is the set of all positive real numbers that are not integers. Its range is the positive real numbers.

### On Your Own

**10. a.** $y = 2$ **b.** $x = -3$ **c.** $\left(2, \frac{3}{5}\right)$

**11. a.** $\{x \mid x \neq -2, 2\}$ **b.** $\{x \mid x \neq -2, 2\}$

**12. a.** $\frac{1}{2}$ **b.** $\frac{1}{2}$ **c.** 0 **d.** 0 **e.** $\infty$

**15. a.** $f(x) = \dfrac{x + 11}{(x + 11)(x + 3)}$ so for all $x \neq -11$ $f(x) = g(x)$. These two functions are not the same, however, because $-11$ does not belong to the domain of $f(x)$. **b.** The graphs look the same on the calculator because the hole is not visible, but if you look at the table you will see that the function is undefined at $x = -11$.

## Lesson 7.08

### Check Your Understanding

**1.** $y = -\frac{1}{2} + \frac{1}{4}(x - 2)$ **2.** Since $f(x) = \frac{1}{x}$ and $g(x) = -\frac{1}{x}$ are reflections of each other over the $x$-axis, their tangents at $x = 2$ will also be reflections of each other over the $x$-axis. **3.** The equation of the tangent at $(a, h(a))$ is $y = \frac{1}{a^2} + \frac{-2}{a^3}(x - a)$.

**4.**

| $x$ | Slope of tangent to $f$ | Slope of tangent to $h$ |
|---|---|---|
| $\frac{1}{10}$ | $-100$ | $-2000$ |
| $\frac{1}{4}$ | $-16$ | $-128$ |
| $\frac{1}{2}$ | $-4$ | $-16$ |
| 1 | $-1$ | $-2$ |
| 2 | $-\frac{1}{4}$ | $-\frac{1}{4}$ |
| 4 | $-\frac{1}{16}$ | $-\frac{1}{32}$ |
| 10 | $-\frac{1}{100}$ | $-\frac{1}{500}$ |

This makes sense because the slope of the tangent to the graph of $f$ must be negative everywhere, but the slope of the tangent to the graph of $h$ will be positive for negative $x$-values and negative for positive $x$-values.

**5.** $y = 2(x + 2) - 7$ **6.** $A = 6, B = -2$

**7. a.** The slope of the line tangent to $f$ at $x = 4$ is $-\frac{3}{2}$.

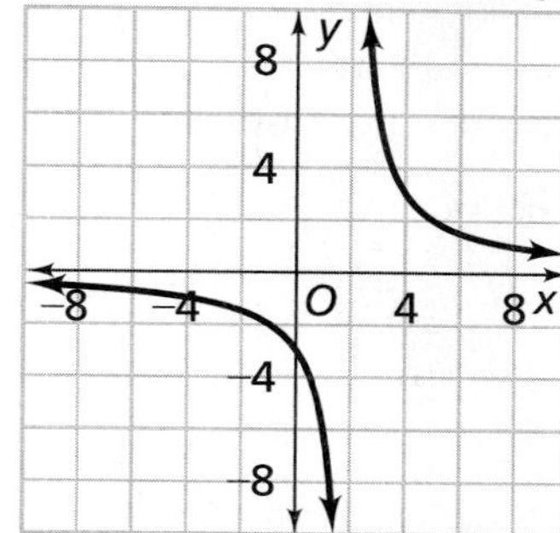

**b.** The slope of the line tangent to $g$ at $x = 4$ is 2.

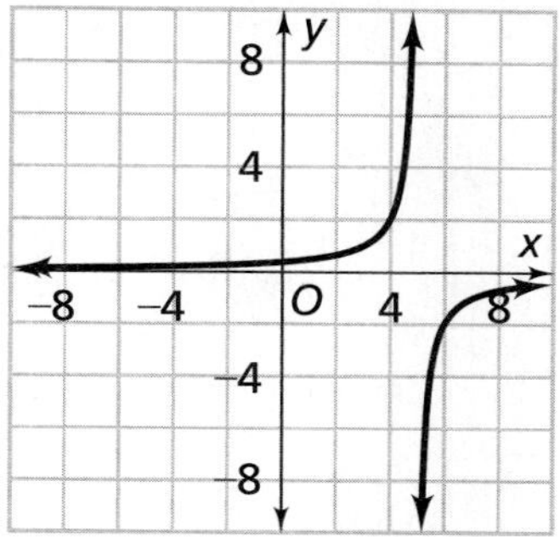

**c.** The slope of the line tangent to $h$ at $x = 4$ is $\frac{1}{2}$.

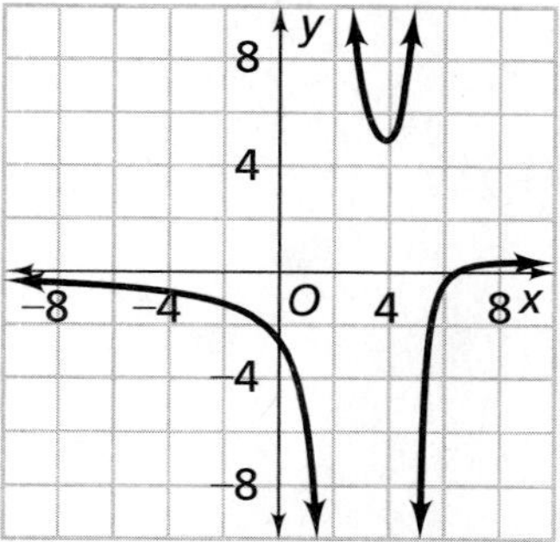

### On Your Own

**9.** $y = 1 - \frac{3}{13}(x - 3)$

**10.**

| $x$ | Slope of tangent to $f$ | Slope of tangent to $g$ |
|---|---|---|
| $-2$ | $-\frac{1}{4}$ | $\frac{3}{4}$ |
| $-1$ | $-1$ | 0 |
| $-\frac{1}{2}$ | $-4$ | $-3$ |
| 0 | undefined | undefined |
| $\frac{1}{2}$ | $-4$ | $-3$ |
| 1 | $-1$ | 0 |
| 2 | $-\frac{1}{4}$ | $\frac{3}{4}$ |
| 3 | $-\frac{1}{9}$ | $\frac{8}{9}$ |

**11. a.** The slope of the line tangent to $j(x)$ at $x = 2$ is $-\frac{4}{25}$. **b.** The slope of the line tangent to $j(x)$ at $x = -2$ is $\frac{4}{25}$. **c.** The answers to parts (a) and (b) are opposites, because $j(x)$ is symmetric across the $y$-axis.
**12.** $y = \frac{b}{d} + \frac{ad - bc}{d^2}x$

**Lesson 7.09**
**On Your Own**

**10.**

| $n$ | $t(n)$ |
|---|---|
| 0 | 1 |
| 1 | 3 |
| 2 | 9 |
| 3 | 27 |
| 4 | 81 |
| 5 | 243 |
| 6 | 729 |
| 7 | 2187 |
| 8 | 6561 |
| 9 | 19,683 |
| 10 | 54,049 |

$t(n) = 3^n$; $t(103) \approx 1.39 \times 10^{49}$, $t(104) \approx 4.17 \times 10^{49}$, $t(245) \approx 7.8 \times 10^{116}$.

**11.**

| $n$ | $j(n)$ |
|---|---|
| 0 | 1 |
| 1 | 4 |
| 2 | 9 |
| 3 | 16 |
| 4 | 25 |
| 5 | 36 |
| 6 | 49 |
| 7 | 64 |
| 8 | 81 |
| 9 | 100 |
| 10 | 121 |

$j(n) = (n + 1)^2$; $j(103) = 10,816$, $j(104) = 11,025$, $j(245) = 60,516$.

**13.**

| $n$ | $d(n)$ |
|---|---|
| 0 | 1 |
| 1 | 1 |
| 2 | 2 |
| 3 | 6 |
| 4 | 24 |
| 5 | 120 |
| 6 | 720 |
| 7 | 5040 |
| 8 | 40,320 |
| 9 | 362,880 |
| 10 | 3,628,800 |

$$d(n) = \begin{cases} 1 & \text{if } n = 0 \\ n \cdot d(n-1) & \text{if } n > 0 \end{cases}$$

**Lesson 7.10**
**Check Your Understanding**

**1.** \$6390.74 **2.** no **3a.** \$269.74 **b.** \$250.51 **c.** \$207.26 **4.** \$8341.43 **5.** about 0.9%

**On Your Own**

**7.** Answers may vary. Sample: For cars that cost less than \$33,200, you would pay less over the life of the loan if you chose the rebate deal. For cars that cost more than \$33,200, you would pay less if you chose the low interest rate deal. The deals are the same if the car costs \$33,200.

**Lesson 7.11**
**Check Your Understanding**

**1.**

| $n$ | $g(n)$ |
|---|---|
| 2 | 2 |
| 3 | 3 |
| 4 | 4 |
| 5 | 5 |
| 6 | 6 |
| 7 | 7 |
| 8 | 8 |
| 9 | 9 |
| 10 | 10 |

$g(n) = n$

**2.**

| $n$ | $h(n)$ |
|---|---|
| 3 | 6 |
| 4 | 12 |
| 5 | 20 |
| 6 | 30 |
| 7 | 42 |
| 8 | 56 |
| 9 | 72 |
| 10 | 90 |

$h(n) = n(n - 1)$ **3.** $k(n) = \frac{n!}{(n-4)!}$
**4.** $q(n) = (n!)^2$ **5a.** 1 **b.** 2 **c.** 4

### On Your Own

**6a.** 8 **7.** $f(n) = \begin{cases} 2 & \text{if } n = 1 \\ n \cdot f(n-1) & \text{if } n > 1 \end{cases}$

**10a.**

| $n$ | $r(n)$ |
|---|---|
| 1 | 1 |
| 2 | 3 |
| 3 | 6 |
| 4 | 10 |
| 5 | 15 |

**b.** $r(n) = \begin{cases} 1 & \text{if } n = 1 \\ r(n-1) + n & \text{if } n > 1 \end{cases}$

**c.** $r(n) = \frac{n(n+1)}{2}$

**12a.**

| $n$ | $t(n)$ |
|---|---|
| 1 | 3 |
| 2 | 15 |
| 3 | 105 |
| 4 | 945 |
| 5 | 10,395 |

**b.** $t(n) = \begin{cases} 2 & \text{if } n = 1 \\ t(n-1) \cdot (2n+1) & \text{if } n > 1 \end{cases}$

## Chapter 8
### Lesson 8.01
### On Your Own

**11a.** $\pm\sqrt{5}$ **b.** 2.32

**12.**

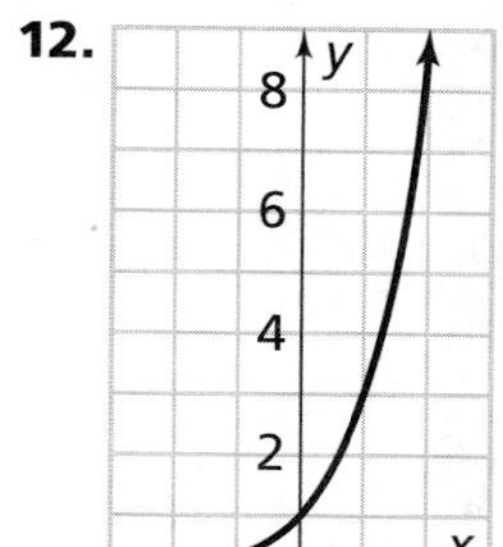


**15a.** outputs: $\frac{3}{4}, \frac{3}{2}, 3, 6, 12$
**16b.** $L(h) = 100 \cdot \left(\frac{1}{2}\right)^h$

### Lesson 8.02
### Check Your Understanding

**1a.** $f(x) = -3 \cdot 2^x$ **b.** $f(x) = 3 \cdot \left(\frac{1}{2}\right)^x$
**c.** $f(x) = 3 \cdot 2^x$ **d.** $f(x) = 3 \cdot 5^x$

**2a.** $f(x) = 12 \cdot \left(\frac{1}{2}\right)^x$ **b.** $f(x) = 48 \cdot \left(\frac{1}{2}\right)^x$
**3a.** Answers may vary. Sample: $f(x) = 2 \cdot 6^x$, $g(x) = 8 \cdot 3^x$ **b.** $f(x) = a \cdot \left(\sqrt{\frac{72}{a}}\right)^x$

**4.** Lemma: The proof uses the fact that $b^x$ is strictly decreasing for nonnegative integer inputs. Let $x = \frac{p}{q}$ for some positive integers $p$ and $q$, and then suppose that $b^{\frac{1}{q}} \geq 1$. Then $b = (b^{\frac{1}{q}})^q \geq 1^q = 1$, which implies $b \geq 1$. But this contradicts the hypothesis of the lemma that $b < 1$. Thus $b^{\frac{1}{q}} < 1$, and therefore $b^x = (b^{\frac{p}{q}}) = (b^{\frac{1}{q}})^p < 1^p = 1$. So, $b^x < 1$.

Theorem: Let $s$ and $t$ be rational numbers such that $s > t$. Then $s - t > 0$, so (using the Lemma) $b^{s-t} < 1$. Since $b^t > 0$, multiplying both sides of the inequality by $b^t$ does not reverse the inequality symbol. So,
$b^{s-t} \cdot b^t < 1 \cdot b^t$
$b^{s-t+t} < b^t$
$b^s < b^t$
Thus, if $s > t$, then $f(s) < f(t)$, which means that $f$ is strictly decreasing on rational number inputs.
**5.** Answers may vary. Sample: If $f(x) = 2^x$, then $f(-x) = 2^{-x} = \frac{1}{2^x} = \left(\frac{1}{2}\right)^x = g(x)$.
**6.** 2.807 **7.** 2.807

Selected Answers

**8a.** 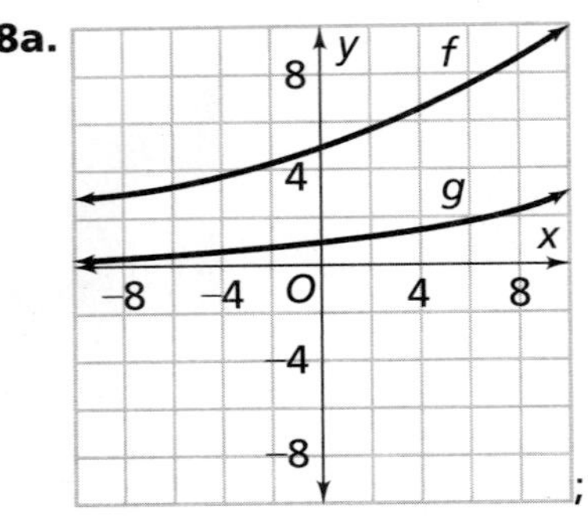

; no

**b.** one **9a.** 4 **b.** Yes; $\left(2^{\sqrt{2}}\right)^{\sqrt{2}} = 2^{\sqrt{2}\cdot\sqrt{2}} = 2^2 = 4$ **10.** Answers may vary. Sample: A calculator gives error messages because $b^a$ is not defined for $b < 0$.

**On Your Own**

**11.** $f(0) = a \cdot b^0 = a \cdot 1 = a$, so the graph contains $(0, a)$. **13a.** \$4.11, \$4.23 **15.** $2 < \sqrt{6} < 3$, so $3^2 < 3^{\sqrt{6}} < 3^3$ or $9 < 3^{\sqrt{6}} < 27$. **18a.** outputs: $\frac{1}{4}, -\frac{1}{2}, 1, -2, 4, -8$

**Lesson 8.03**

**Check Your Understanding**

**1a.** $A(n) = 18 \cdot \left(\frac{1}{3}\right)^n$ **b.** $B(x) = -2 \cdot (4)^n$ **c.** No exponential function fits the table because the ratio between consecutive outputs is not constant. **d.** $D(z) = \frac{1}{3} \cdot 6^z$

**2a.** $A(n) = \begin{cases} 18 & \text{if } n = 0 \\ \frac{1}{3} \cdot A(n-1) & \text{if } n > 0 \end{cases}$

**b.** $B(x) = \begin{cases} -2 & \text{if } x = 0 \\ 4 \cdot B(x-1) & \text{if } x > 0 \end{cases}$

**c.** not an exponential function

**d.** $D(z) = \begin{cases} \frac{1}{3} & \text{if } z = 0 \\ 6 \cdot D(z-1) & \text{if } z > 0 \end{cases}$

**3.** $q(x) = 12{,}500 \cdot \left(\frac{1}{5}\right)^x$ **4.** Disagree; a value of $-\frac{1}{5}$ for $b$ is not possible because the base of an exponential function must be positive. **5.** Answers may vary. Sample: $f(x) = 2x + 16$; $f(x) = (10 \cdot 2^{\frac{3}{5}})(2^{\frac{1}{5}})^x$ **6a.** $a = 100$, $b = 3^{\frac{1}{5}}$

**b.**

| x | T(x) | ÷ |
|---|---|---|
| 0 | 100 | **≈1.246** |
| 1 | **≈124.57** | **≈1.246** |
| 2 | **≈155.18** | **≈1.246** |
| 3 | **≈193.32** | **≈1.246** |
| 4 | **≈240.82** | **≈1.246** |
| 5 | 300 | |

**7a.** \$16,000; \$12,800; \$10,240 **b.** $V(n) = 20{,}000 \cdot (0.8)^n$ **c.** Yes; $V(14) = \$879.61$, so after 14 yr the car will be worth less than \$1000.

**8.** $y = y_1^{\frac{-x_2}{x_1 - x_2}} \cdot y_2^{\frac{x_1}{x_1 - x_2}} \cdot \left(\left(\frac{y_1}{y_2}\right)^{\frac{1}{x_1 - x_2}}\right)^x$

**On Your Own**

**10.** $M(n) = 24, 36, 54, 81$; $M(n) = 16 \cdot \left(\frac{3}{2}\right)^n$,

$M(n) = \begin{cases} 16 & \text{if } n = 0 \\ \frac{3}{2} \cdot M(n-1) & \text{if } n > 0 \end{cases}$

**12b.** $y = -5^{\frac{1}{4}} \cdot \left(5^{\frac{1}{4}}\right)^x$ or $y = -5^{\frac{x+1}{4}}$

**Lesson 8.04**

**Check Your Understanding**

**1.** Multiply $a$ by the power $b^x$. **2.** Divide $C$ by the power $b^x$. **3.** Find the $\frac{1}{x}$ power of the quotient $C \div a$. **4.** Find $C \div a$, and then find the power of $b$ that results in the value $C \div a$.

**5a.**

| x | f(x) = 2^x |
|---|---|
| 0 | 1 |
| 1 | 2 |
| 1.5850 | 3 |
| **2** | 4 |
| 2.3219 | 5 |
| **2.5850** | 6 |
| | 7 |
| **3** | 8 |
| **3.1700** | 9 |
| **3.3219** | 10 |

**b.** 2.8074

**6a.** $f(x + y) = \frac{f(x) \cdot f(y)}{a}$ **b.** $f(x - y) = a \cdot \frac{f(x)}{f(y)}$ **c.** $f(xy) = a^{1-y} \cdot (f(x))^y$ **7a.** 3.162 **b.** $\sqrt{10}$ **c.** \$4743.42 **8a.** 2.154 **b.** $\sqrt[3]{10}$ **c.** \$6962.38

**9.** If $x = 1$, then $x^y = 1$ for all real number values of $y$; if $x = -1$, then $x^y = 1$ for all even values of $y$, or for all fractions $\frac{p}{q}$ where $p$ and $q$ are relatively prime and $p$ is even; if $y = 0$, then $x^y = 1$ for all values of $x$ except $x = 0$.

**On Your Own**

**10a.** 2 **d.** no solution **12a.** 11.9 yr

**13.**

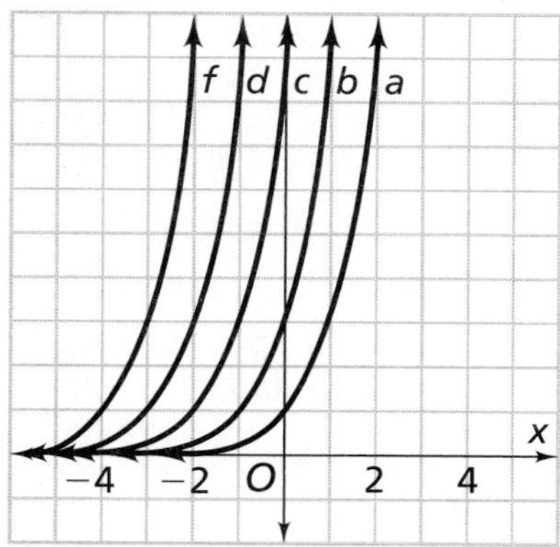


The graphs are all horizontal translations of each other. Answers may vary. Sample: Each function can be written in the form $F(x) = 3^{x+n}$, which represents a horizontal translation of $a(x) = 3^x$. For example, $c(x) = 9 \cdot 3^x = 3^2 + 3^x = 3^{2+x}$, so the graph of $c(x) = 3^{x+2}$ is a horizontal translation of two units to left of the graph of $a(x) = 3^x$.

**16a.** Plan 1: 2 yr, Plan 2: 3 yr

**Lesson 8.05**

**Check Your Understanding**

**1.** domain: positive real numbers, range: all real numbers **2a.** 2 **b.** 0 **c.** 6 **d.** 3 **e.** −2

**3a.** 1.1610 **b.** 1.5 **c.** 2.6610 **d.** 0.3390

**4.**

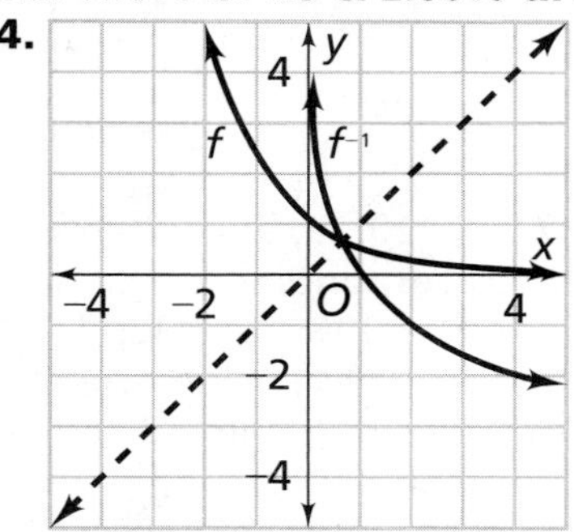


**5a.** the mean of $f(3)$ and $f(5)$ **b.** the mean of $f(5)$ and $f(7)$ **c.** the mean of $f(-4)$ and $f(-2)$ **d.** the mean of $f(x)$ and $f(y)$

**6a.**

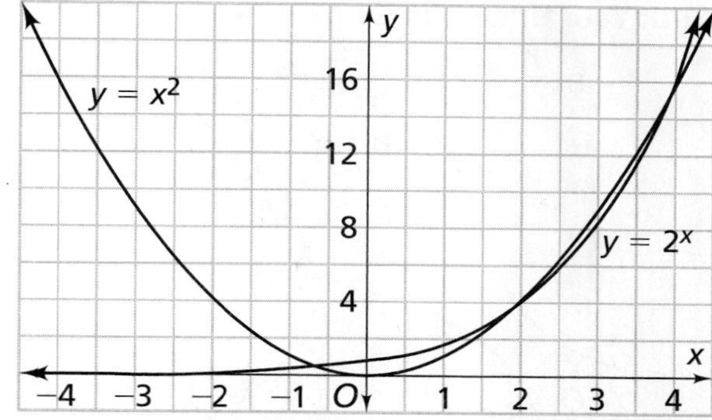


**b.** 3 solutions **7.** no **8a.** no **b.** no **c.** yes

**9.** $b \approx 1.4$; about (2.7, 2.7)

**On Your Own**

**10.** Yes; $L_2(x)$ is the inverse of $f(x) = 2^x$. Since $f(x)$ is one-to-one, its inverse is one-to-one.

**12.**

| $x$ | $L_2(x)$ |
|---|---|
| 1 | 0 |
| 2 | 1 |
| 3 | 1.5850 |
| 4 | **2** |
| 5 | **2.3219** |
| 6 | **2.5850** |
| 7 | **2.8074** |
| 8 | **3** |
| 9 | **3.1699** |

**13b.** $8^{\frac{1}{3}} = 2$, so $L_8(2) = \frac{1}{3}$. **15.** 8 yr

**Lesson 8.06**

**On Your Own**

**11a.** 2 **12a.** 2 **14a.** 5 **d.** $\frac{5}{2}$

**16.**

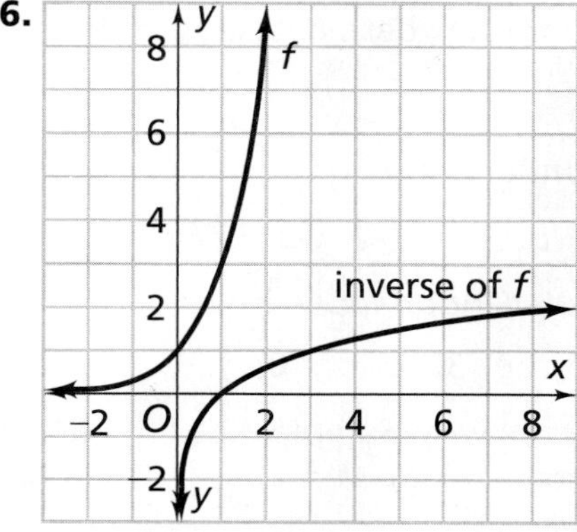


**18a.** 4.3 **b.** 3.2

**Lesson 8.07**
**Check Your Understanding**

**1a.**

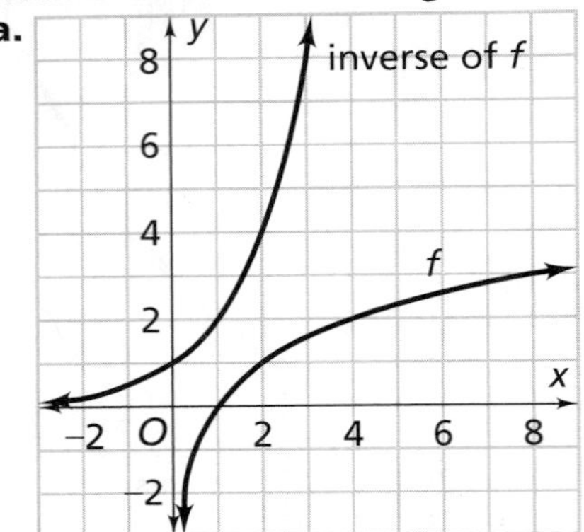


**b.** $f^{-1}(x) = 2^x$ **2.** C **3a.** $\frac{1}{2}$ **b.** 3 **c.** 3 **d.** $\frac{3}{2}$ **e.** 2 **f.** 2 **4.** If $\log_b 0 = x$, then $b^x = 0$. But $b^x = 0$ only when $b = 0$. Since $b = 0$ is not a valid base for logarithms, $\log_b 0$ does not exist. **5.** $\log_2 0.1$, $\log_5 \frac{1}{5}$, $\log_{73} 1$, $\log_{100} 10$, $\log 99$, $\log_4 18$, $\log_2 18$ **6a.** $b^4 = 9$ **b.** $\sqrt{3}$ **7.** 75 **8a.** 2 **b.** 3 **c.** 6 **d.** 27 **e.** 3.49 **f.** 6.42 **9.** 2.322 **10.** Answers may vary. Sample: The characteristic of $\log M$ is a good indicator of the size of the number $M$. For example, if $\log M = 3.6435$, then the characteristic 3 means $M$ is between $10^3 = 1000$ and $10^4 = 10{,}000$. The mantissa of $\log M$ is always the logarithm of the number between 1 and 10 that $10^{\text{characteristic}}$ is multiplied by to get $M$. For example, the number 0.6465 in $\log M = 3.6435$ tells us that $10^{0.6435}$ is the number that must be multiplied by $10^3$ to get $M$. The mantissa in combination with the characteristic provides a way to find $M$ from a logarithm table that gives logarithms of numbers between 1 and 10.

**On Your Own**

**12.** $b^0 = 1$ for any nonzero value of $b$, so $\log_b 1 = 0$ for any base $b$. **13a.** $y = 2x$ **16a.** 2.085

**Lesson 8.08**
**Check Your Understanding**

**1a.** 4 **b.** 7 **c.** 1 **d.** 21 **e.** $\frac{7}{2}$ **2.** 4 **3.** $\frac{\log_2 32}{\log_2 8} \neq \log_2 \frac{32}{8}$, so you cannot apply the rule for $\log_b \frac{M}{N}$ to get $\log_2 32 - \log_2 8$; $\frac{5}{3}$.

**4a.** Answers may vary. Sample: Let $b^x = M$ and $b^y = N$ so $x = \log_b M$ and $y = \log_b N$. Then $\log_b \frac{M}{N} = \log_b \frac{b^x}{b^y}$ $= \log_b b^{x-y} = x - y = \log_b M - \log_b N$.

**b.** Answers may vary. Sample: $\log_b \frac{M}{N}$ $= \log_b \left(M \cdot \frac{1}{N}\right) = \log_b M + \log_b \frac{1}{N}$ $= \log_b M + \log_b N^{-1} = \log_b M + (-1) \cdot \log_b N = \log_b M - \log_b N$. **5a–c.** Answers may vary. Samples are given. **a.** $b^0 = 1$ for any base $b$, so $\log_b 1 = 0$. **b.** $b^1 = b$ for any base $b$, so $\log_b b = 1$. **c.** Start with $\log_b (N \cdot \frac{1}{N}) = \log_b 1$. Rewrite the left side as $\log_b N + \log_b \frac{1}{N}$. The right side is 0, so $\log_b N + \log_b \frac{1}{N} = 0$ and $\log_b \frac{1}{N} = -\log_b N$. **6a.** $C(n) = 3.99 \cdot 1.03^n$ **b.** 55 yr **7.** $\frac{\log 3.5}{\log 5}$; 0.778 **8.** $\frac{\log \frac{c}{a}}{\log b}$ or $\frac{\log c - \log a}{\log b}$ **9.** $\frac{\log \frac{7}{2}}{\log \frac{5}{3}}$; 2.452 **10.** $\frac{\log \frac{c}{a}}{\log \frac{b}{d}}$ or $\frac{\log c - \log a}{\log b - \log d}$

**11.** Answers may vary. Sample: If $6^x = 35$, then $x = \frac{\log 35}{\log 6}$, while if $35^x = 6$ then $x = \frac{\log 6}{\log 35}$; the fractions are reciprocals. **12a.** 2 **b.** $-3, 2$ **c.** all real numbers greater than 0 **d.** 5 **e.** no solution **13.** If $\log 2 = 0.3$ then $5 \cdot \log 2 = 1.5$, and if $\log 3 = 0.5$ then $3 \cdot \log 3 = 1.5$. Then $5 \cdot \log 2 = 3 \cdot \log 3$, so $\log 2^5 = \log 3^3$, which implies that $32 = 27$. Subtracting 27 from each side gives $5 = 0$. Dividing each side by 5 gives $1 = 0$. **14.** If $r$ is the annual interest rate, then the situation of doubling an amount $A$ can be written as $2A = A\left(1 + \frac{r}{100}\right)^y$ or $2 = \left(1 + \frac{r}{100}\right)^y$. Then $\log 2 = y \cdot \log\left(1 + \frac{r}{100}\right)$ and $y = \frac{\log 2}{\log\left(1 + \frac{r}{100}\right)}$. By letting $r$ take the values 6, 7, 8, 9, 10, 11, and 12, you can calculate the corresponding $y$-values 11.8957, 10.2448, 9.0065, 8.0432, 7.2725, 6.6419, and 6.1163. These values are very close to the results given by the Rule of 72 (listed in Exercise 17, Lesson 8.05).

**On Your Own**

**15.** $\log_5 135$; $5^3 = 125$, so $\log_5 135 > 3$. $7^3 = 343$, and $\log_7 300 < 3$. Thus, $\log_5 135 > \log_7 300$. **16.** $\log_3 x = 1$, 1.2619, 1.4650, 1.6309, 1.7712, 1.8928, 2 **17.** D **19a.** $a + b$ **23a.** 1

Lesson 8.09

Check Your Understanding

**1.** 2.6 **2a.** $\ln 1 = 0$; $\ln 0$ is undefined.
**b.** about 2.71728.

**3a.**

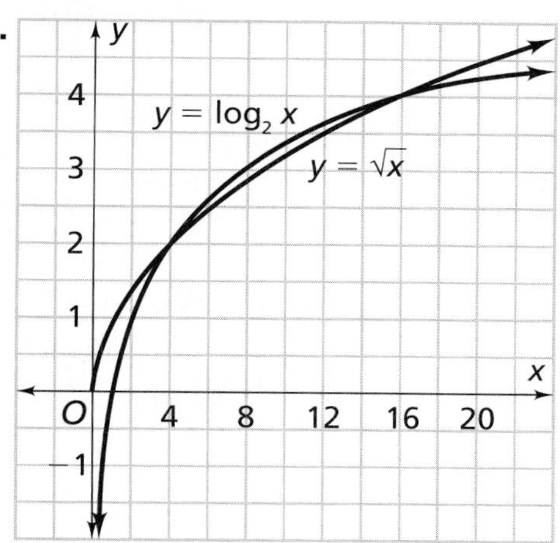


**b.** 2 **4.** no **5a.** no **b.** no **c.** yes **6a.** 1 **b.** 1 **c.** 2 **d.** 0 **e.** 2 **7.** $b \approx 1.4447$, intersect at about (2.7183, 2.7183)

On Your Own

**8a.** 0.468 **9.** Disagree; the graphs are not the same because the domain of $f(x) = \log x^2$ is all real numbers except 0, while the domain of $g(x) = 2 \log x$ is only the positive real numbers.

**10a.**

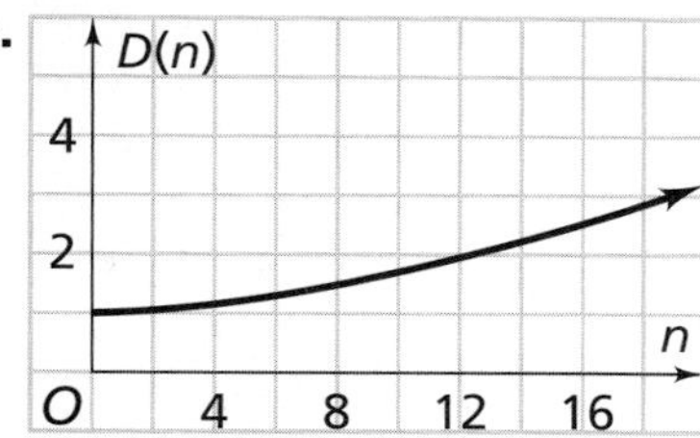


**13a.**

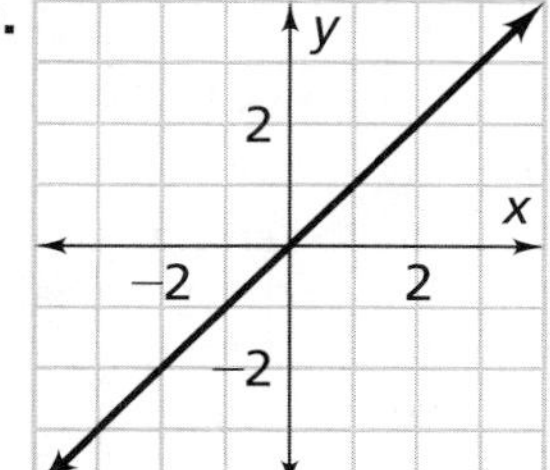


$y = x$; since $\log 10^x = x$ for all real numbers $x$, the graph of $y = \log 10^x$ is the same as the graph of $y = x$.

Lesson 8.10

Check Your Understanding

**1.** Less frequent; about 1 out of 10 integers are prime up to $10^5$, but only 1 out of 22 are prime up to $10^{10}$.

**2.**

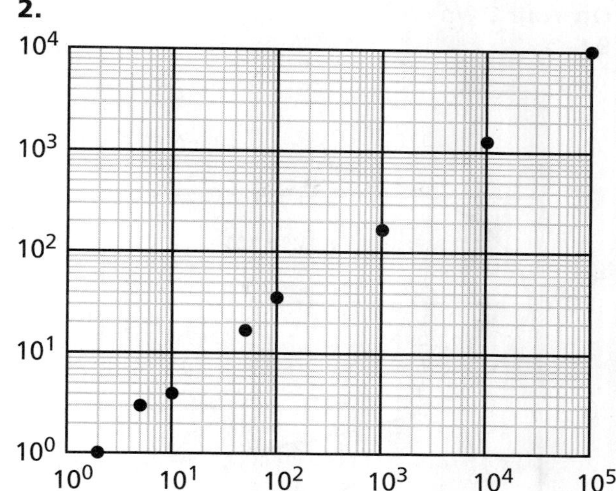


The points appear to lie on a line.

**3.**

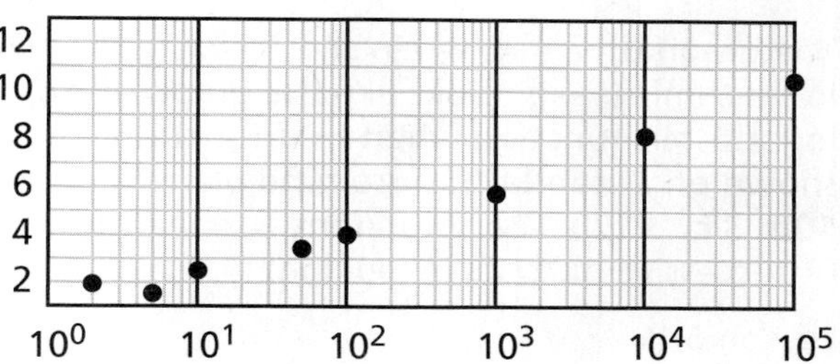


The points appear to lie on a line, especially as the values of $x$ get larger. **4.** Logarithmic; on the vertical axis, equal differences are not represented by equal distances.

**5a.** Suppose $y = \log_b x$ with $b > 0$, $b \neq 1$. Rewrite the equation as $b^y = x$, and take the logarithm of each side: $\log b^y = \log x$. Then $y \cdot \log b = \log x$, so $y = \frac{1}{\log b} \cdot \log x$. Since $\frac{1}{\log b}$ is a constant, say $B$, the equation becomes $y = B \cdot \log x$, which is in linear form. **b.** $\frac{1}{\log b}$

**6a.** If $y = a \cdot x^b$, then $\log y = \log (a \cdot x^b)$. So, $\log y = \log a + b \cdot \log x$. But $\log a$ is a constant, say $A$, so the equation becomes $\log y = A + b \cdot \log x$, which is in linear form. **b.** $b$ **7.** The intersection of $y = x^2$ and $y = 10x^2$ is (0, 0). Because there is no value of 0 on the logarithmic axes, the intersection is not shown.

**On Your Own**

**9a–b.**

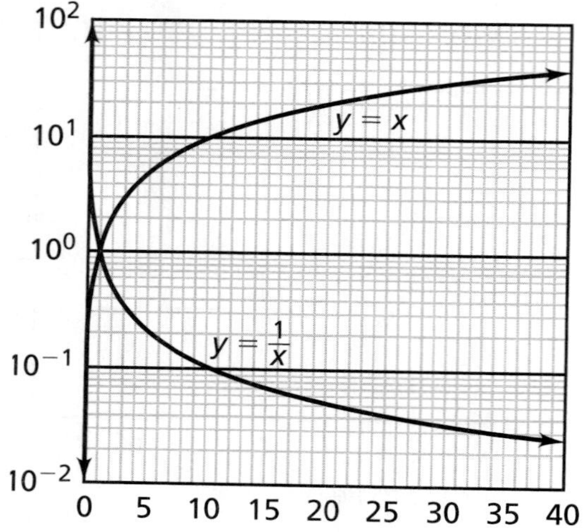


The graph of $y = x$, when shown using a logarithmic $y$-axis, looks like the graph of a logarithmic function when that function is shown on a standard coordinate plane. **10b.** 3 **c.** $\pm 100$ **12a.** Exponential; the ratio of successive outputs is constant.

**Lesson 8.11**

**On Your Own**

**8. a.**

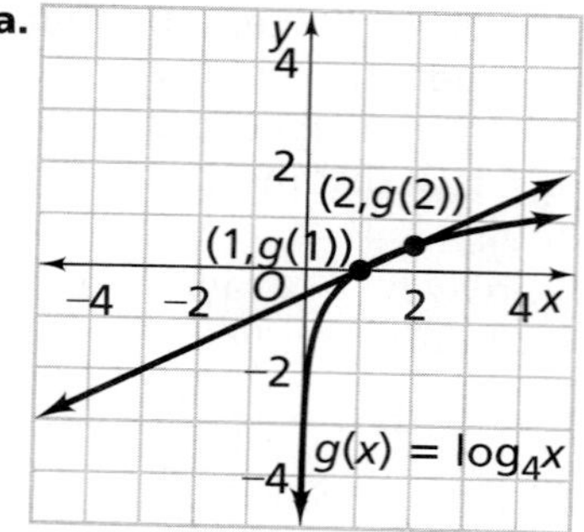


The slope of the secant is 0.5.

**b.** Since the slope is positive and a little more than 0.5, a good estimate might be 0.7.

**9.**

| Base $b$ | Slope of tangent to $f(x) = \log_b x$ at $x = 1$ |
|---|---|
| 2 | 1.443 |
| 3 | 0.910 |
| 4 | 0.721 |
| 5 | 0.621 |
| 8 | 0.481 |
| 10 | 0.434 |

**Lesson 8.12**

**Check Your Understanding**

**1. a.** \$400; \$800; $100(2)^t$ **b.** \$596.05; \$1455.19; $100(2.441406)^t$ **c.** \$2008.55 **2. a.** \$106.00; \$112.36; $100(1.06)^t$ **b.** \$106.09; \$112.55; $100(1.03)^{2n} = 100(1.0609)^n$ **c.** The 100 is the amount Jamie invested. The 1.005 is $1 + \frac{0.06}{12}$, 0.06 is the interest rate expressed as a decimal, 12 is the number of times it is compounded in a year (monthly). $36 = 12 \cdot 3$ is (number of times compounded in a year)(number of years).

**3.** $B = P\left(1 + \frac{0.05}{n}\right)^{nt}$ **4. a.** \$105.09 **b.** \$105.12 **c.** \$105.13 **d.** \$105.13 **5. a.** \$128.40 **b.** \$164.87 **c.** \$271.83 **d.** \$738.91 **6. a.** $\$128.40 \approx 47.237e$ **b.** $\$164.87 \approx 60.653e$ **c.** $\$271.83 \approx 100e$ **d.** $\$738.91 \approx 271.828e$

**7. a.**
$$\frac{1}{K} = \frac{x}{n}$$
$$n \cdot \frac{1}{K} = n \cdot \frac{x}{n}$$
$$\frac{n}{K} = x$$
$$n = Kx$$

**b.** $\left(1 + \frac{x}{n}\right)^n = \left(1 + \frac{1}{K}\right)^{Kx}$

**c.** The two limits are the same because as $n \to \infty$, $K \to \infty$.

**d.**
$$\lim_{K\to\infty}\left(1 + \frac{1}{K}\right)^{Kx} = \lim_{K\to\infty}\left(\left(1 + \frac{1}{K}\right)^K\right)^x = \left(\lim_{K\to\infty}\left(1 + \frac{1}{K}\right)^K\right)^x = e^x$$

**8.**
$$\lim_{n\to\infty} P\left(1 + \frac{r}{n}\right)^{nt} = P\left(\lim_{n\to\infty}\left(1 + \frac{r}{n}\right)^n\right)^t = P(e^r)^t = Pe^{rt}$$

**On Your Own**

**10. a.** Her balance is \$2000; It is multiplied by a factor of 10. **b.** \$2718.28

**11. a.** $B(3) = \$1197.22$; $B(5) = \$1349.86$; $B(t) = 1000 \cdot e^{0.06 \cdot t}$ dollars **b.** It will take approximately 11.55 years for the balance to double. **c.** It will take approximately 23.1 years for the balance to become \$4000. **12.** The better investment is the account at 6% APR compounded annually.

**14.** $m = 0.055$

**Lesson 8.13**

**Check Your Understanding**

**1. a.** $1 + \frac{1}{1!} + \frac{1}{2!} + \frac{1}{3!} + \cdots + \frac{1}{13!} \approx 2.7182818285$; fourteen terms ($k = 13$).

**b.** $\left(1 + \frac{1}{10^7}\right)^{10^7} \approx 2.71828169255$; six

**2. a.** $q(0.05) = 1.05125$ and $e^{0.05} = 1.05127$; approximately $-0.02\%$ **b.** $q(0.5) = 1.625$ and $e^{0.05} = 1.64872$; approximately $-1.44\%$

**c.** $q(-1) = 0.5$ and $e^{-1} = 0.36788$; approximately 35.91%

**3.** $x \approx 0.693$ **4. a.** (0.693, 2) **b.** (1.099, 3)

**5. a.** $\sum_{k=0}^{\infty} \frac{(-1)^k}{k!} \approx 0.36788$ **b.** The summation gives the same rule as $e^x$ where $x = -1$. So it should equal $e^{-1}$, and it does.

**6. a.**

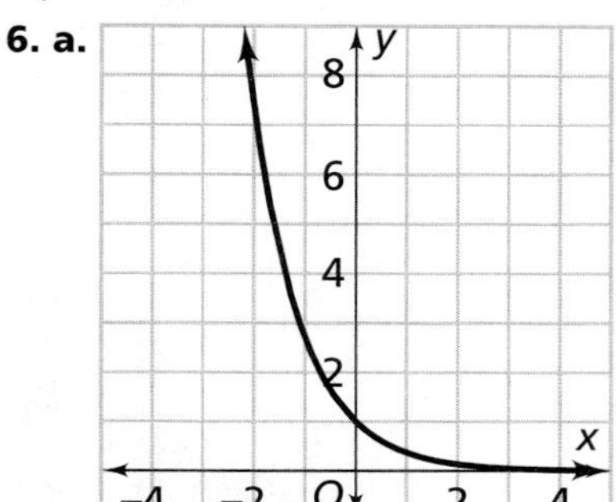

**b.**

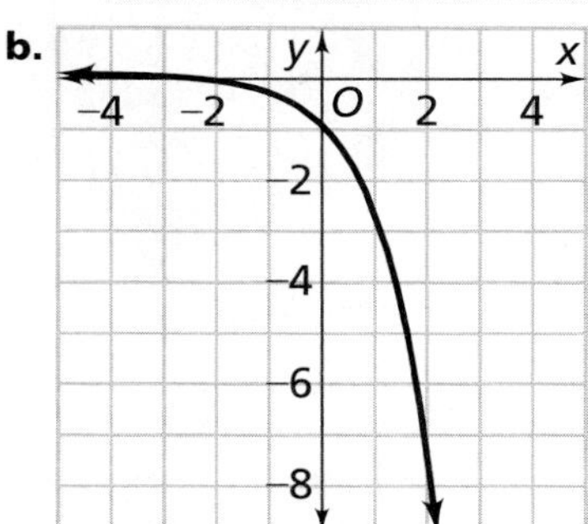

**c.**

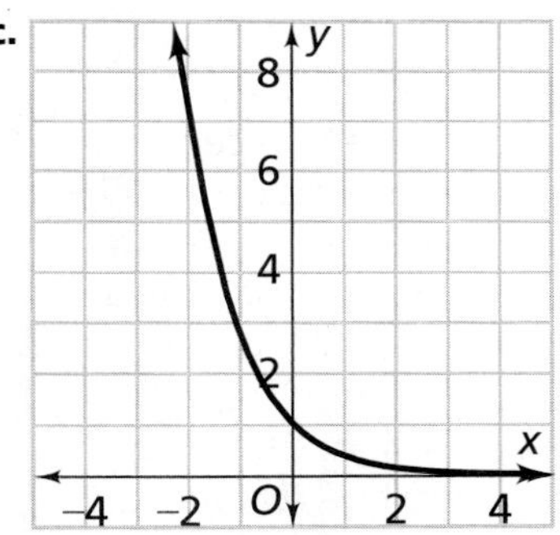

### On Your Own

**8. a.** $c(0.1) = 1.10516666667$ and $f(0.1) = 1.10517091808$; $-0.00038\%$

**b.** $c(0.2) = 1.22133333333$ and $f(0.2) = 1.22140275816$; $-0.00568\%$

$c(0.5) = 1.64583333333$ and $f(0.5) = 1.6487212707$; $-0.17516\%$

$c(1) = 2.666666666667$ and $f(1) = 2.71828182846$; $-1.89882\%$

$c(2) = 6.33333333$ and $f(2) = 7.38905609893$; $-14.28765\%$

**c.** The graphs are very close together for small values of $x$. As $x$ gets larger, the graphs are farther apart.

**d.** There are two solutions: $x = -0.00017$ and $x = -0.00015$.

**9.** $e^2$ **10. a.** $k \approx 1.09861$ **c.** $n \approx 2.70805$

**e.** no solution

### Lesson 8.14

### Check Your Understanding

**1.** 6.931 **2. a.** $p = 4$; $M = 3$ **b.** $\frac{1}{3} \ln 2$

**c.** $-2 \ln 5$ **3. a.** 2 **b.** 10 **c.** $-1$ **d.** 5

**4. a.** $\ln 3$ **b.** $m = \ln 5$ **c.** $e^{x \ln 2} = e^{\ln 2^x} = 2^x$

**5.** $a^x = e^{\ln a^x} = e^{x \ln a} = e^{kx}$ where $k = \ln a$.

**6. a.** $x \approx 2.807$ **b.** $z \approx 2.990$ **c.** $x \approx -1.672$

**d.** $x = \frac{\ln c - \ln a}{\ln b - \ln d} = \frac{\ln \frac{c}{a}}{\ln \frac{b}{d}}$ **7. a.** (3, ln 3) **b.** (ln 3, 3)

**c.** $(2, e^2)$ **d.** $(e^2, 2)$ **e.** $g = e^4$ **f.** $p = \ln 4$

### On Your Own

**8. a.** 1.099 **e.** 0.511 **f.** undefined **9. a.** \$134.99; \$182.21; \$332.01 **d.** $t = \frac{\ln \frac{B}{100}}{0.06}$; 38.38 years

**10. a.** 34.7 years **b.** 23.1 years **f.** $\frac{\ln 2}{0.01p}$ years

### Lesson 8.15

### Check Your Understanding

**1. a.** The slope of the tangent at any point is equal to the $y$-value of that point. **b.** The slope of the tangent at any point is equal to the $y$-value of that point times 2. **c.** The slope of the tangent at any point is equal to the $y$-value of that point times 5. **d.** The slope of the tangent at any point is equal to the $y$-value of that point times $\ln 2$.

**2. a.** $\ln 2$ **b.** $\ln 16$ **c.** $\ln 5^5$

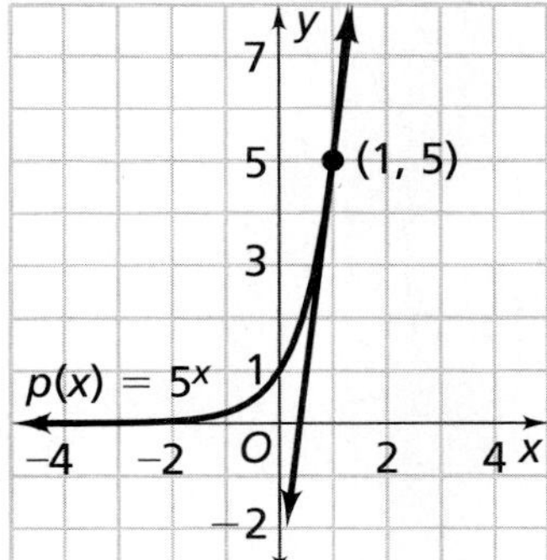


**3. a.** $5^0 \ln 5 = \ln 5$ **b.** $\ln 8 = \ln 2^3 = 3 \ln 2$

**c.** Base $e$, because $e^0 \ln e = 1$. **d.** $b = 1$, but this is just a horizontal line: $y = 1^x \rightarrow y = 1$. **4. a.** This is the definition of logarithm. **b.** $2^y = x \Rightarrow \ln 2^y = \ln x \Rightarrow y \ln 2 = \ln x$ **c.** Divide both sides by $\ln 2$ to get $y = \frac{\ln x}{\ln 2}$. Since $\log_2 x = y$, $\log_2 x = y = \frac{\ln x}{\ln 2}$.

**5. a.** The slope is 3 times the reciprocal of the $x$-value.

**b.** The slope is the reciprocal of the $x$-value.

**c.** The slope is the reciprocal of the $x$-value times $\frac{1}{5}$.

**d.** The slope is the reciprocal of the $x$-value times $\frac{1}{\ln 2}$.

Selected Answers

**6. a.** $\frac{1}{\ln 2} \approx 1.443$ **b.** $\frac{1}{4 \ln 2} \approx 0.361$
**c.** $\frac{1}{5 \ln 5} \approx 0.124$

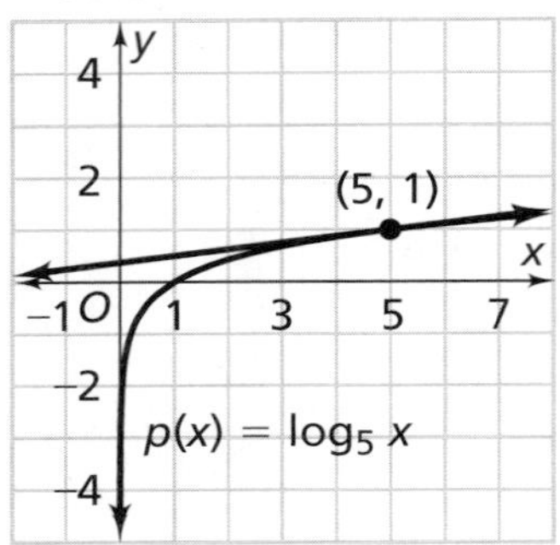


**7. a.** $\frac{1}{\ln 5} \approx 0.621$ **b.** The output for base 8 will be $\frac{1}{\ln 8} = \frac{1}{\ln 2^3} = \frac{1}{3 \ln 2} = \frac{1}{3}\left(\frac{1}{\ln 2}\right)$ and $\frac{1}{\ln 2}$ is the output for base 2. **c.** The slope of the tangent will be 1 if $\frac{1}{\ln b} = 1 \Rightarrow \ln b = 1 \Rightarrow b = e$. **d.** The slope of the tangent will never be zero.

**On Your Own**

**8. a.** $(\ln 8, 8)$ **b.** The $y$-intercept is $-8 \ln 8 + 8 \approx -8.636$, which is negative. **9.** $y = ex$; $(1, e)$
**10.** *slope* $= Abe^{bx} = b \cdot p(x)$ **11.** *slope* $= \frac{A}{x}$

## Chapter 9

### Lesson 9.0

### Check Your Understanding

**1. a.** $|y - 2| = 3$

**b.**

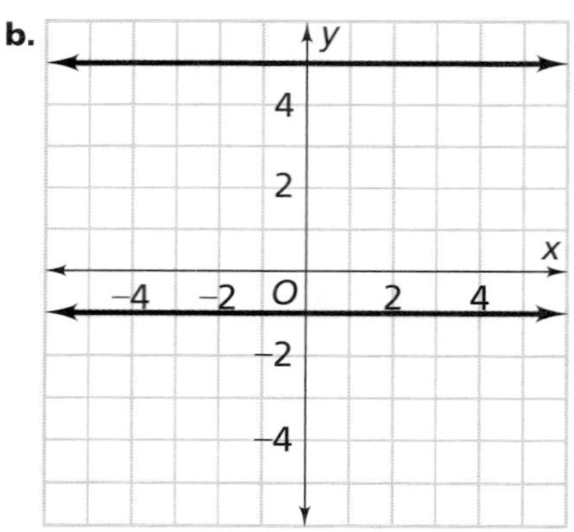


**2. a.** no **b.** yes **c.** If $a < 0$, this point must be closer to the $y$-axis than to (4, 0) since (4, 0) will be on the opposite side of the axis. Therefore, the distances could never be equal. **d.** $y^2 = 8x - 16$
**3. a.** No; the distance from (5, 3) to (15, 0) is $\sqrt{109}$, and the distance from (5, 3) to (6, 0) is $\sqrt{10}$.
**b.** (9, 0) and (−3, 0)
**c.** $36 = (x - 3)^2 + y^2$
**d.** The graph is a circle with center at (3, 0) and radius 6.
**4. a.** $y = 2x - 9$ **b.** $y = -\frac{3}{2}x + \frac{19}{2}$ **c.** $x = \frac{37}{7}$
**5. a.** Answers may vary. Sample: Any $(x, y, z)$ fitting the equation $5 = \sqrt{(x - 2)^2 + (y - 3)^2 + (z - 4)^2}$ is in this set. Some examples include: (7, 3, 4), (2, 3, 9), (2, 0, 0), (−2, 0, 4), and (2, −2, 4).
**b.** Answers may vary. Sample: Any $(x, y, z)$ not fitting the equation in part (a) is not part of this set.
**c.** $(x - 2)^2 + (y - 3)^2 + (z - 4)^2 = 25$
**6. a.** a plane **b.** Yes, this point is part of the set.
**c.** $x + 2y + 3z = 14$ **d.** Yes, this point is part of the set.
**e.**

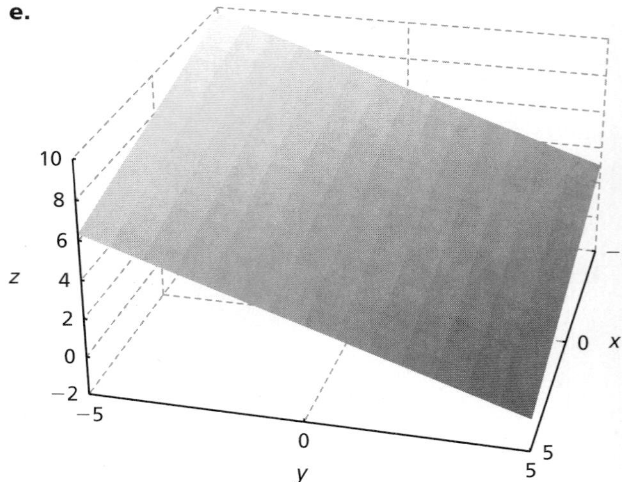


**On Your Own**

**7. a.** $y = -\frac{1}{3}x + \frac{10}{3}$ **11. b.** circle centered at (0, 0) with radius 5

### Lesson 9.01

**On Your Own**

**5.** Answers may vary. Sample: You can use a ruler or odometer readings on a car. On the coordinate plane, you can use the Distance Formula. **7a.** The following description uses L, R, U, and D for the words *left*, *right*, *up*, and *down*, respectively: D2L2D4R1U2R3D2R7D2L2U1. **b.** 28 units
**c.** Answers may vary. Sample: R7D7 has length 14 units, D7R7 has length 14 units, and R1D8L1U1R7 has length 18 units. **d.** 14 units; to get from $A$ to $B$ with no backtracking, the horizontal moves must always be to the right, and the vertical moves must always be down. Since $B$ is 7 units below and 7 units to the right of $A$, nothing less than 14 units will do. The first two sample paths in part (c) show that paths 14 units long are possible. **e.** No; see the answer for part (d). **8a.** $4\sqrt{2}$; 8 **b.** $3\sqrt{10}$; 12
**c.** $\sqrt{113}$; 15

### Lesson 9.02

#### Check Your Understanding

**1.** $50(\sqrt{5} + \sqrt{29})$ ft $\approx$ 381 ft;
$(\sqrt{x^2 + 100^2} + \sqrt{(300 - x)^2 + 100^2})$ ft

**2.** $Q$ is 200 ft downstream from $P'$. The side lengths are the same, so $DP = QF$ and $PF = DQ$. $Q$ would be $(300 - 2x)$ ft downstream from $P$.

**3.**

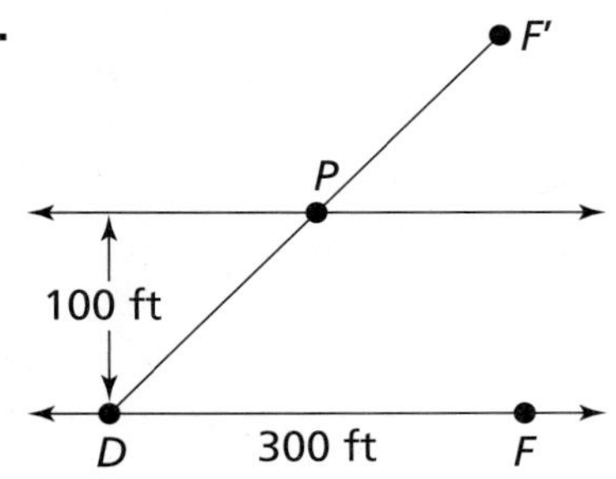


150 ft; no

#### On Your Own

**5c.** $4\sqrt{5} \approx 8.9$ **7.** $D = \sqrt{5}|x - 1|$; $x = 1$
**8.** The shortest path is the shortest perpendicular segment from $M$ to a side; to a side.

### Lesson 9.03

#### Check Your Understanding

**1.**

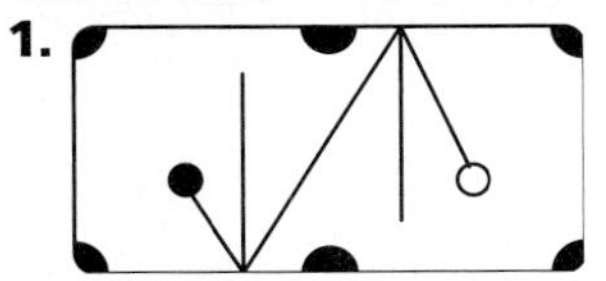

**2.** Answers may vary.
**3.** Refer to the following figure.

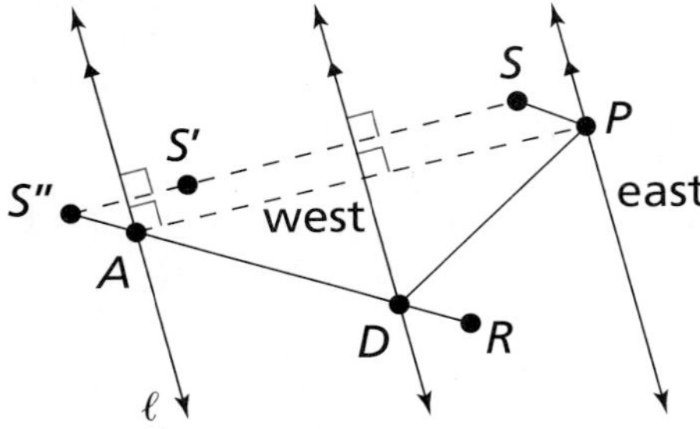


Line $\ell$ and $S'$ result from reflecting east bank and $S$ across west bank. $S''$ results from reflecting $S'$ across line $\ell$. Draw $\overline{S''R}$. Reflect $A$ across west bank to get $P$. The points $D$ and $P$ are the drop-off and pickup points, respectively.

#### On Your Own

**5.** Answers may vary. Sample: Find the best place on each side of the pool and then measure each path to find the shortest one. **8.** Let $d$ be the distance from the starting point to the finish point. The point for the left trough is $\frac{d}{4}$ units above the starting line. The point for the right trough is $\frac{d}{4}$ units below the finish line.

### Lesson 9.04

#### On Your Own

**6a.** old perimeter = 12, new perimeter = 14, old area = 5, new area = 6
**b.** old perimeter = 12, new perimeter = 12, old area = 5, new area = 6
**c.** old perimeter = 16, new perimeter = 14, old area = 8, new area = 9
**d.** old perimeter = 16, new perimeter = 12, old area = 8, new area = 9
**8a.** old surface area = 18, new surface area = 22, old volume = 4, new volume = 5
**b.** old surface area = 24, new surface area = 26, old volume = 6, new volume = 7
**c.** old surface area = 32, new surface area = 32, old volume = 10, new volume = 11 **d.** old surface area = 42, new surface area = 40, old volume = 15, new volume = 16 **e.** old surface area = 46, new surface area = 42, old volume = 17, new volume = 18 **f.** old surface area = 60, new surface area = 54, old volume = 26, new volume = 27

### Lesson 9.05

#### Check Your Understanding

**1a.** 10.247 in.$^2$ (exact area: $\sqrt{105}$ in.$^2$)
**b.** 10.825 in.$^2$ (exact area: $\frac{25\sqrt{3}}{4}$ in.$^2$)
**c.** 10.062 in.$^2$ (exact area: $\frac{9\sqrt{5}}{2}$ in.$^2$) **d.** For a given triangular perimeter, an equilateral triangle encloses the maximum area. **2.** 13 cm and 13 cm; 60 cm$^2$ **3.** A square; the argument in the For You to Do questions can easily be generalized to work not just for the perimeter 128 but for any given perimeter $p$.

#### On Your Own

**6.** 13 m by 11.5 m
**8a.** $h^2 + (5 + a)^2 = (13 + b)^2$, $h^2 + (5 - a)^2 = (13 - b)^2$ **b.** $a = 2.6b$
**c.** $h = \sqrt{144 - 5.76b^2}$ **d.** $h$ is greatest when $144 - 5.76b^2$ is greatest, and this occurs when $b = 0$. But when $b = 0$, both $13 + b$ and $13 - b$ equal 13, which means that the triangle is isosceles. **11.** $16\sqrt{3}$ in.$^2$; 36 in.$^2$; the area of the rectangle

**Lesson 9.06**

**Check Your Understanding**

**1.** The first polygon. Answers may vary. Sample: Cut up the second polygon and show that it fits inside the first polygon with some left over. **2.** Label the polygon $ABCDE$ starting with the bottom left vertex and ending with the bottom right vertex. Draw $\overleftrightarrow{BD}$ and reflect point $C$ across $\overleftrightarrow{BD}$ to $C'$. Draw $ABC'DE$. **3.** A rectangle with side lengths 20, 30, 20, and 30; suppose $ABCD$ is a parallelogram with $AB = 20$ and $AD = 30$. Let $h$ be the length of the perpendicular segment from $B$ to $\overleftrightarrow{AD}$. If $\angle A$ is acute, then $h = 20 \sin A$; so $h < 20$ since $\sin A < 1$. If $\angle A$ is obtuse, then $h = 20 \sin (180° - m\angle A)$; so $h < 20$ since $\sin (180° - m\angle A) < 1$. If $\angle A$ is a right angle, then $h = AB = 20$. In this last case, $h$ has its maximum possible value and the parallelogram has its maximum possible area.

**On Your Own**

**8.** A trapezoid formed by dividing a regular hexagon in half with a line through two opposite vertices gives the maximum area. The sides made with fencing will both be 280 ft long, and the side along the stone wall will be 560 ft long. **9.** Answers may vary. Sample: One reason is that the legs are perpendicular. The perpendicular is the shortest path from a point to a line, so any other path must be longer.

**Lesson 9.07**

**Check Your Understanding**

**1.** 540 **2.** He needed only 2 bags of seed for the small field. **3a.** about 31 cm$^2$ or 4.8 in.$^2$ **b.** about 70 cm$^2$ or 11 in.$^2$

**On Your Own**

**4a.** $\sqrt{12}$ or $\frac{\sqrt{12}}{12}$ **b.** $\sqrt{12}$ or $\frac{\sqrt{12}}{12}$ **5.** The area of the scaled copy is $\frac{1}{16}$ times the area of the original. **7.** 68 in.$^2$

**Lesson 9.08**

**On Your Own**

**6.** $x = 16$

**8. c.**

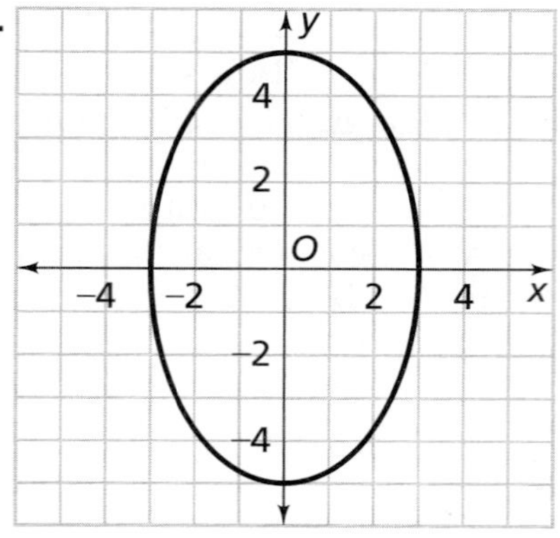


**Lesson 9.09**

**Check Your Understanding**

**1. a.** Answers may vary. Sample: The pins should be placed fairly close together. **b.** The pins should be placed far apart, a little shorter than the string length $s$ but larger than $\frac{s}{2}$. **c.** If both pins are placed in the same spot, a circle will result. **2. a.** $b = 4, -4$ **b.** $a = 5, -5$ **c.** No; the sum of the distances between this point and the foci does not equal 10. **d.** $\sqrt{(x-3)^2 + y^2} + \sqrt{(x+3)^2 + y^2} = 10$ **3.** Your sketch should look like the one on page 471 but points $D$ and $E$ will coincide at the center of the circle. This will also be the point where the two spheres are tangent to the plane of the sliced circle. **4. a.** Answers may vary. Sample:

Any point that satisfies the equation $\left|\sqrt{(x-3)^2 + y^2} - \sqrt{(x+3)^2 + y^2}\right| = 4$.

**b.**

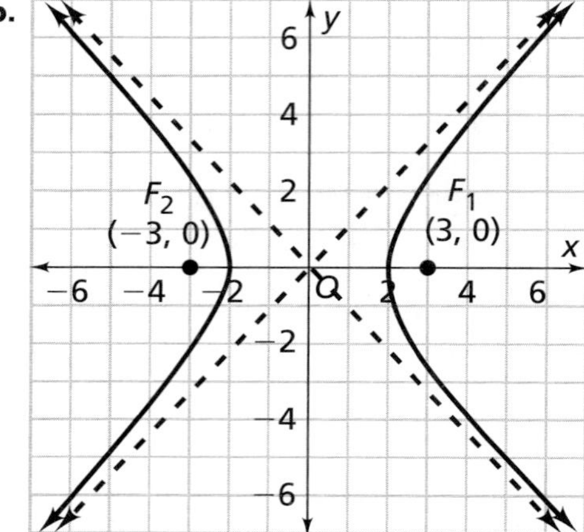


**c.** $\frac{x^2}{4} - \frac{y^2}{5} = 1$ **5.** If $P$ is any point noncollinear with $A$ and $B$, then the triangle inequality applies: if the shorter of $PA$ or $PB$ has length $x$, then the longer cannot be more than $x + 6$. So $|PA - PB| < 6$ is required. If $P$ is collinear with $A$ and $B$, then $|PA - PB| = 6$ is possible but no more. In the entire plane, no point $P$ can satisfy $|PA - PB| = 10$.

**On Your Own**

**6. a.** no **b.** no **c.** yes **d.** no **9.** $x = \frac{1}{4}y^2$

**10. a.** Answers may vary. Sample: $3x + 25 = 5\sqrt{(x+3)^2 + y^2}$

**Lesson 9.10**

**Check Your Understanding**

**1. a.** $25 \cdot (0)^2 + 169 \cdot (5)^2 = 4225$

$169 \cdot 25 = 4225$

**b.** Answers may vary. Sample: Any point satisfying the equation $\frac{x^2}{169} + \frac{y^2}{5} = 1$. **c.** The major axis is formed by the points (13, 0) and (−13, 0). The distance between these points is 26. **d.** $c = 12$

**e.**

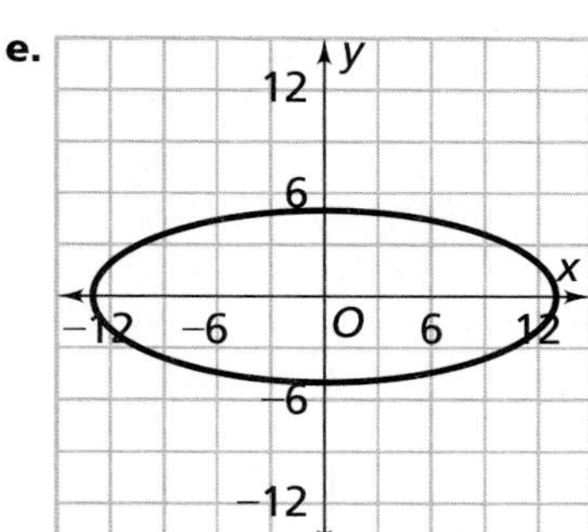


**2. a.** Answers may vary. Sample: Any points satisfying the equation $\frac{x^2}{9} + \frac{y^2}{25} = 1$. **b.** The major axis is formed by the points (0, 5) and (0, −5). The distance between these points is 10. **c.** $c = 4$

**d.**

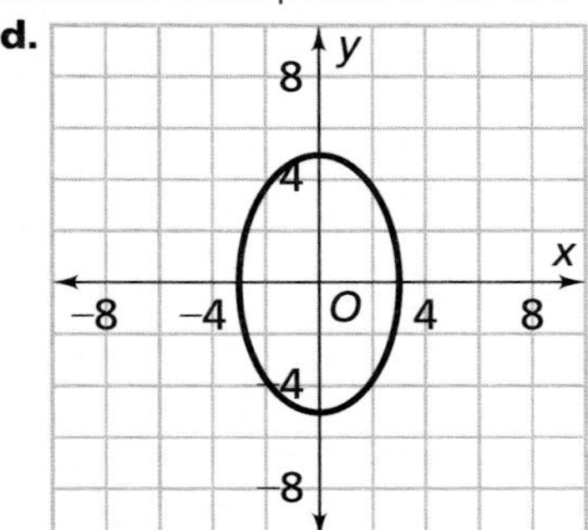


**3.** The graph will pass through the points $(a, 0)$, $(-a, 0)$, $(0, b)$, and $(0, -b)$.

If $a = b$, then this graph is a circle centered at the origin.

If $a > b$, the graph is an ellipse with major axis along the $x$-axis with foci points at $(\pm\sqrt{a^2 - b^2}, 0)$.

If $a < b$, the graph is an ellipse with major axis along the $y$-axis with foci points at $(0, \pm\sqrt{b^2 - a^2})$.

**4. a.** $y^2 - 9x^2 = 36$

$(\pm 6)^2 - 9 \cdot (0)^2 = 36$

**b.** $y = \pm 6.7082$ **c.** $y = \pm 16.1555$

**d.** $y = \pm 300.0600$

**e.** As $x$ grows larger, the ratio of $\frac{y}{x}$ approaches 3 or −3 and the points on the parabola approach asymptotes defined by the lines $y = 3x$ and $y = -3x$.

**5. a.** This graph is a hyperbola that is a dilation with scale factor $\frac{1}{2}$ from the original in Exercise 5.

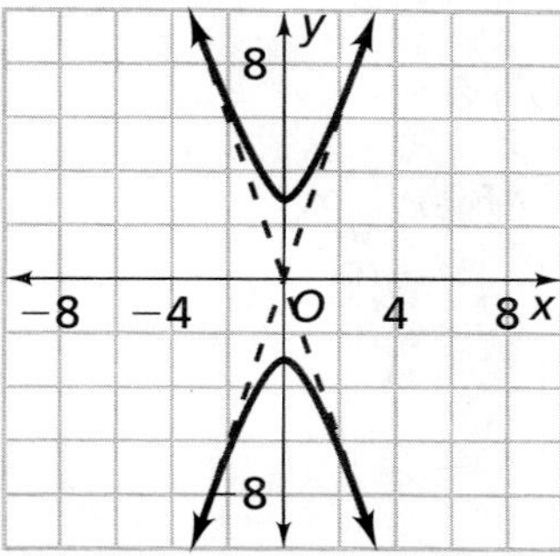


**b.** This graph is a hyperbola, even closer to the origin.

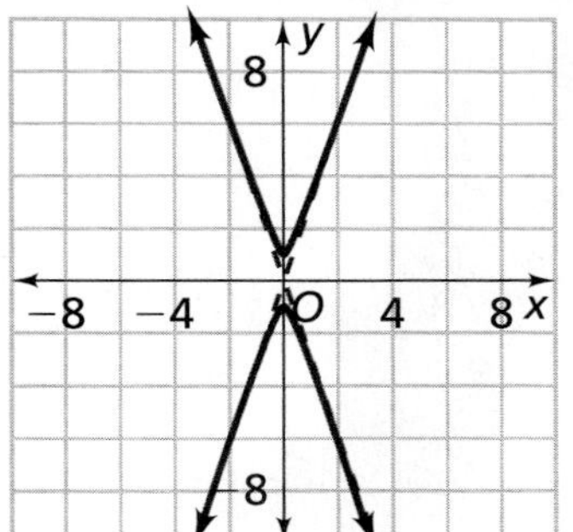


**c.**

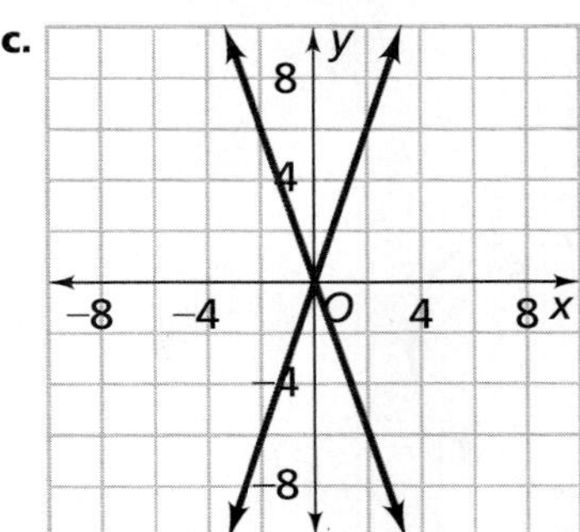


**6. a.** $x^2 - 2xy + y^2 + 20x + 20y - 100 = 0$

**b.** (−5, 5) and (−5, 35)

**c.**

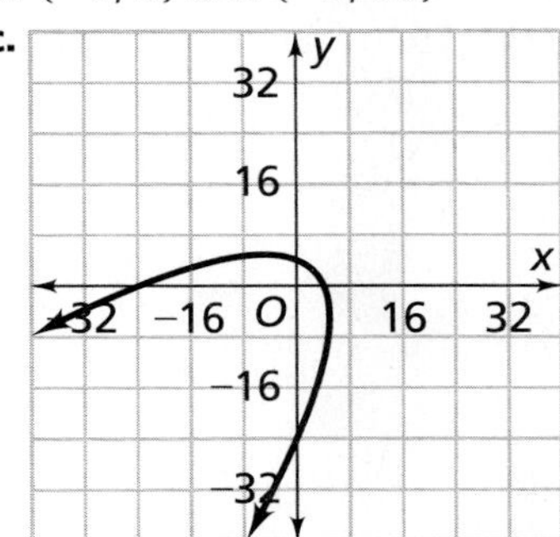

**On Your Own**

**7.** $x = -\frac{1}{8}y^2$ **8. c.** The ratio $\frac{y}{x}$ approaches $\frac{3}{4}$.

**Lesson 9.11**

**Check Your Understanding**

**1. a.** (3, 2)

**b.**

| $x$ | $y$ |
|---|---|
| 6 | undefined |
| 7 | 2 |
| 8 | 4.25 |
| 9 | 5.3541 |
| 11 | 7.1962 |
| 13 | 8.8739 |
| 23 | 16.6969 |
| 43 | 31.8496 |
| 103 | 76.9400 |
| 1003 | 751.9940 |

**c.** The graph becomes asymptotic to the line $y - 2 = \frac{3}{4}(x - 3)$.

**2. a.**

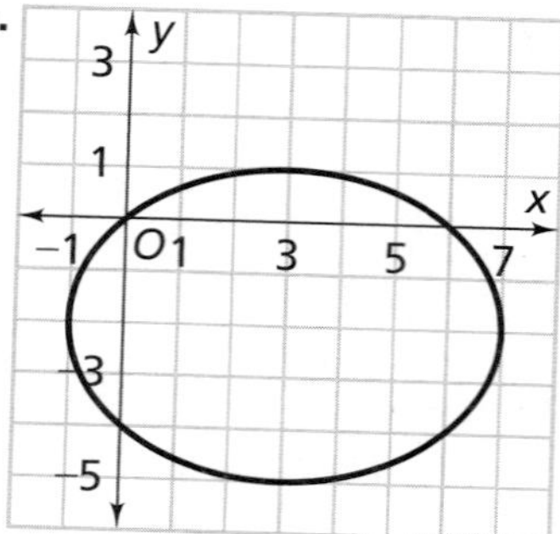

**b.** no

**c.**

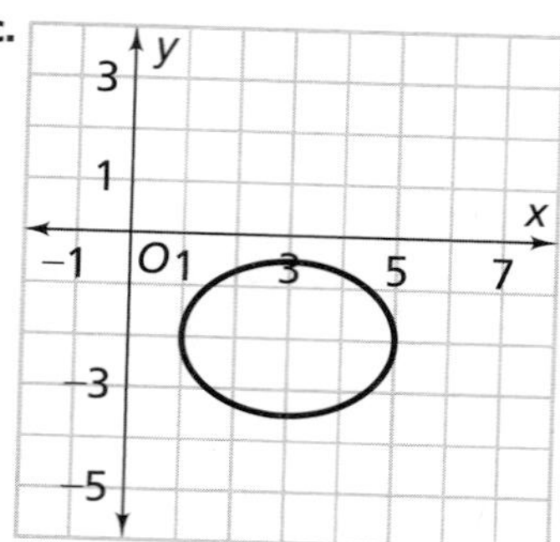

**d.**

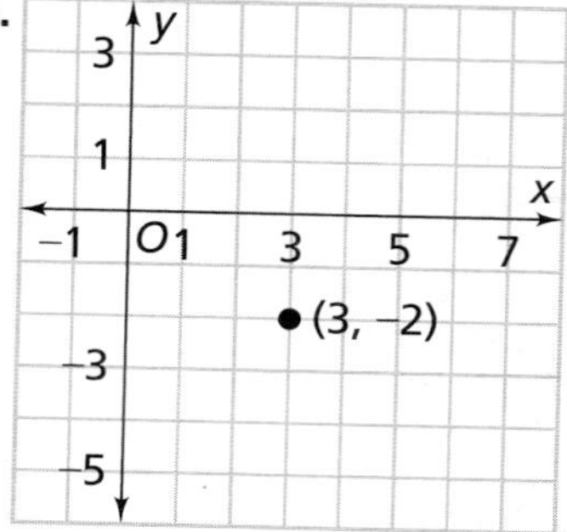


**e.** No graph, since the equation has no solution.

**f.** $N = 916$

**3. a.** Yes; hyperbola

**b.**

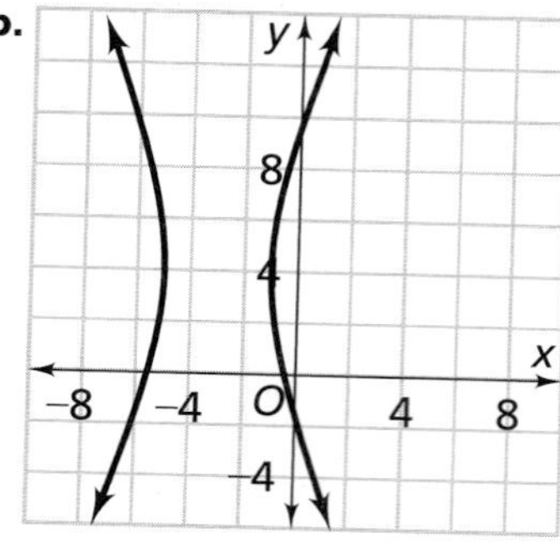

**4. a.** No; this equation is a single point

**b.**

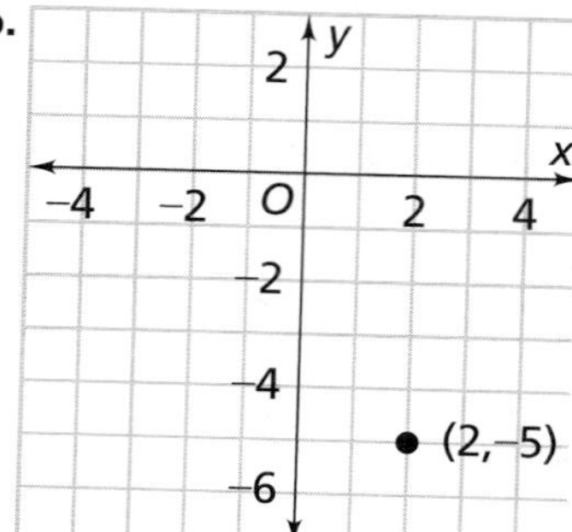


**5. a.** $(y - 2)^2 = 4(x + 3)^2 - 16$ **b.** The next step in solving this equation is to take a square root, which results in two answers (a positive and negative root).

**c.** $f_1(x) = 2 + \sqrt{4(x + 3)^2 - 16}$

$f_2(x) = 2 - \sqrt{4(x + 3)^2 - 16}$

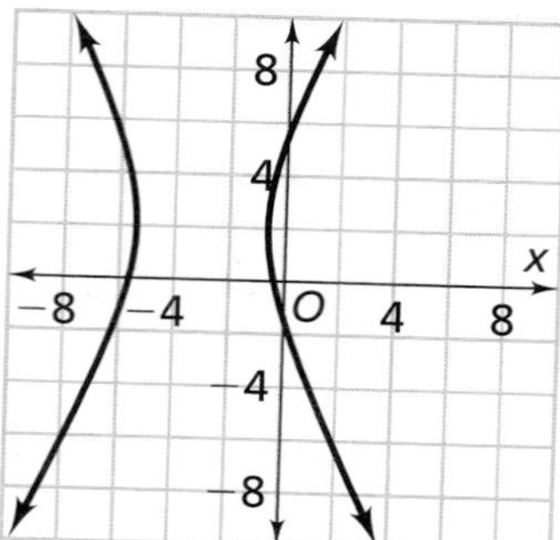

6.

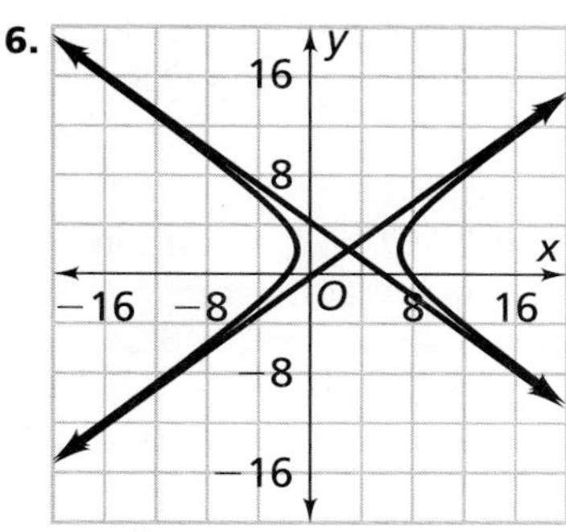


7. $y = \frac{1}{x}$

### On Your Own

**8.** Answers may vary. Sample: The first equation is the sum of squares, and squares can never be negative. The second equation is the difference of squares, and that can be negative. **10. a.** $x \leq -16$ or $x \geq -2$ **11.** (4, 10) and (4, 0)

### Lesson 9.12

### Check Your Understanding

**1. a.** $\frac{3}{5}$ **b.** $\frac{4}{5}$ **c.** $\frac{1}{5}$ **d.** $\frac{\sqrt{3}}{2}$ **2.** $\frac{(x-8)^2}{16} + \frac{y^2}{12} = 1$

**3.** $\frac{(x-8)^2}{16} + \frac{y^2}{12} = 1$; Center = (8, 0)

**4. a.** Center = (−6, 5); vertices = (−12, 5) and (0, 5); foci = (−15, 5) and (3, 5) **b.** $e = 1.5$

**c.**

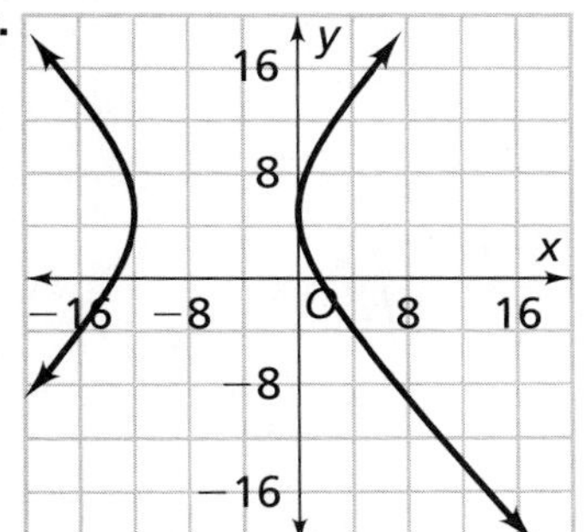


**5.** $e = 3$ **6. a.** If $e = 1$, the definition gives $PF = Pd$, which matches the locus definition of a parabola given in Lesson 9.09. **b.** Let $e < 1$ and use the distance formula to determine the equation of the ellipse.

$$\sqrt{x^2 + (y-1)^2} = e|y+1|$$

Solving this equation yields

$$\frac{x^2}{\frac{1-e^2}{4e^2}} + \frac{\left(y - \frac{1+e^2}{1-e^2}\right)^2}{\frac{(1-e^2)^2}{4e^2}} = 1$$

Based on this equation, $a = \frac{2e}{1-e^2}$ and $b = \frac{2e}{\sqrt{1-e^2}}$, therefore $c = \frac{2e^2}{1-e^2}$.

The eccentricity is given by $\frac{c}{a} = \frac{2e^2/(1-e^2)}{2e/(1-e^2)} = e$.

**c.** Using the same methods, find $a = \frac{2e}{e^2 - 1}$, $b = \frac{2e}{\sqrt{e^2-1}}$, $c = \frac{2e^2}{e^2-1}$ to show that $\frac{c}{a} = e$.

**7.**

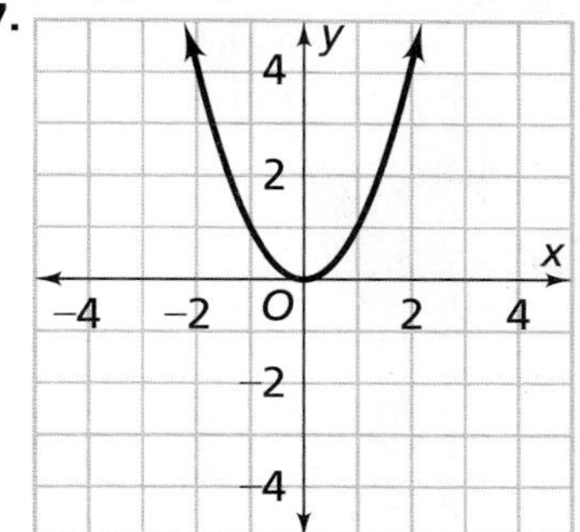


**a.** The graph looks very similar to $y = x^2$. **b.** Answers may vary. Sample: The ellipse must have a very high eccentricity and a vertex at (0, 0).

### On Your Own

**10. a.** $e = 6$ **12.** (−5,7)

## Honors Appendix

### Lesson H.01

### On Your Own

**7. a.** 2 **8. b.** sec $x$ is larger for $0 < x < \frac{\pi}{2}$. By definition, $\tan x = \frac{\sin x}{\cos x}$ and $\sec x = \frac{1}{\cos x}$. For $0 < x < \frac{\pi}{2}$, we have $\frac{\sin x}{\cos x} < \frac{1}{\cos x}$ since $\sin x < 1$. Therefore $\tan x < \sec x$.

### Lesson H.02

### Check Your Understanding

**1. a.**

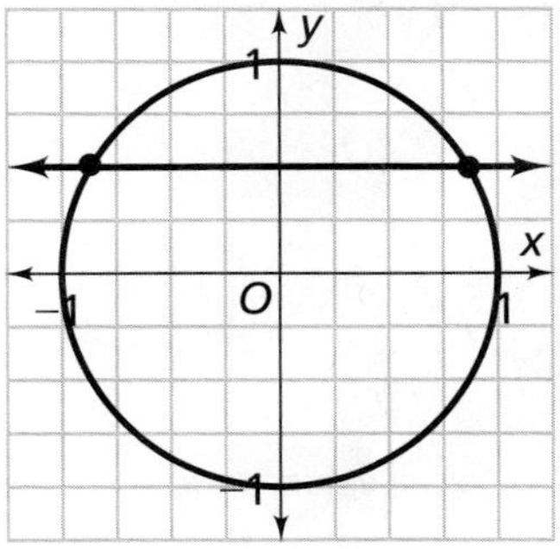

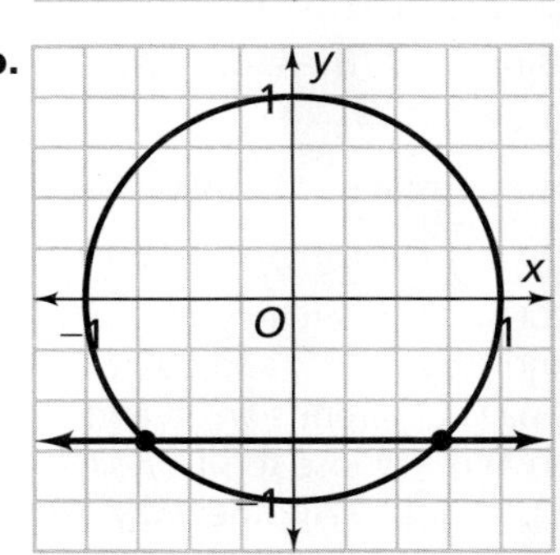


**b.**

c.

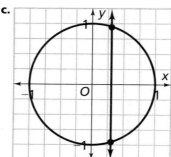

d.

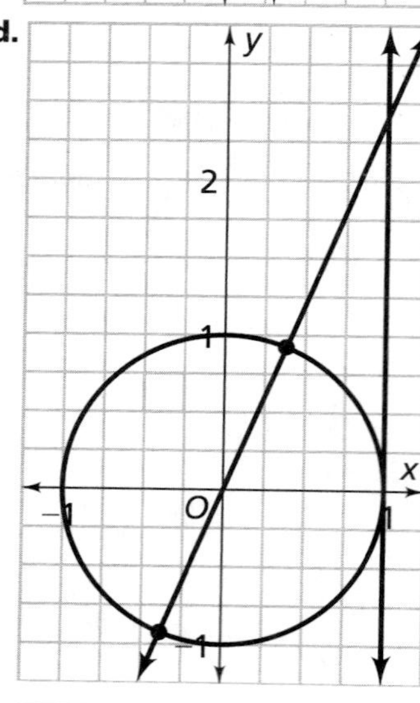


e.

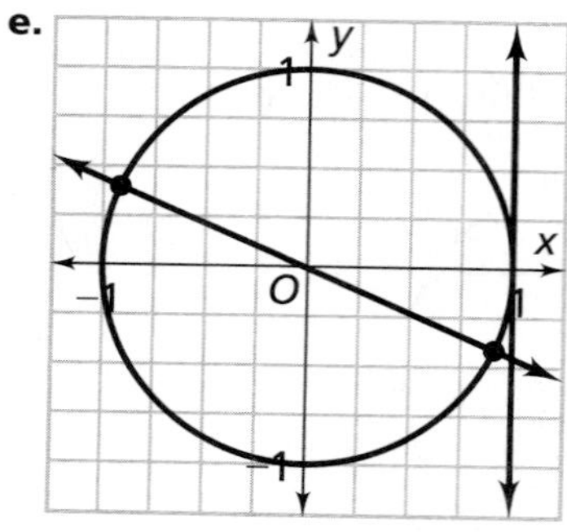


**2.** $\cos^2 x + \sin^2 x = 1$ for all values of $x$, so $\cos x = \pm\sqrt{1 - \sin^2 x}$. Since $0 < 0.38 < \frac{\pi}{2}$, $\cos 0.38 = \sqrt{1 - \sin^2 0.38}$. Therefore, use the calculator to evaluate $\frac{\sin 0.38}{\sqrt{1 - \sin^2 0.38}}$.
**3.** $\tan\left(\frac{\pi}{2} + x\right)$ is the opposite of the reciprocal of $\tan x$, that is, $\tan\left(\frac{\pi}{2} + x\right) = -\frac{1}{\tan x}$. **4.** Quadrants II and IV; one way: By definition, $\tan x = \frac{\sin x}{\cos x}$. So $\tan x$ is negative if and only if $\sin x$ and $\cos x$ have different signs. They have different signs if and only if $x$ corresponds to an angle whose terminal side is in Quadrant II or Quadrant IV. Another way: We know from the In-Class Experiment that $\tan x$ is the $y$-coordinate of the point where the line through the origin and $(\cos x, \sin x)$ intersects the graph of $x = 1$. The line through the origin and $(\cos x, \sin x)$ intersects the graph of $x = 1$ below the $x$-axis if and only if $(\cos x, \sin x)$ is in Quadrant II or Quadrant IV.
**5.** Yes; answers may vary. Sample: $x = 1.57$
**6. a.** $\tan\frac{\pi}{6} = \frac{\sqrt{3}}{3}$ and $\frac{\sqrt{3}}{3} > \frac{\pi}{6}$; $\tan\frac{\pi}{4} = 1$ and $1 > \frac{\pi}{4}$; $\tan 1 \approx 1.557$ and $1.557 > 1$. So for the three given values of $x$, it is true that $\tan x > x$. Other examples may vary. Samples: $\tan 0.5 \approx 0.546$ and $0.546 > 0.5$; $\tan 0.75 \approx 0.932$ and $0.932 > 0.75$; $\tan 0.1 \approx 0.1003$ and $0.1003 > 0.1$. **b.** $\frac{1}{2}\tan x$, $\frac{x}{2}$ **c.** The sector lies inside the triangle, so the area of the sector is less than the area of the triangle, that is, $\frac{x}{2} < \frac{1}{2}\tan x$. Therefore, $x < \tan x$.

### On Your Own

**9. a.** Both are equal to $\frac{1}{2}$. **10.** $\tan\left(\frac{\pi}{2} - x\right) = \frac{\sin\left(\frac{\pi}{2} - x\right)}{\cos\left(\frac{\pi}{2} - x\right)} = \frac{\cos x}{\sin x} = \cot x$; $\tan\left(\frac{\pi}{2} - x\right)$ and $\tan x$ are reciprocals for all values of $x$ for which both a re defined.

### Lesson H.03

### Check Your Understanding

**1. a.** $\frac{\pi}{2}$ **b.** $2\pi$ **2. a.** about 1.249 **b.** Infinitely many; approximately, real numbers of the form $1.249 + \pi n$ ($n$ an integer)

**3. a.**

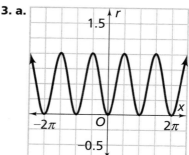

**b.** $\pi$ **c.** Since $\sin(\pi + x) = -\sin x$, it follows that $\sin^2(\pi + x) = (-\sin x)^2 = \sin^2 x$. Hence the period of $r(x)$ is not greater than $\pi$. Since the zeros of $r(x)$ are all of the form $\pi n$ ($n$ an integer), the period of $r(x)$ is not less than $\pi$. Therefore, the period of $r(x)$ is equal to $\pi$.

**4. a.**

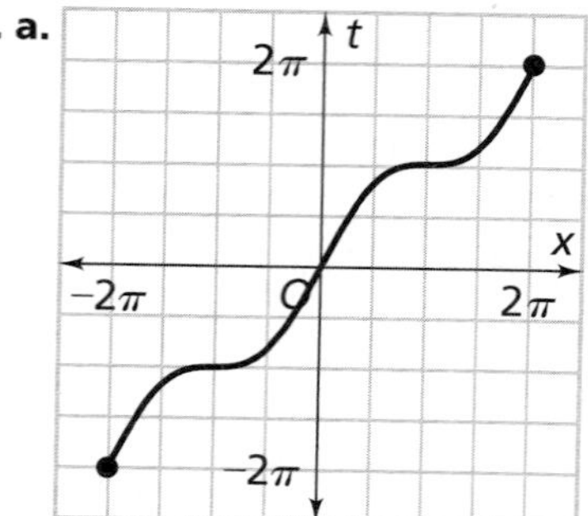


**b.** No; if $x > 1$, then $t(x) > \sin x + 1 \geq 0$. This means the value $t(0) = 0$ is not repeated for $x > 1$, although it would have to be repeated for $t(x)$ to be periodic. **5. a.** $4\pi$ **b.** For $B > 0$, the period of $\sin Bx$

is $\frac{2\pi}{B}$. For example, the period of sin $2x$ is $\pi$, and the period of sin $\frac{1}{2}x$ is $4\pi$.

### On Your Own

**8.** The graphs are the same. **9.** Yes; $2\pi$
**10. c.** $h(x) = 3$ for all $x \neq \frac{\pi}{2} \cdot n$ ($n$ an integer); $h(x)$ is undefined at all the excluded values of $x$.

## Lesson H.04

### Check Your Understanding

**1. a.** all the numbers $-\sin^{-1}\left(\frac{2}{3}\right) + 2n\pi$ and $\sin^{-1}\left(\frac{2}{3}\right) + (2n+1)\pi$ ($n$ an integer) **b.** no solutions **c.** all the numbers $\tan^{-1}\left(-\frac{13}{2}\right) + n\pi$ ($n$ an integer) **d.** no solutions **2. a.** Answers may vary. Sample: $\tan^{-1}0.75 \approx 0.644$ **b.** at $x$-values that are $n\pi$ units ($n$ an integer) from the solution in part (a) **c.** for the solution in part (a): $\pi + \tan^{-1}0.75 \approx 3.785$ **3. a.** Answers may vary. Sample: $\cos^{-1}0.8 \approx 0.644$ **b.** the $x$-values $2n\pi \pm \cos^{-1}0.8$ **c.** for the solution in part (a): $2\pi - \cos^{-1}0.8 \approx 5.640$ **4. a.** Answers may vary. Sample: $\sin^{-1}0.6 \approx 0.644$ **b.** the $x$-values $\sin^{-1}0.6 + 2n\pi$ and $(2n+1)\pi - \sin^{-1}0.6$ ($n$ an integer) **c.** for the solutions in part (a): $\pi - \sin^{-1}0.6 \approx 2.498$ **5. a.** $\frac{\pi}{6}$ **b.** $\frac{\pi}{2}$ **c.** $\frac{\pi}{4}$ **d.** 120° **e.** 2.14 **f.** $\frac{\pi}{6}$ **6. a.** $\frac{24}{25}$ **b.** $\frac{24}{25}$

### On Your Own

**7. c.** the numbers $\frac{11}{2} + 2n$ ($n$ an integer) **9. b.** $\frac{\pi}{2}$
**12. a.** Answers may vary. Sample: $t(x) = 8\sin x + 19$

## Lesson H.05

### Check Your Understanding

**1. a.** $\frac{\pi}{6}$ and $\frac{5\pi}{6}$ **b.** $\frac{\pi}{6}$ and $\frac{7\pi}{6}$ **c.** $0$, $\pi$, and $2\pi$ **d.** $0$, $\pi$, and $2\pi$ **2. a.** $f(30°) = \frac{16}{3}$, $g(30°) = \frac{16}{3}$ **b.** $f\left(\frac{\pi}{4}\right) = 4$, $g\left(\frac{\pi}{4}\right) = 4$ **c.** $f(60°) = \frac{16}{3}$, $g(60°) = \frac{16}{3}$ **d.** $f(120°) = \frac{16}{3}$, $g(120°) = \frac{16}{3}$ **e.** $f(2) \approx 6.9838$, $g(2) \approx 6.9838$ **3.** $f(x) = \sec^2 x + \csc^2 x = \frac{1}{\cos^2 x} + \frac{1}{\sin^2 x} = \frac{\sin^2 x + \cos^2 x}{(\cos^2 x)(\sin^2 x)} = \frac{1}{(\cos^2 x)(\sin^2 x)} = \sec^2 x \cdot \csc^2 x = g(x)$
**4. a.** Answers may vary. Sample: Use $\theta = 60°$.
**b.** Answers may vary. Sample: Use $\theta = 60°$.
**c.** Use the equations $\cos\theta = \sin(90° - \theta)$ and $\sin\theta = \cos(90° - \theta)$.

$$\tan(90° - \theta) = \frac{\sin(90° - \theta)}{\cos(90° - \theta)} = \frac{\cos\theta}{\sin\theta} = \cot\theta$$

**d.** $\sec(90° - \theta) = \frac{1}{\cos(90° - \theta)} = \frac{1}{\sin\theta} = \csc\theta$
**5. a.** $\triangle OSB$ and $\triangle OAT$ are right triangles that share the acute angle with vertex $O$. Hence the acute angles $\angle OBS$ and $\angle OTA$ are congruent. If the angles of one triangle are congruent to those of another triangle, then the triangles are similar. So $\triangle OSB \sim \triangle OAT$.
**b.** By definition, $\sec\alpha = \sec\angle TOS = \frac{\text{hypotenuse}}{\text{adjacent}}$. So $\sec\alpha = \frac{OT}{1} = OT$. **6.** D **7.** B

### On Your Own

**8. a.** domain $= \{x \mid x \neq (2n+1)\frac{\pi}{2}$ ($n$ an integer)$\}$, range $= \{x \mid x \leq -1$ or $x \geq 1\}$
**11. b.** $1 + \cot^2 x = \csc^2 x$ **12.** $\triangle OAT$ is a right triangle, so $OA^2 + AT^2 = OT^2$. But $OA = 1$, $AT = \tan\alpha$, and $OT = \sec\alpha$. So $1 + \tan^2\alpha = \sec^2\alpha$.

## Lesson H.06

### On Your Own

**11.** D **15.** $\cot x$ **18.** $\frac{\pi}{6}, \frac{5\pi}{6}, \frac{7\pi}{6}, \frac{11\pi}{6}$

## Lesson H.07

### Check Your Understanding

**1.** Answers may vary. Sample:
$\cos 3x = \cos^3 x - 3\sin^2 x\cos x$,
$\sin 3x = 3\sin x\cos^2 x - \sin^3 x$
**2. a.** Answers may vary. Sample: $\frac{\sqrt{2}}{2} + \frac{\sqrt{2}}{2}i$ and $\frac{\sqrt{3}}{2} + \frac{1}{2}i$ **b.** $\cos 75° = \frac{\sqrt{6} - \sqrt{2}}{4}$, $\sin 75° = \frac{\sqrt{6} + \sqrt{2}}{4}$ **c.** $\frac{1}{2}$ **3. a.** $\frac{16}{65} + \frac{63}{65}i$ **b.** $\frac{63}{65}$
**4. a.** $\cos(\alpha + \beta) + \cos(\alpha - \beta) = \cos\alpha\cos\beta - \sin\alpha\sin\beta + \cos\alpha\cos(-\beta) - \sin\alpha\sin(-\beta) = \cos\alpha\cos\beta - \sin\alpha\sin\beta + \cos\alpha\cos\beta + \sin\alpha\sin\beta = 2\cos\alpha\cos\beta$ **b.** $\sin(\alpha + \beta) + \sin(\alpha - \beta) = 2\sin\alpha\cos\beta$
**5.** Check students' work. **6.** $\tan(\alpha + \beta) = \frac{\tan\alpha + \tan\beta}{1 - \tan\alpha\tan\beta}$
**7.** $\cos(\alpha + \beta + \gamma) = \cos\alpha\cos\beta\cos\gamma - \cos\alpha\sin\beta\sin\gamma - \sin\alpha\cos\beta\sin\gamma - \sin\alpha\sin\beta\cos\gamma$
$\sin(\alpha + \beta + \gamma) = \cos\alpha\cos\beta\sin\gamma + \cos\alpha\sin\beta\cos\gamma + \sin\alpha\cos\beta\cos\gamma - \sin\alpha\sin\beta\cos\gamma$

### On Your Own

**8. c.** $\cos\left(x + \frac{\pi}{4}\right) = \frac{\sqrt{2}}{2}\cos x - \frac{\sqrt{2}}{2}\sin x$,
$\sin\left(x + \frac{\pi}{4}\right) = \frac{\sqrt{2}}{2}\sin x + \frac{\sqrt{2}}{2}\cos x$
**11. a.** $\tan 2x = \frac{2\tan x}{1 - \tan^2 x}$
**13. a.** $\frac{6 - \sqrt{35}}{12} + \frac{2\sqrt{7} + 3\sqrt{5}}{12}i$

## Lesson H.08

### Check Your Understanding

**1. a.**

$$\begin{aligned}\tan^2 x - \sin^2 x &= \frac{\sin^2 x}{\cos^2 x} - \sin^2 x \\ &= \left(\frac{1}{\cos^2 x} - 1\right)\sin^2 x \\ &= \left(\frac{1 - \cos^2 x}{\cos^2 x}\right)\sin^2 x \\ &= \frac{\sin^2 x}{\cos^2 x} \cdot \sin^2 x \\ &= \tan^2 x\sin^2 x\end{aligned}$$

**b.** $$\frac{\cos x}{1-\sin x} = \frac{\cos x}{1-\sin x}\cdot\frac{1+\sin x}{1+\sin x} = \frac{\cos x(1+\sin x)}{1-\sin^2 x} = \frac{\cos x(1+\sin x)}{\cos^2 x} = \frac{1+\sin x}{\cos x}$$

**c.** $$\cot^2 x - \cos^2 x = \frac{\cos^2 x}{\sin^2 x} - \cos^2 x = \left(\frac{1}{\sin^2 x} - 1\right)\cos^2 x = \left(\frac{1-\sin^2 x}{\sin^2 x}\right)\cos^2 x = \frac{\cos^2 x}{\sin^2 x}\cdot\cos^2 x = \cot^2 x\cos^2 x$$

**d.** $$\frac{\sin x}{1-\cos x} = \frac{\sin x}{1-\cos x}\cdot\frac{1+\cos x}{1+\cos x} = \frac{\sin x(1+\cos x)}{1-\cos^2 x} = \frac{\sin x(1+\cos x)}{\sin^2 x} = \frac{1+\cos x}{\sin x}$$

**2.** The second equation is an identity. $(\cos x + \sin x)^2 = \cos^2 x + 2\cos x \sin x + \sin^2 x = 2\cos x\sin x + 1 = \sin 2x + 1$

**3.** Since $\cos(\alpha+\beta) + \cos(\alpha-\beta) = 2\cos\alpha\cos\beta$ is an identity, $\cos 5x + \cos 3x = 2\cos 4x\cos x$. Hence $\cos 5x = 2\cos x\cos 4x - \cos 3x$.

**4.** This identity follows directly from the identity $\cos(\alpha+\beta) + \cos(\alpha-\beta) = 2\cos\alpha\cos\beta$ if you let $\alpha = (n+1)x$ and $\beta = (n-1)x$.

**5. a.** $$(\sec x\sin x)^2 - (\sec x + 1)(\sec x - 1) = \frac{\sin^2 x}{\cos^2 x} - \left(\sec^2 x - 1\right) = \tan^2 x - \tan^2 x = 0$$

**b.** Since $(\sec x\sin x)^2 - (\sec x + 1)(\sec x - 1) = 0$ is an identity, you obtain an identity if you add $(\sec x + 1)(\sec x - 1)$ to both sides.

**On Your Own**

**6. b.** Use the formula in Exercise 4, and let $n = 2$ to get $\cos 3x = 2\cos x\cos 2x - \cos x$. On the right side of this equation, replace $\cos 2x$ with $2\cos^2 x - 1$ and simplify to get $\cos 3x = 4\cos^3 x - 3\cos x$.

**9. a.** $$\frac{\sec x + 1}{\tan x} = \frac{\sec x + 1}{\tan x}\cdot\frac{\sec x - 1}{\sec x - 1} = \frac{\sec^2 x - 1}{\tan x(\sec x - 1)} = \frac{\tan^2 x}{\tan x(\sec x - 1)} = \frac{\tan x}{\sec x - 1}$$

# Index



Index

# D



# E

## F



## G

Index

## Q



## R



## S

Index

# Acknowledgments

## Staff Credits

The Pearson people on the CME Project team—representing design, editorial, editorial services, digital product development, publishing services, and technical operations—are listed below. Bold type denotes the core team members.

Ernest Albanese, Scott Andrews, Carolyn Artin, Michael Avidon, Margaret Banker, Suzanne Biron, Beth Blumberg, Stacie Cartwright, Carolyn Chappo, Casey Clark, Bob Craton, Sheila DeFazio, Patty Fagan, **Frederick Fellows**, **Patti Fromkin**, Paul J. Gagnon, Cynthia Harvey, Gillian Kahn, Jonathan Kier, Jennifer King, Elizabeth Krieble, Sara Levendusky, Lisa Lin, Clay Martin, **Carolyn McGuire**, Rich McMahon, Eve Melnechuk, Cynthia Metallides, **Hope Morley**, Christine Nevola, Jen Paley, Mairead Reddin, Marcy Rose, Rashid Ross, Carol Roy, Jewel Simmons, Ted Smykal, Kara Stokes, Richard Sullivan, Tiffany Taylor-Sullivan, Catherine Terwilliger, Mark Tricca, Lauren Van Wart, Paula Vergith, **Joe Will**, **Kristin Winters**, Allison Wyss

## Additional Credits

Gina Choe, Lillian Pelaggi, Deborah Savona

### Cover Design and Illustration
9 Surf Studios

### Cover Photography
Peter Sterling/Getty Images, Inc.

### Interior Design
Pronk&Associates

### Illustration
Rich McMahon, Ted Smykal

### Photography
Unless otherwise indicated, all photos are the property of Pearson Education, Inc.

**Table of Contents: vi,** Jim Richardson/CORBIS; **viii,** All Canada Photos/Alamy; **xi,** Roger Ressmeyer/CORBIS; **xiii,** Philip Gould/CORBIS

**Chapter 1: Pages 10 frame,** Photodisc/SuperStock; **10,** Rob Lewine/Corbis; **2–3,** Corbis/William Sallaz; **12,** Animals Animals/Richard Shiell; **16,** Getty/ML Harris; **22,** AP Images/ Charles Krupa; **21,** Granger; **30,** Dreamstime; **32,** iStockphoto; **39,** iStockphoto; **47,** Alamy/Ellen McKnight; **48,** Newscom/Bo Rader; **51,** Corbis/Dirk Anschütz; **51,** SuperStock/PhotoDisc; **64,** Getty Images/S. Meltzer; **69,** iStockphoto.

**Chapter 2: Pages 79,** Kara Stokes; **76–77,** Getty Images/Ian Mckinnell; **86,** Corbis/Tobbe; **101,** Dreamstime; **103,** John Moore; **104,** Newscom; **114,** North Wind; **118,** Dreamstime; **126,** AP Images/Ann Heisenfelt; **134,** Alamy; **153,** Alamy/Dusty Dingo; **156,** John Moore; **168,** John Moore.

**Chapter 3: Pages 172–173,** Paolo Curto/Getty Images; **174–175,** Gallo Images-Anthony/age footstock; **177,** John Gillmoure/CORBIS; **206,** Kevin Schafer/Getty Images; **208,** Court Mast/Getty Images; **215,** James W. Porter/CORBIS; **218,** UPI Photo/Brian Kersey/drr.net; **272,** Paul Katz/photolibrary.com; **282,** University Library, UGent

**Chapter 4: Pages 298–299,** Alamy/Michael Jenner; **306,** Getty Images/Joe Sohm; **310,** AP Images/Sue Ogrocki; **325,** Alamy/John Pitcher; **331,** istockphoto; **332,** Photo Researchers; **351,** Alamy; **342,** Getty Images/Grant V. Faint; **352,** Newscom/Benjamin M. Arnao; **357,** Getty Images/Bruce Dale; **373,** Getty Images/Howard Shooter; **382,** AP Images/Matt Ferguson; **386,** Newscom/Benjamin M. Arnao.

**Chapter 5: Pages 392–393,** Paul Chesley/Getty Images; **394,** Gilbert Iundt; Jean-Yves Ruszniewski/TempSport/Corbis; **403,** Arnulf Husmo/Getty Images; **413,** Jim Richardson/CORBIS; **418,** Patrik Giardino/CORBIS; **420,** Jeffrey Greenberg/Photo Researchers, Inc.; **423,** Siephoto/Masterfile; **437,** Bettmann/CORBIS; **441,** Ray Coleman/Photo Researchers, Inc.; **501,** Gerald Hoberman/drr.net; **774,** 123luftbild/Peter Arnold, Inc.; **787,** Image Source Pink/Alamy; **793,** Lori Lee Miller/Alamy.

**Chapter 6: Pages 446–447,** CORBIS; **446,** Gregory Sams/Photo Researchers, Inc.; **456,** Image Farm Inc./Alamy; **469,** GIPhotostock/Photo Researchers, Inc.; **470,** Iain Masterson/Alamy; **477,** The Granger Collection, New York; **486,** The Granger Collection, New York; **490,** FoodCollection/SuperStock; **500,** travelstock44/Alamy.

**Chapter 7: Pages 504–505,** Last Resort/Digital Vision/Getty Images; **506,** Peter Arnold, Inc./Alamy; **526,** Jim Craigmyle/CORBIS; **544,** Jim Sugar/CORBIS; **559,** All Canada Photos/Alamy; **568,** Corbis/LIII K. **571,** Fundamental Photographs; **579,** Kara Stokes; **581,** Corbis; **683,** Russell Illig/age footstock; **685,** The Granger Collection, New York.

**Chapter 8: Pages 586–587 both,** Getty Images/Craig Mitchelldyer; **588,** Alamy/David Lyons; **599,** Veer; **612,** AP Images/Richard Drew; **624,** Alamy/Kevin Schafer; **631,** istockphoto.com; **641** Dreamstime; **652,** Photo Researchers/Eckhard Slawik; **657,** Veer; **658,** Michael Maslan Historic Photographs/CORBIS; **658,** Gérard Boutin/zefa/Corbis.

**Chapter 9: Pages 690–691,** USPS; **698,** Heather Wright; **713,** Heather Wright; **714,** AP Photo/Daily Southtown, Brett Roseman, File; **733,** David McNew/Getty Images, Inc.; **734,** Jim West/Alamy; **736,** William Manning/Alamy; **758,** Martin Dohrn/Photo Researchers, Inc.

**Honors Appendix A: Pages 774,** 123/uftbild/peter Arnold, Inc.; **787,** Image source Pink/Alamy; **793,** Lori Lee Miller/Alamy.

**Honors Appendix B: Pages 800,** Perry Mastrovito/Corbis; **812,** Grant Faint/Getty Images; **816,** Eddie Gerald/Alamy.

### Additional Credits
Peter Sterling/Getty Images, Inc.

**Chapter 1:** Investigations 1A, 1B, and 1C taken from *CME Project: Algebra 2* Investigations 2B, 2C, and 2D, respectively. Lesson 1.0 taken from *CME Project: Algebra 1* Lesson 7.6.

**Chapter 2:** Whole chapter taken from *CME Project: Algebra 2* Chapter 7, except Lesson 2.0 taken from *CME Project: Algebra 2* Lesson 1.2.

**Chapter 3:** Whole chapter taken from *CME Project: Precalculus* Chapter 7, except Lesson 3.11 taken from *CME Project: Algebra 2 Common Core Additional Lessons* Lesson 3, and Lessons 3.13 and 3.14 taken from *CME Project: Precalculus Common Core Additional Lessons* Lessons 3 and 4, respectively.

**Chapter 4:** Whole chapter taken from *CME Project: Algebra 2* Chapter 8.

**Chapter 5:** Investigations 5A and 5B taken from *CME Project: Precalculus* Investigations 1A and 1C, respectively.

**Chapter 6:** Investigations 6A, Investigation 6B, and Chapter 6 Project taken from *CME Project: Precalculus* Investigations 2A, Investigation 2C, and the Chapter 1 Project, respectively.

**Chapter 7:** Investigations 7A and 7B taken from *CME Project: Precalculus* Investigations 3A and 3B. Investigation 7C taken from *CME Project: Algebra 2* Investigation 1C.

**Chapter 8:** Investigations 8A and 8B taken from *CME Project: Algebra 2* Investigations 5B and 5C, respectively. Investigation 8C taken from *CME Project: Precalculus* Investigation 3C.

**Chapter 9:** Investigations 9A and 9B taken from *CME Project: Geometry* Investigations 8A and 8B. Lesson 9.0 and Investigation 9C taken from *CME Project: Precalculus* Lesson 6.2 and Investigation 6B, respectively.

**Honors Appendix:** Appendix A and Appendix B taken from *CME Project: Precalculus* Investigation 1B and Investigation 2B, respectively.

**Note:** Every effort has been made to locate the copyright owner of material reprinted in this book. Omissions brought to our attention will be corrected in subsequent editions.